Halsbury's Statutes
of
England and Wales

Fourth Edition

Volume 15

Halsbury's Statutes
of
England and Wales

Fourth Edition

Volume 15

Education
Elections
Electricity

London
Butterworths
1986

United Kingdom	Butterworth & Co (Publishers) Ltd, 88 Kingsway, LONDON WC2B 6AB, and 61A North Castle Street, EDINBURGH EH2 3LJ
Australia	Butterworths Pty Ltd, SYDNEY, MELBOURNE, BRISBANE, ADELAIDE, PERTH, CANBERRA and HOBART
Canada	Butterworth & Co (Canada) Ltd, TORONTO and VANCOUVER
New Zealand	Butterworths of New Zealand Ltd, WELLINGTON and AUCKLAND
Singapore	Butterworth & Co (Asia) Pte Ltd, SINGAPORE
South Africa	Butterworth Publishers (Pty) Ltd, DURBAN and PRETORIA
USA	Butterworth Legal Publishers, ST PAUL, Minnesota; SEATTLE, Washington; BOSTON, Massachusetts; AUSTIN, Texas and D and S Publishers, CLEARWATER, Florida

---

First Edition
Published between 1929 and 1930

Second Edition
Published between 1948 and 1951

Third Edition
Published between 1968 and 1972

ISBN for the complete set of volumes: 0 406 21409 3
for this volume: 0 406 21424 7

Typeset by CCC, printed and bound in Great Britain
by William Clowes Limited,
Beccles and London

This volume states the law as at 1 August 1985, although later developments have been
noted wherever possible

Arrangement of Titles by Volume

(N) after the name of a title indicates that that title consists of a note only
and contains no statutes

[7]

[8]

TABLE OF CONTENTS

A detailed Table of Contents for each title appears at the beginning of the title

References and Abbreviations

Note 1
The abbreviations of Reports used in this volume are listed in Vol 1 pp [17] et seq.

Note 2
Statutes are cited by the short title, Statutory Rules and Orders and Statutory Instruments are cited by the short title, if any, followed by the year and number.

Note 3
Where references are made to other publications, the volume number precedes the name of the publication and the edition and page number follow it; eg, the reference "1 Court Forms (2nd edn) (1984 issue), 35" refers to Volume 1 of the 2nd Edition of the Encyclopaedia of Court Forms, page 35.

A-G	Attorney-General
App	Appendix
art	article
B	Baron
c	chapter (number of an Act)
CA	Court of Appeal
CCA	Court of Criminal Appeal
CCR	County Court Rules 1981, SI 1981/1687, as subsequently amended
Cf	compare
Cmd; Cmnd	Command Paper
Court Forms	Encyclopaedia of Court Forms in Civil Proceedings. See Note 3, above
DC	Divisional Court
E	England
EAT	Employment Appeal Tribunal
ECSC	European Coal and Steel Community
EEC	European Economic Community
edn	edition
Euratom	European Atomic Energy Community
Forms and Precedents	Encyclopaedia of Forms and Precedents other than Court Forms. See Note 3, above
HL	House of Lords
H of C	House of Commons
Halsbury's Laws	Halsbury's Laws of England. See Note 3, above
J	Justice
LC	Lord Chancellor
LCJ	Lord Chief Justice
LJ	Lord Justice of Appeal
MR	Master of the Rolls
n	note
NI	Northern Ireland
Ord	Order
P	President
PAT	Patents Appeal Tribunal
PC	Judicial Committee of the Privy Council
para	paragraph
r	rule
RSC	Rules of the Supreme Court 1965, SI 1965/1776, as subsequently amended
RSC (NI)	Rules of the Supreme Court (Northern Ireland) 1980, SR 1980/346, as subsequently amended
reg	regulation
s	section
SI	Statutory Instruments published by authority
SLR Act	Statute Law Revision Act
SL(R) Act	Statute Law (Repeals) Act
SR	Statutory Rules of Northern Ireland published by authority

SR & O	Statutory Rules and Orders published by authority
SR & O (NI)	Statutory Rules and Orders of the Government of Northern Ireland published by authority
SR & O Rev 1904	Revised Edition comprising all Public and General Statutory Rules and Orders in force on 31 December 1903
SR & O Rev 1948	Revised Edition comprising all Public and General Statutory Rules and Orders and Statutory Instruments in force on 31 December 1948
Sch	Schedule
Sess	Session
Statutes Revised, 2nd edn	The Statutes, Second Revised Edition, published by authority (1888–1929)
Statutes Revised, 3rd edn	The Statutes, Third Revised Edition, published by authority (1950)
sub-s	subsection
VC	Vice-Chancellor

TABLE OF STATUTES

Part 1. Alphabetical List of Statutes printed in this Volume

Part 2. Chronological List of Statutes printed in this Volume

Table of Statutory Instruments

This table lists all those statutory instruments appearing in the annotations to the Acts in this volume; the Acts are listed alphabetically, and references are to the section of the Act in the notes to which the instrument appears. the references to 'IN' are references to the first note to the relevant Act.

Section

Table of Cases

A

B

G

H

N

O

P

R

Y

EDUCATION

Outline Table of Contents

Cross References

For Apprenticeship	*See title*	Employment	
Charitable Trusts	,,	Charities	
Child Health	,,	Children; Medicine and Pharmacy; Mental Health; Public Health	
Church Schools	,,	Ecclesiastical Law (Pt 1(a))	
Community Homes	,,	Children	
Contracts of Employment	,,	Employment	
Discrimination	,,	Civil Rights and Liberties	
Employment of Children	,,	Children; Health and Safety at Work	
Examinations, Professional	,,	Architects and Engineers; Medicine and Pharmacy; Solicitors	
Income Tax	,,	Taxation	
Land, Acquisition	,,	Compulsory Acquisition	
Libraries and Museums	,,	Libraries and Other Cultural and Scientific Institutions	
Local Authorities	,,	Local Government; London	
Nurseries	,,	Children	
Pensions, Increase	,,	Pensions and Superannuation	
Physical Training	,,	Public Health	
Rating of School Buildings	,,	Rating	
Remand centres	,,	Prisons	
School buses	,,	Road Traffic	
Schools, Infection in	,,	Public Health	
Schools, Polling in	,,	Elections	
Youth custody centres	,,	Prisons	

Alphabetical List of Statutes

Preliminary Note

The law relating to education is in substance statutory. At common law a parent was under no obligation to educate his child, and equity gave only indirect assistance to the advancement of education generally by recognising a trust for public education as charitable.

Provision for the educational needs of the country at large was made in 1833 by a system of grants in aid, administered at first by the Treasury and continued by a committee of the Privy Council. This committee of the Privy Council on Education was constituted by Order in Council dated 10 April 1839, and later became known as the Education Department.

A general system of public education was first introduced by the Elementary Education Act 1870 (repealed); this Act required school boards to be established to provide schools, the necessary funds to be raised by a rate.

The powers and duties of the Education Department were transferred to the Board of Education by the Board of Education Act 1899, s 2 (repealed), and the duties of the school boards were transferred to local authorities by the Education Act 1902 (repealed). The Education Act 1944, s 1 made provision for the appointment of a Minister of Education. That section has been amended and responsibility for matters relating to education is now in the hands of the Secretary of State for Education and Science or the Secretary of State for Wales; see the Introductory Note to the 1944 Act.

The statutes in this title have been divided into four groups, namely: (1) Universities and Public Schools; (2) The Education Acts; (3) Acquisition of land; (4) Teachers' superannuation and pensions.

Part 1: Universities and Public Schools

The organisation and subsequent reorganisation of the Universities of Oxford, Cambridge, Durham and London is set out in the Acts applicable to those universities respectively, whilst the newer universities are granted privileges for their graduates similar to those already existing in favour of graduates of the older universities (see eg the Leeds University Act 1904 and the Sheffield University Act 1914). The Public Schools Acts 1868 to 1873 (as to which, see the Introductory Note to the Public Schools Act 1868), reorganised the seven public schools—Eton, Winchester, Westminster, Charterhouse, Harrow, Rugby and Shrewsbury. In modern usage the term "public school" is no longer restricted to these seven schools, but includes any and every school represented on the Headmasters' Conference.

The Universities Tests Act 1871 removed certain religious restrictions attached to the holding of various offices or degrees at Oxford, Cambridge and Durham.

The Universities and College Estates Act 1925 applies to the Universities of Oxford, Cambridge and Durham, with the colleges therein, and the Colleges of Winchester and Eton. It conferred extensive powers to deal with land similar to those in the Settled Land Act 1925, Vol 48, title Trusts and Settlements (Pt 2).

The Universities and College Estates Act 1964 made changes in the law relating to property held by or on behalf of certain universities and colleges; the most important of those changes were—

  (i) to release the land transactions of colleges and halls in universities in England and Wales from the restrictions imposed by various Ecclesiastical Leases Acts;
  (ii) to enable the Universities of Oxford, Cambridge and Durham and the colleges and halls therein (but not the colleges of Winchester and Eton) to execute most transactions relating to land without the control of the Minister of Agriculture, Fisheries and Food, for which provision was made in the Universities and College Estates Act 1925; and
  (iii) to make provision for the transfer to the three universities mentioned in (ii) above, and their colleges and halls of all capital money held on their behalf

by the Minister of Agriculture, Fisheries and Food, and to enable them to receive and apply, free from Ministerial control, capital moneys derived from their land transactions.

The Universities and Colleges (Trusts) Act 1943 applies to the Universities of Oxford and Cambridge, with the colleges therein, and to Winchester College. The Act provides for the making of schemes to simplify the administration of trusts; all trust property included in a scheme may be administered as a single fund.

Part 2: The Education Acts

The foundation of the modern law of education in England and Wales was laid in the Education Act 1944. Several important changes have been made to the system of education, particularly as a result of the policies of different governments towards comprehensive secondary education. The law is now to be found almost entirely in the Education Acts 1944 to 1985 (as to which, see the Introductory Note to the Education Act 1944).

The Secretary of State for Education and Science

The Secretary of State for Education and Science is charged with the duty of promoting the education of the people of England and Wales, and of securing the effective execution by local authorities, under his control and direction, of the national policy for providing a varied and comprehensive educational service (see s 1 of the 1944 Act). Duties imposed on him by the 1944 Act include the duty to make sufficient provision for the training of teachers (s 62), the duty to prescribe standards for school premises (s 10) and to arrange for inspection of those premises (s 77(2)), and the duty to make regulations empowering local education authorities to pay grants, scholarships etc (s 81). By virtue of the Education (Grants and Awards) Act 1984, he may make education support grants to local education authorities. He also exercises important functions in relation to the establishment, discontinuance and alteration of schools; see the Education Act 1980, ss 12–15 and the Education Act 1981, s 14. As to the powers of the Secretary of State to prevent the unreasonable exercise by a local education authority or school governors of their functions, and his power to act when they are in default, see ss 68 and 99 of the 1944 Act. As to the exercise of the functions of the Secretary of State in relation to Wales, see the note to the Education Act 1944, s 2.

There are two Central Advisory Councils, one for England and one for Wales, who advise the Secretary of State on such matters concerned with educational theory and practice as they think fit, and on any questions referred to them by him (Education Act 1944, ss 4, 5).

Administration

The local administration of the statutory system of education is undertaken by the local education authority, which is normally the county council or district council (see s 6 of the 1944 Act). As to the Inner London Education Authority, see the Local Government Act 1985, s 18, Vol 25, title Local Government. It is the duty of the local education authority to secure the provision of primary and secondary schools (see s 8 of the 1944 Act) and to ensure that a parent complies with the duty imposed on him by s 36 of the 1944 Act to cause a child of compulsory school age to receive full-time education; see the Education Act 1944, s 37, the Education Act 1980, ss 10, 11 and (in relation to children with special educational needs) the Education Act 1981, ss 15, 16.

As to the appointment of school governors and their functions, see the Education Act 1944, ss 17–22 and the Education Act 1980, ss 1–5, and for the duties of governors and local education authorities in relation to the maintenance of voluntary schools, see the Education Act 1946, s 3, Sch 1. For provisions relating to the governors of colleges of further education, of other institutions providing further education, and of special schools, see the Education (No 2) Act 1968.

The governors of aided or special agreement schools receive assistance from public funds in respect of maintenance of the premises etc; see the Education Act 1944, ss 102, 103, 105. For provisions as to awards and grants, see, inter alia, the Education Act 1944, s 100, the Education Act 1962, ss 1–4, the Education Act 1980, ss 17–21, the Education (Fees and Awards) Act 1983, and the Education (Grants and Awards) Act 1984.

The 1944 Act contains provisions relating to various ancillary services, including medical inspection and cleanliness (ss 48, 54), provision of board and lodging otherwise than at boarding schools (s 50) and provision of transport (s 55).

The Education Act 1968, s 1 was passed as a result of the decision in *Bradbury v London Borough of Enfield* [1967] 3 All ER 434, [1967] 1 WLR 1311, CA, that changing the fundamental character of a school amounted to ceasing to maintain it and establishing a new one so as to fall within the Education Act 1944, s 13. That decision necessitated the retrospective validation of certain changes in the character of schools, made since the 1944 Act came into force but without compliance with s 13 of the Act. S 13 was repealed by the Education Act 1980 and replaced by ss 12–14 of that Act.

The Education Act 1973 confers on the Secretary of State power in certain circumstances to vary educational trusts, including trusts for religious education.

The Further Education Act 1985 empowers local education authorities to supply goods and services through further education establishments.

General principles and system of education

The general principle to be observed by the Secretary of State and local education authorities is that pupils are to be educated in accordance with the wishes of their parents (s 76 of the 1944 Act; for the extent of the duty, see the cases noted to that section). It is the duty of a local education authority to enable a parent to express a preference as to the school at which a child is to be educated and, subject to certain exceptions, to comply with that preference (Education Act 1980, ss 6–8).

The 1944 Act provided for education to be organised in three successive stages known as primary education, normally for junior pupils, ie children up to twelve years of age; secondary education, normally for senior pupils, ie children aged twelve years or over; and further education for persons over the compulsory school age (ss 7, 8, 41). The compulsory school age is sixteen; see s 35 of the 1944 Act, as amended by the Raising of the School Leaving Age Order 1972, SI 1972/444. Under the Education Act 1964, s 1, as amended, proposals submitted under the Education Act 1980, ss 12 or 13 for the establishment of a county or voluntary school may specify an age below ten years and six months and an age above twelve years and provide that the school is to be established for providing full-time education suitable to the requirements of pupils whose ages are between those specified; accordingly many local education authorities have adopted a system of first, middle and upper schools. The duty to give effect to the comprehensive principle in secondary education was laid down in the Education Act 1976, ss 1–3, which were repealed by the Education Act 1979.

Primary and secondary schools maintained by a local education authority, not being nursery schools or special schools, if established by a local education authority, are known as county schools and, if established otherwise than by such an authority, are known as voluntary schools (s 9(2) of the 1944 Act). Voluntary schools are classified as controlled, aided or special agreement schools (s 15 of the 1944 Act). Primary schools for children over two and under five are known as nursery schools (s 9(4) of the 1944 Act). Local education authorities are under no duty to provide nursery education, but have the power to do so (Education Act 1980, s 24). Schools organised to make special educational provision for pupils with special educational needs are known as special schools (Education Act 1944, s 9(5)). As to the assessment and education of such children, see the Education Act 1981. For provisions relating to access for handicapped people to university and school buildings, see the Chronically Sick and Disabled Persons Act 1970, ss 8, 28 and 29. In extraordinary circumstances a local education authority may make special arrangements for a child or young person who is unable to attend a suitable school to be educated otherwise than at school; see the Education Act 1944, s 56. Under the Education (Miscellaneous Provisions) Act 1953, s 6 post, a local education authority may pay the fees of pupils at non-maintained schools. No fees are to be charged in respect of admission to any school maintained by a local education authority; see the Education Act 1944, s 61.

It is the duty of every local education authority, so far as their powers extend, to contribute towards the spiritual, moral, mental and physical development of the community by securing that efficient education throughout the three stages is available to meet the needs of the population of their area (s 7 of the 1944 Act).

Religious instruction is to be given in all schools maintained by a local education authority, and the school day in all such schools must begin with collective worship, unless this is impracticable (s 25 of the 1944 Act). For further provisions as to religious education, see ss 26–30 of the 1944 Act.

Teachers

The Secretary of State may make such arrangements as he considers expedient for securing facilities for the training of teachers; and he may direct local education authorities to provide training colleges (s 62 of the 1944 Act).

The Remuneration of Teachers Act 1965 makes provision for the determination of the remuneration to be paid to teachers by local education authorities. Such remuneration is primarily to be determined by negotiation and provision is to be made for arbitration failing agreement, though the recommendations of arbitrators need not be given effect to if each House of Parliament resolves that national economic circumstances so require.

The appointment and dismissal of teachers in county schools and, with reservations, in controlled and special agreement schools is under the control of the local education authority. In aided schools the appointment and dismissal of teachers is regulated by the articles of government (Education Act 1944, s 24).

For provisions relating to the Commonwealth Scholarship Commission and to educational co-operation between Commonwealth countries, see the Overseas Development and Co-operation Act 1980, ss 14–19.

Independent Schools

An independent school is one at which full-time education is provided for five or more pupils of compulsory school age, not being a school maintained by a local education authority or a special school not maintained by a local education authority (s 114(1) of the 1944 Act). Ss 70–75 of the 1944 Act deal with independent schools and regulations for the registration of independent schools have been made; there are, too, rules with respect to proceedings before an Independent Schools Tribunal, where a complaint against a school has been made by the Secretary of State. For provisions relating to assisted places at independent schools, see the Education Act 1980, ss 17, 18.

Employment of Children and Young Persons

Any person who is not over compulsory school age is to be deemed to be a child for the purposes of any enactment relating to the prohibition or regulation of the employment of children; see s 58 of the 1944 Act, and for such enactments see the note to that section.

The local education authority is authorised to prohibit or restrict employment of children if such employment appears prejudicial to the child's health, etc (s 59 of the 1944 Act). An authority may arrange for children to have work experience, as part of their education, in the last year of compulsory schooling; see the Education (Work

Experience) Act 1973. It is the duty of each local education authority to provide careers services in accordance with the Employment and Training Act 1973, ss 8–10, Vol 16, title Employment.

Part 3: Acquisition of Land

The School Sites Acts (for which, see the Introductory Note to the School Sites Act 1841) afford facilities for persons and bodies who might otherwise be under disabilities to convey or hold land for certain prescribed educational purposes. Such disabilities existed under the Mortmain and Charitable Uses Act 1888, which was repealed, with savings, by the Charities Act 1960, ss 38, 48(2), Sch 7, Pt II, Vol 5, title Charities; the powers are therefore no longer necessary but much land was conveyed under those Acts and their provisions continue to apply to that land. Under the School Sites Acts, grants of land may be made, either absolutely or for a term of years, as a site for a school or otherwise for the education of poor persons. The grants are limited as to area, according to the particular educational purpose for which they are intended, and except in the case of grants for teachers' training colleges, the Acts provide that the land granted is to revert to the grantor on failure of the purposes of the grant. See generally 15 Halsbury's Laws (4th edn) para 276.

Another method of providing land for educational purposes is contained in the Education Act 1944, s 85. Under that provision property may be vested in a local education authority as trustees.

A local education authority may also acquire land compulsorily under the Education Act 1944, s 90, in accordance with the procedural provisions of the Acquisition of Land Act 1981, Vol 9, title Compulsory Acquisition.

The Technical and Industrial Institutions Act 1892 is only of limited application. It is "an Act to facilitate the acquisition and holding of land by institutions for promoting technical and industrial instruction and training". The institutions to which the Act applies are defined in s 2; subject to qualifications, they must be open to the public (s 8).

Part 4: Teachers' Superannuation and Pensions

The Elementary School Teachers (Superannuation) Act 1898 (as amended by the 1912 Act of like title, and as applied to Jersey by the Elementary School Teachers Superannuation (Jersey) Act 1900) applied only to certificated teachers in primary schools. Three kinds of pension were created—a deferred annuity, a superannuation allowance and a disablement allowance. This scheme has been amended and modified from time to time.

Apart from the above, teachers' superannuation and pensions were, until 1965, governed mainly by the Teachers (Superannuation) Acts 1918 to 1946. The Teachers' Superannuation Act 1965 repealed most of the provisions of the Acts of 1918 to 1946, and provided instead for the making of superannuation regulations by the Secretary of State governing teachers' superannuation benefits and introducing pensions for the widows and other dependants of teachers. That Act, and certain earlier enactments on the subject, were repealed by, and consolidated in, the Teachers' Superannuation Act 1967, which was itself repealed with savings by the Superannuation Act 1972, s 29, Sch 7, para 6, Sch 8, Vol 33, title Pensions and Superannuation. Teachers' superannuation is now governed by regulations made under s 9 of the 1972 Act. The current regulations are the Teachers' Superannuation Regulations 1976, SI 1976/1987.

For provisions granting increases of certain pensions payable under the Acts within this title, see the Pensions (Increases) Act 1971, Vol 33, title Pensions and Superannuation.

Part 1

Universities and Public Schools

Table of Contents

OXFORD AND CAMBRIDGE ACT 1571

(13 Eliz 1 c 29)

ARRANGEMENT OF SECTIONS

An Acte for Thincorporation of bothe Thunyversities

The short title to this Act was given by the SLR Act 1948.

The words in square brackets to which there are no specific annotations are modern equivalents of the words originally used, and the numbered notes to ss 1, 3 indicate differences in the available sources from which this version is derived.

So much of this Act as imposes upon the mayor, etc, of Oxford the obligation of taking any oath for the conservation of the liberties and privileges of the University of Oxford, or any such oath as was in the repealing Act referred to, was repealed by 22 & 23 Vict c 19 (1859), s 1 (not printed in this work).

The repeal by 22 & 23 Vict c 19 (1859) also extended to letters patent dated 29 May 1247 (32 Hen 3) whereby the King granted to the scholars at Oxford University, amongst other things, that so often and whensoever the Mayor and Bailiffs of Oxford should take their oath of fealty the commonalty of the town should inform the Chancellor in order that, if he wished, he might himself be present or be represented at the taking of the oath. S 2 of the repealing statute (22 & 23 Vict c 19 (1859) also provided that neither the Mayor, Aldermen and Citizens of Oxford nor any of them, nor any municipal officer of the City of Oxford should thereafter be required to take any oath or to make any declaration for the conservation of the liberty and privileges of the University of Oxford; provided that "the Mayor, Aldermen and Citizens of Oxford, and all officers of the same City, should observe and keep all manner of lawful liberties and customs which the Chancellor, Masters and Scholars of the said University have reasonably used, without any gainsaying".

For confirming the priviledges of the two universities

For the greate love and favor that the Queenes most excellent [Majesty] beareth towardes her Highnes universities of Oxford and Cambridge, and for the greate zeale and care that the lords and comons of this present [Parliament] have for the mayntenaunce of good and godly literature and the vertuouse education of youth within either of the same universities; and to thentent that the auncient priveleges liberties and fraunchises of either of the said universities [here before[1]] graunted ratified and confirmed by the Queenes Highnes and her most noble progenitors may be had in greater estymation and be of greater force and strengthe, for the better increase of larning and the further suppressing of vice:

NOTE
[1] heretofore O.

[1] The chancellor, masters and scholars of the Universities of Oxford and Cambridge incorporated

The right honorable Robert Erle of Leicester nowe chauncellor of the said Universitie of Oxford and his successors for ever, and the masters and schollers of the same Universitie of Oxford for the tyme being, shalbe incorporated and have a [perpetual] succession in facte dede and name, by the name of the Chauncellor Masters and Schollers of the Universitie of Oxford, and that the same chauncellor maisters and schollers of the same Universitie of Oxford for the tyme being, from henceforth by the name of Chauncellor Maisters and Schollers of the Universitie of Oxford, and by none other name or names, shalbe called and named for evermore: And that they shall have a comon seale to serve for their necessarie causes touching and concerning the said chauncellor maysters and schollers of the said Universitie of Oxford and their successors: And likewyse that the right honorable Sr William Cicill Knight Baron of Burghley nowe [chancellor] of the said Universitie of Cambridg and his successors for ever, and the masters and schollers of the same Universite of Cambridg for the tyme being, shalbe incorporated and have a [perpetual] succession in fact deede and name, by the name of the Chauncellor Maisters and Schollers of the Universitie of Cambridge, and that the same chauncellor masters and schollers of the said Universitie of Cambridg for the tyme being, from henceforth by the name of Chauncellor Maisters & Schollers of the Universitie of Cambridg, and by none other name or names, shalbe called & named for evermore: And that they shall have a comon seale to serve for their necessarye causes touching and concerning the said chauncellor maisters and schollers of the said Universitie of Cambridg and their successors: and further that aswell the chauncellor maiesters and schollers of the said Universitie of Oxford and their successors, by the name of Chauncellor Masters and Schollers of the Universitie of Oxford, as the chauncelor maisters and schollers of the sayd Universitie of Cambridge and theire successors, by the name of Chauncellor Maisters and Schollers of the Universitie of Cambridg, may severally impleade and be ympleaded and sue or be sued, for all manner of causes quarels actions realles [personal] and mixt of whatsoever kynde qualitie or nature they be, and shall and maye challeng and demaunde all manner of liberties & fraunchises, and also aunswere and defend themselves, under and by the name aforesaid in the same causes quarels and [actions], for every thinge and things whatsoever, for the proffit and right of either of the foresaid universities to be don, before any manner of judge either [spiritual] or temporall in any courtes and [places] [within] the Queenes Highnes domynions whatsoever they be.

NOTES

Incorporation. The Universities of Oxford and Cambridge were not originally founded by charter, but were subsequently incorporated by charters. The actual dates of foundation are unknown, that of Oxford is usually said to be 1133 or 1167, and that of Cambridge 1209 or 1224. Oxford appears to have been incorporated by charter of Edward III in 1375. By the present Act the charters of incorporation are confirmed. For corporations generally, see 9 Halsbury's Laws (4th edn) paras 1201 et seq.

Cases. Certain cases regarding Universities are worth noting: *Lord North's Case* (1594) Moore KB 361, dealt with the extent of University liberties; the court will take judicial notice that the University of Oxford is a national institution for the advancement of religion and learning (*Oxford Poor Rate Case* (1857) 8 E & B 184); the Corporations of the Universities are lay corporations, and the Crown cannot take away from them any rights that have been formerly subsisting in them under old charters or prescriptive usage (*R v Vice-Chancellor of Cambridge* [1558–1774] All ER Rep (1765) 3 Burr 1647). The court will grant a mandamus to the master of a college to compel him to take the oaths of the fellows as prescribed by statute (*R v St John's College, Cambridge* (1693) 4 Mod Rep 233), or to affix the college seal to a pleading in Chancery (*R v Windham* [1775–1802] All ER Rep 362 (1776) 1 Cowp 377), or to permit inspection of charter etc (*R v President, Fellows and Scholars of St John's College, Oxford* (1845) 5 LTOS 221), or to admit a scholar to a college (*R v St John's College, Oxford* (1694) Holt KB 437). But mandamus does not lie for restoration of a person against whom a sentence of only banishment from the University is pronounced by Vice-Chancellor's Court (*R v Chancellor etc of Cambridge University* (1794) 6 Term Rep 89). As to University and College usage, see *Ex parte Lamprey* (1737) West temp Hard 209. As to lay corporations being subject to temporal jurisdiction, see *R v Gregory* (1772) 4 Term Rep 240n.

Assignment of fellowship. A fellow may assign the profits of his fellowship by way of mortgage (*Feistel v King's College, Cambridge* (1847) 10 Beav 491, 16 LJ Ch 339).

2 Letters patent to Universities of Oxford and Cambridge confirmed

And ... the letters patents of the Queenes Highnes most noble father Kinge Henry Theight made and graunted to the chauncellor and schollers of the Universitie of Oxford, bearing date the first daye of Aprill in the foureteine yere of his raigne, and the [letters] patentes of the Queenes [Majesty] that nowe is, made and graunted unto the chauncellor maisters and schollers of the Universitie of Cambridge, bearing date the sixe and twentie daye of Aprill in the third yeare of her Highnes most gratious raigne, and also all other [letters] patents by any of the progenitors or predicessors of our said soveraigne ladye, made to either of the said corporated bodies severally or to anye of their predecessors of either of the said universities, by whatsoever name or names the said chauncellor masters and schollers of either of the saide universities in anye of the said [letters] patentes have ben heretofore named, shall fromhenceforth be good effectuall and avaylable in the lawe, to all intentes constructions and [purposes], to the foresaid nowe chauncellor maisters & schollers of either of the said universities and to their successors for evermore, after and according to ye fourme wordes [sentences] and true meaning of every of the same [letters] patents, as amply fullye and largely as yf the same [letters] patentes were recited verbatim in this present Acte of [Parliament]; any thing to the contrary in any wyse notwithstandinge.

NOTES

The words omitted were repealed by the SLR Act 1888.

Letters patent. The letters patent of 1 April 1522 (14 Hen 8) were issued at the desire of Wolsey, and the University was (inter alia) empowered to make corporations of tradesmen and frame regulations for them. The Chancellor was allowed a prison and granted exclusive jurisdiction in any part of the kingdom over all persons enjoying the privileges of the University; he was also given confiscated goods of felons and all treasure trove in Oxford. The University was placed in a position of absolute supremacy over all persons in Oxford. For the present status of the Vice-Chancellor's Court, see 10 Halsbury's Laws (4th edn) para 981.

Former charters were: (1) Oxford: 1244 (28 Hen 3), civil rights; 1400 (2 Hen 4), 1331 (5 Edw 3), criminal jurisdiction. (2) Cambridge: 1383 (7 Ric 2); 1561 (3 Eliz); and Royal Letters in 1231 and 1233.

3 All possessions and privileges of the said universities confirmed to them, being so incorporated

And ... the chauncellor masters and schollers of either of the said universities severally, and their successors forever, by the same name of Chauncellor Maisters and Schollors of either of the said universities of Oxforde and Cambridge, shall and may severally have hold [possesse[1]] enjoye and use, to them and to their successors for ever more, all mannor of mannors lorshippes rectories [parsonages] lands tenements rentes services annuyties advousons of churches possessions [pensions portions] and hereditamentes, and all manner of liberties fraunchises immunytes [quietances] and [privileges], view of frankpledge lawedaies and other things whatsoever they be, the [which] either of the said corporated bodies of either of the said universities had held occupied or enjoyed, or of right ought to have had used occupied and enjoyed at any tyme or tymes before the making of this Acte of Parlyament; according to the true intent and meaninge aswell of the said [letters] patentes made by the said noble prynce King Henrye Theight, made and graunted to the chauncellor and schollers of the Unyversitie of Oxford bearing date as is aforesaid, as of the [letters] patentes of the Queenes [Majesty] made and graunted unto the chauncellor masters and schollers of the Universitie of Cambridge bearing date as aforesaid, and as accordinge to the true intent and meaninge of all [other the[2]] foresaid [letters] patentes whatsoever; any statute or other thinge or things whatsoever heretofore made or don to the contrary in anye manner of wyse notwithstandinge.

NOTES

[1] possede O   [2] the other O.

The words omitted were repealed by the SLR Act 1888.

Advowsons. An advowson is the right of patronage which is exercised by its owner or patron in presenting a clergyman to a church or benefice. It is included in the definition of "land" for the purposes of the Law of Property Act 1925; see s 205(1)(ix) of that Act, Vol 37, title Real Property. As to advowsons and rights of patronage generally, see 14 Halsbury's Laws (4th edn) paras 776 et seq.

View of frankpledge, lawedaies. View of frankpledge or lawday is another name for the court leet which is a manorial court of record still extant but virtually extinct; see 10 Halsbury's Laws (4th edn) para 980.

Said letters patent. See the note to s 2 ante.

4 All deeds, obligations, etc, made to the said universities, by any former description, declared valid

And ... all manner of instruments [indentures] [obligations] writings obligatory and recognisaunses, made or knowledged by any [person] or [persons] or body corporate to either of the said corporated bodies of either of the said universities, by what name or names [soever] the said chauncellor maisters and schollers of either of the said universities have ben heretofore called, in any of the said instrumentes [indentures] [obligations] writings obligatori or recognizaunces, shalbe from henceforth avaylable stand and contynue of good [perfect] and full force and strength, to the nowe chauncellor maisters and schollers of either of the said universities and to their successors, to all intents [constructions] and purposes; althoughe they or their predecessors or any of them, in any of the said instruments [indentures] [obligations] writings obligatory or recognyzaunzes, be named by any name contrary or dyverse to the name of the nowe chauncellor maisters and schollers of either of the said universities.

NOTE

The words omitted were repealed by the SLR Act 1888.

5 Patents and liberties granted the universities, by any former description, declared valid, and ratified

And ... aswell the said [letters] patentes of the Queenes Highnes said father Kinge Henry Theight bearing date as is before [expressed], made and graunted to the said corporate bodye of the said Universitie of Oxon, as the letters patentes of the Queens [Majesty] aforesaid, graunted to the chauncellor maisters and schollers of the Universitie of Cambridg bearing date as aforesaid, and all other [letters] patents by any of the progenitors or predecessors of her Highnes, and all manner of liberties fraunchises immunyties [quietances] and [privileges] letes lawedayes, and other things whatsoever therein expressed, geven or graunted to the said chauncellor maisters and schollers of either of the said universities or to anye of their predecessors of either of the said universities, by whatsoever name the said chauncellor maisters and schollers of either of the said universities in any of the said letters patentes be named, in and by vertue of this present Acte shalbe from henceforth ratyfied stablished and confirmed unto the said chauncellor maisters and schollers of either of the said universities and to their successors for ever; any statute lawe usage custom construcc or other thing to the contrary in any wyse notwithstanding.

NOTES

The words omitted were repealed by the SLR Act 1888.
Letes, lawedays. See the third note to s 3 ante.

6 Proviso for title of strangers, lessees etc

Savinge to all and every person and [persons] and bodies politike and incorporate their heyres and successors, and the heirs and successors of every of them, other then to the Quenes [Majesty] her heires & successors, all such titles interests entrees leases conditions [charges] and demaundes, [which] they and every of them have might or should have had, of in or to any the mannors lordshippes rectories [parsonages] landes tenementes rents [services] anuyties advousons of churches [pensions] [portions] hereditamentes, and all other things in the said [letters] patentes or in any of them [mentioned] or comprysed, by reason of any right title charge interest or condicion, to them or any of them or to the auncestors or predecessors of them or any of them devolute or growne, before the several dates of the same [letters] patents, or by reason of any gyfte graunte demyse or other acte or actes at any tyme made or don betwene the said chauncelor maisters and schollers of either of the said universities of Cambridge and Oxford or any of them & others, by what name or names soever the same were made or don, in like manner and fourme as they and every of them had or might have had the same before the making of this Acte; any thinge, &c.

NOTE

Advowsons. See the note to s 3 ante.

7 Proviso for liberties of mayor, bailiffs and burgesses of Cambridge and Oxford

Provyded alwaies . . . that this Acte or anye thinge therin contayned shall not extend to the prejudice or hurt of the liberties & [privileges] of right belonging to the maior bayliffes & burgeses of the towne of Cambridge and cittie of Oxford; but that they ye said maiors bayliffes and burgeses and every of them and their successors shalbe and contynew fre in such sort and degree, and enjoye such liberties fredomes and ymmunyties, as they or any of them lawfully may or might have don before the making of this present Acte; any thing contayned in this present Acte to the contrary notwithstandinge.

NOTE

The words omitted were repealed by the SLR Act 1888.

OXFORD UNIVERSITY ACT 1854

(17 & 18 Vict c 81)

ARRANGEMENT OF SECTIONS

An Act to make further provision for the good Government and Extension of the University of Oxford, of the Colleges therein ... [7 August 1854]

The words omitted from the long title were repealed by the SLR Act 1892.
The short title was given to this Act by the Short Titles Act 1896.
Acquisition of land. With exceptions, the Lands Clauses Consolidation Act 1845, Vol 9, title Compulsory Acquisition, is incorporated with this Act; see the Oxford University Act 1857, s 4 (this part of this title post.

1–4 *(Repealed by the SLR Act 1875.)*

5 Constitution of the University—Establishment of Hebdomadal Council

... Upon the fifteenth day of the Michaelmas term one thousand eight hundred and fifty-four there shall be elected in manner herein-after mentioned a council, which shall be called the Hebdomadal Council, to which shall be transferred immediately after the election thereof all powers, privileges, and functions now possessed or exercised by the hebdomadal board of the said University.

NOTE

The words omitted were repealed by the SLR Act 1892.

6 Composition of Hebdomadal Council

The Hebdomadal Council shall consist of the Chancellor, the Vice-Chancellor, the proctors, six heads of colleges or halls, six professors of the University, and six members of Convocation of not less than five years standing, such heads of colleges, or halls, professors, and members of Convocation to be elected by the Congregation herein-after mentioned of the said University; and the Chancellor, or in his absence the Vice-Chancellor, or his deputy, being a member of the Hebdomadal Council, shall be the president of such Hebdomadal Council: Provided always, that nothing herein contained shall be held to prevent the head of any college or hall who is a professor being returned or continuing to sit as one of the six professors, or the head of any college or hall, or a professor, being returned or continuing to sit as one of the six members of Convocation; and if any person shall be elected a member of the Hebdomadal Council in two or more classes, he shall, when he first takes his seat in the council, declare under which class he desires to sit, and his seat for the other shall be forthwith vacated.

NOTES

Convocation. Convocation consists of all MAs, DDs, DCLs, and MDs, whether resident or not. Convocation, by means of "decrees", transacts much of the ordinary University business; it confers honorary degrees and those granted by decree or diploma.
Congregation. For the composition of Congregation, see s 16 post.

7 *(Repealed by the SLR Act 1875.)*

8 Vacating of seats on the Council

Of the six persons to be then elected together out of each of the classes of heads of colleges or halls, professors, and members of Convocation, the three juniors of each class in academical standing, reckoned from matriculation, shall vacate their seats at the expiration of the third year from such day within the then current academical year as shall be named by the Hebdomadal Council in that behalf; and all the other persons to be then elected shall vacate their seats at the expiration of the sixth year from the said day; and all other persons elected from time to time, except such as shall be so elected upon casual vacancies, shall vacate their seats at the expiration of six years; and the election to supply the places of the persons so vacating their seats shall be made upon the day on which seats are vacated.

NOTES

Matriculation. This is the formal enrolment on the register (matricula) of the University.
Re-election. Persons vacating seats are eligible for re-election; see s 9 post.
Casual vacancies. See s 10 post.
Convocation. See the note to s 6 ante.

9 Members may be re-elected

All such persons whatsoever shall be capable of re-election.

10 Filling up of casual vacancies

Any casual vacancy occurring by death, resignation, or otherwise among such persons shall be filled by the election of a qualified person, according to the directions of this Act; but the person so elected shall be subject to the same rules and conditions in all respects as the person to whose place he succeeds would have been subject to if no such vacancy had taken place.

11 Vice-Chancellor, if not an elected member, to continue a member for a time on the expiration of his term of office

If the Vice-Chancellor for the time being shall not be also an elected member of the said council, then, on the expiration of his term of office, he shall in virtue of his late office continue to be a member thereof until the next triennial election, or for the space of, one year, if such election shall take place at an earlier period.

12 No professors ineligible

No professor shall be ineligible for the said council by reason of anything contained in the statutes of his foundation.

13 Non-residence to vacate seat

If any of the members of the Hebdomadal Council other than the Chancellor of the University shall reside for less than twenty-four weeks during term time in any year, his seat shall at or before the close of such year be declared by the Vice-Chancellor and shall thereupon become vacant.

NOTE

Residents. Cf the definition in s 48 post.

14 Vice-Chancellor to make a register of members of Congregation, and regulations respecting such register and the election, etc, of the Hebdomadal Council

The Vice-Chancellor shall before the twenty-fifth day of September . . . in each . . . year, make and promulgate a register of the persons qualified to the best of his knowledge to be members of the Congregation of the University of Oxford according to this Act, and shall also make and promulgate all such regulations as to the said register, and as to all matters relating to the voting for, election, resignation, and return of members of the

Hebdomadal Council as may be necessary for the assembling together of the Congregation and for the election and assembling together of the said Hebdomadal Council according to this Act, and for keeping the number of such council complete, and shall appoint the time of the day and place at which they shall so assemble together;
... and no persons shall be admitted to vote in the election of members of the Hebdomadal Council but those included in such register, and mentioned or described in the sixteenth section and the schedule therein referred to.

NOTES

The words omitted were repealed by the SLR Act 1875 and the SLR Act 1892.
Congregation. See s 16 post.
Schedule therein referred to. Ie Schedule A to this Act post.

15 Hebdomadal Council may make rules for the regulation of its own proceedings, and revise regulations etc, of Vice-Chancellor

Subject to the provisions of this Act, and without prejudice to the rights of Congregation and Convocation in the making of statutes for the University of Oxford, the Hebdomadal Council shall have power to make, from time to time, rules for the regulation of its own proceedings, and to revise the regulations and register herein-before directed to be made by the Vice-Chancellor.

NOTES

Statutes for the University. The Hebdomadal Council initiates legislation which then goes to Congregation and subsequently to Convocation; see s 17 post.
Congregation. See s 16 post.
Convocation. See the note to s 6 ante.

16 Composition of Congregation—Congregation may frame regulations as to its own proceedings

... The Congregation of the University of Oxford shall be composed of the following persons only, the said persons being members of Convocation:

1. The Chancellor.
2. The High Steward.
3. The heads of colleges and halls.
4. The canons of Christ Church.
5. The proctors.
6. The members of the Hebdomadal Council.
7. The officers named in schedule (A) to this Act annexed.
8. The professors.
9. Assistant or deputy professors.
10. The public examiners.
11. All residents.
12. All such persons as shall be provided to be added by election or otherwise to the said Congregation by any statute of the University approved by the commissioners, or (after the expiry of the commission) passed by licence of the Crown.

The Chancellor, or in his absence the Vice-Chancellor, or his deputy, shall preside in the said Congregation, and the Congregation so constituted as aforesaid shall have power to frame regulations for the order of its own proceedings, but subject to any statute which the University may make in respect thereof.

17 Promulgation, etc of statutes framed by the Council

Every statute framed by the Hebdomadal Council shall, after due notice of the contents thereof, be promulgated in Congregation, and shall also be proposed there for acceptance or rejection after an interval of seven days, or such other interval as the University by statute may appoint, and if accepted by Congregation shall be, after an interval of fourteen days, or such other interval as the University by Statute may appoint, submitted to Convocation for final adoption or rejection as a statute of the University.

NOTES
The Hebdomadal Council alone initiates legislation. A new statute sent down by it must be promulgated in Congregation, which may adopt, reject, or amend it. If not rejected, it goes in its approved form to Convocation who may adopt or reject but cannot amend.

Alteration of statutes. As to the alteration and repeal of University Statutes, see the Oxford University Act 1862, s 9 and the Universities of Oxford and Cambridge Act 1923, s 7, both this part of this title post. See also s 39 of this Act post.

18 Proposal of amendments to statutes

Any member of Congregation may, upon the promulgation of any such statute, propose, in writing, amendments thereof to the Hebdomadal Council, which the said council shall consider, and thereupon may adopt, alter, or reject.

19 If any change be made, statute shall be re-promulgated

If after the promulgation of a statute the said council shall make any change in it, it shall thereupon be promulgated afresh in manner aforesaid.

NOTE
Promulgation. See s 17 ante.

20 Members of Congregation may on promulgation of any statute speak in English

The members of Congregation shall upon the occasion of the promulgation of any statute have the right to speak thereon in the English tongue, but without the power of moving any amendment, and subject to such regulations as the University may make by statute for the due order of debate.

NOTES
English tongue. Formerly Latin only could be used.
Congregation. See s 16 ante.

21 Votes at election of members of Hebdomadal Council

Upon any occasion of electing members of the Hebdomadal Council, every person entitled to vote in such election shall have the power of giving votes in each class as follows; for one vacancy, one vote; for two or three vacancies, two votes; for four vacancies, three votes; for five or six vacancies, four votes; Provided always, that no elector shall give more than one vote for any one candidate.

NOTE
Election of members. See s 6 ante.

22 Saving of powers of Convocation

The Convocation of the University of Oxford shall not, save as herein provided, be deprived of any of the powers by it now lawfully possessed.

NOTE
Convocation. See the note to s 6 ante.

23 Provisions for votes by proxy at election of Chancellor

It shall be lawful for the University to provide by statute, if it shall think fit, that votes may be given either personally or by proxies, being members of convocation authorised by writing under the hand of the member of convocation nominating such proxy, at any election of a chancellor of the University.

24 Certain oaths illegal

Every oath directly or indirectly binding the juror—

> Not to disclose any matter or thing relating to his college, although required so to do by lawful authority:
> To resist or not concur in any change in the statutes of the University or college:
> To do or forbear from doing anything the doing or the not doing of which would tend to any such concealment, resistance, or non-concurrence:

shall . . . be an illegal oath in the said University and the colleges thereof; and no such oath shall hereafter be administered or taken.

NOTE
The words omitted were repealed by the SLR Act 1892.

25 Members of Convocation may obtain licences to open their residences for reception of students

It shall be lawful for any member of Convocation, of such standing and qualifications as may be provided by any statute hereafter to be made, to obtain a licence from the Vice-Chancellor to open his residence, if situate within one mile and a half of Carfax, for the reception of students, who shall be matriculated and admitted to all the privileges of the University without being of necessity entered as members of any college or existing hall; . . .

NOTES
The words omitted were repealed by the SLR Act 1875.
Convocation. See the note to s 6 ante.

26 Such persons shall be called licensed masters, and their residences private halls

Every person to whom such licence is granted shall be called a licensed master, and his residence so opened as aforesaid shall be called a private hall.

NOTE

   Private hall. A private hall at Oxford corresponds to a hostel at Cambridge; see the Cambridge University Act 1856, s 24; see also the Universities Tests Act 1871, s 2. Both sections are in this part of this title post.

27–38 (*Repealed by the SLR Act 1875.*)

39 Repeal or alteration of statutes made by University or colleges

Every statute made by the University of Oxford, ... by virtue of the powers of this Act, shall be subject to repeal or alteration in the same manner and to the same extent, but not otherwise, in and to which other statutes of the said University ... are or may be subject to repeal or alteration by the authorities thereof.

NOTE

   The words omitted were repealed by the SLR Act 1892.

40 Repeal or alteration of provisions of this Act as to Hebdomadal Council and Congregation

... All provisions herein-before contained respecting the election, constitution, powers, and proceedings of the Hebdomadal Council, and respecting the constitution, powers, and proceedings of the Congregation, shall be subject to repeal and alteration by the University ... with the approval of her Majesty in Council.

NOTES

   The words omitted were repealed by the SLR Act 1892.
   Hebdomadal Council. See s 5 ante.
   Congregation. See s 16 ante.

41 Christ Church to be deemed a college

For the purposes of this Act, the cathedral or house of Christ Church in Oxford shall be considered to be to all intents and purposes a college of the University.

42 (*Repealed by the SLR Act 1875.*)

43 No declaration or oath necessary on matriculation

... It shall not be necessary for any person, upon matriculating in the University of Oxford, to make or subscribe any declaration, or to take any oath, any law or statute to the contrary notwithstanding.

NOTES

   The words omitted were repealed by the SLR Act 1892.
   Matriculation. See the note to s 8 ante.

44–46 (*Ss 44, 46 repealed by the SLR Act 1875; s 45 repealed by the Oxford University Act 1862, s 12.*)

47 Saving of powers of University and colleges

Except in so far as they are expressly altered or taken away by the provisions of this Act, the powers and privileges of the University and its officers, and of the colleges and their officers, shall continue in full force.

48 Interpretation of terms

In the construction of this Act, the expression "University or college emolument" shall include all fellowships, studentships, scholarships, exhibitions, demyships, postmaster-ships, taberdarships, Bible clerkships, servitorships, and every other such place of emolument payable out of the revenues of the University, or of any college, or to be held and enjoyed by the members of any college or hall as such within the University; the word "scholarship" shall include the bursaries appropriated to any college in Scotland; and the word "school" shall include colleges in Scotland; and the words "professor" and "professorship" shall be taken to include respectively public readers, praelectors, and their several officers; and the words "public examiner" shall be taken to include moderators and masters of the schools; and the word "hall" shall be taken to mean all halls other than affiliated halls, or such private halls as are authorized by this Act; and the governing body of any college shall mean and include the head and all actual fellows thereof, being graduates, but in the case of Christ Church shall mean the dean and canons thereof; and the word "residents" shall mean and include all members of Convocation who shall have resided twenty weeks within one mile and a half of Carfax during the year that shall expire on the first day of September next preceding the making and promulgation of the register as directed by the fourteenth section of this Act.

NOTES

University or college emolument. Demyships are held at Magdalen College: postmasterships at Merton: bible clerkships at Oriel and Queen's (those at All Soul's have been discontinued). A studentship is a University emolument. Taberdarships are held at Queen's. Servitorships are now obsolete; the holders of them used to wait at table. See also the Oxford University Act 1860, this part of this title post for Craven scholarships ranking as University emoluments.

Residents. There must be an actual as distinct from a constructive residence (*R v Vice-Chancellor of Oxford* (1872) LR 7 QB 471, 26 LT 506.).

SCHEDULES

SCHEDULE A

Section 16

Deputy Steward.

Public Orator.

Keeper of the Archives.

Assessor of the Vice-Chancellor's Court.

Registrar of the University.

Counsel to the University.

Bodley's Librarian.

Radcliffe Librarian.

Radcliffe Observer.

Librarians and Sub-Librarians of University Libraries.
Keepers of University Museums and Repositories of
  Art or Science. } If authorized for the purposes of this schedule by statute of the University.

CAMBRIDGE UNIVERSITY ACT 1856
(19 & 20 Vict c 88)

ARRANGEMENT OF SECTIONS

An Act to make further Provision for the good Government and Extension of the University of Cambridge, of the Colleges therein, and of the College of King Henry the Sixth at Eton
[29 July 1856]

The short title to this Act was given by the Short Titles Act 1896.

Police authority. The police authority for any police area consisting of or including the City of Cambridge must include five persons representing the University of Cambridge; see the Police Act 1964, s 25(5), Vol 33, title Police.

1–4 *(Repealed by the SLR Act 1875.)*

5 Constitution of the University—Establishment of Council of the Senate

. . . Upon the seventh day of . . . the month of November one thousand eight hundred and fifty-six there shall be elected in manner herein-after mentioned a Council, which shall be called the Council of the Senate, and which shall consider and prepare all graces to be offered to the Senate, whether proceeding from individual members of the Senate or from syndicates; and no grace shall be offered to the senate without the sanction of the major part of those voting upon it in the Council.

NOTES

The words omitted were repealed by the SLR Act 1892.

Senate. This is the legislative body of the University. The Council offers to the Senate proposals for confirmation or rejection.

Syndicates. These are appointed by the University to administer various departments of University business.

6 Composition of Council

The Council of the Senate shall consist of the Chancellor, the Vice-Chancellor, four heads of colleges, four professors of the University, and eight other members of the Senate, such eight members to be chosen from the electoral roll herein-after mentioned, and such heads of colleges, professors, and members of the Senate to be elected by the persons whose names shall be on such electoral roll: Provided always, that there shall never be more than two members of the same college among such eight elected members.

NOTE

Electoral roll. See ss 7 and 8 post.

7 Annual list of resident members of Senate

The Vice-Chancellor shall ... on or before the second Monday in October in every year, cause to be promulgated, in such way as may to him seem expedient for the purpose of giving publicity thereto, a list of the members of the Senate whom he shall ascertain to have resided within one mile and a half of Great St. Mary's Church for fourteen weeks at the least between the first day of the preceding Michaelmas term and the first day of the said month of October; and such list, together with the following persons, (that is to say,) all officers of the University being members of the Senate, the heads of houses, the professors, and the public examiners, shall be the electoral roll of the University for the purposes of this Act.

NOTES

The words omitted were repealed by the SLR Act 1892.

Electoral roll. As to notice of objection to the electoral roll, see the Universities of Oxford and Cambridge Act 1877, s 61 post.

8 Such lists to be the electoral roll for a year

The Vice-Chancellor shall at the same time fix some convenient time and place, not more than fourteen nor less than seven days from the time of such promulgation, for publicly hearing objections to the said list, which any member of the Senate may make on the ground of any person being improperly placed on or omitted from the said list; and if any such objections shall appear to the Vice-Chancellor to be well founded, he shall correct the said list accordingly, and he shall thereupon sign and promulgate the said list, which shall thenceforth be the electoral roll for the year thence next ensuing, and until a new roll shall in like manner have been promulgated.

NOTE

As to notice of objection to electoral roll, see further the Universities of Oxford and Cambridge Act 1877, s 61, this part of this title post.

9 *(Repealed by the SLR Act 1875.)*

10 Supply of vacancies in Council

The places of the members of the Council vacating their seats shall be supplied by a new election, to be made on the seventh of November, or in case the seventh of November should be Sunday on the eighth of November, in every other year, in the same manner as is herein-before prescribed as to the election to take place on the seventh day of November one thousand eight hundred and fifty-six, save only that all members of the Council to be then elected shall be elected to hold office for four years; and all members so vacating their seats shall (if otherwise eligible) be capable of re-election.

11 Casual vacancies

Any casual vacancy occurring by death, resignation, or otherwise among the members of the Council shall be filled by the election of a qualified person, according to the directions of this Act, upon a day not later than twenty-one days or sooner than seven days after such occurrence, to be fixed by the Vice-Chancellor, and publicly notified by him; but, if such vacancy shall occur during vacation, the occurrence shall be deemed for the purpose of such notice to have taken place on the first day of the ensuing term; and the person so elected shall be subject to the same rules and conditions as to the tenure of office, and in all other respects, as the person to whose place he succeeds would have been subject to if no such vacancy had taken place.

12 Votes of electors

In all elections of members of the Council every elector may vote for any number of persons, being heads of colleges, professors, or members of the Senate as aforesaid respectively, not exceeding the number of heads of colleges, professors, or members of the Senate respectively to be then chosen; and in case of an equality of votes for any two or more of such heads of colleges, professors, or members of the Senate respectively, the Vice-Chancellor shall name from amongst those persons for whom the number of votes shall be equal as many as shall be requisite to complete the number of heads of colleges, professors, or members of the Senate to be then chosen.

13 Absence from meetings for one term to create a vacancy

If any member of the Council, other than the Chancellor or the Vice-Chancellor, shall have been absent from all the meetings of the Council during the whole of one term, his seat shall at the close of such term become and shall be declared by the Vice-Chancellor to be vacant.

14 Member of Council becoming Vice-Chancellor, etc, not to vacate seat

If any member of the Council shall become Vice-Chancellor, his seat shall not thereby become vacant, nor shall the seat of any member of the Council become vacant by reason that after his election he may have become or may have ceased to be a professor or a head of a college: Provided always, that if any of the eight members of the Senate chosen from the electoral roll as aforesaid shall afterwards cease to be on the electoral roll, his seat shall thereupon become and be declared to be vacant.

15 All professors eligible

No professor shall be ineligible for the Council by reason of anything contained in the statutes of his foundation.

NOTE
>   **Professors.** See s 50 post.

---

16 *(Repealed by the SLR Act 1875.)*

17 Power to Council to make rules and to appoint committees

Subject to the provisions of this Act, and without prejudice to the rights of the Senate in the making of statutes, regulations, and ordinances for the University of Cambridge, the Council shall have power from time to time to make rules for the regulation of its own proceedings, and to revise or alter the regulations herein-before directed to be made by the Vice-Chancellor, or, in the case of his failing to do so, by the Commissioners, and also to appoint committees for the purpose of examining all questions referred to them by the said Council.

NOTES
>   **Regulations . . . made by the Vice-Chancellor.** By s 16 (repealed) the Vice-Chancellor was to make regulations respecting the Council, and in his default they were to be made by the Commissioners.
>   **Commissioners.** These were appointed under s 1 (repealed). Their powers were to continue until 1 January 1860, at the latest.

---

18 *(Repealed by the SLR Act 1875.)*

19 President of the Council

The President of the Council shall be the Chancellor, or in his absence the Vice-Chancellor, or a member of the Council appointed by the Vice-Chancellor to act as his deputy, or if at any Council duly convened and assembled neither the Chancellor nor the Vice-Chancellor nor any deputy so appointed shall be present, then some member to be chosen by the members of the Council then assembled.

20 Quorum of Council

No business shall be transacted in the Council unless five members at least be present; and all questions in the Council shall be decided by the majority of the votes of the members present, and the President shall have a second or casting vote when the votes are equally divided: Provided always, that in case of a difference of opinion between the Chancellor, or the Vice-Chancellor, or his deputy, and the majority of the members present at any meeting of the Council, the question as to which such difference may exist shall not be deemed to be carried by such majority unless the same shall constitute a majority of the whole Council, but in such case the question shall be adjourned to the next meeting of the Council, and such adjourned question shall be finally decided by the majority of the members of Council then present.

21 Council to nominate two persons to Senate for each office

The Council shall nominate two qualified persons to the Senate, of whom the Senate shall choose one, in the manner heretofore accustomed, to fill every vacant office in the University to which the heads of colleges have heretofore nominated two persons to the Senate; Provided always, that the persons nominated as aforesaid to the office of Vice-Chancellor shall be heads of colleges.

22 Certain oaths illegal

Every oath directly or indirectly binding the juror—

Not to disclose any matter or thing relating to his college, although required so to do by lawful authority;

To resist or not concur in any change in the statutes of the University or college;

To do or forbear from doing anything the doing or the not doing of which would tend to any such concealment, resistance, or non-occurrence;

shall from the time of the passing of this Act be an illegal oath in the said University and the colleges thereof; and no such oath shall hereafter be administered or taken.

23 Licence by Vice-Chancellor to members of the University to receive students

Any member of the University, of such standing and qualifications as may be provided by any statute hereafter to be made, may obtain a licence from the Vice-Chancellor to open his residence, if situate within one mile and a half of Great Saint Mary's Church, for the reception of students, who shall be matriculated and admitted to all the privileges of the University, without being of necessity entered as members of any college; . . .

NOTES

The words omitted were repealed by the SLR Act 1875.

Matriculation. This is effected by signing the University register.

24 Licencees to be called principals

Every person to whom such licence is granted shall be called a principal; and his residence so opened as aforesaid shall be called a hostel.

NOTE

Hostel. A hostel corresponds to a private hall at Oxford; see the Oxford University Act 1854, this part of this title ante.

25–31 (Repealed by the SLR Act 1875.)

32 University may provide that members of Senate may vote at election of Chancellor or High Steward by proxy

The University may provide by statute that members of the Senate may vote at any election of a Chancellor or High Steward of the University by proxy, such proxy being a member of the Senate authorized by an instrument in writing signed by the member nominating such proxy; but no member shall be entitled to vote as a proxy unless the instrument appointing him has been transmitted to the Vice-Chancellor not less than forty-eight hours before the time appointed for holding such election of a Chancellor or High Steward, as the case may be; and such instrument may be in the form contained in the schedule to this Act annexed.

33–35 (Repealed by the SLR Act 1875.)

36 Westminster exhibitions at Trinity College

. . . No such exhibition shall be held for more than three years and a quarter, and no such exhibitioner shall by holding such exhibition be disqualified from being elected a scholar of the said college.

NOTES

The words omitted were repealed by the SLR Act 1875.

Such exhibition. Ie an exhibition from Westminster School to Trinity College, referred to in the repealed part of this section, which also provided that not more than three exhibitioners may be received annually at Trinity College from Westminster School.

37–41 (*Repealed by the SLR Act 1875.*)

42 Power to the Chancellor to settle doubts as to meaning of University statutes

If any doubt shall arise with respect to the true intent and meaning of any of the new statutes of the University framed and approved as aforesaid, or of any statute which may hereafter be approved in the manner herein-after mentioned for amending or altering the same, the Council may apply to the Chancellor of the University for the time being, and it shall be lawful for him to declare in writing the intent and meaning of the statute on the matter submitted to him; and such declaration shall be registered by the registrary of the University, and the intent and meaning of the statute, as therein declared, shall be deemed the true intent and meaning thereof.

NOTES

This and the next section were repealed by the SLR Act 1892, but revived by the SLR (No 2) Act 1893, s 3.

New Statutes. These were to be framed under s 30 (repealed). See also the Universities of Oxford and Cambridge Act 1877, s 52, this part of this title post.

43 Statutes, etc, to be subject to appeal, etc

Every statute made in pursuance of the provisions of this Act by the University, or by any college, or by the Commissioners, and likewise all provisions herein-before contained respecting the election, constitution, powers, and proceedings of the Council of the Senate, or respecting hostels, shall be subject to repeal, amendment, and alteration from time to time by the University or college, as the case may be, with the approval of Her Majesty in Council.

NOTES

See the first note to s 42 ante.

Commissioners. See the note to s 17 ante.

44 (*Repealed by the SLR Act 1875.*)

45 No oath on matriculation

. . . No person shall be required, upon matriculating, . . . in the said University, to take any oath or to make any declaration or subscription whatever: . . .

NOTES

The words omitted were repealed by the SLR Act 1892, the SLR Act 1875, and the Universities Tests Act 1871.

Matriculation. See the note to s 23 ante.

46 No declaration as to religious belief on obtaining any exhibition, etc

. . . It shall not be necessary for any person, on obtaining any exhibition, scholarship, or other college emolument available for the assistance of an undergraduate student in his academical education, to make or subscribe any declaration of his religious opinion or belief, or to take any oath, any law or statute to the contrary notwithstanding.

NOTE
The words omitted were repealed by the SLR Act 1892.

47, 48 (*S 47 repealed by the SLR Act 1875, s 48 repealed by the Universities and College Estates Act 1858, s 5.*)

49 Powers of University and colleges to continue in force, except as altered by this Act

Except in so far as they are expressly altered or taken away by the provisions of this Act, the powers and privileges of the University and its officers, and of the colleges and their officers, shall continue in full force.

50 Interpretation

In the construction of this Act, the expression "University or college emolument" shall include all headships, Downing professorships, fellowships, bye-fellowships, scholarships, exhibitions, Bible clerkships, sizarships, subsizarships, and every other such place of emolument payable out of the revenues of the University, or of any college, or to be held and enjoyed by the members of any college as such within the University; and the word "professor" shall be taken to include the three royal professors of Hebrew, Greek, and divinity, and public readers or lecturers in the University, except the Barnaby lecturers; and the governing body of any college shall mean the head and all actual fellows thereof, bye-fellows excepted, being graduates, and in Downing College shall mean the head, professors, and all actual fellows thereof, bye-fellows excepted, being graduates; and the word "statutes" shall be taken to include all ordinances and regulations of the University, and all ordinances and regulations contained in any charter, deed of composition, or other instrument of foundation or endowment of a college, and all bye-laws, ordinances, and regulations; and the word "vacation" shall be taken to include that part of Easter term which falls after the division of term.

NOTE
Downing professorships. The professorship in medicine has been discontinued, but there is a Downing Professorship of the Law of England, which is entirely a University professorship.

51 Acquisition of lands, etc, and penalties

The Lands Clauses Consolidation Act 1845, except the parts and enactments of that Act with respect to the purchase and taking of lands otherwise than by agreement, and with respect to the recovery of forfeitures, penalties, and costs, and with respect to lands required by the promoters of the undertaking, but which shall not be wanted for the purposes thereof, shall be incorporated with and form part of this Act, so far as relates to land within the town of Cambridge required for the erection of any buildings for the extension of the buildings of the said University, or of any college therein, and as if the corporate name of the University or college, as the case may be, had been inserted therein instead of the expression "the promoters of the undertaking."

NOTES

   Acquisition of lands. See also the Universities and College Estates Act 1925, s 34, this part of this title post.
   Lands Clauses Consolidation Act 1845. See Vol 9, title Compulsory Acquisition.

52, 53 (*Repealed by the SLR Act 1875.*)

SCHEDULE
Section 32

A.B.,   , a member of the Senate, doth hereby appoint *C.D.,*   , a member of the Senate, to be the proxy of the said *A.B.* in his absence, and to vote in his name at the election of a Chancellor, *or* High Steward, *as the case may be*, for the University of Cambridge, on the   day of   next, in such manner as he the said *C.D.* may think proper. In witness whereof the said *A.B.*   hath hereunto set his hand, the   day of

(Signature)   *A.B.*

OXFORD UNIVERSITY ACT 1857
(20 & 21 Vict c 25)

An Act to continue the Powers of the Commissioners under an Act of the Seventeenth and Eighteenth years of Her Majesty concerning the University of Oxford and the College of St. Mary Winchester, and further to amend the said Act   [10 August 1857]

   The short title to this Act was given by the Short Titles Act 1896.

1, 2 (*Repealed by the SLR Act 1875.*)

3 Colleges may apply property held for purchase of advowsons

It shall be lawful for any college within the University from time to time, with consent of the visitor, to appropriate and apply any property, or the income of any property, held by or in trust for the college, for the purpose that the same, or the income thereof, may be applied in purchasing advowsons for the benefit of the college, to the augmentation of the endowment of livings in the patronage of the college to such amount as may be by law allowed, or towards the building of fit and suitable parsonage houses on any livings in the patronage of the college, or to the foundation or augmentation of scholarships or exhibitions, or to other purposes for the advancement of religion, learning, and education within the college; and in exercise of this power the college may annex to any living in the patronage of the college (by way of augmentation of the endowment of such living) any tithe rentcharge which may be vested in the college, or any portion thereof, in consideration of the appropriation to other purposes of the college of a part of the trust property or income, not exceeding the amount which the visitor shall adjudge to be an adequate consideration for the tithe rentcharge so to be annexed: Provided that this power shall not extend to property or income applicable to the purchase of advowsons for the benefit of scholars or exhibitioners on any particular foundation within a college.

NOTES

Advowsons. As to advowsons, see the note to the Oxford and Cambridge Act 1571, s 3, this part of this title ante and, as to the restriction on sale of patronage rights, see the Benefices Act 1898 (Amendment) Measure 1923, Vol 14, title Ecclesiastical Law (Pt 3(b)).

Tithe rentcharge. By the Tithe Act 1936, s 1, Vol 14, title Ecclesiastical Law (Pt 9), tithe rentcharge was extinguished and a redemption annuity issued as compensation.

4 Incorporation of 8 & 9 Vict c 18

The Lands Clauses Consolidation Act 1845, except the parts and enactments of that Act with respect to the purchase and taking of lands otherwise than by agreement, and with respect to the recovery of forfeitures, penalties, and costs, and with respect to lands required by the promoters of the undertaking, but which shall not be wanted for the purposes thereof, shall be incorporated with and form part of this Act and of the Oxford University Act 1854, so far as relates to land within one mile and a half of Carfax in the City of Oxford required for the erection of any buildings for the extension of the buildings of the said University or of any college or hall therein, or for purposes of utility or recreation relating to the said University or to any college or hall therein, and as if the corporate name of the University or college, as the case may be, had been inserted therein instead of the expression "the promoters of the undertaking."

NOTES

Acquisition of land. See also the University and College Estates Act 1925, s 34, this part of this title post.
Lands Clauses Consolidation Act 1845. See Vol 9, title Compulsory Acquisition.
Oxford University Act 1854. See this part of this title ante.

OXFORD UNIVERSITY ACT 1860

(23 & 24 Vict c 91)

An Act for removing Doubts respecting the Craven Scholarships in the University of Oxford, and for enabling the University to retain the Custody of certain Testamentary Documents   [13 August 1860]

The short title was given to this Act by the Short Titles Act 1896.
Northern Ireland. This Act does not apply.

1 Scholarships founded by the will of Lord Craven to be deemed University emoluments within 17 & 18 Vict c 81

. . . The Craven Scholarships shall be deemed to be University emoluments within the meaning of the said Act; and . . . all statutes or regulations which heretofore and since the passing of the said Act have been made by the University and approved by Her Majesty in Council, conformably to the conditions and provisions of the said Act, in relation to the said Craven Scholarships, shall have the same force and effect as if the said Scholarships had been expressly named and included in the said Act as University emoluments; and in elections to the said Scholarships no person shall be entitled to preference by reason of his being of the name or kindred of the founder: Provided that nothing herein or in the said Act or in such statutes or regulations contained shall preclude the [High Court] from augmenting from time to time the number of scholars, whenever the increased income of the foundation shall permit.

NOTES

The words omitted were repealed by the SLR Act 1892.

The reference to the High Court was substituted by virtue of the Supreme Court of Judicature (Consolidation) Act 1925, s 224(1) (repealed).

Craven Scholarships. Craven Scholarships are six in number and of the value of £80 a year each, tenable for two years. Candidates must not have exceeded twelve terms (three terms to a year) from matriculation. The scholarships are given for classics.

University scholarships. University scholarships are not, like College scholarships, awarded to persons intending to become members of the University, but are given after examination or competition, which is generally open only to members of the University of a specified standing.

University emoluments. See the definition in the Oxford University Act 1854, s 48, this part of this title ante.

Said Act. The Act referred to is the Oxford University Act 1854, this part of this title ante.

---

2 (*Repealed by the Supreme Court of Judicature (Consolidation) Act 1925, s 226, Sch 6.*)

OXFORD UNIVERSITY ACT 1862

(25 & 26 Vict c 26)

ARRANGEMENT OF SECTIONS

An Act to extend the Power of making Statutes possessed by the University of Oxford, and to make further Provision for the Administration of Justice in the Court of the Chancellor of the said University   [30 June 1862]

Construction. This Act is to be construed together with the Oxford University, Vinerian Foundation, Act 1865; see s 2 of that Act, this part of this title post, and the note thereto for meaning and effect of that provision.

1 Power to University to make regulations as to professorships specified in schedule

The University of Oxford may make statutes for the regulation of the professorships specified in the schedule annexed hereto in respect of the following matters; that is to say:—

> 1.   The functions and duties of each of the professors holding the said professorships:
>
> 2.   The fees, if any, to be charged for admittance to the lectures of each professor:
>
> 3.   The determination of the periods during which each professor is to reside in the University; the authority in whom a power of granting leave of absence is to be vested; and the mode of enforcing the required residence:

4. The appointment of a temporary substitute for each professor in case of his illness or temporary absence with leave, and of a permanent substitute in case of his being permanently incapacitated by old age or infirmity:

5. The remuneration of any such temporary or permanent substitute out of the income of the professor in whose place he is substituted:

6. The constitution of a court or other authority empowered to admonish and, if necessary, remove a professor guilty of notable negligence or inefficiency in conducting the duties of his office, or of immorality.

NOTE

Making of statutes. As to the method of making statutes, see the Oxford University Act 1854, s 17, this part of this title ante. For procedure under this Act, see s 7 post.

2 University may determine mode of election, etc, to professorships

The University may by statute determine in respect of each of the professorships specified in the said schedule (other than the Professorship of Political Economy and the Sherard Professorship of Botany) how and by whom upon the occasion of the next or any subsequent avoidance of such professorship the professor is to be elected; and in the case of the Sherard Professorship of Botany therein named, the professor shall be appointed by the President and Council for the time being of the Royal College of Physicians of London; and the said University may, with the consent of the said President and Council of the College of Physicians, vary and define the qualifications of candidates for election to the said Sherard Professorship.

NOTE

Professor, professorship. For definitions, see s 11 post.

3 Power to suppress certain professorships, etc

If at any time hereafter a new professorship of political economy, chemistry, geology or mineralogy is established in the University of Oxford, it shall be lawful for the University by statute to suppress the existing professorship of that science for which provision is made by a new professorship; and after the suppression of any professorship authorized to be suppressed by this section, the annual sum now payable by the University as a salary to the professor holding the suppressed professorship shall be applied in promoting and assisting, by the purchase of materials or apparatus, by the support of assistant teachers, or by such other means as the University may by statute determine, the study and cultivation in the University of the science which forms the subject matter of the suppressed professorship: Provided, that if the Professorship of Mineralogy is suppressed, the annual sum thereby rendered disposable may, if it be thought fit, be applied in manner aforesaid to the promotion of the study of geology or any branch thereof; and if the Professorship of Geology be suppressed, the annual sum may, if it be thought fit, be applied to the promotion of the study of mineralogy or any branch thereof.

NOTE

Professor, professorship. For definitions, see s 11 post.

4 Power of suppression to extend to professorships attached to a college

The power hereby given to the University of suppressing any of the said Professorships of Political Economy, Chemistry, Geology, or Mineralogy may be exercised although the new professorship substituted for any suppressed professorship is a professorship attached to a college, and established under a statute of such college now in force, if the functions and duties of such new professorship are subject to regulation by the University, and are not confined to the instruction of members of the college.

NOTE

Professorship. For definition, see s 11 post.

5 Elections to certain professorships may be declared subject to power of suppression

The election or appointment of any person who may be hereafter elected or appointed to any of the said Professorships of Political Economy, Chemistry, Geology, and Mineralogy may if it be thought fit, be declared by statute of the University to be subject to the operation of any statute for the suppression of the professorship that may afterwards be made or come into operation.

NOTE

Professorship. For definition, see s 11 post.

6 Variation of the trusts of certain scholarships

The University may vary by statute the directions, trusts, or regulations relating to the Kennicott Scholarships, and to the Johnson Scholarships, and to the Denyer Theological Prizes, with a view of promoting the study of theology, Hebrew, and mathematics respectively, and may for that purpose, if it be deemed advisable, convert the Denyer Theological Prizes into a theological scholarship or scholarships.

NOTE

Scholarships affected. At the present time one Kennicott Hebrew Fellow may be elected every three years. The Denyer and Johnson Senior Theological Scholarship is awarded every other year. The Denyer and Johnson Junior Scholarship is now the Denyer and Johnson Prize, value £100, awarded annually. The Senior Mathematical Scholarship is now a prize, one or two prizes may be awarded annually, and the value of the award is increased by the "Johnson University Prize".

7 Approbation of statutes by Her Majesty in Council, etc

Every statute passed by the University by virtue of this Act shall with all convenient speed after the passing thereof be laid before Her Majesty in Council, and forthwith published in the London Gazette; and any person or body corporate affected thereby may within a month after the publication thereof petition Her Majesty in Council against the same or any part thereof; and every such petition shall be referred by Her Majesty by Order in Council for the consideration and advice of five members of Her Privy Council, of whom two, not including the Lord President, shall be members of the Judicial Committee; and such five members may, if they think fit, admit any petitioner to be heard by counsel in support of his petition; and if, no such petition having been presented, or if, after any petition so presented has been referred and considered, such five members of the Privy Council, or the major part thereof, shall report to Her Majesty their opinion that such statute should be approved with or without modifications, the said statute or modified statute shall be forthwith laid before both Houses of Parliament, if Parliament be then sitting, or, if not, then within three weeks after the commencement of the then next ensuing session of Parliament, and, unless an address be within forty days presented by one or other of the said Houses, praying Her Majesty to withhold her consent from such statute or modified statute, or any part thereof, it shall be lawful for Her Majesty, if she think fit, to declare by Order in Council her approbation of the statute or modified statute; and the same shall thereupon become a statute of the University of Oxford, notwithstanding any Act of Parliament, decree or order, deed or instrument of foundation or endowment; and if the statute or any part thereof is not so approved by Her Majesty, the University may frame and pass another statute in the matter, and so on from time to time as often as occasion requires.

NOTE

Judicial Committee. The Judicial Committee of the Privy Council was set up by the Judicial Committee Act 1833, s 1, Vol 11, title Courts. It consists of the President of the Privy Council, the Lord Keeper or first Lord Commissioner of the Great Seal of England and all privy councillors who have held these offices or hold or have held high judicial office. As to its constitution, jurisdiction and fund, and generally, see 10 Halsbury's Laws (4th edn) paras 767–838.

8 Power of altering statutes made under this Act

Every statute made by the University by virtue of this Act shall be subject to alteration or repeal by the University, with the approval of Her Majesty in Council.

9 Alteration and repeal of University statutes

Every statute of the University made in pursuance of the Oxford University Act 1854, which has been approved by Her Majesty in Council, shall . . . be subject to alteration and repeal by the University, with the approval of Her Majesty in Council.

NOTES

The words omitted were repealed by the SLR Act 1893.
Oxford University Act 1854. See this part of this title ante.

10 Saving of powers and rights

This Act shall not be construed to take away or affect any power of making statutes or regulations now possessed by the University or by any college therein, nor shall it prejudice or affect any interest vested in any member of the University previously to the passing of this Act.

11 Interpretation of terms

In the construction of this Act the words "professor" and "professorship" respectively shall include public readers and praelectors, and their several offices.

12 Power to Vice-Chancellor to make rules for regulation of his Court

. . . The Vice Chancellor of the said University may from time to time, with the approval of any three of the judges of Her Majesty's Superior Courts, make rules for regulating the practice and forms of procedure in all proceedings within the jurisdiction of the Court of the Chancellor of the said University commonly called the Vice-Chancellor's Court, and may from time to time, with the like approval, annul, alter, or add to any such rules.

NOTES

The words omitted were repealed by the SLR Act 1893.
Jurisdiction of the Vice-Chancellor's Court. See 10 Halsbury's Laws (4th edn) para 981.

13 Short title

This Act may be cited for all purposes as "The Oxford University Act 1862".

SCHEDULE

Section 1

The Professorship of Political Economy.

The Readership in Experimental Philosophy.

The Sherard Professorship of Botany.

The Aldrich Professorship of Chemistry.

The Readership in Geology.

The Readership in Mineralogy.

OXFORD UNIVERSITY, VINERIAN FOUNDATION, ACT 1865

(28 & 29 Vict c 55)

An Act to empower the University of Oxford to make statutes as to the Vinerian Foundation in that University   [29 June 1865]

1 Statutes as to the Vinerian foundation

... The said University may, with the view of better promoting the teaching and study of the law in the said University, vary by statute all or any of the directions, trusts, and regulations now in force relating to the Vinerian professorship and the Vinerian fellowship and scholarships respectively, and to the application of the funds held in trust by the said University under the will of Charles Viner, Esquire, deceased: Provided, that part of the income of such funds shall always be applied to the teaching of law, and the residue towards encouraging the study of the law, by means of fellowships or scholarships, or both, and that the name of the said Charles Viner, or the title Vinerian, shall always be retained in connexion with the said foundation: ...

NOTES

The words omitted were repealed by the SLR Act 1893.

Vinerian professorship. The professor's proper title is "The Vinerian Professor of English Law".

Vinerian scholarship. The Vinerian Scholarship is a University Scholarship, the subject matter of which is law, and it is intended for a legal student.

2 Application of 25 & 26 Vict c 26

All the provisions of the Oxford University Act 1862, as to statutes of the University passed by virtue thereof, shall extend and apply to statutes of the University made by virtue of this Act; and the Oxford University Act 1862, and this Act, shall be construed together as one Act.

NOTES

Construed together. Ie the enactments in question are to be construed as if they were contained in one Act, unless there is some manifest discrepancy; see eg *Phillips v Parnaby* [1934] 2 KB 299 at 302. Accordingly, definitions in the earlier Act may be relevant to the construction of provisions of this Act (see *Solomons v R Gertzenstein Ltd* [1954] 2 QB 243, [1954] 2 All ER 625, CA; *Crowe (Valuation Officer) v Lloyds British Testing Co Ltd* [1960] 1 QB 592, [1960] 1 All ER 411, CA).

Oxford University Act 1862. See this part of this title ante.

3 Short title

This Act may be cited for all purposes as "The Oxford University, Vinerian Foundation, Act 1865".

PUBLIC SCHOOLS ACT 1868

(31 & 32 Vict c 118)

ARRANGEMENT OF SECTIONS

Preliminary

An Act to make further provision for the good government and extension of certain public schools in England   [31 July 1868]

The Public Schools Acts 1868 to 1873, apply only to the schools mentioned in s 3 of this Act post (see 15 Halsbury's Laws (4th edn) paras 296–299).

Public Schools Acts 1868 to 1873. By virtue of the Short Titles Act 1896, Vol 41, title Statutes, the following Acts may be cited together by this collective title: the Public Schools Act 1868 (this Act); the Public Schools Act 1869; the Public Schools Act 1871; the Public Schools (Shrewsbury and Harrow Schools Property) Act 1873; and the Public Schools (Eton College Property) Act 1873 (repealed). These Acts are all printed in this part of this title post.

Construction. This Act is to be construed as one with the Public Schools Act 1869; see s 4 of that Act, this part of this title post.

Preliminary

1 Short title

This Act may be cited for all purposes as "The Public Schools Act 1868".

2 "School"

"School" includes, in the case of Eton and Winchester, Eton College and Winchester College.

3 Definition of "existing governing body": "new governing body"

"Existing governing Body" of a school shall for the purposes of this Act mean—

(1) At Eton, the provost and fellows:

(2) At Winchester, the warden and fellows:

(3) At Westminster, the dean and chapter of Westminster, the dean of Christ Church, Oxford, and the master of Trinity College, Cambridge:

(4) At Charterhouse, the governors:

(5) At Harrow, the governors:

(6) At Rugby, the trustees:

(7) At Shrewsbury, the trustees:

"New governing body of a school" shall for the purposes of this Act mean a governing body the constitution of which has been altered in pursuance of this Act, or, if no alteration shall have been made, the governing body which shall be in existence at the end of the time assigned by this Act for making such alteration, or a body which has been established under this Act as the new governing body of a school.

NOTE

Foundation of schools. The seven schools mentioned in this section were founded as follows:

(1) Eton (The College of the Blessed Mary of Eton) by Henry VI in 1440.
(2) Winchester (The Saint Mary College of Winchester) by William of Wykeham in 1382.
(3) Westminster (St Peter's College) before 1339, and refounded by Queen Elizabeth in 1561.
(4) Charterhouse by Thomas Sutton in 1611.
(5) Harrow by John Lyon in 1571.
(6) Rugby by Lawrence Sheriff in 1567.
(7) Shrewsbury by Edward VI in 1552.

---

4 Definition of "boys on the foundation"

Boys on the foundation shall for the purposes of this Act mean—

(1) At Eton, the King's scholars or scholars belonging to the College of Eton:

(2) At Winchester, the scholars belonging to the College of St. Mary, Winchester:

(3) At Westminster, the Queen's scholars:

(4) At Charterhouse, the foundation scholars or boys nominated by the governors, and entitled to receive gratuitous education:

(5) At Harrow, the boys entitled to education wholly or partially gratuitous:

(6) At Rugby, the boys entitled to education wholly or partially gratuitous by reason of their being sons of residents in Rugby or within a certain distance of Rugby:

(7) At Shrewsbury, the boys entitled to education wholly or partially gratuitous by reason of their being sons of burgesses.

NOTE

Rugby. As to qualifications for admission of scholars to Rugby, see *Re Rugby School* (1839) 1 Beav 457.

Statutes by Governing Bodies

5 Powers to governing bodies of schools to which this Act applies to alter their constitutions—Governing body of Westminster

... Any governing body established for Westminster school shall be a body corporate, with a perpetual succession and a common seal ..., and subject to the provisions of this Act shall, as to leasing their land, have the same powers and be subject to the same disabilities as may be possessed by or attached to the dean and chapter of Westminster in respect of lands in their possession.

NOTES

The words omitted in the first place were repealed by the SL(R) Act 1973, Schedule, Pt XI, Vol 41, title Statutes, with a saving in respect of any statute or scheme which, immediately before 18 July 1973, was in force by virtue of this section; the words omitted in the second place were repealed by the Charities Act 1960, s 48(2), Sch 7, Pt II.

Governing body as body corporate. By the Public Schools Act 1869, s 2, this part of this title post, the governing body of any of the schools to which this Act applies (see s 3 ante) is to be a body corporate.

6 (*Repealed with a saving in respect of any statute or scheme which, immediately before 18 July 1973 was in force, by the SL(R) Act 1973, Schedule, Pt XI, Vol 41, title* Statutes.)

7 Power to governing bodies to consolidate and amend existing statutes and regulations

The new governing body of any school to which this Act applies may, by statute made in manner herein provided, consolidate and amend any existing statutes or regulations relating to such school, whether in force by Act of Parliament, charter, judicial decree, instrument of endowment, or otherwise, with power to repeal any statute or regulation that has in the opinion of that body become obsolete, or has become incapable of observance by reason of changes authorized to be made under this Act.

NOTES

New governing body. See s 3 ante.

Statute made in manner herein provided. Ie by s 6 of this Act; that section was repealed, as from 18 July 1973, by the SL(R) Act 1973, Schedule, Pt XI, Vol 41, title Statutes, with a saving in respect of any statute or scheme which immediately before that date was in force by virtue of that section. Accordingly this section and ss 8–11 post now only have effect in relation to such statutes and schemes.

A list of the Statutes approved by Orders in Council under this power, and in force on 1 January 1893, is given in the Second (1893) Edn of the Index to SR & O, Appendix XXIII (Public Schools, England).

8 Restrictions on making statutes, as herein stated

The following restrictions shall be imposed on any governing body of a school making statutes under this Act:

(1) Where two or more schools are interested in any scholarship, exhibition, or emolument, a statute made by the governing body of one school shall not affect the interest of any other school, except with the consent of a majority of the governors, trustees, or other governing body of the last-mentioned school:

(2) Where any statute proposed to be made by any governing body of a school affects any scholarship, exhibition or emolument attached to any college in either of the Universities of Oxford and Cambridge, notice in writing of such intended statute shall be given to the head of such college ...

(3) Where any statute proposed to be made by any governing body of a school affects the interests of any person or class of persons deriving benefit under the institutions in force with respect to the same, a copy of such proposed statute shall be deposited in some convenient place for public inspection in the locality in which such school is situated; and notice of such copy having been so deposited shall be given in some newspaper circulating in such locality ... ; and the said governing body shall hear all objections which such persons or class of persons may be desirous of urging against the same:

(4) No statute made by any governing body of a school under this Act shall be of any validity until the same has been approved by Her Majesty in Council as herein-after mentioned, but when so approved all the requisitions of this Act in respect thereto shall be deemed to have been duly complied with, and the statute shall be of the same force as if it had been contained in this Act, subject nevertheless to the power of alteration or repeal herein-after conferred.

NOTES

The words omitted were repealed by the SL(R) Act 1973.

Statutes under this Act. See the note "Statute made in manner herein provided" to s 7 ante.

Two or more schools interested. For a case where two or more schools were interested in exhibitions, see *A-G v Dean and Chapter of Christ Church, Oxford* [1894] 3 Ch 524, 63 LJ Ch 901.

Approval by Privy Council. See s 9 post.

9 All statutes after approval by Special Commissioners to be laid before Privy Council

All statutes made by any governing body of a school under the powers herein contained shall ... be laid before Her Majesty in Council, and be forthwith published in the London Gazette; and it shall be lawful for the trustees of any scholarship, exhibition, or emolument to which such statute may relate, or for any person or body corporate directly affected thereby, within two months after such publication in the London Gazette, to petition Her Majesty in Council, praying Her Majesty to withhold her approval from the whole or any part of such statute. The petition shall be referred by Her Majesty by Order in Council for the consideration and advice of five members at the least of her Privy Council, of whom two, not including the Lord President, shall be members of the Judicial Committee, and such five members may, if they think fit, admit any petitioner or petitioners to be heard by counsel in support of his or their petition.

Any petition not proceeded with in accordance with the regulations made with respect to petitions presented to the Judicial Committee of the Privy Council shall be deemed to be withdrawn.

NOTES

The words omitted were repealed by the SL(R) Act 1973.

Statutes. See the note "Statute made in manner herein provided" to s 7 ante.

10 Her Majesty in Council may approve or disapprove statutes

It shall be lawful for Her Majesty in Council to signify her approval or disapproval of any statute or part of a statute made by any governing body of a school in pursuance of this Act at the times following; that is to say, where a petition has been presented against such statute, at any time after the hearing or withdrawal of such petition, and where no such petition has been presented, at any time after the expiration of the time limited by this Act for the presentation of a petition. If Her Majesty signify her disapproval of any statute, or any part thereof, the governing body of the school which framed the statute may frame another statute in that behalf, subject to the same conditions as to the approval ... of Her Majesty in Council as are imposed by this Act in relation to the making of original statutes by any governing body of a school, and so on from time to time, as often as occasion requires ...

NOTES

The words omitted were repealed by the SL(R) Act 1973.
Statutes. See the note "Statute made in manner herein provided" to s 7 ante.

11 As to repeal or alteration of statutes made in exercise of powers of this Act

Any statute made in exercise of the powers of this Act may at any time or times ... be repealed or altered by the governing body for the time being, in the same manner, and subject to the same provisions ... in and subject to which statutes may be made by the governing body.

NOTES

The words omitted were repealed by the SL(R) Act 1973.
Statutes. See the note "Statute made in manner herein provided" to s 7 ante.

Regulations by Governing Bodies

12 General powers of new governing bodies to make, order, or annul regulations as to matters herein specified

It shall be lawful for the new governing body of every school to which this Act applies, notwithstanding anything contained in any existing Act of Parliament, charter, statute, decree, instrument of foundation or endowment, or other instrument, and notwithstanding any custom, from time to time to make, alter, or annul such regulations as they may deem it expedient to make, alter, or annul with respect to any of the following matters:

(1) With respect to the number of boys, other than boys on the foundation, in the school, their ages, and the conditions of admission to the school:

(2) With respect to the mode in which the boys, whether on the foundation or not, are to be boarded and lodged, and the conditions on which leave to keep a boarding house should be given:

(3) With respect to the payments to be made for the maintenance and education of the boys, other than boys on the foundation, including fees and charges of all kinds, and to payments by boys on the foundation in respect of anything which they are not entitled to receive gratuitously; and with respect to the application of the monies to be derived from those sources, and of monies paid out of the income of the foundation on account of the instruction of boys on the foundation:

(4) With respect to attendance at divine service, and where the school has a chapel of its own, with respect to the chapel services and the appointment of preachers:

(5) With respect to the times and length of the ordinary holidays:

(6) With respect to the sanitary condition of the school, and of the premises connected therewith:

(7) With respect to the introduction of new branches of study, and the suppression of old ones, and the relative importance to be assigned to each branch of study:

(8) With respect to the number, position, and rank in the school, and salaries and emoluments, of the masters, in so far as such masters are not affected by any statute made in accordance with the provisions herein-before contained:

(9) With respect to giving facilities for the education of boys whose parents or guardians wish to withdraw them from the religious instruction given in the school:

(10) With respect to giving facilities for boys other than boarders to attend at the school, and participate in the educational advantages thereof:

(11) With respect to the powers committed to the headmaster:

Provided, that the charges made for the maintenance and education of the boys shall be kept distinct: Provided, that the new governing body, in all cases where the head master is not a member of the body making the regulations, shall before making any such regulations consult the head master in such a manner as to give him full opportunity for the expression of his views: Provided, that it shall be lawful for the head master from time to time to submit proposals for making, altering, or annulling any such regulations, or any other matter affecting the condition of the school, to the governing body, who shall proceed to consider, and, if they think fit, adopt the same.

NOTES

New governing body. See s 3 ante.
Boys on the foundation. See s 4 ante.

Masters

13 Appointment and tenure of office of head and other masters

The head master of every school to which this Act applies shall be appointed by and hold his office at the pleasure of the new governing body. All other masters shall be appointed by and hold their offices at the pleasure of the head master. No candidate for any mastership shall be entitled to preference by reason of his having been a scholar of or educated at the school at which he desires to be master.

NOTES

New governing body. See s 3 ante.
Dismissal of headmaster. The court will not interfere in the case of dismissal of a headmaster (*Hayman v Governors of Rugby School* (1874) LR 18 Eq 28, 43 LJ Ch 834).

14–19 (*S 14 repealed by the SL(R) Act 1973; ss 15–19 repealed by the SLR Act 1893.*)

Miscellaneous

20 Provisions as to Westminster School

The following provisions shall be made with respect to Westminster School; that is to say,

(1) There shall be paid to the governing body of Westminster School for the time being by the Ecclesiastical Commissioners, for the support of the school, an

annual sum of not less than three thousand five hundred pounds, and a capital sum of fifteen thousand pounds:

(2) The annual sum of three thousand five hundred pounds shall be paid by equal half-yearly payments on the twenty-fifth day of March and the twenty-ninth day of September in every year, the first half-yearly payment to be made on the twenty-fifth day of March next after the passing of this Act, and the said capital sum of fifteen thousand pounds on the twenty-ninth day of September next:

(3) The Ecclesiastical Commissioners shall take steps as soon as they can conveniently for transferring to and vesting in the governing body for the time being of Westminster School, and their successors in fee simple, for the support of the school, such a portion of the estates then vested in the Commissioners as may be adequate to produce an annual income of not less than three thousand five hundred pounds, after deducting all expenses of management:

(4) Upon such transfer as aforesaid being effected, the payment of the said annual sum of three thousand five hundred pounds by the Ecclesiastical Commissioners shall cease:

(5) The said capital sum of fifteen thousand pounds shall be invested by the governing body of the school in three pound per centum Bank annuities, and shall be applied in manner herein-after mentioned:

(6) ... There shall vest in the governing body for the time being of Westminster School, for the use of the school, the playground in Vincent Square, with the lodge on such playground, the dormitory with its appurtenances, the school and class rooms, the houses and premises of the head master and under master, the three boarding houses, and the gymnasium, excepting the crypts:

(7) All the said buildings shall be held by the said governing body for the use of the school, and it shall be incumbent on the said governing body to keep as an open space for the recreation of the boys, and for no other purpose, the said playground in Vincent Square:

(8) The hall and the playground in Dean's Yard shall continue to be used in the same manner as heretofore by the scholars of Westminster School:

(9) The dean and chapter of Westminster shall transfer to and vest in the governing body of Westminster School in fee simple the houses following, on the request of such governing body, at such times and upon payment of such sums as are herein-after mentioned; that is to say,

First. The house in Great Dean's Yard now occupied by the rector canon of Saint John the Evangelist, on the next avoidance of the said canonry, and on payment of the sum of four thousand pounds to the Ecclesiastical Commissioners:

Second. The house now occupied by the sub-dean, on the next avoidance of the canonry held by the said sub-dean, and on payment to the said Commissioners of the like sum of four thousand pounds:

Third. The house now occupied by Mr. Turle on the next vacancy in the office of organist of the Collegiate Church, Westminster, and on payment to the said Commissioners of the sum of two thousand pounds:

(10) The governing body of the school shall be at liberty to make the foregoing payments of four thousand pounds, four thousand pounds, and two thousand pounds, or such of them as may be required, out of the said sum of fifteen thousand pounds, and may apply the residue of the said sum in erecting new buildings or improving old buildings, or otherwise in making improvements in or about the property of the school, and they may apply the income arising from any securities on which the said sum of fifteen thousand pounds may for

the time being be invested in the same manner in which the residue of their income is applicable:

(11) The monies paid to the Ecclesiastical Commissioners in respect of the said canonry houses, or either of them, shall be held by the said Commissioners on trust for the dean and chapter of Westminster, to be expended in building on the college gardens, according to plans to be approved by the dean of Westminster for the time being, houses or a house equivalent to the houses or house in respect of which such payments may be made; and in the meantime the Ecclesiastical Commissioners shall allow and pay to the canon or canons who would have been entitled to the occupation of such house or houses if the same had not been so taken for the purposes of Westminster School interest after the rate of three pounds per centum per annum on such monies, or the balances thereof from time to time remaining in the Commissioners hands:

(12) The monies paid to the Ecclesiastical Commissioners in respect of the house now occupied by Mr. Turle, the organist of the Collegiate Church of Westminster, shall be held by the Commissioners in trust for the dean and chapter of Westminster, who shall be entitled to interest thereon after the like rate of three pounds per centum per annum until such capital monies and all balances thereof shall have been expended by the dean and chapter in providing another residence for the organist of their church:

(13) If the dean and chapter of Westminster and the governing body for the time being of Westminster School agree that it would be for the benefit of the school that any premises not herein-before mentioned, and being at the time of such agreement part of the property of the dean and chapter, should become the property of the school, the dean and chapter may convey the same to the school at a price to be agreed upon, or to be settled by an arbitrator to be appointed by the President for the time being of Her Majesty's Most Honourable Privy Council:

(14) Any transfers of lands which in pursuance of this Act may be made by the Ecclesiastical Commissioners to the governing body of Westminster School may be effected under the provisions of a scheme prepared by the Ecclesiastical Commissioners, and approved and ratified by Order of Her Majesty in Council, and published in the London Gazette, and such scheme shall be effectual for transferring to and vesting in the governing body of the school all estates and interests which it purports to transfer, without any conveyance, assurance, or act in the law:

(15) In consideration of the above-mentioned payments of three thousand five hundred pounds per annum and of fifteen thousand pounds, all annual or other sums of money which if this Act had not been passed would have been paid to Westminster School by the said dean and chapter after the twenty-ninth day of September next shall belong and be paid to the Ecclesiastical Commissioners . . . :

(16) In the event of Westminster School being removed beyond the City of Westminster, all the property and income derived by the school from the Ecclesiastical Commissioners, or the dean and chapter of Westminster, or their estates, shall revert to and become vested in the Ecclesiastical Commissioners:

NOTES

The words omitted were repealed by the SLR Act 1893.

Ecclesiastical Commissioners. The functions of this body were transferred to the Church Commissioners by the Church Commissioners Measure 1947, Vol 14, title Ecclesiastical Law (Pt 5(c)).

21 Schemes for additions to or alterations of school buildings

The new governing body of any of the schools to which this Act applies may at any time before the first day of January one thousand eight hundred and seventy, or such further time as may be determined by Her Majesty in Council as herein-after mentioned, submit to the Special Commissioners and, if approved of by any of them, may lay a scheme before Her Majesty in Council for making any additions to or alterations in the buildings of the school, and for raising monies for that purpose by mortgage of any property belonging to or held in trust for the school, with power to suspend any scholarships or exhibitions payable out of such property; they may also in any such scheme make provisions for exchanging any lands belonging to such school for other lands, and for purchasing any land that may be required for making such additions or alterations as aforesaid; and every such scheme shall be subject to the same provisions, and, if approved, shall take effect and be subject to alteration in the same manner as statutes made by a governing body.

NOTES

New governing body. See s 3 ante.

Special Commissioners. The duties of this body terminated on 25 February 1874, by virtue of the Public Schools Act 1872, s 3 (repealed).

Statutes. See the note to s 9 ante.

22–24 *(Ss 22, 24 repealed by the SL(R) Act 1973; s 23 repealed by the SLR Act 1893.)*

25 General provisions as to schemes—Incorporation of parts of the Land Clauses Act

Any scheme authorized to be made under this Act may contain all powers and provisions that may be thought expedient for carrying into effect its objects; and where any scheme authorizes the purchase or acquisition of any lands, there shall be deemed to be incorporated with such scheme the Lands Clauses Consolidation Act 1845, with the exception of the provisions relating to the purchase of lands otherwise than by agreement, and of the provisions relating to entry upon land, to intersected lands, and to the recovery of forfeitures, penalties, and costs, and of the provisions relating to access to the special Act.

NOTES

Acquisition of land. Cf the University and College Estates Act 1925, s 34, this part of this title post.

Lands Clauses Consolidation Act 1845. See Vol 9, title Compulsory Acquisition.

26 Power to remove Shrewsbury School to another site

The new governing body of Shrewsbury School may, if they deem it expedient, at any time ... lay a scheme before Her Majesty in Council for the removal of the school from its actual site to some other place, and may provide in such scheme for the sale or mortgage of any property belonging to or held in trust for such school, and for its appropriation to building or other purposes, with power to suspend any scholarships or exhibitions payable out of such property, and for the purchase of other property, and for the erection of new buildings on the property so purchased, and generally for all matters (including the sale of any surplus property that may be purchased, and the investment of the money which may be produced by such sale,) required to effect such removal in a convenient manner, to the same extent as if such governing body were the absolute owners of any property they may be dealing with under this section as purchasers, vendors, or otherwise; and any such scheme shall be subject to the same provisions, and, if approved, shall take effect and be subject to alteration in the same manner, as statutes made by a governing body . . .

NOTES

The words omitted in the first place were repealed by the SLR Act 1893, and those omitted in the second place were repealed by the SL(R) Act 1973.

Removal of the school. The school was removed by virtue of this section to Kingsland, near Shrewsbury.

New governing body. See s 3 ante.

27 Certain rights of parties interested as herein stated not to be affected

. . . Nothing contained in this Act or done in pursuance of the powers thereof shall affect the dean and chapter of Westminster or any member of that body, except in so far as relates to their status as [a part of] the governing body of Westminster School, or is herein-before expressly provided with respect to the property to be appropriated to or for the use of the said school.

NOTES

The words omitted were repealed by the SLR Act 1893.

The words in square brackets were substituted by the Public Schools Act 1869, s 3 for the words "apart from" printed in error.

28 Saving of existing powers of governing bodies, and provision for future exercise of such powers

Subject to any alterations made by this Act, or by any scheme or statute made in pursuance of this Act, all powers vested by Act of Parliament, charter, instrument of endowment, custom, or otherwise, in the existing governing body of a school to which this Act applies, in relation to such school or the government thereof, shall continue in force, and may be exercised by such governing body until a new governing body is appointed, and after the appointment of a new governing body by the new governing body, in the same manner in which they might have been exercised if this Act had not passed.

NOTES

Governing body. See s 3 ante.

Statute under this Act. See the note "Statute made in manner herein provided" to s 7 ante.

29 Change of corporate name of Governors of Charterhouse

. . . The corporation known by the name of "The Governors of the Lands, Possessions, Revenues, and Goods of the Hospital of King James founded in Charterhouse within the County of Middlesex at the humble Petition and only Costs and Charges of Thomas Sutton, Esquire" shall bear the corporate name of "The Governors of Sutton's Hospital in Charterhouse", but such change of name shall not in any way affect the position, rights, or obligations of the said governors, or cause any action, suit, or other legal proceeding carried on by or against them to abate; and, except so far as the above-mentioned change of name is concerned, nothing in this Act contained shall affect the private Act passed in the session of thirtieth and thirty-first years of the reign of Her present Majesty, chapter eight, intituled "An Act for enabling the governors of the lands, possessions, revenues, and goods of the hospital of King James founded in Charterhouse within the county of Middlesex at the humble petition and only costs and charges of Thomas Sutton Esquire to sell the site of the school of the said hospital and other lands, to acquire a new site for the school, and to erect a new school thereon, and for other purposes".

NOTES

The words omitted were repealed by the SLR Act 1893.

Within the county of Middlesex. Charterhouse School was in 1872 removed from Charterhouse Square, London, to Godalming, Surrey.

Act of 30 & 31 Vict. The Act referred to is 30 & 31 Vict c viii (1867), not printed in this work.

30 (*Repealed by the SLR Act 1893.*)

31 Provision as to school chapels

The chapel of every school to which this Act applies shall be deemed to be a chapel dedicated and allowed by the ecclesiastical law of this Realm for the performance of public worship and the administration of the sacraments according to the Liturgy of the Church of England, and to be free from the jurisdiction or control of the incumbent of the parish in which such chapel is situate ...

NOTES

The words omitted were repealed by the SLR Act 1893.

This section is saved by the Extra-Parochial Ministry Measure 1967, s 2(5), Vol 14, title Ecclesiastical Law (Pt 3(b)).

32 Power to remove Westminster School to another site

Subject to the conditions in this Act contained with respect to the forfeiture of property, the governing body for the time of Westminster School may lay a scheme before Her Majesty in Council for the removal of the school to some other site; and any such scheme shall be subject to the same provisions, and, if approved, shall take effect and be subject to alterations in the same manner, as statutes made by a governing body ...

NOTES

The words omitted were repealed by the SL(R) Act 1973.

Conditions with respect to forfeiture of property. See s 20(16) ante.

Statutes. See the note "Statute made in manner herein provided" to s 7 ante.

PUBLIC SCHOOLS ACT 1869

(32 & 33 Vict c 58)

An Act for amending the Public Schools Act 1868   [9 August 1869]

1 (*Repealed by the SLR Act 1883.*)

2 Governing bodies to be bodies corporate

Any governing body established for any of the schools to which the said Act applies shall, as in the case of Westminster School, be a body corporate, with perpetual succession and a common seal ...

NOTES

The words omitted were repealed by the Charities Act 1960, s 48(2), Sch 7, Pt II.
Said Act. Ie the Public Schools Act 1868, this part of this title ante; see, as to Westminster School, s 5 of that Act.

---

3 (*Amends the Public Schools Act 1868, s 27, this part of this title ante.*)

4 Short title and construction

This Act may be cited for all purposes as "The Public Schools Act 1869" and shall, so far as is consistent with the tenor thereof, be construed as one with the Public Schools Act 1868.

NOTES

Construed as one. Ie the enactments in question are to be construed as if they were contained in one Act, unless there is some manifest discrepancy; see eg *Phillips v Parnaby* [1934] 2 KB 299 at 302. Accordingly, definitions in the earlier Act may be relevant to the construction of provisions of this Act (see *Solomons v R Gertzenstein Ltd* [1954] 2 QB 243, [1954] 2 All ER 625, CA; *Crowe (Valuation Officer) v Lloyds British Testing Co Ltd* [1960] 1 QB 592, [1960] 1 All ER 411, CA).

Public Schools Acts 1868 to 1873. For the Acts, including this Act, which may be cited by this collective title, see the Introductory Note to the Public Schools Act 1868, this part of this title ante.

UNIVERSITIES TESTS ACT 1871

(34 & 35 Vict c 26)

An Act to alter the law respecting Religious Tests in the Universities of Oxford, Cambridge, and Durham and in the Halls and Colleges of those Universities   [16 June 1871]

1 Short title

This Act may be cited as "The Universities Tests Act 1871".

2 Interpretation

In the construction of this Act—

The word "college" includes the cathedral or house of Christ Church in Oxford, and any hall not being a private hall established under the Oxford University Act 1854, nor being a hostel established under the Cambridge University Act 1856.

The word "office" includes every professorship other than professorships of divinity, every assistant or deputy professorship, public readership, prelectorship, lectureship, headship of a college or hall, fellowship, studentship, tutorship, scholarship, and exhibition, and also any office or emolument not in this section specified, the income of which is payable out of the revenues of any of the said universities, or of any college within the said universities, or which is held or enjoyed by any member as such of any of the said universities, or of any college within any of the said universities.

NOTES

Office. As regards new theological offices, see the Universities of Oxford and Cambridge Act 1877, s 58, this part of this title ante.

Oxford University Act 1854; Cambridge University Act 1856. See this part of this title ante.

3 No person to be required to subscribe any formulary of faith, etc

... No person shall be required, upon taking or to enable him to take any degree (other than a degree in divinity) within the Universities of Oxford, Cambridge, and Durham, or any of them, or upon exercising or to enable him to exercise any of the rights and privileges which may heretofore have been or may hereafter be exercised by graduates in the said universities or any of them, or in any college subsisting at the time of the passing of this Act in any of the said universities, or upon taking or holding, or to enable him to take or hold any office in any of the said universities or any such college as aforesaid, or upon teaching or to enable him to teach within any of the said universities or any such college as aforesaid, or upon opening or to enable him to open a private hall or hostel in any of the said universities for the reception of students, to subscribe any article or formulary of faith, or to make any declaration or take any oath respecting his religious belief or profession, or to conform to any religious observance, or to attend or abstain from attending any form of public worship, or to belong to any specific church, sect, or denomination; nor shall any person be compelled, in any of the said universities or any such college as aforesaid, to attend the public worship of any church, sect, or denomination to which he does not belong: Provided that—

(1) Nothing in this section shall render a layman or a person not a member of the Church of England eligible to any office or capable of exercising any right or privilege in any of the said universities or colleges, which office, right or privilege, under the authority of any Act of Parliament, or any statute or ordinance of such university or college in force at the time of the passing of this Act, is restricted to persons in holy orders, or shall remove any obligation to enter into holy orders which is by such authority attached to any such office.

(2) Nothing in this section shall open any office (not being an office mentioned in this section) to any person who is not a member of the Church of England, where such office is at the passing of this Act confined to members of the said Church by reason of any such degree as aforesaid being a qualification for holding that office.

NOTES

The words omitted were repealed by the SLR (No 2) Act 1893.

Any college subsisting at the time of the passing of this Act. This phrase was discussed in *R v Hertford College* (1878) 3 QBD 693, 47 LJQB 649 (college founded after passing of the Universities Tests Act 1871, not a "subsisting college" within the meaning of that Act, the operation of which is confined to colleges then already subsisting).

Private hall or hostel. The right to open private halls at Oxford and hostels at Cambridge was granted by the Oxford University Act 1854, ss 25, 26, and the Cambridge University Act 1856, ss 23, 24, respectively, this part of this title ante.

Office confined to members of the said church. The chancellorship of a diocese is such an office as is mentioned in proviso (2); see 14 Halsbury's Laws (4th edn) paras 1275 et seq.

Office. For definition, see s 2 ante.

4 Act not to interfere with lawfully established system of religious instruction, worship and discipline

Nothing in this Act shall interfere with or affect, any further or otherwise than is hereby expressly enacted, the system of religious instruction, worship, and discipline which now is or which may hereafter be lawfully established in the said universities respectively, or in the colleges thereof or any of them, or the statutes and ordinances of the said universities and colleges respectively relating to such instruction, worship, and discipline.

5 Religious instruction

The governing body of every college subsisting at the time of the passing of this Act in any of the said universities shall provide sufficient religious instruction for all members thereof in statu pupillari belonging to the Established Church.

6 Chapel services

The Morning and Evening Prayer according to the Order of the Book of Common Prayer shall continue to be used daily as heretofore in the chapel of every college subsisting at the time of the passing of this Act in any of the said universities; but . . . it shall be lawful for the visitor of any such college, on the request of the governing body thereof, to authorize from time to time, in writing, the use . . . of any abridgment or adaptation of the said Morning and Evening Prayer in the chapel of such college instead of the Order set forth in the Book of Common Prayer.

NOTE

The words omitted were repealed by the Church of England (Worship and Doctrine) Measure 1974, Sch 2.

7 Attendance at lectures

No person shall be required to attend any college or university lecture to which he, if he be of full age, or, if he be not of full age, his parent or guardian, shall object upon religious grounds.

8 Repeal

. . . Any provision in any Act of Parliament, or in any statute or ordinance of the said universities or colleges, so far as it is inconsistent with this Act, shall be repealed.

NOTE

The words omitted were repealed by the SLR Act 1883.

(Schedule repealed by the SLR Act 1883.)

PUBLIC SCHOOLS ACT 1871

(34 & 35 Vict c 60)

An Act to amend the Public Schools Act 1868   [31 July 1871]

1 Short title

This Act may be cited for all purposes as "The Public Schools Act 1871".

NOTE

Public Schools Acts 1868 to 1873. For the Acts, including this Act, which may be cited by this collective title, see the Introductory Note to the Public Schools Act 1868, this part of this title ante.

2 *(Repealed by the SLR Act 1883.)*

3 ... Provided that the holding of any such fellowship as a member of the governing body shall not interfere with the right of holding any other fellowship or preferment.

NOTES

The words omitted were repealed by the SLR Act 1883.

Any such fellowship. The repealed words enacted that statutes under the Public Schools Acts might provide that members of the governing bodies of Eton and Winchester should be fellows of those colleges.

4 *(Repealed by the SLR Act 1883.)*

COLLEGE CHARTER ACT 1871
(34 & 35 Vict c 63)

An Act to amend the Law respecting the granting of Charters in certain cases   [31 July 1871]

Northern Ireland. This Act applies.

1 Short title

This Act may be cited for all purposes as "The College Charter Act 1871".

2 Copy of college charter to be laid before Parliament

A copy of any application for a charter for the foundation of any college or university, which ... may be referred by Her Majesty in Council for the consideration and report of any Committee of Her Majesty's Privy Council, shall, together with a copy of the draft of the charter applied for, be laid before both Houses of Parliament for a period of not less than thirty days before any such report shall be submitted to Her Majesty.

NOTES

The words omitted were repealed by the SLR (No 2) Act 1893.

London University. This Act was applied by the University of London Act 1926, s 7(2) (repealed).

Laid before Parliament. For meaning, see the Laying of Documents before Parliament (Interpretation) Act 1948, s 1(1), Vol 41, title Statutes.

3 Definition of "college or university"

In this Act the expression "college or university" shall include any institution in the nature of a college or university.

PUBLIC SCHOOLS (SHREWSBURY AND HARROW SCHOOLS PROPERTY) ACT 1873
(36 & 37 Vict c 41)

An Act to amend the Public Schools Act 1868, as to the Property of Shrewsbury and Harrow schools   [21 July 1873]

1 Short title

This Act may be cited for all purposes as "The Public Schools (Shrewsbury and Harrow Schools Property) Act 1873".

NOTE

Public Schools Acts 1868 to 1873. For the Acts, including this Act, which may be cited by this collective title, see the Introductory Note to the Public Schools Act 1868, this part of this title ante.

2 Interpretation

The term "old corporation" shall mean, ... with reference to Harrow School the corporate body entitled "the Keepers and Governors of the Possessions, Revenues, and Goods of the Free Grammar School of John Lyon, within the town of Harrow-on-the-Hill".

NOTE

The words omitted were repealed by the SLR Act 1883.

3, 4 *(Repealed by the SLR Act 1883.)*

5 New governing body of Harrow School

The new governing body of Harrow School shall ... be deemed to be incorporated by the name of "The Keepers and Governors of the Possessions, Revenues, and Goods of the Free Grammar School of John Lyon, within the town of Harrow-on-the-Hill in the county of Middlesex," and shall be entitled to use as their common seal the seal of the old corporation.

NOTE

The words omitted were repealed by the SLR (No 2) Act 1893.

6–8 *(Repealed by the SLR Act 1883.)*

UNIVERSITIES OF OXFORD AND CAMBRIDGE ACT 1877
(40 & 41 Vict c 48)

ARRANGEMENT OF SECTIONS

An Act to make Further Provision respecting the Universities of Oxford and Cambridge and the Colleges therein   [10 August 1877]

Preliminary

1 Short title

This Act may be cited as the Universities of Oxford and Cambridge Act 1877 ...

NOTE

The words omitted were repealed by the SLR Act 1894.

2 Interpretation

In this Act—

"The University" means the University of Oxford and the University of Cambridge respectively, or one of them separately (as the case may require):

"The Senate" means the Senate of the University of Cambridge:

"College" means a College in the University, and includes the Cathedral or House of Christ Church in Oxford:

"Hall" means one of the following Halls, namely, St. Mary Hall, St. Edmund Hall, St. Alban Hall, New Inn Hall, in the University of Oxford:

"The Governing Body" of a College means, as regards the Colleges in the University of Oxford, except Christ Church, the head and all actual fellows of the College, being graduates, and as regards Christ Church means the dean, canons, and senior students:

"The Governing Body" of a College means, as regards the Colleges in the University of Cambridge, except Downing College, the head and all actual fellows of the College, bye-fellows excepted, being graduates, and as regards Downing College, the head, professors, and all actual fellows thereof, bye-fellows excepted, being graduates:

. . . . .

"Office" has the same meaning in the sections in which the Universities Tests Act 1871, is mentioned as it has in that Act:

. . . . .

"Professor" includes Regius and other professor, and reader, and teacher;

. . . . .

NOTES

The words omitted were repealed by the SLR Act 1883.

Modified application. The provisions of this section have been reproduced with modifications by the Universities of Oxford and Cambridge Act 1923, ss 7(3), 10 and Schedule, this part of this title post.

Hall. The only hall now existing at Oxford is St Edmund Hall, which is, all but in name, a college.

Universities Tests Act 1871. See this part of this title ante.

3–23 *(Repealed by the SLR Act 1883.)*

24 Saving respecting Snell Exhibitions at Oxford

No statute or ordinance shall be made under this Act affecting the trusts, conditions, or directions of the will of John Snell, Esquire, deceased, or any scheme approved by the Court of Chancery relating thereto, without the consent in writing of the University Court of the University of Glasgow.

NOTE

Snell Exhibitions. The Snell Exhibitions at Balliol are awarded annually on the nomination of the Senatus of Glasgow University. The award to the first Snell Exhibition winner is now supplemented by the Newlands Scholarship.

25–43 *(Repealed by the SLR Act 1883.)*

Universities Committee of Privy Council

44 Constitution of Universities Committee of Privy Council

There shall be a Committee of Her Majesty's Privy Council, styled The Universities Committee of the Privy Council (in this Act referred to as the Universities Committee).

The Universities Committee shall consist of the President for the time being of the Privy Council, the Archbishop of Canterbury for the time being, the Lord Chancellor, the Chancellor of the University of Oxford for the time being, if a member of the Privy Council, the Chancellor of the University of Cambridge for the time being, if a member of the Privy Council, and such other member or two members of the Privy Council as Her Majesty from time to time thinks fit to appoint in that behalf, that other member, or one at least of those two other members, being a member of the Judicial Committee of the Privy Council.

The powers and duties of the Universities Committee may be exercised and discharged by any three or more of the members of the Committee, one of whom shall be the Lord Chancellor or a member of the Judicial Committee of the Privy Council.

NOTE

Judicial Committee of the Privy Council. For the constitution of the Judicial Committee, see the Judicial Committee Act 1833, s 1, and the other enactments noted thereto, Vol 11, title Courts.

45–50 (*Repealed by the SLR Act 1883.*)

Effect of Statutes

51 (*Repealed by the SLR Act 1883.*)

52 Power in Cambridge for Chancellor to settle doubts as to meaning of University Statutes

If any doubt arises with respect to the true meaning of any statute made by the Commissioners for the University of Cambridge, the Council of the Senate may apply to the Chancellor of the University for the time being, and he may declare in writing the meaning of the statute on the matter submitted to him, and his declaration shall be registered by the Registry of the University, and the meaning of the statute as therein declared shall be deemed to be the true meaning thereof.

NOTES

Modified application. The provisions of this section have been reproduced with modifications by the Universities of Oxford and Cambridge Act 1923, ss 7(3), 10 and Schedule, this part of this title post.
University of Cambridge Commissioners. See the note to s 53 post.
Council of the Senate. This was established by the Cambridge University Act 1856, s 5, this part of this title ante.

Alteration of Statutes

53 Power for University to alter Commissioners statutes

A statute made by the Commissioners for the University or for a Hall shall be subject to alteration from time to time by statute made by the University under this Act and not otherwise.

But where and as far as a statute made by the Commissioners for the University affects a College, the same shall not be subject to alteration under this section, except with the consent of the College.

NOTE

Commissioners. The University of Oxford Commissioners and the University of Cambridge Commissioners were set up by s 3 (repealed). By s 7 (repealed) the powers of the Commissioners could not continue beyond the end of 1881.

54 Power for Colleges to alter Commissioners statutes

A statute made by the Commissioners for a College, and any statute, ordinance, or regulation made by or in relation to a College under any authority other than that of this Act, shall be subject to alteration from time to time by statute made by the College under this Act and not otherwise, the same being passed at a general meeting of the Governing Body of the College, specially summoned for this purpose, by the votes of not less than two-thirds of the number of persons present and voting.

But where and as far as a statute made by the Commissioners for a College affects the University, the same shall not be subject to alteration under this section except with the consent of the University.

NOTE
Commissioners. See the note to s 53 ante.

55 Confirmation or disallowance of altering statutes

Every statute made by the University or a College under either of the two next preceding sections of this Act shall be submitted to the Queen in Council, and be proceeded on and have effect as if it were a statute made by the Commissioners, with the substitution only of the University or the College for the Commissioners in the provisions of this Act in that behalf.

NOTE
Commissioners. See the note to s 53 ante.

56 *(Repealed by the SLR Act 1883.)*

Tests

57 Saving for Tests Act

Nothing in this Act shall be construed to repeal any provision of the Universities Tests Act 1871.

NOTES
Application of section. The provisions of this section have been reproduced by the Universities of Oxford and Cambridge Act 1923, ss 7(3), 10 and Schedule, this part of this title post.
Universities Tests Act 1871. See this part of this title ante.

58 Operation of Tests Act as regards new theological offices

Where the Commissioners, by any statute made by them, erect or endow an office declared by them in the statute to require in the incumbent thereof the possession of theological learning, which (notwithstanding anything in this Act) they are hereby empowered to do, provided the office be not a headship or fellowship of a College, then the Universities Tests Act 1871, shall, with reference to that office, be read and have effect as if the statute had been made before and was in operation at the passing of the Universities Tests Act 1871.

NOTES
Theological offices. See *Re Pauncefort, Sons of Clergy Corporation v Christ Church, Oxford* (1889) 42 Ch D 624, 58 LJ Ch 578 (condition as to holy orders omitted from statute made by Commissioners).
Commissioners. See the note to s 53 ante.
Universities Tests Act 1871. See this part of this title ante.

59, 60 *(S 59 repealed by the SLR Act 1883; s 60 repealed by the Charities Act 1960, s 48(2), Sch 7, Pt II.)*

Electoral Roll, Cambridge

61 Notice of Objection as to Electoral Roll to be given

No objection to the list of members of the Electoral Roll of the University of Cambridge, promulgated in accordance with section seven of the Cambridge University Act 1856, made on the ground of any person being improperly placed on or omitted from that list, shall be entertained unless notice of it is given in writing to the Vice-Chancellor at least four days before the day for publicly hearing objections to that list; and the Vice-Chancellor shall, at least two days before such day, cause to be promulgated a list of all the objections of which notice has been given.

NOTE

Cambridge University Act 1856, s 7. See this part of this title ante.

(Schedule repealed by the SLR Act 1894.)

VICTORIA UNIVERSITY ACT 1888

(51 & 52 Vict c 45)

An Act to extend the privileges of the Graduates of the Victoria University
[24 December 1888]

1 Extension of privileges of graduates of Victoria University

Wherever any office is or shall be open to graduates of the Universities of Oxford, Cambridge, and London, or wherever any privilege or exemption has been or shall be given by any Act of Parliament or regulation of any public authority to graduates of the Universities of Oxford, Cambridge, and London, graduates of the Victoria University having the degree which would be a qualification if it had been granted by the University of Oxford, Cambridge, or London, may become candidates for and may hold any such office and shall be entitled to all such privileges as fully as graduates of any of the last-mentioned Universities.

2 Short title

This Act may be cited as the Victoria University Act 1888.

UNIVERSITY OF WALES ACT 1902

(2 Edw 7 c 14)

An Act to extend the privileges of the Graduates of the University of Wales   [22 July 1902]

1 Extension of privileges of graduates of the University of Wales

Wherever any office is or shall be open to graduates of the Universities of Oxford, Cambridge and London, and of the Victoria University, or wherever any privilege or exemption has been or shall be given, by any Act of Parliament or regulation of any public authority, to graduates of the Universities of Oxford, Cambridge and London, and the Victoria University, graduates of the University of Wales, having the degree which would be a qualification if it had been granted by the University of Oxford, Cambridge or London, or the Victoria University, may become candidates for, and may hold, any such office, and shall be entitled to all such privileges as fully as graduates of any of the last-mentioned Universities.

2 Short title

This Act may be cited as the University of Wales Act 1902.

UNIVERSITY OF LIVERPOOL ACT 1904

(4 Edw 7 c 11)

An Act to extend the privileges of the Graduates of the University of Liverpool
[15 August 1904]

1 Extension of privileges of graduates of Liverpool University

Wherever any office is or shall be open to graduates of the Universities of Oxford, Cambridge and London and of the Victoria University of Manchester, or wherever any privilege or exemption has been or shall be given by any Act of Parliament or regulation of any public authority to graduates of the Universities of Oxford, Cambridge and London and the Victoria University of Manchester, graduates of the University of Liverpool, having the degree which would be a qualification if it had been granted by the University of Oxford, Cambridge or London or the Victoria University of Manchester, may become candidates for and may hold any such office and shall be entitled to all such privileges as fully as graduates of any of the last-mentioned universities.

2 Short title

This Act may be cited as the University of Liverpool Act 1904.

LEEDS UNIVERSITY ACT 1904

(4 Edw 7 c 12)

An Act to extend the Privileges of the Graduates of the University of Leeds [15 August 1904]

1 Extension of privileges of graduates of Leeds University

Wherever any office is or shall be open to graduates of the Universities of Oxford, Cambridge and London and of the Victoria University of Manchester, or wherever any privilege or exemption has been or shall be given by any Act of Parliament or regulation of any public authority to graduates of the Universities of Oxford, Cambridge and London and the Victoria University of Manchester, graduates of the University of Leeds, having the degree which would be a qualification if it had been granted by the University of Oxford, Cambridge or London or the Victoria University of Manchester, may become candidates for and may hold any such office and shall be entitled to all such privileges as fully as graduates of any of the last-mentioned universities.

2 Short title

This Act may be cited as the Leeds University Act 1904.

SHEFFIELD UNIVERSITY ACT 1914

(4 & 5 Geo c 4)

An Act to extend the privileges of the graduates of the University of Sheffield   [31 July 1914]

1 Extension of privileges of graduates of Sheffield University

Wherever any office is or shall be open to graduates of the Universities of Oxford, Cambridge, and London, the Victoria University of Manchester, the University of Liverpool, and the University of Leeds, or wherever any privilege or exemption has been or shall be given by any Act of Parliament or regulation of any public authority to graduates of the Universities of Oxford, Cambridge, and London, the Victoria University of Manchester, the University of Liverpool, and the University of Leeds, graduates of the University of Sheffield, having the degree which would be a qualification if it had been granted by the University of Oxford, Cambridge, or London, the Victoria University of Manchester, the University of Liverpool, or the University of Leeds, may become candidates for and may hold any such office, and shall be entitled to all such privileges, as fully as graduates of any of the last-mentioned universities.

2 Short title

This Act may be cited as the Sheffield University Act 1914.

SEX DISQUALIFICATION (REMOVAL) ACT 1919

(9 & 10 Geo 5 c 71)

An Act to amend the Law with respect to disqualification on account of sex
[23 December 1919]

Northern Ireland. This Act applies. As respects Northern Ireland, s 4 was repealed in part by the Juries (Northern Ireland) Order 1974, SI 1974/2143, art 9(2), Sch 5.

1, 2 (*For s 1, see Vol 16, title* Employment*; s 2 repealed by the Solicitors Act 1932, s 82, Sch 4 and the Solicitors Act (Northern Ireland) 1938, ss 4(2), 59, Sch 3.*)

3 Power to universities to admit women to membership, etc

Nothing in the statutes or charter of any university shall be deemed to preclude the authorities of such university from making such provision as they shall think fit for the admission of women to membership thereof, or to any degree, right, or privilege therein or in connection therewith.

4 Short title and repeal

(1) This Act may be cited as the Sex Disqualification (Removal) Act 1919.

(2) ... Any other enactment, Order in Council, Royal Charter, or provision, so far as inconsistent with the provisions of this Act, shall cease to have effect, ...

NOTE

The words omitted in the first place were repealed by the SLR Act 1927, and from the second place so indicated by the Criminal Justice Act 1972, s 64(2), Sch 6, Pt I.

(Schedule repealed by the SLR Act 1927.)

UNIVERSITIES OF OXFORD AND CAMBRIDGE ACT 1923

(13 & 14 Geo 5 c 33)

ARRANGEMENT OF SECTIONS

An Act to make further Provision with respect to the Universities of Oxford and Cambridge and the Colleges therein   [31 July 1923]

Whereas the Commissioners appointed by His Majesty's Warrant bearing date the fourteenth day of November, nineteen hundred and nineteen, to consider the applications which have been made by the Universities of Oxford and Cambridge for financial assistance from the State, and for that purpose to enquire into the financial resources of the Universities and of the colleges and halls therein, into the administration and application of these resources, into the government of the Universities and into the relations of the colleges and halls to the Universities and to each other, have in their Report (in this Act referred to as "the Report of the Royal Commission") made recommendations with respect to the matters aforesaid and in particular have recommended that Statutory Commissions should be set up to carry out the changes in University and College statutes consequent on the recommendations of the Commissioners and where necessary to revise trusts:

1 Establishment of Commissions

(1) There shall be two bodies of Commissioners to be styled respectively "the University of Oxford Commissioners" and "The University of Cambridge Commissioners."

(2) The provisions of this Act referring to the Commissioners shall be construed as applying to those two bodies respectively, or to one of those bodies separately, as the case may require.

NOTE

This section is spent, by virtue of s 5 post, but is printed as an aid to the construction of this Act.

2–4 *(Repealed by the SL(R) Act 1978.)*

5 Duration of Commissions

The powers of the Commissioners shall continue in force until the end of the year nineteen hundred and twenty-five and no longer:

Provided that His Majesty in Council may, on the application of the Commissioners, continue their powers for such further period as His Majesty may think fit, but not beyond the end of the year nineteen hundred and twenty-seven.

NOTE

Commissioners. See s 1 ante. The powers of the Oxford University Commissioners were extended until 31 December 1926 (SR & O 1925/607; see the London Gazette, 28 July 1925), and those of the Cambridge Commissioners until 31 December 1927 (SR & O 1925/630).

6 Duties of Commissioners

(1) Subject to the provisions of this Act, the Commissioners shall, from and after the first day of January, nineteen hundred and twenty-five, make statutes and regulations for the University, its colleges and halls, and any emoluments, endowments, trusts, foundations, gifts, offices, or institutions in or connected with the University in general accordance with the recommendations contained in the Report of the Royal Commission, but with such modifications (not being modifications directly dealing with the curriculum or course of study in the University) as may, after the consideration of any representations made to them, appear to them expedient.

(2) In making any statutes or regulations under this Act, the Commissioners shall have regard to the need of facilitating the admission of poorer students to the Universities and colleges.

NOTES

Report of the Royal Commission. See the preamble ante.
Commissioners. See s 1 ante and the note to s 5 ante.

7 Power of Universities and colleges to alter statutes

(1) After the cesser of the powers of the Commissioners, a statute affecting the University made by the Commissioners or by any other authority, not being a statute made for a college, shall be subject to alteration from time to time by statute made by the University under this Act, but, if and in so far as any such statute (not being a statute prescribing the scale or basis of assessment of the contributions to be made by the colleges to University purposes) affects a college, it shall not be subject to alteration except with the consent of the college.

(2) After the cesser of the powers of the Commissioners, a statute for a college made by the Commissioners, and any statute, ordinance or regulation made by or in relation to a college under any authority other than that of this Act, shall be subject to alteration from time to time by statute made by the college under this Act and passed at a general meeting of the governing body of the college specially summoned for the purpose by the votes of not less than two-thirds of the number of persons present and voting:

Provided that—

    (a) notice of any proposed statute for a college shall be given to the University before the statute is submitted to His Majesty in Council; and

    (b) a statute made for a college which affects the University shall not be altered except with the consent of the University.

(3) The provisions contained in this Act (including the provisions of the Schedule to this Act other than the section numbered thirty-five therein) with respect to the making

of statutes by the Commissioners and to the proceedings to be taken after the making thereof in connection with statutes made by the Commissioners, and to the effect thereof after approval, shall, with the necessary substitutions, apply to the making of statutes by the University or by a college and to the proceedings to be taken in connection with statutes made by the University or a college, and to the effect of such statutes.

NOTE

Commissioners. See s 1 ante and the note to s 5 ante.

8 Statutes relating to trusts and college contributions to University purposes

(1) No statute shall be made under any of the provisions of this Act for altering a trust, except with the consent of the trustees or governing body of the trust, unless sixty years have elapsed since the date on which the instrument creating the trust came into operation, but nothing in this subsection shall prevent the making of a statute increasing the endowment of any emolument or otherwise improving the position of the holder thereof.

(2) In the making of any statute, whether by the Commissioners or by the University, prescribing or altering the scale or basis of assessment of contributions to be made by the colleges to University purposes, regard shall be had in the first place to the needs of the several colleges in themselves for educational and other collegiate purposes.

NOTES

Trusts. For powers of the Universities to make schemes for administering university and college trusts, see the Universities and Colleges (Trusts) Act 1943, this part of this title post.

Commissioners. See the note to s 5 ante.

Date of instruments. As to the time when deeds come into operation, see, generally, 12 Halsbury's Laws (4th edn) para 1356. Provisions in a will do not take effect until the testator's death, at which time the will becomes operative; cf *Berkeley v Berkeley* [1946] AC 555 at 569, [1946] 2 All ER 154 at 159, HL.

9 *(Repealed by the Charities Act 1960, s 48(2), Sch 7, Pt II.)*

10 Application for purposes of the Act of certain provisions of 40 & 41 Vict c 48

The provisions of the Universities of Oxford and Cambridge Act 1877 shall, as set out with modifications in the Schedule to this Act, apply to the Commissioners appointed under this Act and to their procedure, powers and duties and to any statutes made by them as if they were re-enacted with the said modifications in this Act.

NOTES

Commissioners. See s 1 ante and the note to s 5 ante.

Universities of Oxford and Cambridge Act 1877. See this part of this title ante.

11 Power to establish superannuation funds for certain university and college employees

(1) It shall be lawful for the University to make a scheme for establishing a superannuation fund for the benefit of persons in the employment of the University, not being members of its administrative or teaching staff, and for a college to adopt in relation to persons in the employment of the college, not being members of its administrative or teaching staff, any scheme so made.

(2) The provisions of this Act relating to the making of statutes, ordinances and

regulations by the University or a college shall not apply to any statutes, ordinances or regulations made for the purposes of this section.

(3) Nothing in this section shall be taken to be in derogation of or to affect the duties of the commissioners or the powers of the University or a college under the foregoing provisions of this Act.

NOTE

Commissioners. See s 1 ante and the note to s 5 ante.

12 Short title

This Act may be cited as the Universities of Oxford and Cambridge Act 1923.

SCHEDULE

Sections 7, 10

Provisions of the Universities of Oxford and Cambridge Act 1877 applied for purposes of this Act

2. Interpretation.—In this Act—

"The University" means the University of Oxford and the University of Cambridge respectively, or one of them separately (as the case may require):

"The Senate" means the Senate of the University of Cambridge:

"College" means a College in the University, and includes the Cathedral or House of Christ Church in Oxford, and also includes Keble College, Oxford, and the Public Hostel known as Selwyn College, Cambridge:

"Hall" means St Edmund Hall, in the University of Oxford:

"The Governing Body" of a College means, as regards the Colleges in the University of Oxford, except Christ Church and Keble College, the head and all actual fellows of the College, being graduates, and as regards Christ Church, means the dean, canons, and students, and as regards Keble College, means the Council of that College:

"The Governing Body" of a College means, as regards the Colleges in the University of Cambridge, except Downing College and Selwyn College, the head and all actual fellows of the College, bye-fellows excepted, being graduates, and as regards Downing College, the head, professors, and all actual fellows thereof, bye-fellows excepted, being graduates, and as regards Selwyn College, the Council of that College:

"Emolument" includes—

(1) A headship, professorship, lectureship, readership, prælectorship, fellowship, bye-fellowship, tutorship, studentship, scholarship, exhibition, demyship, post-mastership, taberdarship, Bible clerkship, servitorship, sizarship, subsizarship, or other place in the University or a College or the Hall, having attached thereto an income payable out of the revenues of the University or of a College or the Hall, or being a place to be held and enjoyed by a head or other member of a College or the Hall as such, or having attached thereto an income to be so held and enjoyed, arising wholly or in part from an endowment, benefaction, or trust; and

(2) The income aforesaid, and all benefits and advantages of every nature and kind belonging to the place, and any endowment belonging to, or held by, or for the benefit of, or enjoyed by, a head or other member of a College or the Hall as such, and any fund, endowment, or property held by or on behalf of the University or a College or the Hall, for the purpose of advancing, rewarding, or otherwise providing for any member of the University or College or Hall, or of purchasing any advowson, benefice, or property to be held for the like purpose, or to be in any manner applied for the promotion of any such member; and

(3) As regards the University of Oxford a bursary appropriated to any College in Scotland:

"School" means a school or other place of education beyond the precincts of the University, and includes a College in Scotland:

"Advowson" includes right of patronage, exclusive or alternate.

6. Vacancies among Commissioners.—If any person nominated a Commissioner by this Act dies, resigns, or becomes incapable of acting as a Commissioner, it shall be lawful for His Majesty to appoint a person to fill his place, and so from time to time as regards every person appointed under this section:

Provided that the name of every person so appointed shall be laid before the Houses of Parliament within ten days after the appointment, if Parliament is then sitting, or if not, then ten days after the next meeting of Parliament.

8. Chairmen and meetings of Commissioners.—The Commissioner first named in this Act, as regards each of the two bodies of Commissioners, shall be the Chairman of the respective body of Commissioners; and in case of his ceasing from any cause to be a Commissioner, or of his absence from any meeting, the Commissioners present at each meeting shall choose a chairman.

The powers of the Commissioners may be exercised at a meeting at which three or more Commissioners are present.

In case of an equality of votes on a question at a meeting, the chairman of the meeting shall have a second or casting vote in respect of that question.

9. Seals of Commissioners.—The Commissioners shall have a common seal, which shall be judicially noticed.

10. Vacancies not to invalidate acts.—Any act of the Commissioners shall not be invalid by reason only of any vacancy in their body, but if at any time, and as long as, the number of persons acting as Commissioners is less than four, the Commissioners shall discontinue the exercise of their powers.

11. Power for University and Colleges to make statutes.—Until the end of the year one thousand nine hundred and twenty-four, the University and the Governing Body of a College shall have the like powers in all respects of making statutes for the University or the College respectively, and of making statutes for altering or repealing statutes made by them, as are, from and after the end of that year, conferred on the Commissioners by this Act, but every statute so made shall, before the end of that year, be laid before the Commissioners, and the same, if approved before or after the end of that year by the Commissioners by writing under their seal, but not otherwise, shall, as regards the force and operation of the statute, and as regards proceedings prescribed by this Act to be taken respecting a statute by the Commissioners after (but not before) the statute is made, be deemed to be a statute made by the Commissioners.

If within one month after a statute so made by a College is laid before the Commissioners, a member of the Governing Body of the College makes a representation in writing to the Commissioners respecting the statute, the Commissioners, before approving of the statute, shall take the representation into consideration.

In considering a statute so made by a College, the Commissioners shall have regard to the interests of the University and the Colleges therein as a whole.

14. Regard to main design of founder.—The Commissioners, in exercising their power to make a statute shall have regard to the main design of the founder of any institution or emolument which will be affected by the statute, except where that design has ceased to be observed before the passing of this Act, or where the trusts, conditions, or directions affecting the institution or emolument have been altered in substance by or under any other Act.

15. Provision for education, religion, etc.—The Commissioners, in making a statute, shall have regard to the interests of education, religion, learning and research, and in the case of a statute which affects a College or the Hall shall have regard, in the first instance, to the maintenance of the College or Hall for those purposes.

20. Power to allow continuance of voluntary payments.—Nothing in or done under this Act shall prevent the Commissioners from making in any statute made by them for a College such provisions as they think expedient for the voluntary continuance of any voluntary payment that has been used to be made out of the revenues of the College in connection with the College estates or property.

30. Distinction of University and College Statutes.—A statute made by the Commissioners may, if the Commissioners think fit, be in part a statute for the University, and in part a statute for a College or the Hall.

The Commissioners shall in each statute made by them declare whether the same is a statute, wholly or in any and what part, for the University or for a College or the Hall therein named; and the declaration in that behalf of the Commissioners shall be conclusive, to all intents.

If any statute is in part a statute for a College or the Hall, it shall, for the purposes of the provisions of this Act relative to the representation of Colleges and the Hall, and of the other provisions of this Act regulating proceedings on the statute, be proceeded on as a statute for the College or Hall.

31. Communication of proposed statutes for University, etc, to Council etc.—Where the Commissioners contemplate making a statute for the University or a statute for a College or the Hall containing a provision for any purpose relative to the University, or a statute otherwise affecting the interests of the University, they shall, one month at least (exclusive of any University vacation) before adopting any final resolution in that behalf, communicate the proposed statute in the University of Oxford to the Hebdomadal Council, and to the Head and to the Visitor of the College affected thereby, or to the Principal of the Hall, and in the University of Cambridge to the Council of the Senate and to the Governing Body of the College affected thereby.

The Commissioners shall take into consideration any representation made to them by the Council, College, Visitor, Principal, or Governing Body respecting the proposed statute.

Within seven days after receipt of such communication by the Council, the Vice-Chancellor of the University shall give public notice thereof in the University.

NOTES
Hebdomadal Council. See the Oxford University Act 1854, s 5, this part of this title ante.
Council of the Senate. See the Cambridge University Act 1856, s 5, this part of this title ante.

32. Publication of proposed statutes for Colleges and Halls.—Where the Commissioners contemplate making a statute for a College or the Hall, they shall, one month at least (exclusive of any University vacation) before adopting any final resolution in that behalf, communicate the proposed statute to the Vice-Chancellor of the University and to the Head, and in the University of Oxford the Visitor, of the College, and to the Principal of the Hall.

Within seven days after receipt of such communication the Vice-Chancellor shall give public notice thereof in the University.

33. Suspension of elections.—The Commissioners may, if they think fit, by writing under their seal, from time to time authorise and direct the University or any College or the Hall to suspend the election or appointment to, or limit the tenure of, any emolument therein mentioned for a time therein mentioned within the continuance of the powers of the Commissioners as then ascertained; and the election or appointment thereto or tenure thereof shall be suspended or limited accordingly.

34. Saving for existing interest.—Any statute made by the Commissioners shall operate without prejudice to any interest possessed by any person by virtue of his having, before the statute comes into operation, become a member of a College or the Hall, or been elected or appointed to a University or College emolument, or acquired a vested right to be elected or appointed thereto.

35. Production of documents, etc.—The Commissioners, in the exercise of their authority, may take evidence, and for that purpose may require from any officer of the University or of a College or the Hall the production of any documents or accounts relating to the University or to the College or Hall (as the case may be), and any information relating to the revenues, statutes, usages, or practice thereof, and generally may send for persons, papers, and records.

36. Election of Commissioners by College. For Hall, Principal to be Commissioner.—Eight weeks at least (exclusive of any University vacation) before the Commissioners, in the first instance, enter on the consideration of a statute to be made by the Commissioners for a College or the Hall, they shall, by writing under their seal, give notice to the Governing Body of the College, and in the University of Oxford to the Visitor of the College, and in the case of the Hall to the Principal thereof, of their intention to do so.

The Governing Body of the College, at any time after receipt of the notice, may, at an ordinary general meeting, or at a general meeting specially summoned for this purpose, elect three persons to be Commissioners to represent the College in relation to the making by the Commissioners of statutes for the College.

But, in the case of a College, any actual member of the foundation whereof is nominated a Commissioner in this Act, no more than two persons shall be so elected, while that member is a Commissioner.

If during the continuance of the powers of the Commissioners a vacancy happens by death, resignation, or otherwise, among the persons so elected, the same may be filled up by a like election; and so from time to time.

Each person entitled to vote at an election shall have one vote for every place to be then filled by election, and may give his votes to one or more of the candidates for election, as he thinks fit.

The persons elected to represent a College, and the Principal of the Hall, shall be, to all intents, Commissioners in relation to the making by the Commissioners of statutes for the College or Hall, before and after the making thereof, but not further or otherwise, save that they shall not be counted as Commissioners for the purposes of the provisions of this Act requiring four Commissioners to be acting and three to be present at a meeting.

37. Notice to College or Hall of meeting.—Where the Commissioners propose at any meeting, not being an adjourned meeting, to make a statute for a College or the Hall, they shall give to the Governing Body of the College or to the Principal of the Hall, by writing under the seal of the Commissioners, or under the hand of their secretary, fourteen days' notice of the meeting.

38. Validity of acts as regards Colleges and Hall.—Any act of the Commissioners shall not be invalid by reason only of any failure to elect any person to be a Commissioner to represent a College, or the failure of any person elected to represent a College, or of the Principal of the Hall, to attend a meeting of the Commissioners.

45. Submission of statutes to His Majesty in Council.—The Commissioners, within one month after making a statute, shall cause it to be submitted to His Majesty in Council, and notice of it having been so submitted shall be published in the London Gazette (in this Act referred to as the gazetting of a statute).

The subsequent proceedings under this Act respecting the statute shall not be affected by the cesser of the powers of the Commissioners.

46. Petition against statute.—At any time within eight weeks (exclusive of any University vacation) after the gazetting of a statute, the University or the Governing Body of a College, or the trustees, governors, or patron of a University or College emolument, or the Principal of the Hall, or the Governing Body of a School, or any other person or body, in case the University, College, emolument, Hall, school, person, or body, is directly affected by the statute, may petition His Majesty in Council for disallowance of the statute, or of any part thereof.

47. Reference to Committee.—It shall be lawful for His Majesty in Council to refer any statute petitioned against under this Act to the Universities Committee.

The petitioners shall be entitled to be heard by themselves or counsel in support of their petition.

It shall be lawful for His Majesty in Council to make from time to time, rules of procedure and practice for regulating proceedings on such petitions.

The costs of all parties of and incident to such proceedings shall be in the discretion of the Universities Committee; and the orders of the Committee respecting costs shall be enforceable as if they were orders of a Division of the High Court of Justice.

NOTE

The Universities Committee. This was set up by the Universities of Oxford and Cambridge Act 1877, s 44, this part of this title ante.

---

48. Disallowance by Order in Council, or remitting to Commissioners.—If the Universities Committee report their opinion that a statute referred to them, or any part thereof, ought to be disallowed, it shall be lawful for His Majesty in Council to disallow the statute or that part, and thereupon the statute or that part shall be of no effect.

If, during the continuance of the powers of the Commissioners, the Universities Committee report their opinion that a statute referred to them ought to be remitted to the Commissioners with a declaration, it shall be lawful for His Majesty in Council to remit the same accordingly; and the Commissioners shall reconsider the statute, with the declaration, and the statute, if and as modified by the Commissioners, shall be proceeded on as an original statute is proceeded on, and so from time to time.

49. Statutes not referred, or not disallowed or remitted, to be laid before Houses of Parliament.—If a statute is not referred to the Universities Committee, then, within one month after the expiration of the time for petitioning against it, the statute shall be laid before both Houses of Parliament, if Parliament is then sitting, and if not, then within fourteen days after the next meeting of Parliament.

If a statute is referred to the Universities Committee, and the Committee do not report that the same ought to be wholly disallowed or to be remitted to the Commissioners, then, as soon as conveniently may be after the report of the Universities Committee thereon, the statute, or such part thereof as is not disallowed by Order in Council, shall be laid before both Houses of Parliament.

50. Approval of statutes by Order in Council.—If neither House of Parliament, within four weeks (exclusive of any period of prorogation) after a statute or part of a statute is laid before it, presents an address praying His Majesty to withhold his consent thereto, it shall be lawful for His Majesty in Council by Order to approve the same.

51. Statutes to be binding and effectual. Every statute or part of a statute made by the Commissioners, and approved by Order in Council, shall be binding on the University and on every College and on the Hall, and shall be effectual notwithstanding any instrument of foundation or any Act of Parliament, Order in Council, decree, order, statute, or other instrument, or thing constituting wholly or in part an instrument of foundation, or confirming or varying a foundation, or endowment, or otherwise regulating the University or a College or the Hall.

52. Power in Cambridge for Chancellor to settle doubts as to meaning of University statutes.—If after the cesser of the powers of the Commissioners any doubt arises with respect to the true meaning of any statute made by the Commissioners for the University of Cambridge, the Council of the Senate may apply to the Chancellor of the University for the time being, and he may declare in writing the meaning of the statute on the matter submitted to him, and his declaration shall be registered by the Registrary of the University, and the meaning of the statute as therein declared shall be deemed to be the true meaning thereof.

NOTE

Chancellor to settle doubts. See the Universities of Oxford and Cambridge Act 1877, s 52, this part of this title ante.

---

56. Statutes awaiting submission to His Majesty in Council, or made before cesser of powers of Commissioners.—Every statute, ordinance, and regulation made as follows, namely:—

(1) Every statute, ordinance, and regulation made by or in relation to the University or a College under any former Act before the passing of this Act, and required by any former Act to be submitted to His Majesty in Council, but not so submitted before the passing of this Act; and

(2) Every statute, ordinance, and regulation made by or in relation to the University or a College under any former Act after the passing of this Act, and before the cesser of the powers of the Commissioners, and required by any former Act to be submitted to His Majesty in Council; and

(3) Every statute, ordinance, and regulation made by or in relation to a College under any former Act or any ordinance since the first day of January, one thousand nine hundred and twenty-three, and before the passing of this Act,

shall, in lieu of being submitted to His Majesty in Council under and according to any former Act or any ordinance, and whether or not a submission to His Majesty in Council is required under any former Act or any ordinance, be, with the consent of the Commissioners in writing under their seal, but not otherwise, submitted to His Majesty in Council under this Act, and be proceeded on as if it were a statute made by the Commissioners, with the substitution only of the University or the College for the Commissioners in the provisions of this Act in that behalf; and the same, if and as far as it is approved by Order in Council under this Act, shall have effect as if it had been submitted and proceeded on under any former Act or any ordinance.

57. Saving for Tests Act.—Nothing in this Act shall be construed to repeal any provision of the Universities Tests Act 1871.

NOTE

Universities Tests Act 1871. See this part of this title ante.

UNIVERSITIES AND COLLEGE ESTATES ACT 1925

(15 & 16 Geo 5 c 24)

ARRANGEMENT OF SECTIONS

An Act to consolidate the Universities and College Estates Acts 1858 to 1898 and enactments amending those Acts   **[9 April 1925]**

Cross references are inserted to sections of this Act which correspond to sections of the Settled Land Act 1925, Vol 48, title Trusts and Settlements (Pt 2). Reference may be made to the notes thereto.

Subject to modification, this Act is applied to property comprised in a fund established under the Universities and Colleges (Trusts) Act 1943 by s 2(3), (5) of that Act, this part of this title post.

Universities and College Estates Acts 1925 and 1964. By the Universities and College Estates Act 1964, s 5(1), this part of this title post, that Act and this Act may be cited together by the above collective title.

Applications and modifications. For the power of universities and colleges to which this Act applies (see s 1 post), to enter into forestry dedication covenants, see the Forestry Act 1967, s 5(4), Sch 2, para 2, Vol 18, title Forestry, and for the power to enter into agreements for use of land for cattle-grids or by-passes, see the Highways Act 1980, s 87(5), Vol 20, title Highways, Streets and Bridges.

1 Universities and Colleges to which the Act applies

The universities and colleges to which this Act applies are the Universities of Oxford, Cambridge and Durham, and the colleges or halls in those universities, and the Colleges of Saint Mary of Winchester, near Winchester, and of King Henry the Sixth at Eton, and for the purposes of this Act the Cathedral or House of Christ Church in Oxford shall be considered to be a college in the University of Oxford.

NOTE

By the Universities of Durham and Newcastle upon Tyne Act 1969, s 19 (not printed in this work) this Act does not apply to the University of Newcastle (which was formerly King's College, Durham).

Sale and Exchange

2 Powers of sale and exchange

(1) A university or college—

(i) May sell any land belonging to the university or college, or any easement, right or privilege of any kind, over or in relation to such land; and

(ii) ...

(iii) May make an exchange of any land belonging to the university or college, or of any easement, right, or privilege of any kind, whether or not newly created, over or in relation to such land, for other land, or for any easement, right or privilege of any kind, whether or not newly created, over or in relation to other land, including an exchange in consideration of money paid for equality of exchange.

(2) *A sale or exchange under this section or any other provision of this Act shall not be made except with the consent of the Minister.*

(3) On a sale or exchange by a university or college under the powers of this Act, any restriction or reservation with respect to building on or other user of land, or with respect to mines and minerals, or with respect to or for the purpose of the more beneficial working thereof, or with respect to any other thing, may be imposed or reserved and made binding, as far as the law permits, by covenant, condition or otherwise, on the university or college and land belonging to it, or on the other party and any land sold or given in exchange to him.

NOTES

Sub-s 1(ii) was repealed by the SL(R) Act 1969.

Sub-s (2) is repealed except in relation to Winchester and Eton by the Universities and College Estates Act 1964, s 2, Sch 1, Pt I, para 1.

Consent of Minister. See s 38(1) post. Cf the Settled Land Act 1925, s 38, Vol 48, title Trusts and Settlements (Pt 2).

Definitions. For "land", "manor", "mines and minerals" and "Minister", see s 43 post.

---

3 Regulations respecting sales

(1) Save as herein-after provided, every sale shall be made for the best consideration in money that can reasonably be obtained.

(2) A sale may be made in consideration wholly or partially of a perpetual rent, or a terminable rent consisting of principal and interest combined, payable yearly or half yearly to be secured upon the land sold, or the land to which the easement, right or privilege sold is to be annexed in enjoyment, or an adequate part thereof:

In the case of a terminable rent, the conveyance shall distinguish the part attributable to principal and that attributable to interest; and the part attributable to principal shall, *when received by the university or college, be paid to the Minister and* be capital money:

Provided that, unless the part of the terminable rent attributable to interest varies according to the amount of the principal repaid, [the university or college concerned] shall, during the subsistence of the rent, accumulate the income of the said capital money in the way of compound interest by investing the same and the resulting income thereof in securities authorised for the investment of capital money and add the accumulations to capital.

(3) The rent to be reserved on any such sale shall be the best rent that can reasonably be obtained, regard being had to any money paid as part of the consideration, or laid out, or to be laid out, for the benefit of any land belonging to the university or college, and generally to the circumstances of the case, but a peppercorn rent, or a nominal or

other rent less than the rent ultimately payable, may be made payable during any period not exceeding five years from the date of the conveyance.

(4) Where a sale is made in consideration of a rent, the following provisions shall have effect:—

(i) The conveyance shall contain a covenant by the purchaser for payment of the rent, and [the statutory powers and remedies for the recovery of rent shall apply]:

(ii) A duplicate of the conveyance shall be executed by the purchaser and delivered to the university or college, of which execution and delivery the execution of the conveyance by the university or college shall be sufficient evidence:

(iii) A statement contained in the conveyance, or in an indorsement thereon signed by or on behalf of the university or college, respecting any matter of fact or of calculation under this Act in relation to the sale, shall, in favour of the purchaser and of those claiming under him, be sufficient evidence of the matter stated.

(5) A sale may be made in one lot or in several lots, and either by auction or by private contract, and may be made subject to any stipulations respecting title or evidence of title or other things.

(6) On a sale the university or college may fix reserve biddings and buy in at an auction.

NOTES

In sub-s (2) the words in italics were repealed except in relation to Winchester and Eton, and the words in square brackets were substituted for the words "the Minister", except in relation to those colleges by the Universities and College Estates Act 1964, s 3(1), Sch 1, Pt II, para 1.

The words in square brackets in sub-s (4) were substituted by the Law of Property (Amendment) Act 1926, s 7, Schedule.

Regulations respecting sales. Cf the Settled Land Act 1925, s 39, Vol 48, title Trusts and Settlements (Pt 2).

Investment of capital money. For methods of investment, see s 26 post.

Definitions. For "conveyance" and "rent", see s 43 post.

4 Regulations respecting exchanges

(1) Save as hereinafter provided every exchange shall be made for the best consideration in land or in land and money that can reasonably be obtained.

(2) An exchange may be made subject to any stipulations respecting title, or evidence of title, or other things.

(3) Land in England or Wales shall not be given by a university or college in exchange for land out of England and Wales.

NOTES

Cf the Settled Land Act 1925, s 40, Vol 48, title Trusts and Settlements (Pt 2).

Land. For definition, see s 43 post.

5 Payment to Minister of money payable on sale or exchange

Any money (not being rent) payable as consideration on a sale or exchange effected by a university or college under this Act shall be capital money *and be paid to the Minister.*

NOTES

The words in italics were repealed except in relation to Winchester and Eton, by the Universities and College Estates Act 1964, s 3(1), Sch 1, Pt II, para 2.

General Note. Cf the Settled Land Act 1925, s 75, Vol 48, title Trusts and Settlements (Pt 2).

Leasehold reform. Where the landlord is a university or college to which this Act applies (see s 1 ante), this section is extended to the purchase price or compensation payable to a landlord under the Leasehold Reform Act 1967 by s 24(1)(*b*) of that Act, Vol 23, title Landlord and Tenant (Pt 2).

Minister. This is the Minister of Agriculture, Fisheries and Food; see s 43(viii) post.

Where any person has power under this Act to lease land for agricultural purposes he may lease it for the purposes of smallholdings on certain specified terms; see the Agricultural Act 1970, s 61(6), Vol 2, title Allotments and Smallholdings.

Nothing in the Ecclesiastical Leases Act 1571, Vol 14, title Ecclesiastical Law (Pt 5(a)), operates to restrict the powers of leasing conferred by this Act; see *Eton College v Minister of Agriculture, Fisheries and Food* [1964] Ch 274, [1962] 3 All ER 290, and the Universities and College Estates Act 1964, s 1, this part of this title post.

Leasing Powers

6 Power to lease for building or mining or ordinary purposes

A university or college may lease any land belonging to the university or college, or any easement, right, or privilege of any kind, over or in relation to the same, for any purpose whatever, whether involving waste or not, for any term not exceeding—

    (i) In case of a building lease, ninety-nine years:

    (ii) In case of a mining lease, sixty years:

    (iii) In case of any other lease, twenty-one years.

NOTES

Cf the Settled Land Act 1925, s 41, Vol 48, title Trusts and Settlements (Pt 2); but the terms allowed by this section are those allowed by the Settled Land Act 1882, s 6 (repealed).

Definitions. For "building lease" and "land", see s 43 post.

---

7 Regulations respecting leases generally

(1) Save as hereinafter provided:—

    (i) Every lease shall be by deed, and be made to take effect in possession not later than twelve months after its date:

    (ii) Every lease shall reserve the best rent that can reasonably be obtained, regard being had to any fine taken, and to any money laid out or to be laid out for the benefit of any land belonging to the university or college, and generally to the circumstances of the case:

    (iii) Every lease shall contain a covenant by the lessee for payment of the rent, and a condition of re-entry on the rent not being paid within a time therein specified not exceeding thirty days.

(2) A counterpart of every lease shall be executed by the lessee and delivered to the university or college, of which execution and delivery the execution of the lease by the university or college shall be sufficient evidence.

(3) A statement, contained in a lease or in an indorsement thereon, signed by or on behalf of the university or college, respecting any matter of fact or of calculation under this Act in relation to the lease, shall, in favour of the lessee and of those claiming under him, be sufficient evidence of the matter stated.

(4) A fine received on the grant of a lease under any power conferred by this Act shall be capital money *and be paid to the Minister.*

NOTES

The words in italics in sub-s (4) were repealed except in relation to Winchester and Eton by the Universities and College Estates Act 1964, s 3(1), Sch 1, Pt II, para 3.

General Note. Cf the Settled Land Act 1925, s 42, Vol 48, title Trusts and Settlements (Pt 2).

Rent. For definition, see s 43(ix) post.

8 Leasing powers for special objects

The leasing power of a university or college extends to the making of—

(i) a lease for giving effect (in such manner and so far as the law permits) to a covenant of renewal, performance whereof could be enforced against the owner for the time being of the land belonging to the university or college; and

(ii) a lease for confirming, as far as may be, a previous lease being void or voidable; but so that every lease, as and when confirmed, shall be such a lease as might at the date of the original lease have been lawfully granted under this Act, or otherwise, as the case may require.

NOTE

Cf the Settled Land Act 1925, s 43, Vol 48, title Trusts and Settlements (Pt 2).

9 Regulations respecting building leases

(1) Every building lease shall be made partly in consideration of the lessee, or some person by whose direction the lease is granted, or some other person, having erected, or agreeing to erect, buildings, new or additional, or having improved or repaired, or agreeing to improve or repair, buildings, or having executed, or agreeing to execute, on the land leased, an improvement authorised by this Act for or in connexion with building purposes.

(2) A peppercorn rent or a nominal or other rent less than the rent ultimately payable, may be made payable for the first five years or any less part of the term.

(3) Where the land is contracted to be leased in lots, the entire amount of rent to be ultimately payable may be apportioned among the lots in any manner; save that—

(i) the annual rent reserved by any lease shall not be less than [50p]; and

(ii) the total amount of the rents reserved on all leases for the time being granted shall not be less than the total amount of the rents which, in order that the leases may be in conformity with this Act, ought to be reserved in respect of the whole land for the time being leased; and

(iii) the rent reserved by any lease shall not exceed one-fifth part of the full annual value of the land comprised in that lease with the buildings thereon when completed.

NOTES

The figure in square brackets in sub-s (3) is substituted by virtue of the Decimal Currency Act 1969, s 10(1), Vol 10, title Constitutional Law (Pt 3).

General Note. Cf the Settled Land Act 1925, s 44, Vol 48, title Trusts and Settlements (Pt 2).

Definitions. For "building purposes", "building leases", "land" and "rent", see s 43 post.

10 Regulations respecting mining leases

(1) In a mining lease—

(i) the rent may be made to be ascertainable by or to vary according to the [area] worked, or by or according to the quantities of any mineral or substance gotten, made merchantable, converted, carried away, or disposed of, in or from any land belonging to the university or college, or any other land, or by or according to any facilities given in that behalf; and

(ii) the rent may also be made to vary according to the price of the minerals or substances gotten, or any of them, and such price may be the saleable value, or the price or value appearing in any trade or market or other price list or return from time to time, or may be the marketable value as ascertained in any manner prescribed by the lease (including a reference to arbitration), or may be an average of any such prices or values taken during a specified period; and

(iii) a fixed or minimum rent may be made payable, with or without power for the lessee, in case the rent, according to [area] or quantity or otherwise, in any specified period does not produce an amount equal to the fixed or minimum rent, to make up the deficiency in any subsequent specified period, free of rent other than the fixed or minimum rent.

(2) A lease may be made partly in consideration of the lessee having executed, or his agreeing to execute, on the land leased, an improvement authorised by this Act for or in connexion with mining purposes.

NOTES

The words in square brackets in sub-s (1) were substituted by the Universities and College Estates Act 1925 (Amendment) Regulations 1978, SI 1978/443.

General Note. Cf the Settled Land Act 1925, s 45, Vol 48, title Trusts and Settlements (Pt 2).

Improvements authorised by this Act. See Sch 1, Pts I, II post.

Definitions. For "mining lease" and "rent", see s 43 post.

11 Variation of building or mining lease according to circumstances of district

Where it is shown to the Minister with respect to the district in which any land belonging to a university or college is situate, either—

(i) that it is the custom for land therein to be leased for building or mining purposes for a longer term or on other conditions than the term or conditions specified in that behalf in this Act; or

(ii) that it is difficult to make leases for building or mining purposes of land therein, except for a longer term or on other conditions than the term and conditions specified in that behalf in this Act;

the Minister may, if he thinks fit, authorise generally the university or college to make from time to time leases of or affecting land in that district for any term or on any conditions as in the authority expressed, or may, if he thinks fit, authorise the university or college to make any such lease in any particular case, and thereupon the university or college, subject to any direction in the authority to the contrary, may make in any case, or in the particular case, a lease of the land in conformity with the authority.

NOTES

Cf the Settled Land Act 1925, s 46, Vol 48, title Trusts and Settlements (Pt 2).

Definitions. For "building lease", "land", "mining lease" and "Minister", see s 43 post.

12 Application of mineral rents, etc.

The net rents, tolls, duties, royalties, and reservations which may be received by a university or college, for or in respect of any mining lease to be granted under this Act or any enactment hereby repealed, shall be applied and disposed of by the university or college in manner following; (that is to say),—

(a) one equal third part of such net rents, tolls, duties, royalties, and reservations, shall be applicable and be applied by the university or college as part of their ordinary income, and

(b) the remaining two equal third parts thereof shall be applicable and be applied by the university or college in or upon any of the purposes following; (that is to say,) in the purchase of lands to be conveyed to or for the benefit of the university or college, or in the erection of new buildings, or in the addition to and enlargement of any existing buildings, or in the drainage, or other permanent and lasting improvement of any lands belonging to the university or college, or in the purchase of any wayleaves, or other easements, in, over, or upon any lands adjoining, or near to any such lands; and, in the meantime, until such two equal third parts shall be applied in or upon any of the purposes aforesaid, the same shall be invested by the university or college in the purchase of Government stocks, funds or securities, and the interest, dividends, and annual proceeds thereof shall be received by the university or college, and be applicable as part of their ordinary income.

NOTES

Cf the Settled Land Act 1925, s 47, Vol 48, title Trusts and Settlements (Pt 2).
Definitions. For "land", "mining lease" and "rent", see s 43 post.

Surrenders and Regrants

13 Surrenders and regrants

(1) A university or college may accept, with or without consideration, a surrender of any lease of land belonging to the university or college, whether made under this Act or not, or a regrant of any land granted in fee simple, whether under this Act or not, in respect of the whole land leased or granted, or any part thereof, with or without an exception of all or any of the mines and minerals therein, or in respect of mines and minerals, or any of them, and with or without an exception of any easement, right or privilege of any kind over or in relation to the land surrendered or regranted.

(2) On a surrender of a lease, or a regrant of land granted in fee simple, in respect of part only of the land or mines and minerals leased or granted, the rent may be apportioned.

(3) On a surrender or regrant, the university or college may in relation to the land or mines and minerals surrendered or regranted, or of any part thereof make a new or other lease or grant in fee simple, or new or other leases or grants in fee simple in lots.

(4) A new or other lease, or grant in fee simple, may comprise additional land or mines and minerals, and may reserve any apportioned or other rent.

(5) On a surrender or regrant, and the making of a new or other lease, whether for the same or for any extended or other term, or of a new or other grant in fee simple, and whether or not subject to the same or to any other covenants, provisions, or conditions, the value of the lessee's or grantee's interest in the lease surrendered, or the land regranted, may be taken into account in the determination of the amount of the rent to be reserved, and of any fine or consideration in money to be taken, and of the nature of the covenants, provisions, and conditions to be inserted in the new or other lease, or grant in fee simple.

(6) Every new or other lease, or grant in fee simple, shall be in conformity with this Act.

(7) All money (not being rent) received on the exercise by a university or college of

the powers conferred by this section, *shall be paid to the Minister*, and shall, unless the Minister (upon an application made within six months after the receipt thereof or within such further time as the Minister may in special circumstances allow) otherwise directs, be capital money.

(8) In this section "land granted in fee simple" means land so granted with or subject to a reservation thereout of a perpetual or terminable rent which is or forms part of land belonging to the university or college, and "grant in fee simple" has a corresponding meaning.

NOTES

The words in italics in sub-s (7) were repealed, except in relation to Winchester and Eton, by the Universities and College Estates Act 1964, s 3(1), Sch 1, Pt II, para 4.
General Note. Cf the Settled Land Act 1925, s 52, Vol 48, title Trusts and Settlements (Pt 2).
Definitions. For "land", "mines and minerals", "Minister" and "rent", see s 43 post.

Miscellaneous Powers

14 Power to grant water rights to statutory bodies

(1) For the development, improvement, or general benefit of land belonging to the university or college, a university or college may make a grant in fee simple or absolutely or a lease for any term of years absolute, for a nominal price or rent, or for less than the best price or rent that can reasonably be obtained, or gratuitously, to any statutory authority, of any water or streams or springs of water in, upon, or under land belonging to the university or college, and of any rights of taking, using, enjoying and conveying water, and of laying, constructing, maintaining, and repairing mains, pipes, reservoirs, dams, weirs and other works of any kind proper for the supply and distribution of water, and of any land belonging to the university or college which is required as a site for any of the aforesaid works, and of any easement, right or privilege over or in relation to land belonging to the university or college in connexion with any of the aforesaid works.

(2) This section does not authorise the creation of any greater rights than could have been created by a person absolutely entitled for his own benefit to the land affected.

(3) In this section "statutory authority" means an authority or company for the time being empowered by any Act of Parliament, public, general, or local or private, or by any order or certificate having the force of an Act of Parliament, to provide with a supply of water any town, parish or place in which the land belonging to the university or college is situated.

(4) All money (not being rent) received on the exercise of any power conferred by this section shall be capital money, *and be paid to the Minister.*

NOTES

The words in italics in sub-s (4) were repealed, except in relation to Winchester and Eton, by the Universities and College Estates Act 1964, s 3(1), Sch 1, Pt II, para 5.
General Note. Cf the Settled Land Act 1925, s 54, Vol 48, title Trusts and Settlements (Pt 2).
Payment to Minister. See the note to s 23 post.
Definitions. For "land", "rent", "term of years absolute" and "Minister", see s 43 post.

15 Power to grant land for public and charitable purposes

(1) For the development, improvement or general benefit of land belonging to the university or college, a university or college may *with the consent of the Minister* make a grant in fee simple or absolutely, or a lease for any term of years absolute, for a nominal

price or rent, or for less than the best price or rent that can reasonably be obtained, or gratuitously, of any land belonging to the university or college, with or without any easement, right or privilege over or in relation to land belonging to the university or college, for all or any one or more of the following purposes, namely:—

(i) For the site or the extension of any existing site of a place of religious worship, residence for a minister of religion, school house, town hall, market house, public library, public baths, museum, hospital, infirmary, or other public building, literary or scientific institution, drill hall, working-men's club, parish room, reading room or village institute, with or without in any case any yard, garden, or other ground to be held with any such building; or

(ii) For the construction, enlargement, or improvement of any railway, canal, road (public or private), dock, sea-wall, embankment, drain, watercourse, or reservoir; or

(iii) For any other public or charitable purpose in connexion with land belonging to the university or college, or tending to the benefit of the persons residing, or for whom dwellings may be erected, on such land:

Not more than [0.40 hectare] shall in any particular case be conveyed for any purpose mentioned in paragraphs (i) and (iii) of this subsection, nor more than [two hectares] for any purpose mentioned in paragraph (ii) of this subsection, unless the full consideration be paid or reserved in respect of the excess.

(2) All money (not being rent) received on the exercise of any power conferred by this section shall be capital money, *and be paid to the Minister.*

NOTES

The words in square brackets in sub-s (1) were substituted by the Universities and College Estates Act 1925 (Amendment) Regulations 1978, SI 1978/443.

The words in italics in sub-ss (1), (2) were repealed, except in relation to Winchester and Eton, by the Universities and College Estates Act 1964, ss 2, 3(1), Sch 1, Pt I, para 2, Pt II, para 6.

General Note. Cf the Settled Land Act 1925, s 55, Vol 48, title Trusts and Settlements (Pt 2).

Payment to Minister. See the note to s 23 post.

Definitions. For "land", "Minister", "rent" and "term of years absolute", see s 43 post.

16 Dedication for streets, open spaces, etc

(1) On or after or in connexion with a sale or grant for building purposes, or a building lease or the development as a building estate of land belonging to the university or college, or at any other reasonable time, the university or college, for the general benefit of the residents on land belonging to the university or college—

(i) may cause or require any parts of such land to be appropriated and laid out for streets, roads, paths, squares, gardens, or other open spaces, for the use, gratuitously or on payment of the public or of individuals, with sewers, drains, watercourses, fencing, paving, or other works necessary or proper in connexion therewith; and

(ii) may provide that the parts so appropriated shall be conveyed to or vested in trustees or any company or public body, on trusts or subject to provisions for securing the continued appropriation thereof to the purposes aforesaid, and the continued repair or maintenance of streets and other places and works aforesaid, with or without provision for appointment of new trustees when required; and

(iii) may execute any general or other deed necessary or proper for giving effect to the provisions of this section (which deed may be inrolled in the Central Office of the Supreme Court of Judicature), and thereby declare the mode, terms, and conditions of the appropriation, and the manner in which and the persons by whom the benefit thereof is to be enjoyed, and the nature and extent of the privileges and conveniences granted.

(2) In regard to the dedication of land for public purposes a university or college shall be in the same position as if it were an absolute owner.

(3) A university or college shall have power—

(*a*) to enter into any agreement for the recompense to be made for any land belonging to the university or college which is required for the widening of a highway under [the Highways Act 1980], or otherwise; and

(*b*) to consent to the diversion of any highway over land belonging to the university or college under [the Highways Act 1980] or otherwise; and

(*c*) ...

and any agreement or consent so made or given shall be as valid and effectual, for all purposes, as if made or given by an individual who is the absolute owner of the land.

(4) All money (not being rent) received on the exercise of any power conferred by this section shall be capital money, *and be paid to the Minister.*

NOTES

The words in square brackets in sub-s (3) were substituted by the Highways Act 1980, s 343(2), Sch 24, para 3.

Sub-s (3)(*c*) was repealed by the Highways Act 1959, s 312(2), Sch 25, and the London Government Act 1963, ss 16(2), 93(1), Sch 6, para 70, Sch 18, Pt II.

The words in italics in sub-s (4) were repealed, except in relation to Winchester and Eton, by the Universities and College Estates Act 1964, s 3(1), Sch 1, Pt II, para 7.

Enrolment. See RSC Ord 63, r 10.

Payment to Minister. See the note to s 23 post.

Forestry dedication convenant. For the power of universities and colleges to which this Act applies (see s 1 ante) to enter into forestry dedication convenants, see the Forestry Act 1967, s 5(4), Sch 2, para 2, Vol 18, title Forestry.

Cattle-grids or by-passes. For the power to enter into agreements for the use of land for cattle-grids or by-passes, see the Highways Act 1980, s 87(5), Vol 20, title Highways, Streets and Bridges.

Definitions. For "building purposes", "building lease", "land", "Minister" and "rent", see s 43 post.

Highways Act 1980. See Vol 20, title Highways, Streets and Bridges.

17 Power to compromise claims and release restrictions, etc

(1) A university or college may, *with the consent of the Minister*, either with or without giving or taking any consideration in money or otherwise, compromise, compound, abandon, submit to arbitration, or otherwise settle any claim, dispute, or question whatsoever relating to land belonging to the university or college, including in particular claims, disputes or questions as to boundaries, the ownership of mines and minerals, rights and powers of working mines and minerals, local laws and customs relative to the working of mines and minerals and other matters, manorial incidents, easements, and restrictive covenants, and for any of those purposes may enter into, give, execute, and do such agreements, assurances, releases, and other things as the university or college may, *with such consent as aforesaid*, think proper.

(2) A university or college may, *with the consent of the Minister*, at any time, either with or without consideration in money or otherwise, release, waive, or modify, or agree to release, waive, or modify, any covenant, agreement or restriction imposed on any other land for the benefit of land belonging to the university or college, or release, or agree to release, any other land from any easement, right or privilege, including a right of pre-emption, affecting the same for the benefit of land belonging to the university or college.

(3) A university or college may contract that a transaction effected before or after the commencement of this Act, which (subject or not to any variation authorised by this

subsection) is affected by section seventy-eight of the Railway Clauses Consolidation Act 1845, or by section twenty-two of the Waterworks Clauses Act 1847 (relating to support by minerals) shall take effect as if some other distance than forty yards or the prescribed distance had been mentioned in such sections or had been otherwise prescribed:

Provided that in any case where section seventy-eight aforesaid has effect as amended and re-enacted by Part II of the Mines (Working Facilities and Support) Act 1923, a university or college may make any agreement authorised by section 85A of the Railway Clauses Consolidation Act 1845, as enacted in the said Part II.

NOTES

The words in italics in sub-ss (1), (2) were repealed, except in relation to Winchester and Eton, by the Universities and College Estates Act 1964, s 2, Sch 1, Pt I, para 3.

General Note. Cf the Settled Land Act 1925, s 58, Vol 48, title Trusts and Settlements (Pt 2).

Commencement of this Act. The Act came into operation on 1 January 1926 by virtue of s 45(2) (repealed) of this Act.

Consideration in money or otherwise. See s 20(2) post.

Definitions. For "land", "mines and minerals" and "Minister", see s 43 post.

Railway Clauses Consolidation Act 1845, ss 78, 85A; Mines (Working Facilities and Support) Act 1923. See Vol 36, title Railways, Inland Waterways and Pipelines.

Waterworks Clauses Act 1847, s 22. That Act was repealed by the Water Act 1945, s 62, Sch 5, but previously existing water undertakers may still operate under the repealed Act; see the Water Act 1945, s 32, Sch 3, ss 13, 14, Vol 49, title Water.

18 Power to vary leases and grants

A university or college may, at any time, by deed, either with or without consideration in money or otherwise, vary, release, waive or modify, either absolutely or otherwise, the terms of any lease whenever made of land belonging to the university or college, or any covenants or conditions contained in any grant in fee simple whenever made of land with or subject to a reservation thereout of a rent payable to the university or college, and in either case in respect of the whole or any part of the land comprised in any such lease or grant, but so that every such lease or grant shall, after such variation, release, waiver or modification as aforesaid, be such a lease or grant as might then have been lawfully made under this Act if the lease had been surrendered, or the land comprised in the grant have never been so comprised, or had been regranted.

NOTES

Cf the Settled Land Act 1925, s 59(1), Vol 48, title Trusts and Settlements (Pt 2).

Consideration in money or otherwise. See s 20(2) post.

Surrender and regrant. See s 13 ante.

Definitions. For "land" and "rent", see s 43 post.

19 Power to apportion rents

(1) A university or college may, at any time, by deed, either with or without consideration in money or otherwise, agree for the apportionment of any rent reserved or created by any such lease or grant as mentioned in the last preceding section, or any rent payable to the university or college, so that the apportioned parts of such rent shall thenceforth be payable exclusively out of or in respect of such respective portions of the land subject thereto as may be thought proper, and also agree that any covenants, agreements, powers, or remedies for securing such rent and any other covenants or agreements by the lessee or grantee and any conditions shall also be apportioned and made applicable exclusively to the respective portions of the land out of or in respect of which the apportioned parts of such rent shall thenceforth be payable.

(2) Where the land, or any part thereof, is held or derived under a lease, or under a grant reserving rent, or subject to covenants, agreements or conditions (whether such lease or grant comprises other land or not), the university or college may, at any time, by deed, with or without giving or taking any consideration in money or otherwise, procure the variation, release, waiver, or modification, either absolutely or otherwise, of the terms, covenants, agreements or conditions contained in such lease or grant, in respect of the whole or any part of the land, including the apportionment of any rent, covenants, agreements, conditions, and provisions reserved, or created by, or contained in, such lease or grant.

(3) This section applies to leases or grants made either before or after the commencement of this Act.

NOTES

Cf the Settled Land Act 1925, s 60, Vol 48, title Trusts and Settlements (Pt 2).
Consideration in money or otherwise. See s 20(2) post.
Definitions. For "land" and "rent", see s 43 post.

20 Provisions as to consideration

(1) All money (not being rent) payable by the university or college in respect of any transaction to which any of the three last preceding sections relates may be paid out of capital money, and all money (not being rent) received on the exercise by the university or college of the powers conferred by any of those sections, *shall be paid to the Minister and* shall, unless the Minister (upon an application made within six months after the receipt thereof or within such further time as the Minister may in special circumstances allow) otherwise directs, be capital money.

(2) For the purpose of the three last preceding sections "consideration in money or otherwise" means—

(a) a capital sum of money or a rent;

(b) land being freehold or leasehold for any term of years whereof not less than sixty years shall be unexpired;

(c) any easement, right or privilege over or in relation to land belonging to the university or college, or any other land;

(d) the benefit of any restrictive covenant or condition; and

(e) the release of land belonging to the university or college, or any other land, from any easement, right or privilege, including a right of pre-emption or from the burden of any restrictive covenant or condition affecting the same.

NOTES

The words in italics in sub-s (1) were repealed, except in relation to Winchester and Eton, by the Universities and College Estates Act 1964, s 3(1), Sch 1, Pt II, para 8.
General Note. Cf the Settled Land Act 1925, s 61, Vol 48, title Trusts and Settlements (Pt 2).
Payment to Minister. See the note to s 23 post.
Definitions. For "land", "Minister" and "rent", see s 43 post

21 General power to effect any transaction under an order of the Minister

(1) Any transaction affecting or concerning land belonging to a university or college, or any other land, not otherwise authorised by this Act, which in the opinion of the Minister would be for the benefit of land belonging to the university or college, may, under an order of the Minister, be effected by a university or college: Provided that the transaction is one which could have been validly effected by an absolute owner.

(2) In this section "transaction" includes any sale, extinguishment of manorial

incidents, exchange, assurance, grant, lease, surrender, reconveyance, release, reservation, or other disposition, and any purchase or other acquisition, and any covenant, contract, or option, and any application of capital money (except as herein-after mentioned), and any compromise or other dealing, or arrangement; but does not include an application of capital money in payment for any improvement not authorised by this Act; and "effected" has the meaning appropriate to a particular transaction; and the references to land extend and apply to restrictions and burdens affecting land.

(3) If a question arises or a doubt is entertained as to the intended exercise by a university or college of any power conferred by this Act, the university or college or any other person interested, may apply to the Minister for his decision, opinion, advice or directions thereon, or for the sanction of the Minister to any conditional contract for such exercise, and the Minister may make such order as he thinks fit.

NOTES

Cf the Settled Land Act 1925, s 64, Vol 48, title Trusts and Settlements (Pt 2).
Improvements. For improvements authorised by this Act, see Sch 1 post.
Definitions. For "land" and "Minister", see s 43 post.

22 Separate dealing with surface and minerals, with or without wayleaves, etc

A sale, exchange, lease or other authorised disposition by a university or college, may be made either of land, with or without an exception or reservation of all or any of the mines and minerals therein, or of any mines and minerals, and in any such case with or without a grant or reservation of powers of working, wayleaves or rights of way, rights of water and drainage, and other powers, easements, rights, and privileges for or incident to or connected with mining purposes, in relation to land belonging to the university or college, or any other land.

NOTES

Cf the Settled Land Act 1925, s 50, Vol 48, title Trusts and Settlements (Pt 2).
Definitions. For "land" and "mines and minerals", see s 43 post.

23 Power to grant options

(1) A university or college may at any time, *with the consent of the Minister*, either with or without consideration, grant by writing an option to purchase or take a lease of land belonging to the university or college, or any easement, right, or privilege over or in relation to the same at a price or rent fixed at the time of the granting of the option.

(2) Every such option shall be made exercisable within an agreed number of years not exceeding ten.

(3) The price or rent shall be the best which, having regard to all the circumstances, can reasonably be obtained and either—

(a) may be a specified sum of money or rent, or at a specified rate according to the superficial area of the land with respect to which the option is exercised, or the frontage thereof or otherwise; or

(b) in the case of an option to purchase contained in a lease or agreement for a lease, may be a stated number of years' purchase of the highest rent reserved by the lease or agreement; or

(c) if the option is exercisable as regards part of the land comprised in the lease or agreement, may be a proportionate part of such highest rent;

and any aggregate price or rent may be made to be apportionable in any manner, or according to any system, or by reference to arbitration.

(4) An option to take a mining lease may be coupled with the grant of a licence to search for and prove any mines or minerals under land belonging to the university or college, pending the exercise of the option.

(5) The consideration (if any) for the grant of the option shall be capital money *and be paid to the Minister.*

NOTES

The words in italics in sub-ss (1), (5) were repealed, except in relation to Winchester and Eton, by the Universities and College Estates Act 1964, ss 2, 3(1), Sch 1, Pt I, para 4.

General Note. Cf the Settled Land Act 1925, s 51, Vol 48, title Trusts and Settlements (Pt 2).

Payment to Minister. This payment is excluded from schemes made under the Universities and College (Trusts) Act 1943, s 2; see s 2(3), (5) of that Act post.

Definitions. For "land", "mines and minerals", "Minister" and "rent", see s 43 post.

24 Power to enter into contracts.

(1) A university or college—

(i) may contract to make any sale, exchange, mortgage, charge or other disposition authorised by this Act; and

(ii) may vary or rescind, with or without consideration, the contract in the like cases and manner in which, if the university or college were absolute owner of the land, it might lawfully vary or rescind the same, but so that the contract as varied be in conformity with this Act; and

(iii) may contract to make any lease; and in making the lease may vary the terms, with or without consideration, but so that the lease be in conformity with this Act; and

(iv) may accept a surrender of a contract for a lease or a grant in fee simple at a rent, in like manner and on the like terms in and on which it might accept a surrender of a lease or a regrant; and thereupon may make a new or other contract for or relative to a lease or leases, or a grant or grants in fee simple at a rent, in like manner and on the like terms in and on which it might make a new or other lease or grant, or new or other leases or grants, where a lease or a grant in fee simple at a rent had been executed; and

(v) may enter into a contract for or relating to the execution of any improvement authorised by this Act, and may vary or rescind the same; and

(vi) may, in any other case, enter into a contract to do any act for carrying into effect any of the purposes of this Act, and may vary or rescind the same.

(2) Every contract, including a contract arising by reason of the exercise of an option, shall be binding on and shall enure for the benefit of the land belonging to the university or college.

(3) The Minister may, on the application of the university or college or of any person interested in any contract, give directions respecting the enforcing, carrying into effect, varying, or rescinding thereof.

(4) A preliminary contract under this Act for or relating to a lease, and a contract conferring an option, shall not form part of a title or evidence of the title of any person to the lease, or to the benefit thereof, or to the land the subject of the option.

(5) All money (not being rent) received on the exercise by the university or college of the powers conferred by subsection (1) of this section, *shall be paid to the Minister, and*

shall, unless the Minister (upon an application made within six months after the receipt thereof or within such further time as the court may in special circumstances allow) otherwise directs, be capital money.

NOTES

The words in italics in sub-s (5) were repealed, except in relation to Winchester and Eton, by the Universities and College Estates Act 1964, s 3(1), Sch 1, Pt II, para 10.

General Note. Cf the Settled Land Act 1925, s 90, Vol 48, title Trusts and Settlements (Pt 2).

Sale etc authorised by Act. See s 2 ante.

Lease in conformity with Act. See s 7 ante.

Surrender and regrant. See s 13 ante.

Improvement authorised by Act. See Sch 1 post.

Payment to Minister. See the note to s 23 ante.

Definitions. For "disposition", "Minister" and "rent", see s 43 post.

25 Exercise of powers: limitation of provisions, etc.

(1) Where a power of sale, exchange, leasing, mortgaging, charging, or other power is exercised by a university or college, the university or college may execute, make and do all deeds, instruments, and things necessary or proper in that behalf.

(2) Where any provision in this Act refers to sale, purchase, exchange, leasing, or other disposition or dealing, or to any power, consent, payment, receipt, deed, assurance, contract, expenses, act, or transaction, the same shall be construed to extend only (unless it is otherwise expressed) to sales, purchases, exchanges, leasings, dispositions, dealings, powers, consents, payments, receipts, deeds, assurances, contracts, expenses, acts, and transactions under this Act.

NOTE

Cf the Settled Land Act 1925, s 112, Vol 48, title Trusts and Settlements (Pt 2).

Investment or other application of Capital Money

26 Modes of investment or application of capital money

(1) Capital money paid, whether before or after the commencement of this Act, to the Minister under this Act, or under any enactment hereby repealed [or paid to a university or college under this Act], and the proceeds of sale of securities representing any such money, may, *with the consent of the Minister*, be applied by a university or college to any of the following purposes:—

(i) In investment on securities in which trustees are by law authorised to invest trust money, with power to vary the investment into or for any other such securities;

(ii) In discharge, purchase, or redemption of incumbrances affecting the inheritance of land belonging to the university or college, or of . . . , rentcharge in lieu of tithe, Crown rent, chief rent, or quit rent, charged on or payable out of the land, or of any charge in respect of an improvement created on an holding under the Agricultural Holdings Act 1923 or any similar previous enactment;

(iii) In payment as for an improvement authorised by this Act of any money expended and costs incurred by a landlord under or in pursuance of the Agricultural Holdings Act 1923 or any similar previous enactment, or under custom or agreement or otherwise, in or about the execution of any improvement comprised in Part I or Part II of the First Schedule to the said Agricultural Holdings Act;

(iv) In payment for equality of exchange of land belonging to the university or college;

(v), (vi) . . .

(vii) In redemption of any compensation rentcharge created in respect of the extinguishment of manorial incidents, and affecting land belonging to the university or college;

(viii) In commuting any additional rent made payable on the conversion of a perpetually renewable leasehold interest into a long term, and in satisfying any claim for compensation on such conversion by any officer, solicitor, or other agent of the lessor in respect of fees or remuneration which would have been payable by the lessee or under-lessee on any renewal;

(ix) In purchase of the freehold reversion in fee of any land expectant on the determination of any interest in the land belonging to the university or college;

(x) In purchase of land in fee simple, or of leasehold land held for sixty years or more unexpired at the time of purchase, subject or not to any exception or reservation of or in respect of mines or minerals therein, or of or in respect of rights or powers relative to the working of mines or minerals therein, or in other land;

(xi) In purchase either in fee simple, or for a term of sixty years or more, of mines and minerals convenient to be held or worked with land belonging to the university or college, or of any easement, right, or privilege convenient to be held with that land for mining or other purposes;

(xii) In purchase of the interest of a lessee under a lease from the university or college;

(xiii) In payment of the costs and expenses of all plans, surveys, and schemes, including schemes under the Town Planning Act 1925, or any similar previous Act, made with a view to, or in connexion with, the improvement or development of any land belonging to the university or college, or any part thereof, or the exercise of any statutory powers, and of all negotiations entered into by the university or college with a view to the exercise of any of the said powers, notwithstanding that such negotiations may prove abortive, and in payment of the costs and expenses of opposing any such proposed scheme as aforesaid affecting land belonging to the university or college, whether or not the scheme is made;

(xiv) In the purchase of an annuity charged under section four of the Tithe Act 1918 on any land belonging to the university or college or any part thereof, or in the discharge of such part of any such annuity as does not represent interest;

(xv) In payment to a local or other authority of such sum as may be agreed in consideration of such authority taking over and becoming liable to repair a private road on land belonging to the university or college or a road for the maintenance whereof the university or college is liable ratione tenurae;

(xvi) In or towards the restoration or rebuilding of the chancel of any church which the university or college is by law liable to restore or rebuild;

(xvii) In payment of costs, charges, and expenses of or incidental to the exercise of any of the powers, or the execution of any of the provisions of this Act or any enactment hereby repealed, including the costs and expenses incidental to any of the matters referred to in this section.

(2) Any such capital money or proceeds may be applied *with the consent of the Minister* in repayment of any money borrowed under this Act or any Act repealed by this Act or to any of the purposes to which money so borrowed is applicable under this Act:

Provided that—

(a) where any capital money is applied in repayment of a loan, it shall be replaced within or at the expiration of the period limited for the repayment of the loan *and on the terms mentioned in the order consenting to the loan,* and that where capital money is applied to any purpose to which money borrowed is applicable under this Act, the like provision shall be made by the university or college for replacing the same as is by this Act required to be made for the repayment of money borrowed under this Act; and

(b) where capital money is applied in payment for an improvement mentioned in Part II of the First Schedule to this Act it shall be replaced by not more than fifty half-yearly instalments, the first instalment being payable at the expiration of six months from the date when the work or operation in payment for which the capital money was applied was completed.

(3) The income of any securities on which capital money is invested under this section shall, except where it is by or under this Act required to be accumulated, be paid or applied as the income of the land represented by the securities would have been payable or applicable.

(4) Land purchased under this section shall be conveyed to the university or college to be held upon trusts corresponding to the purposes for which the capital money or proceeds of sale of securities applied in the purchase were held.

(5) Where the purpose to which money may be applied under this section is of such a nature that, in the opinion of the [university or college concerned], provision ought to be made for replacing the money within a limited time, [the university or college shall make such provision accordingly].

NOTES

The words omitted from sub-s (1)(ii) were repealed by the Finance Act 1963, s 73(8), Sch 14, Pt VI.

Sub-s (1)(v), (vi) were repealed by the SLR Act 1969.

The words in italics in sub-ss (1), (2) were repealed, except in relation to Winchester and Eton, and the words in square brackets in that subsection were inserted, except in relation to those colleges, by the Universities and College Estates Act 1964, ss 2, 3(1), Sch 1, Pt I, para 5, Pt II, para 11. The words in the first pair of square brackets in sub-s (5) were substituted, except in relation to Winchester and Eton, for the word "Minister", and the words in the second pair of square brackets were substituted, except in relation to Winchester and Eton, for the words "the Minister shall, in giving his consent to the application, require provision to be so made" by the Universities and College Estates Act 1964, ss 2, 3(1), Sch 1, Pt II, para 11.

General Note. Cf the Settled Land Act 1925, s 73, Vol 48, title Trusts and Settlements (Pt 2).

Application of capital money. The purposes for which capital money may be applied under this section are extended by the following Acts: the Landlord and Tenant Act 1927, s 13(1), Vol 23, title Landlord and Tenant (Pt 1) (to include certain payments by a landlord in connection with improvements); the Coast Protection Act 1949, s 11(2)(a), Vol 49, title Water (to include payment of coast protection charges and expenses); the Landlord and Tenant Act 1954, s 8(5), Sch 2, para 6, Vol 23, title Landlord and Tenant (Pt 2) (to include payment of expenses incurred in carrying out initial repairs etc); the Coal-Mining (Subsidence) Act 1957, s 11(7), Vol 29, title Mines, Minerals and Quarries (to include payment of expenditure as a result of subsidence damage); the Town and Country Planning Act 1971, s 275, Vol 46, title Town and Country Planning (to include payment of compensation on subsequent development, development charges etc); the Land Commission Act 1967, s 92, Vol 46, title Town and Country Planning (to include payment of betterment levy); the Leasehold Reform Act 1967, ss 17, 18, Sch 2, para 9(2), Vol 23, title Landlord and Tenant (Pt 1) (to include payment of compensation to a tenant under s 17 of that Act), and s 24(1)(b) thereof (to include purchase price for a house and compensation to a landlord); the Mines and Quarries (Tips) Act 1969, s 32(2)(a), Vol 29, title Mines, Minerals and Quarries (to include relevant expenditure under Pt II of that Act); and the Housing Act 1985, s 507(3)(b), Vol 21, title Housing (to include voluntary repayment of grants made under Pt VII of that Act).

Consent of Minister. As to consents by the Minister, see s 38 post.

Sub-s (2) proviso (a). For the extension of this proviso in relation to sinking funds, see the Universities and College Estates Act 1964, s 3(5), Sch 2, para 4, this part of this title post.

Definitions. For "land", "mines and minerals" and "Minister", see s 43 post.

Agricultural Holdings Act 1923, Sch 1. That Act was repealed by the Agricultural Holdings Act 1948, ss 98–100, Sch 8. For provisions corresponding to Sch 1 thereof, see now s 81(2) of, and Sch 3 to, that Act, Vol 1, title Agriculture (Pt 3).

Town Planning Act 1925. That Act was repealed by the Town and Country Planning Act 1932, s 54, Sch 5. See now the Town and Country Planning Act 1971, Vol 46, title Town and Country Planning.

Tithe Act 1918, s 4. See Vol 14, title Ecclesiastical Law (Pt 9).

27 Provisions as to money in court

The provisions of this Act as to capital money shall also apply to money belonging solely to a university or college which may have arisen from the sale, enfranchisement, or exchange under any other Act of Parliament, or otherwise howsoever, of any lands belonging to the university or college and which may for the time being be standing to the account or credit of any cause or matter in the Supreme Court or in the names of trustees nominated in pursuance of any Act of Parliament.

28 Provision as to money payable into court or to trustees

(1) Where the purchase, consideration, or compensation money payable in respect of any land belonging to a university or college is directed by any Act of Parliament to be paid into court, or either into court or to trustees, the money shall, at the option of the university or college, be paid either as directed by the Act or to [the university or college].

(2) Where any such money has been paid either before or after the commencement of this Act either into court or to trustees on behalf of a university or college, that sum, or the securities representing it, may, if in court on the application of, and if held by trustees by the direction of, the university or college, be paid or transferred to [the university or college].

(3) Money paid and securities transferred to [a university or college under this section shall be treated as capital money under this Act and as securities representing such capital money].

NOTES

The words in square brackets in sub-ss (1), (2) were substituted in each case, except in relation to Winchester and Eton, for the words "the Minister" and the words in square brackets in sub-s (3) were substituted, except in relation to those colleges, for the words "the Minister under this section on behalf of a university or college shall be treated as capital money paid to the Minister under this Act and as securities representing money so paid", by the Universities and College Estates Act 1964, s 3(1), Sch 1, Pt II, para 12.

Payment to Minister. See the note to s 23 ante.

Definitions. For "land" and "Minister", see s 43 post.

29 Application of money paid for lease or reversion

Where capital money payable [to a university or college under this Act], is purchase money paid in respect of a lease for years, or in respect of any other estate or interest in land less than the fee simple, or in respect of a reversion dependent on any such lease, estate, or interest, [the university or college concerned shall] cause the same to be laid out, invested, accumulated, and paid in such manner as, in the judgment of [the university or college], [is appropriate to make a proper allocation thereof as between capital and income].

NOTES

The words in the first, second and third pairs of square brackets were substituted, except in relation to Winchester and Eton, for the words "to the Minister under this Act, or any enactment hereby repealed", "the Minister may, notwithstanding anything in this Act, require and" and "the Minister" respectively, and the words in the final pair of square brackets were substituted, except in relation to those colleges, by the Universities and College Estates Act 1964, ss 3(1), 4(1), Sch 1, Pt II, para 13.

General Note. Cf the Settled Land Act 1925, s 79, Vol 48, title Trusts and Settlements (Pt 2).

Definitions. For "land" and "Minister", see s 43 post.

Power of raising money

30 Power to raise money with consent of the Minister for improvements

(1) A university or college may, *with the consent of the Minister*, raise by mortgage of any lands belonging to the university or college, such sums of money (together with all reasonable costs and expenses incidental to such raising and the application thereof) as may be certified by the surveyor of the university or college to be properly required, *and may be authorised by the Minister, carrying interest at a rate not exceeding the rate to be specified in the order evidencing the consent of the Minister.*

(2) The sums so raised shall be applied for or towards the restoration and improvement and (if need be) enlargement of any house or building forming part of or connected with or otherwise belonging to the university or college, or for or towards the erection of new or additional houses or buildings, or for the extension and improvement of any existing houses or buildings upon any lands belonging to the university or college, or for the execution of any improvement specified in the First Schedule to this Act or for any other permanent and lasting improvement of any lands belonging to the university or college.

NOTES

The words in italics in sub-s (1) were repealed, except in relation to Winchester and Eton, by the Universities and College Estates Act 1964, s 2, Sch 1, Pt I, para 6.

Consent of Minister. See s 38(3) post.

Extension of section. The purposes for which capital may be raised and applied under this section have been extended by the Landlord and Tenant (War Damage) Act 1939, s 3(*d*), Vol 23, title Landlord and Tenant (Pt 1) (to include making good war damage, such payment to be deemed an improvement under Pt I of Sch 1 to this Act); the Coast Protection Act 1949, s 11(2)(*a*), Vol 49, title Water (to include payment of coast protection charges and expenses); the Landlord and Tenant Act 1954, s 8(5), Sch 2, para 6, Vol 23, title Landlord and Tenant (Pt 2) (to include payment of expenses incurred in carrying out initial repairs etc); the Coal-Mining (Subsidence) Act 1957, s 11(7), Vol 29, title Mines, Minerals and Quarries (to include payment of expenditure as a result of subsidence damage); the Town and Country Planning Act 1971, s 275, Vol 46, title Town and Country Planning (to include payment of compensation on subsequent development, development charges etc); the Land Commission Act 1967, s 92, Vol 46, title Town and Country Planning (to include payment of betterment levy); the Mines and Quarries (Tips) Act 1969, s 32(2)(*b*), Vol 29, title Mines, Minerals and Quarries (to include relevant expenditure under Pt II of that Act).

Definitions. For "land" and "Minister", see s 43 post.

31 Power to raise money by way of compensation for loss of fines on non-renewal of leases

(1) Whenever any lease of land belonging to a university or college, the leases of which have been customarily renewed on payment of a fine, from any cause whatever (other than such as is hereinafter mentioned) remains unrenewed at any customary period of renewal, or whenever any loss of fines has been occasioned by the surrender of any lease upon any transaction by way of sale or exchange between the university or college and its lessees, it shall be lawful for the university or college, *with the consent of the Minister*, to raise by mortgage of any land belonging to the university or college such sums of money (together with all reasonable costs and expenses incidental to such raising) as may be required, *and be stated in the order evidencing the consent of the Minister, carrying interest at a rate not exceeding the rate to be specified in the order*, for the purpose of paying, by way of indemnity, to the then existing members of the university or college the same amount of money as would have accrued to the said members if any such lease had been renewed in manner theretofore accustomed: Provided that—

    (*a*) the power of raising money under this section shall not be exercised for the purpose of providing for the loss of more than two fines in respect of the same land; and

(b) upon the creation of any such mortgage provision shall be made by the university or college, *with the approval of the Minister*, for the discharge of the borrowed money within or at the expiration of thirty years from the borrowing thereof; and

(c) after any sum has been raised under the power hereinbefore contained in lieu of the fines payable in respect of any lease of any land no fine shall henceforth be taken for the renewal of any lease of that land.

(2) This section does not apply where the non-renewal is due to the refusal of the university or college entitled to the reversion of the land to accept such sum of money by way of fine [as is reasonable], and may be tendered by the lessee at the first and each successive time of renewal after the sixth day of August, eighteen hundred and sixty, or within three months of such time, for the renewal of any lease theretofore regularly renewed.

NOTES

The words in italics were repealed, except in relation to Winchester and Eton, and the words in square brackets in sub-s (2) were substituted, except in relation to those colleges, for the words "as may be deemed reasonable by the Minister" by the Universities and College Estates Act 1964, s 2, Sch 1, Pt I, para 7.

Extension of section. The purposes for which money may be raised on mortgage under this section have been extended by the Leasehold Reform Act 1967, ss 17, 18, Sch 2, para 9(2), Vol 23, title Landlord and Tenant (Pt 1), to include payment of compensation to a tenant under s 17 of that Act.

Definitions. For "land" and "Minister", see s 43 post.

32 Provision for the discharge of money borrowed on mortgage

(1) When money has been raised by a mortgage made by a university or college under this Act, or under any enactment repealed by this Act, the university or college shall, *in such manner as may be approved by the Minister*, make provision, either by the grant of an annuity to the lender or by the creation of a sinking or redemption fund or otherwise, for the discharge, within such time not exceeding fifty years [as the university or college think fit], of the money borrowed, and for the payment of interest due thereon.

(2) The maximum time allowed for the repayment of the loan—

(a) in the case of a mortgage to secure money borrowed before the twelfth day of October, eighteen hundred and ninety-eight, shall not exceed thirty years from the date of the original borrowing; and

(b) in the case of a loan raised for the purposes of an improvement, mentioned in Part II of the First Schedule to this Act, shall not exceed twenty-five years from the date when the work or operation in payment for which the money was borrowed was completed.

NOTES

In sub-s (1), the words in italics were repealed, except in relation to Winchester and Eton, and the words in square brackets were substituted, except in relation to those colleges, for the words "as may be sanctioned by the Minister" by the Universities and College Estates Act 1964, s 2, Sch 1, Pt I, para 8.

Sub-s (1). For the extension of this subsection in relation to sinking funds, see the Universities and College Estates Act 1964, s 3(5), Sch 2, para 4 post.

Minister. Ie the Minister of Agriculture, Fisheries and Food; see s 43(viii) post.

Special Provisions as to Advowsons, etc

33 Power to sell advowsons, etc

(1) Arrangements may be made under the authority of the Ecclesiastical Commissioners to enable a university or college—

(a) to sell any benefices, with or without cure of souls, rights of patronage, impropriate rectories, or any other lands or hereditaments, annexed or belonging to or held, either wholly or partly by, or in trust for, the university or college, or the head or other member of the college;

(b) to sell rights of patronage of benefices, the patronage whereof is vested in any person in trust for the university or college, or for the benefit of the head or any other member of the college;

(c) to invest the proceeds of any such sale in the purchase of land in fee simple or any parliamentary or public stocks or funds of Great Britain or other securities, to be settled, held, applied, and disposed of in such manner as may be arranged and determined by the university or college and the Ecclesiastical Commissioners, with proper provision, in cases where the benefice is annexed or, belongs to or is held in trust for, the head or other member of the college, for the payment of the interest thereof to the head or such other member of the college upon his resigning the benefice; and

(d) to annex the whole or any part of the endowments belonging to any such benefice being a benefice without cure of souls or impropriate rectory, or other lands or hereditaments as aforesaid, or to apply the proceeds of sale thereof, or to apply the proceeds of sale of any rights of patronage, or any part thereof, whether made under this section or otherwise, or any money, stocks, funds, or securities belonging to the university or college, or to any head or to any other member thereof, by way of endowment or augmentation of any benefice with cure of souls, the patronage whereof belongs to, or is held in trust for, or for the benefit of, the university or college or the head or other member of the college:

Provided that the powers conferred by this section shall not be exercised to the prejudice of the existing interest of any such head or other member of a college without his consent; and in case of any diminution being occasioned in the income of any such head or other member of a college by any sale, annexation, purchase, or investment that may be made under the provisions of this section, arrangements may be made under the authority of the said Commissioners for giving to such head or other member adequate compensation for such diminution of his income out of the revenues of the college, or out of the proceeds of any such sale or investment.

(2) Every endowment or augmentation which may be made by a university or college of any benefice with cure of souls under the authority of this section, or by virtue of the provisions of the Augmentation of Benefices Act 1831, or any other Act shall be valid notwithstanding the clear annual value of such benefice may at the time of such endowment or augmentation exceed or be thereby made to exceed the limits prescribed by section sixteen of the said Act of 1831 or by any other Act:

Provided that no such augmentation or endowment beyond the clear annual value of five hundred pounds shall be made under the said Act of 1831, except with the consent of the said Commissioners in addition to such other consents as may be otherwise required thereto.

(3) On the sale or annexation under this section of any benefice without cure of souls, or of any impropriate rectory to which any right of patronage belongs, such right of patronage, if not intended to be included in such sale or to accompany such annexation, shall immediately after such sale or annexation be separated from and be no longer exercised by the holder of such benefice without cure of souls, or impropriate rectory, but shall by force of this Act be absolutely transferred to and vested in the university or college, the former patrons or owners of the benefice or impropriate rectory.

(4) For the purposes of this section the expression "benefice" includes any canonry, ecclesiastical rectory, prebend, or other preferment.

(5) Any authority or consent of the Ecclesiastical Commissioners under this or the next succeeding section shall be evidenced in writing under their common seal.

NOTES

Rights of patronage. As to restriction on sale of patronage rights, see the Benefices Act 1898 (Amendment) Measure 1923, Vol 14, title Ecclesiastical Law (Pt 3).

Advowsons. An advowson is the right of patronage which is exercised by its owner or patron in presenting a clergyman to a church or benefice. It is included in the definition of "land" for the purposes of the Law of Property Act 1925; see s 205(1)(ix) of that Act, Vol 37, title Real Property. As to advowsons and rights of patronage generally, see 14 Halsbury's Laws (4th edn) paras 776 et seq.

Ecclesiastical Commissioners. The functions of this body were transferred to the Church Commissioners by the Church Commissioners Measure 1947, Vol 14, title Ecclesiastical Law (Pt 5).

Definitions. For "hereditaments" and "land", see s 43 post.

Augmentation of Benefices Act 1831, s 16. Repealed by the SL(R) Act 1971.

34 Power to purchase advowsons, etc

(1) Arrangements may be made under the authority of the Ecclesiastical Commissioners to enable a university or college to purchase, out of any of the corporate funds or revenues thereof, advowsons of benefices and any rights of perpetual presentation or nomination to benefices, whether such benefices are or are not annexed to, or held by, or in trust for, the university or college, or the head or other member of the college.

(2) The Lands Clauses Consolidation Act 1845 (except such parts thereof as relate to the purchase of lands otherwise than by agreement, and to the recovery of forfeitures, penalties, and costs, and to the sale of superfluous lands) shall be incorporated with and form part of this section, and as if the university or college in each particular case had been inserted therein instead of "the promoters of the undertaking": Provided that the powers by the said Act vested in the promoters of the undertaking shall be exercised only by a university or college with the consent of the Ecclesiastical Commissioners.

NOTES

Advowsons; Ecclesiastical Commissioners. See the notes to s 33 ante and as to consents of the commissioners, see s 33(5) ante.

Lands Clauses Consolidation Act 1845. See Vol 9, title Compulsory Acquisition.

35 Power to substitute lands, etc, for rents, etc, as endowments of benefices

(1) Where any rent or annual sum of money granted, reserved, or made payable, whether before or after the commencement of this Act, under any of the powers of the Augmentation of Benefices Act 1854 or of the several Acts therein mentioned or otherwise, to the incumbent of any church, by way of endowment, or in augmentation of the endowment of any church or chapel, is charged upon or made payable out of any revenues, lands, or other hereditaments belonging to a university or college, it shall be lawful—

> (a) for the university or college, with the consent of the incumbent for the time being of the church, and also with the consent of the bishop of the diocese within which the church is situate, and of the patron thereof, and notwithstanding any statute or law to the contrary, by deed to appropriate and annex in perpetuity to the church any land, tithe rentcharge, or other hereditaments belonging to the university or college, to the intent that the same may be held and enjoyed by the incumbent for the time being of the church in lieu of and substitution for such rent or annual sum of money as aforesaid; and

(*b*) for the incumbent for the time being to accept to him, and his successors such substituted endowment or augmentation, and by the same or any other deed, to release any revenues, lands, or other hereditaments theretofore charged with the said rent or annual sum of money;

and the premises so released shall be thenceforth wholly discharged from the said rent or sum of money, and from all powers and remedies for the recovery thereof.

(2) A bishop shall not give his consent to any such annexation and release as aforesaid unless it is proved to his satisfaction that the substituted endowment or augmentation will produce an income which will exceed or be fully equal to the rent or annual sum of money for which the same is to be substituted.

(3) Such deed or deeds as aforesaid shall be executed by the patron and bishop whose consent is so required as aforesaid, and shall state that such proof as aforesaid has been given to the satisfaction of the bishop.

NOTES

Tithe rentcharge. By the Tithe Act 1936, s 1, Vol 14, title Ecclesiastical Law (Pt 9), tithe rentcharge was extinguished and a redemption annuity issued as compensation.

Definitions. For "hereditaments", "land" and "rent" see s 43 post.

Augmentation of Benefices Act 1854. Repealed by the SL(R) Act 1971.

36 Severance of benefices from headships of colleges

Where a benefice is by statute or otherwise annexed to the headship of a college as part of the endowment of the headship, and it appears that the endowments of the benefice are sufficient to bear such a charge as is hereinafter mentioned, the college may by deed charge the whole or any part of the land or other endowments of the benefice with the payment to the head of the college for the time being of such an annual sum, not exceeding one half of such endowments, as is in the opinion of the Ecclesiastical Commissioners and the bishop of the diocese proper and adequate, regard being had to the value of the benefice, the requirements of the college, and, in the case of a parochial benefice, the population and other circumstances of the parish, and thereupon the advowson and right of presentation of and in such benefice shall be vested in the college freed and discharged from any trust in favour of the head for the time being.

NOTE

Ecclesiastical Commissioners. See the note to s 33 ante.

37 Power to transfer advowsons, etc, gratuitously

It shall be lawful for a university or college to transfer gratuitously to a bishop, dean and chapter, or other ecclesiastical corporation willing to accept the same, any right of patronage belonging to the university or college.

NOTE

Advowsons. See the note to s 33 ante.

Provisions as to the Minister

38 Provisions as to consents by Minister

(1) The consent required by this Act to be given by the Minister to any sale or exchange by a university or college shall be evidenced in manner following (that is to say); the Minister,

upon consideration of the proposed transaction, and the report thereon of the surveyor of the university or college, and being satisfied as to the propriety thereof, shall issue an order under his official seal authorising the proposed sale or exchange to be carried into effect by the university or the college.

(2) The consent of the Minister to the investment of capital money in the purchase of other lands, shall also be evidenced by a similar order, to be issued by the Minister in manner aforesaid, approving of the proposed purchase, and authorising the university or college to carry the same into effect.

(3) The consent of the Minister to the raising of money by mortgage shall be evidenced by a similar order authorising the proposed mortgage to be effected by the university or college.

(4) It shall not in any case be necessary that the Minister should be made party to, or should execute any conveyance, assignment, or other assurance or instrument to be made or executed by a university or college for effecting any sale, exchange, purchase, mortgage or other transaction under this Act, or satisfy himself as to the title of any lands, the subject of any such transaction.

(5) Notwithstanding anything herein contained, the Minister may require a valuation to be made by any surveyor to be selected or approved by him, and also a plan to be furnished of the lands, the subject of any *such* sale, exchange, purchase, or mortgage [proposed to be made under an order of the Minister under section 21 of the Act], and all costs and expenses of and incidental to obtaining any such [valuation or plan] shall be borne by the university or college.

(6) The Minister may, if he thinks fit, in giving his consent to a sale, exchange, purchase, or redemption of any land tax, tithe rentcharge, Crown rent, chief rent, quit rent or other periodical payment, by a university or college, dispense with a report from the surveyor of the university or college.

NOTES

Except in relation to Winchester and Eton, sub-ss (1)–(3), (6), and the word in italics in sub-s (5) were repealed, the words in the first pair of square brackets in sub-s (5) were inserted, and the words in the second pair of square brackets in sub-s (5) were substituted for the word "consent", by the Universities and College Estates Act 1964, s 2, Sch 1, Pt I, para 9.

Extension of section. This section was applied to purchases under a scheme under the Universities and College (Trusts) Act 1943; see s 2(2), (5) of that Act post.

Tithe rentcharge. See the note to s 35 ante.

Definitions. For "land" and "Minister", see s 43 post.

39 *(Repealed by the Agriculture (Miscellaneous Provisions) Act 1963, s 28, Schedule, Pt II.)*

Supplemental Provisions

40 Power to transfer to the university or college lands vested in individual members thereof

When any lands are vested in any person being a member of a university or college in trust or for the benefit of the university or college, or the head or any other member thereof, it shall be lawful for such person *with the consent of the Minister* to convey and transfer such lands in such manner as that the same may be vested in the university or college in its corporate capacity, upon the trusts nevertheless affecting the same lands respectively.

NOTES

The words in italics were repealed, except in relation to Winchester and Eton, by the Universities and College Estates Act 1964, s 2, Sch 1, Pt I, para 10.

Trusts. For the power to make schemes to administer trust property of certain universities and colleges, see the Universities and Colleges (Trusts) Act 1943, s 2, this part of this title post.

Consent of Minister. As to provisions governing the consent of the Minister, see s 38 ante.

Definitions. For "land" and "Minister", see s 43 post.

41 Land to which Act applies and mode of exercise of powers

(1) The powers and provisions of this Act relating to land belonging to a university or college shall extend and be applicable not only to land vested in the university or college, or in any body constituted for holding land belonging to the university or college, and held as the property or for the general purposes of the university or college, but also to land so vested which may be held upon any trusts, or for any special endowment or other purposes, connected with the university or college.

(2) The powers conferred by this Act on a university or college may as respects each particular university or college be exercised by such body and in such manner as may be provided by the statutes regulating that university or college.

NOTE

Land. For meaning, see s 43(iv) post.

42 Saving of existing powers

Nothing in this Act contained shall restrain a university or college, or other body constituted for holding land belonging to a university or college, from exercising any powers of sale, exchange, purchase, or borrowing, or from granting any leases or making any grants, whether by way of renewal or otherwise, which the university or college might have exercised or granted under the provisions of any Act of Parliament, whether public general or local or private, or under any other authority, or in any other manner whatsoever, in case this Act had not been passed: Provided that, upon any exchange being effected under the provisions of the Inclosure Acts 1845 to 1882, it shall be lawful for the Minister to authorise any money by way of equality of exchange to be received by the university or college, and any money so received shall be capital money *and be paid to the Minister*, and, until [the money (if any) to be paid by way of equality of exchange has been paid to the university or college], no order of exchange shall be finally confirmed by the Minister, and a recital of such payment in the order of exchange shall be conclusive evidence thereof.

NOTES

The words in italics were repealed, except in relation to Winchester and Eton, and the words in square brackets were substituted, except in relation to those colleges, for the words "such payment as agreed", by the Universities and College Estates Act 1964, s 3(1), Sch 1, Pt II, para 14.

Land. For meaning, see s 43 post.

Minister. This means the Minister of Agriculture, Fisheries and Food (see s 43 post); but, except so far as this section provides for the payment of money to that Minister, the Minister's functions under this section were transferred to the Minister of Housing and Local Government or, in relation to Wales, the Secretary of State, by virtue of the Minister of Land and Natural Resources Order 1965, SI 1965/143, art 2(1)(b), Schedule, and the Ministry of Land and Natural Resources (Dissolution) Order 1967, SI 1967/156, art 2(2), (5). The functions of the Minister of Housing and Local Government under this section were transferred to the Secretary of State by virtue of the Secretary of State for the Environment Order 1970, SI 1970/1681, art 2(1).

Inclosure Acts 1845 to 1882. For the Acts which may be cited by this collective title, see the Introductory Note to the Inclosure Act 1845, Vol 6, title Commons.

43 Definitions

In this Act unless the context otherwise requires, the following expressions have the meanings hereby assigned to them respectively, that is to say:—

(i) "Building purposes" include the erecting and the improving of, and the adding to, and the repairing of buildings; and a "building lease" is a lease for any building purposes or purposes connected therewith;

(ii) "Disposition" and "conveyance" include a mortgage, charge by way of legal mortgage, lease, assent, vesting declaration, vesting instrument, disclaimer, release and every other assurance except a will, and "dispose of" or "convey" has a corresponding meaning;

(iii) "Hereditaments" mean real property which on an intestacy might before the commencement of the Law of Property Act 1922 have devolved on an heir;

(iv) "Land" includes land of any tenure, and mines and minerals whether or not held apart from the surface, buildings or parts of buildings (whether the division is horizontal, vertical or otherwise) and all other corporeal hereditaments; also a manor, an advowson, and a rent and all other incorporeal hereditaments, and an easement, right, privilege, or benefit in, over, or derived from land, but not an undivided share in land;

(v) "Lease" includes an agreement for a lease;

(vi) "Manor" includes lordship, and reputed manor or lordship; and "manorial incidents" has the same meaning as in the Law of Property Act 1922;

(vii) "Mines and minerals" mean mines and minerals whether already opened or in work or not, and include all minerals and substances in, on, or under the land, obtainable by underground or by surface working; and "mining purposes" include the sinking and searching for, winning, working, getting, making merchantable, smelting or otherwise converting or working for the purposes of any manufacture, carrying away, and disposing of mines and minerals, in or under [any] land, and the erection of buildings, and the execution of engineering and other works suitable for those purposes and a "mining lease" is a lease for any mining purposes, or purposes connected therewith, and includes a grant or licence for any mining purposes;

(viii) "Minister" means [the Minister of Agriculture, Fisheries and Food];

(ix) "Rent" includes yearly or other rent, and toll, duty, royalty, or other reservation, by the acre, or the ton, or otherwise; and, in relation to rent, "payment" includes delivery; and "fine" includes premium or fore-gift, and any payment, consideration, or benefit in the nature of a fine, premium, or fore-gift;

(x) A "term of years absolute" means a term of years, taking effect either in possession or in reversion, with or without impeachment for waste, whether at a rent or not, and whether subject or not to another legal estate, and whether certain or liable to determination by notice, re-entry, operation of law, or by a provision for cesser on redemption, or in any other event (other than the dropping of a life, or the determination of a determinable life interest), but does not include any term of years determinable with life or lives or with the cesser of a determinable life interest, nor, if created after the commencement of this Act, a term of years which is not expressed to take effect in possession within twenty-one years after the creation thereof where required by statute to take effect within that period; and in this definition the expression "term of years" includes a term for less than a year, or for a year or years and a fraction of a year or from year to year.

NOTES

The word in square brackets in para (vii) was substituted by the Universities and College Estates Act 1964, s 4(1), Sch 3, Pt II.

The words in square brackets in para (viii) are substituted by virtue of the Transfer of Functions (Ministry of Food) Order 1955, SI 1955/554.

Commencement of the Law of Property Act 1922. This was 1 January 1926 by virtue of s 191(2) (repealed) of that Act and the Law of Property Act (Postponement) Act 1924 (repealed).
Land. For land to which this Act applies, see s 41 ante.
Manorial incidents. These have, with certain exceptions, been extinguished by the Law of Property Act 1922, s 128 (repealed). See generally 9 Halsbury's Laws (4th edn) paras 787, 788.
Law of Property Act 1922. See the note "Manorial incidents" above.

44 Repeals

(1) ... nothing in this repeal shall affect the validity of anything done before the commencement of this Act, or shall affect any consent, order, authority, or direction given under any enactment so repealed; but any such consent, order, authority, or direction shall have effect as if made under the corresponding provisions of this Act.

(2) References in any document to any enactment repealed by this Act shall be construed as references to this Act or the corresponding provisions of this Act.

NOTES
The words omitted from sub-s (1) were repealed by the SLR Act 1950.
Commencement of this Act. This was 1 January 1926 by virtue of s 45(2) (repealed) of this Act.

45 Short title and commencement

(1) This Act may be cited as the Universities and College Estates Act 1925.

(2) ...

NOTE
Sub-s (2) was repealed by the SLR Act 1950.

SCHEDULES

FIRST SCHEDULE

Section 30

Part I

IMPROVEMENTS FOR WHICH A UNIVERSITY COLLEGE MAY BORROW OR APPLY CAPITAL MONEY

(i) Drainage, including the straightening, widening, or deepening of drains, streams, and watercourses:

(ii) Bridges:

(iii) Irrigation; warping:

(iv) Drains, pipes, and machinery for supply and distribution of sewage as manure:

(v) Embanking or weiring from a river or lake, or from the sea, or a tidal water:

(vi) Groynes; sea walls; defences against water:

(vii) Inclosing; straightening of fences; re-division of fields:

(viii) Reclamation; dry warping:

(ix) Farm roads; private roads; roads or streets in villages or towns:

(x) Clearing; trenching; planting:

(xi) Cottages for labourers, farm-servants, and artisans, employed on the land or not:

(xii) Farmhouses, offices, and outbuildings, and other buildings for farm purposes:

(xiii) Saw-mills, scutch-mills, and other mills, water-wheels, engine-houses, and kilns, which will increase the value of the land belonging to the university or college for agricultural purposes or as woodland or otherwise:

(xiv) Reservoirs, tanks, conduits, watercourses, pipes, wells, ponds, shafts, dams, weirs, sluices, and other works and machinery for supply and distribution of water for agricultural, manufacturing, or other purposes, or for domestic or other consumption:

(xv) Tramways; railways; canals; docks:

(xvi) Jetties, piers, and landing places on rivers, lakes, the sea, or tidal waters, for facilitating transport of persons and of agricultural stock and produce, and of manure and other things required for agricultural purposes, and of minerals, and of things required for mining purposes:

(xvii) Markets and market-places:

(xviii) Streets, roads, paths, squares, gardens, or other open spaces for the use, gratuitously or on payment, of the public or of individuals, or for dedication to the public, the same being necessary or proper in connexion with the conversion of land into building land:

(xix) Sewers, drains, watercourses, pipe-making, fencing, paving, brick-making, tile-making, and other works necessary or proper in connexion with any of the objects aforesaid:

(xx) Trial pits for mines, and other preliminary works necessary or proper in connexion with development of mines:

(xxi) Additions to or alterations in buildings reasonably necessary or proper to enable the same to be let:

(xxii) Erection of buildings in substitution for buildings within an urban sanitary district taken by a local or other public authority, or for buildings taken under compulsory powers, but so that no more money be expended than the amount received for the buildings taken and the site thereof:

(xxiii) Residential houses for land or mineral agents, managers, clerks, bailiffs, woodmen, gamekeepers and other persons employed on land belonging to the university or college, or in connexion with the management or development thereof:

(xxiv) Any offices, workshops and other buildings of a permanent nature required in connexion with the management or development of land belonging to the university or college:

(xxv) The erection and building of dwelling-houses, shops, buildings for religious, educational, literary, scientific, or public purposes, market places, market houses, places of amusement and entertainment, gasworks, electric light or power works, or any other works necessary or proper in connexion with the development of the land belonging to the university or college as a building estate:

(xxvi) Restoration or reconstruction of buildings damaged or destroyed by dry rot:

(xxvii) Structural additions to or alterations in buildings reasonably required, whether the buildings are intended to be let or not, or are already let:

(xxviii) Boring for water and other preliminary works in connexion therewith:

(xxix) Reconstruction, enlargement or improvement of any of the works authorised by this Schedule.

NOTES

Cf the Settled Land Act 1925, Sch 3, Pt I, Vol 48, title Trusts and Settlements (Pt 2).

War damage. The making good of war damage is deemed to be an improvement authorised by this Part of this Schedule; see the Landlord and Tenant (War Damage) Act 1939, s 3, Vol 23, title Landlord and Tenant (Pt 1).

PART II

IMPROVEMENTS FOR WHICH A UNIVERSITY OR COLLEGE MAY BORROW MONEY OR APPLY CAPITAL MONEY SUBJECT TO SPECIAL PROVISIONS AS TO REPLACEMENT THEREOF

(xxx) Heating, hydraulic or electric power apparatus for buildings, and engines, pumps, lifts, rams, boilers, flues and other works required or used in connexion therewith:

(xxxi) Engine houses, engines, gasometers, dynamos, accumulators, cables, pipes, wiring, switchboards, plant and other works required for the installation of electric, gas, or other artificial light, in connexion with any ... house or buildings; but not electric lamps, gas fittings, or decorative fittings required in any such house or building:

(xxxii) Steam rollers, traction engines, motor lorries and moveable machinery for farming or other purposes.

NOTES

The words omitted from para (xxxi) were repealed by the Universities and College Estates Act 1964, s 4, Sch 3, Pt II, Sch 4.

Cf the Settled Land Act 1925, Sch 3, Pt III, Vol 48, title Trusts and Settlements (Pt 2).

(Sch 2 repealed by the SLR Act 1950.)

UNIVERSITIES AND COLLEGES (TRUSTS) ACT 1943
(6 & 7 Geo 6 c 9)

An Act to make provision as to trust property held by or on behalf of certain universities and colleges or for purposes connected with those universities and colleges   [11 March 1943]

1 Universities and colleges to which the Act applies

(1) This Act shall apply to the Universities of Oxford and Cambridge and to the colleges in those universities, and to the College of St. Mary of Winchester, near Winchester, and the expressions "university" and "college" shall be construed accordingly.

(2) For the purposes of this Act, the Cathedral or House of Christ Church in Oxford, Keble College, St. Peter's Hall, Somerville College, Lady Margaret Hall, St. Hugh's College and St. Hilda's College, shall be deemed to be colleges in the University of Oxford, and Selwyn College, Girton College and Newnham College shall be deemed to be colleges in the University of Cambridge.

2 Schemes for administering university and college trusts

(1) A university or college may make a scheme providing, in relation to that university or college, as the case may be, for the following matters:—

(a) for the application of the scheme to such trusts as may be specified therein, being trusts which are administered by the university or college or which are administered by other trustees for purposes connected with the university or college and are included in the scheme with the consent of those trustees;

(b) for enabling all the property held by the university or college on any trust to which the scheme applies, with such exceptions as may be specified in the scheme, to be administered by the university or college as a single fund (hereafter referred to as "the Fund");

(c) for enabling the trustees of any trust to which the scheme applies which is not administered by the university or college to transfer to the university or college all the property comprised in the trust, with such exceptions as may be specified in the scheme, and for its administration as part of the Fund;

(d) for enabling [the Minister of Agriculture, Fisheries and Food] to transfer to the university or college any property held by him on behalf of the university or college on any trust to which the scheme applies, and for its administration as part of the Fund;

(e) for valuing the Fund and determining the shares of the various trusts therein;

(f) for distributing the income of the Fund in accordance with the said shares, and for enabling, in the case of any trust, advances of capital to be made out of the Fund, up to an amount not exceeding the share of that trust, for any purpose for which capital is authorised by the terms of the trust to be advanced;

(g) for authorising, in such circumstances as may be specified in the scheme, a part of the income for any year to be placed to a reserve account for the purpose of eliminating or reducing fluctuations of income;

(h) for conferring upon the university or college powers of investment with respect to property comprised in the Fund, including powers to invest in the purchase of land;

(i) for enabling the scheme to be extended to trusts administered by or for purposes connected with the university or college, being trusts created after the coming into operation of the scheme or excluded from the scheme for other reasons, unless the terms of the trust expressly provide to the contrary or (in the case of trusts not administered by the university or college) the consent of the trustees is withheld;

(k) for any incidental, consequential and supplementary matters for which the university or college considers it expedient to provide.

(2) Any power conferred by any such scheme on a university or college to purchase land shall not be exercised without the consent of [the Minister of Agriculture, Fisheries and Food], and sections thirty-eight . . . of the Universities and College Estates Act 1925 shall apply to any such consent.

(3) The Universities and College Estates Act 1925 shall, in the case of a scheme made under this section by a university or by a college to which that Act applies, apply to property comprised in the Fund established by the scheme, subject to the modification that so much of the said Act as requires money arising from any sale or exchange of land or other transaction affecting land to be paid to [the Minister of Agriculture, Fisheries and Food] shall not apply in relation to such property as aforesaid; and any scheme made by a college to which the said Act does not apply may apply any of the provisions of the said Act to property comprised in the Fund established by that scheme, subject to the modification aforesaid.

(4) A university or college may make different schemes under this section in relation to different classes of trusts.

[(5) Subsection (2) of this section shall not have effect in relation to any university or college to which section 2 of the Universities and College Estates Act 1964 (in this subsection referred to as "the Act of 1964") applies; and in subsection (3) of this section—

(a) in its application to any university or college to which section 2 of the Act of 1964 applies, any reference to the Universities and College Estates Act 1925 (in this subsection referred to as "the Act of 1925") shall be construed as a reference to that Act as modified by Schedule 1, and amended by Schedule 3, to the Act of 1964, and the words from "subject to the modification" to "such property as aforesaid" shall be omitted;

(b) in its application to any college to which the Act of 1925 applies, but section 2 of the Act of 1964 does not apply, any reference to the Act of 1925 shall be construed as a reference to that Act as amended by Schedule 3 to the Act of 1964; and

(c) in its application to any college to which the Act of 1925 does not apply, the reference to applying any of the provisions of that Act shall be construed as a reference to applying any of the provisions of that Act as modified by Schedule 1, and amended by Schedule 3, to the Act of 1964, and the words "subject to the modification aforesaid" shall be omitted.]

NOTES

The words omitted from sub-s (2) were repealed by the Agriculture (Miscellaneous Provisions) Act 1963, s 28, Schedule, Pt II. Sub-s (5) was added by the Universities and College Estates Act 1964, s 4(1), Sch 3, Pt I, and the other words in square brackets in the section are substituted by virtue of the Transfer of Functions (Ministry of Food) Order 1955, SI 1955/554.

Universities and College Estates Act 1925, s 38. See this part of this title ante.

Universities and College Estates Act 1964, s 2, Schs 1,3. See this part of this title post.

Incidental, consequential and supplementary matters. The Act is concerned with administrative matters only and does not authorise alteration of a beneficial trust; see *Re Freeston's Charity, Sylvester v Master and Fellows of University College, Oxford* [1979] 1 All ER 51, [1978] 1 WLR 741, CA.

3 Submission and approval of schemes

(1) A scheme made under the last foregoing section shall not come into operation until it has been submitted to His Majesty in Council for approval, and has been approved by Order in Council.

(2) Before any such scheme is submitted to His Majesty in Council, a copy thereof shall be laid before each House of Parliament for a period of forty days, and if either House within that period resolves that the scheme shall not be proceeded with, no further proceedings shall be taken thereon, without prejudice to the making of a new scheme.

(3) In reckoning for the purposes of the last foregoing subsection the period of forty days therein mentioned, no account shall be taken of any time during which Parliament is dissolved or prorogued or during which both Houses are adjourned for more than four days.

(4) A scheme approved under this section shall have effect notwithstanding any instrument (including an Act of Parliament) relating to any trust to which the scheme applies.

(5) A scheme approved under this section may be varied or revoked by a subsequent scheme made and approved in like manner and subject to the like conditions.

NOTE

Schemes under this Act. Such schemes are not printed in the SR & O/SI series.

4 Power to charge certain contributions on trust funds

It is hereby declared, for the removal of doubts, that, where any college in a university is required by a statute of the university to make contributions for universities purposes in respect of income arising from any property held on trust by or on behalf of the college or for purposes connected with the college, the amount of the contributions may be charged on the trust property.

5 Short title

This Act may be cited as the Universities and Colleges (Trusts) Act 1943.

MARSHALL AID COMMEMORATION ACT 1953

(1 & 2 Eliz 2 c 39)

An Act to make provision for the granting of Scholarships in commemoration of the assistance received by the United Kingdom under the European Recovery Programme and known as Marshall Aid; and for purposes connected with the matter aforesaid   [31 July 1953]

Marshall Aid Commemoration Acts 1953 and 1959. By the Marshall Scholarships Act 1959, s 2, this part of this title post, the Marshall Aid Commemoration Act 1953 (this Act) and the 1959 Act may be cited together by this collective title.
Northern Ireland. This Act applies.

1 Marshall scholarships

For the purpose of providing, in each year, up to [thirty] scholarships (to be known as Marshall scholarships) tenable at universities or university colleges in the United Kingdom by citizens of the United States of America who are graduates of recognised institutions of higher learning in the United States of America, the Secretary of State may make, out of moneys provided by Parliament, grants to the commission established by this Act to defray the expenditure of the commission incurred for the said purpose, including administrative expenses incurred in connection therewith.

NOTES

The word in square brackets was substituted by the Marshall Scholarships Order 1972, SI 1972/961, art 2.
United Kingdom. Ie Great Britain and Northern Ireland; see the Interpretation Act 1978, s 5, Sch 1, Vol 41, title Statutes. "Great Britain" means England, Scotland and Wales by virtue of the Union with Scotland Act 1706, preamble, Art I, Vol 10, title Constitutional Law (Pt 1), as read with s 22(1) of, and Sch 2, para 5(a) to, the 1978 Act. Neither the Channel Islands nor the Isle of Man is within the United Kingdom.
Commission established by this Act. Ie the Marshall Aid Commemoration Commission established by s 2 post.

2 The Marshall Aid Commemoration Commission

(1) There shall be a commission, to be known as the Marshall Aid Commemoration Commission, to give effect to arrangements made by or with the approval of the Secretary of State—

(a) for administering the grants provided under the foregoing section,
(b) for the selection of the persons to receive Marshall scholarships, and
(c) for the placing of the holders of Marshall scholarships in universities or university colleges in the United Kingdom,

and to discharge such other functions in connection with Marshall scholarships as may be conferred on them by such arrangements.

(2) The Marshall Aid Commemoration Commission (hereinafter referred to as "the Commission") shall consist of not less than seven nor more than ten members appointed by the Secretary of State, of whom not less than two shall be chosen as persons of eminence in academic matters, and such one of the members as the Secretary of State may designate shall be chairman of the Commission.

(3) The quorum of the Commission shall be four.

(4) Subject to the provisions of the last foregoing subsection, the Commission shall have power to act notwithstanding any vacancy in their number.

(5) The terms of office of members of the Commission shall be such as may be determined by the Secretary of State, and a member of the Commission on vacating office shall be eligible for re-appointment.

(6) The Commission shall, as soon as possible after the thirtieth day of September in each year, make to the Secretary of State a report on the discharge by them of their functions during the period of twelve months ending with that day, and the Secretary of State shall lay a copy of every report of the Commission under this section before each House of Parliament.

(7) As respects each financial year the Commission shall prepare accounts of their expenditure in such form as the Secretary of State may with the approval of the Treasury direct, and shall submit the accounts to the Secretary of State at such time as he may direct; and—

(a) the Secretary of State shall, on or before the thirtieth day of November in any year, transmit to the Comptroller and Auditor General the accounts prepared by the Commission under this section for the financial year last ended;

(b) the Comptroller and Auditor General shall examine and certify the accounts of the Commission transmitted to him under this section and lay before Parliament copies of the accounts, together with his report thereon.

NOTES

United Kingdom. See the note to s 1 ante.
Lay ... before ... Parliament. For meaning, see the Laying of Documents before Parliament (Interpretation) Act 1948, s 1(1), Vol 41, title Statutes.

3 Short title

This Act may be cited as the Marshall Aid Commemoration Act 1953.

MARSHALL SCHOLARSHIPS ACT 1959

(8 & 9 Eliz 2 c 3)

An Act to increase the number of Marshall Scholarships which may be provided in each year
[17 December 1959]

Northern Ireland. This Act applies.

1 Increase in maximum number of Marshall scholarships

(1) Section one of the Marshall Aid Commemoration Act 1953 shall have effect with the substitution for the reference to twelve scholarships of a reference to twenty-four or such greater number as Her Majesty may by Order in Council from time to time determine.

(2) Any Order in Council under this section shall be subject to annulment in pursuance of a resolution of either House of Parliament.

NOTES

Marshall Aid Commemoration Act 1953, s 1. See this part of this title ante.
Order in Council ... subject to annulment. The power to make Orders in Council is exercisable by

statutory instrument; see the Statutory Instruments Act 1946, s 1(1), Vol 41, title Statutes. As to statutory instruments which are subject to annulment, see ss 5(1), 7(1) of that Act.

Order in Council under this section. The Marshall Scholarships Order 1972, SI 1972/961 increased the number of scholarships to thirty.

2 Short title and construction

This Act may be cited as the Marshall Scholarships Act 1959 and this Act and the Marshall Aid Commemoration Act 1953 may be cited together as the Marshall Aid Commemoration Acts 1953 and 1959.

NOTE

Marshall Aid Commemoration Act 1953. See this part of this title ante.

UNIVERSITIES AND COLLEGE ESTATES ACT 1964

(1964 c 51)

An Act to amend the law relating to property held by or on behalf of universities and colleges, and for purposes connected therewith   [16 July 1964]

Northern Ireland. This Act does not apply; see s 5(2), (3) post.

1 Ecclesiastical Leases Acts

(1) The Ecclesiastical Leases Act 1571, the Ecclesiastical Leases Act 1572, the Ecclesiastical Leases Act 1575 and the Ecclesiastical Leases Act 1836 shall not have effect in relation to any college in any university.

(2) In this Act "college" includes a hall; and for the purposes of this Act the Cathedral or House of Christ Church in Oxford shall be considered to be a college in the University of Oxford.

NOTES

University. The meaning of "university" was considered in *St David's College, Lampeter v Ministry of Education* [1951] 1 All ER 599, [1951] 1 TLR 656 (where St David's College, Lampeter, was held not to be a university).

In this Act, etc. The first branch of sub-s (2) may be compared with the reference in the Universities and College Estates Act 1925, s 1, this part of this title ante, to the colleges or halls in the universities mentioned in that section. The second branch of sub-s (2) is taken verbatim from that section; see also, in particular, the definition of "college" in the Universities of Oxford and Cambridge Act 1877, s 2 , this part of this title ante.

Ecclesiastical Leases Acts 1571 to 1836. See Vol 14, title Ecclesiastical Law (Pt 5(a)).

2 Removal of restrictions in Universities and College Estates Act 1925

(1) This section applies to the following universities and colleges, that is to say—

    (*a*) the universities to which the Universities and College Estates Act 1925 (in this Act referred to as "the Act of 1925") applies, and

    (*b*) all colleges in those universities.

(2) In relation to universities and colleges to which this section applies, the Act of 1925 shall have effect subject to the exceptions and modifications specified in Part I of Schedule 1 to this Act (being exceptions and modifications for removing restrictions on the powers of those universities and colleges).

NOTES

College. For the meaning of this expression, see s 1(2) ante.

Universities and College Estates Act 1925. See this part of this title ante. That Act applies to the Universities of Oxford, Cambridge and Durham, the colleges or halls therein (including the Cathedral or House of Christ Church in Oxford), Winchester College and Eton College; see s 1 of that Act. Note, however, that Eton College and Winchester College, not being colleges in those universities, are excluded from the provisions of this section by the wording of sub-s (1)(*b*) above.

3 Capital money

(1) In relation to universities and colleges to which the last preceding section applies, the Act of 1925 shall have effect subject to the further exceptions and modifications specified in Part II of Schedule 1 to this Act (being exceptions and modifications relating to the receipt and application of capital money).

(2) Where at the commencement of this Act any capital money belonging to a university or college to which the last preceding section applies is held by the Minister of Agriculture, Fisheries and Food, that Minister shall pay or transfer it to that university or college, or to a person designated for the purpose by that university or college.

(3) Any capital money which in pursuance of the last preceding subsection is paid or transferred to a university or college, or to a person designated by a university or college, shall be held by that university or college, or by that person, as the case may be, on the like trusts (if any) and subject to the like provisions (whether having effect by virtue of an enactment or otherwise) as the capital money so paid or transferred would have been subject to if it had continued to be held as mentioned in the last preceding subsection.

(4) Any stamp duty payable on, or other expenses of or incidental to, the payment or transfer of any capital money in pursuance of this section shall be paid by the university or college to whom the capital money belongs.

(5) The provisions of Schedule 2 to this Act shall have effect with respect to sinking funds.

(6) In this section "capital money" includes any property representing capital money, and "property" includes any investment, any estate or interest in real or personal property, any negotiable instrument, debt or other chose in action and any other right or interest whether in possession or not; and for the purposes of this section capital money shall be taken to belong to a university or college if it is held on behalf of that university or college, whether for the general purposes thereof or for any special endowment or other special purpose connected with that university or college.

NOTES

Commencement of this Act. See s 5(4) post.

Trusts. For power to make schemes to administer trust property of certain universities and colleges, including those to which s 2 ante applies, see the Universities and College (Trusts) Act 1943, s 2, this part of this title ante.

In this section etc. Sub-s (6) is applied for the purposes of Sch 2 post by para 5(2) of that Schedule.

Capital money. For methods of investment or application of capital money, see the Universities and College Estates Act 1925, s 26, this part of this title ante.

Definitions. For "college", see s 1(2) ante. Note as to "capital money" and "property", sub-s (6) above.

Act of 1925. Ie the Universities and College Estates Act 1925, this part of this title ante; see s 2(1)(*a*) ante.

4 Amendment and repeal of enactments

(1) The enactments specified in Schedule 3 to this Act shall have effect subject to the amendments specified in that Schedule (being minor amendments or amendments consequential upon the preceding provisions of this Act).

(2) . . .

NOTE

Sub-s (2) was repealed by the SL(R) Act 1974.

5 Short title, citation, extent and commencement

(1) This Act may be cited as the Universities and College Estates Act 1964; and the Universities and College Estates Act 1925 and this Act may be cited together as the Universities and College Estates Acts 1925 and 1964.

(2) This Act shall not extend to Scotland or to Northern Ireland.

(3) In so far as any enactment contained in this Act, or amended or modified by this Act, is capable of applying, as part of the law of England and Wales, to land in Scotland or in Northern Ireland, the last preceding subsection shall not affect the operation of that enactment, as part of that law, in relation to any such land.

(4) This Act shall come into operation at the end of the period of one month beginning with the day on which it is passed.

NOTES

Beginning with the day on which it is passed. This Act was passed, ie received the Royal Assent, on 16 July 1964, and therefore came into force on 16 August 1964, as in calculating the period the date on which the Act was passed is included; see *Hare v Gocher* [1962] 2 QB 641, [1962] 2 All ER 763, and *Trow v Ind Coope (West Midlands) Ltd* [1967] 2 QB 899 at 909, [1967] 2 All ER 900, CA. See also *Dodds v Walker* [1981] 2 All ER 609, [1981] 1 WLR 1027, HL, as to the day of expiry of periods of a month or a specified number of months.

Universities and College Estates Act 1925. See this part of this title ante.

SCHEDULES

(*Sch 1 amends the Universities and College Estates Act 1925, this part of this title ante, except in relation to Winchester and Eton; see the notes to that Act.*)

SCHEDULE 2

Section 3

SINKING FUNDS

1. The provisions of this Schedule shall have effect where any capital money belonging to a university or college, which is required to be paid or transferred under section 3(2) of this Act, is comprised in a sinking fund maintained in pursuance of a direction given by the Minister under the Act of 1925.

2. Until that capital money is so paid or transferred, the university or college shall continue to pay to the Minister any sums which, in accordance with the direction, are required to be so paid for the purpose of maintaining the sinking fund; and any sums so paid, and (in so far as the direction so requires) any income accruing from property comprised in the sinking fund, shall be dealt with as an accretion to that fund.

3. After the capital money has been so paid or transferred, the university or college shall continue to maintain the sinking fund in accordance with the direction until the end of the period for which it was directed to be maintained.

4. For the purposes of this Schedule—

(*a*) any approval or sanction of the Minister in pursuance of paragraph (*a*) of the proviso to section 26(2) of the Act of 1925, or under section 32 (1) of that Act,

(*b*) any condition imposed by the Minister in giving his consent to any transaction under that Act (whether that condition was contained in any order evidencing that consent or not), and

(*c*) any condition attached to a direction given by the Minister under that Act,

shall be treated as a direction given by the Minister under that Act.

5.—(1) In this Schedule "the Minister" means the Minister of Agriculture, Fisheries and Food.

(2) Subsection (6) of section 3 of this Act shall apply for the purposes of this Schedule as it applies for the purposes of that section.

NOTES

For "capital money" and "property", see s 3(6) ante, in conjunction with para 5(2) above; for "college", see s 1(2) ante. Note as to "the Minister", para 5(1) above.

Act of 1925. Ie the Universities and College Estates Act 1925; see s 2(1) (*a*) ante. For ss 26(2)(*a*), 32(1) of that Act, see this title ante.

(*Sch 3 repealed in part by the SL(R) Act 1974 and the SL(R) Act 1981; the remainder amends the Kendal Corn Rent Act 1932 (22 & 23 Geo 5 c lxiv; not printed in this work), ss 10, 11; the Universities and Colleges (Trusts) Act 1943, s 2 ante; the Agricultural Holdings Act 1948, s 81, Vol 1, title Agriculture (Pt 3); the Universities and College Estates Act 1925, ss 29, 43, Sch 1, para (xxxi) ante; the Coast Protection Act 1949, s 11(2)(a), Vol 49, title Water; the Landlord and Tenant Act 1954, Sch 2, para 6, Vol 23, title Landlord and Tenant (Pt 2); the Coal-Mining (Subsidence) Act 1957, s 11(7), Vol 29, title Mines, Minerals and Quarries; and the Town and Country Planning Act 1962, s 206(1) (repealed). Sch 4 repealed by the SL(R) Act 1974.)*

Part 2

The Education Acts

Table of Contents

ARMY SCHOOLS ACT 1891

(54 & 55 Vict c 16)

An Act to extend to Army Schools the benefit of certain Educational Endowments

[11 May 1891]

Northern Ireland. This Act was repealed in relation to Northern Ireland by the Education (Northern Ireland) Order 1980, SI 1980/1958, arts 10, 11, Schedule.

1 Extension to Army schools of provisions of schemes relating to educational endowments

(1) Where any scheme in force for the regulation of any endowed charity or charities, established or approved before or after the passing of this Act, includes any provision for

the benefit of children who are or have been scholars in a public elementary school, an army school shall be deemed a public elementary school within the meaning of those provisions.

(2) In this Act the expression "army school" means a school established for the purpose of affording education to children of non-commissioned officers and men of Her Majesty's regular land forces, and conducted under the authority of a Secretary of State . . ., and a certificate of the Director General of Military Education or of the Inspector of Naval Schools, as the case may require, shall be sufficient evidence that a school is an army school within the meaning of this Act.

NOTES

The words omitted from sub-s (2) were repealed by the Defence (Transfer of Functions) (No 1) Order 1964, SI 1964/488, art 2, Sch 1, Pt II.

Schemes relating to educational endowments. Such schemes were formerly made under the Endowed Schools Acts 1869 to 1948 (repealed with savings in respect of existing schemes by the Education Act 1973, s 1(1)(b), (3), (4), Sch 1, para 2, Sch 2, Pt II post); they may now be amended or made under ss 1, 2 of the 1973 Act, this part of this title post.

Public elementary school. References to "public elementary school" in sub-s (1) are to be construed as references to a county school or voluntary school by virtue of the Education Act 1944, s 120(1)(a), this part of this title post.

2 Short title

This Act may be cited as the Army Schools Act 1891.

EDUCATION ACT 1918

(8 & 9 Geo 5 c 39)

An Act to make further provision with respect to Education in England and Wales and for purposes connected therewith   [8 August 1918]

Northern Ireland. This Act does not apply; see s 52(2) post.

1–44 (*Ss 1–13, 15–41, 43, 44 repealed by the Education Act 1921, s 172, Sch 7; s 14 repealed by the Education Act 1973, s 1(4), Sch 2, Pt I; s 42 repealed by the Education Act 1944, s 101(4)(b).*)

EDUCATIONAL TRUSTS

45, 46 (*S 45 repealed by the Charities Act 1960, s 48(2), Sch 7, Pt II; s 46 repealed by the Education Act 1921, s 172, Sch 7.*)

47 Appointment of new trustees under scheme

Where, under any scheme made before the passing of this Act relating to an educational charity, the approval of the Board of Education is required to the exercise by the trustees under the scheme of a power of appointing new trustees, the scheme shall . . . have effect as if no such approval was required thereunder . . .

NOTES

The words omitted were repealed by the Education Act 1973, s 1(4), Sch 2, Pt I.

Scheme relating to an educational charity. The Endowed Schools Acts 1869–1948 made provision for such schemes. Insofar as they were still in force, they were repealed by the Education Act 1973, s 1(1)(*b*), (3), (4), Sch 1, para 2, Sch 2, Pt II, this part of this title post with a saving in certain cases in respect of existing schemes.

Board of Education. References to the Board of Education are now construed as references to the Secretary of State for Education and Science, the Secretary of State for Wales, or the Department of Education and Science, as the case may be; see the Education Act 1944, s 2(1), this part of this title post, and the note "Minister of Education" thereto.

48–51 (*Repealed by the Education Act 1921, s 172, Sch 7.*)

52 Short title, construction, extent and commencement

(1) This Act may be cited as the Education Act 1918 ...

(2) This Act shall not extend to Scotland or Ireland.

(3) ...

NOTES

The words omitted from sub-s (1) were repealed by the Education Act 1973, s 1(4), Sch 2, Pt I. Sub-s (3) was repealed by the SLR Act 1927.

(*Schs 1, 2 repealed by the Education Act 1921, s 172, Sch 7.*)

EDUCATION ACT 1944

(7 & 8 Geo 6 c 31)

ARRANGEMENT OF SECTIONS

Part I

CENTRAL ADMINISTRATION

Part II

THE STATUTORY SYSTEM OF EDUCATION

Local Administration

The Three Stages of the System

Primary and Secondary Education

Provision and Maintenance of Primary and Secondary Schools

PART V

SUPPLEMENTAL

An Act to reform the law relating to education in England and Wales   [3 August 1944]

Education Acts 1944 to 1985. By virtue of the Further Education Act 1985, s 8(2), this part of this title post, the following Acts may be cited together by this collective title—the Education Act 1944 (this Act), the Education Act 1946, the Education (Miscellaneous Provisions) Act 1948, the Education (Miscellaneous Provisions) Act 1953, the Education Act 1959, the Education Act 1962, the Education Act 1964, the Remuneration of Teachers Act 1965, the Education Act 1967, the Education Act 1968, the Education (No 2) Act 1968, the Education (Handicapped Children) Act 1970, the Education Act 1973, the Education (Work Experience) Act 1973, the Education Act 1975, the Education (School-Leaving Dates) Act 1976, the Education Act 1976, the Education Act 1979, the Education Act 1980, the Education Act 1981, the Education (Fees and Awards) Act 1983, the Education (Grants and Awards) Act 1984, and the Further Education Act 1985 (except ss 4 and 5 thereof). All these Acts are printed in this part of this title post.

Northern Ireland. This Act does not apply; see s 122(2) post.

PART I

CENTRAL ADMINISTRATION

1 ...

(1) [It shall be the duty of the Secretary of State for Education and Science] to promote the education of the people of England and Wales and the progressive development of institutions devoted to that purpose, and to secure the effective execution by local authorities, under his control and direction, of the national policy for providing a varied and comprehensive educational service in every area.

[(2) The Secretary of State for Education and Science shall for all purposes be a corporation sole under the name of the Secretary of State for Education and Science.]

(3), (4) ...

NOTES

The words in square brackets in sub-s (1) and the whole of sub-s (2) were substituted, and sub-ss (3), (4) were repealed, by the Secretary of State for Education and Science Order 1964, SI 1964/490, art 3(1), Schedule. As the marginal note is no longer applicable to the amended section, it is omitted.

Secretary of State for Education and Science. The Secretary of State was appointed by Her Majesty and all the functions of the Minister of Education and the Minister for Science and certain research functions of the Lord President of the Council were transferred to the Secretary of State; see the Secretary of State for Education and Science Order 1964, SI 1964/490.

The functions of the Secretary of State for Education and Science in relation to primary and secondary education in Wales were transferred to the Secretary of State for Wales by the Transfer of Functions (Wales) Order 1970, SI 1970/1536. This transfer included the power to make orders under Sch 1, Pt II, para 3 to this Act post, but otherwise the power to make regulations under the Education Acts 1944 to 1970, so far as relates to primary or secondary education, was transferred to the Secretary of State for Education and Science and the Secretary of State for Wales jointly. The 1970 Order did not confer on the Secretary of State for Wales functions in relation to the qualifications (including disqualification), training, supply, remuneration or superannuation of teachers or to the appointment of Her Majesty's Inspectors. As to the exercise of the functions under ss 70–74 of this Act, see the note "Secretary of State" to those sections.

By virtue of the Transfer of Functions (Wales) (No 2) Order 1978, SI 1978/274, the functions of the Secretary of State for Education and Science, in relation to Wales, in connection with further education (excluding universities) and in connection with the training and supply of teachers for primary and secondary education were transferred to the Secretary of State. The powers to make regulations which had been transferred by SI 1970/1536 to the Secretary of State for Education and Science and the Secretary of State for Wales jointly, were transferred to the Secretary of State. The functions conferred on the Secretary of State by the 1978 Order do not include functions relating to the qualification (including medical fitness), probation, misconduct, remuneration or superannuation of teachers, or to the appointment of Her Majesty's Inspectors. These functions are exercisable in relation to both England and Wales by the Secretary of State for Education and Science (whether they relate to primary, secondary or further education). The 1978 Order does not transfer any functions of the Secretary of State for Education and Science under the Education Act 1962, this part of this title post, except the power to make regulations under s 3 of that Act in respect of persons ordinarily resident in Wales, and to pay grants under such regulations.

Corporation sole. As to the meaning of this term, see 9 Halsbury's Laws (4th edn) para 1206.

Proceedings by and against the Secretary of State. See the Crown Proceedings Act 1947, Vol 13, title Crown Proceedings.

Parliamentary Commissioner. For the powers of this Commissioner to investigate the administrative actions of the Department of Education and Science, see the Parliamentary Commissioner Act 1967, s 4, Sch 2, Vol 10, title Constitutional Law (Pt 4).

2 Transfer of property and functions to Minister and construction of Acts and documents

(1) All property which, immediately before the date declared by His Majesty in Council to be the date on which the first appointment under this Act of a Minister of Education took effect, was held by the Board of Education constituted under the Board of Education Act 1899 and all functions exercisable by that Board or the President thereof immediately before that date, and all rights and liabilities, whether vested or contingent, to which the Board or the President thereof were entitled or subject immediately before that date, shall, by virtue of this Act, be transferred to the Minister; and, except where the context otherwise requires, references in any enactment or other document to the Board of Education, the President of the Board of Education, the Education Department, or the Department of Science and Art shall be construed as references to the Minister, or, where the case so requires, as references to the Ministry of Education.

(2) ...

NOTES

Sub-s (2) was repealed by the Education (Miscellaneous Provisions) Act 1948, s 11, Sch 2.

First appointment of a Minister of Education. The first appointment of a Minister of Education took effect on 10 August 1944 (Education (Date of Appointment of Minister) Order 1944, SR & O 1944/937).

Minister of Education. The property and functions of the Minister of Education and the Ministry of Education were transferred to the Secretary of State for Education and Science, and the Department of Education and Science, respectively, by the Secretary of State for Education and Science Order 1964, SI 1964/490. See now the note "Secretary of State for Education and Science" to s 1 ante.

Board of Education Act 1899. Repealed by s 121 of this Act as from 10 August 1944 (the date of the first appointment of a Minister of Education).

3 Seal and acts of [Secretary of State]

(1) [The Secretary of State for Education and Science] shall have an official seal which shall be authenticated by the signature of [the Secretary of State for Education and Science] or of a secretary to [the Department of the Secretary of State] or of any person authorised by [the Secretary of State for Education and Science] to authenticate the seal.

(2) The seal of [the Secretary of State for Education and Science] shall be officially and judicially noticed, and every document purporting to be an instrument made or issued by [the Secretary of State for Education and Science] and either to be sealed with the seal of [the Secretary of State for Education and Science] authenticated in the manner provided by this section, or to be signed by a secretary to [the Department of the Secretary of State] or by any other officer of [the Department of the Secretary of State] authorised to sign it, shall in any legal proceedings be deemed to be so made or issued without further proof, unless the contrary is shown.

(3) A certificate signed by [the Secretary of State for Education and Science] certifying that any instrument purporting to be made or issued by him was so made or issued shall be conclusive evidence of the fact certified.

(4) ...

NOTES

The words in square brackets in sub-ss (1)–(3) were substituted, and sub-s (4) was repealed, by the Secretary of State for Education and Science Order 1964, SI 1964/490, art 3(1), Schedule, Pt I.

Secretary of State for Education and Science. See the note to s 1 ante.

Evidence. For further provisions as to evidence, see s 95 post, and the Documentary Evidence Act 1868, as extended, Vol 17, title Evidence.

4 Central Advisory Councils

(1) There shall be two Central Advisory Councils for Education, one for England and the other for Wales and Monmouthshire, and it shall be the duty of those Councils to advise [the Secretary of State] upon such matters connected with educational theory and practice as they think fit, and upon any questions referred to them by him.

(2) The members of each Council shall be appointed by [the Secretary of State] and [the Secretary of State] shall appoint a member of each Council to be Chairman thereof and shall appoint an officer of [the Department of the Secretary of State] to be secretary thereto.

(3) Each Council shall include persons who have had experience of the statutory system of public education as well as persons who have had experience of educational institutions not forming part of that system.

(4) [The Secretary of State] shall by regulations make provision as to the term of office and conditions of retirement of the members of each Council, and regulations made by [the Secretary of State] for either Council may provide for periodical or other meetings of the Council and as to the procedure thereof, but, subject to the provisions of any such regulations, the meetings and procedure of each Council shall be such as may be determined by them.

NOTES

The words in square brackets are substituted by virtue of the Secretary of State for Education and Science Order 1964, SI 1964/490, art 3(2).

Central Advisory Councils. By s 5 post the Secretary of State is bound to include in his annual report to Parliament details of the composition and proceedings of the Councils.

As to appointment to the Central Advisory Council for Wales, see the Transfer of Functions (Wales) Order 1970, SI 1970/1536, art 4.

Wales and Monmouthshire. Wales, including the administrative county of Monmouthshire and the county borough of Newport, was divided into new local government areas as from 1 April 1974 by the Local Government Act 1972, s 20, Sch 4, Pts I, II, Vol 25, title Local Government.

Secretary of State. Ie the Secretary of State for Education and Science; see the note to s 1 ante.

Regulations under this section. The Central Advisory Councils for Education Regulations 1945, SR & O 1945/152, as amended by SI 1951/1742.

5 Annual report to Parliament

[The Secretary of State] shall make to Parliament an annual report giving an account of the exercise and performance of the powers and duties conferred and imposed upon him by this Act and of the composition and proceedings of the Central Advisory Councils for Education.

NOTES

The words in square brackets are substituted by virtue of the Secretary of State for Education and Science Order 1964, SI 1964/490.

Secretary of State. Ie the Secretary of State for Education and Science; see the note to s 1 ante.

Central Advisory Councils. See s 4 ante.

PART II

THE STATUTORY SYSTEM OF EDUCATION

LOCAL ADMINISTRATION

6 Local education authorities

(1) Subject to the provisions of Part I of the First Schedule to this Act, the local education authority for each county shall be the council of the county, and the local education authority for each county borough shall be the council of the county borough.

(2) The local administration of the statutory system of public education shall be conducted in accordance with the provisions of Part II . . . of the said Schedule.

(3) All property which immediately before the date of the commencement of this Part of this Act was held by the council of any county district solely or mainly for the purposes of any functions exercisable by them under the Education Acts 1921 to 1939 and all rights and liabilities, whether vested or contingent, to which any such council were entitled or subject immediately before the said date by reason of the exercise of such functions shall, save as may be otherwise directed by the Minister under the powers conferred on him by this Act, be transferred by virtue of this section to the local education authority for the county in which the county district is situated.

(4) All officers who immediately before the said date were employed by the council of any county district solely or mainly for the purposes of any such functions as aforesaid shall by virtue of this section be transferred to and become officers of the local education authority for the county in which the county district is situated, and shall be employed by that authority upon the terms and conditions upon which they were employed by the council of the county district immediately before that date.

NOTES

The words omitted from sub-s (2) were repealed by the Local Government Act 1972, s 272(1), Sch 30.

Local education authority. Consequent upon the reorganisation of local government under the Local Government Act 1972, outside Greater London the local education authority for each non-metropolitan county is now the council of the county, and the local education authority for each metropolitan district is now the council of the district; see s 192 of the 1972 Act, Vol 25, title Local Government. As to the transfer of functions from the old authorities to the new, see s 192(5), (6) of the 1972 Act. By virtue of the London Government Act 1963, s 30(1), Vol 26, title London, any reference in this Act to the local education authority is to be construed, in relation to any outer London borough (as defined in s 1(1)(*b*) of that Act) as a reference to the council of that borough. In relation to Greater London exclusive of the outer London Boroughs the local education authority is the Inner London Education Authority established by the Local Government Act 1985, s 18, Vol 25, title Local Government.

County. The counties existing immediately before 1 April 1974 were abolished on that date by the Local Government Act 1972, ss 1(10), 20(6), Vol 25, title Local Government, and by virtue of s 179(1), (2) of that Act, the reference to a county is to be construed as a county established by ss 1(1), (2), 20(1), (2) of, and Sch 1, Pts I, II, Sch 4, Pt I to, the 1972 Act.

County borough. The boroughs, other than London boroughs, existing immediately before 1 April 1974 were abolished on that date by the Local Government Act 1972, ss 1(9), (10), 20(6), Vol 25, title Local Government, and the reference to a borough no longer has any effect.

Commencement of this Part of this Act. The date of the commencement of Pt II (ss 6–69) was 1 April 1945 by virtue of s 119 (repealed).

County district. The council of a rural district was incapable under the Education Act 1921 of possessing powers relating to either higher or elementary education; accordingly this expression refers only to non-county boroughs and urban districts in existence on 1 April 1945 (see the previous note).

Rights and liabilities. See the further provisions as to transfer in s 96(2)–(5) post.

Contingent liability. The duty imposed upon the local education authority by this Act is not confined to the maintenance of schools under their authority, but extends to keeping the school and premises belonging thereto in a proper condition for the purposes of the schools; see *Morris v Carnarvon CC* [1910] 1 KB 840, 79 LJKB 670.

Save as may be otherwise directed by the Minister. S 96(1) post enabled the Minister to direct that certain trust property should not be deemed to have been transferred by virtue of this section. The Minister was the Minister of Education appointed under s 1 ante as originally enacted. The Secretary of State for Education and Science was substituted for that Minister by the Secretary of State for Education and Science Order 1964, SI 1964/490, but as the transfers by virtue of this section and any exceptions to them under s 96(1) post must have occurred well before 1964, effect has not been given to that substitution in this section.

Concurrent functions. Where a local authority under Pt III of the Child Care Act 1980 and a local education authority have concurrent functions, the allocation of those functions may be determined by regulations made under s 30 of the 1980 Act, Vol 6, title Children.

Careers services. As to the duties of local education authorities with regard to the provision of careers services, see the Employment and Training Act 1973, ss 8–10, Vol 16, title Employment.

Application to Scilly Isles. See s 118 post.

Education Acts 1921 to 1939. Repealed.

THE THREE STAGES OF THE SYSTEM

7 Stages and purposes of statutory system of education

The statutory system of public education shall be organised in three progressive stages to be known as primary education, secondary education, and further education; and it shall be the duty of the local education authority for every area, so far as their powers extend, to contribute towards the spiritual, moral, mental, and physical development of the community by securing that efficient education throughout those stages shall be available to meet the needs of the population of their area.

NOTES

Enforcement. As to the enforcement of the duty imposed by the present section, see s 99 post.

Exclusion of section. This section is excluded by the Education Act 1964, s 1(3)(*a*) post.

So far as their powers extend. A local education authority has no locus standi to sue to establish a charitable trust (*Re Belling, London Borough of Enfield v Public Trustee* [1967] Ch 425, [1967] 1 All ER 105).

Physical development. For provision of facilities for physical training, see s 53 post.

Definitions. For "further education", "local education authority", "primary education" and "secondary education", see s 114(1) post.

PRIMARY AND SECONDARY EDUCATION

Provision and Maintenance of Primary and Secondary Schools

8 Duty of local education authorities to secure provision of primary and secondary schools

(1) It shall be the duty of every local education authority to secure that there shall be available for their area sufficient schools—

(a) for providing [primary education, that is to say, full-time education suitable to the requirements of junior pupils who have not attained the age of ten years and six months, and full-time education suitable to the requirements of junior pupils who have attained that age and whom it is expedient to educate together with junior pupils who have not attained that age]; and

(b) for providing secondary education, that is to say, full-time education suitable to the requirements of senior pupils, other than such full-time education as may be provided for senior pupils in pursuance of a scheme made under the provisions of this Act relating to further education [and full-time education suitable to the requirements of junior pupils who have attained the age of ten years and six months and whom it is expedient to educate together with senior pupils];

and the schools available for an area shall not be deemed to be sufficient unless they are sufficient in number, character, and equipment to afford for all pupils opportunities for education offering such variety of instruction and training as may be desirable in view of their different ages, abilities, and aptitudes, and of the different periods for which they may be expected to remain at school, including practical instruction and training appropriate to their respective needs.

(2) In fulfilling their duties under this section, a local education authority shall, in particular, have regard—

(a) to the need for securing that primary and secondary education are provided in separate schools;

(b) . . .

[(c) to the need for securing that special educational provision is made for pupils who have special educational needs; and]

(d) to the expediency of securing the provision of boarding accommodation, either in boarding schools or otherwise, for pupils for whom education as boarders is considered by their parents and by the authority to be desirable:

Provided that paragraph (a) of this subsection shall not have effect with respect to special schools.

NOTES

The words in square brackets in sub-s (1)(a) were substituted, and the words in square brackets in sub-s (1)(b) were added, by the Education (Miscellaneous Provisions) Act 1948, s 3.

Sub-s (2)(b) was repealed by the Education Act 1980, s 38(6), Sch 7.

Sub-s (2)(c) was substituted by the Education Act 1981, s 2(1).

General Note. For provision as to the transfer of junior pupils from primary to secondary schools, see the Education (Miscellaneous Provisions) Act 1948, s 4(1), this part of this title post.

It shall be the duty, etc. The general duty to secure that sufficient schools for the area are available is amplified by sub-s (2) above and restricted by s 4(2) of the 1948 Act, this part of this title post. The local education authority is not itself required to provide all the schools required, but to secure that they are available. As to the powers of the Secretary of State in the event of default by the local education authority, see s 99 post. The exercise and performance of all powers and duties conferred and imposed on the Secretary of State and upon local education authorities by this Act are subject to the guiding principle imposed by s 76 post, that so far as is compatible with the provision of efficient instruction and training and the avoidance of unreasonable public expenditure, pupils are to be educated in accordance with the wishes of their parents. A local education authority may, under the Education (Miscellaneous Provisions) Act 1953, s 6, this part of this title post, make arrangements for the provision of education at non-maintained schools and the payment of tuition and boarding fees.

The duties of a local education authority do not extend to require the authority to secure the provision of schools for children or young persons from outside the area of the authority, even though it may be convenient for a child or young person to attend a school in an area other than that in which he lives. The Education Act 1980, s 31, this part of this title post, provides, however, for the recoupment to local authorities of the cost of providing education for persons not belonging to their area.

The question whether the authority's closure of schools is a breach of statutory duty should be determined at the trial of the action, not in interlocutory proceedings, except in most exceptional circumstances; see *Meade v London Borough of Haringey* [1979] 2 All ER 1016, [1979] 1 WLR 637, CA. In that case, schools were closed in an industrial dispute. It was held that such a closure would be unlawful if it was made without just cause or excuse, eg if the authority was affected by considerations not relevant to the educational field (per Eveleigh LJ) or acted from improper motives or for inadequate reasons (per Sir Stanley Rees).

Local education authority. For meaning, see s 114(1) post and the note thereto.

Shall be available. On the meaning of the expression "available", see *Gateshead Union Guardians v Durham CC* [1918] 1 Ch 146 at 160, 87 LJ Ch 113 at 117, CA per Swinfen Eady LJ ("the accommodation in the school cannot be said to be made "available" for children if they are refused admission unless and until their parents comply with some request to pay money which the statutes do not confer upon the local education authority any right to demand").

Full-time education. This term is nowhere defined in this Act, but s 23 post provides that the power to control the secular instruction in schools given by sub-ss (1), (2) of that section includes power (inter alia) to determine the times at which the school session is to begin and end on any day, to determine the times at which the school terms are to begin and end and to determine the school holidays. The Education Act 1980, s 27(1)(e), this part of this title post, empowers the Secretary of State to make regulations concerning the duration of the school day and school year; see now the Education (Schools and Further Education) Regulations 1981, SI 1981/1086, reg 10.

For their area. The duties of a local education authority do not extend to requiring the authority to provide schools for children or young persons from outside the area of the authority. The Education Act 1980, s 31, this part of this title post, provides, however, for the recoupment to local authorities of the cost of providing education for persons not belonging to their area.

Age of children. As to evidence of age, see s 95 post and the note thereto.

Separate school. In the Education Act 1946, s 2(1), this part of this title post, a school organised in two or more separate departments is treated as a single school, but it appears from sub-s (7) of that section that complete physical separation is not required to constitute separate schools.

Boarding accommodation. In certain circumstances, the local education authority has a duty to pay a pupil's boarding fees at a non-maintained school; see the Education (Miscellaneous Provisions) Act 1953, s 6, this part of this title post.

Remedy for breach of duty. The principal remedy for breach of duty under this section is by complaint to the Secretary of State under s 99 post (*Watt v Kesteven CC* [1955] 1 QB 408, [1955] 1 All ER 473, CA) but this does not exclude any other remedy available in the courts when a person has suffered damage; see *Meade v London Borough of Haringey* [1979] 2 All ER 1016, [1979] 1 WLR 637, CA.

Parental preferences. A local education authority must enable the parent of a child in that area to express a preference as to which school the child should attend, and the authority has a duty to comply with the parent's wishes except in certain specified circumstances; see the Education Act 1980, s 6, this part of this title post.

Nursery education. There is no duty on a local education authority to provide education for children under five although it is enabled to do so; see s 9(4) post and the Education Act 1980, s 24, this part of this title post.

Definitions. For "further education", "junior pupil", "school", "senior pupil", see s 114(1) post. For "special educational needs" and "special educational provision", see, by virtue of s 114(1) post, the Education Act 1981, s 1, this part of this title post.

9 County schools, voluntary schools, nursery schools, and special schools

(1) For the purpose of fulfilling their duties under this Act, a local education authority shall have power to establish primary and secondary schools, to maintain such schools whether established by them or otherwise, and ... to assist any such school which is not maintained by them.

(2) Primary and secondary schools maintained by a local education authority, not being nursery schools or special schools, shall, if established by a local education authority or by a former authority, be known as county schools and, if established otherwise than by such an authority, be known as voluntary schools:

Provided that any school which by virtue of any enactment repealed by this Act was to be deemed to be, or was to be treated as, a school provided by a former authority shall, notwithstanding that it was not in fact established by such an authority as aforesaid, be a county school.

(3) Subject to the provisions hereinafter contained as to the discontinuance of voluntary schools, every school which immediately before the commencement of this Part of this Act was, within the meaning of the enactments repealed by this Act, a public elementary school provided otherwise than by a former authority shall, if it was then maintained by a former authority, be maintained as a voluntary school by the local education authority for the area in which the school is situated.

(4) Primary schools which are used mainly for the purpose of providing education for children who have attained the age of two years but have not attained the age of five years shall be known as nursery schools.

[(5) Schools which are specially organised to make special educational provision for pupils with special educational needs and which are for the time being approved by the Secretary of State as special schools shall be known as special schools.]

(6) The powers conferred by subsection (1) of this section on local education authorities shall be construed as including power to establish maintain and assist schools outside as well as inside their areas.

NOTES

The words omitted from sub-s (1) were repealed by the Education Act 1980, s 38(6), Sch 7.

Sub-s (5) was substituted by the Education Act 1981, s 11. For transitional provisions in relation to any approval given under sub-s (5) before the coming into force of s 12 of the 1981 Act, see s 21 of, and Sch 2, para 1 to, the 1981 Act, this part of this title post.

Assist any such school. See the Education (Miscellaneous Provisions) Act 1953, s 6, this part of this title post.

Voluntary schools. For general provisions as to the maintenance of voluntary schools, see the Education Act 1946, s 3, Sch 1, this part of this title post. The Charities Act 1960, s 37, Vol 5, title Charities, does not affect the trusteeship, control or management of a voluntary school within the meaning of this Act; see s 37(7) of that Act. For provisions as to the discontinuance of voluntary schools, see s 14 post and the Education Act 1980, s 12, this part of this title post.

Commencement of this Part of this Act. Ss 6–43, 45–69 came into operation on 1 April 1945 by virtue of s 119 (repealed); as to s 44, see sub-s (1) thereof and the notes thereto.

Age of children. As to evidence of age, see s 95 post and the note thereto.

Nursery schools. As to the provision of nursery schools and nursery classes by a local education authority, see the Education Act 1980, s 24, this part of this title post.

Special schools. As to requirements to be complied with by special schools, see the Education Act 1981, s 12, this part of this title post and the regulations made thereunder.

Secretary of State. Ie the Secretary of State for Education and Science; see the note to s 1 ante.

Valuation for rating of county and voluntary schools. See the General Rate Act 1967, s 30, Vol 36, title Rating.

Greater London. As to the maintenance by local education authorities for areas in Greater London (within the meaning of the London Government Act 1963, s 2(1), Vol 26, title London) of county and voluntary schools which were maintained immediately before 1 April 1965 by the former education authority for that area, see s 31(5), (6) of that Act; and for a restriction of the grounds for refusing a pupil admission to, or excluding a pupil from, any county or voluntary school maintained by a local education authority in Greater London, see s 31(8) of that Act.

Definitions. For "assist", "former authority", "local education authority", "maintain", "primary school", "pupil", "school" and "secondary school", see s 114(1) post.

10 Requirements as to school premises

(1) [The Secretary of State] shall make regulations prescribing the standards to which the premises of schools maintained by local education authorities are to conform, and such regulations may prescribe different standards for such descriptions of schools as may be specified in the regulations.

(2) Subject as hereinafter provided, it shall be the duty of a local education authority to secure that the premises of every school maintained by them conform to the standards prescribed for schools of the description to which the school belongs:

[Provided that, if [the Secretary of State] is satisfied with respect to any school—

    (a) that having regard to the nature of the existing site or to any existing buildings thereon or to other special circumstances affecting the school premises it would be unreasonable to require conformity with a requirement of the regulations as to any matter, or

    (b) where the school is to have an additional or new site that, having regard to shortage of suitable sites it would be unreasonable to require conformity with a requirement of the regulations relating to sites, or

(c) where the school is to have additional buildings or is to be transferred to a new site, and existing buildings not theretofore part of the school premises, or temporary buildings, are to be used for that purpose, that [having regard to the need to control public expenditure in the interests of the national economy] it would be unreasonable to require conformity with a requirement of the regulations relating to buildings,

he may give a direction that, notwithstanding that that requirement is not satisfied, the school premises shall, whilst the direction remains in force, be deemed to conform to the prescribed standards as respects matters with which the direction deals if such conditions, if any, as may be specified in the direction as respects those matters are observed.]

NOTES

The words "the Secretary of State" in this section are substituted by virtue of the Secretary of State for Education and Science Order 1964, SI 1964/490, art 3(2)(a). The proviso to sub-s (2) was substituted by the Education (Miscellaneous Provisions) Act 1948, s 7(1). The words in square brackets in para (c) of the proviso to sub-s (2) were substituted by the Education Act 1968, s 3(3).

General Note. Where proposals are made under the Education Act 1980, ss 12, 13, this part of this title post for the establishment of a school, the maintenance of a school as a county or voluntary school or the making of a significant change in the character, or significant enlargement of the premises, of a school, the Secretary of State must approve the proposals concerning the premises; see s 14 of that Act post.

Secretary of State. Ie the Secretary of State for Education and Science; see the note to s 1 ante.

Local education authority. For meaning, see s 114(1) post and the note thereto.

Duty ... to conform to the standards prescribed. The duty to conform to the prescribed standards under sub-s (2) above is absolute and the test as to whether they have been conformed to is objective (*Reggell v Surrey CC* [1964] 1 All ER 743, [1964] 1 WLR 358). As to the Secretary of State's powers of enforcement of local authorities' duties, see s 99 post. These powers do not exclude any other remedy available in the courts; see *Reggell v Surrey CC* cited above, *Bradbury v London Borough of Enfield* [1967] 3 All ER 434, [1967] 1 WLR 1311, *Ward v Hertfordshire CC* [1969] 2 All ER 807, [1969] 1 WLR 790, and *Meade v London Borough of Haringey* [1979] 2 All ER 1016, [1979] 1 WLR 637, CA.

Definitions. For "maintained", "premises" and "school", see s 114(1) post; and for "site", see the Education Act 1946, s 16(1), this part of this title post.

Regulations under this section. The Education (School Premises) Regulations 1981, SI 1981/909. For general provisions as to regulations under this Act, see s 112 post.

11–13 (*Repealed by the Education Act 1980, s 38(6), Sch 7.*)

14 Restrictions on discontinuance of voluntary schools by ... governors

(1) Subject to the provisions of this section, the ... governors of a voluntary school shall not discontinue the school except after serving on [the Secretary of State] and on the local education authority by whom the school is maintained not less than two years' notice of their intention to do so:

[Provided that, except by leave of [the Secretary of State], no such notice as aforesaid shall be served by the ... governors of any voluntary school in respect of the premises of which expenditure has been incurred otherwise than in connection with repairs by [the Secretary of State] or by any local education authority or former authority.

If [the Secretary of State] grants such leave, he may impose such requirements as he thinks just—

(a) in regard to the repayment of the whole or any part of the amount of the expenditure so incurred by [the Secretary of State];
(b) where [the Secretary of State] is satisfied that the local education authority will require, for any purpose connected with education, any premises which are for the time being used for the purposes of the school in regard to the conveyance of those premises to the authority;

(c) in regard to the payment by the local education authority of such part of the value of any premises so conveyed as is just having regard to the extent to which those premises were provided otherwise than at the expense of the authority or a former authority;

(d) where any premises for the time being used for the purposes of the school are not to be so conveyed, in regard to the payment to the authority by the ... governors of the school of such part of the value of those premises as is just having regard to the extent to which they were provided at the expense of the authority or a former authority.]

(2) No such notice as aforesaid shall be withdrawn except with the consent of the local education authority.

(3) If, while any such notice as aforesaid is in force with respect to a voluntary school, the ... governors of the school inform the local education authority that they are unable or unwilling to carry on the school until the expiration of the notice, the authority may conduct the school during the whole or any part of the unexpired period of the notice as if it were a county school, and shall be entitled to the use of the school premises, free of charge, for that purpose.

(4) While any school is being conducted by a local education authority as a county school under the last foregoing subsection, the authority shall keep the school premises in good repair, and for all purposes relating to the condition of the school premises, the occupation and use thereof, and the making of alterations thereto, any interest in the said premises which is held for the purposes of the school shall be deemed to be vested in the authority:

Provided that the ... governors of the school shall be entitled to the use of the school premises or any part thereof when not required for the purposes of the school to the like extent as if they had continued to carry on the school during the unexpired period of the notice.

(5) Where any school is discontinued in accordance with the provisions of this section, the duty of the local education authority to maintain the school as a voluntary school shall be extinguished.

NOTES

The words "the Secretary of State" are substituted by virtue of the Secretary of State for Education and Science Order 1964, SI 1964/490, art 3(2)(a).

The proviso to sub-s (1) was substituted by the Education Act 1946, s 14(1), Sch 2, Pt II.

The words omitted from the marginal note are repealed by virtue of the Education Act 1980, s 1(1), (2), (4) and the other words omitted were repealed by s 1(3) of, and Sch 1, para 1 to, that Act.

General Note. This section provides a procedure for the closure of voluntary schools by the governors. (For alternative procedures for closure, see s 16(2) post in conjunction with s 13(2) ante, and the Education Act 1980, s 12, this part of this title post.) Where the premises of a voluntary school are held on trust by the governors or a body of trustees failure to comply with this section would generally constitute a breach of trust. In certain circumstances therefore an application for advice should be made to the Secretary of State under the Charities Act 1960, s 24(1), Vol 5, title Charities. This confers considerable indemnity; see s 24(2) of that Act.

Notice. As to special procedure at governors' meetings in relation to a decision to serve such notice, see the Education Act 1980, s 4(5), this part of this title post.

Local inquiries. The Secretary of State may order a local inquiry to be held for the purpose of the exercise of his functions under this section; see s 93 post.

Application to Greater London. As to the application of this section to Greater London, see the London Government Act 1963, s 31(5), Vol 26, title London.

Definitions. For "county school" and "voluntary school", see s 9(2) ante; for "former authority", "local education authority", "premises" and "school", see s 114(1) post.

15 Classification of voluntary schools as controlled schools, aided schools, or special agreement schools

(1) Voluntary schools shall be of three categories, that is to say, controlled schools, aided schools, and special agreement schools, and in schools of those several categories

the management of the school, the secular instruction and religious education, and the appointment and dismissal of teachers, shall be regulated in accordance with the provisions hereinafter contained relating to those matters in controlled schools aided schools and special agreement schools respectively.

(2) Upon application being duly made to him with respect to any voluntary school, [the Secretary of State] may by order direct that the school shall be a controlled school an aided school or a special agreement school, and where he is satisfied that the ... governors of the school will be able and willing, with the assistance of the maintenance contribution payable by [the Secretary of State] under this Act, to defray the expenses which would fall to be borne by them under paragraph (a) of the next following subsection, the order shall direct that the school shall be an aided school, or, in the case of a school with respect to which a special agreement has been made under the Third Schedule to this Act, a special agreement school:

Provided that, subject to the provisions of this section, any application for an order directing that a school shall be an aided school or a special agreement school must be made, in the case of a school which became a voluntary school by virtue of subsection (3) of section nine of this Act not later than six months after the date on which the ... governors of the school received notice of the approval of the development plan for the area, and in any other case not later than the submission to [the Secretary of State] of the proposals that the school should be maintained by the local education authority as a voluntary school; and, subject to the transitional provisions of this Act as to the management and maintenance of voluntary schools, a voluntary school with respect to which no order is in force under this section directing that it shall be an aided school or a special agreement school shall be a controlled school.

(3) The ... governors of a controlled school shall not be responsible for any of the expenses of maintaining the school, but the following provisions shall have effect with respect to the maintenance of aided schools and special agreement schools:

(a) the following expenses shall be payable by the ... governors of the school, that is to say, the expenses of discharging any liability incurred by them or on their behalf or by or on behalf of any former ... governors of the school or any trustees thereof [in connection with the provision of premises or equipment for the purposes of the school], any expenses incurred in effecting such alterations to the school buildings as may be required by the local education authority for the purpose of securing that the school premises should conform to the prescribed standards, and any expenses incurred in effecting repairs to the [school buildings] not being repairs which are excluded from their responsibility by the following paragraph:

[(b) the ... governors of the school shall not be responsible for repairs to the interior of the school buildings, or for repairs to those buildings necessary in consequence of the use of the school premises, in pursuance of any direction or requirement of the authority, for purposes other than those of the school.]

(4) If at any time the ... governors of an aided school or a special agreement school are unable or unwilling to carry out their obligations under paragraph (a) of the last foregoing subsection, it shall be their duty to apply to [the Secretary of State] for an order revoking the order by virtue of which the school is an aided school or a special agreement school, and upon such an application being made to him [the Secretary of State] shall revoke the order.

(5) If at any time [the Secretary of State] is satisfied that the grant made in respect of a special agreement school in pursuance of the special agreement made with respect to the school under this Act has been repaid to the local education authority by which the school is maintained, [the Secretary of State] shall, upon application being made to him for that purpose by the ... governors of the school, by order revoke the order by virtue of which the school is a special agreement school and, if satisfied that the ... governors

of the school will be able and willing, with the assistance of the maintenance contribution payable by [the Secretary of State] under this Act, to defray the expenses which would fall to be borne by them under paragraph (*a*) of subsection (3) of this section, shall by order direct that the school shall be an aided school.

(6) ...

NOTES

The words "the Secretary of State" are substituted by virtue of the Secretary of State for Education and Science Order 1964, SI 1964/490, art 3(2)(*a*).

The words in square brackets in sub-s (3) were substituted, and sub-s (6) was repealed, by the Education Act 1946, s 14(1), Sch 2, Pt II.

The words omitted from sub-ss (2)–(5) were repealed by the Education Act 1980, s 1(3), Sch 1, para 1.

Sub-s (1): Management. Ss 17–22 post regulate the management of those schools.

As to financial provision for aided schools and special agreement schools, see ss 102, 103, 105 post, and the Education Act 1967, s 1(2), this part of this title post. As to financial assistance for Church of England aided schools and Church of England special agreement schools, see the Church Schools (Assistance by Church Commissioners) Measure 1958, Vol 14, title Ecclesiastical Law (Pt 5).

Secular instruction. See s 23 post.

Religious education. See ss 25–30 post.

Appointment and dismissal of teachers. See s 24 post.

Sub-s (2): Secretary of State for Educational Science. See the note to s 1 ante.

Maintenance contribution. See s 102 post.

Not later than six months after. The general rule in cases where an act is to be done within a specified time is that the day from which it runs is not to be counted; see *Goldsmiths' Co v West Metropolitan Rly Co* [1904] 1 KB 1, [1900–3] All ER Rep 667, CA; *Stewart v Chapman* [1951] 2 KB 792, [1951] 2 All ER 613. See also *Dodds v Walker* [1981] 2 All ER 609, [1981] 1 WLR 1027, HL, as to the day of expiry of periods of a month or a specified number of months.

Notice. As to the service of notices, see s 113 post.

Development plan. Under s 11 of this Act (repealed), each local education authority was required to submit to the Secretary of State a development plan showing the authority's proposals for providing sufficient primary and secondary schools in that area.

Transitional provisions of this Act. These provisions, formerly contained in s 32, are now repealed.

Sub-s (3): maintaining the school. As to the duties of the managers and governors in relation to the maintenance of such schools, see the Education Act 1946, s 3, Sch 1, this part of this title post.

For the purposes of this Act the expenses of maintaining voluntary schools include payment of rates; see the Rating and Valuation Act 1961, s 12(6), Vol 36, title Rating.

Prescribed standards. For requirements as to school premises, see s 10 ante and the note "Regulations under this section" thereto.

Other purposes. As to the powers of local education authorities relating to the use of voluntary school premises, see s 22 post.

Sub-s (4): Order. The references to an order by virtue of which a school is an aided school include references to a direction that the school is an aided school under the Education Act 1946, s 2; see s 2(5) of that Act, this part of this title post.

Sub-s (5): Grant made in pursuance of special agreement. As to the making of such grants, see Sch 3, paras 4, 5 post. As to the repayment thereof, see para 9 of that Schedule.

Maintenance contribution. See s 102 post.

Definitions. For "alterations", "local education authority", "maintain" and "premises", see s 114(1) post; and for "voluntary school", see s 9(2) ante. For "school buildings", see the Education Act 1946, s 4(2) post.

Orders under this section. Orders under this section, being local, are not noted in this work. As to variation and revocation of orders under this Act, see s 111 post.

16 Transfer of county and voluntary schools to new sites, and substitution of new voluntary schools for old ones

(1) Where [the Secretary of State] is satisfied that it is expedient that any county school or any voluntary school should be transferred to a new site either because it is not reasonably practicable to make to the existing premises of the school the alterations necessary for securing that they should conform to the prescribed standards, or in consequence of any movement of population or of any action taken or proposed to be taken under the enactments relating to housing or to town and country planning, [the Secretary of State] may by order authorise the transfer of the school to the new site; [and

a voluntary school shall not be transferred to a new site without the authority of an order under this subsection].

(2) Where in connection with any proposals submitted to [the Secretary of State] under [section 13 of the Education Act 1980] it is claimed that any school or schools thereby proposed to be established should be maintained by the local education authority as a voluntary school in substitution for another school at the time being maintained by a local education authority as a voluntary school or for two or more such schools which is or are to be discontinued, then, if [the Secretary of State] is satisfied that the school or schools proposed to be established will be so maintained, he may, if he approves the proposals with or without modifications, by order direct that the school or schools proposed to be established shall be established in substitution for the school or schools to be discontinued, and where such an order is made, the provisions of this Act relating to the discontinuance of voluntary schools shall not apply with respect to the discontinuance of the school or schools to be discontinued.

(3) Before making any order under this section, [the Secretary of State] shall consult any local education authority which will, in his opinion, be affected by the making of the order, and the ... governors of any voluntary school which in his opinion will be so affected; and any such order may impose such conditions on any such local education authority or ... governors and may contain such incidental and consequential provisions as [the Secretary of State] thinks fit.

NOTES

The words "the Secretary of State" are substituted by virtue of the Secretary of State for Education and Science Order 1964, SI 1964/490, art 3(2)(a).

The words in the third pair of square brackets in sub-s (1) were substituted by the Education Act 1968, s 1(3), Sch 1, para 1.

The words in the second pair of square brackets in sub-s (2) were substituted, and the words omitted from sub-s (3) were repealed, by the Education Act 1980, ss 1(3), 16(4), Sch 1, para 1, Sch 3, para 1.

Secretary of State. See the note "Secretary of State for Education and Science" to s 1 ante.

Prescribed standards. For requirements as to school premises, see s 10 ante and the note "Regulations under this section" thereto.

Enactments relating to housing or to town and country planning. See Vol 21, title Housing, and Vol 46, title Town and Country Planning.

Proposals submitted to the Secretary of State. Where the Secretary of State approves a proposal, or makes an order under this section, he may by order make such consequential modifications of any trust deed or other instrument as, after consultation, appear to him to be requisite; see the Education Act 1973, s 1(2), this part of this title post.

Local education authority. For meaning, see s 114 post and the note thereto.

Provisions ... relating to the discontinuance of voluntary schools. Ie s 14 ante.

Governors. As to the duties of governors of aided or special agreement schools when an order is made under this section, see the Education Act 1946, s 3, Sch 1, para 1, this part of this title post.

Definitions. For "alterations", "maintain" and "premises", see s 114(1) post; and for "county school" and "voluntary school", see s 9(2) ante.

Orders under this section. Orders under this section, being local, are not noted in this work. For revocation and variation of orders, see s 111 post.

[Government] of Primary Schools and Government of Secondary Schools

17 Constitution of ... governors and conduct of county schools and voluntary schools

(1) For every county school and for every voluntary school there shall be an instrument providing for the constitution of the body of [governors of the school in accordance with the provisions of this Act, and the instrument providing for the constitution of the body of governors is in this Act referred to as an instrument of government.]

(2) [The instrument of government] shall be made in the case of a county school by

an order of the local education authority and in the case of a voluntary school by an order of [the Secretary of State].

(3) Subject to the provisions of this Act and of any trust deed relating to the school:—

(a) every county primary school and every voluntary primary school shall be conducted in accordance with [articles of government] made by an order of the local education authority; and

(b) every county secondary school and every voluntary secondary school shall be conducted in accordance with articles of government made in the case of a county school by an order of the local education authority and approved by [the Secretary of State], and in the case of a voluntary school by an order of [the Secretary of State]; and such articles shall in particular determine the functions to be exercised in relation to the school by the local education authority, the body of governors, and the head teacher respectively.

(4) Where it appears to [the Secretary of State] that any provision included or proposed to be included in the ... instrument of government, or articles of government, for a county school or a voluntary school is in any respect inconsistent with the provisions of any trust deed relating to the school, and that it is expedient in the interests of the school that the provisions of the trust deed should be modified for the purpose of removing the inconsistency, he may by order make such modifications in the provisions of the trust deed as appear to him to be just and expedient for that purpose.

(5) Before making any order under this section in respect of any school, [the Secretary of State] shall afford to the local education authority and to any other persons appearing to him to be concerned with the ... government of the school an opportunity of making representations to him with respect thereto, and in making any such order [the Secretary of State] shall have regard to all the circumstances of the school, and in particular to the question whether the school is, or is to be, a primary or secondary school, and, in the case of an existing school, shall have regard to the manner in which the school has been conducted theretofore.

[(6) Where proposals for a significant change in the character of a voluntary school are approved under [section 13 of the Education Act 1980] then, without prejudice to the power to vary orders conferred by section 111, the Secretary of State may by order make such variations of the articles of government (if the school is a secondary school) ... as appear to him to be required in consequence of the proposed change in the character of the school; and so much of subsection (5) of this section as relates to the making of representations with respect to orders under this section shall not apply to an order made in pursuance only of the power conferred by this subsection.]

NOTES

The words omitted from the marginal note are repealed, and the word in square brackets in the preceding cross-heading is substituted, by virtue of the Education Act 1980, s 1(1), (2), (4).

The words "the Secretary of State" are substituted by virtue of the Secretary of State for Education and Science Order 1964, SI 1964/490, art 3(2)(a).

The words in square brackets in sub-s (1), the words in the first pair of square brackets in sub-s (2), and the words in the first pair of square brackets in sub-s (3) were substituted by the Education Act 1980, s 1(3), Sch 1, para 2.

Sub-s (6) was added by the Education Act 1968, s 1(3), Sch 1, para 2, the words in the inner pair of square brackets were substituted by the Education Act 1980, s 16(4), Sch 3, para 2, and the words omitted were repealed by the Education Act 1973, s 1(3), (4), Sch 1, para 3, Sch 2, Pt II, with a saving in respect of any order made under the provisions repealed or the operation in relation to any such order of section 111 post.

Governors; instrument of governors. These were formerly known, in relation to primary schools, as managers and instruments of management; see now the Education Act 1980, s 1, this part of this title post. Any reference in any other enactment or document is to be amended in accordance with this change in nomenclature; see s 1(4) of that Act.

As to the functions and proceedings of governors, see ss 18–21, Sch 4 post and the Education Act 1980, ss 1–5 post. As to the relationship of the governors of a voluntary school with the local education authority, see the remarks of Lord Haldane, LC in *Gillow v Durham CC* [1913] AC 54, 82 LJKB 206.

Local education authority. For meaning, see s 114(1) post and the note thereto.

Secretary of State. See the note "Secretary of State for Education and Science" to s 1 ante.

Subject to the provisions of this Act. See, in particular, ss 23, 24 post.

Trust deed. As to modification of the trust deed, see the Charities Act 1960, s 24(1), Vol 5, title Charities.

Shall be conducted. As to the powers of the Secretary of State in relation to the enforcement of the duties of the governors, see s 99 post, and as to the determination of disputes, see s 67 post. S 68 post gives the Secretary of State power to prevent the governors of a school from exercising their functions unreasonably.

Opportunity of making representations. In *Lee v Secretary of State for Education and Science* (1967) 66 LGR 211, 111 Sol Jo 756, a period of five days was held to be insufficient for representations to be made to the Secretary of State under this section and that a period of four weeks would have been reasonable.

Application to London. See the note to s 20 post.

Exclusion of this section. Where an arrangement for the grouping of schools under a single governing body is in force, this section is excluded; see s 20(6) post and the Education Act 1980, s 3(7), this part of this title post.

Definitions. For "county school" and "voluntary school", see s 9(2) ante; and for "primary school", "secondary school" and "significant", see s 114(1) post.

Education Act 1980, s 13. See this part of this title post.

Orders under this section. Orders under this section, being local, are not noted in this work. For revocation and variation of orders, see s 111 post.

18 [Governors] of primary schools

(1) The [instrument of government] for every county primary school serving an area in which there is a minor authority shall provide for the constitution of a body of [governors] consisting of such number of persons, not being less than six, as the local education authority may determine:

Provided that two-thirds of the [governors] shall be appointed by the local education authority and one-third shall be appointed by the minor authority.

(2) The [instrument of government] for every county primary school serving an area in which there is no minor authority shall provide for the constitution of a body of [governors] constituted in such manner as the local education authority may determine.

(3) The [instrument of government] for every voluntary primary school shall provide for the constitution of a body of [governors] consisting of such number of persons not being less than six as [the Secretary of State] may, after consultation with the local education authority, determine:

Provided that—

    (*a*) if the school is an aided school or a special agreement school, two-thirds of the [governors] shall be foundation [governors] and, if the school is a controlled school, one-third of the [governors] shall be foundation [governors];

    (*b*) where the school serves an area in which there is a minor authority, then of the [governors] who are not foundation [governors] not less than one-third nor more than one-half shall be appointed by the minor authority and the remainder shall be appointed by the local education authority; and

    (*c*) where the school serves an area in which there is no minor authority, all the [governors] who are not foundation [governors] shall be appointed by the local education authority.

NOTES

The word in square brackets in the marginal note is substituted by virtue of the Education Act 1980, s 1(1), (2), (4), this part of this title post.

The words "the Secretary of State" in sub-s (3) are substituted by the Secretary of State for Education and Science Order 1964, SI 1964/490, art 3(2)(*a*). All other words in square brackets were substituted by the Education Act 1980, s 1(3), Sch 1, para 3.

Instrument of government. The requirement that there shall be an instrument of government providing for the constitution of a body of governors for every county primary school and voluntary primary school is imposed by s 17(1) ante. As to the manner in which the instrument of government is to be made, see s 17(2) ante. See also sub-s (4) thereof ante as to the modification of the provisions of any trust deed with which the instrument of government is inconsistent.

Note that the instrument of government only deals with the constitution of the body of governors; see s 17(1) ante. The conduct of a primary school (whether a county school or a voluntary school) is controlled by articles of government; see s 17(3)(*a*) ante.

Local education authority. For meaning, see s 114(1) post and the note thereto.

Secretary of State. See the note "Secretary of State for Education and Science" to s 1 ante.

Secretary of State's powers to act in default. Where it appears to the Secretary of State that by reason of the default of any person there is no properly constituted body of governors of any county or voluntary school, he may take such steps as are specified in s 99(2) post. See also s 68 post for the Secretary of State's powers where, in his view a local education authority has acted, or proposes to, act, unreasonably.

Exclusion of this section. This section and s 19 post do not apply to any school to which the Education Act 1980, s 2, this part of this title post applies (see sub-ss (11), (12) thereof), nor where an arrangement for the grouping of schools under one governing body is in force under s 20 post (see sub-s (6) thereof) or under s 3 of the 1980 Act (see sub-s (7) thereof).

Definitions. For "aided school", "controlled school" and "special agreement school", see s 15 ante; for "county school" and "voluntary school", see s 9(2) ante; and for "foundation governors", "minor authority" and "primary school", see s 114(1) post.

19 Governors of secondary schools

(1) The instrument of government for every county secondary school shall provide for the constitution of a body of governors consisting of such number of persons appointed in such manner as the local education authority may determine.

(2) The instrument of government for every voluntary secondary school shall provide for the constitution of a body of governors of the school consisting of such number of persons as [the Secretary of State] may after consultation with the local education authority determine:

Provided that—

   (*a*)   where the school is a controlled school, one-third of the governors shall be foundation governors and two-thirds of the governors shall be appointed by the local education authority;

   (*b*)   where the school is an aided school or a special agreement school, two-thirds of the governors shall be foundation governors and one-third of the governors shall be appointed by the local education authority.

NOTES

The words in square brackets in sub-s (2) are substituted by virtue of the Secretary of State for Education and Science Order 1964, SI 1964/490, art 3(2)(*a*).

Instrument of government. See the note to s 18 ante.

Secretary of State's powers to act in default. See the note to s 18 ante.

Exclusion of this section. See the note to s 18 ante.

Definitions. For "aided school", "controlled school" and "special agreement school", see s 15 ante; for "county school" and "voluntary school", see s 9(2) ante; for "foundation governors" and "secondary school", see s 114(1) post; for "local education authority", see s 114(1) post and the note thereto.

20 Grouping of schools under one [governing body]

(1) A local education authority may make an arrangement for the constitution of a single governing body for any two or more county schools or voluntary schools maintained by them, and any such arrangement may relate exclusively to primary schools, or exclusively to secondary schools or partly to primary schools and partly to secondary schools:

Provided that an authority shall not make any such arrangement with respect to a voluntary school except with the consent of the ... governors thereof.

(2) The governing body constituted in pursuance of any such arrangement as aforesaid shall, if all the schools to which the arrangement relates are county schools,

consist of such number of persons appointed in such manner as the local education authority may determine.

(3) Where all or any of the schools to which any such arrangement relates are voluntary schools, the governing body constituted in pursuance of the arrangement shall consist of such number of persons appointed in such manner as may be determined by agreement between the local education authority and the ... governors of those schools, or, in default of such agreement, by [the Secretary of State].

(4) The local education authority, in making any such arrangement as aforesaid which relates to a primary school serving an area in which there is a minor authority, shall make provision for securing that the minor authority is adequately represented upon the governing body constituted in pursuance of the arrangement.

(5) Every arrangement made under this section may, if it does not relate to any voluntary school, be terminated at any time by the local education authority by which it was made, and any such arrangement which relates to such a school may be terminated by agreement between the local education authority and the governing body constituted in pursuance of the arrangement, or, in default of such agreement, by one year's notice served by the local education authority on the said governing body or by one year's notice served by the said governing body on the local education authority.

(6) While an arrangement under this section is in force with respect to any schools, the provisions of the last three foregoing sections as to the constitution of the body of ... governors shall not apply to the schools, and for the purposes of any enactment the governing body constituted in accordance with the arrangement shall be deemed to be the body of ... governors of each of those schools, and references to a ... governor in any enactment shall, in relation to every such school, be construed accordingly.

NOTES

The words in square brackets in the marginal note are substituted by virtue of the Education Act 1980, s 1(1), (2), (4) and the words omitted from sub-ss (1), (3), (6) were repealed by s 1(3) of, and Sch 1, para 4 to, that Act, this part of this title post.

The words in square brackets in sub-s (3) are substituted by virtue of the Secretary of State for Education and Science Order 1964, SI 1964/490, art 3(2)(*a*).

General Note. New provision as to the grouping of schools under a single governing body was made by the Education Act 1980, s 3, this part of this title post, which applies to schools having an instrument of government made after 1 July 1981 and schools in relation to which an order has been made under s 2(11)(*b*) of the 1980 Act (see s 3(8) thereof). Where s 3 applies, the provisions of this section are excluded (see sub-s (9) thereof).

Local education authority; minor authority. For meaning, see s 114(1) post and the note thereto.

Secretary of State. See the note "Secretary of State for Education and Science" to s 1 ante.

Adequately represented. No indication is given of the meaning of the term "adequately represented", but it presumably means that, as far as possible, the proportionate representation of the minor authority upon bodies of managers of single schools under s 18 ante should be maintained.

Service of notice. As to the service of notices, see s 113 post.

Application to London. As to the continued operation of any instrument or articles of government made by an order under s 17 ante, any arrangement made under this section, any direction of the local education authority under s 22 post, and any agreed syllabus under s 29 post, in the case of any school maintained immediately before 1 April 1965 by a local education authority who, in consequence of the London Government Act 1963, Vol 26, title London, did not continue to maintain it on and after that date, see s 31(7) of the 1963 Act.

Definitions. For "county school" and "voluntary school", see s 9(2) ante; and for "maintain", "primary school" and "secondary school", see s 114(1) post.

21 Proceedings of ... governors of county and voluntary schools

(1) Any ... governor of a county school or of a voluntary school may resign his office, and any such ... governor appointed by a local education authority or by a minor authority shall be removable by the authority by whom he was appointed.

(2) ...

(3) The minutes of the proceedings of the ... governors of any county school or voluntary school shall be open to inspection by the local education authority.

NOTES

Sub-s (2) and the words omitted from sub-ss (1), (3) were repealed by the Education Act 1980, s 1(3), 38(6), Sch 1, para 5, Sch 7. The words omitted from the marginal note are repealed by virtue of s 1(1), (2), (4) of the 1980 Act, this part of this title post.

County school. For meaning, see s 9(2) ante. A special school maintained by a local education authority is treated as a county school for the purposes of sub-ss (1), (3) above.

Governors' proceedings and tenure of office. Provision for these matters is made by the Education Act 1980, s 4, this part of this title post and regulations made thereunder.

Definitions. For "voluntary school", see s 9(2) ante; and for "local education authority" and "minor authority", see s 114(1) post and the notes thereto.

22 Powers of local education authority as to use and care of premises of voluntary schools

(1) The ... governors of a controlled school shall be entitled to determine the use to which the school premises or any part thereof shall be put on Saturdays, except when required to be used on Saturdays for the purposes of the school or for any purpose connected with education or with the welfare of the young for which the local education authority desire to provide accommodation on the premises or on that part thereof, and the ... foundation governors shall be entitled to determine the use to which the school premises or any part thereof shall be put on Sundays, but save as aforesaid the local education authority may give such directions as to the occupation and use of the school premises of a controlled school as they think fit.

(2) If the local education authority desire to provide accommodation for any purpose connected with education or with the welfare of the young and are satisfied that there is no suitable alternative accommodation in their area for that purpose, they may direct the ... governors of any aided school or special agreement school to provide free of charge accommodation for that purpose on the school premises or any part thereof on any week-day when not required for the purposes of the school, so, however, that the ... governors shall not be directed to provide such accommodation on more than three days in any week.

(3) Subject to any directions given by a local education authority under the foregoing provisions of this section and to the requirements of any enactment other than this Act or the regulations made thereunder, the occupation and use of the school premises of any voluntary school shall be under the control of the ... governors thereof.

(4) At any controlled school or special agreement school the persons employed for the purposes of the care and maintenance of the school premises shall be appointed and dismissed by the local education authority, and the local education authority may give directions to the ... governors of an aided school as to the number and conditions of service of persons employed at the school for such purposes.

(5) In relation to any school with respect to which the trust deed provides for any person other than the ... governors of the school being entitled to control the occupation and use of the school premises, this section shall have effect as if for the references to the ... governors there were substituted references to that person.

NOTES

The words omitted were repealed by the Education Act 1980, s 1(3), Sch 1, para 6.

Directions. As to the power of the Secretary of State to prevent unreasonable exercise of functions, see s 68 post. As to the revocation or variation of directions, see s 111 post.

Application to London. See the note to s 20 ante.

Definitions. For "voluntary school", see s 9(2) ante; for "aided school", "controlled school" and "special agreement school", see s 15 ante; for "governors", "premises" and "trust deed", see s 114(1) post; and for "local education authority", see s 114(1) post and the note thereto.

Secular Instruction and Appointment and Dismissal of Teachers in County and Voluntary Schools

23 Secular instruction in county schools and in voluntary schools

(1) In every county school and, subject to the provisions hereinafter contained as to religious education, in every voluntary school except an aided secondary school, the secular instruction to be given to the pupils shall, save in so far as may be otherwise provided by the ... articles of government for the school, be under the control of the local education authority.

(2) Subject to the provisions hereinafter contained as to religious education, the secular instruction to be given to the pupils in every aided secondary school shall, save in so far as may be otherwise provided by the articles of government for the school, be under the control of the governors of the school.

(3) Save in so far as may be otherwise provided by the ... articles of government for the school, the power to control the secular instruction provided in any county school or voluntary school shall include power to determine the times at which the school session shall begin and end on any day, to determine the times at which the school terms shall begin and end, to determine the school holidays, and to require that pupils in attendance at the school shall attend any class not conducted on the school premises for the purpose of receiving instruction or training included in the secular curriculum of the school.

NOTES

The words omitted from sub-ss (1), (3) were repealed by the Education Act 1980, s 1(3), Sch 1, para 7.

Provisions ... as to religious education. See ss 25–30 post.

Articles of government. See s 17(3) ante.

Governors. See ss 17, 19 ante and the Education Act 1980, ss 2, 4, this part of this title post.

School session. As to the hours of secular instruction to be comprised in each session, see the Education (Schools and Further Education) Regulations 1981, SI 1981/1086, reg 10.

Definitions. For "aided schools", see s 15 ante; for "county school" and "voluntary school", see s 9(2) ante; for "premises", "pupil" and "secondary school", see s 114(1) post; for "local education authority", see s 114(1) post and the note thereto.

24 Appointment and dismissal of teachers in county schools and in voluntary schools

(1) In every county school and, subject to the provisions hereinafter contained as to religious education, in every controlled school and special agreement school, the appointment of teachers shall, save in so far as may be otherwise provided by the ... articles of government for the school, be under the control of the local education authority, and no teacher shall be dismissed except by the authority.

(2) In every aided school the respective functions of the local education authority and of the ... governors of the school with respect to the appointment of teachers, and, subject to the provisions hereinafter contained as to religious education, with respect to the dismissal of teachers, shall be regulated by the ... articles of government for the school:

Provided that the ... articles of government for every aided school—

(a) shall make provision for the appointment of the teachers by the ... governors of the school, for enabling the local education authority to determine the number of teachers to be employed, and for enabling the authority, except for reasons for which the . . . governors are expressly empowered by this Act to dismiss teachers without such consent, to prohibit the dismissal of teachers without the consent of the authority and to require the dismissal of any teacher; and

(b) may make such provision as may be agreed between the local education authority and the . . . governors of the school, or in default of such agreement as may be determined by [the Secretary of State], for enabling the authority to prohibit the appointment, without the consent of the authority, of teachers to be employed for giving secular instruction, and for enabling the authority to give directions as to the educational qualifications of the teachers to be so employed.

(3) . . .

NOTES

The words omitted from sub-ss (1), (2) were repealed by the Education Act 1980, s 1(3), Sch 1, para 8.

The words in square brackets in sub-s (2)(b) are substituted by virtue of the Secretary of State for Education and Science Order 1964, SI 1964/490, art 3(2)(a).

Sub-s (3) was repealed by the Sex Discrimination Act 1975, s 83(3)–(5), Sch 6.

County school. For meaning, see s 9(2) ante. A special school maintained by a local education authority under s 9(5) ante is treated as a county school for the purposes of this section; see the Education (No 2) Act 1968, s 2(5), this part of this title post.

Provisions . . . as to religious education. See ss 25–30 post.

Teachers. This term is not defined in the Act. As to the training and remuneration of teachers, see s 62 post and the Remuneration of Teachers Act 1965, this part of this title post. As to the religious opinions of teachers, see s 30 post. As to the effect of failure to communicate a resolution of appointment, see *Powell v Lee* (1908) 99 LT 284.

Articles of government. See s 17(3) ante.

Expressly empowered by this Act to dismiss teachers. As to the application of the Employment Protection (Consolidation) Act 1978, Pt V (Unfair Dismissal), where a teacher is dismissed in pursuance of a requirement under para (a) of the proviso to sub-s (2) above, see s 80 of that Act, Vol 16, title Employment.

The governors of an aided school may, without the consent of the local education authority dismiss a teacher appointed to give religious instruction other than in accordance with an agreed syllabus on the ground that he has failed to give such instruction efficiently and suitably (s 28(2) post).

Determined by the Secretary of State. In addition to this reference to the Secretary of State, s 67(1) post makes provision for the settlement by the Secretary of State of disputes between the local education authority and the governors of a school.

As to the Secretary of State, see the note to s 1 ante.

Secular instruction. This term is not defined in the Act, but includes the matters specified in s 23(3) ante.

Directions. As to the revocation or variation of directions given by a local education authority, see s 111 post.

General power to appoint staff. As to the general power of a local authority to appoint such officers as they think necessary, see the Local Government Act 1972, s 112, Vol 25, title Local Government.

Definitions. For "aided school", "controlled school" and "special agreement school", see s 15 ante; for "county school" and "voluntary school", see s 9(2) ante; for "school", see s 114(1) post; and for "local education authority", see s 114(1) post and the note thereto.

Religious Education in County and Voluntary Schools

25 General provisions as to religious education in county and in voluntary schools

(1) Subject to the provisions of this section, the school day in every county school and in every voluntary school shall begin with collective worship on the part of all pupils in attendance at the school, and the arrangements made therefor shall provide for a single act of worship attended by all such pupils unless, in the opinion of the local education authority or, in the case of a voluntary school, of the . . . governors thereof, the school premises are such as to make it impracticable to assemble them for that purpose.

(2) Subject to the provisions of this section, religious instruction shall be given in every county school and in every voluntary school.

(3) It shall not be required, as a condition of any pupil attending any county school or any voluntary school, that he shall attend or abstain from attending any Sunday school or any place of religious worship.

(4) If the parent of any pupil in attendance at any county school or any voluntary school requests that he be wholly or partly excused from attendance at religious worship in the school, or from attendance at religious instruction in the school, or from attendance at both religious worship and religious instruction in the school, then, until the request is withdrawn, the pupil shall be excused from such attendance accordingly.

(5) Where any pupil has been wholly or partly excused from attendance at religious worship or instruction in any school in accordance with the provisions of this section, and the local education authority are satisfied:—

(a) that the parent of the pupil desires him to receive religious instruction of a kind which is not provided in the school during the periods during which he is excused from such attendance;

(b) that the pupil cannot with reasonable convenience be sent to another county or voluntary school where religious instruction of the kind desired by the parent is provided; and

(c) that arrangements have been made for him to receive religious instruction during school hours elsewhere,

the pupil may be withdrawn from the school during such periods as are reasonably necessary for the purpose of enabling him to receive religious instruction in accordance with the arrangements:

Provided that the pupil shall not be so withdrawn unless the local education authority are satisfied that the arrangements are such as will not interfere with the attendance of the pupil at school on any day except at the beginning or end of the school session on that day.

(6) No directions shall be given by the local education authority as to the secular instruction to be given to pupils in attendance at a voluntary school so as to interfere with the provision of reasonable facilities for religious instruction in the school during school hours; and no such direction shall be given so as to prevent a pupil from receiving religious instruction in accordance with the provisions of this section during the hours normally set apart for that purpose, unless arrangements are made whereby the pupil shall receive such instruction in the school at some other time.

(7) Where the parent of any pupil who is a boarder at a county school or at a voluntary school requests that the pupil is permitted to attend worship in accordance with the tenets of a particular religious denomination on Sundays or other days exclusively set apart for religious observance by the religious body to which his parent belongs, or to receive religious instruction in accordance with such tenets outside school hours, the ... governors of the school shall make arrangements for affording to the pupil reasonable opportunities for so doing and such arrangements may provide for affording facilities for such worship or instruction on the school premises, so however that such arrangements shall not entail expenditure by the local education authority.

NOTES

The words omitted from sub-ss (1), (7) were repealed by the Education Act 1980, s 1(3), Sch 1, para 1.

School day. As to the power to determine the times on which the school day shall begin and end, see s 23(3) ante and the Education (Schools and Further Education) Regulations 1981, SI 1981/1086, reg 10.

Shall begin. As to the enforcement of this requirement, see s 99 post.

Collective worship. The act of collective worship must take place on the school premises, except that in the case of an aided school or a special agreement school it may take place elsewhere on special occasions; see the Education Act 1946, s 7, this part of this title post. In a county school religious worship must not be distinctive of any particular religious denomination; see s 26 post.

Opinion. Statutory powers are often conferred in subjective terms, the competent authority being entitled to act, eg, when in its "opinion", or when it "appears" to it or it is "satisfied" that, a prescribed state of affairs exists, but the inherent jurisdiction of the courts to determine whether such powers have been exceeded is not readily ousted by the use of such language; see, further, 1 Halsbury's Laws (4th edn) para 22.

Governors. As to the appointment and proceedings of governors, see ss 17–21 ante and the Education Act 1980, ss 1–5, this part of this title post.

Religious instruction. As to religious instruction in county schools, see s 26 post; in controlled schools, see s 27(6) post; in aided schools and special agreement schools, see s 28(1) post. As to the provisions of this Act relating to the inspection of religious education, see s 77(5), (6) post.

Excused from attendance. A pupil excused from attendance at religious worship and religious instruction remains subject to the provisions relating to compulsory school attendance (ss 35–37, 39, 40); he may be withdrawn from school only within the provisions of sub-s (5) of this section.

Sub-s (6). Disputes between an authority and the managers and governors of a voluntary school must be determined by the Secretary of State. The jurisdiction of the courts is excluded (*Blencowe v Northamptonshire CC* [1907] 1 Ch 504, 76 LJ Ch 276.

Directions. As to the revocation or variation of directions given by a local education authority, see s 111 post.

Secular instruction. This term is not defined in the Act, but includes the matters specified in s 23(3) ante.

Other days exclusively set apart for religious observance. Ascension day is a day thus exclusively set apart by the Church of England (*Marshall v Graham, Bell v Graham* [1907] 2 KB 112, 76 LJKB 690).

Definitions. For "county school" and "voluntary school", see s 9(2) ante; for "parent", "premises" and "pupil", see s 114(1) post; and for "local education authority", see s 114(1) post and the note thereto.

26 Special provisions as to religious education in county schools

Subject as hereinafter provided, the collective worship required by subsection (1) of the last foregoing section shall not, in any county school, be distinctive of any particular religious denomination, and the religious instruction given to any pupils in attendance at a county school in conformity with the requirements of subsection (2) of the said section shall be given in accordance with an agreed syllabus adopted for the school or for those pupils and shall not include any catechism or formulary which is distinctive of any particular religious denomination:

Provided that, where a county secondary school is so situated that arrangements cannot conveniently be made for the withdrawal of pupils from the school in accordance with the provisions of this Act to receive religious instruction elsewhere, then, if the local education authority are satisfied:—

(*a*) that the parents of pupils in attendance at the school desire them to receive religious instruction in the school in accordance with the tenets of a particular religious denomination; and

(*b*) that satisfactory arrangements have been made for the provision of such instruction to those pupils in the school, and for securing that the cost of providing such instruction to those pupils in the school will not fall upon the authority;

the authority shall, unless they are satisfied that owing to any special circumstances it would be unreasonable so to do, provide facilities for the carrying out of those arrangements.

NOTES

Collective worship. See the note to s 25 ante.

Shall not. As to the enforcement of this requirement, see s 99 post.

Catechism or formulary distinctive of any particular religious denomination. This phrase reproduces the so-called "Cowper-Temple" clause which appeared in the Elementary Education Act 1870, s 14(2), and in the Education Act 1921, s 28(2) (both repealed), and which prohibited the use in provided schools of any religious catechism or religious formulary which is distinctive of any particular denomination.

Withdrawal of pupils from school. As to the withdrawal of pupils from school to receive religious instruction elsewhere, see s 25(5) ante.

Definitions. For "agreed syllabus", "parent", "pupil" and "secondary school", see s 114(1) post; and for "county school", see s 9(2) ante; for "local education authority", see s 114(1) post and the note thereto.

27 Special provisions as to religious education in controlled schools

(1) Where the parents of any pupils in attendance at a controlled school request that they may receive religious instruction in accordance with the provisions of the trust deed relating to the school, or where provision for that purpose is not made by such a deed in accordance with the practice observed in the school before it became a controlled school, the ... foundation governors shall, unless they are satisfied that owing to special circumstances it would be unreasonable so to do, make arrangements for securing that such religious instruction is given to those pupils at the school during not more than two periods in each week.

(2) Without prejudice to the duty to make such arrangements as aforesaid whatever the number of the teaching staff of the school, where the number of the teaching staff of a controlled school exceeds two the teaching staff shall include persons (hereinafter referred to as "reserved teachers") selected for their fitness and competence to give such religious instruction as is required to be given under such arrangements and specifically appointed to do so:

Provided that the number of reserved teachers in any controlled school shall not exceed one-fifth of the number of the teaching staff of the school including the head teacher, so, however, that where the number of the teaching staff is not a multiple of five it shall be treated for the purposes of this subsection as if it were the next higher multiple thereof.

(3) The head teacher of a controlled school shall not, while holding that position, be a reserved teacher, but before appointing any person to be the head teacher of such a school the local education authority shall inform the ... governors of the school as to the person whom they propose to appoint and shall consider any representations made by the ... governors with respect to the proposed appointment.

(4) Where the local education authority propose to appoint any person to be a reserved teacher in a controlled school, the authority shall consult the ... foundation governors of the school, and, unless the said ... governors are satisfied as to that person's fitness and competence to give such religious instruction as is required in pursuance of such arrangements as aforesaid the authority shall not appoint that person to be a reserved teacher.

(5) If the ... foundation governors of a controlled school are of opinion that any reserved teacher has failed to give such religious instruction as aforesaid efficiently and suitably, they may require the authority to dismiss him from employment as a reserved teacher in the school.

(6) Subject to any arrangements made under subsection (1) of this section, the religious instruction given to the pupils in attendance at a controlled school shall be given in accordance with an agreed syllabus adopted for the school or for those pupils.

NOTES

The words omitted from sub-ss (1), (3)–(5) were repealed by the Education Act 1980, s 1(3), Sch 1, para 9.

Religious education. See the general provisions in s 25 ante.

Before it became a controlled school. As to the time at which and the manner in which a school becomes a controlled school, see s 15 ante.

The teaching staff shall include. As to the enforcement of this and other requirements in this section, see s 99(1) post.

Dismissal of reserved teacher. There is no reason why a reserved teacher dismissed under sub-s (5) should not continue to be employed, if the local education authority thinks fit, as a reserved teacher in another controlled school or in a special agreement school (subject to sub-s (4) above or s 28(3) post) or even as a non-reserved teacher in the same school.

Appointment and dismissal of teachers. See the general provisions in s 24 ante.

Definitions. For "controlled school", see s 15 ante; for "agreed syllabus", "foundation governors", "parent", "pupil" and "trust deed", see s 114(1) post; for "local education authority", see s 114(1) post and the note thereto.

28 Special provisions as to religious education in aided schools and in special agreement schools

(1) The religious instruction given to the pupils in attendance at an aided school or at a special agreement school shall be under the control of the ... governors of the school and shall be in accordance with any provisions of the trust deed relating to the school, or, where provision for that purpose is not made by such a deed, in accordance with the practice observed in the school before it became a voluntary school:

Provided that where the parents of pupils in attendance at the school desire them to receive religious instruction in accordance with any agreed syllabus adopted by the local education authority and cannot with reasonable convenience cause those pupils to attend any school at which that syllabus is in use, then, unless the authority are satisfied that owing to any special circumstances it would be unreasonable so to do, arrangements shall be made for religious instruction in accordance with that syllabus to be given to those pupils in the school during the times set apart for the giving of religious instruction therein, and such arrangements shall be made by the ... governors of the school, so, however, that if the local education authority are satisifed that the ... governors are unwilling to make such arrangements, the arrangements shall be made by the authority.

(2) If a teacher appointed to give in an aided school religious instruction, other than instruction in accordance with an agreed syllabus, fails to give such instruction efficiently and suitably, he may be dismissed on that ground by the ... governors of the school without the consent of the local education authority.

(3) Where the special agreement made with respect to any special agreement school provides for the employment of reserved teachers, the local education authority shall, when they propose to appoint any person to be such a teacher in the school, consult the ... foundation governors of the school, and unless the said ... governors are satisfied as to that person's fitness and competence to give such religious instruction as aforesaid, the authority shall not appoint that person to be such a teacher.

(4) If the ... foundation governors of a special agreement school are of opinion that any such reserved teacher as aforesaid has failed to give, efficiently and suitably, such religious instruction as he was appointed to give, they may require the authority to dismiss him from employment as a reserved teacher in the school.

NOTES

The words omitted were repealed by the Education Act 1980, s 1(3), Sch 1, para 9.

Religious education. See the general provisions in s 25 ante.

Arrangements shall be made. As to the power of the Secretary of State to prevent the unreasonable exercise of this function, see s 68 post.

Reserved teacher. As to the dismissal of reserved teachers, see the note to s 27 ante.

Appointment and dismissal of teachers. See the general provisions in s 24 ante.

Definitions. For "aided school" and "special agreement school", see s 15 ante; for "agreed syllabus", "foundation governors", "parent", "pupil" and "trust deed", see s 114(1) post; for "local education authority", see s 114(1) post and the note thereto.

29 Provisions as to religious instruction in accordance with agreed syllabus

(1) The provisions of the Fifth Schedule to this Act shall have effect with respect to the preparation, adoption, and reconsideration, of an agreed syllabus of religious instruction.

(2) A local education authority shall have power to constitute a standing advisory council on religious education to advise the authority upon matters connected with the religious instruction to be given in accordance with an agreed syllabus and, in particular, as to methods of teaching, the choice of books, and the provision of lectures for teachers.

(3) The method of appointment of the members of any council constituted under the last foregoing subsection and the term of office and conditions of retirement of the members thereof shall be such as may be determined by the local education authority.

(4) A local education authority shall have regard to any unanimous recommendations which may be made to them by any conference convened in accordance with the provisions of the said Fifth Schedule with respect to the expediency of constituting such an advisory council as aforesaid or with respect to the method by which or the terms and conditions upon which members of any such council shall be appointed.

NOTES

Agreed syllabus. For meaning, see s 114(1) post.

Local education authority. For meaning, see s 114(1) post and the note thereto.

Have regard to any unanimous recommendations. A local education authority must consider such recommendations, but it is probably not bound to adopt them. In the event of an unreasonable rejection the Minister has powers of direction under s 68 post.

Application to London. See the note to s 20 ante.

30 Saving as to position of teachers

Subject as hereinafter provided, no person shall be disqualified by reason of his religious opinions, or of his attending or omitting to attend religious worship, from being a teacher in a county school or in any voluntary school, or from being otherwise employed for the purposes of such a school; and no teacher in any such school shall be required to give religious instruction or receive any less emolument or be deprived of, or disqualified for, any promotion or other advantage by reason of the fact that he does or does not give religious instruction or by reason of his religious opinions or of his attending or omitting to attend religious worship:

Provided that, save in so far as they require that a teacher shall not receive any less emolument or be deprived of, or disqualified for, any promotion or other advantage by reason of the fact that he gives religious instruction or by reason of his religious opinions or of his attending religious worship, the provisions of this section shall not apply with respect to a teacher in an aided school or with respect to a reserved teacher in any controlled school or special agreement school.

NOTES

Religious instruction. See the general provisions in s 25 ante.

Any less emolument. As to the remuneration of teachers, see the Remuneration of Teachers Act 1965 post.

Attending religious worship. Where a teacher was dismissed because he took time off during school hours to attend religious services, the dismissal was not by reason of his religious opinions but because of a failure to fulfil his contract of employment; see *Ahmad v Inner London Education Authority* [1978] QB 36, [1978] 1 All ER 574, CA.

Appointment and dismissal of teachers. See the general provisions in s 24 ante.

Definitions. For "aided school", "controlled school" and "special agreement school", see s 15 ante; for "county school" and "voluntary school", see s 9(2) ante; and for "reserved teacher", see s 27(2) ante.

Transitional Provisions as to County and Voluntary Schools

31 Transitional provisions as to the separation of primary and secondary schools

(1) ...

(2) Save as may be otherwise directed by [the Secretary of State], every county school

and voluntary school which immediately before the commencement of this Part of this Act was used for providing primary education shall be managed and conducted as a primary school, every such school which was used for providing secondary education shall be managed and conducted as a secondary school, and every such school which was used for providing primary and secondary education indiscriminately shall be managed and conducted as if it were a primary school.

(3) If it appears to [the Secretary of State] to be expedient that any county school or voluntary school should be managed and conducted otherwise than in accordance with the provisions of the last foregoing subsection, he may direct that the school be managed and conducted as a primary school or as a secondary school as the case may be:

Provided that no such direction shall be given except after consultation with the local education authority and, in the case of a voluntary school, with the . . . governors of the school.

(4) Where it appears to a local education authority that the process of securing that primary and secondary education shall be provided in separate schools can be accelerated by the giving of a direction under this section, it shall be the duty of the authority to apply to [the Secretary of State] for such a direction.

NOTES

Sub-s (1), and the words omitted from sub-s (3), were repealed by the Education Act 1980, ss 1(3), Sch 1, para 1(2), Sch 7.

The references to the Secretary of State are substituted by virtue of the Secretary of State for Education and Science Order 1964, SI 1964/490, art 3(2)(a).

Save as may be otherwise directed. Ie under sub-s (3) above.

Commencement of this Part of this Act. See the note to s 9 ante.

Separate schools. The duty of securing that primary and secondary education must be provided in separate schools is imposed by s 8(2)(a) ante. As to the division of existing schools into two or more separate schools, see the Education Act 1946, this part of this title post.

Revocation and variation of directions. As to the revocation and variation of directions given by the Secretary of State under this Act, see s 111 post.

Enforcement of duties. The duties imposed under this section may be enforced by the Secretary of State under s 99 post.

Definitions. For "county school" and "voluntary school", see s 9(2) ante; for "primary education", "primary school", "secondary education" and "secondary school", see s 114(1) post; for "local education authority", see s 114(1) post and the note thereto.

32–34 (S 32 repealed by the Education Act 1980, s 38(6), Sch 7; ss 33, 34 repealed by the Education Act 1981, s 21, Sch 4.)

Compulsory Attendance at Primary and Secondary Schools

35 Compulsory school age

In this Act the expression "compulsory school age" means any age between five years and [sixteen] years, and accordingly a person shall be deemed to be of compulsory school age if he has attained the age of five years and has not attained the age of [sixteen] years and a person shall be deemed to be over compulsory school age as soon as he has attained the age of [sixteen] years:

.   .   .   .   .

NOTES

The words in square brackets are substituted by virtue of the Raising of the School Leaving Age Order 1972, SI 1972/444, art 2, and the words omitted, which made provision for the raising of the school leaving age are spent.

Date of attaining school leaving age. See the Education Act 1962, s 9, this part of this title post.

Application. The meaning of compulsory school age within the meaning of this section is applied by the

Affiliation Proceedings Act 1957, s 6, Vol 6, title Children; the Children and Young Persons Act 1963, s 38, Vol 6, title Children; the Travel Concessions Act 1964, s 1, Vol 38, title Road Traffic; the Guardianship of Minors Act 1971, s 12, Vol 6, title Children; the Matrimonial Causes Act 1973, s 29, Vol 27, title Matrimonial Law (Pt 3); the Sex Discrimination Act 1975, s 82, Vol 6, title Civil Rights and Liberties; the Children Act 1975, s 34B, Vol 6, title Children; the Race Relations Act 1976, s 78, Vol 6, title Civil Rights and Liberties; the Domestic Proceedings and Magistrates' Courts Act 1978, s 5, Vol 27, title Matrimonial Law (Pt 3); and the Child Care Act 1980, s 87, Vol 6, title Children.

Order under this section. The Raising of the School Leaving Age Order 1972, SI 1972/444.

36 Duty of parents to secure the education of their children

It shall be the duty of the parent of every child of compulsory school age to cause him to receive efficient full-time education suitable to his age, ability, and aptitude [and to any special educational needs he may have], either by regular attendance at school or otherwise.

NOTES

The words in square brackets were inserted by the Education Act 1981, s 17.

Duty of parents. As to the action to be taken by the local education authority if it appears that the parent is failing to perform this duty, see s 37 post. Where the proprietor of a school is not under any obligation to admit children as registered pupils otherwise than at the beginning of the school term, parents are not under any duty to cause children to receive full-time education during that term, if it would be impracticable to do so; see the Education (Miscellaneous Provisions) Act 1948, s 4(2), this part of this title post.

Compulsory school age. See s 35 ante and the notes thereto.

Full-time education. This term is not defined in the Act. Presumably attendance at a county school or voluntary school in accordance with the school sessions and school terms fixed under s 23 ante, constitutes full-time education.

Regular attendance at school or otherwise. The only specific indication as to what may in certain circumstances constitute regular attendance is contained in s 39(3) post. As to full-time education otherwise than at school the following cases decided under corresponding provisions of the previous law may be of value: *Bevan v Shears* [1911] 2 KB 936, 80 LJKB 1325 (efficiency of education provided); *R v West Riding of Yorkshire Justices, ex p Broadbent* [1910] 2 KB 192, 79 LJKB 731 (efficiency of alternative education); *R v Walton etc Justices, ex p Dutton* (1911) 75 JP 558, 27 TLR 569 (admissibility of evidence as to state of child's education), and *Osborne v Martin* (1927) 91 JP 197, 138 LT 268 (withdrawal from school for piano lessons).

For a case under the present law, see *Baker v Earl* (1960) Times, 6 February, where an appellant disapproved of schools and did not give her children any lessons or prescribed course of study but encouraged them to follow any subject in which they were interested, it was held that the parent had failed to satisfy the local education authority, the magistrates and the appeals committee that the children were receiving full time efficient education.

See also the note "Fails to attend regularly" to s 39 post.

Definitions. For "child", "compulsory school age", "parent" and "school", see s 114(1) post; for "special educational needs", see, by virtue of s 114(1) post, the Education Act 1981, s 1, this part of this title post.

37 School attendance orders

(1) If it appears to a local education authority that the parent of any child of compulsory school age in their area is failing to perform the duty imposed on him by the last foregoing section, it shall be the duty of the authority to serve upon the parent a notice requiring him, within such time as may be specified in the notice not being less than fourteen days from the service thereof, to satisfy the authority that the child is receiving efficient full-time education suitable to his age, ability, and aptitude [and to any special educational needs he may have] either by regular attendance at school or otherwise.

(2) If, after such a notice has been served upon a parent by a local education authority, the parent fails to satisfy the authority in accordance with the requirements of the notice that the child to whom the notice relates is receiving efficient full-time education suitable to his age, ability, and aptitude [and to any special educational needs he may have], then, if in the opinion of the authority it is expedient that he should attend school, the authority shall serve upon the parent an order in the prescribed form (hereinafter

referred to as a "school attendance order") requiring him to cause the child to become a registered pupil at a school named in the order:

(3) ...

(4) If at any time while a school attendance order is in force with respect to any child the parent of the child makes application to the local education authority by whom the order was made ... requesting that the order be revoked on the ground that arrangements have been made for the child to receive efficient full-time education suitable to his age, ability, and aptitude [and to any special educational needs he may have] otherwise than at school, the authority shall ... revoke the order in compliance with the request unless they are of opinion ... that no satisfactory arrangements have been made for the education of the child otherwise than at school ... and if a parent is aggrieved by a refusal of the authority to comply with any such request, he may refer the question to [the Secretary of State], who shall give such direction thereon as he thinks fit.

(5) If any person upon whom a school attendance order is served fails to comply with the requirements of the order, he shall be guilty of an offence against this section unless he proves that he is causing the child to receive efficient full-time education suitable to his age, ability, and aptitude [and to any special educational needs he may have] otherwise than at school.

(6) If in proceedings against any person for a failure to comply with a school attendance order that person is acquitted, the court may direct that the school attendance order shall cease to be in force, but without prejudice to the duty of the local education authority to take further action under this section if at any time the authority are of opinion that having regard to any change of circumstances it is expedient so to do.

(7) Save as provided by the last foregoing subsection, a school attendance order made with respect to any child shall, subject to any amendment thereof which may be made by the local education authority, continue in force so long as he is of compulsory school age unless revoked by that authority.

NOTES

The words in square brackets in sub-ss (1), (2), (5) were inserted, the words in the first pair of square brackets in sub-s (4) were substituted, and sub-s (3) and the words omitted from sub-ss (2), (4) were repealed, by the Education Act 1981, s 21, Schs 3, 4. As to transitional provisions in relation to a child who is not in need of special educational treatment where notice of intention to serve a school attendance order was served under sub-s (2)(a) before 1 July 1982, or where application for the amendment of a school attendance order was made under sub-s (4) before 1 July 1982, see the Education Act 1981 (Commencement No 2) Order 1983, SI 1983/7, art 4, Schedule, para 4(3), (4).

The words "the Secretary of State" in sub-s (4) are substituted by virtue of the Secretary of State for Education and Science Order 1964, SI 1964/490, art 3(2)(a).

Compulsory school age. See s 35 ante and the notes thereto. For the purposes of a prosecution of the parent of a child for an offence against this section, in so far as the child's having been of compulsory school age at any time is material, the child is presumed to have been of compulsory school age at that time unless the parent proves the contrary; see the Education (Miscellaneous Provisions) Act 1948, s 9(1), this part of this title post.

It shall be the duty. Under s 68 post the Secretary of State may take steps to prevent the unreasonable exercise of this duty.

To serve ... a notice. As to the service of notice, see s 113 post.

Not less than fourteen days. The words "not less than" indicate that fourteen clear days must intervene between the day on which the notice is given and that on which the parent provides a satisfactory reply; see *R v Turner* [1910] 1 KB 346; *Re Hector Whaling Ltd* [1936] Ch 208, [1935] All ER Rep 302.

Full-time education; regular attendance at school or otherwise. See s 36 ante and the notes thereto.

Authority shall serve an order. Children should not be made wards of court as a means of enforcing a school attendance order (*Re B (Infants)* [1962] Ch 201, sub nom *Re Baker (Infants)* [1961] 3 All ER 276).

As to the school to be named in, and amendment of, the order, see the Education Act 1980, ss 10, 11, this part of this title post. As to the revocation and variation of orders, see s 111 post.

Prescribed. Ie prescribed by regulations made under this section; see the note below.

Secretary of State. Ie the Secretary of State for Education and Science; see the note to s 1 ante.

Thinks fit. Statutory powers are often conferred in subjective terms, the competent authority being entitled to act, eg, when it "thinks fit", or when it is "satisfied" or it "appears" to it that a prescribed state of affairs exists, but the inherent jurisdiction of the courts to determine whether such powers have been exceeded is not readily ousted by the use of such language; see further 1 Halsbury's Laws (4th edn) para 22.

Offence against this section. As to the proceedings and penalties in respect of such an offence, see s 40 post.

Unless he proves. The burden of proof laid on the defendant is less onerous than that resting on the prosecutor and may be discharged by satisfying the court of the preponderance of probability of what the defendant is called on to prove; see *R v Carr-Briant* [1943] KB 605, [1943] 2 All ER 156, and *R v Dunbar* [1958] 1 QB 1, [1957] 2 All ER 737.

Definitions. For "child", "compulsory school age", "parent" and "registered pupil", see s 114(1) post; for "local education authority", see s 114(1) post and the note thereto; for "special educational needs", see, by virtue of s 114(1) post, the Education Act 1981, s 1, this part of this title post.

Regulations under this section. The School Attendance Order Regulations 1944, SR & O 1944/1470. For general provisions as to regulations under this Act, see s 112 post.

---

38 (*Repealed by the Education Act 1981, s 21, Sch 4.*)

39 Duty of parents to secure regular attendance of registered pupils

(1) If any child of compulsory school age who is a registered pupil at a school fails to attend regularly thereat, the parent of the child shall be guilty of an offence against this section.

(2) In any proceedings for an offence against this section in respect of a child who is not a boarder at the school at which he is a registered pupil, the child shall not be deemed to have failed to attend regularly at the school by reason of his absence therefrom with leave or—

(a) at any time when he was prevented from attending by reason of sickness or any unavoidable cause;

(b) on any day exclusively set apart for religious observance by the religious body to which his parent belongs;

(c) if the parent proves that the school at which the child is a registered pupil is not within walking distance of the child's home, and that no suitable arrangements have been made by the local education authority either for his transport to and from the school or for boarding accommodation for him at or near the school or for enabling him to become a registered pupil at a school nearer to his home.

(3) Where in any proceedings for an offence against this section it is proved that the child has no fixed abode, paragraph (c) of the last foregoing subsection shall not apply, but if the parent proves that he is engaged in any trade or business of such a nature as to require him to travel from place to place and that the child has attended at a school at which he was a registered pupil as regularly as the nature of the trade or business of the parent permits, the parent shall be acquitted:

Provided that, in the case of a child who has attained the age of six years, the parent shall not be entitled to be acquitted under this subsection unless he proves that the child has made at least two hundred attendances during the period of twelve months ending with the date on which the proceedings were instituted.

(4) In any proceedings for an offence against this section in respect of a child who is a boarder at the school at which he is a registered pupil, the child shall be deemed to have failed to attend regularly at the school if he is absent therefrom without leave during any part of the school term at a time when he was not prevented from being present by reason of sickness or any unavoidable cause.

(5) In this section the expression "leave" in relation to any school means leave granted by any person authorised in that behalf by the . . . governors or proprietor of the school,

and the expression "walking distance" means, in relation to a child who has not attained the age of eight years two miles, and in the case of any other child three miles, measured by the nearest available route.

NOTES

The word omitted from sub-s (5) was repealed by the Education Act 1980, s 1(3), Sch 1, para 10.

Compulsory school age. See s 35 ante and the note thereto. For the purposes of a prosecution of the parent of a child for an offence against this section, in so far as the child's having been of compulsory school age at any time is material, the child is presumed to have been of compulsory school age at that time unless the parent proves the contrary; see the Education (Miscellaneous Provisions) Act 1948, s 9(1), this part of this title post.

Fails to attend regularly. A child who is sent to school dressed in such a way that it is known that the head teacher will, as a matter of discipline, refuse him admission, fails to attend school regularly, see *Spiers v Warrington Corpn* [1954] 1 QB 61, [1953] 2 All ER 1052.

The regular attendance of a child at school is regular attendance for the times prescribed by the local education authority; absence at the time when the attendance register closed is failure in regular attendance (*Hinchley v Rankin* [1961] 1 All ER 692, [1961] 1 WLR 421).

An additional defence to those enumerated in sub-s (2) above is given by s 54(7) post to pupils who have been excluded from school under that section.

The meaning of "attend regularly" is applied by the Children and Young Persons Act 1969, s 2(8)(*b*)(ii), Vol 6, title Children.

Offence against this section. As to the proceedings and penalties in respect of such an offence, see s 40 post.

Absence. The words "unavoidable cause" (in sub-s (2)(*a*)) refer to a cause relating to the child, so that the fact that a child is kept at home to do the house-work in a domestic emergency will not provide a defence (*Jenkins v Howells* [1949] 2 KB 218, [1949] 1 All ER 942). See also *LCC v Hearn* (1909) 78 LJKB 414, 100 LT 438.

Exclusively set apart for religious observance. See the note to s 25 ante.

Within walking distance. Where a local education authority has provided free transport under the belief that the distance involved is over three miles, it is bound to review this service of its discretion when this belief proves to be mistaken; see *Rootkin v Kent CC* [1981] 2 All ER 227, [1981] 1 WLR 1186, CA.

Suitable arrangements. Arrangements whereby an authority paid to parents the cost of the fare necessary to bring the child within the three mile limit were not "suitable arrangements", see *Surrey CC v Ministry of Education* [1953] 1 All ER 705, [1953] 1 WLR 516.

To and from the school. Ie to and from the child's home to the school (*Surrey CC v Ministry of Education* cited above).

As to the provision of transport by a local education authority, see s 55 post.

Nearest available route. Distance not safety is the test for ascertaining the nearest available route. If there is a route which children can walk and which is not more than the stipulated length it is within walking distance even if the parents think it unsafe for unescorted children (*Shaxted v Ward* [1954] 1 All ER 336, 118 JP 168, distinguished in *Rogers v Essex CC* [1985] 2 All ER 39, where it was held that a route which the interests of the children demand that they should not use is not to be regarded as the shortest walking distance; what is to be measured is a route which children can walk without parents who allow them to walk it acting irresponsibly).

Definitions. For "child", "parent", "registered pupil" and "school", see s 114(1) post; for "leave" and "walking distance", note sub-s (5) above.

40 Enforcement of school attendance

(1) Subject to the provisions of this section, any person guilty of an offence against section thirty-seven or section thirty-nine of this Act shall be liable on summary conviction, [to a fine not exceeding level 3 on the standard scale] or to imprisonment for a term not exceeding one month or to both such fine and such imprisonment.

[(2) Proceedings for such offences as aforesaid shall not be instituted except by a local education authority; and before instituting such proceedings the authority shall consider whether it would be appropriate, instead of or as well as instituting the proceedings, to bring the child in question before a juvenile court under section 1 of the Children and Young Persons Act 1969.

(3) The court by which a person is convicted of an offence against section 37 of this Act or before which a person is charged with an offence against section 39 of this Act may if it thinks fit direct the authority who instituted the proceedings to bring the child

to whom the proceedings relate before a juvenile court under the said section 1; and it shall be the duty of the authority to comply with the direction.

(4) Where a child in respect of whom a school attendance order is in force is brought before a juvenile court by a local education authority under the said section 1 and the court finds that the condition set out in subsection (2) (e) of that section is not satisfied with respect to him, the court may direct that the order shall cease to be in force.]

NOTES

Sub-s (1) as originally enacted specified that a person convicted of an offence against s 37 or s 39 ante should be liable "in the case of a first offence against that section to a fine not exceeding one pound, in the case of a second offence against that section to a fine not exceeding five pounds, and in the case of a third or subsequent offence against that section to a fine not exceeding ten pounds or to imprisonment for a term not exceeding one month or to both such fine and such imprisonment". The fine was increased to £10 for a first offence and £20 for a second or subsequent offence by virtue of the Criminal Justice Act 1967, s 92(1), Sch 3, Pt I and subsequently increased to £200 for a first or any subsequent offence by the Criminal Law Act 1977, s 31, Sch 6. The reference to level 3 on the standard scale was then substituted by virtue of the Criminal Justice Act 1982, s 46, Vol 27, title Magistrates.

Sub-ss (2)–(4) were substituted by the Children and Young Persons Act 1969, s 72(3), Sch 5, para 13.

Summary conviction. Summary jurisdiction and procedure are mainly governed by the Magistrates' Courts Act 1980, Vol 27, title Magistrates, and by rules made under s 144 of that Act.

Standard scale. By the Criminal Justice Act 1982, ss 37(3), 75, Vol 27, title Magistrates, this means the standard scale set out in s 37(2) of that Act as amended by order made under the Magistrates' Courts Act 1980, s 143(1), in the same title. The scale as amended by the Criminal Penalties etc (Increase) Order 1984, SI 1984/447, art 3(4), Sch 4, is: level 1: £50; level 2: £100; level 3: £400; level 4: £1,000; and level 5: £2,000.

The authority shall consider. For the powers of the Secretary of State in default of the local education authority, see s 99(1) post.

Juvenile court. For the constitution of and other provisions relating to juvenile courts, see the Children and Young Persons Act 1933, ss 45–49, Sch 2, Vol 6, title Children, and the Magistrates' Courts Act 1980, s 146, Vol 25, title Magistrates. The courts sit for the purpose of hearing any charge against a child or young person and for the purpose of exercising any other jurisdiction conferred on juvenile courts by or under any enactment; see s 45 of the 1933 Act.

School attendance order. See s 37 ante. An attempt to enforce a school attendance order by making the children wards of court, rather than under this section, failed in *Re B (Infants)* [1962] Ch 201, sub nom *Re Baker (Infants)* [1961] 3 All ER 276.

Procedure. For procedural provisions in connection with the juvenile court, see the Magistrates' Courts (Children and Young Persons) Rules 1970, SI 1970/1792, as amended by SI 1976/1769, SI 1978/869, SI 1983/526, SI 1983/1793 and SI 1984/567.

Definitions. For "child", see s 114(1) post; for "local education authority", see s 114(1) post and the note thereto.

Children and Young Persons Act 1969, s 1. See Vol 6, title Children.

40A *(Inserted by the Children and Young Persons Act 1969, s 64(1), Sch 3, para 36, and subsequently repealed by the Children and Young Persons Act 1969, s 72(4), Sch 6.)*

FURTHER EDUCATION

41 General duties of local education authorities with respect to further education

Subject as hereinafter provided, it shall be the duty of every local education authority to secure the provision for their area of adequate facilities for further education, that is to say:—

(a) full-time and part-time education for persons over compulsory school age; and

(b) leisure-time occupation, in such organized cultural training and recreative activities as are suited to their requirements, for any persons over compulsory school age who are able and willing to profit by the facilities provided for that purpose:

Provided that the provisions of this section shall not empower or require local education authorities to secure the provision of facilities for further education otherwise than in accordance with schemes of further education or at county colleges.

NOTES

Local education authority. See s 114(1) post and the note thereto.

Duty to secure the provision of adequate facilities. This section does not require a local education authority to provide adequate facilities for further education, but to secure the provision of such facilities. (For the duty to establish and maintain county colleges, see s 43 post). Power to enforce the execution of the local education authority's functions with respect to further education is given to the Secretary of State by s 99 post.

By s 53 post every local education authority must secure that the facilities for further education provided for its area include adequate facilities for recreation and social and physical training.

The facilities for further education that may be provided under this section are to be deemed to include and always to have included facilities for vocational and industrial training; see the Industrial Training Act 1964, s 16, this part of this title post.

Compulsory school age. See, subject to s 38 ante, s 35 ante and the note thereto.

Schemes of further education. For details of such schemes, see s 42 post.

Instrument of government. As to the duty of providing instruments of government for institutions of further education, other than colleges of education, providing full-time education pursuant to a scheme of further education approved under s 42 post, see the Education (No 2) Act 1968, s 1, this part of this title post.

London. For the provision of further education in Greater London, and as to the recoupment of the cost to such an authority of the provision of further education for persons not belonging to their area, see the London Government Act 1963, s 31(8), Vol 26, title London.

42 Schemes of further education

(1) Every local education authority shall, at such times and in such form as [the Secretary of State] may direct, prepare and submit to [the Secretary of State] schemes of further education for their area, giving particulars of the provision which the authority propose to make for fulfilling such of their duties with respect to further education, other than duties with respect to county colleges, as may be specified in the direction.

(2) Where a scheme of further education has been submitted to [the Secretary of State] by a local education authority, [the Secretary of State] may, after making in the scheme such modifications if any as after consultation with the authority he thinks expedient, approve the scheme, and thereupon it shall be the duty of the local education authority to take such measures as [the Secretary of State] may from time to time, after consultation with the authority, direct for the purpose of giving effect to the scheme.

(3) A scheme of further education approved by [the Secretary of State] in accordance with the provisions of this section may be modified supplemented or replaced by a further scheme prepared submitted and approved in accordance with those provisions, and [the Secretary of State] may give directions revoking any scheme of further education, or any provision contained in such a scheme, as from such dates as may be specified in the directions, but without prejudice to the preparation submission and approval of further schemes.

(4) A local education authority shall, when preparing any scheme of further education, have regard to any facilities for further education provided for their area by universities, educational associations, and other bodies, and shall consult any such bodies as aforesaid and the local education authorities for adjacent areas; and the scheme, as approved by [the Secretary of State], may include such provisions as to the co-operation of any such bodies or authorities as may have been agreed between them and the authority by whom the scheme was submitted.

NOTES

The words in square brackets are substituted by virtue of the Education and Science Order 1964, SI 1964/490, art 3(2)(*a*).

Further education. See s 41 ante.

Local education authority. See s 114(1) post and the note thereto.

Secretary of State. See the note "Secretary of State for Education and Science" to s 1 ante.

County colleges. See s 43 post.

Thinks expedient. See the note "Thinks fit" to s 37 ante.

London. As to the continued operation and restatement of schemes under this section in force immediately before 1 April 1965 and relating to areas in Greater London, see the London Government Act 1963, s 31(1)(*c*), Vol 26, title London.

Enforcement of directions. As to the enforcement of a direction to a local education authority by the Secretary of State, see s 99(1) post; as to the revocation or variation of such an order, see s 111 post.

Instrument of government. See the note to s 41 ante.

Disabled persons. Institutions established under this section must contain means of access and facilities suitable for disabled persons using the institutions; see the Chronically Sick and Disabled Persons Act 1970, s 8, this part of this title post.

43 County colleges

(1) . . . it shall be the duty of every local education authority to establish and maintain county colleges, that is to say, centres approved by [the Secretary of State] for providing for young persons who are not in full time attendance at any school or other educational institution such further education, including physical practical and vocational training, as will enable them to develop their various aptitudes and capacities and will prepare them for the responsibilities of citizenship.

(2) As soon after the date of the commencement of this Part of this Act as [the Secretary of State] considers it practicable so to do, he shall direct every local education authority to estimate the immediate and prospective needs of their area with respect to county colleges having regard to the provisions of this Act, and to prepare and submit to him within such time and in such form as may be specified in the direction a plan showing the provision which the authority propose to make for such colleges for their area, and the plan shall contain such particulars as to the colleges proposed to be established as may be specified in the direction.

(3) [The Secretary of State] shall, after considering the plan submitted by a local education authority and after consultation with them, make an order for the area of the authority specifying the county colleges which it is the duty of the authority to maintain, and the order shall require the authority to make such provision for boarding accommodation at county colleges as [the Secretary of State] considers to be expedient: the order so made for any area shall continue to regulate the duties of the local education authority in respect of the matters therein mentioned and shall be amended by [the Secretary of State], after consultation with the authority, whenever, in his opinion, the amendment thereof is expedient by reason of any change or proposed change of circumstances.

(4) [The Secretary of State] may make regulations as to the maintenance government and conduct of county colleges and as to the further education to be given therein.

NOTES

The words omitted from sub-s (1) were repealed by the SLR Act 1950.

The words in square brackets are substituted by virtue of the Secretary of State for Education and Science Order 1964, SI 1964/490, art 3(2)(*a*).

Duty . . . to establish and maintain county colleges. As to the enforcement of this duty by the Secretary of State, see s 99(1) post.

Secretary of State. See the note "Secretary of State for Education and Science" to s 1 ante.

Full time attendance. See the note "Full-time education" to s 36 ante.

Further education. As to the general duties of local education authorities with respect to further education, see s 41 ante.

Commencement of this Part of this Act. For the reference in this section to the date of the commencement of this Part of this Act there was substituted, by the Compulsory School Age (Postponement) Order 1944, SR & O 1944/979, reference to the date of the expiry of that order (ie 1 April 1947).

Considers it practicable; considers to be expedient. Cf the note "Thinks fit" to s 37 ante.

Boarding accommodation. As to the provision of boarding accommodation otherwise than at college, see s 50(1) post.

Instrument of government. As to the duty of local education authorities to provide instruments of government for institutions of further education, see the Education (No 2) Act 1968, s 1 post.

Definitions. For "maintain", "school" and "young person", see s 114(1) post; for "local education authority", see s 114(1) post and the note thereto.

Regulations under this section. No regulations had been made under this section up to 1 August 1985. For general provisions as to regulations under this Act, see s 112 post.

44 Duty to attend county colleges in accordance with college attendance notices

(1) This section shall come into operation on such date as soon as practicable after the date determined by Order in Council under the last foregoing section as [the Secretary of State] may by order direct.

(2) It shall be the duty of the local education authority to serve upon every young person residing in their area who is not exempt from compulsory attendance for further education a notice (hereinafter referred to as a "college attendance notice") directing him to attend at a county college, and it shall be the duty of every young person upon whom such a notice is served to attend at the county college named in the notice in accordance with the requirements specified therein.

(3) Subject to the provisions of the next following subsection, the requirements specified in a college attendance notice shall be such as to secure the attendance of the person upon whom it is served at a county college—

(*a*) for one whole day, or two half-days, in each of forty-four weeks in every year while he remains a young person; or

(*b*) where the authority are satisfied that continuous attendance would be more suitable in the case of that young person, for one continuous period of eight weeks, or two continuous periods of four weeks each, in every such year;

and in this section the expression "year" means, in relation to any young person, in the case of the first year the period of twelve months beginning with the first day on which he is required by a college attendance notice served on him to attend a county college, and in the case of every subsequent year the period of twelve months beginning immediately after the expiration of the last preceding year:

Provided that in respect of the year in which the young person attains the age of eighteen the requirements specified in the notice shall be reduced to such extent as the local education authority think expedient for securing that the attendances required of him until he attains that age shall be as nearly as may be proportionate to those which would have been required of him during a full period of twelve months.

(4) If, by reason of the nature of the employment of any young person or of other circumstances affecting him, the local education authority are satisfied that attendance in accordance with the provisions of the last foregoing subsection would not be suitable in his case, a college attendance notice may, with the consent of the young person, require his attendance in accordance with such other arrangements as may be specified in the notice, so, however, that the requirements specified in the notice in accordance with such arrangements as aforesaid shall be such as to secure the attendance of the young person for periods amounting in the aggregate to three hundred and thirty hours in each year, or, in the case of the year in which he attains the age of eighteen, to the proportionately reduced number of hours.

(5) Except where continuous attendance is required, no college attendance notice shall require a young person to attend a county college on a Sunday or on any day or

part of a day exclusively set apart for religious observance by the religious body to which he belongs, or during any holiday or half-holiday to which by any enactment regulating his employment or by agreement he is entitled, or, so far as practicable, during any holiday or half-holiday which is allowed in accordance with any custom of his employment, or between the hours of six in the evening and half past eight in the morning:

Provided that [the Secretary of State] may, on the application of any local education authority, direct that in relation to young persons in their area or in any part thereof employed at night or otherwise employed at abnormal times this subsection shall have effect as if for the reference to the hours of six in the evening and half past eight in the morning there were substituted a reference to such other times as may be specified in the direction.

(6) The place, days, times, and periods, of attendance required of a young person, and the period for which the notice is to be in force, shall be specified in any college attendance notice served on him; and the requirements of any such notice in force in the case of a young person may be amended as occasion may require either by the authority by whom it was served on him or by any other local education authority in whose area he may for the time being reside, so, however, that the provisions of every such notice shall be such as to secure that the requirements imposed on the young person during each year while he remains a young person shall comply with the provisions of the last three foregoing subsections.

(7) In determining what requirements shall be imposed upon a young person by a college attendance notice or by any amendments to such a notice, the local education authority shall have regard, so far as practicable, to any preference which he, and in the case of a young person under the age of sixteen years his parent, may express, to the circumstances of his employment or prospective employment, and to any representations that may be made to the authority by his employer or any person proposing to employ him.

(8) The following persons shall be exempt from compulsory attendance for further education, that is to say—

(a) any person who is in full time attendance at any school or other educational institution (not being a county college);

(b) any person who is shown to the satisfaction of the local education authority to be receiving suitable and efficient instruction either full time or for such times as in the opinion of the authority are equivalent to not less than three hundred and thirty hours instruction in a period of twelve months;

(c) any person who having been exempt under either of the last two foregoing paragraphs did not cease to be so exempt until after he had attained the age of seventeen years and eight months;

(d) any person who is undergoing a course of training for the mercantile marine or the sea fishing industry approved by [the Secretary of State] or who, having completed such a course, is engaged in the mercantile marine or in the said industry;

(e) any person to whom, by reason of section one hundred and fifteen or section one hundred and and sixteen of this Act, the duties of local education authorities do not relate;

(f) any person who attained the age of fifteen years before the date on which this section comes into operation, not being a person who immediately before that date was required to attend a continuation school under the provisions of the Education Act 1921.

If any person is aggrieved by a decision of a local education authority given under paragraph (b) of this subsection, he may refer the question to [the Secretary of State], who shall give such direction thereon as he thinks fit.

(9) If any young person upon whom a college attendance notice has been served fails to comply with any requirement of the notice, he shall be guilty of an offence against this section unless he proves either—

    (*a*) that he was at the material time exempt from compulsory attendance for further education; or

    (*b*) that he was prevented from complying with the requirement by reason of sickness or any unavoidable cause; or

    (*c*) that the requirement does not comply with the provisions of this section.

NOTES

The words in square brackets are substituted by virtue of the Secretary of State for Education and Science Order 1964, SI 1964/490, art 3(2)(*a*).

Commencement. Up to 1 August 1985 no order had been made under sub-s (1). The County Colleges Order 1947, SR & O 1947/527 (spent) fixed 1 April 1947 as the date for the establishment of county colleges under s 43 ante.

It shall be the duty. As to enforcement of this duty, see s 99(1) post.

Young person. For meaning, see s 114(1) post. Where a person attains the age of eighteen during the term of his county college, he is deemed, for the purposes of this Act, not to have attained that age until the end of term; see the Education Act 1946, s 8(3), this part of this title post.

Further education. As to the general duties of local education authorities with respect to further education, see s 41 ante.

College attendance notice. As to the service of notices, see s 113 post and of copies upon employers, see s 45(2) post. As to the enforcement of attendance at county colleges, see s 46 post.

Continuous attendance. As to the provision of boarding accommodation, see s 43(3) ante and s 50(1) post.

Exemption from compulsory attendance. Exclusion from college under a direction by the medical officer constitutes an additional ground of exemption; see s 54(7) post.

The burden of proving the existence of an exemption is placed by sub-s (9) above on the defendant; but on the production of a certificate of exemption under s 45(5) post, the burden of proof is transferred back to the prosecution.

Offence against this section. For penalties, see s 46 post.

Unless he proves. See the note to s 37 ante.

Definitions. For "parent" and "school", see s 114(1) post. For "local education authority", see s 114(1) post and the note thereto.

Education Act 1921. The provisions of this Act relating to continuation schools (ss 75–79, 93) were repealed with a saving by s 121 of, and Sch 9, Pt I to, this Act. The saving was repealed by the Education Act 1973, s 1(4).

Order under this section. No order had been made under this section up to 1 August 1985.

45 Administrative provisions for securing attendance at county colleges

(1) For the purpose of facilitating the execution by local education authorities of their functions under the last foregoing section, the following provisions shall, on and after the date on which that section comes into operation, have effect, that is to say:—

    (*a*) every young person who is not exempt from compulsory attendance for further education shall at all times keep the local education authority in whose area he resides informed of his proper address;

    (*b*) any person by whom such a young person as aforesaid is employed otherwise than by way of casual employment shall notify the local education authority for the area in which the young person resides when the young person enters his employment and again when he ceases to be employed by him, and shall also notify the authority of any change of address of the employer, and, if known to him, of the young person, which occurs during the continuance of the employment;

and any person who fails to perform any duty imposed on him by the foregoing provisions of this section shall be guilty of an offence against this section.

(2) The local education authority by whom a college attendance notice is served

upon any young person shall serve a copy thereof upon any person who notifies the authority that the young person is employed by him.

(3) [The Secretary of State] may by regulations make provision as to the form of college attendance notices, as to consultation and the exchange of information between different local education authorities, as to the issue of certificates of exemption in respect of young persons who are exempt from compulsory attendance for further education, and generally for the purpose of facilitating the administration by local authorities of the provisions of this Part of this Act as to attendance at county colleges.

(4) [The Secretary of State] and [the Secretary of State for Employment] shall issue instructions to local education authorities and to local offices of [the Department of Employment] respectively for ensuring due consultation and exchange of information between such authorities and offices.

(5) Any certificate of exemption in the prescribed form purporting to be authenticated in the prescribed manner shall be received in evidence in any legal proceeding, and shall unless the contrary is proved, be sufficient evidence of the fact therein stated.

NOTES

The words "the Secretary of State" in sub-ss (3), (4) are substituted by virtue of the Secretary of State for Education and Science Order 1964, SI 1964/490, art 3(2)(a).

The words in the second and third pairs of square brackets in sub-s (4) were substituted by the Secretary of State for Employment and Productivity Order 1968, SI 1968/729, art 3(2)(a), and the Secretary of State for Trade and Industry Order 1970, SI 1970/1537, art 3(2).

Date on which that section comes into operation. S 44 had not been brought into operation as at 1 August 1985; see sub-s (1) thereof and the note "Order under this section" thereto.

Compulsory attendance at college. See s 44 ante. As to exemption from compulsory attendance, see sub-s (8) thereof and the note "Exemption from compulsory attendance" thereto.

Further education. As to the general duties of local education authorities with respect to further education, see s 41 ante.

Offence against this section. For penalties, see s 46 post.

College attendance notice. See s 44 ante. As to the service of notices, see s 113 post.

Secretary of State. See the note "Secretary of State for Education and Science" to s 1 ante.

County colleges. As to the position of county colleges under this Act, see s 43 ante.

Definitions. For "prescribe" and "young person", see s 114(1) post; for "local education authority", see s 114(1) post and the note thereto.

Regulations under this section. No regulations had been made under this section up to 1 August 1985. For general provisions as to regulations made under this Act, see s 112 post.

46 Enforcement of attendance at county colleges

(1) Any person guilty of an offence against either of the last two foregoing sections shall be liable on summary conviction [to a fine not exceeding level 1 on the standard scale] or to imprisonment for a term not exceeding one month or to both such fine and such imprisonment.

(2) It shall be the duty of the local education authority in whose area the young person in question resides to institute proceedings for such offences as aforesaid wherever, in their opinion, the institution of such proceedings is expedient, and no such proceedings shall be instituted except by or on behalf of a local education authority.

(3) If, in furnishing any information for the purposes of either of the last two foregoing sections, any person makes any statement which he knows to be false in any material particular, or recklessly makes any statement which is false in any material particular, he shall be liable on summary conviction to a fine not exceeding [level 2 on the standard scale] or to imprisonment for a term not exceeding three months or to both such fine and such imprisonment.

(4) Without prejudice to the provisions of any enactment or rule of law relating to the aiding and abetting of offences, if the parent of a young person or any person by whom a young person is employed or the servant or agent of any such person has

conduced to or connived at any offence committed by the young person against either of the last two foregoing sections, the person who has conduced to or connived at the offence shall, whether or not any person is proceeded against or convicted in respect of the offence conduced to or connived at, be guilty of the like offence and punishable accordingly.

NOTES

Sub-s (1) as originally enacted specified that a person convicted of an offence under s 44 or s 45 ante should be liable "in the case of a first offence against that section to a fine not exceeding one pound, in the case of a second offence against that section to a fine not exceeding five pounds, and in the case of a third or subsequent offence against that section to a fine not exceeding ten pounds or to imprisonment for a term not exceeding one month or to both such fine and such imprisonment". The fine was increased to £25 for a first or subsequent offence by the Criminal Law Act 1977, s 31(6), (7), and now a reference to level 1 on the standard scale is substituted by virtue of the Criminal Justice Act 1982, ss 38(4), 46, Vol 27, title Magistrates.

The reference in sub-s (3) to level 2 on the standard scale is substituted by virtue of the Criminal Justice Act 1982, s 46, Vol 27, title Magistrates. The fine was previously increased to £50 by the Criminal Law Act 1977, ss 30, 31.

Summary conviction; standard scale. See the notes to s 40 ante.

It shall be the duty. Where the performance of a duty is, as here, made contingent upon the opinion of the authority, the Secretary of State may, under s 68 post, give such directions as he thinks expedient to prevent any unreasonable action by a local education authority. The Secretary of State's power under s 99 post to enforce the execution of a duty under this Act will not usually be available under this section as the duty is contingent upon the opinion of the authority.

Knows. Knowledge is an essential ingredient of the offence and must be proved by the prosecution; see, in particular, *Gaumont British Distributors Ltd v Henry* [1939] 2 KB 711, [1939] 2 All ER 808.

Knowledge includes the state of mind of a person who shuts his eyes to the obvious; see *James & Son Ltd v Smee* [1955] 1 QB 78 at 91, [1954] 3 All ER 273 at 278 per Parker J. Moreover, there is authority for saying that where a person deliberately refrains from making inquiries the results of which he might not care to have, this constitutes in law actual knowledge of the facts in question; see *Knox v Boyd* 1941 JC 82 at 86, and *Taylor's Central Garages (Exeter) Ltd v Roper* (1951) 115 JP 445 at 449, 450, [1951] WN 383 per Devlin J; and see also, in particular, *Mallon v Allon* [1964] 1 QB 385 at 394, [1963] 3 All ER 843 at 847. Yet mere neglect to ascertain what could have been found out by making reasonable inquiries is not tantamount to knowledge; *Taylor's Central Garages (Exeter) Ltd v Roper* supra per Devlin J, and cf *London Computator Ltd v Seymour* [1944] 2 All ER 11; but see also *Mallon v Allon* supra.

As to when the knowledge of an employee or agent may be imputed to his employer or principal, see 11 Halsbury's Laws (4th edn) para 54.

False. A statement may be false on account of what it omits even though it is literally true; see *R v Lord Kylsant* [1932] 1 KB 442, [1931] All ER Rep 179, and *R v Bishirgian* [1936] 1 All ER 586; and cf *Curtis v Chemical Cleaning and Dyeing Co Ltd* [1951] 1 KB 805 at 808, 809, [1951] 1 All ER 631 at 634, CA. Whether or not gain or advantage accrues from the false statement is irrelevant; see *Jones v Meatyard* [1939] 1 All ER 140; *Stevens & Steeds Ltd and Evans v King* [1943] 1 All ER 314; *Clear v Smith* [1981] 1 WLR 399, [1980] Crim LR 246; and *Barrass v Reeve* [1980] 3 All ER 705, [1981] 1 WLR 408.

Material particular. A particular may be material on the ground that it renders another statement more credible; see *R v Tyson* (1867) LR 1 CCR 107. As to whether evidence should be adduced to show why a piece of information was a material particular, see *R v Mallett* [1978] 3 All ER 10, [1978] 1 WLR 820, CA.

Recklessly. In *R v Caldwell* [1982] AC 341, [1981] 1 All ER 961, HL (applied in *R v Lawrence* [1982] AC 510, [1981] 1 All ER 974, HL; and see also *R v Pigg* [1982] 2 All ER 591, CA; revsd on another point [1983] 1 All ER 56, HL, and *Elliott v C* [1983] 2 All ER 1005, [1983] 1 WLR 939; and *Goldman v Thai Airways International Ltd* [1983] 3 All ER 693) it was held that when used in criminal enactments, the term "reckless" was used not as a term of legal art but in the popular or dictionary sense of meaning "careless, regardless or heedless of the possible harmful consequences of one's acts". As such the term encompassed both a decision to ignore a risk of harmful consequences flowing from an act which the accused had recognised as existing and also a failure to give any thought to whether there was any risk in circumstances where, if any thought were given to the matter, it would be obvious that there was. On the meaning of "recklessly", see also 11 Halsbury's Laws (4th edn) para 14, and 4 Words and Phrases (2nd edn) 272, 273, and the cases there cited.

Any enactment . . . relating to the aiding and abetting of offences. See the Accessories and Abettors Act 1861, Vol 12, title Criminal Law.

Has conduced to. "What has conduced to an offence must in some sense have caused it or contributed to it", see *Cunnington v Cunnington and Noble* (1859) 34 LTOS 45, 28 LJ P & M 101 per Lord Campbell CJ.

Defence. When a pupil is directed to be excluded from a county college on the grounds that his clothing is verminous, such direction is a defence in proceedings under this section; see s 54(7) post.

Evidence. For provisions as to evidence in proceedings, see s 95 post.

Definitions. For "parent" and "young person", see s 114(1) post; for "local education authority", see s 114(1) post and the note thereto.

47 Interim provisions as to further education

Until the date upon which a scheme of further education is first approved by the Minister for the area of a local education authority under the foregoing provisions of this Part of this Act, the authority shall, unless the Minister otherwise directs, continue to maintain or assist any school or other educational institution which, immediately before the date of the commencement of this Part of this Act, was maintained or assisted by them or by the council of any county district within their area, under the powers conferred by section seventy of the Education Act 1921, not being a school or institution which under this Act is maintained or assisted as a secondary school, and may, in accordance with arrangements approved by the Minister, provide such additional facilities for further education, other than education at county colleges, as appear to the authority to be expedient for meeting the needs of their area.

NOTES

Scheme of further education. As to the duty of local education authorities to prepare schemes of further education, see s 42 ante.

Minister. See the note "Secretary of State for Education and Science" to s 1 ante.

Commencement of this Part of this Act. See the note to s 9 ante.

County district. The urban districts and rural districts existing immediately before 1 April 1974 were abolished on that date by the Local Government Act 1972, ss 1(10), 20(6), Vol 25, title Local Government, and by virtue of s 179(1), (3) of that Act, the reference to a county district is to be construed as a reference to a district established by ss 1(1), (3), (4), 20(1), (3) of, and Sch I, Pt I, Sch 4, Pt II to, the 1972 Act.

County college. As to the position of county colleges under the Act, see s 43 ante.

Education Act 1921, s 70. Repealed by s 121 of, and Sch 9 to, this Act. That section gave a general power to county councils and county borough councils to supply or aid the supply of higher education, and a limited power to councils of non-county boroughs or urban districts.

Definitions. For "secondary school" and "school", see s 114(1) post; for "local education authority", see s 114(1) post and the note thereto.

SUPPLEMENTARY PROVISIONS AS TO PRIMARY, SECONDARY AND FURTHER EDUCATION

Ancillary Services

48 Medical inspection and treatment of pupils

(1)–(3) . . .

(4) It shall be the duty of every local education authority to make arrangements for encouraging and assisting pupils to take advantage of [the provision for medical and dental inspection and treatment made for them in pursuance of [section 5(1) of the National Health Service Act 1977 or paragraph 1(*a*)(i) of Schedule 1 to that Act]]:

Provided that if the parent of any pupil gives to the authority notice that he objects to the pupil availing himself of any [of the provision so made], the pupil shall not be encouraged or assisted so to do.

(5) . . .

NOTES

Sub-ss (1)–(3), (5) were repealed by the National Health Service Reorganisation Act 1973, s 57, Sch 5.

In sub-s (4) the words in the outer pair of square brackets in the first paragraph and the words in square brackets in the proviso to that subsection were substituted by the National Health Service Reorganisation Act 1973, s 57, Sch 5 and the words in the inner pair of square brackets in the first paragraph were substituted by the National Health Service Act 1977, s 129, Sch 15, para 2.

General Note. The Secretary of State for Social Services is empowered by the Health Services and Public Health Act 1968, s 63(1)(*b*), (2)(*a*), (3)–(8), Vol 30, title National Health Service, either directly or in arrangement with others, to make arrangements for instructions to be given to certain persons for the efficient carrying out of the duty imposed by this section and, with the approval of the Treasury, for the defrayment of the charges and costs etc in connection therewith.

Definitions. For "pupil" and "parent", see s 114(1) post; for "local education authority", see s 114(1) post and the note thereto.

49 *(Repealed by the Education Act 1980, s 38(6), Sch 7.)*

50 Provision of board and lodging otherwise than at boarding schools or colleges

(1) Where the local education authority are satisfied with respect to any [pupil] that primary or secondary education suitable to his age, ability and aptitude [and to any special educational needs he may have] can best be provided by them for him at any particular county school, voluntary school, or special school, or are satisfied with respect to any young person that further education should in his case be provided by requiring his continuous attendance at a county college, but that such education cannot be so provided unless boarding accommodation is provided for him otherwise than at the school or college, [and where a local education authority are satisfied, with respect to a pupil [having special educational needs], that provision for him of board and lodging is necessary for enabling him to receive the required special educational [provision]] the authority may provide such board and lodging for him under such arrangements as they think fit.

(2) In making any arrangements under this section for any [pupil] or young person, a local education authority shall, so far as practicable, give effect to the wishes of the parent of the [pupil] or to the wishes of the young person, as the case may be, with respect to the religious denomination of the person with whom he will reside.

NOTES

The word "pupil" was substituted wherever it occurs by the Education Act 1946, s 14(1), Sch 2, Pt I.

The words in the second pair of square brackets in sub-s (1) were substituted by the Education Act 1981, s 21, Sch 3, para 3(a), and those in the third pair of square brackets were inserted by the Education (Miscellaneous Provisions) Act 1948, s 11(1), Sch 1, Pt I and the words "having special educational needs" and "provision" were substituted by s 21 of, and Sch 3, para 3(b), (c) to, the 1981 Act.

Continuous attendance. As to the circumstances in which and the extent to which continuous attendance may be required, see s 44(3) ante.

Boarding accommodation. As to the provision of boarding accommodation at primary and secondary schools, see s 8(2)(d) ante, and at county colleges, see s 43(3) ante. As to the recovery of cost of boarding accommodation, see s 52 post.

Definitions. For "county college", see s 43 ante; for "county school" and "voluntary school", see s 9(2) ante; for "further education", see s 41 ante; for "parent", "primary education", "pupil", "secondary education" and "young person", see s 114(1) post; for "local education authority", see s 114(1) post and the note thereto; and for "special educational needs" and "special educational provision", see, by virtue of s 114(1) post, the Education Act 1981, s 1 post.

51 *(Repealed by the Education (Miscellaneous Provisions) Act 1948, s 11, Sch 2; see now, as to the provision of clothing, s 5 of that Act, this part of this title post.)*

52 Recovery of cost of boarding accommodation . . .

(1) Where a local education authority have, under the powers conferred by the foregoing provisions of this Act, provided a pupil with board and lodging otherwise than at a boarding school or college . . . the authority shall require the parent to pay to the authority in respect thereof such sums, if any, as in the opinion of the authority he is able without financial hardship to pay:

Provided that—

(a) where the board and lodging provided for the pupil were so provided under arrangements made by the local education authority on the ground that in their opinion education suitable to his age ability and aptitude [or special educational needs] could not otherwise be provided by the authority for him, no sum shall be recoverable in respect thereof under this section; and

(b) where the board and lodging have been so provided for a pupil in attendance at a county college, the authority, if satisfied that the pupil is in a financial position to pay the whole or any part of a sum recoverable from the parent under this section, may recover that sum or that part thereof from the pupil instead of from the parent.

(2) The sums recoverable under this section shall not exceed the cost to the local education authority of providing the board and lodging ...

(3) Any sums payable by virtue of this section may be recovered summarily as a civil debt.

NOTES

The words omitted (which related to clothing) were repealed by the Education (Miscellaneous Provisions) Act 1948, s 11, Sch 2; see now s 5 of that Act post.

The words in square brackets in sub-s (1) were inserted by the Education Act 1981, s 21, Sch 3, para 4.

Foregoing provisions of this Act. See s 50 ante.

Board and lodging. For the provision of board and lodging, see s 50 ante.

Shall require. Where, as here, the performance by the local education authority of a duty is made contingent upon the opinion of the authority, s 68 post enables the Secretary of State to give such directions as he thinks expedient to prevent the unreasonable exercise of the duty.

Recovered summarily as a civil debt. As to the recovery of civil debts in courts of summary jurisdiction, see the Magistrates' Courts Act 1980, s 50(2), Vol 27, title Magistrates.

Definitions. For "county college", see s 43 ante; for "parent" and "pupil", see s 114(1) post; for "local education authority", see s 114(1) post and the note thereto; and for "special educational needs", see, by virtue of s 114(1) post, the Education Act 1981, s 1, this part of this title post.

53 Provision of facilities for recreation and social and physical training

(1) It shall be the duty of every local education authority to secure that the facilities for primary secondary and further education provided for their area include adequate facilities for recreation and social and physical training, and for that purpose a local education authority ... may establish maintain and manage, or assist the establishment, maintenance, and management of camps, holiday classes, playing fields, play centres, and other places (including playgrounds, gymnasiums, and swimming baths not appropriated to any school or college), at which facilities for recreation and for such training as aforesaid are [available for persons receiving primary secondary or further education], and may organise games expeditions and other activities for such persons, and may defray or contribute towards the expenses thereof.

(2) A local education authority, in making arrangements for the provision of facilities or the organisation of activities under the powers conferred on them by the last foregoing subsection shall, in particular, have regard to the expediency of co-operating with any voluntary societies or bodies whose objects include the provision of facilities or the organisation of activities of a similar character.

(3), (4) ...

NOTES

The words omitted from sub-s (1) were repealed by the Education Act 1980, ss 30(1), (2), 38(6), Sch 7.

The words in square brackets in sub-s (1) were substituted, and sub-s (3) was repealed, by the Education (Miscellaneous Provisions) Act 1948, s 11, Sch 2.

Sub-s (4) was repealed by the SLR Act 1950.

General Note. By the Education (Miscellaneous Provisions) Act 1948, s 5(3)(b), this part of this title post, the Secretary of State may make regulations empowering a local education authority to provide clothing suitable for physical training for persons using facilities available under sub-s (1) above.

Duty of local education authority. For the enforcement of this duty, see s 99(1) post.

Play centres. The Nurseries and Child-Minders Regulation Act 1948 does not apply to the reception of children in any play centre maintained or assisted by a local education authority under this section; see s 8(3) of that Act, Vol 6, title Children.

County college. As to the position of county colleges under this Act, see s 43 ante.

Definitions. For "further education", "primary education", "pupil", "secondary education", and "school", see s 114(1) post; and for "local education authority", see s 114(1) post and the note thereto.

54 Power to ensure cleanliness

(1) A local education authority may, by directions in writing issued with respect to all schools maintained by them or with respect to any of such schools named in the directions, authorise a medical officer of the authority to cause examinations of the persons and clothing of pupils in attendance at such schools to be made whenever in his opinion such examinations are necessary in the interests of cleanliness; and if a medical officer of a local education authority has reasonable cause to suspect that the person or clothing of a pupil in attendance at any county college is infested with vermin or in a foul condition, he may cause an examination thereof to be made.

(2) Any such examination as aforesaid shall be made by a person authorised by the local education authority to make such examinations, and if the person or clothing of any pupil is found upon such an examination to be infested with vermin or in a foul condition, any officer of the authority may serve upon the parent of the pupil, or in the case of a pupil in attendance at a county college upon the pupil, a notice requiring him to cause the person and clothing of the pupil to be cleansed.

(3) A notice served under the last foregoing subsection shall inform the person upon whom it is served that unless within the period limited by the notice, not being less than twenty-four hours after the service thereof, the person and clothing of the pupil to whom the notice relates are cleansed to the satisfaction of such person as may be specified in the notice the cleansing thereof will be carried out under arrangements made by the local education authority; and if, upon a report being made to him by that person at the expiration of that period, a medical officer of the authority is not satisfied that the person and clothing of the pupil have been properly cleansed, the medical officer may issue an order directing that the person and clothing of the pupil be cleansed under such arrangements.

(4) It shall be the duty of the local education authority to make arrangements for securing that any person or clothing required under this section to be cleansed may be cleansed (whether at the request of a parent or pupil or in pursuance of an order issued under this section) at suitable premises by suitable persons and with suitable appliances; and where the council of any county district in the area of the authority are entitled to the use of any premises or appliances for cleansing the person or clothing of persons infested with vermin, the authority may require the council to permit the authority to use those premises or appliances for such purposes upon such terms as may be determined by agreement between the authority and the council or, in default of such agreement, by the Minister of Health.

(5) Where an order has been issued by a medical officer under this section directing that the person and clothing of a pupil be cleansed under arrangements made by a local education authority, the order shall be sufficient to authorise any officer of the authority to cause the person and clothing of the pupil named in the order to be cleansed in accordance with arrangements made under the last foregoing subsection, and for that purpose to convey him to, and detain him at, any premises provided in accordance with such arrangements.

(6) If, after the cleansing of the person or clothing of any pupil has been carried out

under this section, his person or clothing is again found to be infested with vermin or in a foul condition at any time while he is in attendance at a school maintained by a local education authority or at a county college, and it is proved that the condition of his person or clothing is due to neglect on the part of his parent, or in the case of a pupil in attendance at a county college to his own neglect, the parent or the pupil, as the case may be, shall be liable on summary conviction to a fine not exceeding [level 1 on the standard scale].

(7) Where a medical officer of a local education authority suspects that the person or clothing of any pupil in attendance at a school maintained by the authority or at any county college is infested with vermin or in a foul condition, but action for the examination or cleansing thereof cannot immediately be taken, he may, if he considers it necessary so to do either in the interest of the pupil or of other pupils in attendance at the school or college, direct that the pupil be excluded from the school or college until such action has been taken; and such a direction shall be a defence to any proceedings under this Act in respect of the failure of the pupil to attend school or to comply with the requirements of a college attendance notice, as the case may be, on any day on which he is excluded in pursuance of the direction, unless it is proved that the issue of the direction was necessitated by the wilful default of the pupil or his parent.

(8) No girl shall be examined or cleansed under the powers conferred by this section except by a duly qualified medical practitioner or by a woman authorised for that purpose by a local education authority.

NOTES

The reference in sub-s (6) to level 1 on the standard scale is substituted by virtue of the Criminal Justice Act 1982, s 46, Vol 27, title Magistrates. The maximum fine was previously increased to £25 by the Criminal Law Act 1977, s 31(6).

Directions. As to the revocation or variation of such directions, see s 111 post.

Writing. Unless the contrary intention appears this includes other modes of representing or reproducing words in a visible form; see the Interpretation Act 1978, s 5, Sch 1, Vol 41, title Statutes.

County college. As to the position of county colleges under this Act, see s 43 ante.

Obligation to submit to examination for vermin. See *Fox v Burgess* [1922] 1 KB 623, [1922] All ER Rep 754.

Notice. As to the service of notices, see s 113 post.

Responsibility of parent for cleanliness of pupil. It was held in *LCC v Stansell* (1935) 154 LT 241, 100 JP 54 that "parent" refers only to the father and does not include the mother. But this case was doubted and not followed in *Plunkett v Alker* [1954] 1 QB 420, [1954] 1 All ER 396, where it was held that "parent" includes the mother. See also the definition of "parent" in s 114(1) post.

Duty of local education authority. As to the enforcement of this duty, see s 99 post.

County district. See the note to s 47 ante.

Minister of Health. The functions of the Minister of Health were transferred to the Secretary of State and this section has effect as if for a reference to the Minister of Health there were substituted a reference to the Secretary of State, by virtue of the Secretary of State for Social Services Order 1968, SI 1968/1699.

Summary conviction; standard scale. See the notes to s 40 ante.

Failure of pupil to attend school. For enforcement proceedings, see s 40 ante.

The requirements of a college attendance notice. See ss 44–46 ante.

Application to London. This section is applied to the Inner London Education Authority with substitution of "the council of any inner London borough or the Common Council of the City of London" for the words "the council of any county district in the area of the authority" in sub-s (4); see the London Government Act 1963, s 32(7), Vol 26, title London.

Definitions. "County college" is defined in s 43 ante; for "clothing", "medical officer", "parent", "pupil" and "school", see s 114(1) post and for "local education authority", see s 114(1) post and the note thereto.

55 Provision of transport and other facilities

(1) A local education authority shall make such arrangements for the provision of transport and otherwise as they consider necessary or as [the Secretary of State] may direct for the purpose of facilitating the attendance of pupils at schools or county colleges or at any course or class provided in pursuance of a scheme of further education in force

for their area, and any transport provided in pursuance of such arrangements shall be provided free of charge.

(2) A local education authority [may pay the whole or any part, as the authority think fit, of the reasonable travelling expenses] of any pupil in attendance at any school or county college or at any such course or class as aforesaid for whose transport no arrangements are made under this section.

NOTES

The words in square brackets in sub-s (1) are substituted by virtue of the Secretary of State for Education and Science Order 1964, SI 1964/490, art 3(2)(a), and the words in square brackets in sub-s (2) were substituted by the Education (Miscellaneous Provisions) Act 1948, s 11, Sch 1, Pt I.

Provision of transport. Information as to the general arrangements for the transport of pupils to and from school must be included in the development plan for the area; see s 11(2)(g) ante. As to the liability of a local education authority for the safety of pupils for whom transport is provided, see *Shrimpton v Hertfordshire CC* (1911) 104 LT 145, [1911–13] All ER Rep 359. A local authority, which operates a school bus, owes a duty to see that the bus is reasonably safe for children who are going on the bus and this includes the provision of supervision if it is necessary. The standard to be adopted is that of the reasonable parent; see *Jacques v Oxfordshire CC* (1967) 66 LGR 440.

Vacant places in transport provided for the free transport of pupils under sub-s (1) may be occupied, in certain circumstances, by farepaying persons and a school bus may be used in a local bus service when not in use for free school transport; see the Public Passenger Vehicles Act 1981, s 46, Vol 38, title Road Traffic. By virtue of sub-s (1) thereof school buses are exempt from various requirements of that Act.

Cf the provisions of the Public Service Vehicles (Travel Concessions) Act 1955, s 1, Vol 38, title Road Traffic.

Scheme of further education. For details of such schemes, see s 42 ante.

Reasonable travelling expenses. Arrangements under sub-s (2) must be "suitable" within the meaning of s 39(2)(c) ante and if a child lives more than three miles from his school the authority must provide for his transport for the full distance (*Surrey CC v Minister of Education* [1953] 1 All ER 705, [1953] 1 WLR 516). See also the note "Within walking distance" to s 39 ante.

County college. As to the position of county colleges under this Act, see s 43 ante.

Definitions. For "pupil" and "school", see s 114(1) post; and for "local education authority", see s 114(1) post and the note thereto.

56 Power to provide primary and secondary education otherwise than at school

If a local education authority are satisfied that by reason of any extraordinary circumstances a child or young person is unable to attend a suitable school for the purpose of receiving primary or secondary education, [they shall have power with the approval of [the Secretary of State] to make special arrangements for him to receive education otherwise than at school, being primary or secondary education, as the case may require, or, if the authority are satisfied that it is impracticable for him to receive full-time education and [the Secretary of State] approves, education similar in other respects but less than full-time].

NOTES

The words in square brackets were substituted by the Education (Miscellaneous Provisions) Act 1948, s 11, Sch 1, Pt I, and the words "the Secretary of State" therein are substituted by virtue of the Secretary of State for Education and Science Order 1964, SI 1964/490, art 3(2)(a).

Extraordinary circumstances. Mere distance from a suitable school would presumably not be a sufficient reason to justify the exercise of the powers given by this section, since such a case would be adequately covered by s 50 ante.

Definitions. For "child", "primary education", "school", "secondary education" and "young person", see s 114(1) post; and for "local education authority", see s 114(1) post and the note thereto.

57–57B (*These sections were substituted for the original s 57 by the Mental Health Act 1959, ss 11, 153(1), (2), Sch 2, and were subsequently repealed by the Education (Handicapped Children) Act 1970, s 2, Schedule.*)

Employment of Children and Young Persons

58 Adaptation of enactments relating to the employment of children or young persons

For the purposes of any enactment relating to the prohibition or regulation of the employment of children or young persons, any person who is not for the purposes of this act over compulsory school age shall be deemed to be a child within the meaning of that enactment.

NOTES

General Note. The purpose of this section is to effect the necessary modifications of the various enactments relating to the employment of children which are necessitated by the raising of the school leaving age to sixteen years under s 35 ante. The enactments referred to include the Children and Young Persons Act 1933, ss 18–30, the Young Persons (Employment) Act 1938, ss 1–7, 9, 10, the Factories Act 1961, ss 86–119, the Children and Young Persons Act 1963, Pt II, and the Employment of Children Act 1973; the 1961 Act is printed in Vol 19, title Health and Safety at Work, and the other Acts are all printed in Vol 6, title Children.

Definitions. For "child", "compulsory school age" and "young person", see s 114(1) post.

59 Power of local education authorities to prohibit or restrict employment of children

(1) *If it appears to a local education authority that any child who is a registered pupil at a county school, voluntary school, or special school is being employed in such manner as to be prejudicial to his health or otherwise to render him unfit to obtain the full benefit of the education provided for him, the authority may, by notice in writing served upon the employer, prohibit him from employing the child, or impose such restrictions upon his employment of the child as appear to them to be expedient in the interests of the child.*

(2) *A local education authority may, by notice in writing served upon the parent or employer of any child who is a registered pupil at a county school, voluntary school, or special school, require the parent or employer to provide the authority, within such period as may be specified in the notice, with such information as appears to the authority to be necessary for the purpose of enabling them to ascertain whether the child is being employed in such a manner as to render him unfit to obtain the full benefit of the education provided for him.*

(3) *Any person who employs a child in contravention of any prohibition or restriction imposed under subsection (1) of this section, or who fails to comply with the requirements of a notice served under subsection (2) of this section, shall be guilty of an offence against this section and liable on summary conviction, [to a fine not exceeding level 1 on the standard scale] or to imprisonment for a term not exceeding one month or to both such fine and such imprisonment.*

(4) *Subsection (1) and subsection (3) of section twenty-eight of the Children and Young Persons Act 1933 (which relate to powers of entry for the enforcement of the provisions of Part II of that Act with respect to the employment of children) shall apply with respect to the provisions of any notice served under this section as they apply with respect to the provisions of the said Part II.*

NOTES

Prospective repeal. This section is prospectively repealed by the Employment of Children Act 1973, s 3(3), Sch 2, as from a day to be appointed under s 3(4) of that Act, Vol 6, title Children.

The reference in sub-s (3) to level 1 on the standard scale is substituted by virtue of the Criminal Justice Act 1982, s 46, Vol 27, title Magistrates. The maximum fine was previously increased to £25 on first or any subsequent conviction by the Criminal Law Act 1977, s 31(6).

Prohibition of employment. A local education authority must produce the report or other evidence on which they based their resolution to prohibit the employment of a child; see *Margerison v Hind & Co* [1922] 1 KB 214, 91 LJKB 160.

Notice. As to the service of notices, see s 113 post.

Writing. See the note to s 54 ante.

Summary conviction; standard scale. See the notes to s 40 ante.

Evidence. For the provisions as to evidence in proceedings under this section, see s 95 post.

Definitions. For "child", "parent" and "registered pupil", see s 114(1) post; for "local education authority", see s 114(1) post and the note thereto; for "county school" and "voluntary school", see s 9(2) ante; and for "special school", see s 9(5) ante.

Children and Young Persons Act 1933, s 28. See Vol 6, title Children.

60 Effect of college attendance notices on computation of working hours

(1) Where a young person is employed in any employment with respect to which a limitation upon the number of working hours during which he may be employed in that employment otherwise than by way of overtime in any week is imposed by or under any enactment, any period of attendance at a county college required of him during that week by a college attendance notice served on him shall, for the purposes of the limitation, be deemed to be time during which he has been so employed in that week.

(2) Where a young person employed in any employment is entitled by or under the provisions of any enactment or of any agreement to overtime rates of pay in respect of any time during which he is employed in that employment on any day or in any week in excess of any specified number of hours or before or after any specified hour, any period of attendance at a county college required of him during that week or on that day by a college attendance notice served on him shall, for the purposes of those provisions, be deemed to be a period during which he was employed in that employment otherwise than in excess of the specified number of hours, or otherwise than before or after the specified hour, as the case may be.

NOTES

Young person. For definition, see s 114(1) post.

College attendance notice. As to the duty to attend county colleges in accordance with college attendance notices, see s 44 ante.

County college. As to the position of county colleges under this Act, see s 43 ante.

Miscellaneous Provisions

61 Prohibition of fees in schools maintained by local education authorities and in county colleges

(1) No fees shall be charged in respect of admission to any school maintained by a local education authority or to any county college, or in respect of the education provided in any such school or college.

(2) Subject as hereinafter provided, where any pupil in attendance at any such school or college is provided at the school or college with board and lodging at the expense of the local education authority, fees shall be payable in respect of the board and lodging

. . .

Provided that—

    (a) where the board and lodging provided for the pupil are so provided under arrangements made by the local education authority on the ground that, in their opinion, education suitable to his age ability and aptitude [and to any special educational needs he may have] cannot otherwise be provided by the authority for him, the authority shall remit the whole of the fees payable under this subsection; and

    (b) where the local education authority are satisfied that payment of the full fees payable under this subsection would involve financial hardship to the person liable to pay them, the authority shall remit such part of the fees as they consider ought to be remitted in order to avoid such hardship, or, if in the opinion of the authority, such hardship cannot otherwise be avoided, shall remit the whole of the fees.

(3) Any sums payable under the last foregoing subsection in respect of a pupil shall be payable by his parent, so, however, that where the local education authority are satisfied in the case of any young person in attendance at a county college that his financial circumstances are such that the sums so payable in respect of the board and lodging provided for him ought to be defrayed by him, those sums shall be payable by him instead of by his parent; and any sums so payable shall be recoverable summarily as a civil debt.

NOTES

The words omitted from sub-s (2) were repealed by the Education Act 1980, ss 30(1), (2), 38(6), Sch 7, and the words in square brackets in that subsection were inserted by the Education Act 1981, s 21, Sch 3, para 5.

No fees shall be charged. See *R v Hereford and Worcester Local Education Authority, ex p Jones* [1981] 1 WLR 768, 125 Sol Jo 219 (where a local education authority decided that individual music tuition should be included in the curriculum provided in the schools, the mandatory terms of sub-s (1) precluded any fees from being charged).

School maintained by a local education authority. This phrase includes county schools and voluntary schools (see s 9(2) ante); it also includes nursery schools and special schools, if they are maintained by a local education authority (see s 9(4), (5) ante). It does not apply to other schools, whether they are in receipt of grants or assistance from the Secretary of State or a local education authority or not; see s 114(1), (2) post.

Board and lodging. As to the recovery of the cost of the provision of board and lodging otherwise than at a boarding school, see s 52 ante.

Recoverable summarily as a civil debt. See the note to s 52 ante.

Definitions. For "county college", see s 43 ante; for "parent", "pupil" and "young person", see s 114(1) post; for "local education authority", see s 114(1) post and the note thereto.

62 Duties of [Secretary of State] and of local education authorities as to the training of teachers

(1) In execution of the duties imposed on him by this Act, [the Secretary of State] shall, in particular, make such arrangements as he considers expedient for securing that there shall be available sufficient facilities for the training of teachers for service in schools colleges and other establishments maintained by local education authorities, and for that purpose [the Secretary of State] may give to any local education authority such directions as he thinks necessary requiring them to establish maintain or assist any training college or other institution or to provide or assist the provision of any other facilities specified in the direction.

(2) Where by any direction given under this section a local education authority are required to perform any such functions as aforesaid, [the Secretary of State] may give such directions to other local education authorities requiring them to contribute towards the expenses incurred in performing those functions as he thinks just.

NOTES

The words in square brackets are substituted by virtue of the Secretary of State for Education and Science Order 1964, SI 1964/490, art 3(2)(a).

Secretary of State. See the note "Secretary of State for Education and Science" to s 1 ante.

Direction by the Secretary of State. As to the enforcement of a direction to a local education authority by the Secretary of State, see s 99(1) post; as to the revocation or variation of such a direction, see s 111 post.

As to further financial provisions relating to expenditure incurred in pursuance of directions under this section, see the Local Government Act 1974, s 2(2), Sch 2, para 3, Vol 25, title Local Government.

Definitions. For "assist", "maintain" and "school", see s 114(1) post; and for "local education authority", see s 114(1) post and the note thereto.

63 Exemption from building byelaws of buildings approved by the Secretary of State

(1) ...

(2) Where plans for any building required for the purposes of any school or other educational establishment are approved by [the Secretary of State], he may by order direct that any provision of any local Act or of any byelaw made under such an Act shall not apply in relation to the building or shall apply in relation thereto with such modifications as may be specified in the order.

NOTES

Sub-s (1) was repealed by the Building Act 1984, s 133(2), Sch 7.

The words in square brackets in sub-s (2) are substituted by virtue of the Secretary of State for Education and Science Order 1964, SI 1964/490, art 3(2)(a).

Plans ... approved. This term includes particulars submitted and approved under the Education Act 1980, s 14, this part of this title post (see sub-s (4) thereof) or under regulations made under s 27(4) of that Act (see s 27(5) thereof).

Secretary of State. See the note "Secretary of State for Education and Science" to s 1 ante.

Definitions. For "school", see s 114(1) post, and for "educational establishment", see s 77(1) post.

Orders under this section. Orders under this section, being local, are not noted in this work. As to variation and revocation of orders, see s 111 post.

64 *(Repealed with savings by the Rating and Valuation Act 1961, ss 12(1), (2), (4), 29(2), Sch 5, Pt I; see now the General Rate Act 1967, ss 30, 40, Vol 36, title* Rating.)

65 Endowments for maintenance of voluntary schools

Where any sums which accrue after the date of the commencement of this Part of this Act in respect of the income of any endowment are required by virtue of the provisions of any trust deed to be applied towards the maintenance of a school which a local education authority are required to maintain as a voluntary school, the said sums shall not be payable to the local education authority, but shall be applied by the ... governors of the school towards the discharge of their obligations, if any, with respect to the maintenance of the school, or in such other manner, if any, as may be determined by a scheme for the administration of the endowment made after the date of the commencement of this Part of this Act.

NOTES

The words omitted were repealed by the Education Act 1980, s 1(3), Sch 1, para 1.

Date of commencement of this Part of this Act. The date of the commencement of Pt II (ss 6–69) was 1 April 1945 by virtue of s 119 (repealed).

Endowment. Endowments relating to schools were formerly subject to the provisions of the Endowed Schools Act 1869 to 1948 (repealed by the Education Act 1973, s 1, Sch 1, para 2, Sch 2, Pt II).

Endowed schools are charities and are therefore subject to the Charities Act 1960, Vol 5, title Charities. Voluntary schools, which are not charities but have no permanent endowment other than premises, are exempted from registration by the Charities (Exception of Voluntary Schools from Registration) Regulations 1960, SI 1960/2366.

Governors' obligations with respect to maintenance. The governors of a controlled school are not responsible for any of the expenses of maintaining the school; but in the case of aided schools and special agreement schools the governors are responsible for the expenses referred to in s 15(3) ante.

Scheme for the administration of the endowment. As to the making of such schemes, see the Charities Act 1960, ss 18, 19, Vol 5, title Charities and the Education Act 1973, ss 1, 2, this part of this title post.

Definitions. For "maintain", "school" and "trust deed", see s 114(1) post; for "local education authority", see s 114(1) and the note thereto; and for "voluntary school", see s 9(2) ante.

66 *(Repealed by the Education Act 1980, s 38(6), Sch 7.)*

67 Determination of disputes and questions

(1) Save as otherwise expressly provided by this Act, any dispute between a local education authority and the ... governors of any school with respect to the exercise of any power conferred or the performance of any duty imposed by or under this Act, may, notwithstanding any enactment rendering the exercise of the power or the performance of the duty contingent upon the opinion of the authority or of the ... governors, be referred to [the Secretary of State]; and any such dispute so referred shall be determined by him.

(2) Any dispute between two or more local education authorities as to which of them is responsible for the provision of education for any pupil, or whether contributions in respect of the provision of education for any pupil are payable under this Act by one local education authority to another, shall be determined by [the Secretary of State].

(3) Where any trust deed relating to a voluntary school makes provision whereby a bishop or any other ecclesiastical or denominational authority has power to decide whether the religious instruction given in the school which purports to be in accordance with the provisions of the trust deed does or does not accord with those provisions, that question shall be determined in accordance with the provisions of the trust deed.

[(4) If in the case of a county or voluntary school a question arises whether a change in the character of the school or enlargement of the school premises would be a significant change or enlargement, that question shall be determined by the Secretary of State.]

NOTES

The words omitted from sub-s (1) were repealed by the Education Act 1980, s 1(3), Sch 1, para 1.

The words in square brackets in sub-ss (1), (2) are substituted by virtue of the Secretary of State for Education and Science Order 1964, SI 1964/490, art 3(2)(a).

Sub-s (4) was substituted by the Education Act 1968, s 1(3), Sch 1, para 3.

Sub-s (1): Dispute. As to the meaning of "dispute" the following cases decided under corresponding provisions of the previous law may be of value: *Blencowe v Northamptonshire CC* [1907] 1 Ch 504, 76 LJ Ch 276; *Wilford v West Riding of Yorkshire CC* [1908] 1 KB 685, 77 LJKB 436 (a change of character of a non-provided school, against the managers' wishes, was not a matter for the Board's decision); *Board of Education v Rice* [1911] AC 179, [1911–13] All ER Rep 36; *West Suffolk CC v Olorenshaw* [1918] 2 KB 687, 88 LJKB 384 (the county court has no jurisdiction in any matter reserved for the determination of the Board).

Governors. As to governors and their functions, see ss 17–22 ante.

The performance of any duty. As to the enforcement of duties imposed on local education authorities and upon managers or governors by or under this Act, see s 99 post.

Secretary of State. See the note "Secretary of State for Education and Science" to s 1 ante.

Sub-s (2): Contributions. See the Education Act 1980, s 31, this part of this title post.

Sub-s (3): Religious instruction. As to religious education in county and voluntary schools, see ss 25–30 ante.

In accordance with the provisions of the trust deed. As to the giving of such religious instruction in controlled schools, see s 27 ante, and in aided and special agreement schools, see s 28 ante.

Sub-s (4): Significant change in the character. See the note to the Education Act 1968, s 1, this part of this title post.

Application. As to the application of this section and of ss 68 and 99 post, in relation to establishments to which the Education (No 2) Act 1968, this part of this title post applies (as to which, see s 1(1) thereof post) and governors of those establishments, see s 3(3), (4) of that Act.

Definitions. For "alterations", "enlargement", "premises", "school", "significant" and "trust deed", see s 114(1) post; for "local education authority", see s 114(1) post and the note thereto; and for "county school" and "voluntary school", see s 9(2) ante.

68 Power of [Secretary of State] to prevent unreasonable exercise of functions

If [the Secretary of State] is satisfied, either on complaint by any person or otherwise, that any local education authority or the ... governors of any county or voluntary school have acted or are proposing to act unreasonably with respect to the exercise of any power conferred or the performance of any duty imposed by or under this Act, he may, notwithstanding any enactment rendering the exercise of the power or the performance of the duty contingent upon the opinion of the authority or of the ... governors, give such directions as to the exercise of the power or the performance of the duty as appear to him to be expedient. [In this section, references to a local education authority shall be construed as including references to any body of persons authorised, in accordance with the First Schedule to this Act ... to exercise functions of such an authority.]

NOTES

The words "the Secretary of State" are substituted by virtue of the Secretary of State for Education and Science Order 1964, SI 1964/490, art 3(2)(a).

The words omitted in the first and second places were repealed by the Education Act 1980, s 1(3), Sch 1, para 1.

The words in the second pair of square brackets were added by the Education Act 1946, s 14(1), Sch 2, Pt I.

The words omitted in the third place were repealed by the Local Government Act 1972, s 272(1), Sch 30.

Secretary of State. See the note "Secretary of State for Education and Science" to s 1 ante.

Complaint by any person. The right of complaint under this section excludes resort to the courts where the alleged impropriety is a wrong exercise of discretion, but not where the educational body is alleged to be acting ultra vires; a breach of the rules of natural justice is more fundamental than mere wrong exercise of discretion; see *Herring v Templeman* [1973] 2 All ER 581, 137 JP 514, affd [1973] 3 All ER 569, 173 JP 519, CA (although the question of jurisdiction was not discussed in the Court of Appeal).

Proposing to act unreasonably. In order to intervene, it is not sufficient that the Secretary of State should disagree with the policy; the authority must be acting in a way in which no reasonable authority would act; see *Secretary of State for Education and Science v Tameside Metropolitan BC* [1976] 3 All ER 679, [1976] 3 WLR 662, HL. Dicta of Lord Wilberforce in that case applied in *Norwich City Council v Secretary of State for the Environment* [1982] 1 All ER 737, [1982] 2 WLR 580, CA.

Duty imposed. For the power of the Secretary of State in default of local education authorities or governors, see s 99 post.

Directions. As to revocation and variation of any such directions, see s 111 post.

Application. See the note to s 67 ante.

Definitions. For "county school" and "voluntary school", see s 9(2) ante; and for "local education authority", see s 114(1) post and the note thereto.

69 Powers of [Secretary of State] as to medical examinations and inspections

(1) ...

(2) Where any question is referred to [the Secretary of State] under this Part of this Act, then, if in the opinion of [the Secretary of State] the examination of any pupil by a duly qualified medical practitioner appointed for the purpose by him would assist the determination of the question referred to him, [the Secretary of State] may by notice in writing served on the parent of that pupil, or if that pupil is in attendance at a county college upon him, require the parent to submit him, or require him to submit himself, as the case may be, for examination by such a practitioner; and if any person on whom such a notice is served fails without reasonable excuse to comply with the requirements thereof, he shall be liable on summary conviction to a fine not exceeding [level 1 on the standard scale].

NOTES

Sub-s (1) was repealed by the National Health Service Reorganisation Act 1973, s 57, Sch 5.

The words "the Secretary of State" are substituted by virtue of the Secretary of State for Education and Science Order 1964, SI 1964/490, art 3(2)(a).

The reference to level 1 on the standard scale is substituted by virtue of the Criminal Justice Act 1982, ss 38, 46, Vol 27, title Magistrates. The maximum fine was previously increased to £10 by the Criminal Justice Act 1967, s 92(1), Sch 3, Pt I.

Secretary of State. See the note "Secretary of State for Education and Science" to s 1 ante.

Duly qualified medical practitioner. For meaning, see the note "Medical officer" to s 114(1) post.

Notice. As to the service of notices, see s 113 post.

Writing. See the note to s 54 ante.
Summary conviction; standard scale. See the notes to s 40 ante.
Definitions. For "county college", see s 43 ante; for "parent", "prescribe" and "pupil", see s 114(1) post.

PART III

INDEPENDENT SCHOOLS

70 Registration of independent schools

(1) [The Secretary of State] shall appoint one of his officers to be Registrar of Independent Schools; and it shall be the duty of the Registrar of Independent Schools to keep a register of all independent schools, which shall be open to public inspection at all reasonable times, and, subject as hereinafter provided, to register therein any independent school of which the proprietor makes application for the purpose in the prescribed manner and furnishes the prescribed particulars:

Provided that—

(a) no independent school shall be registered if, by virtue of an order made under the provisions hereinafter contained, the proprietor is disqualified from being the proprietor of an independent school or the school premises are disqualified from being used as a school, or if the school premises are used or proposed to be used for any purpose for which they are disqualified by virtue of any such order; and

(b) the registration of any school shall be provisional only until [the Secretary of State], after the school has been inspected on his behalf under the provisions of Part IV of this Act, gives notice to the proprietor that the registration is final.

(2) ...

(3) If after the expiration of six months from the date of the commencement of this Part of this Act any person—

(a) conducts an independent school (whether established before or after the commencement of that Part) which is not a registered school or a provisionally registered school; or

(b) being the proprietor of an independent school does any act calculated to lead to the belief that the school is a registered school while it is a provisionally registered school;

he shall be liable on summary conviction to a fine not exceeding [level 4 on the standard scale or to imprisonment for a term not exceeding three months or to both such imprisonment and such fine].

[(3A) A person shall not be guilty of an offence under subsection (3) (a) above by reason of conducting a school at any time within the period of one month from the date on which it was first conducted (whether by that person or another) if an application for the registration of the school has been duly made within that period.

(4) The Secretary of State may by regulations make provision for requiring the proprietor of a registered or provisionally registered school to furnish the Registrar from time to time with such particulars relating to the school as may be prescribed and for enabling the Secretary of State to order the deletion from the register of the name of any school in respect of which any requirement imposed by or under the regulations is not complied with.

(5) The power to make regulations under this section shall be exercisable by the Secretary of State for Education and Science in relation to schools in England and by the Secretary of State for Wales in relation to schools in Wales.]

NOTES

The words "the Secretary of State" in sub-s (1) are substituted by virtue of the Secretary of State for Education and Science Order 1964, SI 1964/490, art 3(2)(a).

Sub-s (2) was repealed, sub-s (3A) was inserted, and sub-ss (4), (5) were substituted for the original sub-s (4), by the Education Act 1980, s 34(2), (6), (7), respectively.

The words in square brackets in sub-s (3) are substituted by virtue of the Criminal Justice Act 1982, ss 39, 46, Sch 3, Vol 27, title Magistrates. The maximum fine for a first offence had previously been increased from £20 to £50 by the Criminal Law Act 1977, s 31(6). The maximum fine for a second or subsequent offence was not affected by the 1977 Act, and accordingly that amendment effectively abolished enhanced penalties for subsequent offences under sub-s (3) above.

Sub-s (1): Secretary of State. See the note "Secretary of State for Education and Science" to s 1 ante. The functions of the Secretary of State for Education and Science under sub-ss (1), (2) above, in relation to independent schools in Wales, were transferred to the Secretary of State for Wales, and the power under sub-s (4) above is exercisable by the Secretary of State for Education and Science in relation to the register of independent schools in England and by the Secretary of State for Wales in relation to the register of independent schools in Wales; see the Transfer of Functions (Wales) Order 1970, SI 1970/1536.

Registrar of Independent Schools. Ie the Registrar of Independent Schools for England in relation to schools in England and the Registrar of Independent Schools for Wales in relation to schools in Wales; see the Education Act 1980, s 34(5), this part of this title post. The Registrars had power to register certain schools without any application in that behalf, as a consequence of the amendments made to this Act by s 34 of the 1980 Act; see sub-ss (3), (4) thereof.

The proprietor is disqualified; school premises are disqualified. See s 72(2) post.

After the school ... Part IV of this Act. S 77 post imposes a duty upon the Secretary of State to cause inspections to be made of every educational establishment (as defined by sub-s (1) of that section) at such intervals as appear to him to be appropriate. As to the penalty for obstructing an inspector, see sub-s (4) of that section.

Notice. As to the service of notices, see s 113 post.

Sub-s (3): Six months from; one month from. As a general rule the effect of defining a period in such a manner is to exclude the day on which the event in question occurs. See *Dodds v Walker* [1981] 2 All ER 609, [1981] 1 WLR 1027, HL, as to the day of expiry of periods of a month or a specified number of months.

Date of commencement of this Part of this Act. The date of the commencement of Pt III (ss 70–75) was 30 September 1957 by virtue of the Education Act 1944 (Commencement of Part III) Order 1957, SI 1957/96. Accordingly the relevant date under sub-s (3) is 1 April 1945.

Summary conviction; standard scale. See the notes to s 40 ante.

Definitions. For "independent school", "prescribe", "proprietor" and "registered school", see s 114(1) post.

Regulations under sub-s (4). The Education (Particulars of Independent Schools) Regulations 1982, SI 1982/1730. For general provisions as to regulations under this Act, see s 112 post.

---

71 Complaints

(1) If at any time [the Secretary of State] is satisfied that any registered or provisionally registered school is objectionable upon all or any of the following grounds—

(a) that the school premises or any parts thereof are unsuitable for a school;

(b) that the accommodation provided at the school premises is inadequate or unsuitable having regard to the number, ages, and sex of the pupils attending the school;

(c) that efficient and suitable instruction is not being provided at the school having regard to the ages and sex of the pupils attending thereat;

(d) that the proprietor of the school or any teacher employed therein is not a proper person to be the proprietor of an independent school or to be a teacher in any school, as the case may be;

[the Secretary of State] shall serve upon the proprietor of the school a notice of complaint stating the grounds of complaint together with full particulars of the matters complained of, and, unless any of such matters are stated in the notice to be in the opinion of [the Secretary of State] irremediable, the notice shall specify the measures necessary in the opinion of [the Secretary of State] to remedy the matters complained of, and shall specify the time, not being less than six months after the service of the notice, within which such measures are thereby required to be taken.

(2) If it is alleged by any notice of complaint served under this section that any person employed as a teacher at the school is not a proper person to be a teacher in any school,

that person shall be named in the notice and the particulars contained in the notice shall specify the grounds of the allegation, and a copy of the notice shall be served upon him.

(3) Every notice of complaint served under this section and every copy of such a notice so served shall limit the time, not being less than one month after the service of the notice or copy, within which the complaint may be referred to an Independent Schools Tribunal under the provisions hereinafter contained.

NOTES

The words in square brackets are substituted by virtue of the Secretary of State for Education and Science Order 1964, SI 1964/490, art 3(2)(a).

Secretary of State. See the note "Secretary of State for Education and Science" to s 1 ante. The functions of the Secretary of State for Education and Science under this section and ss 72, 73 post, in relation to independent schools in Wales, were transferred to the Secretary of State for Wales by the Transfer of Functions (Wales) Order 1970, SI 1970/1536.

Satisfied. Statutory powers are often conferred in subjective terms, the competent authority being entitled to act, eg, when it is "satisfied" or it "appears" to it that, or when in its "opinion", a prescribed state of affairs exists, but the inherent jurisdiction of the courts to determine whether such powers have been exceeded is not readily ousted by the use of such language; see, further, 1 Halsbury's Laws (4th edn), para 22.

Notice. As to the service of notices, see s 113 post.

Not less than six months after; not less than one month after. See the note "Six months from" to s 70 ante.

Independent Schools Tribunals. As to the constitution of such Tribunals and as to proceedings before them, see ss 72, 75, Sch 6 post.

Definitions. For "premises", "proprietor", "provisionally registered school", "pupil", "registered school" and "school", see s 114(1) post.

72 Determination of complaints

(1) Any person upon whom a notice of complaint or a copy of such a notice is served under the last foregoing section may, within the time limited by the notice, appeal therefrom by referring the complaint, in such manner as may be provided by rules made under this Part of this Act, to an Independent Schools Tribunal constituted in accordance with the provisions of the Sixth Schedule to this Act.

(2) Upon a complaint being referred to an Independent Schools Tribunal, the tribunal shall, after affording to all parties concerned an opportunity of being heard, and after considering such evidence as may be tendered by them or on their behalf, have power—

    (a) to order that the complaint be annulled:

    (b) to order that the school in respect of which the notice of complaint was served be struck off the register:

    (c) to order that the school be so struck off unless the requirements of the notice, subject to such modifications, if any, as may be specified in the order are complied with to the satisfaction of [the Secretary of State] before the expiration of such time as may be specified in the order:

    (d) if satisfied that the premises alleged by the notice of complaint to be unsuitable for use as a school or any part of such premises are in fact unsuitable for such use, by order to disqualify the premises or part from being so used, or, if satisfied that the accommodation provided at the school premises is inadequate or unsuitable having regard to the number, ages and sex of the pupils attending the school, by order to disqualify the premises from being used as a school for pupils exceeding such number or of such age or sex as may be specified in the order:

    (e) if satisfied that any person alleged by the notice of complaint to be a person who is not proper to be the proprietor of an independent school or to be a teacher in any school is in fact such a person, by order to disqualify that person from being the proprietor of any independent school or from being a teacher in any school, as the case may be.

(3) Where a notice of complaint has been served under this Act on the proprietor of any school and the complaint is not referred by him to an Independent Schools Tribunal within the time limited in that behalf by the notice, [the Secretary of State] shall have power to make any order which such a tribunal would have had power to make if the complaint had been so referred:

Provided that, if it was alleged by the notice of complaint that any person employed as a teacher at the school is not a proper person to be a teacher in any school and that person has, within the time limited in that behalf by the copy of the notice served upon him, referred the complaint to an Independent Schools Tribunal, [the Secretary of State] shall not have power to make an order requiring his dismissal or disqualifying him from being a teacher in any school.

(4) Where by virtue of an order made by an Independent Schools Tribunal or by [the Secretary of State] any person is disqualified either from being the proprietor of an independent school or from being a teacher in any school, then, unless the order otherwise directs, that person shall, by virtue of the order, be disqualified both from being the proprietor of an independent school and from being a teacher in any school.

NOTES

The words in square brackets are substituted by virtue of the Secretary of State for Education and Science Order 1964, SI 1964/490, art 3(2)(a).

Notice. As to the service of notices, see s 113 post.

Within the time limited. By s 71(3) ante the time so limited is not to be less than one month after the service of the notice or copy thereof.

Rules made under this Part. As to the making of such rules, and the purpose for which they may be made (including the manner of making appeals), see s 75(1) post and the notes thereto.

Independent Schools Tribunal. The Independent Schools Tribunals constituted under this section and Sch 6 post are under the direct supervision of the Council on Tribunals in accordance with the Tribunals and Inquiries Act 1971, Vol 10, title Constitutional Law (Pt 4).

After affording to all parties concerned an opportunity of being heard. See the Independent Schools Tribunal Rules 1958, SI 1958/519, rr 7–10 as amended (made under s 75 post) for procedure at the hearing etc.

Secretary of State. See the note "Secretary of State for Education and Science" to s 1 ante and the note to s 71 ante.

Enforcement of orders under sub-ss (2), (3). See s 73 post. For removal of disqualifications imposed, see s 74 post. For registration of orders, see s 75(3) post.

Definitions. For "independent school", "premises", "proprietor", "pupil" and "school", see s 114(1) post.

---

73 Enforcement

(1) Where an order is made by [the Secretary of State] or by an Independent Schools Tribunal directing that any school be struck off the register, the Registrar of Independent Schools shall as from the date on which the direction takes effect strike the school off the register.

(2) If any person uses any premises for purposes for which they are disqualified by virtue of any order made under this Part of this Act, that person shall be liable on summary conviction to a fine not exceeding [level 4 on the standard scale or to imprisonment for a term not exceeding three months or to both such imprisonment and such fine].

(3) If any person acts as the proprietor of an independent school, or accepts or endeavours to obtain employment as a teacher in any school, while he is disqualified from so acting or from being so employed by virtue of any such order as aforesaid, he shall be liable on summary conviction to a fine not exceeding [level 4 on the standard scale or to imprisonment for a term not exceeding three months or to both such imprisonment and such fine].

(4) No proceedings shall be instituted for an offence against this Part of this Act except by or on behalf of [the Secretary of State].

[(5) For the purposes of the foregoing provisions of this Part of this Act, a person who is disqualified by an order made under Part IV of the Education (Scotland) Act 1945 from being the proprietor of an independent school or from being a teacher in any school shall be deemed to be so disqualified by virtue of an order made under this Part of this Act.]

NOTES

The words in square brackets in sub-ss (1), (4) are substituted by virtue of the Secretary of State for Education and Science Order 1964, SI 1964/490, art 3(2)(a).

The words in square brackets in sub-ss (2), (3) are substituted by virtue of the Criminal Justice Act 1982, ss 39, 46, Sch 3, Vol 27, title Magistrates. The maximum fine for a first offence had previously been increased from £20 to £50 by the Criminal Law Act 1977, s 31(6). The maximum fine for a second or subsequent offence was not affected by the 1977 Act, and accordingly that amendment effectively abolished enhanced penalties for subsequent offences.

Sub-s (5) was added by the Education Act 1946, s 14(1), Sch 2, Pt I.

Secretary of State. See the note "Secretary of State for Education and Science" to s 1 ante and the note to s 71 ante.

Independent Schools Tribunal. As to the constitution of such Tribunals and as to proceedings before them, see ss 72, 75, Sch 6 post.

Registrar of Independent Schools. As to the appointment and duties of the Registrar of Independent Schools, see s 70 ante.

Disqualified. As to the power to disqualify premises or persons, see s 72(2) ante.

Summary conviction; standard scale. See the notes to s 40 ante.

Definitions. For "independent school", "premises", "proprietor" and "school", see s 114(1) post.

Education (Scotland) Act 1945. 8 & 9 Geo 6 c 37; not printed in this work.

74 Removal of disqualifications

(1) If on the application of any person [the Secretary of State] is satisfied that any disqualification imposed by an order made under this Part of this Act is, by reason of any change of circumstances, no longer necessary, [the Secretary of State] may by order remove the disqualification.

(2) Any person who is aggrieved by the refusal of [the Secretary of State] to remove a disqualification so imposed may, within such time after the refusal has been communicated to him as may be limited by rules made under this Part of this Act, appeal to an Independent Schools Tribunal.

NOTES

The words in square brackets are substituted by virtue of the Secretary of State for Education and Science Order 1964, SI 1964/490, art 3(2)(a).

Secretary of State. The power under this section to remove a disqualification imposed on a person is now exercised by the Secretary of State for Education and Science or by the Secretary of State for Wales, as the case may be; see the Transfer of Functions (Wales) Order 1970, SI 1970/1536, art 5(1).

Secretary of State. See the note "Secretary of State for Education and Science" to s 1 ante. The power under this section to remove a disqualification imposed on a person is now exercisable by the Secretary of State for Education and Science or by the Secretary of State for Wales, according as to whether the disqualification originated in England or in Wales; see the Transfer of Functions (Wales) Order 1970, SI 1970/1536. art 5(1).

Order imposing disqualification. See s 72(2), (3) ante.

Rules made under this Part. See the note to s 75 post. For variation and revocation of orders, see s 111 post.

Independent Schools Tribunal. See s 72(1) ante and the notes thereto; as to the proceedings before such Tribunals, see s 75 post.

75 Proceedings before Independent School Tribunals and matters relating thereto

(1) The Lord Chancellor may, with the concurrence of the Lord President of the Council, make rules as to the practice and procedure to be followed with respect to the constitution of Independent Schools Tribunals, as to the manner of making appeals to such tribunals, and as to proceedings before such tribunals and matters incidental to or consequential on such proceedings, and, in particular, such rules may make provision requiring any such tribunal to sit at such places as may be directed in accordance with the rules, and may make provision as to appearance before such tribunals by counsel or solicitor . . .

(2) The provisions of the Arbitration Acts 1889 to 1934 shall not apply to any proceedings before an Independent Schools Tribunal except so far as any provisions thereof may be applied thereto with or without modifications by rules made under this section.

(3) Every order of an Independent Schools Tribunal shall be registered by the Registrar of Independent Schools and shall be open to public inspection at all reasonable times.

NOTES

The words omitted from sub-s (1) were repealed by the Education Act 1976, s 6(2).
Constitution of Independent Schools Tribunals. See s 72 ante and Sch 6 post, in conjunction with r 3 of the Rules referred to in the note "Rules under this section" below.
Appeals to such tribunals. See ss 72(1), 74(2) ante and as to the manner of making such appeals, see rr 2, 5 of the Rules referred to in the last note to this section below.
Sit at such places. See r 4 of the Rules referred to in the note "Rules under this section" below.
Appearance before such tribunals by counsel or solicitor. See r 7 of the Rules referred to in the last note below.
Registrar of Independent Schools. As to the appointment and duties of the Registrar of Independent Schools, see s 70 ante.
Arbitration Acts 1889 to 1934. Repealed by the Arbitration Act 1950, s 44(3); see now the provisions of that Act, Vol 2, title Arbitration.
Rules under this section. The Independent Schools Tribunal Rules 1958, SI 1958/519, as amended by SI 1968/588, SI 1972/42, SI 1974/563, SI 1974/1972, SI 1975/854 and SI 1975/1298.

PART IV

GENERAL

GENERAL PRINCIPLE TO BE OBSERVED BY [SECRETARY OF STATE] AND LOCAL EDUCATION AUTHORITIES

76 Pupils to be educated in accordance with the wishes of their parents

In the exercise and performance of all powers and duties conferred and imposed on them by this Act [the Secretary of State] and local education authorities shall have regard to the general principle that, so far as is compatible with the provision of efficient instruction and training and the avoidance of unreasonable public expenditure, pupils are to be educated in accordance with the wishes of their parents.

NOTES

The words in square brackets are substituted by virtue of the Secretary of State for Education and Science Order 1964, SI 1964/490, art 3(2)(a).
General Note. For the duty of a local education authority to comply with the preference of a parent as to the school his child should attend, see the Education Act 1980, s 6, this part of this title post.
Secretary of State. See the note "Secretary of State for Education and Science" to s 1 ante.
Shall have regard. Breach of duty under this section would normally give rise only to a complaint under s 99 post; see *Watt v Kesteven CC* [1955] 1 QB 408, [1955] 1 All ER 473, CA, considered and dicta applied

in *Wood v London Borough of Ealing* [1966] 3 All ER 514, [1966] 3 WLR 1209 and in *Cumings v Birkenhead Corpn* [1972] Ch 12, [1970] 3 All ER 302, affd [1972] Ch 30, [1971] 2 All ER 881, CA. As to enforcement of a duty under the Act where a person suffers damage by reason of an ultra vires action, see *Meade v London Borough of Haringey* [1979] 2 All ER 1016, [1979] 1 WLR 637, CA, noted to s 8 ante.

Definitions. For "parent" and "pupil", see s 114(1) post; for "local education authority", see s 114(1) post and the note thereto.

MISCELLANEOUS PROVISIONS

77 Inspection of educational establishments

(1) In this section the expression "educational establishment" means a school, a county college, any establishment which under a scheme of further education made and approved under this Act is used for further education, and any training college or other institution being a training college or other institution maintained by a local education authority; and if the persons responsible for the management of any institution which is not an educational establishment within the foregoing definition request [the Secretary of State] or any local education authority to cause an inspection of that institution to be made under the powers conferred by this section, the institution shall, for the purposes of that inspection, be deemed to be also included within that definition.

(2) It shall be the duty of [the Secretary of State] to cause inspections to be made of every educational establishment at such intervals as appear to him to be appropriate, and to cause a special inspection of any such establishment to be made whenever he considers such an inspection to be desirable; and for the purposes of enabling such inspections to be made on behalf of [the Secretary of State] inspectors may be appointed by His Majesty on the recommendation of [the Secretary of State], and persons may be authorised by [the Secretary of State] to assist such inspectors and to act as additional inspectors:

Provided that [the Secretary of State] shall not be required by virtue of this subsection to cause inspections to be made of any educational establishment during any period during which he is satisfied that suitable arrangements are in force for the inspection of that establishment otherwise than in accordance with this subsection.

(3) Any local education authority may cause an inspection to be made of any educational establishment maintained by the authority, and such inspections shall be made by officers appointed by the local education authority.

(4) If any person obstructs any person authorised to make an inspection in pursuance of the provisions of this section in the execution of his duty, he shall be liable on summary conviction to a fine not exceeding [level 4 on the standard scale or to imprisonment for a term not exceeding three months or to both such imprisonment and such fine].

(5) Subject as hereinafter provided, the religious instruction given in any school maintained by a local education authority shall not be subject to inspection except by one of His Majesty's Inspectors or by a person ordinarily employed for the purpose of inspecting secular instruction either as an additional inspector appointed by [the Secretary of State] or as an officer in the wholetime employment of a local education authority:

Provided that the religious instruction given in a voluntary school otherwise than in accordance with an agreed syllabus shall not be subject to such inspection as aforesaid, but may be inspected under arrangements made for that purpose by the ... governors of the school, or, in the case of a controlled school, by the ... foundation governors thereof so, however, that such inspections shall not be made on more than two days in any year and not less than fourteen days' notice of the dates fixed therefor shall be given to the local education authority.

(6) No pupil who has been excused from attendance at religious worship or

instruction in a voluntary school in accordance with the provisions of this Act shall be required to attend the school on a day fixed for an inspection by arrangements made under the proviso to the last foregoing subsection.

NOTES

The words "the Secretary of State" are substituted in sub-ss (1), (2) and (5) by virtue of the Secretary of State for Education and Science Order 1964, SI 1964/490, art 3(2)(*a*).

The words in square brackets in sub-s (4) are substituted by virtue of the Criminal Justice Act 1982, ss 39, 46, Sch 3, Vol 27, title Magistrates. The maximum fine for a first offence had previously been increased from £20 to £50 by the Criminal Law Act 1977, s 31(6). The maximum fine for a second or subsequent offence was not affected by the 1977 Act, and accordingly that amendment effectively abolished enhanced penalties for subsequent offences.

The words omitted from sub-s (5) were repealed by the Education Act 1980, s 1(3), Sch 1, para 11.

Scheme of further education. For details of such schemes, see s 42 ante.

Training college. As to the provision of training colleges by local education authorities, see s 62 ante.

Secretary of State. See the note "Secretary of State for Education and Science" to s 1 ante.

Otherwise than in accordance with this subsection. See sub-s (3) above.

Summary conviction; standard scale. See the notes to s 40 ante.

Otherwise than in accordance with an agreed syllabus. As to the provision of denominational instruction, see ss 27(1) (controlled schools), 28(1) (aided schools and special agreement schools) ante.

Fourteen days' notice. As to the service of notices, see s 113 post. As to the computation of time, see the note "Not less than fourteen days" to s 37 ante.

Pupil excused from attendance at religious worship or instruction. A pupil may be excused from attendance in accordance with the provisions in s 25(4) ante.

Evidence. For provisions as to evidence in prosecutions under sub-s (4), see s 95 post.

Saving. Provisions relating to inspection of certain schools are made by the Education (Grant) Regulations 1983, SI 1983/74, without prejudice to this section (see reg 24(2)).

Definitions. For "agreed syllabus", "foundation governors", "maintain", "pupil" and "school", see s 114(1) post; for "local education authority", see s 114(1) post and the note thereto; for "controlled school", see s 15(1) ante; for "county college", see s 43 ante; and for "voluntary school", see s 9(2) ante.

78 Provision of certain ancillary services for pupils not in attendance at schools maintained by local education authorities

(1) ...

(2) A local education authority may, with the consent of the proprietor of any school in their area which is not a school maintained by the authority, and upon such financial and other terms, if any, as may be determined by agreement between the authority and the proprietor of the school, make arrangements for securing—

    (*a*) the provision of milk, meals and other refreshment for pupils in attendance at the school; ...

    (*b*) ...

Provided that any arrangements made under this subsection shall be such as to secure, so far as is practicable, that the expense incurred by the authority in connection with the provision under the arrangements of any service or article shall not exceed the expense which would have been incurred by them in the provision thereof if the pupil had been a pupil at a school maintained by them.

NOTES

Sub-s (1), and the words omitted from sub-s (2) in the third place were repealed by the National Health Service Reorganisation Act 1973, ss 57, 58, Sch 5. The other words omitted from sub-s (2) were repealed by the Education (Miscellaneous Provisions) Act 1948, s 11, Sch 2.

Local education authority. For meaning, see s 114(1) post and the note thereto. As to the transfer of certain functions under this section from the local education authority to the Secretary of State, see the National Health Service Reorganisation Act 1973, s 16(3), Vol 30, title National Health Service.

Provision of milk, etc. As to the provision of milk, meals and other refreshments at maintained schools, see the Education Act 1980, s 22 post.

Application. As to the application of sub-s (2) above in relation to compulsory use of special designations in specified areas, and provisions as to licences for specified areas, see the Food Act 1984, s 47, Vol 18, title Food.

Definitions. For "maintain", "proprietor", "pupil" and "school", see s 114(1) post.

79 (*Repealed by the National Health Service Reorganisation Act 1973, s 57, Sch 5.*)

80 Registration of pupils at schools

(1) The proprietor of every school (that is to say in the case of a county school or voluntary school the ... governors thereof) shall cause to be kept in accordance with regulations made by [the Secretary of State] a register containing the prescribed particulars with respect to all persons ... who are pupils at the school, and such regulations may make provision for enabling such registers to be inspected, for enabling extracts therefrom to be taken for the purposes of this Act by persons duly authorised in that behalf under the regulations, and for requiring the persons by whom any such register is required to be kept to make to [the Secretary of State], and to local education authorities, such periodical or other returns as to the contents thereof as may be prescribed.

(2) If any person contravenes or fails to comply with any requirement imposed on him by regulations made under this section, he shall be liable on summary conviction to a fine not exceeding [level 1 on the standard scale].

(3) ...

NOTES

The words omitted from sub-s (1) in the first place were repealed by the Education Act 1980, s 1(3), Sch 1, para 1 and those omitted in the second place were repealed by the Education (Miscellaneous Provisions) Act 1948, ss 4(4), 11, Sch 2.

The words "the Secretary of State" in sub-s (1) are substituted by virtue of the Secretary of State for Education and Science Order 1964, SI 1964/490, art 3(2)(*a*).

The reference in sub-s (2) to level 1 on the standard scale is substituted by virtue of the Criminal Justice Act 1982, s 46, Vol 27, title Magistrates. The maximum fine was previously increased to £25 by the Criminal Law Act 1977, s 31(6).

Sub-s (3) was repealed by the Education (Miscellaneous Provisions) Act 1948, ss 4(5), 11, Sch 2.

Secretary of State. See the note "Secretary of State for Education and Science" to s 1 ante.

Summary conviction; standard scale. See the notes to s 40 ante.

Extension of application. Regulations under this section are to prescribe the grounds on which names are to be deleted from a register kept hereunder; see the Education (Miscellaneous Provisions) Act 1948, s 4(6), this part of this title post.

Evidence. For provisions as to evidence in proceedings under this section, see s 95 post.

Definitions. For "county school" and "voluntary school", see s 9(2) ante; for "proprietor", "pupil" and "school", see s 114(1) post.

Regulations under this section. The Pupils' Registration Regulations 1956, SI 1956/357. For general provisions as to regulations under this Act, see s 112 post.

81 Power of local education authorities to give assistance by means of scholarships and otherwise

Regulations shall be made by [the Secretary of State] empowering local education authorities, for the purpose of enabling pupils to take advantage without hardship to themselves or their parents of any educational facilities available to them—

    (*a*) to defray such expenses of children attending county schools, voluntary schools, or special schools, as may be necessary to enable them to take part in any school activities:

    (*b*) to pay the whole or any part of the fees and expenses payable in respect of children attending schools at which fees are payable:

(c) to grant scholarships, exhibitions, bursaries, and other allowances in respect of pupils over compulsory school age, including pupils undergoing training as teachers:

(d) to grant allowances in respect of any child in respect of whom any scholarship exhibition bursary or other allowance has been granted by a former authority before the date of the commencement of this Part of this Act.

NOTES

The words in square brackets are substituted by virtue of the Secretary of State for Education and Science Order 1964, SI 1964/490, art 3(2)(a).

General Note. The provisions of para (c) are superseded by the Education Act 1962, ss 1, 2 in so far as they require regulations to be made for the purpose of empowering local education authorities to grant scholarships, exhibitions, bursaries and other allowances in respect of pupils over compulsory school age in connection with their attendance at courses to which s 1 or 2(1) of that Act applied, or in connection with their undergoing training as teachers. The provisions of any regulations made under the section in so far as they provide for the granting of such scholarships, exhibitions, bursaries and other allowances are likewise superseded. By virtue of s 4(4)–(6) of the 1962 Act, para (c) above ceased to have effect in so far as it imposed any such requirement or made any such provision as is mentioned above. Ss 1–4 of the 1962 Act, this part of this title post were substituted by the Education Act 1980, s 19, Sch 5. These provisions do not explicitly supersede the provisions of para (c) above but would appear to do so by implication.

Secretary of State. See the note "Secretary of State for Education and Science" to s 1 ante.

Schools at which fees are payable. Cf s 61 ante and the notes thereto.

Exclusion. Sums payable by virtue of regulations made under this section are to be disregarded when ascertaining weekly income for the purposes of any housing benefit; see the Housing Benefits Regulations 1982, SI 1982/1124, reg 14(1)(b), Sch 2, para 5.

Definitions. For "compulsory school age", "former authority", "parent" and "pupil", see s 114(1) post; for "county school" and "voluntary school", see s 9(2) ante; and for "special school", see s 9(5) ante.

Regulations under this section. The Scholarships and Other Benefits Regulations 1977, SI 1977/1443, as amended by SI 1979/260 and SI 1979/542 and the Direct Grant Grammar Schools (Cessation of Grant) Regulations 1975, SI 1975/1198, as amended by SI 1977/1443, SI 1979/1552 and SI 1981/1788. For general provisions as to regulations under this Act, see s 112 post.

82 Powers of local education authorities as to educational research

A local education authority may ... make such provision for conducting or assisting the conduct of research as appears to the authority to be desirable for the purpose of improving the educational facilities provided for their area.

NOTES

The words omitted were repealed by the Education Act 1980, ss 30(1), (2), 38(6), Sch 7.

The purpose ... area. S 84 post in addition enables local education authorities, for the purpose of improving the facilities for further education available for their area, to provide financial assistance to any university or university college.

Grants to persons other than local educational authorities. For provisions relating to such grants, see s 100(1)(b) post and the regulations made thereunder.

Local education authority. For meaning, see s 114(1) post and the note thereto.

83 Powers of local education authorities as to educational conferences

... a local education authority may organise, or participate in the organisation of, conferences for the discussion of questions relating to education, and may expend such sums as may be reasonable in paying or contributing towards any expenditure incurred in connection with conferences for the discussion of such questions, including the expenses of any person authorised by them to attend any such conference.

NOTES

The words omitted were repealed by the Education Act 1980, ss 30(1), (2), 38(6), Sch 7.

Local education authority. For meaning, see s 114(1) post and the note thereto.

Regulations under this section. No regulations are now in force under this section.

84 Power of local education authorities to make grants to universities and university colleges

A local education authority may ... provide financial assistance to any university or university college for the purpose of improving the facilities for further education available for their area.

NOTES

The words omitted were repealed by the Education Act 1980, ss 30(1), (2), 38(6), Sch 7.

Local education authority. For meaning, see s 114(1) post and the note thereto.

Further education. As to the general duties of local education authorities with respect to further education, see s 41 ante.

85 Power of local education authorities to accept gifts for educational purposes

(1) Subject to the provisions of this section, a local education authority shall have power, and any such authority or any former authority shall be deemed always to have had power, to accept hold and administer any property upon trust for purposes connected with education.

[(2) Any intention on the part of a local education authority that a school for providing primary or secondary education (other than a nursery school or a special school) should be vested in the authority as trustees shall be treated for the purposes of subsection (1) of section 12 of the Education Act 1980 as an intention on the part of the authority to maintain the school as a county school; and accordingly proposals for that purpose shall be published and submitted as required by that section, and the other provisions of that section and of sections 14 and 16 of that Act shall apply as in a case where a local education authority intend to maintain a school as a county school.

(3) Any school for providing primary or secondary education which in accordance with subsection (2) above is vested in a local education authority as trustees shall be a county school.]

NOTES

Sub-ss (2), (3) were substituted by the Education Act 1980, s 16(4), Sch 3, para 3.

Power to accept hold and administer property. As to the application of an endowment of an existing school on its transfer to a local education authority, see *Re Poplar and Blackwall Free School* (1878) 8 Ch D 543, 39 LT 88. See generally, as to the acceptance of gifts of property by local authorities, the Local Government Act 1972, s 139, Vol 25, title Local Government.

Definitions. For "county school", "nursery school" and "special school", see s 9 ante; for "former authority", "maintain", "primary education", "school", "secondary education", see s 114(1) post; and for "local education authority", see s 114(1) post and the note thereto.

Education Act 1980, ss 12(1), 14, 16. See this part of this title post.

86, 87 *(S 86 repealed by the Education Act 1973, s 1(4), Sch 2, Pt II; s 87 repealed by the Charities Act 1960, ss 38(1), 48(2), Sch 7, Pt II.)*

ADMINISTRATIVE PROVISIONS

88 Appointment of chief education officers of local education authorities

The duties of a local education authority with respect to the appointment of officers under the provisions of the Local Government Act 1933 shall, without prejudice to the generality of those provisions, include the duty of appointing a fit person to be the chief education officer of the authority ...

NOTES

The words omitted were repealed by the Local Government Act 1972, s 272(1), Sch 30.

Local education authority. For meaning, see s 114(1) post and the note thereto.

Enforcement. The Secretary of State may enforce compliance with the requirements of this section by virtue of s 99 post.

Local Government Act 1933. The 1933 Act was repealed by the Local Government Act 1972, Vol 25, title Local Government, and replaced by provisions of that Act. As to the provisions of that Act relating to the appointment of officers, see ss 112–119 thereof.

89 *(Repealed by the Remuneration of Teachers Act 1965, s 7(6).)*

90 Compulsory purchase of land and other dealings in land by local education authorities

(1) A local education authority may be authorised [by [the Secretary of State]] to purchase compulsorily any land, whether situate within or without the area of the authority, which is required for the purposes of any school or college which is, or is to be, maintained by them [or which they have power to assist], or otherwise for the purposes of their functions under this Act; ...

Provided that [the Secretary of State] shall not [authorise] the purchase of any land required for the purposes of a voluntary school unless he is satisfied that the arrangements made as to the vesting of the land to be purchased, and as to the appropriation thereof for those purposes, are such as to secure that the expenditure ultimately borne by the local education authority will not include any expenditure which, if the land had been purchased by the ... governors of the school, would have fallen to be borne by the ... governors.

(2), (3) ...

NOTES

The words "the Secretary of State" are substituted by virtue of the Secretary of State for Education and Science Order 1964, SI 1964/490, art 3(2)(*a*). The words "or which they have power to assist" were inserted by the Education (Miscellaneous Provisions) Act 1948, s 10(1). The other words in square brackets were substituted by the Acquisition of Land (Authorisation Procedure) Act 1946, s 6, Sch 4.

The words omitted in the first place were repealed by the Acquisition of Land (Authorisation Procedure) Act 1946, ss 6, 10, Schs 4, 6, and those omitted in the second and third places were repealed by the Education Act 1980, s 1(3), Sch 1, para 1. Sub-ss (2), (3) were repealed by s 38(6) of, and Sch 7 to, the 1980 Act.

Compulsory purchase of land. As to the procedure for authorising the compulsory purchase of land by local education authorities, see the Acquisition of Land Act 1981, Vol 9, title Compulsory Acquisition. See also the Compulsory Purchase Act 1965, in the same title.

Secretary of State. See the note "Secretary of State for Education and Science" to s 1 ante.

Definitions. For "assist", "maintain" and "school", see s 114(1) post; for "local education authority", see s 114(1) post and the note thereto; and for "voluntary school", see s 9(2) ante.

91 *(Repealed by the Local Government Act 1972, s 272, Sch 30.)*

92 Reports and returns

Every local education authority shall make to [the Secretary of State] such reports and returns and give to him such information as he may require for the purpose of the exercise of his functions under this Act.

NOTES

The words in square brackets are substituted by virtue of the Secretary of State for Education and Science Order 1964, SI 1964/490, art 3(2)(*a*).

Local education authority. For definition, see s 114(1) post and the note thereto.

Secretary of State. See the note "Secretary of State for Education and Science" to s 1 ante.

93 Power of [Secretary of State] to direct local inquiries

[The Secretary of State] may cause a local inquiry to be held for the purpose of the exercise of any of his functions under this Act; and the provisions of subsections (2), (3), (4) and (5) of section two hundred and ninety of the Local Government Act 1933 shall have effect with respect to any such inquiry as if [the Secretary of State] were a department for the purposes of that section.

NOTES

The words in square brackets are substituted by virtue of the Secretary of State for Education and Science Order 1964, SI 1964/490, art 3(2)(a).

Secretary of State. See the note "Secretary of State for Education and Science" to s 1 ante.

Local inquiry. Inquiries held under this section are subject to the Tribunals and Inquiries Act 1971, ss 1, 11, 12, Vol 10, title Constitutional Law (Pt 4); see the Tribunals and Inquiries (Discretionary Inquiries) Order 1975, SI 1975/1379, arts 3, 4, Schedule, Pt I.

Local Government Act 1933, s 290. Repealed by the Local Government Act 1972, s 272(1), Sch 30; see now s 250 of that Act, Vol 25, title Local Government.

94 Certificates of birth and registrars' returns

(1) Where the age of any person is required to be proved for the purposes of this Act or of any enactment relating to the employment of children or young persons, the registrar having the custody of the register of births and deaths containing the entry relating to the birth of that person shall, upon being presented by any person with a written requisition in such form and containing such particulars as may be determined by regulations made by the Minister of Health and upon payment of a fee of [£1.50], supply that person with a copy of the entry certified under his hand.

Every registrar shall, upon being requested so to do, supply free of charge a form of requisition for the purposes of this subsection.

(2) Every registrar shall supply to a local education authority such particulars of the entries contained in any register of births and deaths in his custody, and in such form, as, subject to any regulations made by the Minister of Health, the authority may from time to time require; . . .

(3) In this section, the expression "register of births and deaths" means a register of births and deaths kept in pursuance of the Births and Deaths Registration Acts 1836 to 1929, and the expression "registrar" includes a registrar of births and deaths and a superintendent registrar.

NOTES

The figures in square brackets in sub-s (1) were substituted by the Registration of Births, Deaths and Marriages (Fees) Order 1982, SI 1982/222, art 2, Schedule.

The words omitted from sub-s (2) were repealed by the Registration of Births, Deaths and Marriages (Fees) Order 1968, SI 1968/1242, Sch 2.

Proof of age. Proof of age for the purposes of this Act may be required by ss 35–37, 39, 44, 58, 59 ante. Enactments relating to the employment of children and young persons include the Children and Young Persons Acts 1933 to 1969, the Young Persons (Employment) Act 1938 and the Employment of Children Act 1973, all Vol 6, title Children.

As to proof of age in legal proceedings under this Act, see s 95 post and also (in relation to proceedings to enforce school attendance), the Education (Miscellaneous Provisions) Act 1948, s 9, this part of this title post.

Minister of Health. See the note to s 54 ante.

Fee. The fee under this section may be varied by orders made under the Public Expenditure and Receipts Act 1968, s 5, Sch 3, para 1(a), Vol 30, title Money (Pt 1). By virtue of the Registration of Births, Deaths and Marriages (Fees) Order 1983, SI 1983/1778, s 2, Schedule, the present fee is maintained at £1.50.

Definitions. For "child" and "young person", see s 114(1) post; for "local education authority", see s 114(1) post and the note thereto.

Births and Deaths Registration Acts 1836 to 1929. Those Acts are now largely consolidated in the Births and Deaths Registration Act 1953 and the Registration Service Act 1953, Vol 37, title Registration

Concerning the Individual. As to the provisions of registers of births and deaths, see s 25 of the first-mentioned 1953 Act.

Regulations under this section. No regulations had been made under this section up to 1 September 1985. The Certificates of Births, Deaths and Marriages (Requisition) Regulations 1937, SR & O 1937/885, made under the Education Act 1921, s 135 (repealed), are still in force by virtue of the saving in s 121 post. For general provisions as to regulations under this Act, see s 112 post.

95 Provisions as to evidence

(1) Where in any proceedings under this Act the person by whom the proceedings are brought alleges that any person whose age is material to the proceedings is under, of, or over, any age, and satisfies the court that having used all reasonable diligence to obtain evidence as to the age of that person he has been unable to do so, then, unless the contrary is proved, the court may presume that person to be under, of, or over, the age alleged.

(2) In any legal proceedings any document purporting to be—

(a) a document issued by a local education authority, and to be signed by the clerk of that authority or by the chief education officer of that authority or by any other officer of the authority authorised to sign it;

(b) an extract from the minutes of the proceedings of the . . . governors of any county school or voluntary school, and to be signed by the chairman of the . . . governors or by their clerk;

(c) a certificate giving particulars of the attendance of a child or young person at a school or at a county college, and to be signed by the head teacher of the school or college; or

(d) a certificate issued by a medical officer of a local education authority and to be signed by such an officer;

shall be received in evidence and shall, unless the contrary is proved, be deemed to be the document which it purports to be, and to have been signed by the person by whom it purports to have been signed, without proof of his identity, signature, or official capacity, and any such extract or certificate as is mentioned in paragraph (b) (c) or (d) of this subsection shall be evidence of the matters therein stated.

NOTES

The words omitted from sub-s (2)(b) were repealed by the Education Act 1980, s 1(3), Sch 1, para 1.

Proceedings under this Act. Proceedings may be brought under ss 37, 39, 44, 45, 59 and 80 ante. In proceedings to enforce attendance at school under ss 37, 39 ante, see the Education (Miscellaneous Provisions) Act 1948, s 9, this part of this title post which supersedes sub-s (1) above for those purposes.

Certificate issued by medical officer. See *R v De Grey, ex p Fitzgerald* (1913) 109 LT 871, 77 JP 463 (magistrate bound by medical certificate, unless certificate disputed).

Unless the contrary is proved. The burden of proof resting on the accused is not so onerous as that which is, in general, laid on the prosecutor as regards proving an offence and may be discharged by satisfying the court of the probability or rather the preponderance of probability, of what the accused is called on to prove; see *R v Carr-Briant* [1943] KB 607, [1943] 2 All ER 156; *R v Dunbar* [1958] 1 QB 1, [1957] 2 All ER 737; and *R v Hudson* [1966] 1 QB 448, [1965] 1 All ER 721.

Documents issued by a divisional executive. These are placed in a similar position to the documents mentioned in sub-s (2) by the Education Act 1946, s 13(1), this part of this title post.

Definitions. For "county school" and "voluntary school", see s 9(2) ante; for "county college", see s 43 ante; for "child", "medical officer", "school" and "young person", see s 114(1) post; and for "local education authority", see s 114(1) post and the note thereto.

96 Provisions consequential on cessation of functions of former authorities

(1) If upon the application of a former authority the Minister is satisfied with respect to any property which was immediately before the date of the commencement of Part II of this Act held by that authority for the purposes of functions exercisable by them under the Education Acts 1921 to 1939 that, although the property was so held, it was held upon trust for purposes of such a nature that the transfer thereof to a local education

authority would be inexpedient, the Minister may by order direct that the property shall be deemed not to have been transferred by virtue of section six of this Act to the local education authority for the county in which the area of the former authority is situated.

(2) Where any question arises as to whether any officers, property, rights, or liabilities, have been transferred by virtue of this Act from a former authority to a local education authority, that question shall be determined by the Minister.

(3) Where any officers, property, rights, or liabilities, have been transferred by virtue of this Act from a former authority to a local education authority, the local education authority and the former authority may by agreement provide for the making of such adjustments in relation to their respective property, rights and liabilities, as appear to the authorities to be desirable having regard to the transfer, and any such agreement may, in particular provide for the making of payments by either party thereto.

(4) Where it appears to the Minister that having regard to any such transfer it is desirable that any such adjustment as aforesaid (including any payment by either of the authorities concerned) should be made, he may, subject to any agreement made under the last foregoing subsection, by directions make provision for that adjustment.

(5) Where at the commencement of Part II of this Act any former authority were parties to any proceedings pending with respect to any property, rights, or liabilities, which by virtue of this Act are transferred from the former authority to a local education authority, the proceedings may be carried on thereafter with the substitution of the local education authority for the former as parties thereto.

NOTES

General Note. This section is largely spent; see the next note below. Sub-s (2) excludes the court's jurisdiction to make a declaration (*Gillingham Corpn v Kent CC* [1953] Ch 37, [1952] 2 All ER 1107).

The Minister. Ie the Minister of Education appointed under s 1 ante as originally enacted. The Secretary of State for Education and Science has been substituted for that Minister by the Secretary of State for Education and Science Order 1964, SI 1964/490, but as the transfers under s 6 ante and any exceptions to them under this section must have occurred well before 1964, effect has not been given to that substitution in this section.

Date of commencement of Part II of this Act. The date of the commencement of Pt II (ss 6–69) was 1 April 1945 by virtue of s 119 (repealed).

Definitions. For "former authority" and "local education authority", see s 114(1) post.

Education Acts 1921 to 1939. By the Education (Emergency) Act 1939, s 2 (repealed), the following Acts might be cited together by this collective title: the Education Act 1921 (repealed); the Education (Institution Children) Act 1923 (repealed); the Education (Local Authorities) Act 1931 (repealed); the Education (Necessity of Schools) Act 1933 (repealed); the Education Act 1936 (repealed); the Education (Deaf Children) Act 1937 (repealed); the Education (Emergency) Act 1939 (repealed).

Orders. Orders under this section, being local, are not recorded in this work. As to variation or revocation of orders, see s 111 post.

97 (*Repealed by the Education Act 1980, s 38(6), Sch 7.*)

98 Compensation of persons prejudicially affected by this Act

(1) If in consequence of the extinguishment or transfer by this Act of any functions exercisable by the council of any county district, or the transfer by this act of any officers employed by any such council, any person who, immediately before the date of the commencement of Part II of this Act, was an officer employed by that council or by the council of the county in which the county district is situated suffers direct pecuniary loss by reason of the determination of his appointment or the diminution of his emoluments, he shall, unless provision for his compensation for that loss is made by or under any other enactment for the time being in force, be entitled to receive compensation under this subsection from the local education authority for the area in which the county district is situated; and, for the purposes of any claim for compensation under this

subsection, the provisions of subsections (2) and (3) of section one hundred and fifty of the Local Government Act 1933, shall have effect as if:—

(a) the extinguishment or transfer had been effected by virtue of an order made by the Minister of Health under Part VI of the said Act of 1933 and coming into operation upon the date of the commencement of Part II of this Act; and

(b) the expression "existing officer," in those subsections, meant any person who, immediately before the said date, was an officer employed by the council of a county or county district in connection with any functions exercisable by that council under any enactment repealed or amended by this Act.

(2) If, in consequence of any school becoming a special agreement school or a controlled school, or in consequence of the discontinuance within six years after the passing of this Act of any school maintained by a local education authority, any person who was a teacher in the school immediately before it became a special agreement school or a controlled school, or before the school was discontinued, as the case may be, suffers direct pecuniary loss by reason of his dismissal or the diminution of his emoluments, he shall, unless provision for his compensation for that loss is made by or under any other enactment for the time being in force, be entitled to receive compensation from the authority under this section.

(3) For the purposes of the determination and payment of compensation under this section, the provisions of the Fourth Schedule to the Local Government Act 1933, shall have effect subject to the following modifications, that is to say:—

(a) references therein to the Minister shall be construed as references to the Minister of Education, and sub-paragraph (1) of paragraph 1 thereof shall have effect as if after the word "prescribed" there were inserted the words "by the Minister of Education";

(b) references therein to a scheme or order shall be construed as references to this Act; and

(c) any period during which a person has been engaged in war service within the meaning of the Local Government Staffs (War Service) Act 1939, shall be reckoned for the purposes of the said Schedule as a period of service in his office, and where any such period is so reckoned, his emoluments during that period shall, for the purposes of sub-paragraph (2) of paragraph 4 of the said Schedule, be deemed to be such as he would have received if he had not been engaged in war service.

NOTES

This section is largely spent; see the General Note below.

General Note. This section deals with compensation payable to officers employed by the council of any county district before 1 April 1945 (sub-s (1)) and teachers employed before 3 August 1950 (sub-s (2)), where they have suffered loss as a result of the reorganisation described in sub-ss (1), (2). It is largely spent.

Date of commencement of Part II of this Act. The date of the commencement of Pt II (ss 6–69) was 1 April 1945 by virtue of s 119 (repealed).

Within six years after the passing of this Act. The Act was passed, ie received the Royal Assent, on 3 August 1944.

Minister of Education. See the note "The Minister" to s 96 ante.

Local Government Act 1933, s 150(2), (3), Sch 4. Repealed by the Local Government Act 1972, s 272(1), Sch 30.

Local Government Staffs (War Service) Act 1939. Repealed by the SL(R) Act 1975.

Regulations under this section. The Education (Compensation Forms) Regulations 1945, SR & O 1945/1705 are spent.

99 Powers of [Secretary of State] in default of local education authorities or ... governors

(1) If [the Secretary of State] is satisfied, either upon complaint by any person interested or otherwise, that any local education authority, or the ... governors of any

county school or voluntary school, have failed to discharge any duty imposed upon them by or for the purposes of this Act, [the Secretary of State] may make an order declaring the authority, or the ... governors, as the case may be, to be in default in respect of that duty, and giving such directions for the purpose of enforcing the execution thereof as appear to [the Secretary of State] to be expedient; and any such directions shall be enforceable, on an application made on behalf of [the Secretary of State], by mandamus.

(2) Where it appears to [the Secretary of State] that by reason of the default of any person there is no properly constituted body of ... governors of any county school or voluntary school, [the Secretary of State] may make such appointments and give such directions as he thinks desirable for the purpose of securing that there is a properly constituted body of ... governors thereof, and may give directions rendering valid any acts or proceedings which in his opinion are invalid or otherwise defective by reason of the default.

(3) Where it appears to [the Secretary of State] that a local education authority have made default in the discharge of their duties relating to the maintenance of a voluntary school, [the Secretary of State] may direct that any act done by or on behalf of the ... governors of the school for the purpose of securing the proper maintenance thereof shall be deemed to have been done by or on behalf of the authority, and may reimburse to the ... governors any sums which in his opinion they have properly expended for that purpose; and the amount of any sum so reimbursed shall be a debt due to the Crown from the authority, and, without prejudice to any other method of recovery, the whole or any part of such a sum may be deducted from any sums payable to the authority by [the Secretary of State] in pursuance of any regulations relating to the payments of grants.

NOTES

The words in square brackets are substituted by virtue of the Secretary of State for Education and Science Order 1964, SI 1964/490, art 3(2)(a) and the words omitted were repealed by the Education Act 1980, s 1(3), Sch 1, para 1.

Secretary of State. See the note "Secretary of State for Education and Science" to s 1 ante.

Complaint by any person interested. The existence of the remedy of complaint under this section does not exclude any other remedy available in the courts at the suit of a person who has suffered special damage; see *Meade v London Borough of Haringey* [1979] 2 All ER 1016, [1979] 1 WLR 637, CA, where the court considered an application for damages or an injunction against a local education authority's failure to perform their statutory duty under s 8 to keep schools open.

The Secretary of State may make an order. Before making an order under sub-s (1) the Secretary of State may, but is not bound to, hold a local inquiry under s 93 ante.

Properly constituted body of governors. See s 17 ante.

Other method of recovery of debt due to the Crown. See the Crown Proceedings Act 1947, ss 13, 15, Vol 13, title Crown Proceedings.

Regulations relating to the payment of grants. See s 100 post and the regulations noted thereto.

Application. Sub-s (1) is applied to any failure to discharge a duty imposed by regulations made under the Local Government Act 1966, s 4(2), Vol 25, title Local Government; see s 4(4) of the 1966 Act.

The powers of the Secretary of State under this section are applied by the Sex Discrimination Act 1975, s 25(2) and the Race Relations Act 1976, s 19(2), both Vol 6, title Civil Rights and Liberties.

Definitions. For "county school" and "voluntary school", see s 9(2) ante; for "maintain", see s 114(1) post; and for "local education authority", see s 114(1) post and the note thereto.

Orders. As to the revocation and variation of orders and directions, see s 111 post.

FINANCIAL PROVISIONS

100 Grants in aid of educational services

(1) [The Secretary of State] shall by regulations make provision:—

　(a) for the payment by him to local education authorities of annual grants in respect of the expenditure incurred by such authorities,

　　(i)–(iii) ...

(b) for the payment by him to persons other than local education authorities of grants in respect of expenditure incurred or to be incurred for the purposes of educational services provided by them or on their behalf or under their management or for the purposes of educational research; and

(c) for the payment by him, for the purpose of enabling pupils to take advantage without hardship to themselves or their parents of any educational facilities available to them, of the whole or any part of the fees and expenses payable in respect of children attending schools at which fees are payable . . .

(2) . . .

(3) Any regulations made by [the Secretary of State] . . . under this section may make provision whereby the making of payments by him in pursuance thereof is dependent upon the fulfilment of such conditions as may be determined by or in accordance with the regulations, and may also make provision for requiring local education authorities and other persons to whom payments have been made in pursuance thereof to comply with such requirements as may be so determined.

(4) . . .

(5) Nothing in this section shall affect any grants in aid of university education payable out of moneys provided by Parliament otherwise than in accordance with the provisions of this Act.

NOTES

The words "the Secretary of State" in square brackets are substituted in sub-ss (1), (3) by virtue of the Secretary of State for Education and Science Order 1964, SI 1964/490, art 3(2)(a).

In sub-s (1), para (a)(i), (ii) were repealed by the Education Act 1980, s 38(6), Sch 7, para (a)(iii) was repealed by the Education Act 1944 (Termination of Grants) Order 1980, SI 1980/660 and the words omitted from para (c) were repealed with savings by the Education Act 1962, s 13(1), Sch 2 post; see now s 3 of that Act post.

Sub-s (2), and the words omitted from sub-s (3), were repealed by the Local Government Act 1958, s 67(a), Sch 9, Pt II.

Sub-s (4) was repealed by the Education Act 1973, s 1(4), Sch 2, Pt II; as to savings in respect of orders made under this section, see s 1(3), and Sch 1, para 3 to that Act, this part of this title post.

Secretary of State. See the note "Secretary of State for Education and Science" to s 1 ante.

Grants . . . for the purposes of educational research. Cf s 82 ante which enables a local education authority to make provision for conducting or assisting the conduct of research.

Payment . . . of fees. Cf s 81 ante which enables a local education authority to give similar assistance by means of scholarships and otherwise.

As to payment by a local education authority of fees in respect of pupils at non-maintained schools receiving grants under sub-s (1)(b) above, see the Education (Miscellaneous Provisions) Act 1953, s 6(2), this part of this title post.

Grants in aid of university education. Grants in aid of university education otherwise than in accordance with the provisions of this Act are made by the Treasury through the University Grants Committee.

Students having no connection with the United Kingdom. For the power of the Secretary of State to make regulations requiring or authorising the charging of fees which are higher in the case of students not having a connection with the United Kingdom; see the Education (Fees and Awards) Act 1983, s 1, this part of this title post.

Sex discrimination. As to the prohibition of sex discrimination in education, see the Sex Discrimination Act 1975, ss 22–28, Sch 2, Vol 6, title Civil Rights and Liberties. Regulations under sub-s (1)(b) above may provide for the making of transitional exemption orders in respect of discriminatory admissions; see s 27(1) of, and Sch 2, para 3 to, that Act.

Registration as a Residential Care Home. This is not required in respect of any establishment to which the Secretary of State has made a payment of maintenance grant under regulations made by virtue of sub-s (1)(b) above; however an establishment to which the Secretary of State has made payment of grant under such regulations is only excluded until the end of the period of 12 months from the date on which the Secretary of State made the payment; see the Registered Homes Act 1984, s 1(5)(g), (7), Vol 35, title Public Health.

Definitions. For "pupil", "school" and "trust deed", see s 114(1) post; for "local education authority", see s 114(1) post and the note thereto.

Regulations under this section. The Direct Grant Schools Regulations 1959, SI 1959/1832, as amended by SI 1963/1379, SI 1965/1, SI 1968/1148, SI 1973/1535, SI 1978/1145, SI 1980/1861, SI 1981/1788 and SI 1983/74; the Direct Grant Grammar Schools (Cessation of Grant) Regulations 1975, SI 1975/1198 as amended by SI 1977/1443, SI 1979/1552 and SI 1981/1788; the Scholarships and Other Benefits Regulations 1977, SI 1977/1443 as amended by SI 1979/260, and SI 1979/542; the Education (Schools and Further Education) Regulations 1981, SI 1981/1086 as amended by SI 1983/262; the Education (Teachers) Regulations 1982, SI 1982/106; the Education (Grant) Regulations 1983, SI 1983/74; and the Education (Grants) (Music and Ballet Schools) Regulations 1985, SI 1985/684.

101 (*Repealed by the Local Government Act 1958, s 67, Sch 9, Pt II.*)

102 Maintenance contributions payable by the [Secretary of State] in respect of aided schools and special agreement schools

[The Secretary of State] shall pay to the ... governors of every aided school and of every special agreement school maintenance contributions equal to [85 per cent] of any sums expended by them in carrying out their obligations under paragraph (*a*) of subsection (3) of section fifteen of this Act in respect of alterations [and repairs] to the school buildings ... [and may pay the ... governors of any aided school or special agreement school maintenance contributions not exceeding [85 per cent] of any sums expended by them on the provision of a site or of school buildings in pursuance of proposals approved under [section 13 of the Education Act 1980] for a significant enlargement of the school premises].

Provided that no maintenance contribution shall be payable under this section in respect of any expenditure incurred by the ... governors of a special agreement school in the execution of repairs or alterations for the execution of which provision is made by the special agreement relating to the school [nor shall a maintenance contribution be payable under this section in respect of any expenditure incurred by the ... governors of a special agreement school in pursuance of proposals for a significant enlargement of the school premises, being proposals to which the special agreement for the school relates].

NOTES

The words "the Secretary of State" are substituted by virtue of the Secretary of State for Education and Science Order 1964, SI 1964/490, art 3(2)(*a*).

The words omitted in the second place were repealed, and the words "and repairs" were inserted, by the Education Act 1946, s 14(1), Sch 2, Pt II.

The other words omitted were repealed by the Education Act 1980, s 1(3), Sch 1, para 1, and the words "section 13 of the Education Act 1980" were substituted by s 16(4) of, and Sch 3, para 3 to, that Act.

The references to "85 per cent" were substituted by the Education Act 1975, s 3.

The words from "and may pay" to "premises" and those from "nor shall" to "relates" were substituted by the Education Act 1968, s 1(3), (5), Sch 1, para 4(1).

Secretary of State. See the note "Secretary of State for Education and Science" to s 1 ante.

Definitions. For "aided school" and "special agreement school", see s 15 ante; for "alterations", "enlargement", "premises", "significant" and "special agreement", see s 114(1) post; and for "school buildings", see the Education Act 1946, s 4(2) post.

Education Act 1980, s 13. See this part of this title post.

103 Power of the [Secretary of State] to make grants in respect of aided schools and special agreement schools transferred to new sites or established in substitution for former schools

(1) Where [the Secretary of State] by an order made under section sixteen of this Act authorises the transfer of any voluntary school to a new site ... then, if the school to be transferred ... in pursuance of the order is to be maintained as an aided school or a special agreement school, [the Secretary of State] may pay to the ... governors of the school in respect of any sums expended by them in the construction of the school a grant not exceeding [85 per cent] thereof:

Provided that no grant shall be payable under this section to the ... governors of a special agreement school in respect of any sums expended by them in the execution of proposals to which the special agreement for the school relates.

(2) ...

(3) Without prejudice to the general discretion of [the Secretary of State] as to the making of any grant under this section and as to the amount of any such grant, [the Secretary of State] shall, in determining the amount of any such grant, take into account any sums which may accrue to the ... governors or trustees of the school in respect of the disposal of the site from which the school is to be transferred ...

NOTES

The words "the Secretary of State" in square brackets are substituted by virtue of the Secretary of State for Education and Science Order 1964, SI 1964/490, art 3(2)(a).

The words omitted in the first and second places in sub-s (1) were repealed by the Education Act 1967, s 1(5)(a), (6) and those omitted in the third and fourth places were repealed by the Education Act 1980, s 1(3), Sch 1, para 12. The reference to "85 per cent" in that subsection was substituted by the Education Act 1975, s 3.

Sub-s (2) was repealed by the Education (Miscellaneous Provisions) Act 1953, s 17(2), Sch 2.

The words omitted in the first place in sub-s (3) were repealed by the Education Act 1980, s 1(3), Sch 1, para 2 and those omitted in the second place were repealed by the Education Act 1967, s 1(5)(a), (6).

Secretary of State. See the note "Secretary of State for Education and Science" to s 1 ante.

Construction of the school. The effect of the Education (Miscellaneous Provisions) Act 1953, s 8(1)(a), this part of this title post is that there must be substituted for this reference to the construction of the school a reference to the provision (whether before or after 14 July 1953, the date of passing of that Act) of the school buildings.

Disposal of the site. As to the power of the trustees of a school to sell or exchange the site of the school, see the School Sites Act 1841, s 14, Pt 3 of this title post and as to the application of the proceeds of sale in certain cases, see the Education Act 1946, Sch 1, para 8, this part of this title post.

Application of sub-s (3). This subsection is applied to grants under the Education Act 1967, s 1(2), this part of this title post by s 1(3), (4) thereof.

Definitions. For "voluntary school", see s 9 ante; for "aided school" and "special agreement school", see s 15 ante; for "maintain", "special agreement" and "school", see s 114(1) post.

104 (Repealed by the Education Act 1967, s 1(5)(b).)

105 Power of the [Secretary of State] to make loans to aided schools and special agreement schools in respect of initial expenditure

(1) If upon the application of the ... governors of any aided school or special agreement school [the Secretary of State] is satisfied after consultation with persons representing them that their share of any initial expenses required in connection with the school premises will involve capital expenditure which, in his opinion having regard to all the circumstances of the case, ought properly to be met by borrowing, he may make to the ... governors of the school for the purpose of helping them to meet that expenditure, a loan of such amount at such rate of interest and otherwise on such terms and conditions as may be specified in an agreement made between him and them with the consent of the Treasury.

(2) For the purposes of this section, the expression "initial expenses" means in relation to any school premises—

    (a) expenses to be incurred in defraying the cost of any alterations required by the development plan approved by [the Secretary of State] for the area;

    (b) expenses to be incurred in pursuance of any special agreement;

    [(c) (i) expenses to be incurred in providing a site or school buildings on a significant enlargement of the school premises, being expenses in respect of which a maintenance contribution may be paid;

    (ii) expenses to be incurred in providing school buildings on a site to which the school is to be transferred under the authority of an order under section 16 (1) of this Act;

    (iii) expenses to be incurred in providing a site or school buildings for a new school which by virtue of an order under section 16 (2) of this Act is deemed to be in substitution for a discontinued school or schools.]

   (d) expenses certified by [the Secretary of State] under the last foregoing section as being attributable to the provisions of education for displaced pupils;

and the ... governors' share of any such initial expenses shall be taken to be so much thereof as remains to be borne by them after taking into account the amount of any maintenance contribution, grant under a special agreement, or grant under either of the last two foregoing sections, as may be paid or payable in respect of those expenses.

(3) If upon an application being made to him under subsection (2) of section fifteen of this Act for an order directing that a school shall be an aided school or a special agreement school it appears to [the Secretary of State] that the area served by the school will not be also served by any county school or controlled school, then, unless he is satisfied that the ... governors of the school will be able to defray the expenses which would fall to be borne by them under paragraph (a) subsection (3) of that section without the assistance of a loan under this section, [the Secretary of State] shall consult such persons or bodies of persons as appear to him to be representative of any religious denomination which, in his opinion having regard to the circumstances of the area, is likely to be concerned; and, unless after such consultation he is satisfied that the holding of a local inquiry is unnecessary, shall cause such inquiry to be held before determining the application.

NOTES

The words "the Secretary of State" in square brackets are substituted by virtue of the Secretary of State for Education and Science Order 1964, SI 1964/490, art 3(2)(a), sub-s (2)(c) was substituted by the Education Act 1968, s 1(2), Sch 1, para 4(2) and the words omitted were repealed by the Education Act 1980, s 1(3), Sch 1, para 1.

Secretary of State. See the note "Secretary of State for Education and Science" to s 1 ante.

Initial expenses. To the list of these expenses must now, by virtue of the Education Act 1967, s 1(4), this part of this title post, be added a reference to any expenses in respect of which the Secretary of State may make a grant under s 1(2) of that Act which gives the Secretary of State power to pay grants towards the cost of providing sites and school buildings for certain new aided schools or special agreement schools. That same subsection further provides that in determining the governors' share of the initial expenses the amount of any such grant paid or payable in respect of them must be taken into account in the same way as grants under s 103 ante.

Required by the development plan approved by the Secretary of State. By virtue of s 11 of this Act (repealed), every Local Education Authority was obliged to prepare, and submit to the Secretary of State, development plans as to primary and secondary schools.

The reference in sub-s (2)(a) to expenses to be incurred in defraying the cost of any alterations required by the development plan approved by the Secretary of State for the area must be read as including a reference to expenses, whether incurred before or after the passing of the Education (Miscellaneous Provisions) Act 1953, this part of this title post (ie 14 July 1953), in defraying the cost of any alterations specified in that plan as submitted to the Secretary of State being alterations to the carrying out of which the Secretary of State had given approval before the approval by him of the plan; see s 8(3)(a) of the 1953 Act this part of this title post.

Enlargement of school premises. See the note "Significant change in character" to the Education Act 1968, s 1, this part of this title post.

Maintenance contribution. As to the maintenance contribution payable by the Secretary of State to the governors of every aided school and every special agreement school, see s 102 ante.

Local inquiry. As to the powers of the Secretary of State in relation to the holding of local inquiries, see s 93 ante.

Definitions. For "aided school", "controlled school" and "special agreement school", see s 15 ante; for "alterations", "enlargement", "premises" and "significant", see s 114(1) post; for "county school", see s 9(2) ante, and for "development plan", see s 11 ante.

106, 107 (S 106 repealed by the SL(R) Act 1975; s 107 repealed by the SL(R) Act 1978.)

PART V

SUPPLEMENTAL

108–110 *(Repealed by the SL(R) Act 1975.)*

111 Revocation and variation of orders and directions

Any order made or directions given by [the Secretary of State], the Minister of Health, or a local education authority under the provisions of this Act may be varied or revoked by a further order or further directions made or given by [the Secretary of State], the Minister of Health, or that authority, as the case may be:

Provided that where the power to make or give such order or directions is exercisable only upon the application or with the consent of any person or body of persons, or after consultation with any person or body of persons, or otherwise subject to any conditions, no order or directions made or given thereunder shall be varied or revoked except under the like application, with the like consent, after the like consultation, or subject to the like conditions, as the case may be.

NOTES

The words in square brackets are substituted by virtue of the Secretary of State for Education and Science Order 1964, SI 1964/490, art 3(2)(*a*).

Secretary of State. See the note "Secretary of State for Education and Science" to s 1 ante.

Minister of Health. See the note to s 54 ante.

Saving. The repeals made to ss 17, 100 ante by the Education Act 1973 do not affect any order made under those sections or the operation of this section in relation to such orders; see s 1(3) of, and Sch 1, para 3 to, that Act, this part of this title post.

112 Regulations to be laid before Parliament

All regulations made under this Act shall be laid before Parliament as soon as may be after they are made, and if either House of Parliament, within the period of forty days beginning with the day on which any such regulations are laid before it, resolves that the regulations be annulled the regulations shall cease to have effect, but without prejudice to anything previously done thereunder or to the making of any new regulations.

In reckoning any such period of forty days no account shall be taken of any time during which Parliament is dissolved or prorogued or during which both Houses are adjourned for more than four days.

NOTES

Laid before Parliament. For meaning, see the Laying of Documents before Parliament (Interpretation) Act 1948, s 1(1), Vol 41, title Statutes.

Saving. By s 121 post any regulation in force under any enactment repealed by this Act is to continue in force and have effect as if made under this Act and may be varied or revoked accordingly.

113 Notices

Any [order, notice or other document] required or authorised by this Act to be served upon any person may be served by delivering it to that person, or by leaving it at his usual or last known place of residence, or by sending it in a pre-paid letter addressed to him at that place.

NOTES

The words in square brackets were substituted by the Education Act 1946, s 14(1), Sch 2, Pt I.

Served. See also the Interpretation Act 1978, s 7, Vol 41, title Statutes. It was decided in *Walthamstow UDC v Henwood* [1897] 1 Ch 41, 66 LJ Ch 31, that prepayment of the letter must be proved in order to prove service. It has also been held (*R v Westminster Unions Assessment Committee, ex p Woodward & Sons* [1917] 1 KB 832, 86 LJKB 698) that the presumption that a notice has been received when properly addressed, prepaid and delivered to the post office is not merely a presumption of fact unless the contrary is shown, but is a presumption of law whether in fact the notice was received by the addressee or not.

Person. Unless the contrary intention appears this includes a body of persons corporate or unincorporate; see the Interpretation Act 1978, s 5, Sch 1, Vol 41, title Statutes.

Leaving it at his last known place of residence. If a notice is served in this way it must be left in a manner in which a reasonable person, minded to bring the document to the attention of the person to whom it is addressed, would adopt; see *Lord Newborough v Jones* [1975] Ch 90, [1974] 3 All ER 17, CA.

Though as a general rule an address which the person concerned is known to have left is not a proper address for service (*White v Weston* [1968] 2 QB 647, [1968] 2 All ER 842, CA), the position is otherwise where the use of the last known address is expressly authorised (*Re Follick, ex p Trustee* (1907) 97 LT 645). However, service at the last known address in England or Wales is not good if a later address abroad is known (*R v Farmer* [1892] 1 QB 637, [1891–4] All ER Rep 921, CA). For other relevant cases, see *Hanrott's Trustees v Evans* (1887) 4 TLR 128; *R v Webb* [1896] 1 QB 487; *Berry v Farrow* [1914] 1 KB 632; *Stylo Shoes Ltd v Prices Tailors Ltd* [1960] Ch 396, [1959] 3 All ER 901; and *McGlynn v Stewart* 1974 SLT 230.

Residence. As to the meaning of the word "residence", see *Blackwell v England* (1857) 27 LJQB 124, 30 LTOS 148; *R v Braithwaite* [1918] 2 KB 319, [1918–19] All ER Rep 1145; and *R v Hastings Justices, ex p Mitchell* (1925) 89 JP Jo 86.

114 Interpretation

(1) In this Act, unless the context otherwise requires, the following expressions have the meanings hereby respectively assigned to them, that is to say:—

"Agreed syllabus" means, subject to the provisions of subsection (4) of this section, an agreed syllabus of religious instruction prepared in accordance with the provisions of the Fifth Schedule to this Act and adopted or deemed to be adopted thereunder;

["alterations", in relation to any school premises, includes improvements, extensions and additions, but does not include any significant enlargement of the school premises];

"Assist", in relation to any school, college or institution, has the meaning assigned to it by subsection (2) of this section;

"Child" means a person who is not over compulsory school age;

"Clothing" includes boots and other footwear;

"Compulsory school age" has ... the meaning assigned to it by section thirty-five of this Act;

"County" means an administrative county within the meaning of the Local Government Act, 1933;

["enlargement", in relation to any school premises, includes any modification of the existing premises which has the effect of increasing the number of pupils for whom accommodation can be provided, and "enlarge" shall be construed accordingly];

"Former authority" means any authority which was a local education authority within the meaning of any enactment repealed by this Act or any previous Act;

["Foundation governors," means, in relation to any voluntary school governors appointed] otherwise than by a local education authority or a minor authority for the purpose of securing, so far as is practicable, that the character of the school as a voluntary school is preserved and developed, and, in particular, that the school is conducted in accordance with the provisions of any trust deed relating thereto; and, unless the context otherwise requires, references in this Act to ... "governors" shall, in relation to any function thereby conferred or imposed exclusively on . . . foundation governors, be construed as references to such . . . governors;

"Further education" has the meaning assigned to it by section forty-one of this Act;

"Independent school" means any school at which full-time education is provided for five or more pupils of compulsory school age (whether or not such education is also provided for pupils under or over that age), not being a school maintained by a local education authority or [a special school not maintained by a local education authority];

"Junior pupil" means a child who has not attained the age of twelve years;

"Local education authority" means, in relation to any area for which a joint education board is constituted as the local education authority under the provisions of Part I of the First Schedule to this Act, the board so constituted, and, save as aforesaid, means, [in relation to a non-metropolitan county, the council of the county, and in relation to a metropolitan district, the council of the district];

.   .   .   .   .

"Local government elector" has the meaning assigned to it by section three hundred and five of the Local Government Act 1933; and in relation to the area of any joint education board constituted under Part I of the First Schedule to this Act a local government elector for the area of any council by whom members are appointed to the board shall be deemed to be a local government elector for the area of the authority;

"Maintain" in relation to any school or county college has the meaning assigned to it by subsection (2) of this section;

"Maintenance contribution", in relation to any voluntary school, means a contribution payable under section one hundred and two of this Act;

.   .   .   .   .

"Medical officer" means, in relation to any local education authority, a duly qualified medical practitioner employed or engaged, whether regularly or for the purposes of any particular case by that authority [or whose services are made available to that authority by the Secretary of State];

.   .   .   .   .

["minor authority" means, in relation to a school maintained by a local education authority,—

(a) where the area which appears to the local education authority to be served by the school is a parish or community, the parish or community council or, in the case of a parish which has no council, the parish meeting;

(b) where the said area is a community having no community council or is an area in England which is not within a parish and is not situated in a metropolitan county, the council of the district for the area concerned;

(c) where the said area comprises two or more of the following, a parish, a community or an area in England which is not within a parish and is not situated in a metropolitan county—

(i) the parish or community council or councils, if any;
(ii) in the case of a parish which has no council, the parish meeting;
(iii) in the case of an area which is a community having no community council or which is in England and is not within a parish, the council of the district concerned;

acting jointly.]

"Parent", in relation to any child or young person, includes a guardian and every person who has the actual custody of the child or young person;

"Premises", in relation to any school, includes any detached playing fields, but, except where otherwise expressly provided, does not include a teacher's dwelling-house;

"Prescribed" means prescribed by regulations made by [the Secretary of State];

"Primary education" has the meaning assigned to it by section eight of this Act;

"Primary school" means . . . a school for providing primary education;

"Proprietor", in relation to any school, means the person or body of persons responsible for the management of the school, and for the purposes of the provisions of this Act relating to applications for the registration of independent schools, includes any person or body of persons proposing to be so responsible;

"Provisionally registered school" means an independent school registered in the register of independent schools, whereof the registration is provisional only;

"Pupil", where used without qualification, means a person of any age for whom education is required to be provided under this Act [but includes a junior pupil who has not attained the age of five years];

"Registered pupil" means, in relation to any school, a pupil registered as such in the register kept in accordance with the requirements of this Act . . .

"Registered school" means an independent school registered in the register of independent schools, whereof the registration is final;

"School" means an institution for providing primary or secondary education or both primary and secondary education, being a school maintained by a local education authority, an independent school, or [a special school not maintained by a local education authority]; and the expression "school" where used without qualification includes any such school or all such schools as the context may require;

"Secondary education" has the meaning assigned to it by section eight of this Act;

"Secondary school" means, subject to the provisions of subsection (3) of this section, a school for providing secondary education;

"Senior pupil" means a person who has attained the age of twelve years but has not attained the age of nineteen years;

["significant", in relation to a change in the character of a school or an enlargement of school premises, implies that there is a substantial change in the function or size of the school];

"Special agreement" means an agreement made under the provisions of the Third Schedule to this Act;

["special educational needs" and "special educational provision" have the meanings given to them by section 1 of the Education Act 1981];

.   .   .   .   .

"Trust deed", in relation to any voluntary school, includes any instrument (not being an . . . instrument of government, . . . or articles of government, made under this Act) regulating the maintenance, management or conduct of the school or the constitution of the body of . . . governors thereof;

"Young person" means a person over compulsory school age who has not attained the age of eighteen years.

(2) For the purposes of this Act:—

(a) the duty of a local education authority to maintain a school or county college shall include the duty of defraying all the expenses of maintaining the school or college except, in the case of an aided school or a special agreement school, any expenses that by virtue of any provision of this Act or of any special agreement made thereunder are payable by the . . . governors of the school, and the expression "maintain" shall be construed accordingly; and

(b)   where a local education authority make to the proprietor of any school which is not maintained by the authority, or to the persons responsible for the maintenance of any training college or other institution which is not so maintained, any grant in respect of the school college or institution or any payment in consideration of the provision of educational facilities thereat, the school college or institution shall be deemed to be assisted by the authority.

(3)–(6) . . .

(7) Where at any time before the date of the commencement of Part II of this Act the premises of any school which was for the time being a public elementary school within the meaning of the enactments repealed by this Act have ceased by reason of war damage, or by reason of any action taken in contemplation or in consequence of war, to be used for the purposes of a school, then, for the purposes of this Act, the school, unless it has been closed in accordance with those enactments, shall be deemed to have been a public elementary school within the meaning of those enactments immediately before that date and, if it was maintained by a former authority immediately before the premises ceased to be used for the purposes of a school, to have been maintained by such an authority immediately before that date.

(8) In this Act, unless the context otherwise requires, references to any enactment or any provision of any enactment shall be construed as references to that enactment or provision as amended by any subsequent enactment, including this Act.

NOTES

The words "the Secretary of State" wherever they occur in square brackets are substituted by virtue of the Secretary of State for Education and Science Order 1964, SI 1964/490, art 3(2)(a).

The definition of "alterations" was substituted by the Education Act 1968, s 1(3), Sch 1, para 5.

The words omitted from the definition of "Compulsory school age" were repealed by the Education (School-leaving Dates) Act 1976, s 3(3), Schedule.

The definition of "enlargement" was inserted by the Education Act 1968, s 1(3), Sch 1, para 5.

In the definition "Foundation governors", the words in square brackets were substituted, and the words omitted were repealed, by the Education Act 1980, s 1(3), Sch 1.

In the definition "Independent school", the words in square brackets were substituted by the Education Act 1980, s 34(1).

In the definition "Local education authority", the words in square brackets were substituted by the Local Authorities etc (Miscellaneous Provision) Order 1977, SI 1977/293, art 4(1).

The definition "Local education order" was repealed by the Education Act 1980, s 38(6), Sch 7.

The definitions of "Medical inspection" and "Medical treatment" were repealed by the National Health Service Reorganisation Act 1973, ss 57, 58, Sch 5.

In the definition "Medical officer", the words in square brackets were added by the National Health Service Reorganisation Act 1973, ss 57, 58, Sch 4, para 8.

The definition "minor authority" was substituted by the Local Government Act 1972, s 192(4).

The words omitted from the definition "Primary school" were repealed by the Education Act 1980, s 38(6), Sch 7, and in the definition "Pupil", the words in square brackets were inserted by s 24(3) of that Act.

The words omitted from the definition of "Registered pupil" were repealed by the Education (Miscellaneous Provisions) Act 1948, s 11, Sch 2.

The definition "significant" was inserted by the Education Act 1968, s 1(3), Sch 1.

The definitions "special educational needs" and "special educational provision" were substituted by the Education Act 1981, s 21, Sch 3.

The definition "special educational treatment" was inserted by virtue of the Education Act 1981 (Commencement No 2) Order 1983, SI 1983/7, art 4, Schedule, para 3(2) for a period of twelve months from 1 April 1983; it is accordingly spent.

The words omitted from the definition "Trust deed" were repealed by the Education Act 1980, s 1(3), Sch 1.

Sub-s (3) and the words omitted from sub-s (2) were repealed by the Education Act 1980, ss 1(3), 38(6), Sch 7.

Sub-s (4) was repealed by the SL(R) Act 1975.

Sub-s (5) was repealed by the Education Act 1946, s 8(4).

Sub-s (6) was repealed by the Education (School-leaving Dates) Act 1976, s 3(3), Schedule.

Sub-s (1): Clothing. As to the provision of clothing by local education authorities, see the Education (Miscellaneous Provisions) Act 1948, s 5, this part of this title post.

Compulsory school age. School leaving dates were altered as from the beginning of September 1963 by the Education Act 1962, s 9, this part of this title post; see, further, the notes thereto.

County. The counties existing immediately before 1 April 1974 were abolished on that date by the Local Government Act 1972, ss 1(10), 20(6), Vol 25, title Local Government, and by virtue of s 179(1), (2) of that Act, the reference to a county is to be construed as a county established by ss 1(1), (2), 20(1), (2) of, and Sch 1, Pts I, II, Sch 4, Pt I to, the 1972 Act.

See also the note "Local Government Act 1933" below.

Former authority. A borough council who under the Education Act 1921 were a local education authority for elementary education only come within this term (*Gillingham Corpn v Kent CC* [1953] Ch 37, [1952] 2 All ER 1107; applied in *Healey v Ministry of Health* [1954] 2 QB 221, [1954] 2 All ER 580).

Foundation governors. Foundation governors exist in relation to voluntary schools (defined in s 9(2) ante) and form only a proportion of the governors of such schools (see ss 18, 19 ante).

Special school. As to such schools, see s 9(5) ante.

Local education authority. As to transitional provisions in relation to things done by old education authorities outside Greater London, see the Local Government Act 1972, s 192(5), (6), Vol 25, title Local Government.

The reference to local education authority in this Act is now construed in relation to any outer London borough (as defined by the London Government Act 1963, s 1(1)(*b*), Sch 1, Pt I, Vol 26, title London) as a reference to the council of that borough. In relation to Greater London exclusive of the outer London Boroughs the local education authority is the Inner London Education Authority established by the Local Government Act 1985, s 18, Vol 25, title Local Government.

County college. See s 43 ante.

Duly qualified medical practitioner. This expression means, by virtue of the Medical Act 1983, s 56, Sch 6, para 11, Vol 28, title Medicine and Pharmacy (Pt 1), a fully registered person as defined in s 55 of that Act.

Parish. As to the parishes in England and their meetings and councils, see the Local Government Act 1972, ss 1(6)–(9), 9 et seq, Sch 1, Pts IV, V, Vol 25, title Local Government.

Community. As to the communities in Wales and their meetings and councils, see the Local Government Act 1972, ss 20(4), 27 et seq, Sch 4, Pt III, Vol 25, title Local Government.

Metropolitan county. As to the metropolitan counties, see the Local Government Act 1972, s 1(1), (2), Sch 1, Pt I, Vol 25, title Local Government.

District. As to the districts in England and Wales and their councils, see the Local Government Act 1972, ss 1(1), (3), (4), 2(2), (3), 20(1), (3), 21(2), (3), Sch 1, Pt I, Sch 4, Pt II, Vol 25, title Local Government.

Premises. As to the prescribed standards to which the premises of schools maintained by local authorities have to conform, see s 10 ante and the regulations made thereunder. See also the definition of "school buildings" in the Education Act 1946, s 4(2), this part of this title post, and see sub-s (7) above.

Primary school. As to financial assistance for primary schools which are Church of England aided schools, see the Church Schools (Assistance by Church Commissioners) Measure 1958, Vol 14, title Ecclesiastical Law (Pt 5).

As to the designation of new county and voluntary schools as primary schools, see the Education Act 1964, s 1(2), this part of this title post.

Applications for the registration of independent schools. For the provisions relating to such applications, see ss 70–75 ante.

Registered pupil. As to the registration of pupils at schools, see s 80 ante.

Register of independent schools. See s 70 ante.

School. New school buildings must contain means of access and facilities suitable for disabled persons using the buildings; see the Chronically Sick and Disabled Persons Act 1970, s 8, this part of this title post. Such buildings are excluded from the provisions of s 4 of that Act, Vol 35, title Public Health by s 4(2) thereof.

Registration under the Registered Homes Act 1984, Pt I, Vol 35, title Public Health, is not required in respect of any school, as defined in this section; however an independent school which provides accommodation for 50 or less children under the age of 18 which is not for the time being approved by the Secretary of State under the Education Act 1981, s 11(3)(*a*), this part of this title post, is not excluded; see s 1(5)(*f*), (6) of the 1984 Act.

A school within the meaning of this section is not a children's home for the purposes of the Children's Homes Act 1982 unless it is an independent school within the meaning of this Act providing accommodation for 50 children or less which is not for the time being approved by the Secretary of State under s 11(3)(*a*) of the 1981 Act; see the Children's Homes Act 1982, s 1(2)(*f*), (3), as from a date to be appointed under s 16(2) of that Act, Vol 6, title Children.

Secondary school. As to the financial assistance for secondary schools which are Church of England aided schools or Church of England special agreement schools, see the Church Schools (Assistance by Church Commissioners) Measure 1958, Vol 14, title Ecclesiastical Law (Pt 5).

It should be noted that the words "subject to subsection (3) of this section" now have no effect as sub-s (3) was repealed by the Education Act 1980.

Significant ... change or enlargement. Any question as to whether a change in the character of a school or enlargement of the school premises would be a significant change or enlargement is determinable by the Secretary of State for Education and Science; see s 67(4) ante and the notes thereto.

Instrument of government. See ss 17–19 ante.

Articles of government. As to the making of such articles, see s 17(3) ante.

Young person. As to a young person attaining the age of eighteen during term, see the Education Act 1946, s 8(3) and the Education Act 1962, s 9, both this part of this title post.

Sub-s (2): Maintain. As to the duties of a local education authority in relation to the maintenance of primary and secondary schools, including county schools, nursery schools, special schools and voluntary schools, see ss 9, 15 ante; as to the maintenance of voluntary schools, see the Education Act 1946, s 3, Sch 1, this part of this title post; and as regards the maintenance of county colleges, see s 43 ante. The expenses of maintaining a voluntary school include the payment of rates; see the Rating and Valuation Act 1961, s 12(6), Vol 36, title Rating. As to the execution of work for the purposes of controlled schools by a local education authority, see the Education Act 1946, s 6, this part of this title post.

An aided school or special agreement school. As to the classification of voluntary schools as controlled, aided and special agreement schools, see s 15 ante.

Assisted. Power to assist a school not maintained by the local education authority is given by s 9(1) ante.

Sub-s (7): Date of the commencement of Part II. Pt II (ss 6–69) came into force on 1 April 1945 by virtue of s 119 (repealed).

Local Government Act 1933. Repealed by the Local Government Act 1972, s 272(1), Sch 30, and replaced by provisions of that Act, Vol 25, title Local Government. Sch 29, para 1(2) to the 1972 Act provides that any reference to any local authority within the meaning of the 1933 Act is now to be construed as a reference to a local authority within the meaning of the 1972 Act. "Local government election" is now defined in s 270 of the 1972 Act.

Education Act 1981. See this part of this title post.

115 Saving as to persons in the service of the Crown

No power or duty conferred or imposed by this Act on [the Secretary of State], on local education authorities, or on parents, shall be construed as relating to any person who is employed by or under the Crown in any service or capacity with respect to which [the Secretary of State] certifies that, by reason of the arrangements made for the education of children and young persons employed therein, the exercise and performance of those powers and duties with respect to such children and young persons is unnecessary.

NOTES

The words in square brackets are substituted by virtue of the Secretary of State for Education and Science Order 1964, SI 1964/490, art 3(2)(a).

Secretary of State. See the note "Secretary of State for Education and Science" to s 1 ante.

Definitions. For "child", "parent" and "young person", see s 114(1) ante; for "local education authority", see s 114(1) ante and the note thereto.

116 Saving as to persons of unsound mind and persons detained by order of a court

No power or duty conferred or imposed by this Act on [the Secretary of State], on local education authorities, or on parents, shall be construed as relating … to any person who is detained in pursuance of an order made by any court [or of an order of recall made by the Prison Commissioners, but a local education authority shall have power to make arrangements for a person who is detained in pursuance of an order made by a court, or of such an order of recall, to receive the benefit of educational facilities provided by the authority.

Where a child or young person is being educated as a boarder at a school, the fact that he is required to be at the school by virtue of an order made by a court under the Children and Young Persons Act 1933, or by virtue of anything done under such an order, or by virtue of a requirement of a probation order or by virtue of anything done under such a requirement, shall not render him a person detained in pursuance of an order made by a court within the meaning of those words in this section].

NOTES

The words "Secretary of State" in square brackets are substituted by virtue of the Secretary of State for Education and Science Order 1964, SI 1964/490, art 3(2)(*a*).

The words omitted were repealed by the Education (Handicapped Children) Act 1970, s 2, Schedule.

The words in the second pair of square brackets were substituted by the Education (Miscellaneous Provisions) Act 1948, s 11, Sch 1, Pt I.

Secretary of State. See the note "Secretary of State for Education and Science" to s 1 ante.

Order of recall made by the Prison Commissioners. The Prison Commissioners were dissolved by the Prison Commissioners Dissolution Order 1963, SI 1963/597, art 2(1). The power to recall any person who is subject to a licence is now vested in the Secretary of State for the Home Department; see the Criminal Justice Act 1967, s 62 and the notes thereto, Vol 34, title Prisons.

Probation order. See, generally, as to probation orders, 11 Halsbury's Laws (4th edn) paras 526–538.

Definitions. For "child", "parent" and "young person", see s 114(1) ante; for "local education authority", see s 114(1) ante and the note thereto.

Children and Young Persons Act 1933. See Vol 6, title Children.

---

117 (*Repealed by the London Government Act 1963, s 93(1), Sch 18, Pt II.*)

118 Application to Isles of Scilly

[The Secretary of State] shall by order provide for the application of this Act to the Isles of Scilly as if those isles were [a separate non-metropolitan county], and any such order may provide for the application of this Act to those isles subject to such modifications as may be specified in the order.

NOTES

The words in the first pair of square brackets are substituted by virtue of the Secretary of State for Education and Science Order 1964, SI 1964/490, art 3(2)(*a*).

The words in the second pair of square brackets were substituted by the Local Authorities etc (Miscellaneous Provisions) Order 1977, SI 1977/293, art 4(1).

Secretary of State. See the note "Secretary of State for Education and Science" to s 1 ante.

Order under this section. The Isles of Scilly (Local Education Authority) Order 1945, SR & O 1945/360, as amended by SI 1977/293, applies this Act, except s 88 ante and Sch 1, Pt III (repealed) to the Isles of Scilly.

---

119 (*Repealed by the Education Act 1973, s 1(4), Sch 2, Pt I.*)

120 Amendment of enactments

(1) On and after the date of the commencement of Part II of this Act any enactment passed before that date shall, unless the context otherwise requires, be construed as if:—

(*a*) for references therein to an elementary school or to a public elementary school (whether or not any reference is made therein to the payment of parliamentary grants in respect of the school) there were substituted references to a county school or voluntary school as the context may require;

(*b*) for references therein to a school certified by the Board of Education, in accordance with the provisions of Part V of the Education Act 1921, as suitable for providing education for blind deaf defective or epileptic children, there were substituted references to a special school;

(*c*) for references therein to the managers of a school there were substituted, in relation to a county ... school or a voluntary ... school, references to the governors of the school;

(*d*) for references therein to elementary education or to higher education there were substituted references to such education as may be provided by a local education authority in the exercise of their functions under Part II of this Act;

(*e*) for references therein to a local education authority, to a local education authority for elementary education, or to a local education authority for higher education, there were substituted references to a local education authority within the meaning of this Act.

(2) ...

(3) The enactments mentioned in the first column of the Eighth Schedule to this Act shall, except in so far as any of them extend to Scotland, have effect subject to the amendments specified in the second column of that Schedule:

Provided that Part I of the said Schedule shall come into operation on the date of the commencement of Part II of this Act ...

(4) Where by virtue of this Act any functions cease to be exercisable by the council of a county district under the Children and Young Persons Acts 1933 and 1938, the following provisions of this Act, that is to say:—

(*a*) subsections (3) and (4) of section six; and
(*b*) section ninety-seven;

shall have effect as if those functions had been exercisable under the Education Acts 1921 and 1939; and, in relation to any such functions, the provisions of section ninety-six and of subsection (3) of section ninety-eight of this Act shall have effect as if for the references therein to the Minister of Education there were substituted references to the Secretary of State.

(5) For the purposes of any byelaws under Part II of the Children and Young Persons Act 1933, the expression "child" shall have the same meaning as it has for the purposes of the said Part II; and any byelaws made by the council of a county district under the said Part II which are in force immediately before the date of the commencement of Part II of this Act shall, in relation to the area to which they extend, continue in operation on and after that date as if they had been made by the local education authority for the area in which the county district is situated, and may be varied or revoked accordingly.

NOTES

The words omitted from sub-s (1)(*c*) were repealed by the Education Act 1980, s 1(3), Sch 1, para 14.

Sub-s (2) and the words omitted from sub-s (3) were repealed by the SL(R) Act 1978.

Date of commencement of Part II of this Act. The date of the commencement of Pt II (ss 6–69) was 1 April 1945 by virtue of s 119 (repealed).

Definitions. For "county school" and "voluntary school", see s 9(2) ante; for "special school", see s 9(5) ante; for "governors of secondary schools", see s 19 ante; for "young person", see s 114(1) ante; and for "local education authority", see s 114(1) ante and the note thereto.

Education Act 1921, Part V. Repealed by s 121, Sch 9 post.

Children and Young Persons Acts 1933 and 1938. For the Children and Young Persons Act 1933, see Vol 6, title Children. As to byelaws under Pt II of that Act, see ss 18, 21, 27 and 29 thereof and the notes thereto. The Children and Young Persons Act 1938 was repealed by the Children and Young Persons Act 1969, s 72(4), Sch 6.

---

121 Repeal of enactments

... any regulation Order in Council order or other instrument in force under any enactment hereby repealed shall continue in operation and have effect as if made under this Act and may be varied or revoked accordingly ...

NOTE

The words omitted were repealed by the Education Act 1973, s 1(4), Sch 2, Pt I.

---

122 Short title and extent

(1) This Act may be cited as the Education Act 1944.

(2) This Act shall not extend to Scotland or to Northern Ireland.

SCHEDULES

FIRST SCHEDULE

Section 6

Local Administration

Part I

Joint Education Boards

1. Where it appears to [the Secretary of State] that the establishment of a joint board as the local education authority for the areas of two or more councils to whom this Part of this Schedule applies would tend to diminish expense, or to increase efficiency or would otherwise be of public advantage, [the Secretary of State] may by order constitute a joint board (in this Act referred to as a "joint education board"), consisting of members appointed by those councils, and direct that the board shall be the local education authority for the areas of those councils:

Provided that [the Secretary of State] shall not make such an order except after a local inquiry, unless all the councils for the areas of which the board are to be the local education authority have consented to the making of the order.

2. A joint education board so constituted shall be a body corporate with perpetual succession and a common seal ...

3. An order constituting a joint education board:—

   (a) may ... provide for regulating the appointment and term of office of members of the board, for regulating the meetings and proceedings of the board, and for determining the manner in which the expenses of the board are to be defrayed;

   (b) may contain such other provisions (including provision for the transfer of officers, property, and liabilities, and for the adjustment of accounts and apportionment of liabilities) as appear to [the Secretary of State] to be expedient for enabling the board to exercise their functions;

   (c) may provide for securing that where in consequence of the establishment of the board as the local education authority for the area of any council any person who was an officer of that council immediately before the date on which the board became the local education authority for the area thereof suffers direct pecuniary loss by reason of the determination of his appointment or the diminution of his emoluments, he shall, unless provision for his compensation for that loss is made by or under any other enactment for the time being in force, be entitled to receive compensation therefor from the board, and for securing that the provisions of subsections (2) and (3) of section one hundred and fifty of the Local Government Act, 1933, and of the Fourth Schedule to that Act shall have effect for the purposes of any claim for such compensation and for the purposes of the determination and payment of the compensation, subject to such modifications and adaptations as appear to [the Secretary of State] to be necessary; and

   (d) may, with the consent of the council of any county or county borough for the area for which the board is to be the local education authority, provide for the transfer to the board of any functions exercisable by that council under the Children and Young Persons Acts 1933 and 1938, otherwise than as a local education authority.

4. An order constituting a joint education board shall be laid before Parliament as soon as may be after it is made.

5. This Part of this Schedule applies to the council of any county, to the council of any county borough, and to the council of any other borough of which the population was not less than half of the population of the county in which the borough is situated, according to the last census before the passing of this Act.

NOTES

The words "the Secretary of State" in square brackets in paras 1, 3 are substituted by virtue of the Secretary of State for Education and Science Order 1964, SI 1964/490, art 3(2)(*a*).

The words omitted from para 2 were repealed by the Charities Act 1960, s 48(2), Sch 7, Pt II.

The words omitted from para 3(*a*) were repealed by the Education Act 1980, s 38(6), Sch 7.

Secretary of State. See the note "Secretary of State for Education and Science" to s 1 ante.

Constitute a joint education board. A joint education board constituted under this Part of this Schedule is an authority to whom the Town and Country Planning Act 1959, Pt II, Vol 25, title Local Government applies, see s 22(4) of, and Sch 4, Pt I, para 4 to, the 1959 Act.

Local inquiry. As to the power of the Secretary of State to direct local inquiries, see s 93 ante.

County. The counties existing immediately before 1 April 1974 were abolished on that date by the Local Government Act 1972, ss 1(10), 20(6), Vol 25, title Local Government, and by virtue of s 179(1), (2) of that Act, the reference to a county is to be construed as a county established by ss 1(1), (2), 20(1), (2) of, and Sch 1, Pts I, II, Sch 4, Pt I to, the 1972 Act.

County borough. The boroughs, other than London boroughs, existing immediately before 1 April 1974 were abolished on that date by the Local Government Act 1972, ss 1(9), (10), 20(6), Vol 25, title Local Government, and the reference to a county borough no longer has any effect.

Laid before Parliament after being made. As to statutory instruments which are required to be laid before Parliament after being made, see the Statutory Instruments Act 1946, s 4(1), (2), and see also the Laying of Documents before Parliament (Interpretation) Act 1948, both Vol 41, title Statutes.

Local Government Act 1933, s 150(2), (3), Sch 4. The 1933 Act was repealed by the Local Government Act 1972, s 272(1), Sch 30. For provisions relating to compensation for loss of office, see now s 259 of the 1972 Act, Vol 25, title Local Government.

Children and Young Persons Acts 1933 and 1938. See the note to s 120 ante.

Orders constituting joint education boards. Orders under this Part, being local, are not noted in this work. For revocation and variation of orders, see s 111 ante.

Part II

Education Committees

1. Every local education authority shall, in accordance with arrangements approved by [the Secretary of State], establish such education committees as they think it expedient to establish for the efficient discharge of their functions with respect to education.

2. . . .

3. Where it appears to [the Secretary of State] to be expedient that two or more local education authorities should combine for the purpose of exercising some but not all of their functions with respect to education and that those authorities should establish a joint committee for that purpose, [the Secretary of State] may after consultation with the authorities by order establish a joint education committee of those authorities and provide for the reference to the committee of such questions relating to those functions as in the opinion of [the Secretary of State] should be so referred; and any such order may provide for authorising the joint education committee to exercise any of those functions on behalf of the authorities concerned, and may include such incidental and consequential provisions, including provisions with respect to the appointment and functions of sub-committees, as [the Secretary of State] thinks desirable.

4. In the following provisions of this Part of this Schedule the expression "education committee" includes a joint education committee.

5. Every education committee of a local education authority shall include persons of experience in education and persons acquainted with the educational conditions prevailing in the area for which the committee acts.

6. At least a majority of every education committee of a local education authority shall be members of the authority:

Provided that in the case of a joint education committee, the provisions of this paragraph shall be deemed to have been complied with if the committee consists, as to more than one half of the members thereof, of persons who are members of any of the authorities for which the committee is established.

7. Every local education authority shall consider a report from an education committee of the authority before exercising any of their functions with respect to education:

Provided that an authority may dispense with such a report if, in their opinion, the matter is urgent . . .

8. A local education authority may authorise an education committee of the authority to exercise on their behalf any of their functions with respect to education, except the power to borrow money or to raise a rate.

9. The minutes of proceedings of an education committee of the local education authority shall be open to the inspection of any local government elector for the area on payment of a fee not exceeding [5p] and any such local government elector may make a copy thereof or an extract therefrom.

10. Every education committee of a local education authority may, subject to any restrictions imposed by the local education authority or the order of [the Secretary of State] by which the committee was established:—

(a) appoint such sub-committees constituted in such manner as the committee may determine; and

(b) authorise any such sub-committees to exercise any of the functions of the committee on their behalf.

11. Nothing in this Part of this Schedule shall require the reference to any education committee of a local education authority, or to any sub-committee of such a committee, of any matter which under any enactment for the time being in force is referred to any committee of the authority other than an education committee.

NOTES

The words in square brackets in paras 1, 3, 10 are substituted by virtue of the Secretary of State for Education and Science Order 1964, SI 1964/490, art 3(2)(a).

Para 2, and the words omitted from para 7, were repealed by the Local Government Act 1972, s 272(1), Sch 30.

The figure in square brackets in para 9 is substituted by virtue of the Decimal Currency Act 1969, s 10(1), Vol 10, title Constitutional Law (Pt 3).

General Note. Joint education committees established under para 2 or 3 above, the members of which are not all representatives of local authorities, are included among the bodies the members of which are entitled, under the Local Government Act 1972, ss 173–178, Vol 25, title Local Government, to financial loss, travelling and subsistence allowances; see the Local Government (Allowances to Members) (Prescribed Bodies) Regulations 1967, SI 1967/1875 (amended by SI 1970/1109) which continue in force by virtue of the Local Authorities etc (Miscellaneous Provision) Order 1974, SI 1974/482.

Secretary of State. Ie the Secretary of State for Education and Science; see the note to s 1 ante. In connection with primary and secondary education in matters only affecting Wales, the power to make orders under para 3 was transferred to the Secretary of State for Wales by the Transfer of Functions (Wales) Order 1970, SI 1970/1536, arts 2(1), 3(1)(a).

Report from an education committee. An education committee may not delegate to its chairman the decision as to what recommendation to make to the full council; see *R v Liverpool City Council, ex p Professional Association of Teachers* 82 LGR 648. See also the discussion in that case of what constitutes a report.

Inspection of minutes. Para 9 applies to education committees the obligation imposed regarding local authorities in general by the Local Government Act 1972, s 228, Vol 25, title Local Government. As to what may be inspected, see *Williams v Manchester Corpn* (1897) 45 WR 412, 13 TLR 299. As to the extent of the right to inspect minutes, see *Stevens v Berwick-upon-Tweed Corpn* (1835) 4 Dowl 277; *R v Wimbledon UDC, ex p Hatton* (1897) 77 LT 599, 62 JP 84; *R v Bradford-on-Avon RDC, ex p Thornton* (1908) 99 LT 89, 72 JP 348; and *R v Godstone RC* [1911] 2 KB 465, 80 LJKB 1184. As to the production of the minute book in the absence of the clerk, see *R v Andover RDC, ex p Thornhill* (1913) 77 JP 296, 29 TLR 419.

Delegation of functions. As to the revocation of delegated powers and the exercise of such powers without revoking the delegation, see *Huth v Clarke* (1890) 25 QBD 391, [1886–90] All ER Rep 542. As to the ratification by a local authority of powers exercised without express delegation, see *Firth v Staines* [1897] 2 QB 70, 66 LJQB 510; *Hussey v Exeter Corpn* (1918) 87 LJ Ch 443, 118 LT 13; and *R v Chapman, ex p Arlidge* [1918] 2 KB 298, 87 LJKB 1142. As to the extent of the power of delegation, see *Young v Cuthbert* [1906] 1 Ch 451, 75 LJ Ch 217; and *Richardson v Abertillery UDC, Thomas v Abertillery UDC* (1928) 138 LT 688, 92 JP 59.

Accounts of joint education committees. For provisions relating to the auditing of accounts, see the Local Government Finance Act 1982, s 12(1)(c), Vol 25, title Local Government and the Accounts and Audit Regulations 1983, SI 1983/1761.

Orders establishing joint education committees. Orders under this Part, being local, are not printed in this work. For revocation and variation of orders, see s 111 ante.

(*Pt III repealed by the Local Government Act 1972, s 272(1), Sch 30.*)

SECOND SCHEDULE
Section 13
TRANSFER TO A LOCAL EDUCATION AUTHORITY OF AN INTEREST IN THE PREMISES OF A VOLUNTARY SCHOOL

1. A local education authority and the ... governors of any voluntary school maintained by the authority may, subject to and in accordance with the provisions of this Schedule, make an agreement for the transfer to the authority of any interest in the school premises held by any persons for the purposes of any trust deed relating to the school.

2. No such agreement shall take effect unless it has been approved by [the Secretary of State].

3. [The Secretary of State] shall not approve any such agreement unless he is satisfied—

   (a) that due notice of the agreement has been given to any persons other than the ... governors of the school who, by virtue of any trust deed relating to the school, have an interest therein and to any other persons who appear to [the Secretary of State] to be concerned; and

   (b) that the execution of the agreement will effect the transfer of all interests necessary for the purpose of enabling the authority to maintain the school as a county school.

4. Before approving any such agreement, [the Secretary of State] shall consider any representations made to him by or on behalf of any persons appearing to [the Secretary of State] to be concerned with the proposed transfer.

5. An agreement under this Schedule may provide for the transfer to the authority, subject to such conditions, reservations and restrictions, if any, as may be specified in the agreement, of the whole of the interest in the premises held by any persons for the purposes of any trust deed relating to the school, or of any less interest in the premises, and may include such other provisions, whether relating to the consideration for the said transfer or otherwise, as may be agreed upon between the authority and the ... governors of the school.

6. Where any agreement made under this Schedule has been approved by [the Secretary of State], the ... governors of the school may, whether or not the interest to be transferred to the authority by virtue of the agreement is vested in them, convey that interest to the authority.

7. Where any person other than the ... governors of the school has a right to the occupation or use of the school premises or any part thereof for any particular purpose, no provision of any agreement made under this Schedule shall affect that right unless he has consented thereto.

8. In this Schedule, the expression "premises" includes a teacher's dwelling-house.

NOTES

The words omitted were repealed by the Education Act 1980, s 1(3), Sch 1, para 1.

The words in square brackets are substituted by virtue of the Secretary of State for Education and Science Order 1964, SI 1964/490, art 3(2)(a).

General Note. There were a number of cases decided upon the construction of or otherwise relating to the provisions replaced by this Schedule or earlier equivalent provisions which may still have some relevance; see, for example, *Re Burnham National Schools* (1873) LR 17 Eq 241, 43 LJ Ch 340; *London School Board v Faulconer* (1878) 8 Ch D 571, 48 LJ Ch 41; *National Society v London School Board, A-G v English* (1874) LR 18 Eq 608, 44 LJ Ch 229; and *Llanbadarnfawr School Board v Charitable Funds (Official Trustee)* [1901] 1 KB 430, 70 LJKB 307.

Agreement for the transfer. Where an aided or special agreement school has an instrument made after 1 July 1981, any decision to make an agreement under this Schedule is subject to the provisions of the Education Act 1980, s 4(4), (5)(e) post.

Secretary of State. See the note "Secretary of State for Education and Science" to s 1 ante.

Satisfied. Statutory powers are often conferred in subjective terms, the competent authority being entitled to act, eg, when it is "satisfied" or it "appears" to it that, or when in its "opinion", a prescribed state of affairs exists, but the inherent jurisdiction of the courts to determine whether such powers have been exceeded is not readily ousted by the use of such language; see, further, 1 Halsbury's Laws (4th edn), para 22.

Notice. As to the service of notices, see s 113 ante.

A right to the occupation or use. See s 22 ante.

Definitions. For "maintain", "premises" and "trust deed", see s 114(1) ante; for "local education authority", see s 114(1) ante and the note thereto; and for "voluntary school", see s 9(2) ante. Note the extension of "premises" in para 8 of this Schedule.

THIRD SCHEDULE

Section 15

SPECIAL AGREEMENTS IN RESPECT OF CERTAIN VOLUNTARY SCHOOLS

1. Where proposals for the establishment of a school or for the alteration of the premises of a school have been submitted to a former authority, within the time limited by subsection (2) of section eight of the Education Act 1936, with a view to the making of an agreement under that section, but the said proposals have not been carried out before the date of the commencement of Part II of this Act, a local education authority shall have power to make an agreement in accordance with the provisions of this Schedule in respect of those proposals or in respect of any revised proposals submitted to the authority in accordance with those provisions:

Provided that no such agreement shall have effect unless it is approved by [the Secretary of State], and no such agreement shall be made or approved unless the authority and [the Secretary of State] are satisfied that the performance thereof will facilitate the execution of provisions relating to school accommodation for senior pupils contained or proposed to be contained in the development plan for the area.

2. If upon the application of any persons interested in any such proposals [the Secretary of State] is satisfied that by reason of the passing of this Act or the making of any regulations thereunder, or by reason of movement of population or of any action taken or proposed to be taken under the enactments relating to housing or to town and country planning, or by reason of war damage, it is desirable that the proposals should be revised, [the Secretary of State] may give directions authorising a local education authority, in lieu of making an agreement in accordance with the provisions of this Schedule with respect to those proposals, to make such an agreement with respect to any revised proposals submitted to the authority before the expiration of such period as may be specified in the directions, being proposals which appear to the authority to serve substantially the same purpose as the proposals originally submitted.

3. ...

4. Any such agreement shall provide for the making of a grant by the local education authority to persons specified in the agreement in consideration of the execution by those persons of the proposals to which the agreement relates.

5. The amount of the grant to be made in pursuance of any such agreement shall not be less than one half or more than three quarters of the cost of executing the proposals to which the agreement relates.

[Provided that, where the proposals include proposals for establishing a playing field or any buildings of a kind which it is, under [section 13(6) of the Education Act 1980], the duty of the local education authority to provide,—

(a) if the proposals as respects the playing field or buildings are to be executed by the persons specified in the agreement, the amount of the grant so far as attributable to the cost thereof, shall be equal to the whole of that cost; and

(b) if the proposals as respects the playing field or buildings are to be executed by the local education authority, the cost thereof shall be borne by them and excluded in computing the amount of the grant.]

6. Where the agreement relates to proposals for the establishment of a school submitted to the local education authority for the County Borough of Liverpool, the authority may, if the agreement so provides, discharge their liabilities under the agreement by providing premises for the school and executing a lease of those premises to such persons as may be specified in the agreement for the purpose of enabling a voluntary school to be conducted thereon.

Any such lease shall provide for the reservation of a yearly rent of an amount not less than one nor more than two per cent of the cost incurred by the authority in providing the premises for the school.

7. Any agreement made under this Schedule may provide for the giving of religious instruction in the school in accordance with the provisions of the trust deed relating to the school, or, where provision for that purpose is not made by such a deed, in accordance with the practice observed in the school before it became a voluntary school, and for the employment in the school, for the purpose of giving such religious instruction, of such number of reserved teachers as may be specified in the agreement.

8. Any agreement made by a local education authority under this Schedule may be varied by a further agreement between the authority and the ... governors of the school to which the agreement relates, or in such other manner, if any, as may be specified in the agreement.

9. Where a grant has been made in respect of any school in pursuance of an agreement made under this Schedule, the ... governors of the school may, at any time while the school is a special agreement school, repay the grant to the local education authority by which the school is maintained.

10. Where an agreement has been made under this Schedule in relation to any school, then, until the proposals to which the agreement relates have been carried out, the provisions of this Act relating to the respective obligations of the ... governors of voluntary schools and the local education authority in respect of repairs and alterations to the premises of the school shall not have effect in relation to that school, but the respective obligations of the ... governors of the school and the local education authority in relation to those matters shall be such as may be determined by agreement between the ... governors and the authority, or in default of such agreement, by [the Secretary of State].

11. Where any local authority have, before the date of the commencement of Part II of this Act, made an agreement under the powers conferred by section eight of the Education Act 1936, with respect to proposals submitted to the authority within the time limited by subsection (2) of that section, then:—

> (a) if the said proposals have been carried out before that date the agreement shall be deemed to have been made under this Schedule, and the provisions of this Act relating to special agreements shall have effect accordingly;
>
> (b) if the said proposals have not been carried out before that date, the agreement shall cease to have effect, but without prejudice to the making of a further agreement under this Schedule with respect to those proposals or with respect to any revised proposals submitted to the authority in accordance with the provisions of this Schedule.

NOTES

The words "the Secretary of State" wherever they occur in square brackets are substituted by virtue of the Secretary of State for Education and Science Order 1964, SI 1964/490, art 3(2)(a).

Para 3 and the words omitted from paras 8–10 were repealed by the Education Act 1980, ss 1(3), 38(6), Sch 1, para 1, Sch 7.

The proviso to para 5 was added by the Education (Miscellaneous Provisions) Act 1948, s 11, Sch 1, Pt I, and the words in square brackets in that proviso were substituted by the Education Act 1980, s 16(4), Sch 3, para 5.

Date of commencement of Part II of this Act. By virtue of s 119 (repealed), the date of the commencement of Pt II (ss 6–69) of this Act was 1 April 1945.

Secretary of State. See the note "Secretary of State for Education and Science" to s 1 ante.

Satisfied. See the note to Sch 2 ante.

Development plan. By virtue of s 11 (repealed) each local education authority was required to prepare and submit to the Secretary of State a plan relating to the development of primary and secondary education in that area.

Directions. As to the revocation or variation of such directions, see s 111 ante.

County Borough of Liverpool. This is now a district in the metropolitan county of Merseyside; see the Local Government Act 1972, s 1, Sch 1, Pt I, Vol 25, title Local Government.

Religious instruction. Special provision is made in s 28 ante with regard to religious education in special agreement schools. See also the Education Act 1946, s 7, this part of this title post, which permits the collective worship of pupils in special agreement schools to take place elsewhere than on the school premises on special occasions.

Reserved teachers. See s 28(3) ante.

The provisions of this Act. The reference is to s 15(3) ante.

Definitions. For "alteration", "former authority", "premises", "senior pupils" and "trust deed", see s 114(1) ante; for "local education authority", see s 114(1) ante and the note thereto; and for "voluntary school", see s 9(2) ante.

Education Act 1936, s 8. Repealed by s 121 ante and Sch 9, Pt I (repealed) to this Act.

Education Act 1980, s 13(6). See this part of this title post.

(Sch 4 repealed by the Education Act 1980, s 38(6), Sch 7.)

FIFTH SCHEDULE

Section 29

PROCEDURE FOR PREPARING AND BRINGING INTO OPERATION AN AGREED SYLLABUS OF RELIGIOUS INSTRUCTION

1. For the purpose of preparing any syllabus of religious instruction to be adopted by a local education authority, the authority shall cause to be convened a conference constituted in accordance with the provisions of this Schedule.

2. For the purpose of constituting such a conference as aforesaid, the local education authority shall appoint constituent bodies (hereinafter referred to as "committees") consisting of persons representing respectively—

(a) such religious denominations as, in the opinion of the authority, ought, having regard to the circumstances of the area, to be represented;

(b) except in the case of an area in Wales or Monmouthshire, the Church of England;

(c) such associations representing teachers as, in the opinion of the authority, ought, having regard to the circumstances of the area, to be represented; and

(d) the authority:

Provided that where a committee is appointed consisting of persons representing the Church of England, the committee of persons appointed to represent other religious denominations shall not include persons appointed to represent that Church.

3. Before appointing a person to represent any denomination or associations as a member of any such committee, a local education authority shall take all reasonable steps to assure themselves that he is representative thereof, but no proceedings under this Schedule shall be invalidated on the ground that a member of such a committee did not represent the denomination or associations which he was appointed to represent unless it is shown that the local education authority failed to take such steps as aforesaid.

4. A person so appointed may resign his membership of any such committee or may be withdrawn therefrom by the local education authority if in the opinion of the authority he ceases to be representative of the religious denomination or associations which he was appointed to represent, or of the authority, as the case may be; and where a vacancy occurs among the persons so appointed the authority shall fill the vacancy in like manner as they made the original appointment.

5. The conference shall consist of the committees aforesaid and it shall be the duty of the conference to seek unanimous agreement upon a syllabus of religious instruction to be recommended for adoption by the local education authority.

6. Where the local education authority propose to adopt more than one syllabus of religious instruction for use in schools maintained by them, the authority shall inform the conference as to the schools in which, or in the case of a syllabus intended to be used for certain pupils only, the class or description of pupils for which, the syllabus to be prepared by the conference is to be used.

7. Any sub-committees appointed by the conference shall include at least one member of each of the committees constituting the conference.

8. Upon any question to be decided by the conference or by any sub-committee thereof one vote only shall be given for each of the committees constituting the conference.

9. If the conference unanimously recommend any syllabus of religious instruction, the authority may adopt it for use in the schools for which, or for the class or description of pupils for which, it was prepared.

10. If the authority report to [the Secretary of State] that the conference are unable to reach unanimous agreement as aforesaid, or if it appears to [the Secretary of State] that an authority have failed to adopt any syllabus unanimously recommended to them by the conference, [the Secretary of State] shall appoint to prepare a syllabus of religious instruction a body of persons having experience in religious instruction which shall, so far as is practicable, be of the like representative character as is required by paragraph 2 of this Schedule in the case of a conference.

11. The body of persons so appointed:—

(a) shall give to the authority, the conference, and every committee constituting the conference, an opportunity of making representations to it, but, save as aforesaid, may conduct the proceedings in such manner as it thinks fit;

(b) shall, after considering any such representations made to it, prepare a syllabus of religious instruction;

(c) shall transmit a copy of the said syllabus to the authority and to [the Secretary of State],

and as from such date as [the Secretary of State] may direct, the syllabus so prepared shall be deemed to be the agreed syllabus adopted for use in the schools for which, or for the class or description of pupils for which, it was prepared until a further syllabus is prepared for use in those schools, or for pupils of that class or description, in accordance with the provisions of this Schedule.

12. Whenever a local education authority are of opinion (whether upon representations made to them or otherwise) that any agreed syllabus for the time being adopted by them ought to be reconsidered, the authority shall cause to be convened for that purpose a conference constituted in accordance with the provisions of this Schedule. If the conference convened for the reconsideration of any syllabus unanimously recommend that the existing syllabus should continue to be the agreed syllabus or that a new syllabus should be adopted in substitution therefor, the authority may give effect to the recommendation of the conference, but if the authority report to [the Secretary of State] that the conference are unable to reach unanimous agreement, or if it appears to [the Secretary of State] that the authority have failed to give effect to the unanimous recommendation of the conference, [the Secretary of State] shall proceed in accordance with the provisions of paragraph 10 of this Schedule, and paragraph 11 thereof shall apply accordingly.

NOTES

The words in square brackets are substituted by the Secretary of State for Education and Science Order 1964, SI 1964/490, art 3(2)(a).

Agreed syllabus. For the provisions relating to the giving of religious instruction in county schools and voluntary schools in accordance with an agreed syllabus, see ss 26–28 ante.

The authority shall. The obligations imposed in para 1 of this Schedule and in later paragraphs thereof may be enforced by the Secretary of State under s 99 ante. The Secretary of State may also take steps under s 68 ante, to prevent the unreasonable exercise by a local education authority of any of its functions under this Act.

See also the note "Complaint by any person interested" to s 99 ante.

As the Secretary of State may direct. As to the revocation or variation of such a direction, see s 111 ante.

As to the exercise of the functions of the Secretary of State, see the note "Secretary of State for Education and Science" to s 1 ante.

Definitions. For "maintain" and "pupils", see s 114(1) ante; for "local education authority", see s 114(1) ante and the note thereto.

SIXTH SCHEDULE

Section 72

CONSTITUTION OF INDEPENDENT SCHOOLS TRIBUNALS

1. For the purpose of enabling Independent Schools Tribunals to be constituted as occasion may require there shall be appointed two panels, that is to say—

(a) a panel (hereinafter referred to as the "legal panel") appointed by the Lord Chancellor, of persons who will be available to act when required as chairman of any such tribunal; and

(b) a panel (hereinafter referred to as the "educational panel") appointed by the Lord President of the Council, of persons who will be available to act when required as members of any such tribunal.

2. No person shall be qualified to be appointed to the legal panel unless he possesses such legal qualifications as the Lord Chancellor considers suitable, and no person shall be qualified to be appointed to the educational panel unless he has had such experience in teaching or in the conduct management or administration of schools as the Lord President of the Council considers suitable.

An officer of any government department and a person employed by a local education authority otherwise than as a teacher shall be disqualified from being appointed to either of the said panels.

3. Any person appointed to be a member of either of the said panels shall hold office as such

subject to such conditions as to the period of his membership and otherwise as may be determined by the Lord Chancellor or the Lord President of the Council, as the case may be.

4. Where any appeal is required to be determined by an Independent Schools Tribunal the tribunal shall consist of a chairman being a member of the legal panel and two other members being members of the educational panel, and the chairman and other members of the tribunal shall be impartial persons appointed from those panels by the Lord Chancellor and the Lord President of the Council respectively.

NOTES

General Note. Independent Schools Tribunals constituted under this Schedule are under the direct supervision of the Council on Tribunals in accordance with the Tribunals and Inquiries Act 1971, Vol 10, title Constitutional Law (Pt 4).

Members of the Tribunal are disqualified for membership of the House of Commons by the House of Commons Disqualification Act 1975, s 1(1)(*f*), Sch 1, Pt III, Vol 32, title Parliament.

Local education authority. See s 114(1) ante and the note thereto.

Any appeal. This refers not only to appeals under s 72(1) ante, but also to appeals under s 74(2) ante against the refusal of the Secretary of State to remove disqualifications imposed under Pt III of this Act.

(Sch 7 repealed by the SL(R) Act 1975; Sch 8, Pt I repealed in part by the SL(R) Act 1978, the remainder amends the Children and Young Persons Act 1933, ss 10, 96, Vol 6, title Children; Pt II repealed by the 1978 Act; Sch 9 repealed by the Education Act 1973, s 1(4), Sch 2, Pt I.)

EDUCATION ACT 1946

(9 & 10 Geo 6 c 50)

ARRANGEMENT OF SECTIONS

An Act to amend and supplement the law relating to education, and to amend the law relating to the execution of the Public Libraries Acts 1892 to 1919   [22 May 1946]

Education Acts 1944 to 1985. This Act is one of the Acts which may be cited by this collective title; see the Introductory Note to the Education Act 1944, this part of this title ante.

Northern Ireland. This Act does not apply; see s 17(3) post.

1 Enlargement of controlled schools

[(1) If upon the application of a local education authority and the . . . governors of a controlled school maintained by the authority the Secretary of State is satisfied—

    (*a*) that there should be a significant enlargement of the school premises; and

(b) either—

 (i) that the enlargement is wholly or mainly required for the purpose of providing accommodation for pupils for whom accommodation would have been provided in some other voluntary school if that other school had not been discontinued or had not otherwise ceased to be available for the purpose; or

 (ii) that the enlargement is desirable for the better provision of primary or secondary education at the premises to be enlarged or for securing that there is available for the area of the authority a sufficiency of suitable primary or secondary schools or for both those reasons;

then, if proposals for carrying out the enlargement are thereafter approved under [section 13 of the Education Act 1980] (hereinafter referred to as "the principal Act"), the Secretary of State may by order direct that the expense of giving effect to those proposals shall be paid by the local education authority.]

(2) ...

NOTES

This section (which had been heavily amended before 1968) is printed as set out in the Education Act 1968, Sch 3, and subsequent amendments are described below.

The words omitted from sub-s (1) are repealed by virtue of the Education Act 1980, s 1(1), (2), (4) post.

The words in square brackets in sub-s (1) were substituted by the Education Act 1980, s 16(4), Sch 3, para 6 for the words "section 13 of the Education Act 1944"; notwithstanding the juxtaposition of the substituted words and the words "hereinafter referred to as 'the principal Act'", references in this Act to "the principal Act" should be taken as references to the Education Act 1944.

Significant enlargement of the premises. See the note "Significant change in the character" to the Education Act 1968, s 1, this part of this title post.

Definitions. By virtue of s 16(2) post, for "enlargement", "maintain", "premises", "pupils" and "significant", see the Education Act 1944, s 114(1) ante; for "local education authority", see s 114(1) of that Act and the note thereto; and for "voluntary school" and "controlled school", see ss 9(2), 15 of the 1944 Act this part of this title ante.

Education Act 1980, s 13. See this part of this title post.

Principal Act. This is a reference to the Education Act 1944, this part of this title ante, not this Act; see the third paragraph of the first note above.

Orders under this section. Orders under this section, being local, are not printed in this work. For revocation and variation of orders, see the Education Act 1944, s 111, this part of this title ante.

---

2 Division of a single school into two or more schools

(1) Where a county school, an aided school or a controlled school is organized in two or more separate departments, and proposals are submitted to [the Secretary of State]—

 (a) in the case of a county school by the local education authority; and
 (b) in the case of an aided school or a controlled school, by the ... governors of the school after consultation with the local education authority;

that the school should be divided into two or more separate schools, [the Secretary of State] may by order direct—

 (i) if the school is a county school, that the school shall be divided into two or more separate county schools; and
 (ii) if the school is an aided school or a controlled school, that the school shall be divided into two or more separate voluntary schools;

and when any such order comes into operation it shall become the duty of the local education authority to maintain each of the separate schools constituted by the order as a county school or as a voluntary school, as the case may be.

(2) The constitution of a separate school in pursuance of any such order shall not, for the purposes of [section 12 or 13 of the Education Act 1980,] be deemed to amount to the establishment of a new school.

(3) Where any such order is made upon proposals submitted by the ... governors of a controlled school, the order shall direct that each of the schools constituted in pursuance of the order shall be a controlled school.

(4) Where any such order is made upon proposals submitted by the ... governors of an aided school, the order shall direct that each of the schools constituted in pursuance of the order shall be an aided school:

Provided that if the ... governors of the original school have requested [the Secretary of State] to direct that all or any of the schools constituted in pursuance of the order shall be controlled schools, the order shall direct accordingly.

(5) Subsection (4) of section fifteen of the principal Act (which relates to the circumstances in which an order directing that a school is to be an aided school is to be revoked) shall have effect as if the references therein to an order by virtue of which a school is an aided school included references to a direction that a school shall be an aided school under this section.

(6) Where an order is made under this section upon proposals submitted by the ... governors of a voluntary school which is being conducted in accordance with the transitional provisions contained in section thirty-two of the principal Act, the provisions of that section shall continue to have effect with respect to each of the schools constituted in pursuance of the order until the question whether that school shall be a controlled school, an aided school or a special agreement school is determined by an order made under subsection (2) of section fifteen of the principal Act.

(7) Any order made under this section shall come into operation upon such date as may be specified in the order and may contain such incidental, consequential and supplemental provisions as appear to [the Secretary of State] to be expedient, and, without prejudice to the generality of the preceding provisions of this subsection, may in particular provide for defining the premises of each of the separate schools to be constituted in pursuance of the order.

(8) No order shall be made under this section for the division of any school with respect to which a special agreement is in force.

NOTES

The words "the Secretary of State" wherever they appear in square brackets are substituted by virtue of the Secretary of State for Education and Science Order 1964, SI 1964/490, art 3(2)(a).

The words omitted from sub-ss (1), (3), (4), and (6) were repealed by the Education Act 1980, s 1(3), Sch 1, para 15.

The words in square brackets in sub-s (2) were substituted by the Education Act 1980, s 16(4), Sch 3, para 7.

Single school; separate school. These terms are not defined. It appears from sub-s (7) that complete physical separation is not required to constitute separate schools.

Secretary of State. See the note "Secretary of State for Education and Science" to the Education Act 1944, s 1 ante.

Definitions. By virtue of s 16(2) post for "aided school", "controlled school", "special agreement school", see the Education Act 1944, s 15 this part of this title ante; for "county school", see s 9(2) of that Act; for "maintain", "premises", "school" and "special agreement", see s 114(1) thereof; and for "local education authority", see s 114(1) thereof and the note thereto. For "department", see s 16(1) post.

Education Act 1980, ss 12, 13. See this part of this title post.

Ss 15, 32 of the principal Act. The principal Act is the Education Act 1944; see the third paragraph of the first note to s 1 ante. For s 15, see this part of this title ante; s 32 was repealed by the Education Act 1980, s 38(6), Sch 7.

3 Maintenance of voluntary schools

(1) In relation to the maintenance of voluntary schools, the duties of local education authorities and of the ... governors of such schools shall be performed in accordance with the provisions of the First Schedule to this Act.

(2) This section and the said First Schedule shall be deemed to have come into operation on the first day of April, nineteen hundred and forty-five.

NOTES

The words omitted from sub-s (1) were repealed by the Education Act 1980, s 1(3), Sch 1, para 16.

1st April 1945. This was the date on which Pt II (ss 6–69) and Pt IV (ss 76–107) of the Education Act 1944, came into operation by virtue of s 119 (repealed) of that Act.

Local education authority. For meaning, see, by virtue of s 16(2) post, the Education Act 1944, s 114(1), this part of this title ante and the note thereto.

Definitions. By virtue of s 16(2) post, for "maintain", see the Education Act 1944, s 114(1), this part of this title ante; and for "voluntary school", see ss 9(2) and 15 of that Act.

4 Letting or hiring of school premises other than school buildings and definition of "school buildings"

(1) Any sum received after the passing of this Act by the ... governors or trustees of a voluntary school, so far as it is paid in respect of the letting or hiring of any part of the school premises other than school buildings, shall be paid over to the local education authority.

(2) In this Act the expression "school buildings", in relation to any school, means any building or part of a building forming part of the school premises, except that it does not include any building or part of a building required only—

    (a) as a caretaker's dwelling;

    (b) for use in connection with playing fields;

    (c) for affording facilities for enabling the [Secretary of State to carry out the functions conferred on him by [paragraph (a) of section 5(1) of the National Health Service Act 1977 and Schedule 1 to that Act]];

    (d) for affording facilities for providing milk, meals or other refreshment for pupils in attendance at the school;

and in the principal Act the said expression shall be deemed always to have had the meaning assigned to it by this section.

NOTES

The word omitted from sub-s (1) was repealed by the Education Act 1980, s 1(3), Sch 1, para 17.

In sub-s (2) the words in the outer pair of square brackets were substituted by the National Health Service Reorganisation Act 1973, ss 57, 58, Sch 4, para 9, and the words in the inner pair of square brackets were substituted by the National Health Service Act 1977, s 129, Sch 15, para 3.

General Note. In the case of a controlled school the local education authority is responsible for providing and maintaining the whole of the school premises; in the case of an aided or special agreement school, the authority is responsible for providing the site and buildings other than school buildings and for all maintenance expenses, other than those expressly imposed on the governors of the school (see the Education Act 1944, s 15 and the notes thereto, this part of this title ante).

Local education authority. For meaning, see, by virtue of s 16(2) post, the Education Act 1944, s 114(1), this part of this title ante and the note thereto.

Caretaker's dwelling. As to the appointment and dismissal of caretakers, see the Education Act 1944, s 22(4), this part of this title ante.

Playing fields. As to the duty to provide playing fields, see the Education Act 1944, s 53(1), this part of this title ante.

Provision of milk and meals. As to the power of local education authorities to provide milk, meals and other refreshment, see the Education Act 1980, s 22, this part of this title post.

Definitions. By virtue of s 16(2) post, for "premises", see the Education Act 1944, s 114(1), this part of this title ante; and for "voluntary school", see ss 9(2) and 15 of that Act.

National Health Service Act 1977, s 5(1), Sch 1. See Vol 30, title National Health Service.

Principal Act. Ie the Education Act 1944; see the third paragraph of the first note to s 1 ante.

5 (*Repealed by the SL(R) Act 1975.*)

6 Power of local education authorities to execute work for the purposes of controlled schools

Where a local education authority are liable to pay the expense of carrying out any building work, repair work or work of a similar character which is required for the purposes of a controlled school, that work shall, if the local authority so determine, be carried out by persons employed by the authority; and it shall be the duty of the ... governors of the school and of any trustees thereof to provide the authority and any such persons with all such facilities as they may reasonably require for the purpose of securing that any such work is properly executed.

NOTES

The words omitted were repealed by the Education Act 1980, s 1(3), Sch 1, para 15.

General Note. As to a local education authority's obligations to carry out work for the purposes of a controlled school, see the Education Act 1944, ss 9, 15(3), 114(2), this part of this title ante, and Sch 1 post.

Definitions. By virtue of s 16(2) post, for "controlled school", see the Education Act 1944, s 15, this part of this title ante; and for "local education authority", see s 114(1) of that Act and the note thereto.

7 Additional provisions relating to religious worship

(1) Subject to the provisions of this section, the collective worship with which the school day in county schools and voluntary schools is required to begin shall take place on the school premises.

(2) If the ... governors of an aided school or a special agreement school are of opinion that it is desirable that a school day should, on any special occasion, begin with collective worship elsewhere than on the school premises, they may make such arrangements for that purpose as they think appropriate:

Provided that the powers of ... governors under this subsection shall not be so exercised as to derogate from the rule that, in every aided school and special agreement school, the collective worship with which the school day is required to begin must normally take place on the school premises.

(3) Any reference in the principal Act to religious worship in any school shall be construed as including a reference to religious worship which, under the provisions of the last preceding subsection, takes place otherwise than on the school premises.

NOTES

The words omitted were repealed by the Education Act 1980, s 1(3), Sch 1, para 18.

Definitions. By virtue of s 16(2) post, for "aided school" and "special agreement school", see the Education Act 1944, s 15, this part of this title ante; for "county school" and "voluntary school", see s 9(2) of that Act; and for "school premises", see the definition of "premises in relation to any school" in s 114(1) of that Act.

Principal Act. Ie the Education Act 1944; see the third paragraph of the first note to s 1 ante.

8 Provisions for avoiding broken terms

(1), (2) ...

(3) Where a person attains the age of eighteen years during the term of any county college which, when he attains that age, he is for the time being required to attend by a college attendance notice, he shall, for the purposes of the provisions of the principal Act relating to the period during which a person remains a young person, be deemed not to have attained that age until the end of the term, and the attendance required of him by

any such notice may extend until the end of the term in which he has attained or will attain that age.

(4) ...

NOTES

Sub-ss (1), (2) were repealed by the Education Act 1962, ss 9(5), (6), 13(1), Sch 2.

Sub-s (4) was repealed by the SL(R) Act 1978.

Attains the age, etc. A person attains a given age expressed in years at the commencement of the relevant anniversary of the date of his birth; see the Family Law Reform Act 1969, s 9, Vol 6, title Children.

End of the term. As to power to determine when a school term ends, see the Education Act 1944, s 23(3), this part of this title ante.

Definitions. By virtue of s 16(2) post, for "college attendance notice", see the Education Act 1944, s 44(2), this part of this title ante; and for "young person", see s 114(1) of that Act.

Principal Act. Ie the Education Act 1944; see the third paragraph of the first note to s 1 ante.

9–12 (*S 9 repealed by the Education (Miscellaneous Provisions) Act 1948, s 11(2), Sch 2; ss 10, 12 repealed by the Local Government Act 1972, s 272(1), Sch 30; s 11 repealed by the Local Government Act 1948, s 147, Sch 2.*)

13 Additional provisions relating to local administration

(1) In any legal proceedings any document purporting to be a document issued by a divisional executive and to be signed by a person authorised by the executive to sign it shall be received in evidence and shall, unless the contrary is proved, be deemed to be the document which it purports to be and to be signed by the person by whom it purports to have been signed without proof of his identity, signature or official capacity.

(2) ...

NOTES

Sub-s (2) was repealed by the Local Government Act 1972, s 272(1), Sch 30.

Divisional executive. Provisions for establishing divisional executives were formerly contained in the Education Act 1944, Sch 1, Pt III. Those provisions and the definition in s 16 of this Act of "divisional executive" were repealed by the Local Government Act 1972, ss 192(2), 272(1), Sch 30.

14 Miscellaneous amendments of enactments

(1) The provisions of the principal Act specified in the first column of the Second Schedule to this Act shall have effect subject to the amendments specified in the second column of that Schedule, and the said amendments, so far as they are contained in Part II of the said Schedule, shall be deemed to have had effect since the commencement of Part II of the principal Act.

(2), (3) ...

NOTES

Sub-s (2) was repealed by the Local Government Act 1972, s 272(1), Sch 30.

Sub-s (3) was repealed by the Public Libraries and Museums Act 1964, s 26(2), Sch 3.

Principal Act. Ie the Education Act 1944; see the third paragraph to the first note to s 1 ante.

15 (*Repealed by the SL(R) Act 1978.*)

16 Interpretation, etc

(1) In this Act, unless the context otherwise requires, the following expressions have the meanings hereby respectively assigned to them, that is to say:—

"department" means such part, if any, of a school as is organised under a separate head teacher;

. . . . .

"site", in relation to any school, does not include playing fields, but, save as aforesaid, includes any site which is to form part of the school premises.

(2) This Act shall be construed as one with the principal Act.

NOTES

The words omitted were repealed by the Local Government Act 1972, s 272(1), Sch 30.

Definitions. By virtue of sub-s (2), "premises" and "school" are defined in the Education Act 1944, s 114(1), this part of this title ante.

Construed as one. Ie the enactments in question are to be construed as if they were contained in one Act, unless there is some manifest discrepancy; see eg *Phillips v Parnaby* [1934] 2 KB 299 at 302. Accordingly, definitions in the earlier Act may be relevant to the construction of provisions of this Act (see *Solomons v R Gertzenstein Ltd* [1954] 2 QB 243, [1954] 2 All ER 625, CA; *Crowe (Valuation Officer) v Lloyds British Testing Co Ltd* [1960] 1 QB 592, [1960] 1 All ER 411, CA).

Principal Act. Ie the Education Act 1944; see the third paragraph of the first note to s 1 ante.

17 Short title, citation and extent

(1) This Act may be cited as the Education Act 1946.

(2) This Act and the Education Act 1944 may be cited together as the Education Acts 1944 and 1946.

(3) This Act shall not extend to Scotland or to Northern Ireland.

NOTE

Education Act 1944. See this part of this title ante.

SCHEDULES

FIRST SCHEDULE

Section 3

MAINTENANCE OF VOLUNTARY SCHOOLS

1. The duty of a local education authority to maintain a voluntary school under the principal Act shall include the duty of providing any site which is to be provided for the school in addition to, or instead of, the whole or any part of the existing site of the school, and shall, in the case of a controlled school, include the duty of providing any buildings which are to form part of the school premises:

Provided that nothing in this paragraph shall require a local education authority—

(a) to perform any duties which, under [section 13 of the Education Act 1980] (which includes provisions relating to the establishment of new schools and to the procedure by which a school which is not a voluntary school may become such a school) are required to be performed by any persons other than the authority; or

(b) to execute any proposals which are required to be executed under a special agreement made under the Third Schedule to the principal Act.

2. Where under subsection (1) of section sixteen of the principal Act [the Secretary of State] has made an order authorising the transfer to a new site of an aided school or a special agreement school, the duties of the ... governors of the school shall include the duty of defraying, with the assistance of any grant which may be made in accordance with section one hundred and three of the principal Act, the expenses of providing any school buildings to be provided on the new site, and accordingly—

(a) [the Secretary of State] shall not direct that a school shall be an aided school or a special agreement school unless he is satisfied that the ... governors of the school will be able and willing to defray any such expenses;

(b) the duty of the local education authority to maintain an aided school or a special agreement school shall not include the duty of defraying any such expenses; and

(c) if at any time the ... governors of an aided school or a special agreement school are unable or unwilling to carry out their obligations under this paragraph, it shall be their duty to apply to [the Secretary of State] for an order revoking the order or direction by virtue of which the school is an aided school or a special agreement school, and upon such an application being made to him [the Secretary of State] shall revoke the order or direction.

3. If when a local education authority provide a site for an aided school or a special agreement school in accordance with paragraph 1 of this Schedule, any work is required to be done to the site for the purpose of clearing it or making it suitable for building purposes, the authority and the ... governors of the school may by agreement provide for the making of such payments, or of such other adjustments of their respective rights and liabilities, as will secure that the cost of that work is borne by the local education authority.

4. If when a local education authority provide a site for an aided school or a special agreement school in accordance with paragraph 1 of this Schedule there are, on the site so provided, any buildings which are of value for the purposes of the school, the authority and the ... governors of the school may by agreement provide for the making of such payments, or of such other adjustments of their respective rights and liabilities, as appear to be desirable having regard to the duties of the ... governors with respect to the school buildings.

5. Where it appears to [the Secretary of State] that provision for any payment or other adjustment ought to have been made under either of the last two preceding paragraphs, but that such provision has not been made, he may by directions provide for the making of such payment or other adjustment as he thinks proper in the circumstances.

6. Where a local education authority provide a site for a school in accordance with the preceding provisions of this Schedule, it shall be the duty of the authority to convey their interest in the site and in any buildings on the site which are to form part of the school premises to the trustees of the school to be held on trust for the purposes of the school.

If any doubt or dispute arises as to the persons to whom a local education authority are required to make a conveyance under this paragraph, the conveyance shall be made to such persons as [the Secretary of State] thinks proper.

7. Where an interest in any premises which are to be used for the purposes of a controlled school is conveyed in accordance with the last preceding paragraph to any persons who possess, or are or may become entitled to, any sum representing proceeds of the sale of other premises which have been used for the purposes of the school, those persons or their successors shall pay to the local education authority so much of that sum as [the Secretary of State] may determine to be just having regard to the value of the interest so conveyed; and any sum so paid shall be deemed for the purposes of section fourteen of the School Sites Act 1841 (which relates to the sale or exchange of land held on trust for the purposes of a school) to be a sum applied in the purchase of a site for the school.

In this paragraph the expression "sale" includes the creation or disposition of any kind of interest.

8. Where in accordance with paragraph 6 of this Schedule a local education authority convey premises to be held on trust for the purposes of any voluntary school, and any person thereafter acquires the premises or any part thereof from the trustees, whether compulsorily or otherwise, [the Secretary of State] may require the trustees or their successors to pay to the authority so much of the compensation or purchase money paid in respect of the acquisition as he thinks just having regard to—

(a) the value of the premises conveyed by the authority in accordance with the said paragraph 6; and

(b) any sums which have been received by the authority in respect of the premises under the preceding provisions of this Schedule.

In this paragraph the expression "premises" includes any interest in premises.

NOTES

The words in square brackets in para 1(a) were substituted by the Education Act 1980, s 16(4), Sch 3, para 8.

The words "the Secretary of State" in square brackets are substituted by virtue of the Secretary of State for Education and Science Order 1964, SI 1964/490, art 3(2)(a).

The words omitted from paras 2, 3 and 4 are repealed by virtue of the Education Act 1980, s 1(1), (2), (4) this part of this title post.

General Note. This Schedule does not apply in relation to temporary accommodation provided by virtue of the Education Act 1968, s 3(4), this part of this title post.

Local education authority. For meaning, see, by virtue of s 16(2) ante, the Education Act 1944, s 114(1), this part of this title ante and the note thereto.

Duty of the local education authority. As to the enforcement of this duty, see the Education Act 1944, s 99(1), this part of this title ante and the notes thereto.

Definitions. By virtue of s 16(2) ante, for "aided school", "controlled school", "special agreement school" and "voluntary school", see the Education Act 1944, ss 9(2), 15, this part of this title ante; and for "maintain" and "premises", see s 114(1) of that Act. For "site", see s 16(1) ante; for "school buildings", see s 4(2) ante. Note the scope of "sale" and "premises" in paras 7, 8 above.

Principal Act. Ie the Education Act 1944; see the third paragraph of the first note to s 1 ante. For ss 16(1), 103 of, and Sch 3 to, that Act, see this part of this title ante.

School Sites Act 1841. See Pt 3 of this title post.

(Sch 2 repealed in part by the Education Act 1968, s 1(3), Sch 2, the Local Government Act 1972, s 272(1), Sch 30, the SL(R) Act 1975, the SL(R) Act 1978 and the Education Act 1980, s 38(6), Sch 7; the remainder amends the Education Act 1944, ss 14, 15, 34, 50, 73, 102, 113, 114, this part of this title ante.)

POLISH RESETTLEMENT ACT 1947

(10 & 11 Geo 6 c 19)

An Act to provide for the application of the Royal Warrant as to pensions, etc, for the military forces to certain Polish forces, to enable the Assistance Board to meet the needs of, and to provide accommodation in camps or other establishments for, certain Poles and others associated with Polish forces, to provide for their requirements as respects health and educational services, to provide for making arrangements and meeting expenses in connection with their emigration, to modify as respects the Polish resettlement forces and past members of certain Polish forces provisions relating to the service of aliens in the forces of the Crown, to provide for the discipline and internal administration of certain Polish forces and to affirm the operation up to the passing of this Act of provision previously made therefor, and for purposes connected therewith and consequential thereon

[27 March 1947]

Northern Ireland. This Act applies subject to the modifications in s 12 post.

1–5 *(For s 1, see Vol 3, title* Armed Forces *(Pt 4); for ss 2, 3, see Vol 40, title* Social Security; *for s 4, see Vol 30, title* National Health Service; *s 5 repealed by the SLR Act 1953.)*

6 Provision by the [Secretary of State for Education] of educational services

(1) [The Secretary of State] may, for meeting the educational needs of persons being of any description [for whom the Secretary of State has power] to provide accommodation under section three of this Act . . . provide any such services and do any such things as a local education authority or [the Secretary of State] are or is authorised or required to provide or do, or may be authorised or required to provide or do, by or under the Education Acts 1944 and 1946.

(2) [The Secretary of State] may make arrangements with any other government

department or other authority or person for the provision of services or the doing of things under this section, on his behalf and at his expense, by that authority or person.

(3) The expenses of [the Secretary of State] under this section shall be defrayed out of moneys provided by Parliament.

NOTES

The words "the Secretary of State" wherever they occur are substituted by virtue of the Secretary of State for Education and Science Order 1964, SI 1964/490, art 3(2)(a).

The words in the second pair of square brackets in sub-s (1) were substituted by the Social Security Act 1980, s 20, Sch 4, para 1.

The words omitted from sub-s (1) were repealed by the SLR Act 1953.

Secretary of State. See the note "Secretary of State for Education and Science" to the Education Act 1944, s 1, this part of this title ante.

Provide such services and do such things. Where a question arises as to whether, if a person were otherwise entitled to or eligible for any benefit or advantage under this Act or any instrument made by virtue of any provision of this Act, he would be precluded by virtue of the forfeiture rule, from receiving the whole or part of the benefit or advantage, that question is to be determined by a Social Security Commissioner; see the Forfeiture Act 1982, ss 1, 4, Vol 12, title Criminal Law.

Local education authority. See the Education Act 1944, s 114(1), this part of this title ante and the note thereto.

S 3 of this Act. See Vol 40, title Social Security.

Education Acts 1944 and 1946. See this part of this title ante.

7–9 *(For s 7, see Vol 3, title* Armed Forces (Pt 4); *ss 8, 9 repealed by the SLR Act 1953.)*

10 Interpretation

(1) In this Act, unless the context otherwise requires, the following expressions have the meanings hereby assigned to them respectively, that is to say,—

> "Pole" means a person registered under the Aliens Order 1920 as being a Pole;
> "Polish resettlement forces" means the Polish Re-Settlement Corps, the Polish Re-Settlement Corps (Royal Air Force), the Polish Re-Settlement Section of the Auxiliary Territorial Service, and the Polish Re-Settlement Section of the Women's Auxiliary Air Force;

.   .   .   .   .

(2) References in this Act to any other enactment shall, unless the context requires, be construed as references to that enactment as amended by or under any other enactment and references in this Act to the Royal Warrant mentioned in section one thereof and to the Aliens Order 1920 shall be construed respectively as references to that Warrant or Order as for the time being in force and to any Royal Warrant or Order substituted therefor.

NOTES

The words omitted were repealed by the SLR Act 1953.

Aliens Order 1920. This Order was replaced by the Aliens Order 1953 which is spent.

11 *(Applies to Scotland only.)*

12 Application to Northern Ireland

(1) The provisions of this section shall have effect for the purpose of the application of this Act to Northern Ireland.

(2) . . .

[(3) References in sections 4 to 7 of this Act to persons of any description for whom the Secretary of State has power to provide accommodation under section 3 of this Act shall include references to persons in Northern Ireland of any description for whom he would have power so to provide if those persons were in Great Britain.]

NOTES

Sub-s (2) was repealed by the SLR Act 1953.

Sub-s (3) was substituted by the Social Security Act 1980, s 20, Sch 4, para 1.

Great Britain. Ie England, Scotland and Wales; see the Union with Scotland Act 1706, preamble, Art I, Vol 10, title Constitutional Law (Pt 1), as read with the Interpretation Act 1978, s 22(1), Sch 2, para 5(*a*), Vol 41, title Statutes.

Sections 3, 4 to 7 of this Act. For s 3, see Vol 40, title Social Security; for s 4, see Vol 30, title National Health Service; s 5 was repealed by the SLR Act 1953; and for s 7, see Vol 3, title Armed Forces (Pt 4).

13 Short title

This Act may be cited as the Polish Resettlement Act 1947.

(For Schedule, see Vol 40, title Social Security.)

EDUCATION (MISCELLANEOUS PROVISIONS) ACT 1948

(11 & 12 Geo 6 c 40)

ARRANGEMENT OF SECTIONS

An Act to amend the Education Acts 1944 and 1946, the Endowed Schools Acts 1869 to 1908, the Provisions of the Mental Deficiency Act 1913, as to Children incapable of receiving education, and the Provision of the Children and Young Persons Act 1933, as to the minimum age of employment   [30 June 1948]

Education Acts 1944 to 1985. This Act is one of the Acts which may be cited by this collective title; see s 14(2) post and the Introductory Note to the Education Act 1944, this part of this title ante.

Northern Ireland. This Act does not apply; see s 14(5) post.

1–3 (*S 1 repealed by the Charities Act 1960, s 48(2), Sch 7, Pt I; s 2 repealed by the Education Act 1973, s 1(4), Sch 2, Pt II; s 3 amends the Education Act 1944, s 8(1), this part of this title ante.)*

4 Provisions as to pupils becoming registered pupils at, and being withdrawn from, schools

(1) A local education authority shall have power to make arrangements with respect to a primary school maintained by them, not being a school which is for the time being organised for the provision of both primary and secondary education, under which any junior pupils who have attained the age of ten years and six months and who are

registered pupils at the school may be required to be withdrawn therefrom for the purpose of receiving secondary education.

(2) The provision of section eight of the principal Act which renders it the duty of every local education authority to secure that there shall be available for their area sufficient schools for providing primary and secondary education shall not be construed as imposing any obligation on proprietors of schools to admit children as registered pupils otherwise than at the beginning of a school term, except as regards admission at a school during the currency of a school term of a child who was prevented from entering the school at the beginning of the term—

    (a) by his being ill or by other circumstances beyond his parent's control; or

    (b) by his parent's having been then resident at a place whence the school was not accessible with reasonable facility;

and, notwithstanding anything in section thirty-six of the principal Act, the parent of a child shall not be under any duty to cause him to receive full-time education during any period during which, having regard to the preceding provisions of this subsection, it is not practicable for the parent to arrange for him to become a registered pupil at a school.

(3) In cases not falling within the exception mentioned in the last preceding subsection, the . . . governors of schools maintained by a local education authority shall comply, as respects the time of admission of children as registered pupils, with any general directions given by the authority in that behalf.

(4), (5) . . .

(6) The regulations made under the said section eighty shall prescribe the grounds on which names are to be deleted from a register kept thereunder, and the name of a person entered in such a register as a registered pupil shall be deleted therefrom when occasion arises on some one or other of the prescribed grounds and shall not be deleted therefrom on any other ground.

NOTES

The words omitted from sub-s (3) were repealed by the Education Act 1980, s 1(3), Sch 1, para 19.

Sub-ss (4), (5) amend the Education Act 1944, s 80, this part of this title ante.

Local education authority. By virtue of s 14(3) post, for meaning, see the Education Act 1944, s 114(1), this part of this title ante and the note thereto.

Definitions. By virtue of s 14(3) post, for "child", "junior pupil", "maintain", "parent", "primary school", "primary education", "secondary education", "proprietor" and "registered pupil", see the Education Act 1944, s 114(1), this part of this title ante.

Principal Act. By s 1(6) of this Act (repealed), the Act referred to is the Education Act 1944, this part of this title ante.

Regulations made under the said s 80. Ie the Pupils' Registration Regulations 1956, SI 1956/357.

---

5 Amendment and consolidation of enactments as to provision of clothing

    (1) A local education authority may provide clothing—

        (a) for any pupil who is a boarder at any educational institution maintained by the authority;

        (b) for any pupil at a nursery school so maintained; or

        (c) for any pupil in a nursery class at any school so maintained

[and they may also provide clothing for a pupil for whom they are providing board and lodging elsewhere than at an educational institution so maintained, being a pupil [for whom special educational provision is made in pursuance of arrangements made by them]].

    (2) Where it appears to a local education authority that—

        (a) a pupil not falling within the preceding subsection at a school maintained by them, or

(b) a pupil not falling within the preceding subsection at a special school whether maintained by them or not,

is unable by reason of the inadequacy or unsuitability of his clothing to take full advantage of the education provided at the school, the authority may provide him with such clothing as in the opinion of the authority is necessary for the purpose of ensuring that he is sufficiently and suitably clad while he remains a pupil at the school.

(3) [A local education authority may provide]—

(a) for pupils at a school maintained by them, or at a county college or other establishment for further education so maintained, and

(b) for persons who make use of facilities for physical training made available for them by the authority under subsection (1) of section fifty-three of the principal Act,

such articles of clothing [as may be determined by the authority] suitable for the physical training provided at the school, college or other establishment, or under the facilities so made available.

(4) A local education authority may, with the consent of the proprietor of a school not maintained by the authority other than a special school, and upon such financial and other terms, if any, as may be determined by agreement between the authority and the proprietor of the school, make arrangements for securing, for any pupil at the school who is unable by reason of the inadequacy or unsuitability of his clothing to take full advantage of the education provided at the school, the provision of such clothing as is necessary for the purpose of ensuring that he is sufficiently and suitably clad while he remains a pupil at the school:

Provided that any arrangements made under this subsection shall be such as to secure, so far as is practicable, that the expense incurred by the authority in connection with the provision of any article under the arrangements shall not exceed the expense which would have been incurred by them in the provision thereof if the pupil had been a pupil at a school maintained by them.

(5) Provision of clothing under any of the powers conferred by this section may be made in such way as to confer either a right of property in the clothing or a right of user only, at the option of the providing authority except in any circumstances for which the adoption of one or other way of making such provision is prescribed.

(6) Where a local education authority have, under the powers conferred by this section, provided a person with clothing, then, in such circumstances respectively as may be prescribed—

(a) the authority shall be under obligation to require the parent to pay to them in respect thereof such sum, if any, as in the opinion of the authority he is able without financial hardship to pay, not exceeding the cost to the authority of the provision;

(b) the authority shall have power to require the parent to pay to them in respect thereof such sums as aforesaid or any less sums; or

(c) the parent shall not be required to pay any sum in respect thereof.

Any sum which a parent is duly required to pay by virtue of paragraph (a) or (b) of this subsection may be recovered summarily as a civil debt.

[(6A) Where a person who has attained the age of eighteen years (other than a registered pupil at a school) is provided with clothing under this section any reference in subsection (6) above to his parent shall be construed as a reference to that person.]

(7) The preceding provisions of this section shall be in substitution for the provisions of the Education Acts 1944 and 1946 relating to the provision of clothing.

NOTES

In sub-s (1), the words in the outer pair of square brackets were added by the Education (Miscellaneous Provisions) Act 1953, s 17(1), Sch 1, and the words in the inner pair of square brackets were substituted by the Education Act 1981, s 21, Sch 3.

The words in square brackets in sub-s (3) were substituted, and sub-s (6A) was inserted, by the Education Act 1980, s 29(1), (2).

Local education authority. For meaning, see, by virtue of s 14(3) post, the Education Act 1944, s 114(1), this part of this title ante and the note thereto.

Civil debt. As to the recovery of civil debts in courts of summary jurisdiction, see the Magistrates' Courts Act 1980, s 58, Vol 27, title Magistrates.

Attains the age, etc. A person attains a given age expressed in years at the commencement of the relevant anniversary of the date of his birth; see the Family Law Reform Act 1969, s 9, Vol 6, title Children.

Definitions. By virtue of s 14(3) post, for "clothing", "further education", "maintain", "parent", "proprietor" and "pupil", see the Education Act 1944, s 114(1), this part of this title ante; for "county college", see s 43 of that Act; and for "nursery school" and "special school", see s 9 thereof.

S 53(1) of the principal Act. By s 1(6) of this Act (repealed), the Act referred to is the Education Act 1944, this part of this title ante.

Education Acts 1944 and 1946. For the Acts which may be cited by this collective title, see the Education Act 1946, s 17(2), this part of this title ante. The provisions in those Acts relating to clothing were repealed by s 11 of, and Sch 2 to, this Act.

Regulations under this section. The Education (Provision of Clothing) Regulations 1980, SI 1980/545.

6–8 (*S 6 repealed by the Education Act 1980, s 38(6), Sch 7; s 7(1), (3) substitute the proviso to the Education Act 1944, s 10(2); sub-ss (2), (2A) repealed by the Education Act 1980, s 38(6), Sch 7; s 8 repealed by the Mental Health Act 1959, s 149(2), Sch 8, Pt I.*)

9 Presumption of age in proceedings to enforce attendance at school

(1) For the purposes of a prosecution of the parent of a child for an offence against section thirty-seven or section thirty-nine of the principal Act (which relate respectively to failure to comply with a school attendance order and to failure of a child to attend regularly at school), in so far as the child's having been of compulsory school age at any time is material, the child shall be presumed to have been of compulsory school age at that time unless the parent proves the contrary.

(2) An obligation under the preceding subsection to presume a child to have been of compulsory school age at any time shall be in substitution, so far as regards the purposes for which that presumption is required to be made, for the power conferred on the court by subsection (1) of section ninety-five of the principal Act (which is a power to presume a person to be under, of, or over, an age alleged by the person by whom any proceedings under the principal Act are brought on his satisfying the court that, having used all reasonable diligence to obtain evidence as to the age of that person, he has been unable to do so).

NOTES

Definitions. By virtue of s 14(3) post, for "child", "compulsory school age" and "parent", see the Education Act 1944, s 114(1), this part of this title ante.

Principal Act. By s 1(6) of this Act (repealed), the Act referred to is the Education Act 1944, this part of this title ante.

---

10 Provisions as to power of local education authorities to acquire land by agreement

(1) ...

(2) For the removal of doubt it is hereby declared that the rendering available of land for the purposes of a school, college or other institution which is, or is to be, maintained by a local education authority, or which they have power to assist, is a function of the authority within the meaning of section one hundred and fifty-seven of the Local

Government Act 1933 ... (which relate to the acquisition by a local authority by agreement of land for the purpose of any of their functions), notwithstanding that the land will not be held by the authority.

(3) A local education authority shall not acquire by agreement any land required for the purposes of a voluntary school unless they are satisfied that the arrangements made as to the vesting of the land to be acquired, and as to the appropriation thereof for those purposes, are such as to secure that the expenditure ultimately borne by them will not include any expenditure which, if the land had been acquired by the ... governors of the school, would have fallen to be borne by the ... governors.

NOTES

Sub-s (1) amends the Education Act 1944, s 90(1).
The words omitted from sub-s (2) were repealed by the London Government Act 1963, s 93(1), Sch 18, Pt II.
The words omitted from sub-s (3) were repealed by the Education Act 1980, s 1(3), Sch 1, para 9.
Acquisition of land. As to compulsory purchase of land by local education authorities, see the Education Act 1944, s 90, this part of this title ante.
Definitions. By virtue of s 14(3) post, for "school", see the Education Act 1944, s 114(1), this part of this title ante; for "local education authority", see s 114(1) of that Act and the note thereto; and for "voluntary school", see s 9(2) of that Act.
Local Government Act 1933, s 157. Repealed by the Local Government Act 1972, s 272, Sch 30, and replaced by s 120 of that Act, Vol 25, title Local Government.

11 Miscellaneous amendments and repeals

(1) The provisions of the principal Act specified in the first column of Part I of the First Schedule to this Act, ... shall have effect subject to the amendments specified in the second column of that Schedule (being amendments which relate to minor matters and consequential amendments).

(2) ...

NOTES

The words omitted from sub-s (1) were repealed by the Education Act 1973, s 1(4), Sch 2, Pt II.
Sub-s (2) was repealed by the SLR Act 1950.

12 Provisions as to regulations

Regulations made for any of the purposes of this Act, save in so far as they are subject to corresponding provision by virtue of their being made under a power conferred by the principal Act, shall be made by statutory instrument and shall be subject to annulment in pursuance of resolution of either House of Parliament.

NOTES

Statutory instrument; subject to annulment. For provisions as to statutory instruments generally, see the Statutory Instruments Act 1946, Vol 41, title Statutes, and as to statutory instruments which are subject to annulment, see ss 5(1), 7(1) of that Act.
Principal Act. By s 1(6) of this Act (repealed), the Act referred to is the Education Act 1944 ante.

13 *(Repealed by the SL(R) Act 1978.)*

14 Short title, citation, construction and extent

(1) This Act may be cited as the Education (Miscellaneous Provisions) Act 1948.

(2) This Act ... and the Education Acts 1944 and 1946 may be cited together as the Education Acts 1944 to 1948 ...

(3) This Act ... shall be construed as one with the Education Acts 1944 and 1946 ...

(4) References in this Act to any other enactment shall, except so far as the context otherwise requires, be construed as references to that enactment as amended by or under any other enactment, including this Act.

(5) This Act shall not extend to Scotland or Northern Ireland.

NOTES

The words omitted from sub-ss (2), (3) were repealed by the Education Act 1973, s 1(4), Sch 2, Pt II.

Construed as one. Ie the enactments in question are to be construed as if they were contained in one Act, unless there is some manifest discrepancy; see eg *Phillips v Parnaby* [1934] 2 KB 299 at 302. Accordingly definitions in the earlier Act may be relevant to the construction of provisions of this Act (see *Solomons v R Gertzenstein Ltd* [1954] 2 QB 243, [1954] 2 All ER 625, CA; *Crowe (Valuation Officer) v Lloyds British Testing Co Ltd* [1960] 1 QB 592, [1960] 1 All ER 411, CA), though this principle should not be pressed too far in construing revenue Acts (see the opinion of Lord Simonds in *Fendoch Investment Trust Co v IRC* [1945] 2 All ER 140, HL).

A later Act may not be referred to for the purpose of interpreting clear terms of an earlier Act which the later Act does not amend, even though both Acts are by the express provision of the later Act to be construed as one; but if the earlier Act is ambiguous the later Act may be used to throw light on its interpretation; see *Kirkness (Inspector of Taxes) v John Hudson & Co Ltd* [1955] AC 696, [1955] 2 All ER 345, HL.

Education Acts 1944 and 1946. For the Acts which may now be cited by the collective title "the Education Acts 1944 to 1985" (which includes those Acts), see the Introductory Note to the Education Act 1944, this part of this title ante.

(Sch 1 repealed in part by the Education (Miscellaneous Provisions) Act 1953, s 17(2), Sch 2, the Mental Health Act 1959, s 149(2), Sch 8, Pt I, the Children and Young Persons Act 1969, s 72(4), Sch 6, the Children Act 1972, s 2(2), Schedule, the Education Act 1973, s 1(4), Sch 2, Pt II, the SL(R) Act 1978, the Education Act 1980, s 38(6), Sch 7. The remainder amends the Education Act 1944, ss 33, 50, 53, 55, 56, 116, Sch 3, para 5, Sch 4, para 4, this part of this title ante. Sch 2 repealed by the SLR Act 1950.)

EDUCATION (MISCELLANEOUS PROVISIONS) ACT 1953

(1 & 2 Eliz 2 c 33)

ARRANGEMENT OF SECTIONS

An Act to amend the law relating to education in England and Wales; and to make further

Provision with respect to the duties of education authorities in Scotland as to dental treatment   **[14 July 1953]**

Education Acts 1944 to 1985. This Act is one of the Acts which may be cited by this collective title; see the Introductory Note to the Education Act 1944, this part of this title ante.
Northern Ireland. This Act does not apply; see s 20(6) post.

1 *(Repealed by the Education Act 1967, s 1(5)(c), (6).)*

2 Power of [Secretary of State], in certain circumstances to require local education authority to defray expenses of establishing a controlled school

Where—

(*a*) any persons submit, under [section 13 of the Education Act 1980] to [the Secretary of State] proposals for the establishment by them, or by persons whom they represent, of a new school ... and for its maintenance by the local education authority as a voluntary school; and

(*b*) the persons who submit the proposals and the local education authority show to the satisfaction of [the Secretary of State] that the establishment of the school is required for the purpose of providing accommodation for pupils for whom accommodation would have been provided in some other voluntary school if that other school had not been discontinued or had not otherwise ceased to be available for the purpose; and

(*c*) no application is made under subsection (2) of section fifteen of the principal Act to [the Secretary of State] for an order directing that the school shall be an aided school or a special agreement school;

[the Secretary of State] may by order direct that the whole, or a specified part, of so much of the cost incurred in the establishment of the school as would, apart from the order, fall to be defrayed by the persons who establish it shall be defrayed by the local education authority.

NOTES

The words "the Secretary of State" wherever they occur are substituted by virtue of the Secretary of State for Education and Science Order 1964, SI 1964/490, art 3(2)(*a*).

The words in the first pair of square brackets in sub-s (1) were substituted by the Education Act 1980, s 16(4), Sch 3, para 9.

The words omitted from sub-s (1) were repealed by the Education Act 1968, s 1(3), Sch 2.

General Note. Where persons other than a local authority submit proposals under the Education Act 1980, s 13, this part of this title post, for the establishment of a new school and its maintenance by the local education authority as a voluntary school, and the proposals make provision as mentioned in the Education Act 1964, s 1(1), this part of this title post, para (*b*) of this section is to have effect as if after the words "for whom" there were inserted the words "or for a substantial proportion of whom"; see the Education Act 1967, s 3, this part of this title post.

Secretary of State. See the note "Secretary of State for Education and Science" to the Education Act 1944, s 1, this part of this title ante.

Discontinued. Provisions as to discontinuance of voluntary schools are contained in the Education Act 1944, s 14, this part of this title ante and the Education Act 1980, ss 12–14, this part of this title post.

Definitions. By virtue of s 20(3) post, for "aided school" and "special agreement school", see the Education Act 1944, s 15, this part of this title ante; for "maintain", "pupil" and "school", see s 114(1) of that Act; for "local education authority", see s 114(1) of that Act and the note thereto; and for "voluntary school", see s 9(2) of that Act.

Education Act 1980, s 13. See this part of this title post.

Principal Act. By s 1 of this Act (repealed), the Act referred to is the Education Act 1944, this part of this title ante.

Orders under this section. Orders under this section, being local, are not printed in this work. For variation and revocation of orders, see, by virtue of s 20(3) post, the Education Act 1944, s 111, this part of this title ante.

3–5 *(S 3 amends the Education Act 1946, s 1(1), this part of this title ante; s 4 repealed by* *the National Health Service Reorganisation Act 1973, ss 57, 58, Sch 5; s 5 repealed by the Education (Scotland) Act 1956, ss 6(3), 13(2), Sch 2.)*

6 Provision of education at non-maintained schools and payment of tuition and boarding fees for pupils attending thereat

(1) . . . a local education authority shall have, and be deemed always to have had, power to make . . . arrangements for the provision of primary and secondary education for pupils at a school not maintained by them or another local education authority.

(2) Where, in pursuance of arrangements made by a local education authority by virtue of the foregoing subsection or [the Education Act 1981], primary or secondary education is provided for a pupil at a school not maintained by them or another local education authority, the authority by whom the arrangements are made—

> (*a*) shall, in the following cases, that is to say—
>> (i) where the pupil fills a place in the school which the proprietors of the school have put at the disposal of the authority and the school is one in respect of which grants are made by [the Secretary of State] under paragraph (*b*) of subsection (1) of section one hundred of the principal Act,
>> (ii) Where the authority are satisfied that, by reason of a shortage of places in schools maintained by them and schools maintained by other local education authorities, being schools to which the pupil could be sent with reasonable convenience, education suitable to the age, ability and aptitude of the pupil [and any special educational needs he may have] cannot be provided by them for him except at a school not maintained by them or another local education authority,
>> [(iii) where, in a case not falling within either of the two foregoing sub-paragraphs, the authority are satisfied that the pupil has special educational needs and that it is expedient in his interests that the required special educational provision should be made for him at a school not maintained by them or another local education authority],
>
> pay the whole of the fees payable in respect of the education provided in pursuance of the arrangements;
> (*b*) shall, where board and lodging are provided for the pupil at the school, and the authority are satisfied that education suitable to his age, ability and aptitude [and to any special educational needs he may have] cannot be provided by them for him at any school unless board and lodging are also provided for him (either at school or elsewhere), pay the whole of the fees payable in respect of the board and lodging.

(3) The powers conferred on a local education authority by subsection (1) of this section shall be in addition to and not in derogation of the powers conferred on them by the principal Act.

NOTES

The words omitted from sub-s (1) were repealed by the Education Act 1980, ss 28(1), (2), 38(6), Sch 7.

The words in the second pair of square brackets in sub-s (2) are substituted by the Secretary of State for Education and Science Order 1964, SI 1964/490, art 3(2)(*a*).

The words in the other pairs of square brackets in sub-s (2) were substituted or inserted by the Education Act 1981, s 21, Sch 3, para 8; but note that the first amendment (which replaces a reference to the Education Act 1944, s 33) does not have effect in relation to the provision of primary or secondary education in pursuance of arrangements made by virtue of s 33 of the Education Act 1944; see the Education Act 1981 (Commencement No 2) Order 1983, SI 1983/7, art 4, Schedule, para 3(3).

Duties under the principal Act. See, in particular, the Education Act 1944, ss 8, 76, this part of this title ante. Where an authority has fulfilled its duty under the Education Act 1944, s 8 ante to secure that sufficient schools are available for its area by making arrangements for the payment of full tuition fees at an independent school there is no obligation on it to pay the whole tuition fees at some other independent school chosen by a parent (*Watt v Kesteven CC* [1955] QB 408, [1955] 1 All ER 473, CA; dicta of Denning LJ in that case applied in *Cumings v Birkenhead Corpn* [1972] Ch 12, [1970] 3 All ER 302.

Secretary of State. See the note "Secretary of State for Education and Science" to the Education Act 1944, s 1, this part of this title ante.

Suitable to the age, ability and aptitude. Cf the Education Act 1944, ss 36, 61(2)(*a*), this part of this title ante.

Definitions. By virtue of s 20(3) post, for "maintain", "primary education", "proprietor", "pupil", "school", and "secondary education", see the Education Act 1944, s 114(1), this part of this title ante; for "local education authority", see s 114(1) of that Act and the note thereto; and by virtue of that section, for "special educational needs" and "special educational provision", see the Education Act 1981, s 1, this part of this title post; for "special school", see the Education Act 1944, s 9(5), this part of this title ante.

Education Act 1981. See this part of this title post.

Principal Act. By virtue of s 1 of this Act (repealed), this means the Education Act 1944, this part of this title ante.

---

7 (*Repealed by the Education Act 1980, s 38(6), Sch 7.*)

8 Amendments of ss 103 to 105 of principal Act as to matters in respect of which [Secretary of State] may make grants and loans

(1) Subsection (1) of section one hundred and three of the principal Act (which empowers [the Secretary of State] to pay to the ... governors of a voluntary school proposed to be transferred to a new site or established in substitution for any discontinued school or schools and to be maintained as an aided school or a special agreement school a grant not exceeding one-half of any sums expended by them in the construction of the school) shall—

    (*a*) in relation to a school of which the transfer has been authorised by [the Secretary of State], have effect as if, for the reference therein to the construction of the school, there were substituted a reference to the provision (whether before or after the passing of this Act) of the school buildings; ...

(2) ...

(3) Section one hundred and five of the principal Act (which empowers [the Secretary of State] to make to the ... governors of an aided school or a special agreement school a loan for the purpose of helping them to meet capital expenditure involved in defraying their share of the initial expenses relating to the school specified in subsection (2) of that section) shall have effect—

    (*a*) as if the reference in paragraph (*a*) of that subsection to expenses to be incurred in defraying the cost of any alterations required by the development plan approved by [the Secretary of State] for the area included a reference to expenses incurred before the passing of this Act or to be incurred thereafter in defraying the cost of any alterations specified in that plan as submitted to [the Secretary of State], being alterations to the carrying out of which [the Secretary of State] has given approval before the approval by him of the plan;

    ...

NOTES

The words in square brackets are substituted by virtue of the Secretary of State for Education and Science Order 1964, SI 1964/490, art 3(2)(*a*).

The words omitted from sub-s (1) in the first place were repealed by the Education Act 1980, s 1(3), Sch 1, para 21, and those omitted in the second place were repealed with savings by the Education Act 1967, s 1(5)(*c*), (6) ante.

Sub-s (2) was repealed with savings by the Education Act 1967, s 1(5)(*c*), (6), this part of this title ante.

The words omitted from sub-s (3) in the first place were repealed by the Education Act 1980, s 1(3), Sch 1, para 21, and those omitted in the second place were repealed by the Education Act 1968, s 1(3), Sch 2.

Secretary of State. See the note "Secretary of State for Education and Science" to the Education Act 1944, s 1 ante.

Site. In the case of the transfer of a voluntary school, the local education authority has to provide the site by virtue of the Education Act 1946, s 3, Sch 1, para 1, this part of this title ante.

Development plan. By virtue of the Education Act 1944, s 11 (repealed), each local education authority had to prepare plans for the development of primary and secondary education in that area.

Passing of this Act. Ie 14 July 1953, the date on which the Act received the Royal Assent.

Definitions. By virtue of s 20(3) post, for "aided school" and "special agreement school", see the Education Act 1944, s 15, this part of this title ante; for "alterations" and "school", see s 114(1) of that Act; for "school buildings", see the Education Act 1946, s 4(2), this part of this title ante, and for "voluntary school", see s 9(2) of the 1944 Act.

Principal Act. By virtue of s 1 of this Act (repealed) this means the Education Act 1944, this part of this title ante.

9–16 *(Ss 9, 16 repealed by the Education Act 1980, s 38(6), Sch 7; s 10 amends the Education Act 1944, s 37(2), proviso, this part of this title ante; s 11 repealed by the Children and Young Persons Act 1969, s 72(4), Sch 6; s 12 repealed with a saving by the Transport Act 1980, ss 32(5), 69, Sch 9, Pt I, Vol 38, title Road Traffic; s 13 repealed by the SL(R) Act 1978; s 14 repealed by the Education Act 1973, s 1(4), Sch 2, Pt I; s 15 repealed by the Charities Act 1960, s 48(2), Sch 4, Pt II.)*

17 Miscellaneous amendments and repeals

(1) The provisions of the principal Act and the Education (Miscellaneous Provisions) Act 1948 specified in the first column of the First Schedule to this Act shall have effect subject to the amendments specified in the second column of that Schedule (being amendments relating to minor matters and amendments consequential on the provisions of this Act).

(2) ...

NOTES

Sub-s (2) was repealed by the Education Act 1973, s 1(4), Sch 2, Pt I.

Principal Act. By virtue of s 1 of this Act (repealed) this means the Education Act 1944, this part of this title ante.

Education (Miscellaneous Provisions) Act 1948. See this part of this title ante.

18 Provisions as to regulations

Any power conferred by this Act on [the Secretary of State] to make regulations shall be exercisable by statutory instrument which shall be subject to annulment in pursuance of a resolution of either House of Parliament.

NOTES

The words in square brackets are substituted by virtue of the Secretary of State for Education and Science Order 1964, SI 1964/490, art 3(2)(a).

Secretary of State. See the note "Secretary of State for Education and Science" to the Education Act 1944, s 1 ante.

Statutory instrument; subject to annulment. For provisions as to statutory instruments generally, see the Statutory Instruments Act 1946, Vol 41, title Statutes, and as to statutory instruments which are subject to annulment, see ss 5(1), 7(1) of that Act.

19 *(Repealed by the SL(R) Act 1978.)*

20 Short title, citation, construction and extent

(1) This Act may be cited as the Education (Miscellaneous Provisions) Act 1953.

(2) This Act ... and the Education Acts 1944 to 1948 may be cited together as the Education Acts 1944 to 1953.

(3) This Act ... shall be construed as one with the Education Acts 1944 to 1948.

(4) References in this Act to any other enactment shall, except so far as the context otherwise requires, be construed as references to that enactment as amended by or under any other enactment, including this Act.

(5) This Act . . . shall not extend to Scotland.

(6) This Act shall not extend to Northern Ireland.

NOTES

The words omitted were repealed by the Education (Scotland) Act 1956, s 13(2) and Sch 2.

Construed as one. Ie the enactments in question are to be construed as if they were contained in one Act, unless there is some manifest discrepancy; see eg *Phillips v Parnaby* [1934] 2 KB 299 at 302. Accordingly definitions in the earlier Act may be relevant to the construction of provisions of this Act (see *Solomons v R Gertzenstein Ltd* [1954] 2 QB 243, [1954] 2 All ER 625, CA; *Crowe (Valuation Officer) v Lloyds British Testing Co Ltd* [1960] 1 QB 592, [1960] 1 All ER 411, CA), though this principle should not be pressed too far in construing revenue Acts (see the opinion of Lord Simonds in *Fendoch Investment Trust Co v IRC* [1945] 2 All ER 140, HL).

A later Act may not be referred to for the purpose of interpreting clear terms of an earlier Act which the later Act does not amend, even though both Acts are by the express provision of the later Act to be construed as one; but if the earlier Act is ambiguous the later Act may be used to throw light on its interpretation; see *Kirkness (Inspector of Taxes) v John Hudson & Co Ltd* [1955] AC 696, [1955] 2 All ER 345, HL.

Education Acts 1944 to 1948. For the Acts which may now be cited by the collective title "the Education Acts 1944 to 1985" (which includes those Acts), see the Introductory Note to the Education Act 1944, this part of this title ante.

(Sch 1 repealed in part by the Local Government Act 1958, s 67, Sch 9, Pt II, the National Health Service Reorganisation Act 1973, ss 57, 58, Sch 5, the Education Act 1976, s 10(2), and the Education Act 1980, s 38(6), Sch 7. The remainder amends the Education (Miscellaneous Provisions) Act 1948, s 5(1). Sch 2 repealed by the Education Act 1973, s 1(4), Sch 2, Pt I.)

EDUCATION ACT 1959

(7 & 8 Eliz 2 c 60)

An Act to enlarge the powers of the Minister of Education to make contributions, grants and loans in respect of aided Schools and Special agreement schools, and for purposes connected therewith   [29 July 1959]

Education Acts 1944 to 1985. This Act is one of the Acts which may be cited by this collective title; see the Introductory Note to the Education Act 1944, this part of this title ante.

Northern Ireland. This Act does not apply; see s 2(2) post.

1 Extended powers to make contributions, etc

(1)–(3) . . .

(4) For the purposes of section one hundred and five of the Education Act 1944 (which authorises [the Secretary of State] to make loans to the . . . governors of aided schools and special agreement schools for certain initial expenses involving capital expenditure), any expenses in respect of which [the Secretary of State] may make a grant under subsection (2) of this section shall be included in the expression "initial expenses", and in determining the governors' share of any initial expenses the amount of any such grant paid or payable in respect of them shall be taken into account in the same way as grants under sections one hundred and three and one hundred and four of that Act.

(5)–(8) . . .

NOTES

Sub-ss (1)–(3), (5)–(8) were repealed with a saving by the Education Act 1967, s 1(5)(*d*), (6), this part of this title post.

The words in square brackets in sub-s (4) are substituted by virtue of the Secretary of State for Education and Science Order 1964, SI 1964/490, art 3(2)(*a*), and the words omitted from that subsection were repealed by the Education Act 1980, s 1(3), Sch 1, para 22.

Secretary of State. See the note "Secretary of State for Education and Science" to the Education Act 1944, s 1, this part of this title ante.

Definitions. For "aided school" and "special agreement school", see the Education Act 1944, s 15, this part of this title ante.

Education Act 1944, s 105. See this part of this title ante.

2 Short title, citation and extent

(1) This Act may be cited as the Education Act 1959, and this Act and the Education Acts 1944 to 1953 may be cited together as the Education Acts 1944 to 1959.

(2) This Act does not extend to Scotland or to Northern Ireland.

NOTE

Education Acts 1944 to 1953. For the Acts which may now be cited by the collective title "the Education Acts 1944 to 1985" (which includes those Acts), see the Introductory Note to the Education Act 1944, this part of this title ante.

EDUCATION ACT 1962

(10 & 11 Eliz 2 c 12)

ARRANGEMENT OF SECTIONS

Awards and grants by local education authorities and Secretary of State in England and Wales

An Act to make further provision with respect to awards and grants by local education authorities and the Minister of Education in England and Wales, and by education authorities and the Secretary of State in Scotland, and to enable the General Grant Order 1960 and the General Grant (Scotland) Order 1960 to be varied so as to take account of additional or reduced expenditure resulting from action (including anticipatory action) taken in accordance with that provision; to make further provision as to school leaving dates; and for purposes connected with the matters aforesaid   [29 March 1962]

Education Acts 1944 to 1985. This Act is one of the Acts which may be cited by this collective title; see the Introductory Note to the Education Act 1944, this part of this title ante.
Northern Ireland. This Act does not apply; see s 14(6) post.

Awards and grants by local education authorities and Secretary of State in England and Wales

[1 Local education authority awards for designated courses

(1) It shall be the duty of every local education authority, subject to and in accordance with regulations made under this Act, to bestow on persons who are ordinarily resident in the area of the authority awards in respect of their attendance at courses to which this section applies.

(2) This section applies to any course which—

(*a*) is provided by a university, college or other institution in the United Kingdom or by such a university, college or institution in conjunction with a university, college or other institution in another country; and

(*b*) is designated by or under the regulations for the purposes of this section as being such a course as is mentioned in subsection (3) of this section.

(3) The courses referred to in subsection (2)(*b*) of this section are—

(*a*) full-time courses which are either first degree courses or comparable to first degree courses;

(*b*) full-time courses for the diploma of higher education;

(*c*) courses for the initial training of teachers;

(*d*) full-time courses for the higher national diploma, [or for the higher national diploma of the body corporate known at the passing of the Education (Grants and Awards) Act 1984 as the Business and Technician Education Council].

(4) A local education authority shall not be under a duty under subsection (1) above to bestow an award on a person in respect of a course designated as comparable to a first degree course unless he possesses such educational qualifications as may be prescribed by or under the regulations, either generally or with respect to that course or a class of courses which includes that course.

(5) Regulations made for the purposes of subsection (1) of this section shall prescribe the conditions and exceptions subject to which the duty imposed by that subsection is to have effect, and the descriptions of payment to be made in pursuance of awards bestowed thereunder, and, with respect to each description of payments, shall—

(*a*) prescribe the circumstances in which it is to be payable, and the amount of the payment or the sales or other provisions by reference to which that amount is to be determined, and

(*b*) indicate whether the payment is to be obligatory or is to be at the discretion of the authority bestowing the award;

and, subject to the exercise of any power conferred by the regulations to suspend or terminate awards, a local education authority by whom an award has been bestowed under subsection (1) of this section shall be under a duty, or shall have power, as the case may be, to make such payments as they are required or authorised to make in accordance with the regulations.

(6) Without prejudice to the duty imposed by subsection (1) of this section, a local education authority shall have power to bestow an award on any person in respect of his attendance at a course to which this section applies, where he is not eligible for an award under subsection (1) of this section in respect of that course.

(7) The provisions of subsection (5) of this section and of the regulations made in accordance with that subsection (except so much of those provisions as relates to the conditions and exceptions subject to which the duty imposed by subsection (1) of this section is to have effect) shall apply in relation to awards under the last preceding subsection as they apply in relation to awards under subsection (1) of this section.

(8) The reference in subsection (1) of this section to persons who are ordinarily resident in the area of a local education authority is a reference to persons who, in accordance with the provisions of Schedule 1 to this Act, are to be treated as being so resident.]

NOTES

This section was substituted by the Education Act 1980, s 19, Sch 5.

The words in square brackets in sub-s (3)(d) were substituted by the Education (Grants and Awards) Act 1984, s 4.

Sub-s (1): It shall be the duty, etc. By virtue of s 14(4) post, see the Education Act 1944, s 68, this part of this title ante, concerning the power of the Secretary of State to prevent the unreasonable exercise of a duty, and s 99(1) of that Act concerning the power of the Secretary of State to enforce the execution of a duty.

Local education authority. See, by virtue of s 14(4) post, the Education Act 1944, s 114(1), this part of this title ante and the note thereto.

Ordinarily resident. See also sub-s (8) above, and Sch 1 post.

Students with indefinite leave to remain in the United Kingdom are "ordinarily resident", but those with students' entry certificates which have to be renewed annually are not, and are accordingly not entitled to awards under this section; *R v London Borough of Barnet, ex p Shah* [1980] 3 All ER 679; affd [1982] QB 688, [1982] 1 All ER 698, CA; on appeal sub nom *Shah v Barnet London BC* [1983] 1 All ER 226, [1983] 2 WLR 16, HL overruling *Cicutti v Suffolk CC* [1980] 3 All ER 689, 125 Sol Jo 134.

Awards. The designation of an award and the terms in which it is bestowed are immaterial; see s 4(1) post.

For the power of the Secretary of State, as respects any awards under sub-s (6) above or s 2 post, to make regulations authorising the adoption of rules of eligibility which confine the awards to persons having such connection with the United Kingdom as may be specified, see the Education (Fees and Awards) Act 1983, s 2, this part of this title post, and the Education (Fees and Awards) Regulations 1983, SI 1983/973, as amended by SI 1984/1021 (made under that section).

As to the supplementation by the Secretary of State of awards with allowances in respect of a wife, husband or child, see the Education Act 1973, s 3, this part of this title post, and the regulations noted thereto.

Sub-s (2): United Kingdom. Ie Great Britain and Northern Ireland; see the Interpretation Act 1978, s 5, Sch 1, Vol 41, title Statutes. "Great Britain" means England, Scotland and Wales by virtue of the Union with Scotland Act 1706, preamble, Art I, Vol 10, title Constitutional Law (Pt 1), as read with s 22(1) of, and Sch 2, para 5(a) to, the 1978 Act. Neither the Channel Islands nor the Isle of Man is within the United Kingdom.

Central government grants. Expenditure under sub-s (1) above and s 2(3) post is not "relevant expenditure" for purposes of determining rate support grants under the Local Government Act 1974, Pt I, Vol 25, title Local Government (see ss 1(4)(b), (5)(b) of that Act), or under the Local Government, Planning and Land Act 1980, ss 53 et seq, in the same title (which supersede the system of rate support grants in Pt I of the 1980 Act) (see s 54(5)(ii), (6)(b) of the 1980 Act), but the Secretary of State is required to make specific grants to local education authorities in respect of such expenditure (s 8(2) of the 1974 Act).

Expenditure under sub-s (1) or in pursuance of s 2(3) post is excluded for the purposes of calculating the limit on expenditure under the Education (Grants and Awards) Act 1984, s 2, this part of this title post; see sub-s (2) of that section.

Education (Grants and Awards) Act 1984. See this part of this title post. The date of the passing of that Act (ie the date of Royal Assent) was 12 April 1984.

Regulations under this section. The Education (Mandatory Awards) Regulations 1985, SI 1985/1126 (made under this section, s 4(2) and Sch 1, paras 3, 4 post).

For general provisions as to regulations, see s 4(2), (4) post.

[2 Local education authority awards for other courses

(1) A local education authority shall have power to bestow awards on persons over compulsory school age (including persons undergoing training as teachers) in respect of their attendance at courses to which this section applies and to make such payments as are payable in pursuance of such awards.

(2) Subject to subsection (3) of this section, this section applies to any course of full-time or part-time education (whether held in Great Britain or elsewhere) which is not a course of primary or secondary education, or (in the case of a course held outside Great Britain) is not a course of education comparable to primary or secondary education in Great Britain, and is not a course to which section 1 of this Act applies.

(3) Except in the case of a person undergoing training as a teacher who attends the course as such training, this section does not apply to any course provided by a university, college or other institution which is for the time being designated by or under regulations made for the purposes of this section as being a postgraduate course or comparable to a postgraduate course.]

NOTES

This section was substituted by the Education Act 1980, s 19, Sch 5.

Awards. See the note to s 1 ante.

Great Britain. Ie England, Scotland and Wales; see the Union with Scotland Act 1706, preamble, Art I, Vol 10, title Constitutional Law (Pt 1), as read with the Interpretation Act 1978, s 22(1), Sch 2, para 5(a), Vol 41, title Statutes.

Central government grants. See the note to s 1 ante.

Definitions. For "training" and "undergoing training", see s 4(5) post. By virtue of s 14(4) post, for "primary education" and "secondary education", see the Education Act 1944, s 8(1), this part of this title ante; for "compulsory school age", see s 114(1) of the 1944 Act; and for "local education authority", see s 114(1) of the 1944 Act and the note thereto.

Regulations under this section. Up to 1 August 1985 no regulations had been made under sub-s (3), and there are none which could have effect under that subsection.

For general provisions as to regulations, see s 4(2), (4) post.

[3 Awards by Secretary of State

Provision may be made by regulations under this Act for authorising the Secretary of State—

(a) to pay grants to or in respect of persons undergoing training as teachers;

(b) to bestow awards on persons in respect of their attendance at such courses provided by universities, colleges or other institutions (whether in Great Britain or elsewhere) as may for the time being be designated by or under the regulations for the purposes of this section as being postgraduate courses or comparable to postgraduate courses;

(c) to bestow awards on persons who, at such time as may be prescribed by the regulations, have attained such age as may be so prescribed, being awards in respect of their attendance at courses provided by any institution which—

   (i) is in receipt of payments under section 100 of the Education Act 1944 or section 75 of the Education (Scotland) Act 1962; and

   (ii) is designated by or under the regulations as a college providing long-term residential courses of full-time education for adults;

and in the case of awards bestowed in accordance with paragraph (b) or (c) of this section, for authorising the Secretary of State to make such payments as are payable in pursuance of the awards.]

NOTES

This section was substituted by the Education Act 1980, s 19, Sch 5.

Secretary of State. See the note "Secretary of State for Education and Science" to the Education Act 1944, s 1, this part of this title ante.

Awards. The designation of an award and the terms in which it is bestowed are immaterial; see s 4(1) post.

Great Britain. See the note to s 3 ante.

Attained such age. A person attains a given age expressed in years at the commencement of the relevant anniversary of the date of his birth; see the Family Law Reform Act 1969, s 9, Vol 6, title Children.

Definitions. For "training" and "undergoing training", see s 4(5) post.

Education Act 1944, s 100. See this part of this title ante.

Education (Scotland) Act 1962. 1962 c 47; not printed in this work.

Regulations under this section. The State Awards Regulations 1978, SI 1978/1096, as amended by SI 1979/333, SI 1983/188 and SI 1983/920 and State Awards (State Bursaries for Adult Education) (Wales) Regulations 1979, SI 1979/333, as amended by SI 1983/1274 and SI 1983/1747, which were made under this section as originally enacted, continue to have effect under this section. The Education (Teacher Training Scholarships) Regulations 1981, SI 1981/1328; the Education (Teacher Training Awards) Regulations 1983, SI 1983/481, as amended by SI 1984/893, SI 1985/1220; the Education (Grants for Teacher Training) Regulations 1985, SI 1985/741.

For general provisions as to regulations, see s 4(2), (4) post.

[4 Provisions supplementary to ss 1 to 3

(1) For the purposes of the exercise of any power or the performance of any duty conferred or imposed by or under any of the provisions of sections 1 to 3 of this Act, it is immaterial—

    (*a*) whether an award is designated by that name or as a scholarship, studentship, exhibition or bursary or by any similar description, or

    (*b*) in what terms the bestowal of an award is expressed.

(2) Any enactment contained in those sections which requires or authorises the making of regulations shall be construed as requiring or authorising regulations to be made by the Secretary of State; and regulations made for the purposes of any such enactment may make different provision for different cases to which that enactment is applicable.

(3) Without prejudice to subsection (2) above, regulations under section 3 (*a*) or (*c*) above may make in relation to persons ordinarily resident in Wales provision different from that made in relation to persons so resident in England.

(4) Any power to make regulations under those sections shall be exercisable by statutory instrument; and any statutory instrument containing any such regulations shall be subject to annulment in pursuance of a resolution of either House of Parliament.

(5) In sections 2 and 3 of this Act "training" (in relation to training as a teacher) includes further training, whether the person undergoing the further training is already qualified as a teacher or not; and any reference to a person undergoing training includes a person admitted or accepted by the appropriate university, college or other authorities for undergoing that training.]

NOTES

This section was substituted by the Education Act 1980, s 19, Sch 5.

Secretary of State. See the note "Secretary of State for Education and Science" to the Education Act 1944, s 1, this part of this title ante.

England; Wales. For meaning, see the Interpretation Act 1978, ss 5, 22(1), Sch 1, Sch 2, para 5(*a*), Vol 41, title Statutes.

Statutory instrument; subject to annulment. For provisions as to statutory instruments generally, see the Statutory Instruments Act 1946, Vol 41, title Statutes, and as to statutory instruments which are subject to annulment, see ss 5(1), 7(1) of that Act.

5–8 (*Ss 5, 6 repealed by the Education (Scotland) Act 1962, ss 147, 148, Schs 8, 9; s 7 repealed by the SL(R) Act 1975; s 8 repealed by the SL(R) Act 1977.*)

School leaving dates

9 School leaving dates in England and Wales

(1) The provisions of subsections (2) to (4) of this section shall have effect in relation to any person who on a date when either—

(*a*) he is a registered pupil at a school, or

(*b*) not being such a pupil, he has been a registered pupil at a school within the preceding period of twelve months,

attains an age which (apart from this section) would in his case be the upper limit of the compulsory school age.

(2) If he attains that age on any date from the beginning of September to the end of January, he shall be deemed not to have attained that age until the end of the appropriate spring term at his school.

[(3) If he attains that age after the end of January but before the next May school-leaving date, he shall be deemed not to have attained that age until that date.

(4) If he attains that age after the May school-leaving date and before the beginning of September next following that date, he shall be deemed to have attained that age on that date.]

(5) The provisions of this section shall have effect for the purposes of the Act of 1944 and for the purposes of any enactment whereby the definition of compulsory school age in that Act is applied or incorporated; and for references in any enactment to section eight of the Education Act 1946 there shall, in relation to compulsory school age, be substituted references to this section:

.   .   .   .   .

(6) ...

(7) In this section "the appropriate spring term", in relation to a person, means the last term at his school which ends before the month of May next following the date on which he attains the age in question ... and any reference to a person's school is a reference to the last school at which he is a registered pupil for a term ending before the said month of May ... or for part of such a term.

[(8) In this section "the May school-leaving date" means the Friday before the last Monday in May.]

NOTES

Sub-ss (3), (4) were substituted, sub-s (8) was added, and sub-s (6) and the words omitted from sub-ss (5), (7) were repealed, by the Education (School-leaving Dates) Act 1976, ss 1, 3(3), Schedule.

Attains an age. See the note "Attained such age" to s 3 ante.

Compulsory school age. See, by virtue of s 14(4) post, the Education Act 1944, s 35, this part of this title ante.

Term. As to the power to determine the times when school terms begin and end, see the Education Act 1944, s 23(3), this part of this title ante.

Definitions. By virtue of s 14(4) post, for "registered pupil" and "school", see the Education Act 1944, s 114(1), this part of this title ante. Note as to "the appropriate spring term", sub-s (7) above, and as to "the May school-leaving date", sub-s (8) above.

Act of 1944. Ie the Education Act 1944, this part of this title ante; see s 12(1) post.

Education Act 1946, s 8. See this part of this title ante.

10 (*Repealed by the Education (Scotland) Act 1962, ss 147, 148, Schs 8, 9.*)

Supplementary provisions

11 (*Repealed by the SL(R) Act 1978.*)

12 Interpretation

(1) In this Act "the Act of 1944" means the Education Act 1944 ...

(2) References in this Act to any enactment shall, except where the context otherwise requires, be construed as references to that enactment as amended by or under any other enactment.

NOTES

The words omitted from sub-s (1) were repealed by the SL(R) Act 1978.
Education Act 1944. See this part of this title ante.

13 Repeals, transitional provisions and savings

(1) ...

(2) Any regulations relating to the training of teachers, in so far as they were made by virtue of the repealed grant provisions, shall continue to have effect notwithstanding the repeal, and may be revoked or varied as if this Act had not been passed.

(3) Any other regulations, in so far as they were made by virtue of the repealed grant provisions, shall continue to have effect notwithstanding the repeal in so far as—

(a) they authorise the making of any payment in respect of a period ending before the first day of September, nineteen hundred and sixty-two, or

(b) they enable scholarships, exhibitions, bursaries or other allowances to be awarded at any time before that day, or authorise the making of any payment (whether before or after that day) in pursuance of a scholarship, exhibition, bursary or other allowance so awarded;

and in so far as any regulations continue to have effect by virtue of this subsection, they may be revoked, or (within the limits subject to which they continue so to have effect) may be varied, as if this Act had not been passed.

(4) Subsection (1) of this section, in so far as it repeals any of the provisions of section eight of the Education Act 1946, shall have effect subject to the provisions of subsections (5) and (6) of section nine of this Act as if it were contained in the said section nine.

(5) In this section "the repealed grant provisions" means so much of section one hundred of the Act of 1944 as is repealed by this Act.

NOTES

Sub-s (1) was repealed by the SL(R) Act 1974.
Education Act 1946, s 8. See this part of this title ante.
Act of 1944. Ie the Education Act 1944, this part of this title ante; see s 12(1) ante.

14 Short title, citation, construction and extent

(1) This Act may be cited as the Education Act 1962.

(2) The Education Acts 1944 to 1959 and this Act (except sections five, six, eight and ten thereof) may be cited together as the Education Acts 1944 to 1962.

(3) ...

(4) This Act shall, in its application to England and Wales, be construed as one with the Education Acts 1944 to 1953.

(5) ... this Act shall not extend to Scotland ...

(6) This Act shall not extend to Northern Ireland.

NOTES

Sub-s (3), and the words omitted from sub-s (5), were repealed by the SL(R) Act 1978.

Construed as one. Ie the enactments in question are to be construed as if they were contained in one Act, unless there is some manifest discrepancy; see eg *Phillips v Parnaby* [1934] 2 KB 299 at 302. Accordingly, definitions in the earlier Act may be relevant to the construction of provisions of this Act (see *Solomons v R Gertzenstein Ltd* [1954] 2 QB 243, [1954] 2 All ER 625, CA; *Crowe (Valuation Officer) v Lloyds British Testing Co Ltd* [1960] 1 QB 592, [1960] 1 All ER 411, CA).

Education Acts 1944 to 1959; Education Acts 1944 to 1953. For the Acts which may now be cited by the collective title "the Education Acts 1944 to 1985" (which include those Acts), see the Introductory Note to the Education Act 1944, this part of this title ante. Ss 5, 6, 8, 10 of this Act were repealed as noted ante.

SCHEDULES

[FIRST SCHEDULE

Ordinary Residence

1. The provisions of this Schedule shall have effect for the purposes of section 1 of this Act.

2. Subject to the following provisions of this Schedule, a person shall be treated for those purposes as ordinarily resident in the area of a local education authority if he would fall to be treated as belonging to that area for the purposes of section 31 (3) of the Education Act 1980.

3. Regulations made under this Act may modify the operation of the last preceding paragraph in relation to cases where a person applies for an award under section 1 of this Act in respect of a course and, at any time within the period of twelve months ending with the date on which that course is due to begin, a change occurs or has occurred in the circumstances by reference to which (apart from this paragraph) his place of ordinary residence would fall to be determined.

4. Regulations made under this Act may make provision whereby a person who under paragraph 2 of this Schedule would fall to be treated for the purposes of section 1 of this Act as not being ordinarily resident in any area is to be treated for those purposes as being ordinarily resident in the area of such local education authority as may be specified by or under the regulations.

5. Subsections (1), (2) and (4) of section 4 of this Act shall have effect in relation to paragraphs 3 and 4 of this Schedule as they have effect in relation to section 1 of this Act.]

NOTES

This Schedule was substituted by the Education Act 1980, s 19, Sch 5.

Local education authority. See, by virtue of s 14(4) ante, the Education Act 1944, s 114(1), this part of this title ante and the note thereto.

If he would fall to be treated . . . for the purposes of s 31(3) of the Education Act 1980. The area to which a person is to be treated as belonging for the purposes of s 31(3) post is to be determined in accordance with regulations made by the Secretary of State and any question under those regulations is to be determined by the Secretary of State; see s 38(5) of that Act.

Award. The designation of an award is immaterial; see s 4(1) ante.

Twelve months ending with. As a general rule the effect of defining a period in such a manner is to include the day on which the event in question occurs. "Months" means calendar months; see the Interpretation Act 1978, s 5, Sch 1, Vol 41, title Statutes.

Regulations under this Schedule. The Education (Mandatory Awards) Regulations 1985, SI 1985/1126 (made under paras 3, 4 above and ss 1, 4(2) ante) (which revoked and replaced with savings the Education (Mandatory Awards) Regulations 1984, SI 1984/1116, as amended by SI 1984/1240).

(Second Schedule repealed by the SL(R) Act 1974.)

INDUSTRIAL TRAINING ACT 1964

(1964 c 16)

An Act to make further provision for industrial and commercial training; to raise the limit on contributions out of the National Insurance Fund towards the expenses of the Minister of Labour in providing training courses; and for purposes connected with those matters

[12 March 1964]

Northern Ireland. This Act does not apply; see s 19(2) post.

1–15 (*Ss 1–10, 12, 14 repealed by the Industrial Training Act 1982, s 20(3), Sch 4, and the Agricultural Training Board Act 1982, s 11(1), Sch 2, and replaced as noted in the destination tables to those Acts, Vol 16, title* Employment, *Vol 1, title* Agriculture (Pt 5), *respectively; ss 11, 13 repealed by the Employment and Training Act 1973, ss 6(1), (3), 14(2), Sch 2, Pt I, para 18(e), Pt III, para 1(f), Sch 4; s 15 repealed by the House of Commons Disqualification Act 1975, s 10(2), Sch 3.*)

16 Powers of education authorities

The facilities for further education that may be provided by a local education authority under section 41 of the Education Act 1944 or by an education authority in Scotland under section 1 of the Education (Scotland) Act 1962 shall be deemed to include and always to have included facilities for vocational and industrial training.

NOTES

Education Act 1944, s 41. See this part of this title ante.
Education (Scotland) Act 1962. 10 & 11 Eliz 2 c 47; not printed in this work.

17, 18 (*S 17 repealed by the Employment and Training Act 1973, ss 6(1), (3), 14(2), Sch 2, Pt I, para 18(e), Pt III, para 1(f), Sch 4; s 18 repealed by the Industrial Training Act 1982, s 20(3), Sch 4, and the Agricultural Training Board Act 1982, s 11(1), Sch 2.*)

19 Short title and extent

(1) *This Act may be cited as the Industrial Training Act 1964.*

(2) *This Act . . . does not extend to Northern Ireland.*

NOTE

This section was repealed by the Industrial Training Act 1982, s 20(3), Sch 4, and the Agricultural Training Board Act 1982, s 11(1), Sch 2, but is printed for ease of interpretation.

(*Schedule repealed by the Industrial Training Act 1982, s 20(3), Sch 4 and the Agricultural Training Board Act 1982, s 11(1), Sch 2, and replaced as noted in the destination tables to those Acts, Vol 16, title* Employment, *Vol 1, title* Agriculture (Pt 5), *respectively.*)

EDUCATION ACT 1964

(1964 c 82)

An Act to enable county schools and voluntary schools to be established for providing full-time education by reference to age-limits differing from those specified in the Education Act 1944, as amended by the Education (Miscellaneous Provisions) Act 1948; to enable maintenance allowances to be granted in respect of pupils at special schools who would be over compulsory school age, or, in Scotland, over school age, but for section 38 (1) of the said Act of 1944 or section 32 (4) of the Education (Scotland) Act 1962; and for purposes connected with the matters aforesaid [31 July 1964]

Education Acts 1944 to 1985. This Act is one of the Acts which may be cited by this collective title; see the Introductory Note to the Education Act 1944, this part of this title ante.
Northern Ireland. This Act does not apply; see s 5(7) post.

Provisions relating to England and Wales

1 New schools with special age-limits

(1) [Where proposals with respect to a school maintained or to be maintained by a local education authority are submitted] to the Secretary of State under [section 12 or 13 of the Education Act 1980,] the proposals may, if the authority or persons submitting the proposals think fit,—

(a) specify an age which is below the age of ten years and six months and an age which is above the age of twelve years, and

(b) provide that the school shall be [a school] for providing full-time education suitable to the requirements of pupils whose ages are between the ages so specified.

[(2) The Secretary of State shall make regulations for determining, or enabling him to determine, whether a school in respect of which proposals making such provision as is mentioned in the preceding subsection are implemented is to be deemed for the purposes of the Education Act 1944 and the other enactments relating to education to be a primary or a secondary school.]

(3) The powers conferred by this section shall be exercisable—

(a) notwithstanding anything contained in the Education Acts 1944 to 1962, and, in particular, in section 7 of the Education Act 1944 (which relates to the stages in which the statutory system of public education is to be organised), but

(b) without prejudice to the exercise of any other power conferred by those Acts.

NOTES

The words in the first and third pairs of square brackets in sub-s (1) were substituted by the Education Act 1968, s 2, consequent on the provision contained therein, this part of this title post.

Sub-s (2), and the words in the second pair of square brackets in sub-s (1), were substituted by the Education Act 1980, s 16(4), Sch 3, para 12.

General Note. Under the Education Act 1944, ss 8(1)(b), 114(1), this part of this title ante, transfer from primary to secondary education takes place at between the ages of $10\frac{1}{2}$ and 12 years. This section enables schools to be established or maintained in pursuance of proposals under s 12 or 13 of the Education Act 1980, this part of this title post which have age limits different from those mentioned above, eg schools with age limits of, say, 5 to 9 years, 9 to 13 years and 13 to 18 years. Any such school will be designated as being either a primary or a secondary school in accordance with regulations made under sub-s (2) above.

Secretary of State. See the note "Secretary of State for Education and Science" to the Education Act 1944, s 1, this part of this title ante.

Thinks fit. Statutory powers are often conferred in subjective terms, the competent authority being entitled to act, eg, when it "thinks fit", or when it is "satisfied" or it "appears" to it that a prescribed state of affairs exists, but the inherent jurisdiction of the courts to determine whether such powers have been exceeded is not readily ousted by the use of such language; see further 1 Halsbury's Laws (4th edn) para 22.

Below the age of ten years and six months. See the Education Act 1944, s 8(1)(*a*), this part of this title ante.

Above the age of twelve years. See the Education Act 1944, s 8(1)(*b*), this part of this title ante in conjunction with the definition of "senior pupil" in s 114(1) of that Act.

Full-time education. This term is not defined in the Education Act 1944, this part of this title ante. Presumably attendance at a county school or voluntary school in accordance with the school sessions and school terms fixed under s 23 of that Act constitutes full-time education.

Definitions. By virtue of s 5(4) post, for "primary school", "pupil", "school" and "secondary school", see the Education Act 1944, s 114(1), this part of this title ante, and for "local education authority", see s 114(1) of that Act and the note thereto.

Education Act 1980, ss 12, 13; Education Act 1944, s 7. See this part of this title post and ante, respectively.

Education Acts 1944 to 1966. For the Acts which may now be cited by the collective title "the Education Acts 1944 to 1985" (which includes those Acts), see the Introductory Note to the Education Act 1944, this part of this title ante.

Regulations under this section. The Education (Middle Schools) Regulations 1980, SI 1980/918.

2, 3 (*S 2 repealed by the Education (School-leaving Dates) Act 1976, s 3(3), Schedule; s 3 repealed by the SL(R) Act 1978.*)

Supplementary provisions

4 (*Repealed by the SL(R) Act 1978.*)

5 Short title, citation, construction and extent

(1) This Act may be cited as the Education Act 1964.

(2) The Education Acts 1944 to 1962 and this Act ... may be cited together as the Education Acts 1944 to 1964.

(3) ...

(4) This Act ... shall be construed as one with the Education Acts 1944 to 1953.

(5) Except in so far as the context otherwise requires, any reference in this Act to an enactment shall be construed as a reference to that enactment as amended or extended by or under any other enactment.

(6) ... this Act shall not extend to Scotland ...

(7) This Act shall not extend to Northern Ireland.

NOTES

Sub-s (3), and the words omitted from sub-ss (2), (4), (6), were repealed by the SL(R) Act 1978.

Construed as one. Ie the enactments in question are to be construed as if they were contained in one Act, unless there is some manifest discrepancy; see eg *Phillips v Parnaby* [1934] 2 KB 299 at 302. Accordingly, definitions in the earlier Act may be relevant to the construction of provisions of this Act (see *Solomons v R Gertzenstein Ltd* [1954] 2 QB 243, [1954] 2 All ER 625, CA; *Crowe (Valuation Officer) v Lloyds British Testing Co Ltd* [1960] 1 QB 592, [1960] 1 All ER 411, CA).

Education Acts 1944 to 1962; Education Acts 1944 to 1953. Cf the note "Education Acts 1944 to 1966" to s 1 ante.

REMUNERATION OF TEACHERS ACT 1965

(1965 c 3)

ARRANGEMENT OF SECTIONS

An Act to make new provision for determining the remuneration of teachers; and for purposes connected therewith   [25 March 1965]

Education Acts 1944 to 1985. This Act is one of the Acts which may be cited by this collective title; see the Introductory Note to the Education Act 1944, this part of this title ante.

Northern Ireland. This Act does not apply; see s 9(5) post.

1 Committees to consider remuneration of teachers

(1) The Secretary of State shall secure that, for the purpose of considering the remuneration payable to teachers by local education authorities, there shall be one or more committees consisting of—

(*a*) a chairman appointed by the Secretary of State as being an independent person;

(*b*) one or more persons nominated from time to time by the Secretary of State to represent him, together with persons representing one or more bodies to which this paragraph applies;

(*c*) persons representing one or more bodies to which this paragraph applies.

(2) The bodies to which paragraph (*b*) of the preceding subsection applies are local education authorities, joint education committees, organisations appearing to the Secretary of State to represent local education authorities and organisations appearing to the Secretary of State to represent education committees; and the bodies to which paragraph (*c*) of that subsection applies are organisations appearing to the Secretary of State to represent teachers or particular descriptions of teachers.

(3) The Secretary of State shall determine which bodies to which paragraph (*b*) or paragraph (*c*) of subsection (1) of this section applies are to be represented on each committee constituted under this section, and the number of persons by whom any such body is to be so represented, and (subject to the following provisions of this section) may from time to time vary or revoke any such determination.

(4) A determination of the Secretary of State whereby a body which is for the time being represented on a committee constituted under this section will cease to be so represented (except in a case where that body will have ceased to exist before the time when the determination is to take effect) shall not have effect unless it is embodied in an order made by the Secretary of State.

(5) Any order under the last preceding subsection may be revoked by a subsequent order made by the Secretary of State.

(6) Any power to make orders under this section shall be exercisable by statutory instrument; and any statutory instrument containing an order under subsection (4) of this section shall be subject to annulment in pursuance of a resolution of either House of Parliament.

(7) Subject to any determination of the Secretary of State under this section, it shall be for each body to which any such determination relates to nominate from time to time the person or persons by whom it is to be represented on a committee constituted under this section.

(8) The Secretary of State, either at the time when a committee is constituted under this section or at any subsequent time, may give directions specifying the descriptions of teachers whose remuneration any such committee are to consider, or allocating, as between two or more such committees, the descriptions of remuneration which they are to consider respectively.

NOTES

Sub-s (1): Secretary of State. See the note "Secretary of State for Education and Science" to the Education Act 1944, this part of this title ante.

Sub-s (2): Joint education committees. Provision for the establishment of joint education committees is made by the Education Act 1944, Sch 1, Pt II, para 3, this part of this title ante.

Sub-s (6): Statutory instrument; subject to annulment. For provisions as to statutory instruments generally, see the Statutory Instruments Act 1946, Vol 41, title Statutes, and as to statutory instruments which are subject to annulment, see ss 5(1), 7(1) of that Act.

Definitions. For "education committee", see s 8(1) post. By virtue of s 9(3) post, for "local education authority", see the Education Act 1944, s 114(1), this part of this title ante and the note thereto.

Orders under this section. The Remuneration of Teachers (Further Education Committee) Order 1966, SI 1966/964; the Remuneration of Teachers (Burnham Committees) Order 1974, SI 1974/959; the Remuneration of Teachers (Burnham Further Education Committee) Order 1976, SI 1976/169; and the Remuneration of Teachers (Primary and Secondary Schools Burnham Committee) (Variation) Order 1979, SI 1979/339.

2 Review of remuneration by committees

(1) It shall be the duty of each committee, whenever they think fit or are required by the Secretary of State to do so, to review the relevant remuneration of teachers as that remuneration exists (whether in pursuance of this Act or of any previous enactment or otherwise) at the time of the review.

(2) Where, in consequence of such a review, a committee agree on any recommendations with respect to the relevant remuneration of teachers, they shall transmit those recommendations to the Secretary of State.

(3) Subject to the following provisions of this section, on the receipt of any recommendations of a committee under the last preceding subsection the Secretary of State shall prepare a draft document, setting out the scales and other provisions required for determining the relevant remuneration of teachers, in the form in which, in his opinion, those scales and provisions should be so as to give effect to the recommendations of the committee.

(4) Where the Secretary of State has prepared a draft document under the last preceding subsection, he shall consult the committee in question with respect to the draft and shall make such modifications of the draft as are requisite for giving effect to any representations made by the committee with respect thereto; and he shall then—

(a) arrange for a document setting out the requisite scales and other provisions in the form of the draft, or in that form as modified under this subsection, as the case may be, to be published by Her Majesty's Stationery Office, and

(b) make an order referring to that document and directing that the relevant remuneration of teachers shall be determined in accordance with the scales and other provisions set out in the document.

(5) If at the time when any recommendations of a committee are transmitted to the Secretary of State under subsection (2) of this section—

(a) an order made under the last preceding subsection is in force with respect to the relevant remuneration of teachers, and

(b) it appears to the Secretary of State that effect could more conveniently be given to those recommendations by amending the scales and other provisions set out in the document referred to in that order, the Secretary of State, instead of preparing a new draft document under subsection (3) of this section, may prepare a draft order setting out the amendments of those scales and other provisions which, in his opinion, are requisite for giving effect to the recommendations.

(6) Where the Secretary of State has prepared a draft order under the last preceding subsection, he shall consult the committee in question with respect to the draft and shall make such modifications of the draft as are requisite for giving effect to any representations made by the committee with respect thereto; and the Secretary of State shall then make the order in the form of the draft, or in that form as modified under this subsection, as the case may be.

NOTES

General Note. As to the Secretary of State's power to refer to arbitration matters in which agreement has not been reached in a committee, see s 3 post.

As to the application of sub-ss (3)–(6) above to the recommendations of arbitrators appointed under s 3 post, see s 4 post.

Secretary of State. See the note "Secretary of State for Education and Science" to the Education Act 1944, s 1, this part of this title ante.

Definitions. For "committee" and "the relevant remuneration of teachers", see s 8(2) post.

Orders under this section. The Remuneration of Teachers (Primary and Secondary Education) Order 1983, SI 1983/1463 (the document entitled "Scales of Salaries for Teachers: Primary and Secondary Education, England and Wales 1983" referred to in that order is amended by SI 1984/1650, SI 1985/38, SI 1985/944, made under this section); and the Remuneration of Teachers (Further Education) Order 1983, SI 1983/1464 (the document entitled "Scales of Salaries for Teachers in Further Education, England and Wales 1983" referred to in this order is amended by SI 1984/2043, SI 1985/495, SI 1985/1248, made under this section).

As to the effect of orders under sub-ss (4), (6) above, see s 5 post.

For supplementary provisions as to orders, see s 7 post.

3 Provision for arbitration

(1) The Secretary of State shall make arrangements whereby, in such circumstances and subject to such exceptions as may be provided by the arrangements, matters in respect of which agreement has not been reached in a committee after they have been considered by the committee in accordance with the preceding provisions of this Act may be referred to arbitration in such manner as may be so provided.

(2) Before making any arrangements under the preceding subsection in relation to a committee, the Secretary of State shall consult the bodies which are to be represented on the committee in accordance with any determinations made by him under section 1 of this Act which are for the time being in force.

(3) Any such arrangements may include provision for the appointment of arbitrators by the [Advisory, Conciliation and Arbitration Service] for the purposes of any reference under this section . . .

(4) The Arbitration Act 1950 shall not apply to any reference under this section.

NOTES

The words in square brackets in sub-s (3) were substituted, and the words omitted from that subsection were repealed, by the Employment Protection Act 1975, s 125(1), (3), Sch 16, Pt IV, para 11, Sch 18.

Secretary of State. See the note "Secretary of State for Education and Science" to the Education Act 1944, s 1, this part of this title ante.

Committee. Ie a committee constituted under s 1 ante; see s 8(2) post.

Referred to arbitration. S 4 post makes provision for the action which may be taken on the recommendation of the arbitrators appointed under this section.

Advisory, Conciliation and Arbitration Service. As to the establishment and functions of this body, see the Employment Protection Act 1975, ss 1 et seq, Vol 16, title Employment.

Arbitration Act 1950. See Vol 2, title Arbitration.

4 Action on recommendations of arbitrators

(1) Any recommendations of the arbitrators, on a reference under section 3 of this Act with respect to any matters considered by a committee, shall be transmitted to the Secretary of State; and, except where those recommendations do not propose any change in the relevant remuneration of teachers, the provisions of subsections (3) to (6) of section 2 of this Act shall (subject to the next following subsection) have effect in relation to the recommendations of the arbitrators as if they were recommendations of that committee.

(2) If, in any case where any recommendations of arbitrators have been transmitted to the Secretary of State under the preceding subsection, each House of Parliament resolves that national economic circumstances require that effect should not be given to the recommendations, the provisions of section 2 of this Act referred to in the preceding subsection shall not have effect as mentioned in that subsection.

(3) Where such a resolution has been passed by each House of Parliament, the Secretary of State, after consultation with the committee in question, shall determine what changes (if any) in the relevant remuneration of teachers are appropriate in the circumstances, and, unless he determines that no such changes are appropriate, shall (subject to the next following subsection) proceed in accordance with subsections (3) and (4) of section 2 of this Act, or (where applicable) in accordance with subsections (5) and (6) of that section, as if the changes determined by him had been recommended by that committee under subsection (2) of that section.

(4) Subsections (4) and (6) of section 2 of this Act, as applied by the last preceding subsection, shall each have effect with the substitution, for the words from "shall make" to "give effect to", of the words "may, if he thinks fit, modify the draft in consequence of".

NOTES

Committee. Ie a committee constituted under s 1 ante; see s 8(2) post.

Secretary of State. See the note "Secretary of State for Education and Science" to the Education Act 1944, s 1, this part of this title ante.

Order under this section. No orders made under this section remain in force as at 1 August 1985.

5 Effect of orders as to remuneration

(1) Where any order made under subsection (4) of section 2 of this Act is for the time being in force, then, subject to the next following subsection, remuneration to which the order applies shall be determined, and shall be paid to teachers by local education authorities, in accordance with the scales and other provisions set out in the document referred to in that order.

(2) Where, at any time while an order under subsection (4) of section 2 of this Act (in this subsection referred to as "the principal order") is in force, an order under subsection (6) of that section relating to remuneration to which the principal order applies (in this subsection referred to as "the amending order") comes into force, then, at any time while the amending order is in force, remuneration to which the principal order applies shall be determined, and shall be paid to teachers by local education authorities, in accordance with the scales and other provisions set out in the document referred to in the principal order as amended by the amending order.

(3) In this section any reference to subsection (4) or subsection (6) of section 2 of this Act includes a reference to that subsection as applied by section 4 of this Act.

NOTE

   Definitions. By virtue of s 9(3) post for "local education authority", see the Education Act 1944, s 114(1), this part of this title ante and the note thereto. Note as to "the amending order" and "the principal order", sub-s (2) above.

6 *(Repealed by the SL(R) Act 1978.)*

7 Supplementary provisions as to orders relating to remuneration and repeals

(1) Any power to make orders under the provisions of sections 2 to 4 of this Act shall be exercisable by statutory instrument.

(2) Any order made under those provisions may be revoked by a subsequent order thereunder.

(3) Any order under those provisions may be made with retrospective effect to any date specified in the order, and the remuneration of teachers to whom the order applies shall be deemed to have been payable accordingly:

Provided that nothing in this subsection shall be construed as authorising the remuneration of any teacher to be reduced retrospectively.

(4) Any order made under those provisions may include provision for revoking any order made under the Remuneration of Teachers Act 1963 which is for the time being in force.

(5) Subject to the proviso to subsection (3) of this section, any order made under those provisions may contain such transitional, supplementary and incidental provisions as the Secretary of State may consider necessary or expedient.

(6) Without prejudice to the operation of any order made (whether before or after the passing of this Act) under the Remuneration of Teachers Act 1963, section 89 of the Education Act 1944 is hereby repealed.

(7) The Remuneration of Teachers Act 1963 is hereby repealed as from the earliest date on which no order made under that Act (whether before or after the passing of this Act) continues to have effect.

NOTES

   Statutory instrument. For provisions as to statutory instruments generally, see the Statutory Instruments Act 1946, Vol 41, title Statutes.

   Revoked. The express power to revoke orders is necessary because the Interpretation Act 1978, s 14, Vol 41, title Statutes, does not extend to powers to make such instruments contained in Acts passed before 1 January 1979; see s 22(1) of, and Sch 2, para 3 to, that Act.

8 Interpretation

(1) In section 1 of this Act "education committee" means an education committee established by a local education authority or a joint education committee established by two or more local education authorities.

(2) In sections 2 to 4 of this Act "committee" means a committee constituted under section 1 of this Act, and "the relevant remuneration of teachers", in relation to such a committee, means the remuneration which, in accordance with any directions under section 1(8) of this Act which are for the time being in force, that committee are required to consider.

(3) Except in so far as the context otherwise requires, any reference in this Act to an enactment shall be construed as a reference to that enactment as amended or extended by or under any other enactment.

NOTES

Education committee. As to the duty to establish education committees, see the Education Act 1944, Sch 1, Pt II, para 1, this part of this title ante.

Joint education committee. See the note to s 1 ante.

Local education authority. By virtue of s 9(3) post, for meaning, see the Education Act 1944, s 114(1), this part of this title ante and the note thereto.

9 Short title, citation, construction and extent

(1) This Act may be cited as the Remuneration of Teachers Act 1965.

(2) The Education Acts 1944 to 1964 and this Act may be cited together as the Education Acts 1944 to 1965.

(3) This Act shall be construed as one with the Education Acts 1944 to 1964.

(4) This Act . . . shall not extend to Scotland.

(5) This Act shall not extend to Northern Ireland.

NOTES

The words omitted from sub-s (4) were repealed by the SL(R) Act 1978.

Construed as one. Ie the enactments in question are to be construed as if they were contained in one Act, unless there is some manifest discrepancy; see eg *Phillips v Parnaby* [1934] 2 KB 299 at 302. Accordingly, definitions in the earlier Act may be relevant to the construction of provisions of this Act (see *Solomons v R Gertzenstein Ltd* [1954] 2 QB 243, [1954] 2 All ER 625, CA; *Crowe (Valuation Officer) v Lloyds British Testing Co Ltd* [1960] 1 QB 592, [1960] 1 All ER 411, CA).

Education Acts 1944 to 1964. For the Acts which may now be cited by the collective title "the Education Acts 1944 to 1985" (which includes those Acts), see the Introductory Note to the Education Act 1944, this part of this title ante.

EDUCATION ACT 1967

(1967 c 3)

An Act to enlarge the powers of the Secretary of State to make contributions, grants and loans in respect of aided schools and special agreement schools and to direct local education authorities to pay the expenses of establishing or enlarging controlled schools; and to provide for loans for capital expenditure incurred for purposes of colleges of education by persons other than local education authorities   [16 February 1967]

Education Acts 1944 to 1985. This Act is one of the Acts which may be cited by this collective title; see the Introductory Note to the Education Act 1944, this part of this title ante.

Northern Ireland. This Act does not apply; see s 6(3) post.

1 Extended powers to make contributions, grants and loans

(1) . . .

(2) Where the Secretary of State—

(*a*) has approved proposals submitted to him under [section 13 of the Education Act 1980] that a school proposed to be established should be maintained by a local education authority as a voluntary school and has directed that the proposed school shall be an aided school or special agreement school; . . .

(*b*) . . .

he may, out of moneys provided by Parliament, pay to the . . . governors of the school, in respect of any sums expended by them on the provision of a site for the school or of the school buildings, a grant not exceeding [85 per cent] of those sums; but no such grant shall be payable to the . . . governors of a special agreement school in respect of any sums expended by them in the execution of proposals to which the special agreement for the school relates.

(3) Subsection (3) of section 103 of the Education Act 1944 (which makes provision for the exercise of the Secretary of State's discretion in determining the amount of grants under that section) shall, with the necessary modifications, apply to grants under subsection (2) of this section.

(4) For the purposes of section 105 of the Education Act 1944 (which authorises the Secretary of State to make loans to the . . . governors of aided schools and special agreement schools for certain initial expenses involving capital expenditure) any expenses in respect of which the Secretary of State may make a grant under subsection (2) of this section shall be included in the expression "initial expenses", and in determining the . . . governors' share of any initial expenses the amount of any such grant paid or payable in respect of them shall be taken into account in the same way as grants under section 103 of that Act.

(5) The following provisions, being superseded by this section, shall cease to have effect (subject to subsection (6) of this section), that is to say—

(*a*) in section 103 of the Education Act 1944, in subsection (1) the words from "or directs" to "discontinued" and the words "or any schools to be established", and in subsection (3) the words from "or of the sites" to the end;

(*b*) section 104 of that Act;

(*c*) section 1 of the Education (Miscellaneous Provisions) Act 1953 and, in section 8 of that Act, paragraph (*b*) of subsection (1) and the word "and" preceding that paragraph, and subsection (2); and

(*d*) section 1 of the Education Act 1959, except subsection (4) of that section.

(6) Nothing in this section shall extend to contributions or grants in respect of expenditure on work which—

(*a*) was begun before 4th July 1966; or

(*b*) was approved by the Secretary of State before that date under section 13 (6) of the Education Act 1944 or under any arrangements relating to work to which that section does not apply; or

(*c*) was included in a programme notified to a local education authority as the main building programme approved by the Secretary of State for the twelve months beginning with April 1966 or for any earlier period;

or in respect of expenditure on the provision of the site on which or buildings to which any such work was done or proposed to be done.

NOTES

Sub-s (1) was repealed, and the words in the second pair of square brackets in sub-s (2) were substituted by the Education Act 1975, ss 4, 5, Schedule.

The words in the first pair of square brackets in sub-s (2) were substituted by the Education Act 1980, s 16(4), Sch 3, para 13.

Sub-s (2)(*b*) and the word "and" immediately preceding it were repealed by the Education Act 1968, s 1(3), Sch 2; the other words omitted from sub-s (2) and the words omitted from sub-s (4) were repealed by the Education Act 1980, s 1(3), Sch 1, para 23.

Secretary of State. See the note "Secretary of State for Education and Science" to the Education Act 1944, s 1, this part of this title ante.

Definitions. By virtue of s 6(2) post, for "maintain" and "school", see the Education Act 1944, s 114(1), this part of this title ante, and for "local education authority", see s 114(1) of that Act and the note thereto; for "voluntary school", see s 9(2) of that Act; for "aided school" and "special agreement school", see s 15 of that Act; for "school buildings", see the Education Act 1946, s 4(2), this part of this title ante, and for "site", see s 16(1) of that Act ante.

Education Act 1980, s 13. See this part of this title post.

Education Act 1944, ss 103, 105; Education (Miscellaneous Provisions) Act 1953, s 8; Education Act 1959, s 1. See this part of this title ante.

2 (*Amends the Education Act 1946, s 1, this part of this title ante.*)

3 Extension of power to require local education authority to defray expenses of establishing controlled middle school

Where [persons submit proposals to the Secretary of State under section 13 of the Education Act 1980] for the establishment of a new school and its maintenance by the local education authority as a voluntary school, and the proposals make provision as mentioned in section 1 (1) of the Education Act 1964 (new schools with special age limits), section 2 of the Education (Miscellaneous Provisions) Act 1953 (power to require local education authority to defray expenses of establishing controlled school) shall apply in relation to the school established in pursuance of the proposals as if in paragraph (*b*) of that section (which limits the power conferred by it to cases where the new school is required for pupils for whom accommodation in some other voluntary school has ceased to be available) after the words "for whom" there were inserted the words "or for a substantial proportion of whom".

NOTES

The words in square brackets were substituted by the Education Act 1980, s 16(4), Sch 3, para 14.

Secretary of State. See the note "Secretary of State for Education and Science" to the Education Act 1944, s 1, this part of this title ante.

Definitions. By virtue of s 6(2) post, for "school" and "maintain", see the Education Act 1944, s 114(1), this part of this title ante, for "local education authority", see s 114(1) of that Act and the note thereto, and for "voluntary school", see s 9(2) of that Act.

Education Act 1980, s 13. See this part of this title post.

Education Act 1964, s 1(1); Education (Miscellaneous Provisions) Act 1953, s 2. See this part of this title ante.

4 Loans for capital expenditure for purposes of colleges of education

(1) The Secretary of State may by regulations make provision for the making by him out of moneys provided by Parliament of loans to persons other than local education authorities for the purpose of helping them to meet capital expenditure incurred or to be incurred by them or on their behalf in connection with the provision, replacement, extension, improvement, furnishing or equipment of colleges for the training of teachers.

(2) Any loan made to any persons in pursuance of regulations under this section shall be made on such terms and conditions as may be specified in an agreement made between the Secretary of State and those persons with the consent of the Treasury.

(3) Regulations under this section may make the making of loans dependent on the fulfilment of such conditions as may be determined by or in accordance with the regulations, and may also make provision for requiring persons to whom loans have

been made in pursuance of the regulations to comply with such requirements as may be so determined.

(4) Regulations under this section shall be made by statutory instrument, which shall be subject to annulment in pursuance of a resolution of either House of Parliament.

NOTES

Secretary of State. See the note "Secretary of State for Education and Science" to the Education Act 1944, s 1, this part of this title ante.

Local education authority. See, by virtue of s 6(2) post, the Education Act 1944, s 114(1), this part of this title ante and the note thereto.

Statutory instrument; subject to annulment. For provisions as to statutory instruments generally, see the Statutory Instruments Act 1946, Vol 41, title Statutes, and as to statutory instruments which are subject to annulment, see ss 5(1), 7(1) of that Act.

Regulations under this section. No regulations made under this section remain in force as at 1 August 1985.

5 Expenses

There shall be defrayed out of moneys provided by Parliament any increase attributable to this Act in the sums so payable under any other enactment.

6 Short title, citation, construction and extent

(1) This Act may be cited as the Education Act 1967 and this Act and the Education Acts 1944 to 1965 may be cited together as the Education Acts 1944 to 1967.

(2) This Act shall be construed as one with the Education Acts 1944 to 1965.

(3) This Act does not extend to Scotland or to Northern Ireland.

NOTES

Construed as one. Ie the enactments in question are to be construed as if they were contained in one Act, unless there is some manifest discrepancy; see eg *Phillips v Parnaby* [1934] 2 KB 299 at 302. Accordingly, definitions in the earlier Act may be relevant to the construction of provisions of this Act (see *Solomons v R Gertzenstein Ltd* [1954] 2 QB 243, [1954] 2 All ER 625, CA; *Crowe (Valuation Officer) v Lloyds British Testing Co Ltd* [1960] 1 QB 592, [1960] 1 All ER 411, CA).

Education Acts 1944 to 1965. For the Acts which may now be cited by the collective title "the Education Acts 1944 to 1985" (which includes those Acts), see the Introductory Note to the Education Act 1944, this part of this title ante.

EDUCATION ACT 1968

(1968 c 17)

An Act to amend the law as to the effect of and procedure for making changes in the character, size or situation of county schools or voluntary schools to enable special age limits to be adopted for existing as well as for new schools, and to make certain other amendments as to the approval or provision of school premises; and for purposes connected therewith
[10 April 1968]

Education Acts 1944 to 1985. This Act is one of the Acts which may be cited by this collective title; see the Introductory Note to the Education Act 1944, this part of this title ante.

Northern Ireland. This Act does not apply; see s 6(3) post.

1 Changes to character, size or situation of schools

(1) For purposes of the Education Acts 1944 to 1967 and any other enactment relating to the duties of a local education authority, references in whatever terms to

discontinuing a school (and, in particular, those in section 13 of the Education Act 1944 [or section 12 of the Education Act 1980] to a local authority ceasing to maintain a county school or a voluntary school), or to establishing a new school, shall not be read as applying by reason of any change which is made to an existing school—

(a) by education beginning or ceasing to be provided for pupils above or below a particular age; or

(b) by education beginning or ceasing to be provided for girls as well as boys, or for boys as well as girls; or

(c) by any enlargement or alteration of the school premises or transfer of the school to a new site;

and the school existing before an event mentioned in paragraph (a), (b) or (c) above shall be regarded as continuing despite that event and as being the same school before and after that event (unless it is to be regarded for other reasons as discontinued).

(2) . . .

(3) In the enactments mentioned in Schedule 1 to this Act there shall be made the amendments provided for by that Schedule, being amendments arising out of or related to the provisions in subsections (1) and (2) above; and the enactments mentioned in Schedule 2 to this Act are hereby repealed to the extent specified in column 3 of that Schedule.

(4) Subsection (1) above shall be deemed to have had effect since the beginning of April 1945 in so far as the effect is—

(a) that a school is to be or have been regarded as being the same school before and after any such event as is there mentioned; or

(b) that anything may be or have been lawfully done without proposals being approved under section 13 of the Education Act 1944.

(5) Subject to subsection (4) above, this section shall not apply in relation to things proposed to be done before the end of the summer term 1968, nor in relation to proposals approved before then under section 13 of the Education Act 1944 or to anything done in pursuance of any such proposals; and for this purpose "summer term" means, in the case of any school, the term ending last before the month of September.

NOTES

The words in square brackets in sub-s (1) were inserted, and sub-s (2) was repealed, by the Education Act 1980, ss 16(4), 38(6), Sch 3, para 15, Sch 7.

Change . . . made to an existing school. But for sub-s (1), a change in the age groups or sex of the pupils or in the premises would have constituted a fundamental change in the character of a school so as to amount to ceasing to maintain a school and establishing a new one under the Education Act 1944, s 13 (repealed) (see *Wilford v West Riding of Yorkshire CC* [1908] 1 KB 685, 77 LJKB 436; and *Bradbury v London Borough of Enfield* [1967] 3 All ER 434, [1967] 1 WLR 1311, CA), with the result that it might have been unlawful for local authorities to continue to maintain schools whose character had been so changed. Similar provisions to those formerly contained in s 13 of the 1944 Act are now contained in the Education Act 1980, s 12, this part of this title post.

Retrospective effect. Sub-s (1) above is given retrospective effect for certain purposes by sub-s (4) above.

Definitions. By virtue of s 6(2) post, for "alterations", "enlargement", "premises" and "school", see the Education Act 1944, s 114(1), this part of this title ante; for "local education authority", see s 114(1) of that Act and the note thereto; and for "county school" and "voluntary school", see ss 9, 15 of the 1944 Act.

Education Acts 1944 to 1967. For the Acts which may now be cited by the collective title "the Education Acts 1944 to 1985" (which includes those Acts), see the Introductory Note to the Education Act 1944, this part of this title ante.

Education Act 1944, s 13. Repealed by the Education Act 1980, s 38(6), Sch 7; see now s 12 of the 1980 Act post.

Education Act 1980, s 12. See this part of this title post.

2 Schools with special age limits

Section 1 of the Education Act 1964 (which enables new county or voluntary schools to be established to provide both primary and secondary education) shall apply where it is proposed that an existing school maintained or to be maintained by a local education authority should provide both primary and secondary education, and accordingly in subsection (1) of that section—

  (a) for the words from "Where a local education authority intend to establish a new county school" to "for that purpose" there shall be substituted the words "Where proposals with respect to a school maintained or to be maintained by a local education authority are submitted"; and

  (b) for the word "established" in paragraph (b) there shall be substituted the words "a school".

NOTES

General Note. Under the Education Act 1944, s 8(1), this part of this title ante, and the definitions of "junior pupil" and "senior pupil" in s 114(1) of that Act, education in a primary school could not continue beyond the age of twelve years and education in a secondary school could not begin before the age of ten years and six months. The Education Act 1964, s 1, this part of this title ante, as originally enacted, enabled the Secretary of State to approve proposals for new county and voluntary schools with age limits different from those mentioned above. This section extended s 1 of the 1964 Act to schools already maintained.

Definitions. By virtue of s 6(2) post, for "county school", see the Education Act 1944, ss 9(2), 15, this part of this title ante; for "primary education" and "secondary education", see s 8(1) of the 1944 Act in conjunction with the definitions of "junior pupil" and "senior pupil" contained in s 114(1) of that Act; for "local education authority", see s 114(1) of that Act and the note thereto.

Education Act 1964, s 1. See this part of this title ante.

3 Approval or provision of school premises (miscellaneous amendments)

  (1)–(3) . . .

  (4) If upon representations made to him by a local education authority the Secretary of State is satisfied—

  (a) that the . . . governors of a voluntary school propose to make a significant enlargement of the school premises or alterations to those premises, and that it is desirable for them to do so for the better provision of primary or secondary education at the premises or for securing that there is available for the area of the authority a sufficiency of suitable primary or secondary schools, or for both those reasons; and

  (b) that, having regard to the need to control public expenditure in the interests of the national economy, it is not reasonably practicable to effect the enlargement or alterations by providing permanent accommodation;

then, subject to proposals for any significant enlargement being approved under [section 13 of the Education Act 1980,] the Secretary of State may authorise the authority to provide, or assist in providing, temporary accommodation in accordance with arrangements approved by him; and Schedule 1 to the Education Act 1946 (which relates to the duties of the local education authority and the . . . governors with regard to the provision of sites and buildings for voluntary schools) shall not apply in relation to temporary accommodation provided by virtue of this subsection.

NOTES

Sub-ss (1), (2) and the words omitted from sub-s (4) were repealed, and the words in square brackets in sub-s (4) were substituted, by the Education Act 1980, ss 1(3), 16(4), 38(6), Sch 1, para 24, Sch 3, para 16, Sch 7.

Sub-s (3) amends the Education Act 1944, s 10(2), this part of this title ante.

Secretary of State. See the note "Secretary of State for Education and Science" to the Education Act 1944, s 1, this part of this title ante.

Significant enlargement of the . . . premises. By the Education Act 1944, s 67(4), this part of this title ante the question whether there is a significant enlargement of the premises is to be determined by the Secretary of State.

Definitions. For "alterations", "enlargement", "premises", "primary school", "secondary school" and "significant", see the Education Act 1944, s 114(1), this part of this title ante; for "primary education" and "secondary education", see s 8(1) of the 1944 Act in conjunction with the definitions of "junior pupil" and "senior pupil" contained in s 114(1) thereof; for "local education authority", see s 114(1) thereof and the note thereto.

Education Act 1980, s 13; Education Act 1946, Sch 1. See this part of this title ante.

4 Expenses

There shall be paid out of moneys provided by Parliament any increase attributable to this Act in the sums so payable under the Education Acts 1944 to 1967.

NOTE

Education Acts 1944 to 1967. See the note to s 1 ante.

5 Text of certain provisions as amended by this Act

(1) In accordance with the provisions of this Act (apart from the transitional provisions in section 1 (5)), the following sections, namely—

section 1 of the Education Act 1946; and

section 7 of the Education (Miscellaneous Provisions) Act 1948;

are to have effect as set out in Schedule 3 to this Act with the amendments made by this Act, by the Secretary of State for Education and Science Order 1964 and by the provisions listed in subsection (2) below, but without prejudice to the operation of any enactment affecting the operation of those sections and not so listed.

(2) The provisions above referred to, . . . as regards provisions by which section 1 of the Education Act 1946 is amended, are—

The Education (Miscellaneous Provisions) Act 1953, section 3; and

The Education Act 1967, section 2.

NOTES

The words omitted were repealed by the Education Act 1980, s 38(6), Sch 7.

All the provisions referred to in this section are printed in this part of this title ante.

6 Short title, citation, construction and extent

(1) This Act may be cited as the Education Act 1968 and this Act and the Education Acts 1944 to 1967 may be cited together as the Education Acts 1944 to 1968.

(2) This Act shall be construed as one with the Education Acts 1944 to 1967.

(3) This Act does not extend to Scotland or to Northern Ireland.

NOTES

Construed as one. Ie the enactments in question are to be construed as if they were contained in one Act, unless there is some manifest discrepancy; see eg *Phillips v Parnaby* [1934] 2 KB 299 at 302. Accordingly, definitions in the earlier Act may be relevant to the construction of provisions of this Act (see *Solomons v R Gertzenstein Ltd* [1954] 2 QB 243, [1954] 2 All ER 625, CA; *Crowe (Valuation Officer) v Lloyds British Testing Co Ltd* [1960] 1 QB 592, [1960] 1 All ER 411, CA).

Education Acts 1944 to 1967. See the note to s 1 ante.

SCHEDULES

(Sch 1 repealed in part by the Education Act 1980, s 38(6), Sch 7; the remainder amends the Education Act 1944, ss 16(1), 17(1), 67(4), 102, 105(2), 114(1), this part of this title ante, the Education Act 1946, s 1(1), this part of this title ante, and the London Government Act 1963, s 31(5), Vol 26, title London.)

SCHEDULE 2

Section 1

REPEALS

Chapter	Short Title	Extent of Repeal
9 & 10 Geo 6 c 50	The Education Act 1946	Section 1(2). In Part II of Schedule 2, the entry relating to section 114 of the Education Act 1944.
1 & 2 Eliz 2 c 33	The Education (Miscellaneous Provisions) Act 1953	In section 2(a), the words "(otherwise than by way of enlargement of an existing school)". Section 8(3)(b), together with the word "and" at the end of section 8(3)(a).
1967 c 3	The Education Act 1967	Section 1(2)(b), together with the word "or" at the end of section 1(2)(a).

(Sch 3 repealed in part by the Education Act 1980, s 38(6), Sch 7; the remainder sets out, with amendments, the Education Act 1946, s 1, and the Education (Miscellaneous Provisions) Act 1948, s 7, both this part of this title ante.)

EDUCATION (NO 2) ACT 1968

(1968 c 37)

An Act to make further provision for the government and conduct of colleges of education and other institutions of further education maintained by local education authorities, and of special schools so maintained   [3 July 1968]

Education Acts 1944 to 1985. This Act is one of the Acts which may be cited by this collective title; see the Introductory Note to the Education Act 1944, this part of this title ante.
Northern Ireland. This Act does not apply; see s 5(3) post.

1 Government and conduct of colleges of education and other institutions providing further education

(1) For every institution maintained by a local education authority, being either—

    (a) a college for the training of teachers (in this section referred to as a college of education); or

    (b) an institution, other than a college of education, providing full-time education pursuant to a scheme of further education approved under section 42 of the Education Act 1944,

there shall be an instrument (to be known as an instrument of government) providing for the constitution of a body of governors of the institution.

(2) The instrument of government for any such institution shall be made, in the case of a college of education, by order of the local education authority with the approval of the Secretary of State, and in any other case by order of the local education authority, and the body of governors to be constituted thereunder shall consist of such number of persons, appointed in such manner, as the local education authority or, in the case of a college of education, that authority with the approval of the Secretary of State may determine.

(3) Every such institution shall be conducted in accordance with articles of government, to be made by order of the local education authority with the approval of the Secretary of State; and those articles shall determine the functions to be exercised respectively, in relation to the institution, by the local education authority, the body of governors, the principal, and the academic board, if any.

(4) A local education authority may, with the approval of the Secretary of State, make an arrangement for the constitution of a single governing body for any two or more such institutions maintained by them as are mentioned in paragraph (b) of subsection (1) of this section; and the governing body constituted in pursuance of any such arrangement shall consist of such number of persons, appointed in such manner, as the local education authority may determine.

NOTES

Local education authority. For meaning, see, by virtue of s 5(2) post, the Education Act 1944, s 114(1), this part of this title ante and the note thereto.

Body of governors. Members of bodies of governors established under this section and s 2 post, and upon which any such body as is mentioned in the Local Government Act 1972, s 177(1)(a), Vol 25, title Local Government, is represented, are entitled to financial loss, travelling and subsistence allowances; see the Local Government (Allowances to Members) (Prescribed Bodies) Regulations 1968, SI 1968/1645.

Articles of government. As to supplemental provisions in relation thereto, see s 3(1) post.

Arrangement. See further as to such arrangements, s 3(2) post.

Education Act 1944, s 42. See this part of this title ante.

2 Government and conduct of special schools

(1) For every special school maintained by a local education authority there shall be an instrument (to be known as an instrument of government) providing for the constitution of a body of governors of the school.

(2) The instrument of government for any such school shall be made by order of the local education authority, and the body of governors to be constituted thereunder shall consist of such number of persons, appointed in such manner, as that authority may determine.

(3) Every such school shall be conducted in accordance with articles of government to be made by order of the local education authority.

(4) A local education authority may make an arrangement for the constitution of a single governing body for any two or more special schools maintained by them; and the governing body constituted in pursuance of any such arrangement shall consist of such number of persons, appointed in such manner, as the local education authority may determine.

(5) For the purposes of [section 21(1) and (3) of the Education Act 1944 (provisions as to governors of county and voluntary schools)] and of section 24 of that Act (appointment and dismissal of teachers in such schools) a special school maintained by a local education authority shall be treated as if it were a county school.

3 Supplemental

(1) The articles of government made under this Act for any establishment may regulate the constitution and functions of committees of the body of governors or of any academic board of that establishment, and of sub-committees of such committees.

(2) Every arrangement made under subsection (4) of section 1 or subsection (4) of section 2 of this Act may be terminated at any time by the local education authority by which it was made; and while such an arrangement is in force with respect to any establishments—

 (a) the foregoing provisions of this Act as to the constitution of the body of governors shall not apply to those establishments; and
 (b) for the purposes of any enactment the governing body constituted in accordance with the arrangement shall be deemed to be the body of governors of each of those establishments, and references to a governor in any enactment shall, in relation to each of those establishments, be construed accordingly.

(3) The following provisions of the Education Act 1944, that is to say—

 (a) subsection (1) of section 67 (determination of disputes between local education authorities and ... governors of schools);
 (b) section 68 (power to prevent unreasonable exercise of functions by local education authorities or by ... governors of county or voluntary schools);
 (c) section 99 (powers of Secretary of State in default of local education authorities or ... governors of county or voluntary schools),

shall apply in relation to establishments to which this Act applies and governors of those establishments as they apply in relation to county schools and governors of county schools.

(4) References in this Act to provisions of the Education Act 1944 are references thereto as amended by or under any subsequent enactment.

4 Commencement

(1) This Act shall come into force on such day as the Secretary of State may by order made by statutory instrument appoint; and different days may be appointed under this section for the purposes of different classes of establishments.

(2) Without prejudice to section 37 of the Interpretation Act 1889, any instrument of government or articles of government to be made under this Act for any establishment and any arrangement under this Act for the constitution of a single governing body for two or more establishments may be made so as to come into force before the date on which this Act comes into force in relation to establishments of that class, and any functions to be exercised under that instrument or arrangement or those articles may be exercised accordingly.

NOTES

Interpretation Act 1889, s 37. Repealed by the Interpretation Act 1978, s 25, Sch 3, Vol 41, title Statutes, and replaced by ss 13, 21(1) of, and Sch 2, para 3 to, that Act.

Orders under this section. The Education (No 2) Act 1968 (Commencement No 1) Order 1969, SI 1969/709 (appointing 1 July 1969 for the coming into force of the Act for the purposes of colleges of education); the Education (No 2) Act 1968 (Commencement No 2) Order 1969, SI 1969/1106 (appointing 1 October 1969 for the coming into force of the Act for the purposes of special schools); and the Education (No 2) Act 1968 (Commencement No 3) Order 1972, SI 1972/212 (appointing 1 September 1972 for the coming into force of the Act for the purposes of establishments of further education).

5 Short title, citation, construction and extent

(1) This Act may be cited as the Education (No 2) Act 1968, and shall be included among the Acts which may be cited together as the Education Acts 1944 to 1968.

(2) This Act shall be construed as one with the Education Acts 1944 to 1968.

(3) This Act does not extend to Scotland or Northern Ireland.

NOTES

Education Acts 1944 to 1968. For the Acts which may now be cited by the collective title "the Education Acts 1944 to 1985" (which includes those Acts), see the Introductory Note to the Education Act 1944, this part of this title ante.

Construed as one. Ie the enactments in question are to be construed as if they were contained in one Act, unless there is some manifest discrepancy; see eg *Phillips v Parnaby* [1934] 2 KB 299 at 302. Accordingly, definitions in the earlier Act may be relevant to the construction of provisions of this Act (see *Solomons v R Gertzenstein Ltd* [1954] 2 QB 243, [1954] 2 All ER 625, CA; *Crowe (Valuation Officer) v Lloyds British Testing Co Ltd* [1960] 1 QB 592, [1960] 1 All ER 411, CA).

CHRONICALLY SICK AND DISABLED PERSONS ACT 1970

(1970 c 44)

An Act to make further provision with respect to the welfare of chronically sick and disabled persons; and for connected purposes   [29 May 1970]

1–7 (*For ss 1, 2, see Vol 40, title* Social Security; *for s 3, see Vol 21, title* Housing; *for ss 4–7, see Vol 35, title* Public Health.)

University and school buildings

8 Access to, and facilities at, university and school buildings

(1) Any person undertaking the provision of a building intended for purposes mentioned in subsection (2) below shall, in the means of access both to and within the building, and in the parking facilities and sanitary conveniences to be available (if any),

make *provision, in so far as it is in the circumstances both practicable and reasonable,* for the needs of persons using the building who are disabled.

(2) The purposes referred to in subsection (1) above are the purposes of any of the following:—

(a) universities, university colleges and colleges, schools and halls of universities;

(b) schools within the meaning of the Education Act 1944, teacher training colleges maintained by local education authorities in England or Wales and other institutions providing further education pursuant to a scheme under section 42 of that Act;

(c) *(applies to Scotland only).*

NOTES

Prospective amendments. In sub-s (1) the words in italics are repealed and the words "appropriate provision" are substituted for those words, and the words:

"unless such body as may be prescribed by the Secretary of State is satisfied, after carrying out any procedures which may be so prescribed, that in the circumstances it is either not practicable to make such provision or not reasonable that such provision should be made; and different bodies and different procedures may be prescribed for different classes of buildings or other premises to which this subsection applies"

are added by the Disabled Persons Act 1981, s 6(1), Vol 35, title Public Health, as from a day to be appointed under s 6(6) of that Act.

The following subsection is inserted by s 6(4) of the 1981 Act as from a day to be appointed under s 6(6) of that Act:

"(1A) In subsection (1) above "appropriate provision" in relation to any case, means provision conforming with so much of the Design Note as is relevant to that case and "prescribed" means prescribed by regulations made by statutory instrument, which shall be subject to annulment in pursuance of a resolution of either House of Parliament; and in the foregoing provisions of this subsection "the Design Note" means Design Note 18 "Access for the Physically Disabled to Educational Buildings", published on behalf of the Secretary of State."

Person. Unless the contrary intention appears this includes a body of persons corporate or unincorporate; see the Interpretation Act 1978, s 5, Sch 1, Vol 41, title Statutes.

Building. It is thought that this expression must be given its ordinary meaning, which, in the words of Byles J, in *Stevens v Gourley* (1859) 7 CB NS 99 at 112, is "a structure of considerable size and intended to be permanent or at least to endure for a considerable time". Perhaps there must also be added, in accordance with the view expressed by Lord Esher MR, in *Moir v Williams* [1892] 1 QB 264 at 270, that the structure must be covered by a roof. It is submitted, however, that contrary to that view, the structure need not consist of bricks and stone-work. In fact a wooden structure of considerable size was held to be a building in *Stevens v Gourley* supra, and in any case the presence of bricks and stone-work seems to be irrelevant in the light of modern technology. Nevertheless, it would seem that a structure cannot be regarded as a building unless it can be said to form part of the realty and change the physical character of the land; see *Cheshire County Council v Woodward* [1962] 2 QB 126, [1962] 1 All ER 517. See also the cases cited in 1 Words and Phrases (2nd edn) 191 et seq.

Disabled. As to the power of the Secretary of State to make provision for the interpretation of this expression, see s 28 post.

Local education authorities. For meaning, see the Education Act 1944, s 114(1), this part of this title ante and the note thereto.

Planning permission. The provisions of this section are to be drawn to the attention of any person to whom planning permission is granted in relation to certain educational buildings; see the Town and Country Planning Act 1971, s 29B, Vol 46, title Town and Country Planning.

Education Act 1944. See this part of this title ante. For the meaning of "school" in that Act, see s 114(4) thereof.

8A–19 (*For ss 8A, 8B, see Vol 35, title* Public Health; *for s 9, see Vol 3, title* Armed Forces (Pt 5); *for s 10, see Vol 21, title* Housing; *s 11 repealed by the Social Security Act 1973, s 100(2)(b), Sch 28, Pt I; for ss 12, 18, see Vol 40, title* Social Security; *for ss 13, 16, see Vol 16, title* Employment; *for s 14, see Vol 34, title* Post Office; *for s 15, see Vol 25, title* Local Government; *for s 17, see Vol 30, title* National Health Service; *s 19 repealed by the National Health Service Reorganisation Act 1973, s 57, Sch 5.)*

Miscellaneous provisions

20–27   (*For ss 20, 21, see Vol 38, title* Road Traffic; *for ss 22, 24, see Vol 30, title* National Health Service; *s 23 amends the Pensions Appeals Tribunals Act 1943, ss 5, 6, 12(1), Vol 33, title* Pensions and Superannuation; *ss 25–27 repealed by the Education Act 1981, s 21, Sch 4.*)

28 Power to define certain expressions

Where it appears to the Secretary of State to be necessary or expedient to do so for the proper operation of any provision of this Act, he may by regulations made by statutory instrument, which shall be subject to annulment in pursuance of a resolution of either House of Parliament, make provision as to the interpretation for the purposes of that provision of any of the following expressions appearing therein, that is to say, "chronically sick", "chronic illness", "disabled" and "disability".

NOTES

Prospective amendment. The letter "(*a*)" is inserted before the words "make provision", and at the end of the section there are added the words "; or

(*b*) amend—

  (i)   the definition of "the Code of Practice for Access for the Disabled to Buildings" in section 4(1A) of this Act; and

  (ii)   the definition of "the Design Note" in section 8(1A) of this Act."

by the Disabled Persons Act 1981, s 6(5), (6), Vol 35, title Public Health, as from a day to be appointed under s 6(7) of that Act.

Statutory instrument; subject to annulment. For provisions as to statutory instruments generally, see the Statutory Instruments Act 1946, Vol 41, title Statutes, and as to statutory instruments which are subject to annulment, see ss 5(1), 7(1) of that Act.

Extension. This section is extended by the Town and Country Planning Act 1971, ss 29A(3), 29B(3), Vol 46, title Town and Country Planning, and by the Local Government (Miscellaneous Provisions) Act 1976, s 20(13), Vol 35, title Public Health.

Regulations under this section. No regulations had been made under this section up to 1 August 1985.

29 Short title, extent and commencement

(1) This Act may be cited as the Chronically Sick and Disabled Persons Act 1970.

(2) (*Applies to Scotland only.*)

(3) Save as otherwise expressly provided by sections 9, 14 and 23, this Act does not extend to Northern Ireland.

(4) This Act shall come into force as follows:—

  (*a*)   sections 1 and 21 shall come into force on the day appointed thereunder;

  (*b*)   sections 4, 5, 6, 7 and 8 shall come into force at the expiration of six months beginning with the date this Act is passed;

  (*c*)   the remainder shall come into force at the expiration of three months beginning with that date.

NOTES

Months. This means calendar months; see the Interpretation Act 1978, s 5, Sch 1, Vol 41, title Statutes.

Beginning with, etc. In calculating the period of six (three) months, the date on which the Act was passed, ie received the Royal Assent, must be included; see *Hare v Gocher* [1962] 2 QB 641, [1962] 2 All ER 763; *Trow v Ind Coope (West Midlands) Ltd* [1967] 2 QB 899, [1967] 2 All ER 900, CA. The Act was passed on 29 May 1970, and accordingly the provisions specified in sub-s (4)(*b*), (*c*) above came into force on 29 November 1970 and 29 August 1970, respectively.

EDUCATION (HANDICAPPED CHILDREN) ACT 1970
(1970 c 52)

An Act to make provision, as respects England and Wales, for discontinuing the classification of handicapped children as unsuitable for education at school, and for purposes connected therewith   [23 July 1970]

Education Acts 1944 to 1985. This Act is one of the Acts which may be cited by this collective title; see the Introductory Note to the Education Act 1944, this part of this title ante.
Northern Ireland. This Act does not apply; see s 2(3) post.

1 Mentally handicapped children

(1) As from such day ("the appointed day") as the Secretary of State may appoint by order made by statutory instrument—

(*a*) no further use shall be made of the powers conferred by section 57 of the Education Act 1944 (that is to say the section having effect as section 57 by virtue of the Mental Health Act 1959) for classifying children suffering from a disability of mind as children unsuitable for education at school; and

(*b*) a local health authority shall not, under section 12 of the Health Services and Public Health Act 1968 have the power or be subject to a duty to make arrangements for training children who suffer from a disability of mind and who are for purposes of the Education Act 1944 of compulsory school age;

and, where immediately before the appointed day a decision under section 57 of the Education Act 1944 was in force with respect to a child, section 34(4) to (6) of that Act shall apply as if the decision had been made, and the examination in consequence of which it was made had been carried out, under section 34.

(2) The Secretary of State shall by order make such provision as appears to him to be necessary or expedient in consequence of subsection (1) above—

(*a*) for the transfer to the employment of local education authorities of persons employed by local health authorities (not being also local education authorities) or by regional hospital boards; and

(*b*) for the protection of the interests of persons who before the appointed day have been employed for the purpose of functions of local health authorities (including those functions of authorities which are also local education authorities) or functions of regional hospital boards; and

(*c*) for the transfer to local education authorities of property, rights and liabilities of local health authorities or regional hospital boards.

(3) The provision to be made under subsection (2)(*b*) above shall include provision—

(*a*) for the payment by a Secretary of State, local health authority or local education authority, subject to such exceptions or conditions as may be prescribed by the order, of compensation to or in respect of any such persons as are referred to in subsection (2)(*b*) who suffer loss of employment or loss or diminution of emoluments which is attributable to the provisions of this section; and

(*b*) as respects any person so referred to who on the appointed day is in consequence of this section employed for the purpose of functions of a local education authority, for securing that, so long as he continues in that authority's employment for the purpose of those functions—

(i) he shall enjoy terms and conditions of employment not less favourable than those he enjoyed immediately before that date, except as regards the scale of his salary or remuneration if on that date or afterwards he ceases to be engaged in duties reasonably comparable to those in which he was engaged immediately before that date; and

(ii) in the event of his ceasing to be so engaged, the scale of his salary or remuneration shall also be not less favourable so long as he has not been served with a statement in writing of new terms and conditions of employment.

A written statement given in accordance with section 4 of the Contracts of Employment Act 1963 shall not be regarded as a statement of new terms and conditions of employment for the purposes of paragraph (b) above unless the statement indicates that it is to be.

(4) An order under subsection (2) above may include provision—

(a) for the determination of questions arising under any such order and as to the manner in which and persons to whom claims for compensation are to be made;

(b) for applying, with or without modifications, any provision made by or under any enactment and relating to the transfer of staff between authorities;

and the provision made under subsection (2)(b) shall have effect notwithstanding, and may amend or repeal, any provision made by or under any enactment and relating to the remuneration of teachers or to superannuation.

(5) Any order under subsection (2) above may be varied or revoked by a subsequent order of the Secretary of State, and the power of the Secretary of State to make orders under that subsection shall be exercisable by statutory instrument which shall be subject to annulment in pursuance of a resolution of either House of Parliament.

(6) There shall be defrayed out of moneys provided by Parliament—

(a) any expenses incurred by a Secretary of State in the payment of compensation under any provision made in accordance with subsection (3)(a) above; and

(b) any increase attributable to this section in the sums payable out of moneys so provided by way of rate support grant.

NOTES

Appointed day. By the Education (Handicapped Children) Act 1970 (Appointed Day) Order 1971, SI 1971/187, the appointed day for the purposes of sub-s (1) is 1 April 1971.

Secretary of State. See the note "Secretary of State for Education and Science" to the Education Act 1944, s 1, this part of this title ante.

Local health authority; regional hospital boards. These bodies were abolished by the National Health Service Reorganisation Act 1973, s 14. As to the reorganisation effected by this Act, see generally 33 Halsbury's Laws (4th edn) paras 7–16.

Compulsory school age. See the Education Act 1944, s 35, this part of this title ante.

Local education authority. See the Education Act 1944, s 114(1), this part of this title ante and the note thereto.

Emoluments. This expression is not defined in this Act, but for judicial consideration of the term, see, eg, *R v Postmaster General* (1878) 3 QBD 428, CA; *Shelford v Mosey* [1917] 1 KB 154 at 159 per Lord Reading CJ; *R v Lyon, ex p Harrison* [1921] 1 KB 203; *Hartland v Diggines* [1926] AC 289, [1926] All ER Rep 578; *Kiddie v Port of London Authority* (1929) 93 JP 203; *Stoke Newington BC v Richards* [1930] 1 KB 222; *Re Wickham and Paddington Corpn's Arbitration* [1946] 2 All ER 68; and *The Acrux* [1965] 2 All ER 323. See also 23 Halsbury's Laws (4th edn) paras 640 et seq.

Written. Expressions referring to writing are, unless the contrary intention appears, to be construed as including references to other modes of representing or reproducing words in a visible form; see the Interpretation Act 1978, s 5, Sch 1, Vol 41, title Statutes.

Varied or revoked. The express power to vary or revoke orders is necessary because the Interpretation Act 1978, s 14, Vol 41, title Statutes, does not extend to powers to make such instruments contained in Acts passed before 1 January 1979; see s 22(1) of, and Sch 2, para 3 to, that Act.

Subject to annulment. As to statutory instruments which are subject to annulment, see the Statutory Instruments Act 1946, ss 5(1), 7(1), Vol 41, title Statutes.

Education Act 1944, ss 34, 57. Repealed by the Education Act 1981, s 21, Sch 4 and by s 2 of, and the Schedule to, this Act respectively.

Health Services and Public Health Act 1968, s 12. Repealed by the National Health Service Act

1977, s 129, Sch 16, and replaced by s 128(1) of, and Sch 8, para 2, Sch 14, paras 12, 15(1) to, that Act, Vol 30, title National Health Service.

Contracts of Employment Act 1963, s 4. Repealed. See now the Employment Protection (Consolidation) Act 1978, s 1, Vol 16, title Employment.

Orders under this section. The Education (Handicapped Children) Act 1970 (Appointed Day) Order 1971, SI 1971/187 (made under sub-s (1)); the Education of Handicapped Children (Transfer of Staff and Property) Order 1971, SI 1971/341 (made under sub-s (2)).

---

2 Citation, repeal and extent

(1) This Act may be cited as the Education (Handicapped Children) Act 1970 ...

(2) As from the appointed day, the enactments mentioned in the Schedule to this Act are hereby repealed to the extent specified in the third column of that Schedule.

(3) Nothing in this Act extends to Scotland or to Northern Ireland.

NOTES

The words omitted from sub-s (1) were repealed by the Education (Milk) Act 1971, s 4(4).
Appointed day. See s 1(1) ante and the note thereto.

SCHEDULE

Section 2

ENACTMENTS REPEALED

Chapter	Short Title	Extent of Repeal
7 & 8 Geo 6 c 31	The Education Act 1944	Sections 57 to 57B (as inserted by the Mental Health Act 1959). In section 116 the words from "to any", where first occurring, down to (but not including) the same words where last occurring.
7 & 8 Eliz 2 c 72	The Mental Health Act 1959	Sections 11 to 13. Schedule 2. Schedule 6, paragraph 2. In Schedule 7, the entry for the Education Act 1944.
1967 c 80	The Criminal Justice Act 1967	In Schedule 3, in Part I, the entries for the Education Act 1944, section 57(2) and for the Mental Health Act 1959 section 12(3), except as respects offences committed before the appointed day.
1968 c 46	The Health Services and Public Health Act 1968	In Schedule 3, in the second paragraph of the entry for the Mental Health Act 1959, the words "and 12(1)".
1970 c 42	The Local Authority Social Services Act 1970	In Schedule 1, in the entry for the Mental Health Act 1959, paragraph (a).

EDUCATION ACT 1973

(1973 c 16)

ARRANGEMENT OF SECTIONS

An Act to make provision for terminating and in part replacing the powers possessed by the Secretary of State for Education and Science and the Secretary of State for Wales under the Charities Act 1960 concurrently with the Charity Commissioners or under the Endowed Schools Acts 1869 to 1948, and enlarging certain other powers of modifying educational trusts, and for supplementing awards under section 1 and restricting awards under section 2 of the Education Act 1962, and for purposes connected therewith
[18 April 1973]

Education Acts 1944 to 1985. This Act is one of the Acts which may be cited by this collective title; see the Introductory Note to the Education Act 1944, this part of this title ante.
Northern Ireland. This Act does not apply; see s 2(3) post.

Educational trusts

1 General provisions as to educational trusts

(1) ...

(2) The Secretary of State may by order—

    (*a*) make such modifications of any trust deed or other instrument relating to a school as, after consultation with the ... governors or other proprietor of the school, appear to him to be requisite in consequence of any [order made by him under section 16 of the Education Act 1944 or proposals falling to be implemented under section 12 or 13 of the Education Act 1980] (which relate to the establishment of and changes affecting schools); and

    (*b*) make such modifications of any trust deed or other instrument relating to a school as, after consultation with the governors or other proprietor of the school, appear to him to be requisite to enable the governors or proprietor to meet any requirement imposed by regulations under [sections 12 and 13 of the Education Act 1981 (approval of schools for purposes of that Act); and]

    (*c*) make such modifications of any trust deed or other instrument relating to or regulating any institution that provides or is concerned in the provision of educational services, or is concerned in educational research, as, after consultation with the persons responsible for the management of the institution, appear to him to be requisite to enable them to fulfil any condition or meet any requirement imposed by regulations under section 100 of the Education Act 1944 (which authorises the making of grants in aid of educational services or research);

and any modification made by an order under this subsection may be made to have permanent effect or to have effect for such period as may be specified in the order.

This subsection shall be construed, and the Education Acts 1944 to 1971 shall have effect, as if this subsection were contained in the Education Act 1944.

(3) In connection with the operation of this section there shall have effect the transitional and other consequential or supplementary provisions contained in Schedule 1 to this Act.

(4) The enactments mentioned in Schedule 2 to this Act (which includes in Part I certain enactments already spent or otherwise no longer required apart from the foregoing provisions of this section) are hereby repealed to the extent specified in column 3 of the Schedule.

(5) Subsection (1)(a) above and Part III of Schedule 2 to this Act shall not come into force until such date as may be appointed by order made by statutory instrument by the Secretary of State.

NOTES

Sub-s (1) repeals the Charities Act 1960, s 2 and the Endowed Schools Acts 1869 to 1948 (ie the Endowed Schools Act 1869, the Endowed Schools Act 1873, the Education (Miscellaneous Provisions) Act 1948, s 2, Sch 1, Pt II). Those provisions are also repealed by sub-s (4) above and Sch 2, Pts II, III post.

The words omitted from sub-s (2)(a) were repealed, and the words in square brackets in that paragraph were substituted by the Education Act 1980, ss 1(3), 16(4), Sch 1, para 26, Sch 3, para 17.

The words in square brackets in sub-s (2)(b) were substituted by the Education Act 1981, s 21, Sch 3, para 10.

Secretary of State. See the note "Secretary of State for Education and Science" to the Education Act 1944, s 1, this part of this title ante.

Statutory instrument. For provisions as to statutory instruments generally, see the Statutory Instruments Act 1946, Vol 41, title Statutes.

Education Act 1944. See this part of this title ante.

Education Act 1980, ss 12, 13; Education Act 1981, ss 12, 13. See this part of this title post.

Education Acts 1944 to 1971. For the Acts that may now be cited by the collective title "the Education Acts 1944 to 1985" (which includes those Acts), see the Introductory Note to the Education Act 1944, this part of this title ante.

Order under this section. The Education Act 1973 (Commencement) Order 1973, SI 1973/1661 (bringing sub-s (1)(a) above and Sch 2, Pt III post into force on 1 February 1974).

2 Special powers as to certain trusts for religious education

(1) Where the premises of a voluntary school have ceased (before or after the coming into force of this section) to be used for a voluntary school, or in the opinion of the Secretary of State it is likely they will cease to be so used, then subject to subsections (2) to (4) below he may by order made by statutory instrument make new provision as to the use of any endowment shown to his satisfaction to be or have been held wholly or partly for or in connection with the provision at the school of religious education in accordance with the tenets of a particular religious denomination; and for purposes of this section "endowment" includes property not subject to any restriction on the expenditure of capital.

(2) No order shall be made under subsection (1) above except on the application of the persons appearing to the Secretary of State to be the appropriate authority of the denomination concerned; and the Secretary of State shall, not less than one month before making an order under that subsection, give notice of the proposed order and of the

right of persons interested to make representations on it, and shall take into account any representations that may be made to him by any person interested therein before the order is made; and the notice shall be given—

    (*a*) by giving to any persons appearing to the Secretary of State to be trustees of an endowment affected by the proposed order a notice of the proposal to make it, together with a draft or summary of the provisions proposed to be included; and

    (*b*) by publishing in such manner as the Secretary of State thinks sufficient for informing any other persons interested a notice of the proposal to make the order and of the place where any person interested may (during a period of not less than a month) inspect such a draft or summary, and by keeping a draft or summary available for inspection in accordance with the notice.

(3) An order under subsection (1) above may require or authorise the disposal by sale or otherwise of any land or other property forming part of an endowment affected by the order, including the premises of the school and any teacher's dwelling-house; and in the case of land liable to revert under the third proviso to section 2 of the School Sites Act 1841 the Secretary of State may by order exclude the operation of that proviso, if he is satisfied either—

    (*a*) that the person to whom the land would revert in accordance with the proviso cannot after due enquiry be found; or

    (*b*) that, if that person can be found, he has consented to relinquish his rights in relation to the land under the proviso and that, if he has consented so to do in consideration of the payment of a sum of money to him, adequate provision can be made for the payment to him of that sum out of the proceeds of disposal of the land.

(4) Subject to subsection (3) above and to any provision affecting the endowments of any public general Act of Parliament, an order under subsection (1) above shall establish and give effect, with a view to enabling the denomination concerned to participate more effectively in the administration of the statutory system of public education, to a scheme or schemes for the endowments dealt with by the order to be used for appropriate educational purposes, either in connection with voluntary schools or partly in connection with voluntary schools and partly in other ways related to the locality served or formerly served by the voluntary school at the premises that have gone or are to go out of use for such a school; and for this purpose "use for appropriate educational purposes" means use for educational purposes in connection with the provision of religious education in accordance with the tenets of the denomination concerned.

(5) A scheme given effect under this section may provide for the retention of the capital of any endowment and application of the accruing income or may authorise the application or expenditure of capital to such extent and subject to such conditions as may be determined by or in accordance with the scheme; and any such scheme may provide for the endowments thereby dealt with or any part of them to be added to any existing endowment applicable for any such purpose as is authorised for the scheme by subsection (4) above.

(6) An order under subsection (1) above may include any such incidental or supplementary provisions as appear to the Secretary of State to be necessary or expedient either for the bringing into force or for the operation of any scheme thereby established, including in particular provisions for the appointment and powers of trustees of the property comprised in the scheme or, if the property is not all applicable for the same purposes, of any part of that property, and for the property or any part of it to vest by virtue of the scheme in the first trustees under the scheme or trustees of any endowment to which it is to be added or, if not so vested, to be transferred to them.

(7) Any order under this section shall have effect notwithstanding any Act of

Parliament (not being a public general Act), letters patent or other instrument relating to, or trust affecting, the endowments dealt with by the order; but section 15(3) of the Charities Act 1960 (by virtue of which the court and the Charity Commissioners may exercise their jurisdiction in relation to charities mentioned in Schedule 4 to the Act notwithstanding that the charities are governed by the Acts or statutory schemes there mentioned) shall have effect as if at the end of paragraph 1(b) of Schedule 4 to the Act there were added the words "or by schemes given effect under section 2 of the Education Act 1973."

(8) This section shall apply where the premises of a non-provided public elementary school ceased before 1st April 1945 to be used for such a school as it applies where the premises of a voluntary school have ceased to be used for a voluntary school.

(9) This section shall be construed, and the Education Acts 1944 to 1971 shall have effect, as if this section were contained in the Education Act 1944.

NOTES

Premises. The term "premises", though originally possessing a very limited meaning, ie the parts of a deed which precede the habendum, is widely used in the popular sense as including land, houses, buildings, etc; see, eg, *Metropolitan Water Board v Paine* [1907] 1 KB 285; *Whitley v Stumbles* [1930] AC 544, HL; *Bracey v Read* [1963] Ch 88, [1962] 3 All ER 472; and *Maunsell v Olins* [1975] AC 373, [1975] 1 All ER 16, HL. In general "premises" would seem to have been construed as meaning a whole property in either one occupation or one ownership according to the context in which it is used; see, eg, *Cadbury Bros Ltd v Sinclair* [1934] 2 KB 389 at 393 (revsd on other grounds (1933) 103 LJKB 29), and *Brickwood & Co v Reynolds* [1898] 1 QB 95.

Voluntary school. For meaning, see the Education Act 1944, s 9(2), this part of this title ante.

Secretary of State. See the note "Secretary of State for Education and Science" to the Education Act 1944, s 1, this part of this title ante.

Statutory instrument. See the note to s 1 ante.

Charity Commissioners. Ie the Charity Commissioners for England and Wales referred to in the Charities Act 1960, s 1, Vol 5, title Charities; see the Interpretation Act 1978, s 5, Sch 1, Vol 41, title Statutes.

School Sites Act 1841, s 2. See Pt 3 of this title post.

Charities Act 1960, s 15(3), Sch 4. See Vol 5, title Charities.

Education Acts 1944 to 1971. See the note to s 1 ante.

Education Act 1944. See this part of this title ante.

Orders under this section. Such orders, being local, are not recorded in this work.

Awards

3 Supplementation by Secretary of State, in special cases, of certain awards by local education authority

(1) The Secretary of State may by regulations make provision for the payment by him, to persons on whom awards have been bestowed by a local education authority under section 1 of the Education Act 1962 (awards for first degree university courses and comparable courses in the United Kingdom), of an allowance in respect of a wife, husband or child for the purpose of enabling those persons to take advantage without hardship of their awards in cases where, in accordance with the regulations having effect under that section, account may not be taken of the wife, husband or child in determining the payments to be made by the authority in pursuance of the award.

(2) The amount of an allowance payable by virtue of this section to the holder of an award in respect of a wife, husband or child shall not exceed the amount by which the payments to be made by the local education authority in pursuance of the award would have been increased if the case had fallen within the provision made with respect to a wife, husband or child by the regulations having effect under section 1 of the Education Act 1962.

(3) Regulations under this section may make different provision for different cases; and the power of the Secretary of State to make regulations under this section shall be

exercisable by statutory instrument which shall be subject to annulment in pursuance of a resolution of either House of Parliament.

(4) Any expenses incurred by the Secretary of State in the payment of allowances under this section shall be defrayed out of moneys provided by Parliament.

(5) In this section references to a person's child include that person's step-child or illegitimate child . . .

NOTES

The words omitted from sub-s (5) were repealed by the Children Act 1975, s 108(1)(*b*), Sch 4.

Secretary of State. See the note "Secretary of State for Education and Science" to the Education Act 1944, s 1, this part of this title ante.

Local education authority. See the Education Act 1944, s 114(1), this part of this title ante and the note thereto.

United Kingdom. Ie Great Britain and Northern Ireland; see the Interpretation Act 1978, s 5, Sch 1, Vol 41, title Statutes. "Great Britain" means England, Scotland and Wales by virtue of the Union with Scotland Act 1706, preamble, Art I, Vol 10, title Constitutional Law (Pt 1), as read with s 22(1) of, and Sch 2, para 5(*a*) to, the 1978 Act. Neither the Channel Islands nor the Isle of Man is within the United Kingdom.

Statutory instrument; subject to annulment. For provisions as to statutory instruments generally, see the Statutory Instruments Act 1946, Vol 41, title Statutes, and as to statutory instruments which are subject to annulment, see ss 5(1), 7(1) of that Act.

Education Act 1962, s 1. See this part of this title ante.

Regulations under this section. The Education (Students' Dependants Allowances) Regulations 1983, SI 1983/1185, as amended by SI 1984/1179, SI 1985/1160.

4 *(Repealed by the Education Act 1980, s 38(6), Sch 7.)*

Supplementary

5 Citation and extent

(1) This Act may be cited as the Education Act 1973, and the Education Acts 1944 to 1971 and this Act may be cited together as the Education Acts 1944 to 1973.

(2) Nothing in this Act extends to Scotland or to Northern Ireland.

NOTE

Education Acts 1944 to 1971; Education Acts 1944 to 1973. See the note "Education Acts 1944 to 1971" to s 1 ante.

SCHEDULES

SCHEDULE 1

TRANSITIONAL AND SUPPLEMENTARY PROVISIONS AS TO CHARITIES ETC

1.—(1) . . .

(2) Section 210(3) of the Local Government Act 1972 (which makes special provision for certain charitable property to vest in local education authorities, if it is held for purposes of a charity registered in a part of the charities register maintained by the Secretary of State by virtue of section 2 of the Charities Act 1960) shall have effect, unless the appointed day is later than the end of March 1974, as if the reference to a charity registered in a part of the register which is maintained by the Secretary of State were a reference to a charity so registered immediately before the appointed day.

(3) Any register, books and documents which on the appointed day are in the possession or custody of the Secretary of State for Education and Science, or of the Secretary of State for Wales, and which in his opinion he requires no longer by reason of the repeal of section 2(1) of the Charities Act 1960, shall be transferred to the Charity Commissioners.

(4) The repeal by this Act of section 2(1) of the Charities Act 1960 shall not affect the operation of section 2(1)—

(a) in conferring on the Charity Commissioners functions belonging at the passing of that Act to the Minister of Education; or

(b) in extending to the Charity Commissioners references to the Secretary of State for Education and Science or the Secretary of State for Wales (or references having effect as if either of them were mentioned) so as to enable the Commissioners to discharge any such functions as aforesaid or to act under or for the purposes of the trusts of a charity;

but on the appointed day any functions so conferred and any reference so extended shall, subject to sub-paragraph (5) below, cease to be functions of or to extend to either Secretary of State.

(5) Where it appears to the Secretary of State for Education and Science or the Secretary of State for Wales that any reference which, in accordance with sub-paragraph (4) above would on the appointed day cease to extend to him, is not related (or not wholly related) to the functions ceasing to belong to him by the repeal of section 2(1) of the Charities Act 1960, he may by order made at any time, whether before the appointed day or not, exclude the operation of that sub-paragraph in relation to the reference and make such modifications of the relevant instrument as appear to him appropriate in the circumstances.

(6) The repeal of section 2(1) of the Charities Act 1960 shall not affect the validity of anything done (or having effect as if done) before the appointed day by or in relation to the Secretary of State for Education and Science or the Secretary of State for Wales, and anything so done (or having effect as if so done) in so far as it could by virtue of section 2(1) have been done by or in relation to the Charity Commissioners shall thereafter have effect as if done by or in relation to them.

(7) In this paragraph "appointed day" means the day appointed under section 1(5) of this Act.

2.—(1) Where before the passing of this Act a scheme under the Endowed Schools Acts 1869 to 1948 has been published as required by section 13 of the Endowed Schools Act 1873, the scheme may be proceeded with as if section 1 of this Act had not been passed.

(2) Where before the passing of this Act a draft scheme under the Endowed Schools Acts 1869 to 1948 has been prepared in a case in which effect might be given to the scheme by order under section 2 of this Act, and the draft scheme has been published as required by section 33 of the Endowed Schools Act 1869, the scheme may be proceeded with in pursuance of section 2 of this Act as if section 2(2)(a) and (b) had been complied with on the date this Act is passed.

3. The repeals made by this Act in sections 17 and 100 of the Education Act 1944 shall not affect any order made by virtue of the provisions repealed, or the operation in relation to any such order of section 111 of that Act (which relates to the revocation and variation of orders).

NOTES

Para 1(1) amends the Charities Act 1960, s 43, Vol 5, title Charities.

Secretary of State. See the note "Secretary of State for Education and Science" to the Education Act 1944, s 1, this part of this title ante.

Charity Commissioners. See the note to s 2 ante.

Appointed day. Ie 1 February 1974; see, by virtue of para 1(2) above, s 1(5) ante and the note thereto.

Local Government Act 1972, s 210(3). See Vol 25, title Local Government.

Endowed Schools Acts 1869 to 1948; Endowed Schools Act 1873, s 13; Endowed Schools Act 1869, s 33. Repealed as noted in the first note to s 1 ante.

Education Act 1944. See this part of this title ante.

Orders under this Schedule. No order had been made under this Schedule up to 1 August 1985.

SCHEDULE 2

REPEALS

PART I

REPEALS OF SPENT ETC ENACTMENTS

Chapter	Short Title	Extent of Repeal
8 & 9 Geo 5 c 39	The Education Act 1918	Section 14. In section 47, the words from "except" to "direct" and the words from "and the Board" onwards. Section 52(1) from the first "and" onwards.
7 & 8 Geo 6 c 31	The Education Act 1944	Section 119. Section 121, except proviso (a). Schedule 9.
1 & 2 Eliz 2 c 33	The Education (Miscellaneous Provisions) Act 1953	Section 14. Section 17(2). Schedule 2.
2 & 3 Eliz 2 c 70	The Mines and Quarries Act 1954	In section 166 the words "section 14 of the Education Act 1918", and the words "the said section 14". In Schedule 4 the entry relating to the Education Act 1918.
8 & 9 Eliz 2 c 58	The Charities Act 1960	Section 4(10). Section 38(1) and (2). Section 39(1). Section 44(3). Section 48(2). Section 49(3). In Schedule 1, paragraph 1(6) and paragraph 2(3). Schedule 5. In Schedule 6 the entry for the Reorganisation Areas Measure 1944. Schedule 7.
9 & 10 Eliz 2 c 34	The Factories Act 1961	In section 167 the words "section 14 of the Education Act 1918".
1963 c 33	The London Government Act 1963	In section 81, subsections (1) to (8) (but not so as to alter the charity trustees of any charity) and subsection (10).

PART II

GENERAL

Chapter	Short Title	Extent of Repeal
32 & 33 Vict c 56	The Endowed Schools Act 1869	The whole Act.
36 & 37 Vict c 86	The Endowed Schools Act 1873	The whole Act.
12 & 13 Geo 5 c 50	The Expiring Laws Continuance Act 1922	In Schedule 1, the entry for the Endowed Schools Act 1869.

Chapter	Short Title	Extent of Repeal
7 & 8 Geo 6 c 31	The Education Act 1944	In section 17(6) (as added by the Education Act 1968) the words from "or such modifications" to "trust deed". Section 86. Section 100(4).
11 & 12 Geo 6 c 40	The Education (Miscellaneous Provisions) Act 1948	Section 2. In section 11(1) the words from the first "and" to the following "Schedule". In section 14, in subsection (2) the words from "(except" to the following "1908)" and the words from "and the said" onwards, and in subsection (3) the words from "(other" to the following "provisions)" and the words from "and the said" onwards. In Schedule 1, Part II.
8 & 9 Eliz 2 c 58	The Charities Act 1960	Section 2(4).
1968 c 17	The Education Act 1968	In Schedule 1, in paragraph 2, the words from "or such modifications" to "trust deed".

Church Assembly Measure

1967 No 2	The Extra-Parochial Ministry Measure 1967	In section 2(5), the words "and section 53 of the Endowed Schools Act 1869" and the words "and endowed".

PART III

REPEALS RELATING TO CHARITIES

Chapter	Short Title	Extent of Repeal
10 & 11 Geo 6 c 44	The Crown Proceedings Act 1947	Section 23(3)(*e*).
8 & 9 Eliz 2 c 58	The Charities Act 1960	Section 2(1), (2), (3) and (5). Section 3(8). In section 4(8) the words "or of the Minister of Education". In section 10(6) the words "and to the Minister of Education". Section 18(13). Section 19(9). Section 20(11). Section 22(12). In section 44, in subsection (1)(*b*) the words "the Minister of Education" and in subsection (2) the words "by the Minister of Education or". In Schedule 6, in the entry relating to section 31 of the New Parishes Measure 1943 the words "or Minister of Education".

Chapter	Short Title	Extent of Repeal
1969 c 22	The Redundant Churches and other Religious Buildings Act 1969	In section 4, in subsection (3) the words "and the Secretary of State for Education and Science" and in subsection (4) the words "and (13)".

Church Assembly Measures

Chapter	Short Title	Extent of Repeal
6 & 7 Geo 6 No 1	The New Parishes Measure 1943	In section 31 the words "or of the Board of Education" and the words "or Minister of Education" inserted by the Charities Act 1960.
1968 No 1	The Pastoral Measure 1968	Section 90(3).

EDUCATION (WORK EXPERIENCE) ACT 1973

(1973 c 23)

An Act to enable education authorties to arrange for children under school-leaving age to have work experience, as part of their education   [23 May 1973]

Education Acts 1944 to 1985. This Act is one of the Acts which may be cited by this collective title; see the Introductory Note to the Education Act 1944 ante.
Northern Ireland. This Act does not apply; see s 2(2) post.

1 Work experience in last year of compulsory schooling

(1) Subject to subsection (2) below, the enactments relating to the prohibition or regulation of the employment of children shall not apply to the employment of a child in his last year of compulsory schooling where the employment is in pursuance of arrangements made or approved by the local education authority or, in Scotland, the education authority with a view to providing him with work experience as part of his education.

(2) Subsection (1) above shall not be taken to permit the employment of any person in any way contrary to—

(*a*) an enactment which in terms applies to persons of less than, or not over, a specified age expressed as a number of years; or

(*b*) section 1(2) of the Employment of Women, Young Persons and Children Act 1920 or (when it comes into force) section 51(1) of the Merchant Shipping Act 1970 (prohibition of employment of children in ships);

(3) No arrangements shall be made under subsection (1) above for a child to be employed in any way which would be contrary to an enactment prohibiting or regulating the employment of young persons if he were a young person (within the meaning of that enactment) and not a child; and where a child is employed in pursuance of arrangements so made, then so much of any enactment as regulates the employment of young persons (whether by excluding them from any description of work, or prescribing the conditions under which they may be permitted to do it, or otherwise howsoever) and would apply in relation to him if he were of an age to be treated as a young person for the purposes of that enactment shall apply in relation to him, in and in respect of the employment arranged for him, in all respects as if he were of an age to be so treated.

(4) In this Act—

"enactment" includes any byelaw, regulation or other provision having effect under an enactment;

other expressions which are also used in the Education Acts shall have the same meaning in this section as in those Acts; and

"the Education Acts" means in England and Wales the Education Acts 1944 to 1973 and, in Scotland, the Education (Scotland) Acts 1939 to 1971;

and for the purposes of subsection (1) above a child is in his last year of compulsory schooling at any time during the period of twelve months before he attains the upper limit of compulsory school age or, in Scotland, school age.

NOTES

Age. A person attains a particular age expressed in years at the commencement of the relevant anniversary of the date of his birth; see the Family Law Reform Act 1969, s 9, Vol 6, title Children.

Definitions. For "child" and "compulsory school age", see, by virtue of sub-s (4), the Education Act 1944, s 114(1), this part of this title ante; for "local education authority", see s 114(1) of that Act and the note thereto. Note, as to "enactment", "the Education Acts" and "last year of compulsory schooling", sub-s (4) above.

Employment of Women, Young Persons and Children Act 1920, s 1(2). See Vol 16, title Employment.

Merchant Shipping Act 1970, s 51(1). See Vol 39, title Shipping and Navigation.

Education Acts 1944 to 1973. For the Acts which may now be cited by the collective title "the Education Acts 1944 to 1985" (which includes those Acts), see the Introductory Note to the Education Act 1944, this part of this title ante.

Education (Scotland) Acts 1939 to 1971. Those Acts are not printed in this work.

2 Citation and extent

(1) This Act may be cited as the Education (Work Experience) Act 1973; and—

(a) in relation to England and Wales, this Act shall be included among the Acts which may be cited together as the Education Acts 1944 to 1973; and

(b) *(applies to Scotland only)*.

(2) Nothing in this Act extends to Northern Ireland.

NOTE

Education Acts 1944 to 1973. See the note to s 1 ante.

EDUCATION ACT 1975

(1975 c 2)

An Act to make further provision with respect to awards and grants by local education authorities; to enable the Secretary of State to bestow awards on students in respect of their attendance at adult education colleges; and to increase the proportion of the expenditure incurred in the maintenance or provision of aided and special agreement schools that can be met by contributions or grants from the Secretary of State   [25 February 1975]

Education Acts 1944 to 1985. This Act is one of the Acts which may be cited by this collective title; see the Introductory Note to the Education Act 1944 ante.

Northern Ireland. This Act does not apply; see s 5(6) post.

1–3 *(Ss 1, 2 repealed by the Education Act 1980, s 38(6), Sch 7; s 3 amends the Education Act 1944, ss 102, 103 and the Education Act 1967, s 1(2), both this part of this title ante.)*

4 Repeals

The enactments mentioned in the Schedule to this Act are hereby repealed to the extent specified in the third column of that Schedule.

5 Citation, interpretation, commencement and extent

(1) This Act may be cited as the Education Act 1975.

(2) The Education Acts 1944 to 1973 and this Act may be cited together as the Education Acts 1944 to 1975.

(3) Any reference in this Act to any enactment is a reference to that enactment as amended by any subsequent enactment.

(4) ...

(5) Nothing in section 3 above or in Part II of the Schedule to this Act affects contributions or grants in respect of expenditure on work which was begun before 6th November 1974 or on the provision of the site on which, or buildings to which, any such work was done.

(6) This Act does not extend to Scotland or Northern Ireland.

NOTES

Sub-s (4) was repealed by the Education Act 1980, s 38(6), Sch 7.

Education Acts 1944 to 1973. For the Acts which may now be cited by the collective title "the Education Acts 1944 to 1985" (which includes those Acts), see the Introductory Note to the Education Act 1944, this part of this title ante.

SCHEDULE

Section 4

REPEALS

PART I

Chapter	Short Title	Extent of Repeal
10 & 11 Eliz 2 c 12	The Education Act 1962	In section 2, in subsection (1) the words "(other than persons undergoing training as teachers)" and subsection (3).
1974 c 7	The Local Government Act 1974	In section 1(5)(b) the words "or section 2(3) (grants to persons undergoing training as teachers)". In section 8(2), paragraph (b) together with the word "and" immediately preceding that paragraph.

PART II

Chapter	Short Title	Extent of Repeal
1967 c 3	The Education Act 1967	Section 1(1).

EDUCATION (SCHOOL-LEAVING DATES) ACT 1976
(1976 c 5)

An Act to make further provision with respect to school-leaving dates; and for connected purposes   [25 March 1976]

Education Acts 1944 to 1985. This Act is one of the Acts which may be cited by this collective title; see the Introductory Note to the Education Act 1944, this part of this title ante.
Northern Ireland. This Act does not apply; see s 3(6) post.

1, 2 (*S 1 amends the Education Act 1962, s 9, this part of this title ante; s 2(1)–(3) repealed by the Child Benefit Act 1975, s 21(2), Sch 5, Pt I, as read with s 3(4) post and the Child Benefit Act 1975 (Commencement No 2) Order 1976, SI 1976/961; s 2(4) amends the Social Security Act 1975, ss 4(2)(a), 7(1), 8(1), Vol 40, title Social Security.*)

3 Citation, repeals, commencement and extent

(1) This Act may be cited as the Education (School-leaving Dates) Act 1976.

(2) The Education Acts 1944 to 1975 and this Act may be cited together as the Education Acts 1944 to 1976.

(3) The enactments mentioned in the Schedule to this Act (which include provisions that are spent in consequence of the Raising of the School Leaving Age Order 1972) are hereby repealed to the extent specified in the third column of that Schedule.

(4) Section 21(2) of the Child Benefit Act 1975 (repeals consequential on the introduction of child benefit) shall have effect as if section 2(1) to (3) above were included among the enactments mentioned in Part I of Schedule 5 to that Act.

(5) Section 2(4) above and so much of the Schedule to this Act as relates to the Social Security Act 1975 shall not come into force until 6th April 1976.

(6) This Act does not extend to Northern Ireland; and section 1 above does not extend to Scotland.

NOTES
Education Acts 1944 to 1975; Education Acts 1944 to 1976. For the Acts that may now be cited by the collective title "the Education Acts 1944 to 1985" (which includes those Acts), see the Introductory Note to the Education Act 1944, this part of this title ante.
Raising of the School Leaving Age Order 1972. SI 1972/444. That order was made under the Education Act 1944, s 35, this part of this title ante.
Child Benefit Act 1975, s 21(2), Sch 5, Pt I; Social Security Act 1975. See Vol 40, title Social Security.

SCHEDULE

Section 3(3)
Repeals

Chapter	Short Title	Extent of Repeal
7 & 8 Geo 6 c 31	The Education Act 1944	Section 38(1). In section 114, in subsection (1) in the definition of "compulsory school age" the words "subject to the provisions of section thirty-eight of this Act" and subsection (6).

Chapter	Short Title	Extent of Repeal
10 & 11 Eliz 2 c 12	The Education Act 1962	In section 9, the proviso to subsection (5), subsection (6) and in subsection (7) the definition of "the appropriate summer term" (together with the word "and" immediately preceding it) and the words "or month of September (as the case may be)".
1964 c 82	The Education Act 1964	Section 2. In section 5(3) and (6) the words "and 2".
1965 c 53	The Family Allowances Act 1965	Section 2(2)(b).
1967 c 90	The Family Allowances and National Insurance Act 1967	Section 2(1) and (2).
1973 c 38	The Social Security Act 1973	In Schedule 27, paragraph 22.
1975 c 14	The Social Security Act 1975	In Schedule 20, the definition of "school-leaving age".
1975 c 61	The Child Benefit Act 1975	In Schedule 4, in paragraph 38, the words "and 'School-leaving age'" (in the opening passage) and the definitions of "School-leaving age" and "The upper limit of compulsory school age." In Schedule 5 the repeal in the Education Act 1962, the repeal of section 2(1) and (2) of the Family Allowances and National Insurance Act 1967 and the repeal of the definition of "School-leaving age" in Schedule 20 to the Social Security Act 1975.

EDUCATION ACT 1976

(1976 c 81)

An Act to amend the law relating to education   [22 November 1976]

Education Acts 1944 to 1985. This Act is one of the Acts which may be cited by this collective title; see the Introductory Note to the Education Act 1944, this part of this title ante.
Northern Ireland. This Act does not apply; see s 12(4) post.

1–3 *(Repealed by the Education Act 1979, s 1(1).)*

Miscellaneous

4, 5 *(Repealed by the Education Act 1980, s 38(6), Sch 7.)*

6 Remuneration of members of Independent Schools Tribunals

(1) The Secretary of State may, out of moneys provided by Parliament, pay to the members of Independent Schools Tribunals such remuneration and allowances as he may with the consent of the Minister for the Civil Service determine.

(2) ...

NOTES

Sub-s (2) amends the Education Act 1944, s 75(1), this part of this title ante.

Secretary of State. See the note "Secretary of State for Education and Science" to the Education Act 1944, s 1, this part of this title ante.

Independent Schools Tribunal. For constitution, see the Education Act 1944, s 72(1), Sch 6, this part of this title ante.

7–10 (*Ss 7–9 repealed by the Education Act 1980, s 38(6), Sch 7; s 10 repealed by the Education Act 1981, s 21, Sch 4.*)

Supplementary

11 Expenses

There shall be paid out of moneys provided by Parliament any increase attributable to this Act in the sums payable out of such moneys under any other Act.

12 Citation, construction and extent

(1) This Act may be cited as the Education Act 1976.

(2) This Act shall be included in the Acts that may be cited as the Education Acts 1944 to 1976.

(3) This Act shall be construed as one with the Education Act 1944.

(4) This Act does not extend to Scotland or Northern Ireland.

NOTES

Construed as one. Ie the enactments in question are to be construed as if they were contained in one Act, unless there is some manifest discrepancy; see eg *Phillips v Parnaby* [1934] 2 KB 299 at 302. Accordingly, definitions in the earlier Act may be relevant to the construction of provisions of this Act (see *Solomons v R Gertzenstein Ltd* [1954] 2 QB 243, [1954] 2 All ER 625, CA; *Crowe (Valuation Officer) v Lloyds British Testing Co Ltd* [1960] 1 QB 592, [1960] 1 All ER 411, CA).

Education Acts 1944 to 1976. For the Acts which may now be cited by the collective title "the Education Acts 1944 to 1985"(which includes those Acts), see the Introductory Note to the Education Act 1944, this part of this title ante.

Education Act 1944. See this part of this title ante.

EDUCATION ACT 1979

(1979 c 49)

An Act to repeal sections 1, 2 and 3 of the Education Act 1976 and to make provision as to certain proposals submitted or transmitted to the Secretary of State under the said section 2 [26 July 1979]

Education Acts 1944 to 1985. This Act is one of the Acts which may be cited by this collective title; see the Introductory Note to the Education Act 1944, this part of this title ante.

Northern Ireland. This Act does not apply; see s 2(4) post.

1 Abolition of duty to give effect to comprehensive principle

(1) ...

(2) The following provisions of this section apply to proposals submitted or

transmitted to the Secretary of State under section 2 which have been treated, by virtue of a direction under subsection (1) of section 3, as if they had been submitted to him by a local education authority under subsection (1) or by the ... governors of a voluntary school under subsection (2) of section 13 of the Education Act 1944 (establishing, maintaining, changing character of, enlarging or ceasing to maintain county school or voluntary school).

(3) Where any proposals to which this subsection applies have been approved under subsection (4) of section 13, the Secretary of State may, on the application of the local education authority, ... or governors concerned, revoke the approval.

(4) Where any proposals to which this subsection applies have not been so approved but public notice of them has been given under subsection (3) of section 13, the local education authority, ... or governors concerned may elect that, notwithstanding the repeals effected by subsection (1) above, the proposals shall continue to be treated as if they had been submitted to the Secretary of State under subsection (1) or (2) of that section; but no such election shall have effect unless it is made in writing to the Secretary of State before 31st December 1979.

NOTES

Sub-s (1) repeals the Education Act 1976, ss 1–3.

The words omitted from sub-ss (2)–(4) were repealed by the Education Act 1980, s 1(3), Sch 1, para 31.

Secretary of State. See the note "Secretary of State for Education and Science" to the Education Act 1944, s 1, this part of this title ante.

Writing. Unless the contrary intention appears this includes other modes of representing or reproducing words in a visible form; see the Interpretation Act 1978, s 5, Sch 1, Vol 41, title Statutes.

Definitions. By virtue of s 2(3) post, for "governors" and "school", see the Education Act 1944, s 114(1), this part of this title ante; for "local education authority", see that section and the note thereto; and for "voluntary school", see s 9(2) of that Act.

Education Act 1944, s 13. See this part of this title ante.

2 Citation, construction and extent

(1) This Act may be cited as the Education Act 1979.

(2) The Education Acts 1944 to 1976 and this Act may be cited together as the Education Acts 1944 to 1979.

(3) This Act shall be construed as one with the Education Act 1944.

(4) This Act does not extend to Scotland or Northern Ireland.

NOTES

Construed as one. Ie the enactments in question are to be construed as if they were contained in one Act, unless there is some manifest discrepancy; see eg *Phillips v Parnaby* [1934] 2 KB 299 at 302. Accordingly, definitions in the earlier Act may be relevant to the construction of provisions of this Act (see *Solomons v R Gertzenstein Ltd* [1954] 2 QB 243, [1954] 2 All ER 625, CA; *Crowe (Valuation Officer) v Lloyds British Testing Co Ltd* [1960] 1 QB 592, [1960] 1 All ER 411, CA).

Education Acts 1944 to 1976. For the Acts which may now be cited by the collective title "the Education Acts 1944 to 1985" (which includes those Acts), see the Introductory Note to the Education Act 1944, this part of this title ante.

Education Act 1944. See this part of this title ante.

EDUCATION ACT 1980

(1980 c 20)

ARRANGEMENT OF SECTIONS

An Act to amend the law relating to education   [3 April 1980]

Commencement. This Act came into force on various dates appointed by order; see s 37 post, the orders noted thereto and the "Commencement" notes throughout the Act.

Education Acts 1944 to 1985. This Act is one of the Acts which may be cited by this collective title; see the Introductory Note to the Education Act 1944 this part of this title ante.

Northern Ireland. Only ss 20, 35, 37 and 38 post apply; see s 38(7) post.

School government

1 Change of nomenclature

(1) The members of the body constituted for a primary school under subsection (1) of section 17 of the Education Act 1944 (governing bodies of county and voluntary schools) shall be known as governors instead of managers and the instrument providing for the constitution of that body as an instrument of government instead of an instrument of management.

(2) The rules in accordance with which a primary school is required to be conducted under subsection (3)(*a*) of that section shall be known as articles of government instead of rules of management.

(3) The enactments mentioned in Schedule 1 to this Act shall have effect with the amendments there specified, being amendments consequential on the provisions of subsections (1) and (2) above.

(4) For any reference in any other enactment or document to the managers, foundation managers, instrument of management or rules of management of any primary school to which the provisions of subsections (1) and (2) above apply there shall be substituted, as respects any time after the coming into force of those provisions, a reference to the governors, foundation governors, instrument of government or articles of government of the school.

NOTES

Commencement. This section was brought into force on 5 May 1980 by the Education Act 1980 (Commencement No 1) Order 1980, SI 1980/489, made under s 37 post.

General Note. This section provides for the same nomenclature as is used with reference to the government of secondary schools to be used with reference to that of primary schools (whether county or voluntary schools).

Primary school. For provisions as to the government of primary schools, see, in particular ss 2–5 post, and the Education Act 1944, ss 17, 18, 20 et seq, this part of this title ante.

Definitions. By virtue of s 38(3) post, for "county school" and "voluntary school", see the Education Act 1944, s 9(2), this part of this title ante, and for "primary school", see s 114(1) of that Act.

Education Act 1944, s 17(1), (3)(a). See this part of this title ante.

---

2 Requirements as to governing bodies

(1) The instrument of government made for a county or voluntary school or for a special school maintained by a local education authority shall contain provisions complying with subsections (2) to (8) below.

(2) The governing body of every such school as is mentioned in subsection (1) above shall include governors appointed by the local education authority by whom it is maintained.

(3) The governing body of a county primary school or voluntary primary school serving an area in which there is a minor authority shall include at least one governor appointed by that authority.

(4) The governing body of a voluntary school shall include foundation governors and—

(a) in the case of a controlled school, at least one-fifth of the members of the governing body shall be foundation governors;

(b) in the case of an aided or special agreement school—

(i) the foundation governors shall outnumber the other members of the governing body by two if that body has eighteen or fewer members and by three if it has more;

(ii) at least one of the foundation governors shall at the time of his appointment be a parent of a registered pupil at the school.

(5) The governing body of a county or controlled school shall include at least two parent governors, that is to say persons who are elected by parents of registered pupils at the school and who are themselves such parents at the time when they are elected; and the governing body of an aided or special agreement school shall include at least one parent governor.

(6) Subsection (5) above shall apply to a special school maintained by a local education authority as it applies to a county or controlled school except that if the school is established in a hospital and it appears to the authority to be impracticable for the governing body to include parent governors it shall include at least two governors who are parents of children of compulsory school age.

(7) The governing body of a county or voluntary school or of a special school maintained by a local education authority shall, if the school has less than three hundred registered pupils, include at least one, and in any other case, at least two teacher governors, that is to say persons who are elected by teachers at the school and who are themselves such teachers at the time when they are elected.

(8) The head teacher of a county or voluntary school or of a special school maintained by a local education authority shall unless he elects otherwise, be a governor of the school by virtue of his office and shall in any event be treated as a member of the governing body for the purposes of subsection (4) above.

(9) It shall be for the local education authority, in the case of a county or controlled school or of a special school maintained by the authority, and for the governors, in the case of an aided or special agreement school—

(a) to determine any question whether, for the purposes of an election of parent governors or teacher governors, a person is a parent of a registered pupil at the school or a teacher at the school; and

(b) to make all necessary arrangements for, and to determine all other matters relating to, any such election (including such matters as qualifying dates and any minimum number of votes required to be cast) but so that any contested election is held by secret ballot.

(10) Nothing in this section shall be construed as preventing the inclusion in the governing body of any school of governors additional to those required by this section.

(11) This section applies to an instrument of government made for a school only if—

(a) the instrument is made after the coming into force of this section; or

(b) an order is made by the Secretary of State applying this section to the school or to schools of a class or description to which the school belongs.

(12) Sections 18 and 19 of the Education Act 1944 (composition of governing bodies of county and voluntary schools) and so much of section 2(2) of the Education (No 2)

Act 1968 as enables the local education authority to determine the size and composition of the governing body of a special school shall not apply to any school in relation to which this section applies.

NOTES

Commencement. This section was brought into force on 1 July 1981 by the Education Act 1980 (Commencement No 3) Order 1981, SI 1981/789, made under s 37 post.

Sub-s (1): Instrument of government. Ie the instrument providing for the constitution of the body of governors of a county school or a voluntary school (Education Act 1944, s 17(1), this part of this title ante) or a special school maintained by a local education authority (Education (No 2) Act 1968, s 2(1), this part of this title ante). Formerly primary schools were managed by a body of managers constituted by an instrument of management but the same nomenclature is now used for primary schools as was used for secondary schools; see s 1(1) ante. Note that the main existing provisions relating to the contents of instruments of government are excluded by sub-s (12) above in the case of schools in relation to which the present section applies (as to which, note sub-s (11) above). See also, as to the contents of instruments of government, s 4(3) post.

Local education authority. These authorities are defined by the Education Act 1944, s 6(1), Sch 1, Pt I, this part of this title ante, as read together with the London Government Act 1963, s 30, Vol 26, title London, the Local Government Act 1972, ss 1(10), 20(6), 192(1), Vol 25, title Local Government, and the Local Government Act 1985, s 18(2), in the same title.

Sub-s (6): Appears. Statutory powers are often conferred in subjective terms, the competent authority being entitled to act, eg, when it "appears" to it or it is "satisfied" that, or when in its "opinion", a prescribed state of affairs exists, but the inherent jurisdiction of the courts to determine whether such powers have been exceeded is not readily ousted by the use of such language. See, further, 1 Halsbury's Laws (4th edn) para 22.

Compulsory school age. By the Education Act 1944, s 35, this part of this title ante, as amended by the Raising of the School Leaving Age Order 1972, SI 1972/444 (made under that section), this means any age between five years and sixteen years, but this must be read subject to the provisions relating to school-leaving dates in the Education Act 1962, s 9, this part of this title ante.

Sub-s (11): Order is made etc. Orders under sub-s (11)(b) above are not statutory instruments and are not recorded in this work.

Secretary of State. See the note "Secretary of State for Education and Science" to the Education Act 1944, s 1, this part of this title ante.

Grouping of schools under single governing body. See s 3 post; and note that by sub-s (7)(a) of that section this section is excluded while an arrangement under that section is in force.

Secretary of State's powers to act in default. Special powers are given to the Secretary of State by the Education Act 1944, s 99(2), this part of this title ante, where, by reason of the default of any person there is no properly constituted body of governors of any county school or voluntary school; and s 99 of the 1944 Act is applied in relation to special schools maintained by local education authorities by the Education (No 2) Act 1968, s 3(3), this part of this title ante.

Definitions. By virtue of s 38(3) post, for "compulsory school age", "foundation governors", "local education authority", "minor authority", "parent", "primary school", "pupil", "registered pupil" and "school", see the Education Act 1944, s 114(1), this part of this title ante; for "maintain", see s 114(2)(a) of that Act; for "county school" and "voluntary school", see s 9(2) of that Act; for "special school", see s 9(5) of that Act; and for "aided school", "controlled school" and "special agreement school", see s 15 of that Act.

Education Act 1944, ss 18, 19; Education (No 2) Act 1968, s 2(2). See this part of this title ante.

3 Grouping of schools under single governing body

(1) Subject to the provisions of this section, a local education authority may make an arrangement for the constitution of a single governing body for any two or more schools maintained by the authority.

(2) Any arrangement under this section, other than one relating only to two primary schools neither of which is a special school, shall require the approval of the Secretary of State.

(3) Any arrangement under this section relating to a voluntary school shall require the consent of the governors or, in the case of a school in respect of which proposals have been submitted under section 13 below and for which no governors have yet been appointed, of the persons submitting the proposals.

(4) The governing body constituted by an arrangement under this section shall include parent governors and teacher governors; and for the purposes of the election of such governors the schools to which the arrangement relates may be treated either separately or as if they were a single school.

(5) Any arrangement under this section may, if it does not relate to any voluntary school, be terminated at any time by the local education authority by whom it was made, and any such arrangement which relates to a voluntary school may be terminated by agreement between the local education authority and the governing body constituted by the arrangement or, in default of agreement, by one year's notice served by the local education authority on the governing body or by one year's notice served by the governing body on the local education authority.

(6) The Secretary of State's approval for the making of any arrangement under this section may be given subject to such conditions as he may specify; and the Secretary of State may at any time terminate any such arrangement either wholly or in relation to any school or schools to which it applies.

(7) While an arrangement under this section is in force in relation to any school—

(a) neither section 2 above nor the provisions as to the constitution of the body of governors in sections 17 to 19 of the Education Act 1944 shall apply to the school; and

(b) for the purposes of any other enactment the governing body constituted by the arrangement and the members of that body shall be deemed to be the governing body and the governors of that school.

(8) This section applies to—

(a) schools having an instrument of government made after the coming into force of section 2 above; and

(b) schools in relation to which an order has been made under subsection (11)(b) of that section.

(9) The provisions of section 20 of the said Act of 1944 and section 2(4) of the Education (No 2) Act 1968 (grouping of schools) shall not apply to any school to which this section applies; and any arrangements made under those provisions shall cease to apply to any school in relation to which an arrangement is made under this section or an order under section 2(11)(b) above comes into force.

NOTES

Commencement. This section was brought into force on 1 July 1981 by the Education Act 1980 (Commencement No 3) Order 1981, SI 1981/789, made under s 37 post.

Sub-s (1): Local education authority. See the note to s 2 ante.

Arrangement. For matters that may be contained therein, see s 4(3) post.

Sub-s (2): Secretary of State. See the note to s 2 ante.

Sub-s (3): Governors. Ie the governors constituted under the Education Act 1944, s 17(1), (2), or under the Education (No 2) Act 1968, s 2(1), (2), both this part of this title ante. As to the instrument of government, see also s 2 ante, or the enactments mentioned in sub-s (12) of that section; and as to governors' proceedings, tenure of office etc, see s 4 post, and s 21(1), (3) of the 1944 Act.

Sub-s (4): Parent governors; teacher governors. Ie parent governors as defined by s 2(5) ante and teacher governors as defined by s 2(7) ante.

Sub-s (5): Notice served. As to the mode of service, see, by virtue of s 38(3) post, the Education Act 1944, s 113, this part of this title ante.

Sub-s (8): Instrument of government. See the note to s 2 ante.

Definitions. By virtue of s 38(3) post, for "primary school" and "school", see the Education Act 1944, s 114(1); for "maintain", see s 114(2)(a) of that Act, this part of this title ante; for "voluntary school", see s 9(2) of that Act; and for "special school", see s 9(5) of that Act.

Education Act 1944, ss 17–20; Education (No 2) Act 1968, s 2(4). See this part of this title ante.

---

4 Governors' proceedings and tenure of office

(1) The Secretary of State may make regulations—

(a) as to the meetings and proceedings of the governors of county and voluntary schools and of special schools maintained by local education authorities and as to the publication of information relating to those meetings and proceedings;

(b) subject to section 21(1) of the Education Act 1944 (resignation and removal of governors), as to the tenure of office and disqualification of the governors of such schools.

(2) Regulations under subsection (1) above shall make provision for the election of a chairman by the governors of any such school.

(3) The instrument of government of any such school and any arrangement made under section 3 above may contain provisions with respect to the matters mentioned in subsection (1) above but any provision relating to a matter dealt with by regulations under that subsection shall have effect subject to the regulations.

(4) Where an aided or special agreement school has an instrument of government made after the coming into force of section 2 above, any decision taken at a meeting of the governors shall, if it is of the kind specified in subsection (5) below, require confirmation at a second meeting of the governors held not less than twenty-eight days after the first.

(5) The decisions referred to in subsection (4) above are—

(a) any decision that would result in the submission of proposals under section 13 below;

(b) any decision to serve a notice under section 14(1) of the Education Act 1944 (discontinuance of school);

(c) any decision that would result in an application under section 15(4) of that Act (revocation of order whereby school is an aided or special agreement school);

(d) any decision to request the making of an order under subsection (2) of section 16 of that Act (discontinuance of school for which another school is substituted) or as to the submissions to be made to the Secretary of State in any consultations under subsections (3) of that section;

(e) any decision to make an agreement under Schedule 2 to that Act (agreement for transfer of interest in school to local education authority).

(6) ...

NOTES

Sub-s (6) repeals the Education Act 1944, s 21(2), Sch 4, and amends the Education (No 2) Act 1968, s 2(5), this part of this title ante.

Commencement. By the Education Act 1980 (Commencement No 3) Order 1981, SI 1981/789, made under s 37 post, sub-ss (1)–(3), (6) were brought into force, subject to the transitional provisions contained in Sch 3 to that Order on 1 August 1981 and sub-ss (4), (5) were brought into force on 1 July 1981.

Sub-s (1): Secretary of State; local education authorities. See the notes to s 2 ante.

Governors. See the note to s 3 ante.

Sub-s (3): Instrument of government. See the note to s 2 ante.

Sub-s (4): Not less than twenty eight days after. The words "not less than" indicate that twenty eight clear days must intervene between the date of the first meeting and that on which the second meeting is held; see *R v Turner* [1910] 1 KB 346; *Re Hector Whaling Ltd* [1936] Ch 208, [1935] All ER Rep 302.

Definitions. By virtue of s 38(3) post, for "school", see the Education Act 1944, s 114(1), this part of this title ante; for "maintain", see s 114(2) of that Act; for "county school" and "voluntary school", see s 9(2) of that Act; for "special school", see s 9(5) of that Act; and for "aided school" and "special agreement school", see s 15 of that Act.

Education Act 1944; Education (No 2) Act 1968, s 2(5). See this part of this title ante.

Regulations under this section. The Education (School Governing Bodies) Regulations 1981, SI 1981/809, as amended by SI 1981/1180.

For general provisions as to regulations, see s 35 post.

---

5 Governors as ex officio trustees

(1) Where a trust deed or other instrument made before the coming into force of section 2 above contains a provision whereby the persons who are for the time being

governors of a voluntary school are by virtue of their office trustees of any property held for the purposes of or in connection with the school, that provision shall have effect as if the governors of the school consisted only of the foundation governors and the governors appointed by the local education authority and any minor authority.

(2) Subsection (1) above is without prejudice to any power to amend any such provision as is mentioned in that subsection.

NOTES

Commencement. This section was brought into force on 1 July 1981 by the Education Act 1980 (Commencement No 3) Order 1981, SI 1981/789, made under s 37 post.

Governors. See the note to s 3 ante.

Local education authority. See the note to s 2 ante.

Definitions. By virtue of s 38(3) post, for "foundation governors", "local education authority", "minor authority", "school" and "trust deed", see the Education Act 1944, s 114(1), this part of this title ante; and for "voluntary school", see s 9(2) of that Act.

Admission to schools

6 Parental preferences

(1) Every local education authority shall make arrangements for enabling the parent of a child in the area of the authority to express a preference as to the school at which he wishes education to be provided for his child in the exercise of the authority's functions and to give reasons for his preference.

(2) Subject to subsection (3) below, it shall be the duty of a local education authority and of the governors of a county or voluntary school to comply with any preference expressed in accordance with the arrangements.

(3) The duty imposed by subsection (2) above does not apply—

(a) if compliance with the preference would prejudice the provision of efficient education or the efficient use of resources;

(b) if the preferred school is an aided or special agreement school and compliance with the preference would be incompatible with any arrangements between the governors and the local education authority in respect of the admission of pupils to the school; or

(c) if the arrangements for admission to the preferred school are based wholly or partly on selection by reference to ability or aptitude and compliance with the preference would be incompatible with selection under the arrangements.

(4) Where the arrangements for the admission of pupils to a school maintained by a local education authority provide for applications for admission to be made to, or to a person acting on behalf of, the governors of the school, a parent who makes such an application shall be regarded for the purposes of subsection (2) above as having expressed a preference for that school in accordance with arrangements made under subsection (1) above.

(5) The duty imposed by subsection (2) above in relation to a preference expressed in accordance with arrangements made under subsection (1) above shall apply also in relation to—

(a) any application for the admission to a school maintained by a local education authority of a child who is not in the area of the authority; and

(b) any application made as mentioned in section 10(3) or 11(1) below;

and references in subsection (3) above to a preference and a preferred school shall be construed accordingly.

NOTES

Commencement. This section and ss 7–9 post were brought into force on 1 October 1980 by the Education Act 1980 (Commencement No 2) Order 1980, SI 1980/959, made under s 37 post. By virtue of that order this section and ss 7, 8 post do not have effect in relation to the admission or proposed admission of a child to a school before the first day of the 1982 autumn term at the school in question.

Local education authority. See the note to s 2 ante.

It shall be the duty etc. Provision for appeals against admission decisions is made by s 7 and Sch 2 post. See also, by virtue of s 38(3) post, the Education Act 1944, s 68, this part of this title ante, concerning the power of the Secretary of State to prevent the unreasonable exercise of a duty, and s 99(1) of that Act concerning the power of the Secretary of State to enforce the execution of a duty.

Governors. See the note to s 3 ante.

Appeals against admission decisions. See s 7 post.

Information as to schools and admission arrangements. As to the duty to publish this information, see s 8 post.

Exclusion. This section does not apply to nursery schools or special schools and is excluded for certain other purposes; see s 9 post.

Definitions. For "child", see s 38(4) post. By virtue of s 38(3) post, for "parent", "pupil" and "school", see the Education Act 1944, s 114(1), this part of this title ante; for "maintain", see s 114(2)(a) of that Act; for "county school" and "voluntary school", see s 9(2) of that Act; for "aided school" and "special agreement school", see s 15 of that Act. Note as to "preference" and "preferred school", sub-s (5) above.

---

7 Appeals against admission decisions

(1) Every local education authority shall make arrangements for enabling the parent of a child to appeal against—

    (a) any decision made by or on behalf of the authority as to the school at which education is to be provided for the child in the exercise of the authority's functions; and

    (b) any decision made by or on behalf of the governors of a county or controlled school maintained by the authority refusing the child admission to such a school.

(2) The governors of every aided or special agreement school shall make arrangements for enabling the parent of a child to appeal against any decision made by or on behalf of the governors refusing the child admission to the school.

(3) Joint arrangements may be made under subsection (2) above by the governors of two or more aided or special agreement schools maintained by the same local education authority.

(4) Any appeal by virtue of this section shall be to an appeal committee constituted in accordance with Part I of Schedule 2 to this Act; and Part II of that Schedule shall have effect in relation to the procedure on any such appeal.

(5) The decision of an appeal committee on any such appeal shall be binding on the local education authority or governors by or on whose behalf the decision under appeal was made and, in the case of a decision made by or on behalf of a local education authority, on the governors of any county or controlled school at which the committee determines that a place should be offered to the child in question.

(6), (7) . . .

NOTES

Sub-s (6) amends the Tribunals and Inquiries Act 1971, s 13(1), Sch 1, Vol 10, title Constitutional Law (Pt 4); sub-s (7) amends the Local Government Act 1974, s 25, Vol 25, title Local Government.

Commencement. See the note to s 6 ante.

Local education authority. See the note to s 2 ante.

Governors. See the note to s 3 ante.

Shall be binding. There is no right of appeal to the High Court from the decision of an appeal committee on a point of law under the Tribunals and Inquiries Act 1971, s 13, Vol 10, title Constitutional Law (Pt 4), as that section is excluded by virtue of the second amendment made by sub-s (6). It is thought however, that the supervisory jurisdiction of the courts is not excluded; see, further, 1 Halsbury's Laws (4th edn) paras 22, 52, 84.

Further provisions. See s 6 ante (parental preferences); s 8 post (information as to schools and admission arrangements); and s 9 post (exclusion of nursery schools and special schools).

Definitions. For "child", see s 38(4) post. By virtue of s 38(3) post, for "parent" and "school", see the Education Act 1944, s 114(1), this part of this title ante; for "maintain", see s 114(2)(a) of that Act; for "county school", see s 9(2) of that Act; and for "aided school", "controlled school" and "special agreement school", see s 15 of that Act.

8 Information as to schools and admission arrangements

(1) Every local education authority shall, for each school year, publish particulars of—

- (a) the arrangements for the admission of pupils to schools maintained by the authority, other than aided or special agreement schools;
- (b) the authority's arrangements for the provision of education at schools maintained by another local education authority or not maintained by a local education authority; and
- (c) the arrangements made by the authority under sections 6(1) and 7(1) above.

(2) The governors of every aided or special agreement school shall, for each school year, publish particulars of—

- (a) the arrangements for the admission of pupils to the school; and
- (b) the arrangements made by them under section 7(2) above.

(3) The particulars to be published under subsections (1)(a) and (2)(a) above shall include particulars of—

- (a) the number of pupils that it is intended to admit in each school year to each school to which the arrangements relate, being pupils in the age group in which pupils are normally admitted or, if there is more than one such group, in each such group;
- (b) the respective admission functions of the local education authority and the governors;
- (c) the policy followed in deciding admissions;
- (d) the arrangements made in respect of pupils not belonging to the area of the local education authority.

(4) The particulars to be published under subsection (1)(b) above shall include particulars of—

- (a) the criteria for offering places at schools not maintained by a local education authority;
- (b) the names of, and number of places at, any such schools in respect of which the authority have standing arrangements.

(5) Every local education authority shall, as respects each school maintained by them other than an aided or special agreement school, and the governors of every aided or special agreement school shall, as respects that school, publish—

- (a) such information as may be required by regulations made by the Secretary of State; and
- (b) such other information, if any, as the authority or governors think fit,

and every local education authority shall also publish such information as may be so required with respect to their policy and arrangements in respect of any matter relating to primary or secondary education in their area.

(6) The local education authority by whom an aided or special agreement school is maintained may, with the agreement of the governors of the school, publish on their behalf the particulars or information relating to the school referred to in subsection (2) or (5) above.

(7) References in this section to publication are references to publication at such time or times and in such manner as may be required by regulations made by the Secretary of State.

NOTES

Commencement. See the note to s 6 ante.

Local education authority; Secretary of State. See the notes to s 2 ante.

School year. Under s 27(1)(*e*) post regulations may be made as to the duration of the school year.

Governors. See the note to s 3 ante.

Pupils not belonging to the area etc. As to the area to which a pupil does not belong, see s 38(5) post, and the regulations noted to that section.

Think fit. Statutory powers are often conferred in subjective terms, the competent authority being entitled to act, eg, when it "thinks fit", or when it is "satisfied" or it "appears" to it that a prescribed state of affairs exists, but the inherent jurisdiction of the courts to determine whether such powers have been exceeded is not readily ousted by the use of such language; see further 1 Halsbury's Laws (4th edn) para 22.

Nursery schools and special schools. In relation to these schools this section is wholly or mainly excluded by s 9 post.

Definitions. By virtue of s 38(3) post, for "pupil" and "school", see the Education Act 1944, s 114(1), this part of this title ante; for "maintain", see s 114(2)(*a*) of that Act; for "primary education" and "secondary education", see s 8(1) of that Act; and for "aided school" and "special agreement school", see s 15 of that Act.

Regulations under this section. The Education (School Information) Regulations 1981, SI 1981/630, as amended by SI 1983/41.

9 Nursery schools and special schools

(1) None of the provisions of sections 6, 7 and 8 above have effect in relation to nursery schools or to children who will not have attained the age of five years at the time of their proposed admission except that where the arrangements for the admission of pupils to a school maintained by a local education authority provide for the admission of children who will attain that age within six months after their admission those sections shall have effect in relation to the admission of such pupils to that school.

(2) None of the provisions of those sections other than subsections (5) and (7) of section 8 have effect in relation to special schools or children [in respect of whom statements are maintained under section 7 of the Education Act 1981 (special educational needs)].

NOTES

The words in square brackets in sub-s (2) were substituted by the Education Act 1981, s 21, Sch 3; for transitional provisions, see the Education Act 1981 (Commencement No 2) Order 1983, SI 1983/7, Schedule, para 3(4).

Commencement. See the note to s 6 ante.

Attained the age. A person attains a given age expressed in years at the commencement of the relevant anniversary of the date of his birth; see the Family Law Reform Act 1969, s 9, Vol 6, title Children.

Local education authority. See the note to s 2 ante.

Within six months after etc. The general rule in cases where an act is to be done within a specified time is that the day from which it runs is not to be counted; see *Goldsmiths' Co v West Metropolitan Rly Co* [1904] 1 KB, [1900–3] All ER Rep 667, CA; *Stewart v Chapman* [1951] 2 KB 792, [1951] 2 All ER 613. See also *Dodds v Walker* [1981] 2 All ER 609, [1981] 1 WLR 1027, HL, as to the day of expiry of periods of a month or a specified number of months.

Definitions. For "child", see s 38(4) post. By virtue of s 38(3) post, for "nursery school" and "special school", see the Education Act 1944, s 9(4), (5), this part of this title ante; for "pupil", see s 114(1) of that Act; and for "maintain", see s 114(2)(*a*) of that Act; for "special educational needs", see the Education Act 1981, s 1, this part of this title post.

School attendance orders

10 Determination of school to be named in order

(1) Before serving a school attendance order on a parent under section 37 of the Education Act 1944 the local education authority shall serve on him a written notice of their intention to serve the order—

(a) specifying the school which they intend to name in the order and, if they think fit, one or more other schools which they regard as suitable alternatives; and

(b) stating the effect of subsections (2) to (4) below;

but no aided or special agreement school shall be specified in the notice without the consent of the governors of the school.

(2) If the notice specifies one or more alternative schools and the parent selects one of them before the expiration of the period of fourteen days beginning with the day after that on which the notice is served, the school selected by him shall be named in the order.

(3) If before the expiration of that period the parent—

(a) applies for the child to be admitted to a school maintained by a local education authority and, if that authority is not the one by whom the notice was served, notifies the latter authority of the application; or

(b) applies to the local education authority by whom the notice was served for education to be provided for the child at a school not maintained by a local education authority,

then, if the child is offered a place at a school as a result of the application mentioned in paragraph (a) above or is offered a place at a school at which the local education authority agree to provide education for him in response to the application mentioned in paragraph (b) above, that school shall be named in the order.

(4) If before the expiration of the period mentioned in subsection (2) above the parent—

(a) applies for the child to be admitted to a school which is not maintained by a local education authority and in respect of which he makes no such application as is mentioned in subsection (3)(b) above; and

(b) notifies the local education authority by whom the notice was served of the application,

then, if as a result of the application the child is offered a place at a school which is suitable to his age, ability and aptitude [and any special educational needs he may have], that school shall be named in the order.

(5) The foregoing provisions of this section do not apply to children [in respect of whom the local education authority maintain a statement under section 7 of the Education Act 1981 (special educational needs)].

(6), (7) . . .

NOTES

The words in square brackets in sub-s (4) were inserted, and in sub-s (5) were added, and sub-ss (6), (7) were repealed by the Education Act 1981, s 21, Sch 3, para 15, Sch 4; for transitional provisions, see the Education Act 1981 (Commencement No 2) Order 1983, SI 1983/7, Schedule, para 3(4).

Commencement. Sub-s (5) was brought into force on 5 May 1980 by the Education Act 1980 (Commencement No 1) Order 1980, SI 1980/489, made under s 37 post. Sub-ss (1)–(4) were brought into force on 1 July 1982 by the Education Act 1980 (Commencement No 2) Order 1980, SI 1980/959, made under s 37 post, with a saving in respect of notices of intention to serve a school attendance order which were served before 1 July 1982.

Sub-s (1): Local education authority. See the note to s 2 ante.

Serve . . . notice. As to mode of service, see, by virtue of s 38(3) post, the Education Act 1944, s 113, this part of this title ante.

Written. Expressions referring to writing are, unless the contrary intention appears, to be construed as including references to other modes of representing or reproducing words in a visible form; see the Interpretation Act 1978, s 5, Sch 1, Vol 41, title Statutes.

Think fit. See the note to s 8 ante.

Governors. See the note to s 3 ante.

Sub-s (2): Fourteen days beginning with. The use of the phrase "beginning with" makes it clear that in computing this period the day from which it runs is to be included; see *Hare v Gocher* [1962] 2 QB 641,

[1962] 2 All ER 763; and *Trow v Ind Coope (West Midlands) Ltd* [1967] 2 QB at 909, [1967] 2 All ER 900, CA.

Sub-s (3): Applies for the child to be admitted to a school. As to parental preference as to a child's admission to school, see s 6 ante (and note, in particular, sub-s (5)(*b*) of that section).

Sub-s (7): Secretary of State. See the note to s 2 ante.

It shall be the duty etc. As to the power of the Secretary of State to enforce the execution of a duty see, by virtue of s 38(3) post, the Education Act 1944, s 99(1), this part of this title ante.

Definitions. By virtue of s 38(3) post, for "child", "parent" and "school", see the Education Act 1944, s 114(1), this part of this title ante; for "maintain", see s 114(2)(*a*) of that Act; for "aided school" and "special agreement school", see s 15 of that Act; and for "special educational treatment", see s 8(2)(*c*) of that Act.

Education Act 1944, s 37. See this part of this title ante.

11 Amendment of order

(1) If at any time while a school attendance order is in force with respect to a child the parent—

> (*a*) applies for the child to be admitted to a school maintained by a local education authority; or
>
> (*b*) applies to the local education authority by whom the order was served for education to be provided for the child at a school not maintained by a local education authority,

being, in either case, a school different from the one named in the order, then, if the child is offered a place at a school as a result of the application mentioned in paragraph (*a*) above or is offered a place at a school at which the local education authority agree to provide education for him in response to the application mentioned in paragraph (*b*) above, the local education authority by whom the order was served shall at the request of the parent amend the order by substituting that school for the one previously named.

(2) If at any time while a school attendance order is in force with respect to a child—

> (*a*) the parent applies for the child to be admitted to a school which is not maintained by a local education authority and in respect of which he makes no such application as is mentioned in subsection (1)(*b*) above, being a school different from the one named in the order; and
>
> (*b*) as a result of the application the child is offered a place at a school which is suitable to his age, ability and aptitude, [and to any special educational needs he may have]

the local education authority by whom the order was served shall at the request of the parent amend the order by substituting that school for the one previously named.

(3) The foregoing provisions of this section do not apply to children [in respect of whom the local education authority maintain a statement under section 7 of the Education Act 1981 (special educational needs)].

NOTES

The words in square brackets in sub-s (2)(*b*) were inserted, and the words in square brackets in sub-s (3) were substituted, by the Education Act 1981, s 21, Sch 3, para 16.

Commencement. This section was brought into force on 1 July 1982 by the Education Act 1980 (Commencement No 2) Order 1980, SI 1980/959, made under s 37 post, with a saving in respect of cases in which application for the amendment of a school attendance order was made in pursuance of the Education Act 1944, s 37(4), this part of this title ante before 1 July 1982.

School attendance order. Ie by virtue of s 38(3) post, an order made under the Education Act 1944, s 37(2), this part of this title ante. As to such orders, see also s 10 ante.

Applies for the child to be admitted to a school. As to parental preference as to a child's admission to a school, see s 6 ante (and note, in particular, sub-s (5)(*b*) of that section).

Local education authority. See the note to s 2 ante.

Definitions. By virtue of s 38(3) post, for "child", "parent" and "school", see the Education Act 1944, s 114(1), this part of this title ante; for "maintain", see s 114(2)(*a*) of that Act; and for "special educational treatment", see s 8(2)(*c*) of that Act.

Education Act 1944, s 37(4). See this part of this title ante.

Establishment, discontinuance and alteration of schools

12 Establishment, discontinuance and alteration of schools by local education authorities

(1) Where a local education authority intend—

(*a*) to establish a new county school;

(*b*) to maintain as a county school any school which is not such a school;

(*c*) to cease to maintain any county school or, except as provided by section 14 of the Education Act 1944, any voluntary school;

(*d*) to make any significant change in the character, or significant enlargement of the premises, of a county school; or

(*e*) to cease to maintain a nursery school established by them or a former authority,

they shall publish their proposals for that purpose in such manner as may be required by regulations made by the Secretary of State and submit to him a copy of the published proposals.

(2) The published proposals shall be accompanied by a statement of the effect of subsection (3) below and shall include particulars of the time or times at which it is intended to implement the proposals and (except where the proposal is to cease to maintain a school) particulars of the number of pupils intended to be admitted to the school in each relevant age group in the first school year in relation to which the proposals have been wholly implemented excluding pupils who will not have attained the age of five years within six months after their admission.

(3) Any ten or more local government electors for the area may within the period of two months after the first publication of the proposals submit an objection to the proposals to the local education authority, and objections to the proposals may also be submitted to the authority within that period by the governors of any voluntary school affected by the proposals and by any other local education authority concerned; and the authority by whom the proposals were published shall within one month after the end of that period transmit to the Secretary of State copies of all objections made (and not withdrawn in writing) in that period, together with their observations on the objections.

(4) Any proposal—

(*a*) for the maintenance as a county school of a school which is for the time being a voluntary school; or

(*b*) for ceasing to maintain a voluntary school,

shall require the approval of the Secretary of State; and he shall not approve proposals for the maintenance as a county school of a school which is for the time being a voluntary school unless he has, in accordance with Schedule 2 to the said Act of 1944, approved an agreement under the powers conferred by that Schedule between the authority and the governors of the school for the transfer to the authority of all necessary interests in the school premises.

(5) Proposals not falling within subsection (4) above shall require the approval of the Secretary of State—

(*a*) if he gives notice to that effect to the local education authority within two months after the submission to him of the published proposals; or

(*b*) if objections have been made as mentioned in subsection (3) above and all objections so made have not been withdrawn as mentioned in that subsection.

(6) If the proposals require the approval of the Secretary of State he may reject them,

approve them without modification or, after consultation with the local education authority, approve them with such modifications as he thinks desirable.

(7) If the proposals do not require the approval of the Secretary of State the local education authority shall determine whether the proposals should be implemented; and the authority shall make that determination not later than four months after the submission of the proposals to the Secretary of State.

(8) A local authority shall notify the Secretary of State of any determination made by them under subsection (7) above.

(9) It shall be the duty of a local education authority to implement—

    (a) any proposals which have been approved by the Secretary of State under this section; and

    (b) any proposals which they have determined to implement in accordance with subsection (7) above;

but the Secretary of State may, at the request of the authority, modify any proposals which they are required to implement by virtue of this subsection.

NOTES

Commencement. This section except sub-ss (1)(a)–(d), (4) was brought into force on 5 May 1980, and the excepted provisions were brought into force on 1 August 1980, by the Education Act 1980 (Commencement No 1) Order 1980, SI 1980/489, made under s 37 post.

General Note. This section and ss 13 and 14 post replaced the Education Act 1944, s 13 (repealed by ss 16(4), 38(6), Sch 7 post, subject to s 16(5) post). These sections have made changed provision as respects proposals by local education authorities, or by the promoters or governors of a voluntary school, for the establishment, discontinuance or significant enlargement of the premises, or change of character, of a school. The principal differences are, first, that, save where a voluntary school is concerned (sub-s (4) above and s 13(4) post), proposals to which no objections are made will require approval by the Secretary of State only if he gives notice to that effect (sub-s (5) above), secondly, that the provisions extend to the discontinuance of nursery schools established by local education authorities (sub-s (1) above) and, thirdly, that only such particulars of premises as the Secretary of State may require (not necessarily full specifications and plans) are to be submitted to him for approval (s 14 post).

Sub-s (1): Local education authority; Secretary of State. See the notes to s 2 ante.

Establish a new county school; maintain as a county school, etc. For the power of a local education authority to establish and maintain schools etc, see the Education Act 1944, s 9, this part of this title ante. See also the next following note.

Cease to maintain any county school, etc. As to the construction of the references to ceasing to maintain a county school or voluntary school and establishing a new school, see the Education Act 1968, s 1(1), this part of this title ante.

Significant change in the character, or significant enlargement etc. Sub-s (1)(d) above is to be read in the light of s 16(2) post and the definitions of "enlargement" and "significant" in the Education Act 1944, s 114(1), this part of this title ante, which apply by virtue of s 38(3) post. Any question whether a change in character or enlargement would be significant is to be determined by the Secretary of State; see by virtue of s 38(3) post, s 67(4) of the 1944 Act.

Publish their proposals . . . and submit to him a copy. As to the need to make an adequate statement of the proposals, see *Legg v Inner London Education Authority* [1972] 3 All ER 177, [1972] 1 WLR 1245 (decided under the Education Act 1944, s 13 (repealed)).

See also the note "Inner London Education Authority" below.

Sub-s (2): School year. See the note to s 8 ante.

Attained the age; within six months after etc. See the notes to s 9 ante.

Sub-s (3): Within . . . two months (one month) after etc. See the note "Within six months after etc" to s 9 ante.

Governors. See the note to s 3 ante.

Writing. See the note "Written" to s 10 ante.

Sub-s (4): Proposal . . . shall require the approval, etc. Only a proposal of which a copy has been submitted to the Secretary of State under sub-s (1) above may be approved (subject to any modification under sub-s (6) above); cf *Legg v Inner London Education Authority* [1972] 3 All ER 177, [1972] 1 WLR 1245.

Sub-s (5): Gives notice. As to the mode of service of notices, see, by virtue of s 38(3) post, the Education Act 1944, s 113, this part of this title ante.

Within two months after etc. See the note "Within six months after etc" to s 9 ante.

Sub-s (6): Consultation. On what constitutes consultation, see, in particular, *Fletcher v Minister of Town and Country Planning* [1947] 2 All ER 496, (1947) 111 JP Jo 542; *Rollo v Minister of Town and Country Planning* [1948] 1 All ER 13, [1948] LJR 817, CA; *Re Union of Whippingham and East Cowes Benefices,*

Derham v Church Comrs for England [1954] AC 245, [1954] 2 All ER 22, PC; and *Agricultural, Horticultural and Forestry Industry Training Board v Aylesbury Mushrooms Ltd* [1972] 1 All ER 280, [1972] 1 WLR 190.

Approve them with such modifications etc. The process involved in modification is one of alteration but throughout the process there has to be the continued existence of the original entity; when the process has reached a stage of wholesale rejection and replacement the process ceases to be one of modification; see *Legg v Inner London Education Authority* [1972] 3 All ER 177, [1972] 1 WLR 1245.

Thinks desirable. See the note "Think fit" to s 8 ante.

Sub-s (7): Not later than four months after etc. See the note "Within six months after etc" to s 9 ante.

Sub-s (9): It shall be the duty etc. See the note to s 10 ante. Sub-s (9) above is to be read subject to s 15(10) post.

Inner London Education Authority. Before publishing any proposals under sub-s (1) above or s 15(3) post, the Inner London Education Authority (as to which, see the Local Government Act 1985, s 18, Vol 25, title Local Government) is required to consult the council of any area which it considers is being, or is to be, served by the school in question; see s 21(6) of the 1985 Act.

Further provisions. See s 13 post (establishment and allocation of voluntary schools); s 14 post (approval of school premises); s 15 post (reduction of school places); and s 16(1)–(5) post (supplementary provisions); and see also the following enactments: the Education Act 1944, s 85(2), the Education Act 1946, s 2, the London Government Act 1963, s 31(10), Vol 26, title London, the Education Act 1964, s 1(1), the Education Act 1973, s 1(2)(a) and the Sex Discrimination Act 1975, Sch 2, para 1, Vol 6, title Civil Rights and Liberties. All of the Education Acts cited are printed in this part of this title ante.

Definitions. For "change in the character of school", see s 16(2) post; for "relevant age group", see s 16(3) post. By virtue of s 38(3) post, for "enlargement", "former authority", "local government elector", "premises", "pupil", "school" and "significant", see the Education Act 1944, s 114(1), this part of this title ante; for "maintain", see s 114(2)(a) of that Act; for "county school" and "voluntary school", see s 9(2) of that Act; and for "nursery school", see s 9(4) of that Act.

Education Act 1944, s 14, Sch 2. See this part of this title ante.

Regulations under this section. The Education (Publication of School Proposals) (No 2) Regulations 1980, SI 1980/658 (partly made under sub-s (1) above).

For general provisions as to regulations, see s 35 post.

13 Establishment and alteration of voluntary schools

(1) Where—

    (a) any persons propose that a school established by them or by persons whom they represent which is not a voluntary school, or any school proposed to be so established, should be maintained by a local education authority as a voluntary school; or

    (b) the governors of a school maintained by a local education authority as a voluntary school intend to make a significant change in the character or significant enlargement of the premises of the school,

they shall, after consultation with the authority, publish proposals for that purpose in such manner as may be required by regulations made by the Secretary of State and submit to him a copy of the published proposals.

(2) Subsection (2) of section 12 above shall apply to proposals published under this section as it applies to proposals published under that section taking the reference to subsection (3) of that section as a reference to subsection (3) below.

(3) Any ten or more local government electors for the area may within the period of two months after the first publication of the proposals submit an objection to the proposals to the Secretary of State, and objections to the proposals may also be submitted to him within that period by the governors of any voluntary school affected by the proposals and by any local education authority concerned.

(4) The proposals shall require the approval of the Secretary of State; and he may reject them, approve them without modification or, after consultation with the persons by whom they were made and the local education authority by whom the school is, or is to be, maintained, approve them with such modifications as he thinks desirable.

(5) Subject to subsections (6) and (7) below, if the proposals are approved by the Secretary of State it shall be the duty of the persons by whom they were made and, in

the case of proposals under subsection (1)(*a*) above, of the local education authority to implement the proposals.

(6) Subject to subsection (7) below, it shall be the duty of the local education authority to implement so much of any proposals approved by the Secretary of State as relates to the provision of playing fields or buildings which are to form part of the school premises but are not to be school buildings.

(7) The Secretary of State may modify any proposals which are required to be implemented under subsection (5) or (6) above but shall not do so in the case of proposals under subsection (1)(*a*) above except at the request of the local education authority or in the case of other proposals except at the request of the persons by whom they were made.

NOTES

Commencement. This section was brought into force on 1 August 1980 by the Education Act 1980 (Commencement No 1) Order 1980, SI 1980/489, made under s 37 post.

General Note. See the General Note to s 12 ante.

Sub-s (1): Persons. See the note "Person" to s 16 post.

Local education authority; Secretary of State. See the notes to s 2 ante.

Governors. See the note to s 3 ante.

Significant change in the character, or significant enlargement etc. See the note to s 12 ante.

Consultation. See the note to s 12 ante.

Sub-s (3): Within . . . two months after etc. See the note "Within six months after etc" to s 9 ante.

Sub-s (4): Thinks desirable. See the note "Think fit" to s 8 ante.

Sub-s (5): It shall be the duty. See the note to s 10 ante. Sub-s (5) above is to be read subject to s 15(10) post.

Further provisions. See s 1(2) ante (establishment, discontinuance and alteration of schools by local education authorities); s 14 post (approval of school premises); s 15 post (reduction of school places); and s 16(1), (2), (4), (5) post (supplementary provisions); and see also the following enactments: the Education Act 1944, ss 16(2), 17(6), 102, Sch 3, para 5, the Education Act 1946, ss 1(1), 2(2), Sch 1, para 1(*a*), the Education (Miscellaneous Provisions) Act 1953, s 2(*a*), the London Government Act 1963, s 31(10), Vol 26, title London, the Education Act 1964, s 1(1), the Education Act 1967, ss 1(2)(*a*), 3, the Education Act 1968, s 3(4), the Education Act 1973, s 1(2)(*a*), and the Sex Discrimination Act 1975, Sch 2, para 1, Vol 6, title Civil Rights and Liberties. All the Education Acts cited are printed in this part of this title ante.

Definitions. For "change in the character of a school", see s 16(2) post. By virtue of s 38(3) post, for "enlargement", "local government elector", "premises", "school" and "significant", see the Education Act 1944, s 114(1), this part of this title ante; for "maintain", see s 114(2)(*a*) of that Act; and for "voluntary school", see s 9(2) of that Act.

Regulations under this section. The Education (Publication of School Proposals) (No 2) Regulations 1980, SI 1980/658 (partly made under sub-s (1) above).

For general provisions as to regulations, see s 35 post.

14 Approval of school premises

(1) Where proposals submitted under section 12 or 13 above are for—

    (*a*) the establishment of a school;

    (*b*) the maintenance of a school as a county or voluntary school; or

    (*c*) the making of a significant change in the character, or significant enlargement of the premises, of a school,

the persons making the proposals shall, at such time and in such form and manner as the Secretary of State may direct, submit to him for his approval such particulars with respect to the premises or proposed premises of the school as he may require.

(2) Before submitting any particulars under this section in respect of a school which is or is to be maintained as a voluntary school, the governors or the persons by whom the school is to be established shall consult the local education authority.

(3) Where particulars with respect to any school are required to be submitted under this section, the persons whose duty it is under section 12 or 13 above to implement the

proposals shall implement them in accordance with the particulars as approved by the Secretary of State.

(4) In ... section 63(2) of the Education Act 1944 (exemption from building regulations etc) references to plans approved by the Secretary of State shall include references to any particulars submitted to and approved by him under this section.

NOTES

The words omitted from sub-s (4) were repealed by the Building Act 1984, s 133(2), Sch 7.

Commencement. This section except sub-s (3) was brought into force on 5 May 1980, and sub-s (3) was brought into force on 1 August 1980, by the Education Act 1980 (Commencement No 1) Order 1980, SI 1980/489, made under s 37 post.

General Note. See the General Note to s 12 ante.

Secretary of State; local education authority. See the notes to s 2 ante.

Significant change in the character, or significant enlargement etc. Cf the note to s 12 ante.

Governors. See the note to s 3 ante.

Consult. See the note "Consultation" to s 12 ante.

Exemption from building regulations. Buildings required for the purposes of a school or other educational establishment erected or to be erected according to plans or particulars approved by the Secretary of State under this section are not subject to building regulations under the Building Act 1984, Pt II; see s 4(1)(a) of that Act, Vol 35, title Public Health.

Supplementary provisions. See s 16(1), (2), (4)–(7) post.

Definitions. For "change in the character of a school", see s 16(2) post. By virtue of s 38(3) post, for "enlargement", "local education authority", "premises", "school" and "significant", see the Education Act 1944, s 114(1), this part of this title ante; for "maintain", see s 114(2)(a) of that Act; and for "county school" and "voluntary school", see s 9(2) of that Act.

Education Act 1944, s 63(2). See this part of this title ante.

15 Reduction of school places

(1) Subject to subsection (2) below, this section has effect where—

(a) a local education authority, in the case of a county school, or the governors, in the case of a voluntary school, intend to reduce the number of pupils in any relevant age group who are to be admitted to the school in any school year ... to a number which is four-fifths or less than four-fifths of the standard number applying under this section to the school in relation to that year and age group; and

(b) in the case of a primary school, the standard number is twenty or more.

(2) Where the age group in question includes children who will not have attained the age of five years within six months after their admission, those children shall be disregarded both in determining the number of pupils who are to be admitted and the standard number applying under this section.

(3) The authority or governors, as the case may be, shall publish their proposals with respect to the reduction in such manner as may be required by regulations made by the Secretary of State and submit to him a copy of the published proposals; and subsections (3), (5), (6), (7) and (8) of section 12 above shall apply to proposals published under this section by a local education authority and subsections (3) and (4) of section 13 above shall apply to proposals published under this section by the governors of a voluntary school as they apply in relation to proposals published under those sections respectively.

(4) The published proposals shall be accompanied by a statement of the effect of section 12(3) or, as the case may be, section 13(3) as applied by subsection (3) above.

(5) Subject to subsections (6), (7) and (8) below, if pupils in any age group were admitted to a school in the school year beginning in 1979, the number admitted in that year shall be the standard number applying to the school for that age group in any subsequent year.

(6) Subject to subsections (7) and (8) below, if proposals under section 13 of the

Education Act 1944 have fallen to be implemented in relation to a school and the first school year in relation to which they are to be wholly implemented begins after 1979, the number of pupils in any age group admitted to the school in the first school year beginning after 1979 in relation to which the proposals have been wholly or partly implemented shall be the standard number applying to the school for that age group in any subsequent year; but where the standard number would fall to be determined under this subsection by reference to a school year in relation to which the proposals have not been wholly implemented the Secretary of State may vary that number in its application to any subsequent school year.

(7) Subject to subsection (8) below, if proposals under section 12 or 13 above have fallen to be implemented in relation to a school, the number stated in the proposals in accordance with subsection (2) of section 12 (or that subsection as applied by section 13) for any school year and age group shall be the standard number applying to the school for that age group in any school year in relation to which the proposals have been wholly implemented and, subject to any variation made by the Secretary of State, in any school year in relation to which they have been partly implemented.

(8) The Secretary of State may by an order applying to any school or to schools of any class or description vary any standard number that would otherwise apply by virtue of the foregoing provisions of this section.

(9) References in subsection (7) above to proposals under section 12 or 13 are references to the proposals with any modifications made by the Secretary of State under either of those sections; and any standard number applying under that subsection is without prejudice to the application under that subsection of a new standard number if further proposals fall to be implemented under those sections.

(10) Neither section 12(9) nor section 13(5) above shall be construed as imposing any duty to admit pupils in accordance with the number stated in the proposals in accordance with subsection (2) of section 12 or that subsection as applied by section 13.

NOTES

The words omitted from sub-s (1) were inserted until 1 August 1981 by the Education Act 1980 (Commencement No 1) Order 1980, SI 1980/489, art 4, Sch 4, para 1 and are accordingly spent.

Commencement. This section was brought into force on 1 August 1980 by the Education Act 1980 (Commencement No 1) Order 1980, SI 1980/489, made under s 37 post.

Sub-s (1): Local education authority. See the note to s 2 ante.

Governors. See the note to s 3 ante.

School year. See the note to s 8 ante.

Sub-s (2): Attained the age; within six months after etc. See the notes to s 9 ante.

Sub-s (3): Secretary of State. See the note to s 2 ante.

Inner London Education Authority. See the note to s 12 ante.

Supplementary provisions. See s 16(1), (3) post; and see also the London Government Act 1963, s 31(10), Vol 26, title London and the note "Inner London Education Authority" to s 12 ante.

Definitions. For "relevant age group", see s 16(3) post. By virtue of s 38(3) post, for "pupil" and "school", see the Education Act 1944, s 114(1), this part of this title ante; and for "county school" and "voluntary school", see s 9(2) of that Act. Note as to "standard number", sub-ss (5)–(8) above.

Education Act 1944, s 13. That section is repealed by ss 16(4) and 38(6) of, and Sch 7 to, this Act post, and it is replaced by ss 12–14 ante.

Regulations and orders under this section. The Education (Publication of School Proposals) (No 2) Regulations 1980, SI 1980/658 (partly made under sub-s (3) above). Up to 1 August 1985, no order had been made under sub-s (8) above and orders relating to particular schools are not recorded in this work.

For general provisions as to orders and regulations, see s 35 post.

16 Provisions supplementary to ss 12 to 15

(1) Neither a local education authority nor any other person shall do or undertake to do anything for which proposals are required to be published and submitted in accordance with any of the provisions of sections 12 to 15 above until those provisions

have been complied with and any necessary approval has been given; but the Secretary of State may in any case allow such steps to be taken pending compliance with those provisions and the giving of any necessary approval as he considers reasonable in the circumstances of the case.

(2) References in sections 12, 13 and 14 above to a change in the character of a school include, in particular, changes in character resulting from education beginning or ceasing to be provided for pupils above or below a particular age, for boys as well as girls or for girls as well as boys, or from the making or alteration of arrangements for the admission of pupils by reference to ability or aptitude.

(3) References in sections 12 and 15 above to a relevant age group are references to an age group in which pupils are or will normally be admitted to the school in question.

(4) Section 13 of the Education Act 1944 (which is superseded by sections 12 to 14 above) shall cease to have effect; and the enactments mentioned in Schedule 3 to this Act shall have effect with the amendments there specified, being amendments consequential on the replacement of that section.

(5) Subsection (4) above does not affect the said section 13, or any enactments referring to it, in relation to any proposals which have been approved or of which public notice has been given under that section before the coming into force of sections 12 to 14 above but any proposals required by virtue of that section to be implemented by a local education authority or by any other person may, at the request of the authority or those persons, be modified by the Secretary of State.

(6) Section 14(1), (2) and (4) above shall apply, and subsection (6) of the said section 13 shall not apply, in relation to proposals for the matters referred to in paragraphs (*a*), (*b*) and (*c*) of section 14(1) above—

> (*a*) which are approved under the said section 13 on or after the date on which this subsection comes into force; or
>
> (*b*) which have then already been approved under that section but in respect of which specifications and plans have not yet been submitted under subsection (6) of that section;

and, in relation to any such proposals, subsection (7) of the said section 13 shall apply as if references to specifications and plans being approved or not required under that section were references to particulars being approved or not required under section 14 above.

(7) In subsection (6) above references to subsection (6) and (7) of the said section 13 include references to those subsections as applied by subsection (9) of that section.

NOTES

Commencement. Sub-ss (1), (6), (7) above were brought into force on 5 May 1980, and the remainder of this section was brought into force on 1 August 1980, by the Education Act 1980 (Commencement No 1) Order 1980, SI 1980/489, made under s 37 post.

Local education authority; Secretary of State. See the notes to s 2 ante.

Person. Unless the contrary intention appears this includes a body of persons corporate or unincorporate; see the Interpretation Act 1978, s 5, Sch 1, Vol 41, title Statutes.

Considers. See the note "Think fit" to s 8 ante.

Definitions. By virtue of s 38(3) post, for "pupil" and "school", see the Education Act 1944, s 114(1), this part of this title ante.

Education Act 1944, s 13. That section is also repealed by s 38(6) of, and Sch 7 to, this Act post.

Awards and grants

17 Assisted places at independent schools

(1) For the purpose of enabling pupils who might otherwise not be able to do so to benefit from education at independent schools, the Secretary of State shall establish and operate a scheme whereby—

(*a*)   participating schools remit fees that would otherwise be chargeable in respect of pupils selected for assisted places under the scheme; and

(*b*)   the Secretary of State reimburses the schools for the fees that are remitted.

(2)   In this section references to a participating school are references to any independent school providing secondary education with which the Secretary of State makes an agreement (a "participation agreement") for the purposes of the scheme; and in determining whether to make a participation agreement with any school the Secretary of State shall have regard to the desirability of securing an equitable distribution of assisted places throughout England and Wales and between boys and girls.

(3)   The fees in relation to which the scheme is to have effect shall be—

(*a*)   tuition and other fees the payment of which is a condition of attendance at a participating school but excluding boarding fees and such other fees, if any, as may be excluded by the participation agreement; and

(*b*)   entrance fees for public examinations paid by a participating school in respect of candidates from the school.

(4)   A participation agreement shall contain provisions with respect to the number of assisted places to be available at the school and may contain conditions to be complied with by the school in addition to those prescribed under subsection (6) below.

(5)   Schedule 4 to this Act shall have effect with respect to the termination of participation agreements.

(6)   The Secretary of State shall by regulations prescribe—

(*a*)   the requirements as to age, residence or otherwise which are to be the conditions of eligibility for selection for an assisted place;

(*b*)   the conditions subject to which, the extent to which, and the arrangements in accordance with which, fees are to be remitted by participating schools;

(*c*)   the time and manner in which participating schools are to claim and receive reimbursements from the Secretary of State;

(*d*)   conditions to be complied with by participating schools with respect to the selection of pupils for assisted places, the admission of pupils, the fees to be charged, the keeping and auditing of accounts and the furnishing of information to the Secretary of State; and

(*e*)   such other matters as appear to him to be requisite for the purposes of the scheme.

(7)   Regulations under subsection (6) above may authorise the Secretary of State to make provision for any purpose specified in the regulations.

(8)   Before making regulations under subsection (6) above the Secretary of State shall consult such bodies as appear to him to be appropriate and to be representative of participating schools or, in the case of regulations made within twelve months of the coming into force of this section, of schools eligible to participate in the scheme.

(9)   Regulations made under subsection (6)(*b*) above shall be reviewed by the Secretary of State in consultation with such bodies as appear to him to be appropriate and to be representative of participating schools—

(*a*)   not later than two years after the date on which the first such regulations are made; and

(*b*)   thereafter at intervals not exceeding two years.

(10)   Except where the context otherwise requires, references in this section and section 18 below to a school include references to the proprietors of the school and persons acting with their authority; and references in this section to an independent school are references to an independent school that is finally registered and conducted for charitable purposes only.

NOTES

Commencement. This section and s 18 post, were brought into force on 1 October 1980 by the Education Act 1980 (Commencement No 2) Order 1980, SI 1980/959, made under s 37 post.

Sub-s (1): Secretary of State. See the note to s 2 ante.

Assisted places. For the payment of incidental expenses of pupils holding assisted places, see s 18 post.

Sub-s (2): England; Wales. For meanings, see the Interpretation Act 1978, s 5, Sch 1, Vol 41, title Statutes.

Sub-s (6): Appear. See the note "Think fit" to s 8 ante.

Sub-s (8): Consult. See the note "Consultation" to s 12 ante.

Within twelve months of etc. See the note "Within six months after etc" to s 9 ante.

Sub-s (9): Not later than two years after. See the note "Within six months after etc" to s 9 ante.

Sub-s (10): Persons. See the note "Person" to s 16 ante.

Independent school that is finally registered. For provisions as to the registration of independent schools, see the Education Act 1944, s 70, this part of this title ante.

Charitable purposes. Charities in the legal sense comprise four principal divisions: trusts for the relief of poverty, trusts for the advancement of education, trusts for the advancement of religion, and trusts for other purposes beneficial to the community not falling under any of the preceding heads; see *Income Tax Special Purposes Comrs v Pemsel* [1891] AC 531 at 583, [1891–4] All ER Rep 28 at 55, HL, per Lord Macnaghten. The essentials of charitable purposes are considered generally in 5 Halsbury's Laws (4th edn) paras 501 et seq, and particular charitable purposes and non-charitable purposes are described in ibid, paras 514 et seq, 550 et seq. As to certain charities which fall within the fourth division mentioned above, see the Recreational Charities Act 1958, Vol 5, title Charities.

Definitions. By virtue of s 38(3) post, for "independent school", "proprietor", "pupil", "school" and "secondary education", see the Education Act 1944, s 114(1), this part of this title ante; and note also as to "independent school" and "school", sub-s (10) above. Note as to "participating school" and "participation agreement", sub-s (2) above.

Regulations under this section. The Education (Assisted Places) Regulations 1985, SI 1985/685.

For general provisions as to regulations, see s 35 post.

---

18 Incidental expenses of pupils holding assisted places

(1) The Secretary of State may make regulations requiring or enabling schools participating in the scheme referred to in section 17 above to make grants in respect of such expenses, and to remit such charges, as may be specified in the regulations, being expenses or charges in respect of matters incidental to or arising out of the attendance at the schools of pupils holding assisted places under the scheme.

(2) Any such regulations shall require any amounts granted or remitted by a school in accordance with the regulations to be reimbursed to the school by the Secretary of State.

(3) Regulations under this section may in particular prescribe—

> (a) the conditions subject to which, the extent to which, and the arrangements in accordance with which, grants and remissions are to be made;
>
> (b) the time and manner in which schools are to claim and receive reimbursements from the Secretary of State.

(4) Regulations under this section may authorise the Secretary of State to make provision for any purpose specified in the regulations.

NOTES

Commencement. See the note to s 17 ante.

Secretary of State. See the note to s 2 ante.

School. For meaning, see s 17(10) ante and, by virtue of s 38(3) post, the Education Act 1944, s 114(1), this part of this title ante.

Regulations under this section. The Education (Assisted Places) (Incidental Expenses) Regulations 1985, SI 1985/830.

For general provisions as to regulations, see s 35 post.

19 Awards for further and higher education

For sections 1 to 4 of the Education Act 1962 and Schedule 1 to that Act (awards for further and higher education) there shall be substituted the provisions set out in Schedule 5 to this Act which—

(*a*) extend the course capable of designation under section 1 to include certain courses provided in conjunction with overseas institutions;

(*b*) incorporate the effect of amendments made by the Education Act 1973, the Education Act 1975 and the Education Act 1976; and

(*c*) omit provisions that are spent or no longer required.

NOTE

Commencement. This section and ss 20 and 21 post were brought into force on 5 May 1980 by the Education Act 1980 (Commencement No 1) Order 1980, SI 1980/489, made under s 37 post.

20 Industrial scholarships

(1) The Secretary of State may award industrial scholarships or make payments to any other person in respect of the award of such scholarships by that person.

(2) In this section "industrial scholarships" means scholarships (however described) tenable by persons undertaking full-time courses of higher education provided by a university, college or other institution in the United Kingdom, being courses which appear to the Secretary of State or, as the case may be, the person awarding the scholarships to be relevant to a career in industry.

(3) In subsection (2) above the reference to a full-time course includes a reference to a course consisting of alternate periods of—

(*a*) full-time study in the university, college or institution in question; and

(*b*) associated industrial, professional or commercial experience;

and the reference in that subsection to a course provided by a university, college or institution in the United Kingdom includes a reference to a course provided by such a university, college or institution in conjunction with a university, college or other institution in another country.

NOTES

Commencement. See the note to s 19 ante.
Secretary of State. See the note to s 2 ante.
Person. See the note to s 16 ante.
United Kingdom. Ie Great Britain and Northern Ireland; see the Interpretation Act 1978, s 5, Sch 1, Vol 41, title Statutes. "Great Britain" means England, Scotland and Wales by virtue of the Union with Scotland Act 1706, preamble, Art I, Vol 10, title Constitutional Law (Pt 1), as read with s 22(1) of, and Sch 2, para 5(*a*) to, the 1978 Act. Neither the Channel Islands nor the Isle of Man is within the United Kingdom.
Appear. See the note "Think fit" to s 8 ante.

21 Grants for education in Welsh

(1) The Secretary of State shall by regulations make provision for the payment by him to local education authorities and other persons of grants in respect of expenditure incurred or to be incurred in, or in connection with, the teaching of the Welsh language or the teaching in that language of other subjects.

(2) Any regulations made by the Secretary of State under this section may make provision whereby the making of payments by him in pursuance of the regulations is dependent on the fulfilment of such conditions as may be determined by or in accordance

with the regulations, and may also make provision for requiring local education authorities and other persons to whom payments have been made in pursuance of the regulations to comply with such requirements as may be so determined.

NOTES

Commencement. See the note to s 19 ante.
Secretary of State; local education authorities. See the corresponding notes to s 2 ante.
Regulations under this section. The Grants for Welsh Language Education Regulations 1980, SI 1980/ 1011.
For general provisions as to regulations, see s 35 post.

School meals

22 School meals: England and Wales

(1) A local education authority—

    (*a*) may provide registered pupils at any school maintained by them with milk, meals or other refreshment; and

    (*b*) shall provide such facilities as the authority consider appropriate for the consumption of any meals or other refreshment brought to the school by such pupils.

(2) a local education authority shall exercise their power under subsection (1)(*a*) above in relation to any pupil whose parents are in receipt of supplementary benefit or family income supplement so as to ensure that such provision is made for him in the middle of the day as appears to the authority to be requisite.

(3) A local education authority—

    (*a*) may make such charges as they think fit for anything provided by them under subsection (1)(*a*) above, except where it is provided by virtue of subsection (2) above; but

    (*b*) shall remit the whole or part of any charge that would otherwise be made if, having regard to the particular circumstances of any pupil or class or description of pupils, they consider it appropriate to do so.

(4) The governors of a school maintained by a local education authority shall—

    (*a*) afford the authority such facilities as they require to enable them to exercise their functions under this section; and

    (*b*) allow the authority to make such use of the premises and equipment of the school and such alterations to the school buildings as the authority consider necessary for that purpose;

but nothing in this subsection shall require the governors of a voluntary school to incur any expenditure.

(5) The power under section 78(2)(*a*) of the Education Act 1944 to make arrangements as to the provision of milk for pupils in attendance at non-maintained schools shall apply in relation to all such pupils . . .

NOTES

The words omitted from sub-s (5) repeal the Education (Milk) Act 1971, s 1(3).
Commencement. This section was brought into force on 14 April 1980 by the Education Act 1980 (Commencement No 1) Order 1980, SI 1980/489, made under s 37 post, subject to a transitional provision which is now spent.
Local education authority. See the note to s 2 ante.
Supplementary benefit. This expression is defined by the Supplementary Benefits Act 1976, s 34(1), Vol 40, title Social Security.

Family income supplement. For meaning, see the Family Income Supplements Act 1970, s 1(2), Vol 40, title Social Security.

Appears; think fit; consider it appropriate. See the note "Think fit" to s 8 ante.

Governors. See the note to s 3 ante.

Special designations. Milk supplied free of charge to the recipient under arrangements made by virtue of this section is subject to the special designations and licensing provisions in the Food Act 1984, ss 39 et seq, Vol 18, title Food; see s 47 of that Act.

Definitions. By virtue of s 38(3) post, for "parent", "premises", "pupil", "registered pupil" and "school", see the Education Act 1944, s 114(1), this part of this title ante; for "maintain", see s 114(2)(a) of that Act; and for "voluntary school", see s 9(2) of that Act.

Education Act 1944, s 78(2)(a). See this part of this title ante.

---

23 (*Repealed by the Education (Scotland) Act 1980, s 136(3), Sch 5.*)

Nursery education

24 Nursery education: England and Wales

(1) A local education authority shall have power to establish nursery schools, to maintain such schools established by them or a former authority and to assist any such school which is not so established.

(2) A local education authority shall not by virtue of section 8(1)(a) of the Education Act 1944 be under any duty in respect of junior pupils who have not attained the age of five years but this subsection shall not affect the power of an authority under section 9(1) of that Act to establish, maintain or assist a school at which education is provided both for such pupils and older pupils, including a school at which there is a nursery class for such junior pupils as aforesaid.

(3) . . .

NOTES

Sub-s (3) amends the definition "pupil" in the Education Act 1944, s 114(1) this part of this title ante.

Commencement. This section and s 26 post were brought into force on 5 May 1980 by the Education Act 1980 (Commencement) (No 1) Order 1980, SI 1980/489 made under s 37 post.

Local education authority. See the note to s 2 ante.

Attained the age. See the note to s 9 ante.

Definitions. By virtue of s 38(3) post, for "former authority", "junior pupil", "pupil" and "school", see the Education Act 1944, s 114(1), this part of this title ante; for "assist" and "maintain", see s 114(2) of that Act; and for "nursery school", see s 9(4) of that Act.

Day nurseries. For provisions relating to day nurseries, see the National Health Service Act 1977, s 21(1), Sch 8, para 1, Vol 30, title National Health Service and s 26 post.

Registration. As to registration etc of nurseries and child-minders, see the Nurseries and Child-Minders Regulation Act 1948, Vol 6, title Children.

Education Act 1944, ss 8(1)(a), 9(1). See this part of this title ante.

---

25 (*Repealed by the Education (Scotland) Act 1980, s 136(3), Sch 5.*)

26 Day nurseries

(1) Subject to subsection (3) below, a local education authority may, in accordance with arrangements made by them in that behalf, make available to any day nursery the services of any teacher who—

(a) is employed by them in a nursery school or in a primary school having one or more nursery classes; and

(b) has agreed to provide his services for the purposes of the arrangements.

(2) Subject to subsection (3) below, the governors of any county or voluntary primary school having one or more nursery classes may, in accordance with arrangements made by them in that behalf, make available to any day nursery the services of any

teacher who is employed by them in the school and has agreed to provide his services for the purposes of the arrangements.

(3) Arrangements made under subsection (1) above in respect of a teacher in a voluntary school shall require the concurrence of the governors of the school; and no arrangements shall be made under subsection (2) above except at the request of the local education authority and on terms approved by them.

(4) Arrangements under this section may make provision—

(a) for the supply of equipment for use in connection with the teaching services made available under the arrangements;

(b) for regulating the respective functions of any teacher whose services are made available under the arrangements, the head teacher of his school and the person in charge of the day nursery;

(c) for any supplementary or incidental matters connected with the arrangements, including, where the teacher's school and the day nursery are in the areas of different local education authorities, financial adjustments between those authorities.

(5) In this section "day nursery" means a day nursery provided under the National Health Service Act 1977 by a local social services authority.

(6) A teacher shall not be regarded as ceasing to be a member of the teaching staff of his school and subject to the general directions of his head teacher by reason only of his services being made available in pursuance of arrangements under this section.

NOTES

Commencement. See the note to s 24 ante.

Local education authority. See the note to s 2 ante.

Governors. See the note to s 3 ante.

Local social services authority. Ie such an authority as defined by the National Health Service Act 1977, s 128(1), Vol 30, title National Health Service.

Definitions. By virtue of s 38(3) post, for "primary school" and "school", see the Education Act 1944, s 114(1), this part of this title ante; for "county school" and "voluntary school", see s 9(2) of that Act; and for "nursery school", see s 9(4) of that Act. Note as to "day nursery", sub-s (5) above.

National Health Service Act 1977. As to the provision of day nurseries, see s 21(1) of, and Sch 8, para 1 to, that Act, Vol 30, title National Health Service.

Miscellaneous

27 School and further education regulations

(1) The Secretary of State may by regulations make provision—

(a) for requiring teachers at schools and further education establishments to which this section applies to possess such qualifications as may be determined by or under the regulations and for requiring such teachers to serve probationary periods;

(b) with respect to the teaching staff to be provided in such schools and establishments;

(c) for requiring the approval of the Secretary of State to be obtained for the use in such schools and establishments of such materials or apparatus as may be specified in the regulations, being materials or apparatus which could or might involve a serious risk to health;

(d) with respect to the keeping, disclosure and transfer of educational records about pupils at such schools and establishments;

(e) with respect to the duration of the school day and school year at, and the granting of leave of absence from, any such schools.

(3) The Secretary of State may by regulations make provision for imposing requirements as to the health and physical capacity of—

    (*a*) teachers at schools and further education establishments to which this section applies;

    (*b*) teachers employed by local education authorities otherwise than at such schools or establishments; and

    (*c*) persons employed by local education authorities in work otherwise than as teachers which brings them regularly into contact with persons who have not attained the age of nineteen years.

(3) The Secretary of State may by regulations make provision for prohibiting or restricting the employment or further employment of persons—

    (*a*) as teachers at schools and further education establishments to which this section applies;

    (*b*) by local education authorities as teachers otherwise than at such schools or establishments; or

    (*c*) by local education authorities in such work as is mentioned in subsection (2)(*c*) above,

on medical grounds, in cases of misconduct and, as respects employment or further employment as a teacher, on educational grounds.

(4) The Secretary of State may by regulations make provision requiring his approval to be obtained for the provision of new premises for, or the alteration of the premises of, any school or further educational establishment to which this section applies or any boarding hostel provided by a local education authority for pupils attending any such school or establishment and for the inspection of any such hostel.

(5) In ... section 63(2) of the Education Act 1944 (exemption from building regulations etc) references to plans approved by the Secretary of State shall include references to any particulars submitted to and approved by him under regulations made by virtue of subsection (4) above.

(6) The Secretary of State may make regulations with respect to the provision of, and the fees to be charged for, courses of further education at further education establishments to which this section applies, including provision for requiring his approval to be obtained for the provision at such establishments of courses designated by or under the regulations as courses of advanced further education and for enabling him to give directions for the discontinuance of any such course at such an establishment or as to the number and categories of students to be admitted to such courses at such establishments.

(7) This section applies to any school maintained by a local education authority, any special school not so maintained, any further education establishment provided by a local education authority and any further education establishment designated by or under the regulations as an establishment substantially dependent for its maintenance on assistance from local education authorities or on grants under section 100(1)(*b*) of the said Act of 1944.

NOTES

The words omitted from sub-s (5) were repealed by the Building Act 1984, s 133(2), Sch 7.

Commencement. This section was brought into force on 1 September 1981 by the Education Act 1980 (Commencement No 4) Order 1981, SI 1981/1064.

Secretary of State; local education authorities. See the corresponding notes to s 2 ante.

Attained the age. See the note to s 9 ante.

Definitions. By virtue of s 38(3) post, for "premises", "pupil" and "school", see the Education Act 1944, s 114(1), this part of this title ante; for "special school", see s 9(5) of that Act; and for "further education", see s 41 of that Act.

Saving. The power of the Secretary of State to make regulations requiring or authorising differential fees from certain overseas students attending British universities and establishments of further education under the Education (Fees and Awards) Act 1983, s 1, is without prejudice to the power conferred under sub-s (6) above; see s 1(6) of the 1983 Act, this part of this title post.

Regulations under this section. See the Education (Schools and Further Education) Regulations 1981, SI 1981/1086, as amended by SI 1983/262.

For general provisions as to regulations, see s 35 post.

28 Provision of education at non-maintained schools

(1) So much of section 9(1) of the Education Act 1944 and section 6(1) of the Education (Miscellaneous Provisions) Act 1953 (arrangements with non-maintained schools) as makes the exercise of the powers of local education authorities under those provisions subject to the approval of the Secretary of State shall cease to have effect.

(2), (3) ...

NOTES

Sub-s (2) amends the Education (Miscellaneous Provisions) Act 1953, s 6(1), this part of this title ante; sub-s (3) repeals the Education Act 1976, s 5(2).

Commencement. This section and s 30 post were brought into force on 5 May 1980 by the Education Act 1980 (Commencement No 1) Order 1980, SI 1980/489, made under s 37 post.

Local education authorities; Secretary of State. See the notes to s 2 ante.

Education Act 1944, s 9(1); Education (Miscellaneous Provisions) Act 1953, s 6(1). See this part of this title ante.

29 (*Amends the Education (Miscellaneous Provisions) Act 1948, s 5, this part of this title ante.*)

30 Relaxation of Ministerial control of local education authorities

(1) So much of the provisions of the Education Act 1944 mentioned in subsection (2) below as makes the exercise of any power by a local education authority subject to the approval or consent of the Secretary of State or subject to the provisions of regulations made by him shall cease to have effect.

(2) The provisions referred to above are—

(*a*) section 53(1) (recreation facilities);
(*b*) section 61(2) (boarding fees);
(*c*) section 82 (educational research);
(*d*) section 83 (education conferences); and
(*e*) section 84 (assistance for universities etc).

(3) ...

NOTES

Sub-s (3) repeals the Education Act 1944, s 12.

Commencement. See the note to s 28 ante.

Local education authority; Secretary of State. See the notes to s 2 ante.

Education Act 1944, ss 53(1), 61(2), 82–84. See this part of this title ante.

31 Recoupment between education authorities

(1) Subject to subsection (2) below, where any provision for primary or secondary education is made by a local education authority in respect of a pupil who belongs to the area of another local education authority, the providing authority shall, on making a claim within the prescribed period, be entitled to recoupment of an amount equal to the cost to them of the provision from the other authority and the amount of the recoupment shall be determined by agreement between the authorities or, in default of agreement, by the Secretary of State.

(2) Subsection (1) above does not apply to any provision for primary education made in respect of a pupil who has not attained the age of five years unless it is made with the consent of the authority from whom recoupment is claimed.

(3) Where any provision for further education is made by a local education authority in respect of a pupil who belongs to the area of another local education authority, and that other authority have consented to the making of the provision, the providing authority shall, on making a claim within the prescribed period, be entitled to recoupment of the amount of the cost to them of the provision from the other authority and the amount of the recoupment shall be determined by agreement between the authorities or, in default of agreement, by the Secretary of State.

(4) A local education authority may make a payment by way of recoupment to another such authority of the cost incurred by the other authority in making any provision for primary, secondary or further education in respect of a pupil belonging to the area of the paying authority notwithstanding that no claim in respect of the cost has been made by the other authority in accordance with subsection (1) or (3) above.

(5) The Secretary of State may make regulations requiring or authorising payments of amounts determined by or under the regulations to be made by one authority to another where—

> (a) the authority receiving the payment makes, in such cases or circumstances as may be specified in the regulations, provision for education in respect of a pupil having such connection with the area of the paying authority as may be so specified; and
>
> (b) one of the authorities is a local education authority and the other an education authority in Scotland.

(6) References in this section to provision for education include references to provision of any benefits or services for which provision is made by or under the enactments relating to education.

(7) References in subsections (3) and (4) above to further education do not include references to further education of a kind such that expenditure on its provision would fall within [paragraph 6 of Schedule 10 to the Local Government, Planning and Land Act 1980] . . .

(8) . . .

NOTES

The words in square brackets in sub-s (7) above were substituted for the words "paragraph 3A of Schedule 2 to the Local Government Act 1974" by the Local Government, Planning and Land Act 1980, s 68(5), and the words "as amended by section 32 below" which appeared immediately after the original words have been omitted as they can no longer have any application.

Sub-s (8) amends the London Government Act 1963, s 31(8), Vol 26, title London.

Commencement. This section was brought into force on 1 August 1980 by the Education Act 1980 (Commencement No 1) Order 1980, SI 1980/489, made under s 37 post.

Sub-s (1): Local education authority; Secretary of State. See the notes to s 2 ante.

Pupil who belongs to the area of another . . . authority. As to the area to which a pupil belongs, see s 38(5) post, and the regulations noted to that section.

Prescribed period. Ie prescribed by regulations made by the Secretary of State; see, by virtue of s 38(3) post, the Education Act 1944, s 114(1), this part of this title ante. By the Education (Areas to which Pupils belong) Regulations 1980, SI 1980/917, reg 27, a local education authority is only entitled to recoupment under sub-s (1) or (3) above in respect of provision made for a school pupil in any year ending with 31 March, or made for a further education pupil in any year ending with 31 July, if a claim is made within 18 months after the end of the year in question.

Sub-s (2): Attained the age. See the note to s 9 ante.

Sub-s (3): Prescribed period. See the note to sub-s (1) above.

Greater London. As to the application of sub-s (3) above in relation to Greater London, see the London Government Act 1963, s 31(8), Vol 26, title London.

Adjustment of block grant. Recoupment between authorities under this section is to be taken account of in adjusting between England and Wales block grants payable under the Local Government Planning and Land Act 1980, s 53, Vol 25, title Local Government; see s 63 of, and Sch 10, paras 1(3), 3(4) to, that Act.

Definitions. By virtue of s 38(3) post, for "further education", "prescribed", "primary education", "pupil" and "secondary education", see the Education Act 1944, s 114(1), this part of this title ante. Note as to "provision for education", sub-s (6) above; and note also as to "further education", sub-s (7) above.
Local Government, Planning and Land Act 1980, Sch 10, para 6. See Vol 25, title Local Government.
Regulations under this section. No regulations had been made under this section up to 1 August 1985. See also the note "Prescribed period" to sub-s (1) above.
For general provisions as to regulations, see s 35 post.

32 Education expenditure and rate support grant

(1) Part I of Schedule 2 to the Local Government Act 1974 (adjustment of needs element of rate support grant by reference to education and other expenditure) shall be amended in accordance with Schedule 6 to this Act.

(2) Regulations under sub-paragraph (4)(a) of paragraph 3 of the said Schedule 2 as amended by this section shall apply that paragraph to—

  (a) expenditure incurred by local education authorities in the making of provision for primary and secondary education in respect of pupils not belonging to the area of any local education authority or to the area of any education authority in Scotland; and

  (b) expenditure, other than that to which paragraph 3A of that Schedule applies, incurred by local education authorities in the making of provision for further education in respect of such pupils.

(3) Regulations under sub-paragraph (4)(a) of paragraph 3 of the said Schedule 2 as amended by this section may be made with retrospective effect to 1st April 1977 insofar as they apply that paragraph to expenditure in making payments to persons who, in consequence of a direction given by the Secretary of State under regulation 3(2) of the Further Education Regulations 1975, have ceased to be employed in colleges for the training of teachers or in institutions having a department for the training of teachers, being—

  (a) payments made by an authority as compensating authority under the Colleges of Education (Compensation) Regulations 1975; or

  (b) the amount by which the salary to which such a person is entitled under a document such as is mentioned in section 5(2) of the Remuneration of Teachers Act 1965 exceeds the salary which would normally be appropriate to the post held by him.

(4) Without prejudice to subsection (3) above, regulations made by virtue of this section under the said Schedule 2 may be made so as to have effect from 1st April 1980 and in relation to regulations made as respects the year beginning on that date under paragraph 3A(2)(a) of that Schedule that paragraph shall have effect as if the words "in advance for each year" were omitted.

NOTES

Commencement. This section was brought into force on 5 May 1980 by the Education Act 1980 (Commencement No 1) Order 1980, SI 1980/489, made under s 37 post, subject to transitional provisions which are now spent.

Prospective repeal. This section, together with Sch 6 post, and the Local Government Act 1974, Sch 2, Vol 25, title Local Government, which they affect, may be repealed by order made by the Secretary of State under the Local Government, Planning and Land Act 1980, s 53(10), (11)(c), Sch 8, Vol 25, title Local Government, consequent upon the introduction by that section of a new system of rate support grants.

Local education authorities; Secretary of State. See the corresponding notes to s 2 ante.

Pupils not belonging to the area of any . . . authority. As to when a pupil is to be treated as not belonging to the area of any authority, see s 38(5) post and the regulations noted thereto.

Definitions. By virtue of s 38(3) post, for "further education", "primary education", "pupil" and "secondary education", see the Education Act 1944, s 114(1), this part of this title ante.

Local Government Act 1974, Sch 2, Part I. See Vol 25, title Local Government. As to the prospective repeal of that Schedule, see the note above.

Further Education Regulations 1975. SI 1975/1054.

Colleges of Education (Compensation) Regulations 1975. SI 1975/1092.
Remuneration of Teachers Act 1965, s 5(2). See this part of this title ante.
Regulations. See the note to Sch 6 post. By the Local Government, Planning and Land Act 1980, s 68(7), Vol 25, title Local Government, any power to amend regulations made under this section includes power to make any such amendments as appear necessary or expedient in consequence of the provisions of ss 53–68 of that Act, in the same title (which introduce a new system of rate support grants).

33 *(Sub-s (1) repealed by the Education Act 1981, s 21, Sch 4; sub-s (2) repealed by the Education (Scotland) Act 1980, s 136(3), Sch 5; sub-s (3) amends the Sex Discrimination Act 1975, Sch 2, Vol 6, title* Civil Rights and Liberties.)

34 Definition and registration of independent schools

(1), (2) . . .

(3) The Registrar of Independent Schools shall, without any application in that behalf, enter in the register kept by him under subsection (1) of the said section 70—

> (*a*) any school which by virtue of subsection (1) above becomes an independent school; and
>
> (*b*) any school which was exempt from registration by virtue of subsection (2) of the said section 70 immediately before the coming into force of this section.

(4) Proviso (*b*) to subsection (1) of the said section 70 (registration of school to be provisional until it has been inspected) shall not apply to the registration of a school under subsection (3) above unless the Registrar has before the coming into force of this section given written notice to the proprietor of the school that the registration will be provisional.

(5) In this section "the Registrar of Independent Schools" means, in relation to any school in England, the Registrar of Independent Schools for England and, in relation to any school in Wales, the Registrar of Independent Schools for Wales.

(6), (7) . . .

NOTES

Sub-s (1) amends the Education Act 1944, s 114(1), this part of this title ante; sub-ss (2), (6), (7) amend s 70 of that Act.
Commencement. This section was brought into force on 1 October 1980 by the Education Act 1980 (Commencement No 2) Order 1980, SI 1980/959, made under s 37 post.
Sub-s (4): Given written notice. As to mode of service, see, by virtue of s 38(3) post, the Education Act 1944, s 113, this part of this title ante, and for the meaning of "Written", see the note to s 10 ante.
Sub-s (5): England; Wales. For meanings, see the Interpretation Act 1978, s 5, Sch 1, Vol 41, title Statutes.
Registrar of Independent Schools for England; Registrar of Independent Schools for Wales. These officers are appointed under the Education Act 1944, s 70(1), this part of this title ante, as read with the Transfer of Functions (Wales) Order 1970, SI 1970/1536, art 5(2).
Definitions. By virtue, where required, of s 37(3) post, for "independent school", "provisionally registered school", "registered school" and "school", see the Education Act 1944, s 114(1), this part of this title ante. Note as to "the Registrar of Independent Schools", sub-s (5) above.
Said section 70. Ie the Education Act 1944, s 70, this part of this title ante.

Supplementary

35 Orders and regulations

(1) Any power of the Secretary of State to make orders or regulations under this Act (other than orders under section 2(11)(*b*) shall be exercisable by statutory instrument.

(2) No regulations shall be made under section 17(6) above unless a draft of the regulations has been laid before and approved by a resolution of each House of Parliament.

(3) Any statutory instrument containing regulations under any provision of this Act other than section 17(6), or an order under section 15(8) above, shall be subject to annulment in pursuance of a resolution of either House of Parliament.

(4) Regulations under this Act may make different provision for different cases or different circumstances and may contain such incidental, supplementary or transitional provisions as the Secretary of State thinks fit.

(5) Without prejudice to subsection (4) above, regulations under any provision of this Act other than section 27(1)(*a*), (2) or (3) or section 38(5) may make in relation to Wales provision different from that made in relation to England.

NOTES

Commencement. This section and ss 36, 37 post, were brought into force on 14 April 1980 by the Education Act 1980 (Commencement No 1) Order 1980, SI 1980/489, made under s 37 post.

Secretary of State. See the note to s 2 ante.

Statutory instrument; subject to annulment. For provisions as to statutory instruments generally, see the Statutory Instruments Act 1946, Vol 41, title Statutes, and as to statutory instruments which are subject to annulment, see ss 5(1), 7(1) of that Act.

Laid before Parliament. For meaning, see the Laying of Documents before Parliament (Interpretation) Act 1948, s 1(1), Vol 41, title Statutes.

Thinks fit. See the note to s 8 ante.

England; Wales. For meanings, see the Interpretation Act 1978, s 5, Sch 1, Vol 41, title Statutes.

36 Expenses

There shall be defrayed out of moneys provided by Parliament—

(*a*) any expenses incurred by the Secretary of State under this Act; and

(*b*) any increase attributable to this Act in the sums payable out of such moneys under any other Act.

NOTES

Commencement. See the note to s 35 ante.

Secretary of State. See the note to s 2 ante.

37 Commencement

(1) This Act shall come into force on such date as the Secretary of State may by order appoint, and different dates may be appointed for different provisions or different purposes.

(2) Any order under this section may make such transitional provision as appears to the Secretary of State to be necessary or expedient in connection with the provisions thereby brought into force, including such adaptations of those provisions, or of any other provisions of this Act then in force, as appear to him to be necessary or expedient for the purpose or in consequence of the operation of any provision of this Act before the coming into force of any other provision.

NOTES

Commencement. See the note to s 35 ante.

Secretary of State. See the note to s 2 ante.

Appears. See the note "Think fit" to s 8 ante.

Orders under this section. The Education Act 1980 (Commencement No 1) Order 1980, SI 1980/489 (bringing certain provisions of this Act into force on 14 April 1980, 5 May 1980 or 1 August 1980, subject in certain cases to transitional provisions, as indicated in the "Commencement" notes to the provisions concerned); the Education Act 1980 (Commencement No 2) Order 1980, SI 1980/959 (bringing certain provisions of this Act into force on 1 October 1980 or 1 July 1982, subject in certain cases to transitional provisions, as indicated in the "Commencement" notes to the provisions concerned); the Education Act 1980 (Commencement No 3) Order 1981, SI 1981/789 (bringing certain provisions of this Act into force on 1

July 1981 or 1 August 1981, subject in certain cases to transitional provisions, as indicated in the "Commencement" notes to the provisions concerned); and the Education Act 1980 (Commencement No 4) Order 1981, SI 1981/1064 (bringing into force on 1 September 1981 all the provisions of the Act not previously brought into force).

For general provisions as to orders, see s 35 ante.

38 Citation, construction, repeals and extent

(1) This Act may be cited as the Education Act 1980.

(2) This Act and the Education Acts 1944 to 1979 may be cited as the Education Acts 1944 to 1980 . . .

(3) Subject to subsection (4) below, this Act shall, in its application to England and Wales, be construed as one with the Education Act 1944 . . .

(4) In the provisions of this Act relating to admissions to schools "child" includes any person who has not attained the age of nineteen years.

(5) For the purposes of this Act an individual shall be treated as belonging to the area of a particular local education authority or education authority or as not belonging to the area of any such authority in accordance with regulations made by the Secretary of State and any question under the regulations shall, in case of dispute, be determined by the Secretary of State.

(6) The enactments mentioned in Schedule 7 to this Act (which include spent provisions) are hereby repealed to the extent specified in the third column of that Schedule.

(7) In this Act—

(a) . . .

(b) sections 20, 35 and 37 and this section extend to Northern Ireland;

but save as aforesaid this Act extends to England and Wales only.

NOTES

The words omitted from sub-ss (2), (3) and (7) were repealed by the Education (Scotland) Act 1980, s 136(3), Sch 5.

Commencement. This section, except sub-ss (4), (5), was brought into force on 14 April 1980, and sub-s (5) was brought into force on 1 August 1980, by the Education Act 1980 (Commencement No 1) Order 1980, SI 1980/489, made under s 37 ante; see, however, as to the commencement of the repeals in Sch 7 post, the "Commencement" note to that Schedule. Sub-s (4) was brought into force on 1 October 1980 by the Education Act 1980 (Commencement No 2) Order 1980, SI 1980/959.

Sub-s (3): England; Wales. For meanings, see the Interpretation Act 1978, s 5, Sch 1, Vol 41, title Statutes.

Construed as one. Ie the enactments in question are to be construed as if they were contained in one Act, unless there is some manifest discrepancy; see eg *Phillips v Parnaby* [1934] 2 KB 299 at 302. Accordingly, definitions in the earlier Act may be relevant to the construction of provisions of this Act (see *Solomons v R Gertzenstein Ltd* [1954] 2 QB 243, [1954] 2 All ER 625, CA; *Crowe (Valuation Officer) v Lloyds British Testing Co Ltd* [1960] 1 QB 592, [1960] 1 All ER 411, CA).

Sub-s (4): Provisions . . . relating to admissions to schools. See ss 6–9 ante, and Sch 2 post.

Attained the age. See the note to s 9 ante.

Sub-s (5). This subsection is applied for the purposes of the Local Government, Planning and Land Act 1980, Sch 10, Vol 25, title Local Government, by para 10 of that Schedule.

Local education authority; Secretary of State. See the notes to s 2 ante.

Education Acts 1944 to 1979; Education Acts 1944 to 1980. For the Acts that may now be cited by the collective title "the Education Acts 1944 to 1985" (which includes those Acts), see the Introductory Note to the Education Act 1944, this part of this title ante.

Education Act 1944. See this part of this title ante.

Regulations under this section. The Education (Areas to which Pupils belong) Regulations 1980, SI 1980/917, as amended by SI 1980/1862 and SI 1983/260 (partly made under sub-s (5) above; applying for the purpose of determining whether a pupil shall be treated (i) as not belonging to the area of a particular local education authority for the purposes of s 8(3)(d) ante, or as belonging to such an area for the purposes of s 31(1), (3) and (4) ante; (ii) as not belonging to the area of any local education authority for the purposes of s 32(2) ante).

For provisions as to regulations generally, see s 35 ante.

SCHEDULES

(Sch 1 makes amendments to the following enactments (which are printed in this part of this title ante unless otherwise indicated) which are consequential upon the change of nomenclature provided for by s 1 ante:

Education Act 1944, ss 14(1), (3), (4), 15(2)–(5), 16(3), 17(1)–(5), 18, 20(1), (3), (6), 21, 22, 23(1), (3), 24(1), (2), 25(1), (7), 27, 28, 31(3), 39(5), 65, 67(1), 68, 77(5), 80(1), 90(1), 95(2)(b), 99, 102, 103(1), (3), 105, 114(1), (2)(a), 120(1)(c), Sch 2, paras 1, 3, 5–7, Sch 3, paras 8–10, Sch 4;
Education Act 1946, ss 2(1)(b), (3), (4), (6), 3(1), 4(1), 6, 7(2);
Education (Miscellaneous Provisions) Act 1948, ss 4(3), 10(3);
Reserve and Auxiliary Forces (Protection of Civil Interests) Act 1951, Sch 2, para 10, Vol 3, title Armed Forces *(Pt 2);*
Education (Miscellaneous Provisions) Act 1953, s 8(1), (3);
Education Act 1959, s 1(4);
Education Act 1967, s 1(2), (4);
Education Act 1968, s 3(4);
Education (No 2) Act 1968, s 3(3);
Education Act 1973, s 1(2)(a);
Sex Discrimination Act 1975, s 22, Vol 6, title Civil Rights and Liberties*;*
Race Relations Act 1976, s 17, Vol 6, title Civil Rights and Liberties*;*
National Health Service Act 1977, Sch 1, para 3, Vol 30, title National Health Service*;*
Employment Protection (Consolidation) Act 1978, s 80(1), Vol 16, title Employment*;*
Education Act 1979, s 1(2), (3), (4).)

SCHEDULE 2

Section 7(4)

School Admission Appeals

Part I

Constitution of Appeal Committees

1.—(1) An appeal pursuant to arrangements made by a local education authority under section 7(1) of this Act shall be to an appeal committee constituted in accordance with this paragraph.

(2) An appeal committee shall consist of three, five or seven members nominated by the authority from among persons appointed by the authority under this paragraph; and sufficient persons may be appointed to enable two or more appeal committees to sit at the same time.

(3) The persons appointed shall comprise—

(a) members of the authority or of any education committee of the authority; and

(b) persons who are not members of the authority or of any education committee of the authority but who have experience in education, are acquainted with the educational conditions in the area of the authority or are parents of registered pupils at a school;

but shall not include any person employed by the authority otherwise than as a teacher.

(4) The members of an appeal committee who are members of the authority or of any education committee of the authority shall not outnumber the others by more than one.

(5) A person who is a member of an education committee of the authority shall not be chairman of an appeal committee.

(6) A person shall not be a member of an appeal committee for the consideration of any appeal against a decision if he was among those who made the decision or took part in discussions as to whether the decision should be made.

(7) A person who is a teacher at a school shall not be a member of an appeal committee for the consideration of an appeal involving a question whether a child is to be admitted to that school.

2.—(1) An appeal pursuant to arrangements made by the governors of an aided or special agreement school under section 7(2) of this Act shall be to an appeal committee constituted in accordance with this paragraph.

(2) An appeal committee shall consist of three, five or seven members nominated by the governors from among persons appointed by them under this paragraph; and sufficient persons may be appointed to enable two or more appeal committees to sit at the same time.

(3) The persons appointed—

    (a) may include one or more of the governors;

    (b) shall include persons appointed from a list drawn up by the local education authority by whom the school is maintained; and

    (c) shall not include any person employed by the authority otherwise than as a teacher.

(4) Half the members of an appeal committee (excluding the chairman) shall be nominated from among such persons as are mentioned in sub-paragraph (3)(b) above.

(5) None of the governors shall be chairman of an appeal committee.

(6) A person shall not be a member of an appeal committee for the consideration of any appeal against a decision if he was among those who made the decision or took part in discussions as to whether the decision should be made.

(7) A person who is a teacher at a school shall not be a member of an appeal committee for the consideration of an appeal involving a question whether a child is to be admitted to that school.

3. An appeal pursuant to joint arrangements made by virtue of section 7(3) of this Act by the governors of two or more schools shall be to an appeal committee constituted as provided in paragraph 2 above, taking references to the governors as references to the governors of both or all the schools.

4. An appeal committee constituted in accordance with paragraph 2 or 3 above shall be included in the bodies to which sections 173(4) and 174 of the Local Government Act 1972 (allowances) apply.

NOTES

Commencement. This Schedule was brought into force on 1 October 1980 by the Education Act 1980 (Commencement No 2) Order 1980, SI 1980/959, made under s 37 ante.

Para 1: Local education authority. See the note to s 2 ante.

Education committee. As to the establishment of education committees, see the Education Act 1944, s 6(2), Sch 1, Pt II, this part of this title ante.

Para 2: Governors. See the note to s 3 ante.

Definitions. For "child", see s 38(4) ante. By virtue of s 38(3) ante, for "parent", "pupil", "registered pupil" and "school", see the Education Act 1944, s 114(1), this part of this title ante; for "maintain", see s 114(2)(a) of that Act; and for "aided school" and "special agreement school", see s 15 of that Act.

Local Government Act 1972, ss 173(4), 174. See Vol 25, title Local Government.

Part II

Procedure

5. An appeal shall be by notice in writing setting out the grounds on which it is made.

6. An appeal committee shall afford the appellant an opportunity of appearing and making oral representations and may allow the appellant to be accompanied by a friend or to be represented.

7. The matters to be taken into account by an appeal committee in considering an appeal shall include—

    (a) any preference expressed by the appellant in respect of the child as mentioned in section 6 of this Act; and

    (b) the arrangements for the admission of pupils published by the local education authority or the governors under section 8 of this Act.

8. In the event of disagreement between the members of an appeal committee the appeal under consideration shall be decided by a simple majority of the votes cast and in the case of an equality of votes the chairman of the committee shall have a second or casting vote.

9. The decision of an appeal committee and the grounds on which it is made shall be communicated by the committee in writing to—

    (a) the appellant and the local education authority; and

(*b*) in the case of an appeal to an appeal committee constituted in accordance with paragraph 2 or 3 above, to the governors by or on whose behalf the decision appealed against was made.

10. Appeals pursuant to arrangements made under section 7 of this Act shall be heard in private except when otherwise directed by the authority or governors by whom the arrangements are made but, without prejudice to paragraph 6 above, a member of the local education authority may attend as an observer any hearing of an appeal by an appeal committee constituted in accordance with paragraph 1 above and a member of the Council on Tribunals may attend as an observer any meeting of any appeal committee at which an appeal is considered.

11. Subject to paragraphs 5 to 10 above, all matters relating to the procedure on appeals pursuant to arrangements made under section 7 of this Act, including the time within which they are to be brought, shall be determined by the authority or governors by whom the arrangements are made; and neither section 106 of the Local Government Act 1972 nor paragraph 44 of Schedule 12 to that Act (procedure of committees of local authorities) shall apply to an appeal committee constituted in accordance with paragraph 1 above.

NOTES

Commencement. See the note to Pt I of this Schedule ante.

Para 5: Writing. See the note "Written" to s 10 ante.

Para 7: Local education authority. See the note to s 2 ante.

Governors. See the note to s 3 ante.

Para 10: Council on Tribunals. As to the constitution etc, of this council, see the Tribunals and Inquiries Act 1971, ss 1–3, Vol 10, title Constitutional Law (Pt 4). Appeal committees constituted under Pt I of this Schedule ante are brought under the direct supervision of the Council on Tribunals by Sch 1, para 6 to the 1971 Act.

Appeals against statement of child's special educational need. This Part is applied with modifications in relation to such appeals; see the Education Act 1981, s 8(3), this part of this title post.

Definitions. For "child", see s 38(4) ante.

Local Government Act 1972, s 106, Sch 12, para 44. See Vol 25, title Local Government.

(*Sch 3 makes amendments to the following enactments (which are printed in this part of this title ante unless otherwise indicated) which are consequential upon the change of nomenclature provided for by s 1 ante:*

Education Act 1944, s 16(2), 17(6), 85, 102, Sch 3, para 5;
Education Act 1946, ss 1(1), 2(2), Sch 1, para 1(a);
Education (Miscellaneous Provisions) Act 1953, s 2(a);
London Government Act 1963, s 31(5), (10), Vol 26, title London;
Education Act 1964, s 1;
Education Act 1967, ss 1, 3;
Education Act 1968, ss 1, 3;
Education Act 1973, s 1(2);
Sex Discrimination Act 1975, Sch 2, para 1, Vol 6, title Civil Rights and Liberties.)

SCHEDULE 4

Section 17(5)

Termination of Participation Agreements

1.—(1) Every participation agreement shall provide that it may be terminated in accordance with this Schedule.

(2) A participation agreement shall not be capable of being terminated by either party otherwise than as aforesaid.

2. The proprietors of the school may terminate a participation agreement by giving three years written notice to the Secretary of State or such shorter notice as he may in any particular case accept.

3. Subject to paragraph 4 below, the Secretary of State may terminate a participation agreement by giving three years written notice to the proprietors of the school.

4.—(1) If the Secretary of State—

(a) is not satisfied that appropriate educational standards are being maintained at the school; or

(b) is satisfied that any condition applying to the school under the agreement or by virtue of regulations made under section 17 of this Act has been contravened,

he may at any time terminate the agreement by written notice to the proprietors of the school.

(2) A notice of termination given under this paragraph may provide that it shall be treated as of no effect if the proprietors of the school satisfy the Secretary of State within such time as may be specified in the notice that they have complied with any condition specified therein.

5. Any notice of termination given under paragraph 3 or 4 above shall contain a statement of the reason for which it is given.

6. The termination of a participation agreement shall not affect the operation of the agreement or of the scheme referred to in section 17 of this Act (including any regulations made under that section) in relation to any pupil holding an assisted place at the school on the date of the termination.

NOTES

Commencement. This Schedule was brought into force on 1 October 1980 by the Education Act 1980 (Commencement No 2) Order 1980, SI 1980/959, made under s 37 ante.

Giving . . . written notice. As to mode of service, see by virtue of s 38(3) ante, the Education Act 1944, this part of this title ante; and for the meaning of "Written", see the note to s 10 ante.

Secretary of State. See the note to s 2 ante.

Satisfied. See the note "Think fit" to s 8 ante.

Definitions. For "participation agreement", see s 17(2) ante. By virtue of s 38(3) post, for "proprietor", "pupil" and "school", see the Education Act 1944, s 114(1), this part of this title ante.

(*Sch 5 sets out ss 1–4 of, and Sch 1 to, the Education Act 1962, this part of this title ante, as substituted by s 19 of this Act; Sch 6 amends the Local Government Act 1974, Sch 2, Vol 25, title* Local Government.)

SCHEDULE 7

Section 38(6)

Repeals

Chapter	Short Title	Extent of Repeal
7 & 8 Geo 6 c 31	The Education Act 1944	Section 8(2)(*b*). In section 9(1) the words "so far as may be authorised by arrangements approved by the Minister". Sections 11, 12 and 13. Section 21(2). Section 31(1). Section 32. Section 49. In section 53(1) the words "with the approval of the Minister". In section 61(2) the words "not exceeding such amounts as may be determined in accordance with scales approved by the Minister". Section 66. In section 82 the words "with the approval of the Minister". In section 83 the words "Subject to any regulations made by the Minister".

Chapter	Short Title	Extent of Repeal
7 & 8 Geo 6 c 31—cont	The Education Act 1944—cont	In section 84 the words "with the consent of the Minister". Section 90(2) and (3). Section 97. Section 100(1)(a)(i) and (ii). In section 114, in subsection (1) the definition of "local education order", in the definition of "primary school" the words "subject to the provisions of subsection (3) of this section", and subsection (3). In Part I of Schedule 1, in paragraph 3(a) the words from "without prejudice" to "joint boards)". In Schedule 3, paragraph 4. Schedule 4.
9 & 10 Geo 6 c 50	The Education Act 1946	In Part II of Schedule 2 the entry relating to section 13 of the Education Act 1944.
11 & 12 Geo 6 c 40	The Education (Miscellaneous Provisions) Act 1948	Section 6. In section 7, subsections (2) and (2A) and in subsection (3) the words "except subsection (2A)". In Part I of Schedule 1, the entry relating to Schedule 4 to the Education Act 1944.
1 & 2 Eliz 2 c 33	The Education (Miscellaneous Provisions) Act 1953	In section 6(1) the words "For the purpose of fulfilling their duties under the principal Act" and "with the approval of the Minister". Section 7. Section 9. Section 16. In Schedule 1 the entry relating to section 13 of the Education Act 1944.
6 & 7 Eliz 2 c 55	The Local Government Act 1958	In Schedule 8, paragraph 16(2)(i) and (ii).
10 & 11 Eliz 2 c 47	The Education (Scotland) Act 1962	Section 53. In section 55 the proviso.
1963 c 33	The London Government Act 1963	Section 31(1)(a) and (b), (2), (3) and (9). Section 33.
1966 c 42	The Local Government Act 1966	Section 14.
1968 c 17	The Education Act 1968	Section 1(2). Section 3(1) and (2). Section 5(1) and (2) so far as relating to section 13 of the Education Act 1944. In Schedule 1, paragraph 7. In Schedule 3, Part A.
1971 c 74	The Education (Milk) Act 1971	The whole Act so far as unrepealed.
1973 c 16	The Education Act 1973	Section 4.

Chapter	Short Title	Extent of Repeal
1975 c 2	The Education Act 1975	Sections 1 and 2. Section 5(4).
1975 c 65	The Sex Discrimination Act 1975	In Schedule 2, paragraph 2.
1976 c 20	The Education (Scotland) Act 1976	Section 3.
1976 c 81	The Education Act 1976	Sections 4 and 5. Sections 7 to 9.

NOTES

Commencement. The repeals in this Schedule have been brought into force by the Education Act 1980 (Commencement No 1) Order 1980, SI 1980/489, made under s 37 ante, to the extent indicated below:—

(1) On 14 April 1980: the repeals of or in the Education Act 1944, s 49, the Education (Scotland) Act 1962, ss 53, 55, the Education (Milk) Act 1971, the Education (Scotland) Act 1976, s 3, and the Education Act 1976, s 9.

(2) On 5 May 1980: the repeals of or in the Education Act 1944, ss 8(2)(b), 9(1), 11, 12, 31(1), 32, 53(1), 61(2), 66, 82–84, 90, 97, 100(1), 114, Sch 1, Pt I, para 3, Sch 3, para 3, the Education (Miscellaneous Provisions) Act 1953, s 6(1), the Local Government Act 1958, Sch 8, para 16(2), the London Government Act 1963, ss 31(1)–(3), 33, the Local Government Act 1966, s 14, the Education Act 1973, s 4, the Education Act 1975, ss 1, 2, 5(4), and the Education Act 1976, ss 5, 7, 8.

(3) On 1 August 1980: the repeals of or in the Education Act 1944, s 13, the Education Act 1946, Sch 2, Pt II, the Education (Miscellaneous Provisions) Act 1948, ss 6, 7, the Education (Miscellaneous Provisions) Act 1953, ss 7, 9, 16, Sch 1, the London Government Act 1963, s 31(9), the Education Act 1968, ss 1(2), 3, 5, Sch 1, para 7, Sch 3, Part A, and the Education Act 1976, s 4.

The repeals of the Education Act 1944, s 21(2), Sch 4 were brought into force on 1 August 1981 by the Education Act 1980 (Commencement No 3) Order 1981, SI 1981/789.

The repeal of the Sex Discrimination Act 1975, Sch 2, para 2 was brought into force on 1 September 1981 by the Education Act 1980 (Commencement No 4) Order 1981, SI 1981/1064.

OVERSEAS DEVELOPMENT AND CO-OPERATION ACT 1980

(1980 c 63)

ARRANGEMENT OF SECTIONS

★   ★   ★   ★   ★

PART IV

EDUCATION

PART V

SUPPLEMENTARY

★   ★   ★   ★   ★

★   ★   ★   ★   ★

(For ss 1–3, 10–13, 18, Schs 1, 2, see Vol 7, title Commonwealth and Other Territories (Pt 4); for ss 4–9, see Vol 30, title Money (Pt 1).)

An Act to consolidate certain enactments relating to overseas development and co-operation and to repeal, as unnecessary, section 16(1) and (2) of the West Indies Act 1967
[13 November 1980]

Northern Ireland. This Act applies; see s 19(3) post.

1–13 (*For ss 1–3 (Pt I), 10–13, see Vol 7, title* Commonwealth and Other Territories (Pt 4); *for ss 4–9 (Pt II), see Vol 30, title* Money (Pt 1).)

PART IV

EDUCATION

14 Provision of teachers for, and for further educational co-operation between, Commonwealth countries

(1) The Secretary of State may from time to time make, out of money provided by Parliament, in accordance with such arrangements as the Secretary of State thinks fit, payments—

(a) for enabling persons from countries and territories of the Commonwealth outside the United Kingdom to attend teacher training courses in the United Kingdom;

(b) for encouraging persons from the United Kingdom or the Republic of Ireland to become temporarily employed in those countries and territories as teachers or in connection with teaching, and for facilitating the return to and resettlement in the United Kingdom or the Republic of Ireland, as the case may be, of persons so employed;

(c) for any purpose which the Secretary of State considers will foster co-operation in educational matters between the United Kingdom and other Commonwealth countries and territories;

(d) for any purpose appearing to the Secretary of State to be incidental or supplemental to any of the purposes mentioned in paragraphs (a) to (c) above.

(2) Payments under this section shall not be made for a purpose mentioned in subsection (1)(c) above or a purpose incidental or supplemental to such a purpose, except with the approval of the Treasury.

NOTES

Secretary of State. Ie one of Her Majesty's Principal Secretaries of State; see the Interpretation Act 1978, s 5, Sch 1, Vol 41, title Statutes.

Commonwealth. As to the meaning of this expression, see 6 Halsbury's Laws (4th edn) para 801.

United Kingdom. Ie Great Britain and Northern Ireland; see the Interpretation Act 1978, s 5, Sch 1, Vol 41, title Statutes.

Note that, by virtue of s 17 post, references to the United Kingdom in this section include references to the Channel Islands and the Isle of Man.

Republic of Ireland. Ie that part of Ireland previously officially known in this country as Eire and originally called the Irish Free State; see the Ireland Act 1949, s 1(1), (3), Vol 7, title Commonwealth and Other Territories (Pt 3) in conjunction with the Eire (Confirmation of Agreements) Act 1938, s 1 (repealed).

15 The Commonwealth Scholarship Commission

(1) There shall continue to be a Commission known as the Commonwealth Scholarship Commission in the United Kingdom (in this section referred to as "the Commission"), charged with the duty of—

    (a) selecting the recipients of awards arising out of the Commonwealth Scholarship and Fellowship Plan to persons coming to the United Kingdom,

    (b) making arrangements for the placing of the recipients at universities, university colleges, colleges of technology or other appropriate establishments in the United Kingdom, and for the supervision of their work during the currency of their awards,

    (c) selecting persons to be put forward as candidates from the United Kingdom for awards arising out of the Plan and to be granted in countries outside the United Kingdom, and

    (d) discharging any other functions under the Plan which the Secretary of State may assign to the Commission.

(2) In subsection (1) above "the Commonwealth Scholarship and Fellowship Plan" means the Plan so named which was put forward by the Commonwealth Development Conference held at Oxford in July 1959.

(3) The persons to be selected under subsection (1)(a) above shall be Commonwealth citizens or British protected persons (within the meaning of [the British Nationality Act 1981]) except where the Commission for special reasons, approved by the Secretary of State, otherwise determine.

(4) The Commission shall consist of a chairman and not less than 9 nor more than 14 other members appointed by the Secretary of State, and not less than 4 of the members shall be persons appointed as the holders of high academic office.

(5) A member of the Commission shall hold and vacate office in accordance with the terms of his appointment, and shall be eligible for re-appointment, but may at any time resign his office by notice in writing to the Secretary of State.

(6) The quorum at any meeting of the Commission shall be 6, but subject as aforesaid the Commission shall have power to act notwithstanding any vacancy in their number or any defect in the appointment of a member.

(7) The Commission may appoint committees to assist them in the discharge of their functions, and may delegate the discharge of any of their functions to a committee so appointed, with or without restrictions or conditions.

(8) Any such committee may include persons who are not members of the Commission.

(9) In the discharge of their functions the Commission shall comply with any directions given to them by the Secretary of State.

(10) No direction shall be given for the selection or rejection of any particular person for an award or as a candidate for an award.

(11) The Secretary of State shall defray the expenses of the Commission, including the payment of travelling and other allowances to members of the Commission or of any committee of the Commission and to persons chosen by the Commission to act as advisers, being allowances of such amounts and payable in such circumstances as he may with the approval of the Minister for the Civil Service determine.

(12) As soon as may be after 30th September in each year the Commission shall make to the Secretary of State a report on the discharge of their functions for the period of 12 months ending with that day, and the Secretary of State shall lay a copy of every such report before Parliament.

NOTES

The words in square brackets in sub-s (3) were substituted by the British Nationality (Modification of Enactments) Order 1982, SI 1982/1832, art 2.

Sub-s (1): Commonwealth Scholarship and Fellowship Plan. This Plan is explained in the White Paper under this title which was published in November 1959 (Cmnd 894).

United Kingdom; Secretary of State. See the notes to s 14 ante.

Sub-s (3): Commonwealth citizen. This expression is defined, for the purposes of enactments passed before 1983, by the British Nationality Act 1981, s 51(1), Vol 31, title Nationality and Immigration.

Sub-s (6): Quorum. "The word 'quorum' in its ordinary signification has reference to the existence of a complete body of persons, of whom a certain specified number is competent to transact the business of the whole"; see *Faure Electric Accumulator Co Ltd v Phillipart* (1888) 58 LT 525 at 527.

Sub-s (12): Lay ... before Parliament. For meaning, see the Laying of Documents before Parliament (Interpretation) Act 1948, s 1(1), Vol 41, title Statutes.

Expenses. See s 16 post.

British Nationality Act 1981. For the meaning of "British protected person" in that Act, see s 38, Vol 31, title Nationality and Immigration.

16 Expenses under Scholarship Plan

The Secretary of State's expenses—

   (*a*) in making such awards as are mentioned in paragraph (*a*) of section 15(1) above;

   (*b*) in supplementing any such awards as are mentioned in paragraph (*c*) of that subsection; and

   (*c*) in defraying the expenses of the Commission (including the allowances mentioned in section 15(11) above),

shall be defrayed out of money provided by Parliament.

NOTES

Secretary of State. See the note to s 1 ante.

The Commission. Ie the Commonwealth Scholarship Commission in the United Kingdom; see s 15(1) ante.

17 Application of Part IV

References to the United Kingdom in this Part of this Act include references to the Channel Islands and the Isle of Man.

NOTE

This Part of this Act. Ie Pt IV (ss 14–17) of this Act.

PART V

SUPPLEMENTARY

18 (*See Vol 7, title* Commonwealth and Other Territories (Pt 4).)

19 Short title, commencement and extent

   (1) This Act may be cited as the Overseas Development and Co-operation Act 1980.

   (2) This Act shall come into force on the expiration of the period of one month from the date on which it is passed.

   (3) It is hereby declared that this Act extends to Northern Ireland.

NOTES

One month from the date etc. As a general rule the effect of defining a period in such a manner is to exclude the day on which the event in question occurs. See *Dodds v Walker* [1981] 2 All ER 609, [1981] 1 WLR 1027, HL, as to the day of expiry of periods of a month or a specified number of months. The Act was passed on 13 November 1980 and accordingly came into force on 14 December 1980.

(*For Schs 1, 2, see Vol 7, title* Commonwealth and Other Territories (Pt 4).)

EDUCATION ACT 1981

(1981 c 60)

ARRANGEMENT OF SECTIONS

Preliminary

An Act to make provision with respect to children with special educational needs

[30 October 1981]

Commencement. Ss 14, 20, 21(1), (2), (5) came into force on 5 January 1982 by virtue of the Education Act 1981 (Commencement No 1) Order 1981, SI 1981/1711. The remainder of the Act came into force on 1 April 1983 by virtue of the Education Act 1981 (Commencement No 2) Order 1983, SI 1983/7. For transitional provisions, see the Schedule to that order.

Education Acts 1944 to 1985. This Act is one of the Acts which may be cited by this collective title; see the Introductory Note to the Education Act 1944, this part of this title ante.

Northern Ireland. This Act does not apply; see s 21(5) post.

Preliminary

1 Meaning of "special educational needs" and "special education provision"

(1) For the purposes of this Act a child has "special educational needs" if he has a learning difficulty which calls for special educational provision to be made for him.

(2) Subject to subsection (4) below, a child has a "learning difficulty" if—

(*a*) he has a significantly greater difficulty in learning than the majority of children of his age; or

(*b*) he has a disability which either prevents or hinders him from making use of educational facilities of a kind generally provided in schools, within the area of the local authority concerned, for children of his age; or

(*c*) he is under the age of five years and is, or would be if special educational provision were not made for him, likely to fall within paragraph (*a*) or (*b*) when over that age.

(3) "Special educational provision" means—

(*a*) in relation to a child who has attained the age of two years, educational provision which is additional to, or otherwise different from, the educational provision made generally for children of his age in schools maintained by the local education authority concerned; and

(*b*) in relation to any child under that age, educational provision of any kind.

(4) A child is not to be taken as having a learning difficulty solely because the language (or form of the language) in which he is, or will be, taught is different from a language (or form of a language) which has at any time been spoken in his home.

NOTES

Commencement. 1 April 1983; see the Introductory Note to this Act.

Age. A person attains a particular age expressed in years at the commencement of the relevant anniversary of the date of his birth; see the Family Law Reform Act 1969, s 9, Vol 6, title Children.

Local education authority. These authorities are defined by the Education Act 1944, ss 6(1), 114(1), Sch 1, Pt I, this part of this title ante, as read with the London Government Act 1963, s 30, Vol 26, title London, the Local Government Act 1972, ss 1(10), 20(6), 192(1), Vol 25 title Local Government, and the Local Government Act 1985, s 18(2), in the same title.

Definitions. For "child", see s 20(1) post; by virtue of s 21(2) post, for "school", see the Education Act 1944, s 114(1), this part of this title ante, and as to "maintain", see s 114(2)(*a*) of that Act. Note as to "learning difficulty", sub-ss (2), (4) above, and as to "special educational provision", sub-s (3) above.

Provision of special education

2 Provision of special education: duties of local education authorities etc

(1) ...

(2) Where a local education authority arrange special educational provision for a child for whom they maintain a statement under section 7 of this Act it shall be the duty

of the authority, if the conditions mentioned in subsection (3) below are satisfied, to secure that he is educated in an ordinary school.

(3) The conditions are that account has been taken, in accordance with section 7, of the views of the child's parent and that educating the child in an ordinary school is compatible with—

(a) his receiving the special educational provision that he requires;
(b) the provision of efficient education for the children with whom he will be educated; and
(c) the efficient use of resources.

(4) It shall be the duty of every local education authority to keep under review the arrangements made by them for special educational provision.

(5) It shall be the duty of the governors, in the case of a county or voluntary school, and of the local education authority by whom the school is maintained, in the case of a maintained nursery school—

(a) to use their best endeavours, in exercising their functions in relation to the school, to secure that if any registered pupil has special educational needs the special educational provision that is required for him is made;
(b) to secure that, where the responsible person has been informed by the local education authority that a registered pupil has special educational needs, those needs are made known to all who are likely to teach him; and
(c) to secure that the teachers in the school are aware of the importance of identifying, and providing for, those registered pupils who have special educational needs.

(6) In subsection (5)(b) above "responsible person" means—

(a) in the case of a county or voluntary school, the head teacher or the appropriate governor (that is to say the chairman of the governors, or, where the governors have designated another governor for the purposes of this paragraph, that other governor); and
(b) in the case of a nursery school, the head teacher.

(7) Where a child who has special educational needs is being educated in an ordinary school maintained by a local education authority it shall be the duty of those concerned with making special educational provision for that child to secure, so far as is both compatible with the objectives mentioned in paragraphs (a) to (c) of subsection (3) above and reasonably practicable, that the child engages in the activities of the school together with children who do not have special educational needs.

NOTES

Sub-s (1) amends the Education Act 1944, s 8.

Commencement. 1 April 1983; see the Introductory Note to this Act.

Sub-s (2): Local education authority. See the note to s 1 ante.

It shall be the duty etc. By virtue of s 21(2) post, see the Education Act 1944, s 68, this part of this title ante, concerning the power of the Secretary of State to prevent the unreasonable exercise of a duty, and s 99(1) of that Act concerning the power of the Secretary of State to enforce the execution of a duty.

Sub-s (6): Governors. Ie the governors constituted under the Education Act 1944, s 17(1), (2), this part of this title ante (see also the Education Act 1980, s 1(1), this part of this title ante). See also, as to the instrument of government, ss 18 and 19 of the 1944 Act or s 2 of the 1980 Act as to grouping of schools under one governing body, s 20 of the 1944 Act, or s 3 of the 1980 Act, and as to governors' proceedings, tenure of office etc, s 21(1), (3) of the 1944 Act and s 4 of the 1980 Act.

Payment of tuition and boarding fees. As to the payment by the local education authority of the tuition and boarding fees of pupils educated at non-maintained schools under arrangements made by virtue of this Act, see the Education (Miscellaneous Provisions) Act 1953, s 6(2), this part of this title ante.

Definitions. For "special educational needs", see s 1(1) ante; for "special educational provision", see s 1(3) ante; for "child" and "ordinary school", see s 20(1) post, and, by virtue of s 21(2) post, for "county school" and "voluntary school", see s 9(2) of the 1944 Act; for "nursery school", see s 9(4) of that Act; for "parent", "pupil" and "registered pupil", see s 114(1) of that Act, and as to "maintain", see s 114(2)(a) of that Act. Note as to "responsible person", sub-s (6) above.

Principal Act. Ie the Education Act 1944, this part of this title ante; see s 20(1) post.

3 Provision of special education otherwise than in schools

If, in relation to any child in their area who has special educational needs, a local education authority are satisfied that it would be inappropriate for the special educational provision required for that child, or for any part of that provision, to be made in a school, they may after consulting the child's parent arrange for it or, as the case may be, for that part of it, to be made otherwise than in a school.

NOTES

Commencement. 1 April 1983; see the Introductory Note to this Act.

Local education authority. See the note to s 1 ante.

Satisfied. Statutory powers are often conferred in subjective terms, the competent authority being entitled to act, eg, when it is "satisfied" or it "appears" to it that, or when in its "opinion", a prescribed state of affairs exists, but the inherent jurisdiction of the courts to determine whether such powers have been exceeded is not readily ousted by the use of such language; see, further, 1 Halsbury's Laws (4th edn) para 22.

Consulting. On what constitutes consultation, see, in particular, *Fletcher v Minister of Town and Country Planning* [1947] 2 All ER 496, (1947) 111 JP Jo 542; *Rollo v Minister of Town and Country Planning* [1948] 1 All ER 13, [1948] LJR 817, CA; *Re Union of Whippingham and East Cowes Benefices, Derham v Church Comrs for England* [1954] AC 245, [1954] 2 All ER 22, PC; and *Agricultural, Horticultural and Forestry Industry Training Board v Aylesbury Mushrooms Ltd* [1972] 1 All ER 280, [1972] 1 WLR 190.

Medical and dental inspection and treatment. As to the provision of medical or dental inspection or treatment for children who under arrangements made by virtue of this Act are receiving education otherwise than at a school, see the National Health Service Act 1977, s 5(1), Sch 1, para 1(a)(ii), Vol 30, title National Health Service.

Definitions. For "special educational needs", see s 1(1) ante; for "special educational provision", see s 1(3) ante; for "child", see s 20(1) post; for "parent" and "school", see by virtue of s 21(2), post, the Education Act 1944, s 114(1), this part of this title ante.

Identification and assessment of children with special educational needs

4 General duty of local education authority towards children for whom they are responsible

(1) It shall be the duty of every local education authority to exercise their powers under this Act with a view to securing that, of the children for whom they are responsible, those with special educational needs which call for the local education authority to determine the special educational provision that should be made for them are identified by the authority.

(2) For the purposes of this Act a local education authority are responsible for a child if he is in their area and—

> (a) he is registered as a pupil at a school maintained by them or is registered as a pupil in pursuance of arrangements made by them by virtue of section 6 of the Education (Miscellaneous Provisions) Act 1953 at a school which is not maintained by them or another local education authority; or
>
> (b) he has been brought to their attention as having, or as probably having, special educational needs and—
>
>> (i) is registered as a pupil at a school but does not fall within paragraph (a) above; or
>> (ii) is not registered as a pupil at a school and is not under the age of two years or over compulsory school age.

NOTES

Commencement. 1 April 1983; see the Introductory Note to this Act.

It shall be the duty etc. See the note to s 2 ante.

Local education authority. See the note to s 1 ante.

Registered as a pupil. As to the registration of pupils at schools, see the Education Act 1944, s 80, this part of this title ante.

Age of two years. See the note "Age" to s 1 ante.

Compulsory school age. By the Education Act 1944, s 35, this part of this title ante, as amended by the Raising of the School Leaving Age Order 1972, SI 1972/444 (made under that section), this means any age between five years and sixteen years, but this must be read subject to the provisions relating to school-leaving dates in the Education Act 1962, s 9, this part of this title ante.

Definitions. For "special educational needs", see s 1(1) ante; for "special educational provision", see s 1(3) ante; for "child", see s 20(1) post; by virtue of s 21(2) post, for "pupil" and "school", see the Education Act 1944, s 114(1), this part of this title ante, and as to "maintain", see s 114(2)(a) of that Act.

Education (Miscellaneous Provisions) Act 1953, s 6. See this part of this title ante.

5 Assessment of special educational needs

(1) Where, in the case of a child for whom a local education authority are responsible, the authority are of the opinion—

  (a) that he has special educational needs which call for the authority to determine the special educational provision that should be made for him; or

  (b) that he probably has such special educational needs;

they shall make an assessment of his educational needs under this section.

(2) Assessments under this section shall be made in accordance with the following provisions of this Act.

(3) If a local education authority propose to make an assessment of the educational needs of a child under this section they shall, before doing so, serve notice on the child's parent informing him—

  (a) that they propose to make an assessment;

  (b) of the procedure to be followed in making it;

  (c) of the name of the officer of the authority from whom further information may be obtained; and

  (d) of his right to make representations, and submit written evidence, to the authority within such period (which shall not be less than 29 days beginning with the date on which the notice is served) as may be specified in the notice.

(4) When a local education authority have served a notice under subsection (3) above and the period specified in the notice in accordance with paragraph (d) has expired, the authority shall, if they consider it appropriate after taking into account any representations made and any evidence submitted to them in response to the notice, assess the educational needs of the child concerned.

(5) Where a local education authority decide to make an assessment under this section they shall notify the child's parent in writing of their decision and of their reasons for making it.

(6) If, after making an assessment of the educational needs of a child under this section, the local education authority decide that they are not required to determine the special educational provision that should be made for him the parent may appeal in writing to the Secretary of State.

(7) In a case falling within subsection (6) above the local education authority shall notify the parent in writing of his right of appeal under that subsection.

(8) On an appeal under subsection (6) above the Secretary of State may, if he thinks fit, direct the local education authority to reconsider their decision.

(9) The provisions of Part I of Schedule 1 to this Act have effect in relation to assessments under this section.

(10) Where, at any time after serving a notice under subsection (3) above, a local education authority decide not to assess the educational needs of the child concerned they shall notify his parent in writing of their decision.

NOTES

Commencement. 1 April 1983; see the Introductory Note to this Act.

Sub-s (1): Child for whom a local education authority are responsible. As to the children for whom a local education authority are responsible, see s 4(2) ante.

Local education authority. See the note to s 1 ante.

Opinion. See the note "Satisfied" to s 3 ante.

Assessment of his educational needs. See also s 7 post (statement of child's special educational needs where assessment has been made under this section and frequency of assessments where statement maintained); s 8 post (appeals against statements under s 7 post); and s 9 post (requests for assessments). Cf also s 6 post (assessment of special educational needs of children under the age of two).

Sub-s (2): Following provisions of this Act. See, in particular, sub-ss (3)–(5), (9) above and Sch 1, Pt II post.

Sub-s (3): Serve notice. As to the mode of service, see, by virtue of s 21(2) post, the Education Act 1944, s 113, this part of this title ante.

Written. Expressions referring to writing are, unless the contrary intention appears, to be construed as including references to other modes of representing or reproducing words in a visible form; see the Interpretation Act 1978, s 5, Sch 1, Vol 41, title Statutes.

Within such period etc. The general rule in cases where an act is to be done within a specified time is that the day from which it runs is not to be counted; see *Goldsmiths' Co v West Metropolitan Rly Co* [1904] 1 KB 1, [1900–3] All ER Rep 667, CA; *Stewart v Chapman* [1951] 2 KB 792, [1951] 2 All ER 613. See also *Dodds v Walker* [1981] 2 All ER 609, [1981] 1 WLR 1027, HL, as to the day of expiry of periods of a month or a specified number of months.

Sub-s (5): Writing. See the note "Written" above. Where in pursuance of sub-s (5) an education authority notify the parent of a child of their decision to make an assessment, they must send copies of the notification to the social services authority and the district health authority; see the Education (Special Educational Needs) Regulations 1983, SI 1983/29, reg 3.

Sub-s (6): Secretary of State. Ie one of Her Majesty's Principal Secretaries of State; see the Interpretation Act 1978, s 5, Sch 1, Vol 41, title Statutes.

Sub-s (8): If he thinks fit. See the note "Satisfied" to s 3 ante.

Definitions. For "special educational needs", see s 1(1) ante; for "special educational provision", see s 1(3) ante; for "child", see s 20(1) post; for "parent", see by virtue of s 21(2) post, the Education Act 1944, s 114(1), this part of this title ante.

Transitional provisions. See s 21(3) and Sch 2, paras 2, 3 post, and the Education Act 1981 (Commencement No 2) Order 1983, SI 1983/7, art 4, Schedule, paras 1, 2.

6 Assessment of special educational needs of children under the age of two

(1) Where, in the case of a child in their area who is under the age of two years, a local education authority are of the opinion—

 (*a*) that he has special educational needs which call for the authority to determine the special educational provision that should be made for him; or

 (*b*) that he probably has such special education needs;

they may, with the consent of the child's parent, make an assessment of his educational needs and shall do so at the request of that parent.

(2) An assessment under this section shall be made in such manner as the local education authority consider appropriate; and after making such an assessment they may make a statement of the child's special educational needs, and maintain that statement in such manner as they consider appropriate.

NOTES

Commencement. 1 April 1983; see the Introductory Note to this Act.

Age of two years. See the note "Age" to s 1 ante.

Local education authority. See the note to s 1 ante.

Opinion. See the note "Satisfied" to s 3 ante.

Assessment of his educational needs. As to the assessment of special educational needs in the case of children not falling within this section, see s 5 ante.

Definitions. For "special educational needs", see s 1(1) ante; for "special educational provision", see s 1(3) ante; for "parent", see, by virtue of s 21(2) post, the Education Act 1944, s 114(1), this part of this title ante.

7 Statement of child's special educational needs

(1) Where an assessment has been made in respect of a child under section 5, the local education authority who are responsible for the child shall, if they are of the opinion that they should determine the special educational provision that should be made for him, make a statement of his special educational needs and maintain that statement in accordance with the following provisions of this Act.

(2) In any case where a local education authority maintain a statement under this section in respect of a child, it shall be the duty of the authority to arrange that the special educational provision specified in the statement is made for him unless his parent has made suitable arrangements.

(3) Before making such a statement a local education authority shall serve on the parent of the child concerned—

 (*a*) a copy of the proposed statement; and
 (*b*) a written explanation of the effect of subsections (4) to (7) below.

(4) If the parent on whom a copy of a proposed statement has been served under subsection (3)(*a*) above disagrees with any part of the proposed statement he may, before the expiry of the appropriate period—

 (*a*) make representations (or futher representations) to the authority about the content of the proposed statement;
 (*b*) require the authority to arrange a meeting between him and an officer of the authority at which the proposed statement can be discussed.

(5) Where a parent, having attended a meeting arranged by a local education authority under subsection (4)(*b*)above, disagrees with any part of the assessment in question he may, before the expiry of the appropriate period, require the authority to arrange one or more meetings under subsection (6) below.

(6) Where a local education authority receive a request duly made under subsection (5) above they shall arrange such meeting or meetings as they consider will enable the parent to discuss the relevant advice with the appropriate person or persons.

In this subsection—

 "relevant advice" means such of the advice given to the authority in connection with the assessment as they consider to be relevant to that part of the assessment with which the parent disagrees; and
 "appropriate person" means the person who gave the relevant advice or any other person who, in the opinion of the authority, is the appropriate person to discuss it with the parent.

(7) In this section "appropriate period" means the period of 15 days beginning—

 (*a*) in the case of a request under subsection (4)(*b*) above, with the date on which the statement mentioned in subsection (3)(*b*) above was served on the parent;
 (*b*) in the case of a request under subsection (5) above, with the date fixed for the meeting arranged under subsection (4)(*b*) above; and
 (*c*) in the case of representations, or futher representations, under subsection (4)(*a*) above—

   (i) with the date mentioned in paragraph (*a*) above; or
   (ii) if one or more meetings have been arranged under the preceding provision of this section, with the date fixed for the last of those meetings.

(8) Where any such representations are made to a local education authority the authority may, after considering those representations—

(*a*) make a statement in the form originally proposed;

(*b*) make a statement in a modified form; or

(*c*) determine not to make a statement;

and shall notify the parent in writing of their decision.

(9) On making a statement under this section a local education authority shall serve on the parent of the child concerned—

(*a*) a copy of the statement;

(*b*) notice in writing of his right under section 8(1) of this Act to appeal against the special educational provision specified in the statement; and

(*c*) notice in writing of the name of the person to whom he may apply for information and advice about the child's special educational needs.

(10) The Secretary of State may by regulations prescribe the frequency with which assessments are to be repeated in respect of children for whom statements are maintained under this section.

(11) The provisions of Part II of Schedule 1 to this Act have effect in relation to statements made under this section.

NOTES

Commencement. 1 April 1983; see the Introductory Note to this Act.

Sub-s (1): Local education authority. See the note to s 1 ante.

Local education authority who are responsible for the child. As to the children for whom a local education authority are responsible, see s 4(2) ante.

Opinion. See the note "Satisfied" to s 3 ante.

Statement of his special educational needs. As to appeals against such statements, see s 8 post; as to the education of a child at an independent school where a statement is maintained for him under this section, see s 11(3) post; and for provisions as to school attendance orders where such a statement is maintained, see ss 15, 16 post.

Following provisions of this Act. See, in particular, sub-ss (3)–(9) and (11) above and Sch 1, Pt II post.

Sub-s (3): Serve . . . a copy, etc. As to the mode of service, see, by virtue of s 21(2) post, the Education Act 1944, s 113, this part of this title ante.

Written. See the note to s 5 ante.

Sub-s (7): 15 days beginning . . . with, etc. The use of the words "beginning with" makes it clear that in computing this period the day from which it runs is to be included; see *Hare v Gocher* [1962] 2 QB 641, [1962] 2 All ER 763, and *Trow v Ind Coope (West Midlands) Ltd* [1967] 2 QB at 909, [1967] 2 All ER 900, CA.

Sub-s (8): Writing. See the note "Written" to s 5 ante.

Sub-s (10): Secretary of State. See the note to s 5 ante.

Assessments. Ie assessments of educational needs made under s 5 ante.

Definitions. For "special educational needs", see s 1(1) ante; for "special educational provision", see s 1(5) ante; for "child", see s 20(1) post; for "parent", see, by virtue of s 21(2) post, the Education Act 1944, s 114(1), this part of this title ante. Note as to "appropriate period", sub-s (7) above.

Regulations under this section. The Education (Special Educational Needs) Regulations 1983, SI 1983/29, made under sub-s (10).

For general provisions as to regulations, see s 19 post.

Transitional provisions. See s 21(3) and Sch 2, paras 2–8 post, and the Education Act 1981 (Commencement No 2) Order 1983, SI 1983/7, art 4, Schedule, paras 1, 2.

---

8 Appeals against statements

(1) Every local education authority shall make arrangements for enabling the parent of a child for whom they maintain a statement under section 7 to appeal, following the first or any subsequent assessment of the child's educational needs under section 5, against the special educational provision specified in the statement.

(2) Any appeal by virtue of this section shall be to an appeal committee constituted in accordance with paragraph 1 of Part I of Schedule 2 to the Education Act 1980.

(3) Part II of that Schedule shall have effect in relation to the procedure on any such appeal but with the following modifications—

    (*a*) paragraph 7 (matters to be taken into account by appeal committee) shall have effect as if for paragraphs (*a*) and (*b*) there were substituted the words "any representations made by the appellant under section 7 of the Education Act 1981";

    (*b*) paragraph 9(*b*) (decision to be communicated to school governors) shall not apply; and

    (*c*) for any reference to section 7 of the 1980 Act there shall be substituted a reference to this section.

(4) An appeal committee hearing an appeal by virtue of this section may—

    (*a*) confirm the special educational provision specified in the statement; or

    (*b*) remit the case to the local education authority for reconsideration in the light of the committee's observations.

(5) When an appeal committee remit a case to a local education authority the authority shall reconsider it in the light of the committee's observations and shall inform the appellant in writing of their decision.

(6) In any case where—

    (*a*) an appeal committee confirm the decision of a local education authority as to the special educational provision to be made for a child; or

    (*b*) a local education authority inform an appellant of their decision in a case which has been remitted to them under subsection (4)(*b*) above;

the appellant may appeal in writing to the Secretary of State.

(7) On an appeal under subsection (6) above the Secretary of State may, after consulting the local education authority concerned—

    (*a*) confirm the special educational provision specified in the statement;

    (*b*) amend the statement so far as it specifies the special educational provision and make such other consequential amendments to the statement as he considers appropriate; or

    (*c*) direct the local education authority to cease to maintain the statement.

NOTES

Commencement. 1 April 1983; see the Introductory Note to this Act.

Sub-s (1): Local education authority. See the note to s 1 ante.

Subsequent assessment. As to the frequency of assessments under s 5 ante, where a statement is maintained under s 7 ante, see s 7(10) ante.

Sub-s (5): Writing. See the note "Written" to s 5 ante.

Sub-s (6): Secretary of State. See the note to s 5 ante.

Sub-s (7): Consulting. See the note to s 3 ante.

Definitions. For "special educational provision", see s 1(3), ante; for "child", see s 20(1) post; for "parent", see, by virtue of s 21(2) post, the Education Act 1944, s 114(1), this part of this title ante.

Education Act 1980, Sch 2. See this part of this title ante.

Transitional provisions. See s 21(3) and Sch 2, paras 2, 7 post, and the Education Act 1981 (Commencement No 2) Order 1983, SI 1983/7, art 4, Schedule, paras 1, 2.

9 Requests for assessments

(1) If the parent of a child for whom a local education authority are responsible but for whom no statement is maintained by the authority under section 7 asks the authority to arrange for an assessment to be made of the child's educational needs the authority shall comply with the request unless it is in their opinion unreasonable.

(2) If the parent of a child for whom a local education authority maintain a statement under section 7 asks the authority to arrange for an assessment of his educational needs

under section 5 and such an assessment has not been made within the period of 6 months ending with the date on which the request is made, the authority shall comply with the request unless they are satisfied that an assessment would be inappropriate.

NOTES

Commencement. 1 April 1983; see the Introductory Note to this Act ante.

Child for whom a local education authority are responsible. As to the children for whom a local education authority are responsible, see s 4(2) ante.

Local education authority. See the note to s 1 ante.

Opinion; satisfied. See the note "Satisfied" to s 3 ante.

Months. Ie calendar months; see the Interpretation Act 1978, s 5, Sch 1, Vol 41, title Statutes.

Definitions. For "child", see s 20(1) post; for "parent", see by virtue of s 21(2) post, the Education Act 1944, s 114(1), this part of this title ante.

10 Duty of health authority to notify parents etc

(1) If an Area or District Health Authority, in the course of exercising any of its functions in relation to a child who is under the age of five years, forms the opinion that he has, or probably has, special educational needs, the Authority shall—

    (*a*) inform his parent of its opinion and of its duty under this section; and

    (*b*) after giving the parent an opportunity to discuss that opinion with an officer of the Authority, bring it to the attention of the appropriate local education authority.

(2) If, in a case falling within subsection (1) above, the Authority are of the opinion that a particular voluntary organisation is likely to be able to give the parent advice or assistance in connection with any special educational needs that the child may have, they shall inform the parent accordingly.

NOTES

Commencement. 1 April 1983; see the Introductory Note to this Act.

Area or District Health Authority. As to the constitution of these authorities and the determination of their areas or districts, see the National Health Service Act 1977, s 8, Sch 5, Pts I, III, as amended, in conjunction with the Health Services Act 1980, s 1, both Vol 30, title National Health Service. By virtue of the orders now in force under s 8 of the 1977 Act only district health authorities now exist.

Age of five years. See the note "Age" to s 1 ante.

Opinion. See the note "Satisfied" to s 3 ante.

Local education authority. See the note to s 1 ante.

Definitions. For "special educational needs", see s 1(1) ante; for "parent", see, by virtue of s 21(2) post, the Education Act 1944, s 114(1), this part of this title ante.

Special schools and approved independent schools

11 Special schools and approved independent schools

(1) ...

(2) The parent of a child who is of compulsory school age and is registered as a pupil at a special school in accordance with arrangements made by a local education authority shall not withdraw the child from that school without the consent of the local education authority; but any such parent aggrieved by a refusal of the authority to give their consent may refer the question to the Secretary of State, who shall give such direction thereon as he thinks fit.

(3) Where a local education authority maintain a statement for a child under section 7 they shall not make arrangements for the provision of education for that child at an independent school unless—

(*a*) the school is for the time being approved by the Secretary of State as suitable for the admission of children for whom statements are maintained under section 7; or

(*b*) the Secretary of State consents to the child being educated there.

NOTES

Sub-s (1) amends the Education Act 1944, s 9.

Commencement. 1 April 1983; see the Introductory Note to this Act.

Secretary of State. See the note to s 5 ante.

Compulsory school age. See the note to s 4 ante.

Registered as a pupil. As to the registration of pupils at schools, see the Education Act 1944, s 80, this part of this title ante.

Local education authority. See the note to s 1 ante.

Refer the question to the Secretary of State. As to examination of the child on such a reference, see s 18 post.

Thinks fit. See the note "Satisfied" to s 3 ante.

Independent school ... approved by the Secretary of State. As to the approval of independent schools, see s 13(1), (2), (4) post.

Secretary of State consents. As to consents under sub-s (3)(*b*) above, see also s 13(3), (4) post.

Definitions. For "child", see s 20(1) post; and by virtue of s 21(2) post, for "special school", see the Education Act 1944, s 9(5), this part of this title ante, and for "compulsory school age", "independent school", "parent" and "pupil", see s 114(1) of that Act.

Transitional provision. See s 21(3) and Sch 2, para 1 post, and the Education Act 1981 (Commencement No 2) Order 1983, SI 1983/7, art 4, Schedule, paras 1, 2.

12 Approval of special schools

(1) The Secretary of State may by regulations make provision as to—

(*a*) the requirements which are to be complied with by any school as a condition of approval of the school as a special school under section 9(5) of the principal Act;

(*b*) the requirements which are to be complied with by a special school while such an approval is in force with respect to it; and

(*c*) the withdrawal of approval from any school—

(i) at the request of the proprietor; or

(ii) on the ground that there has been a failure to comply with any prescribed requirement.

(2) Without prejudice to the generality of subsection (1) above, regulations under that subsection may impose requirements which call for arrangements to be approved by the Secretary of State.

(3) Notwithstanding that the provisions of the principal Act requiring local education authorities to have regard to the need for securing that primary and secondary education are provided in separate schools do not apply with respect to special schools, the regulations may impose requirements as to the organisation of any special school as a primary school or as a secondary school.

(4) Provision shall be made in the regulations to secure that, so far as practicable, every pupil attending a special school will attend religious worship and religious instruction, or will be withdrawn from attendance at such worship or instruction in accordance with the wishes of his parent.

NOTES

Commencement. 1 April 1983; see the Introductory Note to this Act.

Secretary of State. See the note to s 5 ante.

Local education authorities. See the note "Local education authority" to s 1 ante.

Modification of trust deeds. As to the making of modifications to any trust deed or other instrument relating to a school to enable the governors or proprietor to meet any requirement imposed by regulations under this section or s 13 post, see the Education Act 1973, s 1(2)(b), this part of this title ante.

Definitions. By virtue of s 21(2) post, for "primary education" and "secondary education", see the Education Act 1944, s 8(1), this part of this title ante; for "special school", see s 9(5) of that Act ante, and for "parent", "prescribed", "primary school", "proprietor", "pupil", "school" and "secondary school", see s 114(1) of that Act.

Principal Act. Ie the Education Act 1944; see s 20(1) post. For the provisions of that Act requiring local education authorities to have regard to the need for securing that primary and secondary education are provided in separate schools and providing that that requirement shall not apply with respect to special schools, see s 8(2)(a) and the proviso to s 8(2), this part of this title ante.

Regulations under this section. The Education (Approval of Special Schools) Regulations 1983, SI 1983/1499.

For general provisions as to regulations, see s 19 post.

Transitional provisions. See s 21(3) and Sch 2, para 1 post.

13 Approval of independent schools

(1) The Secretary of State may by regulations make provision as to—

    (a) the requirements to be complied with by any school as a condition of approval of the school for the purposes of section 11(3)(a) of this Act;

    (b) the requirements which are to be complied with by any school while such an approval is in force with respect to it; and

    (c) the withdrawal of approval from any school—

        (i) at the request of the proprietor; or

        (ii) on the ground that there has been a failure to comply with any prescribed requirement.

(2) Any approval under section 11(3)(a) may be given subject to such conditions (in addition to those prescribed) as the Secretary of State sees fit to impose.

(3) Any consent under section 11(3)(b) may be given subject to such conditions as the Secretary of State sees fit to impose.

(4) In any case where there is a failure to comply with a condition imposed under subsection (2) or (3) above, the Secretary of State may withdraw his approval or, as the case may be, consent.

NOTES

Commencement. 1 April 1983; see the Introductory Note to this title.

Secretary of State. See the note to s 5 ante.

Sees fit. See the note "Satisfied" to s 3 ante.

Modification of trust deeds. See the note to s 12 ante.

Definitions. By virtue of s 21(2), post, for "prescribed", "proprietor" and "school", see the Education Act 1944, s 114(1), this part of this title ante.

Regulations under this section. No regulations had been made under this section up to 1 August 1985.

For general provisions as to regulations, see s 19 post.

14 Discontinuance of maintained special schools

(1) A local education authority shall not cease to maintain a special school except in accordance with proposals approved by the Secretary of State under this section.

(2) Where a local education authority intend to cease to maintain a special school they shall serve written notice of their proposals on—

    (a) the Secretary of State;

    (b) the parent of every child who is, at the time when notice is served on the Secretary of State, a registered pupil of the school;

    (c) any other local education authority who have arranged for special educational provision to be made at the school for a child in their area; and

    (d) any such other persons as the authority consider appropriate.

(3) The notice shall specify—

(a) the time at which the local education authority intend to implement the proposals; and

(b) a period (which shall not be less than two months beginning with the date on which the notice is served) during which written objections to the proposals may be made to the local education authority.

(4) Before the expiry of the period of one month beginning with the date on which the period for making objections, specified in the last notice to be served under subsection (2) above, expires, the local education authority shall send to the Secretary of State copies of all objections which have been duly made and not withdrawn in writing, together with their observations on those objections.

(5) After considering the proposals and any objections and observations sent to him under subsection (4) above the Secretary of State may approve or reject the proposals.

(6) Where the Secretary of State approves the proposals under this section he may direct that they are to be implemented at a time which is different from that specified in the notice served under subsection (2) above.

(7) Service of any notice under subsection (2) above which is sent by post in accordance with section 113 of the principal Act shall be deemed to have been effected on the second day after the day on which it is posted.

NOTES

Commencement. This section was brought into force on 5 January 1982 by the Education Act 1981 (Commencement No 1) Order 1981, SI 1981/1711, made under s 20(2), (3) post. (The transitional provisions contained in that order are now spent.)

Sub-s (1): Local education authority. See the note to s 1 ante.

Secretary of State. See the note to s 5 ante.

Sub-s (2): Serve . . . notice. As to the mode of service, see, by virtue of s 21(2) post, the Education Act 1944, this part of this title ante; and note sub-s (7) above.

Written. See the note to s 5 ante.

Sub-s (3): Two months beginning with, etc. See the note "15 days beginning . . . with, etc" to s 7 ante. "Months" means calendar months by virtue of the Interpretation Act 1978, s 5, Sch 1, Vol 41, title Statutes.

Sub-s (4): One month beginning with, etc. See the note "15 days beginning . . . with, etc" to s 7 ante.

Writing. See the note "Written" to s 5 ante.

Definitions. For "special educational provision", see s 1(3) ante; for "child", see s 20(1) post; by virtue of s 21(2) post, for "special school", see the Education Act 1944, s 9(5), this part of this title ante, for "parent" and "registered pupil", see s 114(1) of that Act, and as to "maintain", see s 114(2)(a) of that Act.

Principal Act. Ie the Education Act 1944, this part of this title ante; see s 20(1) post.

School attendance orders

15 Proposed school attendance order: choice of school

(1) This section applies in any case where—

(a) a local education authority propose to serve a school attendance order on the parent of a child under section 37 of the principal Act; and

(b) the authority maintain a statement for that child under section 7.

(2) The order shall not be served until the expiry of the period of 15 days beginning with the date on which the authority serve on the parent written notice—

(a) of their intention to serve the order;

(b) stating that if, before the expiry of that period, he selects a school at which he desires the child to become a registered pupil, that school will, unless the Secretary of State otherwise directs, be named in the order.

(3) If, before the expiry of the period mentioned in subsection (2), the parent selects

such a school, that school shall, unless the Secretary of State otherwise directs, be named in the order.

(4) If the local education authority are of the opinion that—

(a) the school selected by the parent as the school to be named in the order is unsuitable to the child's age, ability or aptitude or to his special educational needs; or

(b) that the attendance of the child at the school so selected would prejudice the provision of efficient education or the efficient use of resources;

the authority may, after giving the parent notice of their intention to do so, apply to the Secretary of State for a direction determining what school is to be named in the order.

(5) Any direction under subsection (4) above may require the local education authority to make such amendments in the statement concerned as the Secretary of State considers necessary or expedient in consequence of his determination.

(6) Where the school to be named in the school attendance order in pursuance of a direction given by the Secretary of State under this section is a school maintained by a local education authority, it shall be the duty of the authority and of the governors of the school to admit the child to the school.

NOTES

Commencement. 1 April 1983; see the Introductory Note to this Act.

Sub-s (1): Local education authority. See the note to s 1 ante.

School attendance order. See also s 16 post, as to the amendment or revocation of such orders where the local education authority maintain a statement for the child concerned under s 7 ante.

Sub-s (2): 15 days beginning with, etc. See the note to s 7 ante.

Serve . . . notice. As to the mode of service, see, by virtue of s 21(2), post, the Education Act 1944, s 113, this part of this title ante.

Written; Secretary of State. See the notes to s 5 ante.

Sub-s (4): Opinion. See the note "Satisfied" to s 3 ante.

Sub-s (5): Statement concerned. Ie the relevant statement maintained by the local education authority under s 7 ante.

Sub-s (6): It shall be the duty, etc; governors. See the notes to s 2 ante.

Definitions. For "special educational needs", see s 1(1) ante; by virtue of s 21(2) post, for "school attendance order", see the Education Act 1944, s 37(2), this part of this title ante; for "child", "parent", "registered pupil" and "school", see s 114(1) of that Act, and as to "maintain", see s 114(2)(a) of that Act.

Principal Act. Ie the Education Act 1944, this part of this title ante; see s 20(1) post.

Transitional provisions. See s 21(3) and Sch 2, paras 2, 8 post, and the Education Act 1981 (Commencement No 2) Order 1983, SI 1983/7, art 4, Schedule, paras 1, 2.

16 Amendment and revocation of school attendance orders

(1) This section applies in any case where—

(a) a local education authority have served a school attendance order on the parent of a child under section 37 of the principal Act; and

(b) the authority maintain a statement for that child under section 7.

(2) If at any time while the order is in force the parent applies to the local education authority requesting—

(a) that another school be substituted for that named in the order; or

(b) that the order be revoked on the ground that arrangements have been made for the child to receive efficient full-time education suitable to his age, ability and aptitude and to his special educational needs otherwise than at school;

the authority shall amend or revoke the order in compliance with the request unless they are of the opinion that—

(i) the school selected by the parent as the school to be named in the order is unsuitable to the child's age, ability or aptitude or to his special educational needs or that the proposed change of school is against the interests of the child;

(ii) the attendance of the child at the school so selected would prejudice the provision of efficient education or the efficient use of resources; or

(iii) no satisfactory arrangements have been made for the education of the child otherwise than at school.

(3) If a parent is aggrieved by a refusal of the authority to comply with a request made under subsection (2) above he may refer the question to the Secretary of State, who shall give such direction thereon as he thinks fit.

(4) Any direction under subsection (3) above may require the local education authority to make such amendments in the statement concerned as the Secretary of State considers necessary or expedient in consequence of his determination.

(5) Where, in pursuance of a direction given by the Secretary of State under this section, a school which is to be substituted for that named in the school attendance order is a school maintained by a local education authority, it shall be the duty of the authority and of the governors of the school to admit the child to the school.

NOTES

Commencement. 1 April 1983; see the Introductory Note to this Act.

Sub-s (1): Local education authority. See the note to s 1 ante.

School attendance order. See also s 15 ante, as to choice of school where the local education authority propose to serve such an order and they maintain a statement for the child concerned under s 7 ante.

Sub-s (2): Full-time education. Cf the note to the Education Act 1944, s 36, this part of this title ante.

Opinion. See the note "Satisfied" to s 3 ante.

Sub-s (3): Refer the question to the Secretary of State. As to examination of the child on such a reference, see s 18 post.

Secretary of State. See the note to s 5 ante.

Thinks fit. See the note "Satisfied" to s 3 ante.

Sub-s (4): Statement concerned. Ie the relevant statement maintained by the local education authority under s 7 ante.

Sub-s (5): It shall be the duty, etc; governors. See the notes to s 2 ante.

Definitions. For "special education needs", see s 1(1) ante; by virtue of s 21(2) post, for "school attendance order", see the Education Act 1944, s 37(2), this part of this title ante; for "child", "parent" and "school", see s 114(1) of that Act, and as to "maintain", see s 114(2)(a) of that Act.

Principal Act. Ie the Education Act 1944, this part of this title ante; see s 20(1) post.

Transitional provisions. See s 21(3) and Sch 2, paras 2, 8 post, and the Education Act 1981 (Commencement No 2) Order 1983, SI 1983/7, art 4, Schedule, paras 1, 2.

Miscellaneous

17 (*Amends the Education Act 1944, s 36, this part of this title ante.*)

18 Powers of Secretary of State as to medical and other examinations

(1) Where any question arising under this Act is referred to the Secretary of State then, if in his opinion he would be assisted in determining that question by the advice of a person appointed by him to examine the child concerned, he may serve a notice on the parent of that child requiring the child's attendance for examination in accordance with the provisions of the notice.

(2) Sub-paragraphs (2) and (4) of paragraph 2 of Schedule 1 to this Act apply in relation to an examination under this section as they apply in relation to one under Schedule 1.

NOTES

Commencement. 1 April 1983; see the Introductory Note to this Act.

Question . . . is referred to the Secretary of State. Questions may be referred to the Secretary of State under ss 11(2) and 16(3) ante.

Secretary of State. See the note to s 5 ante.

Serve a notice. As to the mode of service, see, by virtue of s 21(2) post, the Education Act 1944, s 113 ante.

Definitions. For "child", see s 20(1) post, or, by virtue of s 21(2) post, the Education Act 1944, s 114(1), this part of this title ante; for "parent", see by virtue of s 21(2) post, s 114(1) of the 1944 Act.

19 Regulations

Regulations under this Act—

- (*a*) shall be made by statutory instrument;
- (*b*) shall be subject to annulment in pursuance of a resolution of either House of Parliament;
- (*c*) may make different provision for different cases or circumstances;
- (*d*) may contain such incidental, supplemental or transitional provisions as the Secretary of State thinks fit; and
- (*e*) may make in relation to Wales provision different from that made in relation to England.

NOTES

Commencement. 1 April 1983; see the Introductory Note to this Act.

Statutory instrument; subject to annulment. For provisions as to statutory instruments generally, see the Statutory Instruments Act 1946, Vol 41, title Statutes, and as to statutory instruments which are subject to annulment, see ss 5(1), 7(1) of that Act.

Secretary of State. See the note to s 5 ante.

Thinks fit. See the note "Satisfied" to s 3 ante.

England; Wales. For meanings, see the Interpretation Act 1978, s 5, Sch 1, Vol 41, title Statutes.

20 Interpretation and commencement

(1) In this Act—

"child" includes any person who has not attained the age of 19 years and is registered as a pupil at a school;

"ordinary school" means a school which is not a special school;

"principal Act" means the Education Act 1944.

(2) This Act shall come into force on such date as the Secretary of State may by order made by statutory instrument appoint and different dates may be appointed for different provisions or different purposes.

(3) Any order under this section may make such transitional provisions as appear to the Secretary of State to be necessary or expedient in connection with the provisions thereby brought into force, including such adaptations of those provisions, or of any other provisions of this Act then in force, as appear to him to be necessary or expedient for the purpose or in consequence of the operation of any provisions of this Act before the coming into force of any other provision.

NOTES

Commencement. This section was brought into force on 5 January 1982 by the Education Act 1981 (Commencement No 1) Order 1981, SI 1981/1711, made under sub-s (2) above.

Age of 19 years. See the note "Age" to s 1 ante.

Registered as a pupil. As to the registration of pupils at schools, see the Education Act 1944, s 80, this part of this title ante.

Secretary of State. See the note to s 5 ante.

Statutory instrument. For provisions as to statutory instruments generally, see the Statutory Instruments Act 1946, Vol 41, title Statutes.

Definitions. By virtue of s 21(2) post, for "special school", see the Education Act 1944, s 9(5), this part of this title ante, and for "pupil" and "school", see s 114(1) of that Act.

Education Act 1944. See this part of this title ante.

Orders under this section. The Education Act 1981 (Commencement No 1) Order 1981, SI 1981/1711, bringing ss 14, 20 and 21(1), (2), (5) into force on 5 January 1982, and the Education Act 1981 (Commencement No 2) Order 1983, SI 1983/7, bringing the remainder of the Act into force on 1 April 1983.

21 Short title, etc

(1) This Act may be cited as the Education Act 1981, and this Act and the Education Acts 1944 to 1980 may be cited as the Education Acts 1944 to 1981.

(2) This Act shall be construed as one with the principal Act.

(3) The transitional provisions made by Schedule 2 to this Act shall have effect.

(4) The enactments mentioned in Schedule 3 to this Act shall have effect subject to the minor and consequential amendments specified in that Schedule; and the enactments mentioned in Schedule 4 are hereby repealed to the extent specified in the third column.

(5) This Act does not extend to Scotland or Northern Ireland.

NOTES

Commencement. Sub-ss (1), (2), (5) above were brought into force on 5 January 1982 by the Education Act 1981 (Commencement No 1) Order 1981, SI 1981/1711, made under s 20(2) ante. Sub-ss (3), (4) were brought into force on 1 April 1983 by the Education Act 1981 (Commencement No 2) Order 1983, SI 1983/7, made under s 20(2) ante.

Construed as one. Ie the enactments in question are to be construed as if they were contained in one Act, unless there is some manifest discrepancy; see eg *Phillips v Parnaby* [1934] 2 KB 299 at 302. Accordingly, definitions in the earlier Act may be relevant to the construction of provisions of this Act (see *Solomons v R Gertzenstein Ltd* [1954] 2 QB 243, [1954] 2 All ER 625, CA; *Crowe (Valuation Officer) v Lloyds British Testing Co Ltd* [1960] 1 QB 592, [1960] 1 All ER 411, CA).

Principal Act. Ie the Education Act 1944, this part of this title ante; see s 20(1) ante.

Education Acts 1944 to 1981. For the Acts that may be cited by this collective title, see the Introductory Note to the Education Act 1944, this part of this title ante.

SCHEDULES

SCHEDULE 1

Sections 5 and 7

ASSESSMENT AND STATEMENTS OF SPECIAL EDUCATIONAL NEEDS

PART I

ASSESSMENTS

Regulations

1.—(1) The Secretary of State shall by regulations make provision as to the advice which a local education authority are to seek in making assessments.

(2) Without prejudice to the generality of sub-paragraph (1) above, regulations made under that sub-paragraph shall require the local education authority to seek medical, psychological and educational advice and such other advice as may be prescribed.

(3) The Secretary of State may by regulations make provision—

    (a) as to the manner in which assessments are to be conducted; and

    (b) in connection with such other matters relating to the making of assessments as the Secretary of State considers appropriate.

Attendance at examinations

2.—(1) Where a local education authority propose to make an assessment they may serve a notice on the parent of the child to be assessed requiring the child's attendance for examination in accordance with the provisions of the notice.

(2) The parent of a child examined under this paragraph shall be entitled to be present at the examination if he so desires.

(3) A notice under this paragraph shall—

    (*a*) state the purpose of the examination;
    (*b*) state the time and place at which the examination will be held;
    (*c*) name an officer of the authority from whom further information may be obtained;
    (*d*) inform the parent that he may submit such information to the authority as he may wish; and
    (*e*) inform the parent of his right to be present at the examination.

(4) Any parent on whom a notice has been served under this paragraph and who fails without reasonable excuse to comply with any of the requirements of the notice shall, if the notice relates to a child who was not over compulsory school age at the time stated in the notice as the time for holding the examination, be guilty of an offence and liable on summary conviction to a fine not exceeding [level 2 on the standard scale].

NOTES

The reference in para 2(4) to level 2 on the standard scale is substituted by virtue of the Criminal Justice Act 1982, s 46, Vol 27, title Magistrates.

Commencement. 1 April 1983; see the Introductory Note to this Act.

Para 1: Secretary of State. See the note to s 5 ante.

Local education authority. See the note to s 1 ante.

Assessments. Ie assessments of special educational needs made under s 5 ante.

Para 2: Serve a notice. As to the mode of service, see, by virtue of s 21(2) ante, the Education Act 1944, s 114(1), this part of this title ante.

Reasonable excuse. What is a reasonable excuse is largely a question of fact; cf *Leck v Epsom RDC* [1922] 1 KB 383, [1922] All ER Rep 784. Yet it is clear that ignorance of the statutory provisions provides no reasonable excuse (cf *Aldridge v Warwickshire Coal Co Ltd* (1925) 133 LT 439, CA), nor does a mistaken view of the effect of those provisions (*R v Philip Reid* [1973] 3 All ER 1020, [1973] 1 WLR 1283, CA). Quaere whether reliance on the advice of an expert can amount to a reasonable excuse; see *Saddleworth UDC v Aggregate and Sand Ltd* (1970) 69 LGR 103.

Once evidence of a reasonable excuse emerges, it is for the prosecution to eliminate the existence of that defence to the satisfaction of the court; see *R v Clarke* [1969] 2 All ER 1008, [1969] 1 WLR 1109, CA.

Compulsory school age. See the note to s 4 ante.

Summary conviction. Summary jurisdiction and procedure are mainly governed by the Magistrates' Courts Act 1980, Vol 27, title Magistrates, and by rules made under s 144 of that Act.

Standard scale. By the Criminal Justice Act 1982, ss 37(3), 75, Vol 27, title Magistrates, this means the standard scale set out in s 37(2) of that Act as amended by order made under the Magistrates' Courts Act 1980, s 143(1), in the same title. The scale as amended by the Criminal Penalties etc (Increase) Order 1984, SI 1984/447, art 3(4), Sch 4, is: level 1: £50; level 2: £100; level 3: £400; level 4: £1,000; and level 5: £2,000.

Definitions. For "child", see s 20(1) ante; for "parent" and "prescribed", see, by virtue of s 21(2) ante, the Education Act 1944, s 114(1).

Regulations under para 1. The Education (Special Educational Needs) Regulations 1983, SI 1983/29. For general provisions as to regulations, see s 19 ante.

PART II

STATEMENTS

Form of statement

3. A statement shall be in the prescribed form and contain the prescribed information and shall, in particular—

    (*a*) give details of the authority's assessment of the special educational needs of the child; and

(b) specify the special educational provision to be made for the purpose of meeting those needs.

Keeping and disclosure of statements

4. The Secretary of State may by regulations make provision with respect to the keeping, disclosure and transfer of statements.

Review of statements

5. Every statement shall, on the making of an assessment of the educational needs of the child concerned under section 5, be reviewed by the local education authority and shall be reviewed in any event within the period of twelve months beginning with the making of the statement or, as the case may be, with the previous review.

Amendment of statements, etc.

6.—(1) If a local education authority propose to amend, or to cease to maintain, a statement they shall, before doing so, serve on the parent of the child concerned notice in writing of their proposal and of the right of the parent to make representations under this paragraph.

(2) Any parent on whom a notice has been served under this paragraph may, within the period of 15 days beginning with the date on which the notice is served, make representations to the authority about their proposal.

(3) A local education authority shall consider any representations made to them under this paragraph and on taking a decision on the proposal to which those representations relate shall (in writing) inform the parent of their decision.

7. Paragraph 6 above does not apply in any case where a local education authority cease to maintain a statement for a child who has ceased to be their responsibility, or where amendments which are made to a statement are consequential upon the making, amendment or revocation of a school attendance order.

NOTES

Commencement. 1 April 1983; see the Introductory Note to this Act.

Para 3: Statement. Ie a statement of a child's special educational needs made by a local education authority under s 7 ante.

Prescribed form; prescribed information. Ie prescribed by regulations made by the Secretary of State; see, by virtue of s 21(2) ante, the Education Act 1944, s 114(1), this part of this title ante. See the note "Regulations under para 4" below.

Authority's assessment of the special educational needs. Ie the local education authority's assessment made under s 5 ante.

Para 4: Secretary of State. See the note to s 5 ante.

Para 5: Local education authority. See the note to s 1 ante.

Twelve months beginning with, etc. See the note "15 days beginning . . . with, etc" to s 7 ante.

Para 6: Serve . . . notice. As to the mode of service, see by virtue of s 21(2) ante, the Education Act 1944, s 114(1), this part of this title ante.

Writing. See the note "Written" to s 5 ante.

15 Days beginning with, etc. See the note to s 7 ante.

Para 7: Child who has ceased to be their responsibility. As to the children for whom a local education authority are responsible, see s 4(2) ante.

Definitions. For "special educational needs", see s 1(1) ante; for "special educational provision", see s 1(3) ante; for "child", see s 20(1) ante; by virtue of s 21(2) ante, for "school attendance order", see the Education Act 1944, s 37(2), this part of this title ante, and for "parent" and "prescribed", see s 114(1) of that Act.

Regulations under para 4. The Education (Special Educational Needs) Regulations 1983, SI 1983/29.

SCHEDULE 2

Section 21

TRANSITIONAL PROVISIONS

Approval of special schools

1. Any approval given under section 9(5) of the principal Act (special schools) before the commencement of section 12 of this Act and in force immediately before that date shall have

effect for the purposes of the principal Act and of regulations made under section 12 as if it had been given under section 9(5) as amended by this Act.

Special educational treatment

2. The following provisions of this Schedule apply in relation to any child for whom, immediately before the commencement of section 7, a local education authority were providing special educational treatment under the principal Act.

3. The child shall be taken to have special educational needs and the local education authority which arranged the provision of special educational treatment (the "authority") shall be taken to have made an assessment of his educational needs under section 5 and to have formed the opinion, that his special educational needs call for the authority to determine the special educational provision that should be made for him.

4. During the period of 12 months beginning with the commencement of section 7 the authority shall not be under the duty imposed by that section to make and maintain a statement of the child's special educational needs.

5. A statement made in respect of the child under section 7, but before an assessment of his educational needs is made under section 5, need not give details of the authority's assessment of those needs until such time as an assessment has been made under section 5.

6. Until such time as the authority make a statement in respect of the child under section 7 they shall be under a duty to continue to provide the special educational treatment which the child was receiving immediately before the commencement of section 7 unless the child's parent makes suitable arrangements; but this paragraph shall not require the authority to act in any way which would be incompatible with the provisions of a school attendance order in force under section 37 of the principal Act.

7. Section 8 shall not apply in relation to a statement of the child's special educational needs under section 7 unless—

> (a) the special educational provision specified in the statement differs from the special educational treatment which the child was receiving immediately before the commencement of this Schedule (otherwise than to take account of a school attendance order); or
>
> (b) an assessment of the child's educational needs has been made under section 5 following the making of the statement.

8. Sections 15 and 16 apply, at any time before a statement is made for the child under section 7, as if in each of those sections the following were substituted for paragraph (b) of subsection (1)—

> "(b) that local education authority were, immediately before the commencement of section 7, providing special educational treatment for that child under the principal Act.".

NOTES

Commencement. 1 April 1983; see the Introductory Note to this Act.

Para 2: Local education authority. See the note to s 1 ante.

Para 4: 12 months beginning with, etc. See the note "15 days beginning . . . with, etc" to s 7 ante.

Definitions. For "special educational needs", see s 1(1) ante; for "special educational provision", see s 1(3) ante; for "child", see s 20(1) ante; by virtue of s 21(2) ante, for "school attendance order", see the Education Act 1944, s 37(2), this part of this title ante, and for "parent", see s 114(1) of that Act. Note, as to the "authority", para 3 above.

Principal Act. Ie the Education Act 1944, this part of this title ante; see s 20(1) ante.

(Sch 3: para 1 amends the Children and Young Persons Act 1933, s 10(1), Vol 6, title Children; *paras 2–6 amend the Education Act 1944, ss 37, 50, 52, 61, 114, respectively, this part of this title ante; para 6A (which was inserted by the Education Act 1981 (Commencement No 2) Order 1983, SI 1983/7) amended s 114 of the 1944 Act and is now spent; para 7 amends the Education (Miscellaneous Provisions) Act 1948, s 5(1), this part of this title ante; para 8 amends the Education (Miscellaneous Provisions) Act 1953, s 6, this part of this title ante; para 9 amends the Children and Young Persons Act 1969, s 1(2)(e), Vol 6, title* Children; *para 10 amends the Education Act 1973, s 1(2)(b), this part of this title ante; para 11 amends the Sex Discrimination Act 1975, s 23(1), Vol 6, title* Civil Rights and

Liberties; *para 12 amends the Race Relations Act 1976, s 18(1), in the same title; para 13 amends the National Health Service Act 1977, Sch 1, para 1, Vol 30, title* National Health Service; *paras 14–16 amend the Education Act 1980, ss 9(2), 10, 11, this part of this title ante.*)

SCHEDULE 4

Section 21

REPEALS

Chapter	Short Title	Extent of Repeal
7 & 8 Geo 6 c 31	The Education Act 1944	Sections 33 and 34 In section 37, in subsection (2) the words from "provided that" to the end, subsection (3), in subsection (4) the words from "requesting that another" to "order or", the words "amend or", the words from "that the proposed" to "child or" and the words "as the case may be". Section 38.
1970 c 44	The Chronically Sick and Disabled Persons Act 1970	Sections 25 to 27.
1976 c 81	The Education Act 1976	Section 10.
1980 c 20	The Education Act 1980	Section 10(6) and (7). Section 33(1).

NOTE

Commencement. 1 April 1983; see the Introductory Note to this Act.

LOCAL GOVERNMENT (MISCELLANEOUS PROVISIONS) ACT 1982

(1982 c 30)

An Act to make amendments for England and Wales of provisions of that part of the law relating to local authorities or highways which is commonly amended by local Acts; to make provision for the control of sex establishments; to make further provision for the control of refreshment premises and for consultation between local authorities in England and Wales and fire authorities with regard to fire precautions for buildings and caravan sites; to repeal the Theatrical Employers Registration Acts 1925 and 1928; to make further provision as to the enforcement of section 8 of the Public Utilities Street Works Act 1950 and sections 171 and 174 of the Highways Act 1980; to make provision in connection with the computerisation of local land charges registers; to make further provision in connection with the acquisition of land and rights over land by boards constituted in pursuance of section 1 of the Town and Country Planning Act 1971 or reconstituted in pursuance of Schedule 17 to the Local Government Act 1972; to exclude from the definition of "construction or maintenance work" in section 20 of the Local Government, Planning and Land Act 1980 work undertaken by local authorities and development bodies pursuant to certain agreements with the Manpower Services Commission which specify the work to be undertaken and under which the Commission agrees to pay the whole or part of the cost of the work so specified; to define "year" for the purposes of Part III of the said Act of 1980; to amend section 140 of the Local Government Act 1972 and to provide for the insurance by local authorities of persons voluntarily assisting probation committees; to make provision for controlling nuisance and disturbance on educational premises; to amend section 137 of the Local Government Act 1972; to make further provision as to arrangements made by local authorities under the Employment and Training Act 1973; to extend the duration of certain powers to assist industry or employment conferred by local Acts; to make corrections and minor improvements in certain enactments relating to the local administration of health and planning functions; and for connected purposes [13 July 1982]

Northern Ireland. This Act does not apply; see s 49(2) post.

1–32 *((Pts I–IX) For ss 1, 2, see Vol 45, title* Theatres and Other Places of Entertainment; *for s 3, see Vol 47, title* Trade and Industry (Pt 1); *for ss 4–6, see Vol 18, title* Food; *s 7 amends the Late Night Refreshment Houses Act 1969, s 1, Vol 24, title* Licensing and Liquor Duties; *ss 8(1), 24, 25, 28 repealed by the Building Act 1984, s 133(2), Sch 7 and replaced by provisions of that Act, Vol 35, title* Public Health; *s 8(2) amends the Caravan Sites and Control of Development Act 1960, ss 5, 8, 24, 29, Vol 32, title* Open Spaces and Historic Buildings (Pt 4); *for ss 9, 10, 13–17, 29–32, see Vol 35, title* Public Health; *s 11 repeals the Theatrical Employers Registration Acts 1925 and 1928; for s 12, see Vol 25, title* Local Government; *ss 18, 19 repealed by the Food Act 1984, s 134, Sch 11 and replaced by provisions of that Act, Vol 18, title* Food; *s 20 introduces Sch 5 which specifies enactments which have effect subject to amendments concerning amenities for certain highways; s 21(1) amends the Public Utilities Street Works Act 1950, s 30, Vol 20, title* Highways; *s 21(2) amends the Highways Act 1980, s 312, Vol 20, title* Highways; *s 22 amends s 179 of the 1980 Act, Vol 20, title* Highways; *s 23 inserts s 147A in the Highways Act 1980, Vol 20, title* Highways; *s 26(1) amends s 92(1)(d) of the 1936 Act; s 26(2) amends the Clean Air Act 1956, s 16(1), Vol 35, title* Public Health; *s 27(1) substitutes a new s 17 for the original ss 17, 18 of the Public Health Act 1961, Vol 35, title* Public Health; *s 27(2) repeals the Greater London Council (General Powers) Act 1967, s 24.)*

PART XII

MISCELLANEOUS

33–39 *(For s 33, see Vol 37, title* Real Property; *s 34 amends the Local Land Charges Act 1975, ss 3, 8, 10, 16, Vol 37, title* Real Property; *s 35 amends the Local Government, Planning and Land Act 1980, s 119, Vol 46, title* Town and Country Planning; *s 36 inserts s 109A in the Town and Country Planning Act 1971 and amends ss 269, 280 of, and Sch 21, Pt II to, the 1971 Act, Vol 46, title* Town and Country Planning; *for s 37, see Vol 27, title* Markets and Fairs; *s 38 amends the Local Government, Planning and Land Act 1980, s 20, Vol 25, title* Local Government; *s 39(1), amends the Local Government Act 1972, s 140, Vol 25, title* Local Government; *s 39(2) inserts ss 140A–140C in the 1972 Act; s 39(3) amends the Insurance Companies Act 1981, Sch 2, Pt I, Class 1 (repealed).)*

40 Nuisance and disturbance on educational premises

(1) Any person who without lawful authority is present on premises to which this section applies and causes or permits nuisance or disturbance to the annoyance of persons who lawfully use those premises (whether or not any such persons are present at the time) shall be guilty of an offence and shall be liable on summary conviction to a fine not exceeding [level 2 on the standard scale].

(2) This section applies to premises, including playgrounds, playing fields and other premises for outdoor recreation—

(*a*) of a school maintained by a local education authority; or

(*b*) of a further education establishment provided by such an authority.

(3) If—

(*a*) a police constable; or

(*b*) subject to subsection (5) below, a person whom a local education authority have authorised to exercise the power conferred by this subsection,

has reasonable cause to suspect that any person is committing or has committed an offence under this section, he may remove him from the premises.

(4) The power conferred by subsection (3) above may also be exercised, in relation to premises of an aided or special agreement school, by a person whom the schoool governors have authorised to exercise it.

(5) A local education authority may not authorise a person to exercise the power conferred by subsection (3) above in relation to premises of a voluntary school without first obtaining the consent of the school governors.

(6) Except as provided by subsection (7) below, no proceedings under this section shall be brought by any person other than—

(*a*) a police constable; or

(*b*) subject to subsection (8) below, a local education authority.

(7) Proceedings under this section for an offence committed on premises of an aided or special agreement school may be brought by a person whom the school governors have authorised to bring such proceedings.

(8) A local education authority may not bring proceedings under this section for an offence committed on premises of a voluntary school without first obtaining the consent of the school governors.

(9) Expressions used in this section and in the Education Act 1944 have the meanings assigned to them by that Act.

(10) This section shall come into force on the expiry of the period of two months beginning with the date on which this Act is passed.

NOTES

The reference in sub-s (1) to level 2 on the standard scale is substituted by virtue of the Criminal Justice Act 1982, s 46, Vol 27, title Magistrates.

Commencement. This section came into force on 13 September 1982; see sub-s (10) above.

Sub-s (1) : Premises to which this section applies. See sub-s (2) above.

Causes or permits. To "cause" involves some degree of dominance or control, or some express or positive mandate, from the person "causing" (*McLeod (or Houston) v Buchanan* [1940] 2 All ER 179 at 187, HL, per Lord Wright; *Shave v Rosner* [1954] 2 QB 113, [1954] 2 All ER 280; *Lovelace v DPP* [1954] 3 All ER 481, [1954] 1 WLR 1468; *Shulton (Great Britain) Ltd v Slough BC* [1967] 2 QB 471, [1967] 2 All ER 137). A person cannot be said to have "caused" another to do or omit to do something unless he either knows or deliberately chooses not to know what it is that the other is doing or failing to do (*James & Son Ltd v Smee* [1955] 1 QB 78, [1954] 3 All ER 273; *Ross Hillman Ltd v Bond* [1974] QB 435, [1974] 2 All ER 287).

To "permit" denotes a general or particular permission, as distinguished from a mandate, and the permission may be express or implied (*McLeod (or Houston) v Buchanan* ubi supra). To "permit" an offence to be committed involves a knowledge of the facts constituting the offence; but shutting one's eyes to the obvious, or allowing a person to do something in circumstances where a contravention is likely not caring whether a contravention takes place or not, is sufficient (*James & Son Ltd v Smee* supra; *Gray's Haulage Co Ltd v Arnold* [1966] 1 All ER 896, [1966] 1 WLR 534, *Ross Hillman Ltd v Bond* supra). Reasonable grounds for suspicion that the offence will be committed may be sufficient but suspicion itself is not enough (*Sweet v Parsley* [1970] AC 132, [1969] 1 All ER 347, HL; *R v Souter* [1971] 2 All ER 1151, [1971] 1 WLR 1187, CA). But a person cannot permit unless he is in a position to forbid (*Goodbarne v Buck* [1940] 1 KB 771, [1940] 1 All ER 613, CA; *Lloyd v Singleton* [1953] 1 QB 357, [1953] 1 All ER 291) and no one can permit what he cannot control (*Tophams Ltd v Earl of Sefton* [1967] 1 AC 50, [1966] 1 All ER 1039, HL).

For a corporation to be liable for "causing" or "permitting" it must be shown that some person for whose criminal acts the corporation would be liable caused or permitted the commission of the offence. Knowledge on the part of an ordinary employee is not sufficient: it has to be that of someone exercising a directing mind over the company's affairs (*James & Son Ltd v Smee* supra; *Ross Hillman Ltd v Bond* supra; *Tesco Supermarkets Ltd v Nattrass* [1972] AC 153, [1971] 2 All ER 127, HL).

Summary conviction. Summary jurisdiction and procedure are mainly governed by the Magistrates' Courts Act 1980, Vol 27, title Magistrates, and by rules made under s 144 of that Act.

Standard scale. By the Criminal Justice Act 1982, ss 37(3), 75, Vol 27, title Magistrates, this means the standard scale set out in s 37(2) of that Act as amended by order made under the Magistrates' Courts Act 1980, s 143(1), in the same title. The scale as amended by the Criminal Penalties etc (Increase) Order 1984, SI 1984/447, art 3(4), Sch 4, is: level 1: £50; level 2: £100; level 3: £400; level 4: £1,000; and level 5: £2,000.

Sub-s (2): Local education authority. These authorities are defined by the Education Act 1944, ss 6(1), 114(1), Sch 1, Pt I, this part of this title ante, as read with the London Government Act 1963, s 30, Vol 26, title London, the Local Government Act 1972, ss 1(10), 20(6), 192(1), Vol 25, title Local Government, and the Local Government Act 1985, s 18(2), in the same title.

Sub-s (3): Constable. This means any person holding the office of constable (as to which, see 36 Halsbury's Laws (4th edn) paras 201 et seq), not a member of a police force holding the rank of constable. As to the attestation of constables, see the Police Act 1964, s 18, Sch 2, Vol 33, title Police, and as to their jurisdiction, see s 19 of that Act.

Reasonable cause to suspect. It is submitted that these words require not only that the person in question has reasonable cause to suspect but also that he does actually suspect; see *R v Banks* [1916] 2 KB 621, [1916–17] All ER Rep 356, and *R v Harrison* [1938] 3 All ER 134, 159 LT 95; and see also *Nakkuda Ali v Jayaratne* [1951] AC 66, PC.

The existence of the reasonable cause and of the suspicion founded on it is ultimately a question of fact to be tried on evidence and the cause of the suspicion must be sufficient to induce in a reasonable person the required suspicion; see in particular, *McArdle v Egan* (1933) 150 LT 412, [1933] All ER Rep 611, CA; *Nakkuda Ali v Jayaratne* supra; *Registrar of Restrictive Trading Agreements v W H Smith & Son Ltd* [1969] 3 All ER 1065 at 1070, [1969] 1 WLR 1460 at 1468, CA per Lord Denning MR; and *IRC v Rossminster Ltd* [1980] AC 952, [1980] 1 All ER 80 at 84, 92, 103, 104, HL.

Two months beginning with etc. The use of the words "beginning with" make it clear that in computing this period the day from which it runs is to be included; see *Hare v Gocher* [1962] 2 QB 641, [1962] 2 All ER 763, and *Trow v Ind Coope (West Midlands) Ltd* [1967] 2 QB 899 at 909, [1967] 2 All ER 900, CA. See also *Dodds v Walker* [1981] 2 All ER 609, [1981] 1 WLR 1027, HL, as to the day of expiry of periods of a month or a specified number of months. This Act was passed on 13 July 1982 and accordingly this section came into force on 13 September 1982.

Definitions. By virtue of sub-s (9) above for "voluntary school", see the Education Act 1944, s 9(2), this part of this title ante; for "aided school" and "special agreement school", see s 15 of that Act; for "further education", see s 41 of that Act; for "premises" and "school", see s 114(1) of that Act, and for "maintain", see s 114(2)(*a*) of that Act.

Education Act 1944. See this part of this title ante.

41–46 (*For ss 41, 45, 46, see Vol 25, title* Local Government; *s 42 repealed by the Public Health (Control of Disease) Act 1984, s 78, Sch 3; s 43 amends the Local Authorities (Land) Act 1963, s 3, Vol 25, title* Local Government; *s 44 amends the Local Government Act 1972, s 137, Vol 25, title* Local Government.)

Part XIII

Supplementary

47, 48 (*For ss 47(1), 48, see Vol 25, title* Local Government; *for s 47(2), see Vol 25, title* Local Government, *Vol 35, title* Public Health, *Vol 37, title* Real Property *or Vol 45, title* Theatres and Other Places of Entertainment; *for s 47(3) see Vol 45, title* Theatres and Other Places of Entertainment; *s 47(4) applies to Scotland only.*)

49 Citation and extent

(1) This Act may be cited as the Local Government (Miscellaneous Provisions) Act 1982.

(2) Subject to sections 11(2), 38(3) and 47(4) above, and to paragraph 8(2) of Schedule 6 to this Act, this Act extends to England and Wales only.

NOTE

England; Wales. For meanings, see the Interpretation Act 1978, s 5, Sch 1, Vol 41, title Statutes.

(For Schs 1, 3, Sch 7, Pts I, II, IV, see Vol 45, title Theatres and Other Places of Entertainment; Sch 2 makes amendments consequential on s 1 (see Vol 45, title Theatres and Other Places of Entertainment); for Sch 4, see Vol 47, title Trade and Industry (Pt 1); Sch 5, Pt I, inserts Pt VIIA in the Highways Act 1980, Vol 20, title Highways; Sch 5, Pt II, amends s 212 of, and Sch 21, Pt II to, and repeals s 213 of, the Town and Country Planning Act 1971, Vol 46, title Town and Country Planning; Sch 6: paras 1–3, 6 repealed by the Public Health (Control of Disease) Act 1984, s 78, Sch 3; paras 4, 5 amend the Public Health Act 1936, s 267, 346, respectively, Vol 35, title Public Health; para 7 amends the Town and Country Planning Act 1971, ss 7(4), 10(7), 15(3), 15A(6), (7), 23(9), 177(2)(a), 242(3)(f), (h), Sch 4, para 12(2), Vol 46, title Town and Country Planning; para 8 adds sub-s (8) to s 21 of the Local Government Planning and Land Act 1980, Vol 25, title Local Government; for Sch 7, Pts III, VIII–XI, see Vol 35, title Public Health; for Sch 7, Pts V–VII, XIV–XVI, see Vol 25, title Local Government; for Sch 7, Pts XII, XIII, see Vol 37 title Real Property.)

EDUCATION (FEES AND AWARDS) ACT 1983

(1983 c 40)

An Act to make provision with respect to the fees charged by universities and other institutions to students not having the requisite connection with the United Kingdom, the Channel Islands or the Isle of Man and the exclusion of such students from eligibility for certain discretionary awards [13 May 1983]

Commencement. This Act came into force on receiving the Royal Assent on 13 May 1983.

Education Acts 1944 to 1985. This Act is one of those which may be cited by this collective title; see the Further Education Act 1985, s 8(2), this part of this title post, and the Introductory Note to the Education Act 1944, this part of this title ante.

Northern Ireland. This Act does not apply; see s 3(3) post.

1 Fees at universities and further education establishments

(1) The Secretary of State may, as respects any institutions to which this section applies, make regulations requiring or authorising the charging of fees which are higher in the case of students not having such connection with the United Kingdom or any part of it as may be specified in the regulations than in the case of students having such a connection.

(2) The regulations may provide for exceptions and make different provision for different cases or purposes.

(3) This section applies to—

    (*a*) any university, university college or college, school, hall or other institution of a university;

    (*b*) any further education establishment provided by a local education authority or, in Scotland, an education authority; and

    (*c*) any other further education establishment which is substantially dependent for its maintenance on public funds and either is specified in the regulations or is of a class or description so specified.

(4) In this section "fees" includes charges however described (including charges for board and lodging) and "public funds" means assistance from a local authority or, in

Scotland, an education authority or grants under section 100(1)(*b*) of the Education Act 1944 or section 73 of the Education (Scotland) Act 1980.

(5) The power to make regulations under this section shall be exercisable by statutory instrument subject to annulment in pursuance of a resolution of either House of Parliament.

(6) This section is without prejudice to section 27(6) of the Education Act 1980 (regulations as to fees for courses of further education).

NOTES

General Note. The purpose of this section is to return to the position obtaining before the decision of the House of Lords in *Shah v Barnet London Borough Council* [1983] 1 All ER 226, [1983] 2 WLR 16, where it was held that neither the fact that a student had a home overseas nor the fact that he was resident in this country only for a specific and limited purpose, eg to attend school, necessarily prevented him from being "ordinarily resident" for the purposes of the award of educational grants. The fact that the provisions requiring or authorising differential fees are made by statutory instrument brings them within the exception to the discrimination provisions of the Race Relations Act 1976, Vol 6, title Civil Rights and Liberties, which is contained in s 41(1) of that Act.

Sub-s (1): Secretary of State. Ie one of Her Majesty's Principal Secretaries of State; see the Interpretation Act 1978, s 5, Sch 1, Vol 41, title Statutes.

United Kingdom. Ie Great Britain and Northern Ireland; see the Interpretation Act 1978, s 5, Sch 1, Vol 41, title Statutes. "Great Britain" means England, Scotland and Wales by virtue of the Union with Scotland Act 1706, preamble, Art I, Vol 10, title Constitutional Law (Pt 1), as read with s 22(1) of, and Sch 2, para 5(*a*) to, the 1978 Act. The Channel Islands and the Isle of Man are included in references to the United Kingdom in this Act; see s 3(2) post.

Sub-s (3): Local education authority. These authorities are defined by the Education Act 1944, ss 6(1), 114(1), Sch 1, Pt I, this part of this title ante, as read with the London Government Act 1963, s 30, Vol 26, title London, the Local Government Act 1972, ss 1(10), 20(6), 192(1), Vol 25, title Local Government, and the Local Government Act 1985, s 18(2), in the same title ante.

Sub-s (5): Statutory instrument; subject to annulment. For provisions as to statutory instruments generally, see the Statutory Instruments Act 1946, Vol 41, title Statutes, and as to statutory instruments which are subject to annulment, see ss 5(1), 7(1) of that Act.

Education Act 1944, s 100(1)(b); Education Act 1980, s 27(6). See this part of this title ante.

Education (Scotland) Act 1980. 1980 c 44; not printed in this work.

Regulations under this section. The Education (Fees and Awards) Regulations 1983, SI 1983/973, as amended by SI 1984/1201, SI 1985/1219, made under this section and s 2 post.

2 Discretionary awards

(1) The Secretary of State may, as respects any awards to which this section applies, make regulations authorising the adoption of rules of eligibility which confine the awards to persons having such connection with the United Kingdom or any part of it as may be specified in the regulations.

(2) The regulations may provide for exceptions and make different provision for different cases or purposes.

(3) This section applies to—

(*a*) any award under section 1(6) or 2 of the Education Act 1962 (discretionary awards by local education authorities); and

(*b*) such other awards (however described) as may be specified by the regulations, being awards in connection with courses of education or training or the undertaking of research.

(4) The power to make regulations under this section shall be exercisable by statutory instrument subject to annulment in pursuance of a resolution of either House of Parliament.

NOTES

General Note. This section gives the Secretary of State power to make regulations as to eligibility for discretionary awards which differentiate between home and overseas students. Since such power is exercisable by statutory instrument any discrimination resulting from the application of the regulations is exempted from the provisions of the Race Relations Act 1976; see s 41(1) of that Act, Vol 6, title Civil Rights and Liberties.

Secretary of State; United Kingdom; statutory instrument; subject to annulment. See the notes to s 1 ante.

Education Act 1962, ss 1(6), 2. See this part of this title ante.

Regulations under this section. The Education (Fees and Awards) Regulations 1983, SI 1983/973, as amended by SI 1984/1201, SI 1985/1219, made under this section and s 1 ante.

3 Short title, interpretation and extent

(1) This Act may be cited as the Education (Fees and Awards) Act 1983.

(2) In sections 1 and 2 above references to the United Kingdom include references to the Channel Islands and the Isle of Man.

(3) This Act does not extend to Northern Ireland.

NOTE

United Kingdom. See the note to s 1 ante.

EDUCATION (GRANTS AND AWARDS) ACT 1984

(1984 c 11)

An Act to make provision for the payment of education support grants to local education authorities in England and Wales; and to amend section 1(3)(d) of the Education Act 1962 so as to refer to the higher national diploma of the Business & Technician Education Council instead of to the corresponding diplomas of the Councils there mentioned

[12 April 1984]

Commencement. This Act came into force on 12 June 1984, two months after receiving the Royal Assent on 12 April 1984; see s 6(2) post.

Education Acts 1944 to 1985. This Act is one of those which may be cited by this collective title; see the Further Education Act 1985, s 8(2), this part of this title post, and the Introductory Note to the Education Act 1944, this part of this title ante.

Northern Ireland. This Act does not apply; see s 6(3) post.

PART I

EDUCATION SUPPORT GRANTS

1 Education support grants

(1) The Secretary of State may, in accordance with the provisions of this Part of this Act, make grants to be known as education support grants.

(2) Education support grants shall be payable to local education authorities in England and Wales in respect of expenditure incurred or to be incurred by them of any class or description specified in regulations made by the Secretary of State under this section, being expenditure for or in connection with educational purposes which it appears to him that those authorities should be encouraged to incur in the interests of education in England and Wales.

(3) Regulations under this section shall provide that any education support grant payable in pursuance of the regulations—

(a) shall only be payable in respect of prescribed expenditure incurred or to be incurred by a local education authority in a financial year to the extent to which that expenditure is approved for that year by the Secretary of State for the purposes of the regulations; and

(b) shall be payable at such rate, not exceeding 70 per cent of the expenditure so approved, as may be specified in the regulations.

(4) Regulations under this section may provide—

(a) for the time and manner of payment of any education support grant;

(b) that the payment of any such grant shall be dependent on the fulfilment of such conditions as may be determined by or in accordance with the regulations;

(c) for requiring local education authorities to whom payments have been made in pursuance of the regulations to comply with such requirements as may be so determined.

(5) Regulations under this section may provide for expenditure incurred or to be incurred by any local education authority in making payments, whether by way of maintenance, assistance or otherwise, to any body or persons who incur expenditure for or in connection with educational purposes (including another local education authority) to be treated, in such circumstances as may be specified in the regulations, as prescribed expenditure.

(6) References in this section to prescribed expenditure are to expenditure of a class or description for the time being specified under subsection (2) above; and references in this section or section 2 below to a financial year are to the period of twelve months ending with 31st March in any year.

(7) Any function of the Secretary of State under this section or section 2 below may be exercised or performed separately and differently for England and for Wales, and any reference in those sections to local education authorities in England and Wales, or otherwise relating to education in England and Wales, shall be construed accordingly.

NOTES

Sub-s (1): Secretary of State. Ie one of Her Majesty's Principal Secretaries of State; see the Interpretation Act 1978, s 5, Sch 1, Vol 41, title Statutes. See further sub-s (1) above.

This Part of this Act. Ie Pt I (ss 1–3) of this Act.

Sub-s (2): Local education authorities. Local education authorities are defined by the Education Act 1944, ss 6(1), 114(1), Sch 1, Pt I, this part of this title ante, as read with the London Government Act 1963, s 30, Vol 26, title London, the Local Government Act 1972, ss 1(10), 20(6), 192(1), Vol 25, title Local Government, and the Local Government Act 1985, s 18(2), in the same title.

England; Wales. For meanings, see the Interpretation Act 1978, s 5, Sch 1, Vol 41, title Statutes.

Appears. Statutory powers are often conferred in subjective terms, the competent authority being entitled to act, eg, when it "appears" to it or it is "satisfied" that, or when in its "opinion", a prescribed state of affairs exists, but the inherent jurisdiction of the courts to determine whether such powers have been exceeded is not readily ousted by the use of such language. See, further, 1 Halsbury's Laws (4th edn) para 22.

Sub-s (3): Prescribed expenditure. Ie expenditure of a class or description for the time being specified under sub-s (2) above; see sub-s (6) above.

Financial year. Ie the period of 12 months ending with 31 March in any year; see sub-s (6) above.

Expenditure ... approved ... by the Secretary of State. For the determination of the aggregate amount of expenditure which may be approved by the Secretary of State by regulations under sub-s (3)(a) above, see s 2 post.

Regulations under this section. The Education Support Grant Regulations 1984, SI 1984/1098, as amended by SI 1985/1070, made under this section and s 2 post.

For general provisions as to regulations under this section, see s 3 post. Note in particular, as to regulations under sub-s (2) above, s 3(2) post.

---

2 Limit on expenditure approved for grant purposes

(1) The aggregate amount of the expenditure of local education authorities in England and Wales approved for any financial year by the Secretary of State in pursuance

of section 1(3)(*a*) above shall not exceed 0.5 per cent of the amount determined by him for that year in accordance with this section.

(2) For each financial year the Secretary of State shall by regulations determine for the purposes of this section an amount representing the aggregate amount of expenditure for or in connection with educational purposes which it would in his opinion be appropriate for local education authorities in England and Wales to incur in that year, excluding—

(*a*) expenditure under section 1(1) of the Education Act 1962 (awards for university and comparable courses) or in pursuance of section 2(3) of that Act (grants to persons undergoing training as teachers);

(*b*) prescribed expenditure as defined by or by virtue of Schedule 12 to the Local Government, Planning and Land Act 1980 (expenditure of a capital nature); and

(*c*) such other heads of expenditure (if any) as appear to the Secretary of State to be appropriate to be excluded in relation to that year.

(3) Regulations under this section may determine an amount for a financial year for the purposes of this section either—

(*a*) by specifying it; or

(*b*) by providing for it to be ascertained by reference to an amount or amounts specified or to be specified in any Rate Support Grant Report made for that year under section 60 of the said Act of 1980.

(4) Any regulations made in pursuance of subsection (3)(*a*) above shall relate to one financial year only; and in arriving at the amount to be specified for a financial year by any such regulations the Secretary of State shall have regard to the matters mentioned in paragraphs (*a*) to (*d*) of section 54(4) of the said Act of 1980 so far as relating to expenditure for or in connection with educational purposes or to education services in England and Wales.

(5) Any regulations made in pursuance of subsection 3(*b*) above may determine an amount for purposes of this section for each one of a number of financial years.

(6) Regulations under this section shall be made before the beginning of the financial year to which they relate or, if they relate to two or more financial years, before the beginning of the first of those years.

NOTES

Sub-s (1): Local education authorities; England; Wales; Secretary of State. See the notes to s 1 ante.

Financial year. Ie the period of 12 months ending with 31 March in any year; see s 1(6) ante.

Sub-s (2): In his opinion; appear. See the note "Appears" to s 1 ante.

Education Act 1962, ss 1(1), 2(3). See this part of this title ante.

Local Government, Planning and Land Act 1980, ss 54(4), 60, Sch 12. See Vol 25, title Local Government.

Regulations under this section. The Education Support Grants Regulations 1984, SI 1984/1098, as amended by SI 1985/1070, made under this section and s 1 ante.

For general provisions as to regulations under this section, see s 3 post.

3 Regulations

(1) Any regulations under this Part of this Act shall be made by statutory instrument.

(2) No regulations which include provisions authorised by section 1(2) above shall be made unless a draft of the regulations has been laid before and approved by a resolution of each House of Parliament.

(3) A statutory instrument containing regulations under this Part of this Act, not

being regulations to which subsection (2) above applies, shall be subject to annulment in pursuance of a resolution of either House of Parliament.

(4) Regulations under this Part of this Act may make different provision for different cases or circumstances, and may contain such incidental, supplementary or transitional provisions as the Secretary of State thinks fit.

(5) Before making any regulations under this Part of this Act the Secretary of State shall consult such bodies representing local education authorities as appear to him to be appropriate.

NOTES

This Part of this Act. Ie Pt I (ss 1–3).

Statutory instrument; subject to annulment. For provisions as to statutory instruments generally, see the Statutory Instruments Act 1946, Vol 41, title Statutes, and as to statutory instruments which are subject to annulment, see ss 5(1), 7(1) of that Act.

Laid before Parliament. For meaning, see the Laying of Documents before Parliament (Interpretation) Act 1948, s 1(1), Vol 41, title Statutes.

Secretary of State; local education authorities. See the notes to s 1 ante.

Thinks fit; appear. See the note "Appears" to s 1 ante.

Consult. On what constitutes consultation, see, in particular, *Fletcher v Minister of Town and Country Planning* [1947] 2 All ER 496, (1947) 111 JP Jo 542; *Rollo v Minister of Town and Country Planning* [1948] 1 All ER 13, [1948] LJR 817, CA; *Re Union of Whippingham and East Cowes Benefices, Derham v Church Comrs for England* [1954] AC 245, [1954] 2 All ER 22, PC; and *Agricultural, Horticultural and Forestry Industry Training Board v Aylesbury Mushrooms Ltd* [1972] 1 All ER 280, [1972] 1 WLR 190.

4 ((*Pt II*) *Amends the Education Act 1962, s 1(3)(d), this part of this title ante.*)

Part III

General

5 Expenses of Secretary of State

Any expenses incurred by the Secretary of State in consequence of this Act shall be paid out of money provided by Parliament.

NOTES

Secretary of State. See the note to s 1 ante.

England; Wales. See the note to s 1 ante.

6 Short title, commencement and extent

(1) This Act may be cited as the Education (Grants and Awards) Act 1984.

(2) This Act shall come into force at the end of the period of two months beginning with the day on which it is passed.

(3) This Act extends to England and Wales only.

NOTES

Two months beginning with, etc. "Months" means calendar months; see the Interpretation Act 1978, s 5, Sch 1, Vol 41, title Statutes. In calculating this period the day (ie 12 April 1984) on which this Act was passed (ie received the Royal Assent) is reckoned; see *Hare v Gocher* [1962] 2 QB 641, [1962] 2 All ER 763, and *Trow v Ind Coope (West Midlands) Ltd* [1967] 2 QB 899 at 909, [1967] 2 All ER 900, CA. See also *Dodds v Walker* [1981] 2 All ER 609, HL, as to the day of expiry of periods of a month or a specified number of months. Accordingly this Act came into force on 12 June 1984.

England; Wales. See the note to s 1, ante.

FURTHER EDUCATION ACT 1985

(1985 c 47)

ARRANGEMENT OF SECTIONS

An Act to empower local education authorities to supply goods and services through further education establishments and to make loans to certain other persons to enable them to do so; to repeal section 28(b) of the Sex Discrimination Act 1975; and for connected purposes   [16 July 1985]

Education Acts 1944 to 1985. This Act is one of the Acts which may be cited by this collective title; see s 8(2) post and the Introductory Note to the Education Act 1944, this part of this title ante.
Northern Ireland. Save to the extent mentioned in s 6(3) post, this Act does not apply.

Further education establishments

1 Supply of goods and services through further education establishments

(1) For the purposes of this Act goods are supplied through a further education establishment if they result—

(*a*) from its educational activities;

(*b*) from the use of its facilities and the expertise of persons employed at it in the fields in which they are so employed;

(*c*) from ideas of a person employed at it, or of one of its students, arising out of its educational activities.

(2) For the purposes of this Act services are supplied through such an establishment—

(*a*) if they are provided by making available—

(i) its facilities;

(ii) the expertise of persons employed at it in the fields in which they are so employed;

(*b*) if they result—

(i) from its educational activities;

(ii) from ideas such as are mentioned in subsection (1)(*c*) above.

(3) For the purposes of this Act educational activities are—

(*a*) the provision of teaching and industrial and vocational training;

(*b*) the carrying out of research; and

(c) any activity incidental or ancillary to any activity mentioned in paragraph (a) or (b) above.

NOTES

Commencement. This section came into force on 16 September 1985; see s 7(3) post and the note "Two months beginning with, etc" thereto.

Further education. For meaning, see by virtue of s 8(3) post, the Education Act 1944, s 41, this part of this title ante.

2 Powers of local education authorities

(1) A local education authority shall have power—

(a) to enter into an agreement for the supply of goods or services or both through a further education establishment provided by them;

(b) to lend money for the purposes of such an agreement to a body corporate in which they have a holding such as is mentioned in subsection (8) below.

(2) A local education authority shall also have power to lend money—

(a) to a person providing a further education establishment which they are deemed to assist; or

(b) to a body corporate in which such a person has a holding such as is mentioned in subsection (8) below,

if the loan is for the purposes of an agreement for the supply of goods or services or both through the establishment which he provides.

(3) Subject to the following provisions of this section, a local education authority shall not under an agreement under subsection (1)(a) above supply goods or services for less than their open market value.

(4) Subsection (3) above does not apply to the supply of goods or services where the goods are produced, or the goods or services are supplied, in the normal course of any of the educational activities mentioned in section 1(3)(a) above, or where the supply is—

(a) for a body which is a Research Council for the purposes of the Science and Technology Act 1965; or

(b) for a body specified in an order under subsection (5) below.

(5) The Secretary of State may by order made by statutory instrument provide that any person who is specified in the order or is of a description so specified, being a person or description of persons appearing to the Secretary of State to be exercising functions of a public nature, shall be a public body for the purposes of this Act; and any statutory instrument made by virtue of this subsection shall be subject to annulment in pursuance of a resolution of either House of Parliament.

(6) An order under subsection (5) above may contain such provisions as the Secretary of State considers appropriate—

(a) for restricting the application of subsection (4)(b) above to agreements of a description specified in the order;

(b) without prejudice to paragraph (a) above, for securing the inclusion of terms imposing restrictions in any agreement to which subsection (4)(b) above applies and which is made by a body to which the order applies.

(7) For the purposes of this Act the open market value of goods or services shall be taken to be the amount of the consideration in money that would be payable for the supply by a person standing in no such relationship with any person as would affect that consideration.

(8) The holding referred to in subsections (1)(b) and (2)(b) above is a holding of not less than 20 per cent of the issued shares comprised in the share capital of the body

corporate and carrying rights to vote in all circumstances at general meetings of the body corporate.

(9) Money may be lent under this section for the purposes of an agreement either before the agreement is made or during its currency.

(10) Nothing in this section shall be construed as derogating from any powers exercisable by a local education authority apart from this section.

NOTES

Commencement. This section came into force on 16 September 1985; see s 7(3) post and the note "Two months beginning with, etc" thereto.

Sub-s (1): Supply of goods or services. As to the supply of goods through a further education establishment, see s 1(1) ante, and as to services so supplied, see s 1(2) ante.

Body corporate. For the general law relating to corporations, see 9 Halsbury's Laws (4th edn) paras 1201 et seq.

Sub-s (2): Deemed to assist. For the further education establishments which a local education authority is deemed to assist, see (by virtue of s 8(3) post) the Education Act 1944, s 114(2)(b), this part of this title ante.

Sub-s (5): Secretary of State. Ie one of Her Majesty's Principal Secretaries of State; see the Interpretation Act 1978, s 5, Sch 1, Vol 41, title Statutes. The Secretary of State here concerned is the Secretary of State for Education.

Statutory instrument; subject to annulment. For provisions as to statutory instruments generally, see the Statutory Instruments Act 1946, Vol 41, title Statutes, and as to statutory instruments which are subject to annulment, see ss 5(1), 7(1) of that Act.

Definitions. By virtue of s 8(3) post for "further education", see the Education Act 1944, s 41, this part of this title ante, and for "local education authority", see s 114(1) of that Act. Note as to "public body" sub-s (5) above, and as to "open market value" sub-s (7) above.

Science and Technology Act 1965. See Vol 10, title Constitutional Law (Pt 4). For the bodies which are Research Councils for the purposes of that Act, see s 1 thereof.

Orders under this section. Up to 1 August 1985 no orders had been made under sub-s (5) above.

3 Financial and accounting provisions

(1) Loans under this Act shall carry interest at a rate not less than such rate as may be determined by the Secretary of State with the consent of the Treasury.

(2) Without prejudice to the generality of subsection (1) above a rate may be determined in relation—

(a) to all loans under this Act; or

(b) to loans under this Act of a particular category,

and a determination may be made by reference to a rate specified by or under any other statutory provision or a rate ascertainable by such other means as the Secretary of State may with the consent of the Treasury specify.

(3) Before determining a rate the Secretary of State shall consult such bodies representing local education authorities as appear to him to be concerned and any local education authority with whom consultation appears to him to be desirable.

(4) In addition to any accounts or statements of account with they are required to keep by virtue of section 23 of the Local Government Finance Act 1982 a local education authority who exercise powers under this Act shall in respect of their exercise—

(a) keep—

(i) a general revenue account; and

(ii) such other accounts as the Secretary of State may direct; and

(b) prepare such statements of account as he may direct.

(5) Any revenue account kept by an authority under this section and any statement of account prepared by an authority under this section shall show the full cost to the authority of goods or services which are supplied under this Act and which are relevant to that account or statement.

(6) A local education authority shall use their best endeavours to secure that at the end of every year any revenue account kept by them under this section and relating to that year is in surplus.

(7) Income and expenditure attributable to the supply of goods or services in circumstances such as are mentioned in section 2(4) above are to be disregarded for the purposes of subsection (6) above, whether or not the goods or services are supplied for less than their open market value.

(8) If at the end of any year any revenue account kept by a local education authority under this section is in deficit, the amount of the deficit shall be charged—

(a) to the extent that the deficit is attributable to a particular establishment, to any fund set up by the authority for the sole purpose of meeting expenditure in relation to that establishment in connection with the authority's functions under this Act or their other functions as a local education authority;

(b) subject to paragraph (a) above, to any general fund set up by the authority for the sole purpose of meeting expenditure in connection with their functions under this Act or their other functions as a local education authority; and

(c) subject to paragraphs (a) and (b) above, to their rate fund.

(9) Without prejudice to the generality of this section, the powers conferred upon the Secretary of State by this section may be exercised separately and differently as respects England and Wales.

(10) In this section—

"rate fund"—

(a) in relation to the Inner London Education Authority, means any fund for which a precept is issued by the Greater London Council; and

(b) in relation to any other local education authority, means the county fund or general rate fund; and

"year" means a period of twelve months ending with 31st March.

NOTES

Commencement. This section came into force on 16 September 1985; see s 7(3) post and the note "Two months beginning with, etc" thereto.

Sub-s (1): Loans under this Act. Ie a loan made by a local education authority under s 2(1)(b) or s 2(2) ante.

Secretary of State. See the note to s 2 ante.

Treasury. Ie the Commissioners of HM Treasury; see the Interpretation Act 1978, s 5, Sch 1, Vol 41, title Statutes.

Sub-s (3): Consult. On what constitutes consultation, see, in particular, *Fletcher v Minister of Town and Country Planning* [1947] 2 All ER 496, (1947) 111 JP Jo 542; *Rollo v Minister of Town and Country Planning* [1948] 1 All ER 13, [1948] LJR 817, CA; *Re Union of Whippingham and East Cowes Benefices, Derham v Church Comrs for England* [1954] AC 245, [1954] 2 All ER 22, PC; and *Agricultural, Horticultural and Forestry Industry Training Board v Aylesbury Mushrooms Ltd* [1972] 1 All ER 280, [1972] 1 WLR 190.

Sub-s (5): Goods or services which are supplied under this Act. As to the supply of goods or services for the purposes of this Act, see s 1(1), (2) ante.

Sub-s (9): England; Wales. For meanings, see the Interpretation Act 1978, s 5, Sch 1, Vol 41, title Statutes.

Sub-s (10): Inner London Education Authority. For the construction of references to this body, see the Local Government Act 1985, s 18(6), Vol 25, title Local Government.

Greater London Council. This council, constituted under the Local Government Act 1972, s 8, Sch 2 (3rd edn Vol 42, pp 860, 1115), is abolished as from 1 April 1986 by the Local Government Act 1985, s 1(1)(a), Vol 25, title Local Government (most of the functions of the council being reallocated, principally to the London boroughs, by Pt II of that Act).

County fund; general rate fund. As to these funds, see the Local Government Act 1972, s 148, Vol 25, title Local Government.

Months. This means calendar months; see the Interpretation Act 1978, s 5, Sch 1, Vol 41, title Statutes.

Definitions. For "open market value", see s 2(7) ante; for "local education authority", see, by virtue of s 8(3) post, the Education Act 1944, s 114(1), this part of this title ante. Note as to "rate fund" and "year" sub-s (10) above.

Local Government Finance Act 1982, s 23. See Vol 25, title Local Government.

Teachers of physical training

4 Repeal of s 28(b) of Sex Discrimination Act 1975

In section 28 of the Sex Discrimination Act 1975 (which excepts physical training courses from the application of provisions of that Act making sex discrimination in education unlawful), paragraph (*b*) (which relates to courses for teachers of physical training) and the word "or" immediately preceding it shall cease to have effect except in relation to persons admitted to courses in an academic year beginning in a year earlier than the year in which there falls the day appointed for the coming into force of this section.

NOTES

Commencement. This section came into force on 16 September 1985; see the Further Education Act 1985 (Commencement) (No 1) Order 1985, SI 1985/1429 (made under s 7(1) post).

Day appointed for the coming into force of this section. Ie the day appointed by order made under s 7(1) post.

Sex Discrimination Act 1975, s 28. See Vol 6, title Civil Rights and Liberties.

5 Power to make corresponding provision for Northern Ireland

An Order in Council under paragraph 1(1)(*b*) of Schedule 1 to the Northern Ireland Act 1974 (legislation for Northern Ireland in the interim period) which states that it is made only for purposes corresponding to those of section 4 above—

(*a*) shall not be subject to paragraph 1(4) and (5) of that Schedule (affirmative resolution of both Houses of Parliament); but

(*b*) shall be subject to annulment in pursuance of a resolution of either House.

NOTES

Commencement. This section came into force on 16 July 1985; see s 7(2) post and the note "Day this Act is passed" thereto.

Order in Council; subject to annulment. The power to make Orders in Council is exercisable by statutory instrument; see the Statutory Instruments Act 1946, s 1(1), Vol 41, title Statutes. As to statutory instruments which are subject to annulment, see ss 5(1), 7(1) of that Act.

Up to 1 August 1985 no Order in Council had been made by virtue of this section making provision corresponding to s 4 ante in relation to Northern Ireland.

Extent. This section applies to Northern Ireland only; see s 6(3) post.

Northern Ireland Act 1974, Sch 1, para 1(1)(b). See Vol 31, title Northern Ireland (Pt 2).

Supplementary

6 Extent

(1) Sections 1 to 3 above extend to England and Wales only.

(2) Section 4 above extends to England and Wales and Scotland.

(3) Section 5 above extends to Northern Ireland only.

(4) This section and sections 7 and 8 below extend to England and Wales, Scotland and Northern Ireland.

Commencement. This section came into force on 16 July 1985; see s 7(2) post and the note "Day this Act is passed" thereto.
England; Wales. See the note to s 3 ante.

7 Commencement

(1) Section 4 above shall come into force on such day as the Secretary of State may by order made by statutory instrument appoint, and different days may be appointed under this subsection for England and Wales and for Scotland.

(2) Sections 5 and 6 above, this section and section 8 below shall come into force on the day this Act is passed.

(3) Subject to subsections (1) and (2) above, this Act shall come into force at the end of the period of two months beginning with the day on which it is passed.

Commencement. See sub-s (2) above and the note "Day this Act is passed" below.
Secretary of State. See the note to s 2 ante.
Statutory instrument. Cf the note "Statutory instrument; subject to annulment" to s 2 ante.
England; Wales. See the note to s 3 ante.
Day this Act is passed. This Act was passed (ie received the Royal Assent) on 16 July 1985.
Two months beginning with, etc. "Months" means calendar months; see the Interpretation Act 1978, s 5, Sch 1, Vol 41, title Statutes. In calculating this period the day (ie 16 July 1985) on which the Act was passed is reckoned; see *Hare v Gocher* [1962] 2 QB 641, [1962] 2 All ER 763, and *Trow v Ind Coope (West Midlands) Ltd* [1967] 2 QB 899 at 909, [1967] 2 All ER 900, CA. Accordingly ss 5–8 of this Act came into force on 16 September 1985.
Order under this section. The Further Education Act 1985 (Commencement) (No 1) Order 1985, SI 1985/1429 bringing s 4 ante into force on 16 September 1985.

8 Short title

(1) This Act may be cited as the Further Education Act 1985.

(2) The Education Acts 1944 to 1981, the Education (Fees and Awards) Act 1983, the Education (Grants and Awards) Act 1984 and this Act, except sections 4 and 5 above, may be cited together as the Education Acts 1944 to 1985.

(3) This Act, except sections 4 and 5 above, shall be construed as one with the Education Act 1944.

Commencement. This section came into force on 16 July 1985; see s 7(2) ante and the note "Day this Act is passed" thereto.
Education Acts 1944 to 1985. For all the Acts which may be cited by this collective title, see the Introductory Note to the Education Act 1944, this part of this title ante.
Construed as one. Ie the enactments in question are to be construed as if they were contained in one Act, unless there is some manifest discrepancy; see eg *Phillips v Parnaby* [1934] 2 KB 299 at 302. Accordingly, definitions in the earlier Act may be relevant to the construction of provisions of this Act (see *Solomons v R Gertzenstein Ltd* [1954] 2 QB 243, [1954] 2 All ER 625, CA; *Crowe (Valuation Officer) v Lloyds British Testing Co Ltd* [1960] 1 QB 592, [1960] 1 All ER 411, CA).
Education (Fees and Awards) Act 1983; Education (Grants and Awards) Act 1984; Education Act 1944. See this part of this title ante.

Part 3

Acquisition of Land

Table Contents

SCHOOL SITES ACT 1841

(4 & 5 Vict c 38)

ARRANGEMENT OF SECTIONS

An Act to afford further facilities for the Conveyance and Endowment of Sites for Schools
[21 June 1841]

The short title was given to this Act by the Short Titles Act 1896.

Extended application of Act. This Act applies also to schools or colleges for religious or theological training; see the School Sites Act 1852, this part of this title post. As to the application of this Act to conveyances of land for enlargement of churchyards or burial grounds, see the Consecration of Churchyards Act 1867, s 4, Vol 14, title Ecclesiastical Law (Pt 5(a)).

Gifts for educational purposes. As to the power of local education authorities to accept gifts for educational purposes, see the Education Act 1944, s 85, Pt 2 of this title ante.

School Sites Acts. By the Short Titles Act 1896, s 2, Sch 2, Vol 41, title Statutes, the following Acts may be cited together by this collective title: the School Sites Act 1841 (this Act); the School Sites Act 1844; the School Sites Act 1849; the School Sites Act 1851; the School Sites Act 1852. These Acts are all printed in this part of this title.

Construction. By virtue of the School Sites Act 1851, s 2, this part of this title post, that Act is deemed to be part of this Act. For the meaning and effect of that provision, see the note "Construed as a part" to that section.

Interpretation. See the School Sites Act 1849, s 7, this part of this title post.

Northern Ireland. This Act does not apply; see s 21 post.

1 (*Repealed by the SLR Act 1874 (No 2).*)

2 Landlords empowered to convey land to be used as sites for schools, etc

. . . Any person, being seised in fee simple, fee tail, or for life, of and in any manor or lands of freehold, copyhold, or customary tenure, and having the beneficial interest therein, . . . may grant, convey, or enfranchise by way of gift, sale, or exchange, in fee simple or for a term of years, any quantity not exceeding one acre of such land, as a site for a school for the education of poor persons, or for the residence of the schoolmaster or schoolmistress, or otherwise for the purposes of the education of such poor persons in religious and useful knowledge; provided that no such grant made by any person seised only for life of and in any such manor or lands shall be valid, unless the person next entitled to the same in remainder, in fee simple or fee tail, (if legally competent,) shall be a party to and join in such grant: Provided also, that where any portion of waste or commonable land shall be gratuitously conveyed by any lord or lady of a manor for any such purposes as aforesaid, the rights and interest of all persons in the said land shall be barred and divested by such conveyance; Provided also, that upon the said land so granted as aforesaid, or any part thereof, ceasing to be used for the purposes in this Act mentioned, the same shall thereupon immediately revert to and become a portion of the said estate held in fee simple or otherwise, or of any manor or land as aforesaid, as fully to all intents and purposes as if this Act had not been passed, any thing herein contained to the contrary notwithstanding.

NOTES

The words omitted were repealed by the SLR (No 2) Act 1888.

General Note. This section was restricted by the Commons Act 1899, s 22, Sch 1, Vol 6, title Commons, in that the consent of the Ministry of Agriculture, Fisheries and Food was usually required in the case of a grant of common land.

Reversion to grantor under the third proviso. For cases, see *A-G v Shadwell* [1910] 1 Ch 92, 79 LJ Ch 113; *Dennis v Malcolm* [1934] Ch 244, [1933] All ER Rep 293; *Re Cawston's Conveyance, Hassard-Short v Cawston* [1940] Ch 27, [1939] 4 All ER 140; *Re Ingleton Charity, Croft v A-G* [1956] Ch 585, [1956] 2 All ER 881 (whether land held on original trusts by trustees who had retained possession and obtained possessory title).

As soon as a reverter occurs, an equitable interest arises in favour of the estate interest out of which the original conveyance had been carved, and the legal estate remains with the successors in title of the persons to whom the original conveyance in fee simple or otherwise was made; see *Re Clayton's Deed Poll* [1979] 2 All ER 1133, [1979] 3 WLR 351. Cf, however, *Re Rowhook Mission Hall, Horsham* [1984] 3 All ER 179, [1984] 3 WLR 710 (on a reverter under this section, time begins to run in favour of the trustees from the time when the land ceases to be used for the purpose specified in the conveyance, since at that point the possibility of reverter matures into a fee simple absolute).

The proviso as to reverter is saved by the Law of Property Act 1925, s 7(1), Vol 37, title Real Property. It may be excluded in connection with a scheme made under the Education Act 1973, s 2, Pt 2 of this title ante.

3 Chancellor and council of the duchy of Lancaster may grant lands to the trustees of any existing or intended school—If lands cease to be used for the purposes of the Act they shall revert

And whereas it may be expedient and proper that the chancellor and council of her Majesty's duchy of Lancaster, on her Majesty's behalf, should be authorized to grant, convey, or enfranchise, to or in favour of the trustee or trustees of any existing or intended school, lands and hereditaments belonging to her Majesty in right of her said duchy, for the purposes of this Act: . . . it shall and may be lawful for the chancellor and council of her Majesty's duchy of Lancaster for the time being, by any deed or writing under the hand and seal of the chancellor of the said duchy for the time being, attested by the clerk of the council of the said duchy for the time being, for and in the name of her Majesty, ... to grant, convey, or enfranchise, to or in favour of such trustee or trustees, any lands and hereditaments to be used by them for the purposes of this Act, upon such terms and conditions as to the said chancellor and council shall seem meet; and where any sum or sums of money shall be paid as or for the purchase or consideration for such lands or hereditaments so to be granted, conveyed, or enfranchised as aforesaid, the same shall be paid by such trustee or trustees into the hands of the receiver general for the time being of the said duchy, or his deputy, and shall be by him paid, applied, and disposed of according to the provisions and regulations contained in an Act passed in the forty-eighth year of the reign of his late Majesty King George the Third, intituled "An Act to improve the land revenue of the Crown in England, and also of his Majesty's duchy of Lancaster", or any other Act or Acts now in force for that purpose: Provided always, that upon the said land so granted as aforesaid, or any part thereof, ceasing to be used for the purposes in this Act mentioned, the same shall thereupon immediately revert to and become again a portion of the possessions of the said duchy, as fully to all intents and purposes as if this Act or any such grant as aforesaid had not been passed or made; any thing herein contained to the contrary notwithstanding.

NOTES

The words omitted in the first place were repealed by the SLR (No 2) Act 1888, and those omitted in the second place were repealed by the SLR (No 2) Act 1890.

Shall revert to the duchy. The proviso as to reverter is saved by the Law of Property Act 1925, s 7(1), Vol 37, title Real Property.

Act of 48 Geo 3. The Act referred to is 48 Geo 3 c 73 (1808), which was repealed, except as to the Duchy of Lancaster, by the Crown Lands Act 1829, s 1, and is not printed in this work.

4 *(Repealed by the SLR Act 1874 (No 2).)*

5 Persons equitably entitled or under disability may convey lands for the purposes of this Act

... Where any person shall be equitably entitled to any manor or land, but the legal estate therein shall be in some trustee or trustees, it shall be sufficient for such person to convey the same for the purposes of this Act without the trustee or trustees being party to the conveyance thereof: and where any married woman shall be seised or possessed of or entitled to any estate or interest, manorial or otherwise, in land proposed to be conveyed for the purposes of this Act, she ... may convey the same for such purposes by deed, without any acknowledgement thereof; and where it is deemed expedient to purchase any land for the purposes aforesaid belonging to or vested in any infant or [person of unsound mind], such land may be conveyed by the guardian or committee of such infant, or the committee of such [person of unsound mind] respectively, who may receive the purchase money for the same, and give valid and sufficient discharges to the party paying such purchase money, who shall not be required to see to the application thereof.

NOTES

The words omitted in the first place were repealed by the SLR (No 2) Act 1888, and those omitted in the second place were repealed by the Law Reform (Married Women and Tortfeasors) Act 1935, s 5, Sch 2.

The words in square brackets were substituted by the Mental Treatment Act 1930, s 20(5), as saved by the Mental Health Act 1983, s 148, Sch 5, para 29, Vol 28, title Mental Health.

Settled land. For the power of a tenant for life to grant settled land for public purposes, including the site of a school house, see the Settled Land Act 1925, s 55, Vol 48, title Trusts and Settlements (Pt 2); as to the powers of trustees for sale of land, see the Law of Property Act 1925, s 28(1), Vol 37, title Real Property.

Exclusion. This section does not apply to persons as to whom powers are exercisable and have been exercised under the Mental Health Act 1983, s 98, Vol 28, title Mental Health; see s 113 of, and Sch 3 to, that Act.

6 Corporations, justices, trustees etc, may convey lands for the purposes of this Act

... It shall be lawful for any corporation, ecclesiastical or lay, whether sole or aggregate, and for any officers, justices of the peace, trustees, or commissioners, holding land for public, ecclesiastical, parochial, charitable, or other purposes or objects, subject to the provisions next herein-after mentioned, to grant, convey, or enfranchise, for the purposes of this Act, such quantity of land as aforesaid in any manner vested in such corporation, officers, justices, trustees, or commissioners: Provided always, that no ecclesiastical corporation sole, being below the dignity of a bishop, shall be authorized to make such grant without the consent in writing of the bishop of the diocese to whose jurisdiction the said ecclesiastical corporation is subject: Provided also, that no parochial property shall be granted for such purposes without the consent of ... the poor law commissioners, to be testified by their seal being affixed to the deed of conveyance ... ; provided also, that where any officers, trustees, or commissioners, other than parochial trustees, shall make any such grant, it shall be sufficient if a majority or quorum authorized to act of such officers, trustees, or commissioners, assembled at a meeting duly convened, shall assent to such grant, and shall execute the deed of conveyance, although they shall not constitute a majority of the actual body of such officers, trustees, or commissioners ....

NOTES

The words omitted in the first place were repealed by the SLR (No 2) Act 1888, those omitted in the second and third places were repealed by the Local Government Act 1929, s 137, Sch 12, Pt VII, and those omitted at the end of the section were repealed by the Local Government Act 1933, s 307, Sch 11, Pt IV and by the London Government Act 1939, s 207, Sch 8.

General Note. There is no provision for reverter in this section similar to that in s 2 ante.

Poor Law Commissioners. The powers of this body were transferred to the Local Government Board under the Local Government Board Act 1871, s 2, Vol 10, title Constitutional Law (Pt 4), and thence to the Minister of Health under the Ministry of Health Act 1919, s 3(1)(a), (5), Sch 1. The latter provisions were repealed by the Secretary of State for Social Services Order 1968, SI 1968/1699, which order dissolves the Minister of Health and transfers his functions to the Secretary of State.

7 Grants of land may be made to corporations or trustees, to be held by them for school purposes

... All grants of land or buildings, or any interest therein, for the purposes of the education of poor persons, whether taking effect under the authority of this Act or any other authority of law, may be made to any corporation sole or aggregate, or to several corporations sole, or to any trustees whatsoever, to be held by such corporation or corporations or trustees whatsoever, to be held by such corporation or corporations or trustees for the purposes aforesaid: Provided nevertheless, that any such grant may be made to the minister of any parish being a corporation, and the churchwardens or chapelwardens and overseers of the poor, or to the minister and kirk session of the said parish, and their successors; and in such case the land or buildings so granted shall be vested for ever thereafter in the minister, churchwardens, or chapelwardens, and overseers of the poor for the time being, or the minister and kirk session of such parish, but the management, direction, and inspection of the school shall be and remain according to the provisions contained in the deed of conveyance thereof: Provided also, that where any ecclesiastical corporation sole below the dignity of a bishop shall grant any land to trustees, other than the minister, churchwardens or chapelwardens, and overseers, for the purposes aforesaid, such trustees shall be nominated in writing by the bishop of the diocese to whose jurisdiction such corporation shall be subject; provided that where any school shall be intended for any ecclesiastical district not being a parish as hereinafter defined, it shall be sufficient if the grant be made to the minister and church or chapel warden or wardens of the church or chapel of such district, and to hold to them and their successors in office; and such grant shall enure to vest the land, subject to the conditions contained in the deed of conveyance, in such minister and the church or chapel warden or wardens for the time being.

NOTES

The words omitted were repealed by the SLR (No 2) Act 1888.

Churchwardens and overseers. The School Sites Act 1844, s 4, this part of this title post, provides that the overseers need not be made parties to the conveyance. Overseers were abolished (except as to London) by the Rating and Valuation Act 1925, s 62 (repealed in part), Vol 36, title Rating. See the Overseers Order 1927, SR & O 1927/55, as to the transfer of property (other than ecclesiastical property) of churchwardens and overseers. In what was formerly the administrative county of London (now Greater London, by virtue of the Local Law (Greater London Council and Inner London Boroughs) Order 1965, SI 1965/540, art 4) the borough councils were the overseers, under the London Government Act 1899, s 11(1) (repealed); the property of churchwardens (other than ecclesiastical property) and overseers was transferred to borough councils by s 23(3) of that Act (repealed). Metropolitan borough councils were replaced by inner London borough councils; see the London Government Act 1963, s 1(1), Sch 1, Pt I, Vol 26, title London; see also s 4(5) of that Act. In the City of London, the Common Council are the overseers; see the City of London (Union of Parishes) Act 1907, s 11, Vol 36, title Rating. The term overseers has in fact dropped out of current use.

Parish. For definition, see s 20 post.

8 Estates now vested in trustees for the purposes of education, and not subject to 3 & 4 Vict c 77 may be conveyed to the minister and churchwardens

And whereas schools for the education of the poor in the principles of the Established Church, or in religious and useful knowledge, and residences for the masters or mistresses of such schools, have been heretofore erected, and are vested in trustees not having a corporate character: ... it shall be lawful for the trustees for the time being of such last-mentioned schools and residences, not being subject to the provisions of the Act passed in the last session of Parliament, intituled "An Act for improving the conditions and extending the benefits of grammar schools," to convey or assign the same, and all their estate and interest therein, to such ministers and churchwardens and overseers of the poor of the parish within which the same are respectively situate, and their successors as aforesaid, or, being situated within an ecclesiastical district not being a parish as hereinafter defined, then to the minister and church or chapel wardens of the church or chapel of such district, and their successors, in whom the same shall thereafter remain vested accordingly, but subject to and under the existing trusts and provisions respectively affecting the same.

NOTES

The words omitted were repealed by the SLR (No 2) Act 1888.

Churchwardens and overseers. See the note to s 7 ante.

Act passed in the last session of Parliament. The Act referred to is the Grammar Schools Act 1840 (repealed).

Parish. For definition, see s 20 post.

9 Any number of sites may be granted by one person for separate schools, etc

... Any person or persons or corporation may grant any number of sites for distinct and separate schools, and residences for the master or mistress thereof, although the aggregate quantity of land thereby granted by such person or persons or corporation shall exceed the extent of one acre; provided that the site of each school and residence do not exceed that extent: Provided also, that not more than one such site shall be in the same parish.

NOTES

The words omitted were repealed by the SLR (No 2) Act 1888.

Number of sites in the same parish. See the School Sites Act 1849, s 3 post.

Parish. This term is defined for the purposes of this section in the School Sites Act 1851, s 1 post. See also s 20 of this Act post.

10 Forms of grants, etc

... All grants, conveyances, and assurances of any site for a school, or the residence of a schoolmaster or schoolmistress, under the provisions of this Act, in respect of any land, messuages, or buildings, may be made according to the form following, or as near thereto as the circumstances of the case will admit; (that is to say,)

"I [or we, or the corporate title of a corporation], under the authority of an Act passed in the   year of the reign of her Majesty Queen Victoria, intituled 'An Act for affording further facilities for the conveyance and endowment of sites for school,' do hereby freely and voluntarily, and without any valuable consideration, [or do, in consideration of the sum of   to me or us of the said   paid], grant, [alienate,] and convey to   all [description of the premises,] and all [my or our or the right, title and interest of the   ] to and in the same and every part thereof, to hold unto and to the use of the said   and his or their [heirs, or executors, or administrators, or successors,] for the purposes of the said Act, and to be applied as a site for a school for poor persons of and in the parish of and for the residence of the schoolmaster [or schoolmistress] of the said school [or for other purposes of the said school,] and for no other purposes whatever; such school to be under the management and control of [set forth the mode in which and the persons by whom the school is to be managed, directed, and inspected.] [In case the school be conveyed to trustees, a clause providing for the renewal of the trustees, and in cases where the land is purchased, exchanged, or demised, usual covenants or obligations for title, may be added.] In witness whereof the conveying and other parties have hereunto set their hands and seals, this   day of

Signed, sealed, and delivered by the said   in the presence of
                   of   ."

And no bargain and sale or livery of seisin shall be requisite in any conveyance intended to take effect under the provisions of this Act, nor more than one witness to the execution by each party ...

NOTES

The words omitted where indicated by dots in the first place in which they occur were repealed by the SLR (No 2) Act 1888, and in the second place where they occur were repealed by virtue of the Education (Scotland) Act 1945, ss 77, 88, Sch 5.

General Note. As to the acquisition of, and dealings in, land by a local education authority, see the Education Act 1944, s 90, this part of this title ante, and the Local Government Act 1972, ss 120–130, Vol 25, title Local Government.

Heirs. For the statutory authority for the abolition of words of limitation, see the Law of Property Act 1925, s 60, vol 37, title Real Property.

Parish. For definition, see s 20 post.

11 Application of purchase money for land sold by any ecclesiastical corporation sole

... Where any land shall be sold by any ecclesiastical corporation sole for the purposes of this Act, and the purchase money to be paid shall not exceed the sum of twenty pounds, the same may be retained by the party conveying, for his own benefit; but when it shall exceed the sum of twenty pounds, it shall be applied for the benefit of the said corporation, in such manner as the bishop in whose diocese such land shall be situated shall, by writing under his hand, to be registered in the registry of his diocese, direct and appoint; but no person purchasing such land for the purpose aforesaid shall be required to see to the due application of any such purchase money.

NOTE

The words omitted were repealed by the SLR (No 2) Act 1888.

12 (*Repealed by the Education (Scotland) Act 1945, ss 77, 88, Sch 5.*)

13 Ecclesiastical corporations sole to procure a certificate as to the extent of the land conveyed—Form of certificate

... When any ecclesiastical corporation sole below the dignity of a bishop shall grant any land belonging to him in right of his corporation for the purposes of this Act, he shall procure a certificate, under the hands of three beneficed clergymen of the diocese within which the land to be conveyed shall be situate, as to the extent of the land so conveyed, to be endorsed on the said deed; which certificate shall be in the form following; (that is to say,)

"We, A.B. clerk, rectory of the parish of   , C.D. clerk, rector of the parish of   , and E.F. clerk, vicar of the parish of   , being three beneficed clergymen of the diocese of   , do hereby certify, that   clerk, rector of the parish of   within the said diocese of   , being about to convey a portion of land situate in the said parish of   for the purposes of a school, under the powers of the Act passed in   year of the reign of her Majesty Queen Victoria, intituled 'An Act for affording further facilities for the conveyance and endowment of sites for schools,' we have at his request inspected and examined the portion of land, and have ascertained that the same is situate at [here describe the situation], and that the extent thereof does not exceed   acre   . As witness our hands, this   day of   at   in the county of   and diocese of
      Witness   of   ."

And until such certificate shall have been signed no such conveyance shall have any force or validity.

NOTES

The words omitted were repealed by the SLR (No 2) Act 1888.
Parish. For definition, see s 20 post.

14 Trustees of schools may sell or exchange lands or buildings

... When any land or building shall have been or shall be given or acquired under the provisions of the said first-recited Act or this Act, or shall be held in trust for the purposes aforesaid, and it shall be deemed advisable to sell or exchange the same for any other more convenient or eligible site, it shall be lawful for the trustees in whom the legal estate in the said land or building shall be vested, by the direction or with the consent of the managers and directors of the said school, if any such there be, to sell or exchange the said land or building, or part thereof, for other land or building suitable to the purposes of their trust, and to receive on any exchange any sum of money by way of effecting an equality of exchange, and to apply the money arising from such sale or given on such exchange in the purchase of another site, or in the improvement of other premises used or to be used for the purposes of such trust; provided that where the land shall have been given by any ecclesiastical corporation sole, the consent of the bishop of the diocese shall be required to be given to such sale or exchange before the same shall take place: Provided also, that where a portion of any parliamentary grant shall have been or shall be applied towards the erection of any school, no sale or exchange thereof shall take place [unless the Secretary of State consents].

NOTES

The words omitted were repealed by the SLR (No 2) Act 1890; the words in square brackets were substituted by the SL(R) Act 1978.

First recited Act. The Act referred to is 6 & 7 Will 4 c 70 (1836), which was repealed by s 1 (repealed) of this Act.

Secretary of State. Ie one of Her Majesty's Principal Secretaries of State; see the Interpretation Act 1978, s 5, Sch 1, Vol 41, title Statutes. The Secretary of State here concerned is the Secretary of State for Education and Science or the Secretary of State for Wales as the case may be.

15, 16 *(S 15 repealed by the SL(R) Act 1978; s 16 repealed by the SLR Act 1874 (No 2).)*

17 No schoolmaster to acquire a life interest by virtue of his appointment

... No schoolmaster or schoolmistress to be appointed to any school erected upon land conveyed under the powers of this Act shall be deemed to have acquired an interest for life by virtue of such appointment, but shall, in default of any specific engagement, hold his office at the discretion of the trustees of the said school.

NOTE

The words omitted were repealed by the SLR (No 2) Act 1888.

18, 19 *(S 18 repealed by the Rent Act 1965, s 52, Sch 7, Pt II; s 19 repealed by the SL(R) Act 1978.)*

20 Definition of the term "parish"

... The term "parish" in this Act shall be taken to signify every place separately maintaining its own poor, and having its own overseers of the poor and church or chapel wardens.

NOTES

The words omitted were repealed by the SLR (No 2) Act 1888.

Parish. See the School Sites Act 1851, s 1, this part of this title post, for a definition applying specially to s 9 ante.

Overseers of the poor. As to their abolition, see the note "Churchwardens and overseers" to s 7 ante.

21 Extent of Act

This Act shall not extend to Ireland.

22, 23 *(S 22 repealed by the SLR Act 1874 (No 2) and the Education (Scotland) Act, ss 77, 88, Sch 5; s 23 repealed by the SLR Act 1874 (No 2).)*

SCHOOL SITES ACT 1844

(7 & 8 Vict c 37)

An Act to secure the Terms on which Grants are made by Her Majesty out of the Parliamentary Grant for the Education of the Poor; and to explain the Act of the Fifth Year of the Reign of Her present Majesty, for the Conveyance of Sites for Schools   [19 July 1844]

The short title was given to this Act by the Short Titles Act 1896.

Extended application of Act. This Act applies also to schools or colleges for religious or theological training; see the School Sites Act 1852, this part of this title post.

School Sites Acts. For the Acts which may be cited by this collective title, see the Introductory Note to the School Sites Act 1841, this part of this title ante.

Interpretation. See the School Sites Act 1849, s 7, this part of this title post.

Northern Ireland. This Act does not apply.

[1] The terms and conditions upon which parliamentary aid has been given towards the building of schools, if not inserted in deed of conveyance of site, or deed of declaration of trust, to be binding on trustees and managers as if so inserted—Provided they are set forth in some document signed by trustees or donor of site

Where any grant hath been made or shall hereafter be made out of any sums of money heretofore granted or hereafter to be granted by Parliament for the purposes of education in Great Britain, under the advice of any committee of the council on education for the time being, upon terms and conditions to provide for the inspection of the school by an inspector appointed or to be appointed by her Majesty . . . which shall not be inserted in the conveyance of the site of the school, or in the deed declaring the trusts thereof, and such grant shall be made in aid of the purchase of the site, or of the erection, enlargement, or repair of the school, or of the residence of the master or mistress thereof, or of the furnishing of the school, such terms and conditions shall be binding and obligatory upon the trustees or managers of the said school or other the premises for the time being, in like manner and to the like effect as though they had been inserted in the conveyance of the site of the said school, or in the declaration of the trusts thereof; and henceforth all personal obligations entered into for the purpose of securing the fulfilment of such terms and conditions shall, so far as they relate thereto, but no further, be null and void: Provided nevertheless, that such terms and conditions shall have been or shall be set forth in some document in writing, signed by the trustees of the said school or the major part of them, or by the party or parties conveying the site, in the case where there shall have been a voluntary gift thereof.

NOTES

The words omitted were repealed by the SLR Act 1891.

Committee of Council on Education. This committee was constituted by Order in Council, dated 10 April 1839. Later it became known as the Education Department (Interpretation Act 1889, s 12(6) (repealed)), the functions of which were transferred to the Board of Education (Board of Education Act 1899, s 2(1) (repealed)), and from the Board to the Minister of Education (Education Act 1944, s 2(1), Pt 2 of this title ante). The functions of the Minister of Education were transferred to the Secretary of State by the Secretary of State for Education and Science Order 1964, SI 1964/490.

The responsibility for primary and secondary education in Wales has been transferred to the Secretary of State for Wales by the Transfer of Functions (Wales) Order 1970, SI 1970/1536, but under that order the Secretary of State for Education and Science retains functions relating to the qualifications, training, supply, remuneration and superannuation of teachers and the appointment of HM Inspectors. Subsequently by the Transfer of Functions (Wales) (No 2) Order 1978, SI 1978/274 the Secretary of State for Wales was enabled to exercise in relation to Wales the functions of the Secretary of State for Education and Science in connection with further education (excluding universities), as regards training and supply of teachers (excluding matters relating to their qualification (including medical fitness), probation, misconduct, remuneration or superannuation), with regard to making regulations and paying grants thereunder to persons training as teachers and to certain mature students, and regarding nominations to the Ancient Monuments Board for Wales.

2 Trustees of ancient endowed schools may apply for parliamentary aid for rebuilding, etc, and consent to such school being open to inspection

. . . Where the major part of the trustees of any endowed school for the education of the poor duly appointed under the terms of the deed of endowment, or, when such deed cannot be found or cannot be acted upon, of the persons who shall be in the possession of the endowment, and shall be acting in the execution of the trusts or the reputed trusts thereof, shall, and in cases where there shall be a visitor of such school with the consent of such visitor in writing, apply for aid out of such parliamentary grant to enable them to rebuild, repair, or enlarge the school belonging to such endowment, or the residence of the master or mistress thereof, or to furnish such school, and shall in writing assent to the said school being open to inspection on behalf of her Majesty . . . if the said committee shall deem fit to advise that any such grant shall be made, it shall immediately after the making of such grant, and thenceforth from time to time, be lawful for any inspector of schools appointed by her Majesty . . . in conformity with the terms contained in the writing testifying such consent as aforesaid, to enter the said school at all reasonable hours in the day for the purpose of inspecting and examining the state and condition of the school and the scholars thereat, and of making such report thereon as he shall deem fit.

NOTES

The words omitted were repealed by the SLR Act 1891.

Said committee. See the note "Committee of Council on Education" to s 1 ante.

Inspector . . . appointed by her Majesty. This power of appointment is exercised on the recommendation of the Secretary of State by virtue of the Education Act 1944, s 77(2), Pt 2 of this title ante.

3 (Repealed by the Charities Act 1960, s 48(2), Sch 7, Pt II.)

4 Site may be granted under the said Act to the minister and churchwardens and their successors

And whereas it was provided by the said Act that grants of land or buildings, or any interest therein, for the purposes of the education of poor persons, might be made to the minister of any parish, being a corporation, and the churchwardens or chapelwardens and overseers of the poor and their successors, and it is sometimes found inexpedient or impracticable to introduce the overseers as parties to the legal estate: Be it therefor enacted, that such grants may be made to the minister and churchwardens of any parish, such minister being the rector, vicar, or perpetual curate thereof, whether endowed or not, to hold to them and their successors, subject to the provisions contained in the deed of conveyance thereof for the management, direction, and inspection of the school and premises.

NOTES

Said Act. The Act referred to is the School Sites Act 1841, which was mentioned in s 3 of this Act (repealed); see s 7 of that Act ante.

Churchwardens and overseers. See the note to the School Sites Act 1841, s 7, this part of this title ante.

5 Rector, vicar, or perpetual curate may, with consent of patron and bishop, grant part of glebe under the said Act

... If the rector, vicar, or perpetual curate of any parish shall be desirous of making a grant of any land for the purposes and under the powers of the said Act, being part of the glebe or other possessions of his benefice, and shall, with the consent of the patron of the said benefice, and of the bishop of the diocese within which the same shall be situated, grant the same to the minister and church or chapel wardens, or to the minister, church or chapel wardens, and overseers of the poor, of the said parish, such grant shall be valid, and shall thenceforth enure for the purposes of the trust set forth therein, if otherwise lawful, notwithstanding such minister is the party making the grant.

NOTES

The words omitted were repealed by the SLR Act 1891.

General Note. By the Law of Property Act 1925, s 72, Vol 37, title Real Property, a person may convey land to himself jointly with another person.

Overseers. See the note "Churchwardens and overseers" to the School Sites Act 1841, s 7, this part of this title ante.

Said Act. The Act referred to is the School Sites Act 1841, which was mentioned in s 3 of this Act (repealed); see especially s 6 of that Act, this part of this title ante.

6 *(Repealed by the SLR Act 1874 (No 2).)*

SCHOOL SITES ACT 1849

(12 & 13 Vict c 49)

An Act to extend and explain the Provisions of the Acts for the granting of Sites for Schools
[28 July 1849]

The short title was given to this Act by the Short Titles Act 1896.

Extended application of Act. This Act also applies to schools or colleges for religious or theological training; see the School Sites Act 1852, this part of this title post.

As to the application of this Act to conveyances of land for enlargement of churchyards or burial grounds, see the Consecration of Churchyards Act 1867, s 4, Vol 14, title Ecclesiastical Law (Pt 5).

School Sites Acts. For the Acts which may be cited by this collective title, see the Introductory Note to the School Sites Act 1841, this part of this title ante.

Construction. By virtue of the School Sites Act 1851, s 2, this part of this title post, that Act is deemed to be part of this Act. For the meaning and effect of that provision, see the note "Construed as a part" to that section.

Northern Ireland. This Act does not apply.

[1] Apportionment of rents and fines where part only of lands under lease is conveyed

... If part only of any lands comprised in a lease for a term of years unexpired shall be conveyed or agreed to be conveyed for the purposes of the School Sites Act 1841, the rent payable in respect of the lands comprised in such lease, and any fine certain or fixed sum of money to be paid upon any renewals thereof, or either of such payments, may be apportioned between the part of the said lands so conveyed or agreed to be conveyed and the residue thereof; and such apportionment may be settled by agreement between the parties following, that is to say, the lessor or other the owner, subject to such lease, of the lands comprised therein, the lessee or other the party entitled thereto by virtue of such lease or any assignment thereof for the residue of the term thereby created, and the party to whom such conveyance as aforesaid for the purposes of the School Sites Act 1841 is made or agreed to be made; and when such apportionment shall so be made it shall be binding on all underlessees and other persons and corporations whatsoever, whether parties to the said agreement or not.

NOTES

The words omitted were repealed by the SLR Act 1891.
Definitions. For "land", "lease" and "owner", see s 7 post.
School Sites Act 1841. See this part of this title ante.

2 Liabilities of tenants, and remedies of landlords, as to the lands not conveyed

... In case of any such apportionment as aforesaid, and after the lands so conveyed or agreed to be conveyed as aforesaid shall have been conveyed, the lessee, and all parties entitled under him to the lands comprised in the lease not included in such conveyance, shall, as to all future accruing rent, and of all future fines certain or fixed sums of money to be paid upon renewals, be liable only to so much of the rent, and of such fines or sums of money, as shall be apportioned in respect of such last-mentioned lands; and the party entitled to the rent reserved by the lease shall have all the same rights and remedies for the recovery of such portion of the rent as last aforesaid as previously to such apportionment he had for the recovery of the whole rent reserved by such lease; and all the covenants, conditions, and agreements of such lease, except as to the amount of rent to be paid, and of fines or sums of money to be paid upon renewals, in case of any apportionment of the same respectively, shall remain in force with regard to that part of the land comprised in the lease which shall not be so conveyed as aforesaid, in the same manner as they would have done in case such part only of the land had been included in the lease.

NOTES

The words omitted were repealed by the SLR Act 1891.
Definitions. For "land" and "lease", see s 7 post.

3 Limitation of land to be granted in same parish

... Nothing in the said Act contained shall prevent any person or corporation from granting any number of sites for separate and distinct schools in the same parish, provided the aggregate quantity of land granted by such person in the same parish shall not exceed the extent of one acre.

NOTES

The words omitted were repealed by the SLR Act 1891.
Parish. This term is defined, for the purposes of this section, in the School Sites Act 1851, s 1, this part of this title post.
Said Act. The Act referred to is the School Sites Act 1841, mentioned in s 1 ante. See s 9 of that Act, this part of this title ante.

4 Sites for schools for instruction of masters, etc, of elementary schools

... It shall be lawful for all persons, being ... absolute owners or tenants in tail in possession ..., to grant, convey, or enfranchise, by way of gift, sale, or exchange, any quantity of land, not exceeding in the whole five acres, to any corporation sole or aggregate, or to several corporations sole, or to any trustees whatsoever, to be held, applied and used by such corporation or corporations or trustees in and for the erection of school buildings and premises thereon for the purpose of educating and instructing, and of boarding during the time of such education and instruction, persons intended to be masters or mistresses of elementary schools for poor persons, and for the residence of the principal or master or mistress and other officers of such institution; ... Provided always, that it shall be lawful for the trustees of such school buildings and premises to allow the same to be applied and used, concurrently with the education and instruction of such masters or mistresses, for the purpose of boarding other persons, and of educating and instructing the said persons in religious and useful knowledge.

NOTES

The words omitted, except in the last place, were repealed by the SLR Act 1891; those omitted in the last place were repealed by the Charities Act 1960, s 48(2), Sch 7, Pt II.

General Note. This section contains no reverter clause; cf the School Sites Act 1841, s 2, this part of this title ante.

Elementary school. By virtue of the Education Act 1944, s 120(1)(a), Pt 2 of this title ante, this Act is to be construed as if for references to an elementary school there were substituted references to a county or voluntary school.

Tenant in tail. An entailed interest may still subsist as an equitable interest and will then devolve as formerly; see the Law of Property Act 1925, s 130(4), Vol 37, title Real Property.

Definitions. For "land" and "owner", see s 7 post.

5 Power to convey to corporations as trustees

And whereas the absolute owners of land may grant, subject to the regulations and provisions prescribed by the statutes in such behalf, any quantity of such land to trustees, to be held upon charitable purposes; and it would be beneficial that they should be authorized to exercise such power in respect of lands granted for the sites or for the endowment of the last-mentioned schools, or of schools for poor persons, by vesting the same so as to secure it permanently for the purpose of the trust, without the necessity of subsequent renewals of the deeds of trust: Be it therefor enacted, that where any such person shall be lawfully entitled to convey an estate in land to trustees, to hold the same upon any charitable use, and shall be desirous of conveying the same for the purposes of the Acts herein-before referred to, or this Act, or for the endowment of such schools, such person may grant and convey the same to any corporation or corporations as aforesaid, to be held in trust for such purposes, whatever may be the quantity of land or extent of the estate so to be granted and conveyed.

NOTES

Acts herein-before referred to. The repealed preamble to this Act recited the School Sites Act 1841 and the School Sites Act 1844, both this part of this title ante.

Definitions. For "land" and "owner", see s 7 post.

6 (Repealed by the SL(R) Act 1969.)

7 Interpretation

. . . Except in cases where there shall be something in the subject or context repugnant to such construction, words occurring in this Act and the above-recited Acts importing the singular number shall include the plural number, and words importing the plural number shall include the singular number; and words importing the masculine gender only shall include females; and the word "land" shall include messuages, houses, lands, tenements, hereditaments, and heritages, of every tenure; and the word "lease" shall include an under-lease, agreement for a lease, and missive of lease; and the word "owner" shall include any person or corporation enabled under the provisions of the School Sites Act 1841, to convey lands for the purposes thereof.

NOTES

The words omitted were repealed by the SLR Act 1891.

Above-recited Acts. The repealed preamble to this Act recited the School Sites Act 1841 and the School Sites Act 1844, both this part of this title ante.

8 *(Repealed by the SLR Act 1875.)*

SCHOOL SITES ACT 1851
(14 & 15 Vict c 24)

An Act to amend the Acts for the granting of Sites for Schools   [24 July 1851]

The short title was given to this Act by the Short Titles Act 1896.

School Sites Acts. For the Acts which may be cited by this collective title, see the Introductory Note to the School Sites Act 1841, this part of this title ante.

Northern Ireland. This Act does not apply.

1 Definition of parish in recited sections

The word parish in the sections of the Statutes herein referred to shall, in the case of any parish which has heretofore been or shall hereafter be divided by lawful authority into two or more ecclesiastical districts, whether confined to such parish, or comprising also any part of another parish, be construed with reference to such parish to signify each such ecclesiastical district.

NOTE

Statutes herein referred to. The repealed preamble to this Act recited the School Sites Act 1841 (see s 9 of that Act), and the School Sites Act 1849 (see s 3 of that Act), both this part of this title ante.

2 Construction

This Act shall be construed as and be deemed to be a part of the said recited Acts, except so far as it amends the same.

Construed as ... a part. Ie the enactments in question are to be construed as if they were contained in one Act, unless there is some manifest discrepancy; see eg *Phillips v Parnaby* [1934] 2 KB 299 at 302. Accordingly, definitions in the earlier Act may be relevant to the construction of provisions of this Act (see *Solomons v R Gertzenstein Ltd* [1954] 2 QB 243, [1954] 2 All ER 625, CA; *Crowe (Valuation Officer) v Lloyds British Testing Co Ltd* [1960] 1 QB 592, [1960] 1 All ER 411, CA).

Said recited Acts. The repealed preamble to this Act recited the School Sites Act 1841 and the School Sites Act 1849, both this part of this title ante.

SCHOOL SITES ACT 1852

(15 & 16 Vict c 49)

An Act to extend the Provisions of the several Acts passed for the Conveyance of Sites for Schools   [30 June 1852]

The short title was given to this Act by the Short Titles Act 1896.

School Sites Acts. For the Acts which may be cited by this collective title, see the Introductory Note to the School Sites Act 1841, this part of this title ante.

Northern Ireland. This Act does not apply.

[1] Provisions of recited Acts as to conveyances and endowments

... All the provisions contained in the said recited Acts or any of them in relation to the conveyance and endowment of sites for such schools as are contemplated by the provisions of the said Acts respectively, shall apply to and be construed to be applicable to the cases of such schools as are hereinafter specified; (that is to say), schools or colleges for the religious or educational training of the sons of yeomen or tradesmen or others, or for the theological training of candidates for holy orders, which are erected or maintained in part by charitable aid, and which in part are self-supporting, in the same or the like manner as if such schools or colleges as last aforesaid had been expressly specified in the School Sites Act 1841 and the said subsequent Acts, and the same or the like powers had been thereby given for or in relation to the conveyance and endowments of sites for such schools or colleges, and for the residences of schoolmasters, or otherwise in connexion therewith, as are by the said Acts given for or in reference to the conveyance and endowment of sites for schools falling within the provisions of those Acts: Provided always, that no ecclesiastical corporation, sole or aggregate, shall be authorized to grant any site under this Act, except for schools or colleges which shall be conducted upon the principles of and be in union with the Church of England ... as by law established; and that no ecclesiastical corporation, aggregate or sole, shall grant, by way of gift, and without a valuable consideration, for any of the purposes of this Act, any greater quantity of land in the whole than two acres; and that no other person or persons or corporation not coming within the class or description of persons empowered by the second section of the School Sites Act 1841, to convey land for sites as therein mentioned, shall grant, by way of sale for a valuable consideration, for any of the purposes of this Act, any greater quantity of land in the whole than two acres, or shall grant any land whatever for any of the purposes of this Act by way of gift and without a valuable consideration, anything in the said recited Acts or herein-before contained to the contrary notwithstanding.

NOTES

The words omitted were repealed by the SLR Act 1892.

In so far as this Act applies the Trustee Appointment Act 1850 (repealed) (see the note "Said recited Acts" to this section) it ceases to have effect, subject to a saving, by virtue of the Charities Act 1960, s 35(6), Vol 5, title Charities.

Quantity of land. Conveyances under this section are limited to two acres. Cf conveyances under the School Sites Act 1841, s 2, this part of this title ante, which are limited to one acre.

Church of England and Ireland. The union of the churches of England and Ireland effected by the Union with Ireland Act 1800, Vol 31, title Northern Ireland (Pt 2), was dissolved by the Irish Church Act 1869 (not printed in this work).

School Sites Act 1841. See this part of this title ante.

Said recited Acts. The repealed preamble to this Act recited the following Acts: the School Sites Act 1841; the School Sites Act 1844; the School Sites Act 1849; the Trustee Appointment Act 1850 (repealed (except as respects Northern Ireland), with a saving, by the Charities Act 1960, ss 35(6), 48(2), 49(2), Sch 7, Pt I), and the School Sites Act 1851. The Acts of 1841, 1844, 1849 and 1851 are all printed in this part of this title ante.

SCHOOL GRANTS ACT 1855
(18 & 19 Vict c 131)

An Act to render more secure the Conditions upon which Money is advanced out of the Parliamentary Grant for the Purposes of Education   [14 August 1855]

The short title was given to this Act by the Short Titles Act 1896.
Northern Ireland. This Act does not apply.

1 Restriction on sale, etc, of premises, for purchase of which a grant has been made out of money granted by Parliament for education

Where any grant hath been made or shall hereafter be made out of any sums of money heretofore granted or hereafter to be granted by Parliament for the purposes of education in Great Britain, under the advice of any Committee of the Council on Education . . . , to the trustees, managers, or other persons applying on behalf of any school, with the consent of the trustees or persons holding the legal estate thereof, for or towards the purchase of the site, or the erection, enlargement, or repair of the school, or the residence of the master or mistress, or the furnishing such school or residence, no sale, exchange, or mortgage of the premises in respect of which such grant hath been or may hereafter be made, in exercise of any power contained in the conveyance or other deed relating thereto, or under any other legal authority, shall be valid unless either [the Secretary of State gives his written consent] . . . , or the amount of the grant which shall have been made as aforesaid shall be repaid to . . . the Treasury . . . ; and whenever any grant as aforesaid shall be hereafter made, a memorandum, to be signed by one of the Lords Commissioners of the Treasury . . . , shall be endorsed upon some one of the title deeds relating to the school, certifying to the fact of the grant having been made upon such application, and for some such purpose as aforesaid, and referring to this Act; and in any case in which any grant as aforesaid shall have been already made, so soon as such memorandum shall have been endorsed and signed on any such deed, all bonds, covenants, or other personal obligations, heretofore given or entered into to prevent the exercise of any such power of sale, exchange, or mortgage without such consent as aforesaid, shall, so far as they relate to such exercise, but no further, be annulled.

NOTES

The words omitted in the second place were repealed by the SL(R) Act 1981; the other words omitted were repealed by the SLR Act 1892. The words in square brackets were substituted by the SL(R) Act 1978.

Committee of the Council on Education. See the note to the School Sites Act 1844, s 1, this part of this title ante.

Secretary of State. Ie one of Her Majesty's Principal Secretaries of State; see the Interpretation Act 1978, s 5, Sch 1, Vol 41, title Statutes. The Secretary of State here concerned is the Secretary of State for Education and Science or the Secretary of State for Wales as the case may be; see the second paragraph of the note "Committee of Council on Education" to the School Sites Act 1844, s 1, this part of this title ante.

Written. Expressions referring to writing are, unless the contrary intention appears, to be construed as including references to other modes of representing or reproducing words in a visible form; see the Interpretation Act 1978, s 5, Sch 1, Vol 41, title Statutes.

Consent. As to what amounts to consent within the meaning of this section, see *Re Mill Lane Land, Everton, Re Liverpool Education (Emmanuel School Purchase) Order* 1929, *ex p Liverpool Corporation* [1937] 4 All ER 197, 81 Sol Jo 921.

2 Saving as to purchasers for value without notice, etc

Nothing herein contained shall affect any purchaser for a valuable consideration without notice, nor be deemed to apply to any school in respect of any such grant heretofore made without any such bond, covenant, or other personal obligations, or conditions as to sale, exchange, or mortgage, having been entered into by the trustees or persons holding the legal estate in such schools and the Committee of Council on Education.

NOTE

Committee of Council on Education. See the note to the School Sites Act 1844, s 1, this part of this title ante.

TECHNICAL AND INDUSTRIAL INSTITUTIONS ACT 1892

(55 & 56 Vict c 29)

An Act to facilitate the Acquisition and Holding of Land by Institutions for promoting Technical and Industrial Instruction and Training   [27 June 1892]

This Act is saved by the Local Government Act 1972, s 131(1)(*b*), (2)(*a*), Vol 25, title Local Government.
Northern Ireland. This Act was repealed in relation to Northern Ireland by the Education (Northern Ireland) Order 1980, SI 1980/1958, arts 10, 11, Schedule.

1 Short title

This Act may be cited as the Technical and Industrial Institutions Act 1892.

2 Definition of institution

This Act applies to every institution established, whether before or after the passing of this Act, for effecting all or any of the following purposes, that is to say:

(i) To give technical instruction within the meaning of the Technical Instruction Act 1889;

(ii) To provide the training, mental or physical, necessary for the above purpose;

(iii) In connexion with the purposes before mentioned, to provide workshops, tools, scientific apparatus and plant of all kinds, libraries, reading rooms, halls for lectures, exhibitions, and meetings, gymnasiums, and swimming baths, and also general facilities for mental and physical training, recreation, and amusement, and also all necessary and proper accommodation for persons frequenting the institutions;

and every such institution is in this Act referred to as the institution.

NOTES

Institution. A technical trade school has been held to be any institution within the meaning of this section; see *Re Stanley's Trust Deed, Stanley v A-G* (1910) 26 TLR 365.

Technical Instruction Act 1889. Repealed, except as to London, by the Education Act 1902, ss 25(3), 27(1), Sch 4, Pt I (repealed), and as to London, by the Education (London) Act 1903, s 1 (repealed). By virtue of the Education Act 1921, s 171(2) (repealed), references to that Act are to be construed as references to Pt VI (ss 70–79) of the Education Act 1921. The last-mentioned Act was repealed by the Education Act 1944, s 121 ante and Sch 9 (repealed).

3 Governing body

(1) The governing body of the institution may be any body corporate, council, public authority, local authority, commissioners, directors, committee, trustees, or other body of persons, corporate or unincorporate, willing to undertake, or elected or

appointed for the purpose of undertaking, or having, the government and management of the institution.

(2) The governing body may make byelaws and rules for the management and conduct of the institution.

NOTE

The institution. For definition, see s 2 ante.

4 Incorporation of 8 & 9 Vict c 18; 23 & 24 Vict c 106

The Lands Clauses Consolidation Act 1845 and the Lands Clauses Consolidation Acts Amendment Act 1860 (except the provisions of those Acts relating to the purchase and taking of lands otherwise than by agreement, and with respect to the entry upon lands by promoters of the undertaking, and with respect to determining the amount of purchase money by valuation of surveyors), are hereby incorporated in this Act.

NOTES

General Note. As to the acquisition of, and dealings in, land by a local education authority, see the Education Act 1944, s 90, this part of this title ante; and the Local Government Act 1972, ss 120–131, Vol 25, title Local Government.

Lands Clauses Consolidation Act 1845; Lands Clauses Consolidation Acts Amendment Act 1860. See Vol 9, title Compulsory Acquisition.

5 Power to take land by agreement

The governing body of the institution may by agreement enter on, take, and use any land required by them for the purposes of the institution, and such land may be conveyed either to the governing body or to trustees for the governing body.

NOTE

The institution. For definition, see s 2 ante.

6 Conveyance may be by way of sale, exchange, or gift

(1) A conveyance of land may be made to the governing body of the institution or to trustees for the governing body either for valuable consideration in money, or in consideration of a rentcharge, or by way of exchange for other land, or, subject as in this Act provided, by way of free gift, and without any consideration.

(2) A conveyance under this Act by a person having an equitable estate shall operate to pass any bare outstanding legal estate vested in a trustee.

NOTES

Conveyance of land. See *Re Stanley's Trust Deed, Stanley v A-G* (1910) 26 TLR 365 (direction in will to executors to execute conveyance).

The institution. For definition, see s 2 ante.

7 Conveyances by limited owners

(1) A conveyance under this Act by a person not entitled to dispose absolutely for his own benefit of the land proposed to be conveyed (other than a conveyance on a sale or exchange for the best consideration in money, or by way of rent-charge, or in land to be reasonably obtained) shall be subject to the following restrictions and provisions:

(a) It shall not in itself, or in addition to any land conveyed under this Act by the same person, comprise more than two acres in the whole in any one county, city, or borough:

(b) It shall be made either with the consent of the person, if any, entitled to the next estate of freehold in remainder for the time being, or with the approval of the High Court of Justice.

(2) Every application to the Court for an Order approving a conveyance under this Act shall be by summons in chambers, and shall, subject to the Acts regulating the Court, be assigned to the Chancery Division.

(3) On any such application the Court may direct notice to be served on such persons, if any, as it thinks fit.

(4) On any such application the Court shall have regard to the circumstances of the settled estate, the wants of the neighbourhood, and the interests of the persons entitled, in remainder, and the Court, if it thinks fit under all the circumstances of the case, may make an order approving the proposed conveyance. Such order, if the Court thinks fit, may be made on such terms and conditions, if any, as the Court thinks proper; but no such order shall be made if the application is opposed by any person entitled in remainder, unless the Court is of opinion that the opposition is unreasonable, or the interest of the person opposing so remote that it may properly be disregarded.

NOTE

Summons in chambers. As to proceedings in chambers in the Chancery Division, see RSC Ord 32, rr 1, 14.

8 Institution to be public

Every institution for which land has been acquired under an exercise of the powers conferred by this Act shall be open generally either to all persons or to all persons within specified limits as to age, qualification, or otherwise, and either without payment or on specified terms as to times of attendance and payment of subscriptions or fees or otherwise, but so that no preference be given to any person or class of persons within the specified limits.

NOTE

Institution. For definition, see s 2 ante.

9 Site may be sold or exchanged

(1) Land acquired under the powers of this Act shall not be used otherwise than for the purposes of an institution within the meaning of this Act, but, with the consent of the Charity Commissioners, may be sold or may be exchanged for other land.

(2) The governing body or their trustees may execute conveyances and do all acts necessary to effectuate a sale or exchange.

(3) On a sale, the receipt of the governing body or of the trustees for the governing

body shall be a sufficient discharge for the purchase money, and such money shall, as soon as convenient, be invested in the purchase of other land.

(4) Land purchased or taken in exchange under this section shall be devoted to the same purposes and be liable to the same incidents as originally were applicable to or affected the land sold or given in exchange.

(5) Money arising by sale may, until reinvested in the purchase of land, be invested in the names of the governing body or of trustees for the governing body in any manner in which trust money is for the time being by law authorised to be invested; and all dividends and income on investments so made and all the resulting income shall be invested in like manner so as to accumulate in the way of compound interest, and be added to capital until the capital is reinvested in the purchase of land.

NOTES

Charity Commissioners. The powers of the Charity Commissioners relating to charities held solely for educational purposes were transferred to the Board of Education by the Board of Education (Powers) Orders in Council 1900 to 1902, SR & Os 1900/600, 1901/587 and 1902/647; the functions of the Board of Education were transferred to the Minister of Education by the Education Act 1944, s 2, Pt 2 of this title ante.

The Charities Act 1960, s 48(2), Sch 7, Pt I, repealed the above-mentioned Orders in Council and by s 2 of that Act, made provision regarding the exercise of these functions by the Charity Commissioners and the Minister of Education jointly; that section was repealed by the Education Act 1973, s 1, Sch 2, Pt III.

Institution. For interpretation, see s 2 ante.

10 (*Repealed by the Charities Act 1960, s 48(2), Sch 7, Pt II.*)

11 Extent of Act

This Act shall not extend to Scotland.

Part 4

Teachers' Superannuation and Pensions

Table of Contents

ELEMENTARY SCHOOL TEACHERS (SUPERANNUATION) ACT 1898

(61 & 62 Vict c 57)

ARRANGEMENT OF SECTIONS

An Act to provide for Superannuation and other Annuities and Allowances to Elementary School Teachers certificated by the Education Department   [12 August 1898]

Increase of pensions. Pensions payable under the Elementary School Teachers (Superannuation) Acts 1898 to 1912 are subject to increase under the Pension (Increase) Act 1971, ss 4, 5, Sch 2, Pt I, para 17, Vol 33, title Pensions and Superannuation.

Extension of Act. This Act was extended to Jersey by the Elementary School Teachers Superannuation (Jersey) Act 1900, this part of this title post.

Elementary School Teachers (Superannuation) Acts 1898 to 1912. By the Elementary School Teachers (Superannuation) Act 1912, s 4 post, the following Acts may be cited together by this collective title: the Elementary School Teachers (Superannuation) Act 1898 (this Act); the Elementary School Teachers Superannuation (Isle of Man) Act 1900; the Elementary School Teachers Superannuation (Jersey) Act 1900; and the Elementary School Teachers (Superannuation) Act 1912. The Acts of 1900 and 1912 are printed in this part of this title post.

Northern Ireland. This Act does not apply; see s 13 post.

1 Elementary school teachers certificated after commencement of the Act

(1) . . .

(2) In the case of a teacher who becomes a certificated teacher after the commencement of this Act, the following provisions shall, subject to rules under this Act, apply:—

> (*a*) His certificate shall expire on his attaining the age of sixty-five years, or if the Education Department, on account of his special fitness, allow his service to

continue for a further limited time, then on the expiration of that limited time;

(b) The teacher shall, while serving in recorded service, contribute to the deferred annuity fund under this Act at the rate, if a man, of [£3.60], and if a woman, of [£2.40] a year ...

(c) On his attaining the age of sixty-five years, or on any later date at which his certificate expires, he shall be entitled, out of the deferred annuity fund, to such annuity for the remainder of his life in respect of his contributions to that fund as may be fixed by the tables under this Act, but he shall not be entitled to any return of contributions or to any benefits in respect of his contributions other than that annuity;

(d) On his attaining the age of sixty-five years, or on any later date at which his certificate expires, if he has contributed to the deferred annuity fund in accordance with this Act, and his years of recorded service are not less than half the number of years which have elapsed since he became certificated, the Treasury may grant to him, out of moneys provided by Parliament, an annual superannuation allowance calculated at the rate of [one pound] for each complete year of recorded service.

(3), (4) ...

(5) ["Recorded service" means, for the purposes of this Act, such service in the capacity of a certificated teacher in any educational establishment in respect of which grants are paid by the Minister as is recorded by the Minister for the purposes of this Act;] *"Recorded service" for the purposes of this Act shall be such service in the capacity of certificated teacher in a public elementary school, not being an evening school, as is recorded by the Education Department, and may include such service as is so recorded in the capacity, within the meaning of the Education Code, either of a teacher in a training college, or of organising teacher, or of teacher of a central class for pupil teachers, or in such other capacity in or connected with public elementary schools as may be for the time being prescribed, or in the capacity of a certificated teacher in a certified reformatory or industrial school*; but no service after the teacher attains the age of sixty-five years, shall be recorded service for the purpose either of contribution to the deferred annuity fund, or of determining the amount of any allowance under this Act.

NOTES

Sub-s (1) was repealed by the Teachers (Superannuation) Act 1925, s 23(3), and sub-ss (3), (4) were repealed by the Elementary School Teachers (Superannuation) Act 1912, s 1(1).

The words and figures in sub-s (2)(b) were substituted by the Elementary School Teachers (Superannuation) Act 1912, s 1(1) and subsequently changed to decimal currency by virtue of the Decimal Currency Act 1969, s 10(1), Vol 10, title Constitutional Law (Pt 3); the words omitted from that paragraph were repealed by s 1(1) of the 1912 Act. The words in square brackets in sub-s (2)(d) were substituted by s 1(2) of that Act.

The words in square brackets in sub-s (5) were substituted for the words printed in italics by the Teachers (Superannuation) Act 1945, s 11(1); the words in square brackets apply in relation to service on or after 1 April 1945 and the words in italics in relation to service before that date.

Elementary school. References to an elementary school or a public elementary school are to be construed as references to a county school or voluntary school; see the Education Act 1944, s 120(1)(a), Pt 2 of this title ante.

Commencement of this Act. S 14 (repealed) provided that this Act was to come into operation on 1 April 1899.

Education Department. The functions of the Education Department were transferred to the Board of Education (Board of Education Act 1899 (repealed), s 2(1)) and from the Board to the Minister of Education. References to the Education Department were to be construed as references to the Minister of Education or the Ministry of Education (Education Act 1944, s 2(1), Pt 2 of this title ante). The functions and property of the Minister of Education were transferred to the Secretary of State, the Ministry of Education was dissolved, and consequential provision for the construction of enactments, etc was made, by the Secretary of State for Education and Science Order 1964, SI 1964/490. The functions of the Secretary of State in relation to remuneration and superannuation of teachers are not transferred by the Transfer of Functions (Wales) Order 1970, SI 1970/1536 or the Transfer of Functions (Wales) No 2 Order 1978, SI 1978/274.

Sub-s (2)(b): While serving in recorded service. For permission to contribute whilst not so employed, see s 6(1) post.

Sub-s (2)(b), (c): Deferred annuity fund. As from 1 April 1919 the deferred annuity fund ceased to exist, and references to contributions to the deferred annuity fund were substituted by references to contributions towards deferred annuities, and references to payment out of the deferred annuity fund were substituted by references to payment by the National Debt Commissioners (School Teachers (Superannuation) Act 1918, s 12 (repealed)). The Teachers (Superannuation) Act 1956, s 22 (repealed) made provision for the payment of deferred annuities under this Act by the Minister of Education (now the Secretary of State) instead of by the National Debt Commissioners.

Sub-s (2)(d): Superannuation allowance. The superannuation allowance under sub-s (2)(d) is in addition to any annuity under sub-s (2)(c). As to payment of annuities and allowances, see s 9 post. As to forfeiture of allowances for misconduct, see s 8 post.

Definitions. For "certificated teacher", "certificate" and "Education Code", see s 11 post. Note as to "recorded service", sub-s (5) above.

2 Allowances to incapacitated teachers

(1) Where a teacher satisfies the Treasury in the prescribed manner that he—

(a) has served a number of years of recorded service not less than ten and not less than half the years which have elapsed since he became certificated; and

(b) has not at the date of the application been for more than the prescribed time unemployed in recorded service; and

(c) has become permanently incapable, owing to infirmity of mind or body, of being an efficient teacher in a public elementary school; and

(d) is not excluded by the prescribed disqualifications;

the Treasury may, subject to the prescribed conditions and to the provisions of this Act, grant to such teacher out of moneys provided by Parliament an annual allowance (in this Act called "a disablement allowance") not exceeding—

(a) if the teacher is a man, twenty pounds for ten complete years of recorded service, with the addition of [£1.50] for each complete additional year of recorded service; and

(b) if the teacher is a woman, fifteen pounds for ten complete years of recorded service, with the addition of [one pound] for each complete additional year of recorded service; and

(c) in any case, the total annual sum which the teacher might obtain from an annuity and superannuation allowance under this Act by continuing to serve until the age of sixty-five years.

(2) If the grantee of a disablement allowance attains the age of sixty-five years, any annuity which would otherwise be payable to the grantee out of the deferred annuity fund shall, except where the allowance has ceased by reason of the grantee being again employed as a teacher in recorded service, be paid to the Treasury and applied as they direct . . . and, in that case, the Treasury shall not award any superannuation allowance to the grantee.

(3) A disablement allowance shall be reconsidered by the Treasury at intervals not exceeding three years; and the rules shall provide for the suspension, cessation, or reduction of the allowance in whole or in part, if the prescribed conditions are not complied with or the prescribed disqualifications apply, and those disqualifications shall deal with the cases of persons who have caused or increased their infirmity by their own misconduct or default, or who marry or cease to be incapable . . .

NOTES

The words and figures in square brackets in sub-s (1) were substituted by the Elementary School Teachers (Superannuation) Act 1912, s 1(3) and changed to decimal currency by virtue of the Decimal Currency Act 1969, s 10(1), Vol 10, title Constitutional Law (Pt 3). The words omitted from sub-s (2) were repealed by the School Teachers (Superannuation) Act 1918, s 12(4), and those omitted from sub-s (3) were repealed by s 13(3) of that Act.

Sub-s (2): Award of superannuation allowance. This is modified in certain cases by the Elementary School Teachers (Superannuation) Act 1912, s 2(1), this part of this title post.

Sub-s (3): Reconsideration of disablement allowance by the Treasury. Reconsideration at intervals of not more than three years is no longer obligatory where the Treasury so direct; see the Elementary School Teachers (Superannuation) Act 1912, s 2(2), this part of this title post.

Deferred annuity fund. See the note to s 1 ante.

Definitions. For "certificated teacher" and "prescribed", see s 11 post; for "recorded service", see s 1(5) ante.

3 Collection of contributions and deferred annuity fund arising therefrom

(1) The contributions under this Act from certificated teachers shall be paid to the Education Department at the prescribed time and in the prescribed manner by the teachers or their employers; and the receipt of the Education Department for the amount of a contribution paid by the employer of a teacher shall be a good discharge for the like amount of remuneration otherwise payable to the teacher.

(2) The contributions so received by the Education Department shall be paid to the National Debt Commissioners ...

(3)–(6) ...

NOTES

The words omitted were repealed by the School Teachers (Superannuation) Act 1918, s 12(4).

Education Department. See the note to s 1 ante.

Definitions. For "certificated teacher" and "prescribed", see s 11 post.

4, 5 *(S 4 repealed by the School Teachers (Superannuation) Act 1918, s 12(4); s 5 is spent.)*

6 Rules

(1) The Treasury and the Education Department may make rules for carrying into effect this Act, and shall provide thereby—

(a) for permitting certificated teachers to pay contributions to the deferred annuity fund during any interval not exceeding six months in which they are not employed in recorded service, and for reckoning the time in respect of which such contributions are made, as if it were recorded service;

(b) for the application of an annuity or allowance under this Act when payable to a person who is of unsound mind, or otherwise incapable of giving a receipt;

(c) for the suspension of all or any part of an allowance when the grantee is wholly or partly maintained out of any public money; and

(d) for the payment of any sum under [£5,000] due on the death of a person without the production of probate or other proof of the title of the personal representative of such person.

(2) All rules made under this section shall be laid, as soon as may be, before both Houses of Parliament.

NOTES

The reference to £5,000 is substituted for a reference to £1,500 by virtue of the Administration of Estates (Small Payments) (Increase of Limit) Order 1984, SI 1984/539, in relation to deaths occurring after 11 May 1984.

Education Department. See the note to s 1 ante.

Person of unsound mind. Sub-s (1)(b), so far as it applies in relation to persons of unsound mind, was repealed by the Mental Health Act 1959, s 149(2), Sch 8, Pt I (repealed).

£5,000. This figure may be further increased by order; see the Administration of Estates (Small Payments) Act 1965, ss 1(1), 6(1), (2), (4), Vol 17, title Executors and Administrators.

Laid ... before ... Parliament. For meaning, see the Laying of Documents before Parliament (Interpretation) Act 1948, s 1(1), Vol 41, title Statutes.

Definitions. For "certificated teacher", see s 11 post; for "recorded service", see s 1(5) ante.

Rules under this section. Elementary School Teachers Superannuation Rules 1919, SR & O 1920/2298, as amended by SI 1950/60 and by the Administration of Estates (Small Payments) Act 1965, ss 1(1), 7(5) and Sch 1, Pt III, Vol 17, title Executors and Administrators.

7 Decision of Treasury and Education Department

Any question which arises as to the application of any section of this Act to any person, or as to the amount of any annuity or allowance under this Act, or as to the grant, refusal, suspension or cessation of any such allowance, shall be referred to the Treasury, and any question as to the reckoning of any service for any purpose of this Act shall be referred to the Education Department, and the decision of the Treasury or Education Department on any question so referred shall be final.

NOTE

Education Department. See the note to s 1 ante.

8 Forfeiture for misconduct

(1) Where the certificate of a teacher is suspended or cancelled by the Education Department, the teacher shall not be entitled to any disablement allowance under this Act unless the certificate is restored by the Department.

(2) Where the Education Department certify to the Treasury that a recipient of any superannuation allowance, or disablement allowance under this Act, has been proved to them to have been guilty of any act or conduct which, if he had continued to serve as a teacher, would have justified them in suspending or cancelling his certificate, the Treasury shall suspend or determine the allowance in whole or in part.

NOTES

Education Department. See the note to s 1 ante.
Disablement allowance. See s 2 ante.
Certificate. For definition, see s 11 post.

9 As to payment and assignment of annuities and allowances

(1) Every annuity and allowance under this Act shall be payable . . . at such times and payable and apportionable in such manner as the Treasury may fix.

(2) Every assignment of or charge on, and every agreement to assign or charge, any annuity or allowance to a teacher under this Act, whether payable presently or at some future date shall be void, and on the bankruptcy of the teacher the annuity or allowance shall not pass to any trustee or other person acting on behalf of the creditors, but this provision shall be without prejudice to any order of the Court made under section fifty-three of the Bankruptcy Act 1883, or any corresponding enactment in Scotland or Ireland.

NOTES

The word omitted was repealed by the Teachers (Superannuation) Act 1956, s 21.
Bankruptcy Act 1883, s 53. Repealed by the Bankruptcy Act 1914, s 168(1), Sch 6. See now s 51 of that Act, Vol 4, title Bankruptcy and Insolvency.

10 (*Repealed by the Theft Act 1968, s 33(3), Sch 3, Pt I.*)

11 Definitions

In this Act, unless the context otherwise requires—

The expression "certificated teacher" means a teacher who is recognised under the Education Code as a certificated teacher for public elementary schools:

The expression "certificate" includes any document issued by the Education Department, which recognises a teacher as a certificated teacher:

The expression "Education Code" means such minutes of the Education Department as are for the time being in force for the purpose of the Elementary Education Act 1870:

The expression "prescribed" means prescribed by rules under this Act.

NOTES

Construction. This Act is to be construed as one with the Elementary School Teachers (Superannuation) Act 1912; see s 4 of that Act, this part of this title post.

Certificated teacher. This definition applies only in relation to periods before 1 April 1945. In relation to any subsequent period the expression "certificated teacher" was defined by the Teachers (Superannuation) Act 1945, s 11(2) (repealed by the Teachers' Superannuation Act 1965, s 8(1), (2), Sch 3, Pt II), as meaning, for the purposes of this Act, any person who would for the time being have been recognised as a certificated teacher under the regulations of the Minister which were in force with respect to such recognition immediately before 1 April 1945 if those regulations had remained in force thereafter.

Education Department. See the note to s 1 ante.

Elementary Education Act 1870. Repealed.

12 *(Repealed by the Education (Scotland) Superannuation Act 1919, s 10, Schedule.)*

13 Extent of Act

This Act shall not extend to Ireland.

14 *(Repealed by the SLR Act 1908.)*

15 Short title

This Act may be cited as the Elementary School Teachers (Superannuation) Act 1898.

ELEMENTARY SCHOOL TEACHERS SUPERANNUATION (JERSEY) ACT 1900

(63 & 64 Vict c 40)

An Act to extend the Elementary School Teachers (Superannuation) Act 1898 to Teachers serving in the Island of Jersey, and to service as a Teacher in that Island

[6 August 1900]

Increase of pensions. Pensions payable under the Elementary School Teachers (Superannuation) Acts 1898 to 1912 are subject to increase under the Pensions (Increase) Act 1971, ss 4, 5, Sch 2, Pt I, para 17, Vol 33, title Pensions and Superannuation.

1 Extension of 61 & 62 Vict c 57, to service as a teacher in the Island of Jersey

Subject to the provisions of this Act, the Elementary School Teachers (Superannuation) Act 1898 (in this Act referred to as the principal Act), shall apply to teachers serving in the Island of Jersey and to service as a teacher in that Island, as it applies to teachers serving in England or Scotland and to service as a teacher in England or Scotland.

NOTES

General Note. Cf the Elementary School Teachers (Superannuation) Act 1912, s 3, this part of this title post, as to the application of that Act to Jersey.

Elementary School Teachers (Superannuation) Act 1898. See this part of this title ante.

2 Payment by Island of whole or part of superannuation or disablement allowances

Recorded service in the Island of Jersey shall not be reckoned as such service for the purpose of annual superannuation allowances or disablement allowances under the principal Act, unless provision is made and maintained to the satisfaction of the Treasury by the legislature of the Island—

> (i) for the grant and payment of any such allowances, in the case of a teacher the whole of whose recorded service has been service in the Island, by the Government of the Island out of Island Funds; and
>
> (ii) in the case of the grant of any such allowance to a teacher whose recorded service has been partly service in the Island and partly service elsewhere, for the payment by the Government of the Island out of Island Funds of a part of that allowance proportionate or assignable to the period of the recorded service in the Island.

NOTE

Principal Act. This is defined in s 1 ante as the Elementary School Teachers (Superannuation) Act 1898, this part of this title ante.

3 Option of existing teachers to accept Act

Section five of the principal Act (which relates to the application of the Act to existing teachers) shall as respects any such teacher who has been serving in the Island of Jersey at any time after the commencement of the principal Act, and has not already accepted that Act, be read as if the period of twelve months after the commencement of this Act were substituted for the period of one year after the commencement of the principal Act as the maximum time to be prescribed within which the option to accept the principal Act may be exercised.

NOTE

Principal Act. This is defined in s 1 ante as the Elementary School Teachers (Superannuation) Act 1898, this part of this title ante.

4 Supplemental modifications

(1) The power to grant an annual superannuation allowance or a disablement allowance under sections one and two of the principal Act shall be exercised in the case of a teacher the whole of whose recorded service has been service in the Island of Jersey, by or on behalf of the Government of Jersey, instead of by the Treasury, and any allowance granted under the power so exercised shall not be paid out of moneys provided by Parliament.

Paragraph (*d*) of subsection (2) of section one of the principal Act, and sections two, seven, and eight of that Act, shall accordingly be construed as if as respects the superannuation and disablement allowances of such teachers "the Government of Jersey" were substituted for "the Treasury," and "Island Funds" for "moneys provided by Parliament."

(2) Section nine of the principal Act shall apply in the Island of Jersey as if the words "or in the Island of Jersey" were added at the end of the section.

(3) Sub-section three of section five of the principal Act shall be construed as if the words "or the legislature or Government of the Island of Jersey" were added after the word "Parliament."

(4) Section eleven of the principal Act shall be construed as if the words "or as respects the Island of Jersey the corresponding law in force in that Island" were added at the end of the definition of "Education Code."

NOTE

Principal Act. This is defined in s 1 ante as the Elementary School Teachers (Superannuation) Act 1898, this part of this title ante.

---

5 Short title

This Act may be cited as the Elementary School Teachers Superannuation (Jersey) Act 1900.

ELEMENTARY SCHOOL TEACHERS (SUPERANNUATION) ACT 1912

(2 & 3 Geo 5 c 12)

An Act to amend the Elementary School Teachers (Superannuation) Act 1898, as originally enacted and as applied by any other Act   [7 August 1912]

Increase of pensions. See the Introductory Note to the Elementary School Teachers (Superannuation) Act 1898, this part of this title ante.
Northern Ireland. This Act does not apply.

1 (*Amends the Elementary School Teachers (Superannuation) Act 1898, ss 1(2)(b), (d), 2(1), 5(2)(a) ante.*)

2 Supplemental provisions as to annuities and allowances

(1) Where a disablement allowance granted under the principal Act has been determined by the Treasury, whether before or after the passing of this Act, and the person to whom it was granted attained the age of sixty-five on or after the first day of April nineteen hundred and twelve or hereafter attains that age, he shall, notwithstanding anything in subsection (2) of section two of the principal Act, be entitled to the like deferred annuity and may be granted the like superannuation allowance as if no disablement allowance had ever been granted to him.

(2) Notwithstanding anything in subsection (3) of section two of the principal Act a disablement allowance need not be reconsidered at intervals of not [more] than three years in any case where the Treasury so direct.

NOTES

The word in square brackets was substituted by the School Teachers (Superannuation) Act 1918, s 13(4).

Principal Act. This was defined in s 1(1) as the Elementary School Teachers (Superannuation) Act 1898, this part of this title ante.

3 Application to Isle of Man and the Island of Jersey

Nothing in this Act shall affect a teacher serving in the Isle of Man or the Island of Jersey or in respect of his service as a teacher in such Island unless and until the Legislature of the Isle of Man or the Island of Jersey, as the case may be, adopts this Act or any provisions thereof, and, if either such Legislature does adopt this Act or any provisions thereof, the Elementary School Teachers Superannuation (Isle of Man) Act 1900, or the Elementary School Teachers Superannuation (Jersey) Act 1900, as the case may be, shall be construed as if for references therein to the principal Act there were substituted references to the principal Act as amended by this Act or by the provisions adopted, as the case may be ...

NOTES

The words omitted at the end of this section were repealed by the SLR Act 1927.

Elementary School Teachers Superannuation (Isle of Man) Act 1900. Repealed by the SL(R) Act 1977.

Elementary School Teachers Superannuation (Jersey) Act 1900. See this part of this title ante.

4 Short title

This Act may be cited as the Elementary School Teachers (Superannuation) Act 1912, and shall be construed as one with the principal Act, and that Act, the Elementary School Teachers Superannuation (Isle of Man) Act 1900, the Elementary School Teachers Superannuation (Jersey) Act 1900 and this Act may be cited together as the Elementary School Teachers (Superannuation) Acts 1898 to 1912.

NOTES

Construed as one. Ie the enactments in question are to be construed as if they were contained in one Act, unless there is some manifest discrepancy; see eg *Phillips v Parnaby* [1934] 2 KB 299 at 302. Accordingly, definitions in the earlier Act may be relevant to the construction of provisions of this Act (see *Solomons v R Gertzenstein Ltd* [1954] 2 QB 243, [1954] 2 All ER 625, CA; *Crowe (Valuation Officer) v Lloyds British Testing Co Ltd* [1960] 1 QB 592, [1960] 1 All ER 411, CA).

Principal Act. This was defined in s 1(1) as the Elementary School Teachers (Superannuation) Act 1898, this part of this title ante.

Elementary School Teachers Superannuation (Isle of Man) Act 1900. Repealed by the SL(R) Act 1977.

Elementary School Teachers Superannuation (Jersey) Act 1900. See this part of this title ante.

ELECTIONS

Table of Contents

Cross References

Preliminary Note

Parliamentary and local government elections

Parliamentary and local government franchise and its exercise, the conduct of elections and the questioning of elections are wholly governed by statute law and subordinate legislation, the principal statute in this context being the Representation of the People Act 1983 (referred to in this note as "the Act").

The franchise. By virtue of s 1(1) of the Act a person entitled to vote as an elector at a parliamentary election in any constituency is one who (*a*) is resident there on the qualifying date (as to which date, see s 4 of the Act); and (*b*) on that date and on the date of the poll is not subject to any legal incapacity to vote (age apart) and is either a Commonwealth citizen or a citizen of the Republic of Ireland; and (*c*) is of voting age (18 years or older) on the date of the poll. Identical provision is made by s 2(1) of the Act as to persons entitled to vote as electors at a local government election in any electoral area in England or Wales. Ss 14–17 of the Act make special provision to enable members of the forces or those employed outside the United Kingdom in the service of the Crown or by the British Council, and the spouses of such persons, to vote. As to the extension of the franchise to British citizens overseas, see the Representation of the People Act 1985, ss 1–4 post, as from a day to be appointed under s 29(2) of that Act.

Registration. A person is nót entitled to vote as an elector unless registered (ss 1(2), 2(2) of the Act). Registration officers have the duty to prepare and publish in each year registers of parliamentary and local government electors and a person who may be entitled to vote is entitled to be registered therein (ss 8–13 of the Act).

Voting at elections. The place and manner of voting at parliamentary and local government elections are governed by ss 18–30 and 31–40, respectively, of the Act. These sections include provisions as to the division of constituencies and electoral divisions into polling districts; voting in person; absent voters; voting by proxy; and the functions of returning officers. In particular, s 21 provides that parliamentary elections are to be conducted in accordance with the rules set out in Sch 1 to the Act, and s 36 provides that elections of councillors for local government areas are to be conducted in accordance with rules made under that section by the Secretary of State. Supplementary provisions as to local government elections are contained in ss 46–48 of the Act; and ss 49 to 59 of the Act contain further provisions applicable to both parliamentary and local government elections, in particular with regard to the corrupt and illegal practices list, registration expenses and appeals to the county court from decisions of registration officers. Ss 60–66 make provision as to offences by voters, penalties for breach of official duty and the requirement of secrecy.

The election campaign. Pt II (ss 67–119) of the Act contains matters concerning the election campaign itself, covering such matters as election agents, election expenses, publicity by post and broadcasting, and the use of schools and rooms for meetings. Failure to comply with certain of those provisions are described as corrupt or illegal practices.

Election petitions. By virtue of s 120 of the Act, no parliamentary election and no return to Parliament may be questioned except by a parliamentary election petition presented in accordance with Pt III (ss 120–186) thereof. Presentation and service is to be in accordance with s 121 and within the time limits specified by s 122, and the petition is tried by an election court, constituted in accordance with s 123. The validity of an election under the Local Government Act 1972 may be questioned by an election petition in the circumstances mentioned in s 127 of the Act, and where that section applies that is the only method of questioning the petition; presentation is in accordance with s 128 and within the time limits specified by s 129, and the petition is tried by an election court constituted in accordance with s 130. The procedure to be followed on all election petitions is laid down by ss 136–157 of the Act, and at the conclusion of the trial the election court is to determine whether the person (member) whose election (or return) is complained of, or any and what other person, was duly elected (or returned), or whether the election was void; that determination is final to all intents and purposes. Further action, in the case of a parliamentary election petition, is by direction of the House of Commons (s 144(7) of the Act); the consequences of a void local election are stated in s 135 of the Act.

Corrupt and illegal practices. Election offences consist of corrupt practices, illegal practices, and illegal payment, employment or hiring (the third category in certain circumstances constituting illegal practice). The provisions creating the individual offences are listed in the notes to the 1983 Act, s 168 (corrupt practices), s 169 (illegal practices) and s 175 (illegal payments, etc), which sections also prescribe the penalties for those offences. The principal provisions of the Act concerning such offences are ss 158–160 (consequences on the finding by an election court of corrupt or illegal practices); ss 161–163 (duty of the Director of Public Prosecutions to report corrupt practice by certain persons); ss 164–166 (avoidance of elections and striking off voters); s 167 (application for relief); ss 168–173 (prosecutions); s 174 (mitigation and remission of incapacities). General provisions as to prosecutions are contained in ss 176–181 of the Act.

Representation of the People Act 1985. The provisions of the Representation of the People Act 1985 which are printed in this title (which are partly yet to come into force) give effect to proposals for election reform contained in the Government Reply to the First Report of the Home Affairs Committee, Session 1982–83, on the Representation of the People Acts HC 32–1 (Cmnd 9140).

Ss 1–4 extend the parliamentary franchise (including the right to vote at European Assembly elections) to British citizens who are resident abroad for the period of five years after their departure; ss 5–9 replace with modifications the provisions currently contained in ss 19–22 and 32–34 of the Representation of the People Act 1983 relating to the manner of voting at parliamentary elections in the United Kingdom and local government elections in Great Britain; s 10 makes special provision as to absent voters who are in Northern Ireland on election day; s 11 and Sch 2 contain consequential amendments; and s 12 creates offences in connection with overseas voters' declarations and applications for absent votes. Up to 1 August 1985 no order had been made (under s 29(2)) bringing the above provisions into force.

Ss 13, 14 (both of which are in force) amend the 1983 Act by increasing the deposit paid by candidates at parliamentary elections but reducing the number of votes below which the deposit is forfeited, and by increasing certain expense limits, respectively.

Ss 15–17 (of which s 16 only, which relates to certain local elections, is in force) provide for the combination or postponement of polls taking place on the same day; s 18 (in force) changes the ordinary day of local government elections to 8 May for 1986 only and amends the existing power (s 37(b) of the 1983 Act) to make alterations to that day; s 19 (partly in force) makes amendments relating to the timing of elections; s 21 (not in force) permits co-opting at an ordinary election of parish or community councillors; s 22 (in force) relates to the prescribing of Welsh versions of forms; s 23 and Sch 3 (in force) effect amendments to the penalties for certain offences under the 1983 Act; ss 24, 27 and Schs 4, 5 (which are partly in force) make miscellaneous and consequential amendments and repeals.

Elections (Northern Ireland) Act 1985. This title also contains the Elections (Northern Ireland) Act 1985, the principal purpose of which is to strengthen safeguards against personation at elections in Northern Ireland. The Act makes certain amendments to the parliamentary election rules (set out in the Representation of the People Act 1983, Sch 1) and provides for the creation of various offences relating to personation.

Parliamentary constituencies and redistribution of seats

"Constituency" is defined by the House of Commons (Redistribution of Seats) Act 1949, s 4, as an area having separate representation in the House of Commons. The constituencies themselves are set out in Sch 1 to the Representation of the People Act 1948, as affected by Orders in Council made under the 1949 Act, and each returns a single member.

Since the share of the individual voter in representation in the House of Commons is decreased if his constituency, though still only electing one member, should become larger in population in relation to others, provision was made by the House of Commons (Redistribution of Seats) Acts of 1944 and 1947 (both repealed) for establishing permanent boundary commissions for the purpose of the continuous review of the distribution of seats at parliamentary elections. The commissions continue in existence under the House of Commons (Redistribution of Seats) Act 1949, s 1. They are required to keep under review the representation of the electorate in the House of Commons, and to submit to the Secretary of State reports recommending the constituencies into which the United Kingdom should be divided or that no such change is necessary; see ss 2 and 3 of the 1949 Act and the House of Commons (Redistribution of Seats) Act 1958, s 2. The rules for the redistribution of seats are set out in Sch 2 to the 1949 Act, as in part explained by s 3 of the 1958 Act; these rules are amended in their application to Northern Ireland by the House of Commons (Redistribution of Seats) Act 1979, s 1. As to the constitution of the Commissions, see Sch 1, Pt I to the 1949 Act, and s 1 of the 1958 Act. As to the officers and expenses of the Commissions, see Pt II of Sch 1 to the 1949 Act, and as to their procedure, see Pt III of that Schedule and s 4 of the 1958 Act. (For the functions of the Boundary Commissions, other than the Boundary Commission for Northern Ireland, in relation to elections to the Assembly of the European Communities, see the European Assembly Elections Act 1978, Sch 2.)

The European Assembly

The statute law concerning elections to the Assembly of the European Communities is contained in the European Assembly Elections Act 1978, as amended by the European Assembly Elections Act 1981 and by the Representation of the People Act 1983. As to the Assembly constituencies, see Sch 1, para 1 and Sch 2 to the 1978 Act, and the orders noted to Sch 2.

Election to the Assembly is by the simple majority system in Great Britain and by the single transferable vote system in Northern Ireland; see s 3 of, and Sch 1, para 2 to, the 1978 Act. For provisions relating to expenses of Assembly elections, see s 6 of that Act, and for provisions relating to the times of elections and returning officers, see Sch 1, paras 3 and 4 to that Act.

The provisions of the Representation of the People Act 1983 and certain regulations made under that Act are applied with modifications to Assembly elections by the European Assembly Elections Regulations 1984, SI 1984/137, and the European Assembly Elections (Northern Ireland) Regulations 1984, SI 1984/198, both made under para 2 of Sch 1 to the 1978 Act; see generally the Introductory Note to the 1983 Act.

3 EDW 1

(The Statute of Westminster the First) (1275)

Chapters 1–4 (*Cc 1, 3, 4 repealed by the SLR Act 1863 (as respects England) and the SL(I)R Act 1872 (as respects Ireland); c 2 repealed by 7 & 8 Geo 4 c 27 (1827), s 1 (as respects England) and 9 Geo 4 c 53 (1828), s 1 (as respects Ireland).*)

Chapter 5. Freedom of election

And because elections ought to be free, the King commandeth upon great forfeiture, that [no man[1]] by force of arms, nor by malice, or menacing, shall disturb any to make free election.[2]

NOTES

The numbered notes below give alternative wordings which indicate inconsistencies in the sources from which the text of this Act is derived.

[1] No great man nor other.

[2] *MS Tr 1 joins to this sentence the beginning of the next chapter thus,* fre chuesinge, in cite, ne in boruz, ne in toune. The sixte chapittle that no man be amercied, &c.

Great forfeiture. This apparently means "the disturbers to be punished by grievous fines and imprisonment" (2 Co Inst 169). See also provision as to freedom of election in the Bill of Rights (1688) (sess 2 c 2), Vol 10, title Constitutional Law (Pt 1).

Chapters 6–51 (*Cc 6, 28 repealed by the Criminal Law Act 1967, s 10(2), Sch 3 Pt I (as respects England) and the Criminal Law Act (Northern Ireland) 1967, s 15(2), Sch 2, Pt I (as respects Northern Ireland); cc 7, 8, 12, 14, 17, 18, 22, 23, 27, 30, 32, 33, 36–49, 51* *repealed by the SLR Act 1863 (as respects England) and the SL(I)R Act 1872 (as respects Ireland); c 9 repealed in part by the Sheriffs Act 1887, s 39, Sch 3, the remainder by the Coroners Act 1887, s 45, Sch 3 (as respects England) and the Criminal Law Act (Northern Ireland) 1967, s 15(2), Sch 2, Pt I (as respects Northern Ireland); c 10 repealed by the Coroners Act 1887, s 45, Sch 3 (as respects England) and the SLR Act (NI) 1952 (as respects Northern Ireland); cc 11, 13 repealed by 9 Geo 4 c 31 (1828), s 1 (as respects England) and 10 Geo 4 c 34 (1829), s 1 (as respects Ireland); c 15 repealed by the Sheriffs Act 1887, s 39, Sch 3 and was previously repealed by the Criminal Law Act 1826, s 32 (as respects England) and 9 Geo 4 c 53 (1828), s 1 (as respects Ireland); c 16 repealed by the SL(R) Act 1969 (as respects England) and the Judgments (Enforcement) Act (Northern Ireland) 1969, s 132, Sch 6 (as respects Northern Ireland); c 19 repealed by the Statute Law Revision and Civil Procedure Act 1881, s 3, Schedule (as respects England) and the Judgments (Enforcement) Act (Northern Ireland) 1969, s 132, Sch 6 (as respects Northern Ireland); c 20 repealed by 7 & 8 Geo 4 c 27 (1827), s 1 (as respects England) and 9 Geo 4 c 53 (1828), s 1 (as respects Ireland); cc 21, 24, 35 repealed by the Civil Procedure Acts Repeal Act 1879, s 2, Schedule, Pt I; c 25 repealed by the Criminal Law Act 1967, s 13, Sch 4, Pt I (as respects England) and the Criminal Justice (Miscellaneous Provisions) Act (Northern Ireland) 1968, s 16, Sch 4 (as respects Northern Ireland); cc 26, 31 repealed by the Theft Act 1968, s 33(3), Sch 3, Pt I (as respects England) and the Theft Act (Northern Ireland) 1969, s 31(2), Sch 3, Pt I (as respects Northern Ireland); c 29 repealed by the SLR Act 1948; c 34 repealed by the SLR Act 1887; for c 50, see Vol 10, title Constitutional Law (Pt 1).)*

REPRESENTATION OF THE PEOPLE ACT 1867

(30 & 31 Vict c 102)

An Act further to amend the Laws relating to the Representation of the People in England and Wales   [15 August 1867]

Northern Ireland. This Act applies; see the Government of Ireland Act 1920, s 61, Vol 31, title Northern Ireland (Pt 2), and the General Adaptation of Enactments (Northern Ireland) Order 1921, SR & O 1921/1804, art 3.

(Whole Act except ss 7, 51, repealed by the Representation of the People Act 1949, ss 175, 176(2), (3), Sch 9; s 7 repealed by the Rating and Valuation Act 1925, ss 69(1), 70(1), Sch 8 and the Local Government Act 1948, s 147(1), (3), Sch 2, Pt II.)

1 Short title

This Act shall be cited for all purposes as "The Representation of the People Act 1867."

NOTE

This section was repealed as noted but is reproduced here for reference.

51 Demise of Crown not to dissolve Parliament

... The Parliament in being at any future demise of the Crown shall not be determined or dissolved by such demise, but shall continue so long as it would have continued but for such demise, unless it should be sooner prorogued or dissolved by the Crown, anything in the Succession to the Crown Act 1707 in any way notwithstanding.

NOTES

The words omitted were repealed by the SLR Act 1893.

Succession to the Crown Act 1707. See Vol 10, title Constitutional Law (Pt 1); and see especially ss 4, 5 of that Act, which provide for the continuation of Parliament on the death of the reigning sovereign.

PARLIAMENT (ELECTIONS AND MEETING) ACT 1943

(6 & 7 Geo 6 c 48)

An Act to make temporary provision as respects parliamentary elections and the registration of parliamentary electors and, in connection therewith, as respects the dissolution of parliament as from a future date and other matters; to consolidate and amend the law as to the officers to whom writs for parliamentary elections are to be directed, and the persons to whom and the manner in which they are to be conveyed; and to shorten the time required for summoning parliament when prorogued [11 November 1943]

Northern Ireland. The unrepealed provisions of this Act (ss 34, 35 post) apply.

1–33 *(Ss 1–25 repealed by the Representation of the People Act 1948, s 80(7), Sch 13; ss 26–33 repealed by the Representation of the People Act 1949, ss 175, 176(2), (3), Sch 9.)*

PART III

MEETING OF PARLIAMENT WHEN PROROGUED

34 Time for summoning Parliament during prorogation

The date appointed for the meeting of parliament by a proclamation issued under section one of the Meeting of Parliament Act 1797 (which relates to the summoning of parliament when prorogued), may be any day after the date of the proclamation; . . .

NOTES

The words omitted make a consequential amendment to the Meeting of Parliament Act 1797, s 1, Vol 32, title Parliament.

Meeting of Parliament Act 1797, s 1. See Vol 32, title Parliament.

PART IV

GENERAL

35 Short title

This Act may be cited as the Parliament (Elections and Meeting) Act 1943.

(Schs 1, 2, 4, 6 repealed by the Representation of the People Act 1948, s 80(7), Sch 13; Sch 3 repealed by the Representation of the People Act 1945, s 40, Sch 5; Sch 5 repealed by the Representation of the People Act 1949, ss 175, 176(2), (3), Sch 9; Sch 7 repealed by the SLR Act 1950.)

REPRESENTATION OF THE PEOPLE ACT 1948

(11 & 12 Geo 6 c 65)

ARRANGEMENT OF SECTIONS

PART I

PARLIAMENTARY FRANCHISE AND ITS EXERCISE

Parliamentary franchise and distribution of seats

An Act to amend the law relating to parliamentary and local government elections and to corrupt and illegal practices, and for purposes connected therewith   [30 July 1948]

Representation of the People Acts. This Act is one of the Acts which may be cited by this collective title; the others which are still in force are: the House of Commons (Redistribution of Seats) Act 1949, the House of Commons (Redistribution of Seats) Act 1958, the London Government Act 1963, Sch 3, Vol 26, title London, the House of Commons (Redistribution of Seats) Act 1979, the Representation of the People Act 1981, Vol 32, title Parliament, the Representation of the People Act 1983, the Elections (Northern Ireland) Act 1985 and the Representation of the People Act 1985. Unless otherwise indicated, these Acts are printed in this title post.

Northern Ireland. For the application of this Act to Northern Ireland, see ss 55 and 79 post.

PART I

PARLIAMENTARY FRANCHISE AND ITS EXERCISE

Parliamentary franchise and distribution of seats

1 Constituencies and electors

(1) Subject to any Order in Council hereafter made under the House of Commons (Redistribution of Seats) Act 1944, there shall for the purpose of parliamentary elections be the county and borough constituencies, each returning a single member, which are described in the First Schedule to this Act, and no other constituencies.

(2), (3) . . .

NOTES

Sub-s (2), (3) were repealed by the Representation of the People Act 1949, ss 175, 176(2), (3), Sch 9.

Order in Council hereafter made. The House of Commons (Redistribution of Seats) Act 1944 was repealed, with savings as to Orders in Council made under that Act, by the House of Commons (Redistribution of Seats) Act 1949, s 8, Sch 3. The most recent orders made under the House of Commons (Redistribution of Seats) Act 1949, s 3 post are the Parliamentary Constituencies (Northern Ireland) Order 1982, SI 1982/1838; the Parliamentary Constituencies (England) Order 1983, SI 1983/417; the Parliamentary Constituencies (Wales) Order 1983, SI 1983/418; and the Parliamentary Constituencies (Scotland) Order 1983, SI 1983/422. These orders (which superseded all previous constituency orders) substituted the constituencies set out therein for those in existence on 30 March 1983, and have therefore been incorporated in Sch 1 to this Act post.

House of Commons (Redistribution of Seats) Act 1944. Repealed, with savings as to Orders in Council made under that Act, by the House of Commons (Redistribution of Seats) Act 1949, s 8 and Sch 3.

2–31 *(Ss 2, 4–20 and ss 21–31 (Pt II) repealed by the Representation of the People Act 1949, ss 175, 176(2), (3), Sch 9; s 3 repealed by the House of Commons (Redistribution of Seats) Act 1949, ss 8(1), 9(2), Sch 3.)*

PART III

CORRUPT AND ILLEGAL PRACTICES AND OTHER PROVISIONS AS TO ELECTION CAMPAIGN

32–51 *(Repealed by the Representation of the People Act 1949, ss 175, 176(2), (3), Sch 9.)*

Provisions applying to parliamentary and local government elections

52–54 *(Ss 52(1)–(4), (6), 53(1), (2) repealed by the Representation of the People Act 1949, ss 174(2), 175(3), Sch 9; ss 52(5), 53(3), 54 repealed by the Election Commissioners Act 1949, s 21, Schedule; s 52(7) amends the Public Bodies Corrupt Practices Act 1889, s 2(c), (d), Vol 12, title* Criminal Law.)

55 Inter-relation of United Kingdom and Northern Ireland law as to corrupt and illegal practices

(1)–(3) . . .

(4) Where, by reason of anything done in reference to an election, a person is subject to an incapacity with respect to [the Parliament of the United Kingdom], and the incapacity is limited to a particular constituency or constituencies, then the like incapacity imposed by this section with respect to the [Northern Ireland Assembly] shall be limited to any constituency which includes the area or part of the area for which the said election was held.

NOTES

Sub-s (1) was repealed by the SL(R) Act 1978.

Sub-s (2) was repealed by the Representation of the People Act 1949, ss 174(2), 175, 176(2), (3), Sch 9.

Sub-s (3) is spent.

The words in square brackets in sub-s (4) were substituted by the Northern Ireland (Modification of Enactments—No 1) Order 1973, SI 1973/2163, art 14(1), Sch 5, para 14.

United Kingdom. Ie Great Britain and Northern Ireland; see the Interpretation Act 1978, s 5, Sch 1, Vol 41, title Statutes.

Northern Ireland Assembly. This assembly was established by the Northern Ireland Assembly Act 1973, and further relevant provisions are contained in the Northern Ireland Constitution Act 1973, Pts II, IV, both Vol 31, title Northern Ireland (Pt 2). The Assembly, elected under s 2 of the first-mentioned Act, was dissolved by the Northern Ireland Assembly (Dissolution) Order 1975, SI 1975/422 (made under the Northern Ireland Act 1974, s 1(1), Vol 31, title Northern Ireland (Pt 2)). Under Sch 1, para 1, to the 1974 Act, laws for Northern Ireland may be made by Order in Council during the interim period as defined by s 1(4) of that Act. By para 1(7) of that Schedule, references to Measures of the Northern Ireland Assembly include references to such Orders in Council.

A new Assembly was elected by virtue of an election held on 20 October 1982 (ie the day appointed by the Northern Ireland Assembly (Day of Election) Order 1982, SI 1982/1078, made under the Northern Ireland Constitution Act 1973, s 27(7), as applied by s 1(1) of the 1974 Act). Provision for the general or partial suspension of the system of direct rule introduced by Sch 1 to the 1974 Act may now be made by Order in Council made under the Northern Ireland Act 1982, Vol 31, title Northern Ireland (Pt 2), and the effect of any such Order is set out in Sch 1 to that Act. See also, in particular, s 3 of the 1982 Act, as to matters which may be considered by the Assembly pending general suspension of direct rule; s 5 as to the dissolution of the Assembly and revocation of Orders in Council made under s 2 of the Act; and s 6 and Sch 2 for amendments of the 1973 Acts.

56–65 *(Ss 56, 58, 60, 61, 64 repealed by the Representation of the People Act 1949, ss 174(2), 175, 176(2), (3), Sch 9; s 57 repealed by the Local Government Act 1972, s 272(1), Sch 30; s 59 repealed by the London Government Act 1963, s 93(1), Sch 18, Pt I; ss 62, 65 repealed by the Local Government (Scotland) Act 1973, s 237(1), Sch 29; s 63 repealed by the Licensing (Scotland) Act 1959, s 200, Sch 12.)*

PART VI

GENERAL

66–72 *(Ss 66–71 repealed by the Representation of the People Act 1949, ss 174(2), 175, 176(2), (3), Sch 9; s 72 repealed by the Superannuation Act 1972, s 29(4), Sch 8, the Local Government Superannuation Regulations 1974, SI 1974/520, reg M2(1), Sch 19, Pt I, and by the Local Government Superannuation (City of London) Regulations 1977, SI 1977/1341, reg 23, Sch 6, Pt I.)*

Miscellaneous

73 *(Repealed by the Representation of the People Act 1949, ss 174(2), 175, 176(2), (3), Sch 9.)*

74 Adaptation, interpretation and minor amendments of law

(1) The Tenth Schedule to this Act shall have effect with respect to the interpretation and adaptation of Acts other than this Act . . .

(2) The provisions of the said Tenth Schedule may be supplemented in relation to any Act passed before this Act by an order made by the Secretary of State in any particular case where that appears to him necessary for harmonising that Act with this Act.

(3) Any power conferred by this section . . . to make an order shall be exercisable by statutory instrument, and any such instrument shall be subject to annulment by resolution of either House of Parliament.

(4), (5) . . .

NOTES

The words omitted from sub-ss (1), (3) were repealed by the SL(R) Act 1978.

Sub-s (4) was repealed by the Representation of the People Act 1949, ss 174(2), 175, 176(2), (3), Sch 9.

Sub-s (5) was repealed by the SLR Act 1953.

Statutory instrument; subject to annulment. For provisions as to statutory instruments generally, see the Statutory Instruments Act 1946, Vol 41, title Statutes, and as to statutory instruments which are subject to annulment, see ss 5(1), 7(1) of that Act.

Orders under sub-s (2). Such orders, being local, are not noted in this work.

75 *(Sub-s (1) repealed by the SL(R) Act 1978; sub-s (2) is spent; sub-s (3) repealed by the Representation of the People Act 1949, ss 174(2), 175, 176(2), (3), Sch 9.)*

76 General provisions as to interpretation

(1), (2) . . .

(3) References in this Act to any enactment shall, except in so far as the context otherwise requires, be taken as referring to that enactment as amended by any other enactment, including this Act.

(4) . . .

NOTE

Sub-ss (1), (2), (4) were repealed by the Representation of the People Act 1949, ss 174(2), 175, 176(2), (3), Sch 9.

77 Interpretation and application of local government provisions in England and Wales

(1) In this Act unless the context otherwise requires the following expressions have, in relation to England and Wales, the meanings assigned to them by this subsection, that is to say—

.   .   .   .   .

the expression "county" means (subject to subsection (5) of this section) an administrative county;

.   .   .   .

(2)–(4) . . .

(5) This Act shall apply in relation to the Isles of Scilly as if those isles were an administrative county and as if the council of those isles were a county council, . . .

NOTES

The definitions omitted from sub-s (1) as indicated by dots in the first place where they occur were repealed by the London Government Act 1963, s 93(1), Sch 18, Pt I, and in the second place where they occur were repealed by the Representation of the People Act 1949, ss 174(2), 175, 176(2), (3), Sch 9, and by the SL(R) Act 1978.

Sub-ss (2)–(4) and the words omitted from sub-s (5) were repealed by the Representation of the People Act 1949, ss 174(2), 175, 176(2), (3), Sch 9.

County. The counties existing immediately before 1 April 1974 were abolished on that date by the Local Government Act 1972, ss 1(10), 20(6), Vol 25, title Local Government, and by virtue of s 179(1), (2) of that Act, the reference to a county is to be construed as a county established by ss 1(1), (2), 20(1), (2) of, and Sch 1, Pts I, II, Sch 4, Pt I to, the 1972 Act.

The council of those Isles. The Council of the Isles of Scilly is continued in being by the Local Government Act 1972, s 265(1), Vol 25, title Local Government, and is now constituted by the Isles of Scilly Order 1978, SI 1978/1844, art 4 (made under s 265(2) of that Act).

78 *(Sub-ss (1), (2) apply to Scotland only; sub-s (3) repealed by the SL(R) Act 1978; sub-s (4) repealed by the Representation of the People Act 1949, ss 174(2), 175, 176(2), (3), Sch 9.)*

79 General application to Northern Ireland

(1) The following provisions shall, in addition to any express provision for the application to Northern Ireland of any provision of this Act, have effect for the general application of this Act to Northern Ireland, that is to say:—

(*a*), (*b*) ...
(*c*) subject to the next following subsection, a reference to any enactment shall be construed as a reference to that enactment as it applies in Northern Ireland.

(2) Nothing in this Act shall affect the law relating ... to local government in Northern Ireland except so far as is expressly provided by this Act.

(3) ...

NOTES

Sub-s (1)(*a*), (*b*) were repealed by the Representation of the People Act 1949, ss 174(2), 175, 176(2), Sch 9.
Sub-s (3) and the words omitted from sub-s (2) were repealed by the Northern Ireland Constitution Act 1973, s 41(1), Sch 6, Pt I.
Any provision of this Act. See s 55(4) ante.

80 Commencement, repeals, etc

(1)–(6) ...

(7) ... without prejudice to any provision of the Interpretation Act 1889 as to repeals,—

(*a*) the repeal by this Act of any enactment abolishing any ground of incapacity to be registered as an elector or to vote shall not be taken as restoring that ground of incapacity;
(*b*), (*c*) ...
(*d*) any document referring to any Act or enactment repealed by this Act shall be construed as referring to this Act or to the corresponding enactment, if any, in this Act.

(8)–(10) ...

NOTES

Sub-ss (1), (3), (4) were repealed by the Representation of the People Act 1949, ss 174(2), 175, 176(2), (3), Sch 9.
Sub-ss (2), (5), (6), (8)–(10) were repealed by the SL(R) Act 1978.
Sub-s (7)(*c*) was repealed by the SL(R) Act 1978; the other words omitted from sub-s (7) were repealed by the SLR Act 1953.
Saving. The Representation of the People Act 1918, s 9(5) (repealed) so far as saved by sub-s (7)(*a*) above was repealed by the Peerage Act 1963, s 7(2), Sch 2.
Interpretation Act 1889. Repealed by the Interpretation Act 1978, s 25, Sch 3, and replaced by provisions of that Act, Vol 41, title Statutes. For provisions relating to repeals, see ss 16(1), 17(2)(*a*) of, and Sch 2, para 3 to, the 1978 Act.

81 Short title, and citation

This Act may be cited as the Representation of the People Act 1948, and this Act ... shall be included among the Acts which may be cited as the Representation of the People Acts.

NOTES

The words omitted were repealed by the House of Commons (Redistribution of Seats) Act 1949, ss 8, 9, Sch 3.
Representation of the People Acts. For the Acts which may be cited by this collective title, see the Introductory Note to the Representation of the People Act 1948 ante.

SCHEDULES

FIRST SCHEDULE

Section 1

PARLIAMENTARY CONSTITUENCIES

Amendment of Schedule. The constituencies set out below have been substituted by virtue of the orders cited in the note "Order in Council hereafter made" to s 1 ante.

PART I

ENGLAND

AVON

(a) County Constituencies

Northavon

The following wards of the District of Northavon, namely, Almondsbury, Alveston, Badminton, Charfield, Chipping Sodbury, Dodington North, Frampton Cotterell Central, Frampton Cotterell East, Frampton Cotterell West, Hawkesbury, Iron Acton, Marshfield, Oldbury-on-Severn, Olveston, Patchway Callicroft, Patchway Coniston, Patchway Stoke Lodge, Pilning and Severn Beach, Pucklechurch, Thornbury North, Thornbury South, Westerleigh Stanshawes, Westerleigh and Coalpit Heath, Wick and Abson, Wickwar, Winterbourne, Winterbourne Down and Hambrook, Winterbourne Frenchay, Yate Central, Yate North, Yate South and Yate West.

Wansdyke

(i) The following wards of the District of Kingswood, namely, Badminton, Bitton North Common, Bitton Oldland Common, Bitton South, Blackhorse, Bromley Heath, Hanham Abbots East, Hanham Abbots West, Oldland Cadbury Heath, Oldland Longwell Green, Siston and Springfield; and

(ii) the following wards of the District of Wansdyke, namely, Bathampton, Batheaston, Bathford, Camerton, Charlcombe, Freshford, Hinton Charterhouse, Keynsham East, Keynsham North, Keynsham South, Keynsham West, Midsomer Norton Redfield, Newton St Loe, Peasedown St John, Radstock, Saltford and Westfield.

Weston-Super-Mare

The following wards of the District of Woodspring, namely, Banwell, Blagdon, Churchill, Congresbury, Hutton, Locking, Weston-Super-Mare Ashcombe, Weston-Super-Mare East, Weston-Super-Mare Ellenborough, Weston-Super-Mare North, Weston-Super-Mare South, Weston-Super-Mare Uphill, Weston-Super-Mare West, Winscombe, Wrington and Yatton.

Woodspring

(i) The following wards of the District of Wansdyke, namely, Cameley, Chew Magna, Chew Stoke, Clutton, Compton Dando, Farmborough, Harptrees, High Littleton, Paulton, Publow, Stowey Sutton and Timsbury; and

(ii) the following wards of the District of Woodspring, namely, Backwell, Clevedon Central, Clevedon East, Clevedon North, Clevedon South, Clevedon Walton, Clevedon West, Easton-in-Gordano, Gordano, Long Ashton, Nailsea East, Nailsea North and West, North Weston, Portishead Central, Portishead Coast, Portishead South, Portishead West, Winford and Wraxall.

(b) Borough Constituencies

Bath

The City of Bath.

Bristol East

The following wards of the City of Bristol which are constituted by the City of Bristol (Electoral Arrangements) Order 1980 and which come into operation on 5th May 1983, namely, Brislington East, Brislington West, Easton, Eastville, Hengrove, Lawrence Hill and Stockwood.

Bristol North West

(i) The following wards of the City of Bristol which are constituted by the City of Bristol (Electoral Arrangements) Order 1980 and which come into operation on 5th May 1983, namely, Avonmouth, Henbury, Horfield, Kingsweston, Lockleaze, Southmead and Westbury-on-Trym; and

(ii) the following wards of the District of Northavon, namely, Filton Charborough, Filton Conygre, Filton Northville, Stoke Gifford North and Stoke Gifford South.

Bristol South

The following wards of the City of Bristol, which are constituted by the City of Bristol (Electoral Arrangements) Order 1980 and which come into operation on 5th May 1983, namely, Bedminster, Bishopsworth, Filwood, Hartcliffe, Knowle, Southville, Whitchurch Park and Windmill Hill.

Bristol West

The following wards of the City of Bristol which are constituted by the City of Bristol (Electoral Arrangements) Order 1980 and which come into operation on 5th May 1983, namely, Ashley, Bishopston, Cabot, Clifton, Cotham, Henleaze, Redland and Stoke Bishop.

Kingswood

(i) The following wards of the City of Bristol which are constituted by the City of Bristol (Electoral Arrangements) Order 1980 and which come into operation on 5th May 1983, namely, Frome Vale, Hillfields, St George East and St George West; and

(ii) the following wards of the District of Kingswood, namely, Chase, Chiphouse, Downend, Forest, Hanham, Mangotsfield, New Cheltenham, Soundwell, Staple Hill and Woodstock.

BEDFORDSHIRE

(a) County Constituencies

Mid Bedfordshire

(i) The following wards of the District of Mid Bedfordshire, namely, Ampthill, Arlesey, Biggleswade Ivel, Biggleswade Stratton, Blunham, Campton and Meppershall, Clifton and Henlow, Clophill, Haynes and Houghton Conquest, Langford, Maulden, Northill, Old Warden and Southill, Potton, Sandy All Saints, Sandy St Swithuns, Shefford, Shillington and Stondon, Stotfold, Wensley and Wrest; and

(ii) the following wards of the Borough of North Bedfordshire which are constituted by the Borough of North Bedfordshire (Electoral Arrangements) Order 1979 and which come into operation on 5th May 1983, namely, Eastcotts, Great Barford, Kempston East, Kempston Rural, Kempston West, Wilshamstead and Wootton.

North Bedfordshire	The following wards of the Borough of North Bedfordshire which are constituted by the Borough of North Bedfordshire (Electoral Arrangements) Order 1979 and which come into operation on 5th May 1983, namely, Brickhill, Bromham, Carlton, Castle, Cauldwell, Clapham, De Parys, Felmersham, Goldington, Harpur, Harrold, Kingsbrook, Newnham, Oakley, Putnoe, Queens Park, Renhold, Riseley, Roxton and Sharnbrook.
North Luton	(i) The following wards of the Borough of Luton, namely, Bramingham, Challney, Icknield, Leagrave, Lewsey, Limbury and Sundon Park;
	(ii) the following wards of the District of Mid Bedfordshire, namely, Flitton and Pulloxhill, Flitwick East, Flitwick West, Harlington and Westoning; and
	(iii) the following wards of the District of South Bedfordshire, namely, Barton-le-Clay, Streatley and Toddington.
South West Bedfordshire	(i) The following wards of the District of Mid Bedfordshire, namely, Aspley, Cranfield, Marston and Woburn; and
	(ii) the following wards of the District of South Bedfordshire, namely, Beaudesert Brooklands, Dunstable Central, Eaton Bray Heath and Reach, Hockliffe, Houghton Central, Houghton East, Houghton South, Icknield, Kensworth, Linslade, Northfields, Plantation, Priory, Southcott, Stanbridge, Studham, Totternhoe and Watling.

(b) Borough Constituency

Luton South	(i) The following wards of the Borough of Luton, namely, Biscot, Crawley, Dallow, Farley, High Town, Putteridge, Saints, South and Stopsley; and
	(ii) the following wards of the District of South Bedfordshire, namely, Caddington and Slip End.

BERKSHIRE

(a) County Constituencies

East Berkshire	(i) The District of Bracknell; and
	(ii) the following wards of the Royal Borough of Windsor and Maidenhead which are constituted by the Royal Borough of Windsor and Maidenhead (Electoral Arrangements) Order 1980 and which come into operation on 5th May 1983, namely, Datchet, Horton and Wraysbury, Old Windsor, Sunningdale and South Ascot and Sunninghill.
Newbury	The following wards of the District of Newbury which are constituted by the District of Newbury (Electoral Arrangements) Order 1979 and which come into operation on 5th May 1983, namely, Aldermaston, Basildon, Beenham, Bradfield, Bucklebury, Burghfield, Chievely, Cold Ash, Compton, Craven, Downlands, Falklands, Greenham, Hungerford, Kintbury, Lambourn Valley, Mortimer, Northcroft, St John's, Shaw-cum-Donnington, Speen, Thatcham North, Thatcham South, Thatcham West, Turnpike and Winchcombe.

Reading East	(i) The following wards of the Borough of Reading which are constituted by the Borough of Reading (Electoral Arrangements) Order 1979 and which come into operation on 5th May 1983, namely, Abbey, Caversham, Church, Park, Peppard, Redlands, Thames and Whitley; and
	(ii) the following wards of the District of Wokingham, namely, Arborfield, Barkham, Finchampstead, Shinfield and Swallowfield.
Reading West	(i) The following wards of the District of Newbury which are constituted by the District of Newbury (Electoral Arrangements) Order 1979 and which come into operation on 5th May 1983, namely, Calcot, Pangbourne, Purley, Theale and Tilehurst; and
	(ii) the following wards of the Borough of Reading which are constituted by the Borough of Reading (Electoral Arrangements) Order 1979 and which come into operation on 5th May 1983, namely, Battle, Katesgrove, Kentwood, Minster, Norcot, Southcote and Tilehurst.
Windsor and Maidenhead	The following wards of the Royal Borough of Windsor and Maidenhead which are constituted by the Royal Borough of Windsor and Maidenhead (Electoral Arrangements) Order 1980 and which come into operation on 5th May 1983, namely, Belmont, Bisham and Cookham, Boyn Hill, Bray, Castle, Clewer North, Clewer South, Cox Green, Eton North and South, Eton West, Furze Platt, Hurley, Oldfield, Park, Pinkneys Green, St Mary's and Trinity.
Wokingham	The following wards of the District of Wokingham, namely, Bulmershe, California, Charvil, Coronation, Emmbrook, Evendons, Hurst, Little Hungerford, Loddon, Norreys, Redhatch, Remenham and Wargrave, St Sebastian's, Sonning, South Lake, Twyford and Ruscombe, Wescott, Whitegates and Winnersh.

(b) Borough Constituency

Slough	The Borough of Slough.

BUCKINGHAMSHIRE

County Constituencies

Aylesbury	(i) The following wards of the District of Aylesbury Vale, namely, Aston Clinton, Aylesbury Central, Bedgrove, Elmhurst, Gatehouse, Grange, Mandeville, Meadowcroft, Oakfield, Southcourt, Wendover and Weston Turville;
	(ii) the following wards of the District of Chiltern, namely, Ballinger and South Heath, Great Missenden and Prestwood and Heath End; and
	(iii) the following wards of the District of Wycombe which are constituted by the District of Wycombe (Electoral Arrangements) Order 1980 and which come into operation on 5th May 1983, namely, Bledlow-cum-Saunderton, Icknield, Lacey Green and Hampden, Naphill-cum-Bradenham, Princes Risborough and Stokenchurch.

Beaconsfield

(i) The District of South Bucks; and

(ii) the following wards of the District of Wycombe which are constituted by the District of Wycombe (Electoral Arrangements) Order 1980 and which come into operation on 5th May 1983, namely, Bourne End-cum-Hedsor, Flackwell Heath, Loudwater, The Wooburns and Tylers Green.

Buckingham

(i) The following wards of the District of Aylesbury Vale, namely, Bierton, Brill, Buckingham North, Buckingham South, Cheddington, Eddlesborough, Great Brickhill, Great Horwood, Grendon Underwood, Haddenham, Hogshaw, Long Crendon, Luffield Abbey, Marsh Gibbon, Newton Longville, Oakley, Pitstone, Quainton, Steeple Claydon, Stewkley, Stone, Tingewick, Waddesdon, Wing, Wingrave and Winslow; and

(ii) the following wards of the Borough of Milton Keynes, namely, Stony Stratford, Wolverton and Wolverton Stacey Bushes.

Chesham and Amersham

(i) The following wards of the District of Chiltern, namely, Amersham Common, Amersham-on-the-Hill, Amersham Town, Asheridge Vale, Ashley Green and Latimer, Austenwood, Chalfont Common, Chalfont St Giles, Chalfont St Peter Central, Chartridge, Chenies, Chesham Bois and Weedon Hill, Cholesbury and The Lee, Coleshill and Penn Street, Gold Hill, Hilltop, Holmer Green, Little Chalfont, Little Missenden, Lowndes, Newtown, Penn, Pond Park, St Mary's, Seer Green and Jordans, Townsend and Waterside; and

(ii) the following wards of the District of Wycombe which are constituted by the District of Wycombe (Electoral Arrangements) Order 1980 and which come into operation on 5th May 1983, namely, Hazlemere North and Hazlemere South.

Milton Keynes

The following wards of the Borough of Milton Keynes, namely, Bradwell, Church Green, Danesborough, Denbigh, Eaton, Fenny Stratford, Lavendon, Linford, Loughton, Manor Farm, Newport Pagnell, Newton, Olney, Pineham, Sherington, Stantonbury, Whaddon, Woburn Sands and Woughton.

Wycombe

The following wards of the District of Wycombe which are constituted by the District of Wycombe (Electoral Arrangements) Order 1980 and which come into operation on 5th May 1983, namely, Booker and Castlefield, Bowerdean and Daws Hill, Cressex and Frogmoor, Downley, Great Marlow, Green Hill and Totteridge, Hambleden Valley, Hughenden Valley, Keep Hill and Hicks Farm, Kingshill, Lane End and Piddington, Little Marlow, Marlow Bottom, Marlow North, Marlow South, Marsh and Micklefield, Oakridge and Tinkers Wood and West Wycombe and Sands.

CAMBRIDGESHIRE

(a) County Constituencies

Huntingdon

(i) The following wards of the District of Huntingdon, namely, Brampton, Bury, Earith, Ellington, Elton, Farcet, Fenstanton, Godmanchester, Hemingford Abbots and Hilton, Hemingford Grey, Houghton and Wyton, Huntingdon North, Huntingdon West, Kimbolton, Needingworth, Ramsey, Sawtry, Somersham, Stilton, St Ives North, St Ives South, The Stukeleys, Upwood and the Raveleys, Warboys and Yaxley; and

(ii) the following wards of the City of Peterborough, namely, Barnack, Glinton, Northborough, Werrington and Wittering.

North East Cambridgeshire

(i) The following wards of the District of East Cambridgeshire which are constituted by the District of East Cambridgeshire (Electoral Arrangements) Order 1980 and which come into operation on 5th May 1983, namely, Downham, Haddenham, Littleport, Stretham, Sutton and Witchford;

(ii) the District of Fenland; and

(iii) the following wards of the City of Peterborough, namely, Eye, Newborough and Thorney.

South East Cambridgeshire

(i) The following wards of the District of East Cambridgeshire which are constituted by the District of East Cambridgeshire (Electoral Arrangements) Order 1980 and which come into operation on 5th May 1983, namely, Bottisham, Burwell, Cheveley, Dullingham Villages, Ely Northern, Ely Southern, Ely West, Fordham Villages, Isleham, Soham, The Swaffhams and Woodditton; and

(ii) the following wards of the District of South Cambridgeshire, namely, Abington, Balsham, Bar Hill, Castle Camps, Coton, Cottenham, Elsworth, Fulbourn, Girton, Histon, Linton, Longstanton, Milton, Over, Swavesey, Teversham, The Wilbrahams, Waterbeach and Willingham.

South West Cambridgeshire

(i) The following wards of the City of Cambridge, namely, Queen Edith's and Trumpington;

(ii) the following wards of the District of Huntingdon, namely, Buckden, Eaton Ford, Eaton Socon, Eynesbury, Gransden, Paxton, Priory Park, Staughton and The Offords; and

(iii) the following wards of the District of South Cambridgeshire, namely, Arrington, Barrington and Shepreth, Barton, Bassingbourn, Bourn, Comberton, Duxford, Foxton, Gamlingay, Great Shelford, Hardwick, Harston, Haslingfield, Ickleton, Little Shelford, Melbourn, Meldreth, Orwell, Papworth, Sawston, Stapleford, The Mordens and Whittlesford.

(b) Borough Constituencies

Cambridge

The following wards of the City of Cambridge, namely, Abbey, Arbury, Castle, Cherry Hinton, Coleridge, East Chesterton, King's Hedges, Market, Newnham, Petersfield, Romsey and West Chesterton.

Peterborough

The following wards of the City of Peterborough, namely, Bretton, Central, Dogsthorpe, East, Fletton, North, Orton Longueville, Orton Waterville, Park, Paston, Ravensthorpe, Stanground, Walton and West.

CHESHIRE

(a) County Constituencies

City of Chester

The following wards of the City of Chester, namely, Blacon Hall, Boughton, Boughton Heath, Christleton, College, Curzon, Dee Point, Dodleston, Grosvenor, Hoole, Newton, Plas Newton, Sealand, Upton Grange, Upton Heath, Vicars Cross and Westminster.

Congleton

(i) The Borough of Congleton; and

(ii) the following ward of the Borough of Crewe and Nantwich, namely, Haslington.

Crewe and Nantwich

The following wards of the Borough of Crewe and Nantwich, namely, Acton, Alexandra, Audlem, Barony Weaver, Bunbury, Combermere, Coppenhall, Delamere, Grosvenor, Maw Green, Minshull, Peckforton, Queens Park, Ruskin Park, St Barnabas, St Johns, Shavington, Waldron, Wellington, Weston Park, Willaston East, Willaston West, Wistaston, Wrenbury and Wybunbury.

Eddisbury

(i) The following wards of the City of Chester, namely, Barrow, Farndon, Malpas, Tarvin, Tattenhall, Tilston and Waverton; and

(ii) the following wards of the District of Vale Royal, namely, Church, Cuddington and Marton, Davenham and Moulton, Forest, Frodsham East, Frodsham North West, Frodsham South, Gorst Wood, Gravel, Hartford, Helsby Central, Helsby North, Helsby South and Alvanley Ward, Kingsley, Mara, Milton, Oulton, Over One, Over Two, Swanlow, Tarporley, Vale Royal, Weaver and Wharton.

Ellesmere Port and Neston

(i) The following wards of the City of Chester, namely, Elton, Mollington and Saughall; and

(ii) the Borough of Ellesmere Port and Neston.

Halton

The following wards of the Borough of Halton, namely, Appleton, Broadheath, Castlefields, Ditton, Farnworth, Grange, Hale, Halton, Halton Brook, Heath, Hough Green, Kingsway, Mersey, Victoria and Weston.

Macclesfield

The following wards of the Borough of Macclesfield, namely, Alderley Edge, Bollington Central, Bollington East, Bollington West, Disley, Gawsworth, Henbury, Macclesfield Central, Macclesfield East, Macclesfield North East, Macclesfield North West, Macclesfield South, Macclesfield West, Nether Alderley, Poynton Central, Poynton East, Poynton West, Prestbury, Rainow and Sutton.

Tatton

(i) The following wards of the Borough of Macclesfield, namely, Dean Row, Fulshaw, Handforth, High Legh, Hough, Knutsford Nether, Knutsford Over, Knutsford South, Knutsford West, Lacey Green, Mere, Moberley, Morley and Styal and Plumley; and

(ii) the following wards of the District of Vale Royal, namely, Barnton, Castle, Cogshall, Lostock Gralam, Marston and Wincham, Northwich, Rudheath and Whatcroft, Seven Oaks, Shakerley, Winnington, Witton North and Witton South.

(b) Borough Constituencies

Warrington North

The following wards of the Borough of Warrington, namely, Bewsey, Burtonwood, Croft, Culcheth and Glazebury, Fairfield, Howley, Hulme, Longford, Orford, Poulton-with-Fearnhead North, Poulton-with-Fearnhead South, Rixton and Woolston, Whitecross and Winwick.

Warrington South

(i) The following wards of the Borough of Halton, namely, Daresbury and Norton; and

(ii) the following wards of the Borough of Warrington, namely, Appleton and Stretton, Booths Hill, Grappenhall and Thelwall, Great Sankey North, Great Sankey South, Heatley, Latchford, Lymm, Penketh and Cuerdley, Statham, Stockton Heath and Walton and Westy.

CLEVELAND

(a) County Constituencies

Langbaurgh

(i) The following wards of the Borough of Langbaurgh, namely, Belmont, Brotton, Guisborough, Hutton, Lockwood, Loftus, Longbeck, Saltburn, Skelton, Skinningrove and St Germain's; and

(ii) the following wards of the Borough of Middlesbrough, namely, Easterside, Hemlington, Marton, Newham, Nunthorpe, Park End and Stainton and Thornton.

(b) Borough Constituencies

Hartlepool

The Borough of Hartlepool.

Middlesbrough

The following wards of the Borough of Middlesbrough, namely, Acklam, Beckfield, Beechwood, Berwick Hills, Gresham, Grove Hill, Kirby, Linthorpe, North Ormesby, Pallister, Park, St Hilda's, Southfield, Thorntree and Westbourne.

Redcar

The following wards of the Borough of of Landbaurgh, namely, Bankside, Church Lane, Coatham, Dormanstown, Eston, Grangetown, Kirkleatham, Newcomen, Normanby, Ormesby, Overfields, Redcar, South Bank, Teesville and West Dyke.

Stockton North

The following wards of the Borough of Stockton-on-Tees, namely, Blue Hall, Charltons, Elm Tree, Glebe, Grange, Hardwick, Marsh House, Mile House, Newtown, Northfield, Norton, Portrack and Tilery, Roseworth, St Aidan's, St Cuthbert's, Whitton and Wolviston.

Stockton South

(i) The following wards of the Borough of Middlesbrough, namely, Ayresome, Brookfield and Kader; and

(ii) the following wards of the Borough of Stockton-on-Tees, namely, Bishopsgarth, Egglescliffe, Fairfield, Grangefield, Hartburn, Ingleby Barwick, Mandale, Parkfield, Preston, Stainsby, Victoria, Village and Yarm.

CORNWALL AND THE ISLES OF SCILLY

County Constituencies

Falmouth and Cambourne

(i) The following wards of the District of Carrick, namely, Arwenack, Mylor, Penryn, Penwerris, Smithick and Trevethan; and

(ii) the following wards of the District of Kerrier, namely, Camborne North, Camborne South, Camborne West, Constantine, Illogan North, Illogan South, Mabe and St Gluvias, Mawnan and Budock, Redruth North, Redruth South, St Day and Lanner and Stithians.

North Cornwall

(i) The following wards of the District of North Cornwall, namely, Allan, Altarnun, Bodmin St Mary's, Bodmin St Petroc, Bude and Poughill, Camelford, Grenville, Lanivet, Launceston North, Launceston South, Lesnewth, North Petherwin, Ottery, Padstow and St Merryn, Penfound, Rumford, St Breward, St Endellion, St Minver, St Teath, South Petherwin, Stratton, Tintagel, Trigg, Wadebridge and Week St Mary; and

(ii) the following wards of the Borough of Restormel which are constituted by the Borough of Restormel (Electoral Arrangements) Order 1979 and which come into operation on 5th May 1983, namely, Edgcumbe, Gannel, Rialton, St Columb and St Enoder.

St Ives

(i) The following wards of the District of Kerrier, namely, Breage and Germoe, Crowan, Grade-Ruan and Landewednack, Helston North, Helston South, Meneage, Mullion, Porthleven, St Keverne and Wendron and Sithney;

(ii) the District of Penwith; and

(iii) the Isles of Scilly.

South East Cornwall

(i) The District of Caradon;

(ii) the following ward of the District of North Cornwall, namely, Stokeclimsland; and

(iii) the following wards of the Borough of Restormel which are constituted by the Borough of Restormel (Electoral Arrangements) Order 1979 and which come into operation on 5th May 1983, namely, Fowey, Lostwithiel, St Blaise and Tywardreath.

Truro

(i) The following wards of the District of Carrick, namely, Boscawen, Chacewater, Feock, Kea, Kenwyn, Moresk, Newlyn, Perranzabuloe, Probus, Roseland, St Agnes, St Clement, Tregolls and Trehaverne; and

(ii) the following wards of the Borough of Restormel which are constituted by the Borough of Restormel (Electoral Arrangements) Order 1979 and which come into operation on 5th May 1983, namely, Crinis, Mevagissey, Poltair, Rock, St Ewe, St Mewan, St Stephen-in-Brannel, Trevarna and Treverbyn.

CUMBRIA

(a) County Constituencies

Barrow and Furness

(i) The Borough of Barrow-in-Furness; and

(ii) the following wards of the District of South Lakeland, namely, Low Furness, Pennington, Ulverston Central, Ulverston East, Ulverston North, Ulverston South and Ulverston West.

Copeland

The Borough of Copeland.

Penrith and The Border

(i) The following wards of the District of Allerdale, namely, Aspatria, Boltons, Marsh, Silloth, Tarns, Wampool, Warnell, Waver and Wigton;

(ii) the following wards of the City of Carlisle which are constituted by the City of Carlisle (Electoral Arrangements) Order 1979 and which come into operation on 5th May 1983, namely, Arthuret, Brampton, Burgh, Dalston, Great Corby and Geltsdale, Hayton, Irthing, Lyne, St Cuthbert Without, Stanwix Rural and Wetheral; and

(iii) the following wards of the District of Eden, namely, Alston Moor, Appleby, Appleby Bongate, Askham, Brough, Crosby Ravensworth, Dacre, Eamont, Greystoke, Hartside, Hesket, Kirkby Thore, Kirkoswald, Langwathby, Lazonby, Long Marton, Lowther, Penrith East, Penrith North, Penrith South, Penrith West, Skelton, Ullswater and Warcop.

Westmorland and Lonsdale

(i) The following wards of the District of Eden, namely, Kirkby Stephen, Orton with Tebay, Ravenstonedale and Shap; and

(ii) the following wards of the District of South Lakeland, namely, Arnside, Beetham, Broughton, Burneside, Burton and Holme, Cartmel, Cartmel Fell, Colton and Haverthwaite, Coniston, Crake Valley, Endmoor, Grange, Hawkshead, Holker, Hutton, Kendal Castle, Kendal Far Cross, Kendal Fell, Kendal Glebelands, Kendal Heron Hill, Kendal Highgate, Kendal Mintsfeet, Kendal Nether, Kendal Oxenholme, Kendal Stonecross, Kendal Strickland, Kendal Underley, Kirkby Lonsdale, Lakes Ambleside, Lakes Grasmere, Levens, Lyth Valley, Milnthorpe, Sedbergh, Staveley-in-Westmorland, Whinfell, Windermere Applethwaite, Windermere Bowness North, Windermere Bowness South and Windermere Town.

Workington

The following wards of the District of Allerdale, namely, All Saints, Binsey, Broughton, Castle, Clifton, Crummock, Dalton, Dearham, Derwent Valley, Ellen, Ellenborough, Ewanrigg, Flimby, Harrington, Keswick, Moorclose, Netherhall, Northside, St Bridget's, St John's, St Michael's, Salterbeck, Seaton Moor, Stainburn and Westfield.

(b) Borough Constituency

Carlisle

The following wards of the City of Carlisle which are constituted by the City of Carlisle (Electoral Arrangements) Order 1979 and which come into operation on 5th May 1983, namely, Belah, Belle Vue, Botcherby, Currock, Denton Holme, Harraby, Morton, St Aidans, Stanwix Urban, Trinity, Upperby and Yewdale.

DERBYSHIRE

(a) County Constituencies

Amber Valley

(i) The following wards of the District of Amber Valley, namely, Aldercar, Alfreton East, Alfreton West, Codnor, Denby and Horsley Woodhouse, Heage and Ambergate, Heanor East, Heanor and Loscoe, Heanor West, Holbrook and Horsley, Kilburn, Riddings, Ripley, Ripley and Marehay, Shipley Park, Somercotes, Swanwick and Wingfield; and

(ii) the following wards of the Borough of Erewash, namely, Breadsall and Morley, Little Eaton and Stanley.

Bolsover

(i) The District of Bolsover; and

(ii) the following wards of the District of North East Derbyshire, namely, Morton, Pilsley, Shirland and Sutton.

Erewash

The following wards of the Borough of Erewash, namely, Breaston, Cotmanhay, Dale Abbey, Derby Road East, Derby Road West, Draycott, Ilkeston Central, Ilkeston North, Ilkeston South, Kirk Hallam North, Kirk Hallam South, Long Eaton Central, Nottingham Road, Ockbrook and Borrowash, Old Park, Sandiacre North, Sandiacre South, Sawley, Victoria, West Hallam and Wilsthorpe.

High Peak

(i) The Borough of High Peak; and

(ii) the following wards of the District of West Derbyshire, namely, Bradwell, Hathersage and Tideswell.

North East Derbyshire

(i) The following wards of the Borough of Chesterfield, namely, Barrow Hill and Hollingwood and Lowgates and Woodthorpe; and

(ii) the following wards of the District of North East Derbyshire, namely, Ashover, Barlow and Holmesfield, Brampton and Walton, Coal Aston, Clay Cross North, Clay Cross South, Dronfield North, Dronfield South, Dronfield Woodhouse, Eckington North, Eckington South, Gosforth Valley, Hasland, Holmewood and Heath, Killamarsh East, Killamarsh West, North Wingfield Central, Renishaw, Ridgeway and Marsh Lane, Tupton, Unstone and Wingerworth.

South Derbyshire

(i) The following wards of the City of Derby, namely, Boulton, Chellaston and Mickleover; and

(ii) the District of South Derbyshire.

West Derbyshire

(i) The following wards of the District of Amber Valley, namely, Alport, Belper East, Belper North, Belper South, Crich, Duffield and South West Parishes; and

(ii) the following wards of the District of West Derbyshire, namely, All Saints, Ashbourne, Ashford and Longstone, Bakewell, Baslow, Brailsford, Brassington and Parwich, Calver, Clifton and Bradley, Darley Dale, Doveridge, Eyam and Stoney Middleton, Hartington and Dovedale, Hulland, Masson, Norbury, St Giles and Tansley, Stanton, Taddington, Winster and South Darley, Wirksworth and Youlgreave.

(b) Borough Constituencies

Chesterfield
:   The following wards of the Borough of Chesterfield, namely, Brimington North, Brimington South, Brockwell, Dunston, Hasland, Holmebrook, Inkersall, Markham, Middlecroft, Moor, Newbold, New Whittington, Old Whittington, Rother, St Helen's, St Leonard's, Walton and West.

Derby North
:   The following wards of the City of Derby, namely, Abbey, Allestree, Breadsall, Chaddesden, Darley, Derwent, Mackworth and Spondon.

Derby South
:   The following wards of the City of Derby, namely, Alvaston, Babington, Blagreaves, Kingsway, Litchurch, Littleover, Normanton, Osmaston and Sinfin.

DEVON

(a) County Constituencies

Honiton
:   The following wards of the District of East Devon, namely, Axminster Hamlets, Axminster Town, Beer, Budleigh Salterton, Colyton, Edenvale, Exmouth Brixington, Exmouth Halsdon, Exmouth Littleham Rural, Exmouth Littleham Urban, Exmouth Withycombe Raleigh, Exmouth Withycombe Urban, Honiton St Michaels, Honiton St Pauls, Lympstone, Newbridges, Newton, Poppleford and Harpford, Otterhead, Patteson, Raleigh, Seaton, Sidmouth Rural, Sidmouth Town, Sidmouth Woolbrook, Trinity, Upper Axe, Woodbury and Yarty.

North Devon
:   (i) The following wards of the District of Mid Devon, namely, Taw, Taw Vale and West Creedy; and

    (ii) the District of North Devon.

South Hams
:   (i) The following wards of the District of South Hams, namely, Avon and Harbourne, Avonleigh, Bickleigh and Shaugh, Brixton, Charterlands, Cornwood and Harford, Dart Valley, Dartington, Dartmouth Clifton, Dartmouth Hardness, Erme Valley, Garabrook, Ivybridge, Kingsbridge, Kingswear, Malborough, Marldon, Modbury, Newton and Noss, Salcombe, Saltstone, Skerries, South Brent, Sparkwell, Stoke Gabriel, Stokenham, Thurlestone, Totnes, Totnes Bridgetown, Ugborough, West Dart, Wembury and Yealmpton; and

    (ii) the following wards of the Borough of Torbay which are constituted by the Borough of Torbay (Electoral Arrangements) Order 1979 and which come into operation on 5th May 1983, namely, Blatchcombe, Furzeham-with-Churston and St Peter's-with-St Mary's.

Teignbridge
:   (i) The following ward of the District of South Hams, namely, Eastmoor; and

    (ii) the following wards of the District of Teignbridge, namely, Abbotskerswell, Ambrook, Ashburton, Bovey, Bradley, Buckfastleigh, Buckland, Bushell, Chudleigh, College, Dawlish Central, Dawlish North East, Dawlish South West, Haldon, Haytor, Ipplepen, Kingskerswell, Kingsteignton East, Kingsteignton West, Milber, Moorland, Moretonhampstead, Shaldon, Teignhydes, Teignmouth Central, Teignmouth East, Teignmouth North and Teignmouth West.

Tiverton	(i) The following wards of the District of East Devon, namely, Broadclyst, Clystbeare, Clyst Valley, Exe Valley, Ottery St Mary Rural, Ottery St Mary Town and Tale Vale;
	(ii) the following wards of the District of Mid Devon, namely, Boniface, Bradninch, Cadbury, Canal, Canonsleigh, Castle, Clare, Cullompton Outer, Cullompton Town, Culm, East Creedy, Halberton, Lawrence, Lowman, Newbrooke, Paullet, Sandford, Shuttern, Silverton, Upper Culm, Upper Yeo, Westexe North, Westexe South, Willand and Yeo; and
	(iii) the following wards of the District of Teignbridge, namely, Dunsford, Kenn Valley, Powderham, Teign Valley and Whitestone.
Torridge and West Devon	(i) The District of Torridge; and
	(ii) the Borough of West Devon.

(b) Borough Constituencies

Exeter	The City of Exeter.
Plymouth, Devonport	The following wards of the City of Plymouth, namely, Budshead, Estover, Ham, Honicknowle, Keyham, St Budeaux and Southway.
Plymouth, Drake	The following wards of the City of Plymouth, namely, Compton, Drake, St Peter, Stoke, Sutton and Trelawny.
Plymouth, Sutton	The following wards of the City of Plymouth, namely, Efford, Eggbuckland, Mount Gould, Plympton Erle, Plympton St Mary, Plymstock Dunstone and Plymstock Radford.
Torbay	The following wards of the Borough of Torbay which are constituted by the Borough of Torbay (Electoral Arrangements) Order 1979 and which come into operation on 5th May 1983, namely, Cockington-with-Chelston, Coverdale, Ellacombe, Preston, St Marychurch, St Michael's-with-Goodrington, Shiphay, Tormohun and Torwood.

DORSET

(a) County Constituencies

Christchurch	(i) The Borough of Christchurch; and
	(ii) The following wards of the District of Wimborne which are constituted by the District of Wimborne (Electoral Arrangements) Order 1980 and which come into operation on 5th May 1983, namely, Ameysford, Ferndown Central, Golf Links, Longham, St Leonards and St Ives East, St Leonards and St Ives South, St Leonards and St Ives West, Stapehill, Tricketts Cross, Verwood, West Moors North, West Moors South and West Parley.
North Dorset	(i) The District of North Dorset;
	(ii) the following wards of the District of Purbeck, namely, Lytchett Matravers and Lytchett Minster; and

(iii) the following wards of the District of Wimborne which are constituted by the District of Wimborne (Electoral Arrangements) Order 1980 and which come into operation on 5th May 1983, namely, Colehill, Corfe Mullen Central, Corfe Mullen North, Corfe Mullen South, Crane, Holt, Sixpenny Handley, Sturminster Marshall, Vale of Allen and Wimborne Minster.

South Dorset

(i) The following wards of the District of Purbeck, namely, Bere Regis, Castle, Langton, St Martin, Swanage North, Swanage South, Wareham, West Purbeck, Winfrith and Wool;

(ii) the following ward of the District of West Dorset which is constituted by the District of West Dorset (Electoral Arrangements) Order 1980 and which comes into operation on 5th May 1983, namely, Owermoigne; and

(iii) the Borough of Weymouth and Portland.

West Dorset

The following wards of the District of West Dorset which are constituted by the District of West Dorset (Electoral Arrangements) Order 1980 and which come into operation on 5th May 1983, namely, Beaminster, Bothenhampton, Bradford Abbas, Bradpole, Bridport North, Bridport South, Broadmayne, Broadwindsor, Burton Bradstock, Caundle Vale, Cerne Valley, Charminster, Charmouth, Chesil Bank, Chickerell, Dorchester East, Dorchester North, Dorchester South, Dorchester West, Frome Valley, Halstock, Holnest, Loders, Lyme Regis, Maiden Newton, Netherbury, Piddle Valley, Puddletown, Queen Thorne, Sherborne East, Sherborne West, Symondsbury, Thorncombe, Tolpuddle, Whitechurch Canonicorum, Winterborne St Martin and Yetminster.

(b) Borough Constituencies

Bournemouth East

The following wards of the Borough of Bournemouth, namely, Boscombe East, Boscombe West, Central, East Cliff, Littledown, Moordown, Muscliff, Queen's Park, Southbourne, Strouden Park and West Southbourne.

Bournemouth West

(i) The following wards of the Borough of Bournemouth, namely, Ensbury Park, Kinson, Redhill Park, Talbot Woods, Wallisdown, Westbourne, West Cliff and Winton; and

(ii) the following wards of the Borough of Poole which are constituted by the Borough of Poole (Electoral Arrangements) Order 1979 and which come into operation on 5th May 1983, namely, Alderney, Bourne Valley and Canford Magna.

Poole

The following wards of the Borough of Poole which are constituted by the Borough of Poole (Electoral Arrangements) Order 1979 and which come into operation on 5th May 1983, namely, Broadstone, Canford Cliffs, Canford Heath, Creekmoor, Hamworthy, Harbour, Newtown, Oakdale, Parkstone and Penn Hill.

DURHAM

(a) County Constituencies

Bishop Auckland

(i) The following wards of the District of Sedgefield which are constituted by the District of Sedgefield (Electoral Arrangements) Order 1979 and which come into operation on 5th May 1983, namely, Byerley, Middridge, Neville, Shafto, Simpasture, Sunnydale, Thickley, West and Woodham;

(ii) the District of Teesdale; and

(iii) the following wards of the District of Wear Valley which are constituted by the District of Wear Valley (Electoral Arrangements) Order 1979 and which come into operation on 5th May 1983, namely, Bishop Auckland Town, Cockton Hill, Coundon, Coundon Grange, Escomb, Henknowle, St Helen's, West Auckland and Woodhouse Close.

City of Durham

The City of Durham.

Easington

The following wards of the District of Easington, namely, Acre Rigg, Blackhalls, Dawdon, Dene House, Deneside, Easington Colliery, Easington Village, Eden Hill, Haswell, High Colliery, Horden North, Horden South, Howletch, Murton East, Murton West, Park, Passfield, Seaham, Shotton, South and South Hetton.

North Durham

(i) The District of Chester-le-Street; and

(ii) the following wards of the District of Derwentside, namely, Annfield Plain, Burnopfield, Catchgate, Craghead, Dipton, Havannah, South Moor, South Stanley, Stanley Hall and Tanfield.

North West Durham

(i) The following wards of the District of Derwentside, namely, Benfieldside, Blackhill, Burnhope, Castleside, Cornsay, Consett North, Consett South, Crookhall, Delves Lane, Ebchester and Medomsley, Esh, Lanchester and Leadgate; and

(ii) the following wards of the District of Wear Valley which are constituted by the District of Wear Valley (Electoral Arrangements) Order 1979 and which come into operation on 5th May 1983, namely, Crook North, Crook South, Howden, Hunwick, St John's Chapel, Stanhope, Stanley, Tow Law, Wheatbottom and Helmington Row, Willington East, Willington West and Wolsingham.

Sedgefield

(i) The following wards of the Borough of Darlington, namely, Heighington, Hurworth, Middleton St George, Sadberge and Whessoe;

(ii) the following wards of the District of Easington, namely, Deaf Hill, Hutton Henry, Thornley, Wheatley Hill and Wingate; and

(iii) the following wards of the District of Sedgefield which are constituted by the District of Sedgefield (Electoral Arrangements) Order 1979 and which come into operation on 5th May 1983, namely, Bishop Middleham, Broom, Chilton, Cornforth, Ferryhill, Fishburn, Low Spennymoor and Tudhoe Grange, Middlestone, New Trimdon and Trimdon Grange, Old Trimdon, Sedgefield, Spennymoor and Tudhoe.

(b) Borough Constituency

Darlington

The following wards of the Borough of Darlington, namely, Bank Top, Central, Cockerton East, Cockerton West, College, Eastbourne North, Eastbourne South, Harrowgate Hill, Haughton East, Haughton West, Hummersknott, Lascelles, Lingfield, Mowden, Northgate North, Northgate South, North Road, Park East, Park West and Pierremont.

EAST SUSSEX

(a) County Constituencies

Bexhill and Battle

(i) The following wards of the District of Rother which are constituted by the District of Rother (Electoral Arrangements) Order 1980 and which come into operation on 5th May 1983, namely, Ashburnham, Battle, Beckley and Peasmarsh, Bodiam and Ewhurst, Brede and Udimore, Burwash, Catsfield and Crowhurst, Central, Collington, Etchingham and Hurst Green, Northiam, Old Town, Sackville, St Marks, St Michaels, St Stephens, Salehurst, Sedlescombe and Whatlington, Sidley, Ticehurst and Westfield; and

(ii) the following wards of the District of Wealden which are constituted by the District of Wealden (Electoral Arrangements) Order 1979 and which come into operation on 5th May 1983, namely, Herstmonceux, Ninfield and Pevensey and Westham.

Hastings and Rye

(i) The Borough of Hastings; and

(ii) the following wards of the District of Rother which are constituted by the District of Rother (Electoral Arrangements) Order 1980 and which come into operation on 5th May 1983, namely, Camber, Fairlight, Guestling and Pett, Rye and Winchelsea.

Lewes

(i) The District of Lewes; and

(ii) the following wards of the District of Wealden which are constituted by the District of Wealden (Electoral Arrangements) Order 1979 and which come into operation on 5th May 1983, namely, Alfriston, Arlington and East Dean.

Wealden

The following wards of the District of Wealden which are constituted by the District of Wealden (Electoral Arrangements) Order 1979 and which come into operation on 5th May 1983, namely, Buxted, Chiddingly and East Hoathly, Crowborough East, Crowborough North, Crowborough West, Danehill, Fletching, Forest Row, Framfield, Frant, Hailsham Central and North, Hailsham East, Hailsham South and West, Hartfield, Heathfield, Hellingly, Horam, Maresfield, Mayfield, Rotherfield, Uckfield, Wadhurst, Waldron and Withyam.

(b) Borough Constituencies

Brighton, Kemptown

The following wards of the Borough of Brighton which are constituted by the Borough of Brighton (Electoral Arrangements) Order 1980 and which come into operation on 5th May 1983, namely, Hanover, King's Cliff, Marine, Moulsecoomb, Queen's Park, Rottingdean, Tenantry and Woodingdean.

Brighton, Pavilion	The following wards of the Borough of Brighton which are constituted by the Borough of Brighton (Electoral Arrangements) Order 1980 and which come into operation on 5th May 1983, namely, Hollingbury, Patcham, Preston, Regency, St Peter's Seven Dials, Stanmer and Westdene.
Eastbourne	(i) The Borough of Eastbourne; and
	(ii) the following wards of the District of Wealden which are constituted by the District of Wealden (Electoral Arrangements) Order 1979 and which come into operation on 5th May 1983, namely, Polegate North, Polegate South and Willingdon.
Hove	The Borough of Hove.

ESSEX

(a) County Constituencies

Billericay	(i) The following wards of the District of Basildon, namely, Billericay East, Billericay West, Burstead, Laindon, Wickford North and Wickford South; and
	(ii) the following wards of the Borough of Thurrock, namely, Corringham and Fobbing, Orsett, Stanford-le-Hope and The Homesteads.
Braintree	(i) The following wards of the District of Braintree, namely, Black Notley, Bocking North, Bocking South, Braintree Central, Braintree East, Braintree West, Coggeshall, Cressing, Hatfield Peverel, Kelvedon, Panfield, Rayne, Terling, Three Fields, Witham Central, Witham Chipping Hill, Witham North, Witham Silver End and Rivenhall, Witham South and Witham West; and
	(ii) the following wards of the Borough of Chelmsford, namely, Broomfield and Chignall, Good Easter Mashbury and Roxwell, Great and Little Leighs and Little Waltham, Great Waltham and Pleshey and Writtle.
Brentwood and Ongar	(i) The District of Brentwood; and
	(ii) the following wards of the District of Epping Forest, namely, Chipping Ongar, Greensted and Marden Ash, High Ongar, Lambourne, Moreton and Matching, Passingford, Roothing Country and Shelley.
Chelmsford	The following wards of the Borough of Chelmsford, namely, All Saints, Baddow Road, Boreham and Springfield, Cathedral, Danbury and Sandon, East and West Hanningfield, Galleywood, Goat Hall, Great Baddow Village, Highwood and Margaretting, Little Baddow, Mildmays, Moulsham Lodge, Oaklands, Patching Hall, Rothmans, St Andrews, Stock, The Lawns and Waterhouse Farm.
Epping Forest	The following wards of the District of Epping Forest, namely, Broadway, Buckhurst Hill East, Buckhurst Hill West, Chigwell Row, Chigwell Village, Debden Green, Epping Hemnall, Epping Lindsey, Grange Hill, High Beach, Loughton Forest, Loughton Roding, Loughton St John's, Loughton St Mary's, Paternoster, Theydon Bois, Waltham Abbey East and Waltham Abbey West.

Harlow	(i) The following wards of the District of Epping Forest, namely, Nazeing, North Weald Bassett, Roydon and Sheering; and
	(ii) the District of Harlow.
Harwich	The following wards of the District of Tendring, namely, Beaumont and Thorpe, Bockings Elm, Bradfield Wrabness and Wix, Frinton, Golf Green, Great and Little Oakley, Harwich East, Harwich East Central, Harwich West, Harwich West Central, Haven, Holland and Kirby, Little Clacton, Ramsey, Rush Green, Southcliff, St Bartholomews, St James, St John's, St Mary's, St Osyth, Tendring and Weeley and Walton.
North Colchester	(i) The following wards of the Borough of Colchester, namely, Boxted and Langham, Castle, Copford and Eight Ash Green, Dedham, Fordham, Great and Little Horkesley, Great Tey, Lexden, Marks Tey, Mile End, St Andrew's, St Anne's, St John's, St Mary's, Stanway, West Bergholt and Wivenhoe; and
	(ii) the following wards of the District of Tendring, namely, Alresford Thorrington and Frating, Ardleigh, Brightlingsea East, Brightlingsea West, Elmstead, Great Bentley, Great Bromley, Little Bromley and Little Bentley, Lawford and Manningtree and Mistley.
Rochford	(i) The following wards of the Borough of Chelmsford, namely, Ramsden Heath and Downham, Rettendon and South Hanningfield, Runwell, Woodham Ferrers North and Woodham Ferrers South; and
	(ii) the District of Rochford.
Saffron Walden	(i) The following wards of the District of Braintree, namely, Bumpstead, Castle Hedingham, Colne Engaine and Greenstead Green, Earls Colne, Gosfield, Halstead St Andrews, Halstead Trinity, Sible Hedingham, Stour Valley Central, Stour Valley North, Stour Valley South, Upper Colne and Yeldham; and
	(ii) the District of Uttlesford.
South Colchester and Maldon	(i) The following wards of the Borough of Colchester, namely, Berechurch, Birch-Messing, East Donyland, Harbour, New Town, Prettygate, Pyefleet, Shrub End, Tiptree, West Mersea and Winstree; and
	(ii) the District of Maldon.

(b) Borough Constituencies

Basildon	The following wards of the District of Basildon, namely, Fryerns Central, Fryerns East, Langdon Hills, Lee Chapel North, Nethermayne, Pitsea East, Pitsea West and Vange.
Castle Point	The District of Castle Point.
Southend East	The following wards of the Borough of Southend-on-Sea, namely, Milton, St Lukes, Shoebury, Southchurch, Thorpe and Victoria.

Southend West	The following wards of the Borough of Southend-on-Sea, namely, Belfairs, Blenheim, Chalkwell, Eastwood, Leigh, Prittlewell and Westborough.
Thurrock	The following wards of the Borough of Thurrock, namely, Aveley, Belhus, Chadwell St Mary, East Tilbury, Grays Thurrock North, Grays Thurrock Town, Little Thurrock, Ockendon, Stifford, Tilbury and West Thurrock.

GLOUCESTERSHIRE

(a) County Constituencies

Cirencester and Tewkesbury	(i) The following wards of the District of Cotswold, namely, Ampneys, Beacon, Blockley, Bourton-on-the-Water, Campden, Churn Valley, Cirencester Abbey, Cirencester Beeches, Cirencester Chesterton, Cirencester Stratton, Cirencester Watermoor, Coln, Ermin, Evenlode Vale, Fairford, Fossehill, Fosseridge, Hampton, Kempsford, Lechlade, Mickleton, Moreton-in-Marsh, Northleach, Sandywell, Sherborne Brook, Stow-on-the-Wold, Thames Head, Three Rivers, Vale and Water Park; and
	(ii) the following wards of the Borough of Tewkesbury, which are constituted by the Borough of Tewkesbury (Electoral Arrangements) Order 1980 and which come into operation on 5th May 1983, namely, Ashchurch, Bishop's Cleeve East, Bishop's Cleeve North, Bishop's Cleeve South, Cleeve Hill, Coombe Hill, Crickley, Dumbleton, Gotherington, Shurdington, Swindon, Tewkesbury Mitton, Tewkesbury Newton, Tewkesbury Prior's Park, Tewkesbury Town, Twyning and Winchcombe.
Stroud	(i) The following wards of the District of Cotswold, namely, Avening, Grumbold's Ash and Tetbury; and
	(ii) the following wards of the District of Stroud which are constituted by the District of Stroud (Electoral Arrangements) Order 1979 and which come into operation on 5th May 1983, namely, Berkeley, Bisley, Cainscross, Cam, Cambridge, Central, Chalford, Dursley, Eastington, Hinton, King's Stanley, Leonard Stanley, Minchinhampton, Nailsworth, Nibley, Painswick, Parklands, Randwick, Rodborough, Severn, Stonehouse, Thrupp, Trinity, Uley, Uplands, Vale, Whiteshill, Woodfield and Wotton and Kingswood.
West Gloucestershire	(i) The District of Forest of Dean; and
	(ii) the following wards of the Borough of Tewkesbury which are constituted by the Borough of Tewkesbury (Electoral Arrangements) Order 1980 and which come into operation on 5th May 1983, namely, Brockworth Glebe, Brockworth Moorfield, Brockfield Westfield, Churchdown Brookfield, Churchdown Parton, Churchdown Pirton, De Winton, Haw Bridge, Highnam, Horsbere and Innsworth.

(b) Borough Constituencies

Cheltenham	(i) The Borough of Cheltenham; and

(ii) the following wards of the Borough of Tewkesbury which are constituted by the Borough of Tewkesbury (Electoral Arrangements) Order 1980 and which come into operation on 5th May 1983, namely, Leckhampton with Up Hatherley, Prestbury St Mary's and Prestbury St Nicolas.

Gloucester	(i) The City of Gloucester; and
	(ii) the following wards of the District of Stroud which are constituted by the District of Stroud (Electoral Arrangements) Order 1979 and which come into operation on 5th May 1983, namely, Quedgeley and Hardwicke and Upton St Leonards.

GREATER LONDON

Borough Constituencies

Barking	The following wards of the London Borough of Barking and Dagenham, namely, Abbey, Cambell, Eastbury, Gascoigne, Goresbrook, Longbridge, Manor, Parsloes and Thames.
Battersea	The following wards of the London Borough of Wandsworth, namely, Balham, Fairfield, Latchmere, Northcote, Queenstown, St John, St Mary's Park and Shaftesbury.
Beckenham	The following wards of the London Borough of Bromley, namely, Anerley, Clock House, Copers Cope, Eden Park, Kelsey Park, Lawrie Park and Kent House, Penge and Shortlands.
Bethnal Green and Stepney	The following wards of the London Borough of Tower Hamlets, namely, Holy Trinity, Redcoat, St Dunstan's, St James', St Katharine's, St Mary's, St Peter's, Spitalfields and Weavers.
Bexleyheath	The following wards of the London Borough of Bexley, namely, Barnehurst, Barnehurst North, Brampton, Christchurch, Danson, East Wickham, Falconwood, St Michael's and Upton.
Bow and Poplar	The following wards of the London Borough of Tower Hamlets, namely, Blackwall, Bow, Bromley, East India, Grove, Lansbury, Limehouse, Millwall, Park and Shadwell.
Brent East	The following wards of the London Borough of Brent, namely, Brentwater, Brondesbury Park, Carlton, Chamberlayne, Church End, Cricklewood, Gladstone, Kilburn, Mapesbury, Queens Park and Willesden Green.
Brent North	The following wards of the London Borough of Brent, namely, Barnhill, Fryent, Kenton, Kingsbury, Preston, Queensbury, Roe Green, St Andrew's, Sudbury and Sudbury Court.
Brent South	The following wards of the London Borough of Brent, namely, Alperton, Barham, Harlesden, Kensal Rise, Manor, Roundwood, St Raphael's, Stonebridge, Tokyngton and Wembley Central.

Brentford and Isleworth

The following wards of the London Borough of Hounslow, namely, Brentford Clifden, Chiswick Homefields, Chiswick Riverside, Gunnersbury, Hounslow Central, Hounslow South, Isleworth North, Isleworth South, Spring Grove and Turnham Green.

Carshalton and Wallington

The following wards of the London Borough of Sutton, namely, Beddington North, Beddington South, Carshalton Beeches, Carshalton Central, Carshalton North, Clockhouse, St Helier North, St Helier South, Wallington North, Wallington South, Wandle Valley, Woodcote and Wrythe Green.

Chelsea

The following wards of the Royal Borough of Kensington and Chelsea, namely, Abingdon, Brompton, Cheyne, Church, Courtfield, Earls Court, Hans Town, North Stanley, Redcliffe, Royal Hospital and South Stanley.

Chingford

The following wards of the London Borough of Waltham Forest, namely, Chapel End, Chingford Green, Endlebury, Hale End, Hatch Lane, Larkswood and Valley.

Chipping Barnet

The following wards of the London Borough of Barnet, namely, Arkley, Brunswick Park, East Barnet, Hadley and Totteridge.

Chislehurst

The following wards of the London Borough of Bromley, namely, Bickley, Chislehurst, Mottingham, Plaistow and Sundridge and St Paul's Cray.

Croydon Central

The following wards of the London Borough of Croydon, namely, Fairfield, Fieldway, Heathfield, New Addington, Spring Park and Waddon.

Croydon North East

The following wards of the London Borough of Croydon, namely, Addiscombe, Ashburton, Monks Orchard, Rylands, South Norwood, Thornton Heath, Upper Norwood and Woodside.

Croydon North West

The following wards of the London Borough of Croydon, namely, Bensham Manor, Beulah, Broad Green, Norbury, West Thornton and Whitehorse Manor.

Croydon South

The following wards of the London Borough of Croydon, namely, Coulsdon East, Croham, Kenley, Purley, Sanderstead, Selsdon and Woodcote and Coulsdon West.

Dagenham

The following wards of the London Borough of Barking and Dagenham, namely, Alibon, Chadwell Heath, Eastbrook, Fanshawe, Heath, Marks Gate, River, Triptons, Valence and Village.

Dulwich

The following wards of the London Borough of Southwark, namely, Alleyn, Bellenden, College, Lyndhurst, Ruskin, Rye, The Lane and Waverley.

Ealing, Acton

The following wards of the London Borough of Ealing, namely, Ealing Common, Hanger Lane, Heathfield, Pitshanger, Southfield, Springfield, Vale and Victoria.

Ealing North

The following wards of the London Borough of Ealing, namely, Argyle, Costons, Hobbayne, Mandeville, Perivale, Ravenor, West End and Wood End.

Ealing, Southall	The following wards of the London Borough of Ealing, namely, Dormers Wells, Elthorne, Glebe, Mount Pleasant, Northcote, Northfield, Walpole and Waxlow.
Edmonton	The following wards of the London Borough of Enfield, namely, Angel Road, Craig Park, Huxley, Jubilee, Latymer, Raglan, St Alphege, St Marks, St Peters, Village and Weir Hall.
Eltham	The following wards of the London Borough of Greenwich, namely, Avery Hill, Coldharbour, Deansfield, Eltham Park, Herbert, Middle Park, New Eltham, Nightingale, Palace, Sherard, Sutcliffe, Tarn and Well Hall.
Enfield North	The following wards of the London Borough of Enfield, namely, Bullsmoor, Chase, Enfield Lock, Enfield Wash, Green Street, Hoe Lane, Ponders End, Southbury, Town, Willow and Worcesters.
Enfield, Southgate	The following wards of the London Borough of Enfield, namely, Arnos, Bowes, Grange, Grovelands, Highfield, Merryhills, Oakwood, Palmers Green, Southgate Green, Trent and Winchmore Hill.
Erith and Crayford	The following wards of the London Borough of Bexley, namely, Belvedere, Bostall, Crayford, Erith, North End, Northumberland Heath and Thamesmead East.
Feltham and Heston	The following wards of the London Borough of Hounslow, namely, Cranford, East Bedfont, Feltham Central, Feltham North, Feltham South, Hanworth, Heston Central, Heston East, Heston West, Hounslow Heath and Hounslow West.
Finchley	The following wards of the London Borough of Barnet, namely, East Finchley, Finchley, Friern Barnet, St Pauls and Woodhouse.
Fulham	The following wards of the London Borough of Hammersmith and Fulham, namely, Avonmore, Colehill, Crabtree, Eel Brook, Gibbs Green, Margravine, Normand, Palace, Sands End, Sherbrooke, Sulivan, Town and Walham.
Greenwich	The following wards of the London Borough of Greenwich, namely, Blackheath, Charlton, Ferrier, Hornfair, Kidbrooke, Rectory Field, St Alfege, Trafalgar, Vanbrugh and West.
Hackney North and Stoke Newington	The following wards of the London Borough of Hackney, namely, Brownswood, Clissold, Eastdown, Leabridge, New River, North Defoe, Northfield, Northwold, Rectory, South Defoe and Springfield.
Hackney South and Shoreditch	The following wards of the London Borough of Hackney, namely, Chatham, Dalston, De Beauvoir, Haggerston, Homerton, Kings Park, Moorfields, Queensbridge, Victoria, Wenlock, Westdown and Wick.
Hammersmith	The following wards of the London Borough of Hammersmith and Fulham, namely, Addison, Broadway, Brook Green, College Park and Old Oak, Coningham, Grove, Ravenscourt, Starch Green, White City and Shepherds Bush and Wormholt.

Hampstead and Highgate	The following wards of the London Borough of Camden, namely, Adelaide, Belsize, Fitzjohns, Fortune Green, Frognal, Hampstead Town, Highgate, Kilburn, Priory, South End, Swiss Cottage and West End.
Harrow East	The following wards of the London Borough of Harrow, namely, Canons, Centenary, Greenhill, Harrow Weald, Kenton East, Kenton West, Marlborough, Stanmore Park, Stanmore South, Wealdstone and Wemborough.
Harrow West	The following wards of the London Borough of Harrow, namely, Harrow on the Hill, Hatch End, Headstone North, Headstone South, Pinner, Pinner West, Rayners Lane, Ridgeway, Roxbourne and Roxeth.
Hayes and Harlington	The following wards of the London Borough of Hillingdon, namely, Barnhill, Botwell, Charville, Crane, Harlington, Heathrow, Townfield, Wood End and Yeading.
Hendon North	The following wards of the London Borough of Barnet, namely, Burnt Oak, Colindale, Edgware, Hale and Mill Hill.
Hendon South	The following wards of the London Borough of Barnet, namely, Childs Hill, Garden Suburb, Golders Green, Hendon and West Hendon.
Holborn and St Pancras	The following wards of the London Borough of Camden, namely, Bloomsbury, Brunswick, Camden, Castlehaven, Caversham, Chalk Farm, Gospel Oak, Grafton, Holborn, King's Cross, Regent's Park, St John's, St Pancras and Somers Town.
Hornchurch	The following wards of the London Borough of Havering, namely, Airfield, Elm Park, Hacton, Hylands, Rainham, St Andrew's and South Hornchurch.
Hornsey and Wood Green	The following wards of the London Borough of Haringey, namely, Alexandra, Archway, Bowes Park, Crouch End, Fortis Green, Highgate, Hornsey Central, Hornsey Vale, Muswell Hill, Noel Park, South Hornsey and Woodside.
Ilford North	The following wards of the London Borough of Redbridge, namely, Aldborough, Barkingside, Chadwell, Fairlop, Fullwell, Hainault and Seven Kings.
Ilford South	The following wards of the London Borough of Redbridge, namely, Clementswood, Cranbrook, Goodmayes, Loxford, Mayfield, Newbury and Valentines.
Islington North	The following wards of the London Borough of Islington, namely, Gillespie, Highbury, Highview, Hillrise, Junction, Mildmay, Quadrant, St George's, Sussex and Tollington.
Islington South and Finsbury	The following wards of the London Borough of Islington, namely, Barnesbury, Bunhill, Canonbury East, Canonbury West, Clerkenwell, Hillmarton, Holloway, St Mary, St Peter and Thornhill.
Kensington	The following wards of the Royal Borough of Kensington and Chelsea, namely, Avondale, Campden, Colville, Golborne, Holland, Kelfield, Norland, Pembridge, Queen's Gate and St Charles.

Kingston upon Thames	The following wards of the Royal Borough of Kingston upon Thames, namely, Burlington, Cambridge, Canbury, Coombe, Grove, Hill, Malden Manor, Norbiton, Norbiton Park, St James and Tudor.
Lewisham, Deptford	The following wards of the London Borough of Lewisham, namely, Blythe Hill, Crofton Park, Drake, Evelyn, Grinling Gibbons, Ladywell, Marlowe and Pepys.
Lewisham East	The following wards of the London Borough of Lewisham, namely, Blackheath, Churchdown, Downham, Grove Park, Hither Green, Manor Lee, St Margaret, St Mildred and Whitefoot.
Lewisham West	The following wards of the London Borough of Lewisham, namely, Bellingham, Catford, Forest Hill, Horniman, Perry Hill, Rushey Green, St Andrew, Sydenham East and Sydenham West.
Leyton	The following wards of the London Borough of Waltham Forest, namely, Cann Hall, Cathall, Forest, Grove Green, Lea Bridge, Leyton and Leytonstone.
Mitcham and Morden	The following wards of the London Borough of Merton, namely, Colliers Wood, Figge's Marsh, Graveney, Lavender, Longthornton, Lower Morden, Phipps Bridge, Pollards Hill, Ravensbury and St Helier.
Newham North East	The following wards of the London Borough of Newham, namely, Castle, Central, Greatfield, Kensington, Little Ilford, Manor Park, Monega, St Stephens and Wall End.
Newham North West	The following wards of the London Borough of Newham, namely, Forest Gate, New Town, Park, Plashet, Stratford, Upton and West Ham.
Newham South	The following wards of the London Borough of Newham, namely, Beckton, Bemersyde, Canning Town and Grange, Custom House and Silvertown, Hudsons, Ordnance, Plaistow and South.
Norwood	The following wards of the London Borough of Lambeth, namely, Angell, Gipsy Hill, Herne Hill, Knight's Hill, St Martin's, Thurlow Park and Tulse Hill.
Old Bexley and Sidcup	The following wards of the London Borough of Bexley, namely, Blackfen, Blendon and Penhill, Cray, Lamorbey, St Mary's, Sidcup East and Sidcup West.
Orpington	The following wards of the London Borough of Bromley, namely, Chelsfield and Goddington, Crofton, Farnborough, Orpington Central, Petts Wood and Knoll and St Mary Cray.
Peckham	The following wards of the London Borough of Southwark, namely, Barset, Brunswick, Consort, Faraday, Friary, Liddle, Newington and St Giles.
Putney	The following wards of the London Borough of Wandsworth, namely, East Putney, Parkside, Roehampton, Southfield, Thamesfield, West Hill and West Putney.
Ravensbourne	The following wards of the London Borough of Bromley, namely, Biggin Hill, Bromley Common and Keston, Darwin, Hayes, Martins Hill and Town, West Wickham North and West Wickham South.

Richmond and Barnes	The following wards of the London Borough of Richmond upon Thames, namely, Barnes, East Sheen, East Twickenham, Ham and Petersham, Kew, Mortlake, Palewell, Richmond Hill and Richmond Town.
Romford	The following wards of the London Borough of Havering, namely, Brooklands, Chase Cross, Collier Row, Gidea Park, Heath Park, Mawney, Oldchurch, Rise Park and St Edward's.
Ruislip-Northwood	The following wards of the London Borough of Hillingdon, namely, Bourne, Cavendish, Deansfield, Eastcote, Manor, Northwood, Northwood Hills, Ruislip and St Martins.
Southwark and Bermondsey	The following wards of the London Borough of Southwark, namely, Abbey, Bricklayers, Browning, Burgess, Cathedral, Chaucer, Dockyard, Riverside and Rotherhithe.
Streatham	The following wards of the London Borough of Lambeth, namely, Clapham Park, St Leonard's, Streatham Hill, Streatham South, Streatham Wells, Thornton and Town Hall.
Surbiton	The following wards of the Royal Borough of Kingston upon Thames, namely, Berrylands, Chessington North, Chessington South, Hook, St Mark's, Surbiton Hill, Tolworth East, Tolworth South and Tolworth West.
Sutton and Cheam	The following wards of the London Borough of Sutton, namely, Belmont, Cheam South, Cheam West, North Cheam, Rosehill, Sutton Central, Sutton Common, Sutton East, Sutton South, Sutton West, Worcester Park North and Worcester Park South.
The City of London and Westminster South	The City of London, and the following wards of the City of Westminster, namely, Baker Street, Belgrave, Bryanston, Cavendish, Churchill, Hyde Park, Knightsbridge, Millbank, St James's, St George's, Victoria and West End.
Tooting	The following wards of the London Borough of Wandsworth, namely, Bedford, Earlsfield, Furzedown, Graveney, Nightingale, Springfield and Tooting.
Tottenham	The following wards of the London Borough of Haringey, namely, Bruce Grove, Coleraine, Green Lanes, Harringay, High Cross, Park, Seven Sisters, South Tottenham, Tottenham Central, West Green and White Hart Lane.
Twickenham	The following wards of the London Borough of Richmond upon Thames, namely, Central Twickenham, Hampton, Hampton Hill, Hampton Nursery, Hampton Wick, Heathfield, South Twickenham, Teddington, West Twickenham and Whitton.
Upminster	The following wards of the London Borough of Havering, namely, Ardleigh Green, Cranham East, Cranham West, Emerson Park, Gooshays, Harold Wood, Heaton, Hilldene and Upminster.
Uxbridge	The following wards of the London Borough of Hillingdon, namely, Colham, Cowley, Harefield, Hillingdon East, Hillingdon North, Hillingdon West, Ickenham, Uxbridge North, Uxbridge South, West Drayton and Yiewsley.

Vauxhall	The following wards of the London Borough of Lambeth, namely, Bishop's, Clapham Town, Ferndale, Larkhall, Oval, Prince's, Stockwell and Vassall.
Walthamstow	The following wards of the London Borough of Waltham Forest, namely, Higham Hill, High Street, Hoe Street, Lloyd's Park, St James Street and Wood Street.
Wanstead and Woodford	The following wards of the London Borough of Redbridge, namely, Bridge, Church End, Clayhall, Monkhams, Roding, Snaresbrook and Wanstead.
Westminster North	The following wards of the London City of Westminster, namely, Bayswater, Church Street, Hamilton Terrace, Harrow Road, Lancaster Gate, Little Venice, Lords, Maida Vale, Queen's Park, Regent's Park and Westbourne.
Wimbledon	The following wards of the London Borough of Merton, namely, Abbey, Cannon Hill, Dundonald, Durnsford, Hillside, Merton Park, Raynes Park, Trinity, Village and West Barnes.
Woolwich	The following wards of the London Borough of Greenwich, namely, Abbey Wood, Arsenal, Burrage, Eynsham, Glyndon, Lakedale, Plumstead Common, St Mary's, St Nicholas, Shrewsbury, Slade, Thamesmead Moorings and Woolwich Common.

GREATER MANCHESTER

(a) County Constituencies

Bolton West	The following wards of the Borough of Bolton, namely, Blackrod, Deane-Cum-Heaton, Halliwell, Horwich, Hulton Park, Smithills and Westhoughton.
Hazel Grove	The following wards of the Borough of Stockport, namely, Bredbury, Great Moor, Hazel Grove, North Marple, Romiley and South Marple.
Heywood and Middleton	The following wards of the Borough of Rochdale, namely, Heywood North, Heywood South, Heywood West, Middleton Central, Middleton East, Middleton North, Middleton South and Middleton West.
Littleborough and Saddleworth	(i) The following wards of the Borough of Oldham, namely, Crompton, Lees, Saddleworth East, Saddleworth West and Shaw; and (ii) the following wards of the Borough of Rochdale, namely, Littleborough, Milnrow and Wardle.
Makerfield	The following wards of the Borough of Wigan, namely, Abram, Ashton-Golborne, Bryn, Lightshaw, Orrell, Winstanley and Worsley Mesnes.
Stalybridge and Hyde	The following wards of the Borough of Tameside, namely, Dukinfield, Dukinfield Stalybridge, Hyde Godley, Hyde Newton, Hyde Werneth, Longdendale, Stalybridge North and Stalybridge South.

Worsley	(i) The following wards of the City of Salford, namely, Cadishead, Irlam, Little Hulton, Walkden North, Walkden South and Worsley and Boothstown; and
	(ii) the following wards of the Borough of Wigan, namely, Bedford-Astley and Tyldesley East.

(b) Borough Constituencies

Altrincham and Sale	The following wards of the Borough of Trafford, namely, Altrincham, Bowdon, Broadheath, Brooklands, Hale, Sale Moor, Timperley and Village.
Ashton under Lyne	The following wards of the Borough of Tameside, namely, Ashton Hurst, Ashton St Michael's, Ashton St Peter's, Ashton Waterloo, Droylsden East, Droylsden West and Mossley.
Bolton North East	The following wards of the Borough of Bolton, namely, Astley Bridge, Bradshaw, Breightmet, Bromley Cross, Central and Tonge.
Bolton South East	The following wards of the Borough of Bolton, namely, Burnden, Daubhill, Derby, Farnworth, Harper Green, Kearsley and Little Lever.
Bury North	The following wards of the Borough of Bury, namely, Church, East, Elton, Moorside, Ramsbottom, Redvales, Tottington and Unsworth.
Bury South	The following wards of the Borough of Bury, namely, Besses, Holyrood, Pilkington Park, Radcliffe Central, Radcliffe North, Radcliffe South, St Mary's and Sedgley.
Cheadle	The following wards of the Borough of Stockport, namely, Cheadle, Cheadle Hulme North, Cheadle Hulme South, East Bramhall, Heald Green and West Bramhall.
Davyhulme	The following wards of the Borough of Trafford, namely, Bucklow, Davyhulme East, Davyhulme West, Flixton, Mersey St Mary's, Priory, St Martin's and Urmston.
Denton and Reddish	(i) The following wards of the Borough of Stockport, namely, Brinnington, North Reddish and South Reddish; and
	(ii) the following wards of the Borough of Tameside, namely, Audenshaw, Denton North East, Denton South and Denton West.
Eccles	The following wards of the City of Salford, namely, Barton, Eccles, Pendlebury, Swinton North, Swinton South, Weaste and Seedley and Winton.
Leigh	The following wards of the Borough of Wigan, namely, Atherton, Hindley, Hindley Green, Hindsford, Hope Carr, Leigh Central and Leigh East.
Manchester, Blackley	The following wards of the City of Manchester, namely, Blackley, Charlestown, Crumpsall, Harpurhey, Lightbowne and Moston.
Manchester, Central	The following wards of the City of Manchester, namely, Ardwick, Beswick and Clayton, Bradford, Central, Cheetham, Hulme and Newton Heath.
Manchester, Gorton	The following wards of the City of Manchester, namely, Fallowfield, Gorton North, Gorton South, Levenshulme, Longsight and Rusholme.

Manchester, Withington	The following wards of the City of Manchester, namely, Barlow Moor, Burnage, Chorlton, Didsbury, Old Moat and Withington.
Manchester, Wythenshawe	The following wards of the City of Manchester, namely, Baguley, Benchill, Brooklands, Northenden, Sharston and Woodhouse Park.
Oldham Central and Royton	The following wards of the Borough of Oldham, namely, Alexandra, Coldhurst, Royton North, Royton South, St James, St Marys, St Pauls and Waterhead.
Oldham West	The following wards of the Borough of Oldham, namely, Chadderton Central, Chadderton North, Chadderton South, Failsworth East, Failsworth West, Hollinwood and Werneth.
Rochdale	The following wards of the Borough of Rochdale, namely, Balderstone, Brimrod and Deeplish, Castleton, Central and Falinge, Healey, Newbold, Norden and Bamford, Smallbridge and Wardleworth and Spotland.
Salford East	The following wards of the City of Salford, namely, Blackfriars, Broughton, Claremont, Kersal, Langworthy, Ordsall and Pendleton.
Stockport	The following wards of the Borough of Stockport, namely, Cale Green, Davenport, Edgeley, Heaton Mersey, Heaton Moor and Manor.
Stretford	(i) The following wards of the City of Manchester, namely, Moss Side and Whalley Range; and
	(ii) the following wards of the Borough of Trafford, namely, Clifford, Longford, Park, Stretford and Talbot.
Wigan	The following wards of the Borough of Wigan, namely, Aspull-Standish, Beech Hill, Ince, Langtree, Newtown, Norley, Swinley and Whelley.

HAMPSHIRE

(a) County Constituencies

Aldershot	(i) The following wards of the District of Hart, namely, Eversley, Frogmore and Darby Green, Hartley Wintney, Hawley, Whitewater, Yateley East, Yateley North and Yateley West; and
	(ii) the Borough of Rushmoor.
Basingstoke	The following wards of the Borough of Basingstoke and Deane, namely, Basing, Black Dam, Bramley, Brighton Hill, Buckskin, Chapel, Daneshill, Eastrop, Farleigh Wallop, Kempshott, King's Furlong, Norden, North Waltham, Oakley, Pamber, Popley, Sherborne St John, Sherfield on Loddon, Silchester, South Ham, Upton Grey, Viables, Westside and Winklebury.
East Hampshire	(i) The following wards of the District of East Hampshire, namely, Binsted, Bramshott and Liphook, Clanfield and Buriton, East Meon and Langrish, Froyle and Bentley, Froxfield and Steep, Grayshott, Headley, Horndean-Catherington, Horndean-Hazleton, Horndean-Kings, Horndean-Murray, Liss, Petersfield-Heath, Petersfield-St Mary's, Petersfield-St Peters, Rowlands Castle, Selborne, The Hangers, Whitehill-Bordon and Whitehill and Whitehill-Lindford; and

Fareham

(ii) the following wards of the District of Hart, namely, Church Crookham, Crondall, Fleet Courtmoor, Fleet Pondtail, Fleet West, Hook, Long Sutton and Odiham.

(i) The following wards of the Borough of Fareham, namely, Fareham East, Fareham North, Fareham North-West, Fareham South, Fareham West, Locks Heath, Porchester Central, Porchester East, Porchester West, Sarisbury, Titchfield and Warsash; and

(ii) the following wards of the City of Winchester, namely, Boarhunt and Southwick, Curdridge, Denmead, Droxford Soberton and Hambledon, Shedfield, Swanmore, Waltham Chase and Wickham.

New Forest

The following wards of the District of New Forest, namely, Barton, Bashley, Becton, Boldre, Bransgore and Sopley, Brockenhurst, Copythorne South, Downlands, Fordingbridge, Forest North, Forest North West, Forest South, Forest West, Hordle, Lymington Town, Lyndhurst, Milford, Milton, Pennington, Ringwood North, Ringwood South and Sway.

North West Hampshire

(i) The following wards of the Borough of Basingstoke and Deane, namely, Baughurst, Burghclere, East Woodhay, Kingsclere, Overton, St Mary Bourne, Tadley Central, Tadley North, Tadley South and Whitchurch; and

(ii) the following wards of the Borough of Test Valley, namely, Alamein, Anna, Bourne Valley, Dun Valley, Harewood, Harroway, Kings Somborne and Michelmersh, Millway, Nether Wallop and Broughton, Over Wallop, St Mary's, Stockbridge, Tedworth, Weyhill and Winton.

Romsey and Waterside

(i) The following wards of the District of New Forest, namely, Blackfield and Langley, Colbury, Dibden and Hythe North, Dibden Purlieu, Fawley Holbury, Hythe South, Marchwood, Netley Marsh, Totton Central, Totton North and Totton South; and

(ii) the following wards of the Borough of Test Valley, namely, Abbey, Blackwater, Chilworth and Nursling, Cuppernham, Field, North Baddesley, Romsey Extra and Tadburn.

Winchester

(i) The following wards of the District of East Hampshire, namely, Alton-Holybourne, Alton North East, Alton North West, Alton South East, Alton South West and Beech, Farringdon, Four Marks, Medstead, North Downland and Ropley and West Tisted; and

(ii) the following wards of the City of Winchester, namely, Bishops Sutton, Bishops Waltham, Cheriton, Compton, Durley and Upham, Itchen Valley, Littleton, Micheldever, New Alresford, Olivers Battery, Otterbourne and Hursley, Owslebury and Colden Common, St Barnabas, St Bartholomew, St John and All Saints, St Luke, St Michael, St Paul, Sparsholt, The Worthys, Twyford, Upper Meon Valley and Wonston.

(b) Borough Constituencies

Eastleigh

(i) The Borough of Eastleigh; and

(ii) the following ward of the City of Southampton, namely, Woolston.

Gosport	(i) The following wards of the Borough of Fareham, namely, Hill Head and Stubbington; and
	(ii) the Borough of Gosport.
Havant	The following wards of the Borough of Havant, namely, Barncroft, Battins, Bedhampton, Bondfields, Cowplain, Emsworth, Hart Plain, Hayling East, Hayling West, St Faith's, Warren Park and Waterloo.
Portsmouth North	(i) The following wards of the Borough of Havant, namely, Purbrook and Stakes; and
	(ii) the following wards of the City of Portsmouth which are constituted by the City of Portsmouth (Electoral Arrangements) Order 1979 and which come into operation on 5th May 1983, namely, Copnor, Cosham, Drayton and Farlington, Hilsea, Nelson and Paulsgrove.
Portsmouth South	The following wards of the City of Portsmouth which are constituted by the City of Portsmouth (Electoral Arrangements) Order 1979 and which come into operation on 5th May 1983, namely, Charles Dickens, Fratton, Havelock, Highland, Milton, St Jude and St Thomas.
Southampton, Itchen	The following wards of the City of Southampton, namely, Bargate, Bitterne, Bitterne Park, Harefield, Peartree, St Lukes and Sholing.
Southampton, Test	The following wards of the City of Southampton, namely, Bassett, Coxford, Freemantle, Millbrook, Portswood, Redbridge and Shirley.

HEREFORD AND WORCESTER

(a) County Constituencies

Bromsgrove	The District of Bromsgrove.
Hereford	(i) The City of Hereford; and
	(ii) the following wards of the District of South Herefordshire, namely, Backbury, Broad Oak, Dinedor Hill, Doward, Fownhope, Garron, Golden Valley, Gorsley, Gorsty, Harewood End, Hollington, Kingsthorne, Merbach, Olchon, Old Gore, Penyard, Pontrilas, Ross-on-Wye East, Ross-on-Wye West, Stoney Street, Tram Inn, Walford, Whitfield and Wilton.
Leominster	(i) The District of Leominster;
	(ii) the following wards of the District of Malvern Hills, namely, Baldwin, Bringsty, Broadheath, Bromyard, Butterley, Cradley, Frome, Frome Vale, Hallow, Hegdon, Hope End, Laugherne Hill, Leadon Vale, Ledbury, Leigh and Bransford, Marcle Ridge, Martley, Temeside and Woodbury; and
	(iii) the following wards of the District of South Herefordshire, namely, Burghill, Burmarsh, Dinmore Hill, Hagley, Magna, Munstone, Swainshill and Thinghill.
Mid Worcestershire	(i) The Borough of Redditch; and

| | (ii) the following wards of the District of Wychavon, namely, Bowbrook, Claines Central and West, Claines East, Dodderhill, Droitwich Central, Droitwich South, Droitwich West, Hanbury, Hartlebury, Lovett and Ombersley. |

South Worcestershire

(i) The following wards of the District of Malvern Hills, namely, Chase, Kempsey, Langland, Link, Longdon, Morton, Powyke, Priory, Ripple, The Hanleys, Trinity, Upton upon Severn, Wells and West; and

(ii) the following wards of the District of Wychavon, namely, Badsey, Bredon, Bretforton and Offenham, Broadway, Eckington, Elmley Castle, Evesham East, Evesham Hampton, Evesham North, Evesham South, Evesham West, Fladbury, Harvington and Norton, Honeybourne and Pebworth, Pershore Holy Cross, Pershore St Andrews, Somerville, South Bredon Hill, The Littletons and Wickhamford.

Wyre Forest

The District of Wyre Forest.

(b) Borough Constituency

Worcester

(i) The City of Worcester; and

(ii) the following wards of the District of Wychavon, namely, Drakes Broughton, Inkberrow, Lenches, Pinvin, Spetchley and Upton Snodsbury.

HERTFORDSHIRE

(a) County Constituencies

Hertford and Stortford

The following wards of the District of East Hertfordshire, namely, Bishop's Stortford Central, Bishop's Stortford Chantry, Bishop's Stortford Parsonage, Bishop's Stortford Thorley, Braughing, Buntingford, Hertford Bengeo, Hertford Castle, Hertford Kingsmead, Hertford Sele, Hunsdon, Little Hadham, Much Hadham, Sawbridgeworth, Standon St Mary, Stapleford, Tewin, Thundridge, Ware Christchurch, Ware Priory, Ware St Mary's and Ware Trinity.

Hertsmere

(i) The Borough of Hertsmere; and

(ii) the following ward of the City of St Albans, namely, London Colney.

North Hertfordshire

The following wards of the District of North Hertfordshire, namely, Arbury, Ashbrook, Baldock, Bearton, Cadwell, Grange, Highbury, Hitchwood, Hoo, Kimpton, Letchworth East, Letchworth South East, Letchworth South West, Newsells, Offa, Oughton, Priory, Royston East, Royston West, Sandon, Walsworth, Weston and Wilbury.

St Albans

The following wards of the City of St Albans, namely, Ashley, Batchwood, Clarence, Colney Heath, Cunningham, Harpenden East, Harpenden North, Harpenden South, Harpenden West, Marshalswick North, Marshalswick South, Redbourn, St Peters, Sandridge, Sopwell and Verulam.

South West Hertfordshire

(i) The following wards of the District of Dacorum, namely, Berkhamsted Central, Berkhamsted East, Berkhamsted West, Bovingdon and Flaunden, Chipperfield, Kings Langley and Northchurch; and

(ii) the following wards of the District of Three Rivers, namely, Ashridge, Bedmond, Carpenders Park, Chorleywood, Chorleywood West, Croxley Green, Croxley Green North, Croxley Green South, Hayling, Langlebury, Maple Cross and West Hyde, Mill End, Money Hill, Moor Park, Northwick, Oxhey Hall, Rickmansworth and Sarratt.

Stevenage

(i) The following wards of the District of East Hertfordshire, namely, Cottered, Datchworth, Munden, Walkern and Watton-at-Stone.

(ii) the following wards of the District of North Hertfordshire, namely, Codicote and Knebworth; and

(iii) the Borough of Stevenage.

Welwyn Hatfield

(i) The following ward of the City of St Albans, namely, Wheathampstead; and

(ii) the following wards of the District of Welwyn Hatfield, namely, Brookmans Park and Little Heath, Haldens, Handside, Hatfield Central, Hatfield East, Hatfield North, Hatfield South, Hollybush, Howlands, Peartree, Sherrards, Welham Green and Redhall, Welwyn East and Welwyn West.

West Hertfordshire

The following wards of the District of Dacorum, namely, Adeyfield East, Adeyfield West, Aldbury and Wigginton, Ashridge, Bennetts End, Boxmoor, Central, Chaulden, Crabtree, Cupid Green, Flamstead and Markyate, Gadebridge, Grove Hill, Highfield, Leverstock Green, Nash Mills, South, Tring Central, Tring East, Tring West and Warners End.

(b) Borough Constituencies

Broxbourne

(i) The Borough of Broxbourne;

(ii) the following wards of the District of East Hertfordshire, namely, Great Amwell, Little Amwell and Stanstead; and

(iii) the following ward of the District of Welwyn Hatfield, namely, Northaw.

Watford

(i) The following wards of the City of St Albans, namely, Park Street and St Stephens;

(ii) the following wards of the District of Three Rivers, namely, Abbots Langley and Leavesden; and

(iii) the Borough of Watford.

HUMBERSIDE

(a) County Constituencies

Beverley

The following wards of the Borough of the East Yorkshire Borough of Beverley, namely, Anlaby, Brough, Castle, Hessle East, Hessle West, Kirk Ella, Leconfield, Leven, Mill Beck and Croxby, Minster North, Minster South, Molsecroft, Priory, St Mary's East, St Mary's West, Springfield, Swanland, Tickton, Willerby and Woodmansey.

Boothferry

(i) The Borough of Boothferry;

(ii) the following wards of the Borough of East Yorkshire, namely, Battleburn, Garrowby, Market Weighton, Pocklington, Stamford Bridge, Vale, Wilberfosse, Wold and Woodland; and

(iii) the following wards of the Borough of the East Yorkshire Borough of Beverley, namely, Cherry Holme, Skidby and Rowley, South Cave and Walkington.

Bridlington

(i) The following wards of the Borough of East Yorkshire, namely, Bridlington Bessingby, Bridlington Hilderthorpe, Bridlington Old Town East, Bridlington Old Town West, Bridlington Quay North, Bridlington Quay South, Coastal, Driffield North, Driffield South, Hutton Cranswick, Lowland, Nafferton, Roman, St John and Viking; and

(ii) the Borough of Holderness.

Brigg and Cleethorpes

(i) The Borough of Cleethorpes; and

(ii) the following wards of the Borough of Glanford, namely, Abbey, Barton-upon-Humber Bridge, Barton-upon-Humber Park, Brigg, Goxhill, Humber, Kirton, North Ancholme, Scawby, South Ancholme, Ulceby, Wold and Wrawby.

(b) Borough Constituencies

Glanford and Scunthorpe

(i) The following wards of the Borough of Glanford, namely, Bottesford Central, Bottesford East, Bottesford West, Broughton, Burton upon Stather, Gunness, Messingham, North West, Trentside and Winterton; and

(ii) the Borough of Scunthorpe.

Great Grimsby

The Borough of Great Grimsby.

Kingston upon Hull East

The following wards of the City of Kingston upon Hull which are constituted by the City of Kingston upon Hull (Electoral Arrangements) Order 1979 and which come into operation on 5th May 1983, namely, Drypool, Holderness, Ings, Longhill, Marfleet, Southcoates and Sutton.

Kingston upon Hull North

The following wards of the City of Kingston upon Hull which are constituted by the City of Kingston upon Hull (Electoral Arrangements) Order 1979 and which came into operation on 5th May 1983, namely, Avenue, Beverley, Newland, Noddle Hill, Orchard Park, Stoneferry and University.

Kingston upon Hull West

The following wards of the City of Kingston upon Hull which are constituted by the City of Kingston upon Hull (Electoral Arrangements) Order 1979 and which come into operation on 5th May 1983, namely, Boothferry, Derringham, Myton, Newington, Pickering and St Andrews.

ISLE OF WIGHT

County Constituency

Isle of Wight

The administrative county of Isle of Wight.

KENT

(a) County Constituencies

Ashford	The Borough of Ashford.
Canterbury	(i) The following wards of the City of Canterbury, namely, Barham Downs, Barton, Blean Forest, Chartham, Chestfield, Gorrell, Harbledown, Harbour, Little Stour, Marshside, Northgate, North Nailbourne, Seasalter, Stone Street, St Stephens, Sturry North, Sturry South, Swalecliffe, Tankerton, Westgate and Wincheap; and
	(ii) the following wards of the Borough of Swale, namely, Boughton and Courtenay.
Dartford	(i) The Borough of Dartford; and
	(ii) the following wards of the District of Sevenoaks, namely, Ash-cum-Ridley, Fawkham and Hartley, Horton Kirby and Longfield.
Dover	The following wards of the District of Dover, namely, Aylesham, Barton, Buckland, Capel-le-Ferne, Castle, Cornilo, Eastry, Eythorne, Lower Walmer, Lydden and Temple Ewell, Maxton and Elms Vale, Middle Deal, Mill Hill, Mongeham, Noninstone, North Deal, Pineham, Priory, Ringwould, River, St Margaret's at Cliffe, St Radigunds, Shepherdswell with Coldred, Tower Hamlets, Town and Pier and Upper Walmer.
Faversham	The following wards of the Borough of Swale, namely, Abbey, Borden, Davington Priory, East Downs, Eastern, Grove, Iwade and Lower Halstow, Kemsley, Milton Regis, Minster Cliffs, Murston, Newington, Queenborough and Halfway, Roman, St Ann's, Sheerness East, Sheerness West, Sheppey Central, Teynham and Lynsted, Watling, West Downs and Woodstock.
Folkestone and Hythe	The District of Shepway.
Gravesham	The Borough of Gravesham.
Maidstone	The following wards of the Borough of Maidstone, namely, Allington, Barming, Boughton Monchelsea, Bridge, Coxheath, Farleigh, Headcorn, Heath, High Street, Langley, Leeds, Loose, Marden, Park Wood, Shepway East, Shepway West, South, Staplehurst, Sutton Valence and Yalding.
Medway	The following wards of the City of Rochester upon Medway, namely, All Saints, Cuxton and Halling, Earl, Frindsbury, Frindsbury Extra, Hoo St Werburgh, Rede Court, St Margarets and Borstal, Temple Farm, Thames Side, Town, Troy Town and Warren Wood.
Mid Kent	(i) The following wards of the Borough of Maidstone, namely, Bearsted, Boxley, Detling, East, Harrietsham and Lenham, Hollingbourne, North and Thurnham; and
	(ii) the following wards of the City of Rochester upon Medway, namely, Holcombe, Horsted, Lordswood, Luton, Walderslade, Wayfield and Weedswood.
North Thanet	(i) The following wards of the City of Canterbury, namely, Herne, Heron, Reculver and West Bay; and

	(ii) the following wards of the District of Thanet, namely, Birchington East, Birchington West, Cecil, Cliftonville, Dane Park, Ethelbert, Margate West, Marine, Northdown Park, Pier, Salmestone, Thanet Parishes and Westgate-on-Sea.
Sevenoaks	The following wards of the District of Sevenoaks, namely, Brasted, Chevening, Crockenhill and Lullingstone, Dunton Green, Edenbridge North, Edenbridge South, Eynsford, Farningham, Halstead Knockholt and Badgers Mount, Hextable and Swanley Village, Kemsing, Leigh, Otford, Penshurst and Fordcombe, Riverhead, Seal, Sevenoaks Kippington, Sevenoaks Northern, Sevenoaks Town and St John's, Sevenoaks Weald and Under-river, Sevenoaks Wildernesse, Shoreham, Somerden, Sundridge and Ide Hill, Swanley Christchurch, Swanley St Mary's, Swanley White Oak, Westerham and Crockham Hill and West Kingsdown.
South Thanet	(i) The following wards of the District of Dover, namely, Ash, Little Stour, Sandwich, Woodnesborough with Staple and Worth; and
	(ii) the following wards of the District of Thanet, namely, Beacon Road, Bradstowe, Central Eastcliff, Central Westcliff, Kingsgate, Minster Parish, Newington, Northwood, Pierremont, St Lawrence, St Peter's, Sir Moses Montefiore, Southwood and Upton.
Tonbridge and Malling	The District of Tonbridge and Malling.
Tunbridge Wells	The Borough of Tunbridge Wells.

(b) Borough Constituency

Gillingham	(i) The Borough of Gillingham; and
	(ii) the following wards of the Borough of Swale, namely, Hartlip and Upchurch.

LANCASHIRE

(a) County Constituencies

Chorley	(i) The Borough of Chorley; and
	(ii) the following wards of the District of West Lancashire, namely, Parbold and Wrightington.
Fylde	(i) The Borough of Fylde; and
	(ii) the following ward of the Borough of Preston, namely, Preston Rural West.
Lancaster	(i) The following wards of the City of Lancaster, namely, Bulk, Castle, Caton, Ellel, Hornby, John O'Gaunt, Scotforth East, Scotforth West, Skerton Central, Skerton East and Skerton West; and
	(ii) the following wards of the Borough of Wyre, namely, Brock, Calder, Catterall, Duchy, Garstang, Great Eccleston, Pilling and Wyresdale.
Morecambe and Lunesdale	The following wards of the City of Lancaster, namely, Alexandra, Arkholme, Bolton-le-Sands, Carnforth, Halton-with-Aughton, Harbour, Heysham Central, Heysham North, Heysham South, Kellet, Overton, Parks, Poulton, Silverdale, Slyne-with-Hest, Torrisholme, Victoria and Warton.

Ribble Valley	(i) The following wards of the Borough of Preston, namely, Cadley, Greyfriars, Preston Rural East and Sharoe Green; and
	(ii) the Borough of Ribble Valley.
South Ribble	The Borough of South Ribble.
West Lancashire	The following wards of the District of West Lancashire, namely, Aughton Park, Aughton Town Green, Bickerstaffe, Birch Green, Burscough, Derby, Digmoor, Downholland, Halsall, Heskith-with-Becconsall, Knowsley, Lathom, Moorside, Newburgh, North Meols, Rufford, Scarisbrick, Scott, Skelmersdale North, Skelmersdale South, Tanhouse, Tarleton, Upholland North and Upholland South.
Wyre	The following wards of the Borough of Wyre, namely, Bailey, Bourne, Breck, Carleton, Cleveleys Park, Hambleton, Hardhorn, High Cross, Jubilee, Mount, Norcross, Park, Pharos, Preesall, Rossall, Staina, Tithebarn, Victoria and Warren.

(b) Borough Constituencies

Blackburn	The following wards of the Borough of Blackburn, namely, Bank Top, Billinge, Brookhouse, Brownhill, Cathedral, Ewood, Green Bank, Higher Croft, Mill Hill, Moorgate, Pleckgate, Queen's Park, Revidge, Shadsworth and West Rural.
Blackpool North	The following wards of the Borough of Blackpool, namely, Anchorsholme, Bispham, Brunswick, Claremont, Greenlands, Ingthorpe, Layton, Norbreck, Park, Talbot and Warbreck.
Blackpool South	The following wards of the Borough of Blackpool, namely, Alexandra, Clifton, Foxhall, Hawes Side, Highfield, Marton, Squires Gate, Stanley, Tyldesley, Victoria and Waterloo.
Burnley	The Borough of Burnley.
Hyndburn	The Borough of Hyndburn.
Pendle	The Borough of Pendle.
Preston	The following wards of the Borough of Preston, namely, Ashton, Avenham, Brookfield, Central, Deepdale, Fishwick, Ingol, Larches, Moorbrook, Park, Ribbleton, St John's, St Matthew's and Tulketh.
Rossendale and Darwen	(i) The following wards of the Borough of Blackburn, namely, Earcroft, Marsh House, North Turton, Sudell, Sunnyhurst and Whitehall; and
	(ii) the Borough of Rossendale.

LEICESTERSHIRE

(a) County Constituencies

Blaby	(i) The District of Blaby; and

	(ii) the following wards of the District of Harborough which are constituted by the District of Harborough (Electoral Arrangements) Order 1979 and which come into operation on 5th May 1983, namely, Broughton, Dunton, Gilmorton, Kilworth, Lutterworth Linden, Lutterworth St Mary's, Lutterworth Sherrier, Lutterworth Wycliffe, Peatling and Ullesthorpe.

Bosworth

(i) The following ward of the Borough of Charnwood which is constituted by the Borough of Charnwood (Electoral Arrangements) Order 1980 and which comes into operation on 5th May 1983, namely, Bradgate; and

(ii) the Borough of Hinckley and Bosworth.

Harborough

(i) The following wards of the District of Harborough which are constituted by the District of Harborough (Electoral Arrangements) Order 1979 and which come into operation on 5th May 1983, namely, Billesdon, Bosworth, Easton, Fleckney, Glen, Houghton, Kibworth, Langton, Lubenham, Market Harborough Bowden, Market Harborough North, Market Harborough South, Market Harborough West, Scraptoft, Thurnby and Tilton; and

(ii) the Borough of Oadby and Wigston.

Loughborough

The following wards of the Borough of Charnwood which are constituted by the Borough of Charnwood (Electoral Arrangements) Order 1980 and which come into operation on 5th May 1983, namely, Ashby, Barrow upon Soar and Quorndon, Birstall Goscote, Birstall Greengate, Birstall Netherhall, Birstall Riverside, Birstall Stonehill, Garendon, Hastings, Hathern, Lemyngton, Nanpantan, Mountsorrel and Rothley, Outwoods, Sileby, Southfields, Storer, The Wolds, Thurcaston, Woodhouse and Swithland and Woodthorpe.

North West Leicestershire

(i) The following wards of the Borough of Charnwood which are constituted by the Borough of Charnwood (Electoral Arrangements) Order 1980 and which come into operation on 5th May 1983, namely, Shepshed East and Shepshed West; and

(ii) the District of North West Leicestershire.

Rutland and Melton

(i) The following wards of the Borough of Charnwood which are constituted by the Borough of Charnwood (Electoral Arrangements) Order 1980 and which come into operation on 5th May 1983, namely, East Goscote, Queniborough, Six Hills, Syston and Thurmaston;

(ii) the Borough of Melton; and

(iii) the District of Rutland.

(b) Borough Constituencies

Leicester East

The following wards of the City of Leicester which are constituted by the City of Leicester (Electoral Arrangements) Order 1979 and which come into operation on 5th May 1983, namely, Belgrave, Charnwood, Coleman, Evington, Humberstone, Latimer, Rushey Mead, Thurncourt and West Humberstone.

Leicester South	The following wards of the City of Leicester which are constituted by the City of Leicester (Electoral Arrangements) Order 1979 and which come into operation on 5th May 1983, namely, Aylestone, Castle, Crown Hills, East Knighton, Eyres Monsell, Saffron, Spinney Hill, Stoneygate, West Knighton and Wycliffe.
Leicester West	The following wards of the City of Leicester which are constituted by the City of Leicester (Electoral Arrangements) Order 1979 and which come into operation on 5th May 1983, namely, Abbey, Beaumont Leys, Mowmacre, New Parks, North Braunstone, Rowley Fields, St Augustine's, Westcotes and Western Park.

LINCOLNSHIRE

(a) County Constituencies

East Lindsey	The following wards of the District of East Lindsey which are constituted by the District of East Lindsey (Electoral Arrangements) Order 1979 and which come into operation on 5th May 1983, namely, Alford, Burgh le Marsh, Chapel St Leonards, Coningsby, Fotherby, Friskney, Frithville, Grimoldby, Halton Holegate, Hogsthorpe, Holton le Clay, Hundleby, Ingoldmells, Legbourne, Mablethorpe, Mareham le Fen, Marsh Chapel, New Leake, North Holme, North Somercotes, North Thoresby, Partney, Priory, St Clements, St James', St Margaret's, St Michael's, Scarbrough, Seacroft, Sibsey, Spilsby, Sutton and Trusthorpe, Tattershall, Tetford, Tetney, Theddlethorpe St Helen, Trinity, Wainfleet, Willoughby with Sloothby, Winthorpe and Withern with Stain.
Gainsborough and Horncastle	(i) The following wards of the District of East Lindsey which are constituted by the District of East Lindsey (Electoral Arrangements) Order 1979 and which come into operation of 5th May 1983, namely, Binbrook, Donington on Bain, Horncastle, Roughton, Woodhall Spa and Wragby; and
	(ii) the District of West Lindsey.
Grantham	(i) The following wards of the District of North Kesteven, namely, Ashby de la Launde, Bassingham, Billinghay, Brant Broughton and Stragglethorpe, Branston and Mere, Cranwell and Byard's Leap, Eagle and North Scarle, Heckington, Heighington, Helpringham, Leasingham, Martin, Metheringham, Navenby, North Kyme, Osbournby, Ruskington, Sleaford East, Sleaford North, Sleaford South, Sleaford West, Waddington East, Washingborough and Wellingore; and
	(ii) the following wards of the District of South Kesteven, namely, Barrowby, Belmont, Earlesfield, Ermine, Grantham St Johns, Greyfriars, Harrowby, Heath, Loveden, Peascliffe, St Annes, St Wulframs, Saxonwell and Witham Valley.
Holland with Boston	(i) The Borough of Boston; and

(ii) the following wards of the District of South Holland, namely, Donington, Fleet, Gedney, Holbeach Hurn, Holbeach St Johns, Holbeach Town, Long Sutton, Moulton, Sutton Bridge, The Saints and Whaplode.

Stamford and Spalding

(i) The following wards of the District of South Holland, namely, Crowland, Deeping St Nicholas, Gosberton Village, Pinchbeck East, Pinchbeck West, Spalding Central, Spalding East, Spalding North, Spalding South, Spalding West, Surfleet and Weston; and

(ii) the following wards of the District of South Kesteven, namely, All Saints, Aveland, Bourne East, Bourne West, Casewick, Deeping St James, Devon, Forest, Glen Eden, Hillsides, Isaac Newton, Lincrest, Market and West Deeping, Morkery, Ringstone, St Georges, St Marys, Stamford St Johns, Toller and Truesdale.

(b) Borough Constituency

Lincoln

(i) The City of Lincoln; and

(ii) the following wards of the District of North Kesteven, namely, Bracebridge Heath, North Hykeham Central, North Hykeham North, North Hykeham South, Skellingthorpe and Waddington West.

MERSEYSIDE

(a) County Constituencies

Knowsley North

The following wards of the Borough of Knowsley, namely, Cantril Farm, Cherryfield, Kirkby Central, Knowsley Park, Northwood, Park, Prescot East, Prescot West, Tower Hill and Whitefield.

Knowsley South

The following wards of the Borough of Knowsley, namely, Halewood East, Halewood South, Halewood West, Longview, Page Moss, Princess, Roby, St Gabriels, St Michaels, Swanside, Whiston North and Whiston South.

Wirral South

The following wards of the Borough of Wirral, namely, Bebington, Bromborough, Clatterbridge, Eastham and Heswall.

Wirral West

The following wards of the Borough of Wirral, namely, Hoylake, Prenton, Royden, Thurstaston and Upton.

(b) Borough Constituencies

Birkenhead

The following wards of the Borough of Wirral, namely, Bidston, Birkenhead, Claughton, Egerton, Oxton and Tranmere.

Bootle

The following wards of the Borough of Sefton, namely, Church, Derby, Ford, Linacre, Litherland, Netherton, Orrell and St Oswald.

Crosby

The following wards of the Borough of Sefton, namely, Blundellsands, Harington, Manor, Molyneux, Park, Ravenmeols, Sudell and Victoria.

Liverpool, Broadgreen	The following wards of the City of Liverpool, namely, Broadgreen, Childwall, Kensington, Old Swan and Tuebrook.
Liverpool, Garston	The following wards of the City of Liverpool, namely, Allerton, Netherley, St Mary's, Speke, Valley and Woolton.
Liverpool, Mossley Hill	The following wards of the City of Liverpool, namely, Aigburth, Church, Grassendale, Picton and Smithdown.
Liverpool, Riverside	The following wards of the City of Liverpool, namely, Abercromby, Arundel, Dingle, Everton, Granby and Vauxhall.
Liverpool, Walton	The following wards of the City of Liverpool, namely, Anfield, Breckfield, County, Fazakerley, Melrose and Warbreck.
Liverpool, West Derby	The following wards of the City of Liverpool, namely, Clubmoor, Croxteth, Dovecot, Gillmoss and Pirrie.
St Helens North	The following wards of the Borough of St Helens, namely, Billinge and Seneley Green, Blackbrook, Broad Oak, Haydock, Moss Bank, Newton East, Newton West, Rainford and Windle.
St Helens South	The following wards of the Borough of St Helens, namely, Eccleston, Grange Park, Marshalls Cross, Parr and Hardshaw, Queen's Park, Rainhill, Sutton and Bold, Thatto Heath and West Sutton.
Southport	The following wards of the Borough of Sefton, namely, Ainsdale, Birkdale, Cambridge, Duke's, Kew, Meols and Norwood.
Wallasey	The following wards of the Borough of Wirral, namely, Leasowe, Liscard, Moreton, New Brighton, Seacombe and Wallasey.

NORFOLK

(a) County Constituencies

Great Yarmouth	The Borough of Great Yarmouth.
Mid Norfolk	(i) The following wards of the District of Breckland, namely, Beetley and Gressenhall, East Dereham—Neatherd, East Dereham—St Withburga, East Dereham—Toftwood, East Dereham—Town, Eynsford, Hermitage, Launditch, Mattishall, Shipworth, Springvale, Swanton Morley, Taverner, Two Rivers, Upper Wensum and Upper Yare; and
	(ii) the following wards of the District of Broadland, namely, Acle, Aylsham, Blofield, Brundall, Burlingham, Buxton, Cawston, Coltishall, Drayton, Foulsham, Freethorpe, Great Witchingham, Hainford, Hevingham, Horsford, Plumstead, Rackheath, Reedham, Reepham, St Faiths, South Walsham, Spixworth, Taverham and Wroxham.
North Norfolk	The District of North Norfolk.

North West Norfolk

The following wards of the Borough of King's Lynn and West Norfolk which are constituted by the District of West Norfolk (Electoral Arrangements) Order 1979 and which come into operation on 5th May 1983, namely, Burnham, Chase, Clenchwarton, Creake, Dersingham, Docking, Gayton, Gaywood Central, Gaywood North, Gaywood South, Grimston, Heacham, Hunstanton, Lynn Central, Lynn North, Lynn South West, Mershe Lande, Middleton, North Coast, Priory, Rudham, St Lawrence, St Margarets, Snettisham, Spellowfields, The Walpoles, The Woottons, Valley Hill, West Walton, West Winch and Wiggenhall.

South Norfolk

The District of South Norfolk.

South West Norfolk

(i) The following wards of the District of Breckland, namely, All Saints, Besthorpe, Buckenham, Conifer, East Guiltcross, Haggard De Toni, Harling, Haverscroft, Heathlands, Mid-Forest, Nar Valley, Necton, Peddars Way, Queen's, Swaffham, Templar, Thetford—Abbey, Thetford—Barnham Cross, Thetford—Guildhall, Thetford—Saxon, Watton, Wayland, Weeting, West Guiltcross and Wissey; and

(ii) the following wards of the Borough of King's Lynn and West Norfolk which are constituted by the District of West Norfolk (Electoral Arrangements) Order 1979 and which come into operation on 5th May 1983, namely, Airfield, Denton, Denver, Downham Market, Emneth, Ten Mile, Upwell Outwell and Delph, Watlington and Wissey.

(b) Borough Constituencies

Norwich North

(i) The following wards of the District of Broadland, namely, Catton, Hellesdon North, Hellesdon Southeast, Hellesdon West, Sprowston Central, Sprowston East, Sprowston South, Sprowston West, Thorpe St Andrew Northeast, Thorpe St Andrew Northwest and Thorpe St Andrew South; and

(ii) the following wards of the City of Norwich, namely, Catton Grove, Coslany, Crome, Mile Cross and Mousehold.

Norwich South

The following wards of the City of Norwich, namely, Bowthorpe, Eaton, Heigham, Henderson, Lakenham, Mancroft, Nelson, St Stephen, Thorpe Hamlet, Town Close and University.

NORTH YORKSHIRE

(a) County Constituencies

Harrogate

The following wards of the Borough of Harrogate which are constituted by the Borough of Harrogate (Electoral Arrangements) Order 1979 and which come into operation on 5th May 1983, namely, Bilton, Claro, Duchy, East Central, Granby, Harlow, Knaresborough East, Knaresborough West, Marston Moor, Nether Poppleton, New Park, Ouseburn, Pannal, Spofforth, Starbeck, Upper Poppleton, Wedderburn and West Central.

Richmond (Yorks)	(i) The following wards of the District of Hambleton, namely, Appleton Wiske, Bedale, Brompton, Broughton and Greenhow, Carlton Miniott, Crakehall, Great Ayton, Hillside, Leeming, Leeming Bar, Morton-on-Swale, Northallerton North East, Northallerton South East, Northallerton West, Osmotherley, Romanby, Romanby Broomfield, Rudby, Sowerby, Stokesley, Swainby, Tanfield, The Cowtons, The Thorntons, Thirsk, Topcliffe and Whitestonecliffe; and
	(ii) the District of Richmondshire.
Ryedale	(i) The following wards of the District of Hambleton, namely, Crayke, Easingwold, Helperby, Huby-Sutton, Shipton, Stillington and Tollerton;
	(ii) the following wards of the District of Ryedale which are constituted by the District of Ryedale (Electoral Arrangements) Order 1979 and which come into operation on 5th May 1983, namely, Amotherby, Ampleforth, Birdsall, Clifton Without, Dales, Ebberston, Haxby North East, Haxby West, Helmsley, Hovingham, Huntington North, Huntington South, Kirby Misperton, Kirkbymoorside, Malton, New Earswick, Norton, Pickering, Rawcliffe, Rillington, Sherburn, Sheriff Hutton, Skelton, Stockton and Bossall, Strensall, Thornton Dale and Wigginton; and
	(iii) the following wards of the Borough of Scarborough, namely, Filey and Hertford.
Scarborough	The following wards of the Borough of Scarborough, namely, Ayton, Castle, Cayton, Central, Danby, Derwent, Eastfield, Eskdaleside, Falsgrave, Fylingdales, Lindhead, Mayfield, Mulgrave, Newby, Northstead Scalby, Seamer, Streonshalh, Weaponness and Woodlands.
Selby	(i) The following ward of the District of Ryedale which is constituted by the District of Ryedale (Electoral Arrangements) Order 1979 and which comes into operation on 5th May 1983, namely, Osbaldwick and Heworth; and
	(ii) the District of Selby.
Skipton and Ripon	(i) The District of Craven; and
	(ii) the following wards of the Borough of Harrogate which are constituted by the Borough of Harrogate (Electoral Arrangements) Order 1979 and which come into operation on 5th May 1983, namely, Almscliffe, Bishop Monkton, Boroughbridge, Fountains, Killinghall, Kirkby Malzeard, Lower Nidderdale, Mashamshire, Newby, Nidd Valley, Pateley Bridge, Ripon East, Ripon West, Wathvale and Wharfedale Moors.

(b) Borough Constituency

York	The City of York.

NORTHAMPTONSHIRE

(a) County Constituencies

Corby	(i) The District of Corby; and

(ii) the following wards of the District of East Northamptonshire, namely, Barnwell, Brigstock, Drayton, Forest, Irthlingborough, King's Cliffe, Lower Nene, Margaret Beaufort, Oundle, Raunds, Ringstead, Stanwick, Thrapston, Willibrook and Woodford.

Daventry

(i) The following wards of the District of Daventry, namely, Abbey North, Abbey South, Badby, Barby, Brampton, Braunston, Byfield, Crick and West Haddon, Drayton, Everdon, Flore, Guilsborough, Hill, Kilsby, Long Buckby, Ravensthorpe, Spratton, Weedon, Welford, Woodford and Yelvertoft; and

(ii) the following wards of the District of South Northamptonshire, namely, Astwell, Blakesley, Brackley East, Brackley West, Cosgrove, Danvers, Deanshanger, Forest, Grafton, Greatworth, King's Sutton, Kingthorn, Middleton Cheney, Pottersbury, Rainsborough, Slapton, Tove, Towcester and Wardoun.

Kettering

(i) The following wards of the District of Daventry, namely, Boughton and Pitsford, Brixworth, Clipston, Moulton and Overstone and Walgrave; and

(ii) the Borough of Kettering.

Wellingborough

(i) The following wards of the District of Northamptonshire, namely, Higham Ferrers, Rushden East, Rushden North, Rushden South and Rushden West; and

(ii) the Borough of Wellingborough.

(b) Borough Constituencies

Northampton North

The following wards of the Borough of Northampton, namely, Abington, Boughton Green, Dallington and Kings Heath, Headlands, Kingsthorpe, Links, Lumbertubs, Park, St Alban, St George, Thorplands and Welford.

Northampton South

(i) The following wards of the Borough of Northampton, namely, Billing, Castle, Delapre, Nene Valley, New Duston, Old Duston, St Crispin, South and Weston; and

(ii) the following wards of the District of South Northamptonshire, namely, Blisworth, Brafield, Bugbrooke, Cogenhoe, Gayton, Hackleton, Harpole, Heyford, Kislingbury, Milton, Roade, Salcey and Yardley.

NORTHUMBERLAND

(a) County Constituencies

Berwick-upon-Tweed

(i) The District of Alnwick;

(ii) the Borough of Berwick-upon-Tweed; and

(iii) the following wards of the Borough of Castle Morpeth, namely, Chevington, Ellington, Hartburn, Longhorsley, Lynemouth and Ulgham.

Hexham

(i) The following wards of the Borough of Castle Morpeth, namely, Heddon-on-the-Wall, Ponteland East, Ponteland North, Ponteland South, Ponteland West, Stamfordham, Stannington and Whalton; and

(ii) the District of Tynedale.

Wansbeck

(i) The following wards of the Borough of Castle Morpeth, namely, Hebron, Hepscott and Mitford, Morpeth Central, Morpeth Kirkhill, Morpeth North, Morpeth South, Morpeth Stobhill and Pegswood; and

(ii) the District of Wansbeck.

(b) Borough Constituency

Blyth Valley

The Borough of Blyth Valley.

NOTTINGHAMSHIRE

(a) County Constituencies

Ashfield

(i) The following wards of the District of Ashfield, namely, Jacksdale, Kirkby in Ashfield Central, Kirkby in Ashfield East, Kirkby in Ashfield West, Selston, Sutton in Ashfield Central, Sutton in Ashfield East, Sutton in Ashfield North, Sutton in Ashfield West, Underwood and Woodhouse; and

(ii) the following wards of the Borough of Broxtowe, namely, Brinsley, Eastwood East, Eastwood North and Eastwood South.

Bassetlaw

(i) The following wards of the District of Bassetlaw, namely, Beckingham, Blyth, Carlton, Clayworth, Everton, Harworth East, Harworth West, Hodsock, Misterton, Rampton, Ranskill, Sturton, Sutton, Welbeck, Worksop East, Worksop North, Worksop North East, Worksop North West, Worksop South and Worksop South East; and

(ii) the following wards of the District of Mansfield, namely, Birklands and Meden.

Broxtowe

The following wards of the Borough of Broxtowe, namely, Attenborough, Awsworth and Cossall, Beeston Central, Beeston North-East, Beeston North-West, Beeston Rylands, Bramcote, Chilwell East, Chilwell West, Greasley, Kimberley, Nuthall, Stapleford East, Stapleford North, Stapleford West, Strelley and Trowell and Toton.

Gedling

The following wards of the Borough of Gedling, namely, Bonington, Burton Joyce and Stoke Bardolph, Carlton, Carlton Hill, Cavendish, Conway, Gedling, Killisick, Kingswell, Mapperley Plains, Netherfield, Oxclose, Phoenix, Porchester, Priory, St James, St Mary's and Woodthorpe.

Mansfield

The following wards of the District of Mansfield, namely, Berry Hill, Broomhill, Cumberlands, Eakring, Forest Town, Ladybrook, Leeming, Lindhurst, Manor, Northfield, Oakham, Oak Tree, Pleasleyhill, Ravensdale, Sherwood and Titchfield.

Newark

(i) The following wards of the District of Bassetlaw, namely, East Markham, East Retford East, East Retford North, East Retford West, Elkesley, Trent and Tuxford; and

(ii) the following wards of the District of Newark, namely, Beacon, Bridge, Bullpit-Pinfold, Castle, Caunton, Collingham, Devon, Elston, Farndon, Magnus, Meering, Milton-Lowfield, Muskham, Southwell East, Southwell West, Sutton on Trent, Trent and Winthorpe.

Rushcliffe

The Borough of Rushcliffe.

Sherwood

(i) The following wards of the District of Ashfield, namely, Hucknall Central, Hucknall East, Hucknall North and Hicknall West;

(ii) the following wards of the Borough of Gedling, namely, Bestwood Park, Calverton, Lambley, Newstead and Woodborough; and

(iii) the following wards of the District of Newark, namely, Bilsthorpe, Blidworth, Boughton, Clipstone, Dover Beck, Edwinstowe, Farnsfield, Fishpool, Lowdham, Ollerton North, Ollerton South, Rainworth and Rufford.

(b) Borough Constituencies

Nottingham East

The following wards of the City of Nottingham, namely, Basford, Forest, Greenwood, Manvers, Mapperley, Radford, St Ann's, Sherwood and Trent.

Nottingham North

The following wards of the City of Nottingham, namely, Aspley, Beechdale, Bestwood Park, Bilborough, Bulwell East, Bulwell West, Byron, Portland and Strelley.

Nottingham South

The following wards of the City of Nottingham, namely, Abbey, Bridge, Clifton East, Clifton West, Lenton, Park, Robin Hood, Wilford and Wollaton.

OXFORDSHIRE

(a) County Constituencies

Banbury

(i) The following wards of the District of Cherwell, namely, Adderbury, Ambrosden, Ardley, Bicester East, Bicester South, Bicester West, Bloxham, Bodicote, Calthorpe, Chesterton, Cropredy, Deddington, Easington, Fringford, Grimsbury, Hardwick, Heyford, Hook Norton, Hornton, Kirtlington, Launton, Neithrop, Otmoor, Ruscote, Sibford, Steeple Aston and Wroxton; and

(ii) the following wards of the District of West Oxfordshire, namely, Bartons and Tackley and Wootton.

Henley

The following wards of the District of South Oxfordshire which are constituted by the District of South Oxfordshire (Electoral Arrangements) Order 1980 and which come into operation on 5th May 1983, namely, Aston Rowant, Benson, Berinsfield, Chalgrove, Chinnor, Clifton Hampden, Crowmarsh, Dorchester, Forest Hill, Garsington, Goring, Goring Heath, Great Milton, Henley, Kidmore End, Nettlebed, Rotherfield Peppard, Shiplake, Sonning Common, Thame North, Thame South, Watlington, Wheatley and Woodcote.

Oxford West and Abingdon	(i) The following wards of the City of Oxford, namely, Central, Cherwell, North, South, West and Wolvercote; and
	(ii) the following wards of the District of Vale of White Horse, namely, Abbey, Caldecott, Cumnor, Fitzharris, Hinksey, Kennington, Northcourt, Ock, Radley, St Helen Without and Sunningwell and Wootton.
Wantage	(i) The following wards of the District of South Oxfordshire (Electoral Arrangements) Order 1980 and which come into operation on 5th May 1983, namely, Brightwell, Cholsey, Didcot North, Didcot Northbourne, Didcot South, Hagbourne and Wallingford; and
	(ii) the following wards of the District of Vale of White Horse, namely, Appleton, Craven, Drayton, Faringdon and Littleworth, Greendown, Grove, Harwell and Chilton, Hendred, Icknield, Island Villages, Kingston Bagpuize and Southmoor, Longworth, Marcham, Segsbury, Shrivenham, Stanford, Steventon, Sutton Courtenay, The Coxwells and Upton and Blewbury.
Witney	(i) The following wards of the District of Cherwell, namely, Gosford, North West Kidlington, South East Kidlington and Yarnton; and
	(ii) the following wards of the District of West Oxfordshire, namely, Ascott and Shipton, Aston Bampton and Standlake, Bampton, Bladon and Cassington, Brize Norton and Curbridge, Burford, Carterton North, Carterton South, Chadlington, Charlbury, Chipping Norton, Clanfield and Shilton, Combe and Stonesfield, Ducklington, Enstone, Eynsham, Filkins and Langford, Finstock and Leafield, Freeland and Hanborough, Hailey, Kingham, Milton-under-Wychwood, Minster Lovell, North Leigh, Rollright, Stanton Harcourt, Witney East, Witney North, Witney South, Witney West and Woodstock.

(b) Borough Constituency

Oxford East	(i) The following wards of the City of Oxford, namely, Blackbird Leys, East, Headington, Iffley, Marston, Quarry, St Clement's, Temple Cowley and Wood Farm; and
	(ii) the following wards of the District of South Oxfordshire which are constituted by the District of South Oxfordshire (Electoral Arrangements) Order 1980 and which come into operation on 5th May 1983, namely, Littlemore, Marston and Risinghurst.

SHROPSHIRE

(a) County Constituencies

Ludlow	(i) The District of Bridgnorth; and
	(ii) the District of South Shropshire.
North Shropshire	(i) The District of North Shropshire;
	(ii) the Borough of Oswestry; and

| | (iii) the following wards of the District of the Wrekin, namely, Church Aston, Edgmond, Ercall Magna, Newport East, Newport North and Newport West. |
| Shrewsbury and Atcham | The Borough of Shrewsbury and Atcham. |

(b) Borough Constituency

The Wrekin	The following wards of the District of The Wrekin, namely, Arleston, Brookside, College, Cuckoo Oak, Dawley Magna, Donnington, Donnington Wood, Dothill, Ercall, Hadley, Haygate, Hollinswood/Randley, Ironbridge (The Gorge), Ketley, Ketley Bank, Langley, Lawley, Leegomery, Lilleshall, Madeley, Malinslee, Park, Priorslee, Stirchley, Wombridge, Woodside, Wrockwardine and Wrockwardine Wood.

SOMERSET

County Constituencies

Bridgwater	(i) The following wards of the District of Sedgemoor, namely, Cannington and Combwich, Central, Dowsborough, Eastern Quantocks, Eastover, East Poldens, Hamp, Huntspill, Newton Green, North Petherton, Parchey, Pawlett and Puriton, Quantock, Sandford, Sowey, Sydenham, Victoria, Westonzoyland, West Poldens and Woolavington; and
	(ii) the following wards of the District of West Somerset, namely, Alcombe, Aville Vale, Carhampton and Withycombe, Crowcombe and Stogumber, Dunster, East Brendon, Holnicote, Minehead North, Minehead South, Old Cleeve, Porlock and Oare, Quantock Vale, Watchet, West Quantock and Williton.
Somerton and Frome	(i) The following wards of the District of Mendip, namely, Beacon, Beckington and Rode, Coleford, Creech, Frome Badcox, Frome Fromefield, Frome Keyford, Mells, Nordinton, Postlebury, Selwood and Berkley, Stratton and Vale; and
	(ii) the following wards of the District of Yeovil, namely, Blackmoor Vale, Brue, Burrow Hill, Camelot, Cary, Curry Rivel, Islemoor, Ivelchester, Langport and Huish, Martock, Milborne Port, Northstone, Turn Hill, Wessex and Wincanton.
Taunton	(i) The Borough of Taunton Deane; and
	(ii) the following wards of the District of West Somerset, namely, Dulverton and Brushford, Exmoor, Haddon and Quarme.
Wells	(i) The following wards of the District of Mendip, namely, Ashwick, Avalon, Chilcompton and Ston Easton, Ebbor, Glastonbury St Benedict's, Glastonbury St Edmund's, Glastonbury St John's, Glastonbury St Mary's, Moor, Nedge, Pylcombe, Rodney, Sheppey, Shepton Mallet, Street North, Street South, Wells Central, Wells St Cuthbert's and Wells St Thomas; and
	(ii) The following wards of the District of Sedgemoor, namely, Axbridge, Axe Vale, Berrow, Brent, Burnham North, Burnham South, Cheddar, Highbridge, Mark, Shipham and Wedmore.

Yeovil	The following wards of the District of Yeovil, namely, Blackdown, Chard North East, Chard North West, Chard Parish, Chard South East, Chard South West, Chinnock, Coker, Crewkerne Town, Dowlish, Egwood, Hazelbury, Houndstone, Ilminster Town, Lynches, Mudford, Neroche, St Michael's, South Petherton, Stoke, Windwhistle, Yeovil Central, Yeovil East, Yeovil North, Yeovil Preston, Yeovil South and Yeovil West.

SOUTH YORKSHIRE

(a) County Constituencies

Barnsley West and Penistone	The following wards of the Borough of Barnsley, namely, Darton, Dodworth, Hoyland East, Hoyland West, Park, Penistone East, Penistone West and Worsbrough.
Don Valley	The following wards of the Borough of Doncaster, namely, Conisbrough, Edlington and Warmsworth, Mexborough, Richmond, Rossington, South East and Southern Parks.
Doncaster North	The following wards of the Borough of Doncaster, namely, Adwick, Askern, Bentley Central, Bentley North Road, Hatfield, Stainforth and Thorne.
Rother Valley	The following wards of the Borough of Rotherham, namely, Anston and Woodsetts, Aston Orgreave and Ulley, Brinsworth Catcliffe and Treeton, Kiveton Park, Maltby, St John's and Thurcroft and Whiston.
Sheffield, Hallam	The following wards of the City of Sheffield, namely, Broomhill, Dore, Ecclesall, Hallam and Nether Edge.
Sheffield, Hillsborough	The following wards of the City of Sheffield, namely, Chapel Green, Hillsborough, South Wortley, Stocksbridge and Walkley.
Wentworth	The following wards of the Borough of Rotherham, namely, Bramley Ravenfield and Wickersley, Brampton Melton and Wentworth, Dalton Hooton Roberts and Thrybergh, Rawmarsh East, Rawmarsh West, Swinton and Wath.

(b) Borough Constituencies

Barnsley Central	The following wards of the Borough of Barnsley, namely, Ardsley, Central, Monk Bretton, North West, Royston and South West.
Barnsley East	The following wards of the Borough of Barnsley, namely, Brierley, Cudworth, Darfield, Dearne South, Dearne Thurnscoe, Wombwell North and Wombwell South.
Doncaster Central	The following wards of the Borough of Doncaster, namely, Armthorpe, Balby, Bessacarr, Central, Intake, Town Field and Wheatley.
Rotherham	The following wards of the Borough of Rotherham, namely, Boston, Broom, Central, Greasbrough, Herringthorpe, Kimberworth, Park and Thorpe Hesley.
Sheffield, Attercliffe	The following wards of the City of Sheffield, namely, Birley, Darnall, Handsworth and Mosborough.

Sheffield, Brightside	The following wards of the City of Sheffield, namely, Brightside, Firth Park, Nether Shire, Owlerton and Southey Green.
Sheffield Central	The following wards of the City of Sheffield, namely, Burngreave, Castle, Manor, Netherthorpe and Sharrow.
Sheffield, Heeley	The following wards of the City of Sheffield, namely, Beauchief, Heeley, Intake, Norton and Park.

STAFFORDSHIRE

(a) County Constituencies

Burton	The District of East Staffordshire.
Cannock and Burntwood	(i) The following wards of the District of Cannock Chase, namely, Anglesey, Broomhill, Cannock South, Chadsmoor, Heath Hayes, Longford, Norton Canes, Parkside, Pye Green Valley and Rawnsley; and
	(ii) the following wards of the District of Lichfield, namely, All Saints, Boney Hay, Chase Terrace, Chasetown, Hammerwich, Highfield, Redslade and Summerfield.
Mid Staffordshire	(i) The following wards of the District of Cannock Chase, namely, Brereton and Ravenhill, Brindley Heath, Etching Hill, Hagley and Western Springs;
	(ii) the following wards of the District of Lichfield, namely, Armitage with Handsacre, Central, Chadsmead, Colton and Ridwares, Curborough, King's Bromley, Longdon, Leomansley, St John's and Stowe; and
	(iii) the following wards of the Borough of Stafford, namely, Barlaston, Chartley, Fulford, Haywood, Milwich, Oulton, St Michael's, Stonefield and Christchurch and Walton.
South East Staffordshire	(i) The following wards of the District of Lichfield, namely, Alrewas, Bourne Vale, Fazeley, Little Aston, Mease Valley, Shenstone, Stonnall, Tame and Whittington; and
	(ii) the Borough of Tamworth.
South Staffordshire	The District of South Staffordshire.
Stafford	(i) The following wards of the Borough of Newcastle-under-Lyme, namely, Loggerheads, Madeley and Whitmore; and
	(ii) the following wards of the Borough of Stafford, namely, Baswich, Beaconside, Castle, Church Eaton, Common, Coton, Eccleshall, Forebridge, Gnosall, Highfields, Holmcroft, Littleworth, Manor, Milford, Penkside, Rowley, Seighford, Swynnerton, Tillington, Weeping Cross and Woodseaves.
Staffordshire Moorlands	The District of Staffordshire Moorlands.

(b) Borough Constituencies

Newcastle-under-Lyme	The following wards of the Borough of Newcastle-under-Lyme, namely, Audley and Bignall End, Bradwell, Chesterton, Clayton, Cross Heath, Halmerend, Holditch, Keele, May Bank, Porthill, Seabridge, Silverdale, Thistleberry, Town, Westlands and Wolstanton.

Stoke-on-Trent Central	The following wards of the City of Stoke-on-Trent, namely, Abbey, Berryhill, Brookhouse, Hanley Green, Hartshill, Shelton and Stoke West.
Stoke-on-Trent North	(i) The following wards of the Borough of Newcastle-under-Lyme, namely, Butt Lane, Kidsgrove, Newchapel and Talke; and
	(ii) the following wards of the City of Stoke-on-Trent, namely, Burslem Central, Burslem Grange, Chell, East Valley, Norton and Bradeley and Tunstall North.
Stoke-on-Trent South	The following wards of the City of Stoke-on-Trent, namely, Blurton, Fenton Green, Great Fenton, Longton South, Meir Park, Trentham Park and Weston.

SUFFOLK

(a) County Constituencies

Bury St Edmunds	(i) The District of Forest Heath; and
	(ii) the following wards of the Borough of St Edmundsbury, namely, Abbeygate, Barningham, Barrow, Chevington, Eastgate, Fornham, Great Barton, Honington, Horringer, Ixworth, Northgate, Pakenham, Risby, Risbygate, Rougham, St Olaves, Sextons, Southgate, Stanton, Westgate and Whelnetham.
Central Suffolk	(i) The following wards of the Borough of Ipswich, namely, Broom Hill, Castle Hill, White House and Whitton; and
	(ii) the District of Mid Suffolk.
South Suffolk	(i) The District of Babergh; and
	(ii) The following wards of the Borough of St Edmundsbury, namely, Cangle, Castle, Cavendish, Chalkstone, Clare, Clements, Hundon, Kedington, St Mary's and Helions, Wickhambrook and Withersfield.
Suffolk Coastal	The District of Suffolk Coastal.
Waveney	The District of Waveney.

(b) Borough Constituency

Ipswich	The following wards of the Borough of Ipswich, namely, Bixley, Bridge, Chantry, Gainsborough, Priory Heath, Rushmere, St Clement's, St John's, St Margaret's, Sprites, Stoke Park and Town.

SURREY

(a) County Constituencies

East Surrey	The District of Tandridge.
Guildford	(i) The following wards of the Borough of Guildford, namely, Christchurch, Friary and St Nicholas, Holy Trinity, Merrow and Burpham, Onslow, Shalford, Stoke, Stoughton, The Pilgrims, Tongham, Westborough and Worplesdon; and

(ii) the following wards of the District of Waverley which are constituted by the District of Waverley (Electoral Arrangements) Order 1979 and which come into operation on 5th May 1983, namely, Blackheath and Wonersh, Bramley, Cranleigh East, Cranleigh West, Ewhurst and Shamley Green.

Mole Valley

(i) The following ward of the Borough of Guildford, namely, Tillingbourne; and

(ii) the District of Mole Valley.

North West Surrey

(i) The following wards of the Borough of Runnymede, namely, Egham, Englefield Green East, Englefield Green West, Hythe, Thorpe and Virginia Water; and

(ii) the Borough of Surrey Heath.

South West Surrey

The following wards of the District of Waverley which are constituted by the District of Waverley (Electoral Arrangements) Order 1979 and which came into operation on 5th May 1983, namely, Alfold and Dunsfold, Busbridge Hambledon and Hascombe, Chiddingfold, Elstead Peper Harow and Thursley, Farnham Bourne, Farnham Castle, Farnham Hale and Heath End, Farnham Rowledge and Wrecclesham, Farnham Upper Hale, Farnham Waverley, Farnham Weybourne and Badshot Lea, Frensham Dockenfield and Tilford, Godalming North, Godalming North East and South West, Godalming North West, Godalming South East, Haslemere South, Hindhead, Milford, Shottermill and Witley.

Woking

(i) The following wards of the Borough of Guildford, namely, Ash, Ash Vale, Normandy and Pirbright; and

(ii) the Borough of Woking.

(b) Borough Constituencies

Chertsey and Walton

(i) The following wards of the Borough of Elmbridge, namely, Hersham North, Hersham South, Oatlands Park, St George's Hill, Walton Ambleside, Walton Central, Walton North, Walton South, Weybridge North and Weybridge South; and

(ii) the following wards of the Borough of Runnymede, namely, Addlestone Bourneside, Addlestone North, Addlestone St Paul's, Chertsey Meads, Chertsey St Ann's, Foxhills, New Haw and Woodham.

Epsom and Ewell

(i) The Borough of Epsom and Ewell; and

(ii) the following wards of the Borough of Reigate and Banstead, namely, Banstead Village, Nork, Preston and Tattenhams.

Esher

(i) The following wards of the Borough of Elmbridge, namely, Claygate, Cobham and Downside, Cobham Fairmile, Esher, Hinchley Wood, Long Ditton, Molesey East, Molesey North, Molesey South, Oxshott and Stoke D'Abernon, Thames Ditton and Weston Green; and

(ii) the following wards of the Borough of Guildford, namely, Clandon and Horsley, Effingham, Lovelace and Send.

Reigate	The following wards of the Borough of Reigate and Banstead, namely, Chipstead-Hooley and Woodmansterne, Horley East, Horley West, Kingswood with Burgh Heath, Reigate Central, Reigate East, Reigate North, Reigate North Central, Reigate North East, Reigate South Central, Reigate South East, Reigate South West, Salfords and Sidlow and Tadworth and Walton.
Spelthorne	The Borough of Spelthorne.

TYNE AND WEAR

Borough Constituencies

Blaydon	The following wards of the Borough of Gateshead, namely, Birtley, Blaydon, Chopwell and Rowlands Gill, Crawcrook and Greenside, Lamesley, Ryton, Whickham North, Whickham South and Winlaton.
Gateshead East	The following wards of the Borough of Gateshead, namely, Chowdene, Deckham, Felling, High Fell, Leam, Low Fell, Pelaw and Heworth, Saltwell and Wrekendyke.
Houghton and Washington	The following wards of the Borough of Sunderland, namely, Eppleton, Hetton, Houghton, Shiney Row, Washington East, Washington North, Washington South and Washington West.
Jarrow	The following wards of the Borough of South Tyneside, namely, Bede, Biddick Hall, Boldon Colliery, Cleadon and East Boldon, Fellgate and Hedworth, Hebburn Quay, Hebburn South, Monkton, Primrose and Whitburn and Marsden.
Newcastle upon Tyne Central	The following wards of the City of Newcastle upon Tyne, namely, Blakelaw, Fenham, Jesmond, Kenton, Moorside, South Gosforth and Wingrove.
Newcastle upon Tyne East	The following wards of the City of Newcastle upon Tyne, namely, Byker, Dene, Heaton, Monkchester, Sandyford, Walker and Walkergate.
Newcastle upon Tyne North	The following wards of the City of Newcastle upon Tyne, namely, Castle, Denton, Fawdon, Grange, Lemington, Newburn, Westerhope and Woolsington.
South Shields	The following wards of the Borough of South Tyneside, namely, All Saints, Beacon and Bents, Cleadon Park, Harton, Horsley Hill, Rekendyke, Tyne Dock and Simonside, Westoe, West Park and Whiteleas.
Sunderland North	The following wards of the Borough of Sunderland, namely, Castletown, Central, Colliery, Fulwell, Pallion, St Peter's, South Hylton, Southwick and Town End Farm.
Sunderland South	The following wards of the Borough of Sunderland, namely, Grindon, Hendon, Ryhope, St Chad's, St Michael's, Silksworth, Thorney Close and Thornholme.
Tyne Bridge	(i) The following wards of the Borough of Gateshead, namely, Bede, Bensham, Dunston and Teams; and
	(ii) the following wards of the City of Newcastle upon Tyne, namely, Benwell, Elswick, Scotswood and West City.

Tynemouth	The following wards of the Borough of North Tyneside, namely, Chirton, Collingwood, Cullercoats, Monkseaton, North Shields, Riverside, St Mary's, Seatonville, Tynemouth and Whitley Bay.
Wallsend	The following wards of the Borough of North Tyneside, namely, Battle Hill, Benton, Camperdown, Holystone, Howdon, Longbenton, Northumberland, Valley, Wallsend and Weetslade.

WARWICKSHIRE

County Constituencies

North Warwickshire	(i) The Borough of North Warwickshire; and (ii) the following wards of the Borough of Nuneaton and Bedworth, namely, Exhall, Heath, Mount Pleasant and Poplar.
Nuneaton	(i) The following wards of the Borough of Nuneaton and Bedworth, namely, Abbey, Arbury, Attleborough, Bulkington, Camp Hill, Chilvers Coton, Galley Common, St Nicolas, Stockingford, Weddington and Whitestone; and (ii) the following wards of the Borough of Rugby, namely, Earl Craven, Fosse and Wolvey.
Rugby and Kenilworth	(i) The following wards of the Borough of Rugby, namely, Admirals, Benn, Bilton, Brownsover, Caldecott, Clifton and Newton, Dunchurch and Thurlaston, Eastlands, Hillmorton, Knightlow, Lawford, Leam Valley, New Bilton, Newbold, Overslade, Paddox, Ryton-on-Dunsmore, St Mary's and Wolston; and (ii) the following wards of the District of Warwick which are constituted by the District of Warwick (Electoral Arrangements) Order 1979 and which come into operation on 5th May 1983, namely, Abbey, Park Hill, St John's and Stoneleigh.
Stratford-on-Avon	The District of Stratford-on-Avon.
Warwick and Leamington	The following wards of the District of Warwick which are constituted by the District of Warwick (Electoral Arrangements) Order 1979 and which come into operation on 5th May 1983, namely, Bishop's Tachbrook, Brunswick, Budbrooke, Clarendon, Crown, Cubbington, Lapworth, Leek Wootton, Manor, Milverton, Radford Semele, Warwick North, Warwick South, Warwick West, Whitnash and Willes.

WEST MIDLANDS

(a) County Constituencies

Meriden	The following wards of the Borough of Solihull, namely, Bickenhill, Castle Bromwich, Chelmsley Wood, Fordbridge, Kingshurst, Knowles, Meriden, Packwood and Smith's Wood.

(b) Borough Constituencies

Aldridge-Brownhills	The following wards of the Borough of Walsall, namely, Aldridge Central and South, Aldridge North and Walsall Wood, Brownhills, Hatherton Rushall, Pelsall and Streetly.

Birmingham, Edgbaston	The following wards of the City of Birmingham, namely, Edgbaston, Harborne and Quinton.
Birmingham, Erdington	The following wards of the City of Birmingham, namely, Erdington, Kingsbury and Stockland Green.
Birmingham, Hall Green	The following wards of the City of Birmingham, namely, Billesley, Brandwood and Hall Green.
Birmingham, Hodge Hill	The following wards of the City of Birmingham, namely, Hodge Hill, Shard End and Washwood Heath.
Birmingham, Ladywood	The following wards of the City of Birmingham, namely, Ladywood, Sandwell and Soho.
Birmingham, Northfield	The following wards of the City of Birmingham, namely, Bartley Green, Longbridge, Northfield and Weoley.
Birmingham, Perry Barr	The following wards of the City of Birmingham, namely, Handsworth, Kingstanding, Oscott and Perry Barr.
Birmingham, Selly Oak	The following wards of the City of Birmingham, namely, Bournville, King's Norton, Moseley and Selly Oak.
Birmingham, Small Heath	The following wards of the City of Birmingham, namely, Aston, Nechells and Small Heath.
Birmingham, Sparkbrook	The following wards of the City of Birmingham, namely, Fox Hollies, Sparkbrook and Sparkhill.
Birmingham, Yardley	The following wards of the City of Birmingham, namely, Acock's Green, Sheldon and Yardley.
Coventry North East	The following wards of the City of Coventry, namely, Foleshill, Henley, Longford, Upper Stoke and Wyken.
Coventry North West	The following wards of the City of Coventry, namely, Bablake, Holbrook, Radford and Sherbourne.
Coventry South East	The following wards of the City of Coventry, namely, Binley and Willenhall, Cheylesmore, Lower Stoke and St Michael's.
Coventry South West	The following wards of the City of Coventry, namely, Earlsdon, Wainbody, Westwood, Whoberley and Woodlands.
Dudley East	The following wards of the Borough of Dudley, namely, Castle and Priory, Coseley East, Coseley West, Netherton and Woodside, Quarry Bank and Cradley, St Andrew's, St James's and St Thomas's.
Dudley West	The following wards of the Borough of Dudley, namely, Amblecote, Brierley Hill, Brockmoor and Pensnett, Gornal, Kingswinford North and Wall Heath, Kingswinford South, Sedgley and Wordsley.
Halesowen and Stourbridge	The following wards of the Borough of Dudley, namely, Belle Vale and Hasbury, Halesowen North, Halesowen South, Hayley Green, Lye and Wollescote, Norton, Pedmore and Stourbridge East and Wollaston and Stourbridge West.
Solihull	The following wards of the Borough of Solihull, namely, Elmdon, Lyndon, Olton, St Alphege, Shirley East, Shirley South, Shirley West and Silhill.
Sutton Coldfield	The following wards of the City of Birmingham, namely, Sutton Four Oaks, Sutton New Hall and Sutton Vesey.

Walsall North

The following wards of the Borough of Walsall, namely, Birchills Leamore, Blakenall, Bloxwich East, Bloxwich West, Short Heath, Willenhall North and Willenhall South.

Walsall South

The following wards of the Borough of Walsall, namely, Bentley and Darlaston North, Darlaston South, Paddock, Palfrey, Pheasey, Pleck and St Matthew's.

Warley East

The following wards of the Borough of Sandwell, namely, Abbey, Bristnall, Old Warley, St Pauls, Smethwick and Soho and Victoria.

Warley West

The following wards of the Borough of Sandwell, namely, Blackheath, Cradley Heath and Old Hill, Langley, Oldbury, Rowley and Tividale.

West Bromwich East

The following wards of the Borough of Sandwell, namely, Charlemont, Friar Park, Great Barr, Hateley Heath, Newton and West Bromwich Central.

West Bromwich West

The following wards of the Borough of Sandwell, namely, Great Bridge, Greets Green and Lyng, Princes End, Tipton Green, Wednesbury North and Wednesbury South.

Wolverhampton North East

The following wards of the Borough of Wolverhampton, namely, Bushbury, Fallings Park, Heath Town, Low Hill, Oxley, Wednesfield North and Wednesfield South.

Wolverhampton South East

The following wards of the Borough of Wolverhampton, namely, Bilston East, Bilston North, Blakenhall, East Park, Ettingshall and Spring Vale.

Wolverhampton South West

The following wards of the Borough of Wolverhampton, namely, Graiseley, Merry Hill, Park, Penn, St Peter's, Tettenhall Regis and Tettenhall Wightwick.

WEST SUSSEX

(a) County Constituencies

Arundel

The following wards of the District of Arun which are constituted by the District of Arun (Electoral Arrangements) Order 1980 and which come into operation on 5th May 1983, namely, Aldingbourne, Arundel, Barnham, Bersted, Bognor Regis Aldwick, Bognor Regis Central, Bognor Regis Hotham, Bognor Regis North, Bognor Regis South, Bognor Regis West, Felpham East, Felpham West, Littlehampton Beach, Littlehampton Central, Littlehampton Ham, Littlehampton River, Littlehampton Wick, Middleton-on-Sea, Pagham and Walberton.

Chichester

The District of Chichester.

Horsham

The District of Horsham.

Mid Sussex	The following wards of the District of Mid Sussex which are constituted by the District of Mid Sussex (Electoral Arrangements) Order 1980 and which come into operation on 5th May 1983, namely, Ardingly, Bolney, Burgess Hill—Chanctonbury, Burgess Hill—Franklands, Burgess Hill—North, Burgess Hill—St Andrews, Burgess Hill—Town, Burgess Hill—West, Clayton, Cuckfield, East Grinstead East, East Grinstead North, East Grinstead South, East Grinstead West, Haywards Heath Ashenground, Haywards Heath Bentswood, Haywards Heath Franklands, Haywards Heath Harlands, Haywards Heath—Heath, Horsted Keynes, Hurstpierpoint, Keymer, Lindfield Rural, Lindfield Urban and West Hoathly.
Shoreham	(i) The District of Adur; and
	(ii) the following wards of the District of Arun which are constituted by the District of Arun (Electoral Arrangements) Order 1980 and which come into operation on 5th May 1983, namely, Angmering, East Preston and Kingston, Ferring, Findon, Rustington East and Rustington West.

(b) Borough Constituencies

Crawley	(i) The Borough of Crawley; and
	(ii) the following wards of the District of Mid Sussex which are constituted by the District of Mid Sussex (Electoral Arrangements) Order 1980 and which come into operation on 5th May 1983, namely, Balcombe, Copthorne and Worth, Crawley Down, Slaugham and Turners Hill.
Worthing	The Borough of Worthing.

WEST YORKSHIRE

(a) County Constituencies

Calder Valley	The following wards of the Borough of Calderdale, namely, Brighouse, Calder Valley, Elland, Greetland and Stainland, Hipperholme and Lightcliffe, Luddendenfoot, Rastrick, Ryburn and Todmorden.
Colne Valley	The following wards of the Borough of Kirklees, namely, Colne Valley West, Crosland Moor, Golcar, Holme Valley North, Holme Valley South and Lindley.
Dewsbury	The following wards of the Borough of Kirklees, namely, Denby Dale, Dewsbury East, Dewsbury West, Kirkburton, Mirfield and Thornhill.
Elmet	The following wards of the City of Leeds, namely, Barwick and Kippax, Garforth and Swillington, Wetherby and Whinmoor.
Hemsworth	The following wards of the City of Wakefield, namely, Crofton and Ackworth, Featherstone, Hemsworth, South Elmsall and South Kirkby.
Keighley	The following wards of the City of Bradford, namely, Craven, Ilkley, Keighley North, Keighley South, Keighley West and Worth Valley.
Normanton	(i) The following ward of the City of Leeds, namely, Rothwell; and

	(ii) the following wards of the City of Wakefield, namely, Normanton and Sharlston, Ossett, Stanley and Altofts and Stanley and Wrenthorpe.
Pontefract and Castleford	The following wards of the City of Wakefield, namely, Castleford Glasshoughton, Castleford Ferry Fryston, Castleford Whitwood, Knottingley, Pontefract North and Pontefract South.
Shipley	The following wards of the City of Bradford, namely, Baildon, Bingley, Bingley Rural, Rombalds, Shipley East and Shipley West.

(b) Borough Constituencies

Batley and Spen	The following wards of the Borough of Kirklees, namely, Batley East, Batley West, Birstall and Birkenshaw, Cleckheaton, Heckmondwike and Spen.
Bradford North	The following wards of the City of Bradford, namely, Bolton, Bowling, Bradford Moor, Eccleshill, Idle and Undercliffe.
Bradford South	The following wards of the City of Bradford, namely, Great Horton, Odsal, Queensbury, Tong, Wibsey and Wyke.
Bradford West	The following wards of the City of Bradford, namely, Clayton, Heaton, Little Horton, Thornton, Toller and University.
Halifax	The following wards of the Borough of Calderdale, namely, Illingworth, Mixenden, Northowram and Shelf, Ovenden, St John's, Skircoat, Sowerby Bridge, Town and Warley.
Huddersfield	The following wards of the Borough of Kirklees, namely, Almondbury, Birkby, Dalton, Deighton, Newsome and Paddock.
Leeds Central	The following wards of the City of Leeds, namely, Beeston, City and Holbeck, Richmond Hill and University.
Leeds East	The following wards of the City of Leeds, namely, Burmantofts, Halton, Harehills and Seacroft.
Leeds North East	The following wards of the City of Leeds, namely, Chapel Allerton, Moortown, North and Roundhay.
Leeds North West	The following wards of the City of Leeds, namely, Cookridge, Headingley, Otley and Wharfedale and Weetwood.
Leeds West	The following wards of the City of Leeds, namely, Armley, Bramley, Kirkstall and Wortley.
Morley and Leeds South	The following wards of the City of Leeds, namely, Hunslet, Middleton, Morley North and Morley South.
Pudsey	The following wards of the City of Leeds, namely, Aireborough, Horsforth, Pudsey North and Pudsey South.
Wakefield	The following wards of the City of Wakefield, namely, Horbury, Wakefield Central, Wakefield East, Wakefield North, Wakefield Rural and Wakefield South.

WILTSHIRE

(a) County Constituencies

Devizes

    (i) The District of Kennet; and

    (ii) the following wards of the Borough of Thamesdown, namely, Blunsdon, Chiseldon, Covingham, Highworth, Ridgeway, St Margaret, St Philip and Wroughton.

North Wiltshire

    The District of North Wiltshire.

Salisbury

    The following wards of the District of Salisbury, namely, Alderbury, Amesbury, Bemerton, Bishopdown, Bulford, Chalke Valley, Donhead, Downton, Durrington, Ebble, Fisherton and Bemerton Village, Fonthill, Fovant, Harnham, Idmiston, Laverstock, Milford, Nadder, Redlynch, St Edmund, St Mark, St Martin, St Paul, Stratford, Till Valley, Tisbury, Upper Bourne, Whiteparish, Wilton, Winterbourne, Winterslow, Woodford Valley and Wylye.

Westbury

    (i) The following wards of the District of Salisbury, namely, Knoyle, Mere and Western; and

    (ii) the District of West Wiltshire.

(b) Borough Constituency

Swindon

    The following wards of the Borough of Thamesdown, namely, Central, Dorcan, Eastcott, Gorse Hill, Lawns, Moredon, Park, Toothill, Walcot, Western and Whitworth.

PART II

WALES

CLWYD

County Constituencies

Alyn and Deeside

    (i) The District of Alyn and Deeside; and

    (ii) the Borough of Wrexham Maelor wards Nos 13 and 14.

Clwyd North West

    (i) The Borough of Colwyn wards Nos 1 to 12; and

    (ii) The following wards of the Borough of Rhuddlan which are constituted by the Borough of Rhuddlan (Electoral Arrangements) Order 1982 and which come into operation on 5th May 1983, namely, Bodelwyddan, Dyserth, Rhuddlan, Rhyl East, Rhyl South, Rhyl South East, Rhyl South West, Rhyl West, St Asaph East, St Asaph West and Tremeirchion.

Clwyd South West

    (i) The Borough of Colwyn wards Nos 13 to 17;

    (ii) the District of Glyndŵr; and

    (iii) the Borough of Wrexham Maelor wards Nos 15 to 22, 26 and 27.

Delyn

    (i) The Borough of Delyn; and

(ii) the following wards of the Borough of Rhuddlan which are constituted by the Borough of Rhuddlan (Electoral Arrangements) Order 1982 and which come into operation on 5th May 1983, namely, Meliden, Prestatyn Central, Prestatyn East, Prestatyn North and Prestatyn South West.

Wrexham

The Borough of Wrexham Maelor wards Nos 1 to 12, 23 to 25 and 28 to 36.

DYFED

County Constituencies

Carmarthen

(i) The District of Carmarthen; and

(ii) the Borough of Dinefŵr wards Nos 1, 7, 8 and 10 to 24.

Ceredigion and Pembroke North

(i) The District of Ceredigion; and

(ii) the District of Preseli wards Nos 3, 4, 9 to 14, 18 and 21.

Llanelli

(i) The Borough of Dinefŵr wards Nos 2 to 6 and 9; and

(ii) the Borough of Llanelli.

Pembroke

(i) The District of Preseli wards Nos 1, 2, 5 to 8, 15 to 17, 19, 20 and 22 to 31; and

(ii) the District of South Pembrokeshire.

GWENT

County Constituencies

Blaenau Gwent

The Borough of Blaenau Gwent wards Nos 1 to 18.

Islwyn

The Borough of Islwyn.

Monmouth

(i) The Borough of Blaenau Gwent wards Nos 19 and 20;

(ii) the District of Monmouth wards Nos 1 to 13 and 16 to 27; and

(iii) the Borough of Torfaen ward No 13.

Newport East

(i) The District of Monmouth wards Nos 14 and 15; and

(ii) the Borough of Newport wards Nos 2, 4, 7, 9, 11, 13 and 18 to 20.

Newport West

The Borough of Newport wards Nos 1, 3, 5, 6, 8, 10, 12 and 14 to 17.

Torfaen

The Borough of Torfaen wards Nos 1 to 12.

GWYNEDD

County Constituencies

Caernarfon

(i) The Borough of Arfon wards Nos 8 to 12 and 16 to 29; and

(ii) the District of Dwyfor.

Conwy

(i) The Borough of Aberconwy wards Nos 1 to 4, 6 to 13, 15, 16 and 18; and

(ii) the Borough of Arfon wards Nos 1 to 7, 13 to 15 and 30 to 33.

Meirionnydd Nant	(i) The Borough of Aberconwy wards Nos 5, 14, 17 and 19 to 21; and
	(ii) the District of Meirionnydd.
Ynys Môn	The Borough of Ynys Môn—Isle of Anglesey.

MID GLAMORGAN

County Constituencies

Bridgend	The Borough of Ogwr wards Nos 1, 2, 12 to 16, 18 and 20 to 23.
Caerphilly	The District of Rhymney Valley wards Nos 1 to 4, 6 to 13 and 21.
Cynon Valley	The Borough of Cynon Valley.
Merthyr Tydfil and Rhymney	(i) The Borough of Merthyr Tydfil; and
	(ii) the District of Rhymney Valley wards Nos 5 and 14 to 20.
Ogmore	(i) The Borough of Ogwr wards Nos 3 to 11, 17, 19, 24 and 25; and
	(ii) the Borough of Taff-Ely wards Nos 11 and 14 to 16.
Pontypridd	The Borough of Taff-Ely wards Nos 1 to 10, 12 and 13.
Rhondda	The Borough of Rhondda.

POWYS

County Constituencies

Brecon and Radnor	(i) The Borough of Brecknock; and
	(ii) the District of Radnor.
Montgomery	The District of Montgomery.

SOUTH GLAMORGAN

(a) County Constituency

Vale of Glamorgan	The following wards of the Borough of Vale of Glamorgan which are constituted by the Borough of Vale of Glamorgan (Electoral Arrangements) Order 1982 and which come into operation on 5th May 1983, namely, Baruc, Buttrills, Cadoc, Castleland, Court, Cowbridge, Dinas Powys, Dyfan, Gibbonsdown, Illtyd, Llandow, Llantwit Major, Peterson-super-Ely, Rhoose, St Athan, Sully and Wenvoe.

(b) Borough Constituencies

Cardiff Central	The following wards of the City of Cardiff which are constituted by the City of Cardiff (Electoral Arrangements) Order 1982 and which come into operation on 5th May 1983, namely, Adamsdown, Cathays, Cyncoed, Pentwyn, Plasnewydd and Roath.

Cardiff North

The following wards of the City of Cardiff which are constituted by the City of Cardiff (Electoral Arrangements) Order 1982 and which come into operation on 5th May 1983, namely, Gabalfa, Heath, Lisvane and St Mellons, Llandaff North, Llanishen, Rhiwbina and Whitchurch and Tongwynlais.

Cardiff South and Penarth

(i) The following wards of the City of Cardiff which are constituted by the City of Cardiff (Electoral Arrangements) Order 1982 and which come into operation on 5th May 1983, namely, Butetown, Grangetown, Llanrumney, Rumney, Splott and Trowbridge; and

(ii) the following wards of the Borough of Vale of Glamorgan which are constituted by the Borough of Vale of Glamorgan (Electoral Arrangements) Order 1982 and which come into operation on 5th May 1983, namely, Alexandra, Cornerswell, Llandough and Stanwell.

Cardiff West

The following wards of the City of Cardiff which are constituted by the City of Cardiff (Electoral Arrangements) Order 1982 and which come into operation on 5th May 1983, namely, Caerau, Canton, Ely, Fairwater, Llandaff, Radyr and St Fagans and Riverside.

WEST GLAMORGAN

(a) *County Constituencies*

Aberavon

(i) The Borough of Afan; and

(ii) the Borough of Neath wards Nos 3 and 6.

Gower

(i) The Borough of Lliw Valley wards Nos 1 to 3, 5 and 6; and

(ii) the City of Swansea wards Nos 8 and 16 to 20.

Neath

(i) The Borough of Lliw Valley wards Nos 4, 7 and 8; and

(ii) the Borough of Neath wards Nos 1, 2, 4, 5 and 7 to 16.

(b) *Borough Constituencies*

Swansea East

The City of Swansea wards Nos 5 to 7, 9, 11 and 12.

Swansea West

The City of Swansea wards Nos 1 to 4, 10 and 13 to 15.

PART III

SCOTLAND

BORDERS REGION

County Constituencies

Roxburgh and Berwickshire

(1) Roxburgh District;

(2) Berwickshire District.

Tweeddale, Ettrick and Lauderdale

(1) Tweeddale District;

(2) Ettrick and Lauderdale District.

County Constituencies

Clackmannan

(1) Clackmannan District;

(2) electoral division 13 (Carseland) in Stirling District;

(3) electoral division 29 (Kinnaird) in Falkirk District.

Falkirk East

Electoral divisions 19 (Bainsford), 22 (Dundas), 23 (Kalantyre), 24 (Sealock), 25 (Carriden), 26 (Kinneil), 32 (Braes), 33 (Laurmont) and 34 (Avonside) in Falkirk District.

Falkirk West

Electoral divisions 17 (Callendar), 18 (Grahamsdyke), 20 (Glenfuir), 21 (Carmuirs), 27 (Herbertshire), 28 (Tryst), 30 (Carronglen) and 31 (Bonnybridge) in Falkirk District.

Stirling

Stirling District except electoral division 13 (Carseland).

DUMFRIES AND GALLOWAY REGION

County Constituencies

Dumfries

(1) Annandale and Eskdale District;

(2) Nithsdale District except electoral divisions 14 (Kirkconnel), 15 (Sanquhar and Queensberry), 16 (Mid Nithsdale) and 20 (Mabie).

Galloway and Upper Nithsdale

(1) Stewartry District;

(2) Wigtown District;

(3) electoral divisions 14 (Kirkconnel), 15 (Sanquhar and Queensberry), 16 (Mid Nithsdale) and 20 (Mabie) in Nithsdale District.

FIFE REGION

County Constituencies

Central Fife

Electoral divisions 10, 11, 12, 13, 14, 15, 16, 17 and 18 in Kirkcaldy District.

Dunfermline East

(1) Electoral divisions 31, 32, 33, 33, 34, 35, 36, 37 and 45 in Dunfermline District;

(2) electoral division 19 in Kirkcaldy District.

Dunfermline West

Electoral divisions 29, 30, 38, 39, 40, 41, 42, 43 and 44 in Dunfermline District.

Kirkcaldy

Electoral divisions 1, 2, 3, 4, 5, 6, 7, 8 and 9 in Kirkcaldy District.

North East Fife

North East Fife District.

GRAMPIAN REGION

(a) Burgh Constituencies

Aberdeen North	Electoral divisions 25 (Woodside), 26 (St Machar), 27 (Northfield East), 28 (Northfield West), 29 (Kittybrewster), 30 (Seaton), 31 (Mastrick), 32 (Ashgrove), 33 (Summerfield) and 48 (Brimmond) in City of Aberdeen District.
Aberdeen South	Electoral divisions 34 (Rosemount), 35 (Rubislaw), 36 (St Clements), 37 (St Nicholas), 38 (Hazlehead), 39 (Holburn), 40 (Ferryhill), 41 (Torry) and 45 (Nigg) in City of Aberdeen District.

(b) County Constituencies

Banff and Buchan	Banff and Buchan District.
Gordon	(1) Gordon District;
	(2) electoral divisions 47 (West Don) and 49 (East Don) in City of Aberdeen District.
Kincardine and Deeside	(1) Kincardine and Deeside District;
	(2) electoral divisions 42 (Craigton), 43 (Auchinyell), 44 (Kincorth) and 46 (Peterculter) in City of Aberdeen District.
Moray	Moray District.

HIGHLAND REGION

County Constituencies

Caithness and Sutherland	(1) Caithness District;
	(2) Sutherland District.
Inverness, Nairn and Lochaber	(1) Electoral divisions 31 (Merkinch), 32 (Dalneigh-Muirtown), 33 (Ballifeary and Columba), 34 (Ness Central), 35 (Crown-Raigmore), 36 (Old Edinburgh), 37 (Drummond), 38 (Hilton), 39 (Ardersier, Petty and Culloden), 39A (Inverness East) and 40 (Strathdearn, Strathnairn and Loch Ness East) in Inverness District;
	(2) Badenoch and Strathspey District;
	(3) Lochaber District;
	(4) Nairn District.
Ross, Cromarty and Skye	(1) Ross and Cromarty District;
	(2) Skye and Lochalsh District;
	(3) electoral divisions 41 (Aird South), 41A (Charleston) and 42 (Aird North) in Inverness District.

LOTHIAN REGION

(a) Burgh Constituencies

Edinburgh Central	Electoral divisions 20 (Murrayfield/Dean), 21 (New Town/Stockbridge), 27 (Dalry/Shandon), 28 (Haymarket/Tollcross) and 29 (St Giles'/Holyrood) in City of Edinburgh District.
Edinburgh East	(1) Electoral divisions 22 (Calton/Lochend), 30 (Willowbrae/Mountcastle), 31 (Portobello/Milton) and 39 (Niddrie/Craigmillar) in City of Edinburgh District;

	(2) ward 30 (Craigentinny) of City of Edinburgh District.
Edinburgh Leith	(1) Electoral divisions 12 (Pilton/Muirhouse), 13 (Granton/Trinity), 14 (Newhaven/Fort), 17 (Broughton/Inverleith) and 18 (Lorne/Harbour) in City of Edinburgh District;
	(2) ward 29 (Links) of City of Edinburgh District.
Edinburgh Pentlands	Electoral divisions 10 (Balerno/Baberton), 24 (Hailes), 25 (Sighthill/Longstone), 35 (Colinton/Firrhill) and 36 (Braidburn/Fairmilehead) in City of Edinburgh District.
Edinburgh South	Electoral divisions 32 (Merchiston/Morningside), 33 (Sciennes/Marchmont), 34 (Prestonfield/Mayfield), 37 (Alnwickhill/Kaimes) and 38 (Inch/Gilmerton) in City of Edinburgh District.
Edinburgh West	Electoral divisions 11 (Cramond/Parkgrove), 15 (Corstorphine North), 16 (Telford/Blackhall), 19 (Corstorphine South) and 26 (Moat/Stenhouse) in City of Edinburgh District.

(b) County Constituencies

East Lothian	East Lothian District.
Linlithgow	(1) Electoral divisions 1 (Linlithgow), 2 (Bathgate West/Armadale), 3 (Bathgate East/Blackburn) and 4 (Whitburn) in West Lothian District;
	(2) ward 1 (Queensferry) of City of Edinburgh District.
Livingston	(1) Electoral divisions 5 (Livingston (North)), 6 (Livingston (South)), 7 (Broxburn) and 8 (Calders) in West Lothian District;
	(2) ward 2 (Kirkliston) of City of Edinburgh District.
Midlothian	Midlothian District.

STRATHCLYDE REGION

(a) Burgh Constituencies

Glasgow Cathcart	Electoral divisions 36, 37 and 39 in City of Glasgow District.
Glasgow Central	Electoral divisions 21, 34 and 35 in City of Glasgow District.
Glasgow Garscadden	Electoral divisions 9, 10 and 11 in City of Glasgow District.
Glasgow Govan	Electoral divisions 28, 29 and 30 in City of Glasgow District.
Glasgow Hillhead	Electoral divisions 12, 13 and 17 in City of Glasgow District.
Glasgow Maryhill	Electoral divisions 14, 15 and 16 in City of Glasgow District.
Glasgow Pollok	Electoral divisions 31, 32 and 33 in City of Glasgow District.
Glasgow Provan	Electoral divisions 24, 25 and 27 in City of Glasgow District.
Glasgow Rutherglen	Electoral divisions 38, 40 and 41 in City of Glasgow District.

Glasgow Shettleston	Electoral divisions 22, 23 and 26 in City of Glasgow District.
Glasgow Springburn	Electoral divisions 18, 19 and 20 in City of Glasgow District.
Greenock and Port Glasgow	(1) Electoral divisions 85 (Cartsdyke) and 86 (Greenock South West) in Inverclyde District;
	(2) the areas of wards 2 (Port Glasgow East), 3 (Port Glasgow South), 4 (Clune Brae), 5 (Port Glasgow West), 16 (Greenock West Central) and 17 (Greenock West End) of Inverclyde District as these wards are described in the Schedule to the Inverclyde District (Electoral Arrangements) Order 1981 which comes into operation on 3rd May 1984.
Hamilton	Electoral divisions 63 (Hamilton East), 64 (Hamilton West) and 66 (Hamilton North) in Hamilton District.
Monklands East	Electoral divisions 54 (Airdrie East), 55 (Airdrie South and West) and 56 (Chapelhall and Salsburgh) in Monklands District.
Monklands West	(1) Electoral divisions 52 (Coatbridge North) and 53 (Coatbridge South) in Monklands District;
	(2) electoral division 48 (Chryston and Kelvin Valley) in Strathkelvin District.
Motherwell North	Electoral divisions 60 (Fortissat), 61 (Bellshill and Tannochside) and 62 (Clydesdale) in Motherwell District.
Motherwell South	Electoral divisions 57 (Dalziel), 58 (Wishaw) and 59 (Clydevale) in Motherwell District.
Paisley North	Electoral divisions 75 (Paisley Craigielea), 78 (Paisley Abercorn) and 81 (Renfrew) in Renfrew District.
Paisley South	Electoral divisions 76 (Paisley Glennifer), 77 (Paisley Central) and 80 (Johnstone) in Renfrew District.

(b) County Constituencies

Argyll and Bute	Argyll and Bute District.
Ayr	(1) Electoral divisions 97 (Ayr North), 98 (Ayr South) and 100 (North Kyle) in Kyle and Carrick District;
	(2) the areas of wards 11 (St Cuthberts), 12 (St Nicholas) and 13 (Kingcase) of Kyle and Carrick District as these wards are described in the Schedule to the Kyle and Carrick District (Electoral Arrangements) Order 1981 which comes into operation on 3rd May 1984.
Carrick, Cumnock and Doon Valley	(1) Cumnock and Doon Valley District;
	(2) electoral division 101 (Carrick) in Kyle and Carrick District;
	(3) the areas of wards 14 (Annbank, Mossblown and St Quivox) and 15 (Coylton and Kincaidston) of Kyle and Carrick District as these wards are described in the Schedule to the Kyle and Carrick District (Electoral Arrangements) Order 1981 which comes into operation on 3rd May 1984.
Clydebank and Milngavie	(1) Clydebank District;

(2) the areas of wards 1 (Barloch), 2 (Keystone), 3 (Craigdhu) and 4 (Clober) of Bearsden and Milngavie District as these wards are described in the Schedule to the Bearsden and Milngavie District (Electoral Arrangements) Order 1981 which comes into operation on 3rd May 1984.

Clydesdale

(1) Clydesdale District;

(2) electoral division 65 (Larkhall and Stonehouse) in Hamilton District.

Cumbernauld and Kilsyth

Cumbernauld and Kilsyth District.

Cunninghame North

Electoral divisions 91 (Garnock Valley), 92 (Saltcoats and Ardrossan) and 93 (Arran, Largs and West Kilbride) in Cunninghame District.

Cunninghame South

Electoral divisions 88 (Irvine Central), 89 (Irvine South) and 90 (Kilwinning and Stevenston) in Cunninghame District.

Dumbarton

Dumbarton District.

Eastwood

(1) Eastwood District;

(2) electoral division 79 (Barrhead) in Renfrew District.

East Kilbride

East Kilbride District.

Kilmarnock and Loudoun

Kilmarnock and Loudoun District.

Renfrew West and Inverclyde

(1) Electoral divisions 82 (Gryffe) and 83 (Bargarran) in Renfrew District;

(2) the areas of wards 1 (Kilmacolm), 18 (Cardwell Bay), 19 (Gourock) and 20 (Firth) of Inverclyde District as these wards are described in the Schedule to the Inverclyde District (Electoral Arrangements) Order 1981 which comes into operation on 3rd May 1984.

Strathkelvin and Bearsden

(1) Electoral divisions 46 (Kirkintilloch) and 47 (Bishopbriggs) in Strathkelvin District;

(2) electoral division 45 (Bearsden) in Bearsden and Milngavie District;

(3) the area of ward 5 (Kilmardinny) of Bearsden and Milngavie District as that ward is described in the Schedule to the Bearsden and Milngavie District (Electoral Arrangements) Order 1981 which comes into operation on 3rd May 1984.

TAYSIDE REGION

(a) Burgh Constituencies

Dundee East

Electoral divisions 11 (Wellgate/Baxter Park), 12 Craigiebank), 13 (West Ferry/Broughty Ferry), 14 (Balgillo/Eastern), 15 (Douglas/Drumgeith), 16 (Whitfield/Longhaugh), 17 (Fintry), 18 (Caird/Midmill), 19 (Clepington/Maryfield) and 20 (Coldside/Hilltown) in City of Dundee District.

Dundee West

Electoral divisions 21 (Central/Riverside), 22 (Dudhope/Logie), 23 (Law/Ancrum), 24 (Menzieshill/Ninewells), 25 (Gourdie/Pitalpin), 26 (Lochee), 27 (Rockwell/Fairmuir), 28 (Trottick/Gillburn), 29 (Downfield/St Mary's) and 30 (Ardler/Blackshade) in City of Dundee District.

(b) County Constituencies

Angus East

(1) Electoral divisions 1 (Aberbrothock), 2 (Arbroath Elliot), 3 (Arbroath St Vigeans), 4 (Carnoustie), 6 (Montrose Northesk), 9 (Montrose Lunan) and 10 (Brechin) in Angus District;

(2) the area of ward 15 (Eastern Glens) of Angus District as that ward is described in the Schedule to the Angus District (Electoral Arrangements) Order 1980 which comes into operation on 3rd May 1984.

(3) electoral division 31 (Monifieth) in City of Dundee District;

(4) the area of ward 44 (Sidlaw) of City of Dundee District as that ward is described in the Schedule to the City of Dundee District (Electoral Arrangements) Order 1980 which comes into operation on 3rd May 1984.

North Tayside

(1) Electoral divisions 5 (Forfar East and Dunnichen) and 8 (Forfar West and Strathmore) in Angus District;

(2) the areas of wards 13 (Kirriemuir) and 14 (Western Glens) of Angus District as these wards are described in the Schedule to the Angus District (Electoral Arrangements) Order 1980 which comes into operation on 3rd May 1984.

(3) electoral divisions 38 (Atholl, Breadalbane and Rannoch), 39 (Strathhardle), 40 (Strathisla), 43 (Strathtay) and 44 (St Martins) in Perth and Kinross District.

Perth and Kinross

(1) Electoral divisions 33 (Inveralmond), 34 (Moncreiffe), 35 (St Johnstoun), 36 (Viewlands), 37 (Letham), 41 (Strathearn), 42 (Tullibardine), 45 (Gowrie) and 46 (Kinross) in Perth and Kinross District;

(2) the area of ward 43 (Gowrie) of City of Dundee District as that ward is described in the City of Dundee District (Electoral Arrangements) Order 1980 which comes into operation on 3rd May 1984.

ISLANDS AREAS

County Constituencies

Orkney and Shetland

(1) Orkney Islands Area;

(2) Shetland Islands Area.

Western Isles

Western Isles Islands Area.

PART IV

NORTHERN IRELAND

(a) County Constituencies

East Antrim

(i) The local government districts of Carrickfergus and Larne; and

(ii) the following wards of the local government district of Newtownabbey, namely, Bradan, Cloughfern, Coole, Dunanney, Hopefield, Monkstown, Rostulla, Whiteabbey and Whitehouse.

East Londonderry

(i) The local government districts of Coleraine and Limavady; and

	(ii) the following wards of the local government district of Magherafelt, namely, Bellaghy, Castledawson, Gulladuff, Knockcloughrim, Lower Glenshane, Maghera, Swatragh, Tobermore, Town Parks East, Town Parks West, Upperlands and Valley.
Fermanagh and South Tyrone	The local government districts of Dungannon and Fermanagh.
Foyle	(i) The local government district of Londonderry; and
	(ii) the following wards of the local government district of Strabane, namely, Artigarvan, Dunnamanagh, East, North, Slievekirk, South and West.
Lagan Valley	(i) The local government district of Lisburn; and
	(ii) the Carryduff ward of the local government district of Castlereagh.
Mid-Ulster	(i) The local government districts of Cookstown and Omagh;
	(ii) the following wards of the local government district of Magherafelt, namely, Ballymaguigan, Draperstown and Lecumpher; and
	(iii) the following wards of the local government district of Strabane, namely, Castlederg, Clare, Finn, Glenderg, Newtownstewart, Plumbridge, Sion Mills and Victoria Bridge.
Newry and Armagh	(i) The local government district of Armagh; and
	(ii) the following wards of the local government district of Newry and Mourne, namely, Ballybot, Belleek, Bessbrook, Camlough, Creggan, Crossmaglen, Daisy Hill, Derrymore, Drumalane, Drumgullion, Fathom, Forkhill, Newtownhamilton, St Mary's, St Patrick's, Tullyhappy and Windsor Hill.
North Antrim	The local government district of Ballymena, Ballymoney and Moyle.
North Down	(i) The local government district of North Down; and
	(ii) the following wards of the local government district of Castlereagh, namely, Ballyhanwood, Carrowreagh, Dundonald, Enler, Gilnahirk and Tullycarnet.
Strangford	(i) The local government district of Ards; and
	(ii) the following wards of the local government district of Castlereagh, namely, Beechill, Fourwinds, Hillfoot, Lower Braniel, Minnowburn, Moneyreagh, Newtownbreda and Upper Braniel.
South Antrim	(i) The local government district of Antrim; and
	(ii) the following wards of the local government district of Newtownabbey, namely, Ballyclare, Ballyeaston, Ballyhenry, Ballynure, Carnmoney, Doagh, Glengormley, Jordanstown, Mallusk, Mossgrove, Mossley and Whitewell.
South Down	(i) the local government district of Down;
	(ii) the following wards of the local government district of Banbridge, namely, Annaclone, Ballyoolymore, Croob, Dromore, Drumadonnell, Garran, Quilly and Skeagh; and

	(iii) the following wards of the local government districts of Newry and Mourne, namely, Annalong, Ballycrossan, Binnian, Clonallan, Cranfield, Donaghmore, Drumgath, Kilkeel, Lisnacree, Rathfriland, Rostrevor, Seaview and Spelga.
Upper Bann	(i) The local government district of Craigavon; and
	(ii) the following wards of the local government district of Banbridge, namely, Ballydown, Central, Edenderry, Gilford, Lawrencetown, Loughbrickland and Seapatrick.

(b) Borough Constituencies

Belfast East	(i) The following wards of the local government district of Belfast, namely, Ballyhackamore, Ballymacarrett, Belmont, Bloomfield, Island, Orangefield, Shandon, Stormont, Sydenham and The Mount; and
	(ii) the following wards of the local government district of Castlereagh, namely, Cregagh, Downshire, Lisnasharragh and Wynchurch.
Belfast North	The following wards of the local government district of Belfast, namely, Ardoyne, Ballysillan, Bellevue, Castleview, Cavehill, Cliftonville, Crumlin, Duncairn, Fortwilliam, Grove, Legoniel, New Lodge, Shankill and Woodvale.
Belfast South	The following wards of the local government district of Belfast, namely, Ballynafeigh, Cromac, Donegall, Finaghy, Malone, Ormeau, Rosetta, St George's, Stranmillis, University, Upper Malone, Willowfield and Windsor.
Belfast West	The following wards of the local government district of Belfast, namely, Andersonstown, Ballygomartin, Central, Clonard, Court, Falls, Grosvenor, Highfield, Ladybrook, Milltown, North Howard, St James, Suffolk and Whiterock.

(Sch 2 repealed by the House of Commons (Redistribution of Seats) Act 1949, ss 8, 9, Sch 3; Schs 3–5, 8, 9 repealed by the Representation of the People Act 1949, ss 174(2), 175, 176(2), (3), Sch 9; Sch 6 repealed by the Local Government Act 1972, s 272(1), Sch 30; Sch 7 repealed by the Local Government (Scotland) Act 1973, s 237(1), Sch 29.)

TENTH SCHEDULE

Section 74

ADAPTATION AND INTERPRETATION OF ENACTMENTS, ETC

(Pt I: para 1 repealed by the House of Commons (Redistribution of Seats) Act 1949, ss 8(1), 9(2), Sch 3, and the Representation of the People Act 1949, ss 174(2), 175, 176(2), (3), Sch 9; paras 2–4, 6, 7, 8(2) repealed by the Representation of the People Act 1949, ss 174(2), 175, 176(2), (3), Sch 9; para 5 repealed by the Election Commissioners Act 1949, s 21, Schedule; para 8(1) repealed by the SLR Act 1953.)

PART II

SPECIFIC ADAPTATIONS

Elections

(Para 1(1), (2) repealed by the Representation of the People Act 1949, ss 174(2), 175, 176(2), Sch 9; para 1(3) repealed by the Local Government Act 1972, s 272(1), Sch 30; para 2 repealed by the

Representation of the People Act 1949, ss 174(2), 175, 176(2), (3), Sch 9; para 3 repealed by the SLR Act 1953.)

4. In the Sheriffs Act 1887, the expression "writ" shall be taken as not including a writ for a parliamentary election.

NOTE

Sheriffs Act 1887. See Vol 39, title Sheriffs and Bailiffs.

(Para 5 repealed by the Election Commissioners Act 1949, s 21, Schedule; para 6 repealed by the SL(R) Act 1978; para 7(1) repealed by the SLR Act 1950; para 7(2) repealed by the Local Government Act 1972, 272(1), Sch 30, and the Criminal Justice Act 1972, s 64(2), Sch 6, Pt I.)

(Schs 11, 13 repealed by the SLR Act 1953; Sch 12 repealed by the Representation of the People Act 1949, ss 174(2), 175, 176(2), (3), Sch 9.)

HOUSE OF COMMONS (REDISTRIBUTION OF SEATS) ACT 1949

(12, 13 & 14 Geo 6 c 66)

ARRANGEMENT OF SECTIONS

An Act to consolidate the enactments which make permanent provision for the redistribution of seats at parliamentary elections and the provisions of the Representation of the People Act 1948 interpreting statutory references to constituencies   [24 November 1949]

Representation of the People Acts. This Act is one of the Acts which may be cited by this collective title; see the Introductory Note to the Representation of the People Act 1948 ante.

House of Commons (Redistribution of Seats) Acts 1949 to 1979. This Act, the House of Commons (Redistribution of Seats) Act 1958 post, and the House of Commons (Redistribution of Seats) Act 1979 post may be cited together by this collective title; see s 2 of the 1979 Act post.

Northern Ireland. This Act applies to elections for the United Kingdom Parliament.

1 Establishment of permanent Boundary Commissions

(1) For the purpose of the continuous review of the distribution of seats at parliamentary elections, there shall be four permanent Boundary Commissions, namely a Boundary Commission for England, a Boundary Commission for Scotland, a Boundary Commission for Wales and a Boundary Commission for Northern Ireland.

(2) The Boundary Commissions shall be constituted in accordance with the provisions of Part I of the First Schedule to this Act, their assistant Commissioners and other officers

shall be appointed and their expenses shall be defrayed in accordance with the provisions of Part II of that Schedule, and their procedure shall be regulated in accordance with Part III of that Schedule.

(3) For the purposes of this Act [Monmouthshire] shall be taken to be part of Wales and not part of England.

NOTES

The word in square brackets in sub-s (3) was substituted by the House of Commons (Redistribution of Seats) Act 1958, s 5. As to the counties in Wales now, see the Local Government Act 1972, Sch 4, Vol 25, title Local Government.

Shall be constituted. Amendments were made to the constitution of the Boundary Commissions consequential on the provisions of the House of Commons (Redistribution of Seats) Act 1958, s 1 post; see Sch 1 post.

Records of the Commissions. See the note to s 2 post.

2 Periodical reports of Commissions as to redistribution

(1) Each Boundary Commission shall keep under review the representation in the House of Commons of the part of the United Kingdom with which they are concerned and shall, in accordance with the next following subsection, submit to the Secretary of State reports with respect to the whole of that part of the United Kingdom, either—

    (*a*) showing the constituencies into which they recommend that it should be divided in order to give effect to the rules set out in the Second Schedule to this Act; or

    (*b*) stating that, in the opinion of the Commission, no alteration is required to be made in respect of that part of the United Kingdom in order to give effect to the said rules.

(2) ...

(3) Any Boundary Commission may also from time to time submit to the Secretary of State reports with respect to the area comprised in any particular constituency or constituencies in the part of the United Kingdom with which they are concerned, showing the constituencies into which they recommend that that area should be divided in order to give effect to the rules set out in the said Second Schedule.

(4) Where a Commission intend to consider making a report under this Act, they shall, by notice in writing, inform the Secretary of State accordingly, and a copy of the said notice shall be published—

    (*a*) in a case where it was given by the Boundary Commission for England or the Boundary Commission for Wales, in the London Gazette;

    (*b*) (*applies to Scotland only*); and

    (*c*) in a case where it was given by the Boundary Commission for Northern Ireland, in the Belfast Gazette.

(5) As soon as may be after a Boundary Commission have submitted a report to the Secretary of State under this Act, he shall lay the report before Parliament together, except in a case where the report states that no alteration is required to be made in respect of the part of the United Kingdom with which the Commission are concerned, with the draft of an Order in Council for giving effect, whether with or without modifications, to the recommendations contained in the report.

NOTES

Sub-s (2) was repealed by the House of Commons (Redistribution of Seats) Act 1958, ss 2(1), 7(2).

Boundary Commissions. Ie the Commissions established under s 1 ante.

United Kingdom. Ie Great Britain and Northern Ireland; see the Interpretation Act 1978, s 5, Sch 1, Vol 41, title Statutes.

Secretary of State. Ie one of Her Majesty's Principal Secretaries of State; see the Interpretation Act 1978, s 5, Sch 1, Vol 41, title Statutes. The Secretary of State here concerned is the Secretary of State for the Home Department.

Reports. For the requirements as to recommendations in a report, see also s 3(1) post. A Boundary Commissions report is to be submitted not less than ten nor more than fifteen years from the date of the submission of the Commissions' last report; see the House of Commons (Redistribution of Seats) Act 1958, s 2(1) post.

As to a supplementary report to be submitted by the Boundary Commission for Northern Ireland, see the Northern Ireland Constitution Act 1973, s 28(2), Vol 31, title Northern Ireland (Pt 2), as modified by the House of Commons (Redistribution of Seats) Act 1979, s 1(3) post.

As to supplementary reports in relation to European Assembly Constituencies, see the European Assembly Elections Act 1978, Sch 2, paras 1, 3 post.

Constituencies. For definition, see s 4 post.

Give effect to the rules etc. It is not the duty of a Boundary Commission to aim at giving full effect in all circumstances to the rules set out in Sch 2 post; see the House of Commons (Redistribution of Seats) Act 1958, s 2(2) post, as to what the Commissions should generally take into account in giving effect to those rules. Note that it is Parliament alone that can challenge the exercise of a Boundary Commission's discretion in its report recommending the division of constituencies to the Secretary of State; see *Harper v Secretary of State for the Home Department* [1955] Ch 238, [1955] 1 All ER 331.

For an examination of the commission's duty to give effect to the rules, and of the importance of the rules, see *R v Boundary Commission for England, ex p Foot* [1983] QB 600, [1983] 1 All ER 1099, CA.

Writing. Unless the contrary intention appears this includes other modes of representing or reproducing words in a visible form; see the Interpretation Act 1978, s 5, Sch 1, Vol 41, title Statutes.

Lay . . . before Parliament. For meaning, see the Laying of Documents before Parliament (Interpretation) Act 1948, s 1(1), Vol 41, title Statutes.

Order in Council. The power to make Orders in Council is exercisable by statutory instrument; see the Statutory Instruments Act 1946, s 1(1), Vol 41, title Statutes.

Records of the Commissions. Records of the Commissions are public records for the purposes of the Public Records Act 1958, Vol 17, title Evidence; see s 10(1) of, and Sch 1, para 3, Table, Pt II to, that Act.

Application. Sub-ss (4) and (5) above and s 3 post are applied by the Northern Ireland Constitution Act 1973, s 28(4), Vol 31, title Northern Ireland (Pt 2), and, with modifications, by the European Assembly Elections Act 1978, s 3, Sch 2, para 4(1)(*a*), (2)(*a*)–(*c*) post.

3 General provisions as to reports and Orders in Council

(1) A report of a Boundary Commission under this Act showing the constituencies into which they recommend that any area should be divided shall state, as respects each constituency, the name by which they recommend that it should be known, and whether they recommend that it should be a county constituency or a borough constituency.

(2) The draft of any Order in Council laid before Parliament by the Secretary of State under this Act for giving effect, whether with or without modifications, to the recommendations contained in the report of a Boundary Commission may make provision—

(*a*) for any matters which appear to him to be incidental thereto or consequential thereon; . . .

(3) Where any such draft gives effect to any such recommendations with modifications, the Secretary of State shall lay before Parliament together with the draft a statement of the reasons for the modifications.

(4) If any such draft is approved by resolution of each House of Parliament, the Secretary of State shall submit it to His Majesty in Council.

(5) If a motion for the approval of any such draft is rejected by either House of Parliament or withdrawn by leave of the House, the Secretary of State may amend the draft and lay the amended draft before Parliament, and if the draft as so amended is approved by resolution of each House of Parliament, the Secretary of State shall submit it to His Majesty in Council.

(6) Where the draft of an Order in Council is submitted to His Majesty in Council under this Act, His Majesty in Council may make an Order in terms of the draft which shall come into force on such date as may be specified therein and shall have effect notwithstanding anything in any enactment:

Provided that the coming into force of any such Order shall not affect any parliamentary election until a proclamation is issued by His Majesty summoning a new

Parliament, or affect the constitution of the House of Commons until the dissolution of the Parliament then in being.

(7) The validity of any Order in Council purporting to be made under this Act and reciting that a draft thereof has been approved by resolution of each House of Parliament shall not be called in question in any legal proceedings whatsoever.

NOTES

The words omitted from sub-s (2) were repealed by the London Government Act 1963, s 93(1), Sch 18, Pt I.

General Note. See the cases referred to in the note "Give effect to the rules etc" to s 2 ante.

Boundary Commission. Ie the Commission established under s 1 ante.

Constituency. For definition, see s 4 post.

Lay before Parliament; Secretary of State. See the notes to s 2 ante.

Application. See the note to s 2 ante.

Orders in Council. The orders setting out the current constituencies are the Parliamentary Constituencies (Northern Ireland) Order 1982, SI 1982/1838; the Parliamentary Constituencies (England) Order 1983, SI 1983/417; the Parliamentary Constituencies (Wales) Order 1983, SI 1983/418; the Parliamentary Constituencies (Scotland) Order 1983, SI 1983/442; the European Assembly Constituencies (England) Order 1984, SI 1984/544; the European Assembly Constituencies (Wales) Order 1984, SI 1984/545; and the European Assembly Constituencies (Scotland) Order 1984, SI 1984/548.

The power to make Orders in Council is exercisable by statutory instrument; see the Statutory Instruments Act 1946, s 1(1), Vol 41, title Statutes.

4 Meaning of constituency in this Act and future Acts

In this Act, and, except where the context otherwise requires, in any other Act passed after the Representation of the People Act 1948, the expression "constituency" means an area having separate representation in the House of Commons.

NOTE

Representation of the People Act 1948. See this title ante. That Act was passed (ie received the Royal Assent) on 30 July 1948.

5 Amendments of former Acts consequential on disappearance of parliamentary counties and boroughs

(1) The constituencies for the time being established by the Representation of the People Act 1948, and any Order in Council under this Act shall take the place of parliamentary counties and boroughs.

(2) Subject to the next following subsection—

(a) any reference in any former Act to parliamentary counties and boroughs shall be construed as a reference to constituencies;

(b) references in any former Act to a parliamentary county shall be construed as references to a county constituency, and those to a parliamentary borough as references to a borough constituency, and references to a county election or a borough election shall be construed accordingly;

(c) (applies to Scotland only).

(3) Any reference in any former Act to the authority having power to divide a county or borough into polling districts or to appoint polling places for a county or a borough for the purposes of parliamentary elections shall, where the context is such as to show that the last foregoing subsection ought not to apply, be taken as a reference to the county council or the borough council, as the case may be.

(4) The provisions of subsections (2) and (3) of this section shall apply to a reference to any of the matters mentioned therein, whatever the terms used in that reference; but

those provisions may be excluded in whole or in part by an order of the Secretary of State in any particular case where they appear to him to be inappropriate.

(5) The power conferred by this section to make an order shall be exercisable by statutory instrument, and any such instrument shall be subject to annulment by resolution of either House of Parliament.

(6) In this section the expression "former Act" means an Act passed before the Representation of the People Act 1948.

NOTES

Order in Council. Ie an order made under s 3 ante.

Constituency. For definition, see s 4 ante.

Secretary of State. See the note to s 2 ante.

Statutory instrument; subject to annulment. For provisions as to statutory instruments generally, see the Statutory Instruments Act 1946, Vol 41, title Statutes, and as to statutory instruments which are subject to annulment, see ss 5(1), 7(1) of that Act.

Representation of the People Act 1948. See this title ante. That Act was passed (ie received the Royal Assent) on 30 July 1948. For the constituencies established under that Act, see Sch 1 to that Act ante.

6, 7 (*S 6 applies to Scotland only; s 7 repealed by the Northern Ireland Constitution Act 1973, s 41(1), Sch 6, Pt I.*)

8 Repeal and savings

(1) . . .

(2) Nothing in this repeal shall affect any Order in Council made, or any thing whatsoever done, under any enactment repealed by, and re-enacted in, this Act and every such Order in Council or thing and also any order of a Secretary of State under sub-paragraph (1) of paragraph 8 of Part I of the Tenth Schedule to the Representation of the People Act 1948, shall, so far as it could have been made or done under this Act, have effect as if made or done under the corresponding provision of this Act.

(3) Nothing in this repeal shall affect the constitution of the Boundary Commissions established before the commencement of this Act.

(4) Nothing in this repeal shall affect the terms and conditions on and subject to which any person held office immediately before the commencement of this Act.

(5) Any document referring to any Act or enactment repealed by this Act shall be construed as referring to this Act or to the corresponding enactment in this Act.

NOTES

Sub-s (1) was repealed by the SLR Act 1953.

Boundary Commissions. This refers to Commissions established under the enactments repealed by Sch 3 to this Act (repealed).

Representation of the People Act 1948, Sch 10, Pt I, para 8(1). Repealed by the SLR Act 1953.

9 Short title, citation and commencement

(1) This Act may be cited as the House of Commons (Redistribution of Seats) Act 1949, and shall be included among the Acts which may be cited as the Representation of the People Acts.

(2) This Act shall come into force on such day, not before the coming into force of the redistribution of seats effected by subsection (1) of section one of the Representation of the People Act 1948 as the Secretary of State may by statutory instrument appoint.

NOTES

Appointed day. This Act was brought into force on 1 April 1950 by the House of Commons (Redistribution of Seats) Act 1949 (Date of Commencement) Order 1950, SI 1950/371 (spent).

Representation of the People Acts. For the Acts which may be cited by this collective title, see the Introductory Note to the Representation of the People Act 1948 ante.

Representation of the People Act 1948, s 1(1). See this title ante.

SCHEDULES

FIRST SCHEDULE

Sections 1, 7

CONSTITUTION, OFFICERS, EXPENSES AND PROCEDURE OF BOUNDARY COMMISSIONS

PART I

Constitution

1. The Speaker of the House of Commons shall be the chairman of each of the four Commissions.

2. The Commission for England shall consist of the chairman, [a judge as deputy chairman] and two other members of whom one shall be appointed by the Secretary of State and the other by the Minister of Health.

3. (*Applies to Scotland only.*)

4. The Commission for Wales shall consist of the chairman, [a judge as deputy chairman] and two other members of whom one shall be appointed by the Secretary of State and the other by the Minister of Health.

5. The Commission for Northern Ireland shall consist of the chairman, [a judge as deputy chairman] and two other members appointed by the Secretary of State.

6, 7. . . .

8. A member of any Commission appointed by the Secretary of State or Minister of Health shall hold his appointment for such term and on such conditions as may be determined before his appointment by the Secretary of State or Minister of Health, as the case may be.

NOTES

The words in square brackets in paras 2, 4, 5 were substituted, and para 6 was repealed, by the House of Commons (Redistribution of Seats) Act 1958, ss 6, 7(2), Schedule, para 1.

Para 7 was repealed by the House of Commons Disqualification Act 1957, s 14(1), Sch 4.

Secretary of State. See the note to s 2 ante.

Minister of Health. The functions of that Minister under this Act were transferred to the Minister of Housing and Local Government, or in relation to Wales, the Secretary of State for Wales; see the Transfer of Functions (Minister of Health and Minister of Local Government and Planning) (No 2) Order 1951, SI 1951/753, in conjunction with the Minister of Local Government and Planning (Change of Style and Title) Order 1951, SI 1951/1900, and the Secretary of State for Wales and Minister of Land and Natural Resources Order 1965, SI 1965/319. The functions of the Minister of Housing and Local Government under this Act were subsequently transferred to the Secretary of State by virtue of the Secretary of State for the Environment Order 1970, SI 1970/1681, art 2(1).

Disqualification of Commissioners from other office. Boundary Commissioners and Assistant Boundary Commissioners are disqualified from membership of the House of Commons by the House of Commons Disqualification Act 1975, s 1(1)(*f*), Sch 1, Pt III, Vol 32, title Parliament, and are disqualified from membership of the Northern Ireland Assembly by the Northern Ireland Assembly Disqualification Act 1975, s 1, Sch 1, Pt III, Vol 31, title Northern Ireland (Pt 2).

PART II

Officers and expenses

1.—(1) The Secretary of State may, at the request of any Commission, appoint one or more assistant Commissioners to inquire into, and report to the Commission upon, such matters as the Commission think fit.

(2) Any such assistant Commissioner shall be appointed either for a certain term or for the

purposes of a particular inquiry, and on such conditions as to remuneration and otherwise as may be determined before his appointment by the Secretary of State with the approval of the Treasury.

2. The Secretary of State shall appoint a secretary to each of the Commissions, and may appoint such other officers of any Commission as he may determine with the approval of the Treasury, and the term and conditions of any such appointment shall be such as may be so determined.

3. The expenses of each Commission, including the travelling and other expenses of the members thereof, and the remuneration and expenses of the assistant Commissioners, secretary and other officers, shall be defrayed out of moneys provided by Parliament.

NOTES

Expenses. As to the payment of expenses of the Boundary Commissions attributable to the European Assembly Elections Act 1978, see s 7(2)(c) of that Act post.

Secretary of State. See the note to s 2 ante.

Treasury. Ie the Commissioners of HM Treasury; see the Interpretation Act 1978, s 5, Sch 1, Vol 41, title Statutes.

Disqualification of Commissioners from other office. See the note to Pt I of this Schedule ante.

PART III

Procedure

1. A Commission shall have power to act notwithstanding a vacancy among the members thereof, and at any meeting of a Commission two, or such greater number as the Commission may determine, shall be the quorum.

2. For the purpose of considering any matter of common concern, the Commissions, or any two or three of them, may hold joint meetings.

3. Where a Commission have provisionally determined to make recommendations affecting any constituency, they shall publish in at least one newspaper circulating in the constituency a notice stating—

(a) the effect of the proposed recommendations and (except in a case where they propose to recommend that no alteration be made in respect of the constituency) that a copy of the recommendations is open to inspection at a specified place within the constituency; and

(b) that representations with respect to the proposed recommendations may be made to the Commission within one month after the publication of the notice;

and the Commission shall take into consideration any representations duly made in accordance with any such notice.

4. A Commission may, if they think fit, cause a local inquiry to be held in respect of any constituency or constituencies.

5.—(1) Subsections (2) and (3) of section two hundred and ninety of the Local Government Act 1933, (which relate to the attendance of witnesses at inquiries) shall apply in relation to any local inquiry which the Commission for England or the Commission for Wales may cause to be held in pursuance of this Act.

(2) (*Applies to Scotland only.*)

(3) In relation to any local inquiry which the Commission for Northern Ireland may cause to be held as aforesaid, sections nineteen and twenty of the Poor Relief (Ireland) (No 2) Act 1847 shall apply.

6. Subject to the foregoing provisions of this Schedule, each of the Commissions shall have power to regulate their own procedure.

7. Every document purporting to be an instrument made or issued by a Commission and to be signed by the secretary or any person authorised to act in that behalf, shall be received in evidence and shall, until the contrary is proved, be deemed to be an instrument made or issued by the Commission.

NOTES

Quorum. "The word 'quorum' in its ordinary signification has reference to the existence of a complete body of persons, of whom a certain specified number is competent to transact the business of the whole"; see *Faure Electric Accumulator Co Ltd v Phillipart* (1888) 58 LT 525 at 527.

Recommendations. The House of Commons (Redistribution of Seats) Act 1958, s 4(1) post, provides that where a Boundary Commission revises any proposed recommendations after publishing a notice under para 3, the Commission must again comply with the paragraph in relation to the revised recommendations as if no earlier notice had been published.

Newspaper circulating in the constituency. This expression is not restricted to a local newspaper but includes a national newspaper and a newspaper which circulates among a limited class of persons and not among the public generally; see *Re Southern Builders and Contractors (London) Ltd* (1961) Times, 10 October, and *R v Westminster Betting Licensing Committee, ex p Peabody Donation Fund (Governors)* [1963] 2 QB 750, [1963] 2 All ER 544.

Within one month after, etc. The general rule in cases where an act is to be done within a specified time is that the day from which it runs is not to be counted; see *Goldsmiths' Co v West Metropolitan Rly Co* [1904] 1 KB 1, [1900–3] All ER Rep 667, CA; *Stewart v Chapman* [1951] 2 KB 792, [1951] 2 All ER 613. See also *Dodds v Walker* [1981] 2 All ER 609, [1981] 1 WLR 1027, HL, as to the day of expiry of periods of a month or a specified number of months.

Local inquiry. Further provision is made as to local inquiries under this paragraph by the House of Commons (Redistribution of Seats) Act 1958, s 4(2), (3) post.

Application. Para 4 above is applied with modifications by the European Assembly Elections Act 1978, s 3, Sch 2, para 4(1)(*b*), (2)(*a*) post.

Local Government Act 1933, s 290(2), (3). Repealed by the Local Government Act 1972, s 272(1), Sch 30, and replaced by s 250(2), (3) of that Act, Vol 25, title Local Government.

Poor Relief (Ireland) (No 2) Act 1847. 10 & 11 Vict c 90; not printed in this work.

SECOND SCHEDULE

Section 2

RULES FOR REDISTRIBUTION OF SEATS

1. The number of constituencies in the several parts of the United Kingdom set out in the first column of the following table shall be as stated respectively in the second column of that table—

Part of the United Kingdom.	*No of Constituencies.*
Great Britain	Not substantially greater or less than 613
Scotland	Not less than 71
Wales	Not less than 35
Northern Ireland	[Not greater than 18 or less than 16]

2. Every constituency shall return a single member.

3. There shall continue to be a constituency which shall include the whole of the City of London and the name of which shall refer to the City of London.

4.—(1) So far as is practicable having regard to the foregoing rules—

(*a*) in England and Wales,—

(i) no county or any part thereof shall be included in a constituency which includes the whole or part of any other county or the whole or part of a . . . metropolitan borough;

(ii) . . .

(iii) no metropolitan borough or any part thereof shall be included in a constituency which includes the whole or part of any other metropolitan borough;

(iv) . . .

(*b*) (*applies to Scotland only*);

(*c*) in Northern Ireland, no [ward] shall be included partly in one constituency and partly in another.

(2) In paragraph (1) of this rule the following expressions have the following meanings, that is to say:—

"county" means an administrative county . . . ;

.   .   .   .   .

5. The electorate of any constituency shall be as near the electoral quota as is practicable having regard to the foregoing rules; and a Boundary Commission may depart from the strict application of the last foregoing rule if it appears to them that a departure is desirable to avoid an excessive

disparity between the electorate of any constituency and the electoral quota, or between the electorate thereof and that of neighbouring constituencies in the part of the United Kingdom with which they are concerned.

6. A Boundary Commission may depart from the strict application of the last two foregoing rules if special geographical considerations, including in particular the size, shape and accessibility of a constituency, appear to them to render a departure desirable.

[7. In the application of these rules to each of the several parts of the United Kingdom for which there is a Boundary Commission—

(*a*) the expression "electoral quota" means a number obtained by dividing the electorate for that part of the United Kingdom by the number of constituencies in it existing on the enumeration date;

(*b*) the expression "electorate" means—

(i) in relation to a constituency, the number of persons whose names appear on the register of parliamentary electors in force on the enumeration date under the Representation of the People Acts for the constituency;

(ii) in relation to the part of the United Kingdom, the aggregate electorate as hereinbefore defined of all the constituencies therein;

(*c*) the expression "enumeration date" means, in relation to any report of a Boundary Commission under this Act, the date on which the notice with respect to that report is published in accordance with section two of this Act.]

NOTES

The words in square brackets in r 1 were substituted by the House of Commons (Redistribution of Seats) Act 1979, s 1(1).

The words omitted from r 4(1) were repealed by the Local Government Act 1972, ss 251(2), 272(1), Sch 29, Pt II, para 38, Sch 30; and the word in square brackets in that rule was substituted by the Local Government Reorganisation (Consequential Provisions) (Northern Ireland) Order 1973, SI 1973/2095, art 2(7).

The words omitted from r 4(2) as indicated by dots in the first place where they occur were repealed by the London Government Act 1963, s 93(1), Sch 18, Pt II, and in the other places where they occur were repealed by the Local Government Act 1972, s 272(1), Sch 30, and the Local Government Reorganisation (Consequential Provisions) (Northern Ireland) Order 1973, SI 1973/2095, art 5(2), Sch 2.

Para 7 was substituted by the House of Commons (Redistribution of Seats) Act 1958, s 6, Schedule, para 2.

General Note. See the note "Give effect to the rules etc" to s 2 ante.

Constituency. For definition, see s 4 ante. For a list of constituencies, see the Representation of the People Act 1948, Sch 1 ante.

County. As to the counties in England and Wales and their councils, see the Local Government Act 1972, ss 1(1), (2), 2(1), (3), 20(1), (2), 21(1), (3), Sch 1, Pts I, II, Sch 4, Pt I, Vol 25, title Local Government.

Metropolitan borough. This is to be construed as a reference to a London borough; see the London Government Act 1963, s 8(1), Sch 3, para 21, Vol 26, title London. London boroughs are listed in Sch 1 to that Act.

Boundary Commission. Ie one of the Boundary Commissions established under s 1 ante.

United Kingdom. See the note to s 2 ante.

Modification. Rules 1 and 5 of this Schedule are modified in relation to Northern Ireland by the House of Commons (Redistribution of Seats) Act 1979, s 1(2)–(4) post.

Representation of the People Acts. For the Acts which may be cited by this collective title, see the Introductory Note to the Representation of the People Act 1948 ante.

(*Sch 3 repealed by the SLR Act 1953.*)

HOUSE OF COMMONS (REDISTRIBUTION OF SEATS) ACT 1958

(6 & 7 Eliz 2 c 26)

An Act to amend the House of Commons (Redistribution of Seats) Act 1949

[14 May 1958]

Representation of the People Acts. This Act is one of the Acts which may be cited together by this collective title; see the Introductory Note to the Representation of the People Act 1948 ante.

Northern Ireland. This Act applies.

1 Constitution of Boundary Commissions

(1) The deputy chairman of each Boundary Commission under the House of Commons (Redistribution of Seats) Act 1949 (hereinafter referred to as "the principal Act"), shall be a judge who—

(a) in the case of the Commission for England shall be a judge of the High Court appointed by the Lord Chancellor,

(b) in the case of the Commission for Scotland shall be a judge of the Court of Session appointed by the Lord President of the Court of Session,

(c) in the case of the Commission for Wales shall be a judge of the High Court appointed by the Lord Chancellor,

(d) in the case of the Commission for Northern Ireland shall be a judge of the High Court in Northern Ireland appointed by the Lord Chief Justice of Northern Ireland,

and each deputy chairman shall hold his appointment for such term and on such conditions as may be determined before his appointment by the person appointing him.

(2) The officers of each Commission shall include two assessors who shall be—

(a) in the case of the Commission for England, the Registrar General for England and Wales and the Director General of Ordnance Survey,

(b) in the case of the Commission for Scotland, the Registrar General of Births, Deaths and Marriages in Scotland and the Director General of Ordnance Survey,

(c) in the case of the Commission for Wales, the Registrar General for England and Wales and the Director General of Ordnance Survey,

(d) in the case of the Commission for Northern Ireland the Registrar General of Births, Deaths and Marriages for Northern Ireland and the Commissioner of Valuation for Northern Ireland,

and those persons shall cease to be members of the Commissions.

NOTES

Boundary Commission. The Boundary Commissions were established under s 1 of the House of Commons (Redistribution of Seats) Act 1949 ante. For provisions as to their constitution, officers and procedure, see Sch 1 to that Act.

House of Commons (Redistribution of Seats) Act 1949. See this title ante.

---

2 Boundary Commissions' reports

(1) After the coming into force of this Act a Boundary Commission's report under subsection (1) of section two of the principal Act shall be submitted not less than ten or more than fifteen years from the date of the submission of the Commission's last report under that subsection; and subsection (2) of that section (which in general requires reports to be made not less than three or more than seven years from the date of the submission of the Commission's last report) shall cease to have effect.

(2) It shall not be the duty of a Boundary Commission, in discharging their functions under the said section two, to aim at giving full effect in all circumstances to the rules set out in the Second Schedule to the principal Act, but they shall take account, so far as they reasonably can, of the inconveniences attendant on alterations of constituencies other than alterations made for the purposes of rule 4 of those rules, and of any local ties which would be broken by such alterations; and references in that section to giving effect to those rules shall be construed accordingly.

NOTES

Coming into force of this Act. This Act came into force on receiving the Royal Assent on 14 May 1958.

Principal Act. Ie the House of Commons (Redistribution of Seats) Act 1949 ante; see s 1(1) ante.

3 Electoral quotas

In the application of rule 5 of the rules set out in the Second Schedule to the principal Act (under which the electorate of a constituency is to be brought as near the electoral quota as is practicable having regard to the other rules in that Schedule) to a constituency in any of the several parts of the United Kingdom for which there is a Boundary Commission, the expression "electoral quota" shall mean a number obtained by dividing the electorate for that part of the United Kingdom by the number of constituencies in it existing on the enumeration date (and not, as at present in Great Britain, a number obtained by reference to Great Britain as a whole).

NOTES

Several parts. Ie England, Scotland, Wales and Northern Ireland; see the House of Commons (Redistribution of Seats) Act 1949, s 1 ante.

United Kingdom. Ie Great Britain and Northern Ireland; see the Interpretation Act 1978, s 5, Sch 1, Vol 41, title Statutes. "Great Britain" means England, Scotland and Wales by virtue of the Union with Scotland Act 1706, preamble, Art I, Vol 10, title Constitutional Law (Pt 1), as read with s 22(1) of, and Sch 2, para 5(a) to, the 1978 Act. Neither the Channel Islands nor the Isle of Man is within the United Kingdom.

Principal Act. Ie the House of Commons (Redistribution of Seats) Act 1949 ante; see s 1(1) ante.

4 Procedure of Boundary Commissions

(1) Where a Boundary Commission revise any proposed recommendations after publishing a notice of them under paragraph 3 of Part III of the First Schedule to the principal Act, the Commission shall comply again with that paragraph in relation to the revised recommendations, as if no earlier notice had been published.

(2) Where, on the publication of the notice under the said paragraph 3 of a recommendation of a Boundary Commission for the alteration of any constituencies, the Commission receive any representation objecting to the proposed recommendation from an interested authority or from a body of electors numbering one hundred or more, the Commission shall not make the recommendation unless, since the publication of the said notice, a local inquiry has been held in respect of the constituencies under paragraph 4 of the said Part III:

Provided that, where a local inquiry was held in respect of the constituencies before the publication of the said notice, this subsection shall not apply if the Commission, after considering the matters discussed at the local inquiry, the nature of the representations received on the publication of the said notice and any other relevant circumstances, are of opinion that a further local inquiry would not be justified.

(3) In the last foregoing subsection, "interested authority" and "elector" respectively mean, in relation to any recommendation, a local authority whose area is wholly or partly comprised in the constituencies affected by the recommendation, and a

parliamentary elector for any of these constituencies; and for this purpose "local authority" means the council of any county, or any borough . . . or of any urban . . . district.

(4) (*Applies to Scotland only.*)

NOTES

The words omitted from sub-s (3) as indicated by dots in the first place where they occur were repealed by the London Government Act 1963, s 93(1), Sch 18, Pt II, and in the second place where they occur in that subsection were repealed by the Local Government Act 1972, s 272(1), Sch 30.

Parliamentary elector. For qualification to vote as a parliamentary elector, see the Representation of the People Act 1983, s 1 post.

County. As to the counties in England and Wales and their councils, see the Local Government Act 1972, ss 1(1), (2), 2(1), (3), 20(1), (2), 21(1), (3), Sch 1, Pts I, II, Sch 4, Pt I, Vol 25, title Local Government.

Borough. The boroughs, other than London boroughs, existing immediately before 1 April 1974 were abolished on that date by the Local Government Act 1972, ss 1(9), (10), 20(6), Vol 25, title Local Government, and the reference to a borough no longer has any effect.

Urban district. The urban districts and rural districts existing immediately before 1 April 1974 were abolished on that date by the Local Government Act 1972, ss 1(10), 20(6), Vol 25, title Local Government, and by virtue of s 179(1), (2) of that Act, the reference to an urban district is to be construed as a reference to a district established by ss 1(1), (3), (4), 20(1), (3) of, and Sch 1, Pt I, Sch 4, Pt II to, the 1972 Act.

Modification. By the Local Government Reorganisation (Consequential Provisions) (Northern Ireland) Order 1973, SI 1973/2095, arts 1(7), 2(7), in sub-s (2) above "interested authority" in relation to any recommendation means, as respects Northern Ireland, the district council for a district which is wholly or partly comprised in the constituencies affected by the recommendation.

Application. This section is applied, with modifications, by the European Assembly Elections Act 1978, s 3, Sch 2, para 4(1)(*b*), (2)(*d*) post.

Principal Act. Ie the House of Commons (Redistribution of Seats) Act 1949 ante; see s 1(1) ante.

5 (*Amends the House of Commons (Redistribution of Seats) Act 1949, s 1(3) ante.*)

6 Consequential amendments

The principal Act shall have effect subject to the amendments specified in the Schedule to this Act, being amendments consequent on the foregoing provisions of this Act.

NOTE

Principal Act. Ie the House of Commons (Redistribution of Seats) Act 1949 ante; see s 1(1) ante.

7 Short title, repeal and extent

(1) This Act may be cited as the House of Commons (Redistribution of Seats) Act 1958 and shall be included among the Acts which may be cited as the Representation of the People Acts, and this Act and the House of Commons (Redistribution of Seats) Act 1949 may be cited together as the House of Commons (Redistribution of Seats) Acts 1949 and 1958.

(2), (3) . . .

NOTES

Sub-s (2) was repealed by the SL(R) Act 1974.

Sub-s (3) was repealed by the Northern Ireland Constitution Act 1973, s 41(1), Sch 6, Pt I.

Representation of the People Acts. For the Acts which may be cited by this collective title, see the Introductory Note to the Representation of the People Act 1948 ante.

House of Commons (Redistribution of Seats) Act 1949. See this title ante.

(*Schedule amends the House of Commons (Redistribution of Seats) Act 1949, Sch 1, Pt I, paras 2–5, Sch 2, r 7 ante and repeals para 6 in Pt I of Sch 1 to that Act.*)

EUROPEAN ASSEMBLY ELECTIONS ACT 1978

(1978 c 10)

ARRANGEMENT OF SECTIONS

An Act to make provision for and in connection with the election of representatives to the Assembly of the European Communities, and to prevent any treaty providing for any increase in the powers of the Assembly from being ratified by the United Kingdom unless approved by Act of Parliament   [5 May 1978]

Northern Ireland. This Act applies.

1 Election of representatives to the European Assembly

The representatives of the people of the United Kingdom in the Assembly of the European Communities (in this Act referred to as "the Assembly") shall be elected in accordance with this Act.

NOTES

United Kingdom. Ie Great Britain and Northern Ireland; see the Interpretation Act 1978, s 5, Sch 1, Vol 41, title Statutes. "Great Britain" means England, Scotland and Wales by virtue of the Union with Scotland Act 1706, preamble, Art I, Vol 10, title Constitutional Law (Pt 1), as read with s 22(1) of, and Sch 2, para 5(a) to, the 1978 Act. Neither the Channel Islands nor the Isle of Man is within the United Kingdom.

Assembly of the European Communities. Ie the one common Assembly which has served the European Communities since the establishment of the European Economic Community and the European Atomic Energy Community in 1958; see the Convention on Common Institutions, arts 1, 2(1), in conjunction with ECSC Treaty, arts 20–25, EEC Treaty, arts 137–144, and Euratom Treaty, arts 107–114. The Assembly is also known as the European Parliament, although under the treaties it exercises only advisory and supervisory, and not legislative, powers (and note that by s 6 post any treaty increasing the powers of the Assembly requires the approval of an Act of Parliament). The Act annexed to the Decision of the Council of the European Communities concerning the Election of Representatives of the Assembly by Direct Universal Suffrage, 76/787/ECSC, EEC, Euratom, makes new provisions for the composition of the Assembly and for the election of the members thereof and accordingly provides for the lapse of the provisions of the above-mentioned Treaties concerning the composition of the Assembly, viz, ECSC Treaty, art 21(1), (2), EEC Treaty, art 138(1), (2), and Euratom Treaty, art 108(1), (2).

2 Number of representatives

The number of representatives to the Assembly to be elected in the United Kingdom shall be 81; and of those representatives—

    (a) 66 shall be elected in England;

    (b) 8 shall be elected in Scotland;

(*c*) 4 shall be elected in Wales; and
(*d*) 3 shall be elected in Northern Ireland.

NOTES

The Assembly. Ie the Assembly of the European Communities; see s 1 ante and the note thereto.
United Kingdom. See the note to s 1 ante.

3 Method of election

Assembly elections shall be held and conducted in accordance with the provisions of Schedule 1 to this Act (with Schedule 2) under the simple majority system (for Great Britain) and the single transferable vote system (for Northern Ireland).

NOTES

Assembly elections. Ie elections to the Assembly of the European Communities; cf s 1 ante. See also s 8(1) post.
Great Britain. Ie England, Scotland and Wales; see the Union with Scotland Act 1706, preamble, Art I, Vol 10, title Constitutional Law (Pt 1), as read with the Interpretation Act 1978, s 22(1), Sch 2, para 5(*a*), Vol 41, title Statutes.

4 Double voting

(1) Without prejudice to any enactment relating to voting offences as applied by regulations under this Act to elections of representatives to the Assembly held in the United Kingdom, a person shall be guilty of an offence if, on any occasion when under Article 9 elections to the Assembly are held in all the member States, he votes otherwise than as a proxy more than once in those elections, whether in the United Kingdom or elsewhere.

(2) The provisions of the [Representation of the People Act 1983] as applied by regulations under this Act shall have effect in relation to an offence under this section as they have effect in relation to an offence under [section 61(2)] of that Act (double voting); and, without prejudice to the generality of the foregoing provision, [section 61(7)] of that Act (which makes such an offence an illegal practice but allows any incapacity resulting from conviction to be mitigated by the convicting court) and [section 178] of that Act (prosecutions of offences committed outside the United Kingdom) shall apply accordingly.

NOTES

The words in square brackets in sub-s (2) were substituted by the Representation of the People Act 1983, s 206, Sch 8, para 21.
Enactment relating to voting offences. See, in particular, the Representation of the People Act 1983, ss 60, 61 post.
Regulations under this Act. Ie regulations made under s 3 ante and Sch 1, para 2(3), (4) post.
United Kingdom. See the note to s 1 ante.
Member States. Ie States which are members of the European Communities; see the European Communities Act 1972, s 1(2), Sch 1, Pt II, Vol 17, title European Communities, as applied by the Interpretation Act 1978, s 5, Sch 1, Vol 41, title Statutes.
Definitions. For "the Assembly", see s 1 ante; as to "Article 9", see s 8(2)(*a*) post; for "enactment", see s 8(2)(*b*) post.
Representation of the People Act 1983, ss 61, 178. See this title post.

5 (*Sub-s (1) amends the Jurors Act 1974, Sch 1, Pt III, Vol 22, title* Juries *and the* Juries (Northern Ireland) Order 1974, SI 1974/2143, Sch 2; sub-s (2) repealed by the Law Reform (Miscellaneous Provisions) (Scotland) Act 1980, s 28(2), Sch 3.*)

6 Parliamentary approval of treaties increasing Assembly's powers

(1) No treaty which provides for any increase in the powers of the Assembly shall be ratified by the United Kingdom unless it has been approved by an Act of Parliament.

(2) In this section "treaty" includes any international agreement, and any protocol or annex to a treaty or international agreement.

NOTES

The Assembly. Ie the Assembly of the European Communities; see s 1 ante and the note thereto.
United Kingdom. See the note to s 1 ante.

7 Expenses

(1) There shall be charged on, and paid out of, the Consolidated Fund—

    (a) such reasonable charges as returning officers are by virtue of this Act entitled to in connection with Assembly elections; and

    (b) any increase attributable to this Act in the sums charged on and payable out of that Fund under any other enactment.

(2) There shall be paid out of money provided by Parliament—

    (a) any additional sums payable by way of rate support grant because of an increase attributable to this Act in the registration expenses of registration officers in Great Britain;

    (b) any increase so attributable in the sums payable out of money so provided under [section 54(2) of the Representation of the People Act 1983] on account of the registration expenses of registration officers in Northern Ireland; and

    (c) any increase so attributable in the sums payable out of money so provided under the House of Commons (Redistribution of Seats) Act 1949.

NOTES

The words in square brackets in sub-s (2)(b) were substituted by the Representation of the People Act 1983, s 206, Sch 8, para 22.

Consolidated Fund. Ie the Consolidated Fund of the United Kingdom which was established by the Consolidated Fund Act 1816, s 1, Vol 30, title Money (Pt 1). By the Finance Act 1954, s 34(3), Vol 30, title Money (Pt 1), any charge on the Fund extends to the growing produce thereof. See also, as to payment out of the Fund, the Exchequer and Audit Departments Act 1866, s 13, in conjunction with the Exchequer and Audit Departments Act 1957, s 2, and the Finance Act 1975, s 56, all Vol 30, title Money (Pt 1).

Such reasonable charges as returning officers are ... entitled to, etc. As to the returning officers for Assembly elections, see s 3 ante, and Sch 1, para 4 post; and as to the charges of returning officers, see the Representation of the People Act 1983, s 29(3)–(5) post, which applies, with modifications, to Assembly elections by virtue of the European Assembly Elections Regulations 1984, SI 1984/137, reg 3(1), Sch 1.

Assembly elections. Ie elections to the Assembly of the European Communities; cf s 1 ante. See also s 8(1) post.

Enactment. For definition, see s 8(2)(b) post.

Rate support grant. These grants are paid under the Local Government, Planning and Land Act 1980, s 53, Vol 25, title Local Government.

Registration expenses of registration officers. As to the appointment of registration officers, see the Representation of the People Act 1983, s 8 post, and as to their registration expenses, see s 54 of that Act post, which is applied to Assembly elections by virtue of the European Assembly Elections Regulations 1984, SI 1984/137, reg 3(1), Sch 1.

Great Britain. See the note to s 3 ante.

Representation of the People Act 1983, s 54(2). See this title post.

House of Commons (Redistribution of Seats) Act 1949. See this title ante.

8 Interpretation

(1) The provisions of this Act, except section 4, apply only in relation to representatives to the Assembly who fall to be elected in the United Kingdom; and

references in this Act (except section 4) to elections to the Assembly shall be construed accordingly.

(2) In this Act—

(a) any reference to a numbered Article is a reference to the Article so numbered of the Act concerning the election of the representatives of the Assembly by direct universal suffrage annexed to the decision of the Council of the European Communities dated the 20th September 1976, and any reference to a numbered subdivision of a numbered Article shall be construed accordingly;

(b) "enactment" includes an enactment contained in an Act of Parliament of Northern Ireland or an Order in Council made under the Northern Ireland (Temporary Provisions) Act 1972, or in a Measure of the Northern Ireland Assembly.

(3) Except where the context otherwise requires, any reference in this Act to an enactment is a reference to that enactment as amended, and includes a reference to it as applied, by or under any other enactment, including this Act.

NOTES

The Assembly. Ie the Assembly of the European Communities; see s 1 ante and the note thereto.

United Kingdom. See the note to s 1 ante.

Decision of the Council of the European Communities dated the 20th September 1976. Council Decision 76/787/ECSC/EEC/Euratom. The proposals set out in the Act annexed to that Decision were made in pursuance of ECSC Treaty, art 21(3), EEC Treaty, art 138(3), and Euratom Treaty, art 108(3).

Northern Ireland Assembly. This assembly was established by the Northern Ireland Assembly Act 1973, and further relevant provisions are contained in the Northern Ireland Constitution Act 1973, Pts II, IV, both Vol 31, title Northern Ireland (Pt 2). The Assembly, elected under s 2 of the first-mentioned Act, was dissolved by the Northern Ireland Assembly (Dissolution) Order 1975, SI 1975/422 (made under the Northern Ireland Act 1974, s 1(1), Vol 31, title Northern Ireland (Pt 2)). Under Sch 1, para 1, to the 1974 Act, laws for Northern Ireland may be made by Order in Council during the interim period as defined by s 1(4) of that Act. By para 1(7) of that Schedule, references to Measures of the Northern Ireland Assembly include references to such Orders in Council.

A new Assembly has now been elected by virtue of an election held on 20 October 1982 (ie the day appointed by the Northern Ireland Assembly (Day of Election) Order 1982, SI 1982/1078, made under the Northern Ireland Constitution Act 1973, s 27(7), as applied by s 1(1) of the 1974 Act). Provision for the general or partial suspension of the system of direct rule introduced by Sch 1 to the 1974 Act may now be made by Order in Council made under the Northern Ireland Act 1982, Vol 31, title Northern Ireland (Pt 2), and the effect of any such Order is set out in Sch 1 to that Act. See also, in particular, s 3 of the 1982 Act, as to matters which may be considered by the Assembly pending general suspension of direct rule; s 5 as to the dissolution of the Assembly and revocation of Orders in Council made under s 2 of the Act; and s 6 and Sch 2 for amendments of the 1973 Acts.

Northern Ireland (Temporary Provisions) Act 1972. See Vol 31, title Northern Ireland (Pt 2).

9 Citation etc

(1) This Act may be cited as the European Assembly Elections Act 1978.

(2) Any power to make orders or regulations conferred by this Act shall be exercisable by statutory instrument; and any power to make an order under any provision of this Act includes power to vary or revoke a previous order made under that provision.

NOTES

Statutory instrument. For provisions as to statutory instruments generally, see the Statutory Instruments Act 1946, Vol 41, title Statutes.

Vary or revoke. The express power to vary or revoke orders is necessary because the Interpretation Act 1978, s 14, Vol 41, title Statutes, does not extend to powers to make such instruments contained in Acts passed before 1 January 1979; see s 22(1) of, and Sch 2, para 3 to, that Act.

SCHEDULES

SCHEDULE 1

Section 3

Simple Majority System (for Great Britain) with STV (for Northern Ireland)

Assembly constituencies

1.—(1) Representatives to the Assembly shall be elected in Great Britain for the Assembly constituencies for the time being specified in an Order in Council under Schedule 2 to this Act, and in Northern Ireland for a single Assembly constituency comprising the whole of Northern Ireland; and there shall be—

(a) one representative for each such constituency in Great Britain; and
(b) three representatives for the Assembly constituency of Northern Ireland.

(2) There shall be a total of 79 Assembly constituencies, of which—

(a) 66 shall be in England;
(b) 8 shall be in Scotland;
(c) 4 shall be in Wales;
(d) 1 shall be that of Northern Ireland.

NOTES

The Assembly. Ie the Assembly of the European Communities; see s 1 ante and the note thereto.
Great Britain. See the note to s 3 ante.

Assembly elections

2.—(1) The persons entitled to vote as electors at an Assembly election in any particular Assembly constituency shall be—

(a) those who, on the day appointed under paragraph 3 below for the election, would be entitled to vote as electors at a parliamentary election in a parliamentary constituency wholly or partly comprised in the Assembly constituency (excluding any person not registered in the register of parliamentary electors at an address within the Assembly constituency); and
(b) peers who, on that day, would be entitled to vote at a local government election in an electoral area wholly or partly comprised in the Assembly constituency (excluding any peer not registered at an address within the Assembly constituency for the purposes of local government elections).

(2) In an Assembly election in the constituency of Northern Ireland each vote shall be a single transferable vote, that is to say a vote—

(a) capable of being given so as to indicate the voter's order of preference for the candidates for election as representatives for the constituency; and
(b) capable of being transferred to the next choice—

(i) when the vote is not required to give a prior choice the necessary quota of votes; or
(ii) when, owing to the deficiency in the number of votes given for a prior choice, that choice is eliminated from the list of candidates.

(3) Subject to the provisions of this and the following paragraph, the Secretary of State may by regulations make provision—

(a) as to the conduct of Assembly elections (including the registration of electors and the limitation of candidates' election expenses); and
(b) as to the questioning of such an election and the consequences of irregularities.

(4) Regulations under this paragraph may—

(a) apply, with such modifications or exceptions as may be specified in the regulations, any provision of the Representation of the People Acts or of any other enactment relating to parliamentary elections or local government elections, and any provision made under any enactment;

(*b*) amend any form contained in regulations made under the Representation of the People Acts so far as may be necessary to enable it to be used both for the purpose indicated in regulations so made and for the corresponding purpose in relation to Assembly elections;

(*c*) so far as may be necessary in consequence of any provision made by or under this Act, amend any provision made by or under any enactment relating to the registration of parliamentary electors or local government electors.

(5) Section 2(1) of the Welsh Language Act 1967 (power to prescribe Welsh version) shall apply in relation to regulations under this paragraph as it applies in relation to enactments.

(6) No regulations shall be made under this paragraph unless a draft thereof has been laid before Parliament and approved by a resolution of each House of Parliament.

NOTES

Assembly election. Ie an election to the Assembly of the European Communities; cf s 1 ante. See also s 8(1) ante.

Assembly constituency. See para 1 ante, and Sch 2 post.

Electors at a parliamentary election. For the persons who are entitled to vote at parliamentary elections, see the Representation of the People Act 1983, s 1 post.

Parliamentary constituency. The expression "constituency" is defined by the House of Commons (Redistribution of Seats) Act 1949, s 4 ante and the parliamentary constituencies are enumerated in the Representation of the People Act 1948, Sch 1 ante.

Register of parliamentary electors; registered ... for the purposes of local government elections. As to the compilation of the registers of parliamentary electors and of local government electors, see the Representation of the People Act 1983, ss 9 et seq post.

For the extension of the franchise to include persons registered in pursuance of an overseas elector's declaration, see the Representation of the People Act 1985, s 3(1) post, as from a day to be appointed under s 29(2) of that Act.

Peers ... entitled to vote at a local government election. Peers, although legally incapable of voting at parliamentary elections, are entitled to vote at local government elections, provided they are able to comply with the usual requirements and are not subject to any other legal incapacity; see 15 Halsbury's Laws (4th edn) para 410.

See also the Representation of the People Act 1985, s 3(2)–(4) post, as from a day to be appointed under s 29(2) of that Act, which extends the franchise to peers who are not resident in the United Kingdom and who satisfy the other conditions set out in those subsections.

Electoral area. Ie an electoral area as defined by the Representation of the People Act 1983, s 203(1) post.

Constituency of Northern Ireland. See para 1(1), (2)(*d*) ante.

Enactment. For definition, see s 8(2)(*b*) ante.

Laid before Parliament. For meaning, see the Laying of Documents before Parliament (Interpretation) Act 1948, s 1(1), Vol 41, title Statutes.

Representation of the People Acts. For the Acts which may be cited by this collective title, see the Introductory Note to the Representation of the People Act 1948 ante.

Welsh Language Act 1967, s 2(1). See Vol 41, title Statutes. The relevant order made under that section is the European Assembly Elections (Welsh Forms) Order 1979, SI 1979/368.

Regulations under this paragraph. The European Assembly Elections Regulations 1984, SI 1984/137, and the European Assembly Elections (Northern Ireland) Regulations 1984, SI 1984/198.

For general provisions as to regulations, see s 9(2) ante; and note sub-para (6) above.

Northern Ireland. For the construction of sub-para (1) above in relation to Northern Ireland, see the Elections (Northern Ireland) Act 1985, s 5(3) post.

Times of elections

3.—(1) Each general election of representatives to the Assembly shall be held on a day appointed by order of the Secretary of State.

(2) Subject to sub-paragraph (4) below, where, an Assembly election having been held in any particular Assembly constituency, the seat of a representative to the Assembly is or falls vacant, a by-election shall be held to fill the vacancy.

(3) A by-election in pursuance of sub-paragraph (2) above shall be held on a day appointed by order of the Secretary of State, being a day not later than six months after the occurrence of either of the following events, namely—

(*a*) notification of the vacancy by the Assembly under Article 12(2); or
(*b*) declaration of the vacancy by the Secretary of State.

(4) A by-election need not be held if the latest date for holding it would fall on or after the relevant Thursday (that is to say the Thursday with which the next period for holding elections to the Assembly in all the member States would begin in accordance with Article 10(2) in the absence of any determination by the Council thereunder).

(5) A statutory instrument made under this paragraph shall be laid before Parliament after being made.

NOTES

Assembly election. Ie an election to the Assembly of the European Communities; cf s 1 ante. See also s 8(1) ante.

Assembly constituency. See para 1 ante, and Sch 2 post.

Six months after, etc. As a general rule the effect of defining a period in such a manner is to exclude the day on which the event in question occurs. See *Dodds v Walker* [1981] 2 All ER 609, [1981] 1 WLR 1027, HL, as to the day of expiry of periods of a month or a specified number of months.

Member States. See the note to s 4 ante.

The Council. Ie the Council of European Communities.

Statutory instrument; laid before ... Parliament. For provisions as to statutory instruments generally, see the Statutory Instruments Act 1946, Vol 41, title Statutes; and as to statutory instruments which are required to be laid before Parliament after being made, see s 4(1), (2) of that Act, and the Laying of Documents before Parliament (Interpretation) Act 1948, Vol 41, title Statutes.

Definitions. For "the Assembly", see s 1 ante; as to "Assembly election", see s 8(1) ante; as to "Article 10(2)" and "Article 12(2)", see s 8(2)(a) ante.

Orders under this paragraph. The European Assembly Elections (Day of Election) Order 1979, SI 1979/219, and the European Assembly Elections (Day of Election) Order 1983, SI 1983/1152.

Orders appointing days for the holding of by-elections are not recorded in this work.

For general provisions as to orders, see s 9(2) ante; and note sub-para (5) above.

Returning officers, and staff to assist them

4.—(1) In England and Wales the returning officer for an Assembly election in any Assembly constituency shall be the person who is the returning officer for parliamentary elections for such one of the parliamentary constituencies wholly or partly comprised in that Assembly constituency as may be designated in an order made by the Secretary of State.

(2) *(Applies to Scotland only.)*

(3) In Northern Ireland the Chief Electoral Officer shall be the returning officer for every Assembly election.

(4) The council of a local government area wholly or partly situated in an Assembly constituency in England, Wales or Scotland shall place the services of their officers at the disposal of the returning officer for that Assembly constituency for the purpose of assisting him in the discharge of any functions conferred on him in relation to an Assembly election in that Assembly constituency.

(5) In this paragraph "local government area" means—

(a) in England and Wales, a district or London borough;
(b) *(applies to Scotland only)*.

NOTES

Assembly election. Ie an election to the Assembly of the European Communities; cf s 1 ante. See also s 8(1) ante.

Assembly constituency. See para 1 ante, and Sch 2 post.

Returning officer for parliamentary elections. These officers are designated by the Representation of the People Act 1983, s 24 post.

District. As to the districts in England and Wales and their councils, see the Local Government Act 1972, ss 1(1), (3), (4), 2(2), (3), 20(1), (3), 21(2), (3), Sch 1, Pt I, Sch 4, Pt II, Vol 25, title Local Government.

London borough. For definition, see the Interpretation Act 1978, s 5, Sch 1, Vol 41, title Statutes; and as to the London boroughs and their councils, see the London Government Act 1963, s 1, Sch 1, Vol 26, title London, and the Local Government Act 1972, s 8, Sch 2, Vol 25, title Local Government.

Orders under this paragraph. The European Assembly Elections (Returning Officers) (England and Wales) Order 1984, SI 1984/571.

For general provisions as to orders, see s 9(2) ante.

Disqualification for office of representative to Assembly

5.—(1) Subject to sub-paragraph (3) below, and without prejudice to Article 6(1) (incompatibility of office of representative with certain offices in or connected with Community institutions), a person is disqualified for the office of representative to the Assembly if—

> (a) he is disqualified, whether under the House of Commons Disqualification Act 1975 or otherwise, for membership of the House of Commons; or
> (b) he is a Lord of Appeal in Ordinary.

(2) A person is disqualified for the office of representative to the Assembly for a particular Assembly constituency if he is under section 1(2) of the House of Commons Disqualification Act 1975 disqualified for membership of the House of Commons for any particular parliamentary constituency wholly or partly comprised in that Assembly constituency.

(3) A person is not disqualified for office as a representative to the Assembly by reason only—

> (a) that he is a peer, whether of the United Kingdom, Great Britain, England or Scotland; or
> (b) that he has been ordained or is a minister of any religious denomination; or
> (c) that he holds an office mentioned in section 4 of the House of Commons Disqualification Act 1975 (stewardship of Chiltern Hundreds etc); or
> (d) that he holds any of the offices for the time being described in Part II or Part III of Schedule 1 to the House of Commons Disqualification Act 1975 which are for the time being designated in an order by the Secretary of State as non-disqualifying offices in relation to the Assembly.

(4) If any person disqualified under this paragraph for the office of representative to the Assembly, or for the office of representative to the Assembly for a particular Assembly constituency, is elected as a representative to the Assembly or as a representative for that constituency, as the case may be, his election shall be void.

(5) If a representative to the Assembly becomes disqualified under this paragraph for the office of representative to the Assembly or for the office of representative to the Assembly for the Assembly constituency for which he was elected, his seat shall be vacated.

(6) A statutory instrument made under this paragraph shall be subject to annulment in pursuance of a resolution of either House of Parliament.

NOTES

Community institutions. For meaning, see the European Communities Act 1972, Sch 1, Pt II, Vol 17, title European Communities, as applied by the Interpretation Act 1978, s 5, Sch 1, Vol 41, title Statutes.

Disqualified ... otherwise etc. In addition to the classes of persons disqualified under the House of Commons Disqualification Act 1975, the following are disqualified for membership of the House of Commons by other enactments—

Aliens: see the Act of Settlement (1700), s 3, Vol 10, title Constitutional Law (Pt 1).

Bankrupts: see the Bankruptcy (Ireland) Amendment Act 1872, ss 41, 42 (not printed in this work); the Bankruptcy Act 1883, ss 32, 33(1) and the Bankruptcy Act 1890, s 9, both Vol 4, title Bankruptcy and Insolvency; and the Bankruptcy (Scotland) Act 1913, ss 183, 184 (not printed in this work).

Criminal offenders: see the Forfeiture Act 1870, s 2, Vol 12, title Criminal Law (persons convicted of treason); and the Representation of the People Act 1983, ss 159(2), 160(4) post (persons guilty of corrupt or illegal practices at elections).

Persons under the age of 21: see the Parliamentary Elections Act 1695, s 7, Vol 32, title Parliament; and the Parliamentary Elections (Ireland) Act 1823, s 74 (not printed in this work). It should be noted that although in general a person now attains majority at the age of eighteen under the Family Law Reform Act 1969, this does not make it possible for anyone under twenty-one to sit in Parliament; see the 1969 Act, s 1(4), Sch 2, para 2, Vol 6, title Children.

As to the disqualification of persons of unsound mind, see 34 Halsbury's Laws (4th edn) para 1103.

There are also disqualifications affecting peers and clergymen but these are not considered here in view of sub-para (3)(a), (b) above.

Lords of Appeal in Ordinary. Lords of Appeal are appointed under the Appellate Jurisdiction Act 1876, s 6, Vol 11, title Courts.

Assembly constituency. See para 1 ante and Sch 2 post.

Peer, whether of the United Kingdom etc. For the classification of peers, see 35 Halsbury's Laws (4th edn) para 804.

Statutory instrument; subject to annulment. For provisions as to statutory instruments generally, see the Statutory Instruments Act 1946, Vol 41, title Statutes, and as to statutory instruments which are subject to annulment, see ss 5(1), 7(1) of that Act.

Judicial proceedings as to disqualification. See para 6 post.

Definitions. For "the Assembly", see s 1 ante; as to "Article 6(1)", see s 8(2)(a) ante.

House of Commons Disqualification Act 1975, ss 1(2), 4, Sch 1, Parts II, III. See Vol 32, title Parliament.

Orders under this paragraph. No order had been made under sub-para (3)(d) above up to 1 August 1985.

For general provisions as to orders, see s 9(2) ante; and note sub-para (6) above.

Judicial proceedings as to disqualification under paragraph 5

6.—(1) Any person who claims that a person purporting to hold office as a representative to the Assembly is disqualified or was disqualified at the time of, or at any time since, his election may apply to the court for a declaration or, as the case may be, declarator to that effect, and the decision of the court on the application shall be final.

(2) On an application under this paragraph the person in respect of whom the application is made shall be the respondent or, as the case may be, defender; and the applicant shall give such security for the costs or expenses of the proceedings, not exceeding £200, as the court may direct.

(3) No declaration or declarator shall be made under this paragraph in respect of any person on grounds which subsisted at the time of his election if there is pending, or has been tried, an election petition in which his disqualification on those grounds is, or was, in issue.

(4) Any declaration or declarator made by the court on an application under this paragraph shall be certified in writing to the Secretary of State forthwith by the court.

(5) The court for the purposes of this paragraph is the High Court, the Court of Session or the High Court of Justice in Northern Ireland according as the Assembly constituency to which the application relates is in England and Wales, or Scotland, or Northern Ireland; and in this paragraph "disqualified" means disqualified under paragraph 5 above for the office of representative to the Assembly (whether generally or in relation to a particular Assembly constituency).

NOTES

Declaration; declarator. For the general law relating to declarations, see 1 Halsbury's Laws (4th edn) paras 185 et seq. The declarator is the equivalent remedy in Scottish law.

Election petition. As to election petitions, see the Representation of the People Act 1983, s 121 post, applied to Assembly elections by the European Assembly Elections Regulations 1984, SI 1984/137, reg 3(1), Sch 1.

Writing. Unless the contrary intention appears this includes other modes of representing or reproducing words in a visible form; see the Interpretation Act 1978, s 5, Sch 1, Vol 41, title Statutes.

Assembly constituency. See para 1 ante and Sch 2 post.

Definitions. For "the Assembly", see s 1 ante. Note as to "the court" and "disqualified", sub-para (5) above.

SCHEDULE 2

Section 3, Sch 1, para 1

ASSEMBLY CONSTITUENCIES IN GREAT BRITAIN

PART I

Reports of Boundary Commission and Orders in Council

[1. If—

(a) an Order in Council has been made under section 3 of the 1949 Act giving effect, with or without modifications, to the recommendations contained in a report submitted to the Secretary of State under section 2(1) of that Act by the Boundary Commission for any part of Great Britain; or

(b) the Boundary Commission for any part of Great Britain have submitted a report to the Secretary of State under section 2(1) stating that, in the opinion of the Commission, no alteration is required to be made in the parliamentary constituencies into which that part of Great Britain is divided;

the Boundary Commission shall thereupon proceed to consider the representation in the Assembly of the part of Great Britain with which they are concerned and shall as soon as may be after that time submit to the Secretary of State a supplementary report in accordance with paragraph 2 below.]

2. [The supplementary report which the Boundary Commission for any part of Great Britain is required under paragraph 1 above to submit to the Secretary of State shall be a] report either—

(a) showing the Assembly constituencies into which they recommend that that part of Great Britain should be divided in order to give effect to the provisions of paragraph 1(2) of Schedule 1 to this Act and Part II of this Schedule; or

(b) stating that, in the opinion of the Commission, no alteration is required to be made in the Assembly constituencies in that part of Great Britain in order to give effect to those provisions.

[3. If—

(a) an Order in Council has been made under section 3 of the 1949 Act giving effect, with or without modifications, to recommendations for the alteration of any particular parliamentary constituency or constituencies contained in a report submitted to the Secretary of State under section 2(3) of that Act by the Boundary Commission for any part of Great Britain; and

(b) the result of the alterations in parliamentary constituencies made by the Order is that paragraph 9 below is no longer complied with in relation to one or more of the Assembly constituencies into which that part of Great Britain is divided;

the Boundary Commission shall thereupon proceed to consider in what manner the Assembly constituency or constituencies affected should be altered in order that paragraph 9 be complied with and shall as soon as may be after that time submit to the Secretary of State a supplementary report showing the alterations which they recommend should be made in the Assembly constituency or constituencies for that purpose.]

4.—(1) Subject to the following sub-paragraph—

(a) sections 2(4), 2(5) and 3 of the 1949 Act (notice of proposed report of Boundary Commission and implementation of recommendations in report) shall apply in relation to a . . . supplementary report made under this Schedule and a recommendation made or proposed to be made in such a . . . supplementary report; and

(b) paragraph 4 of Part III of Schedule 1 to that Act (local inquiries) and section 4 of the 1958 Act (procedure) shall apply in relation to a supplementary report so made . . . and to a recommendation made or proposed to be made in such a supplementary report.

(2) In their application in accordance with the preceding sub-paragraph the provisions there mentioned shall have effect with the following modifications, that is to say—

(a) references to constituencies shall be read as references to Assembly constituencies;

(b) in section 3(1) of the 1949 Act, the words from "and whether" onwards shall be omitted;

(c) in section 3(6) of the 1949 Act, the proviso shall be omitted; and

(d) in section 4 of the 1958 Act—

(i) references to paragraph 3 of Part III of Schedule 1 to the 1949 Act shall be read as references to paragraph 5 of this Schedule;

(ii) for the words "one hundred or more" in subsection (2) (which specify the number of electors whose objection in a body may make a local inquiry necessary) there shall be substituted the words "five hundred or more"; and

(iii) in subsection (2) "elector" shall mean an elector for any of the Assembly constituencies affected by the recommendation in question (and the definition of "elector" in subsection (3) shall not apply).

5.—(1) Where a Boundary Commission have provisionally determined to make recommendations with respect to any Assembly constituency, they shall publish a notice under this paragraph in such manner as they think best calculated to bring it to the attention of those concerned.

(2) A notice under this paragraph relating to an Assembly constituency shall state—

(a) the effect of the proposed recommendations with respect to that constituency and (except where the proposed recommendations do not involve any alteration in that Assembly constituency) that copies of the recommendations are open to inspection at one or more specified places within each parliamentary constituency included in that Assembly constituency; and

(b) that representations with respect to the proposed recommendations may be made to the Commission within one month after the first publication of the notice,

and the Commission shall take into consideration any representations duly made in accordance with any such notice.

6. Section 250(2) and (3) of the Local Government Act 1972 or, as the case may be, section 210(4) and (5) of the Local Government (Scotland) Act 1973 (attendance of witnesses at inquiries) shall apply in relation to an inquiry held in pursuance of paragraph 4 above.

7. Nothing in paragraph 4 above shall be taken as enabling the Secretary of State to modify any recommendation or draft Order in Council in a manner conflicting with the provisions of Part II of this Schedule.

8.—(1) An Order in Council under the provisions applied by paragraph 4 above shall apply to the first general election of representatives to the Assembly held after the Order comes into force and (subject to any further Order in Council) to any subsequent Assembly election, but shall not affect any earlier election.

(2) The validity of an Assembly election held in an Assembly constituency consisting of an area determined by an Order in Council made under the provisions applied by paragraph 4 above, being an Order which applied to that election, shall not be affected by any alteration made in any parliamentary constituency since the making of that Order.

NOTES

Paras 1, 3 and the words in square brackets in para 2 were substituted by the European Assembly Elections Act 1981, s 1(1)–(3), and the words omitted from para 4 were repealed by s 1(4) of that Act.
   Great Britain. See the note to s 3 ante.
   Parliamentary constituencies. See the note "Parliamentary constituency" to Sch 1, para 2 ante.
   Within one month after, etc. See the note "Six months after, etc" to Sch 1, para 3 ante.
   Definitions. For "the Assembly", see s 1 ante; as to "Assembly election", see s 8(1) ante; for "Boundary Commission", see para 11 in Pt III of this Schedule post.
   The 1949 Act. Ie the House of Commons (Redistribution of Seats) Act 1949 ante; see para 11 in Pt III of this Schedule post.
   The 1958 Act. Ie the House of Commons (Redistribution of Seats) Act 1958 ante; see para 11 in Pt III of this Schedule post.
   Local Government Act 1972, s 250(2), (3). See Vol 25, title Local Government.
   Local Government (Scotland) Act 1973. 1973 c 65; not printed in this work.
   Orders in council. The European Assembly Constituencies (England) Order 1984, SI 1984/544; the European Assembly Constituencies (Wales) Order 1984, SI 1984/545; and the European Assembly Constituencies (Scotland) Order 1984, SI 1984/548 (all made under the House of Commons (Redistribution of Seats) Act 1949, s 3 ante, as applied by para 4 above).

PART II

Division of Great Britain into Assembly Constituencies

9. In Great Britain—

(a) each Assembly constituency shall consist of an area that includes two or more parliamentary constituencies; and

(b) no parliamentary constituency shall be included partly in one Assembly constituency and partly in another.

10. The electorate of any Assembly constituency in Great Britain shall be as near the electoral quota as is reasonably practicable having regard, where appropriate, to special geographical considerations.

NOTES

   Great Britain. See the note to s 3 ante.
   Assembly constituency. See Sch 1, para 1 ante, and Pt I of this Schedule ante.
   Parliamentary constituency. See the note to Sch 1, para 2 ante.
   Definitions. For "electoral quota" and "electorate", see para 12 in Pt III of this Schedule post.

PART III

Interpretation

11. In this Schedule—

"the 1949 Act" means the House of Commons (Redistribution of Seats) Act 1949;
"the 1958 Act" means the House of Commons (Redistribution of Seats) Act 1958;
"Boundary Commission" means a Boundary Commission established by the 1949 Act other than the Boundary Commission for Northern Ireland.

12. In Part II of this Schedule and this paragraph in their application to a part of Great Britain for which there is a Boundary Commission—

"electoral quota" means the number obtained by dividing the electorate of that part of Great Britain by the number of Assembly constituencies specified for that part in paragraph 1(2) of Schedule 1 to this Act;

"electorate" means—

(a) in relation to an Assembly constituency, the number of persons whose names appear on the relevant registers for that Assembly constituency in force on the enumeration date;

(b) in relation to that part of Great Britain, the number of persons whose names appear on the relevant registers for that part of Great Britain in force on the enumeration date;

["enumeration date" means, in relation to any supplementary report of a Boundary Commission under this Schedule, the date on which the notice with respect to that report is published in accordance with section 2(4) of the 1949 Act];

"the relevant registers" means the following registers under the Representation of the People Acts, namely—

(a) in relation to an Assembly constituency, the registers of parliamentary electors to be used at an Assembly election in that Assembly constituency;

(b) in relation to that part of Great Britain, the registers of parliamentary electors for the parliamentary constituencies in that part.

NOTES

The definition "enumeration date" in para 12 was substituted by the European Assembly Elections Act 1981, s 1(5).

Great Britain. See the note to s 3 ante.

Assembly constituencies. See Sch 1, para 1, and Pts I and II of this Schedule ante.

Registers of parliamentary electors to be used at an Assembly election. Ie by virtue of Sch 1, para 2(1)(a) ante. See also the note "Register of parliamentary electors" to that paragraph.

House of Commons (Redistribution of Seats) Act 1949. See this title ante; and as to the Boundary Commissions, see s 1 of, and Sch 1 to, that Act.

House of Commons (Redistribution of Seats) Act 1958. See this title ante.

Representation of the People Acts. For the Acts which may be cited by this collective title, see the Introductory Note to the Representation of the People Act 1948 ante.

HOUSE OF COMMONS (REDISTRIBUTION OF SEATS) ACT 1979

(1979 c 15)

An Act to increase the number of constituencies in Northern Ireland required by rule 1 in Schedule 2 to the House of Commons (Redistribution of Seats) Act 1949

[22 March 1979]

Northern Ireland. This Act applies.

1 Increase of number of constituencies in Northern Ireland

(1) ...

(2) Notwithstanding subsection (1) above, in discharging their functions under

section 2 of the principal Act, the Boundary Commission for Northern Ireland shall read rule 1 as if it required the number of constituencies in Northern Ireland to be 17, unless it appears to the Commission that Northern Ireland should for the time being be divided into 16 or (as the case may be) into 18 constituencies.

(3) In framing their first report after the passing of this Act under section 2(1) of the principal Act, the Boundary Commission for Northern Ireland shall read rule 5 of those rules (under which the electorate of a constituency is to be brought as near the electoral quota as is practicable having regard to the other rules) in accordance with the definitions given in subsection (4) below instead of in accordance with rule 7 of those rules.

(4) In rule 5 as it applies by virtue of subsection (3) above—

   (a) "electoral quota" shall mean a number obtained by dividing the aggregate electorate (as defined in paragraph (b) below) of all the constituencies in Northern Ireland by 17; and

   (b) "electorate" shall mean, in relation to any constituency, the number of persons whose names appear on the register of parliamentary electors in force for the constituency at the passing of this Act under the Representation of the People Acts.

(5) ...

(6) In framing their first supplementary report after the passing of this Act under section 28 (supplementary reports with respect to the number of members to be returned to the Northern Ireland Assembly by each constituency in Northern Ireland), the Boundary Commission for Northern Ireland shall read subsection (3) of that section (which requires the ratio of the electorate of each constituency to the number of members to be returned by that constituency to be as far as practicable the same in every constituency) as if the electorate were defined by reference to the passing of this Act instead of by reference to the enumeration date.

NOTES

Sub-s (1) amends the House of Commons (Redistribution of Seats) Act 1949, Sch 2, r 1 ante; sub-s (5) substitutes the Northern Ireland Constitution Act 1973, s 28(5), (6), Vol 31, title Northern Ireland (Pt 2).

Rule 1; those rules. By virtue of sub-s (1) this means the rules for the redistribution of seats set out in Sch 2 to the House of Commons (Redistribution of Seats) Act 1949 ante.

Principal Act. By virtue of sub-s (1) this means the House of Commons (Redistribution of Seats) Act 1949 ante.

Boundary Commission for Northern Ireland. That Commission is established under the House of Commons (Redistribution of Seats) Act 1949, s 1, Sch 1, Pt I ante.

Constituency. For meaning, see the House of Commons (Redistribution of Seats) Act 1949, s 4 ante.

Passing of this Act. This Act was passed (ie received the Royal Assent) on 22 March 1979.

Register of parliamentary electors. For provisions relating to the compilation of registers of electors, see the Representation of the People Act 1983, ss 8–13 post.

Section 28. Ie the Northern Ireland Constitution Act 1973, s 28, Vol 31, title Northern Ireland (Pt 2).

Northern Ireland Assembly. This assembly was established by the Northern Ireland Assembly Act 1973, and further relevant provisions are contained in the Northern Ireland Constitution Act 1973, Pts II, IV, both Vol 31, title Northern Ireland (Pt 2). The Assembly, elected under s 2 of the first-mentioned Act, was dissolved by the Northern Ireland Assembly (Dissolution) Order 1975, SI 1975/422 (made under the Northern Ireland Act 1974, s 1(1), Vol 31, title Northern Ireland (Pt 2)). Under Sch 1, para 1, to the 1974 Act, laws for Northern Ireland may be made by Order in Council during the interim period as defined by s 1(4) of that Act. By para 1(7) of that Schedule, references to Measures of the Northern Ireland Assembly include references to such Orders in Council.

A new Assembly has now been elected by virtue of an election held on 20 October 1982 (ie the day appointed by the Northern Ireland Assembly (Day of Election) Order 1982, SI 1982/1078, made under the Northern Ireland Constitution Act 1973, s 27(7), as applied by s 1(1) of the 1974 Act). Provision for the general or partial suspension of the system of direct rule introduced by Sch 1 to the 1974 Act may now be made by Order in Council made under the Northern Ireland Act 1982, Vol 31, title Northern Ireland (Pt 2), and the effect of any such Order is set out in Sch 1 to that Act. See also, in particular, s 3 of the 1982 Act, as to matters which may be considered by the Assembly pending general suspension of direct rule; s 5 as to the dissolution of the Assembly and revocation of Orders in Council made under s 2 of the Act; and s 6 and Sch 2 for amendments of the 1973 Acts.

Representation of the People Acts. For the Acts which may be cited together by this collective title, see the Introductory Note to the Representation of the People Act 1948 ante.

2 Citation

This Act may be cited as the House of Commons (Redistribution of Seats) Act 1979, and shall be included among the Acts which may be cited as the Representation of the People Acts, and this Act and the House of Commons (Redistribution of Seats) Acts 1949 and 1958 may be cited together as the House of Commons (Redistribution of Seats) Acts 1949 to 1979.

NOTES

Representation of the People Acts. For the Acts which may be cited by this collective title, see the Introductory Note to the Representation of the People Act 1948.

House of Commons (Redistribution of Seats) Acts 1949 and 1958. See this title ante.

EUROPEAN ASSEMBLY ELECTIONS ACT 1981

(1981 c 8)

An Act to amend the provisions of Schedule 2 to the European Assembly Elections Act 1978 with respect to the supplementary reports affecting Assembly constituencies to be submitted by the Boundary Commission for any part of Great Britain following reviews of parliamentary constituencies [19 March 1981]

1 *(Sub-ss (1), (3) substitute the European Assembly Elections Act 1978, Sch 2, paras 1, 3 ante; sub-ss (2), (4), (5) amend paras 2, 4, 12 of that Schedule.)*

2 Short title

This Act may be cited as the European Assembly Elections Act 1981.

REPRESENTATION OF THE PEOPLE ACT 1983

(1983 c 2)

ARRANGEMENT OF SECTIONS

PART I

PARLIAMENTARY AND LOCAL GOVERNMENT FRANCHISE AND ITS EXERCISE

Parliamentary and local government franchise

PART II

THE ELECTION CAMPAIGN

The election agent

Election expenses

Publicity at parliamentary elections

Election meetings

Agency by election officials and canvassing by police officers

Conveyance of voters to and from poll

Part III

Legal Proceedings

Questioning of a parliamentary election

Questioning of a local election

Procedure on all election petitions

Part IV

Special Provisions as to Other Local Elections

England and Wales, and Scotland

An Act to consolidate the Representation of the People Acts of 1949, 1969, 1977, 1978 and 1980, the Electoral Registers Acts of 1949 and 1953, the Elections (Welsh Forms) Act 1964, Part III of the Local Government Act 1972, sections 6 to 10 of the Local Government (Scotland) Act 1973, the Representation of the People (Armed Forces) Act 1976, the Returning Officers (Scotland) Act 1977, section 3 of the Representation of the People Act 1981, section 62 of and Schedule 2 to the Mental Health (Amendment) Act 1982, and connected provisions; and to repeal as obsolete the Representation of the People Act 1979 and other enactments related to the Representation of the People Acts

[8 February 1983]

Commencement. This Act came into force on 15 March 1983; see s 207(2) post and the order noted thereto.

European Assembly elections. Under the European Assembly Elections Act 1978, s 3, Sch 1, para 2(3), (4) ante the Secretary of State may by regulations make provision as to the conduct of elections to the Assembly of the European Communities (as to which Assembly, see the note to s 1 of the 1978 Act ante) and as to the questioning of such an election and the consequences of irregularities, and such regulations may, inter alia, apply with modifications or exceptions any provision of the Representation of the People Acts or any provision made thereunder. The European Assembly Elections Regulations 1984, SI 1984/137, reg 3(1), Sch 1, accordingly apply certain provisions of this Act to Assembly elections in Great Britain, subject in certain cases to modifications and exceptions which are noted to those provisions which are printed in this work. It should also be noted that certain of these applications no longer have any effect in view of the amendments and repeals made to this Act by the Representation of the People Act 1985. It is understood, however, that new regulations will be made before the next European Assembly elections. The provisions so applied are ss 18(1), (9), 19–23, 24(2), 27(3), 28(4)–(6), 29, 30, 49, 50, 52, 54, 55, 60, 61, 63, 65–70, 72–76, 78–84, 86–89, 91–95, 97–126, 136–144, 146–176, 178–186, 200, 202; Sch 1, rr 1, 2, 5–9, 10(1), 11–50, 53, 54, 55(1), 56, 57, 60 and Appendix (except the form of writ), Sch 3; and Sch 5, paras 1, 5.

Certain provisions of the regulations made under this Act are also applied, with modifications and exceptions in certain cases, to European Assembly elections by reg 3(2) of, and Sch 2 to, the above-mentioned 1984 regulations; the regulations so applied are the Representation of the People Regulations 1983, SI 1983/435, regs 3(1), (4)–(6), 28, 29, 38–67, 69–75, Sch 3, Forms E, F, H, V, W, X.

The above-mentioned provisions of the 1984 regulations must be read in conjunction with the other provisions thereof and, in particular, with the provisions set out below:

Interpretation

2.—(1) Unless the context otherwise requires, in these Regulations and in any provision applied by these Regulations:—

"Act of 1983" means the Representation of the People Act 1983;

"Act of 1978" means the European Assembly Elections Act 1978;

"Assembly" means the Assembly of the European Communities;

"Assembly constituency" means a constituency constituted by an Order in Council under section 3 of the House of Commons (Redistribution of Seats) Act 1949, as applied by paragraph 4 of Schedule 2 to the Act of 1978;

"day of the poll" and "date of the poll" mean the day appointed by order under paragraph 3 of Schedule 1 to the Act of 1978 for the holding of the election;

"elections rules" and "parliamentary elections rules" mean the rules in Schedule 1 to the Act of 1983, as applied by Schedule 1 to these Regulations;

"elector" means a person who under paragraph 2(1) of Schedule 1 to the Act of 1978 is entitled to vote at an Assembly election in a particular Assembly constituency;

"postal proxy" means a person entitled to vote by post as a proxy at an election;

"register" means the register or registers of parliamentary, or in the case of peers local government, electors in force within a particular Assembly constituency at the time of an Assembly election in that constituency;

"registered", in relation to an elector, means a person registered on a register;

"registration officer" means an electoral registration officer appointed under section 8 of the Act of 1983;

. . . .

"representative" means a representative to the Assembly;

"verifying officer" means the officer, appointed by the returning officer, with responsibility for the verification of the ballot paper accounts.

(2) Any reference in these Regulations or in the provisions applied by these Regulations to the time when any proceeding at an Assembly election is due to take place (for example, publication of notice of election) shall be determined in accordance with the timetable in rule 1 of the elections rules.

Application of certain statutory provisions to Assembly elections

3.—(1), (2) . . .

(3) Section 72 of the Post Office Act 1969 and section 11(3) of the Act of 1983 shall apply in relation to an Assembly election as they apply in relation to a parliamentary election, and as though the reference in section 72 to the Act of 1983 was a reference to that Act as applied by these Regulations.

(4) In the provisions applied by Schedules 1 and 2 to these Regulations, any provision relating solely to a local government election and references in connection therewith (including a reference to a petition questioning an election under the local government Act) shall, unless the context otherwise requires, be disregarded.

(5) Unless the context otherwise requires, in the provisions applied by Schedules 1 and 2 to these Regulations:—

(a) any reference to a parliamentary election shall be construed as a reference to an Assembly election and any reference to a general election shall accordingly be construed as a reference to an Assembly general election;

(b) any reference to a constituency shall be construed as a reference to an Assembly constituency;

(c) any reference to a returning officer shall be construed as a reference to such an officer at an Assembly election;

(d) any reference to a member in the context of a Member of Parliament shall be construed as a reference to a representative;

(e) any reference to a parliamentary election petition shall be construed as a reference to an Assembly election petition, except that this construction shall not apply to any reference to the rota for the trial of parliamentary election petitions;

(f) any reference to a return in the context of a return to the writ of election (and a return to

Parliament) shall be construed as a reference to the declaration of result made by the returning officer under rule 50 of the elections rules.

(6) Unless the context otherwise requires, in the provisions applied by Schedules 1 and 2 to these Regulations, any reference to an enactment or instrument made under an enactment shall be construed as a reference to that enactment or instrument as applied by these Regulations.

(7)–(9) . . .

Discharge of duties of returning officer in England and Wales

5.—(1) In England and Wales, the duties of the returning officer at an Assembly election (except those referred to in paragraph (2) below) shall be discharged, as acting returning officer, by the acting returning officer who, by virtue of section 28(1) of the Act of 1983, would discharge the duties of that returning officer at a parliamentary election.

(2) Paragraph (1) above does not apply to any duties under rule 50 of the elections rules which the returning officer reserves to himself and undertakes to perform in person.

(3) The returning officer shall give to the acting returning officer written notice of any duties which he reserves to himself under paragraph (2) above, and that paragraph shall, in the case of any election, apply to the duties (if any) of which notice is given not later than the day following that on which notice of election is published, and to no others.

Applications for voting by post or by proxy

6. In England and Wales, from the date of the publication of the notice of an Assembly election, the functions of a registration officer in connection with applications to vote by post or proxy or by a proxy to vote by post at that election shall be exercised by the returning officer:
Provided that a registration officer shall, on the request of the returning officer, exercise those functions in respect of the area for which he was appointed.

As to the extension of the franchise for European Assembly elections, see the Representation of the People Act 1985, s 3 post, as from a day to be appointed under s 29(2) of that Act.
Representation of the People Acts. This Act is included among the Acts which may be cited by this collective title; see the Introductory Note to the Representation of the People Act 1948 ante.
Northern Ireland. This Act applies to elections in Northern Ireland for the United Kingdom Parliament but it does not apply to elections for the Northern Ireland Assembly nor to local government elections in Northern Ireland. For the general application of this Act to Northern Ireland, see s 205 post.
In relation to European Assembly elections in Northern Ireland, provisions similar to those made by the European Assembly Elections Regulations 1984, SI 1984/137, cited in the note "European Assembly elections" above are made by the European Assembly Elections (Northern Ireland) Regulations 1984, SI 1984/198 (made under the European Assembly Elections Act 1978, Sch 1, para 2 ante); those regulations apply certain provisions of this Act and of the Representation of the People (Northern Ireland) Regulations 1983, SI 1983/436, to European Assembly elections in Northern Ireland and contain ancillary provisions.
This Act is amended in its application to Northern Ireland by the Elections (Northern Ireland) Act 1985; see the notes to s 61 and Sch 1, rr 26, 37–40. The provisions of the 1985 Act which modify this Act are printed in this title post.

PART I

PARLIAMENTARY AND LOCAL GOVERNMENT FRANCHISE AND ITS EXERCISE

This Act has effect as if the Representation of the People Act 1985, ss 1–12, 15–18, 21, Sch 1 post were contained in this Part, and references in any other enactment to this Part includes a reference to those provisions of the 1985 Act; see s 27(2), (3) of the 1985 Act.

Parliamentary and local government franchise

1 Parliamentary electors

(1) A person entitled to vote as an elector at a parliamentary election in any constituency is one who—

>   (*a*) is resident there on the qualifying date (subject to subsection (2) below in relation to Northern Ireland); and
>
>   (*b*) on that date and on the date of the poll—
>
>>   (i) is not subject to any legal incapacity to vote (age apart); and

(ii) is either a Commonwealth citizen or a citizen of the Republic of Ireland; and

(c) is of voting age (that is, 18 years or over) on the date of the poll.

(2) A person is not entitled to vote as an elector at a parliamentary election in any constituency in Northern Ireland unless he was resident in Northern Ireland during the whole of the period of three months ending on the qualifying date for that election.

(3) A person is not entitled to vote as an elector in any constituency unless registered there in the register of parliamentary electors to be used at the election.

(4) A person is not entitled to vote as an elector—

(a) more than once in the same constituency at any parliamentary election;

(b) in more than one constituency at a general election.

NOTES

Sub-s (1) contains provisions formerly in the Representation of the People Act 1949, s 1(1) as amended by the Representation of the People Act 1969, s 24(1), Sch 2, para 1 and as affected by the British Nationality Act 1981, s 51(1) and in s 1(1) of the 1969 Act. Sub-s (2) contains provisions formerly in s 1(2) of the 1949 Act as partly repealed by s 24(4) of, and Sch 3, Pt I to, the 1969 Act. Sub-s (3) contains provisions formerly in the proviso to s 1(1) of the 1949 Act. Sub-s (4) contains provisions formerly in the proviso to s 1(1) and in s 1(3) of the 1949 Act.

Sub-s (1): Entitled to vote. The resolution of a committee of the House of Commons cannot deprive anyone of a right of voting conferred by statute; see *Bulmer v Norris* (1860) 9 CBNS 19, 30 LJCP 25. A candidate may vote for himself or his opponent (*Harwich Case* (1803) 1 Peck 381), and a returning officer has a vote (s 27(3) post). For the definition of "vote", see s 202(1) post.

As an elector. Ss 19–22 post provide that voting as an elector must be done in person, unless voting by proxy or by post is permitted. Those sections are repealed by the Representation of the People Act 1985, s 28, Sch 5 post, as from a day to be appointed under s 29(2) of that Act, and new provision is made, as from that date, as to absent voters and proxies by ss 5–9 of that Act.

An elector's name must be on the register; see sub-s (3) above, s 2(2) post, and the definition of "elector" in s 202(1) post.

Parliamentary election. Ie an election of a Member to serve in Parliament for a constituency; see the Interpretation Act 1978, s 5, Sch 1, Vol 41, title Statutes. As to the extension of the parliamentary franchise to British citizens overseas and registration of such electors, see the Representation of the People Act 1985, ss 1, 2 post, as from a day to be appointed under s 29(2) of that Act.

Constituency. For definition, see the House of Commons (Redistribution of Seats) Act 1949, s 4 ante. Constituencies in England, Wales, Scotland and Northern Ireland are described in Sch 1, Pts I, II, III and IV, respectively, to the Representation of the People Act 1948 ante, as affected by orders made under s 3 of the 1949 Act ante.

Resident. For the meaning of this expression, see s 5 post, and the notes thereto. Where a service declaration is made under s 15 post, the declarant is treated as resident at the address specified in the declaration; see s 17(1)(a) post. Entries in the register are conclusive evidence of residence; see s 49(1)(a) post.

A merchant seaman who is not resident in the United Kingdom, but would have been resident there but for the nature of his occupation, is entitled to be treated for the purposes of this section and s 2 post as resident at any place at which he would otherwise have been resident or at any seamen's hostel or club where he commonly stays; see s 6 post.

A person detained in a mental hospital is not to be treated for the purposes of this section and s 2 post, as resident there; see s 7(1) post. Note, however, that by virtue of s 7(3), (4) post, a voluntary mental patient may make a declaration with a view to registration in the register of electors which entitles him to be treated as resident at the address at which he would otherwise have been resident (see s 7(7) post).

Qualifying date. For this date, see s 4 post.

Commonwealth citizen. In Acts passed after 1982 this means a person who has the status of a Commonwealth citizen under the British Nationality Act 1981; see s 51(2) of the 1981 Act, and for the persons who have that status, see s 37 of, and Sch 3 to, that Act, Vol 31, title Nationality and Immigration.

Republic of Ireland. Ie that part of Ireland previously officially known in this country as Eire and originally called the Irish Free State; see the Ireland Act 1949, s 1(1), (3), Vol 7, title Commonwealth and Other Territories (Pt 3(c)) in conjunction with the Eire (Confirmation of Agreements) Act 1938, s 1 (repealed).

Voting age. For the right of a person who comes of age during the currency of the register of electors to be registered, see s 12(5) post. Note that a person is to be deemed not to have attained a given age until the commencement of the relevant anniversary of his birth; see s 202(2) post.

Sub-s (2): Resident in Northern Ireland. By s 14(2) post, a person ceasing to have a service qualification is treated for the purposes of sub-s (2) above as resident in Northern Ireland during the period in which he had a service qualification.

Months. Ie calendar months; see the Interpretation Act 1978, s 5, Sch 1, Vol 41, title Statutes.

Sub-s (3): Registered . . . in the register . . . to be used. As to the preparation and publication of the register of electors, see ss 9–13 post; and see, in particular, s 13(1), (3) as to the register to be used at any election.

Definitions. For "election", "elector", "legal incapacity" and "vote", see s 202(1) post.

2 Local government electors

(1) A person entitled to vote as an elector at a local government election in any electoral area is one who—

    (*a*) is resident there on the qualifying date; and

    (*b*) on that date and on the date of the poll—

        (i) is not subject to any legal incapacity to vote (age apart); and

        (ii) is either a Commonwealth citizen or a citizen of the Republic of Ireland; and

    (*c*) is of voting age (that is, 18 years or over) on the date of the poll.

(2) A person is not entitled to vote as an elector in any electoral area unless registered there in the register of local government electors to be used at the election.

(3) A person is not entitled to vote as an elector—

    (*a*) more than once in the same electoral area at any local government election; and

    (*b*) in more than one electoral area at an ordinary election for any local government area which is not a single electoral area.

NOTES

Sub-s (1) contains provisions formerly in the Representation of the People Act 1949, s 2(1), as amended by the Representation of the People Act 1969, s 24(1), Sch 2, para 1, and as affected by the British Nationality Act 1981, s 51(1), and in s 1(1) of the 1969 Act. Sub-s (2) contains provisions formerly in the proviso to s 2(1) of the 1949 Act. Sub-s (3) contains provisions formerly in the proviso to s 2(1) and in s 2(2) of the 1949 Act.

As an elector; Commonwealth citizen; Republic of Ireland; voting age; registered . . . in the register . . . to be used. See the notes to s 1 ante.

Resident. Cf the note to s 1 ante, but note that by s 7(9) post a voluntary mental patient may not make a declaration specially for the purpose of local government elections (subject to certain exceptions), but any patient's declaration made for the purpose of parliamentary elections is to have effect also for the purpose of local government elections.

Qualifying date. For this date, see s 4 post.

Definitions. For "election", "elector", "legal incapacity" and "vote", see s 202(1) post; for "electoral area", "local government area" and "local government election", see s 203(1) post.

3 Disfranchisement of offenders in prison etc

(1) A convicted person during the time that he is detained in a penal institution in pursuance of his sentence [or unlawfully at large when he would otherwise be so detained] is legally incapable of voting at any parliamentary or local government election.

(2) For this purpose—

    (*a*) "convicted person" means any person found guilty of an offence (whether under the law of the United Kingdom or not), including a person found guilty by a court-martial under the Army Act 1955, the Air Force Act 1955 or the Naval Discipline Act 1957 or on a summary trial under section 49 of the Naval Discipline Act 1957, or by a Standing Civilian Court established under the Armed Forces Act 1976, but not including a person dealt with by committal or other summary process for contempt of court; and

(b) "penal institution" means an institution to which the Prison Act 1952, the Prisons (Scotland) Act 1952 or the Prison Act (Northern Ireland) 1953 applies; and

(c) a person detained for default in complying with his sentence shall not be treated as detained in pursuance of the sentence, whether or not the sentence provided for detention in the event of default, but a person detained by virtue of a conditional pardon in respect of an offence shall be treated as detained in pursuance of his sentence for the offence.

(3) It is immaterial for the purposes of this section whether a conviction or sentence was before or after the passing of this Act.

NOTES

This section contains provisions formerly in the Representation of the People Act 1969, s 4 as amended, in the case of sub-s (2) thereof, by the Armed Forces Act 1976, s 22(5), Sch 9, para 19.

The words in square brackets in sub-s (1) were inserted by the Representation of the People Act 1985, s 24, Sch 4, para 1.

Parliamentary election. See the note to s 1 ante.

Committal . . . for contempt of court. See generally 9 Halsbury's Laws (4th edn) paras 88 et seq.

Ward elections in the City of London. This section applies; see the City of London (Various Powers) Act 1957, s 8(1), Vol 26, title London.

Definitions. For "local government election", see s 203(1) post. Note as to "convicted person", "penal institution" and "detained in pursuance of the sentence", sub-s (2) above.

Army Act 1955; Air Force Act 1955; Naval Discipline Act 1957. See Vol 3, title Armed Forces (Pt 1).

Armed Forces Act 1976. As to the establishment of Standing Civilian Courts, see s 6 of, and Sch 3 to, this Act, Vol 3, title Armed Forces (Pt 1).

Prison Act 1952. See Vol 34, title Prisons.

Prisons (Scotland) Act 1952. Certain provisions of that Act are printed in Vol 34, title Prisons.

Prison Act (Northern Ireland) 1953. 1953 c 18 (NI); not printed in this work.

4 Qualifying date

(1) In England and Wales and Scotland, 10th October in any year is the qualifying date for a parliamentary or local government election at which the date fixed for the poll falls within the period of twelve months beginning with 16th February in the next following year.

(2) In Northern Ireland, 15th September in any year is the qualifying date for such a parliamentary election as is mentioned above, subject to the Secretary of State's power under section 13(2) below.

NOTES

This section contains provisions formerly in the Electoral Registers Act 1949, s 1(3), (4), as substituted by the Electoral Registers Act 1953, s 1(1).

England; Wales. For meanings, see the Interpretation Act 1978, s 5, Sch 1, Vol 41, title Statutes.

Parliamentary election. See the note to s 1 ante.

Local government election. For meaning, see s 203(1) post.

Twelve months beginning with, etc. The use of the phrase "beginning with" makes it clear that in computing this period the day from which it runs is to be included; see *Hare v Gocher* [1962] 2 QB 641, [1962] 2 All ER 763, and *Trow v Ind Coope (West Midlands) Ltd* [1967] 2 QB 899 at 909, [1967] 2 All ER 900, CA. See also *Dodds v Walker* [1981] 2 All ER 609, [1981] 1 WLR 1027, HL, as to the day of expiry of periods of a month or a specified number of months.

Secretary of State. Ie one of Her Majesty's Principal Secretaries of State; see the Interpretation Act 1978, s 5, Sch 1, Vol 41, title Statutes. The Secretary of State here concerned is the Secretary of State for Northern Ireland.

Delayed publication of register. Where any part of a register is published late this section is to be read subject to s 13(4) post.

5 Residence

(1) For the purposes of sections 1 and 2 above any question as to a person's residence on the qualifying date for an election—

(a) shall be determined in accordance with the general principles formerly applied in determining questions as to a person's residence on a particular day of the qualifying period within the meaning of the Representation of the People Act 1918; and

(b) in particular regard shall be had to the purpose and other circumstances, as well as to the fact, of his presence at or absence from the address in question.

(2) Without prejudice to those general principles, a person's residence in a dwelling house shall not be deemed for the purposes of sections 1 and 2 to have been interrupted—

(a) by reason of that person's absence in the performance of any duty arising from or incidental to any office, service or employment held or undertaken by him, if he intends to resume actual residence within six months of giving it up and will not be prevented by the performance of that duty; or

(b) by reason of permission being given by letting or otherwise for its occupation furnished by some other person—

(i) if the permission is given in the expectation that throughout the period for which it is given the person giving it or his wife or her husband will be absent in the performance of any such duty as is mentioned above; or

(ii) if the first mentioned person intends to resume actual residence within nine weeks of giving it up and will not be prevented by the permission given as mentioned above.

(3) A person who is detained at any place in legal custody shall not by reason thereof be treated for the purposes of sections 1 and 2 as resident there.

NOTES

This section contains provisions formerly in the Representation of the People Act 1949, s 4(1)–(3), as amended, in the case of s 4(3), by the Mental Health (Amendment) Act 1982, s 62(1).

For the purposes of sections 1 and 2 above. This section and ss 6, 7(1) post also apply for the purposes of the Representation of the People Act 1985, ss 1–3 post, which extend the parliamentary and European Assembly franchise to certain British citizens overseas, as from a day to be appointed under s 29(2) of that Act; see s 27(2) of that Act.

Any question as to a person's residence, etc. Actual user of a place as home will constitute residence even if such user is unlawful (*Beal v Ford* (1877) 3 CPD 73, 47 LJQB 56). A person cannot be presumed to reside in a place unless he has a sleeping apartment there which he uses or could use if he wished; conversely, occasional uses of an apartment for sleeping will not by itself constitute residence (*Oldham Case, Cobbett v Hibbert and Platt, Baxter's Case* (1869) 20 LT 302, 308). The circumstances in which and the purposes for which such apartment is maintained must be considered; see *Tewkesbury Case, Whithorn v Thomas* (1844) 14 LJCP 38, Bar & Arn 259; *R v Exeter (Mayor), Wescomb's Case* (1868) LR 4 QB 110, 19 LT 397; *R v Exeter (Mayor), Dipstale's Case* (1868) LR 4 QB 114, 19 LT 432.

If a person has more than one place at which he resides during some portion of the year it will be a question of fact which or whether either of them constitutes his residence or residences on the qualifying day; a man may have two residences; see *R v Exeter (Mayor), Wescomb's Case*, above. Having regard to the ordinary meaning of "resident" and to what is now sub-s (1) above, the following principles have been held to be applicable to the question of residence on the qualifying date for the purpose of s 1 ante: a person can have two residences and be resident in both (though he can only vote at one place; see ss 1(4), 2(3) ante); temporary presence at an address does not make a person resident there but temporary absence does not deprive a person of his residence; and a person is properly resident in a place when his stay there has a considerable degree of permanence; see *Fox v Stirk* [1970] 2 QB 463, [1970] 3 All ER 7, CA. A person may therefore be entitled to be registered in the registers of electors for two areas; see *Fox v Stirk* above (students in residence at university); *Dumble v Electoral Registration Officer for Borders* 1980 SLT (Sh Ct) 60 (person having two careers requiring addresses in separate constituencies); and cf *Scott v Phillips* 1974 SLT 32, and *Scott v Electoral Registration Officer for Kinross and West Perthshire* 1980 SLT (Sh Ct) 126.

In determining whether a person not actually present at a given place is legally resident there, it is relevant to ascertain whether that person then possessed any intention to return on a future date, whether he then had physical liberty to return, and whether or not he could have returned without breach of any public or private obligation to which he was then subject. The following cases relating to absence and its effect on the right to vote, though decided in regard to former law, may be relevant in ascertaining whether or not a person has under this Act a right to vote in a particular constituency: *Durant v Carter* (1873) LR 9 CP 261, 43 LJCP 17 (office holder receiving leave of absence and in consequence absent from his official residence; cf now sub-s (2)(*a*) above); *Evans v Curren* (1913) 48 ILT 176 (office holder absent from his official residence on account of suspension); *Criglington v Gallagher* (1889) 26 LR Ir 134 (absence from home due to arrest on a criminal charge); *Connolly v Riddall* (1888) 24 LR Ir 127; *Martin v Hanrahan* (1888) 24 LR Ir 127; and *Charlton v Morris* [1895] 2 IR 541 (absence from home due to remand in custody); *Kidderminster Case, Powell v Guest* (1864) 18 CBNS 72 (absence from home due to imprisonment or detention consequent on sentence; cf now s 3 ante); *M'Carron v Chambers* (1890) 28 LR Ir 294; and *Holland v Chambers* [1895] 2 IR 551 (absence from home due to imprisonment or detention in default of payment of a fine; cf now s 3(2)(*c*) ante); *Ford v Drew* (1879) 5 CPD 59, 49 LJQB 172; and *Duffy v Chambers* (1890) 26 LR Ir 100 (absence from home due to terms of employment; cf sub-s (2)(*a*) above); *Barrett v Buchanan* (1912) 47 ILT 191 (absence from home due to temporary closing of whole or part thereof).

For the effect on a person's right to vote of the destruction or partial destruction of the premises constituting his home, see *Woodstock Case, Father's Case* (1838) Falc & Fitz 449; *Lyme Regis Case, Hicks's Case* (1842) Bar & Aust 460 at 463; *Whitley v M'Cleane* (1866) 14 LT 899.

See further, as to residence for the purposes of ss 1 and 2, ante, 15 Halsbury's Laws (4th edn) paras 415, 416.

Qualifying date. See s 4 ante.

Qualifying period. This refers to the old law of eligibility. There is now no qualifying period except in Northern Ireland; see s 1(2) ante. The right to vote depends under ss 1(1)(*a*) and 2(1)(*a*) ante, on residence on the qualifying date (as to which, see s 4 ante).

Interrupted. This expression was apt where the law required residence during a qualifying period; the consequence of interruption then was lack of qualification. The same consequence must be taken to be intended now, although the word is not appropriate to the requirement of residence on a qualifying date as distinct from throughout a period.

In the performance of any duty. Special provision is made by s 59(2) post, for reservists or auxiliaries who are absent from their residence on the qualifying day by reason of duty.

Within six months; within nine weeks. In calculating either of these periods the day from which it runs is not to be counted; see, in particular, *Goldsmiths' Co v West Metropolitan Rly Co* [1904] 1 KB 1, [1900–3] All ER Rep 667, CA, and *Stewart v Chapman* [1951] 2 KB 792, [1951] 2 All ER 613. See also *Dodds v Walker* [1981] 2 All ER 609, [1981] 1 WLR 1027, HL, as to the day of expiry of periods of a month or a specified number of months.

Definitions. For "dwelling house" and "election" see s 202(1) post.

Representation of the People Act 1918. That Act was repealed, so far as otherwise unrepealed, by the Representation of the People Act 1985, s 28(1), Sch 5.

6 Residence: merchant seamen

At any time when a merchant seaman is not resident in the United Kingdom and would have been resident there but for the nature of his occupation, he shall be entitled to be treated for the purposes of sections 1 and 2 above as resident—

(a) at any place at which he would have been resident but for the nature of his occupation; or

(b) at any hostel or club providing accommodation for merchant seamen at which he commonly stays in the course of his occupation.

For this purpose "merchant seaman" means any person not having a service qualification whose employment or the greater part of it is carried out on board seagoing ships, and includes any such person while temporarily without employment.

NOTES

This section contains provisions formerly in the Representation of the People Act 1969, s 3(1).

Resident. Cf the note to s 1 ante, and see also s 5 ante, and the notes thereto.

United Kingdom. Ie Great Britain and Northern Ireland; see the Interpretation Act 1978, s 5, Sch 1, Vol 41, title Statutes. "Great Britain" means England, Scotland and Wales by virtue of the Union with Scotland Act 1706, preamble, Art I, Vol 10, title Constitutional Law (Pt 1), as read with s 22(1) of, and Sch 2, para 5(*a*) to, the 1978 Act. Neither the Channel Islands nor the Isle of Man is within the United Kingdom.

For the purposes of sections 1 and 2 above. See the note to s 5 ante.

Service qualification. For those who have a service qualification, see s 14 post.

Ward elections in the City of London. This section applies; see the City of London (Various Powers) Act 1957, s 8(1), Vol 26, title London.

7 Residence: detained and voluntary mental patients

(1) A person who is detained at any place by virtue of any enactment relating to persons suffering from mental disorder shall not by reason thereof be treated for the purposes of sections 1 and 2 above as resident there.

(2) In the following provisions of this section—

"assistance" does not include assistance necessitated by blindness or other physical incapacity;

"mental hospital" means any establishment maintained wholly or mainly for the reception and treatment of persons suffering from any form of mental disorder;

"patient's declaration" means a declaration made under this section by a voluntary mental patient;

"voluntary mental patient" means a person who is a patient in a mental hospital but is not liable to be detained there by virtue of any enactment.

(3) A person who on the qualifying date is a voluntary mental patient shall not be entitled to be registered as mentioned in section 12(1) or (2) below except in pursuance of a declaration made with reference to that date in accordance with subsection (4) below.

This subsection is without prejudice to the registration of a voluntary mental patient by virtue of his residence at an address other than the mental hospital in which he is a patient in any case in which he would be entitled to be so registered apart from this subsection and the following subsections of this section.

(4) A voluntary mental patient may make a declaration under this subsection if he is able to do so without assistance; and a patient's declaration—

(a) shall be made with a view to registration in the register of electors for a particular year and with reference to the qualifying date for that register,

(b) shall be made during the 12 months ending with the qualifying date by reference to which it is made but shall not have effect if after it is made and before that date the declarant ceases to be a voluntary mental patient or cancels the declaration,

(c) may be made by a declarant notwithstanding the fact that by reason of his age he is not yet entitled to vote,

(d) shall state that it was made by the declarant without assistance, and shall state—

(i) the date of the declaration,

(ii) that on that date and, unless it is the qualifying date, on the qualifying date next following the declarant is or will be a voluntary mental patient,

(iii) the address of the mental hospital in which the declarant is a voluntary mental patient,

(iv) the address where the declarant would be resident in the United Kingdom if he were not a voluntary mental patient or, if he cannot give any such address, an address (other than a mental hospital) at which he has resided in the United Kingdom,

(v) that on the date of the declaration the declarant is a Commonwealth citizen or a citizen of the Republic of Ireland, and

(vi) whether the declarant had on the date of the declaration attained the age of 18 years and, if he had not, the date of his birth,

and a patient's declaration shall be attested in the prescribed manner.

(5) If a person—

(a) makes a patient's declaration declaring to more than one address, or

(b) makes more than one patient's declaration bearing the same date and declaring to different addresses,

the declaration or declarations shall be void.

(6) A patient's declaration may at any time be cancelled by the declarant and (subject to subsection (5) above) a patient's declaration bearing a later date shall, without any express cancellation, cancel a declaration bearing an earlier date if it is made with reference to the same qualifying date.

(7) A voluntary mental patient whose patient's declaration is made with reference to the qualifying date for any register shall be treated in relation to that register—

(a) as resident on the qualifying date at the address specified in the declaration pursuant to paragraph (d)(iv) of subsection (4) above;

(b) in the case of registration in Northern Ireland, as resident in Northern Ireland during the whole of the period of 3 months ending on the qualifying date; and

(c) in any case, until the contrary is proved, as being a Commonwealth citizen or a citizen of the Republic of Ireland of the age appearing from the declaration and as not being subject to any legal incapacity except as so appearing.

(8) Where a patient's declaration appearing to be properly made out and attested is transmitted to the registration officer in the proper manner, the declarant shall, until the contrary is proved, be treated for the purposes of registration as having been from the date of the declaration or such later date, if any, as appears from it, and as continuing to be, qualified to be registered as an elector.

(9) No patient's declaration shall be specially made by a person for the purpose of local government elections, and any patient's declaration made for the purpose of parliamentary elections shall have effect also for the purpose of local government elections; but—

(a) a patient's declaration may be made for the purpose of local government elections only by a person who is a peer subject to a legal incapacity to vote at parliamentary elections; and

(b) where so made, shall be marked to show that it is available for local government elections only, but shall in all other respects be the same as any other patient's declaration.

NOTES

Sub-s (1) contains provisions formerly in the Representation of the People Act 1949, s 4(3) as amended by the Mental Health (Amendment) Act 1982, s 62(1). Sub-s (2) contains provisions formerly in Sch 2, paras 1, 3(1), (9), to the 1982 Act. Sub-s (3) contains provisions formerly in Sch 2, para 2, to the 1982 Act. Sub-s (4) contains provisions formerly in Sch 2, para 3(1)–(6), to the 1982 Act. Sub-ss (5), (6) contain provisions formerly in Sch 2, para 3(7), (8), to the 1982 Act. Sub-ss (7), (8) contain provisions formerly in Sch 2, para 4, to the 1982 Act. Sub-s (9) contains provisions formerly in Sch 2, para 5, to the 1982 Act.

Sub-s (1): Detained ... by virtue of ... mental disorder. See, in particular, as to compulsory admission to hospital, the Mental Health Act 1983, Pt II, and as to patients who are concerned in criminal proceedings or under sentence, Pt III of that Act, Vol 28, title Mental Health. The expression "mental disorder" is defined by s 1(2) of the 1983 Act in the same title, for the purposes of that Act.

For the purposes of sections 1 and 2 above. See the note to s 5 ante.

Resident. Cf the note to s 1 ante, and see also s 5 ante, and the notes thereto.

Sub-s (3): Qualifying date. For this date, see s 4 ante.

Sub-s (4): Registration in the register of electors. See s 9 post and the note "Register" thereto.

Months; Commonwealth citizen; Republic of Ireland. See the notes to s 1 ante.

United Kingdom. See the note to s 6 ante.

Age of 18 years. A person is to be deemed not to have attained a given age until the commencement of the relevant anniversary of his birth; see s 202(2) post.

Attested in the prescribed manner. The manner in which a patient's declaration is to be attested is specified in the Representation of the People Regulations 1983, SI 1983/435, reg 10(1), (2), and the Representation of the People (Northern Ireland) Regulations 1983, SI 1983/436, reg 9(1).

Sub-s (8): Transmitted to the registration officer in the proper manner. A patient's declaration is to be transmitted to the appropriate registration officer by or on behalf of the declarant; see the Representation of the People Regulations 1983, SI 1983/435, reg 10(3). See also reg 10(4) of those regulations as to notification of receipt of the declaration, and reg 11 as to the return of an invalid declaration. As respects Northern Ireland the corresponding provisions are the Representation of the People (Northern Ireland) Regulations 1983, SI 1983/436, regs 9(2), (3), 10.

Supplementary provisions. Ss 19(1)(f), (4), 32(1)(e), (4) provide that a patient registered in the register of electors by virtue of a declaration made under this section is excepted from the general requirement to vote in person. Those provisions are repealed by the Representation of the People Act 1985, s 28(1), Sch 5 post, as from a day to be appointed under s 29(2) of that Act, and replaced, as from that date, by s 7(1)(a) of that Act which allows the registration officer to grant an application for an absent vote at a particular election if he is satisfied that the applicant's circumstances on the date of the poll will be or are likely to be such that he cannot reasonably be expected to vote in person.

Offences. For offences relating to declarations made under this section, see s 62 post.

Definitions. For "registration officer", see s 8(1) post; for "legal incapacity" and "prescribed", see s 202(1) post; for "local government election", see s 203(1) post. Note as to "assistance", "mental hospital", "patient's declaration" and "voluntary mental patient", sub-s (2) above.

Registration of parliamentary and local government electors

8 Registration officers

(1) For the registration of electors there shall be electoral registration officers (in this Act referred to as "registration officers").

(2) In England and Wales—

    (a) the council of every district and London borough shall appoint an officer of the council to be registration officer for any constituency or part of a constituency coterminous with or situated in the district or borough, and

    (b) the Common Council shall appoint an officer to be registration officer for the part of the constituency containing the City and the Inner Temple and the Middle Temple.

(3) (*Applies to Scotland only.*)

(4) In Northern Ireland, the Chief Electoral Officer for Northern Ireland is the registration officer for each constituency.

NOTES

Sub-s (1) contains provisions formerly in the Representation of the People Act 1949, s 6(1). Sub-s (2) contains provisions formerly in the Local Government Act 1972, s 39. Sub-s (4) contains provisions formerly in the Local Government Reorganisation (Consequential Provisions) (Northern Ireland) Order 1973, SI 1973/2095, art 2(1).

Electoral registration officers. For the principal duties discharged by registration officers under this Act, see ss 9–11 post (preparation and correction of registers), s 20 post (absent voters), ss 21(5), (8), 34(5) post (proxies), s 28(1) post (discharge of functions of returning officer), s 33(4) post (keeping of record of absent voters) and Sch 1, r 27 post (preparation of absent voters lists, lists of proxies and lists of persons entitled to vote by post as proxies). Note, however, that ss 20, 21, 33, 34, Sch 1, r 27 are repealed by the Representation of the People Act 1985, s 28(1), Sch 5, as from a day to be appointed under s 29(2) of that Act, and the duties of registration officers in relation to applications to vote by post or proxy will then be found in ss 6–9 of that Act post. As to the discharge of registration duties generally, including the appointment of a deputy registration officer for these purposes, see s 52 post; and as to the penalties for breach of these duties, see s 63 post. S 54 post, provides for the payment of registration expenses incurred by registration officers. Appeals lie to the county court from certain decisions of registration officers; see s 56 post.

A registration officer appointed under sub-s (2) above is disqualified for membership of the House of Commons by the House of Commons Disqualification Act 1975, s 1(1)(f), Sch 1, Pt III, Vol 32, title Parliament.

England; Wales. See the note to s 4 ante.

Council of every district. As to the districts in England and Wales and their councils, see the Local Government Act 1972, ss 1(1), (3), (4), 2(2), (3), 20(1), (3), 21(2), (3), Sch 1, Pt I, Sch 4, Pt II, Vol 25, title Local Government.

London borough. For definition, see the Interpretation Act 1978, s 5, Sch 1, Vol 41, title Statutes; and as to the London boroughs and their councils, see the London Government Act 1963, s 1, Sch 1, Vol 26, title London, and the Local Government Act 1972, s 8, Sch 2, Vol 25, title Local Government.

As to the application of Pt I (ss 1–66) of this Act in relation to the City of London, see s 203(2), (3) post.

Constituency. See the note to s 1 ante.

Chief Electoral Officer for Northern Ireland. This officer is appointed under the Electoral Law Act (Northern Ireland) 1962, s 14 (not printed in this work).

Isles of Scilly. Sub-s (2) above and ss 18(2), 22(3)(*b*), 31(1), 35(1), 187(1) and Sch 5, para 3(1) post, are modified in their application to the Isles of Scilly by the Isles of Scilly Order 1978, SI 1978/1844 (made under the Local Government Act 1972, s 265, Vol 25, title Local Government), art 6(4), Schedule, as construed in accordance with the Interpretation Act 1978, ss 17(2)(*a*), 23(2), Vol 41, title Statutes.

Definitions. For "the City" and "Common Council", see s 202(1) post.

Saving. For a saving in respect of sub-s (4) above, see s 206 and Sch 7, para 5 post.

9 Registers of electors

(1) It is every registration officer's duty to prepare and publish in every year—

> (*a*) a register of parliamentary electors for each constituency or part of a constituency in the area for which he acts; and
>
> (*b*) a register of local government electors for the local government areas or parts of local government areas included in the area for which he acts.

(2) The registers of parliamentary electors and of local government electors shall so far as practicable be combined, the names of persons registered only as local government electors being marked to indicate that fact.

(3) A registration officer's general duty to prepare and publish registers of electors in conformity with this Act includes the duty to take reasonable steps to obtain information required by him for that purpose (without prejudice to any specific requirement of this Act or regulations under it).

NOTES

Sub-ss (1), (2) contain provisions formerly in the Representation of the People Act 1949, s 7(1), (2). Sub-s (3) contains provisions formerly in the Representation of the People Act 1969, s 7(1).

Prospective amendment. The words "parliamentary electors or" are inserted after the words "only as" in sub-s (2) by the Representation of the People Act 1985, s 4(1), as from a day to be appointed under s 29(2) of that Act post.

It is every registration officer's duty. As to the appointment of registration officers, see 8 ante; as to the discharge of his functions under this Act, see s 52 post; and as to the penalties for breach of duty, see s 63 post.

Parliamentary electors; local government electors. See ss 1 and 2 ante, respectively.

Register. As to registration of electors, see also, in particular, s 10 post (preparation of registers); s 11 post (correction of registers); s 12 post (right to be registered); s 13 post (publication of registers); ss 14–17 post (service qualifications and declarations for registration); s 49 post (effect of registers); s 50 post (effect of misdescription); s 53 post (power to make regulations as to registration etc); s 54 post (registration expenses); and ss 56, 58 post (registration appeals).

As to the use of the register for jury selection, see the Juries Act 1974, s 3(1), (2), Vol 22, title Juries; and see also s 53(3) and Sch 2, para 2 post.

Constituency. See the note to s 1 ante.

Definitions. For "registration officer", see s 8(1) ante; for "local government area", see s 203(1) post.

10 Preparation of registers

With a view to the preparation of registers, the registration officer shall—

> (*a*) have a house to house or other sufficient inquiry made as to the persons entitled to be registered (excluding persons entitled to be registered in pursuance of a service declaration);
>
> (*b*) have prepared and published electors lists showing the persons appearing to him to be entitled to be registered *together with* their qualifying addresses;
>
> (*c*) determine all claims for registration duly made by any person, and all objections to any person's registration duly made by another person appearing

from the electors lists to be himself entitled to be registered including claims and objections asking for the omission, insertion or alteration of a date as that on which a person will become of voting age and entitled to be treated as an elector.

NOTES

This section contains provisions formerly in the Representation of the People Act 1949, s 9(1) as amended by the Representation of the People Act 1969, s 24(1), Sch 2, para 3 and as partly repealed by the Local Government Reorganisation (Consequential Provisions) (Northern Ireland) Order 1973, SI 1973/2095, art 5(2), Sch 2.

Prospective amendment. In para (a) the words "patient's declaration or overseas elector's declaration" are inserted after the word "declaration", and in para (b) the words "and, subject to any prescribed exceptions" are substituted for the words "together with" by the Representation of the People Act 1985, s 4(2), as from a day to be appointed under s 29(2) of that Act post.

Registration officer. As to the appointment of registration officers, see s 8 ante.

Persons entitled to be registered. See s 12 post.

Service declaration. For those entitled to make a service declaration, see s 15 post.

Electors lists. The form and method of publication of electors lists are governed by the Representation of the People Regulations 1983, SI 1983/435, regs 17, 18, and the Representation of the People (Northern Ireland) Regulations 1983, SI 1983/436, regs 12, 13. As to misdescriptions, see s 50 post.

Qualifying address. This expression is not defined in this Act, but cf ss 1(1)(a), 2(1)(a) ante.

Determine all claims etc. See also the Representation of the People Regulations 1983, SI 1983/435, regs 19–25, and the Representation of the People (Northern Ireland) Regulations 1983, SI 1983/436, reg 14. Appeals from such determinations lie to the county court and thence to the Court of Appeal; see ss 56, 58 post.

Date . . . on which a person will become of voting age. As to the entry in the register of that date, see s 12(5) post; and as to when a person attains a given age, see s 202(2) post.

Definitions. For "voting age", see s 1(1)(c) or 2(1)(c) ante; for "registration officer", see s 8(1) ante; for "elector", see s 202(1) post.

11 Correction of registers

(1) Where a register of electors as published does not carry out the registration officer's intention—

    (a) to include the name of any person shown in the electors lists as a person entitled to be registered, or

    (b) to give or not to give in a person's entry a date as that on which he will attain voting age, or as to the date to be given, or

    (c) to give effect to a decision on a claim or objection made with respect to the electors lists,

then (subject to the decision on any appeal from a decision on a claim or objection) the registration officer on becoming aware of the fact shall make the necessary correction in the register.

[(2) Where in a case in which paragraph (a) of subsection (1) above does not apply—

    (a) a claim is duly made that any person whose name is not included in a register of electors as published is entitled to be registered in that register, and

    (b) having duly disposed of the claim, the registration officer is satisfied that the person in respect of whom the claim is made is entitled to be so registered,

the registration officer shall make the necessary correction in the register.

(3) An alteration made in a register of electors after the last day on which nomination papers nominating candidates at an election may be delivered to the returning officer shall not have effect for the purposes of that election.]

(4) No alteration shall be made in a register of electors as published otherwise than under—

    (a) subsection (1) or subsection (2); or

    (b) the provisions of sections 56 to 58 below relating to appeals.

NOTES

This section, as originally enacted, contained provisions formerly in the Representation of the People Act 1949, s 9(3)–(6), as added by the Representation of the People Act 1980, s 2(1).

Sub-ss (2), (3) were substituted by the Representation of the People Act 1985, s 24, Sch 4, para 2, as from 1 October 1985.

Register of electors. See s 9 ante, and the note "Register" thereto.

Registration officer. As to the appointment of registration officers, see s 8 ante.

Electors lists. As to the preparation and publication of electors lists, see s 10(b) ante and the note thereto.

Person entitled to be registered. See s 12 post.

Give ... in a person's entry a date ... on which he will attain voting age. As to the entry in the register of that date, see s 12(5) post, and as to when a person attains a given age, see s 202(2) post.

Decision on a claim or objection; appeal from a decision on a claim or objection. For the determination by the registration officer of claims and objections made with respect to the electors lists, see s 10(1)(c) ante; see also the Representation of the People Regulations 1983, SI 1983/435, regs 19–25, and the Representation of the People (Northern Ireland) Regulations 1983, SI 1983/436, reg 14. Appeals from such determinations lie to the county court and thence to the Court of Appeal; see ss 56, 58 post.

Correction in the register. As to alterations to a published register, see the Representation of the People Regulations 1983, SI 1983/435, regs 34–37, Sch 3, Forms K, L and the Representation of the People (Northern Ireland) Regulations 1983, SI 1983/436, reg 22.

European Assembly elections. Sub-s (3) above is applied in relation to such elections by the European Assembly Elections Regulations 1984, SI 1984/137, reg 3(3). See further the Introductory Note to this Act.

Definitions. For "voting age", see s 1(1)(c) or 2(1)(c) ante; for "registration officer", see s 8(1) ante.

---

12 Right to be registered

(1) A person who may be entitled to vote as an elector at parliamentary elections for which any register is to be used is entitled to be registered in that register, subject to—

  (a) section 7(3) above, as to a person who on the qualifying date is a voluntary mental patient, and subsections (3) and (4) below as to one who on the qualifying date has a service qualification; and

  (b) any enactment imposing a disqualification for registration as a local government elector.

(2) A person who may be entitled to vote as an elector at local government elections for which any register is to be used is entitled to be registered in that register, subject to—

  (a) section 7(3) above, as to a person who on the qualifying date is a voluntary mental patient, and subsections (3) and (4) below as to one who on the qualifying date has a service qualification; and

  (b) any enactment imposing a disqualification for registration as a local government elector.

(3) A person who on the qualifying date has a service qualification is not entitled to be registered as mentioned in subsection (1) or subsection (2) above except in pursuance of an appropriate service declaration; and in this subsection and in subsection (4) below "appropriate service declaration" means—

  (a) in the case of a person who on the qualifying date is a member of the forces or the wife or husband of such a member, a service declaration made in accordance with section 15 below and in force on that date; and

  (b) in any other case, a service declaration made in accordance with that section with reference to that date.

(4) Subsection (3) above does not apply to a person who on the qualifying date is the wife or husband of a member of the forces if on that date—

  (a) that person has no other service qualification;

  (b) that person is resident in the United Kingdom; and

  (c) no appropriate service declaration is in force in respect of that person.

(5) A person otherwise qualified is entitled to be registered in a register of parliamentary electors or a register of local government electors if he will attain voting age before the end of the twelve months following the day by which the register is required to be published; but, if he will not be of voting age on the first day of those twelve months—

(a) his entry in the register shall give the date on which he will attain that age; and

(b) until the date given in the entry he shall not by virtue of the entry be treated as an elector for any purposes other than purposes of an election at which the day fixed for the poll is that or a later date.

NOTES

Sub-s (1) contains provisions formerly in the Representation of the People Act 1949, s 8(1) as partly repealed by the Representation of the People Act 1980, s 3(2), Schedule. Sub-s (2) contains provisions formerly in s 8(2) of the 1949 Act, as partly repealed by the Representation of the People Act 1969, s 24(1), (4), Sch 2, para 2(2), Sch 3, Pt II and by s 3(2) of, and the Schedule to, the 1980 Act. Sub-ss (3), (4) contain provisions formerly in s 8(2A), (2B) of the 1949 Act, as inserted by s 1(1) of the 1980 Act. Sub-s (5) contains provisions formerly in s 1(2) of the 1969 Act.

Prospective amendment. The words "(aa) section 2(1) of the Representation of the People Act 1985" are inserted after the word "qualification" in sub-s (1)(a) above, by the Representation of the People Act 1985, s 4(3) post, as from a day to be appointed under s 29(2) of that Act.

Sub-s (1): Entitled to vote. For the persons who are entitled to vote at parliamentary elections, see s 1 ante.

Parliamentary elections. See the note "Parliamentary election" to s 1 ante.

Register. See s 9 ante and the note "Register" thereto.

Qualifying date. For this date, see s 4 ante.

Voluntary mental patient. For meaning, see s 7(2) ante.

Service qualification. For the persons who have a service qualification, see s 14 post.

Sub-s (2): Entitled to vote. For the persons who are entitled to vote at local government elections, see s 2 ante.

Sub-s (4): Resident. See the note to s 1 ante, and see also s 5 ante, and the notes thereto.

United Kingdom. See the note to s 6 ante.

Attain voting age. As to when a person attains a given age, see s 202(2) post.

Months. See the note to s 1 ante.

Definitions. For "elector", see s 202(1) post; for "local government election", see s 203(1) post; for "voting age", see s 1(1)(c) or 2(1)(c) ante; for "member of the forces", see s 59(1) post. Note as "appropriate service declaration", sub-s (3) above.

13 Publication of registers

(1) Registers of parliamentary and local government electors or, in Northern Ireland, of parliamentary electors, shall be—

(a) prepared and published once a year, and

(b) published not later than 15th February,

and registers published in any year shall be used for elections at which the date fixed for the poll falls within the period of twelve months beginning with 16th February in that year.

(2) The Secretary of State has power to make regulations altering the interval in Northern Ireland between the qualifying date and the date of publication of the registers of parliamentary electors by changing either date, and any such regulations may make such consequential provisions (including the modification of any enactment contained in this or any other Act) as may appear to the Secretary of State to be necessary.

(3) If any part of a register is not published within the time required by this section, then until the day following that on which it is published the corresponding part of the previous register shall continue in use.

(4) Where any part of the register used at an election is a part continued in force by subsection (3) above, the Representation of the People Acts (including this Act) shall have effect in relation to the election and the area to which that part relates as if the qualifying date by reference to which that part was prepared were the qualifying date for the election.

NOTES

Sub-s (1) contains provisions formerly in the Electoral Registers Act 1949, s 1(1), (2) as substituted, in the case of s 1(2), by the Electoral Registers Act 1953, s 1(1). Sub-s (2) contains provisions formerly in s 1(5) of the 1949 Act. Sub-ss (3), (4) contain provisions formerly in s 1(6) of the 1949 Act.

Registers ... shall be prepared. For the duty of the registration officer to prepare registers of electors, see s 10 ante.

Elector. For meaning, see s 202(1) post.

Twelve months beginning with, etc; Secretary of State. See the notes to s 4 ante.

Qualifying date. For this date, see s 4 ante.

Representation of the People Acts. For the Acts which may be cited by this collective title and are still in force, see the Introductory Note to the Representation of the People Act 1948 ante.

Regulations under this section. Up to 1 August 1985 no regulations had been made under sub-s (2) above, and none have effect thereunder by virtue of the Interpretation Act 1978, s 17(2)(b), Vol 41, title Statutes.

For general provisions as to regulations made under this Act, see s 201 post.

Service qualifications and declarations for registration

14 Service qualification

(1) A person has a service qualification for the purposes of this Act who—

    (a) is a member of the forces,

    (b) (not being such a member) is employed in the service of the Crown in a post outside the United Kingdom of any prescribed class or description,

    (c) is employed by the British Council in a post outside the United Kingdom,

    (d) is the wife or husband of a member of the forces,

    (e) is the wife or husband of a person mentioned in paragraph (b) or paragraph (c) above and is residing outside the United Kingdom to be with her husband or, as the case may be, his wife,

and where a person leaves the United Kingdom to take up employment or residence as mentioned above or returns to the United Kingdom at the end of such employment or residence, the employment or residence shall be deemed to begin from the time of leaving or to continue until the time of returning, as the case may be.

(2) For the purposes of section 1(2) above a person ceasing to have a service qualification shall be treated as if he were resident in Northern Ireland for the period during which he had a service qualification.

NOTES

Sub-s (1) contains provisions formerly in the Representation of the People Act 1949, s 10(1), as amended by the Representation of the People Act 1969, ss 2(3), 24(1), Sch 2, para 4(1), as further amended by the Representation of the People (Armed Forces) Act 1976, s 2. Sub-s (2) contains provisions formerly in s 4(4) of the 1949 Act.

United Kingdom. See the note to s 6 ante.

Prescribed class or description. See the Representation of the People Regulations 1983, SI 1983/435, reg 5, and the Representation of the People (Northern Ireland) Regulations 1983, SI 1983/436, reg 4, which confer a service qualification upon a person employed in the service of the Crown in a post outside the United Kingdom if he is required to devote his whole working time to the duties of the post and the remuneration of it is paid wholly out of moneys provided by Parliament.

Residing. See the note "Resident" to s 1 ante, and see also s 5 ante, and the notes thereto.

Ward elections in the City of London. Sub-s (1) above and ss 15–17 post, apply; see the City of London (Various Powers) Act 1957, s 8(1), Vol 26, title London.

Supplementary provisions. As to the duty of—

(a) the appropriate government department, in the case of persons having a service qualification by virtue of sub-s (1)(a) or (b) above, and

(b) the British Council, in the case of persons having a service qualification by virtue of sub-s (1)(c) above,

to secure that such persons have an effective opportunity of exercising their rights under this Act in relation to the making and cancellation of service declarations, etc, and receive instructions and assistance in connection with the exercise of those rights, see s 59(3), (4) respectively post.

Definitions. For "member of the forces", see s 59(1) post; for "prescribed", see s 202(1) post.

15 Service declaration

(1) A service declaration shall be made only—

(a) by a person who has a service qualification, or

(b) subject to any prescribed conditions, by a person about to leave the United Kingdom in such circumstances as to acquire a service qualification,

and a service declaration may be made by such a person notwithstanding the fact that by reason of his age he is not yet entitled to vote.

(2) A service declaration made by a member of the forces or the wife or husband of such a member shall, if not cancelled, continue in force so long as the declarant has a service qualification, except in so far as regulations provide that the declaration shall cease to be in force on a change in the circumstances giving the service qualification.

(3) A service declaration made by any other person shall be made with a view to registration in the register of electors—

(a) for a particular year; and

(b) with reference to the qualifying date for that register.

(4) A service declaration made with reference to any qualifying date shall be made during the twelve months ending with that date, but shall not have effect if after it is made and before that date—

(a) the declarant ceases to have a service qualification; or

(b) the declarant cancels the declaration; or

(c) in so far as regulations so provide, there is a change in the circumstances giving the service qualification.

(5) No service declaration shall be specially made by a person for the purpose of local government elections, and any service declaration made for the purpose of parliamentary elections shall have effect also for the purpose of local government elections; but—

(a) a service declaration may be made for the purpose of local government elections only by a person who is as a peer subject to a legal incapacity to vote at parliamentary elections; and

(b) where so made, shall be marked to show that it is available for local government elections only, but shall in all other respects be the same as other service declarations.

(6) If a person—

(a) makes a service declaration declaring to more than one address, or

(b) makes more than one service declaration bearing the same date and declaring to different addresses,

the declaration or declarations shall be void.

(7) A service declaration may at any time be cancelled by the declarant and (subject to subsection (6) above) a service declaration bearing a later date shall without any express cancellation cancel a declaration bearing an earlier date [unless the declarations are made with reference to different qualifying dates].

NOTES

Sub-s (1) contains provisions formerly in the Representation of the People Act 1949, s 10(2), (3) as repealed in part, in the case of s 10(3), by the Representation of the People Act 1969, s 24(4), Sch 3, Pt II. Sub-ss (2)–(4) contain provisions formerly in s 10(3A)–(3C) of the 1949 Act as inserted by the Representation of the People (Armed Forces) Act 1976, s 1(2). Sub-ss (5)–(7) contain provisions formerly in s 10(4), (8), (9), respectively, of the 1949 Act, as amended, in the case of s 10(9), by s 24(1) of, and Sch 2, para 4 to, the 1969 Act, as further amended, in the case of s 10(9), by s 3(6) of the 1976 Act.

The words in square brackets in sub-s (7) were substituted by the Representation of the People Act 1985, s 24, Sch 4, para 3.

Sub-s (1): Service declaration. See further, s 16 post, as to the contents of a service declaration, and s 17 post, as to the effect of such a declaration.

Service qualification. For the persons who have a service qualification, see s 14 ante.

Subject to any prescribed conditions, by a person about to leave the United Kingdom. The Representation of the People Regulations 1983, SI 1983/435, reg 9, and the Representation of the People (Northern Ireland) Regulations 1983, SI 1983/436, reg 8, provide that a service declaration made by a person about to leave the United Kingdom in such circumstances as to acquire a service qualification shall be made not more than six weeks before he expects to leave the United Kingdom. As to the meaning of "the United Kingdom", see the note to s 6 ante.

By reason of his age he is not yet entitled to vote. Voting age is attained on a person's eighteenth birthday; see ss 1(1)(c), 2(1)(c) ante, and s 202(2) post.

Sub-s (2): If not cancelled. Ie under sub-s (7) above.

Sub-s (3): Register of electors. See s 9 ante, and the note "Register" thereto.

Qualifying date. For this date, see s 4 ante.

Sub-s (4): Months. See the note to s 1 ante.

Sub-s (5): Parliamentary elections. See the note "Parliamentary election" to s 1 ante.

Person who is as a peer subject to a legal incapacity to vote. As to this incapacity, see 15 Halsbury's Laws (4th edn) para 410.

Ward elections in the City of London; supplementary provisions. See the notes to s 14 ante.

Definitions. For "local government election", see s 203(1) post; for "legal incapacity" and "prescribed", see s 202(1), post; for "member of the forces", see s 59(1) post.

Regulations under this section. The Representation of the People Regulations 1983, SI 1983/435, reg 12(1), and the Representation of the People (Northern Ireland) Regulations 1983, SI 1983/436, reg 11(1) (made under sub-s (2) above). Up to 1 August 1985 no regulations had been made under sub-s (4)(c) above and none have effect thereunder by virtue of the Interpretation Act 1978, s 17(2)(b), Vol 41, title Statutes. See also the note "Subject to any prescribed conditions . . ." above.

For general provisions as to regulations made under this Act, see s 201 post.

---

16 Contents of service declaration

A service declaration shall state—

(a) the date of the declaration,

(b) where the declarant is a member of the forces or the wife or husband of such a member, that on that date the declarant is, or but for the circumstances entitling him to make the declaration would have been, residing in the United Kingdom,

(c) in the case of any other declarant, that on that date and, unless it is a qualifying date, on the qualifying date next following he is or will be, or but for those circumstances would have been, residing in the United Kingdom,

(d) the address where the declarant is or, as the case may be, will be or would have been residing in the United Kingdom or, if he cannot give any such address, an address at which he has resided in the United Kingdom,

(e) that on the date of the declaration the declarant is a Commonwealth citizen or a citizen of the Republic of Ireland,

(f) whether the declarant had on the date of the declaration attained the age of 18 years, and, if he had not, the date of his birth, and

(g) such particulars (if any) as may be prescribed of the declarant's identity and service qualifications,

and (except where the declarant is a member of the forces or the wife or husband of such a member) shall be attested in the prescribed manner.

NOTES

This section contains provisions formerly in the Representation of the People Act 1949, s 10(5) as amended by the Representation of the People Act 1969, s 24(1), Sch 2, para 4(2), by the Representation of the People (Armed Forces) Act 1976, s 3(4) and by the Representation of the People Act 1980, s 1(2).

Service declaration. As to the making of service declarations, see s 15 ante.

Residing. See the note "Resident" to s 1, ante, and see also s 5 ante, and the notes thereto.

United Kingdom. See the note to s 6 ante.

Qualifying date. For this date, see s 4 ante.

Commonwealth citizen; Republic of Ireland. See the notes to s 1 ante.

Age of 18 years. A person is deemed not to have attained a given age until the commencement of the relevant anniversary of his birth; see s 202(2) post.

Such particulars . . . as may be prescribed, etc; attested in the prescribed manner. In addition to the matters specified in paras (*a*)–(*f*) above a service declaration must state the matters specified in the Representation of the People Regulations 1983, SI 1983/435, reg 6. A declaration must be attested in the manner prescribed by reg 7 of those Regulations. As respects Northern Ireland the corresponding provisions are the Representation of the People (Northern Ireland) Regulations 1983, SI 1983/436, regs 5, 6.

As to offences in relation to false statements as to any particulars required by regulations under this section, see s 62 post.

Service qualifications. As to these, see s 14 ante.

Ward elections in the City of London. See the note to s 14 ante; and see also, in connection with the present section, s 191(2) and Sch 6, para 5 post.

Definitions. For "member of the forces", see s 59(1) post; for "prescribed", see s 202(1) post.

17 Effect of service declaration

(1) A member of the forces or the wife or husband of such a member whose service declaration is in force on the qualifying date shall be treated for the purposes of registration, and any other person whose service declaration is made with reference to the qualifying date for any register shall be so treated in relation to that register—

(*a*) as resident on the qualifying date at the address specified in the declaration;

(*b*) in the case of registration in Northern Ireland, as resident in Northern Ireland during the whole of the period of three months ending on the qualifying date; and

(*c*) in any case, until the contrary is proved, as being a Commonwealth citizen or a citizen of the Republic of Ireland of the age appearing from the declaration and as not being subject to any legal incapacity except as so appearing.

(2) Where a service declaration appearing to be properly made out and (where required) attested is transmitted to the registration officer in the proper manner, the declarant shall, until the contrary is proved, be treated for the purposes of registration as having had from the date of the declaration or such later date, if any, as appears from it, and as continuing to have, a service qualification.

NOTES

Sub-s (1) contains provisions formerly in the Representation of the People Act 1949, s 10(6), as substituted by the Representation of the People (Armed Forces) Act 1976, s 3(5). Sub-s (2) contains provisions formerly in s 10(7) of the 1949 Act, as amended by the Representation of the People Act 1980, s 1(2).

Service declaration. As to the making of service declarations, see ss 15, 16 ante.

Qualifying date. For this date, see s 4 ante.

Registration; register. See s 9 ante, and the note "Register" thereto.

Resident. See the note to s 1 ante, and see also s 5 ante, and the notes thereto.

Months; Commonwealth citizen; Republic of Ireland. See the notes to s 1 ante.

(Where required) attested. A service declaration is only to be attested where the declarant is not a member of the forces or the wife or husband of such a member; see the final limb of s 16 ante.

Transmitted to the registration officer in the proper manner. A service declaration is to be transmitted to the appropriate registration officer in accordance with the Representations of the People Regulations 1983, SI 1983/435, reg 8(1)–(3). See also reg 8(4) of those regulations as to notification of receipt of the declaration, and reg 11 as to the return of an invalid declaration. As respects Northern Ireland the corresponding provisions are the Representation of the People (Northern Ireland) Regulations 1983, SI 1983/436, regs 7, 10.

Ward elections in the City of London. See the note to s 14 ante.

Definitions. For "registration officer", see s 8(1) ante; for "legal incapacity", see s 202(1) post; for "member of the forces", see s 59(1) post.

Place and manner of voting at parliamentary elections

18 Polling districts and places at parliamentary elections

(1) Every constituency shall be divided into polling districts and subject to the provisions of this section there shall be a polling place designated for each polling district.

(2) In England and Wales it is the duty of the council of each district or London borough to divide their area into polling districts for the purpose of parliamentary elections for so much of any constituency as is situated in their area, and to designate the polling places for those polling districts, and to keep the polling districts and polling places under review, in accordance with the following rules—

    (*a*) the council shall exercise the powers conferred by this section with a view to giving all electors in so much of the constituency as falls within their area such reasonable facilities for voting as are practicable in the circumstances [and, in particular, they shall, so far as is reasonable and practicable, designate as polling places only places which are accessible to electors who are disabled];

    (*b*) . . . each parish or community shall in the absence of special circumstances be a separate polling district or districts;

    (*c*) the polling place for any polling district shall be an area in that district, except where special circumstances make it desirable to designate an area wholly or partly outside the polling district, and shall be small enough to indicate to electors in different parts of the polling district how they will be able to reach the polling station;

    (*d*) a polling place need not be designated for any polling district, if the size and other circumstances of the district are such that the situation of the polling stations does not materially affect the convenience of the electors or any body of them.

(3) (*Applies to Scotland only.*)

(4) In the case of a polling district for which no polling place is designated the polling district shall be taken to be the polling place for the purposes of this Act.

(5) If any interested authority or not less than 30 electors in a constituency make a representation to the Secretary of State that the powers conferred by this section have not been exercised so as to meet the reasonable requirements of the electors in the constituency or any body of those electors, the Secretary of State shall consider the representation and may, if he thinks fit—

    (*a*) direct the council (or in Scotland, the returning officer) by whom the powers are exercisable, to make any alterations which the Secretary of State thinks necessary in the circumstances, and

    (*b*) if the council or returning officer fails to make those alterations within a month after the direction is given, himself make the alterations,

and any alterations made by the Secretary of State under this subsection shall have effect as if they had been made by the council or returning officer.

In this subsection the expression "interested authority", in relation to any constituency, means—

    (i) as respects England, the council or where there is no such council the parish meeting of a parish which is wholly or partly situated within the constituency;

    (ii) as respects Wales, the council of a community which is so situated;

    (iii) (*applies to Scotland only*).

(6) On the exercise of any power given by this section, the council or returning officer—

(a) shall publish in the constituency a notice showing the boundaries of any polling districts or polling places constituted as a result of the exercise of the power; . . .

(b) . . .

(7) Subsections (2) to (6) above do not apply to Northern Ireland, and in Northern Ireland the polling districts and polling places are those for the time being established under the law relating to [local elections within the meaning of section 130 of the Electoral Law Act (Northern Ireland) 1962].

(8) Regulations—

(a) may provide for adapting the register in force for the time being to any alteration of polling districts, and

(b) may make special provisions for cases where any alteration of polling districts is made between the publication of any electors lists and the coming into force of the register prepared from those lists,

but except in cases for which provision is made by regulations an alteration of polling districts shall not be effective until the coming into force of the first register prepared from electors lists published after the alteration is made.

(9) An election shall not be questioned by reason of—

(a) any non-compliance with the provisions of this section; or

(b) any informality relative to polling districts or polling places.

NOTES

Sub-ss (1), (4), (6), (8), (9) contain provisions formerly in the Representation of the People Act 1949, s 11(1), (3), (5), (7), (8) respectively. Sub-s (2) contains provisions formerly in s 11(2) of the 1949 Act, as repealed in part by the London Government Act 1963, s 93(1), Sch 18, Pt I, and by the Local Government Act 1972, s 272(1), Sch 30, and as amended by s 45 of, and Sch 6, para 5(1), (2) to, the 1972 Act. Sub-s (5) contains provisions formerly in s 11(4) of the 1949 Act, and Sch 6, para 5(3) to the 1972 Act. Sub-s (7) contains provisions formerly in s 11(6) of the 1949 Act, as amended by the Northern Ireland (Modification of Enactments—No 1) Order 1973, SI 1973/2163, art 14(1), Sch 5, para 15(a).

The words in square brackets in sub-s (2)(a) were inserted, the words omitted from sub-ss (2)(b), (6) were repealed, and the words in square brackets in sub-s (7) were substituted, by the Representation of the People Act 1985, ss 24, 28(1), Sch 4, para 4, Sch 5, as from 1 October 1985.

Sub-s (1): Constituency. See the note to s 1 ante.

Polling place. As to the provision of polling stations see s 23(1) and Sch 1, para 25 post.

Sub-s (2): England; Wales. See the note to s 4 ante.

It is the duty etc. As to the remedies for failure to perform a statutory duty, see generally the Preliminary Note to the title Statutes, Vol 41, Halsbury's Laws (4th edn) paras 99, 195, 205 and 44 Halsbury's Laws (4th edn) paras 941 et seq.

Council of each district; London borough. See the corresponding notes to s 8 ante.

Parliamentary elections. See the note "Parliamentary election" to s 1 ante.

Elector. For meaning, see s 202(1) post.

Sub-s (5): Secretary of State. See the note to s 4 ante. The Secretary of State here concerned is the Secretary of State for the Home Department.

Direct; direction. Such directions are not statutory instruments (cf the Statutory Instruments Act 1946, s 1(1), Vol 41, title Statutes) and are not noted in this work.

Within a month after, etc. See the note "Within six months . . ." to s 5 ante.

Council or . . . parish meeting of a parish. As to the parishes in England and their meetings and councils, see the Local Government Act 1972, ss 1(6)–(9) et seq, Sch 1, Pts IV, V, Vol 25, title Local Government.

Council of a community. As to the communities in Wales and their meetings and councils, see the Local Government Act 1972, ss 20(4), 27 et seq, Sch 4, Pt II, Vol 25, title Local Government.

Sub-s (8): Register. As to the register of electors, see s 9 ante and the note "Register" thereto.

Electors lists. See s 10(b) ante and the note "Electors lists" to that section.

Sub-s (9): Election shall not be questioned. As to the questioning of parliamentary elections, see generally ss 120 et seq post.

European Assembly elections. Sub-ss (1) and (9) above are applied to such elections by the European Assembly Elections Regulations 1984, SI 1984/137, reg 3(1), Sch 1, and by those regulations the following subsection also applies to those elections:

"(1A) The polling districts and polling places designated under this section shall be the same as those used or designated for parliamentary elections, except where it appears to those responsible for the designation of parliamentary polling districts and polling places that special circumstances make it desirable for some other polling district or place to be designated."

See further the Introductory Note to this Act.

As to provisions relating to such elections in Northern Ireland, see the Introductory Note to this Act.

Isles of Scilly. See the note to s 8 ante.

Special polling stations in Northern Ireland. This section does not affect the Representation of the People Act 1985, s 10, Sch 1, Pt I, para 1(5); see para 1(6) of that Part of that Schedule post, as from a day to be appointed under s 29(2) of that Act.

Electoral Law Act (Northern Ireland) 1962. 1962 c 14 (NI); not printed in this work.

Regulations under this section. The Representation of the People Regulations 1983, SI 1983/435, reg 32, and the Representation of the People (Northern Ireland) Regulations 1983, SI 1983/436, reg 20 (made under sub-s (8) above).

For general provisions as to the regulations made under this Act, see s 201 post.

---

19 Voting at parliamentary elections

(1) A person voting as an elector at a parliamentary election shall do so in person at the polling station allotted to him under the parliamentary elections rules except in so far as this section makes exceptions for—

(a) those registered as service voters;

(b) those unable or likely to be unable to go in person to the polling station for one of the following reasons—

(i) the general nature of the occupation, service or employment of the person in question;

(ii) that person's service as a member of any of Her Majesty's reserve or auxiliary forces;

(iii) the particular circumstances of that person's employment on the date of the poll either as a constable or, for a purpose connected with the election, by the returning officer;

(iv) at a general election, the candidature in some other constituency of that person or that person's wife or husband;

(v) at a general election, the fact that that person is acting as returning officer for some other constituency;

(vi) at a general election, the particular circumstances of that person's employment on the date of the poll by the returning officer for some other constituency for a purpose connected with the election in that constituency;

(c) those unable or likely to be unable, by reason either of blindness or any other physical incapacity or of religious observance, to go in person to the polling station or, if able to go, to vote unaided;

(d) those unable or likely to be unable to go in person from their qualifying address to the polling station without making a journey by air or sea;

(e) those no longer residing at their qualifying address;

(f) those registered by virtue of a patient's declaration under section 7 above;

(g) those who have a service qualification depending on marriage to, and residence outside the United Kingdom to be with, a person having a service qualification; and

(h) those unable or likely to be unable to go in person to the polling station by reason of the general nature of the occupation, service or employment of, and their resulting absence from their qualifying address to be with, their husband or wife.

(2) A person registered as a service voter may vote by proxy unless he is entitled in pursuance of an application made under subsection (4) below to vote by post.

(3) A person not registered as a service voter if unable or likely to be unable to go in person to the polling station by reason either—

(a) of the general nature of his occupation, service or employment, or

(b) of his service as a member of any of Her Majesty's reserve or auxiliary forces,

may vote by proxy if he applies to be treated as an absent voter and is likely to be at sea or out of the United Kingdom on the date of the poll.

(4) A person mentioned in paragraphs (a) to (f) of subsection (1) above may vote by post if he applies to be treated as an absent voter and provides an address in the United Kingdom to which a ballot paper is to be sent for the purpose, but—

(a) a person shall not be entitled to vote by post if he is not registered as a service voter and there is in force an appointment of a proxy to vote for him; and

(b) a person shall not be entitled to vote by post on the ground that he no longer resides at his qualifying address if at the time of his application he resides at an address in the same area; and

(c) a person registered as a service voter shall not be entitled to vote by post on any ground other than his being so registered.

For the purposes of this subsection an address shall not be treated as in the same area as a qualifying address unless it would be so treated under section 22(3) below for the purposes of that section.

(5) A person who is not registered as a service voter but who either—

(a) has made a service declaration in respect of a qualification depending on marriage as described in subsection (1) above, or

(b) is as a married person unable or likely to be unable to go to the poll by reason of absence in the circumstances there described,

has the like right to vote by proxy and, in the case dealt with by paragraph (b) above, the like right to vote by post as a person unable or likely to be unable to go to the poll by reason of the general nature of his occupation, service or employment.

(6) A person, whether registered as a service voter or not—

(a) may vote in person as an elector notwithstanding any appointment of a proxy to vote for him, if he applies for a ballot paper for the purpose before a ballot paper has been issued for him to vote by proxy; but

(b) shall not be entitled to vote in person as an elector—

(i) where he may vote by proxy by virtue of an appointment for the time being in force and he does not so apply; or

(ii) where he has applied to be treated as an absent voter and is entitled in pursuance of the application to vote by post.

(7) A person not registered as a service voter may vote at any polling station in the constituency if he is entitled to vote in person but unable or likely to be unable to go to the polling station allotted to him by reason of the particular circumstances of his employment on the date of the poll either—

(a) as a constable; or

(b) by the returning officer, for a purpose connected with the election.

(8) Nothing in this section confers a right to vote on a person not having the right apart from this section.

NOTES

Sub-s (1) contains provisions formerly in the Representation of the People Act 1949, s 12(1), as amended by the Representation of the People Act 1969, s 24(1), Sch 2, para 5, in s 5(1) of the 1969 Act, and in the Mental Health (Amendment) Act 1982, Sch 2, para 7(1). Sub-ss (2), (3), (7), (8) contain provisions formerly in s 12(2), (3), (6), (8), respectively, of the 1949 Act, as partly repealed, in the case of s 12(2), by s 24(4) of, and Sch 3, Pt II to, the 1969 Act. Sub-s (4) contains provisions formerly in s 12(4) of the 1949 Act, the Local Government Act 1972, Sch 6, para 6, the Local Government Reorganisation (Consequential Provisions) (Northern Ireland) Order 1973, SI 1973/2095, art 2(4), and Sch 2, para 7(1), to the above-mentioned 1982

Act. Sub-s (5) contains provisions formerly in s 5(2) of the 1969 Act. Sub-s (6) contains provisions formerly in s 6(3) of the 1969 Act.

Prospective repeal. This section and ss 20–22 post are repealed by the Representation of the People Act 1985, s 28(1), Sch 5 post, as from a day to be appointed under s 29(2) of that Act. As from that date, new provision is made as to the manner of voting in parliamentary and local government elections by ss 5–9 of that Act post.

Sub-s (1): Person voting as an elector. Ie a person voting in his own right, as contrasted with a person voting as a proxy for an elector (to whom ss 21 and 22 post apply). For the persons who are entitled to vote as electors at parliamentary elections, see, in particular, s 1 ante.

Parliamentary election; constituency. See the notes to s 1 ante.

Polling station allotted. As to the allocation of polling stations, see Sch 1, r 25 post.

Registered as service voters. For the meaning of "service voter", see s 202(1) post; and as to service qualifications and declarations, see ss 14–17 ante.

Those unable . . . to go in person to the polling station. These words have been held to include those who could not reasonably be expected to go to the polling station for any of the reasons enumerated in sub-s (1)(b) above; see *Moore v Electoral Registration Officer for Borders* 1980 SLT (Sh Ct) 39 (the elector was a student who lived thirty-five miles from his polling station).

General nature of the occupation. In order to qualify as an absent voter on the ground of the general nature of his occupation, an elector's inability to attend his polling station must be due to a fundamental condition of his employment and be liable to recur throughout the continuance of that employment (*Daly v Watson* 1960 SC 216, 1960 SLT 271). A minister of the Church of Scotland summoned to General Assembly (*Craig v Mitchell* 1955 SLT 369) and a managing director having to attend conferences (*Daly v Watson* supra) were accordingly registered as absent voters. But such registration was refused in *Keay v Macleod* 1953 SC 252, 1953 SLT 144, where the circumstances were considered as accidental and extrinsic to the applicant's occupation.

University students who are obliged to vacate halls of residence during the vacation and find alternative accommodation qualify under this exception as absent voters; see *MacCorquodale v Bovack* 1984 SLT 328.

Constable. This means any person holding the office of constable (as to which, see 36 Halsbury's Laws (4th edn) paras 201 et seq), not a member of a police force holding the rank of constable. As to the attestation of constables, see the Police Act 1964, s 18, Sch 2, Vol 33, title Police, and as to their jurisdiction, see s 19 of that Act.

Returning officer. As to the designation of such officers, see ss 24, 26 post.

No longer residing at their qualifying address. The words "no longer" imply more than a temporary absence from home; there has to be a definite abandonment and detention in prison as an untried prisoner cannot be said to have a degree of permanency about it (*Electoral Registration Officer for Strathclyde v Boylan* 1980 SC 266).

The expression "qualifying address" is not defined in this Act, but cf s 1(1)(a) ante.

As to "residing", see the note "Resident" to s 1 ante, and see also s 5 ante, and the notes thereto.

Service qualification. For the persons who have a service qualification, see s 14 ante.

United Kingdom. See the note to s 6 ante.

Sub-s (2): Proxy. For persons eligible to be appointed as proxies at parliamentary elections, see s 21 post; and as to voting as proxy at such elections, see s 22 post.

Sub-s (3): Applies to be treated as an absent voter. As to the procedure for determining the right to be treated as an absent voter, see s 20 post.

Sub-s (4): Ballot paper. As to postal ballot papers, see Sch 1, r 24 post, the Representation of the People Regulations 1983, SI 1983/435, Pt V, and the Representation of the People (Northern Ireland) Regulations 1983, SI 1983/436, Pt V.

Sub-s (5): Service declaration. As to these declarations, see ss 15–17 ante.

Sub-s (7): Unable . . . to go to the polling station allotted . . . by reason . . . of his employment . . . as a constable etc. As to the issue of a certificate of employment for the purposes of sub-s (7) above, see the Representation of the People Regulations 1983, SI 1983/435, reg 47, Sch 3, Form G, as amended by the European Assembly Elections Regulations 1984, SI 1984/137, and the Representation of the People (Northern Ireland) Regulations 1983, SI 1983/436, reg 32, Sch 3, Form D, as amended by the European Assembly Elections (Northern Ireland) Regulations 1984, SI 1984/198.

Sub-s (8): Right to vote. As to the persons possessing this right at parliamentary elections, see s 1 ante.

European Assembly elections. This section and ss 20–23 post, are applied to such elections by the European Assembly Elections Regulations 1984, SI 1984/137, reg 3(1), Sch 1. See further the Introductory Note to this Act, and, in particular, the provisions of reg 6 of those regulations set out in that note.

As to provisions relating to such elections in Northern Ireland, see the Introductory Note to this Act.

Definitions. For "elector", "parliamentary elections rules", "service voter" and "vote", see s 202(1) post.

20 Absent voters at parliamentary elections

(1) An application to be treated as an absent voter at parliamentary elections shall be made to the registration officer and shall be allowed by him if he is satisfied that the applicant is, or will if registered be, entitled under section 19 above to vote as an absent voter.

(2) The application shall be for a particular election only, unless it is based on—

   (a) the general nature of the applicant's occupation, service or employment; or
   (b) the applicant's physical incapacity; or
   (c) the necessity of a journey by sea or air to go from the applicant's qualifying address to his polling station; or
   (d) the ground that the applicant no longer resides at his qualifying address.

(3) An application based on one of the grounds mentioned in subsection (2) above shall be for an indefinite period but where such an application is allowed the applicant shall cease to be entitled to be treated as an absent voter in pursuance of it if—

   (a) he applies to the registration officer to be no longer so treated; or
   (b) he ceases to be registered at the same qualifying address or becomes so registered as a service voter; or
   (c) the registration officer gives notice that he has reason to believe there has been a material change of circumstances, and the prescribed period elapses after the giving of the notice.

(4) This section applies to an application based on the grounds related to the applicant's marriage referred to in paragraphs (g) and (h) of section 19(1) as it applies to an application based on the general nature of the applicant's occupation, service or employment.

(5) The registration officer shall keep a record of absent voters and of the addresses provided by them as the addresses to which their ballot papers are to be sent.

NOTES

Sub-ss (1)–(3), (5) contain provisions formerly in the Representation of the People Act 1949, s 13(1)–(4); in addition sub-ss (1), (2) contain provisions formerly in the Mental Health (Amendment) Act 1982, Sch 2, para 7(3) and (2), respectively. Sub-s (4) contains provisions formerly in the Representation of the People Act 1969, s 5(3).

Prospective repeal. See the note to s 19 ante.

Sub-s (1): Application to be treated as an absent voter. This is regulated by the Representation of the People Regulations 1983, SI 1983/435 (as amended by SI 1984/137), reg 38, Sch 3, Forms M–R, and the Representation of the People (Northern Ireland) Regulations 1983, SI 1983/436 (as amended by SI 1984/198), reg 23, Sch 3, Forms F–L. See also Sch 1, r 5(2) post. As to when an application may be disregarded, see SI 1983/435, reg 44(1), and SI 1983/436, reg 29(1).

Sub-s (2): General nature of the applicant's occupation. See the corresponding note to s 19 ante.

Polling station. The provision of polling stations is regulated by Sch 1, r 25 post.

Resides. See the note "Resident" to s 1 ante, and see also s 5 ante, and the notes thereto.

Qualifying address. The expression is not defined in this Act, but cf s 1(1)(a) ante.

Sub-s (3): Applies . . . to be no longer so treated. As to when an application under sub-s (3)(a) above may be disregarded, see the Representation of the People Regulations 1983, SI 1983/435, reg 44(2), or the Representation of the People (Northern Ireland) Regulations 1983, SI 1983/436, reg 29(2).

Registered as a service voter. For the meaning of "service voter", see s 202(1) post; and as to service qualifications and declarations, see ss 14–17 ante.

Prescribed period. The Representation of the People Regulations 1983, SI 1983/435, reg 38(5), directs that where under sub-s (3)(c) above or s 33(3)(c) post, the registration officer gives notice to an absent voter that he has reason to believe there has been a material change of circumstances, that person shall cease to be treated as an absent voter seven days after the day on which the registration officer sends such notice. The Representation of the People (Northern Ireland) Regulations 1983, SI 1983/436, reg 23(5), contains a similar direction concerning sub-s (3)(c) above only.

Sub-s (5): Record of absent voters. See also s 23(1) and Sch 1, r 27 post, as to the absent voters list.

Ballot papers. See the note to s 19 ante.

European Assembly elections. See the note to s 19 ante.

Appeals. As to appeals from decisions of the registrations officer disallowing an application to be treated as an absent voter where the application is not made for a particular election only, see ss 56, 58 post.

Definitions. For "registration officer", see s 8(1) ante; for "prescribed" and "service voter", see s 202(1) post.

21 Proxies at parliamentary elections

(1) A person is not entitled to have more than one person at a time appointed as a proxy to vote for him at a parliamentary election.

(2) A person is not capable of being appointed to vote or of voting as proxy at a parliamentary election unless—

> *(a) he is not subject (age apart) to any legal incapacity to vote at a parliamentary election as an elector, and*
>
> *(b) he is either a Commonwealth citizen or a citizen of the Republic of Ireland,*

and a person is not entitled to vote as proxy at the same election in any constituency on behalf of more than two electors of whom that person is not the husband, wife, parent, grandparent, brother, sister, child or grandchild.

(3) A person otherwise qualified is capable of voting as proxy at a parliamentary election at which he is of voting age on the date of the poll, and of being appointed proxy for that purpose before he is of voting age.

(4) Subject to the foregoing provisions of this section a person is capable of being appointed proxy to vote at a parliamentary election and may vote in pursuance of the appointment.

(5) The appointment shall be made by the registration officer by means of a proxy paper issued by him on the elector's application, and it is the registration officer's duty to issue a proxy paper in pursuance of any application duly made to him, if he is satisfied—

> *(a) that the applicant is or will be registered for elections to which the application relates and entitled in respect of that registration to have a proxy appointed; and*
>
> *(b) that the proxy is capable of being and willing to be appointed.*

(6) The appointment may be cancelled by the elector by giving notice to the registration officer and shall cease to be in force on the issue of a proxy paper appointing a different person to vote for him, whether in respect of the same registration or elsewhere, but, subject to that, shall remain in force—

> *(a) in the case of an appointment for a person registered as a service voter, for all elections for which he remains registered as a service voter at the same qualifying address; and*
>
> *(b) in the case of an appointment for a person not registered as a service voter, for all elections at which he is entitled to vote by proxy in pursuance of the same application to be treated as an absent voter.*

(7) Stamp duty is not chargeable on any instrument appointing a proxy under this section.

(8) The registration officer shall keep a record of electors for whom proxies have been appointed and of the names and addresses of the persons appointed.

NOTES

Sub-ss (1), (4), (5), (7), (8) contain provisions formerly in the Representation of the People Act 1949, s 14(1), (3), (4), (6), (7), respectively. Sub-ss (2), (6) contain provisions formerly in s 14(2), (5) of the 1949 Act, as amended by the Representation of the People Act 1969, s 24(1), Sch 2, para 6(1), (2). Sub-s (3) contains provisions formerly in s 1(3) of the 1969 Act.

Prospective repeal. See the note to s 19 ante.

Sub-s (1): Parliamentary election. See the note to s 1 ante.

Sub-s (2): Commonwealth citizen; Republic of Ireland; constituency. See the notes to s 1 ante.

Sub-s (5): Appointment shall be made ... by means of a proxy paper etc. As to applications to vote by proxy, see the Representation of the People Regulations 1983, SI 1983/435 (as amended by SI 1984/137), reg 39, Sch 3, Forms S, T; as to the appointment of a proxy, see reg 40 of those regulations; as to the form of proxy paper and the sending of notice to the elector, see reg 41, Sch 3, Form D; and as to when an application may be disregarded, see reg 44(1). As respects Northern Ireland the corresponding provisions are the Representation of the People (Northern Ireland) Regulations 1983, SI 1983/436 (as amended by SI 1984/198), regs 24–26, 29(1), Sch 3, Forms M, N and A.

As to misdescriptions in proxy papers, see s 50 post.

It is the registration officer's duty etc. As to the penalty for breach of this duty, see s 63 post.

Sub-s (6): Appointment may be cancelled etc. See, further, as to the cancellation of a proxy appointment etc, the Representation of the People Regulations 1983, SI 1983/435, reg 42, and as to when a notice cancelling the appointment of a proxy may be disregarded, see reg 44(2) of those regulations. As respects Northern Ireland the corresponding provisions are the Representation of the People (Northern Ireland) Regulations 1983, SI 1983/436, regs 27, 29(2).

Registered as a service voter. For the meaning of "service voter", see s 202(1) post, and as to service qualifications and declarations, see ss 14–17 ante.

Qualifying address. The expression is not defined in this Act, but cf s 1(1)(*a*) ante.

Application to be treated as an absent voter. See, in particular, s 20 ante.

Sub-s (8): Record of electors for whom proxies have been appointed etc. See also s 23(1) and Sch 1, r 27 post, as to the list of proxies.

Local government elections. Sub-ss (5)–(7) above are applied for the purposes of local government elections by s 34(6) post.

European Assembly elections. See the note to s 19 ante.

Definitions. For "voting age", see s 1(1)(*c*) ante; for "registration officer", see s 8(1) ante; for "election", "legal incapacity", "service voter" and "vote", see s 202(1) post.

22 Voting as proxy at parliamentary elections

(1) *A person voting as proxy for an elector at a parliamentary election shall do so in person at the elector's polling station, except in so far as this section entitles the proxy to vote by post.*

(2) *A proxy may exercise the right to vote as such at a parliamentary election by post if—*

(*a*) *he applies so to do and provides an address in the United Kingdom to which a ballot paper is to be sent for the purpose; and*

(*b*) *either—*

(*i*) *he is entitled to vote by post as an absent voter at the election; or*

(*ii*) *that address is not in the same area as the elector's qualifying address.*

(3) *For the purposes of this section, an address shall not be treated as in the same area as a qualifying address unless—*

(*a*) *both addresses are in the same [constituency in Greater London or in a metropolitan county], or*

(*b*) *both addresses are in the same electoral division of a [non-metropolitan county] in England and, if either address is in a parish, both are in the same parish, or*

(*c*) *both addresses are in the same electoral division of a county in Wales and in the same community, or*

(*d*) *(applies to Scotland only),*

(*e*) *both addresses are in the same ward in Northern Ireland.*

(4) *A proxy is not entitled to exercise the right to vote as such in person at any election for which his application to exercise that right by post is allowed.*

(5) *Any such application shall be made to the registration officer and shall be allowed by him in any case where he is satisfied—*

(*a*) *that the elector is or will be registered as such for elections to which the application relates; and*

(*b*) *that there is in force an appointment of the applicant as his proxy to vote in respect of that registration; and*

(*c*) *that the conditions entitling the applicant to vote by post are fulfilled.*

(6) *Where any such application is based on the applicant's right to vote by post as an elector, then—*

(*a*) *if that right extends only to a particular election, the application shall also extend only to that election;*

(*b*) *in any other case, the application shall be for an indefinite period but, where it is allowed, the applicant shall cease to be entitled to vote by post in pursuance of that right if—*

(*i*) *he ceases to have the right to vote by post as an elector, or has that right only by virtue of a new application; or*

(*ii*) *he ceases to be proxy for the elector, or is so only by virtue of a new appointment.*

(7)   Where any such application is based on the situation of the address to which the ballot paper is to be sent, it shall be for an indefinite period but, if it is allowed, the applicant shall cease to be entitled to vote by post in pursuance of it if—

(a)   he applies for a ballot paper not to be sent to that address; or

(b)   he ceases to be proxy for the elector, or is so only by virtue of a new appointment.

(8)   The registration officer shall keep a record of the persons whose applications to vote by post as proxy are for the time being allowed and of the addresses provided by them as the addresses to which their ballot papers are to be sent.

NOTES

Sub-ss (1), (2), (4)–(8) contain provisions formerly in the Representation of the People Act 1949, s 15(1), (2), (4)–(8), as amended, in the case of s 15(2), (5)–(7), and as partly repealed, in the case of s 15(1), (2), (4), by the Representation of the People Act 1969, s 24(1), Sch 2, para 7. Sub-s (3) contains provisions formerly in the Local Government Act 1972, Sch 6, para 6, and the Local Government Reorganisation (Consequential Provisions) (Northern Ireland) Order 1973, SI 1973/2095, art 2(4).

The words in square brackets in sub-s (3)(*a*), (*b*) were substituted by the Local Government Act 1985, s 102(1), Sch 16, para 10, as from 1 April 1986.

Prospective repeal. See the note to s 19 ante.

Sub-s (1): Parliamentary election. See the note to s 1 ante.

Polling station. The provision of polling stations is regulated by Sch 1, r 25 post.

Sub-s (2): Proxy may ... vote ... by post of ... he applies, etc. As to applications by a proxy to vote by post, see the Representation of the People Regulations 1983, SI 1983/435 (as amended by SI 1984/137), reg 43, Sch 3, Form U, and as to when an application may be disregarded, see reg 44(1) of those regulations. As respects Northern Ireland the corresponding provisions are the Representation of the People (Northern Ireland) Regulations 1983, SI 1983/436 (as amended by SI 1984/198), regs 28, 29(1), Sch 3, Form O.

United Kingdom. See the note to s 6 ante.

Ballot paper. See the note to s 19 ante.

Entitled to vote by post as an absent voter. For this entitlement, see s 19(4) ante.

Qualifying address. This expression is not defined in this Act, but cf s 1(1)(*a*) ante.

Sub-s (3): Electoral division. As to the division of Greater London and of counties into electoral divisions for the purposes of the election of councillors, see the Local Government Act 1972, ss 6(2)(*a*), 8(1), 25(2)(*a*), Sch 2, para 7(1)(*a*), Vol 25, title Local Government.

Greater London. Ie the London boroughs, the City of London and the Inner and Middle Temples; see the London Government Act 1963, s 2(1), Vol 26, title London.

County. As to the counties in England and Wales, see the Local Government Act 1972, ss 1(1), (2), 20(1), (2), Sch 1, Pts I, II, Sch 4, Pt I, Vol 25, title Local Government.

Note that by s 203(4) post, this Act applies in general in relation to the Isles of Scilly as if they were a county.

England; Wales. See the note to s 4 ante.

Parish; community. Cf the notes "Council or ... parish meeting of a parish" and "Council of a community" to s 18 ante.

Sub-s (5): Appointment ... as his proxy. See s 21 ante.

Conditions entitling the applicant to vote by post. See s 19(4) ante.

Sub-s (7): Applies for a ballot paper not to be sent. As to when such an application may be ignored, see the Representation of the People Regulations 1983, SI 1983/435, reg 44(3), or the Representation of the People (Northern Ireland) Regulations 1983, SI 1983/436, reg 29(3).

Sub-s (8): Record of the persons whose applications to vote by post as proxy are ... allowed. See also s 23(1) and Sch 1, r 27 post, as to the list of postal proxies.

Local government elections. Sub-ss (4)–(6), (8) above are applied for the purposes of local government elections by s 34(6) post.

European Assembly elections. See the note to s 19 ante.

Isles of Scilly. See the note to s 8 ante.

Appeals. As to appeals from decisions of the registration officer disallowing a person's application to vote by post as proxy where the application is not made for a particular election only, see ss 56, 58 post.

Definitions. For "registration officer", see s 8(1) ante; for "elector", "vote" and "voter", see s 202(1) post.

Conduct of parliamentary elections

23   Rules for parliamentary elections

(1)   The proceedings at a parliamentary election shall be conducted in accordance with the parliamentary elections rules in Schedule 1 to this Act.

(2) It is the returning officer's general duty at a parliamentary election to do all such acts and things as may be necessary for effectually conducting the election in the manner provided by those parliamentary elections rules.

(3) No parliamentary election shall be declared invalid by reason of any act or omission by the returning officer or any other person in breach of his official duty in connection with the election or otherwise of the parliamentary elections rules if it appears to the tribunal having cognizance of the question that—

(a) the election was so conducted as to be substantially in accordance with the law as to elections; and

(b) the act or omission did not affect its result.

NOTES

This section contains provisions formerly in the Representation of the People Act 1949, s 16.

Parliamentary election. See the note to s 1 ante.

Returning officer. As to the designation of such officers, see s 24 post, or, as respects Northern Ireland, see s 26 post. As to returning officers generally and the discharge of their functions, see ss 27, 28 post, and for further provisions, see ss 29, 30 post.

No parliamentary election shall be declared invalid etc. It is for the court to make up its mind on the evidence as a whole whether there was a substantial compliance with the law as to elections or whether the act or omission affected the result; see Re Kensington North Parliamentary Election [1960] 2 All ER 150, [1960] 1 WLR 762, distinguishing Islington, West Division, Case, Medhurst v Lough and Gasguet (1901) 17 TLR 210, 230 (approving Gribbin v Kirker (1873) IR 7 CL 30) where it was stated that the onus rests on the respondent of proving that the result of the election was not affected by the transgression; see also Levers v Morris [1972] 1 QB 221, [1971] 3 All ER 1300.

Where breaches of the election rules, although trivial, have affected the result, that by itself is enough to compel the court to declare the election invalid even though it has been conducted substantially in accordance with the law as to elections; see Morgan v Simpson [1975] QB 151, [1974] 3 All ER 722, CA, and Gunn v Sharpe [1974] QB 808, [1974] 2 All ER 1058. Conversely, if the election was conducted so badly that it was not substantially in accordance with the law as to elections, the election is vitiated, irrespective of whether the result was affected or not; see Morgan v Simpson supra at 164 and 728 respectively, per Lord Denning MR, applying Hackney Case, Gill v Reed and Holms (1874) 31 LT 69.

If owing to a mistake in the notice of election some candidates are misled into delivering their nomination papers too late, and they are rejected by the returning officer for being late, the election will be declared invalid; see Howes v Turner (1876) 1 CPD 670 45 LJQB 550, and R v Glover (1866) 15 LT 289. On the other hand, failure to comply with the timetable set out in Sch 1, r 1 post, as respects the publication of the notice of the election does not render the election void if the result of the election has not been affected by it; see Clare, Eastern Division, Case (1892) 4 O'M & H 162 at 164–166; Longford Case (1870) 2 O'M & H 6; and Athlone Case (1843) Bar & Arn 115 at 122 et seq. The wrongful rejection of the nomination of a candidate will avoid an election; see Haverfordwest Case, Davies v Lord Kensington (1874) LR 9 CP 720, 43 LJCP 370, Mayo Case (1874) 2 O'M & H 191. The inclusion on a ballot paper of the name of a candidate who has withdrawn will avoid an election if the number of votes given to that candidate might affect the result; see Wilson v Ingham (1895) 64 LJQB 775, 72 LT 796.

The marking of the faces of a number of ballot papers with the electors' numbers in the register before delivering them to the voters will not, if the result is unaffected, avoid the election (Woodward v Sarsons (1875) LR 10 CP 733, [1874–80] All ER Rep 262; explained in Morgan v Simpson supra), but the marking in this way of all the ballot papers would avoid the election (Deans v Stevenson 1882 9 R (Ct of Sess) 1077 at 1088).

Failure to open or close the poll at a polling station at the correct time will not avoid an election (Clare, Eastern Division, Case supra; East Kerry Case (1911) 6 O'M & H 58 at 85; Drogheda Borough Case (1874) 2 O'M & H 201; Worcester Borough Case (1880) 3 O'M & H 184) provided that it can be shown that the result was not affected (Islington, West Division, Case (1901) Medhurst and Lough v Gasguet 17 TLR 210, 230); Latham v Glasgow Corpn 1921 SC 694 at 706; Gribbin v Kirker supra; Hackney Case, Gill v Reed and Holms supra).

Failure to count or record the number of ballot papers in each box or mix the whole of the ballot papers before counting (Re Pembroke Election Petition [1908] 2 IR 433), or failure to comply strictly with the provisions as to forwarding documents after the close of the poll (Horsham Second Case (1848) 1 Pow R & D 240; Kidderminster Borough Case (1850) 1 Pow R & D 260 at 262; Barnstaple Borough Case (1853) 2 Pow R & D 206; Clonmell Borough Case (1833) Per & Kn 425; Coleraine Borough Case (1833) Per & Kn 472 at 507), is not sufficient to avoid the election.

The exposure of a few ballot papers by the voters themselves would not invalidate an election in the absence of a conspiracy to nullify the law relating to elections (Louth, Northern Division, Case (1911) 6 O'M & H 103 at 39).

In Ruffle v Rogers (1982) 1 QB 1220, [1982] 3 All ER 157, CA, it was held that failure to stamp four ballot papers with the official mark was an omission which affected the result of the election because it prevented the result of the court from being a tie and accordingly prevented the successful candidate from being chosen by lot.

By s 18(9) ante, a parliamentary election is not to be questioned by reason of non-compliance with that section or any informality relative to polling districts or polling places. Note also s 24(2) post.

Tribunal having cognizance. Ie an election court constituted under s 123 post, or the High Court where a case is stated under s 146 post.

European Assembly elections. See the note to s 19 ante.

24 Returning officers: England and Wales

(1) In England and Wales, the returning officer for a parliamentary election is—

(a) in the case of a county constituency which is coterminous with or wholly contained in a county, the sheriff of the county;

(b) in the case of a borough constituency which is coterminous with or wholly contained in a district, the chairman of the district council;

(c) in the case of any other constituency wholly outside Greater London, such sheriff or chairman of a district council as may be designated in an order by the Secretary of State made by statutory instrument;

(d) in the case of a constituency which is coterminous with or wholly contained in a London borough, the mayor of the borough;

(e) in the case of a constituency wholly or partly in Greater London which is situated partly in one London borough and partly in a district or any other London borough, the mayor of such London borough or the chairman of such district council as may be designated in an order by the Secretary of State made by statutory instrument.

The City, the Inner Temple and the Middle Temple shall be treated for the purposes of this section as if together they formed a London borough.

(2) A parliamentary election is not liable to be questioned by reason of a defect in the title, or want of title, of the person presiding at or conducting the election, if that person was then in actual possession of, or acting in, the office giving the right to preside at or conduct the election.

NOTES

Sub-s (1) contains provisions formerly in the Local Government Act 1972, s 40(1), (2), 266(1). Sub-s (2) contains provisions formerly in s 40(5) of the 1972 Act.

England; Wales. See the note to s 4 ante.

Returning officer. As to the discharge of the returning officer's duties in England and Wales, see s 28 post.

County constituency; borough constituency. The county and borough constituencies are described in the Representation of the People Act 1948, Sch 1 ante; see further the note "Constituency" to s 1 ante.

County; Greater London. See the notes to s 22 ante.

Sheriff of the county. As to the appointment of sheriffs, see the Local Government Act 1972, s 219, Vol 25, title Local Government.

District; chairman of the district council. See the note "Council of every district" to s 8 ante. As to the election of the chairman of a district council, see the Local Government Act 1972, ss 3, 4, 22, 23, Vol 25, title Local Government.

Secretary of State. Cf the note to s 4 ante. The Secretary of State here concerned is the Secretary of State for the Home Department.

Statutory instrument. For provisions as to statutory instruments generally, see the Statutory Instruments Act 1946, Vol 41, title Statutes.

London borough. See the note to s 8 ante.

Mayor of the borough. As to the election of the mayor of a London borough, see the Local Government Act 1972, s 8, Sch 2, paras 2, 3, Vol 25, title Local Government.

European Assembly elections. Sub-s (2) above is applied to such elections by the European Assembly Elections Regulations 1984, SI 1984/137, reg 3(1), Sch 1. See further the Introductory Note to this Act, and, in particular, reg 5 of those regulations set out in that note; and as to the returning officer for an Assembly election, see the European Assembly Elections Act 1978, s 3, Sch 1, para 4(1) ante.

25 (*Applies to Scotland only.*)

26 Returning officer: Northern Ireland

[(1)] In Northern Ireland, the Chief Electoral Officer for Northern Ireland is the returning officer for each constituency.

[(2) Sections 14(5) and 14A(2) and (3) of the Electoral Law Act (Northern Ireland) 1962 (appointment of temporary deputy and delegation to assistants) shall have effect in relation to the Chief Electoral Officer in his capacity as returning officer.]

NOTES

This section, as originally enacted, contained provisions formerly in the Local Government Reorganisation (Consequential Provisions) (Northern Ireland) Order 1973, SI 1973/2095, art 2(1).

Sub-s (2) was added by the Representation of the People Act 1985, s 24, Sch 4, para 5, as from 1 October 1985, and, accordingly, this section, as originally enacted, is numbered sub-s (1).

Chief Electoral Officer for Northern Ireland. See the note to s 8 ante.

European Assembly elections. In Northern Ireland the Chief Electoral Officer is also the returning officer for every Assembly election; see the European Assembly Elections Act 1978, s 3, Sch 1, para 4(3) ante.

Electoral Law Act (Northern Ireland) 1962. 1962 c 14 (NI); not printed in this work.

Saving. See s 206 and Sch 7, para 5 post.

27 Returning officers generally

(1) It is for the returning officer as such to execute the writ for a parliamentary election, and the office of returning officer is a distinct office from that by virtue of which he becomes returning officer.

(2) Where a person takes any office by virtue of which he becomes returning officer, he (and not the outgoing holder of the office) shall complete the execution of any writ for a parliamentary election previously issued and not yet returned.

(3) A person is not subject to any incapacity to vote at a parliamentary election by reason of being or acting as returning officer at that election.

NOTES

This section contains provisions formerly in the Representation of the People Act 1949, s 17(4)–(6).

Returning officer. As to the designation of this officer, see ss 24, 26 ante; and as to the discharge of his functions in England and Wales, see s 28 post.

Writ for a parliamentary election. As to the issue of writs for parliamentary elections, see Sch 1, rr 1, 3, 4 post, and 15 Halsbury's Laws (4th edn) paras 551 et seq. See also the note "Parliamentary election" to s 1 ante.

European Assembly elections. Sub-s (3) is applied to such elections by the European Assembly Elections Regulations 1984, SI 1984/137, reg 3(1), Sch 1. See further the Introductory Note to this Act.

As to provisions relating to such elections in Northern Ireland, see the Introductory Note to this Act.

28 Discharge of returning officer's functions in England and Wales

(1) In England and Wales the duties of the returning officer for a parliamentary election (except those mentioned in subsection (2) below) shall be discharged, as acting returning officer—

> (a) in the case of a constituency for which the chairman of a district council or the mayor of a London borough is returning officer by virtue of section 24(1) above, by the registration officer appointed by that council;

(b) in the case of any other constituency, by such registration officer as may be designated in an order made [by statutory instrument] by the Secretary of State.

(2) The duties excepted from subsection (1) above are—

(a) any duty imposed on a returning officer under rule 3 of the parliamentary elections rules; and

(b) any duty so imposed under rule 50 of those rules which the person (if any) who for the time being holds the office of returning officer reserves to himself and undertakes to perform in person.

(3) The returning officer shall give to the acting returning officer written notice of any duties which he reserves to himself under paragraph (b) of subsection (2) above, and that paragraph shall, in the case of any election, apply to the duties (if any) of which the notice is so given not later than the day following that on which the writ is received, and to no others.

(4) In the discharge of the duties imposed by subsection (1) an acting returning officer has all the powers, obligations, rights and liabilities of the returning officer under this Act, and this Act has effect accordingly.

(5) An acting returning officer has power to appoint deputies to discharge all or any of those duties, [and a district council or London borough council may assign officers to assist in carrying out all or any of those duties].

(6) Section 25 of the Sheriffs Act 1887 (death of sheriff) does not authorise the under-sheriff to discharge the duties of returning officer, and upon a sheriff's death the acting returning officer shall discharge all the sheriff's duties as returning officer until another sheriff is appointed and has made the declaration of office.

NOTES

Sub-ss (1), (2) contain provisions formerly in the Representation of the People Act 1949, s 18(1), (1A), as substituted by the Local Government Act 1972, s 40(3). Sub-ss (3)–(5) contain provisions formerly in s 18(2)–(4) of the 1949 Act, as amended, in the case of s 18(2), by s 45 of, and Sch 6, para 7 to, the 1972 Act. Sub-s (6) contains provisions formerly in s 18(1B) of the 1949 Act, as inserted by s 40(3) of the 1972 Act, and in s 40(4) of the 1972 Act.

The words in square brackets in sub-s (1)(b) were inserted, and those in sub-s (5) were substituted, by the Representation of the People Act 1985, s 24, Sch 4, para 6, as from 1 October 1985.

Sub-s (1): England; Wales. See the note to s 4 ante.

Returning officer. As to the designation of this officer, see ss 24, 26 ante; and as to returning officers generally, see s 27 ante.

Parliamentary election; constituency. See the notes to s 1 ante.

Chairman of a district council. See the note "District; chairman of the district council" to s 24 ante.

Mayor of a London borough. See the notes "London borough" to s 8 ante, and "Mayor of the borough" to s 24 ante.

Registration officer. As to the appointment of registration officers, see s 8 ante.

Statutory instrument. See the note to s 24 ante.

Secretary of State. Cf the note to s 4 ante. The Secretary of State here concerned is the Secretary of State for the Home Department.

Sub-s (2): Duty . . . under r 3 of the parliamentary elections rules. Sch 1, r 3 post must be read subject to Sch 1, r 4 post, which provides for the conveyance of the writ for a parliamentary election to the acting returning officer in certain cases.

Sub-s (3): Written. Expressions referring to writing are, unless the contrary intention appears, to be construed as including references to other modes of representing or reproducing words in a visible form; see the Interpretation Act 1978, s 5, Sch 1, Vol 41, title Statutes.

Sub-s (5): Nomination papers. The receipt of nomination papers and the decision upon objections relating to them are governed by Sch 1, rr 10, 12 post.

Offences. For penalties for neglect of duty on the part of returning officers, see s 63 post.

European Assembly elections. Sub-ss (4)–(6) above are applied to such elections by the European Assembly Elections Regulations 1984, SI 1984/137, reg 3(1), Sch 1, subject to the substitution, in sub-s (4) above, of the words "Regulation 5(1) of the European Assembly Elections Regulations 1984" for the words "subsection (1)". Sub-s (5) was also modified but that modification no longer has any effect in view of the amendment to that subsection.

See further the Introductory Note to this Act and, in particular, the provisions of reg 5 of the 1984 regulations set out in that note.

Definitions. For "registration officer", see s 8(1) ante; for "parliamentary elections rules", see s 202(1) post.
Sheriffs Act 1887, s 25. See Vol 39, title Sheriffs and Bailiffs.
Order under this section. The Returning Officers (Parliamentary Constituencies) (England and Wales) Order 1983, SI 1983/468 (made under sub-s (1)(*b*) above and s 24(1)(*c*), (*e*) ante).

29 Payments by and to returning officer

(1) No consideration shall be given by or to a returning officer for the making out, receipt, delivery or return of the writ for a parliamentary election or, subject to the following provisions of this section, otherwise in connection with its execution.

(2) Nothing in subsection (1) above shall be taken as applying to any inclusive salary payable to a returning officer in respect of the office by virtue of which he becomes returning officer.

(3) The Treasury shall by statutory instrument prescribe a scale of maximum charges in respect of services rendered and expenses incurred by a returning officer for the purposes of or in connection with parliamentary elections, and may revise the scale as and when they think fit.

(4) A returning officer shall be entitled to his reasonable charges, not exceeding the sums specified in that scale, in respect of services and expenses of the several kinds so specified which have been properly rendered or incurred by him for the purposes of or in connection with a parliamentary election.

(5) The amount of any such charges shall be charged on and paid out of the Consolidated Fund on an account being submitted to the Treasury, but the Treasury may if they think fit, before payment, apply for the account to be taxed under the provisions of section 30 below.

(6) Where the superannuation contributions required to be paid by a local authority in respect of any person are increased by any fee paid under this section as part of a returning officer's charges at a parliamentary election, then on an account being submitted to the Treasury a sum equal to the increase shall be charged on and paid out of the Consolidated Fund to the authority.

(7) On the returning officer's request for an advance on account of his charges, the Treasury may, on such terms as they think fit, make such an advance.

(8) The Treasury may make regulations as to the time when and the manner and form in which accounts are to be rendered to them for the purposes of the payment of a returning officer's charges.

NOTES

Sub-ss (1), (2) contain provisions formerly in the Representation of the People Act 1949, s 20(1). Sub-ss (3)–(5), (7), (8) contain provisions formerly in s 20(2)–(6), respectively, of the 1949 Act as partly repealed in the case of s 20(4), by the SLR Act 1963. Sub-s (6) contains provisions formerly in the Representation of the People Act 1969, s 20.

Sub-s (1): Returning officer. As to returning officers, see, in particular, ss 24, 26–28 ante.
Writ for a parliamentary election. See the note to s 27 ante.
Office by virtue of which he becomes returning officer. See ss 24(1) and 26 ante.
Sub-s (3): Treasury. Ie the Commissioners of Her Majesty's Treasury; see the Interpretation Act 1978, s 5, Sch 1, Vol 41, title Statutes.
Statutory instrument. See the note to s 24 ante.
Sub-s (5): Consolidated Fund. Ie the Consolidated Fund of the United Kingdom which was established by the Consolidated Fund Act 1816, s 1, Vol 30, title Money (Pt 1). By the Finance Act 1954, s 34(3), Vol 30, title Money (Pt 1), any charge on the Fund extends to the growing produce thereof. See also, as to payment out of the Fund, the Exchequer and Audit Departments Act 1866, s 13, in conjunction with the

Exchequer and Audit Departments Act 1957, s 2, and the Finance Act 1975, s 56, all Vol 30, title Money (Pt 1).

European Assembly elections. This section is applied to such elections by the European Assembly Elections Regulations 1984, SI 1984/137, reg 3(1), Sch 1, subject to:

(1) the omission of sub-ss (1) and (2) above; and

(2) the substitution, in sub-s (5) above, for the words from the beginning of the subsection to "the Treasury, but", of the words "On an account for such charges being submitted to the Treasury".

See further the Introductory Note to this Act.

As to provisions relating to such elections in Northern Ireland, see the Introductory Note to this Act.

Definitions. For "election" and "prescribe", see s 202(1) post; for "local authority", see s 203(1) post.

Regulations under this section. The Returning Officers' Expenses (England and Wales) Regulations 1984, SI 1984/720; the Returning Officers' Expenses (Northern Ireland) Regulations 1984, SI 1984/722 (both made under sub-s (3) above); the European Assembly Elections (Returning Officers' Expenses) Regulations 1984, SI 1984/723 (made under sub-s (3) above as applied by the European Assembly Elections Regulations 1984, SI 1984/137, reg 3(1), Sch 1); and the European Assembly Elections (Returning Officers' Expenses) (Northern Ireland) Regulations 1984, SI 1984/724 (made under sub-s (3) above as applied by the European Assembly Elections (Northern Ireland) Regulations 1984, SI 1984/198, reg 3(1), Sch 1).

In addition by virtue of the Interpretation Act 1978, s 17(2)(b), Vol 41, title Statutes, the Treasury Regulations dated 30 November 1949, set out in Appendix B to the Memorandum of Guidance for Acting Returning Officers which was enclosed with Home Office Circular RPA 271, dated 10 May 1983, have effect as if made under sub-s (8) above.

For general provisions as to the making of regulations, see s 201 post.

30 Taxation of returning officer's account

(1) An application for a returning officer's account to be taxed shall be made—

(a) where the account relates to an election in a constituency in England or Wales or in Northern Ireland, to the county court,

(b) (applies to Scotland only),

and in this section the expression "the court" means that court . . .

(2) On any such application the court has jurisdiction to tax the account in such manner and at such time and place as the court thinks fit, and finally to determine the amount payable to the returning officer.

(3) On any such application the returning officer may apply to the court to examine any claim made by any person against him in respect of matters charged in the account; and the court, after notice given to the claimant and after giving him an opportunity to be heard and to tender any evidence, may allow or disallow or reduce the claim objected to with or without costs; and the determination of the court shall be final for all purposes and as against all persons.

(4) Any reference in this section to the county court shall be taken, in relation to Northern Ireland, as a reference to the county court having jurisdiction at the place for the delivery of nomination papers at the election in question.

NOTES

This section contains provisions formerly in the Representation of the People Act 1949, s 20(7)–(10).

The words omitted from sub-s (1) where indicated by dots apply to Scotland only.

Returning officer's account. As to the submission of this account, see s 29(5) ante.

Constituency. See the note to s 1 ante.

England; Wales. See the note to s 4 ante.

County court. Ie a court held for a district under the County Courts Act 1984; see the Interpretation Act 1978, s 5, Sch 1, Vol 41, title Statutes. As to county court districts, see ss 1, 2 of the 1984 Act, Vol 11, title County Courts.

In relation to Northern Ireland, note also sub-s (4) above.

Person. For meaning, see s 202(1) post.

Place for the delivery of nomination papers. See Sch 1, r 10 post.

European Assembly elections. This section is applied to such elections by the European Assembly Elections Regulations 1984, SI 1984/137, reg 3(1), Sch 1. See further the Introductory Note to this Act.

As to provisions relating to such elections in Northern Ireland, see the Introductory Note to this title.

Procedure. The procedure on an application for taxation of a returning officer's account is set out in CCR Ord 45, r 1.

Place and manner of voting at local government elections

31 Polling districts and stations at local government elections

(1) For elections of county councillors . . . the county council may divide an electoral division into polling districts, and may alter any polling district, and for elections of London borough or district councillors the London borough or district council may divide the London borough or district or any ward thereof into polling districts, and may alter any polling district.

(2) *(Applies to Scotland only.)*

(3) Any power to constitute polling districts for the purpose of local government elections shall be exercised so that electors from any parliamentary polling district wholly or partly within the electoral area can, in the absence of special circumstances, be allotted to a polling station within the parliamentary polling place for that district unless the parliamentary polling place is outside the electoral area.

(4), (5) . . .

[(6) Any polling district formed for the purpose of the election of councillors for any ward of a London borough shall, if the ward is wholly included in the electoral area for the election of a member of the Inner London Education Authority, be a polling district for the election of a member of that Authority for that electoral area.

(7) If the polling districts in an electoral area for the election of a member of the Inner London Education Authority or any part of such an area are not determined by subsection (6) above—

(*a*) the council of the London borough which includes that electoral area, or

(*b*) in the case of an electoral area which includes the City, the Inner Temple and the Middle Temple, the City of Westminster,

may divide that area or, as the case may be, that part of that area, into polling districts, and may alter any polling district and subsection (3) above applies to any power conferred by this subsection.]

NOTES

Sub-s (1) contains provisions formerly in the Representation of the People Act 1949, s 22(1), as partly repealed by the London Government Act 1963, ss 8(1), 93(1), Sch 3, para 13(4), Sch 18, Pt I, and as amended by the Local Government Act 1972, s 45, Sch 6, para 8, and in Sch 3, Pt III, para 27(1), to the 1963 Act. Sub-s (3) contains provisions formerly in s 22(3) of the 1949 Act.

Sub-ss (4), (5) were repealed by the Local Government Act 1985, s 102(2), Sch 17, as from 1 April 1986 ("the abolition date" within the meaning of s 1(2) of that Act, Vol 25, title Local Government). Sub-ss (6), (7) were added by s 19 of, and Sch 9, Pt I, para 1(2) to, that Act as from 1 September 1985 (see the Local Government Act 1985 (New Authorities) (Appointed Days) Order 1985, SI 1985/1283).

Sub-s (1): County councillors; district councillors; London borough councillors. Elections of councillors for local government areas are conducted in accordance with rules made by the Secretary of State; see s 36 post, and the note "Rules under this section" thereto.

County council. As to the counties in England and Wales and their councils, see the Local Government Act 1972, ss 1(1), (2), 2(1), (3), 20(1), (2), 21(1), (3), Sch 1, Pts I, II, Sch 4, Pt I, Vol 25, title Local Government.

Note that by s 203(4) post, this Act applies in general in relation to the Council of the Isles of Scilly as if it were a county council.

Electoral division. See the note to s 22 ante.

London borough. See the note to s 8 ante.

District council. See the note "Council of every district" to s 8 ante.

Ward. As to the division of London boroughs and districts into wards for the purposes of the election of councillors, see the Local Government Act 1972, ss 6(2)(*b*), (*c*), 8(1), 25(2)(*b*), Sch 2, para 7(1)(*b*), Vol 25, title Local Government.

Sub-s (3): Parliamentary polling district; parliamentary polling place. As to the division of constituencies into polling districts, and the designation of polling places, see s 18 ante.

Polling station. As to the provision of polling stations at local government elections, see the Local Elections (Principal Areas) Rules 1973, SI 1973/79, Sch 2, r 21, and the Local Elections (Parishes and Communities) Rules 1973, SI 1973/1910, Sch 1, r 20.

Sub-s (6): Inner London Education Authority. This is the local education authority for the Inner London Education Area now established by the Local Government Act 1985, s 18, Vol 25, title Local Government. By sub-s (3) of that section the Inner London Education Area consists of Greater London exclusive of the outer London boroughs.

Isles of Scilly. See the note to s 8 ante.

Definitions. For "the City" and "elector", see s 202(1) post; for "electoral area" and "local government election", see s 203(1) post.

32 Voting at local government elections

(1) All persons voting as electors at a local government election shall do so in person at the polling station allotted to them by the rules under section 36 or section 42 below except in so far as this section makes exceptions for—

(a) those registered as service voters;

(b) those unable or likely to be unable to go in person to the polling station for one of the following reasons—

(i) the general nature of the occupation, service or employment of the person in question;

(ii) that person's service as a member of Her Majesty's reserve or auxiliary forces;

(iii) the particular circumstances of that person's employment on the date of the poll either as a constable or, for a purpose connected with the election, by the returning officer;

(iv) at an ordinary election, the fact that that person is acting as returning officer at an ordinary election of councillors for some other electoral area;

(v) at an ordinary election, the particular circumstances of that person's employment on the date of the poll by the returning officer at an ordinary election of councillors for some other electoral area for a purpose connected with the election in that area;

(c) those unable or likely to be unable, by reason either of blindness or any other physical incapacity or of religious observance, to go in person to the polling station or, if able to go, to vote unaided;

(d) those unable or likely to be unable to go in person from their qualifying address to the polling station without making a journey by air or sea;

(e) those registered by virtue of a patient's declaration under section 7 above;

(f) those who have a service qualification depending on marriage to, and residence outside the United Kingdom to be with, a person having a service qualification; and

(g) those unable or likely to be unable to go in person to the polling station by reason of the general nature of the occupation, service or employment of, and their resulting absence from their qualifying address to be with, their husband or wife.

(2) A person registered as a service voter may at any local government election vote by proxy.

(3) Where—

(a) a person is registered at the same qualifying address both as a parliamentary and as a local government elector, and is not so registered as a service voter, and

(b) there is in force an appointment of a proxy to vote for him at parliamentary elections in respect of that registration, being an appointment based on the general nature of his occupation, service or employment,

then, in respect of that registration, at local government elections at which postal voting is allowed he shall be treated as an absent voter and may vote by proxy.

(4) Unless treated as an absent voter under subsection (3) above, any of the persons mentioned in paragraphs (b) to (e) of subsection (1) above who is not registered as a service

voter may vote by post at any local government election at which postal voting is allowed, if he applies to be treated as an absent voter and provides an address in the United Kingdom to which a ballot paper is to be sent for the purpose.

(5) A person who is not registered as a service voter but who either—

(a) has made a service declaration in respect of a qualification depending on marriage as described in subsection (1), or

(b) is as a married person unable or likely to be unable to go to the poll by reason of absence in the circumstances there described,

has the like right to vote by proxy and, in the case dealt with by paragraph (b) above, the like right to vote by post as a person unable or likely to be unable to go to the poll by reason of the general nature of his occupation, service or employment.

(6) A person, whether registered as a service voter or not—

(a) may vote in person as an elector notwithstanding any appointment of a proxy to vote for him, if he applies for a ballot paper for the purpose before a ballot paper has been issued for him to vote by proxy; but

(b) shall not be entitled to vote in person as an elector—

(i) where he may vote by proxy by virtue of an appointment for the time being in force and he does not so apply; or

(ii) where he has applied to be treated as an absent voter and is entitled in pursuance of the application to vote by post.

(7) A person not registered as a service voter, if he is entitled to vote in person, but unable or likely to be unable to go in person to the polling station allotted to him by reason of the particular circumstances of his employment on the date of the poll either as a constable or, for a purpose connected with the election by the returning officer, may vote at any polling station of the electoral area.

(8) Postal voting shall be allowed at all local government elections, except, in England and Wales, elections of parish or community councillors.

(9) Nothing in this section shall be taken as conferring a right to vote on a person not having the right apart from this section.

NOTES

Sub-s (1) contains provisions formerly in the Representation of the People Act 1949, s 23(1) as amended by the Representation of the People Act 1969, s 24(1), Sch 2, para 8(1), in s 5(1) of the 1969 Act, and in the Mental Health (Amendment) Act 1982, Sch 2, para 7(1). Sub-ss (2), (3) contain provisions formerly in s 23(2), (3) of the 1949 Act as partly repealed by s 24(4) of, and Sch 3, Pt II to, the 1969 Act. Sub-s (4) contains provisions formerly in s 23(4) of the 1949 Act, as amended by s 24(1) of, and Sch 2, para 8(2) to, the 1969 Act, and in Sch 2, para 7(1), to the above-mentioned 1982 Act. Sub-ss (5), (6) contain provisions formerly in ss 5(2), 6(3), respectively, of the 1969 Act. Sub-ss (7), (9) contain provisions formerly in s 23(6), (8) of the 1949 Act. Sub-s (8) contains provisions formerly in s 23(7) of the 1949 Act as amended by the Local Government Act 1958, s 28(5), as partly repealed by s 6(5) of the 1969 Act, and as further amended by the Local Authorities etc (Miscellaneous Provisions) Order 1977, SI 1977/293, art 4(2).

Prospective repeal. This section and ss 33, 34 post are repealed by the Representation of the People Act 1985, s 28(1), Sch 5 post, as from a day to be appointed under s 29(2) of that Act. As from that date, new provision is made as to the manner of voting in parliamentary and local government elections by ss 5–9 of that Act post.

Sub-s (1): Persons voting as electors. Ie persons voting in their own right as contrasted with persons voting as a proxy for an elector (to whom s 34 post applies). For the persons who are entitled to vote as electors at local government elections, see, in particular, s 2 ante.

Polling station allotted. As to the allocation of polling stations, see the Local Elections (Principal Areas) Rules 1973, SI 1973/79, Sch 2, r 21 (for elections of councillors of Greater London and London boroughs, and counties and districts in England and Wales), and the Local Elections (Parishes and Communities) Rules 1973, SI 1973/1910, Sch 1, r 20 (for elections of parish councillors in England and community councillors in Wales).

Registered as service voters. For the meaning of "service voter", see s 202(1) post; and as to service qualifications and declarations, see ss 14–17 ante.

Those unable ... to go in person to the polling station; general nature of the occupation; constable. See the notes to s 19 ante.

Returning officer. For the persons who act as returning officers for local government elections, see s 35 post.

Ordinary election. As to ordinary elections of councillors, see the Local Government Act 1972, ss 7(1), (2), (8), 8(1), 16(3), 26(1), (6), 35(2), Sch 2, paras 6(2), (3), Vol 25, title Local Government.

Qualifying address. This expression is not defined in this Act, but cf s 2(1)(*a*) ante.

Service qualification. For the persons who have a service qualification, see s 14 ante.

United Kingdom. See the note to s 6 ante.

Sub-s (2): Proxy. For the appointment of proxies for the purposes of local government elections, see s 34 post.

Sub-s (3): Parliamentary and ... local government elector. For parliamentary qualification, see s 1 ante; and for local government qualification, see s 2 ante.

Appointment of a proxy to vote ... at parliamentary elections. As to proxies at parliamentary elections, see s 21 ante.

Local government elections at which postal voting is allowed. Ie all local government elections except those of parish and community councillors; see sub-s (8) above.

Sub-s (4): Absent voter. For applications to be treated as an absent voter at a local government election, see s 33 post.

Ballot paper. As to postal ballot papers, see the Local Elections (Principal Areas) Rules 1973, SI 1973/79, Sch 2, r 20, the Representation of the People Regulations 1983, SI 1983/435, Pt V, and the Representation of the People (Northern Ireland) Regulations 1983, SI 1983/436, Pt V.

Sub-s (5): Service declaration. As to these declarations, see ss 15–17 ante.

Sub-s (8): England; Wales. See the note to s 4 ante.

Sub-s (9): Right to vote. As to the persons possessing this right at parliamentary elections, see s 2 ante.

Ward elections in the City of London. This section and ss 33 and 34, post, apply with a modification in the case of this section and s 34; see the City of London (Various Powers) Act 1957, s 8(1)–(3), Vol 26, title London.

Definitions. For "elector", "service voter" and "vote", see s 202(1), post; for "electoral area" and "local government election", see s 203(1) post.

33 Absent voters at local government elections

(1) An application to be treated as an absent voter at local government elections shall be made to the registration officer and shall be allowed by him if he is satisfied that the applicant is, or will if registered be, entitled under section 32 above to vote as an absent voter.

(2) The application shall be for a particular election only, if it is based on—

(a) the applicant's service as a member of any of Her Majesty's reserve or auxiliary forces; or

(b) the fact that the applicant is acting as returning officer in some other electoral area; or

(c) the particular circumstances of the applicant's employment on the date of the poll either as a constable or by a returning officer; or

(d) religious observance; or

(e) a patient's declaration under section 7 above.

(3) An application not based on one of the grounds mentioned in subsection (2) above shall be for an indefinite period but, where such an application is allowed, the applicant shall cease to be entitled to be so treated as an absent voter in pursuance of it if—

(a) he applies to the registration officer to be no longer so treated; or

(b) he ceases to be registered at the same qualifying address, or becomes so registered as a service voter; or

(c) the registration officer gives notice that he has reason to believe that there has been a material change of circumstances, and the prescribed period elapses after the giving of notice.

(4) The registration officer shall keep a record of absent voters and of the addresses provided by them as the addresses to which their ballot papers are to be sent.

NOTES

This section contains provisions formerly in the Representation of the People Act 1949, s 24 as amended, in the case of s 24(2), by the Representation of the People Act 1969, s 24(1), Sch 2, para 9, and as partly repealed, in the case of s 24(3), by s 24(4) of, and Sch 3, Pt II to, that Act. In addition sub-ss (1), (2) contain provisions formerly in the Mental Health (Amendment) Act 1982, Sch 2, para 7(3), (2), respectively.

Prospective repeal. See the note to s 32 ante.

Sub-s (1): Application to be treated as an absent voter. See the note to s 20 ante.

Sub-s (2): Acting as returning officer. As to returning officers in England and Wales and the discharge of their functions, see ss 24, 28 ante.

Constable. See the note to s 19 ante.

Sub-s (3): Applies . . . to be no longer so treated; prescribed period. See the notes to s 20 ante.

Qualifying address. This expression is not defined in this Act, but cf s 2(1)(*a*) ante.

Registered as a service voter. For the meaning of "service voter", see s 202(1) post; and as to service qualifications and declarations, see ss 14–17 ante.

Sub-s (4): Record of absent voters. See also the Local Elections (Principal Areas) Rules 1973, SI 1973/79, Sch 2, r 23 as to the absent voters list.

Ballot paper. See the note to s 32 ante.

Ward elections in the City of London. See the note to s 32 ante.

Definitions. For "registration officer", see s 8(1) ante; for "electoral area" and "local government election", see s 203(1) post; for "prescribed", "service voter" and "vote", see s 202(1) post.

34 Proxies at local government elections

(1) Except in the case of a service voter who is as a peer subject to a legal incapacity to vote at parliamentary elections, no person shall be specially appointed proxy to vote at local government elections, but any appointment of a person to vote as proxy at parliamentary elections shall have effect also for the purpose of local government elections.

(2) Subject to subsection (3) below, in the case of a service voter who is as a peer subject to a legal incapacity to vote at parliamentary elections, any person shall be capable of being appointed proxy to vote at local government elections for him and may vote in pursuance of the appointment, but not more than one person at a time shall be appointed on behalf of any service voter.

(3) A person—

(a) is not capable of being appointed under subsection (2) above to vote, or of voting, as proxy at a local government election unless he is not subject (age apart) to any legal incapacity to vote at the election as an elector and is either a Commonwealth citizen or a citizen of the Republic of Ireland;

(b) otherwise qualified is capable of voting as proxy at a local government election at which he is of voting age on the date of the poll, and of being appointed proxy for that purpose before he is of voting age.

(4) A person voting as proxy at a local government election may do so by post if—

(a) he applies to vote as proxy by post and provides an address in the United Kingdom to which a ballot paper is to be sent for the purpose, and

(b) he is entitled to vote by post as an absent voter at the election,

but a person voting as proxy at a local government election, unless entitled to do so by post, shall do so in person at the elector's polling station.

(5) The registration officer shall keep a record of electors for whom proxies have been appointed and of the names and addresses of the persons appointed.

(6) Subsections (5) to (7) of section 21 and subsections (4), (5), (6) and (8) of section 22 above apply for the purposes of local government elections as they apply for the purposes of parliamentary elections.

NOTES

Sub-ss (1), (2), (4)–(6) contain provisions formerly in the Representation of the People Act 1949, s 25(1), (2), (4)–(6), respectively, as partly repealed in the case of s 25(4), (6), by the Representation of the People Act

1969, s 24(4), Sch 3, Pt II. Sub-s (3) contains provisions formerly in s 25(3) of the 1949 Act, as amended by s 24(1) of, and Sch 2, para 10 to, the 1969 Act, and s 1(3) of the 1969 Act.

Prospective repeal. See the note to s 32 ante.

Sub-s (1): Service voter who is as a peer subject to a legal incapacity to vote. As to this incapacity, see 15 Halsbury's Laws (4th edn) para 410.

Parliamentary elections. See the note "Parliamentary election" to s 1 ante.

Proxy at parliamentary elections. For the appointment of proxies at parliamentary elections, see s 21 ante.

Sub-s (3): Commonwealth citizen; Republic of Ireland. See the notes to s 1 ante.

Sub-s (4): Person voting as proxy . . . may do so by post if . . . he applies, etc. See the first note to s 22(2) ante.

United Kingdom. See the note to s 6 ante.

Ballot paper. See the note to s 19 ante.

Entitled to vote by post as an absent voter. For this entitlement, see s 32(4) ante.

Polling station. As to the provision of polling stations, see s 32(1) ante and the note "Polling station allotted" thereto.

Sub-s (5): Record of electors for whom proxies have been appointed, etc. See also the Local Elections (Principal Areas) Rules 1973, SI 1973/79, Sch 2, r 23, and the Local Elections (Parishes and Communities) Rules 1973, SI 1973/1910, Sch 1, r 22, as to the list of proxies and also, in the case of the former rule, the list of postal proxies.

Ward elections in the City of London. See the note to s 32 ante.

Definitions. For "voting age", see s 2(1)(c) ante; for "registration officer", see s 8(1) ante; for "election", "elector", "legal incapacity", "service voter" and "vote", see s 202(1) post; for "local government election", see s 203(1) post.

Conduct of local government elections in England and Wales

35 Returning officers: local elections in England and Wales

(1) In England and Wales [every non-metropolitan council] shall appoint an officer of the council to be the returning officer for elections of councillors of the county and every district council shall appoint an officer of the council to be the returning officer for the elections of councillors of the district and an officer of the council to be the returning officer for elections of councillors of parishes or communities within the district.

(2) . . .

(3) The returning officer at an election of London borough councillors shall be the proper officer of the borough.

[(3A) The returning officer at an election of members of the Inner London Education Authority shall be the proper officer of the borough which includes the electoral division for which the election is held or, in the case of the electoral division which includes the City, the Inner Temple and the Middle Temple, the proper officer of the City of Westminster.]

(4) The returning officer at any election mentioned in subsections (1) to [(3A)] above may by writing under his hand appoint one or more persons to discharge all or any of his functions.

(5) A local government election in England and Wales is not liable to be questioned by reason of a defect in the title, or want of title, of the person presiding at or conducting the election, if that person was then in actual possession of, or acting in, the office giving the right to preside at or conduct the election.

NOTES

This section, as originally enacted, contained provisions formerly in the Local Government Act 1972, s 41.

The words in square brackets in sub-s (1) were substituted by the Local Government Act 1985, s 102(1), Sch 16, para 11, as from 1 April 1986 ("the abolition date" within the meaning of s 1(2) of that Act, Vol 25, title Local Government), and sub-s (2) was repealed by s 102(2) of, and Sch 17 to, that Act, as from that date. Sub-s (3A) was inserted, and the reference to that subsection in sub-s (4) was substituted, by s 19 of, and Sch 9,

Pt I, para 1(3) to, that Act, as from 1 September 1985 (see the Local Government Act 1985 (New Authorities) (Appointed Days) Order 1985, SI 1985/1283).

England; Wales. See the note to s 4 ante.

Elections of councillors of the county; the district; parishes or communities; London borough councillors. As to the election of such councillors, see, in addition to the provisions of this Act, the Local Government Act 1972, ss 6, 7 (relating to county council and district council elections in England), ss 25, 26 (relating to such elections in Wales), s 16 (parish elections), s 35 (community elections), and s 8 and Sch 2, paras 6, 7 (London borough elections), Vol 25, title Local Government.

District council. See the note "Council of every district" to s 8 ante.

Borough. Ie the London borough, as to which, see the note to s 8 ante.

Inner London Education Authority. See the note to s 31 ante.

Writing. See the note "Written" to s 28 ante.

Isles of Scilly. See the note to s 8 ante.

Definitions. For "the City", "election" and "proper officer", see s 202(1) post; for "electoral area" and "local government election", see s 203(1) post.

36 Local elections in England and Wales

(1) Elections of councillors for local government areas in England and Wales shall be conducted in accordance with rules made by the Secretary of State.

(2) Rules made under this section shall apply the parliamentary elections rules in Schedule 1 to this Act, subject to such adaptations, alterations and exceptions as seem appropriate to the Secretary of State.

[(3) Where the polls at—

    (*a*) the ordinary election of district councillors for any district ward or an election to fill a casual vacancy occurring in the office of such a councillor, and

    (*b*) the ordinary election of parish or community councillors for any parish or community or an election to fill a casual vacancy occurring in the office of such a councillor,

are to be taken on the same day and the elections are for related electoral areas, the polls at those elections shall be taken together.

(3A) For the purposes of this section electoral areas are related if they are coterminous or if one is situated within the other.

[(3AA) Where the poll at an ordinary election of members of the Inner London Education Authority for an electoral division, or an election to fill a casual vacancy occurring in the office of member of that Authority for an electoral division, is to be held on the same date as the poll at an ordinary election of councillors for any ward of a London borough which is wholly included in that electoral division, or an election to fill a casual vacancy occurring in the office of councillor for such a ward, the polls at those elections shall be taken together.]

(3B) Where the polls at any elections are combined under this section the cost of taking the combined polls (excluding any cost solely attributable to one election) and any cost attributable to their combination shall be apportioned equally among the elections.

(3C) The Secretary of State may by regulations make such provision as he thinks fit in connection with the combining of polls at any elections under this section including provision modifying the Representation of the People Acts in relation to such elections.]

(4) All expenditure properly incurred by a returning officer in relation to the holding of an election of a councillor for a principal area (that is, a county, . . . a district or a London borough) shall, in so far as it does not, in cases where there is a scale fixed for the purposes of this section by the council for that area, exceed that scale, be paid by that council.

[(4A) All expenditure properly incurred by a returning officer in relation to the holding of an election of members of the Inner London Education Authority shall, in so far as it does not exceed any scale fixed for that election by the Authority, be paid by that Authority.]

(5) All expenditure properly incurred by a returning officer in relation to the holding of an election of a parish or community councillor shall, in so far as it does not, in cases where there is a scale fixed for the purposes of this section by the council of the district in which the parish or the community is situated, exceed that scale, be paid by the district council, but any expenditure so incurred shall be chargeable only on the parish or community for which the election is held.

(6) Before a poll is taken at an election of a councillor for any local government area in England and Wales the council of that area or, in the case of an election of a parish or community councillor, the council who appointed the returning officer shall, at the request of the returning officer or of any person acting as returning officer, advance to him such reasonable sum in respect of his expenses at the election as he may require.

(7) Rules made under this section shall be—

(a) made by statutory instrument;

(b) subject to annulment in pursuance of a resolution of either House of Parliament.

NOTES

Sub-ss (1)–(6), as originally enacted, contained provisions formerly in the Local Government Act 1972, s 42(1), (3)–(7), respectively. Sub-s (7) contains provisions formerly in ss 42(8) and 266(1) of that Act.

Sub-ss (3), (3A), (3B), (3C) were substituted for the original sub-s (3) by the Representation of the People Act 1985, s 17, as from 1 September 1985. The words omitted from sub-s (4) were repealed by the Local Government Act 1985, s 102(2), Sch 17, as from 1 April 1986 ("the abolition date" within the meaning of s 1(2) of that Act, Vol 25, title Local Government). Sub-ss (3AA), (4A) were inserted by s 19 of, and Sch 9, Pt I, para 1(4) to, that Act, as from 1 September 1985 (see the Local Government Act 1985 (New Authorities) (Appointed Days) Order 1985, SI 1985/1283).

Sub-s (1): England; Wales. See the note to s 4 ante.

Secretary of State. Cf the note to s 4 ante. The Secretary of State here concerned is the Secretary of State for the Home Department.

Sub-s (3): Ordinary election of district councillors. As to when such elections take place, see the Local Government Act 1972, s 7(2) (ordinary elections of metropolitan district councillors) and (8) (ordinary elections of non-metropolitan district councillors), and s 26(6) (ordinary elections of district councillors in Wales), Vol 25, title Local Government. For provisions relating to the postponement of a poll at such elections, where the date of that poll is the same as the date of the poll at a parliamentary general election or an Assembly general election, see the Representation of the People Act 1985, s 16 post, as from a day to be appointed under s 29(2) of that Act.

District ward. As to the division of metropolitan and non-metropolitan districts into wards, see the Local Government Act 1972, s 6(2)(b), (c), Vol 25, title Local Government, and as to the division of districts in Wales into wards, see s 25(2)(b) of that Act.

Casual vacancy. For provisions relating to the filling of casual vacancies among parish or community councillors, see the Local Government Act 1972, s 89(6), Vol 25, title Local Government.

Ordinary election of parish or community councillors. As to when such elections take place, see the Local Government Act 1972, ss 16(3), 35(2), respectively, Vol 25, title Local Government.

Sub-s (3AA): Inner London Education Authority. See the note to s 31 ante.

Electoral division. See the note to s 22 ante.

London borough. See the note to s 8 ante.

Sub-s (3C): Representation of the People Acts. For the Acts which may be cited by this collective title, see the Introductory Note to the Representation of the People Act 1948 ante.

Sub-s (4): Returning officer. As to this officer, see s 35 ante.

County. See the note to s 22 ante.

District. See the note "Council of every district" to s 8 ante.

Sub-s (7): Statutory instrument; subject to annulment. For provisions as to statutory instruments generally, see the Statutory Instruments Act 1946, Vol 41, title Statutes, and as to statutory instruments which are subject to annulment, see ss 5(1), 7(1) of that Act.

Computation of time. As to the computation of time for the purposes of rules made under this section, see s 40(3) post.

Validity of local elections. No local government election is to be declared invalid by reason of any breach of rules under this section if it appears that the election was conducted substantially in accordance with the law and that the breach did not affect the result of the election; see s 48 post.

Welsh Sunday polls. Rules under this section have effect in their application to polls under the Licensing

Act 1964, s 66 (Sunday closing in Wales), Vol 24, title Licensing and Liquor Duties, subject to such adaptations, etc as seem appropriate to the Secretary of State; see Sch 8, para 1, to that Act, in the same title.

Filling of casual vacancies among parish or community councillors. Such vacancies are to be filled by election or by the parish or community council in accordance with rules made under this section; see the Local Government Act 1972, s 89(6), Vol 25, title Local Government.

Polls consequent on parish or community meetings. Rules made under this section with respect to the election of parish or community councillors apply to such polls subject to any adaptations, etc, made by rules made by the Secretary of State; see the Local Government Act 1972, Sch 12, paras 18(5), 34(5), Vol 25, title Local Government. The Local Elections (Parishes and Communities) Rules 1973, SI 1973/1910, cited in the note "Rules under this section" below, are adapted for this purpose by the Parish and Community Meetings (Polls) Rules 1973, SI 1973/1911 (as amended by SI 1976/2067 and SI 1983/1151), r 5, Schedule.

Isles of Scilly. By the Isles of Scilly Order 1978, SI 1978/1844 (made under the Local Government Act 1972, s 265, Vol 25, title Local Government; and see s 203(5), post), art 5(2), as construed in accordance with the Interpretation Act 1978, ss 17(2)(a), 23(2), Vol 41, title Statutes, elections of councillors of the Isles of Scilly are to be conducted in accordance with rules made under this section as if such elections were elections of county councillors. See also s 203(4)(b) post, and the last note to that section.

Definitions. For "election" and "parliamentary elections rules", see s 202(1) post; for "electoral area" and "local government area", see s 203(1) post. Note as to "related electoral areas", sub-s (3A) above.

Rules under this section. The following rules have been made under this section or have effect thereunder by virtue of the Interpretation Act 1978, s 17(2)(b), Vol 41, title Statutes: the Local Elections (Principal Areas) Rules 1973, SI 1973/79, as amended by SI 1976/2065 and SI 1983/1154 (which include provisions made by virtue of the Local Government Act 1972, s 83(1), Vol 25, title Local Government, as construed in accordance with s 17(2)(a) of the 1978 Act); the Elections (Welsh Forms) (No 1) Rules 1973, SI 1973/358 (also made under the Welsh Language Act 1967, s 2(2), Vol 41, title Statutes); the Local Elections (Parishes and Communities) Rules 1973, SI 1973/1910, as amended by SI 1974/84, SI 1976/2066 and SI 1983/1153 (which include provisions having effect by virtue of s 90(1)(b) or s 187(1) post, or made by virtue of s 83(4) of the 1972 Act, Vol 25, title Local Government, or by virtue of s 89(6) of that Act); the Parish and Community Meetings (Polls) Rules 1973, SI 1973/1911, as amended by SI 1976/2067 and SI 1983/1151 (which include provisions having effect by virtue of s 187(1) post, or made under the Local Government Act 1972, Sch 12, paras 18(5), 34(5), Vol 25, title Local Government); the Elections (Welsh Forms) (No 2) Rules 1973, SI 1973/2184 (also made under the Welsh Language Act 1967, s 2(2), Vol 41, title Statutes). As to SI 1973/1910 and SI 1973/1911, see also the notes to s 187 post, and the note "Polls consequent on parish or community meetings" above.

Regulations under this section. Up to 1 August 1985, no regulations had been made under sub-s (3C) above. As to regulations generally, see s 201 post.

37 Ordinary day of local elections in England and Wales

In every year the ordinary day of election of councillors is the same for all local government areas in England and Wales and is—

(a) the first Thursday in May;

(b) such other day as may be fixed by the Secretary of State by order made not later than 1st February in the year preceding [the year (or, in the case of an order affecting more than one year, the first year] in which the order is to take effect.

The power to make an order under this section is exercisable by statutory instrument.

NOTES

This section contains provisions formerly in the Local Government Act 1972, ss 43, 266(1).

The words in square brackets in para (b) were substituted by the Representation of the People Act 1985, s 18(2), as from 1 October 1985.

Ordinary day of election. Note s 40(1), (2) post, which makes provision in the event of the ordinary day of election falling on a Sunday, etc.

Local government area. For meaning, see s 203(1) post.

England; Wales. See the note to s 4 ante.

Secretary of State. Cf the note to s 4 ante. The Secretary of State here concerned is the Secretary of State for the Home Department.

Statutory instrument. See the note to s 24 ante.

Orders under this section. Up to 1 August 1985 no order had been made under this section and none has effect thereunder by virtue of the Interpretation Act 1978, s 17(2)(b), Vol 41, title Statutes.

38 Nominations and candidate's death in local election in England and Wales

(1) At local government elections in England and Wales—

    (a) the nomination paper shall give for each person subscribing it his electoral number (that is, his number as an elector for the electoral area); and

    (b) a telegram (or any similar means of communication) consenting to a nomination shall be admissible instead of the candidate's written consent.

(2) If at a contested local government election in England and Wales proof is given to the returning officer's satisfaction before the result of the election is declared that one of the persons named or to be named as a candidate in the ballot papers has died, then the returning officer—

    (a) shall countermand the poll, or

    (b) if polling has begun, shall direct that the poll be abandoned,

and the provisions of section 39(5) below shall apply.

NOTES

Sub-s (1) contains provisions formerly in the Representation of the People Act 1969, Sch 1, Pt II, para 6(1), as partly repealed by the Local Government Act 1972, s 272(1), Sch 30. Sub-s (2) contains provisions formerly in s 13(1)(*b*) of the 1969 Act.

Prospective repeal. This section is repealed by the Representation of the People Act 1985, ss 24, 28(1), Sch 4, para 7, Sch 5 post, as from a day to be appointed under s 29(2) of that Act.

England; Wales. See the note to s 4 ante.

Nomination paper. See, as to the nomination of candidates generally, the Local Elections (Principal Areas) Rules 1973, SI 1973/79 (as amended by SI 1983/1154), Sch 2, rr 5–10, and the Local Elections (Parishes and Communities) Rules 1973, SI 1973/1910 (as amended by SI 1983/1153), Sch 1, rr 5–10.

Telegram (or any similar means of communication). The forerunner of sub-s (1)(*b*) above mentioned only a telegram. The words in parenthesis have been inserted consequent on the abolition of the inland telegram service but the exact nature of the "similar means of communication" referred to is uncertain. Presumably it would include, at any rate, a telemessage. It should be noted that the replaced provision was not amended so as to refer to any similar means of communication.

Written consent. Written consent to nomination is required by the Local Elections (Principal Areas) Rules 1973, SI 1973/79, Sch 2, r 7, as amended by SI 1983/1154, or the Local Elections (Parishes and Communities) Rules 1973, SI 1973/1910, Sch 1, r 7(1), as amended by SI 1983/1153.

Returning officer. As to this officer, see s 35 ante.

Ballot papers. For general provisions relating to ballot papers, see the Local Elections (Principal Areas) Rules 1973, SI 1973/79 (as amended by SI 1983/1154), Sch 2, rr 15, 20, and the Local Elections (Parishes and Communities) Rules 1973, SI 1973/1910, Sch 1, r 15.

Definitions. For "elector", see s 202(1) post; for "electoral area" and "local government election", see s 203(1) post.

39 Local elections void etc in England and Wales

(1) If in England and Wales at an election of a councillor for a local government area—

    (*a*) the poll is countermanded or abandoned for any reason, or

    (*b*) no person is or remains, or an insufficient number of persons are or remain, validly nominated to fill the vacancy or vacancies in respect of which the election is held,

the returning officer . . . shall order an election to fill any vacancy which remains unfilled to be held on a day appointed by him.

That day shall be within the period of *42 days* (computed according to section 40 below) beginning with the day fixed as the day of election for the first-mentioned election.

[(1A) Subsection (1) above shall apply in relation to an election of a member of the Inner London Education Authority with the substitution for the reference to the returning officer of a reference to the proper officer of the Authority.]

(2) If for any other reason an election to an office under the Local Government Act

1972 [or Part III of the Local Government Act 1985], other than that of chairman of a parish or community council or parish meeting or parish or community councillor, is not held on the appointed day or within the appointed time, or fails either wholly or in part or becomes void, the High Court may order an election to be held on a day appointed by the court.

(3) The High Court may order that the costs incurred by any person in connection with proceedings under subsection (2) above shall be paid by the local authority concerned.

(4) In a case not falling within subsection (1) above—

(a) if any difficulty arises with respect to an election of parish or community councillors or of an individual parish or community councillor, or to the first meeting of a parish or community council after an ordinary election of parish or community councillors, or

(b) if a parish or community council is not properly constituted because an election is not held or is defective or for any other reason,

the district council—

(i) may by order make any appointment or do anything which appears to them necessary or expedient for the proper holding of such an election or meeting and properly constituting the council, and

(ii) may, if it appears to them necessary, direct the holding of an election or meeting and fix the date for it.

(5) Where an election is ordered to be held under this section—

(a) rules under section 36 above relating to the notice to be given of an election and the manner in which an election is to be conducted apply in relation to the election so ordered to be held as they applied or would have applied in relation to the election which has not been duly held or has failed or become void;

(b) no fresh nomination is necessary in the case of a candidate who remains validly nominated for that election.

(6) An order made—

(a) under this section may include such modifications of the provisions of—

(i) this Part of this Act (and the rules under section 36), and

(ii) the Local Government Act 1972 [or Part III of the Local Government Act 1985],

as appear to the High Court, or, as the case may be, the district council, necessary or expedient for carrying the order into effect;

(b) by a district council under subsection (4) above with respect to an election of parish or community councillors may modify the provisions of—

(i) this Act (and the rules with respect to such elections under section 36); and

(ii) any other enactment relating to such elections.

(7) In the case of a common parish council under which are grouped, by virtue of section 11(5) of the Local Government Act 1972 (grouping of parishes), parishes situated in different districts, references in subsections (4) and (6) above to the district council shall be construed as references to the council of the district in which there is the greater number of local government electors for the parishes in the group.

(8) ...

(9) If a municipal election in a London borough is not held on the appointed day or within the appointed time or becomes void, the municipal corporation shall not thereby be dissolved or be disabled from acting.

NOTES

Sub-ss (1), (2)–(4), (7), (9) contain provisions formerly in the Local Government Act 1972, s 44(1)–(4), (6), (8), respectively. Sub-s (5) contains provisions formerly in the Representation of the People Act 1949, s 36(2), as partly repealed by the London Government Act 1963, s 93(1), Sch 18, Pt I, as amended by s 45(1) of, and Sch 6, para 10(1) to, the 1972 Act, and by the Local Authorities etc (Miscellaneous Provisions) (No 2) Order 1974, SI 1974/595, art 3(7). Sub-s (6) contains provisions formerly in s 36(4) of the 1949 Act as substituted by s 45(1) of, and Sch 6, para 10(2) to, the 1972 Act, and in s 44(5) of the 1972 Act.

The words omitted from sub-s (1) were repealed by the Local Government Act 1985, s 102(2), Sch 17, as from 1 April 1986 ("the abolition date" within the meaning of s 1(2) of that Act, Vol 25, title Local Government). Sub-s (1A) and the words in square brackets in sub-s (2), (6)(a)(ii) were inserted by s 19 of, and Sch 9, Pt I, para 1(5) to, that Act as from 1 September 1985 (see the Local Government Act 1985 (New Authorities) (Appointed Days) Order 1985, SI 1985/1283).

Sub-s (8) was repealed by the Representation of the People Act 1985, ss 24, 28(1), Sch 4, para 8, Sch 5, as from 1 October 1985.

Prospective amendment. The words "35 days" are substituted for the words "42 days" in sub-s (1) above by the Representation of the People Act 1985, s 19(2) post, as from a day to be appointed under s 29(2) of that Act.

Sub-s (1): England; Wales. See the note to s 4 ante.

Election of a councillor for a local government area. See the note "Elections of councillors of the county; the district; parishes or communities; London borough councillors" to s 35 ante.

Returning officer. As to this officer, see s 35 ante.

42 days . . . beginning with, etc. As stated in sub-s (1) above this is to be computed according to s 40 post (but note the prospective amendment). See also the note "Twelve months beginning with, etc" to s 4 ante.

Sub-s (1A): Inner London Education Authority. See the note to s 31 ante.

Sub-s (2): High Court. Ie Her Majesty's High Court of Justice in England; see the Interpretation Act 1978, s 5, Sch 1, Vol 41, title Statutes. For the constitution of the court, see the Supreme Court Act 1981, s 4, Vol 11, title Courts, and as to its divisions, see ss 5 and 7 of that Act.

As to the exercise of the jurisdiction of the High Court under the Representation of the People Acts, see RSC Ord 94, r 5.

Sub-s (3): High Court may order, etc. See *Re Stratford on Avon Corpn* (1886) 2 TLR 431 (costs of mandamus to hold election ordered to be paid by corporation).

Sub-s (4): Ordinary election of parish or community councillors. See the note to s 36 ante.

District council. See the note "Council of every district" to s 8 ante. Note also sub-s (7) above.

Sub-s (5): Where an election is ordered, etc. This includes a local government election held after a poll has been countermanded or abandoned by the returning officer on the death of a candidate; see s 38(2) ante.

Sub-s (6): This Part of this Act. Ie Pt I (ss 1–66).

Sub-s (9): London borough. See the note to s 8 ante.

Insufficient nominations. In the case of there being an insufficient number of persons who are or remain validly nominated to fill the vacancies in respect of which an ordinary election of parish or community councillors in England and Wales is held, the district may exercise the powers conferred by sub-s (4) above in relation to any vacancies not filled and sub-s (1) does not apply; see the Representation of the People Act 1985, s 21(2)(b), (c) post, as from a day to be appointed under s 29(2) of that Act. Note also that sub-s (7) above applies for the purposes of those provisions.

Supplementary provision. Note s 40 post, which makes provision in the event of a day on which anything is required to be done by this section falling on a Sunday, etc.

Definitions. For "election", "elector" and "proper officer", see s 202(1) post; for "local government area", see s 203(1) post.

Local Government Act 1972; Local Government Act 1985, Part III. See Vol 25, title Local Government.

---

40 Timing as to local elections in England and Wales

(1) When the day on which anything is required to be done by section 37 or section 39 above is a *Sunday, day of the Christmas break, of the Easter break or of a bank holiday*

break or a day appointed for public thanksgiving or mourning, the requirement shall be deemed to relate to the first day thereafter which is not one of the days specified above.

In this subsection—

"bank holiday break" means any bank holiday not included in the Christmas break or the Easter break and the period beginning with the last week day before that bank holiday and ending with the next week day which is not a bank holiday;

"Christmas break" means the period beginning with the last day before Christmas Day and ending with the first week day after Christmas Day which is not a bank holiday;

"Easter break" means the period beginning with the Thursday before and ending with the Tuesday after Easter day.

(2) Where under subsection (1) above the day of election is postponed, the day to which it is postponed shall be treated for the purposes of this Act [the Local Government Act 1972 and Part III of the Local Government Act 1985] as the day of election.

(3) In computing any period of time for the purpose of any rules under section 36 above or for the purposes of section 39 any day specified in subsection (1) shall be disregarded; but where between the giving of a notice of election and the completion of the poll a day is declared to be a bank holiday or day of public thanksgiving or mourning, the foregoing provision, so far as it relates to any such rules, shall not operate to invalidate any act which would have been valid apart from that provision.

This subsection, so far as it relates to any such rules, has effect subject to the provisions of those rules.

NOTES

Sub-s (1) contains provisions formerly in the Local Government Act 1972, ss 243(1), (2), 270(1). Sub-s (2) contains provisions formerly in s 243(3) of the 1972 Act. Sub-s (3) contains provisions formerly in s 243(4), (5) of the 1972 Act.

The words in square brackets in sub-s (2) were substituted by the Local Government Act 1985, s 19, Sch 9, Pt I, para 1(6), as from 1 September 1985 (see the Local Government Act 1985 (New Authorities) (Appointed Days) Order 1985, SI 1985/1283).

Prospective amendment. The following amendments are made to sub-s (1) above by the Representation of the People Act 1985 post, as from a day or days to be appointed under s 29(2) of that Act: after the words "section 39 above", the words "or section 16 of the Representation of the People Act 1985" are inserted by s 16(2) of that Act; the words "Saturday, Sunday, Christmas Eve, Christmas Day, Maundy Thursday, Good Friday, bank holiday" are substituted for the first set of words in italics by s 19(1)(a) of that Act; and the second set of words in italics are repealed by ss 19(1)(b), 28(1) of, and Sch 5 to, that Act.

Bank holiday. As to bank holidays, see the Banking and Financial Dealings Act 1971, s 1, Sch 1, Vol 45, title Time.

First day thereafter. For a case in point, see *Re Counter's Petition, Buckingham v Counter* [1938] 2 KB 90, [1938] 1 All ER 186 (service on the day after Whit Monday of petition alleging illegal practice at election).

For the purposes of section 39. Sub-s (3) also applies for the purposes of the Representation of the People Act 1985, s 21(2) post; see s 21(3) of that Act, as from a day to be appointed under s 29(2) of that Act.

Local Government Act 1972; Local Government Act 1985, Part III. See Vol 25, title Local Government.

41–45 *(Apply to Scotland only; s 44 is repealed by the Representation of the People Act 1985, ss 24, 28(1), Sch 4, para 9, Sch 5 post, as from a day to be appointed under s 29(2) of that Act.)*

Supplemental provisions as to local government elections

46 Further provision as to local election voting

(1) At a local government election for any electoral area no person shall as an elector and no person shall as proxy for any one elector—

(*a*) give more than one vote for any one candidate; or

(*b*) give more votes in all than the total number of councillors to be elected for the electoral area.

(2) No person is subject to any incapacity to vote at a local government election by reason of his being or acting as returning officer at that election.

NOTES

This section contains provisions formerly in the Representation of the People Act 1949, s 33.

Proxy. As to the appointment and voting of proxies at local government elections, see s 34 ante. That section is repealed by the Representation of the People Act 1985, s 28(1), Sch 5 post, as from a day to be appointed under s 29(2) of that Act. New provision is made, as from that date, as to proxies, see ss 8, 9 of that Act.

Give more votes in all than the total number of councillors to be elected. By the Local Elections (Principal Areas) Rules 1973, SI 1973/79, r 3(1), Sch 2, r 43(1) (as amended in the case of r 3(1) by SI 1983/1154), and the Local Elections (Parishes and Communities) Rules 1973, SI 1973/1910, r 3, Sch 1, r 41(1) (as amended in the case of r 3 by SI 1983/1153) (all made or having effect under s 36 ante), any ballot paper on which votes are given for more candidates than the voter is entitled to vote for is void and is not to be counted.

Returning officer. As to this officer, see s 35 ante.

Ward elections in the City of London. This section applies; see the City of London (Various Powers) Act 1957, s 8(1), Vol 26, title London.

Definitions. For "elector" and "vote", see s 202(1) post; for "electoral area" and "local government election", see s 203(1) post.

47 Loan of equipment for local elections

(1) Any ballot boxes, fittings and compartments provided for parliamentary elections out of moneys provided by Parliament, may, on request, be lent to the returning officer at a local government election on such terms and conditions as the Treasury may determine.

(2) Any ballot boxes, fittings and compartments provided by or belonging to—

(*a*) a local authority within the meaning of the Local Government Act 1972, or

(*b*) (*applies to Scotland only*),

as the case may be, shall, on request, and if not required for immediate use by that authority, be lent to the returning officer at an election held under those Acts [or Part III of the Local Government Act 1985] on such terms and conditions as may be agreed.

NOTES

Sub-s (1) contains provisions formerly in the Representation of the People Act 1949, s 35(1). Sub-s (2) contains provisions formerly in s 35(2) of the 1949 Act, as construed in accordance with the Interpretation Act 1978, s 17(2)(*a*) 41, title Statutes.

The words in square brackets were inserted by the Local Government Act 1985, s 19, Sch 9, Pt I, para 1(7), as from 1 September 1985 (see the Local Government Act 1985 (New Authorities) (Appointed Days) Order 1985, SI 1985/1283).

Parliamentary elections. See the note "Parliamentary election" to s 1 ante.

Returning officer. As to this officer, see s 35 ante.

Local government election. For meaning, see s 203(1) post.

Treasury. See the note to s 29 ante.

Local Government Act 1972. For the meaning of "local authority" in that Act, see s 270(1) thereof, Vol 25, title Local Government.

Local Government Act 1985, Part III. See Vol 25, title Local Government.

48 Validity of local elections, and legal costs

(1) No local government election shall be declared invalid by reason of any act or omission of the returning officer or any other person in breach of his official duty in connection with the election or otherwise of rules under section 36 or section 42 above if it appears to the tribunal having cognizance of the question that—

(a) the election was so conducted as to be substantially in accordance with the law as to elections; and

(b) the act or omission did not affect its result.

(2) A local government election, unless questioned by an election petition within the period fixed by law for those proceedings, shall be deemed to have been to all intents a good and valid election.

(3) The council which is required to pay the expenses properly incurred by a returning officer in relation to any local government election may treat those expenses as including all costs properly incurred by the returning officer in connection with or in contemplation of any legal proceedings arising out of the election (including any criminal proceedings against the returning officer), whether or not the proceedings are in fact instituted.

(4) *(Applies to Scotland only.)*

NOTES

Sub-ss (1), (2) contain provisions formerly in the Representation of the People Act 1949, s 37(1), (2). Sub-s (3) contains provisions formerly in the Representation of the People Act 1969, s 19(1).

No local government election shall be declared invalid, etc. Sub-s (1) above corresponds to s 23(3) ante, which governs parliamentary elections, and cases relevant to the interpretation of that subsection may be relevant to the interpretation of this subsection; see, further, the note "No parliamentary election shall be declared invalid, etc" to that section.

Tribunal having cognizance. Ie an election court constituted under s 130 post, or the High Court where a case is stated under s 146 post.

Returning officer. As to this officer, see s 35 ante.

Election petition. This is the method of questioning a local government election; see ss 127 et seq post.

Period fixed by law. As to the time within which an election petition may be presented, see s 129 post.

Application to other local elections. Sub-ss (1), (2) above have effect as if any reference in them to a local government election included a reference to any other election under the Local Government Act 1972 or the Local Government Act 1985, Pt III, both Vol 25, title Local Government; see s 187(2) post.

Definitions. For "election" and "election petition", see s 202(1) post; for "local government election", see s 203(1) post.

Supplemental provisions as to parliamentary and local government elections

49 Effect of registers

(1) The register of parliamentary electors shall for the purposes of this Part of this Act be conclusive on the following questions—

(a) whether or not a person registered in it was on the qualifying date resident at the address shown;

(b) whether or not that address is in any constituency or any particular part of a constituency;

(c) whether or not a person registered as an elector in a constitutuency in Northern Ireland was during the whole of the period of three months ending on the qualifying date resident in Northern Ireland;

(d) . . .

(2) The register of local government electors shall for the purposes of this Part be conclusive on the following questions—

(a) whether or not a person registered in it was on the qualifying date resident at the address shown;

(b) whether or not that address is in any local government area or any particular part of a local government area;

(c) . . .

(3) The relevant special lists prepared under this Act for a parliamentary or local government election shall, for the purposes of this Part, be conclusive on the following questions—

(a) whether or not a person's right to vote at the election is exercisable by post;

(b) whether or not there is in force an appointment of a proxy to vote for any person and (if so) who is appointed.

(4) Any entry in the register of parliamentary or local government electors, if it gives a date as that on which the person named will attain voting age, shall for any purpose of this Part relating to him as elector be conclusive that until the date given in the entry he is not of voting age nor entitled to be treated as an elector except for the purposes of an election at which the day fixed for the poll is that or a later date.

(5) A person registered as a parliamentary or local government elector, or entered in the list of proxies, shall not be excluded from voting on the ground—

(*a*) that he is not a Commonwealth citizen or citizen of the Republic of Ireland, or

(*b*) that he is not of voting age, or

(*c*) that he is otherwise subject to any legal incapacity to vote,

or that on the qualifying date or the date of his appointment, as the case may be—

(i) he was not a Commonwealth citizen or citizen of the Republic of Ireland, or

(ii) he was otherwise subject to any legal incapacity to vote,

but this provision shall not prevent the rejection of the vote on a scrutiny or affect his liability to any penalty for voting.

NOTES

Sub-ss (1), (3) contain provisions formerly in the Representation of the People Act 1949, s 39(1), (3). Sub-s (2) contains provisions formerly in s 39(2) of the 1949 Act as amended and as partly repealed by the Representation of the People Act 1969, s 24(1), (4), Sch 2, para 11(1), Sch 3, Pt II. Sub-s (4) contains provisions formerly in s 39(3A) of the 1949 Act, as inserted by s 24(1) of, and Sch 2, para 11(2) to, the 1969 Act. Sub-s (5) contains provisions formerly in s 39(4) of the 1949 Act, as amended and as partly repealed by s 24(1), (4) of, and Sch 2, para 11(3) to, the 1969 Act, as affected by the British Nationality Act 1981, s 51(1).

Sub-ss (1)(*d*), (2)(*c*) were repealed by the Representation of the People Act 1985, ss 24, 28(1), Sch 4, para 10, Sch 5, as from 1 October 1985.

Prospective amendment. The words "or, in the case of a person registered as a parliamentary elector in pursuance of an overseas elector's declaration, a British citizen" are inserted after the word "Ireland" in sub-s (5)(*a*)(i) above by the Representation of the People Act 1985, s 4(4) post, and sub-s (3) is repealed by s 28(1) of, and Sch 5 to, that Act, as from a day or days to be appointed under s 29(2) of that Act.

Sub-s (1): Register of parliamentary electors. See s 9 ante, and the note "Register" thereto.

This Part of this Act. Ie Pt I (ss 1–66).

Conclusive. Once a register has become conclusive as to any matters specified in sub-ss (1) and (2) above (subject to any right of appeal under s 56 post), it is not permissible to take objection to it before any court, tribunal or person on the ground that it is not correct (whether in reality it be true or false); but as to matters concerning which it is not conclusive, objection may be taken. See, further, *New Sarum Case, Ryder v Hamilton* (1869) LR 4 CP 559, 38 LJCP 260; *Petersfield Case, Stowe v Jolliffe* (1874) LR 9 CP 734, 43 LJCP 173; *Worcester Borough Case* (1880) 3 O'M & H 184; and *Pembroke Boroughs Case* (1901) 5 O'M & H 135.

Qualifying date. For this date, see s 4 ante.

Resident. See the note to s 1 ante, and see also s 5 ante, and the notes thereto.

Constituency; months. See the notes to s 1 ante.

Sub-s (2): Register of local government electors. See s 9 ante and the note "Register" thereto.

Sub-s (3): Special lists. For these lists, see Sch 1, r 27 post, and the Local Elections (Principal Areas) Rules 1973, SI 1973/79, Sch 2, r 23.

Parliamentary . . . election. See the note to s 1 ante.

Right to vote . . . by post. For the right to a postal vote, see ss 19(4), 22(2) (for parliamentary elections) and ss 32(4), (8), 34(4) post (for local government elections other than those for parish or community councillors).

Appointment of a proxy. As to the appointment of proxies at parliamentary and local government elections, see ss 21 and 34 ante, respectively.

Sub-s (5): List of proxies. This list is to be prepared under Sch 1, r 27, post, or the Local Elections (Principal Areas) Rules 1973, SI 1973/79, Sch 2, r 23; see also the Representation of the People Regulations

1983, SI 1983/435, reg 45, and the Representation of the People (Northern Ireland) Regulations 1983, SI 1983/436, reg 30. Note, however, that Sch 1, r 27 is repealed by the Representation of the People Act 1985, s 28(1), Sch 5 post, as from a day to be appointed under s 29(2) of that Act, and it is thought that the rules and regulations mentioned above will also be changed. New provision is made as to proxies by ss 8, 9 of the 1985 Act.

Commonwealth citizen; Republic of Ireland. See the notes to s 1 ante.

Scrutiny. This is an investigation by an election court into the legality of votes cast in order to see which candidate has a legal majority. A scrutiny must be distinguished from a count or re-count of votes made by the returning officer under Sch 1, r 45 or 46 post, the Local Elections (Principal Areas) Rules 1973, SI 1973/79, Sch 2, r 41 or 42, or the Local Elections (Parishes and Communities) Rules 1973, SI 1973/1910, Sch 1, r 39 or 40. As to scrutiny generally, see 15 Halsbury's Laws (4th edn) paras 924 et seq.

Penalty for voting. For offences and penalties under this Act in respect of voting, see ss 60 et seq, 168 et seq post.

European Assembly elections. This section and s 50 post, are applied to such elections by the European Assembly Elections Regulations 1984, SI 1984/137, reg 3(1), Sch 1. See further the Introductory Note to this Act.

As to provisions relating to such elections in Northern Ireland, see the Introductory Note to this Act.

Definitions. For "voting age", see s 1(1)(c) or 2(1)(c) ante; for "elector", "legal incapacity", "service voter" and "vote", see s 202(1) post; for "local government area" and "local government election", see s 203(1) post.

50 Effect of misdescription

No misnomer or inaccurate description of any person or place named—

    (a) in the register of parliamentary electors, or

    (b) in the register of local government electors, or

    (c) in any list, record, proxy paper, nomination paper, ballot paper, notice or other document required for the purposes of this Part of this Act, and the parliamentary elections rules,

affects the full operation of the document with respect to that person or place in any case where the description of the person or place is such as to be commonly understood.

NOTES

This section contains provisions formerly in the Representation of the People Act 1949, s 39(5).

Register of parliamentary electors; register of local electors. See s 9 ante and the note "Register" thereto.

List. See, in particular s 10(b) ante (electors lists) and Sch 1, r 27 post (absent voters lists, lists of proxies and lists of postal proxies) (repealed by the Representation of the People Act 1985, s 28, Sch 5, as from a day to be appointed under s 29 of that Act).

Proxy paper. This is issued under s 21(5) ante, or under that subsection as applied by s 34(6) ante. Those provisions are repealed by the Representation of the People Act 1985, s 28(1), Sch 5 post, as from a day to be appointed under s 29(2) of that Act and new provision is made, as from that date, in relation to proxy papers, by s 8(8) of that Act post.

Nomination paper. For these papers, see Sch 1, rr 6, 7 post, the Local Elections (Principal Areas) Rules 1973, SI 1973/79, Sch 2, rr 5, 6, and the Local Elections (Parishes and Communities) Rules 1973, SI 1973/1910, Sch 1, rr 5, 6.

Ballot paper. As to ballot papers, see Sch 1, rr 19, 20, 24 post, the Local Elections (Principal Areas) Rules 1973, SI 1973/79 (as amended by SI 1976/2065 and SI 1983/1154), Sch 2, rr 15, 16, 20, and the Local Elections (Parishes and Communities) Rules 1973, SI 1973/1910 (as amended by SI 1976/2066), Sch 2, rr 15, 16.

This Part of this Act. Ie Pt I (ss 1–66).

European Assembly elections. See the note to s 49 ante.

Definitions. For "elector" and "parliamentary elections rules", see s 202(1) post.

51 (*Repealed by the Representation of the People Act 1985, ss 24, 28(1), Sch 4, para 11, Sch 5, as from 1 October 1985.*)

52 Discharge of registration duties

    (1) A registration officer shall comply with any general or special directions which may be given by the Secretary of State with respect to the arrangements to be made by the registration officer for carrying out his [functions under this Act].

(2) Any of the duties and powers of a registration officer may be performed and exercised by any deputy for the time being approved . . . by the council which appointed the registration officer, and the provisions of this Act apply to any such deputy so far as respects any duties or powers to be performed or exercised by him as they apply to the registration officer.

(3) In England and Wales, any acts authorised or required to be done by or with respect to the registration officer may, in the event of his incapacity to act or of a vacancy, be done by [or with respect to] the proper officer of the council by whom the registration officer was appointed.

[(4) It shall be the duty—

    (a) in England and Wales, of a district council or London borough council, and
    (b) (applies to Scotland only),

to assign such officers to assist the registration officer as may be required for carrying out his functions under this Act.

(5) Subsection (2) above does not apply in Northern Ireland but sections 14(5) and 14A(2) and (3) of the Electoral Law Act (Northern Ireland) 1962 (appointment of temporary deputy and delegation to assistants) shall have effect in relation to the Chief Electoral Officer for Northern Ireland in his capacity as registration officer.]

NOTES

Sub-ss (1), (2) contain provisions formerly in the Representation of the People Act 1949, s 41(1), (2). Sub-s (3) contains provisions formerly in s 41(4) of the 1949 Act, as amended by the Local Government Act 1972, s 45, Sch 6, para 1, and as partly repealed by the Local Government Reorganisation (Consequential Provisions) (Northern Ireland) Order 1973, SI 1973/2095, art 5(2), Sch 2.

The words in square brackets in sub-s (1) were substituted, the words omitted from sub-s (2) were repealed, the words in square brackets in sub-s (3) were inserted, and sub-ss (4), (5) were substituted by the Representation of the People Act 1985, ss 24, 28(1), Sch 4, para 12, Sch 5, as from 1 October 1985.

Secretary of State. Cf the note to s 4 ante. The Secretary of State here concerned is the Secretary of State for the Home Department.

England; Wales. See the note to s 4 ante.

District council. See the note "Council of every district" to s 8 ante.

London borough council. See the note "London borough" to s 8 ante.

Parliamentary elections. See the note "Parliamentary election" to s 1 ante.

European Assembly elections. This section is applied to such elections by the European Assembly Elections Regulations 1984, SI 1984/137, reg 3(1), Sch 1, subject to the omission of sub-ss (4) and (5). See further the Introductory Note to this Act.

As to provisions relating to such elections in Northern Ireland, see the Introductory Note to this Act.

Definitions. For "registration officer", see s 8(1) ante; for "proper officer", see s 202(1) post.

Electoral Law Act (Northern Ireland) 1962. 1962 c 14 (NI); not printed in this work.

53 Power to make regulations as to registration etc

(1) Provision may be made by regulations—

    (a) with respect to the form of the register of electors and of the electors lists or any special lists or records required by this Act in connection with the register or with any election;

    (b) with respect to the procedure to be followed in the preparation of the register, the electors lists and any such special lists or records as mentioned above, and with respect to the time, place and manner of their publication [(including provision for electors lists which have been published in the form of a draft register to take effect with any necessary amendments as the register and provision with respect to the time at which the register is to be treated as being published in such a case)]; and

    (c) generally with respect to any matters incidental to the provisions of this Act so far as those provisions relate to the registration of electors or to voting by post or proxy.

(2) ...

(3) Without prejudice to the generality of [subsection (1)] above, regulations made with respect to the matters mentioned in [that subsection] may contain any such provisions as are mentioned in Schedule 2 to this Act.

NOTES

This section contains provisions formerly in the Representation of the People Act 1949, s 42.

The words in square brackets in sub-s (1)(b) were inserted, sub-s (2) was repealed, and the words in square brackets in sub-s (3) were substituted, by the Representation of the People Act 1985, ss 24, 28(1), Sch 4, para 13, Sch 5, as from 1 October 1985.

Register of electors. See s 9 ante and the note "Register" thereto.

Electors lists. For the preparation and publication of electors lists, see s 10(b) ante.

Special lists. For these lists, see Sch 1, r 27 post (repealed by the Representation of the People Act 1985, s 28, Sch 5, as from a day to be appointed under s 29 of that Act), and the Local Elections (Principal Areas) Rules 1973, SI 1973/79, Sch 2, r 23.

Voting by post or proxy. For the main provisions relating to these matters, see ss 19–22, 32–34 ante. Those sections are repealed by the Representation of the People Act 1985, s 28(1), Sch 5 post, as from a day to be appointed under s 29(2). New provision is made as to absent votes, as from that date, by ss 6–9 of that Act.

Welsh Sunday polls. Regulations under this section may, so far as they relate to voting by proxy or by post or to matters connected therewith, make special provision in connection with polls under the Licensing Act 1964, s 66 (Sunday closing in Wales), Vol 24, title Licensing and Liquor Duties; see Sch 8, paras 5(1), to that Act, in the same title.

Definitions. For "election" and "elector", see s 202(1) post.

Regulations under this section. The Representation of the People Regulations 1983, SI 1983/435, and the Representation of the People (Northern Ireland) Regulations 1983, SI 1983/436 (both made partly under this section). In addition, by virtue of the Interpretation Act 1978, s 17(2)(b), Vol 41, title Statutes, the Elections (Welsh Forms) Regulations 1975, SI 1975/1329, as amended by SI 1977/106, SI 1979/434, SI 1980/1032 and SI 1981/63, have effect under this section and the Welsh Language Act 1967, s 2(2), Vol 41, title Statutes.

For general provisions as to the making of regulations, see s 201 post.

54 Payment of expenses of registration

(1) Any expenses properly incurred by a registration officer in the performance of his [functions under this Act] (in this Act referred to as "registration expenses") shall (except in Northern Ireland) be paid by the local authority by whom the registration officer was appointed.

(2) The registration expenses of the Chief Electoral Officer for Northern Ireland shall be paid out of moneys provided by Parliament.

(3) Any fees [paid to the registration officer under this Act]—

    (a) shall be accounted for by him and paid to the local authority by whom he was appointed;

    (b) in the case of the Chief Electoral Officer for Northern Ireland, shall be accounted for by him to the Secretary of State and paid into the Consolidated Fund.

(4) On the request of a registration officer for an advance on account of registration expenses—

    (a) the local authority by whom the registration officer was appointed may, if they think fit, make such an advance to him of such an amount and subject to such conditions as they may approve; or

    (b) in the case of the Chief Electoral Officer for Northern Ireland, the Secretary of State may, if he thinks fit, make such an advance to him of such an amount and subject to such conditions as the Secretary of State may approve.

(5) Any registration expenses or contributions to them paid by the Common Council shall be paid out of the general rate and any sums paid to the Common Council under this section shall be placed to the credit of that rate.

NOTES

Sub-s (1) contains provisions formerly in the Representation of the People Act 1949, s 43(1), as partly repealed by the Local Government Act 1958, s 67, Sch 9, Pt II, and as amended and partly repealed by the Local Government Act 1972, ss 45, 272(1), Sch 6, para 2, Sch 30. Sub-s (2) contains provisions formerly in s 43(2) of the 1949 Act, as amended by the Local Government Reorganisation (Consequential Provisions) (Northern Ireland) Order 1973, SI 1973/2095, art 2(1). Sub-s (3) contains provisions formerly in s 43(3) of the 1949 Act, as amended and partly repealed by the Local Government Act 1958, ss 62, 67, Sch 8, paras 31(2), 35, Sch 9, Pt II, and as affected by the Transfer of Functions (Northern Irish Registration Expenses) Order 1962, SI 1962/169, art 2(1), and as amended by s 45 of, and Sch 6, para 2 to, the 1972 Act, and partly repealed by art 5(2) of, and Sch 2 to, the 1973 Order. Sub-s (4) contains provisions formerly in s 43(5) of the 1949 Act, as affected by art 2(1) of the 1962 Order and amended by s 45 of, and Sch 6, para 2 to, the 1972 Act, and art 2(1) of the 1973 Order. Sub-s (5) contains provisions formerly in s 43(7) of the 1949 Act.

The words in square brackets in sub-ss (1), (3) were substituted by the Representation of the People Act 1985, s 24, Sch 4, para 14, as from 1 October 1985.

Sub-s (1): Expenses. As to the expenses incurred in connection with appeals, see s 56(5) post.

Sub-s (2): Chief Electoral Officer for Northern Ireland. By s 8(4) ante, this officer is the registration officer for each constituency in Northern Ireland.

Sub-s (3): Secretary of State. See the note to s 4 ante.

Consolidated Fund. See the note to s 29 ante.

European Assembly elections. This section is applied to such elections by the European Assembly Elections Regulations 1984, SI 1984/137, reg 3(1), Sch 1. See further the Introductory Note to this Act; and see also, as to the payment of expenses of registration pursuant to sub-s (2) above which are attributable to European Assembly elections, the European Assembly Elections Act 1978, s 7(2)(b) ante.

As to provisions relating to such elections in Northern Ireland, see the Introductory Note to this title.

Definitions. For "registration officer", see s 8(1) ante; for "the Common Council", see s 202(1) post; for "local authority", see s 203(1) post. Note as to "registration expenses", sub-s (1) above.

55 (*Repealed by the Representation of the People Act 1985, ss 24, 28(1), Sch 4, para 15, Sch 5, as from 1 October 1985.*)

56 Registration appeals: England and Wales

(1) An appeal lies to the county court—

(a) from any decision under this Act of the registration officer on any claim for registration or objection to a person's registration made to and considered by him,

(b) from any decision under this Act of the registration officer disallowing a person's application to *be treated as an absent voter* or to vote by post as proxy, in any case where the application is not made for a particular election only,

(c) . . .

(d) from any decision under this Act of the registration officer to make or not to make an alteration in a register as published,

but an appeal does not lie where the person desiring to appeal has not availed himself of a prescribed right to be heard by or make representations to the registration officer on the matter which is the subject of the appeal, or has not given the prescribed notice of appeal within the prescribed time.

(2) No appeal lies from the decision of the Court of Appeal on appeal from a decision of the county court under this section.

(3) An appeal to the county court or Court of Appeal by virtue of this section which is pending when notice of an election is given shall not prejudice the operation as respects the election of the decision appealed against, and anything done in pursuance of the

decision shall be as good as if no such appeal had been brought and shall not be affected by the decision of the appeal.

(4) Notice shall be sent to the registration officer in manner provided by rules of court of the decision of the county court or of the Court of Appeal on any appeal by virtue of this section, and the registration officer shall make such alterations in the electors lists or register as may be required to give effect to the decision.

[(4A) Where, as a result of the decision on an appeal, an alteration in the register is made under subsection (4) above on or before the last day on which nomination papers nominating candidates at an election may be delivered to the returning officer, subsection (3) above does not apply to that appeal as respects that election.]

(5) The registration officer shall undertake such duties in connection with appeals brought by virtue of this section as may be prescribed and shall on any such appeal be deemed to be a party to the proceedings, and the registration expenses payable to a registration officer shall include any expenses properly incurred by him by virtue of this subsection.

(6) ...

NOTES

Sub-s (1) contains provisions formerly in the Representation of the People Act 1949, s 45(1), as partly repealed by the Representation of the People Act 1969, s 24(4), Sch 3, Pt II, and as amended by the Representation of the People Act 1980, s 2(2). Sub-ss (2)–(4), (5) contain provision formerly in s 45(2)–(5) of the 1949 Act.

Sub-ss (1)(c), (6) were repealed by the Representation of the People Act 1985, ss 24, 28(1), Sch 4, para 16(a), Sch 5, as from 1 October 1985. Sub-s (4A) was inserted by s 24 of, and Sch 4, para 16(b) to, that Act, as from that date.

Prospective amendment. For the words in italics in sub-s (1)(b) above, the words "vote by proxy or by post as elector" are substituted by the Representation of the People Act 1985, s 11, Sch 2, Pt I, para 1 post, as from a day to be appointed under s 29(2) of that Act.

Sub-s (1): An appeal lies, etc. This section creates rights of appeal in the cases specified in sub-s (1) above; it does not create a general right of appeal. Apart from this section, the High Court might in appropriate cases issue an order of mandamus to a registration officer. For procedural provisions, see CCR Ord 45, rr 2, 3.

An appeal cannot be treated as a test case binding on persons who are not parties to the appeal unless the procedure prescribed by CCR Ord 45, r 3, of giving notice to interested parties is followed (*R v Judge Hurst, ex p Smith* [1960] 2 QB 133, [1960] 2 All ER 385).

An appeal under this section lies at the instance of the party affected. In *Hampshire Parliamentary County Registration Officer v Ainslie* [1933] All ER Rep 847, (1933) 148 LT 496, the Court of Appeal set aside as made without jurisdiction an order made on appeal brought by a political agent. See also *R v Judge Hurst, ex p Smith* supra.

County court. See the note to s 30 ante.

Claim ... or objection. As to the determination of claims and objections of the kinds mentioned in sub-s (1)(a) above, see s 10(c) ante.

Vote by post as proxy. Applications to vote by post as proxy are made under s 22(2) or 34(4) ante. Those provisions are repealed by the Representation of the People Act 1985, s 28(1), Sch 5 post, as from a day to be appointed under s 29(2) of that Act. New provision is made as to voting by post or proxy, as from that date, by ss 6–9 of that Act.

Register. See s 9 ante and the note "Register" thereto.

Alteration in a register as published. As to the correction of a published register of electors, see s 11 ante, the Representation of the People Regulations 1983, SI 1983/435, regs 34–37, and the Representation of the People (Northern Ireland) Regulations 1983, SI 1983/436, reg 22.

Prescribed right to be heard ... or make representations. This refers to the right conferred by the Representation of the People Regulations 1983, SI 1983/435, reg 23; see also the Representation of the People (Northern Ireland) Regulations 1983, SI 1983/436, reg 14.

Prescribed notice of appeal within the prescribed time. By the Representation of the People Regulations 1983, SI 1983/435, reg 68(1), or the Representation of the People (Northern Ireland) Regulations 1983, SI 1983/436, reg 53(1), notice of appeal must be given to the registration officer and to the opposite party (if any) when the decision is given, or within 14 days thereafter, specifying the grounds of appeal. See also SI 1983/435, reg 68(2), (3), SI 1983/436, reg 53(2), (3), and CCR Ord 45, r 2(1).

Sub-s (2): No appeal lies from the decision of the Court of Appeal, etc. Under the County Courts Act 1984, s 77, Vol 11, title County Courts, there is a right of appeal to the Court of Appeal from the determination of the judge of a county court.

See further, as to such appeals in the case of decisions of the county court under this section, 15 Halsbury's Laws (4th edn) paras 472 et seq.

Certiorari will lie to remove into the High Court and to quash a decision of the judge of a county court if he acted without jurisdiction; see *R v Judge Hurst, ex p Smith* [1960] 2 QB 133, [1960] 2 All ER 385.

As to the constitution of the Court of Appeal, see the Supreme Court Act 1981, ss 2, 3, Vol 11, title Courts.

Sub-s (3): Notice of an election. As to this notice, see Sch 1, r 5 post, the Local Elections (Principal Areas) Rules 1973, SI 1973/79, Sch 2, r 4, and the Local Elections (Parishes and Communities) Rules 1973, SI 1973/1910, Sch 1, r 4.

Sub-s (4): Rules of court. The rules of court governing registration appeals are CCR Ord 45, rr 2, 3, and RSC Ord 59, r 19(6). See further *R v Judge Hurst, ex p Smith*, cited in the note "An appeal lies, etc" above.

Electors lists. As to the preparation and publication of electors lists, see s 10(*b*) ante.

Sub-s (5): Such duties . . . as may be prescribed. For the duties referred to in sub-s (5) above, see the Representation of the People Regulations 1983, SI 1983/435, reg 68(2), (3), and the Representation of the People (Northern Ireland) Regulations 1983, SI 1983/436, reg 53(2), (3); and see also CCR Ord 45, r 2(1).

Registration expenses. As to registration expenses generally, see s 54 ante.

Definitions. For "registration officer", see s 8(1) ante; for "election", "elector" and "prescribed", see s 202(1) post; for "registration expenses", see s 54(1) ante.

Northern Ireland. For the application of this section to Northern Ireland, see s 58 post.

57 (*Applies to Scotland only.*)

58 Registration appeals: Northern Ireland

Section 56 above, except [subsection (2) and the words from the beginning to "and" in subsection (4)], applies to Northern Ireland, and—

(*a*) any decision of a county court upon a point of law under section 56(1) shall be appealable in the same way and subject to the same provisions as a corresponding decision under the law relating to the registration of [local electors within the meaning of section 130 of the Electoral Law Act (Northern Ireland) 1962] and the reference in subsection (3) of that section to the Court of Appeal shall be construed accordingly; and

(*b*) any power to make rules of court with respect to appeals under that law applies to appeals under this section.

NOTES

This section, as originally enacted, contained provisions formerly in the Representation of the People Act 1949, s 45(11), as amended by the Northern Ireland (Modification of Enactments—No 1) Order 1973, SI 1973/2163, art 14(1), Sch 5, para 15.

The words in both pairs of square brackets were substituted by the Representation of the People Act 1985, s 24, Sch 4, para 17, as from 1 October 1985.

Electoral Law Act (Northern Ireland) 1962. 1962 c 14 (NI); not printed in this work.

59 Supplemental provisions as to members of forces and service voters

(1) In this Part of this Act, the expression "member of the forces"—

(*a*) means a person serving on full pay as a member of any of the naval, military or air forces of the Crown raised in the United Kingdom; but

(*b*) does not include a person serving only as a member of a reserve or auxiliary force except in so far as regulations provide that it shall include persons so serving during a period of emergency.

(2) Where a person—

(*a*) is not a member of the forces as defined by subsection (1) above, but

(*b*) is, in the performance of his duty as a member of any of Her Majesty's reserve or auxiliary forces, absent on the qualifying date from an address at which he has been residing,

any question arising under section 5(2) above whether his residence at that address has been interrupted on that date by his absence in the performance of that duty shall be determined as if the performance of it did not prevent his resuming actual residence at any time after that date.

(3) Arrangements shall be made by the appropriate government department for securing that (so far as circumstances permit) every person having a service qualification by virtue of paragraph (*a*) or (*b*) of section 14(1) above shall—

(*a*) have an effective opportunity of exercising from time to time as occasion may require the rights conferred on him by this Act in relation to the making and cancellation of service declarations and of appointments of a proxy, and in relation to voting by post; and

(*b*) receive such instructions as to the effect of this Act and any regulations made under it, and such other assistance, as may be reasonably sufficient in connection with the exercise by him and any wife of his or, as the case may be, by her and any husband of hers, of any rights conferred on them as mentioned above.

In this subsection "the appropriate government department" means, in relation to members of the forces, the Ministry of Defence, and in relation to any other person means the government department under which he is employed in the employment giving the service qualification.

(4) In relation to persons having a service qualification by virtue of paragraph (*c*) of section 14(1), the British Council shall be under a corresponding obligation to that imposed by subsection (3) above on the appropriate government department.

NOTES

Sub-ss (1), (2) contain provisions formerly in the Representation of the People Act 1949, s 46(1), (3). Sub-s (3) contains provisions formerly in s 46(4), (5) of the 1949 Act, as amended and as partly repealed, in the case of s 46(4), by the Representation of the People Act 1969, s 24(1), (4), Sch 2, para 12(1), Sch 3, Pt II, and as affected, in the case of s 46(5), by the Defence (Transfer of Functions) Act 1964, s 3(2). Sub-s (4) contains provisions formerly in s 46(4A) of the 1949 Act, as inserted by s 24(1) of, and Sch 2, para 12(2) to, the 1969 Act.

This Part of this Act. Ie Pt I (ss 1–66).

United Kingdom. See the note to s 6 ante.

Qualifying date. For this date, see s 4 ante.

Residing. See the note "Resident" to s 1 ante, and see also s 5 ante, and the notes thereto.

Making and cancellation of service declarations. As to the making and cancellation of such declarations, see s 15 ante.

Appointments of a proxy. See ss 21 and 34 ante. Those sections are repealed by the Representation of the People Act 1985, s 28(1), Sch 5 post, as from a day to be appointed under s 29(2) of that Act, and new provision is made, as from that date, as to absent voters by ss 6–9 of that Act.

Voting by post. For the right of service voters to vote by post, see ss 19(1)(*a*), (4), 32(1)(*a*), (4) ante. Those sections are repealed by the Representation of the People Act 1985, s 28(1), Sch 5 post, as from a day to be appointed under s 29(2) of that Act, and new provisions is made, as from that date, as to absent voters by ss 6–9 of that Act.

Employment giving the service qualification. Ie the employment mentioned in s 14(1)(*b*) ante; see also the note "Prescribed class or description" to s 14 ante.

Ward elections in the City of London. This section applies; see the City of London (Various Powers) Act 1957, s 8(1), Vol 26, title London.

Regulations under this section. Up to 1 August 1985 no regulations had been made under sub-s (1)(*b*) above and none have effect thereunder by virtue of the Interpretation Act 1978, s 17(2)(*b*), Vol 41, title Statutes.

For general provisions as to the making of regulations, see s 201 post.

Offences

60 Personation

(1) A person shall be guilty of a corrupt practice if he commits, or aids, abets, counsels or procures the commission of, the offence of personation.

(2) A person shall be deemed to be guilty of personation at a parliamentary or local government election if he—

(a) votes in person or by post as some other person, whether as an elector or as proxy, and whether that other person is living or dead or is a fictitious person; or

(b) votes in person or by post as proxy—

(i) for a person whom he knows or has reasonable grounds for supposing to be dead or to be a fictitious person; or

(ii) when he knows or has reasonable grounds for supposing that his appointment as proxy is no longer in force.

(3) For the purposes of this section, a person who has applied for a ballot paper for the purpose of voting in person or who has marked, whether validly or not, and returned a ballot paper issued for the purpose of voting by post, shall be deemed to have voted.

NOTES

This section contains provisions formerly in the Representation of the People Act 1949, s 47.

Person shall be guilty, etc. Mens rea must be proved in order to establish an offence, so that a person voting innocently by mistake may commit no offence though the person instigating him to do so will be guilty if he knowingly instigates him to do so; see *Tower Hamlets, Stepney Division Case, Isaacson v Durant* (1886) 54 LT 684, 2 TLR 559.

This section has no application to the case of a person who applies for a ballot paper in a name other than his original name or the name by which he is usually known, if the name in which he applies is the name on the register which was put there for the purpose of giving him a vote; there is no offence committed and his vote is valid (*R v Fox* (1887) 16 Cox CC 166). In *Tower Hamlets, Stepney Division Case, Isaacson v Durant* (1886) supra, a voter voted twice in different divisions of the borough; but in the absence of proof of corrupt intention on his part, the court held that there was no personation involved and that the first vote was valid and the second void.

A House of Commons committee has held payment of money to a man to personate a voter to be bribery (*Lisburn Case* (1863) Wolf & B 221 at 225). Where personation constitutes bribery an election might be void for general corruption under s 164 post, but personation is not mentioned in that section as a ground for avoidance of an election irrespective of liability therefor on the part of the candidate or his agents.

On an election petition, if the person whose name is on the register has not voted, and a vote is shown to have been cast in his name, the vote will be struck off without further inquiry (*Finsbury Central Division Case, Penton v Naoroji* (1892) 4 O'M & H 171).

Corrupt practice. As to prosecutions for corrupt practices, see s 168 post; as to conviction of an illegal practice on a charge of corrupt practice, see s 170 post; as to the incapacities which are imposed on conviction of a corrupt practice on indictment, see s 173 post; as to mitigation and remission of incapacities, see s 174 post; and as to offences by associations, see s 179 post. For the consequences of a report by an election court that a candidate or other person is guilty of a corrupt practice, see ss 158–160 post. See also the note "Related provisions" to s 168 post.

Aids, abets, counsels or procures. As to the difference between "aid and abet" and "counsel and procure", see *Ferguson v Weaving* [1951] 1 KB 814 at 819, [1951] 1 All ER 412 at 413.

Inaction, when positive conduct to prevent the commission of the offence is a duty in the circumstances, may amount to aiding and abetting; see *Du Cros v Lambourne* [1907] 1 KB 40; *Rubie v Faulkner* [1940] 1 KB 571, [1940] 1 All ER 285; and *Tuck v Robson* [1970] 1 All ER 1171, [1970] 1 WLR 741. Yet, mere negligence in the performance of a duty, in consequence of which the opportunity for committing the offence is created, does not of itself constitute aiding and abetting; see *Callow v Tillstone* (1900) 83 LT 411. To be convicted as an aider and abettor a person must know all the circumstances which constitute the offence, but whether he realises that these circumstances constitute an offence is immaterial; see *Ackroyd's Air Travel Ltd v DPP* [1950] 1 All ER 933 at 936, 48 LGR 398; and *Thomas v Lindop* [1950] 1 All ER 966 at 968, per Lord Goddard CJ, [1950] WN 227.

"Procure" has been defined as "obtain by care and effort" and, it has been said, "can be more simply paraphrased as 'see to it'"; see *Re Royal Victoria Pavilion, Ramsgate, Whelan v FTS (Great Britain) Ltd* [1961] Ch 581 at 587, [1961] 3 All ER 83 at 86. Similarly it has been held that "to procure means to produce by endeavour. You procure a thing by setting out to see that it happens and taking the appropriate steps to produce that happening"; see *A-G's Reference (No 1 of 1975)* [1975] QB 773 at 779, [1975] 2 All ER 684 at 686, CA; applied in *R v Broadfoot* [1976] 3 All ER 753, [1977] Crim LR 690, CA. Where a person performs some act which results in another person unwittingly committing an offence which is an absolute offence, the first person may be said to have procured the commission of the offence by the other even though there was no communication between them before the offence was committed; see *A-G's Reference (No 1 of 1975)* supra.

See, further, on secondary parties to crimes, 11 Halsbury's Laws (4th edn) paras 44 et seq.

Parliamentary election. See the note to s 1 ante.

Votes in person or by post . . . as an elector or as proxy. As to the manner of voting at parliamentary elections, see ss 19–22 ante, and as to voting at local government elections, see ss 32–34 ante. Those sections are repealed by the Representation of the People Act 1985, s 28(1), Sch 5 post, as from a day to be appointed under s 29(2) of that Act, and new provision is made, as from that date, as to absent voters by ss 6–9 of that Act.

Knows. Knowledge is an essential ingredient of the offence and must be proved by the prosecution; see, in particular, *Gaumont British Distributors Ltd v Henry* [1939] 2 KB 711, [1939] 2 All ER 808.

Knowledge includes the state of mind of a person who shuts his eyes to the obvious; see *James & Son Ltd v Smee* [1955] 1 QB 78 at 91, [1954] 3 All ER 273 at 278 per Parker J. Moreover, there is authority for saying that where a person deliberately refrains from making inquiries the results of which he might not care to have, this constitutes in law actual knowledge of the facts in question; see *Knox v Boyd* 1941 JC 82 at 86, and *Taylor's Central Garages (Exeter) Ltd v Roper* (1951) 115 JP 445 at 449, 450 per Devlin J, [1951] WN 383; and see also, in particular, *Mallon v Allon* [1964] 1 QB 385 at 394, [1963] 3 All ER 843 at 847. Yet mere neglect to ascertain what could have been found out by making reasonable inquiries is not tantamount to knowledge; *Taylor's Central Garages (Exeter) Ltd v Roper* supra per Devlin J, and cf *London Computator Ltd v Seymour* [1944] 2 All ER 11; but see also *Mallon v Allon* supra.

As to when the knowledge of an employee or agent may be imputed to his employer or principal, see 11 Halsbury's Laws (4th edn) para 54.

Appointment as proxy is no longer in force. As to when this is the case, see ss 21(6), 34(6) ante. Those provisions are repealed by the Representation of the People Act 1985, s 28(1), Sch 5 post, as from a day to be appointed under s 29(2) of that Act. New provision as to the cancellation of such appointment is contained in ss 8(9), 9(11) of the 1985 Act.

Applied for a ballot paper. Ie under Sch 1, r 37 post, the Local Elections (Principal Areas) Rules 1973, SI 1973/79, Sch 2, r 33, or the Local Elections (Parishes and Communities) Rules 1973, SI 1973/1910, Sch 1, r 31.

Ballot paper . . . for . . . voting by post. For the issue of postal ballot papers, see Sch 1, r 24 post, or the Local Elections (Principal Areas) Rules 1973, SI 1973/79, Sch 2, r 20, as amended by SI 1983/1154.

Parish and community elections. This section applies to elections of parish and community councillors subject to any exceptions, modifications and adaptations made by rules made under s 36 ante; see s 187(1) post, and the rules noted thereto.

Municipal elections in the City of London. As to the application of this section to such elections, see ss 191(1), 193 post.

Welsh Sunday polls. This section and s 61 post, except for sub-ss (1) and (4) thereof, apply to a poll under the Licensing Act 1964, s 66 (Sunday closing in Wales), Vol 24, title Licensing and Liquor Duties, as if it were a poll at an ordinary election of district councillors; see the Licensing Act 1964, s 67(5)(a), in the same title.

European Assembly elections. This section and s 61 post, are applied to such elections by the European Assembly Elections Regulations 1984, SI 1984/137, reg 3(1), Sch 1. See further the Introductory Note to this Act.

As to provisions relating to such elections in Northern Ireland, see the Introductory Note to this Act.

Definitions. For "elector" and "vote", see s 202(1) post, for "local government election", see s 203(1) post. Note also, as to "vote", sub-s (3) above.

61 Other voting offences

(1) A person shall be guilty of an offence if—

    (a) he votes in person or by post, whether as an elector or as proxy, or applies to *be treated as an absent voter or to vote by post as proxy, at a parliamentary or local government election, knowing that he is subject to a legal incapacity to vote;* or

    (b) he applies for the appointment of a proxy to vote for him at *parliamentary or local government elections, knowing that he or the person to be appointed is subject to a legal incapacity to vote;* or

    (c) he votes, whether in person or by post, *or applies to vote by post,* as proxy for some other person at a parliamentary or local government election, knowing that that person is subject to a legal incapacity to vote.

For the purposes of this subsection references to a person being subject to a legal incapacity to vote do not, in relation to things done before polling day at the election or first election at or for which they are done, include his being below voting age if he will be of voting age on that day.

(2) A person shall be guilty of an offence if—

   (*a*) he votes as elector otherwise than by proxy either—

      (i) more than once in the same constituency at any parliamentary election, or more than once in the same electoral area at any local government election; or

      (ii) in more than one constituency at a general election, or in more than one electoral area at an ordinary election of councillors for a local government area which is not a single electoral area; or

      (iii) in any constituency at a general election, or in any electoral area at such an ordinary election as mentioned above, when there is in force an appointment of a person to vote as his proxy at the election in some other constituency or electoral area; or

   (*b*) he votes as elector in person at a parliamentary or local government election at which he is entitled to vote by post; or

   (*c*) he votes as elector in person at a parliamentary or local government election, knowing that a person appointed to vote as his proxy at the election either has already voted in person at the election or is entitled to vote by post at the election; or

   (*d*) *not being a service voter*, he applies for a person to be appointed as his proxy to vote for him at parliamentary elections without applying for the cancellation of a previous appointment of a third person then in force or without withdrawing a pending application for such an appointment.

(3) A person shall be guilty of an offence if—

   (*a*) he votes as proxy for the same elector either—

      (i) more than once in the same constituency at any parliamentary election, or more than once in the same electoral area at any local government election; or

      (ii) in more than one constituency at a general election, or in more than one electoral area at an ordinary election of councillors for a local government area which is not a single electoral area; or

   (*b*) he votes in person as proxy for an elector at a parliamentary or local government election at which he is entitled to vote by post as proxy for that elector; or

   (*c*) *he votes in person as proxy for an elector registered as a service voter at a parliamentary or local government election knowing that the elector is entitled to vote by post at the election; or*

   (*d*) he votes in person as proxy for an elector at a parliamentary or local government election knowing that the elector has already voted in person at the election.

(4) A person shall also be guilty of an offence if he votes at a parliamentary election in any constituency as proxy for more than two persons of whom he is not the husband, wife, parent, grandparent, brother, sister, child or grandchild.

(5) A person shall also be guilty of an offence if he knowingly induces or procures some other person to do an act which is, or but for that other person's want of knowledge would be, an offence by that other person under the foregoing subsections of this section.

(6) For the purposes of this section a person who has applied for a ballot paper for the purpose of voting in person, or who has marked, whether validly or not, and returned a ballot paper issued for the purpose of voting by post, shall be deemed to have voted, but for the purpose of determining whether an application for a ballot paper constitutes an offence under subsection (4) above, a previous application made in circumstances which entitle the applicant only to mark a tendered ballot paper shall, if he does not exercise that right, be disregarded.

(7) An offence under this section shall be an illegal practice, but—

    (*a*) the court before whom a person is convicted of any such offence may, if they think it just in the special circumstances of the case, mitigate or entirely remit any incapacity imposed by virtue of section 173 below; and

    (*b*) a candidate shall not be liable, nor shall his election be avoided, for an illegal practice under this section of any agent of his other than an offence under subsection (5) above.

NOTES

Sub-s (1) contains provisions formerly in the Representation of the People Act 1949, s 48(1), as amended and as partly repealed by the Representation of the People Act 1949, s 24(1), (4), Sch 2, para 13(1), Sch 3, Pt II. Sub-ss (2), (3) contain provisions formerly in s 48(2), (3) of the 1949 Act, as amended and as partly repealed by s 24(1) of, and Sch 2, para 13(2) to, the 1969 Act. Sub-ss (4)–(7) contain provisions formerly in s 48(4)–(7), respectively, of the 1949 Act.

This section is amended in relation to Northern Ireland; see the note "Northern Ireland" below.

Prospective amendment. The following amendments are made to this section by the Representation of the People Act 1985, ss 11, 28(1), Sch 2, para 2, Sch 5 post, as from a day or days to be appointed under s 29(2) of that Act:

in sub-s (1)(*a*), the substitution of the words "vote by proxy or by post as elector, at a parliamentary or local government election, or at parliamentary or local government elections, knowing that he is subject to a legal incapacity to vote at the election or, as the case may be, at elections of that kind; or" for the words in italics;

in sub-s (1)(*b*), the substitution of the words "any parliamentary or local government election or at parliamentary or local government elections knowing that he or the person to be appointed is subject to a legal incapacity to vote at the election or, as the case may be, at elections of that kind; or" for the words in italics;

the repeal of the words in italics in sub-ss (1)(*c*), (2)(*d*), and the whole of sub-s (3)(*c*);

in sub-s (2)(*d*), the insertion of the words "in any constituency" after the word "elections", and of the words "in respect of that or another constituency" after both the word "force" and the words "an appointment";

in sub-s (4), the insertion of the words "or at a local government election in any electoral area" after the word "constituency".

Votes in person or by post . . . as an elector or as proxy. As to the manner of voting at parliamentary elections, see ss 19–22 ante, and as to voting at local government elections, see ss 32–34 ante.

Applies to be treated as an absent voter or to vote by post as proxy. As to such applications, see ss 19(3), (4), 20, 22(2), (5)–(7), 32(4), 33, 34(4), (6) ante.

Knowing. See the note "Knows" to s 60 ante.

Applies for the appointment of a proxy. As to such applications, see s 21(5), 34(6) ante.

Parliamentary elections. See the note "Parliamentary election" to s 1 ante.

Sub-s (2): Constituency. See the note to s 1 ante.

Ordinary election of councillors. See the note "Ordinary election" to s 32 ante.

Sub-s (5): Knowingly. See the note "Knows" to s 60 ante.

Procures. See the note "Aids, abets, counsels or procures" to s 60 ante.

Sub-s (6): Applied for a ballot paper; ballot paper . . . for . . . voting by post. See the notes to s 60 ante.

Circumstances which entitle the applicant only to mark a tendered ballot paper. For these circumstances, see Sch 1, r 40 post, the Local Elections (Principal Areas) Rules 1973, SI 1973/79, Sch 2, r 36, and the Local Elections (Parishes and Communities) Rules 1973, SI 1973/1910, r 34.

Sub-s (7): Illegal practice. As to prosecutions for illegal practices, see s 169 post; as to conviction of an illegal practice where the offence amounts to a corrupt practice, see s 170 post; as to the incapacities which are imposed on convictions of an illegal practice, see s 173 post; as to mitigation and remission of incapacities, see s 174 post; and as to offences by associations, see s 179 post. For the consequences of a report by an election court that a candidate or other person is guilty of an illegal practice, see ss 158–160 post. Note that under s 167 post, certain courts may except an innocent act from being an illegal practice, etc. See also the note "Related provisions" to s 169 post.

Municipal elections in the City of London. As to the application of this section to such elections, see ss 191(1), 193 post.

Welsh Sunday polls. See the note to s 60 ante.

European Assembly elections. See the note to s 60 ante; and see further the European Assembly Elections 1978, s 4(2) ante.

As to provisions relating to such elections in Northern Ireland, see the Introductory Note to this Act.

Definitions. For "voting age", see s 1(1)(*c*) or 2(1)(*c*) ante; for "election", "legal incapacity", "service voter" and "vote", see s 202(1) post; for "electoral area" and "local government election", see s 203(1) post. Note also, as to "vote", sub-s (6) above.

Northern Ireland. The following subsection is added after sub-s (6) above by the Elections (Northern Ireland) Act 1985, s 2(5), as from 6 August 1985:

"(6A) Where a person is alleged to have committed an offence under subsection (2)(a)(i) or (3)(a)(i) above by voting on a second or subsequent occasion at a parliamentary election, he shall not be deemed by virtue of subsection (6) above to have voted by applying on a previous occasion for a ballot paper for the purpose of voting in person unless he then marked a tendered ballot paper under rule 40(1C) of the parliamentary elections rules."

62 Offences as to declarations

(1) A person who—

(a) makes a patient's declaration or a service declaration—

(i) when he is not authorised so to do by section 7(4) or section 15(1) above, as the case may be, or

(ii) except as permitted by this Act, when he knows that he is subject to a legal incapacity to vote, or

(iii) when he knows that it contains a statement which is false, or

(b) attests a patient's declaration or a service declaration, as the case may be, when he knows—

(i) that he is not authorised to do so, or

(ii) that it contains a false statement as to any particulars required by paragraph (d) of section 7(4), or by regulations under section [16], as the case may be,

shall be liable [on summary conviction to a fine not exceeding level 5 on the standard scale].

(2) Where the declaration is available only for local government elections the reference in subsection (1) above to a legal incapacity to vote refers to a legal incapacity to vote at local government elections.

NOTES

This section contains provisions formerly in the Representation of the People Act 1949, s 49, as amended, in the case of sub-s (1) thereof, by the Criminal Law Act 1977, ss 15(1), 30(1), (2), Sch 1, para 9, the Criminal Justice Act 1982, ss 37(1), (2), 46(1), and the Mental Health (Amendment) Act 1982, s 62(2), Sch 2, para 6.

The reference to "16" in sub-s (1)(b)(ii) was substituted by the Representation of the People Act 1985, s 24, Sch 4, para 18, as from 16 July 1985, and the other words in square brackets were substituted by s 23 of, and Sch 3, para 1 to, that Act, as from 1 October 1985.

Except as permitted by this Act. A person may make a patient's declaration or service declaration, as the case may be, although he is not yet of voting age; see ss 7(4)(c), 15(1), respectively ante.

Knows. See the note to s 60 ante.

False. A statement may be false on account of what it omits even though it is literally true; see *R v Lord Kylsant* [1932] 1 KB 442, [1931] All ER Rep 179, and *R v Bishirgian* [1936] 1 All ER 586; and cf *Curtis v Chemical Cleaning and Dyeing Co Ltd* [1951] 1 KB 805 at 808, 809, [1951] 1 All ER 631 at 634, CA. Whether or not gain or advantage accrues from the false statement is irrelevant; see *Jones v Meatyard* [1939] 1 All ER 140; *Stevens & Steeds Ltd and Evans v King* [1943] 1 All ER 314; *Clear v Smith* [1981] 1 WLR 399, [1980] Crim LR 246; and *Barrass v Reeve* [1980] 3 All ER 705, [1981] 1 WLR 408.

Attests a ... declaration ... when he knows ... he is not authorised, etc. As to the requirements relating to the attestation of a service declaration or a patient's declaration, see ss 7(4), 16 ante, the Representation of the People Regulations 1983, SI 1983/435, regs 7, 10(1), (2), and the Representation of the People (Northern Ireland) Regulations 1983, SI 1983/436, regs 6, 9(1).

Summary conviction. Summary jurisdiction and procedure are mainly governed by the Magistrates' Courts Act 1980, Vol 27, title Magistrates, and by rules made under s 144 of that Act.

Available only for local government elections. Ie by virtue of s 7(9) or 15(5) ante.

Definitions. For "legal incapacity", "standard scale" and "vote", see s 202(1) post; for "local government election", see s 203(1) post. Note also, as "legal incapacity", sub-s (2) above.

[63 Breach of official duty

(1) If a person to whom this section applies is, without reasonable cause, guilty of any act or omission in breach of his official duty, he shall be liable on summary conviction to a fine not exceeding level 5 on the standard scale.

(2) No person to whom this section applies shall be liable for breach of his official duty to any penalty at common law and no action for damages shall lie in respect of the breach by such a person of his official duty.

(3) The persons to whom this section applies are—

    (a) the Clerk of the Crown (or, in Northern Ireland, the Clerk of the Crown for Northern Ireland),

    (b) any sheriff clerk, registration officer, returning officer or presiding officer,

    (c) any other person whose duty it is to be responsible after a local government election for the used ballot papers and other documents (including returns and declarations as to expenses),

    (d) any postmaster, and

    (e) any deputy of a person mentioned in any of paragraphs (a) to (d) above or any person appointed to assist or in the course of his employment assisting a person so mentioned in connection with his official duties;

and "official duty" shall for the purposes of this section be construed accordingly, but shall not include duties imposed otherwise than by the law relating to parliamentary or local government elections or the registration of parliamentary or local government electors.]

NOTES

This section was substituted for the original ss 63, 64 by the Representation of the People Act 1985, s 24, Sch 4, para 19, in relation to offences committed on or after 1 October 1985.

Without reasonable cause. Cf *Edwards v Jackson and Dingle* [1946] 2 All ER 129 (alteration of nomination paper by returning officer held in the circumstances to be no offence).

Summary conviction. See the note to s 62 ante.

Returning officer. As to these officers, see ss 24, 26–28, 35 ante.

Presiding officer. As to the appointment of this officer, see Sch 1, r 26 post.

European Assembly Elections. This section is applied to such elections by the European Assembly Elections Regulations 1984, SI 1984/137, reg 3(1), Sch 1, subject to the insertion in sub-s (3)(b) above, after the words "returning officer", of the words "verifying officer". See further the Introductory Note to this Act.

Application to other local elections. This section has effect as if any reference in it to a local government election included a reference to any other election under the Local Government Act 1972 or the Local Government Act 1985, Pt III, both Vol 25, title Local Government; see s 187(2) post.

Definitions. For "registration officer", see s 8(1) ante; for "Clerk of the Crown", "election", "elector" and "standard scale", see s 202(1) post. For "local government election", see s 203(1) post. Note as to "official duty", sub-s (3) above.

65 Tampering with nomination papers, ballot papers etc

(1) A person shall be guilty of an offence, if, at a parliamentary or local government election, he—

    (a) fraudulently defaces or fraudulently destroys any nomination paper; or

    (b) fraudulently defaces or fraudulently destroys any ballot paper, or the official mark on any ballot paper, or any declaration of identity or official envelope used in connection with voting by post; or

    (c) without due authority supplies any ballot paper to any person; or

    (d) fraudulently puts into any ballot box any paper other than the ballot paper which he is authorised by law to put in; or

    (e) fraudulently takes out of the polling station any ballot paper; or (*f*) without due authority destroys, takes, opens or otherwise interferes with any ballot box or packet of ballot papers then in use for the purposes of the election; or

(*g*) fraudulently or without due authority, as the case may be, attempts to do any of the foregoing acts.

(2) (*Applies to Scotland only.*)

[(3) If a returning officer, a presiding officer or a clerk appointed to assist in taking the poll, counting the votes or assisting at the proceedings in connection with the issue or receipt of postal ballot papers is guilty of an offence under this section, he shall be liable—

(*a*) on conviction on indictment to a fine, or to imprisonment for a term not exceeding 2 years, or to both;

(*b*) on summary conviction, to a fine not exceeding the statutory maximum, or to imprisonment for a term not exceeding 6 months, or to both.

(4) If any other person is guilty of an offence under this section, he shall be liable on summary conviction to a fine not exceeding level 5 on the standard scale, or to imprisonment for a term not exceeding 6 months, or to both.]

NOTES

This section, as originally enacted, contained provisions formerly in the Representation of the People Act 1949, s 52, as affected, in the case of s 52(3), by the Criminal Law Act 1967, s 1, and as amended in the case of s 52(4), by the Criminal Law Act 1977, s 31(6), and by the Criminal Justice Act 1982, ss 37(1), (2), 46(1), and, in the case of s 52(5), by s 32(1) of the 1977 Act, and by the Magistrates' Courts Act 1980, s 32(2).

Sub-ss (3), (4) were substituted for the original sub-ss (3)–(5) by the Representation of the People Act 1985, s 23, Sch 3, para 2, as from 1 October 1985.

Sub-s (1): Parliamentary election. See the note to s 1 ante.

Nomination paper. As to nomination papers, see Sch 1, rr 6, 7 post, the Local Elections (Principal Areas) Rules 1973, SI 1973/79, Sch 2, rr 5, 6, and the Local Elections (Parishes and Communities) Rules 1973, SI 1973 No 1910, rr 5, 6.

Ballot paper; official mark. As to ballot papers and official marks thereon, see Sch 1, rr 19, 20, 24 post, the Local Elections (Principal Areas) Rules 1973, SI 1973/79 (as amended by SI 1983/1154), Sch 2, rr 15, 16, 20, and the Local Elections (Parishes and Communities) Rules 1973, SI 1973/1910, Sch 1, rr 15, 16.

Declaration of identity; official envelope. Ie the declaration and envelope referred to in Sch 1, r 24 post, or the Local Elections (Principal Areas) Rules 1973, SI 1973/79, Sch 2, r 20, as amended by SI 1983/1154.

Or otherwise interferes. For two relevant cases (both of throwing liquid chemicals into ballot box), see *R v Chapin* (1909) 74 JP 71, 22 Cox CC 10 and *R v Neilan* (1909) Times, 25 November.

Sub-s (3): Returning officer. As to returning officers, see ss 24, 26–28, 35 ante.

Presiding officer. As to the appointment of this officer at parliamentary elections, see Sch 1, r 26 post, and at local government elections, see the Local Elections (Principal Areas) Rules 1973, SI 1973/79, Sch 2, r 22, and the Local Elections (Parishes and Communities) Rules 1973, SI 1973/1910, Sch 1, r 21.

Counting the votes. This includes a reference to counting the ballot papers under the Representation of the People Act 1985, Sch 1 (special polling stations in Northern Ireland); see s 10 of, and Sch 1, Pt IV, para 26 to, that Act post, as from a day to be appointed under s 29(2) thereof.

Issue or receipt of postal ballot papers. For provisions relating to the issue or receipt of such papers, see the Representation of the People Regulations 1983, SI 1983/435, Pt V, and the Representation of the People (Northern Ireland) Regulations 1983, SI 1983/436, Pt V.

Shall be liable, etc. For the procedure for determining the mode of trial of offences triable either summarily or on indictment, see the Magistrates' Courts Act 1980, ss 18 et seq, Vol 27, title Magistrates.

Conviction on indictment. All proceedings on indictment are to be brought before the Crown Court; see the Supreme Court Act 1981, s 46(1), Vol 11, title Courts. As to the trial of indictments generally, see 11 Halsbury's Laws (4th edn) paras 225 et seq.

Fine. There is no specific limit to the amount of the fine which may be imposed on conviction on indictment, but the fine should be within the offender's capacity to pay; see, in particular, *R v Churchill (No 2)* [1967] 1 QB 190, [1966] 2 All ER 215, CCA; revsd on other grounds sub nom *Churchill v Walton* [1967] 2 AC 224, [1967] 1 All ER 497, HL; and see also the Bill of Rights (1688), s 1, Vol 10, title Constitutional Law (Pt 1).

Summary conviction. See the note to s 62 ante.

Welsh Sunday polls. This section applies to a poll under the Licensing Act 1964, s 66 (Sunday closing in Wales), Vol 24, title Licensing and Liquor Duties, as if it were a poll at an ordinary election of district councillors; see the Licensing Act 1964, s 67(5)(*a*), in the same title.

European Assembly elections. This section is applied to such elections by the European Assembly Elections Regulations 1984, SI 1984/137, reg 3(1), Sch 1, subject to a modification which, in view of the substitution of sub-s (3) above, no longer has effect. See further the Introductory Note to this Act.

As to provisions relating to such elections in Northern Ireland, see the Introductory Note to this Act.

Definitions. For "local government election", see s 203(1) post; for "standard scale" and "statutory maximum", see s 202(1) post.

66 Requirement of secrecy

(1) The following persons—

(a) every returning officer and every presiding officer or clerk attending at a polling station,

(b) every candidate or election agent or polling agent so attending,

shall maintain and aid in maintaining the secrecy of voting and shall not, except for some purpose authorised by law, communicate to any person before the poll is closed any information as to—

(i) the name of any elector or proxy for an elector who has or has not applied for a ballot paper or voted at a polling station;

(ii) the number on the register of electors of any elector who, or whose proxy, has or has not applied for a ballot paper or voted at a polling station; or

(iii) the official mark.

(2) Every person attending at the counting of the votes shall maintain and aid in maintaining the secrecy of voting and shall not—

(a) ascertain or attempt to ascertain at the counting of the votes the number on the back of any ballot paper;

(b) communicate any information obtained at the counting of the votes as to the candidate for whom any vote is given on any particular ballot paper.

(3) No person shall—

(a) interfere with or attempt to interfere with a voter when recording his vote;

(b) otherwise obtain or attempt to obtain in a polling station information as to the candidate for whom a voter in that station is about to vote or has voted;

(c) communicate at any time to any person any information obtained in a polling station as to the candidate for whom a voter in that station is about to vote or has voted, or as to the number on the back of the ballot paper given to a voter at that station;

(d) directly or indirectly induce a voter to display his ballot paper after he has marked it so as to make known to any person the name of the candidate for whom he has or has not voted.

(4) Every person attending the proceedings in connection with the issue or the receipt of ballot papers for persons voting by post shall maintain and aid in maintaining the secrecy of the voting and shall not—

(a) except for some purpose authorised by law, communicate, before the poll is closed, to any person any information obtained at those proceedings as to the official mark; or

(b) except for some purpose authorised by law, communicate to any person at any time any information obtained at those proceedings as to the number on the back of the ballot paper sent to any person; or

(c) except for some purpose authorised by law, attempt to ascertain at the proceedings in connection with the receipt of ballot papers the number on the back of any ballot paper; or

(d) attempt to ascertain at the proceedings in connection with the receipt of the ballot papers the candidate for whom any vote is given in any particular ballot paper or communicate any information with respect thereto obtained at those proceedings.

(5) No person having undertaken to assist a blind voter to vote shall communicate at any time to any person any information as to the candidate for whom that voter intends to vote or has voted, or as to the number on the back of the ballot paper given for the use of that voter.

(6) If a person acts in contravention of this section he shall be liable on summary conviction [to a fine not exceeding level 5 on the standard scale or] to imprisonment for a term not exceeding 6 months.

NOTES

This section contains provisions formerly in the Representation of the People Act 1949, s 53.

The words in square brackets in sub-s (6) were substituted by the Representation of the People Act 1985, s 23, Sch 3, para 3, as from 1 October 1985.

Sub-s (1): Returning officer. As to returning officers, see ss 24, 26–28, 35 ante.

Presiding officer; ballot paper; official mark. See the notes to s 65 ante.

Election agent. As to the appointment of election agents, see s 67 post.

Polling agent. As to the appointment of polling agents, see s 72(1) and Sch 1, r 30 post, the Local Elections (Principal Areas) Rules 1973, SI 1973/79, Sch 2, r 26, as amended by SI 1983/1154 and the Local Elections (Parishes and Communities) Rules 1973, SI 1973/1910, Sch 1, r 24.

Proxy. As to proxies, see ss 21, 22 and 34 ante. Those provisions are repealed by the Representation of the People Act 1985, s 28(1), Sch 5, as from a day to be appointed under s 29(2) of that Act. As from that date, new provision is made as to proxies by ss 8, 9 of that Act post.

Number on the register of electors. As to the register of electors, see s 9 ante and the note "Register" thereto; and as to the numbering of names in the register, see the Representation of the People Regulations 1983, SI 1983/435, reg 15(3).

Sub-s (2): Person attending at the counting of the votes. For the persons who may so attend, see Sch 1, r 44(1)–(3) post, the Local Elections (Principal Areas) Rules 1973, SI 1973/79, Sch 2, r 40(1)–(3) and the Local Elections (Parishes and Communities) Rules 1973, SI 1973/1910, Sch 1, r 38(1)–(3).

Attempt. As to when a person may be guilty of an attempt under sub-s (2)(a) or (3)(a) or (b) above, see the Criminal Attempts Act 1981, s 3, Vol 12, title Criminal Law; and for provisions as to trial and evidence, see s 4(2), (4) of that Act. On attempts generally, see 11 Halsbury's Laws (4th edn) paras 63 et seq, which must be read in the light of the provisions of Pt I of the 1981 Act.

Sub-s (3): Attempt. See the note to sub-s (2) above.

Sub-s (4): Issue or the receipt of ballot papers for persons voting by post. See the note "Issue or receipt of postal ballot papers" to s 65 ante.

Sub-s (5): Persons having undertaken to assist a blind voter. As to voting by blind persons, see Sch 1, r 39 post the Local Elections (Principal Areas) Rules 1973, SI 1973/79, Sch 2, r 35, and the Local Elections (Parishes and Communities) Rules 1973, SI 1973/1910, Sch 1, r 33.

Sub-s (6): Summary conviction. See the note to s 62 ante.

Imprisonment. Under the Magistrates' Courts Act 1980, s 34(3), Vol 27, title Magistrates, a fine may be imposed instead of imprisonment provided that it does not exceed the limits there specified (as amended by any order made under s 143 of that Act).

Declaration of secrecy. A declaration promising that the person in question will not do anything forbidden by sub-ss (1)–(3) and (6) above must be made by certain persons before the opening of the poll (Sch 1, r 31 post; Local Elections (Principal Areas) Rules 1973, SI 1973/79, Sch 2, r 27, as amended by SI 1983/1154; Local Elections (Parishes and Communities) Rules 1973, SI 1973/1910, Sch 1, r 25, as amended by SI 1983/1153), and a declaration promising that the person in question will not do anything forbidden by sub-ss (4) and (6) above must be made by persons attending the proceedings on the issue or receipt of postal ballot papers (Representation of the People Regulations 1983, SI 1983/435, reg 52; Representation of the People (Northern Ireland) Regulations 1983, SI 1983/436, reg 37).

European Assembly elections. This section is applied to such elections by the European Assembly Elections Regulations 1984, SI 1984/137, reg 3(1), Sch 1, subject to:

(1) the insertion, in sub-s (2) above, before the word "counting" in the first and third places where that word occurs, of the words "verification of the ballot paper accounts or the", and

(2) the insertion, after sub-s (2) above, of the following subsection:

"(2A) No person attending at the verification of the ballot paper accounts or the counting of the votes shall express to any person an opinion based on information obtained at that verification or count as to the likely outcome of that count."

See further the Introductory Note to this Act.

As to provisions relating to such elections in Northern Ireland, see the Introductory Note to this Act.

Parish and community elections. This section applies to elections of parish and community councillors subject to any exceptions, modifications or adaptations made by rules made under s 36, ante; see s 187(1) post, and the rules noted thereto.

Welsh Sunday polls. This section applies with modifications to a poll under the Licensing Act 1964, s 66 (Sunday closing in Wales), Vol 24, title Licensing and Liquor Duties, as if it were a poll at an ordinary election of district councillors; see s 67(5)(*b*) of and para (i) of the proviso to that subsection. See also Sch 8, para 5(1)(*c*) to that Act, in the same title.

Northern Ireland. For a modification of this section in relation to special polling stations in Northern Ireland, see the Representation of the People Act 1985, s 10, Sch 1, Pt IV, para 27, as from a day to be appointed under s 29(2) of that Act.

Definitions. For "elector", "standard scale", "vote" and "voter", see s 202(1) post.

PART II

THE ELECTION CAMPAIGN

The election agent

67 Appointment of election agent

(1) Not later than the latest time for the delivery of notices of withdrawals for an election, a person shall be named by or on behalf of each candidate as the candidate's election agent, and the name and address of the candidate's election agent shall be declared in writing by the candidate or some other person on his behalf to the appropriate officer not later than that time.

(2) A candidate may name himself as election agent, and upon doing so shall, so far as circumstances admit, be subject to the provisions of this Act both as a candidate and as an election agent, and, except where the context otherwise requires, any reference in this Act to an election agent shall be construed to refer to the candidate acting in his capacity of election agent.

(3) One election agent only shall be appointed for each candidate, but the appointment, whether the election agent appointed be the candidate himself or not, may be revoked.

(4) If whether before, during or after the election the appointment [(or deemed appointment)] of an election agent is revoked or an election agent dies, another election agent shall be appointed forthwith and his name and address declared in writing to the appropriate officer.

(5) The declaration as a candidate's election agent of a person other than the candidate shall be of no effect under this section unless it is made and signed by that person or is accompanied by a written declaration of acceptance signed by him.

(6) Upon the name and address of an election agent being declared to the appropriate officer, the appropriate officer shall forthwith give public notice of that name and address.

(7) In this Part of this Act the expression "appropriate officer" means—

(*a*) in relation to a parliamentary election, the returning officer;
(*b*) in relation to a local government election, the proper officer of the authority for which the election is held.

NOTES

Sub-ss (1)–(4), (6), (7) contain provisions formerly in the Representation of the People Act 1949, s 55(1)–(6), respectively, as affected, in the case of s 55(6), by the Local Government Act 1972, s 270(3). Sub-s (5) contains provisions formerly in the Representation of the People Act 1969, s 11(1).

The words in square brackets in sub-s (4) were inserted by the Representation of the People Act 1985, s 24, Sch 4, para 20, as from 1 October 1985.

Latest time for the delivery of notices of withdrawals. The "latest time" referred to is prescribed by Sch 1, r 1 post, the Local Elections (Principal Areas) Rules 1973, SI 1973/79, Sch 2, r 1, and the Local Elections

(Parishes and Communities) Rules 1973, SI 1973/1910, Sch 1, r 1. As to notice of withdrawal, see Sch 1, r 13 post, SI 1973/79, Sch 2, r 11, and SI 1973/1910, Sch 1, r 11.

Election agent. A sub-agent may be appointed in the case of a parliamentary election for a county constituency; see s 68 post. In default of appointment of an election agent by a candidate, he is deemed to have named himself as his own agent; see s 70 post. An election agent must have an office; see s 69 post. Election agents are not required for elections to which s 71 post, applies. As to the duties of an election agent, see also 15 Halsbury's Laws (4th edn) para 691.

A candidate is responsible for the acts of his agents. It is a "wise and beneficial rule of constitutional law that for the purpose of securing purity and freedom of election, candidates shall be answerable for the acts of their agents as well as for their acts"; see *Coventry Case, Berry v Eaton and Hill* (1869) 20 LT 405 at 409 per Willes J. So too a candidate has been held responsible for the acts of sub-agents appointed under what is now s 68 post; see eg *Plymouth Case, Latimer and Barratt v Bates* (1880) 3 O'M & H 107. Distinction is to be drawn between criminal responsibility and civil responsibility for the purpose of determining the validity of elections; it is the latter to which reference is made here (*Greenock Case* (1869) 1 O'M & H 247). For the consequences of a report by an election court that a candidate has been guilty through his agents of corrupt, etc, practices, see ss 158(3), 159(1) post. An election may be avoided for the employment of a corrupt agent; see s 165 post. See further, as to the liability of a candidate for his agents' conduct, the note "By his agents" to s 159 post, and 15 Halsbury's Laws (4th edn) paras 697 et seq.

Writing. See the note "Written" to s 28 ante.

Forthwith. A provision to the effect that a thing must be done "forthwith" or "immediately" means that it must be done as soon as possible in the circumstances, the nature of the act to be done being taken into account; see *Re Southam, ex p Lamb* (1881) 19 Ch D 169 at 173, [1881–5] All ER Rep 391, CA; *Re Muscovitch, ex p Muscovitch* [1939] Ch 694 at 679, 698, [1939] 1 All ER 135 at 139, CA; and *Sameen v Abeyewickrema* [1963] AC 597, [1963] 3 All ER 382, PC. Provided, however, that no harm is done, "forthwith" means "at any reasonable time thereafter", and in the absence of some detriment suffered by the person affected failure to act "forthwith" does not invalidate the action taken; see *Hillingdon London Borough v Cutler* [1968] 1 QB 124, [1967] 2 All ER 361, CA. See, further, 2 Words and Phrases (2nd edn) 273–275.

Public notice. For the method in which this notice is to be given, see s 200(1), (1A) post, and as to the statement in it of the address of the election agent's office, see s 69(1)(*b*) post.

Parliamentary election. See the note to s 1 ante.

Returning officer. As to these officers, see ss 24, 26–28 ante.

Parish and community elections. So far as they apply to an election in England and Wales of parish or community councillors, or the chairman of a parish or community council or a parish meeting, this Part (ss 67–119) and Pt III (ss 120–186) post, have effect subject to any adaptations, modifications or exceptions which may be made by rules under s 36 ante, but this is not to affect s 96 or 100 post; see s 187(1) post and for the relevant rules, see the notes to that section. In this connection it should be noted that this section and ss 68–70, 73–75 and 78–89 post, do not apply to elections of parish and community councillors; see ss 71 and 90(1)(*b*) post.

Municipal elections in City of London. As to the application of this Part (ss 67–119) except ss 96 and 99 post, and Pt III (ss 120–186) to municipal elections in the City, see ss 191(1), 194–196 post.

Exclusion. This section and ss 68–70 post, do not apply to elections of the kinds mentioned in s 71 post.

European Assembly elections. This section is applied to such elections by the European Assembly Elections Regulations 1984, SI 1984/137, reg 3(1), Sch 1. See further the Introductory Note to this Act.

As to provision relating to such elections in Northern Ireland, see the Introductory Note to this Act.

Definitions. For "candidate", see s 118 post; for "election" and "proper officer", see s 202(1) post; for "local government election", see s 203(1) post. Note as to "appropriate officer", sub-s (7) above.

68 Nomination of sub-agent at parliamentary elections

(1) In the case of a parliamentary election for a county constituency an election agent for a candidate may appoint to act in any part of the constituency one, but not more than one, deputy election agent (in this Act referred to as a sub-agent).

(2) As regards matters in a part of the constituency for which there is a sub-agent the election agent may act by the sub-agent and—

   (*a*) anything done for the purposes of this Act by or to the sub-agent in his part of the constituency shall be deemed to be done by or to the election agent; and

   (*b*) any act or default of a sub-agent which, if he were the election agent, would be an illegal practice or other offence against this Act shall be an illegal practice and offence against this Act committed by the sub-agent, and the sub-agent shall be liable to punishment accordingly; and (*c*) the candidate shall suffer the like incapacity as if that act or default had been the election agent's act or default.

(3) [Not later than the second day] before the day of the poll the election agent shall declare in writing the name and address of every sub-agent to the appropriate officer, and the appropriate officer shall forthwith give public notice of the name and address of every sub-agent so declared.

(4) The appointment of a sub-agent—

(*a*) shall not be vacated by the election agent who appointed him ceasing to be election agent, but

(*b*) may be revoked by whoever is for the time being the candidate's election agent,

and in the event of the revocation of the appointment or of the death of a sub-agent another sub-agent may be appointed, and his name and address shall be forthwith declared in writing to the appropriate officer, who shall forthwith give public notice of the name and address so declared.

(5) The declaration to be made to the appropriate officer, and the notice to be given by him, under subsection (3) or subsection (4) above shall specify the part of the constituency within which any sub-agent is appointed to act.

NOTES

Sub-s (1) contains provisions formerly in the Representation of the People Act 1949, s 56(1), as amended by the Representation of the People Act 1969, s 24(1), Sch 2, para 14(*a*), and in s 11(2) of the 1969 Act. Sub-ss (2)–(5) contain provisions formerly in s 56(2)–(5) of the 1949 Act, as amended and as partly repealed, in the case of s 56(2), by s 24(1) of, and Sch 2, para 14(*b*) to, the 1969 Act, and as added, in the case of s 56(5), by s 24(1) of, and Sch 2, para 14(*c*), to, that Act.

The words in square brackets in sub-s (3) were substituted by the Representation of the People Act 1985, s 24, Sch 4, para 21, as from 1 October 1985.

Sub-s (1): Parliamentary election. See the note to s 1 ante.

County constituency. See the note "County constituency; borough constituency" to s 24 ante.

Election agent. As to the appointment of election agents, see s 67 ante.

Sub-agent. A sub-agent must have an office; see s 69 post. As to the liability of a candidate for the acts of sub-agents, see the second paragraph of the note "Election agent" to s 67 ante.

Sub-s (2): Illegal practice or other offence against this Act. The offences that election agents are liable to commit under this Act are: failure to deliver or send declaration of expenses (s 75(5) post); unauthorised payment of claims (s 78(3) post); failure to make return and declaration of expenses (s 84 post); broadcasting from outside the United Kingdom (s 92 post); payments for conveyance of voters (s 102 post); false statements as to candidates (s 106(1) post); illegal hiring of committee rooms (s 108 post); payment for exhibition of election notices (s 109 post); bribery, treating and undue influence (ss 113–115 post). For the penalties for these offences, see ss 168, 169, 175 post.

Incapacity. Ie the candidate's election shall be void and he shall be liable to the penalties specified in s 159 post.

Sub-s (3): Writing. See the note "Written" to s 28 ante.

Forthwith. See the note to s 67 ante.

Public notice. For the method in which this notice is to be given, see s 200(1) post; and as to the statement in it of the address of the sub-agent's office, see s 69(1)(*b*) post.

Parish and community elections; municipal elections in City of London; exclusion. See the notes to s 67 ante.

European Assembly elections. This section is applied to such elections by the European Assembly Elections Regulations 1984, SI 1984/137, reg 3(1), Sch 1, subject to the omission, from sub-s (1) above, of the words "In the case of a parliamentary election for a county constituency". See further the Introductory Note to this Act.

As to provisions relating to such elections in Northern Ireland, see the Introductory Note to this Act.

Definitions. For "appropriate officer", see s 67(7) ante; for "candidate", see s 118 post; for "election", see s 202(1) post. Note as to "sub-agent", sub-s (1) above.

69 Office of election agent and sub-agent

(1) Every election agent and every sub-agent shall have an office to which all claims, notices, writs, summonses and documents may be sent, and the address of the office shall be—

    (a) declared to the appropriate officer at the same time as the appointment of the agent [is declared to him]; and

    (b) stated in the public notice of the name of the agent.

(2) The office—

    (a) of the election agent for a parliamentary election shall be within the constituency or an adjoining constituency or in a London borough or district which is partly comprised in or adjoins the constituency, and that of a sub-agent shall be in the area within which he is appointed to act; and

    (b) of an election agent for a local government election shall be within the local government area or in the constituency or one of the constituencies in which the area is comprised or in a London borough or district which adjoins it.

(3) Any claim, notice, writ, summons or document delivered at the office of the election agent or sub-agent and addressed to him, shall be deemed to have been served on him and every election agent or sub-agent may in respect of any matter connected with the election in which he is acting be sued in any court having jurisdiction at the place where his office is situated.

NOTES

Sub-ss (1), (3) contains provisions formerly in the Representation of the People Act 1949, s 57(1), (3). Sub-s (2) contains provisions formerly in the Representation of the People Act 1969, s 11(3), as amended by the Local Government Act 1972, s 45, Sch 6, para 14.

The words in square brackets in sub-s (1)(a) were inserted by the Representation of the People Act 1985, s 24, Sch 4, para 22, as from 1 October 1985.

Election agent; sub-agent. As to the appointment of election agents, see s 67 ante; and as to the appointment of sub-agents, see s 68 ante.

Public notice. Ie the notices referred to in ss 67(6), 68(3) ante. For the method in which this notice is to be given, see s 200(1), (1A) post.

Parliamentary election; constituency. See the notes to s 1 ante.

London borough. See the note to s 8 ante.

District. See the note "Council of every district" to s 8 ante.

Parish and community elections; municipal elections in City of London; exclusion. See the notes to s 67 ante.

European Assembly elections. This section and ss 70 and 72 post, are applied to such elections by the European Assembly Elections Regulations 1984, SI 1984/137, reg 3(1), Sch 1. See further the Introductory Note to this Act.

As to provisions relating to such elections in Northern Ireland, see the Introductory Note to this Act.

Definitions. For "appropriate officer", see s 67(7) ante; for "sub-agent", see s 68(1) ante; for "local government area" and "local government election", see s 203(1) post.

70 Effect of default in election agent's appointment

(1) If no person's name and address is given as required by section 67 above as the election agent of a candidate who remains validly nominated at the latest time for delivery of notices of withdrawals, the candidate shall be deemed at that time to have named himself as election agent and to have revoked any appointment of another person as his election agent.

(2) If—

    (a) the person whose name and address have been so given as those of the candidate's election agent (not being the candidate himself) dies, and

(b) a new appointment is not made on the day of the death or on the following day,

the candidate shall be deemed to have appointed himself as from the time of death.

(3) If the appointment of a candidate's election agent is revoked without a new appointment being made, the candidate himself shall be deemed to have been appointed (or re-appointed) election agent.

[(3A) The deemed appointment of a candidate as his own election agent may be revoked as if it were an actual appointment.]

(4) Where a candidate is by virtue of this section to be treated as his own election agent, he shall be deemed to have his office—

(a) at his address as given in the statement as to persons nominated; or
(b) if that address is outside the permitted area for the office, at the qualifying address of the person (or first person) named in that statement as his proposer.

(5) (*Applies to Scotland only.*)

(6) The appropriate officer on being satisfied that a candidate is by virtue of this section to be treated as his own election agent, shall forthwith proceed to publish the like notice as if the name and address of the candidate and the address of his office had been duly given to him under sections 67 and 69 above.

NOTES

Sub-ss (1)–(3), (4) contain provisions formerly in the Representation of the People Act 1949, s 58(1)–(4), as amended, in the case of s 58(4), by the Representation of the People Act 1969, s 24(1), Sch 2, para 5. Sub-s (6) contains provisions formerly in s 58(5) of the 1949 Act.

Sub-s (3A) was inserted by the Representation of the People Act 1985, s 24, Sch 4, para 23, as from 1 October 1985.

Sub-s (1): Validly nominated. As to the nomination of candidates, see Sch 1, rr 6–17 post, the Local Elections (Principal Areas) Rules 1973, SI 1973/79 (as amended by SI 1983/1154), Sch 2, rr 5–12, and the Local Elections (Parishes and Communities) Rules 1973, SI 1973/1910 (as amended by SI 1983/1153), Sch 1, rr 5–12.

Latest time for delivery of notices of withdrawals. See the note to s 67 ante.

Sub-s (4): Statement as to persons nominated. For this statement, see Sch 1, r 14 post, the Local Elections (Principal Areas) Rules 1973, SI 1973/79, Sch 2, r 9, and the Local Elections (Parishes and Communities) Rules 1973, SI 1973/1910, Sch 1, r 9.

Permitted area for the office. See s 69(2) ante.

Qualifying address. The expression is not defined but cf s 1(1)(a), 2(1)(a) ante.

Sub-s (6): Forthwith. See the note to s 67 ante.

Like notice. As to this notice, see ss 67(6), 68(3) ante; and as to its publication, see s 200(1), (1A) post.

Parish and community elections; municipal elections in City of London; exclusion. See the notes to s 67 ante.

European Assembly elections. See the note to s 69 ante.

Definitions. For "appropriate officer", see s 67(7) ante; for "candidate", see s 118 post.

71 Elections where election agent not required

A candidate—

(a) at an election in England of parish councillors, or in Wales of community councillors, or
(b) at any election under the local government Act which is not a local government election,

need not have an election agent, and accordingly the foregoing provisions of this Part of this Act do not apply to those elections.

NOTES

This section contains provisions formerly in the Representation of the People Act 1949, s 59.

England; Wales. See the note to s 4 ante.

Election under the local government Act; local government election. As to the difference in the scope of these expressions, see the note on the former expression to s 202 post.

Foregoing provisions of this Part of this Act. Ie ss 67–70 ante.

Expenses. For provisions relating to expenses at elections where an election agent is not required, see s 90 post.

Definitions. For "election", see s 202(1) post; for "local government Act" and "local government election", see s 203(1) post.

Election expenses

72 Making of contracts through election agent

(1) The election agent of a candidate shall appoint every polling agent, clerk and messenger employed for payment on behalf of the candidate at an election, and hire every committee room hired on behalf of the candidate.

(2) A contract by which any election expenses are incurred shall not be enforceable against a candidate at the election unless made by the candidate himself or by his election agent, but this subsection does not relieve the candidate from the consequences of any corrupt or illegal practice having been committed by his agent.

(3) The references in this section to an election agent shall, in relation to a parliamentary election where sub-agents are allowed, be taken as references to the election agent acting by himself or a sub-agent.

NOTES

This section contains provisions formerly in the Representation of the People Act 1949, s 60.

Election agent. As to election agents, see s 67 ante, and the notes thereto. Under that section or s 70 ante, a candidate may be his own agent. Note also sub-s (3) above.

Polling agent. As to the appointment of polling agents, see also Sch 1, r 30 post, the Local Elections (Principal Areas) Rules 1973, SI 1973/79, Sch 2, r 26, as amended by SI 1983/1154, and the Local Elections (Parishes and Communities) Rules 1973, SI 1973/1910, Sch 1, r 24.

Hire every committee room. Hiring of committee rooms is subject to the restrictions imposed by s 108 post.

Corrupt or illegal practice. As to prosecutions for such practices, see ss 168–170, 173 post, and for the consequences of a candidate being reported guilty of such a practice by an election court, see s 159 post.

Parliamentary election. See the note to s 1 ante.

Where sub-agents are allowed. As to the appointment of sub-agents at parliamentary elections, see s 68 ante.

Parish and community elections; municipal elections in City of London. See the notes to s 67 ante.

European Assembly elections. See the note to s 69 ante.

Exclusion. This section, ss 73–75 and 78–89 post, do not apply to elections of parish and community councillors, but the provisions of Sch 4 post, apply in their place; see s 90(1)(b) post.

Note also that this section and ss 73–89 post, do not apply to elections under the Local Government Act 1972, Vol 25, title Local Government, other than local government elections; see s 90(2) post.

Saving for rights of creditors. See s 116 post.

Definitions. For "candidate", "committee room" and "election expenses", see s 118 post; for "election", see s 202(1) post. Note as to "election agent", sub-s (3) above.

---

73 Payment of expenses through election agent

(1) Except as permitted by section 74 below, or in pursuance of section 78 or section 79 below, no payment and no advance or deposit shall be made—

(a) by a candidate, or

(b) by any agent on behalf of a candidate, or

(c) by any other person,

at any time in respect of election expenses otherwise than by or through the candidate's election agent.

(2) Every payment made by an election agent in respect of any election expenses shall, except where less than [£20], be vouched for by a bill stating the particulars and by a receipt.

(3) The references in the foregoing provisions of this section to an election agent shall, in relation to a parliamentary election where sub-agents are allowed, be taken as references to the election agent acting by himself or a sub-agent.

(4) All money provided by any person other than the candidate for any election expenses, whether as gift, loan, advance or deposit, shall be paid to the candidate or his election agent and not otherwise.

(5) The foregoing provisions of this section shall not be deemed to apply to any sum disbursed by any person out of his own money for any small expense legally incurred by him if the sum is not repaid to him.

(6) A person who makes any payment, advance or deposit in contravention of subsection (1) above, or pays in contravention of subsection (4) above any money so provided as mentioned above, shall be guilty of an illegal practice.

NOTES

This section, as originally enacted, contained provisions formerly in the Representation of the People Act 1949, s 61, as affected, in the case of s 61(2), by the Decimal Currency Act 1969, s 10(1).

The reference to "£20" in sub-s (2) was substituted by the Representation of the People Act 1985, s 14(1), as from 1 October 1985 (see further the note "£20" below).

Sub-s (1): Any agent. For the circumstances establishing agency, see the note "By his agents" to s 159 post. The word "agent" in sub-s (1) above should be construed in accordance with the principles set out in that note.

Election agent. As to election agents, see s 67 ante and the notes thereto. Under that section or s 70 ante, a candidate may be his own election agent. Note also sub-s (3) above.

Sub-s (2): £20. For the power of the Secretary of State to vary this sum, see s 76A post.

Sub-s (3): Parliamentary election. See the note to s 1 ante.

Where sub-agents are allowed. As to the appointment of sub-agents at parliamentary elections, see s 68 ante.

Sub-s (5): Small expense legally incurred. This applies to such small payments as the hire of a taxi by a canvasser (where no use is made of it for the purpose of taking voters to the poll) or for postage where the payer is not and does not expect to be paid (*Norwich Case, Birkbeck v Bullard* (1886) 54 LT 625).

Sub-s (6): Illegal practice. See the note to s 61 ante. In *Re Worcester City Case, ex p Williamson* (1906) 51 Sol Jo 14, and *Re Worcester (Borough) Case, ex p Caldecote* (1907) 51 Sol Jo 593, payment of a candidate's expenses was made by his friend at his request in ignorance of the law requiring payment to be made by an election agent; relief was granted to both parties under what is now s 167 post.

Parish and community elections; municipal elections in City of London. See the notes to s 67 ante.

European Assembly elections. This section is applied to such elections by the European Assembly Elections Regulations 1984, SI 1984/137, reg 3(1), Sch 1, subject to a modification that no longer has any effect in view of the amendment to sub-s (2) above. See further the Introductory Note to this Act.

Exclusion. See the note to s 72 ante.

Saving for rights of creditors. See s 116 post.

Definitions. For "candidate" and "election expenses", see s 118 post; for "election", see s 202(1) post. Note as to "election agent", sub-s (3) above.

74 Candidate's personal expenses, and petty expenses

(1) The candidate at an election may pay any personal expenses incurred by him on account of or in connection with or incidental to the election, but the amount which a candidate at a parliamentary election may pay shall not exceed [£600], and any further personal expenses so incurred by him shall be paid by his election agent.

(2) The candidate shall send to his election agent within the time limited by this Act for sending in claims a written statement of the amount of personal expenses paid as mentioned above by the candidate.

(3) Any person may, if so authorised in writing by the candidate's election agent, pay any necessary expenses for stationery, postage, telegrams (or any similar means of communication) and other petty expenses, to a total amount not exceeding that named in the authority, but any excess above the total amount so named shall be paid by the election agent.

(4) A statement of the particulars of payments made by any person so authorised shall be sent to the election agent within the time limited by this Act for sending in claims, and shall be vouched for by a bill containing that person's receipt.

NOTES

This section contains provisions formerly in the Representation of the People Act 1949, s 62.

The reference to "£600" in sub-s (1) was substituted by the Representation of the People Act 1985, s 14(2), as from 1 October 1985 (see further the note "£600" below).

On account of ... the election. For the scope of these words, cf the note "On account of ... the conduct or management of the election" to s 76 post.

Parliamentary election. See the note to s 1 ante.

£600. For the power of the Secretary of State to vary this sum, see s 76A post.

Election agent. As to election agents, see s 67 ante and the notes thereto.

Time limited by this Act. Ie within twenty-one days after the day on which the result of the election is declared; see s 78(1) post and the note thereto.

Written. See the note to s 28 ante.

Parish and community elections; municipal elections in City of London. See the notes to s 67 ante.

European Assembly elections. This section is applied to such elections by the European Assembly Elections Regulations 1984, SI 1984/137, reg 3(1), Sch 1, subject to a modification that no longer has any effect in view of the amendment to sub-s (1) above. See further the Introductory Note to this Act.

As to provisions relating to such elections in Northern Ireland, see the Introductory Note to this Act.

Exclusion. See the note to s 72 ante.

Definitions. For "candidate" and "personal expenses", see s 118 post; for "election", see s 202(1) post.

---

75 Prohibition of expenses not authorised by election agent

(1) No expenses shall, with a view to promoting or procuring the election of a candidate at an election, be incurred by any person other than the candidate, his election agent and persons authorised in writing by the election agent on account—

(a) of holding public meetings or organising any public display; or

(b) of issuing advertisements, circulars or publications; or

(c) of otherwise presenting to the electors the candidate or his views or the extent or nature of his backing or disparaging another candidate,

but paragraph (c) of this subsection shall not—

(i) restrict the publication of any matter relating to the election in a newspaper or other periodical or in a broadcast made by the British Broadcasting Corporation or the Independent Broadcasting Authority [or in a programme included in a cable programme service which is or does not require to be licensed]; or

(ii) apply to any expenses not exceeding in the aggregate the sum of [£5] which may be incurred by an individual and are not incurred in pursuance of a plan suggested by or concerted with others, or to expenses incurred by any person in travelling or in living away from home or similar personal expenses.

(2) Where a person incurs any expenses required by this section to be authorised by the election agent—

(a) that person shall [within 21 days after the day on which the result of the election is declared deliver] to the appropriate officer a return of the amount of those expenses, stating the election at which and the candidate in whose support they were incurred, and

(b) the return shall be accompanied by a declaration made by that person (or in the case of an association or body of persons, by a director, general manager, secretary or other similar officer of the association or body) verifying the return and giving particulars of the matters for which the expenses were incurred, but this subsection does not apply to any person engaged or employed for payment or promise of payment by the candidate or his election agent.

(3) The return and declaration under the foregoing provisions of this section shall be in the prescribed form, and the authority received from the election agent shall be annexed to and deemed to form part of the return.

(4) A copy of every return and declaration made under subsection (2) above in relation to a parliamentary election in England, Wales or Northern Ireland shall be sent to the Clerk of the Crown within [21 days after the day on which the result of the election is declared] by the person making the return or declaration, and rule 57 of the parliamentary elections rules applies to any documents sent to the Clerk of the Crown under this subsection.

In this subsection references to the Clerk of the Crown in relation to an election in Northern Ireland are references to the Clerk of the Crown for Northern Ireland.

(5) If a person—

    (a) incurs, or aids, abets, counsels or procures any other person to incur, any expenses in contravention of this section, or

    (b) knowingly makes the declaration required by subsection (2) falsely,

he shall be guilty of a corrupt practice; and if a person fails to [deliver or] send any declaration or return or a copy of it as required by this section he shall be guilty of an illegal practice, but—

    (i) the court before whom a person is convicted under this subsection may, if they think it just in the special circumstances of the case, mitigate or entirely remit any incapacity imposed by virtue of section 173 below; and

    (ii) a candidate shall not be liable, nor shall his election be avoided, for a corrupt or illegal practice under this subsection committed by an agent without his consent or connivance.

(6) Where any act or omission of an association or body of persons, corporate or unincorporate, is an offence declared to be a corrupt or illegal practice by this section, any person who at the time of the act or omission was a director, general manager, secretary or other similar officer of the association or body, or was purporting to act in any such capacity, shall be deemed to be guilty of that offence, unless he proves—

    (a) that the act or omission took place without his consent or connivance; and

    (b) that he exercised all such diligence to prevent the commission of the offence as he ought to have exercised having regard to the nature of his functions in that capacity and to all the circumstances.

NOTES

Sub-s (1) contains provisions formerly in the Representation of the People Act 1949, s 63(1), as amended by the Representation of the People Act 1969, s 9(4), and as affected by the Decimal Currency Act 1969, s 10(1), and further amended by the Broadcasting Act 1981, s 65(3), Sch 8, para 7. Sub-ss (2)–(6) contain provisions formerly in s 63(2)–(6) of the 1949 Act.

The words in square brackets in sub-s (1)(i) were inserted by the Cable and Broadcasting Act 1984, s 57(1), Sch 5, para 44(1), and the reference to "£5" in sub-s (1)(ii) was substituted by the Representation of the People Act 1985, s 14(3), as from 1 October 1985 (see further the note "£5" below). The words in square brackets in sub-ss (2)(a), (4), (5) were substituted or inserted by s 24 of, and Sch 4, para 24 to, the 1985 Act, as from 1 October 1985.

Sub-s (1): With a view to. In *Grieve v Douglas-Home* 1965 SLT 186 at 190 it was stated that the maxim that a person must be taken to have intended the consequences of his acts does not apply in construing the words "with a view to". What has to be considered is the intention or motive in the mind of the person who occasioned the expense; if there is more than one motive, then it is the dominant one that has to be looked at; see *Grieve v Douglas-Home* supra at 190; but see *DPP v Luft* [1977] AC 962 at 983, [1976] 2 All ER 569 at 574, HL, per Lord Diplock ("For my part I prefer to omit the adjective 'dominant'. In my view the offence . . . is committed by the accused if his desire to promote or procure the election of a candidate was one of the reasons which played a part in inducing him to incur the expense").

Promoting or procuring the election of a candidate. It has been held that if a person disparages one candidate and tries to induce the electors not to vote for that candidate, he is, in effect, promoting the election of one or another of the other candidates; see *R v Hailwood and Ackroyds Ltd* [1928] 2 KB 277, [1928] All ER Rep 529, CCA, and *DPP v Luft* cited above.

The insertion of an advertisement in a national newspaper which contained criticisms of one party's financial policy, and which might have been held to advance the prospects of the opposing party's cause at a pending general election, has been held not to constitute an offence under these provisions (*R v Tronoh Mines Ltd* [1952] 1 All ER 697, 116 JP 180, CCA) but the distribution of pamphlets in three constituencies urging voters not to vote for the candidates of a certain political party in those constituencies has been held to constitute such an offence, as an intention to prevent the election of one candidate will involve also an intention to improve the collective chances of the remaining candidates (*DPP v Luft* cited above).

Election agent. As to election agents, see s 67 ante and the notes thereto.

Writing. See the note "Written" to s 28 ante.

Advertisements, circulars or publications. See the second paragraph of the note "Promoting or procuring the election of a candidate" above.

Disparaging. This is to be understood in its ordinary and natural meaning; a person may be disparaged by attacks on the political views he holds as well as by attacks on his personal conduct; see *DPP v Luft* cited above per Lord Diplock.

Broadcast. For restrictions on broadcasting, see ss 92 and 93 post.

British Broadcasting Corporation. This body was originally incorporated by Royal Charter on 20 December 1926 and its existence has been extended by subsequent charters. It operates under a licence from the Secretary of State.

Independent Broadcasting Authority. This body is now constituted under the Broadcasting Act 1981, s 1, Sch 1, Vol 45, title Telecommunications and Broadcasting.

£5. For the power of the Secretary of State to vary this sum, see s 76A post.

Sub-s (2): Within 21 days after, etc. For the computation of time, see s 119 post. See also the note "Within six months . . ." to s 5 ante.

Publication of the result. Ie in accordance with Sch 1, r 50 post, the Local Elections (Principal Areas) Rules 1973, SI 1973/79, Sch 2, r 46, or the Local Elections (Parishes and Communities) Rules 1973, SI 1973/1910, Sch 1, r 44.

Return; declaration. For general provisions as to returns to be made by the election agent, see s 81 post, and as to the inspection of returns and declarations, see s 89 post.

Sub-s (3): Prescribed form. For the relevant forms, see the Representation of the People Regulations 1983, SI 1983/435, reg 70(1), Sch 3, Forms V, W, or the Representation of the People (Northern Ireland) Regulations 1983, SI 1983/436, reg 55(1), Sch 3, Forms P, Q.

Sub-s (4): Parliamentary election. See the note to s 1 ante.

England; Wales. See the note to s 4 ante.

Sub-s (5): Aids, abets, counsels or procures. See the note to s 60 ante.

Knowingly. See the note "Knows" to s 60 ante.

Falsely. Cf the note "False" to s 62 ante.

Corrupt practice. See note to s 60 ante. Note also that ss 122(3)–(5) and 129(3)–(6) post (time for presentation or amendment of election petition) apply to a corrupt practice under this section as if it were an illegal practice; see sub-ss (6) and (7) of those sections, respectively.

Illegal practice. See the note to s 61 ante.

Agent. Cf the note "Any agent" to s 73 ante.

Consent. There is authority for saying that this presupposes knowledge; see *Re Caughey, ex p Ford* (1876) 1 Ch D 521 at 528, CA, per Jessel MR, and *Lamb v Wright & Co* [1924] 1 KB 857 at 864, [1924] All ER Rep 220 at 223. It is thought, however, that actual knowledge is not necessary; cf *Knox v Boyd* 1941 JC 82 at 86; *Taylor's Central Garages (Exeter) Ltd v Roper* (1951) 115 JP 445 at 449, 450, per Devlin J, [1951] WN 383; *James & Son Ltd v Smee* [1955] 1 QB 78 at 91, [1954] 3 All ER 273 at 278 per Parker J; and *Mallon v Allon* [1964] 1 QB 385 at 394, [1963] 3 All ER 843 at 847.

Connivance. Though there are many decisions on the meaning of this word in matrimonial law (see *Godfrey v Godfrey* [1965] AC 444, [1964] 3 All ER 154, HL, especially the speech of Lord Guest in which earlier decisions are reviewed), there is little authority as to its meaning in the context in which it appears in this section (see *Gregory v Walker* (1912) 77 JP 55, 29 TLR 51, and Glanville Williams, Criminal Law: The General Part, para 222). It is thought that the word implies knowledge of, and acquiescence in, the offence committed. Yet it seems that here again positive knowledge is not necessary and that suspicion is enough although mere negligence or inattention is not; see *Rogers v Rogers* (1830) 3 Hag Ecc 57 (but note the express reference to neglect in this section).

Sub-s (6): Where any act . . . is an offence, etc. Except where the penalty is inappropriate or where, by the nature of the offence, it must be committed by an individual, a corporation may be convicted for the criminal acts of the directors and managers who represent the directing mind and will of the corporation and control what it does; see *DPP v Kent and Sussex Contractors Ltd* [1944] KB 146, [1944] 1 All ER 119; *R v ICR Haulage Ltd* [1944] KB 551, [1944] 1 All ER 691, CCA; and *Tesco Supermarkets Ltd v Nattrass* [1972] AC 153, [1971] 2 All ER 127, HL.

As to the prosecution of members of associations and bodies of persons, see s 179 post; and for the general law relating to corporations, see 9 Halsbury's Laws (4th edn) paras 1201 et seq.

Purporting to act. The reference to any person who was purporting to act in any such capacity is introduced in view of *Dean v Hiesler* [1942] 2 All ER 340, where a director who had not been duly appointed was held not liable for an offence committed by the company.

Unless he proves, etc. The burden of proof resting on the accused is not so onerous as that which is, in general, laid on the prosecutor as regards proving an offence and may be discharged by satisfying the court of the probability or rather the preponderance of probability, of what the accused is called on to prove; see *R v Carr-Briant* [1943] KB 607, [1943] 2 All ER 156; *R v Dunbar* [1958] 1 QB 1, [1957] 2 All ER 737; and *R v Hudson* [1966] 1 QB 448, [1965] 1 All ER 721.

Exercised all such diligence. Whether or not the accused has exercised all due diligence is a question of fact, but on a case stated the High Court will interfere if there was no evidence to support a finding on this point; see *R C Hammett Ltd v Crabb* (1931) 145 LT 638, [1931] All ER Rep 70.

The failure of the directors of a limited company to exercise due diligence is the failure of the company; see *Pearce v Cullen* (1952) 96 Sol Jo 132. But the failure of subordinate managers and similar employees in a company with large-scale business to exercise due diligence is not necessarily the failure of the company; see *Tesco Supermarkets Ltd v Nattrass* [1972] AC 153, [1971] 2 All ER 127, HL.

It has been said that a contractual obligation to exercise due diligence is indistinguishable from an obligation to exercise reasonable care; see *Riverstone Meat Co Pty Ltd v Lancashire Shipping Co Ltd* [1960] 1 QB 536 at 581, [1960] 1 All ER 193 at 291, CA per Willmer LJ (revsd on other grounds [1961] AC 807, [1961] 1 All ER 495, HL).

Parish and community elections; municipal elections in City of London. See the notes to s 67 ante.

European Assembly elections. This section is applied to such elections by the European Assembly Elections Regulations 1984, SI 1984/137, reg 3(1), Sch 1, subject to the omission of sub-s (4), and a modification that no longer has any effect in view of the amendment of sub-s (1)(ii) above.

See further the Introductory Note to this Act.

As to provisions relating to such elections in Northern Ireland, see the Introductory Note to this Act.

Exclusion. See the note to s 72 ante.

Saving for rights of creditors. See s 116 post.

Definitions. For "appropriate officer", see s 67(7) ante; for "candidate" and "personal expenses", see s 118 post; for "Clerk of the Crown"; "election" and "parliamentary elections rules", see s 202(1) post (and note also as to "Clerk of the Crown", the second paragraph of sub-s (4) above). For "programme", see the Cable and Broadcasting Act 1984, s 56(2), Vol 45, title Telecommunications and Broadcasting, and, by virtue of that section, for "cable programme service" and "licensed", see ss 2(1) and 4 respectively of that Act, in the same title.

---

76 Limitation of election expenses

(1) No sum shall be paid and no expense shall be incurred by a candidate at an election or his election agent, whether before, during or after an election, on account of or in respect of the conduct or management of the election, in excess of the maximum amount specified in this section, and a candidate or election agent knowingly acting in contravention of this subsection shall be guilty of an illegal practice.

(2) That maximum amount is—

(*a*) for a candidate at a parliamentary election—

    (i) in a county constituency, £2,700 together with an additional 3.1p for every entry in the register of electors to be used at the election (as first published); and

    (ii) in a borough constituency, £2,700 together with an additional 2.3p for every entry in the register of electors to be used at the election (as first published);

(*b*) for a candidate at a local government election—

    (i) . . .

    [(ia) at an election to the Inner London Education Authority, £620 together with an additional 3.7p for every entry in the register of electors to be used at the election (as first published);]

    (ii) at any other local government election, £120 together with an additional 2.4p for every entry in the register of electors to be used at the election (as first published).

(3) . . .

(4) If the register to be used at the election is not published before the day of publication of the notice of election then for any reference in subsection (2) above to an entry in that register there shall be substituted a reference to an entry in the electors lists for that register as first published which gives the name of a person appearing from those lists to be entitled to be registered.

(5) The maximum amount mentioned above for a candidate at a parliamentary election is not required to cover the candidate's personal expenses.

(6) Where at an election a poll is countermanded or abandoned by reason of a candidate's death, the maximum amount of election expenses shall, for any of the other candidates who then remain validly nominated, be twice or, if there has been a previous increase under this subsection, three times what it would have been but for any increase under this subsection; but the maximum amount shall not be affected for any candidate by the change in the timing of the election or of any step in the proceedings at the election.

NOTES

Sub-ss (1), (4), (5) contain provisions formerly in the Representation of the People Act 1949, s 64(1), (3), (4), respectively. Sub-s (2)(*a*) contains provisions formerly in s 64(2)(*a*) of the 1949 Act, as substituted by the Representation of the People Act 1978, s 1, and as amended by the Representation of the People (Variation of Limits of Candidates' Election Expenses) Order 1982, SI 1982/363, arts 2, 3. Sub-s (2)(*b*), as originally enacted, contained provisions formerly in s 64(2)(*b*) of the 1949 Act, as substituted by the Representation of the People Act 1977, s 1(1), and as amended, by the Representation of the People (Variation of Limits of Candidates' Election Expenses) Order 1981, SI 1981/191, art 2, and by art 4 of the 1982 Order. Sub-s (6) contains provisions formerly in s 64(4A) of the 1949 Act, as inserted by s 24(1) of, and Sch 2, para 16 to, the 1969 Act.

Sub-s (2)(*b*)(i) was repealed by the Local Government Act 1985, s 102(2), Sch 17, as from 1 April 1986 ("the abolition date" within the meaning of s 1(2) of that Act), and sub-s (2)(*b*)(ia) was inserted by s 19 of, and Sch 9, Pt I, para 1(8) to, that Act as from 1 September 1985 (see the Local Government Act 1985 (New Authorities) (Appointed Days) Order 1985, SI 1985/1263).

Sub-s (3) was repealed by the Representation of the People Act 1985, ss 24, 28(1), Sch 4, para 25, Sch 5, as from 1 October 1985.

Sub-s (1): Candidate. For special provisions applicable to joint candidatures in local government elections, see s 77 post.

Election agent. As to election agents, see s 67 ante and the notes thereto. For the position in relation to parish and community council elections, see s 90(1)(*a*) post.

On account of . . . the conduct or management of the election. The extent of these words has been the subject of much judicial consideration. It is a question of fact as to when an election "begins" for the purpose of rendering candidates and their agents responsible for breaches of election laws governing candidatures (*Lambeth, Kennington Division Case, Crossman v Davis* (1886) 54 LT 628; *Lancaster County, Lancaster Division, Case, Bradshaw and Kaye v Foster* (1896) 5 O'M & H 39). In parliamentary cases it is usually immaterial to consider either the date of dissolution of Parliament, or the issue of writs or nomination day (*Walsall Borough Case, Hateley, Moss and Mason v James* (1892) 4 O'M & H 123), as in the majority of cases a candidature will have begun at an earlier date. When a person has with his own consent been adopted as a candidate by a political association to stand at a definite election or has put himself in the running by announcing himself as a candidate for election at a definite election (whether as an independent or as a person hoping for a party nomination) this section will apply to him for the future whether or not the time of the election at which he will stand is definitely known (*Great Yarmouth Borough Case, White v Fell* (1906) 5 O'M & H 176; *Maidstone Borough Case, Evans v Viscount Castlereagh* (1906) 5 O'M & H 200; *Bodmin Division Case* (1906) 5 O'M & H 225). This section does not attach merely on account of a person forming the desire or intention to be a candidate, but it will attach as soon as active steps are taken by him or on his behalf with a view to promoting his candidature (*Stafford County, Lichfield Division Case, Wolseley, Levett, Atkin and Shaw v Fulford* (1895) 5 O'M & H 27; *Maidstone Case* supra; *Dorsetshire, Eastern Division Case, Lambert and Bond v Guest* (1910) 6 O'M & H 22).

A distinction must be drawn between expenses incurred with a view to procuring the election of a particular person (which are within the scope of the section) and expenses incurred for general political purposes (which are not) (*Shoreditch, Haggerston Division Case, Cremer v Lowles* (1896) 5 O'M & H 68; *Great Yarmouth Case*, cited above). See also *Cumberland, Cockermouth Division Case, Armstrong, Brooksbank, Brown, Beck, Cooper and Henderson v Randles* (1901) 5 O'M & H 155 (Liberal Unionist tea held in the circumstances not to be connected with election of a candidate).

This section does not apply to expenses incurred by third parties for the purpose of procuring a candidate or for inducing a person to be candidate at a time when it is not known whether the person they have in mind will accept nomination or not (*Norwich Case, Birkbeck v Bullard* (1886) 54 LT 625).

In excess of the maximum amount. The offence is excusable under s 167 post. In *Ex p Ayrton* (1885) 2 TLR 214, relief was granted for exceeding the then permitted maximum for parliamentary candidates by £97 19s 6d; this sum had been expended mainly in contradicting reports about the candidate. In *Ex p Hughes* (1897) 42 Sol Jo 163, leave was granted to pay £8 11s 6d which had been incurred in excess of the then permitted maximum in a municipal election; this sum had been incurred by an agent stated to be experienced in election law who had forgotten to include a sum paid for the use of committee rooms and who had been in the habit of acting at elections where a larger maximum was allowed and had not appreciated how the printing expenses had mounted up. In *Re Hackney Central Division Municipal Election, ex p Wood and Stuart* (1898) 42 Sol Jo 396, relief was granted for exceeding the maximum by £43 spent on extra printing being an unforeseen outlay consequent upon postponement of the poll following the death of one of the candidates.

Note that in certain cases the cost of access by sea to a polling place may be allowed in addition to the maximum amount of expenses; see s 105(1), (2) post.

Knowingly. This word is not mere surplusage. It means knowing at the time payment is made, or the expense incurred, that it is an election expense; and if, when the total of those expenses is added up, that total is in excess of the maximum, then the offence is complete. It is not necessary to prove that when a particular payment was made or expense incurred the candidate or election agent was aware that the maximum amount had been exceeded (*Northumberland, Berwick-upon-Tweed Division, Case* (1923) 7 O'M & H 1 at 19, 20; *Oxford Borough Case* (1924) 7 O'M & H 49 at 67). See also the note "Knows" to s 60 ante.

Illegal practice. See the note to s 61 ante.

Sub-s (2): Maximum amount. For the power of the Secretary of State to vary a maximum amount specified in this subsection, see s 76A post.

Parliamentary election. See the note to s 1 ante. For a modification of this section in relation to the summoning of a new Parliament on the demise of the Crown, see the Representation of the People Act 1985, s 20(5), Vol 32, title Parliament.

County constituency; borough constituency. See the note to s 24 ante.

Register of electors. See s 9 ante and the note "Register" thereto.

Inner London Education Authority. See the note to s 31 ante.

Sub-s (4): Notice of election. As to the publication of this notice, see Sch 1, r 5 post, the Local Elections (Principal Areas) Rules 1973, SI 1973/79, Sch 2, r 4, and the Local Elections (Parishes and Communities) Rules 1973, SI 1973/1910, Sch 1, r 4.

Electors lists. As to the preparation and publication of electors lists, see s 10(*b*) ante and the note thereto.

Sub-s (5): Candidates' personal expenses. As to those, see s 74 ante.

Sub-s (6): Nominated. As to the nomination of candidates for parliamentary and local government elections, see Sch 1, rr 6–17 post, the Local Elections (Principal Areas) Rules 1973, SI 1973/79 (as amended by SI 1983/1154), Sch 2, rr 5–12, and the Local Elections (Parishes and Communities) Rules 1973, SI 1973/1910 (as amended by SI 1983/1153), Sch 1, rr 5–12.

Parish and community elections; municipal elections in City of London. See the notes to s 67 ante, and note, in particular, the special provisions relating to expenses at ward elections and elections by liverymen in common hall in the City of London in s 197 post.

European Assembly elections. This section is applied to such elections by the European Assembly Elections Regulations 1984, SI 1984/137, reg 3(1), Sch 1, subject to modifications which appear no longer to have any effect in view of the amendments to this section.

See further the Introductory Note to this Act.

As to such elections in Northern Ireland, see the Introductory Note to this Act.

Exclusion. See the note to s 72 ante.

Saving for rights of creditors. See s 116 post.

Definitions. For "candidate", "election expenses", "money" and "personal expenses", see s 118 post; for "election" and "elector", see s 202(1) post; for "local government election", see s 203(1) post.

[76A   Power to vary provisions concerning election expenses

(1) The Secretary of State may by order made by statutory instrument vary the sum specified in section 73(2), 74(1) or 75(1) above or a maximum amount of candidate's election expenses specified in section 76(2) above where in his opinion there has been a change in the value of money since the last occasion on which that sum or, as the case may be, amount was fixed (whether by such an order or otherwise) and the variation shall be such as in his opinion is justified by that change.

(2) An order under subsection (1) above shall not be made unless a draft of the order has been laid before, and approved by a resolution of, each House of Parliament.]

77 Expenses limit for joint candidates at local election

(1) Where there are two or more joint candidates at a local government election the maximum amount mentioned in section 76 above shall, for each of those joint candidates, be reduced by a quarter or, if there are more than two joint candidates, by one-third.

(2) Where two or more candidates appoint the same election agent, or by themselves or any agent or agents—

(a) employ or use the services of the same clerks or messengers at the election, or

(b) hire or use the same committee rooms for the election, or

(c) publish a joint address, circular or notice at the election,

those candidates shall for the purposes of this section be deemed to be joint candidates; but—

(i) the employment and use of the same clerk, messenger or committee room, if accidental or casual, or of a trivial and unimportant character, shall not be deemed of itself to constitute persons joint candidates;

(ii) nothing in this subsection shall prevent candidates from ceasing to be joint candidates.

(3) Where—

(a) any excess of expenses above the maximum allowed for one of two or more joint candidates has arisen owing to his having ceased to be a joint candidate, or to his having become a joint candidate after having begun to conduct his election as a separate candidate,

(b) the change was made in good faith,

(c) the excess is not more than under the circumstances is reasonable, and

(d) the total election expenses of the candidate do not exceed the maximum amount allowed for a separate candidate,

the excess shall be deemed to have arisen from a reasonable cause for the purposes of section 167 below.

78 Time for sending in and paying claims

(1) Every claim against a candidate or his election agent in respect of election expenses which is not sent in to the election agent within [21 days] after the day on which the result of the election is declared shall be barred and not paid.

(2) All election expenses shall be paid within 28 days after that day.

(3) An election agent who pays a claim in contravention of subsection (1) or makes a payment in contravention of subsection (2) above shall be guilty of an illegal practice; but where the election court reports that it has been proved to the court by the candidate that any payment was made by an election agent without the sanction or connivance of the candidate—

(a) the candidate's election shall not be void, nor
(b) shall he be subject to any incapacity under this Act by reason only of that payment having been made in contravention of this section.

(4) The claimant or the candidate or his election agent may apply to the High Court or to a county court for leave to pay a claim for any election expenses, although sent in after that period of [21 days] or although sent in to the candidate and not to the election agent, and the court on cause shown to their satisfaction may by order grant the leave.

.   .   .   .   .

(5) Any sum specified in the order of leave may be paid by the candidate or his election agent and when paid in pursuance of the leave shall not be deemed to be in contravention of subsection (2) above.

(6) Except in Scotland, the jurisdiction vested by subsection (4) above in the High Court in matters relating to parliamentary elections shall, subject to rules of court, be exercised by—

(a) one of the judges for the time being on the rota for the trial of parliamentary election petitions,
(b) in Northern Ireland, one of the judges of the High Court or the Court of Appeal for the time being selected under section 108 of the Judicature (Northern Ireland) Act 1978,

sitting either in court or at chambers, or by a master of the Supreme Court in manner directed by and subject to an appeal to those judges.

(7) The jurisdiction vested by subsection (4) in a county court may, except in Northern Ireland, be exercised otherwise than in open court and, in Northern Ireland, shall be exercised in such manner as may be provided by rules of court.

An appeal lies to the High Court from any order of a county court made by virtue of subsection (4).

NOTES

This section contains provisions formerly in the Representation of the People Act 1949, s 66, as partly repealed, in the case of s 66(6), by the Representation of the People Act 1969, s 24(4), Sch 3, Pt I, and as amended, in the case of that subsection, by the Judicature (Northern Ireland) Act 1978, s 122(1), Sch 5, Pt II.

The words omitted from sub-s (4) where indicated by dots apply to Scotland only.

The references to "21 days" in sub-ss (1), (4) were substituted by the Representation of the People Act 1985, s 24, Sch 4, para 26, as from 1 October 1985.

Sub-s (1): Election agent. As to election agents, see s 67 ante and the notes thereto; and as to an election agent's claim for his remuneration, see s 80 post.

Within 21 days after, etc. For the computation of time, see s 119 post. See also the note "Within six months . . ." to s 5 ante.

Result . . . is declared. See the note to s 81 post.

Sub-s (2): Within 28 days after, etc. See the note "Within 21 days after, etc" above.

Sub-s (3): Illegal practice. See the note to s 61 ante. In *Re Preston, Fishwick Ward Councillor, Re Hubberstey* (1899) 43 Sol Jo 826, relief was granted under what is now s 167 post, for making a payment out of time where the successful candidate at a local government election (a solicitor) stated that he had not appreciated the correct time limit after consulting a text book on elections.

Election court. For the constitution of election courts, see s 123 or 130 post.

Reports. As to the reports of election courts, see ss 144, 145, 158 post.

Connivance. See the note to s 75 ante.

Incapacity. For the incapacities of candidates reported guilty of an illegal practice, see ss 159(2), (3), 160(5) post.

Sub-s (4): High Court. See the note to s 39 ante; and note sub-s (6) above.

County court. See the note to s 30 ante.

Leave to pay. In *Ex p Morris* (1897) 42 Sol Jo 163, leave was granted to pay bills which had been inadvertently omitted from the candidate's return; the default arose in consequence of the illness of an agent who had been unable to check the accounts. In *Ex p Polson* (1923) 39 TLR 231, the candidate was given leave to pay £75 11s 1d outstanding for printing, clerks, committee rooms, and personal expenses, as the court took the view that all the irregularities in the case were due to the election agent.

Sub-s (6): Parliamentary elections. See the note "Parliamentary election" to s 1 ante.

Rules of court. As to such rules, see s 182 post and the notes thereto.

Rota. As to the selection of judges for the rota for the trial of parliamentary election petitions, see the Supreme Court Act 1981, s 142, Vol 11, title Courts.

Disputed claims. As to disputed claims, see s 79 post.

Parish and community elections; municipal elections in City of London. See the notes to s 67 ante.

European Assembly elections. This section and ss 79–84, 86–88 post, are applied to such elections by the European Assembly Elections Regulations 1984, SI 1984/137, reg 3(1), Sch 1. See further the Introductory Note to this Act.

As to provisions relating to such elections in Northern Ireland, see the Introductory Note to this Act.

Exclusion. See the note to s 72 ante.

Saving for rights of creditors. See s 116 post.

Definitions. For "candidate" and "election expenses", see s 118 post; for "election", "election court" and "parliamentary election petition", see s 202(1) post.

Judicature (Northern Ireland) Act 1978, s 108. See Vol 31, title Northern Ireland (Pt 2).

79 Disputed claims

(1) If the election agent disputes any claim sent in to him within the period of [21 days] mentioned in section 78 above or refuses or fails to pay the claim within the period of 28 days so mentioned, the claim shall be deemed to be a disputed claim.

(2) The claimant may, if he thinks fit, bring an action for a disputed claim in any competent court, and any sum paid by the candidate or his agent in pursuance of the judgment or order of the court shall not be deemed to be in contravention of section 73(1) above or of section 78(2).

(3) If the defendant in the action admits his liability but disputes the amount of the claim, that amount shall, unless the court on the plaintiff's application otherwise directs, be forthwith referred for taxation—

(a) to a Circuit judge nominated under subsection (1)(a) of section 68 of the Supreme Court Act 1981, or

(b) to the master, registrar or other proper officer of the court,

and the amount found due on the taxation shall be the amount to be recovered in the action in respect of the claim.

(4) Subsections (4) to (7) of section 78 apply in relation to a disputed claim as they apply in relation to a claim for election expenses sent in after that period of [21 days].

NOTES

This section contains provisions formerly in the Representation of the People Act 1949, s 67, as amended, in the case of s 67(3), by the Supreme Court Act 1981, s 68(7).

The references to "21 days" in sub-ss (1), (4) were substituted by the Representation of the People Act 1985, s 24, Sch 4, para 26, as from 1 October 1985.

Election agent. As to election agents, see s 67 ante and the notes thereto; and as to an election agent's claim for his remuneration, see s 80 post.

Within the period of 21 (28) days, etc. For the computation of time, see s 119 post. See also the note "Within six months . . ." to s 5 ante.

Disputed claim. Under s 80 post, an election agent's claim for his remuneration may also be a "disputed claim".

Forthwith. See the note to s 67 ante.

Notice of application. In *Re Salop Southern or Ludlow Division Case* (1886) 54 LT 129, an application was refused on account of lack of sufficient notice of intention to make application. The court said notice should be given to the other candidate, and to the returning officer and to the constituency by advertisement or otherwise.

Leave to pay disputed claims. In *Re South Shropshire Case* (1886) 34 WR 352, which is the subsequent proceeding to the case reported sub nom *Re Salop Southern or Ludlow Division Case* (1886) 54 LT 129, leave was given to a candidate to pay about £300 to sub-agents for their charges although the time for payment had passed; the reason for delay was that at first the candidate thought the charges unreasonable then changed his mind. In the *Re Chelsea Case* (1886) 2 TLR 375, the candidate was refused leave to pay £41 for the hire of a conveyance in respect of which he was not liable as it had been hired by a clerk without authority.

In *Re Parliamentary Election* (1887) 4 TLR 38, the facts were that a member of Parliament instructed his agent to prepare canvassing books for a general election and then did not employ him as election agent for that election at which he was returned unopposed. The former agent sent in his claim to the member for preparing the canvassing books which he returned in his election return as a "disputed claim". The former agent then brought an action for damages for breach of an alleged agreement to employ him as election agent. The action was referred to arbitration and the arbitrator awarded £60 for the preparation of the canvassing books. In this application, leave to pay the sum awarded in the arbitration was granted.

Parish and community elections; municipal elections in City of London. See the notes to s 67 ante.

European Assembly elections. See the note to s 78 ante.

Exclusion. See the note to s 72 ante.

Definitions. For "candidate" and "election expenses", see s 118 post. Note as to "disputed claim", sub-s (1) above.

Supreme Court Act 1981, s 68(1)(a). See Vol 11, title Courts.

80 Election agent's claim

So far as circumstances admit, this Act applies to an election agent's claim for his remuneration and to its payment in like manner as if he were any other creditor, and if any difference arises about the amount of the claim, the claim shall be a disputed claim within the meaning of this Act and be dealt with accordingly.

NOTES

This section contains provisions formerly in the Representation of the People Act 1949, s 68.

Election agent. As to election agents, see s 67 ante and the notes thereto.

Disputed claim. This expression is defined by s 79(1) ante. As to the settlement of such claims, see s 79(2), (3) ante, and s 78(4)–(7) ante, as applied by s 79(4) ante.

Parish and community elections; municipal elections in City of London. See the notes to s 67 ante.

European Assembly elections. See the note to s 78 ante.

Exclusion. See the note to s 72 ante.

81 Return as to election expenses

(1) Within 35 days after the day on which the result of the election is declared, the election agent of every candidate at the election shall [deliver] to the appropriate officer a true return in the form set out in Schedule 3 to this Act, or to the like effect, containing as respects that candidate a statement of all payments made by the election agent together with all the bills and receipts.

(2) The return shall deal under a separate heading or subsection with any expenses included in it—

(a) as respects which a return is required to be made under section 75(2) above; or

(b) which are on account of the remuneration or expenses of speakers at public meetings.

(3) The return shall also contain as respects that candidate—

(a) a statement of the amount of personal expenses, if any, paid by the candidate;

(b) a statement of all disputed claims of which the election agent is aware;

(c) a statement of all the unpaid claims, if any, of which the election agent is aware, in respect of which application has been or is about to be made to the High Court or county court;

(d) a statement of all money, securities and equivalent of money received by the election agent from the candidate or any other person for the purposes of election expenses incurred or to be incurred, with a statement of the name of every person from whom they may have been received.

(4) Where the candidate is his own election agent, a statement of all money, securities and equivalent of money paid by the candidate shall be substituted in the return as to election expenses for the statement of money, securities and equivalent of money received by the election agent from the candidate.

(5) Where after the date at which the return as to election expenses is [delivered], leave is given by the court under section 78(4) above for any claim to be paid, the candidate or his election agent shall, within seven days after its payment, [deliver] to the appropriate officer a return of the sums paid in pursuance of the leave, accompanied by a copy of the order of the court giving the leave, and in default he shall be deemed to have failed to comply with the requirements of this section without such authorised excuse as is mentioned in section 86 below.

NOTES

This section contains provisions formerly in the Representation of the People Act 1949, s 69.

The words in square brackets in sub-ss (1), (5) were substituted by the Representation of the People Act 1985, s 24, Sch 4, para 27, as from 1 October 1985.

Sub-s (1): Within 35 days after, etc. For the computation of time, see s 119 post. See also the note "Within six months . . ." to s 5 ante.

Result . . . is declared. As to the declaration of an election result, see Sch 1, r 50 post, the Local Elections (Principal Areas) Rules 1973, SI 1973/79, Sch 2, r 46 and the Local Elections (Parishes and Communities) Rules 1973, SI 1973/1910, Sch 1, r 44.

Election agent. As to election agents, see s 67 ante and the notes thereto.

Every candidate. Note that candidates of the kind specified in s 83 post are not required to make a return under this section.

True return. Errors in a return do not necessarily affect its validity as a return but may be made the subject of an application for relief under s 86 post (*Mackinnon v Clark* [1898] 2 QB 251, 67 LJQB 763, CA).

It does not seem to have been judicially decided that a return of no expenses must be made in parliamentary elections but it has been so decided in relation to municipal elections (*Ex p Robson* (1886) 18 QBD 336, 3 TLR 274; *Ex p Pennington* (1898) 46 WR 415; *Nichol v Fearby* [1923] 1 KB 480, [1922] All ER Rep 790).

Declarations as to election expenses must also be delivered; see s 82 post.

All payments made by the election agent. All payments by or on behalf of a candidate in respect of election expenses must be made by or through the election agent; see s 73 ante, which regulates the making of payments.

Sub-s (3): Disputed claims. Ie claims governed by s 79 or 80 ante.

Unpaid claims. This refers to claims governed by s 78(4) ante.

High Court. See the note to s 39 ante.

County court. See the note to s 30 ante.

Sub-s (4): Candidate is his own election agent. Ie by virtue of s 67(2) or 70 ante.

Penalties. For penalties for failure to comply with the requirements of this section, see ss 84, 85 post, but note that the candidate or election agent may have an authorised excuse under s 86 post. See also s 87 post.

Inspection of returns. See ss 88, 89 post.

Parish and community elections; municipal elections in City of London. See the notes to s 67 ante.

European Assembly elections. See the note to s 78 ante.

Exclusion. See the note to s 72 ante.

Definitions. For "appropriate officer", see s 67(7) ante; for "disputed claim", see ss 79(1), 80 ante; for "candidate", "election expenses", "money", "payment" and "personal expenses", see s 118 post; for "election" and "person", see s 202(1) post.

---

82 Declarations as to election expenses

(1) The return [delivered] under section 81(1) above shall be accompanied by a declaration made by the election agent in the form in Schedule 3 to this Act.

(2) At the same time that the election agent [delivers] that return, or within seven days afterwards, the candidate shall [deliver] to the appropriate officer a declaration made by him in the form in that Schedule.

(3) Where the candidate is out of the United Kingdom when the return is so [delivered]—

    (*a*) the declaration required by subsection (2) above may be made by him within 14 days after his return to the United Kingdom, and

    (*b*) in that case, the declaration shall be forthwith [delivered] to the appropriate officer,

but the delay authorised by this provision in making the declaration shall not exonerate the election agent from complying with the provisions of this Act relating to the return and declaration as to election expenses.

(4) An election agent's or a candidate's declaration as to election expenses under this section may be made either before a justice of the peace or before any person who is—

    (*a*) in England and Wales, the chairman or proper officer of ... [... the Inner London Education Authority], a county council or a district council, or the mayor or proper officer of a London borough;

    (*b*) (*applies to Scotland only*);

    (*c*) in Northern Ireland, the clerk of a district council.

(5) Where the candidate is his own election agent, the declaration by an election agent as to election expenses need not be made and the declaration by the candidate as to election expenses shall be modified as specified in the form in Schedule 3.

(6) If a candidate or election agent knowingly makes the declaration required by this section falsely, he shall be guilty of a corrupt practice.

NOTES

Sub-ss (1), (2) contain provisions formerly in the Representation of the People Act 1949, s 70(1), (2) as partly repealed by the Representation of the People Act 1969, s 24(4), Sch 3, Pt II. Sub-s (3) contains provisions formerly in the proviso to s 70(2) of the 1949 Act. Sub-s (4) contains provision formerly in s 8(4) of the 1969 Act, as partly repealed by the Local Government Act 1972, s 272(1), Sch 30, and as amended by the Local Government Reorganisation (Consequential Provisions) (Northern Ireland) Order 1973, SI 1973/2095, art 2(6). Sub-s (5), (6) contain provisions formerly in s 70(3), (4) of the 1949 Act.

The words in square brackets in sub-ss (1), (2), (3) were substituted by the Representation of the People Act 1985, s 24, Sch 4, para 28, as from 1 October 1985. The words omitted from sub-s (4)(*a*) were repealed by the Local Government Act 1985, s 102(2), Sch 17, as from 1 April 1986 ("the abolition date" within the meaning of s 1(2) of that Act), and the words in square brackets in that subsection were inserted by s 19 of, and Sch 9, Pt I, para 1(9) to, that Act, as from 1 September 1985 (see the Local Government Act 1985 (New Authorities) (Appointed Days) Order 1985, SI 1985/1263).

Sub-s (1): Election agent. As to election agents, see s 67 ante and the notes thereto.

Sub-s (2): Within seven days afterwards, etc. For the computation of time, see s 119 post. See also the note "Within six months ..." to s 5 ante.

Candidate. Note that candidates of the kind specified in s 83 post are not required to make a declaration under this section.

Sub-s (3): United Kingdom. See the note to s 6 ante.

Forthwith. See the note to s 67 ante.

Provisions ... relating to the return and declaration as to election expenses. See, in particular, sub-s (1) above and s 81 ante.

Sub-s (4): Justice of the peace. A justice of the peace may be either a lay justice or a stipendiary magistrate. The main provisions relating to justices of the peace (including stipendiary magistrates), covering such matters as appointment, removal and organisation, will be found in the Justices of the Peace Act 1979, Vol 27, title Magistrates, and the office and jurisdiction of justices are considered generally in 29 Halsbury's Laws (4th edn) paras 201 et seq.

England; Wales. See the note to s 4 ante.

Inner London Education Authority; county council. See the note to s 31 ante.

District council. See the note "Council of every district" to s 8 ante.

London borough. See the note to s 8 ante.

Sub-s (5): Candidate is his own election agent. Ie by virtue of s 67(2) or 70 ante.

Sub-s (6): Knowingly. See the note "Knows" to s 60 ante.

Falsely. Cf the note "False" to s 62 ante.

Corrupt practice. See the note to s 60 ante.

Penalties. For penalties for failure to comply with the requirements of this section, see ss 84, 85 post, but note that the candidate or election agent may have an authorised excuse under s 86 post. See also s 87 post.

Inspection of declarations. See ss 88, 89 post.

Parish and community elections; municipal elections in City of London. See the notes to s 67 ante.

European Assembly elections. See the note to s 78 ante.

Exclusion. See the note to s 72 ante.

Definitions. For "appropriate officer", see s 67(7) ante; for "candidate", "declaration as to election expenses", "election expenses" and "return as to election expenses", see s 118 post; for "proper officer", see s 202(1) post.

83 Where no return and declarations needed at parliamentary elections

Notwithstanding anything in sections 81 and 82 above, no return or declaration as to election expenses shall be required in the case of a person—

(a) who is a candidate at a parliamentary election, but is so only because he has been declared by others to be a candidate; and

(b) who has not consented to the declaration or taken any part as a candidate in the election.

NOTES

This section contains provisions formerly in the Representation of the People Act 1949, s 71.

Parish and community elections; municipal elections in City of London. See the notes to s 67 ante.

European Assembly elections. See the note to s 78 ante.

Exclusion. See the note to s 72 ante.

Definitions. For "candidate", "declaration as to election expenses", "election expenses" and "return as to election expenses", see s 118 post.

84 Penalty for failure as respects return or declarations

Subject to the provisions of section 86 below, if a candidate or election agent fails to comply with the requirements of section 81 or section 82 above he shall be guilty of an illegal practice.

NOTES

This section contains provisions formerly in the Representation of the People Act 1949, s 72.

Candidate. For meaning, see s 118 post.

Election agent. As to election agents, see s 67 ante and the notes thereto.

Illegal practice. See the note to s 61 ante; and note also the provision for relief in s 86 post.

Parish and community elections; municipal elections in City of London. See the notes to s 67 ante.

European Assembly elections. See the note to s 78 ante.

Exclusion. See the note to s 72 ante.

85 Penalty for sitting or voting where no return and declarations transmitted

(1) If, in the case of any candidate, the return and declarations as to election expenses are not [delivered] before the expiry of the time limited for the purpose, that candidate shall not, after the expiry of that time, sit or vote in the House of Commons as member for the constituency for which the election was held until—

(a) either that return and those declarations have been [delivered], or

(b) the date of the allowance of an authorised excuse for the failure to [deliver] that return and those declarations, and if he sits or votes in contravention of this subsection he shall forfeit £100 for every day on which he so sits or votes.

(2) In the application of subsection (1) above to a candidate at a local government election—

(a) the reference to sitting or voting in the House of Commons for the constituency for which the election was held shall be taken as a reference to sitting or voting in the council for the local government area for which the election was held; and

(b) £50 shall be substituted for £100 and, instead of civil proceedings for a penalty, summary proceedings may be instituted under the Magistrates' Courts Act 1980, or, in Scotland, in the sheriff court, and the person charged shall be liable on conviction to a fine not exceeding the amount of the penalty which would be recoverable in civil proceedings.

[(3) Civil proceedings for a penalty under this section shall be commenced within the period of one year beginning with the day in respect of which the penalty is alleged to have been incurred.]

(4) For the purposes of subsection (3) above—

(a) where the service or execution of the writ or other process on or against the alleged offender is prevented by the absconding or concealment or act of the alleged offender, the issue of a writ or other process shall be deemed to be a commencement of a proceeding; but,

(b) where paragraph (a) does not apply, the service or execution of the writ or other process on or against the alleged offender, and not its issue, shall be deemed to be the commencement of the proceeding.

(5) Subsections (3) and (4) above do not apply in Scotland.

NOTES

Sub-ss (1), (2) contain provisions formerly in the Representation of the People Act 1949, s 73(1), (2). Sub-s (4) contains provisions formerly in s 73(3) of the 1949 Act, as partly repealed by the Representation of the People Act 1969, s 24(4), Sch 3, Pt II.

The words in square brackets in sub-s (1), and the whole of sub-s (3), were substituted by the Representation of the People Act 1985, s 24, Sch 4, para 29, as from 1 October 1985.

Sub-s (1): Time limited. See ss 81(1), 82(1)–(3) ante.

Constituency. See the note to s 1 ante.

Authorised excuse. See s 86 post for allowance of excuses for failures as to returns and declarations.

Forfeit. This penalty belongs to the Crown since this Act does not give it to any other person (*Bradlaugh v Clarke* (1883) 8 App Cas 354, [1881–5] All ER Rep 1002).

As to evidence in proceedings for penalties under this section, see s 180 post.

Sub-s (2): Summary proceedings. See the note "Summary conviction" to s 62 ante.

Sub-s (3): Within one year after, etc. For the computation of time, see s 119 post; and note sub-s (4) above. See also the note "Within six months . . ." to s 5 ante.

Parish and community elections; municipal elections in City of London. See the notes to s 67 ante.

Exclusion. See the note to s 72 ante.

Definitions. For "candidate", "declaration as to election expenses", "election expenses" and "return as to election expenses", see s 118 post; for "election", see s 202(1) post; for "local government area" and "local government election", see s 203(1) post.

Magistrates' Courts Act 1980. See Vol 27, title Magistrates.

---

86 Authorised excuses for failures as to return and declarations

(1) A candidate or his election agent may apply for relief under this section to—

(a) the High Court, except in relation to a local government election in Scotland;
(b) an election court; or
(c) a county court.

[(1A) Where a person makes an application under this section he shall notify the

Director of Public Prosecutions of the application and the Director or his assistant or any barrister, advocate or solicitor duly appointed as the Director's representative may attend the hearing of the application and make representations at the hearing in respect of it.]

(2) Relief under this section may be granted—

(a) to a candidate, in respect of any failure to [deliver] the return and declarations as to election expenses, or any part of them, or in respect of any error or false statement in them; or

(b) to an election agent, in respect of the failure to [deliver] the return and declarations which he was required to [deliver], or any part of them, or in respect of any error or false statement in them.

(3) The application for relief may be made on the ground that the failure, error or false statement arose—

(a) by reason of the applicant's illness; or

(b) where the applicant is the candidate, by reason of the absence, death, illness or misconduct of his election agent or sub-agent or of any clerk or officer of such agent; or

(c) where the applicant is the election agent, by reason of the death or illness of any prior election agent of the candidate, or of the absence, death, illness or misconduct of any sub-agent, clerk or officer of any election agent of the candidate; or

(d) by reason of inadvertence or any reasonable cause of a like nature,

and not by reason of any want of good faith on the applicant's part.

(4) The court may—

(a) after such notice of the application in the constituency or local government area, as the case may be, as it considers fit, and

(b) on production of such evidence of the grounds stated in the application and of the good faith of the application, and otherwise, as it considers fit,

make such order for allowing an authorised excuse for the failure, error or false statement as it considers just.

(5) Where it is proved to the court by the candidate—

(a) that any act or omission of the election agent in relation to the return and declarations was without the sanction or connivance of the candidate, and

(b) that the candidate took all reasonable means for preventing the act or omission,

the court shall relieve the candidate from the consequences of the act or omission of his election agent.

(6) An order under subsection (4) above may make the allowance conditional on the making of the return and declaration in a modified form or within an extended time, and upon the compliance with such other terms as to the court seem best calculated for carrying into effect the objects of this Part of this Act.

(7) An order under subsection (4) shall relieve the applicant for the order from any liability or consequences under this Act in respect of the matter excused by the order.

(8) The date of the order, or if conditions and terms are to be complied with, the date at which the applicant fully complies with them, is referred to in this Act as the date of the allowance of the excuse.

(9) Except in Scotland, the jurisdiction vested by the foregoing provisions of this section in the High Court in matters relating to parliamentary elections shall, subject to rules of court, be exercised by—

(a) one of the judges for the time being on the rota for the trial of parliamentary election petitions,

(b) in Northern Ireland, one of the judges of the High Court or the Court of Appeal for the time being selected under section 108 of the Judicature (Northern Ireland) Act 1978,

sitting either in court or at chambers, but shall not be exercisable by a master.

(10) The jurisdiction vested by this section in a county court may, except in Northern Ireland, be exercised otherwise than in open court and, in Northern Ireland, shall be exercised in such manner as may be provided by rules of court.

(11) An appeal lies to the High Court from any order of a county court made by virtue of this section.

NOTES

Sub-ss (1), (2)–(8) contain provisions formerly in the Representation of the People Act 1949, s 74(1)–(8). Sub-s (9) contains provisions formerly in s 74(9) of the 1949 Act, as partly repealed by the Representation of the People Act 1969, s 24(4), Sch 3, Pt II, and as amended by the Judicature (Northern Ireland) Act 1978, s 122(1), Sch 5, Pt I. Sub-ss (10), (11) contain provisions formerly in s 74(10) of the 1949 Act.

Sub-s (1A) was inserted, and the words in square brackets in sub-s (2) were substituted, by the Representation of the People Act 1985, s 24, Sch 4, para 30, as from 1 October 1985.

Sub-s (1): Election agent. As to election agents, see s 67 ante and the notes thereto.

Apply for relief. There is no stipulated time for granting relief and the fact that proceedings have been taken to recover a penalty (see ss 84, 85 ante) does not prevent the court from granting relief (*Nichol v Fearby* [1923] 1 KB 480, [1922] All ER Rep 790). See also the note "Application for relief" to s 167 post.

High Court. See the note to s 39 ante; and note sub-s (9) above.

Election court. For the constitution of these courts, see s 123 or 130 post.

County court. See the note to s 30 ante; and note sub-ss (10), (11) above.

Sub-s (1A): Director of Public Prosecutions. See the note to s 148 post.

Sub-s (2): False. See the note to s 62 ante.

Sub-s (3): Sub-agent. As to the appointment of sub-agents, see s 68 ante and the notes thereto.

Sub-s (4): Notice of the application. Want of sufficient notice is ground for refusing an application or postponing consideration thereof. Notice should be given to the returning officer and the other candidates (if any) and to the constituency or local government area affected. It is for the court to decide what notice of application is sufficient. See, further, the note "Such notice of the application . . . as seems fit" to s 167 post.

Constituency. See the note to s 1 ante.

On production of such evidence, etc. A mere assertion of facts unsupported by evidence is insufficient to establish a claim to relief (*Ex p Haseldine* (1895) 59 JP 71).

Order for allowing an authorised excuse. The court will make some allowance for ignorance of the law on the part of candidates or their election agents especially if they have not been candidates or agents on a previous occasion, and this is so even if either person is legally qualified. Reliance on misleading or inaccurate text books of an imposing appearance has been taken into account (see the note "Inadvertence" to s 167 post) and the court will show some indulgence to candidates who rely on their election agents, particularly so in the matter of returns where the duty of making returns is cast on the election agent. If, however, a person is shown to have been engaged on election work or as an election agent on a previous occasion, the court expects him to have acquired an acquaintance with the legal duties of his post and will not be inclined to show him much favour. See *Smith and Sloan v Mackenzie* 1919 SC 546 (candidate and election agent excused for ignorance); *Munro and M'Mullen v Mackintosh* 1920 SC 218 (relief granted to candidate and election agent). Contrast *Re Pole and Scanlon* 1921 SC 98 (candidate excused for failure to lodge return and declaration; election agent refused relief, as he had had previous electioneering experience and it was his default that occasioned the failure); and *Ex p Polson* (1923) 39 TLR 231 (court considered that all the defaults in the case were due to the election agent; candidate excused but not the agent except in relation to failure to render accounts).

The court will excuse inadvertent failure to send in all the documents required (*Clark v Sutherland* 1897 24 R (Ct of Sess) 821, 4 SLT 363); but it will not excuse persons guilty of knowingly making false returns (*West Ham, North Division Case* (1911) 6 O'M & H 392; *Northumberland, Berwick-upon-Tweed Division Case* (1923) 7 O'M & H 1; *Oxford Borough Case* (1924) 7 O'M & H 49).

For cases when failure was due to illness, see *Re Ipswich Case* (1887) 3 TLR 397 (municipal election; failure occasioned mainly by illness of sub-agent; relief granted; costs refused to persons opposing relief); and *Re Application of Right Hon David Lloyd George* (1932) 76 Sol Jo 166 (parliamentary election; failure to transmit declaration of expenses due to illness and absence abroad recuperating; unintentional inadvertence on return; relief granted).

There will also be occasions when insufficient or inaccurate returns are made where there has been doubt as to what should or should not be returned as "election expenses".

Sub-s (5): Where it is proved. The burden of proof on the candidate is not so onerous as that resting on a prosecutor as regards proving an offence and may be discharged by satisfying the court of the preponderance of probability of what he is called upon to prove; cf *R v Carr-Briant* [1943] KB 607, [1943] 2 All ER 156 and *R v Dunbar* [1958] 1 QB 1, [1957] 2 All ER 737.

Connivance. See the note to s 75 ante.

Sub-s (6): This Part of this Act. Ie Pt II (ss 67–119) of this Act.

Sub-s (7): Order . . . shall relieve the applicant. Contrast s 167(4) post, by which an order under that section relieves any person whether the applicant or not.

Liability or consequences under this Act. See, in particular, ss 84, 85 ante, and the note "Illegal practice" to s 61 ante.

Sub-s (9): Rules of court. As to such rules, see s 182 post and the notes thereto.

Rota. As to the selection of judges for the rota for the trial of parliamentary election petitions, see the Supreme Court Act 1981, s 142, Vol 11, title Courts.

Power to require information from election agent or sub-agent. See s 87 post.

Parish and community elections; municipal elections in City of London. See the notes to s 67 ante.

European Assembly elections. See the note to s 78 ante.

Exclusion. See the note to s 72 ante.

Definitions. For "sub-agent", see s 68(1) ante; for "candidate", "declaration as to election expenses", "election expenses" and "return as to election expenses", see s 118 post; for "election", "election court" and "parliamentary election petition", see s 202(1) post; for "local government area" and "local government election", see s 203(1) post.

Judicature (Northern Ireland) Act 1978, s 108. See Vol 31, title Northern Ireland (Pt 2).

---

87 Court's power to require information from election agent or sub-agent

(1) Where on an application under section 86 above it appears to the court that any person who is or has been an election agent or sub-agent has refused or failed to make such return, or to supply such particulars, as will enable the candidate and his election agent respectively to comply with the provisions of this Act as to the return or declarations as to election expenses, the court, before making an order under that section, shall order that person to attend before the court.

(2) The court shall on the attendance of that person, unless he shows cause to the contrary, order him—

(*a*) to make the return and declaration, or

(*b*) to deliver a statement of the particulars required to be contained in the return,

as the court considers just, within such time, to such person and in such manner as it may direct, or may order him to be examined with respect to the particulars.

(3) If a person fails to comply with any order of the court under this section, the court may order him to pay a fine not exceeding [the amount of the maximum fine to which he would be liable if at the time the order is made he were convicted of a summary offence on conviction of which he was liable to a fine of level 5 on the standard scale].

NOTES

This section contains provisions formerly in the Representation of the People Act 1949, s 75.

The words in square brackets in sub-s (3) were substituted by the Representation of the People Act 1985, s 24, Sch 4, para 31, as from 1 October 1985.

Election agent; sub-agent. As to these, see ss 67 and 68 respectively, ante, and the notes thereto.

Order that person to attend. As to the method of service of process requiring such attendance, see s 69(3) ante.

Parish and community elections; municipal elections in City of London. See the notes to s 67 ante.

European Assembly elections. See the note to s 78 ante.

Exclusion. See the note to s 72 ante.

Definitions. For "sub-agent", see s 68(1) ante; for "candidate", "declaration as to election expenses", "election expenses" and "return as to election expenses", see s 118 post; for "standard scale", see s 202(1) post.

88 Publication of time and place for inspection of returns and declarations

At a parliamentary election—

(a) the returning officer shall, within 10 days after the end of the time allowed for [delivering] to him returns as to election expenses, publish in not less than two newspapers circulating in the constituency for which the election was held, and shall send to each of the election agents, a notice of the time and place at which the returns and declarations (including the accompanying documents) can be inspected; but

(b) if any return or declaration has not been received by the returning officer before the notice is despatched for publication, the notice shall so state, and a like notice about that return or declaration, if afterwards received, shall within 10 days after the receipt be published in like manner and sent to each of the election agents other than the agent who is in default or is agent for the candidate in default.

NOTES

This section contains provisions formerly in the Representation of the People Act 1969, s 8(5).

The word in square brackets in para (a) was substituted by the Representation of the People Act 1985, s 24, Sch 4, para 32, as from 1 October 1985.

Parliamentary elections. See the note to s 1 ante.

Returning officer. As to this officer, see ss 24, 26–28 ante.

Within 10 days after, etc. For the computation of time, see s 119 post. See also the note "Within six months . . ." to s 5 ante.

Time allowed for delivering . . . returns. See s 81(1) ante.

Newspapers circulating in the constituency. It appears from *Re Southern Builders and Contractors (London) Ltd* (1961) Times, 10 October, that a national newspaper is a newspaper so circulating. On the meaning of this expression, cf also *R v Westminster Betting Licensing Committee, ex p Peabody Donation Fund (Governors)* [1963] 2 QB 750, [1963] 2 All ER 544.

As to the meaning of "constituency", see the note to s 1 ante.

Election agents. As to election agents, see s 67 ante and the note thereto.

Parish and community elections; municipal elections in City of London. See the notes to s 67 ante.

European Assembly elections. See the note to s 78 ante.

Exclusion. See the note to s 72 ante.

Definitions. For "candidate", "election expenses" and "return as to election expenses", see s 118 post; for "election", see s 202(1) post.

89 Inspection of returns and declarations

(1) Any returns or declarations (including the accompanying documents) [delivered] to the appropriate officer under section 75, section 81 or section 82 above—

(a) shall be kept at the appropriate officer's office or some convenient place appointed by him, and

(b) shall at all reasonable times during the two years next after they are received by him be open to inspection by any person on payment of the prescribed fee,

and the appropriate officer shall on demand and at the prescribed fee provide copies of them or any part of them.

(2) After the expiry of those two years the appropriate officer—

(a) may cause those returns and declarations (including the accompanying documents) to be destroyed, or

(b) if the candidate or his election agent so require, shall return them to the candidate.

(3) Any returns or declarations [delivered] under section 75 shall be returned not to the candidate (if he or his election agent so require) but to the person [delivering] them, if he so requires.

NOTES

Sub-s (1) contains provisions formerly in the Representation of the People Act 1949, s 77(1), as amended by the Representation of the People Act 1969, s 8(6). Sub-ss (2), (3) contain provisions formerly in s 77(2) of the 1949 Act.

The words in square brackets in sub-ss (1), (3) were substituted by the Representation of the People Act 1985, s 24, Sch 4, para 33, as from 1 October 1985.

At all reasonable times. What is a reasonable time is a question of fact. The time during which the premises in question are open for business purposes will ordinarily be deemed reasonable (cf *Davies v Winstanley* (1930) 144 LT 433) and presumably a person would not be justified, except in special circumstances, in demanding that premises should be opened at an unusual hour (*Small v Bickley* (1875) 32 LT 726).

Prescribed fee. By the Representation of the People Regulations 1983, SI 1983/435, reg 70(2), (3), and the Representation of the People (Northern Ireland) Regulations 1983, SI 1983/436, reg 55(1), (2), the fee for inspection is £1 and the price of a copy is 10p for each side of each page.

Election agent. As to election agents, see s 67 ante and the notes thereto.

Parish and community elections; municipal elections in City of London. See the notes to s 67 ante.

European Assembly elections. This section is applied to such elections by the European Assembly Elections Regulations 1984, SI 1984/137, reg 3(1), Sch 1, subject to the substitution, in sub-ss (1) and (2) above, for the words "two years", in each place where they occur, of the words "12 months". See further the Introductory Note to this Act.

As to provisions relating to such elections in Northern Ireland, see the Introductory Note to this Act.

Exclusion. See the note to s 72 ante.

Definitions. For "appropriate officer", see s 67(7) ante; for "candidate", see s 118 post; for "person", see s 202(1) post.

---

90   Election expenses at elections where election agent not required

(1) In relation to an election of parish councillors in England or of community councillors in Wales—

(a)   section 76(1) above has effect as if for the references to an election agent there were substituted references to any agent of the candidate;

(b)   sections 72 to 75 and 78 to 89 above do not apply, and instead the provisions of Schedule 4 to this Act have effect but the form of declaration as to election expenses shall be that prescribed by rules under section 36 above relating to the election of parish or, as the case may be, community councillors, or a form to the like effect;

[(c)   section 76A(1) has effect as if for the reference to the sum specified in section 73(2), 74(1) or 75(1) above there were substituted a reference to the sum specified in paragraph 3 of Schedule 4 to this Act].

(2)   At an election under the local government Act which is not a local government election, sections 72 to 89 do not apply, and if a candidate at that election or any person on behalf of a candidate at that election knowingly pays any sum or incurs any expense, whether before, during or after that election, on account of or in respect of the conduct or management of the election he shall be guilty of an illegal practice.

NOTES

Sub-s (1), as originally enacted, contained provisions formerly in the Representation of the People Act 1949, s 78(1), as amended by the Local Government Act 1958, s 28(5), Sch 7, para 7(1), (6), and as affected by the Local Government Act 1972, s 42(2). Sub-s (2) contains provisions formerly in s 78(2) of the 1949 Act.

Sub-s (1)(c) was added by the Representation of the People Act 1985, s 14(5), as from 1 October 1985.

England; Wales. See the note to s 4 ante.

Form of declaration as to election expenses. This is prescribed by the Local Elections (Parishes and Communities) Rules 1973, SI 1973/1910, r 5(2), Sch 2, Pt II (having effect under s 36 ante, and sub-s (1)(b) above).

Election under the local government Act; local government election. As to the difference in the scope of these expressions, see the note on the former expression to s 202 post.

Knowingly. See the note "Knows" to s 60 ante.

On account of . . . the conduct or management of the election. See the note to s 76 ante.

Illegal practice. See the note to s 61 ante.

Municipal elections in City of London. For the application of this section to certain such elections, see s 197(2) post.

Definitions. For "candidate" and "election expenses", see s 118 post; for "election" and "prescribed", see s 202(1) post; for "local government Act" and "local government election", see s 203(1) post.

Publicity at parliamentary elections

91 Candidate's right to send election address post free

(1) A candidate at a parliamentary election is, subject to Post Office regulations, entitled to send free of any charge for postage to each elector one postal communication containing matter relating to the election only and not exceeding 2 ounces in weight.

(2) He is also, subject as mentioned above, entitled to send free of any charge for postage to each person entered in the list of proxies for the election one such communication as mentioned above for each appointment in respect of which that person is so entered.

(3) A person shall not be deemed to be a candidate for the purposes of this section unless he is shown as standing nominated in the statement of persons nominated, but until the publication of that statement any person who declares himself to be a candidate shall be entitled to exercise the right of free postage conferred by this section if he gives such security as may be required by the Post Office for the payment of postage should he not be shown as standing nominated as mentioned above.

(4) For the purposes of this section, "elector" means a person—

  (*a*) who is registered as a parliamentary elector in the constituency in the register to be used at the election, or

  (*b*) who, pending the publication of that register, appears in the electors lists for that register (as corrected by the registration officer) to be entitled to be so registered,

and accordingly includes a person shown in the register or electors lists as below voting age if it appears from that register or those lists that he will be of voting age on the day fixed for the poll, but not otherwise.

NOTES

This section contains provisions formerly in the Representation of the People Act 1949, s 79, as amended, in the case of s 79(4), by the Representation of the People Act 1969, s 24(1), Sch 2, para 17, and as further amended, in the case of s 79(1) and (3), by the Post Office Act 1969, s 76, Sch 4, Pt II, para 47(1).

Prospective amendment. The following subsection is substituted for sub-s (1) above by the Representation of the People Act 1985, s 24, Sch 4, para 34 post, as from a day to be appointed under s 29(2) of that Act:—

"(1) A candidate at a parliamentary election is, subject to Post Office regulations, entitled to send free of charge for postage either—

  (*a*) one unaddressed postal communication, containing matter relating to the election only and not exceeding 60 grammes in weight, to each place in the constituency which, in accordance with those regulations, constitutes a delivery point for the purposes of this subsection; or

  (*b*) one such postal communication addressed to each elector."

Cross-heading. The cross-heading "Publicity at parliamentary elections" which appears above this section is inaccurate since both ss 92 and 93 post (which appear below that heading) relate to local government elections as well as parliamentary elections.

Sub-s (1): Candidate. For meaning, see s 118 post, but note sub-s (3) above.

Parliamentary election. See the note to s 1 ante.

Post Office. This public authority is constituted under the Post Office Act 1969, s 6, Sch 1, Vol 34, title Post Office.

Regulations. These regulations are not made by statutory instrument and are not noted in this work.

Free of charge. See, however, as to the remuneration of the Post Office out of the Consolidated Fund, the Post Office Act 1969, s 72, Vol 34, title Post Office.

Sub-s (2): List of proxies. This is prepared under Sch 1, r 27(*b*) post. That rule is repealed by the

Representation of the People Act 1985, s 28(1), Sch 5 post, as from a day to be appointed under s 29(2) of that Act. As from that date, new provision is made as to proxies by ss 8, 9 of that Act post.

Sub-s (3): Statement of persons nominated. This is prepared under Sch 1, r 14 post.

Sub-s (4): Registered as a parliamentary elector. As to parliamentary electors, see s 1 ante, and as to their registration, see ss 9 et seq ante.

Constituency. See the note to s 1 ante.

Electors lists. For the preparation and publication of electors lists, see s 10(b) ante, and the note thereto.

European Assembly elections. This section is applied to such elections by the European Assembly Elections Regulations 1984, SI 1984/137, reg 3(1), Sch 1, subject to the substitution, for sub-s (4) above, of the following subsection:

"(4) For the purposes of this section, "elector" means a person—

(a) who is registered in any of the registers to be used at the election in the Assembly constituency (excluding any person not registered at an address within the Assembly constituency), or

(b) who, pending the publication of those registers appears in the electors lists for those registers (as corrected by the registration officer) to be entitled to be so registered at an address within the Assembly constituency,

and accordingly includes a person shown in any of those registers or electors lists as below voting age if it appears from those registers or lists that he will be of voting age on the day of the poll, but not otherwise."

See further the Introductory Notes to this Act ante, and note, in particular, that the Post Office Act 1969, s 72, cited in the note "Free of charge" above, is applied to Assembly elections by reg 3(3) of the above-mentioned regulations, which is set out in the Introductory Note.

As to provisions relating to such elections in Northern Ireland, see the Introductory Note to this Act.

Definitions. For "voting age", see s 1(1)(c) ante; for "registration officer", see s 8(1) ante; for "candidate", see s 118 post (and note sub-s (3) above). Note as to "elector", sub-s (4) above.

92 Broadcasting from outside United Kingdom

(1) No person shall, with intent to influence persons to give or refrain from giving their votes at a parliamentary or local government election, use, or aid, abet, counsel or procure the use of, any television or other wireless transmitting station outside the United Kingdom for the transmission of any matter having reference to the election otherwise than in pursuance of—

(a) arrangements made with the British Broadcasting Corporation for it to be received and re-transmitted by that Corporation; or

(b) arrangements made with the Independent Broadcasting Authority or a programme contractor (within the meaning of the Broadcasting Act 1981) for it to be received by the Authority or contractor and re-transmitted by the Authority.

(2) An offence under this section shall be an illegal practice, but the court before whom a person is convicted of an offence under this section may, if they think it just in the special circumstances of the case, mitigate or entirely remit any incapacity imposed by virtue of section 173 below.

(3) Where any act or omission of an association or body of persons, corporate or unincorporate, is an illegal practice under this section, any person who at the time of the act or omission was a director, general manager, secretary or other similar officer of the association or body, or was purporting to act in any such capacity, shall be deemed to be guilty of the illegal practice, unless he proves—

(a) that the act or omission took place without his consent or connivance; and

(b) that he exercised all such diligence to prevent the commission of the illegal practice as he ought to have exercised having regard to the nature of his functions in that capacity and to all the circumstances.

NOTES

Sub-s (1) contains provisions formerly in the Representation of the People Act 1949, s 80(1), as amended by the Representation of the People Act 1969, s 9(5), and as further amended by the Broadcasting Act 1981, s 65(3), Sch 8, para 7. Sub-ss (2), (3) contain provisions formerly in s 80(2), (3) of the 1949 Act.

Parliamentary election. See the note to s 1 ante.

Aid, abet, counsel or procure. See the note to s 60 ante.

United Kingdom. See the note to s 6 ante.

British Broadcasting Corporation; Independent Broadcasting Authority; purporting to act; unless he proves; consent; connivance; exercised all such diligence. See the notes to s 75 ante.

Illegal practice. See the note to s 61 ante.

Where any act . . . is an illegal practice, etc. See the note "Where any act . . . is an offence, etc" to s 75 ante.

Parish and community elections; municipal elections in City of London. See the notes to s 67 ante; but note that by s 194(*a*) post, this section does not apply to municipal elections in the City of London other than ward elections.

European Assembly elections. This section is applied to such elections by the European Assembly Elections Regulations 1984, SI 1984/137, reg 3(1), Sch 1. See further the Introductory Note to this Act.

As to provisions relating to such elections in Northern Ireland, the Introductory Note to this Act.

Definitions. For "election" and "person", see s 202(1), post; for "local government election", see s 203(1), post.

Broadcasting Act 1981. For the meaning of "programme contractor", see s 2(3) of that Act, Vol 45, title Telecommunications and Broadcasting.

93 Broadcasting during elections

(1) In relation to a parliamentary or local government election—

(*a*) pending such an election it shall not be lawful for any item about the constituency or electoral area to be broadcast from a television or other wireless transmitting station in the United Kingdom if any of the persons who are for the time being candidates at the election takes part in the item and the broadcast is not made with his consent; and

(*b*) where an item about a constituency or electoral area is so broadcast pending such an election there, then if the broadcast either is made before the latest time for delivery of nomination papers, or is made after that time but without the consent of any candidate remaining validly nominated, any person taking part in the item for the purpose of promoting or procuring his election shall be guilty of an illegal practice, unless the broadcast is so made without his consent.

(2) For the purposes of subsection (1) above—

(*a*) a parliamentary election shall be deemed to be pending during the period ending with the close of the poll and beginning—

(i) at a general election, with the date of the dissolution of Parliament or any earlier time at which Her Majesty's intention to dissolve Parliament is announced; or

(ii) at a by-election, with the date of the issue of the writ for the election or any earlier date on which a certificate of the vacancy is notified in the London Gazette in accordance with the Recess Elections Act 1975; and

(*b*) a local government election shall be deemed to be pending during the period ending with the close of the poll and beginning [with the last date on which notice of the election may be published in accordance with rules made under section 36 or, in Scotland, section 42 above].

[(3) References in this section to items being broadcast from a television or other wireless telegraphy transmitting station in the United Kingdom include references to items being included in a cable programme service; and references in this section to the making of broadcasts shall be construed accordingly.]

NOTES

This section, as originally enacted, contained provisions formerly in the Representation of the People Act 1969, s 9(1), (2), as construed, in the case of s 9(2), in accordance with the Local Government Act 1972, s 272(2).

The words in square brackets in sub-s (2) were substituted by the Representation of the People Act 1985, s 24, Sch 4, para 35, in relation to offences committed, or alleged to have been committed, on or after 1 October 1985.

Sub-s (3) was added by the Cable and Broadcasting Act 1984, s 57(1), Sch 5, para 44(2).

Parliamentary election; constituency. See the notes to s 1 ante.

United Kingdom. See the note to s 6 ante.

Take part in. Where a candidate has merely been shown in, and has not actively participated in the item, the broadcast does not require his consent; see *Marshall v BBC* [1979] 3 All ER 80, [1979] 1 WLR 1071, CA.

Consent. See the note to s 75 ante.

Latest time for delivery of nomination papers; close of the poll. The times of these are set out in the timetables in Sch 1, r 1 post, the Local Elections (Principal Areas) Rules 1973, SI 1973/79, Sch 2, r 1, and the Local Elections (Parishes and Communities) Rules 1973, SI 1973/1910, Sch 1, r 1.

Nominated. See the note to s 76 ante.

For the purpose of promoting or procuring his election. Cf the notes "With a view to" and "Promoting or procuring the election of a candidate" to s 75 ante.

Illegal practice. See the note to s 61 ante.

Parish and community elections; municipal elections in City of London. See the notes to s 67 ante; but note that by s 194(*a*) post, this section does not apply to municipal elections in the City of London other than ward elections. As to when a ward election is to be deemed to be pending for the purposes of sub-s (1) above, see s 194(*b*) post.

European Assembly elections. This section is applied to such elections by the European Assembly Elections Regulations 1984, SI 1984/137, reg 3(1), Sch 1, subject to the substitution for sub-s (2) above of the following subsection:

"(2) For the purposes of subsection (1) above, an Assembly election shall be deemed to be pending for the period of 6 weeks ending on the day of the poll."

See further the Introductory Note to this Act.

As to provisions relating to such elections in Northern Ireland, see the Introductory Note to this Act.

Definitions. For "candidate", see s 118 post; for "election", see s 202(1) post; for "electoral area" and "local government election", see s 203(1) post. For "cable programme service", see, by virtue of the Cable and Broadcasting Act 1984, s 56(2), Vol 45, title Telecommunications and Broadcasting, s 2(1) of the Act, in the same title. Note as to "pending", sub-s (2) above.

Recess Elections Act 1975. See Vol 32, title Parliament.

94 Imitation poll cards

[(1)] No person shall for the purpose of promoting or procuring the election of any candidate at a parliamentary election [or a local government election to which this section applies] issue any poll card or document so closely resembling an official poll card as to be calculated to deceive, and subsections (2) and (3) of section 92 above apply as if an offence under this section were an offence under that section.

[(2) This section applies to any local government election in relation to which rules made under section 36 or, in Scotland, section 42 above require an official poll card to be sent to electors in a form prescribed by the rules.]

NOTES

This section, as originally enacted, contained provisions formerly in the Representation of the People Act 1949, s 81.

The words in square brackets in sub-s (1) were inserted, and sub-s (2) was added by the Representation of the People Act 1985, s 24, Sch 4, para 36, as from 1 October 1985. Accordingly, this section, as originally enacted, has been numbered as sub-s (1).

For the purpose of promoting or procuring the election of any candidate. Cf the notes "With a view to" and "Promoting or procuring the election of a candidate" to s 75 ante.

Parliamentary election. See the note to s 1 ante.

Poll card. The issue of official poll cards for parliamentary elections is governed by Sch 1, r 28 post.

Calculated. The word "calculated" is not free from ambiguity, for it may mean "likely" or "intended" (cf 82 JP Jo 447 and 103 JP Jo 734), but it is thought that here the word has the former meaning; cf, in particular, *Eno v Dunn* (1890) 15 App Cas 252; *Re McGlennon's Application for Registration of Shamrock* (1908) 25 TLR 23; and *Re Royal Worcester Corset Co's Application* [1909] 1 Ch 459. See also *North Cheshire and Manchester Brewery Co v Manchester Brewery Co* [1889] AC 83; *McDowell v Standard Oil Co (New Jersey)* [1927] AC 632; *Collett v Co-op Wholesale Society Ltd* [1970] 1 All ER 274, 68 LGR 158; *R v Davison* [1972] 3 All ER 1121, [1972] 1 WLR 1540, CA; and *Turner v Shearer* [1973] 1 All ER 397, [1972] 1 WLR 1387.

Deceive. To deceive is, in the well-known words of Buckley J (as he then was) in *Re London and Globe Finance Corporation Ltd* [1903] 1 Ch 728 at 732, [1900–3] All ER Rep 891 at 893 (modified in the light of the observations of Lord Radcliffe in *Welham v DPP* [1961] AC 103 at 126, 127, [1960] 1 All ER 805 at 810, HL), to induce a man to believe a thing is true which is false, or a thing is false which is true, contrary to what the person practising the deceit knows or believes to be the case.

European Assembly elections. This section is applied to such elections by the European Assembly Elections Regulations 1984, SI 1984/137, reg 3(1), Sch 1. See further the Introductory Note to this Act.

As to provisions relating to such elections in Northern Ireland, see the Introductory Note to this Act.

Definitions. For "candidate", see s 118 post; for "election" and "person", see s 202(1) post; for "local government election", see s 203(1) post.

Election meetings

95 Schools and rooms for parliamentary election meetings

(1) Subject to the provisions of this section, a candidate at a parliamentary election is entitled for the purpose of holding public meetings in furtherance of his candidature to the use [free of charge] at reasonable times between the receipt of the writ and [the day preceding] the date of the poll of—

(a) a suitable room in the premises of a school to which this section applies;

(b) any meeting room to which this section applies.

(2) This section applies—

(a) in England and Wales, to county schools and voluntary schools of which the premises are situated in the constituency or an adjoining constituency, and

(b) *(applies to Scotland only),*

but a candidate is not entitled under this section to the use of a room in school premises outside the constituency if there is a suitable room in other premises in the constituency which are reasonably accessible from the same parts of the constituency as those outside and are premises of a school to which this section applies.

(3) This section applies to meeting rooms situated in the constituency, the expense of maintaining which is payable wholly or mainly out of public funds or out of any rate, or by a body whose expenses are so payable.

(4) Where a room is used for a meeting in pursuance of the rights conferred by this section, the person by whom or on whose behalf the meeting is convened—

(a) [shall defray any expenses] incurred in preparing, warming, lighting and cleaning the room and providing attendance for the meeting and restoring the room to its usual condition after the meeting; and

(b) shall defray any damage done to the room or the premises in which it is situated, or to the furniture, fittings or apparatus in the room or premises.

(5) A candidate is not entitled to exercise the rights conferred by this section except on reasonable notice; and this section does not authorise any interference with the hours during which a room in school premises is used for educational purposes, or any interference with the use of a meeting room either for the purposes of the person maintaining it or under a prior agreement for its letting for any purpose.

(6) The provisions of Schedule 5 to this Act have effect with respect to the rights conferred by this section and the arrangements to be made for their exercise.

(7) For the purposes of this section (except those of paragraph (b) of subsection (4) above), the premises of a school shall not be taken to include any private dwelling house, and in this section—

(a) the expression "meeting room" means any room which it is the practice to let for public meetings; and

(b) the expression "room" includes a hall, gallery or gymnasium.

(8) This section does not apply to Northern Ireland.

NOTES

This section contains provisions formerly in the Representation of the People Act 1949, s 82.

The words in square brackets in sub-s (1) were inserted, and those in sub-s (4)(a) were substituted, by the Representation of the People Act 1985, s 24, Sch 4, para 37, as from 1 October 1985.

Sub-s (1): Parliamentary election. See the note to s 1 ante.

At reasonable times. Note the provisions of sub-s (5) above.

Receipt of the writ. As to the issue of the writ for a parliamentary election, see Sch 1, r 3 post.

Date of the poll. The date of the poll at parliamentary elections is fixed in accordance with Sch 1, r 1 post.

Sub-s (2): England; Wales. See the note to s 4 ante.

County schools; voluntary schools. As to this classification, see the Education Act 1944, s 9, title Education (Pt 2) ante.

Constituency. See the note to s 1 ante.

Sub-s (3): Wholly or mainly. The word "mainly" probably means "more than half" though there is nothing to indicate by reference to what this is to be calculated; cf *Fawcett Properties Ltd v Buckingham County Council* [1961] AC 636 at 669, [1960] 3 All ER 503 at 512, HL per Lord Morton of Henryton. See also on the meaning of "wholly or mainly" (or "exclusively or mainly"), *Re Hatschek's Patents, ex p Zerenner* [1909] 2 Ch 68; *Miller v Ottilie (Owners)* [1944] 1 KB 188, [1944] 1 All ER 277; *Franklin v Gramophone Co Ltd* [1948] 1 KB 542 at 555, [1948] 1 All ER 353 at 358, CA per Somervell LJ; and *Berthelemy v Neale* [1952] 1 All ER 437, 96 Sol Jo 165, CA.

Local election meetings. For the application of sub-ss (4), (5), (7) above to schools and rooms for such meetings, see s 96(4) post.

European Assembly elections. This section is applied to such elections by the European Assembly Elections Regulations 1984, SI 1984/137, reg 3(1), Sch 1, subject to the substitution, in sub-s (1) above, for the words "receipt of the writ", of the words "publication of notice of election". See further the Introductory Note to this Act.

Definitions. For "candidate", see s 118 post; for "dwelling house" and "election", see s 202(1) post. Note as to "meeting room" and "room", sub-s (7) above.

[96 Schools and rooms for local election meetings

(1) Subject to the provisions of this section, a candidate at a local government election is entitled for the purpose of holding public meetings in furtherance of his candidature to the use free of charge at reasonable times between the last day on which notice of the election may be published in accordance with rules made under section 36 or, in Scotland, section 42 above and the day preceding the day of election of—

(a) a suitable room in the premises of a school to which this section applies; or

(b) a meeting room to which this section applies.

(2) This section applies—

(a) in England and Wales, to a county or voluntary school situated in the electoral area for which the candidate is standing (or, if there is no such school in the area, in any such school in an adjacent electoral area) or in a parish or community, as the case may be, in part comprised in that electoral area; and

(b) (applies to Scotland only).

(3) This section applies—

(a) in England and Wales, to any meeting room situated in the electoral area for which the candidate is standing or in a parish or community, as the case may be, in part comprised in that electoral area, the expense of maintaining which is payable wholly or mainly out of public funds or out of any rate, or by a body whose expenses are so payable;

(b) (applies to Scotland only).

(4) Subsections (4), (5) and (7) of section 95 above and paragraph 1(1) of Schedule 5 to this Act shall apply for the purposes of this section as they apply for the purposes of that section, and any person stating himself to be, or to be authorised by, a candidate at a local government election in respect of an electoral area which falls (or partly falls) within a constituency, or his election agent, shall be entitled to inspect the lists prepared

under Schedule 5 to this Act in relation to the constituency or a copy of them at all reasonable hours during the period beginning with the day on which notice of the election is published and ending with the day preceding the day of election.]

NOTES

This section was substituted by the Representation of the People Act 1985, s 24, Sch 4, para 38, in relation to elections in respect of which the notice is published on or after 1 October 1985.

Notice of election. This is governed by the Local Elections (Principal Areas) Rules 1973, SI 1973/79, Sch 2, r 4, and the Local Elections (Parishes and Communities) Rules 1973, SI 1973/1910, Sch 1, r 4.

England; Wales. See the note to s 4 ante.

County schools; voluntary schools. As to this classification, see the Education Act 1944, s 9, title Education (Pt 2) ante.

Wholly or mainly. See the note to s 95 ante.

Definitions. For "candidate", see s 118 post; for "election", see s 202(1) post; for "electoral area" and "local government election", see s 203(1) post.

97 Disturbances at election meetings

(1) A person who at a lawful public meeting to which this section applies acts, or incites others to act, in a disorderly manner for the purpose of preventing the transaction of the business for which the meeting was called together shall be guilty of an illegal practice.

(2) This section applies to—

(*a*) a political meeting held in any constituency between the date of the issue of a writ for the return of a member of Parliament for the constituency and the date at which a return to the writ is made;

(*b*) a meeting held with reference to a local government election in the electoral area for that election [in the period beginning with the last date on which notice of the election may be published in accordance with rules made under section 36 or, in Scotland, section 42 above and ending with] the day of election.

(3) If a constable reasonably suspects any person of committing an offence under subsection (1) above, he may if requested so to do by the chairman of the meeting require that person to declare to him immediately his name and address and, if that person refuses or fails so to declare his name and address or gives a false name and address, he shall be liable on summary conviction to a fine not exceeding level 1 on the standard scale, *and*—

(a) if he refuses or fails so to declare his name and address or

(b) if the constable reasonably suspects him of giving a false name and address,

the constable may without warrant arrest him.

This subsection does not apply in Northern Ireland.

NOTES

This section contains provisions formerly in the Representation of the People Act 1949, s 84, as amended, in the case of s 84(3), by the Criminal Law Act 1977, s 31(6), and by the Criminal Justice Act 1982, ss 37(1), (2), 46(1).

The words in square brackets in sub-s (2)(*b*) were substituted by the Representation of the People Act 1985, s 24, Sch 4, para 39, as from 1 October 1985.

Prospective repeal. The words printed in italics in sub-s (3) above are repealed by the Police and Criminal Evidence Act 1984, ss 26(1), 119(2), Sch 7, Pt I, Vol 12, title Criminal Law, as from a day to be appointed under s 121 of that Act, Vol 12, title Criminal Law.

Lawful public meeting. A meeting is not unlawful merely because it is held on a public highway; see *Burden v Rigler* [1911] 1 KB 337, 80 LJKB 100. Note that the Public Meeting Act 1908, s 1, Vol 12, title Criminal Law, does not apply to meetings to which this section applies; see s 1(4) of that Act.

Illegal practice. See the note to s 61 ante.

Constituency. See the note to s 1 ante.

Issue of a writ; return to the writ. See Sch 1, rr 3 and 51 post, respectively.

Constable. See the note to s 19 ante.

Summary conviction. See the note to s 62 ante.

Without warrant arrest him. As to what constitutes an arrest, the necessity of making the ground of arrest known, etc, see 11 Halsbury's Laws (4th edn) paras 99 et seq; and as to the position of persons purporting to arrest without warrant under a statutory power, the handing over of the person arrested, etc, see ibid, paras 116 et seq.

For provisions as to bail on arrest without warrant, see the Magistrates' Courts Act 1980, s 43, Vol 27, title Magistrates, and for special provisions which apply where a child or young person is arrested, see the Children and Young Persons Act 1933, s 34(2), and the Children and Young Persons Act 1969, ss 28(4), (5), 29, both Vol 6, title Children.

Parish and community elections; municipal elections in City of London. See the notes to s 67 ante; and note in particular the modifications to this section as it applies to municipal elections in the City of London contained in s 195 post.

European Assembly elections. This section is applied to such elections by the European Assembly Elections Regulations 1984, SI 1984/137, reg 3(1), Sch 1, subject to the substitution, for sub-s (2) above, of the following subsection.

"(2) This section applies to a political meeting held in any Assembly constituency in connection with an Assembly election between the date of publication of notice of election and the date of the poll."

See further the Introductory Note to this Act.

As to provisions relating to such elections in Northern Ireland, see the Introductory Note to this Act.

Definitions. For "standard scale", see s 202(1) post; for "electoral area" and "local government election", see s 203(1) post.

98 Premises not affected for rates

The use of any premises for the holding of public meetings in furtherance of any person's candidature at a parliamentary or local government election does not render any person liable to be rated or to pay any rate for the premises.

NOTES

This section contains provisions formerly in the Representation of the People Act 1949, s 85.

Parliamentary election. See the note to s 1 ante.

Local government election. For meaning, see s 203(1) post.

Parish and community elections; municipal elections in City of London. See the notes to s 67 ante.

European Assembly elections. This section and ss 99–104 post, are applied to such elections by the European Assembly Elections Regulations 1984, SI 1984/137, reg 3(1), Sch 1. See further the Introductory Note to this Act.

As to provisions relating to such elections in Northern Ireland, see the Introductory Note to this Act.

Agency by election officials and canvassing by police officers

99 Officials not to act for candidates

(1) If—

    (*a*) any returning officer at a parliamentary or local government election, or

    (*b*) any officer or clerk appointed under the parliamentary elections rules, or the rules under section 36 or section 42 above, as the case may be, or

    (*c*) any partner or clerk of any such person,

acts as a candidate's agent in the conduct or management of the election, he shall be guilty of an offence, but nothing in this subsection prevents a candidate from acting as his own election agent.

[(2) A person guilty of an offence under this section shall be liable on summary conviction to a fine not exceeding level 4 on the standard scale.]

NOTES   •

Sub-s (1) contains provisions formerly in the Representation of the People Act 1949, s 86(1), as affected by the Criminal Law Act 1967, s 1.

Sub-s (2) was substituted by the Representation of the People Act 1985, s 23, Sch 3, para 4, as from 1 October 1985.

Returning officer. As to returning officers, see ss 24, 26–28, 35 ante.

Parliamentary election. See the note to s 1 ante.

Candidate's agent. See the note "Any agent" to s 73 ante.

Acting as his own election agent. Ie by virtue of s 67(2) or 70 ante.

Summary conviction. See the note to s 62 ante.

Parish and community elections. See the note to s 67 ante, and the rules noted to s 187 post.

European Assembly elections. See the note to s 98 ante.

Definitions. For "candidate", see s 118 post; for "election", "parliamentary elections rules" and "standard scale", see s 202(1) post; for "local government election", see s 203(1) post.

100 Illegal canvassing by police officers

(1) No member of a police force shall by word, message, writing or in any other manner, endeavour to persuade any person to give, or dissuade any person from giving, his vote, whether as an elector or as proxy—

(*a*) at any parliamentary election for a constituency, or

(*b*) at any local government election for any electoral area,

wholly or partly within the police area.

(2) A person acting in contravention of subsection (1) above shall be liable [on summary conviction to a fine not exceeding level 3 on the standard scale, but] nothing in that subsection shall subject a member of a police force to any penalty for anything done in the discharge of his duty as a member of the force.

(3) In this section references to a member of a police force and to a police area are to be taken in relation to Northern Ireland as references to a member of the Royal Ulster Constabulary and to Northern Ireland.

NOTES

Sub-ss (1), (2) contain provisions formerly in the Representation of the People Act 1949, s 87(1), as amended by the Criminal Justice Act 1982, ss 37(1), (2), 38(1), (6), (8), 46(1). Sub-s (3) contains provisions formerly in s 87(3) of the 1949 Act, as partly repealed by the Police Act 1964, s 64(3), Sch 10, Pt I.

The words in square brackets in sub-s (2) were substituted by the Representation of the People Act 1985, s 23, Sch 3, para 5, as from 1 October 1985.

Police force; police area. For meanings, see the Police Act 1964, s 62, Sch 8, Vol 33, title Police, as applied by the Interpretation Act 1978, s 5, Sch 1, Vol 41, title Statutes. Note also sub-s (3) above.

Writing. See the note "Written" to s 28 ante.

Proxy. For the appointment of proxies for parliamentary elections, see s 21 ante, and for local government elections, see s 34 ante. These provisions are repealed by the Representation of the People Act 1985, s 28(1), Sch 5 post, as from a day to be appointed under s 29(2) of that Act. As from that date, new provision is made as to proxies by ss 8, 9 of that Act.

Parliamentary election; constituency. See the notes to s 1 ante.

Summary conviction. See the note to s 62 ante.

Parish and community elections; municipal elections in City of London. See the notes to s 67 ante, and the rules noted to s 187 post.

European Assembly elections. See the note to s 98 ante.

Definitions. For "election", "elector", "standard scale" and "vote", see s 202(1) post; for "electoral area" and "local government election", see s 203(1) post.

Conveyance of voters to and from poll

101 No hiring of vehicles to convey voters

(1) A person shall not let, lend, or employ any public vehicle for the purpose of the conveyance of electors or their proxies to or from the poll at an election, and if he does so knowing that the public vehicle is intended to be used for that purpose he shall be guilty of an illegal hiring.

(2) A person shall not hire, borrow or use for the purpose of the conveyance of electors or their proxies to or from the poll at an election any public vehicle the owner of which he knows to be prohibited by subsection (1) above from letting, lending or employing for that purpose, and if he does so he shall be guilty of an illegal hiring.

(3) In this section "public vehicle" means any public stage or hackney carriage or any carriage kept or used for the purpose of letting out for hiring.

NOTES

Sub-ss (1), (3) contain provisions formerly in the Representation of the People Act 1949, s 89(1). Sub-s (2) contains provisions formerly in s 89(2) of the 1949 Act.

Proxies. For the appointment of proxies for parliamentary elections, see s 21 ante, and for local government elections, see s 34 ante. Those sections are repealed by the Representation of the People Act 1985, s 28(1), Sch 5 post, as from a day to be appointed under s 29(2) of that Act. As from that date, new provision is made as to proxies by ss 8, 9 of that Act.

Knowing. See the note "Knows" to s 60 ante.

Illegal hiring. For the penalty for illegal hiring and as to the circumstances in which an illegal hiring may constitute an illegal practice, etc, see s 175 post. Note that under s 167 post, certain courts may except an innocent act from being an illegal hiring. See *Ex p Forster* (1903) 89 LT 18, 19 TLR 525 (candidate hired two horses temporarily in substitution for his own to drive voters to the poll in his carriage; relief granted under what is now s 167 post, but with costs to respondent opposing the applicant); and see *Re County Councillors' Election* (1904) 68 JP 208. See also the note "Further provisions" to s 175 post.

Parish and community elections; municipal elections in City of London. See the notes to s 67 ante.

European Assembly elections. See the note to s 98 ante.

Supplemental provisions. See s 103 post.

Application to horses, etc. See s 104(*b*) post.

Definitions. For "carriage", see s 104(*a*) post; for "election", "elector" and "person", see s 202(1) post. Note as to "public vehicle", sub-s (3) above in conjunction with s 104 post.

---

102 No payments for conveyance of voters

If any payment or contract for payment is knowingly made, either before, during or after an election, for the purpose of promoting or procuring the election of a candidate on account of the conveyance of electors or their proxies to or from the poll, whether for the hire of carriages, or for railway fares, or otherwise—

(*a*) the person making the payment or contract, and
(*b*) if he knew it to be in contravention of this Act, any person receiving the payment or being a party to the contract,

shall be guilty of an illegal practice.

NOTES

This section contains provisions formerly in the Representation of the People Act 1949, s 89(3).

Knowingly. See the note "Knows" to s 60 ante.

For the purpose of promoting or procuring, etc. See the notes "With a view to" and "Promoting or procuring the election of a candidate" to s 75 ante.

Railway fares. Independently of the provisions of this section, paying a voter's railway fare can constitute bribery (as to which, see s 113 post) (*Cooper v Slade* (1858) 6 HL Cas 746, [1843–60] All ER Rep 446; *Nottingham Town Case, Whitchurch and Taylor's Case* (1866) 15 LT 89; *Northallerton Case* (1869) 1 O'M & H 167; *Bolton Case, Ormerod v Cross* (1874) 31 LT 194, 20 M & H 188; *Horsham Case, Aldridge v Hurst* (1876) 3 O'M & H 52; *Harwich Case, Tomline v Tyler* (1880) 44 LT 187; *Salisbury Case, Rigden v Passmore,*

Edwards and Grenfell (1880) 44 LT 192; *Ipswich Case, Packard v Collings and West* (1886) 54 LT 619, 2 TLR 477; and *Southampton Borough Case, Austin and Rowland v Chamberlayne and Simeon* (1895) 5 O'M & H 17).
   Illegal practice. See the note to s 61 ante.
   Parish and community elections; municipal elections in City of London. See the notes to s 67 ante.
   European Assembly elections. See the note to s 98 ante.
   Supplemental provisions. See s 103 post.
   Application to horses, etc. See s 104(*b*) post.
   Saving for rights of creditors. See s 116 post.
   Definitions. For "candidate" and "payment", see s 118 post; for "carriage", see s 104(*a*) post; for "election", "elector" and "person", see s 202(1) post.

103 Provisions supplemental to ss 101 and 102

   (1) Nothing in sections 101 and 102 above prevents a carriage being let, hired, employed or used by an elector or his proxy or several electors or their proxies at their joint cost, for the purpose of being conveyed to or from the poll.

   (2) . . .

NOTES

   Sub-s (1) contains provisions formerly in the Representation of the People Act 1949, s 90(1).
   Sub-s (2) was repealed by the Representation of the People Act 1985, ss 24, 28(1), Sch 4, para 40, Sch 5, as from 1 October 1985.
   Proxy. See the note "Proxy" to s 101 ante.
   Parish and community elections; municipal elections in City of London. See the notes to s 67 ante.
   European Assembly elections. See the note to s 98 ante.
   Application to horses, etc. See s 104(*b*) post.
   Definitions. For "carriage", see s 104(*a*) post; for "elector", see s 202(1) post.

104 "Carriage" in ss 101 to 103

In sections 101 to 103 above—

   (*a*) "carriage" includes for the purposes of those sections—

   (i) any mechanically propelled vehicle intended or adapted for use on roads, and
   (ii) and any vehicle drawn by such a vehicle,

   and any such vehicle as so described shall be deemed to be a public vehicle for the purposes of section 101 if used as such; and

   (*b*) the provisions of those sections . . . apply in relation to horses or other animals as they apply in relation to carriages, and any reference in section 101 to a public vehicle includes a reference to horses or other animals kept or used for drawing such vehicles.

NOTES

   This section contains provisions formerly in the Representation of the People Act 1949, s 90(2), (3).
   The words omitted from para (*b*) were repealed by the Representation of the People Act 1985, s 28(1), Sch 5, as from 1 October 1985.
   Parish and community elections; municipal elections in City of London. See the notes to s 67 ante.
   European Assembly elections. See the note to s 98 ante.

105 Access to polling place by sea

   (1) Where the nature of a county constituency is such that any electors or proxies for electors resident there are unable at a parliamentary election for that constituency to

reach their polling place without crossing the sea or a branch or arm of the sea, nothing in this Act prevents the provision of means for conveying those electors or proxies by sea to their polling place.

(2) The amount of any payment for such means of conveyance as are mentioned in subsection (1) above may be in addition to the maximum amount of expenses allowed by this Act.

(3) (*Applies to Scotland only.*)

NOTES

This section contains provisions formerly in the Representation of the People Act 1949, s 90(4).
County constituency. See the note "County constituency; borough constituency" to s 24 ante.
Proxies. See the note "Proxy" to s 101 ante.
Resident. See the note to s 1 ante, and see also s 5 ante and the notes thereto.
Parliamentary election. See the note to s 1 ante.
Polling place. As to polling places for parliamentary elections, see s 18(1) ante.
Maximum amount. Ie the amount calculated in accordance with s 76(2)(*a*) ante.
European Assembly elections. This section is applied to such elections by the European Assembly Elections Regulations 1984, SI 1984/137, reg 3(1), Sch 1, subject to the omission, from sub-s (1) above, of the word "county". See further the Introductory Note to this Act.
As to provisions relating to such elections in Northern Ireland, see the Introductory Note to this Act.
Definitions. For "election" and "elector", see s 202(1) post.

Other illegal practices, payments, employments or hirings

106 False statements as to candidates

(1) A person who, or any director of any body or association corporate which—

(*a*) before or during an election,
(*b*) for the purpose of affecting the return of any candidate at the election,

makes or publishes any false statement of fact in relation to the candidate's personal character or conduct shall be guilty of an illegal practice, unless he can show that he had reasonable grounds for believing, and did believe, the statement to be true.

(2) A candidate shall not be liable nor shall his election be avoided for any illegal practice under subsection (1) above committed by his agent other than his election agent unless—

(*a*) it can be shown that the candidate or his election agent has authorised or consented to the committing of the illegal practice by the other agent or has paid for the circulation of the false statement constituting the illegal practice; or

(*b*) an election court find and report that the election of the candidate was procured or materially assisted in consequence of the making or publishing of such false statements.

(3) A person making or publishing any false statement of fact as mentioned above may be restrained by interim or perpetual injunction by the High Court or the county court from any repetition of that false statement or of a false statement of a similar character in relation to the candidate and, for the purpose of granting an interim injunction, prima facie proof of the falsity of the statement shall be sufficient.

(4) . . .

(5) Any person who, before or during an election, knowingly publishes a false statement of a candidate's withdrawal at the election for the purpose of promoting or procuring the election of another candidate shall be guilty of an illegal practice.

(6) A candidate shall not be liable, nor shall his election be avoided, for an illegal

practice under subsection (5) above committed by his agent other than his election agent.

(7) In the application of this section to an election where a candidate is not required to have an election agent, references to an election agent shall be omitted and the reference in subsection (6) above to an illegal practice committed by an agent of the candidate shall be taken as a reference to an illegal practice committed without the candidate's knowledge and consent.

(8) Except in Scotland, the jurisdiction vested by subsection (3) above in the High Court in matters relating to parliamentary elections shall, subject to rules of court, be exercised by—

(a) one of the judges for the time being on the rota for the trial of parliamentary election petitions,

(b) in Northern Ireland, one of the judges of the High Court or the Court of Appeal for the time being selected under section 108 of the Judicature (Northern Ireland) Act 1978,

sitting either in court or at chambers, or by a master of the Supreme Court in manner directed by and subject to an appeal to those judges.

(9) The jurisdiction vested by subsection (3) in a county court may, except in Northern Ireland, be exercised otherwise than in open court, and, in Northern Ireland, shall be exercised in accordance with rules of court.

An appeal lies to the High Court from any order of a county court made by virtue of subsection (3).

NOTES

Sub-ss (1), (2) contain provisions formerly in the Representation of the People Act 1949, s 91(1). Sub-ss (3), (7)–(9) contain provisions formerly in s 91(2), (5)–(7), respectively, of the 1949 Act, as partly repealed, in the case of s 91(6), by the Representation of the People Act 1969, s 24(4), Sch 3, Pt I. Sub-ss (5), (6) contain provisions formerly in s 91(4) of the 1949 Act.

Sub-s (4) was repealed by the Representation of the People Act 1985, ss 24, 28(1), Sch 4, para 41, Sch 5, as from 1 October 1985.

Sub-s (1): Makes and publishes. As to what constitutes publication, see *Tower Hamlets, St George's Division, Case, Benn v Marks* (1896) 5 O'M & H 89, 104–107.

Any false statement of fact. Ie not merely an expression of opinion (*Sunderland Borough Case* (1896) 5 O'M & H 53 at 65; *Silver v Benn* (1896) 12 TLR 199; *Ellis v National Union of Conservative and Constitutional Associations, Middleton and Southall* (1900) 44 Sol Jo 750). See, further, the note "False" to s 62 ante. Sub-s (1) above applies whether or not the statement objected to is libellous (*Tower Hamlets, St George's Division, Case, Benn v Marks* (1896) 5 O'M & H 89, 104–107). If a false statement is made by a person having no reasonable ground for believing it to be true, it is not material for the purposes of this section that the statement is made by way of countercharge to an original charge or that the candidate affected has in some way by his speech or publication provoked the making of the statement. These matters might be relevant in an action for defamation (*Tower Hamlets, St George's Division, Case, Benn v Marks* (1896) 5 O'M & H 89, 103–107; *Monmouth Boroughs Case, Embrey and Sweeting v Harris* (1901) 5 O'M & H 166, 173, 174). For a municipal election case, see *Mills v Drummond* (1934) 78 Sol Jo 192, in which an injunction was granted against publication of statements suggesting that a person was the sort of individual to use or had used his position as chairman of the LCC Entertainments Committee to further the showing or exploitation of wild animals at circuses whether or not for his own personal gain.

Personal character. This section does not apply to a candidate's public acts or conduct (*Bayley v Edmunds, Byron and Marshall* (1895) 11 TLR 537, CA; *Cumberland, Cockermouth Division, Case, Armstrong, Brooksbank, Brown, Beck, Cooper and Henderson v Randles* (1901) 5 O'M & H 155; *Sheffield, Attercliffe Division, Case, Wilson v Langley* (1906) 5 O'M & H 218). It has been held that calling a person a Communist does not amount to making a "false statement as to his personal character" (*Burns v Associated Newspapers Ltd* (1925) 89 JP 205, 42 TLR 37).

Illegal practice. See the note to s 61 ante.

Unless he can show. See the note "Unless he proves, etc" to s 75 ante.

Sub-s (2): By his agent. See the note to s 159 post.

Election agent. As to the appointment of election agents, see s 67 ante and the notes thereto.

Consented. See the note "Consent" to s 75 ante.

Procured. See the note "Aids, abets, counsels or procures", to s 60 ante.

Election court. For the constitution of election courts, see s 123 or 140 post.

Report. As to the reports of election courts, see ss 144, 145, 158 post.

Sub-s (3): Interim ... injunction. Where justification is pleaded in answer to an action for libel, an interim injunction under sub-s (3) above ought not to be granted unless the court is satisfied that the defendants have every reasonable prospect of success at the trial (*Burns v Associated Newspapers Ltd* (1925) 89 JP 205, 42 TLR 37).

High Court. See the note to s 39 ante; and note sub-s (8) above.

County court. See the note to s 30 ante.

Sub-s (5): Knowingly. See the note "Knows" to s 60 ante.

For the purpose of promoting, etc. Cf the notes "With a view to" and "Promoting or procuring the election of a candidate" to s 75 ante.

Sub-s (7): Election where a candidate is not required to have an election agent. Ie an election to which s 71 ante applies.

Sub-s (8): Rules of court. As to such rules, see s 182 post and the notes thereto.

Rota. As to the rota for the trial of parliamentary election petitions, see the Supreme Court Act 1981, s 142, Vol 11, title Courts.

Parish and community elections; municipal elections in City of London. See the notes to s 67 ante.

European Assembly elections. This section and ss 107–117 post, are applied to such elections by the European Assembly Elections Regulations 1984, SI 1984/137, reg 3(1), Sch 1. See further the Introductory Note to this Act.

As to provisions relating to such elections in Northern Ireland, see the Introductory Note to this Act.

Definitions. For "candidate", see s 118 post; for "election", "election court", "parliamentary election petition" and "person", see s 202(1) post.

Judicature (Northern Ireland) Act 1978, s 108. See Vol 31, title Northern Ireland (Pt 2).

107 Corrupt withdrawal from candidature

Any person who corruptly induces or procures any other person to withdraw from being a candidate at an election, in consideration of any payment or promise of payment, and any person withdrawing in pursuance of the inducement or procurement, shall be guilty of an illegal payment.

NOTES

This section contains provisions formerly in the Representation of the People Act 1949, s 92.

Procures. Cf the note "Aids, abets, counsels or procures" to s 60 ante.

Illegal payment. For the penalty for illegal payment and as to the circumstances in which an illegal payment may constitute an illegal practice, etc, see s 175 post. Note that under s 167 post certain courts may except an innocent act from being an illegal payment. See also the note "Further provisions" to s 175 post.

Parish and community elections; municipal elections in City of London. See the notes to s 67 ante.

European Assembly elections. See the note to s 106 ante.

Definitions. For "candidate" and "payment", see s 118 post; for "election" and "person", see s 202(1) post.

108 Premises not to be used as committee rooms

(1) If a person—

    (*a*) hires or uses any premises to which this section applies, or any part of them, for a committee room for the purpose of promoting or procuring the election of a candidate, or

    (*b*) lets any premises to which this section applies or any part of them knowing that it was intended to use them or that part as a committee room,

he shall be guilty of an illegal hiring.

(2) Where the election is an election under the local government Act, the reference in subsection (1) above to letting any premises or part of premises includes a reference to permitting the use of any premises or part of premises.

(3) ...

(4) This section ... applies—

(a) in England and Wales, to the premises of all schools maintained or assisted by a local education authority and all other schools in respect of which grants are made out of moneys provided by Parliament to the person or body of persons responsible for the management of the school;

(b) (applies to Scotland only); and

(c) in Northern Ireland, to the premises of all schools other than independent schools within the meaning of the Education and Libraries (Northern Ireland) Order 1972.

For the purposes of this section, the premises of a school shall be taken to include any dwelling house which forms part of the school and is occupied by a person employed for the purposes of the school.

NOTES

Sub-ss (1), (2) contain provisions formerly in the Representation of the People Act 1949, s 93(1). Sub-s (4) contains provisions formerly in s 93(2), (3) of the 1949 Act.

Sub-s (3) and the word omitted from sub-s (4) were repealed by the Representation of the People Act 1985, ss 24, 28(1), Sch 4, para 42, Sch 5, as from 1 October 1985.

For the purpose of promoting, etc. Cf the notes "With a view to" and "Promoting or procuring the election of a candidate" to s 75 ante.

Knowing. See the note "Knows" to s 60 ante.

Illegal hiring. For the penalty for illegal hiring and as to the circumstances in which an illegal hiring may constitute an illegal practice, etc, see s 175 post. Note that under s 167 post certain courts may except an innocent act from being an illegal hiring. For instances of unsuccessful objection to the use of premises for a committee room, see *Devonport Case, Pascoe v Puleston* (1886) 54 LT 733, 2 TLR 345; *Cumberland, Cockermouth Division, Case, Armstrong, Brooksbank, Brown, Beck, Cooper and Henderson v Randles* (1901) 5 O'M & H 155. See also the note "Further provisions" to s 175 post.

England; Wales. See the note to s 4 ante.

Local education authority. These authorities are defined by the Education Act 1944, s 6(1), Sch 1, Pt I, title Education (Pt 2) ante, as read together with the London Government Act 1963, s 30, Vol 26, title London, and the Local Government Act 1972, ss 1(10), 20(6), 192(1), Vol 25, title Local Government.

Parish and community elections; municipal elections in City of London. See the notes to s 67 ante.

European Assembly elections. See the note to s 106 ante.

Definitions. For "candidate" and "committee room", see s 118 post; for "dwelling house" and "election", see s 202(1) post; for "local government Act", see s 203(1) post.

Education and Libraries (Northern Ireland) Order 1972. SI 1972/1263.

109 Payments for exhibition of election notices

(1) No payment or contract for payment shall for the purpose of promoting or procuring the election of a candidate at an election be made to an elector or his proxy on account of the exhibition of, or the use of any house, land, building or premises for the exhibition of, any address, bill or notice, unless—

(a) it is the ordinary business of the elector or proxy as an advertising agent to exhibit for payment bills and advertisements; and

(b) the payment or contract is made in the ordinary course of that business.

(2) If any payment or contract for payment is knowingly made in contravention of this section either before, during or after an election—

(a) the person making the payment or contract, and

(b) if he knew it to be in contravention of this Act, any person receiving the payment or being a party to the contract,

shall be guilty of an illegal practice.

NOTES

This section contains provisions formerly in the Representation of the People Act 1949, s 94.

For the purpose of promoting, etc. Cf the notes "With a view to" and "Promoting or procuring the election of a candidate" to s 75 ante.

Proxy. For the appointment of proxies for parliamentary elections, see s 21 ante, and for local government elections, see s 34 ante. Those sections are repealed by the Representation of the People Act 1985, s 28(1), Sch 5 post, as from a day to be appointed under s 29(2) of that Act. As from that date, new provision is made as to proxies by ss 8, 9 of that Act.

Knowingly; knew. See the note "Knows" to s 60 ante.

Illegal practice. See the note to s 61 ante.

Parish and community elections; municipal elections in City of London. See the notes to s 67 ante.

European Assembly elections. See the note to s 106 ante.

Saving for rights of creditors. See s 116 post.

Definitions. For "candidate" and "payment", see s 118 post; for "election", "elector" and "person", see s 202(1) post.

110 Printer's name and address on election publications

(1) A person shall not—

    (a) print or publish, or cause to be printed or published, any bill, placard or poster having reference to an election or any printed document distributed for the purpose of promoting or procuring the election of a candidate, or

    (b) post or cause to be posted any such bill, placard or poster as mentioned above, or

    (c) distribute or cause to be distributed any printed document for that purpose,

unless the bill, placard, poster or document bears upon its face the name and address of the printer and publisher.

(2) For the purposes of this section, any process for multiplying copies of a document, other than copying it by hand, shall be deemed to be printing and the expression "printer" shall be construed accordingly.

(3) A candidate or election agent acting in contravention of this section shall be guilty of an illegal practice, and any other person so acting shall on summary conviction be [liable to a fine not exceeding level 5 on the standard scale].

In relation to an election where candidates are not required to have election agents the reference to an election agent shall be omitted and the reference to any person other than the candidate shall be construed accordingly.

NOTES

This section contains provisions formerly in the Representation of the People Act 1949, s 95.

The words in square brackets in sub-s (3) were substituted by the Representation of the People Act 1985, s 23, Sch 3, para 6, as from 1 October 1985.

Cause to be printed or published. For the evidence necessary to procure a conviction of a principal where the act complained of was done by an alleged agent, see *Bettesworth v Allingham* (1885) 16 QBD 44 (in this case the appellant had been convicted of two offences and fined one single sum; the High Court found no evidence to support one charge and, as the conviction and sentence were indivisible, allowed the appeal entirely and quashed the conviction.

For the purpose of promoting or procuring, etc. Cf the notes "With a view to" and "Promoting or procuring the election of a candidate" to s 75 ante.

Candidate. For definition, see s 118 post; and see *Alcott v Emden* (1904) 68 JP 434, 20 TLR 487 (conviction upheld for circulating a document bearing no printer's name and address relating to forthcoming election of mayor).

Election agent. See s 67 ante and the notes thereto, as to the appointment of election agents.

Illegal practice. See the note to s 61 ante. An innocent act may be excepted by the court from being an illegal practice under s 167 post; see, eg, *Re Shipston-on-Stour Rural District Council Election* (1953) Times, 9 June (duplicated letter distributed without name of printer or publisher; held to be so done through inadvertence and excusable on that ground). The court will excuse trivial offences (*Cumberland, Cockermouth Division, Case, Armstrong, Brooksbank, Brown, Beck, Cooper and Henderson v Randles* (1901) 5 O'M & H 155 (election address printed on the back of a photograph which bore only the printer's impress)). Want of sufficient notice under s 167(2)(c) post, is ground for refusing relief; notice claiming relief should be precise, and want of precision is good ground for allowing costs to a person opposing relief (*Re County Councillors' Elections, Byrch's Case* (1889) 5 TLR 195). The court may in suitable cases grant relief although a petition is threatened (*Re County Councillors' Elections, Stephen's Case* (1889) 5 TLR 203), but if the applicant has been elected and a petition is pending, it will usually decline to adjudicate (*Ex p Wilks* (1885) 16 QBD 114, 50 JP 487 followed in *Re County Councils' Elections, Evans' Case* (1889) 5 TLR 206).

It is always a point in favour of an applicant for relief that so soon as he became aware of an illegality he took steps to remedy it (if it was capable of remedy), eg in the case of offences under this section by withdrawal of the offending bills, placards, posters or documents. However, in some cases the court will grant relief although placards and posters are not immediately withdrawn; see *Re County Councillors' Elections, Birley's Case* (1889) 5 TLR 220 (relief granted and the costs of opposition to application refused where the posters objected to remained up from 9 November to 2 January). See also *Ex p Smith and Ward* (1898) 42 Sol Jo 254 (relief granted in respect of posters issued with the printer's name but not his address, and of tickets issued without the printer's name; the candidate had approved the draft of the posters and tickets, but on being informed that the printer's foreman was used to election matters had instructed him to correct the proofs and not to submit them for correction; as soon as the mistake was discovered the posters were cancelled and the tickets as far as possible withdrawn from circulation); *Re Pembroke CC Case* (1889) 5 TLR 272 (relief refused; affidavit asserting want of knowledge was prima facie incorrect and the fact was not explained). The court will decline to grant relief in respect of documents containing libels (*Re County Council Elections, ex p Lenanton, ex p Pierce* (1889) 53 JP 263, 5 TLR 173 (applicant refused relief and ordered to pay costs of opposing the application); contrast *Re County Councillors' Elections, Birley's Case* (1889) 5 TLR 220 (relief was granted to applicant; opponent's charge of "scurrility" in a letter contained in a circular rejected). In *Re Droitwich Elective Auditors' Case, ex p Tolley, ex p Slater* (1907) 71 JP 236, 23 TLR 372, relief was refused in respect of cards containing an attack upon a candidate.

Any other person. It is not an "illegal practice" for the printer to contravene this section, and he cannot apply for relief under s 167 post (*Re County Councils' Elections, ex p Lenanton, ex p Pierce* (1889) 53 JP 263, 5 TLR 173) but if the candidate or his election agent obtains relief, then the printer is exonerated under sub-s (2) of that section.

Summary conviction. See the note to s 62 ante.

Election where candidates are not required to have election agents. Ie an election to which s 71 ante applies.

Prosecution. As to the time limit for prosecution, see s 176 post; and as to offences by associations, etc, see s 179 post.

If a prosecution is commenced it is a reasonable course to apply for an adjournment so that application for relief can be made under s 167 post; see *Re Huntingdon Borough Municipal Election, ex p Clark* (1885) 52 LT 260, 1 TLR 243.

Parish and community elections; municipal elections in City of London. See the notes to s 67 ante.

European Assembly elections. See the note to s 106 ante.

Definitions. For "candidate", see s 118 post; for "election" and "standard scale", see s 202(1) post. Note as to "printer", sub-s (2) above.

---

111 Prohibition of paid canvassers

If a person is, either before, during or after an election, engaged or employed for payment or promise of payment as a canvasser for the purpose of promoting or procuring a candidate's election—

    (*a*) the person so engaging or employing him, and

    (*b*) the person so engaged or employed,

shall be guilty of illegal employment.

NOTES

This section contains provisions formerly in the Representation of the People Act 1949, s 96.

If a person is ... engaged or employed, etc. Employment of paid canvassers can constitute bribery under s 113 post (*Bradford Case (No 1), Haley v Ripley* (1869) 19 LT 718). Note also that if corrupt persons are engaged, the candidates may become incapable of being elected; see s 165 post.

For the purpose of promoting, etc. Cf the notes "With a view to" and "Promoting or procuring the election of a candidate" to s 75 ante.

Illegal employment. For the penalty for illegal employment and as to the circumstances in which illegal employment may constitute an illegal practice, etc, see s 175 post. Note that under s 167 post certain courts may except an innocent act from being illegal employment. In *Ex p Thomas* (1889) 60 LT 728, CA, the Court of Appeal, reversing the Divisional Court, allowed relief in respect of the employment of four paid canvassers who had been paid £1 19s. The main ground for the decision was that the court had jurisdiction to review the matter as the applicant had been unsuccessful at the election which was held after the date of the Divisional Court's decision. See also the note "Further provisions" to s 175 post.

Parish and community elections; municipal elections in City of London. See the notes to s 67 ante.

European Assembly elections. See the note to s 106 ante.
Saving for rights of creditors. See s 116 post.
Definitions. For "candidate" and "payment", see s 118 post; for "election" and "person", see s 202(1) post.

112 Providing money for illegal purposes

Where a person knowingly provides money—

(a) for any payment which is contrary to the provisions of this Act, or

(b) for any expenses incurred in excess of the maximum amount allowed by this Act, or

(c) for replacing any money expended in any such payment or expenses,

except where the payment or the incurring of the expenses may have been previously allowed in pursuance of section 167 below to be an exception, that person shall be guilty of an illegal payment.

NOTES

This section contains provisions formerly in the Representation of the People Act 1949, s 98.

Knowingly. See the note "Knows" to s 60 ante.

Payment . . . contrary to the provisions of this Act. This includes the following payments: payments not through election agent (s 73 ante); expenses not authorised by election agent (s 75 ante); expenses in excess of maximum amount (s 76 ante); payment of claims not made in due time (s 78 ante); payment for conveyance of voters (s 102 ante); payment for exhibition of election notices (s 109 ante); payment of canvassers (s 111 ante); payment of bribes (s 113 post); and treating (s 114 post).

Maximum amount. Ie the amounts specified in s 76 ante, or, as respects certain elections in the City of London, s 197 post.

Illegal payment. For the penalty for illegal payment, and as to the circumstances in which an illegal payment is also an illegal practice, etc, see s 175 post. Note that under s 167 post certain courts may except an innocent act from being an illegal payment. See also the note "Further provisions" to s 175 post.

Parish and community elections; municipal elections in City of London. See the notes to s 67 ante.

European Assembly elections. See the note to s 106 ante.

Saving for rights of creditors. See s 116 post.

Definitions. For "money" and "payment", see s 118 post; for "person", see s 202(1) post.

Bribery, treating and undue influence

113 Bribery

(1) A person shall be guilty of a corrupt practice if he is guilty of bribery.

(2) A person shall be guilty of bribery if he, directly or indirectly, by himself or by any other person on his behalf—

(a) gives any money or procures any office to or for any voter or to or for any other person on behalf of any voter or to or for any other person in order to induce any voter to vote or refrain from voting, or

(b) corruptly does any such act as mentioned above on account of any voter having voted or refrained from voting, or

(c) makes any such gift or procurement as mentioned above to or for any person in order to induce that person to procure, or endeavour to procure, the return of any person at an election or the vote of any voter,

or if upon or in consequence of any such gift or procurement as mentioned above he procures or engages, promises or endeavours to procure the return of any person at an election or the vote of any voter.

For the purposes of this subsection—

(i) references to giving money include references to giving, lending, agreeing to give or lend, offering, promising, or promising to procure or endeavour to procure any money or valuable consideration; and

(ii) references to procuring any office include references to giving, procuring, agreeing to give or procure, offering, promising, or promising to procure or to endeavour to procure any office, place or employment.

(3) A person shall be guilty of bribery if he advances or pays or causes to be paid any money to or for the use of any other person with the intent that that money or any part of it shall be expended in bribery at any election or knowingly pays or causes to be paid any money to any person in discharge or repayment of any money wholly or in part expended in bribery at any election.

(4) The foregoing provisions of this section shall not extend or be construed to extend to any money paid or agreed to be paid for or on account of any legal expenses incurred in good faith at or concerning an election.

(5) A voter shall be guilty of bribery if before or during an election he directly or indirectly by himself or by any other person on his behalf receives, agrees, or contracts for any money, gift, loan or valuable consideration, office, place or employment for himself or for any other person for voting or agreeing to vote or for refraining or agreeing to refrain from voting.

(6) A person shall be guilty of bribery if after an election he directly or indirectly by himself or by any other person on his behalf receives any money or valuable consideration on account of any person having voted or refrained from voting or having induced any other person to vote or refrain from voting.

(7) In this section the expression "voter" includes any person who has or claims to have a right to vote.

NOTES

This section contains provisions formerly in the Representation of the People Act 1949, s 99.

General Note. This section does not affect acts which are not done with a view to influencing the voter, or which do not relate to any vote which has been cast or which are not related to the particular objectives enumerated in the section. Thus payment of an arrested debtor's debts in order to procure his release would be bribery if it were done with a view to influencing his vote (*Londonderry Borough Case* (1869) 1 O'M & H 274), but paying an acknowledged supporter's debts to procure his release would not be bribery if the payment of the debt had no effect on his vote (*Ashburton Case, Dicker's Case* (1859) Wolf & B 1). For other instances of acts not constituting bribery, see *Belfast Borough Case* (1869) 1 O'M & H 281 (subscription to Orange Lodge); *Cashel Borough Case* (1869) 1 O'M & H 286 at 289; *Oldham Case, Cobbett v Hibbert and Platt* (1869) 20 LT 302 (payment of voter's rates to enable him to be registered as a voter); *Hastings Case, Calthorpe and Sutton v Brassey and North* (1869) 21 LT 234 (lavish personal expenditure for the purpose of gaining influence); *Youghal Case* (1869) 21 LT 306 (offer of a loan having no relation to voter's vote; overpayments to agents); *Tower Hamlets, St George's Division Case, Benn v Marks* (1896) 5 O'M & H 89, 90 (payment to shout for candidate).

In determining whether there has been bribery the court will always look to the essence of the transaction. For examples of acts done with a view to influencing a voter in relation to his vote, or on account of a vote cast by him and so contrary to law, see *Sulston v Norton* (1761) 3 Burr 1235 (colourable transaction amounting to a gift); *Huddersfield Case, Priestley's Case* (1859) Wolf & B 28 (buying pigs and horses above their value); *New Windsor Case* (1866) 15 LT 105 (hiring of 23 public houses at ten or twenty guineas each for no ostensible purpose); *Boston Case, Buxton v Garfit* (1880) 44 LT 287 (colourable hiring to perform valueless services).

Charitable gifts are not bribery and a person may give gifts to the electorate whom he represents (*Stafford Borough Case, Chawner v Meller* (1869) 21 LT 210; *Windsor Case, Herbert v Gardiner* (1874) 31 LT 133; *Plymouth Case, Latimer and Barratt v Bates* (1880) 3 O'M & H 107). The court must decide whether ostensible charity is only a cloak for bribery.

For the circumstances in which "treating" can constitute bribery, see *Bodmin Case* (1869) 20 LT 989. Payment of a voter's fares or employment of paid canvassers may also constitute bribery; see the note "Railway fares" to s 102 ante, and the note "If a person is . . . engaged or employed, etc" to s 111 ante.

Sub-s (1) : Corrupt practice. See the note to s 60 ante. Note that a candidate's election will be void under s 159(1) post if he is reported by an election court personally guilty or guilty by his agents of a single act of bribery, and s 158(3) post does not apply as it does in the case of treating or undue influence by agents so as to enable a candidate to claim exoneration in respect of the act of his agent. A candidate is not liable for bribery by persons not his agents, but the election would be void under s 164(1) post if bribery on his behalf has occurred on so extensive a scale as to have affected the result.

As to the striking off of votes of persons who have been bribed, see s 166 post. Note also the provisions of s 163 post relating to holders of licences or certificates under the Licensing Acts.

Sub-s (2): Procures. Cf the note "Aids, abets, counsels or procures" to s 60 ante.

In order to induce any voter to vote, etc. See the General Note above.

Procure the return of any person. In *Britt v Robinson* (1870) LR 5 CP 503, 39 LJCP 265, a test ballot was held to decide who should be Liberal candidate. In the circumstances of the case it was a certainty that the winner of the test ballot would be returned by the electors. After the writ for the election had been received, two agents of the successful candidate had given money and one agent had given drink to others participating in the test ballot. This was held to contravene what is now sub-s (2)(*c*) above and the election was declared void.

Valuable consideration. For examples of considerations to which this section applies, see *Northallerton Case* (1866) 14 LT 304 (promise to excuse rent); *Boston Case, Malcolm v Parry* (1874) LR 9 CP 610, 43 LJCP 331 (distribution of coal); *Re Launceston Case, Drinkwater v Deakin* (1874) LR 9 CP 626, 43 LJCP 355 (landlord, being candidate, giving leave to his tenants to trap and shoot rabbits on his estate); *Gravesend Case, Truscott v Bevan* (1880) 44 LT 64 (giving of paid holiday); *Bewdley Case, Spencer v Harrison* (1880) 44 LT 283 (release from liability on share in a building society).

Office. Eg the office of town councillor (*Waterford Borough Case* (1870) 2 O'M & H 24).

Place. Eg a place in a hospital (*Staleybridge Case* (1869) 20 LT 75).

Sub-s (3): Intent. As to proof of criminal intent, see the Criminal Justice Act 1967, s 8, Vol 12, title Criminal Law.

Knowingly. See the note "Knows" to s 60 ante.

Sub-s (4): Legal expenses. This expression refers to election expenses which a candidate is allowed to incur and not to those of any voter or other person; see *Coventry Case, Berry v Eaton and Hill* (1869) 20 LT 405. See, further, 15 Halsbury's Laws (4th edn) para 778; and as to election expenses generally, see ss 72 et seq ante.

Sub-s (5): Receives, agrees or contracts for. This expression does not cover an offer by a voter to sell his vote which is not accepted (*Mallow Borough Case* (1870) 2 O'M & H 18); but an offer made to a voter is contrary to sub-s (2) above.

Sub-s (6): After an election. In the absence of evidence to connect a payment after the election with an agreement or understanding with a voter before the poll, a payment after the election is not bribery. For relevant cases, see *Dublin Case* (1836) Falc & Fitz 88, 204; *Newcastle-under-Lyme Case* (1842) Bar & Aust 436; and *Caldicott v Corrupt Practices Comrs* (1907) 21 Cox CC 404.

Parish and community elections; municipal elections in City of London. See the notes to s 67 ante.

European Assembly elections. See the note to s 106 ante.

Saving for rights of creditors. See s 116 post.

Welsh Sunday polls. This section applies with modifications to a poll under the Licensing Act 1964, s 66 (Sunday closing in Wales), Vol 24, title Licensing and Liquor Duties, as if it were a poll at an ordinary election of district councillors; see the Licensing Act 1964, s 67(5)(*c*), and para (ii) of the proviso to that subsection, in the same title.

Definitions. For "election", "person" and "vote", see s 202(1) post; for "voter", see s 202(1) post, but note also sub-s (7) above.

114 Treating

(1) A person shall be guilty of a corrupt practice if he is guilty of treating.

(2) A person shall be guilty of treating if he corruptly, by himself or by any other person, either before, during or after an election, directly or indirectly gives or provides, or pays wholly or in part the expense of giving or providing, any meat, drink, entertainment or provision to or for any person—

(*a*) for the purpose of corruptly influencing that person or any other person to vote or refrain from voting; or

(*b*) on account of that person or any other person having voted or refrained from voting, or being about to vote or refrain from voting.

(3) Every elector or his proxy who corruptly accepts or takes any such meat, drink, entertainment or provision shall also be guilty of treating.

NOTES

This section contains provisions formerly in the Representation of the People Act 1949, s 100.

Corrupt practice. See the note to s 60 ante. Note that if a candidate is reported by an election court personally guilty of treating his election will be void; see s 159(1) post. If an agent is guilty of treating the candidate's election will also be void under that subsection unless the circumstances come within those specified in s 158(3) post. A candidate is not liable for treating by persons who are not his agents but, even if the candidate or his agents were not responsible, an election would be void under s 164(1) post if treating had occurred on so extensive a scale as to have affected the result.

As to the striking off of votes of persons who have been treated, see s 166 post. Note also the provisions of s 163 post, relating to holders of licences or certificates under the Licensing Acts.

Corruptly. Proof of a corrupt intention is essential (*Bewdley Case* (1869) 19 LT 676; *Wallingford Case* (1869) 19 LT 766; *Tamworth Case, Hill and Walton v Peel and Bulwer* (1869) 20 LT 181). A corrupt intention is not to be presumed merely from the fact of entertainment; see *New Windsor Case, Hunt's Case* (1866) 15 LT 108 (if open air treating is alleged, the exact locality where it is stated to have occurred must be specified); *Windsor Case, Richardson-Gardner v Eykyn* (1869) 19 LT 613 (candidate attending a dinner of a non-political society at which electors were present, he also supplying wines; held undesirable but prima facie not treating); *Bradford Case (No 2), Storey and Garnett v Forster* (1869) 19 LT 723 (hiring of rooms in public houses for committee rooms; strong partisan asked supporter of rival candidate to come to talk matter over at a public house and gave him some beer; large number of voters alleged to agent that the other side was treating, agent told landlady to give them beer to keep them quiet; refreshment given to persons engaged on actual business of election; all acts were held not treating); *Westminster Borough Case* (1869) 20 LT 238 (volunteer canvasser occasionally paid for wine and liquors at public houses where friends and supporters of the candidate were present; respondent on one occasion present at a meeting of a political association in a public house where landlord gave free drinks; held, not treating); *Coventry Case, Berry v Eaton and Hill, Ince's Case* (1869) 20 LT 405 (invitation to drink ruled not to be treating merely because an election is in progress, but if invitations were numerous that would be evidence of corrupt intention tending to establish proof of treating); *Hereford Borough Case, Thomas v Clive and Wyllie* (1869) 21 LT 117 (breakfast given before poll to which everyone was invited; candidate sent letter thanking the provider for his action; this was held to go a considerable way to prove agency); *Hastings Case, Calthorpe and Sutton v Brassey and North* (1869) 21 LT 234 (refreshment provided for persons attending revising barrister's court; held, unwise but not treating); *Norfolk, Northern Division, Case Colman v Walpole and Lacon* (1869) 21 LT 264 (discussion on the legality of giving post-election feasts); *Brecon Borough Case, Watkins and Watkins v Holford* (1871) 2 O'M & H 43 (discussion of the law); *Poole Case, Hurdle and Stark v Waring, Young and Rennison v Waring* (1874) 31 LT 171 (supply of beer, consideration of what constitutes "general treating"; election declared void); *Rochester Borough Case, Barry and Varrall v Davis* (1892) 4 O'M & H 156 (provision of refreshment is not in itself treating); *Lancaster County, Lancaster Division, Case, Bradshaw and Kaye v Foster* (1896) 5 O'M & H 39 (concert given by political association; unwise but in the circumstances not objected to); *Bodmin Division Case* (1906) 5 O'M & H 225 (giving of garden party held to be treating in this particular case).

In the absence of evidence connecting them with any votes cast or with abstention from voting, post-election festivities are not treating (*Carrickfergus Borough Case* (1880) 3 O'M & H 90; *Cork, Eastern Division, Case* (1911) 6 O'M & H 318).

For the circumstances in which treating can also constitute bribery, see *Bodmin Case* (1869) 20 LT 989.

See generally, as to proof of criminal intent, the Criminal Justice Act 1967, s 8, Vol 12, title Criminal Law.

Proxy. For the appointment of proxies for parliamentary elections, see s 21 ante, and for local government elections, see s 34 ante. Those sections are repealed by the Representation of the People Act 1985, s 28(1), Sch 5 post, as from a day to be appointed under s 29(2) of that Act. As from that date, new provision is made as to proxies by ss 8, 9 of that Act.

Parish and community elections; municipal elections in City of London. See the notes to s 67 ante.

European Assembly elections. See the note to s 106 ante.

Saving for rights of creditors. See s 116 post.

Welsh Sunday polls. This section and s 115 post, apply to a poll under the Licensing Act 1964, s 66 (Sunday closing in Wales), Vol 24, title Licensing and Liquor Duties, as if it were a poll at an ordinary election of district councillors; see the Licensing Act 1964, s 67(5)(*c*), in the same title.

Definitions. For "election", "person" and "vote", see s 202(1) post.

115 Undue influence

(1) A person shall be guilty of a corrupt practice if he is guilty of undue influence.

(2) A person shall be guilty of undue influence—

    (*a*) if he, directly or indirectly, by himself or by any other person on his behalf, makes use of or threatens to make use of any force, violence or restraint, or inflicts or threatens to inflict, by himself or by any other person, any temporal or spiritual injury, damage, harm or loss upon or against any person in order to induce or compel that person to vote or refrain from voting, or on account of that person having voted or refrained from voting; or

(b) if, by abduction, duress or any fraudulent device or contrivance, he impedes or prevents the free exercise of the franchise of an elector or proxy for an elector, or so compels, induces or prevails upon an elector or proxy for an elector either to vote or to refrain from voting.

NOTES

This section contains provisions formerly in the Representation of the People Act 1949, s 101.

Corrupt practice. See the note to s 60 ante. Note that if a candidate is reported by an election court personally guilty of undue influence his election will be void; see s 159(1) post. If an agent is guilty of undue influence the candidate's election will also be void under that subsection unless the circumstances come within those specified in s 158(3) post. A candidate is not liable for undue influence by persons who are not his agents but, even if the candidate or his agents were not guilty of undue influence, his election would be void under s 164(1) post if undue influence had occurred on such a scale as to have affected the result.

As to the striking off of votes of persons who have been unduly influenced, see s 166 post.

Spiritual injury. For a case of spiritual influence not improperly exercised, see *Galway Borough Case* (1869) 22 LT 75; and for discussion of the law as to the legitimate use of spiritual influence, see *Longford Case* (1870) 2 O'M & H 6.

Damage, harm or loss. For instances, see *R v Barnwell* (1857) 29 LTOS 107, 21 JP 323 (threat to withdraw custom from tradesmen); *Wareham Case, Harris' Case* (1857) Wolf & D 85 (threat to dismiss servant). Contrast *Westbury Case, Eyers' Case* (1869) 20 LT 16 (harsh conduct to a political adversary held not intimidation); *Tamworth Case, Hill and Walton v Peel and Bulwer* (1869) 20 LT 181 (eviction of tenants held in the circumstances not oppressive); *Windsor Case, Herbert v Gardiner* (1874) 31 LT 133 (eviction of tenants held not undue influence in the absence of evidence of pre-election threat to evict). For discussion of the law, see *Blackburn Case, Potter and Feilden v Hornby and Feilden* (1869) 20 LT 823; and *Norfolk, Northern Division, Case, Colman v Walpole and Lacon* (1869) 21 LT 264.

It does not have to be shown that the undue influence exercised attained its objective in order to establish the offence under sub-s (2)(a) above, but under sub-s (2)(b) above proof of such success is necessary.

Fraudulent device. Pairing by voters so that neither votes is not such a device (*Northallerton Case, Johns v Hutton* (1869) 21 LT 113).

Parish and community elections; municipal elections in City of London. See the notes to s 67 ante.

European Assembly elections. See the note to s 106 ante.

Welsh Sunday polls. See the note to s 114 ante.

Definitions. For "election", "person" and "vote", see s 202(1) post.

Supplemental

116 Rights of creditors

The provisions of this Part of this Act prohibiting—

(a) payments and contracts for payments,

(b) the payment or incurring of election expenses in excess of the maximum amount allowed by this Act; or

(c) the incurring of expenses not authorised by the election agent,

do not affect the right of any creditor, who, when the contract was made or the expense was incurred, was ignorant of that contract or expense being in contravention of this Act.

NOTES

This section contains provisions formerly in the Representation of the People Act 1949, s 105.

This Part of this Act. Ie Pt II (ss 67–119).

Payments and contracts for payments. For payments which are contrary to this Part of this Act, see the note "Payment . . . contrary to the provisions of this Act" to s 112 ante.

Maximum amount. Ie the amounts specified in s 76 ante, or as respects certain elections in the City of London, those specified in s 197 post.

Election agent. As to the appointment of election agents, see s 67 ante and the notes thereto.

Expenses not authorised by the election agent. See ss 73, 75 ante.

Parish and community elections; municipal elections in City of London. See the notes to s 67 ante.

European Assembly elections. See the note to s 106 ante.

Definitions. For "election expenses" and "payment", see s 118 post.

117 Savings as to parliamentary elections

(1) Where a person has been declared by others to be a candidate at a parliamentary election without his consent, nothing in this Part of this Act shall be construed to impose any liability on that person, unless he has afterwards given his assent to the declaration or has been nominated.

(2) Nothing in this Part makes it illegal for an employer to permit parliamentary electors or their proxies to absent themselves from his employment for a reasonable time for the purpose of voting at the poll at a parliamentary election without having any deduction from their salaries or wages on account of their absence, if the permission—

(a) is (so far as practicable without injury to the employer's business) given equally to all persons alike who are at the time in his employment, and

(b) is not given with a view to inducing any person to record his vote for any particular candidate at the election, and

(c) is not refused to any person for the purpose of preventing him from recording his vote for any particular candidate at the election,

but this subsection shall not be construed as making illegal any act which would not be illegal apart from this subsection.

NOTES

This section contains provisions formerly in the Representation of the People Act 1949, s 104.

Parliamentary election. See the note to s 1 ante.

This Part of this Act. Ie Pt II (ss 67–119).

Nominated. As to the nomination of candidates at parliamentary elections, see Sch 1, rr 6–17 post.

Parliamentary electors. See s 1 ante.

Proxies. For the appointment of proxies for parliamentary elections, see s 21 ante. That section is repealed by the Representation of the People Act 1985, s 28(1), Sch 5 post, as from a day to be appointed under s 29(2) of that Act. New provision is made as to proxies, as from that date, by ss 8, 9 of that Act.

Absent . . . from his employment. See also *Gravesend Case, Truscott v Bevan* (1880) 44 LT 64, as to the circumstances in which giving a holiday with pay would be bribery.

European Assembly elections. See the note to s 106 ante.

Definitions. For "candidate", see s 118 post; for "election", "elector" and "vote", see s 202(1) post.

118 Interpretation of Part II

In this Part of this Act, unless the context otherwise requires—

"appropriate officer" has the meaning given by section 67(7) above;

"candidate"—

(a) in relation to a parliamentary election, means a person who is elected to serve in Parliament at the election or a person who is nominated as a candidate at the election, or is declared by himself or by others to be a candidate on or after the day of the issue of the writ for the election, or after the dissolution or vacancy in consequence of which the writ was issued;

(b) in relation to an election under the local government Act, means a person elected or having been nominated or having declared himself a candidate for election, to the office to be filled at the election;

"committee room" does not include any house or room occupied by a candidate as a dwelling, by reason only of the candidate transacting business there with his agents in relation to the election, and no room or building shall be deemed to be a committee room by reason only of the candidate or any agent of the candidate addressing in it electors, committee members or others;

"date of the allowance of an authorised excuse" has the meaning given by section 86(8) above, or paragraph 7 of Schedule 4 to this Act, as the case may be;

"declaration as to election expenses" means a declaration made under section 82 above, or, as the case may be, paragraph 3 of Schedule 4 to this Act;

"disputed claim" has the meaning given by section 79(1) above as extended by section 80 above.

"election expenses" in relation to an election means expenses incurred, whether before, during or after the election, on account of or in respect of the conduct or management of the election;

"money" and "pecuniary reward" shall (except in sections 113 and 114 above) be deemed to include—

(a) any office, place or employment, and

(b) any valuable security or other equivalent of money, and

(c) any valuable consideration,

and expressions referring to money shall be construed accordingly;

"payment" includes any pecuniary or other reward;

"personal expenses" as used with respect to the expenditure of any candidate in relation to any election includes the reasonable travelling expenses of the candidate, and the reasonable expenses of his living at hotels or elsewhere for the purposes of and in relation to the election;

"return as to election expenses" means a return (including the bills and receipts to be [delivered] with it) to be made under section 81(1) above, or, as the case may be, paragraph 3 of Schedule 4 to this Act.

NOTES

This section contains provisions formerly in the Representation of the People Act 1949, s 103.

The word in square brackets in the definition of "return as to election expenses" was substituted by the Representation of the People Act 1985, s 24, Sch 4, para 43, as from 1 October 1985.

This Part of this Act. Ie Pt II (ss 67–119).

Parliamentary election. See the note to s 1 ante.

Nominated. As to the nomination of candidates, see Sch 1, rr 6–17 post, the Local Elections (Principal Areas) Rules 1973, SI 1973/79 (as amended by SI 1983/1154), Sch 2, rr 5–12, and the Local Elections (Parishes and Communities) Rules 1973, SI 1973/1910 (as amended by SI 1983/1153), Sch 1, rr 5–12.

Writ. As to the issue of the writ for parliamentary elections, see Sch 1, r 3 post.

Valuable consideration. See the note to s 113 ante.

Election expenses. These do not include expenses incurred on advertisements designed to support the interests of a particular political party generally in all constituencies as against furthering the interests of a particular candidate in his constituency; see *R v Tronoh Mines Ltd* [1952] 1 All ER 697.

Parish and community elections; municipal elections in City of London. See the notes to s 67 ante.

European Assembly elections. This section is applied to such elections by the European Assembly Elections Regulations 1984, SI 1984/137, reg 3(1), Sch 1, subject to the substitution, in the definition of "candidate", for the word "Parliament" of the words "the Assembly", and for the words from "day of the issue" to the end of the definition of the words "date of publication of notice of election". See further the Introductory Note to this Act.

As to provisions relating to such elections in Northern Ireland, see the Introductory Note to this Act.

Definitions. For "election", see s 202(1) post; for "local government Act", see s 203(1) post.

119 Computation of time for purposes of Part II

(1) Where the day or last day on which anything is required or permitted to be done by or in pursuance of this Part of this Act is any of the days mentioned in subsection (2) below—

(a) the requirement or permission shall be deemed to relate to the first day thereafter which is not one of those days; and

(b) in computing any period of not more than 7 days for the purposes of this Part any of the days so mentioned shall be disregarded.

(2) The days referred to in subsection (1) above are—

(a) a Sunday;

(b) a day of the Christmas break, of the Easter break, or of a bank holiday break; and

(c) a day appointed for public thanksgiving or mourning.

(3) In this section—

"bank holiday break" means any bank holiday under the Banking and Financial Dealings Act 1971 (in England and Wales, in Scotland or in Northern Ireland, as the case may be) which is not included in the Christmas break or the Easter break and the period beginning with the last weekday before that bank holiday and ending with the next weekday which is not a bank holiday under that Act,

"Christmas break" means the period beginning with the last weekday before Christmas Day and ending with the first weekday after Christmas Day which is not a bank holiday,

"Easter break" means the period beginning with the Thursday before and ending with the Tuesday after Easter Day,

but so much of this subsection as includes in a bank holiday break a period before and after a bank holiday does not apply in Scotland or Northern Ireland to a bank holiday which is not also a bank holiday in England and Wales, except in Scotland New Year's Day.

NOTES

This section contains provisions formerly in the Representation of the People Act 1949, s 106, as amended, in the case of s 106(2), and as inserted, in the case of s 106(3), by the Representation of the People Act 1969, s 24(1), Sch 2, para 18, and as affected, in the case of s 106(3), by the Banking and Financial Dealings Act 1971, s 4(1).

Prospective amendment. The following subsections are substituted for sub-ss (2), (3) above by the Representation of the People Act 1985, s 19(4) post, as from a day to be appointed under s 29(2) of that Act:

"(2) The days referred to in subsection (1) above are Saturday, Sunday, Christmas Eve, Christmas Day, Maundy Thursday, Good Friday, a bank holiday or a day appointed for public thanksgiving or mourning.

(3) In this section 'bank holiday', in relation to any election, means a day which is a bank holiday in the part of the United Kingdom in which the constituency or, as the case may be, electoral area is situated."

This Part of this Act. Ie Pt II (ss 67–119). This section also applies to Pt III (ss 120–186) post; see s 186 post.

England; Wales. See the note to s 4 ante.

Parish and community elections; municipal elections in City of London. See the notes to s 67 ante.

European Assembly elections. This section and s 120 and 121 post, are applied to such elections by the European Assembly Elections Regulations 1984, SI 1984/137, reg 3(1), Sch 1. See further the Introductory Note to this Act.

As to provisions relating to such elections in Northern Ireland, see the Introductory Note to this Act.

Banking and Financial Dealings Act 1971. See Vol 45, title Time.

PART III

LEGAL PROCEEDINGS

Questioning of a parliamentary election

120 Method of questioning parliamentary election

(1) No parliamentary election and no return to Parliament shall be questioned except by a petition complaining of an undue election or undue return ("a parliamentary election petition") presented in accordance with this Part of this Act.

(2) A petition complaining of no return shall be deemed to be a parliamentary election petition and the High Court—

(*a*) may make such order on the petition as they think expedient for compelling a return to be made; or

(b) may allow the petition to be heard by an election court as provided with respect to ordinary election petitions.

NOTES

This section contains provisions formerly in the Representation of the People Act 1949, s 107.

Parliamentary election. See the note to s 1 ante.

Return to Parliament. As to the return to the writ for a parliamentary election, see Sch 1, r 51 post.

Presented in accordance with this Part. See, in particular, ss 121, 122 post.

High Court. See the note to s 39 ante; and for provisions as to appeals and jurisdiction under this Part of this Act, see s 157 post.

Election court. For meaning, see s 202(1) post; and as to its constitution, etc, see s 123 post.

European Assembly elections. See the note to s 119 ante.

Definitions. For "election court" and "election petition", see s 202(1) post. Note as to "parliamentary election petition", sub-s (1) above.

121 Presentation and service of parliamentary election petition

(1) A parliamentary election petition may be presented by one or more of the following persons—

(a) a person who voted as an elector at the election or who had a right so to vote; or

(b) a person claiming to have had a right to be elected or returned at the election; or

(c) a person alleging himself to have been a candidate at the election.

(2) The member whose election or return is complained of is hereinafter referred to as the respondent, but if the petition complains of the conduct of a returning officer, the returning officer shall for the purposes of this Part of this Act be deemed to be a respondent.

(3) The petition shall be in the prescribed form, state the prescribed matters and be signed by the petitioner, or all the petitioners if more than one, and shall be presented to the High Court, or to the Court of Session, or to the High Court of Northern Ireland depending on whether the constituency to which it relates is in England and Wales, or Scotland or Northern Ireland.

(4) The petition shall be presented by delivering it to the prescribed officer or otherwise dealing with it in the prescribed manner; and the prescribed officer shall send a copy of it to the returning officer of the constituency to which the petition relates, who shall forthwith publish it in that constituency.

(5) The petition shall be served as nearly as may be in the manner in which a writ or summons is served or in such other manner as may be prescribed.

NOTES

This section contains provisions formerly in the Representation of the People Act 1949, s 108.

Sub-s (1): Voted. It does not appear to have been decided judicially whether the right to petition depends on the casting of a valid vote or whether a person actually voting is entitled to petition even though this vote is void; see 15 Halsbury's Laws (4th edn) para 839, note 1.

As an elector. Ie in his own right and not as proxy for another elector. For the persons who are entitled to vote as electors at parliamentary elections, see, in particular, s 1 ante.

Or who had a right so to vote. This refers to a person entitled under s 1 ante to vote whose name was in the register of electors but who did not exercise his right.

Returned. Ie under Sch 1, r 51 post.

Sub-s (2): Returning officer. As to returning officers at parliamentary elections, see ss 24, 26–28 ante.

Sub-s (3): Prescribed form; prescribed matters. These are prescribed by the Election Petition Rules 1960, SI 1960/543, r 4(1), Schedule.

High Court. See the notes to ss 39 and 120 ante.

Constituency. See the note to s 1 ante.

Sub-s (4): Prescribed officer. Ie the officer specified in s 157(4) post.

Prescribed manner. Ie the manner prescribed by the Election Petition Rules 1960, SI 1960/543, r 4(2).

Forthwith. See the note to s 67 ante.

Sub-s (5): Petition shall be served, etc. The relevant provisions as to service will be found in the Election Petition Rules 1960, SI 1960/543, r 5, as substituted by SI 1985/1278.

European Assembly elections. See the note to s 119 ante.

Legal aid. See the note to s 154 post.

Definitions. For "parliamentary election petition", see s 120 ante; for "prescribed", see s 185 post; for "candidate", see, by virtue of s 185 post, s 118 ante; for "elector" and "vote", see s 202(1) post.

122 Time for presentation or amendment of parliamentary election petition

(1) Subject to the provisions of this section, a parliamentary election petition shall be presented within 21 days after the return has been made to the Clerk of the Crown, or to the Clerk of the Crown for Northern Ireland, as the case may be, of the member to whose election the petition relates.

(2) If the petition questions the election or return upon an allegation of corrupt practices and specifically alleges a payment of money or other reward to have been made by the member or on his account or with his privity since the time of that return in pursuance or in furtherance of the alleged corrupt practice, it may be presented within 28 days after the date of the payment.

(3) A petition questioning the election or return upon an allegation of an illegal practice may, so far as respects that illegal practice, be presented—

    (*a*) within 21 days after the day specified in subsection (4) below; or

    (*b*) if specifically alleging a payment of money or some other act to have been made or done since the day so specified by the member to whose election the petition relates or an agent of his, or with the privity of that member or his election agent, in pursuance or in furtherance of the alleged illegal practice, within 28 days after the date of the payment or other act.

(4) The day referred to in subsection (3) above is the tenth day after the end of the time allowed for [delivering] to the returning officer returns as to election expenses at the election or, if later—

    (*a*) that on which the returning officer receives the return and declarations as to election expenses by that member and his election agent; or

    (*b*) where the return and declarations are received on different days, the last of those days; or

    (*c*) where there is an authorised excuse for failing to make the return and declarations, the date of the allowance of the excuse, or if there was a failure as regards two or more of them, and the excuse was allowed at different times, the date of the allowance of the last excuse.

(5) An election petition presented within the time limited by subsection (1) or subsection (2) above may, for the purpose of questioning the election or return upon an allegation of an illegal practice, be amended with the leave of the High Court within the time within which a petition questioning the election upon the allegation of that illegal practice could be presented under subsection (3).

(6) Subsections (3), (4) and (5) above apply—

    (*a*) notwithstanding that the act constituting the alleged illegal practice amounted to a corrupt practice; and

    (*b*) to a corrupt practice under section 75 above, as if it were an illegal practice.

(7) For the purposes of this section, an allegation that an election is avoided under section 164 below shall be deemed to be an allegation of corrupt practices, notwithstanding that the offences alleged are or include offences other than corrupt practices.

(8) Except in Scotland, the jurisdiction vested by subsection (5) in the High Court shall, subject to rules of court, be exercised—

(a) by one of the judges for the time being on the rota for the trial of parliamentary election petitions,

(b) in Northern Ireland, by one of the judges of the High Court or the Court of Appeal for the time being selected under section 108 of the Judicature (Northern Ireland) Act 1978,

sitting either in court or at chambers, or by a master of the Supreme Court in manner directed by and subject to an appeal to those judges.

NOTES

This section contains provisions formerly in the Representation of the People Act 1949, s 109, as amended, in the case of s 109(3) and (4), by the Representation of the People Act 1969, s 24(1), Sch 2, para 1, and as partly repealed, in the case of s 109(8), by s 24(4) of, and Sch 3, Pt I to, the 1969 Act, and as amended, in the case of s 109(8), by the Judicature (Northern Ireland) Act 1978, s 122(1), Sch 5, Pt II.

The word in square brackets in sub-s (4) was substituted by the Representation of the People Act 1985, s 24, Sch 4, para 44, as from 1 October 1985.

Sub-s (1): Within 21 days after, etc. For the computation of time, see s 119 ante, as applied by s 186 post, together with the Election Petition Rules 1960, SI 1960/543, r 19(2). See also the note "Within six months ..." to s 5 ante.

Return has been made. Ie under Sch 1, r 51 post. A return is "made" when it is received, not when it is sent (*Re Poole Case, Hurdle v Waring* (1874) LR 9 CP 435, LJCP 209).

Sub-s (2): Corrupt practices. For the corrupt practices created by this Act, see the note to s 168 post, and for the consequences of a report by an election court that a candidate or other person is guilty of a corrupt practice, see ss 158–160 post. Note also sub-s (7) above.

Within 28 days after, etc. See the note "Within 21 days after, etc" above.

Sub-s (3): Illegal practice. For the illegal practices created by this Act see the note to s 169 post; and for the consequences of a report by an election court that a candidate or other person is guilty of an illegal practice, see ss 158–160 post. Note also sub-s (6) above.

Agent. See the note "Any agent" to s 73 ante.

Election agent. As to the appointment of election agents, see s 67 ante and the notes thereto.

Sub-s (4): Returning officer. As to returning officers at parliamentary elections, see ss 24, 26–28 ante.

Returns as to election expenses. These are required under s 81 ante. As to the time allowed for delivering the return, see sub-s (1) of that section.

Declarations as to election expenses. These are required by s 82 ante.

Authorised excuse. As to authorised excuses for failure to make returns and declarations as to election expenses, see 86 ante.

Sub-s (5): High Court. See the notes to ss 39 and 120 ante; and note sub-s (8) above.

Sub-s (8): Rules of court. As to such rules, see s 182 post and the notes thereto.

Rota. See the note to s 123 post.

European Assembly elections. This section is applied to such elections by the European Assembly Elections Regulations 1984, SI 1984/137, reg 3(1), Sch 1, subject to:

(1) the substitution, in sub-s (1) above, for the words from "the return" to the end of the subsection, of the words "the day on which the relevant result was declared in accordance with rule 50 of the elections rules"; and

(2) the substitution, in sub-s (2) above, for the words "that return", of the words "that declaration of the result of the election".

See further the Introductory Note to this Act.

As to provisions relating to such elections in Northern Ireland, see the Introductory Note to this Act.

Definitions. For "parliamentary election petition", see s 120 ante; for "date of the allowance of an authorised excuse", "declaration as to election expenses", "money", "payment" and "return as to election expenses", see s 185 post; for "Clerk of the Crown", see s 202(1) post.

Judicature (Northern Ireland) Act 1978, s 108. See Vol 31, title Northern Ireland (Pt 2).

123 Constitution of election court and place of trial

(1) A parliamentary election petition shall be tried by—

(a) two judges on the rota for the trial of parliamentary election petitions, and the judges for the time being on that rota shall, unless they otherwise agree, try the election petitions standing for trial according to their seniority,

(b) in Northern Ireland, the two judges of the High Court or the Court of Appeal for the time being selected under section 108 of the Judicature (Northern Ireland) Act 1978,

and the judges presiding at the trial of a parliamentary election petition are hereinafter referred to as the election court.

(2) The election court has, subject to the provisions of this Act, the same powers, jurisdiction and authority as a judge of the High Court . . . and shall be a court of record.

(3) The place of trial shall be within the constituency for which the election was held, but—

(a) the High Court may, on being satisfied that special circumstances exist rendering it desirable that the petition should be tried elsewhere, appoint some other convenient place for the trial; and

(b) if that constituency is wholly or partly in Greater London, the petition may be heard at such place within Greater London as the High Court may appoint.

(4) The election court may adjourn the trial from one place to another within the constituency.

NOTES

This section contains provisions formerly in the Representation of the People Act 1949, s 110, as amended, in the case of s 110(3), by the London Government Act 1963, s 8(1), Sch 3, para 31, and as amended, in the case of s 110(1) by the Judicature (Northern Ireland) Act 1978, s 122(1), Sch 5, Pt II.

The words omitted from sub-s (2) apply to Scotland only.

Rota. As to the selection of judges for the rota for the trial of parliamentary election petitions, see the Supreme Court Act 1981, s 142, Vol 11, title Courts.

Subject to the provisions of this Act. For instances in which the jurisdiction of an election court is limited, see *Wallingford Case, Wells v Wren* (1880) 5 CPD 546, 49 LJQB 681, in which it was decided that interrogatories could not be administered to a sitting member; see also *Salisbury Case, Moore v Kennard* (1883) 10 QBD 290, 52 LJQB 285 (order for production and inspection of documents was refused); *Norwich Case, Birbeck v Bullard* (1886) 54 LT 625 (no jurisdiction to allow new charge after expiry of the statutory time limits imposed by s 122 ante, which must be observed). For the powers and functions of an election court, see also s 157(2), (3) post.

It has not yet been decided whether a parliamentary election court is subject to judicial review; see *R v Election Court, ex p Sheppard* [1975] 2 All ER 723, [1975] 1 WLR 1319; and *R v Cripps, ex p Muldoon* [1984] QB 68, [1983] 3 All ER 72 (and for the position in so far as a local election court is concerned, see the second paragraph of the note to s 130(5) post).

High Court. See the notes to ss 39 and 120 ante.

Court of record. As to courts of record and courts not of record, see 10 Halsbury's Laws (4th edn) para 709.

Constituency. See the note to s 1 ante.

Special circumstances. See *Sligo Borough Case* (1869) 1 O'M & H 300 (systematic intimidation and violence prior to election continued until and during trial; venue changed); *Tewkesbury Case, Collins v Price* (1880) 5 CPD 544, 49 LJQB 685 (an order transferring the trial from Tewkesbury to Gloucester had been made in chambers by one judge and as doubts arose concerning the validity of the order, the application was renewed in the Commons Pleas; that court expressed the view that such orders should be made by the court, but eventually concurred in the order though doubting the sufficiency of the grounds upon which it was made, namely, want of suitable accommodation for an election court at Tewkesbury); *Cirencester Case, Lawson v Chester Master* [1893] 1 QB 245, 62 LJQB 231 (the place of trial had been changed once; application made to remove the trial to the metropolis in order to avoid expense; court refused the application). Cf *Arch v Bentinck* (1887) 18 QBD 548, 56 LJQB 458, where the court allowed a removal to London where a petition had been presented in respect of one act which the respondent admitted but denied to be an illegal practice, which was the point in issue. For a further case in which a removal was allowed, see *Cork, Eastern Division, Case* (1911) 6 O'M & H 318.

Greater London. See the note to s 22 ante.

Special case for High Court. As to the statement of an election petition as a special case for the High Court and the reference of any question of law to that court, see s 146(1), (2), (4) post.

Appeals and jurisdiction. See s 157 post.

Evidence. The records of election courts are, by virtue of sub-s (2) above, public records for the purposes of the Public Records Act 1958; see s 10(1) of, and Sch 1, para 4(1)(a), to, the 1958 Act, Vol 17, title Evidence.

European Assembly elections. This section and s 124 post, are applied to such elections by the European Assembly Elections Regulations 1984, SI 1984/137, reg 3(1), Sch 1. See further the Introductory Note to this Act.

As to provisions relating to such elections in Northern Ireland, see the Introductory Note to this Act.

Definitions. For "parliamentary election petition", see s 120 ante. Note as to "election court", sub-s (1) above.

Judicature (Northern Ireland) Act 1978, s 108. See Vol 31, title Northern Ireland (Pt 2).

124 Judges' expenses and reception: England and Wales and Northern Ireland

In relation to the trial of a parliamentary election petition—

(a) in England and Wales and Northern Ireland, the travelling and other expenses of the judges and all expenses properly incurred in . . . providing them with necessary accommodation and with a proper court shall be defrayed by the Treasury out of moneys provided by Parliament;

(b) . . .

NOTES

Para (a) contains provisions formerly in the Representation of the People Act 1949, s 111(3), as partly repealed by the Courts Act 1971, s 56(4), Sch 11, Pt IV.

The words omitted were repealed by the Representation of the People Act 1985, ss 24, 28(1), Sch 4, para 45, Sch 5, as from 1 October 1985.

Parliamentary election petition. For meaning, see s 120 ante.

England; Wales. See the note to s 4 ante.

Treasury. See the note to s 29 ante.

Witnesses' expenses. See s 143 post.

European Assembly elections. See the note to s 123 ante.

125 (Applies to Scotland only.)

126 Attendance of House of Commons shorthand writer

(1) The shorthand writer of the House of Commons or his deputy shall attend the trial and shall be sworn by one of the judges of the election court faithfully and truly to take down the evidence given at the trial and from time to time as occasion requires to transcribe that evidence or cause it to be transcribed.

(2) The shorthand writer shall take down the evidence and from time to time transcribe it or cause it to be transcribed and a copy of the evidence shall accompany the certificate given by the election court to the Speaker.

(3) In Scotland and Northern Ireland the expenses of the shorthand writer shall be deemed to be part of the expenses occurred in receiving the judges.

NOTES

This section contains provisions formerly in the Representation of the People Act 1949, s 111(5)–(7), as repealed as respects England and Wales, in the case of s 111(7), by the Courts Act 1971, s 56(4), Sch 11, Pt IV.

Certificate given . . . to the Speaker. This certificate is to be given under s 144(2) post.

European Assembly elections. This section is applied to such elections by the European Assembly Elections Regulations 1984, SI 1984/137, reg 3(1), Sch 1, subject to:

(1) the substitution, in sub-s (1) above, for the words "The shorthand writer of the House of Commons or his deputy", of the words "A shorthand writer";

(2) the substitution, in sub-s (2) above, for the word "Speaker", of the words "Secretary of State".

See further the Introductory Note to this Act.

As to provisions relating to such elections in Northern Ireland, see the Introductory Note to this Act.

Definitions. For "election court", see s 123(1) ante; for "Speaker", see s 185 post.

Questioning of a local election

127 Method of questioning local election

An election under the local government Act may be questioned on the ground that the person whose election is questioned—

(*a*) was at the time of the election disqualified, or

(*b*) was not duly elected,

or on the ground that the election was avoided by corrupt or illegal practices or on the grounds provided by section 164 or section 165 below, and shall not be questioned on any of those grounds except by an election petition.

NOTES

This section contains provisions formerly in the Representation of the People Act 1949, s 112.

Election under the local government Act. See the note to s 202 post.

Disqualified. As to qualifications and disqualifications for being elected or being a member of a local authority, see the Local Government Act 1972, ss 79–81, Vol 25, title Local Government.

Corrupt or illegal practices. Cf the notes "Corrupt practices" and "Illegal practice" to s 122 ante.

Parish and community elections; municipal elections in City of London. See the notes to s 67 ante.

Definitions. For "election petition", see s 202(1) post; for "local government Act", see s 203(1) post.

128 Presentation of petition questioning local election

(1) A petition questioning an election under the local government Act may be presented either by four or more persons who voted as electors at the election or had a right so to vote, or by a person alleging himself to have been a candidate at the election.

(2) A person whose election is questioned by the petition, and any returning officer of whose conduct the petition complains, may be made a respondent to the petition.

(3) The petition shall be in the prescribed form signed by the petitioner and shall be presented in the prescribed manner—

(*a*) in England and Wales, to the High Court;

(*b*) (*applies to Scotland only*).

(4) In England and Wales the prescribed officer shall send a copy of the petition to the proper officer of the authority for which the election was held, who shall forthwith publish it in the area of that authority.

NOTES

This section contains provisions formerly in the Representation of the People Act 1949, s 113, as affected, in the case of s 113(4), by the Local Government Act 1972, s 251(1), Sch 29, Pt I, para 4(1).

Election under the local government Act. See the note to s 202 post.

Voted. See the note to s 121 ante.

As electors. Ie in their own right and not as proxies for other electors. For the persons who are entitled to vote as electors at local government elections, see s 2 ante.

Or who had a right so to vote. This refers to a person entitled under s 2 ante to vote whose name was in the register of electors but who did not exercise his right.

Returning officer. As to returning officers at local government elections, see s 35 ante.

Respondent. As to the respondents to a local election petition, see also s 138(3) post.

Prescribed form; prescribed manner. For the prescribed form, see the Election Petition Rules 1960, SI 1960/543, r 4(1), Schedule, and for the prescribed manner of presenting a petition, see r 4(2) of those rules.

England; Wales. See the note to s 4 ante.

High Court. See the notes to ss 39 and 120 ante.

Prescribed officer. By the Election Petition Rules 1960, SI 1960/543, r 2(3) (having effect under s 157(6) post), as construed in accordance with the Interpretation Act 1978, ss 17(2)(*a*), 23(2), Vol 41, title Statutes, the master of the Supreme Court (Queen's Bench Division) nominated under s 157(4) post as the prescribed officer in relation to parliamentary elections is also to be the prescribed officer in relation to elections under the Local Government Act 1972, Vol 25, title Local Government.

Forthwith. See the note to s 67 ante.

Parish and community elections; municipal elections in City of London. See the notes to s 67 ante.

Legal aid. See the note to s 154 post.

Definitions. For "prescribed", see s 185 post; for "candidate", see, by virtue of s 185 post, s 118 ante; for "elector", "proper officer" and "vote", see s 202(1) post; for "local government Act"; see s 203(1) post.

129 Time for presentation or amendment of petition questioning local election

(1) Subject to the provisions of this section, a petition questioning an election under the local government Act shall be presented within 21 days after the day on which the election was held.

(2) If the petition complains of the election—

    (a) on the ground of a corrupt practice, and

    (b) specifically alleges that a payment of money or other reward has been made or promised since the election by a candidate elected at the election, or on his account or with his privity, in pursuance or furtherance of that corrupt practice,

it may be presented at any time within 28 days after the date of the alleged payment or promise, whether or not any other petition against that person has been previously presented or tried.

(3) If the petition complains of the election—

    (a) on the ground of an illegal practice, and

    (b) specifically alleges a payment of money or other act made or done since the election by the candidate elected at the election, or by an agent of the candidate or with the privity of the candidate or his election agent, in pursuance or in furtherance of that illegal practice,

it may be presented at any time within 28 days after the date of that payment or act, whether or not any other petition against that person has been previously presented or tried.

(4) If the petition complains of an election where election expenses are allowed on the ground of an illegal practice, it may be presented at any time within 14 days after the day specified in subsection (5) below.

(5) The day referred to in subsection (4) above is—

    (a) that on which the appropriate officer receives the return and declarations as to election expenses by that candidate and his election agent; or

    (b) where the return and declarations are received on different days, the last of those days; or

    (c) where there is an authorised excuse for failing to make the return and declarations, the date of the allowance of the excuse, or if there was a failure as regards two or more of them and the excuse was allowed at different times, the date of the allowance of the last excuse.

(6) An election petition presented within the time limited by subsection (1) or subsection (2) above may for the purpose of complaining of the election upon an allegation of an illegal practice, be amended with the leave of the High Court within the time within which a petition complaining of the election on the ground of that illegal practice could, under this section, be presented.

(7) Subsections (3), (4), (5) and (6) above apply—

    (a) notwithstanding that the act constituting the alleged illegal practice amounted to a corrupt practice; and

    (b) to a corrupt practice under section 75 above as if it were an illegal practice.

(8) For the purposes of this section, an allegation that an election is avoided under section 164 below shall be deemed to be an allegation of corrupt practices, notwithstanding that the offences alleged are or include offences other than corrupt practices.

(9) In relation to an election where candidates are not required to have election agents there shall be omitted—

(a) the references in subsection (3) and paragraph (a) of subsection (5) above to an election agent; and

(b) paragraphs (b) and (c) of subsection (5).

NOTES

This section contains provisions formerly in the Representation of the People Act 1949, s 114.

The words omitted from sub-s (6) where indicated by dots apply to Scotland only.

Sub-s (1): Election under the local government Act. See the note to s 202 post.

Within 21 days after, etc. For the computation of time, see s 119 ante, as applied by s 186 post, together with the Election Petition Rules 1960, SI 1960/543, r 19(2). See also the note "Within six months . . ." to s 5 ante.

Sub-s (2): Corrupt practice. See the note to "Corrupt practices" to s 122 ante (but here sub-s (8) above applies instead of s 122(7) ante).

Within 28 days after, etc. See the note "Within 21 days after, etc" above.

Sub-s (3): Illegal practice. See the note to s 122 ante (but here sub-s (7) above applies instead of s 122(6) ante).

Agent. See the note "Any agent" to s 73 ante.

Election agent. As to the appointment of election agents, see s 67 ante and the notes thereto.

Sub-s (5): Return and declarations as to election expenses. These are required under ss 81, 82 ante.

Authorised excuse. As to authorised excuses for failure to make returns and declarations as to election expenses, see s 86 ante.

Sub-s (6): High Court. See the notes to ss 39 and 120 ante.

Sub-s (9): Election where candidates are not required to have election agents. See s 71 ante.

Parish and community elections; municipal elections in City of London. See the notes to s 67 ante.

Definitions. For "date of the allowance of an authorised excuse", "declaration as to election expenses", "money", "payment" and "return as to election expenses", see s 185 post; by virtue of s 185 post, for "appropriate officer", see s 67(7) ante, and for "candidate", see s 118 ante; for "local government Act", see s 203(1) post.

130 Election court for local election in England and Wales, and place of trial

(1) A petition questioning an election in England and Wales under the local government Act shall be tried by an election court consisting of a barrister qualified and appointed as provided by this section.

(2) A barrister shall not be qualified to constitute an election court—

(a) if he is of less than 15 years standing, or

(b) if the court is for the trial of an election petition relating to any local government area—

(i) in which he resides; or

(ii) which is included in a circuit on which he practises as a barrister.

(3) The judges for the time being on the rota for the trial of parliamentary election petitions, or any two of those judges—

(a) may annually appoint as many barristers, not exceeding five, as they may think necessary as commissioners for the trial of petitions questioning elections in England and Wales under the local government Act; and

(b) shall from time to time assign the petitions to be tried by each commissioner.

(4) If the commissioner to whom the trial of a petition is assigned dies, or declines to act or becomes incapable of acting, those judges or two of them may assign the trial to

be conducted or continued by any other of the commissioners appointed under this section.

(5) The election court has for the purposes of the trial the same powers and privileges as a judge on the trial of a parliamentary election petition.

(6) The place of trial shall be within the area of the authority for which the election was held, except that the High Court may, on being satisfied that special circumstances exist rendering it desirable that the petition should be tried elsewhere, appoint some other convenient place for the trial.

(7) The election court may in its discretion adjourn the trial from one place to another within the local government area or place where it is held.

NOTES

Sub-ss (1), (3)–(7) contain provisions formerly in the Representation of the People Act 1949, s 115(1), (4)–(8), as partly repealed, in the case of s 115(6), by the Administration of Justice Act 1960, s 19(2), Sch 4. Sub-s (2) contains provisions formerly in s 115(2) of the 1949 Act, as partly repealed by the House of Commons Disqualification Act 1957, s 14(1), Sch 4, Pt I, and by the Representation of the People Act 1969, ss 22(1), 24(4), Sch 3, Pt II, and s 115(3) of the 1949 Act as substituted by the Courts Act 1971, s 56(1), Sch 8, Pt II.

Sub-s (1): Election ... under the local government Act. See the note to s 202 post.

England; Wales. See the note to s 4 ante.

Sub-s (2): Barrister ... of less than 15 years standing. See, however, as to barristers who have been solicitors, the Barristers (Qualification for Office) Act 1961, s 1, Vol 4, title Barristers.

Resides. "Residence" is defined in s 5 ante for the purpose of ascertaining the right to the franchise. See also the notes to that section.

Sub-s (3): Rota. See the note to s 123 ante.

Commissioners. As to the commissioners' remuneration and allowances, see ss 132, 133 post.

Sub-s (5): Same powers and privileges as ... on ... a parliamentary election petition. See, as to the powers of such a judge, s 123(2) ante, and s 157(2), (3) post; and see also the note "Subject to the provisions of this Act" to s 123 ante.

In *R v Cripps ex p Muldoon* [1984] 2 All ER 705, [1984] 3 WLR 53, CA, it was held (i) that a local election court ceased to exist when the trial for which it was convened was concluded; accordingly a commissioner had no further power to reconsider or vary his decision, whether under RSC Ord 20, r 11 (the "slip rule") or otherwise, and (ii) that certiorari would issue to quash an order purportedly made by the commissioner after the conclusion of the trial.

Sub-s (6): High Court. See the notes to ss 39 and 120 ante.

Special circumstances. There do not appear to have been any reported cases of applications for change of venue referred to in sub-s (6) above, but for cases applying to parliamentary election petitions, see the note to s 123 ante.

Special case for High Court. As to the statement of an election petition as a special case for the High Court and the reference of any question of law to that court, see s 146(1), (3), (4) post.

Appeals and jurisdiction. See s 157 post.

Parish and community elections; municipal elections in City of London. See the notes to s 67 ante.

Definitions. For "parliamentary election petition", see s 120 ante; for "local government Act" and "local government area", see s 203(1) post.

---

131 Accommodation of and attendance on court

(1) The proper officer of the authority for which the election was held shall provide suitable accommodation for holding the election court constituted under section 130 above and any expenses incurred by him for the purposes of this section and section 132 below shall be paid by that authority.

(2) The election court so constituted may employ officers and clerks as prescribed, and all constables and bailiffs shall give their assistance to the court in the execution of its duties.

(3) A shorthand writer (whose expenses, according to a prescribed scale, shall be treated as part of the expenses incurred in receiving the election court) shall attend the trial before that court, and—

(*a*) shall be sworn by the court faithfully and truly to take down the evidence given at the trial, and

(*b*) shall take down such evidence at length,

and a transcript of the notes of the evidence taken down by him shall, if the election court so directs, accompany the court's certificate.

NOTES

Sub-s (1) contains provisions formerly in the Representation of the People Act 1949, s 116(1), as affected by the Local Government Act 1972, s 251(1), Sch 29, Pt I, para 4(1). Sub-s (2) contains provisions formerly in s 116(2), (3) of the 1949 Act, as partly repealed, in the case of s 116(2), by the London Government Act 1963, s 93(1), Sch 18, Pt II, and the Representation of the People Act 1969, s 24(4), Sch 3, Pt I. Sub-s (3) contains provisions formerly in s 116(4) of the 1949 Act.

Officers and clerks as prescribed; prescribed scale. The relevant provisions are contained in the Election Petition Rules 1960, SI 1960/543, r 18.

Constables. See the note "Constable" to s 19 ante.

Certificate. Ie the certificate given under s 145(2) post.

Further provisions. See s 132 post (remuneration and allowances); s 133 post (repayments under this section and s 132); and s 143 post (witnesses' expenses).

Parish and community elections; municipal elections in City of London. See the notes to s 67 ante.

Definitions. For "prescribed", see s 185 post; for "proper officer", see s 202(1) post.

132 Remuneration and allowances

(1) The remuneration and allowances to be paid to the commissioner for his services in respect of that trial and to any officers, clerks or shorthand writers employed under section 131 above in relation to that trial shall be fixed by a scale made and varied   by the judges on the rota for the trial of parliamentary election petitions, with the Treasury's approval.

(2) The remuneration and allowances shall be paid in the first instance by the Treasury and shall be repaid to the Treasury on their certificate by the authority for which the election was held.

NOTES

This section contains provisions formerly in the Representation of the People Act 1949, s 116(5), as partly repealed by the Local Authorities etc (Miscellaneous Provisions) (No 2) Order 1974, SI 1974/595, art 3(22), Sch 1, Pt I.

Commissioner. Ie the commissioner appointed under s 130(3) ante.

Rota. See the note to s 123 ante.

Treasury. See the note to s 29 ante.

Further provisions. See s 131(1) ante (payment of expenses), and s 133 post (repayments under this section and s 131 ante).

Parish and community elections; municipal elections in City of London. See the notes to s 67 ante; and see, in particular, as to municipal elections in the City, s 196 post.

133 Repayments under ss 131 and 132

(1) The election court constituted under section 130 above may in its discretion order that—

(*a*) the expenses referred to in section 131 above, incurred by the proper officer of the authority for receiving the court, or

(*b*) the remuneration and allowances referred to in section 132 above,

shall be repaid, wholly or in part, to the proper officer of the authority or to the Treasury, as the case may be—

(i) when, in the opinion of the election court, the petition is frivolous and vexatious, by the petitioner;

(ii) when, in the opinion of the election court, the respondent has been personally guilty of corrupt practices at the election, by that respondent.

(2) The order so made for the repayment of any sum by a petitioner or respondent may be enforced as an order for payment of costs, but a deposit made or a security given under this Part of this Act shall not be applied for any such repayment until all costs and expenses payable by the petitioner or respondent to any party to the petition have been satisfied.

NOTES

This section contains provisions formerly in the Representation of the People Act 1949, s 116(6), (7), as affected in the case of s 116(6), by the Local Government Act 1972, s 251(1), Sch 29, Pt I, para 4(1).

Proper officer. For meaning, see s 202(1) post.

Treasury. See the note to s 29 ante.

Corrupt practices. See the note to s 122 ante.

Enforced as an order for . . . costs. Ie in accordance with s 183(2) post.

Security. This refers to security required under s 136 post.

This Part of this Act. Ie Pt III (ss 120–186).

Parish and community elections; municipal elections in City of London. See the notes to s 67 ante.

134 (*Applies to Scotland only.*)

135 Consequences of local election declared void

(1) Where on a petition questioning an election under the local government Act—

(*a*) the election of any person has been declared void, and

(*b*) no other person has been declared elected in his place,

a new election shall be held to fill the vacancy in the same manner as on a casual vacancy.

(2) For the purposes of that election any duties to be performed by any officer shall, if he has been declared not elected, be performed by a deputy or other person who might have acted for him if he had been incapacitated by illness.

(3) This section does not apply to Scotland.

NOTES

Sub-ss (1), (2) contain provisions formerly in the Representation of the People Act 1949, s 118(1). Sub-s (3) contains provisions formerly in s 118(3) of that Act.

Election under the local government Act. See the note to s 202 post; and for the meaning of "local government Act", see s 203(1) post.

Election . . . has been declared void. As to when the election of a candidate is void, see s 159(1) post.

Election . . . as on a casual vacancy. Ie in accordance with the Local Government Act 1972, s 89, Vol 25, title Local Government.

Parish and community elections; municipal elections in City of London. See the notes to s 67 ante; and see, also as to avoidance of election to a corporate office in the City, s 198 post.

Procedure on all election petitions

136 Security for costs

(1) At the time of presenting an election petition or within three days afterwards the petitioner shall give security for all costs which may become payable by him to any witness summoned on his behalf or to any respondent.

(2) The security shall be—

(*a*) in the case of a parliamentary election petition, [such amount not exceeding £5,000 as the High Court or a judge of the High Court, on summons, directs]; and

(b) in the case of a petition questioning an election under the local government Act, such amount not exceeding [£2,500] as the High Court, or a judge of the High Court, on summons, directs,

and shall be given in the prescribed manner by recognisance entered into by any number of sureties not exceeding four or by a deposit of money, or partly in one way and partly in the other; . . .

[(3) Within the prescribed time after giving the security the petitioner shall serve on the respondent in the prescribed manner—

(a) a notice of the presentation of the petition and of the amount and nature of the security, and

(b) a copy of the petition.]

(4) Within a further prescribed time, . . . , the respondent may object in writing to any recognisance on the ground that any surety is insufficient or is dead or cannot be found or ascertained for want of a sufficient description in the recognisance, or that a person named in the recognisance has not duly acknowledged the recognisance.

(5) . . .

(6) An objection to a recognisance shall be decided in the prescribed manner.

(7) If the objection is allowed, the petitioner may within a further prescribed time . . ., remove it by a deposit in the prescribed manner of such sum of money as will, in the opinion of the court or officer having cognisance of the matter, make the security sufficient.

(8) If no security is given as required by this section or any objection is allowed and not removed as mentioned above, no further proceedings shall be had on the petition.

NOTES

Sub-ss (1), (2), (4), (6)–(8) contain provisions formerly in the Representation of the People Act 1949, s 119(1), (2), (4), (6)–(8).

The words omitted from sub-s (2) where indicated by dots apply to Scotland only.

The words in square brackets in sub-s (2)(a), (b), and the whole of sub-s (3), were substituted, and the words omitted from sub-ss (4), (7), and the whole of sub-s (5), were repealed by the Representation of the People Act 1985, ss 24, 28(1), Sch 4, para 48, Sch 5, as from 1 October 1985.

Sub-s (1): Presenting an election petition. For the method of and time for, presentation, see ss 121, 122 ante (parliamentary election), and ss 128, 129 ante (local election).

Within three days. For the computation of time, see s 119 ante, as applied by s 186 post. See also the note "Within six months . . ." to s 5 ante.

Shall give security. It seems that there is no power to exempt a petitioner from liability to give security; see *Everett v Griffiths (No 2)* [1923] 1 KB 130, 92 LJKB 293.

Witness summoned. As to the summoning of witnesses, see s 140 post.

Sub-s (2): Election under the local government Act. See the note to s 202 post.

Such amount not exceeding £2,500, etc. Where, in the case of a local election petition, the petitioner proposes to give the maximum amount under sub-s (2)(b) above, an application to fix the security at the amount may be made ex parte by summons to a master (Election Petition Rules 1960, SI 1960/543, r 6(1), as substituted by SI 1985/1278). There do not appear to be any reported English judicial decisions on increasing of security but there are Irish cases; see *Bandon Case, Buckley v Walsh* (1899) 33 ILT 121 (petitioner's means alleged to be insufficient to meet costs; security increased from £50 to £100); *Daly v Monks, Re Arranquay Case* (1903) 37 ILT 96 (increase of security ordered where petitioners appeared to be of small means and litigation was likely to be protracted on account of the extent of the charges made); and *Redmond v Manly* (1908) 42 ILT 181 (increase of security ordered where petitioners had small means, and illegal practice was alleged against the candidates elected, and also irregularities were charged against the returning officer).

In its application to an election of the chairman and councillors of a parish or community council, and to the election of the chairman of a parish meeting or a poll consequent on a parish or community meeting, sub-s (2)(b) above is modified as noted to s 187 post.

High Court. See the notes to ss 39 and 120 ante.

Prescribed manner. For the procedure relating to the recognisance referred to in this section, see the Election Petition Rules 1960, SI 1960/543, r 6(2), (3), as substituted by SI 1985/1278.

Recognisance. As to the forfeiture of such recognisances, see s 155(2) post.

Sureties. One surety is sufficient (*Hereford City Election Petition, Preece v Pulley and Reid* (1880) 49 LJQB

686) petitioners should not be sureties; but a security given by them is not invalid in itself, though it is liable to rejection as insufficient (*Hull Case, Pease v Norwood* (1869) LR 4 CP 235, 38 LJCP 161).

Sub-s (3): Prescribed time. Ie in the case of a parliamentary election petition within fourteen days after its presentation; see the Election Petition Rules 1960, SI 1960/543, r 5(1), as substituted by SI 1985/1278.

Sub-s (4): Further prescribed time. Ie within fourteen days after service of notice of the parliamentary election petition; see the Election Petition Rules 1960, SI 1960/543, r 7(1), as amended by SI 1985/1278.

Writing. See the note "Written" to s 28 ante.

Sub-ss (6), (7): Prescribed manner; further prescribed time. The relevant provisions are contained in the Election Petition Rules 1960, SI 1960/543, rr 5–7, as amended by SI 1985/1278; see also r 19(1) (as so amended) of those rules as to the computation of periods of time prescribed by rr 5–7.

Parish and community elections; municipal elections in City of London. See the notes to s 67 ante, and the rules noted to s 187 post.

European Assembly elections. This section and ss 137 and 138 post, are applied to such elections by the European Assembly Elections Regulations 1984, SI 1984/137, reg 3(1), Sch 1. See further the Introductory Note to this Act.

As to provisions relating to such elections in Northern Ireland, see the Introductory Note to this Act.

Definitions. For "parliamentary election petition", see s 120 ante; for "respondent", see s 121(2) or 128(2) ante; for "prescribed", see s 185 post; for "election petition", see s 202(1) post; for "local government Act", see s 203(1) post.

137 Petition at issue

The petition shall be at issue—

> (*a*) on the expiry of the time limited for objections; or
> (*b*) if an objection is made, on that objection being disallowed or removed, whichever happens last.

NOTES

This section contains provisions formerly in the Representation of the People Act 1949, s 120.

Time limited for objections. See s 136(4) ante.

Objection . . . removed. As to the removal of objections, see s 136(7) ante.

Parish and community elections; municipal elections in City of London. See the notes to s 67 ante.

European Assembly elections. See the note to s 136 ante.

138 List of petitions

(1) The prescribed officer shall—

> (*a*) as soon as may be, make out a list of all election petitions at issue presented to the court of which he is officer, placing them in the order in which they were presented, and
> (*b*) keep at his office a copy of the list, open to inspection in the prescribed manner,

and the petitions questioning elections under the local government Act shall be in a separate list, a copy of which shall be sent to each of the judges for the time being on the rota for the trial of parliamentary election petitions.

(2) The petitions shall, so far as convenient, be tried in the order in which they stand in the list.

(3) In the case of a petition questioning an election under the local government Act, two or more candidates may be made respondents to the same petition, and their cases may be tried at the same time, but for the purposes of this Part of this Act the petition shall be deemed to be a separate petition against each respondent.

(4) Where more petitions than one are presented relating to the same election or to elections under the local government Act held at the same time for more than one electoral area in the same local government area, all those petitions shall be bracketed

together in the election list and shall be dealt with as one petition, standing, unless the High Court otherwise direct, in the election list in the place where the last of them would have stood if it had been the only petition presented.

(5) (*Applies to Scotland only.*)

NOTES

This section contains provisions formerly in the Representation of the People Act 1949, s 121.

Prescribed officer. In relation to parliamentary elections this is the officer specified in s 157(4) post, and in relation to local elections the same person is the prescribed officer; see the note to s 128 ante.

Election petitions at issue. See s 137 ante.

Prescribed manner. The list of petitions is to be open to inspection as provided by the Election Petition Rules 1960, SI 1960/543, r 8.

Elections under the local government Act. See the corresponding note to s 202 post.

Rota. See the note to s 123 ante.

Respondents. As to the respondents to a local election petition, see also s 128(2) ante.

This Part of this Act. Ie Pt III (ss 120–186).

High Court. See the notes to ss 39 and 120 ante.

Parish and community elections; municipal elections in City of London. See the notes to s 67 ante.

European Assembly elections. See the note to s 136 ante.

Definitions. For "parliamentary election petition", see s 120 ante; for "prescribed", see s 185 post; for "candidate", see, by virtue of s 185 post, s 118 ante; for "election petition", see s 202(1) post; for "electoral area", "local government Act" and "local government area", see s 203(1) post.

139 Trial of petition

(1) An election petition shall be tried in open court, without a jury, and notice of the time and place of trial shall be given in the prescribed manner, not less than, in the case of a parliamentary election petition, 14 days and in any other case, seven days, before the day of trial.

(2) The election court may in its discretion adjourn the trial from time to time, but the trial shall, so far as is practicable consistently with the interests of justice in respect of the trial, be continued from day to day on every lawful day until its conclusion.

(3) The trial of a parliamentary election petition shall be proceeded with notwithstanding the acceptance by the respondent of an office vacating his seat in Parliament and notwithstanding the prorogation of Parliament; and the trial of a petition questioning an election under the local government Act shall be proceeded with notwithstanding that the respondent has ceased to hold the office his election to which is questioned by the petition.

(4) On the trial of a petition, unless the court otherwise directs, any charge of a corrupt practice may be gone into, and evidence in relation to it received, before any proof has been given of agency on behalf of any candidate in respect of the corrupt practice.

In relation to an election in England and Wales under the local government Act, this subsection applies as if corrupt practices included illegal practices.

(5) On the trial of a petition complaining of an undue election and claiming the seat or office for some person, the respondent may give evidence to prove that that person was not duly elected, in the same manner as if he had presented a petition against the election of that person.

(6) If the petition relates to an election conducted under the parliamentary elections rules or the rules under section 36 or section 42 above and it appears that there is an equality of votes between any candidates at the election, and that the addition of a vote would entitle any of those candidates to be declared elected then—

(a) any decision under the provisions as to equality of votes in the parliamentary elections rules or the rules under section 36 or section 42, as the case may be, shall in so far as it determines the question between those candidates, be effective also for the purposes of the petition; and

(b) in so far as that question is not determined by such a decision, the court shall decide between them by lot and proceed as if the one on whom the lot then falls had received an additional vote.

NOTES

This section contains provisions formerly in the Representation of the People Act 1949, s 122, as amended, in the case of s 122(3), by the Representation of the People Act 1969, s 22(2).

Sub-s (1): Prescribed manner. Notice of the trial is to be given in accordance with the Election Petition Rules 1960, SI 1960/543, r 9(3), (4).

Not less than . . . 14 (seven) days. The words "not less than" indicate that 14 (or seven) clear days must intervene between the day on which notice is given and the day of trial; see *R v Turner* [1910] 1 KB 346; *Re Hector Whaling Ltd* [1936] Ch 208, [1935] All ER Rep 302. See also s 119 ante, as applied by s 186 post.

Sub-s (3): Prorogation. For the effect of a dissolution of Parliament, see *Exeter Case, Carter v Mills* (1874) LR 9 CP 117, 43 LJCP 111 (petition unheard; abated), and *Taunton Case, Marshall v James* (1874) LR 9 CP 702, 43 LJCP 281 (petition heard and judgment delivered; taxation of costs held permissible).

Election under the local government Act. See the note to s 202 post.

Sub-s (4): Corrupt practice; illegal practices. See the corresponding notes to s 122 ante.

England; Wales. See the note to s 4 ante.

Sub-s (6): Provisions as to equality of votes. For the provisions mentioned in sub-s (6)(a) above, see Sch 1, r 49 post, the Local Elections (Principal Areas) Rules 1973, SI 1973/79, Sch 2, r 45, and the Local Elections (Parishes and Communities) Rules 1973, SI 1973/1910, Sch 1, r 43.

Lot. For a decision by lot by the court, see *Lovers v Morris* [1972] 1 QB 221, [1971] 3 All ER 1300.

Attendance of Director of Public Prosecutions. See s 181(2) post.

Parish and community elections; municipal elections in City of London. See the notes to s 67 ante.

European Assembly elections. This section is applied to such elections by the European Assembly Elections Regulations 1984, SI 1984/137, reg 3(1), Sch 1, subject to the substitution, in sub-s (3) above, for the words from "the acceptance" to the end of the subsection, of the words "that the representative has resigned from the Assembly". See further the Introductory Note to this Act.

As to provisions relating to such elections in Northern Ireland, see the Introductory Note to this Act.

Definitions. For "parliamentary election petition", see s 120 ante; for "respondent"; see s 121(2) or 128(2) ante; for "candidate", see, by virtue of s 185 post, s 118 ante; for "election court", "election petition", "parliamentary elections rules" and "vote", see s 202(1) post; for "local government Act", see s 203(1) post.

140 Witnesses

(1) Witnesses shall be summoned and sworn in the same manner as nearly as circumstances admit as in an action tried in the High Court, but this subsection does not apply to Scotland in relation to an election of councillors.

(2) On the trial a member of the election court may, by order signed by him, require any person who appears to him to have been concerned in the election to attend as a witness, and any person refusing to obey the order shall be guilty of contempt of court.

(3) The election court may examine any person so required to attend or who is in court although he is not called and examined by any party to the petition.

(4) A witness may, after his examination by the court, be cross-examined by or on behalf of the petitioner and respondent, or either of them.

(5) . . .

(6) The Director of Public Prosecutions shall without any direction from the court cause any person appearing to him to be able to give material evidence as to the subject of the trial to attend the trial and shall, with the leave of the court, examine him as a witness.

(7) *(Applies to Scotland only.)*

NOTES

This section contains provisions formerly in the Representation of the People Act 1949, s 123(1)–(6), as amended, in the case of s 123(1), by the Courts Acts 1971, s 56(1), Sch 8, Pt II, para 30(2), and by the Judicature (Northern Ireland) Act 1978, s 122(1), Sch 5, Pt II.

Sub-s (5) was repealed by the Representation of the People Act 1985, ss 24, 28(1), Sch 4, para 49(*a*), Sch 5, as from 1 October 1985.

Sub-s (1): Same manner . . . as in an action, etc. As to enforcing the attendance and as to the swearing of witnesses, see 17 Halsbury's Laws (4th edn) paras 243 et seq.

High Court. See the notes to ss 39 and 120 ante.

Sub-s (2): Require any person . . . to attend as a witness. For instances of compelling attendance, see *Norwich Case, Tillett v Stracey* (1869) 19 LT 615; *Waterford Case* (1870) 2 O'M & H 3; and *Galway County Case* (1872) 2 O'M & H 48, 50, 51.

Contempt of court. As to the punishment of contempt of court consisting of disobedience to orders of the court (ie civil contempt), see 9 Halsbury's Laws (4th edn) paras 101 et seq.

Sub-s (6): Director of Public Prosecutions. See the note to s 148 post.

Able to give material evidence. It is not part of the Director's duty to call evidence with respect to matters at issue in the petition, but he should intervene if he thinks there has been a collusive withholding of evidence. For a discussion of the duties of the Director, see *Rochester Borough Case, Barry and Varrall v Davis* (1892) 4 O'M & H 156, and *Montgomery Boroughs Case, George v Pryce-Jones* (1892) 4 O'M & H 167.

Further provisions. For further provisions as to witnesses, see ss 141, 143 post.

Parish and community elections; municipal elections in City of London. See the notes to s 67 ante.

European Assembly elections. This section and ss 141, 143 post, are applied to such elections by the European Assembly Elections Regulations 1984, SI 1984/137, reg 3(1), Sch 1. See further the Introductory Note to this Act.

As to provisions relating to such elections in Northern Ireland, see the Introductory Note to this Act.

Definitions. For "respondent", see s 121(2) or 128(2) ante; for "election court", see s 202(1) post.

141 Duty to answer relevant questions

(1) A person called as a witness respecting an election before any election court shall not be excused from answering any question relating to any offence at or connected with the election—

    (*a*) on the ground that the answer to it may incriminate or tend to incriminate—

        (i) that person or that person's husband or wife, or
        (ii) *(applies to Scotland only)*;

    (*b*) on the ground of privilege.

(2) An answer by a person to a question put by or before any election court shall not, except in the case of any criminal proceeding for perjury in respect of the evidence, be in any proceeding, civil or criminal, admissible in evidence against—

    (*a*) that person or that person's husband or wife; or
    (*b*) *(applies to Scotland only)*.

(3), (4) . . .

NOTES

Sub-ss (1), (2) contain provisions formerly in the Representation of the People Act 1949, s 123(7), as amended by the Civil Evidence Act 1968, s 17(3), Schedule, and the Civil Evidence Act (Northern Ireland) 1971, s 13, Schedule.

Sub-ss (3), (4) were repealed by the Representation of the People Act 1985, ss 24, 28(1), Sch 4, para 50, Sch 5, as from 1 October 1985.

Shall not be excused from answering, etc. As to refusal to answer questions on the grounds mentioned in sub-s (1) above, see 11 Halsbury's Laws (4th edn) para 464 and 17 Halsbury's Laws (4th edn) paras 235 et seq.

Perjury. As to the punishment of perjury, see the Perjury Act 1911, s 1, Vol 12, title Criminal Law.

In respect of the evidence. These words qualify the preceding word "perjury". Answers to questions governed by sub-s (2) are not admissible in proceedings for perjury alleged to have been committed before another court; cf *R v Buttle* (1870) LR 1 CCR 248, 39 LJMC 115.

Parish and community elections; municipal elections in City of London. See the notes to s 67 ante.

European Assembly elections. See the note to s 140 ante.
Definitions. For "election" and "election court", see s 202(1) post.

---

142 *(Repealed by the Representation of the People Act 1985, ss 24, 28(1), Sch 4, para 50, Sch 5, as from 1 October 1985.)*

143 Expenses of witnesses

(1) The reasonable expenses incurred by any person in appearing to give evidence at the trial of an election petition, according to the scale allowed to witnesses on the trial of civil actions, may be allowed to him by a certificate of the election court or of the prescribed officer.

(2) If the witness was called and examined by virtue of section 140(2) above, the expenses referred to in subsection (1) above shall be deemed part of the expenses of providing a court, but otherwise they shall be deemed costs of the petition.

.   .   .   .   .

NOTES

This section contains provisions formerly in the Representation of the People Act 1949, s 123(11).
The words omitted from sub-s (2) where indicated by dots apply to Scotland only.
Reasonable expenses . . . according to the scale . . . on the trial of civil actions. As to witnesses' expenses in civil actions, see 17 Halsbury's Laws (4th edn) paras 254 et seq.
Prescribed officer. See the note to s 138 ante.
Expenses of providing a court. As to the defrayal of such expenses, see s 124(a) or 131(1) ante.
Costs of the petition. As to the defrayal of such costs, see ss 154–156 post.
Parish and community elections; municipal elections in City of London. See the notes to s 67 ante.
European Assembly elections. See the note to s 140 ante.
Definitions. For "costs", see s 185 post; for "election petition", see s 202(1) post.

---

144 Conclusion of trial of parliamentary election petition

(1) At the conclusion of the trial of a parliamentary election petition, the election court shall determine whether the member whose election or return is complained of, or any and what other person, was duly returned or elected or whether the election was void, and the determination so certified shall be final to all intents as to the matters at issue on the petition.

(2) The election court shall forthwith certify in writing the determination to the Speaker.

(3) If the judges constituting the election court—

(a) differ as to whether the member whose election or return is complained of was duly elected or returned, they shall certify that difference and the member shall be deemed to be duly elected or returned;

(b) determine that the member was not duly elected or returned but differ as to the rest of the determination, they shall certify that difference and the election shall be deemed to be void.

(4) Where any charge is made in the petition of any corrupt or illegal practice having been committed at the election the court shall, in addition to giving a certificate, and at the same time, make a report to the Speaker as required by sections 158 and 160 below and also stating whether corrupt or illegal practices have, or whether there is reason to believe that corrupt or illegal practices have, extensively prevailed at the election.

(5) The election court may at the same time make a special report to the Speaker as

to matters arising in the course of the trial an account of which in the judgment of the court ought to be submitted to the House of Commons.

(6) Every report sent to the Speaker under this section shall be signed by both judges of the election court and if the judges differ as to the subject of the report, they shall certify that difference and make no report on the subject on which they so differ.

(7) The House of Commons, on being informed by the Speaker of a certificate and any report of an election court, shall order the certificate and report (if any) to be entered in their Journals and shall give the necessary direction—

    (*a*) for confirming or altering the return, or
    (*b*) for issuing a writ for a new election, or
    (*c*) for carrying the determination into execution as the circumstances may require,

and where the court make a special report, the House of Commons may make such order in respect of that report as they think proper.

NOTES

Sub-ss (1)–(3) contain provisions formerly in the Representation of the People Act 1949, s 124(1). Sub-ss (4)–(7) contain provisions formerly in s 124(2)–(5) of that Act.

Sub-s (1): Shall be final. Subject to the general rule depriving of effect judgments obtained by fraud or collusion, a determination certified under this section is final and cannot be questioned by a subsequent petition (*Taunton Case, Waygood v James* (1869) LR 4 CP 361, 38 LJCP 195).

Sub-s (2): Forthwith. See the note to s 67 ante.

Certify. A copy of the evidence is to accompany the certificate; see s 126(2) ante. As to postponing the granting of a certificate until a question of law has been determined by the High Court, see s 146(4) post.

Writing. See the note "Written" to s 28 ante.

Sub-s (4): Corrupt or illegal practice. See the notes "Corrupt practices" and "Illegal practice" to s 122 ante.

Corrupt or illegal practices have ... extensively prevailed. As to the avoidance of an election for general corruption, see s 164 post.

Sub-s (6): Both judges. For the constitution of election courts for parliamentary election petitions, see s 123(1) ante.

Sub-s (7). This subsection is saved by the House of Commons Disqualification Act 1975, s 6(3), Vol 32, title Parliament.

European Assembly elections. This section is applied to such elections by the European Assembly Elections Regulations 1984, SI 1984/137, reg 3(1), Sch 1, subject to:

(1) the substitution in sub-ss (2), (4) and (6) above for any reference to "Speaker" of a reference to "Secretary of State"; and
(2) the omission of sub-ss (5) and (7) above.

See further the Introductory Note to this Act.

As to provisions relating to such elections in Northern Ireland, see the Introductory Note to this Act.

Definitions. For "parliamentary election petition", see s 120 ante; for "Speaker", see s 185 post; for "election court", see s 202(1) post.

---

145 Conclusion of trial of local election petition

(1) At the conclusion of the trial of a petition questioning an election under the local government Act, the election court shall determine whether the person whose election is complained of, or any and what other person, was duly elected, or whether the election was void, and the determination so certified shall be final to all intents as to the matters at issue on the petition.

(2) The election court shall forthwith certify in writing the determination to the High Court.

(3) Where a charge is made in the petition of any corrupt or illegal practice having been committed at the election the court shall, in addition to giving a certificate, and at the same time, make a report in writing to the High Court as required by sections 158 and 160 below and also stating whether any corrupt practices have, or whether there is reason to believe that any corrupt practices have, extensively prevailed at the election in

the area of the authority for which the election was held or in any electoral area of that authority's area.

(4) The election court may at the same time make a special report to the High Court as to matters arising in the course of the trial an account of which in the judgment of the court ought to be submitted to the High Court.

(5) A copy of any certificate or report made to the High Court shall be sent by the High Court to the Secretary of State.

(6) The High Court shall by the signatures of two or more of its judges certify a copy of the certificate mentioned in subsection (5) above to the proper officer of the authority for which the election was held.

(7) (*Applies to Scotland only.*)

NOTES

This section contains provisions formerly in the Representation of the People Act 1949, s 125, as affected, in the case of s 125(6), by the Local Government Act 1972, s 251(1), Sch 29, Pt I, para 4(1).

Sub-s (1): Election under the local government Act. See the note to s 202 post.

Shall be final. See the note to s 144 ante.

Sub-s (2): Forthwith. See the note to s 67 ante.

Certify. A transcript of the evidence is to accompany the certificate; see s 131(3) ante. As to postponing the grant of a certificate until a question of law has been determined by the High Court, see s 146(4) post.

Writing. See the note "Written" to s 28 ante.

High Court. See the notes to ss 39 and 120 ante.

Sub-s (3): Corrupt or illegal practice. See the notes "Corrupt practices" and "Illegal practice" to s 122 ante.

Corrupt practices have . . . extensively prevailed. As to the avoidance of an election for general corruption, see s 164 post.

Sub-s (5): Secretary of State. Cf the note to s 4 ante. The Secretary of State here concerned is the Secretary of State for the Home Department.

Parish and community elections; municipal elections in City of London. See the notes to s 67 ante; and see also, in relation to the City, s 198 post.

Definitions. For "election court" and "proper officer", see s 202(1) post; for "electoral area" and "local government Act", see s 203(1) post.

146 Special case for determination of High Court

(1) If, on the application of any party to a petition made in the prescribed manner to the High Court, it appears to the High Court that the case raised by the petition can be conveniently stated as a special case, the High Court may direct it to be stated accordingly and the special case shall be heard before the High Court.

(2) In the case of a parliamentary election petition, the High Court shall certify to the Speaker its decision on the special case.

(3) In the case of a petition questioning an election in England and Wales under the local government Act, a statement of the decision on the special case shall be sent by the High Court to the Secretary of State and the High Court shall by the signatures of two or more of its judges also certify that statement to the proper officer of the authority for which the election was held.

(4) If it appears to the election court on the trial of an election petition that any question of law as to the admissibility of evidence or otherwise requires further consideration by the High Court, the election court may postpone the granting of a certificate until the question has been determined by the High Court, and for this purpose may reserve the question by stating a case for the decision of the High Court.

In the application of this subsection to Northern Ireland the references to the High Court are to the Court of Appeal.

(5) (*Applies to Scotland only.*)

NOTES

Sub-ss (1)–(3) contain provisions formerly in the Representation of the People Act 1949, s 126(1), as affected by the Local Government Act 1972, s 251(1), Sch 29, Pt I, para 4(1). Sub-s (4) contains provisions formerly in s 126(2) of the 1949 Act, as amended by the Judicature (Northern Ireland) Act 1978, s 122(1), Sch 5, Pt II.

Sub-s (1): Application . . . in the prescribed manner. Application is made by motion to a Divisional Court; see the Election Petition Rules 1960, SI 1960/543, r 11.

High Court. See the notes to ss 39 and 120 ante.

Special case. Usually only one counsel on either side is allowed (*Re Gloucestershire, Thornbury Division, Case, Ackers v Howard* (1886) 16 QBD 739, 55 LJQB 273).

In proceedings by way of special case stated before the election court, it is not open to respondents, as it is open to them in appeals by way of case stated by justices, to seek to uphold the decision given in their favour on grounds not relied on when it was made; see *Evans v Thomas* [1962] 2 QB 350 at 370, [1962] 3 All ER 108 at 118 per Winn J.

Sub-s (3): Election . . . under the local government Act. See the note to s 202 post.

England; Wales. See the note to s 4 ante.

Secretary of State. See the note to s 145 ante.

Sub-s (4): Granting of a certificate. This refers to the certificate granted under s 144(1), (2) or 145(1), (2) ante

Reserve the question by stating a case. For the general principles followed, see *Britt v Robinson* (1870) LR 5 CP 503, 39 LJCP 265 (treating at a test ballot); *Taunton Borough Case, Marshall and Brannan v James* (1874) 30 LT 125 (a reserved point should be one the decision on which affects the whole case); *Tipperary Case* (1875) 3 O'M & H 19, 41 (votes cast away); *Horsham Case, Aldridge v Hurst* (1876) 3 O'M & H 52 (reference refused; court entertained no doubt about its own decision); *Tower Hamlets, Stepney Division, Case, Isaacson v Durant* (1886) 54 LT 684, 2 TLR 559 (validity of votes cast by voters born in Hanover); *Re Gloucestershire, Thornbury Division, Election Petition, Ackers v Howard* (1886) 16 QBD 739, 55 LJQB 273 (question should not be reserved merely because it is difficult to decide); *Sheffield, Attercliffe Division, Case* (1906) 5 O'M & H 218 (no reservation where no question of law involved).

Parish and community elections; municipal elections in City of London. See the notes to s 67 ante; and see also, in relation to the City, s 198 post.

European Assembly elections. This section is applied to such elections by the European Assembly Elections Regulations 1984, SI 1984/137, reg 3(1), Sch 1, subject to the substitution, in sub-s (2) above, for the word "Speaker" of the words "Secretary of State". See further the Introductory Note to this Act.

As to provisions relating to such elections in Northern Ireland, see the Introductory Note to this Act.

Appeals and jurisdiction. See s 157 post.

Definitions. For "parliamentary election petition", see s 120 ante; for "prescribed" and "Speaker", see s 185 post; for "election court" and "proper officer", see s 202(1) post; for "local government Act", see s 203(1) post.

147 Withdrawal of petition

(1) A petitioner shall not withdraw an election petition without the leave of the election court or High Court on special application, made in the prescribed manner and at the prescribed time and place.

. . . . . .

(2) The application shall not be made until the prescribed notice of the intention to make it has been given in the constituency or local government area to which the petition relates.

(3) Where there are more petitioners than one, the application shall not be made except with the consent of all the petitioners.

(4) If a petition is withdrawn the petitioner shall be liable to pay the costs of the respondent.

NOTES

This section contains provisions formerly in the Representation of the People Act 1949, s 127.

The words omitted from sub-s (1) where indicated by dots apply to Scotland only.

Shall not withdraw. In *Hartlepool Election Petition* (1869) 19 LT 821, the election court declined to allow withdrawal of a petition without public notice first being given as required by what is now this section, but in at least ten reported cases the election courts appear to have sanctioned a withdrawal of a petition without such notice; see *Tower Hamlets, St George's Division, Case, Benn v Marks* (1896) 5 O'M & H 89; *York City Case, Furness v Beresford* (1898) 5 O'M & H 118; *Pembroke Boroughs Case* (1901) 5 O'M & H 135; *Christchurch Case, Brassey v Balfour* (1901) 5 O'M & H 147; *Westmorland, Appleby Division, Case, Kerry (Earl) v Jones*

(1906) 5 O'M & H 237; *Denbighshire Boroughs Case, Edwards v Ormsby-Gore* (1910) 6 O'M & H 57; *Wiltshire, North Western (Chippenham) Division, Case, Freeman v Terrell* (1911) 6 O'M & H 99; and *Tower Hamlets, Mile End Division, Case, Straus v Lawson* (1911) 6 O'M & H 100, 102. "Withdrawal" presumably refers only to a withdrawal which does not amount to an adjudication upon charges put forward, and excludes a withdrawal by leave of the court which in effect amounts to an adjudication and dismissal of the petition for want of proof, and which would be pleadable in bar of a subsequent petition if one were presented.

High Court. See the notes to ss 39 and 120 ante.

Prescribed manner; prescribed time and place; prescribed notice. For the procedure on an application to withdraw a petition, see the Election Petition Rules 1960, SI 1960/543, r 12.

Constituency. See the note to s 1 ante.

Costs. For further provisions as to costs, see ss 154–156, 183 post.

Further provisions. For further provisions relating to the withdrawal of a petition, see s 148 post (evidence required for withdrawal); s 149 post (penalty for corrupt withdrawal and breach of s 148); s 150 post (substitution of new petitioner on application for leave to withdraw), and s 151 post (report by court on withdrawal); and cf also s 152 post (abatement of petition on death of petitioner), and s 153 post (withdrawal and substitution of respondents before trial).

Parish and community elections; municipal elections in City of London. See the notes to s 67 ante.

European Assembly elections. This section and ss 148–150 post, are applied to such elections by the European Assembly Elections Regulations 1984, SI 1984/137, reg 3(1), Sch 1. See further the Introductory Note to this Act.

Definitions. For "respondent", see s 121(2) or 128(2) ante; for "costs" and "prescribed", see s 185 post; for "election court" and "election petition", see s 202(1) post; for "local government area", see s 203(1) post.

148 Evidence required for withdrawal of petition

(1) Before leave for the withdrawal of an election petition is granted, there shall be produced affidavits—

    (*a*) by all the parties to the petition and their solicitors, and

    (*b*) if the election was an election at which candidates are required to have election agents, by the election agents of all of those parties who were candidates at the election,

but the High Court may on cause shown dispense with the affidavit of any particular person if it seems to the court on special grounds just so to do.

(2) Each affidavit shall state that, to the best of the deponent's knowledge and belief—

    (*a*) no agreement or terms of any kind whatsoever has or have been made, and

    (*b*) no undertaking has been entered into, in relation to the withdrawal of the petition,

but if any lawful agreement has been made with respect to the withdrawal of the petition, the affidavit shall set forth that agreement and shall make the foregoing statement subject to what appears from the affidavit.

(3) The affidavits of the applicant and his solicitor shall further state the ground on which the petition is sought to be withdrawn.

(4) Copies of those affidavits shall be delivered to the Director of Public Prosecutions a reasonable time before the application for the withdrawal is heard, and the court—

    (*a*) may hear the Director of Public Prosecutions or his assistant or other representative . . . in opposition to the allowance of the withdrawal of the petition; and

    (*b*) shall have power to receive the evidence on oath of any person or persons whose evidence the Director of Public Prosecutions or his assistant, or other representative, may consider material.

(5) Where more than one solicitor is concerned for the petitioner or respondent, whether as agent for another solicitor or otherwise, the affidavit shall be made by all such solicitors.

(6) Except in Scotland, the jurisdiction vested by subsection (1) above in the High Court in matters relating to parliamentary elections shall, subject to rules of court, be exercised—

    (*a*) by one of the judges for the time being on the rota for the trial of parliamentary election petitions,

    (*b*) in Northern Ireland, by one of the judges of the High Court or the Court of Appeal for the time being selected under section 108 of the Judicature (Northern Ireland) Act 1978,

sitting either in court or at chambers, or may be exercised by a master of the Supreme Court in manner directed by and subject to appeal to those judges.

NOTES

This section contains provisions formerly in the Representation of the People Act 1949, s 128, as partly repealed, in the case of s 128(6), by the Representation of the People Act 1969, s 24(4), Sch 3, Pt I, and as amended, in the case of that subsection, by the Judicature (Northern Ireland) Act 1978, s 122(1), Sch 5, Pt II.

The words omitted from sub-s (1), and those omitted in the second place from sub-s (4), apply to Scotland only, and those omitted in the first place from sub-s (4) were repealed by the Representation of the People Act 1985, s 28(1), Sch 5, as from 1 October 1985.

Sub-s (1): Leave for the withdrawal of an election petition. This is required by s 147 ante.

Candidates are required to have election agents. Candidates are required to have election agents at all elections except those mentioned in s 71 ante.

Election agents. As to the appointment of election agents, see s 67 ante and the notes thereto.

High Court. See the notes to ss 39 and 120 ante; and note sub-s (6) above.

Sub-s (4): Director of Public Prosecutions. Provision for the appointment of the Director of Public Prosecutions and Assistant Director is currently made by the Prosecution of Offences Act 1979, s 1, Vol 12, title Criminal Law; by sub-s (4) of that section an Assistant Director may do any act or thing which the Director is required or authorised to do.

The 1979 Act is repealed by the Prosecution of Offences Act 1985, Vol 12, title Criminal Law, as from a day to be appointed under s 31(2) thereof. New provision is made as to the appointment of the Director by s 2 of that Act, and as to the establishment of a Crown Prosecution Service for England and Wales by ss 1–10. In particular, by s 1(6), every Crown Prosecutor has all the powers of the Director as to the institution and conduct of proceedings but exercises those powers under his direction.

The courts have held that costs cannot be granted to the Director if a petition is withdrawn; see the note to s 181(6) post.

In relation to Northern Ireland references in this Act to the Director of Public Prosecutions are references to the Director of Public Prosecutions for Northern Ireland; see s 205(1)(*aa*) post.

Sub-s (6): Parliamentary elections. See the note "Parliamentary election" to s 1 ante.

Rules of court. As to such rules, see s 182 post and the notes thereto.

Rota. See the note to s 123 ante.

Penalties. See s 149 post.

Parish and community elections; municipal elections in City of London. See the notes to s 67 ante.

European Assembly elections. See the note to s 147 ante.

Definitions. For "parliamentary election petition", see s 120 ante; for "respondent", see s 121(2) or s 128(2) ante; for "candidate", see, by virtue of s 185 post, s 118 ante; for "Attorney General", "election" and "election petition", see s 202(1) post (and see also, as to "Attorney General", s 205(1)(*a*) post).

Judicature (Northern Ireland) Act 1978, s 108. See Vol 31, title Northern Ireland (Pt 2).

149 Penalty for corrupt withdrawal and breach of s 148

If a person makes any agreement or terms, or enters into any undertaking, in relation to the withdrawal of an election petition, and such agreement, terms or undertaking—

    (*a*) is or are for the withdrawal of the election petition in consideration of any payment, or in consideration that the seat or office should at any time be vacated, or in consideration of the withdrawal of any other election petition, or

    (*b*) is or are (whether lawful or unlawful) not mentioned in the affidavits referred to in section 148 above,

he shall be [liable—

(i) on conviction on indictment, to imprisonment for a term not exceeding one year, or to a fine, or to both;

(ii) on summary conviction, to imprisonment for a term not exceeding 6 months, or to a fine not exceeding the statutory maximum, or to both].

NOTES

This section, as originally enacted, contained provisions formerly in the Representation of the People Act 1949, s 129, as partly repealed by the Criminal Law Act 1967, s 10(2), Sch 3, Pt III, and as affected by the Criminal Law Act 1977, s 32(1).

The words in square brackets were substituted by the Representation of the People Act 1985, s 23, Sch 3, para 7, as from 1 October 1985.

Withdrawal of an election petition. As to such withdrawal, see s 147 ante and the enactments mentioned in the note "Further provisions" thereto.

Conviction on indictment. See the note to s 65 ante. As to the time limit for prosecutions, see s 176 post.

Fine. See the note to s 65 ante.

Summary conviction. See the note to s 62 ante.

Parish and community elections; municipal elections in City of London. See the notes to s 67 ante.

European Assembly elections. See the note to s 147 ante.

Definitions. For "payment", see s 185 post; for "election petition", "person" and "statutory maximum", see s 202(1) post.

150 Substitution of new petitioner

(1) On the hearing of the application for leave to withdraw, any person who might have been a petitioner in respect of the election may apply to the court to be substituted as a petitioner, and the court may, if they think fit, substitute him accordingly.

(2) If the proposed withdrawal is in the opinion of the court the result of any agreement, terms or undertaking prohibited by section 149 above or induced by any corrupt bargain or consideration, the court may by order direct—

(a) that the security given on behalf of the original petitioner shall remain as security for any costs that may be incurred by the substituted petitioner, and

(b) that, to the extent of the sum named in the security, the original petitioner and his sureties shall be liable to pay the costs of the substituted petitioner.

(3) If the court does not so direct, then security to the same amount as would be required in the case of a new petition, and subject to the like conditions, shall be given on behalf of the substituted petitioner before he proceeds with his petition and within the prescribed time after the order of substitution.

(4) Subject to the above provisions, a substituted petitioner shall, as nearly as may be, stand in the same position and be subject to the same liabilities as the original petitioner.

NOTES

This section contains provisions formerly in the Representation of the People Act 1949, s 130.

Application for leave to withdraw. Ie an application made under s 147 ante.

Person who might have been a petitioner. See s 121(1) or 128(1) ante.

Security. Ie security given under s 136 ante.

Costs. For further provisions as to costs, see ss 154–156, 183 post.

Prescribed time. Ie three days after the order of substitution; see the Election Petition Rules 1960, SI 1960/543, r 12(5).

Parish and community elections; municipal elections in City of London. See the notes to s 67 ante.

European Assembly elections. See the note to s 147 ante.

Definitions. For "costs" and "prescribed", see s 185 post; for "election", see s 202(1) post.

151 Report on withdrawal

(1) In every case of the withdrawal—

    (a) of a parliamentary election petition, the court giving leave for the withdrawal shall make a report to the Speaker as required by subsection (2) below; and

    (b) by leave of the election court, of a petition questioning an election in England and Wales under the local government Act, that court shall make a report in writing to the High Court as so required.

(2) The report shall state whether in the court's opinion the withdrawal of the petition was—

    (a) the result of any agreement, terms or undertaking, or

    (b) in consideration of any payment, or in consideration that the seat or office should at any time be vacated or in consideration of the withdrawal of any other election petition or for any other consideration,

and, if so, shall state the circumstances attending the withdrawal.

NOTES

This section contains provisions formerly in the Representation of the People Act 1949, s 131.

Withdrawal . . . of a . . . petition. As to such withdrawal, see s 147 ante, and the enactments mentioned in the note "Further provisions" thereto.

Election . . . under the local government Act. See the note to s 202 post.

England; Wales. See the note to s 4 ante.

Writing. See the note "Written" to s 28 ante.

High Court. See the notes to ss 39 and 120 ante.

Parish and community elections; municipal elections in City of London. See the notes to s 67 ante.

European Assembly elections. This section is applied to such elections by the European Assembly Elections Regulations 1984, SI 1984/137, reg 3(1), Sch 1, subject to the substitution, in sub-s (1)(a) above, for the word "Speaker" of the words "Secretary of State". See further the Introductory Note to this Act.

As to provisions relating to such elections in Northern Ireland, see the Introductory Note to this Act.

Definitions. For "parliamentary election petition", see s 120 ante, for "payment" and "Speaker", see s 185 post; for "election court" and "election petition", see s 202(1) post; for "local government Act", see s 203(1) post.

152 Abatement of petition

(1) An election petition shall be abated by the death of a sole petitioner or of the survivor of several petitioners.

(2) The abatement shall not affect the liability of the petitioner or any other person to the payment of costs previously incurred.

(3) On the abatement the prescribed notice of it shall be given in the constituency or local government area to which the petition relates; and within the prescribed time after the notice is given, any person who might have been a petitioner in respect of the election may apply to the election court or High Court in the prescribed manner and in the prescribed time and place to be substituted as a petitioner; and the court may, if it thinks fit, substitute him accordingly.

(4) Security shall be given on behalf of a petitioner so substituted, as in the case of a new petition.

(5) (*Applies to Scotland only.*)

NOTES

This section contains provisions formerly in the Representation of the People Act 1949, s 133.

Costs. For provisions as to costs, see ss 154–156, 183 post.

Prescribed notice; prescribed time (and place); prescribed manner. The matters to be prescribed mentioned in sub-s (3) are all prescribed by the Election Petition Rules 1960, SI 1960/543, r 14.

Constituency. See the note to s 1 ante.

Person who might have been a petitioner. See s 121(1) or 128(1) ante.

High Court. See the notes to ss 39 and 120 ante.

Security. As to the giving of security for costs, see s 136 ante.

Parish and community elections; municipal elections in City of London. See the notes to s 67 ante.

European Assembly elections. This section is applied to such elections by the European Assembly Elections Regulations 1984, SI 1984/137, reg 3(1), Sch 1. See further the Introductory Note to this Act.

As to provisions relating to such elections in Northern Ireland, see the Introductory Note to this Act.

Definitions. For "costs" and "prescribed", see s 185 post; for "election", "election court" and "election petition", see s 202(1) post; for "local government area", see s 203(1) post.

---

153 Withdrawal and substitution of respondents before trial

(1) If before the trial of an election petition a respondent other than a returning officer—

    (a) gives the prescribed notice that he does not intend to oppose the petition or dies, or

    (b) where the petition questions a parliamentary election or return, is summoned to Parliament as a peer by a writ issued under the Great Seal of the United Kingdom or the House of Commons have resolved that his seat is vacant, or

    (c) where the petition questions an election under the local government Act, resigns or otherwise ceases to hold the office to which the petition relates,

notice of any of those matters shall be given in the constituency or local government area to which the petition relates, and, within the prescribed time after the notice is given, any person who might have been a petitioner in respect of the election may apply to a member of the election court or to the High Court to be admitted as a respondent to oppose the petition, and shall be admitted accordingly, except that the number of persons so admitted shall not exceed three.

(2) The notice to be given under subsection (1) above in any local government area shall be such as may be prescribed.

(3) A respondent who has given the prescribed notice that he does not intend to oppose the petition shall not be allowed to appear or act as a party against the petition in any proceedings on the petition, and if the petition relates to a parliamentary election he shall not sit or vote in the House of Commons until the House of Commons has been informed of the report on the petition.

(4) Where a respondent to a parliamentary election petition has given that notice in the prescribed time and manner, the High Court or either of the judges constituting the election court shall report that fact to the Speaker.

(5) (*Applies to Scotland only.*)

NOTES

Sub-ss (1), (2) contain provisions formerly in the Representation of the People Act 1949, s 134(1). Sub-ss (3), (4) contain provisions formerly in s 134(2) of that Act.

Returning officer. As to returning officers, see ss 24, 26–28, 35 ante.

Prescribed notice; prescribed time; such as may be prescribed. The matters to be prescribed mentioned in sub-ss (1), (2) above are prescribed by the Election Petitions Rules 1960, SI 1960/543, rr 15, 16.

Parliamentary election; constituency. See the notes to s 1 ante.

Election under the local government Act. See the note to s 202 post.

Person who might have been a petitioner. See s 121(1) or 128(1) ante.

High Court. See the notes to ss 39 and 120 ante.

Parish and community elections; municipal elections in City of London. See the notes to s 67 ante.

European Assembly elections. This section is applied to such elections by the European Assembly Elections Regulations 1984, SI 1984/137, reg 3(1), Sch 1, subject to:

(1) the substitution for sub-s (1)(*b*) and (*c*) above of the following paragraph:

"(*b*) resigns or otherwise ceases to hold the office of representative";

(2) the omission from sub-s (3) above of the words from "and if the petition" to the end of the subsection; and

(3) the substitution in sub-s (4) above for the word "Speaker" of the words "Secretary of State".

See further the Introductory Note to this Act.

As to provisions relating to such elections in Northern Ireland, see the Introductory Note to this Act.

Definitions. For "parliamentary election petition", see s 120 ante; for "respondent", see s 121(2) or 128(2) ante; for "prescribed" and "Speaker", see s 185 post; for "election", "election court" and "election petition", see s 202(1) post; for "local government Act" and "local government area", see s 203(1) post.

154 Costs of petition

(1) All costs of and incidental to the presentation of an election petition and the proceedings consequent on it, except such as are by this Act otherwise provided for, shall be defrayed by the parties to the petition in such manner and in such proportions as the election court or High Court may determine.

(2) In particular—

(*a*) any costs which in the opinion of the election court or High Court have been caused by vexatious conduct, unfounded allegations or unfounded objections on the part either of the petitioner or of the respondent, and

(*b*) any needless expense incurred or caused on the part of the petitioner or respondent,

may be ordered to be defrayed by the parties by whom it has been incurred or caused whether or not they are on the whole successful.

(3) (*Applies to Scotland only.*)

NOTES

Sub-ss (1), (2) contain provisions formerly in the Representation of the People Act 1949, s 135(1).

Except such as are . . . otherwise provided for. See, in particular, s 124 ante (judges' expenses on parliamentary election petition); s 126(3) ante (shorthand writers' expenses on parliamentary election petition in Northern Ireland); ss 131–133 ante (expenses incurred on local election petition); s 143 ante (expenses of witnesses); and s 156 post (costs to be paid by person engaged in corrupt practices).

In such proportions as the election court . . . may determine. The general rule is that costs follow the event, but there is a large body of case law governing the circumstances in which this rule may or should not be observed; see 15 Halsbury's Laws (4th edn) paras 961, 962.

The discretion of the election court in dealing with costs is absolute and cannot be reviewed by the High Court; see *Maidenhead Case, Lovering v Dawson (No 2)* (1875) LR 10 CP 726, 44 LJCP 321. There is no provision in this Act for an appeal from the election court to the High Court except by way of case stated under s 146 ante. There is provision, however, for an appeal from the High Court; see s 157(1) post. It does not follow, therefore, that the above-mentioned cases would apply to a decision of the High Court as to costs.

High Court. See the notes to ss 39 and 120 ante.

Further provisions. As to costs, see also the provisions mentioned in the note, "Except such as are . . . otherwise provided for" above and s 155 post (neglect or refusal to pay costs) and s 183 post (supplemental provisions as to costs).

Parish and community elections; municipal elections in City of London. See the notes to s 67 ante.

European Assembly elections. This section and ss 155, 156 post, are applied to such elections by the European Assembly Elections Regulations 1984, SI 1984/137, reg 3(1), Sch 1. See further the Introductory Note to this Act.

As to provisions relating to such elections in Northern Ireland, see the Introductory Note to this Act.

Legal aid. Legal aid is not available in connection with election petitions under this Act; see the Legal Aid Act 1974, s 7(1), Sch 1, Pt II, para 5, Vol 24, title Legal Aid, as construed in accordance with the Interpretation Act 1978, s 17(2)(*a*), Vol 41, title Statutes.

Definitions. For "respondent", see s 121(2) or 128(2) ante; for "costs", see s 185 post; for "election court" and "election petition", see s 202(1) post.

155 Neglect or refusal to pay costs

(1) Subsection (2) below applies if a petitioner neglects or refuses—

  (a) in the case of a parliamentary election petition, for six months after demand, and

  (b) in the case of a petition questioning an election under the local government Act, for three months after demand,

to pay to any person summoned as a witness on his behalf or to the respondent any sum certified to be due to that person or the respondent for his costs, and the neglect or refusal is, within one year after the demand, proved to the satisfaction of the High Court, or, in Scotland, the election court.

(2) Where subsection (1) above applies, every person who under this Act entered into a recognisance relating to that petition shall be held to be in default of the recognisance, and—

  (a) the prescribed officer shall thereupon certify the recognisance to be forfeited, and

  (b) it shall be dealt with as if forfeited by the Crown Court, or, in Northern Ireland, under the Fines Act (Ireland) 1851, as the case may be,

· · · · · ·

NOTES

This section contains provisions formerly in the Representation of the People Act 1949, s 135(2), as amended by the Courts Act 1971, s 56(1), Sch 8, Pt II, para 30(3).

The words omitted from sub-s (2) where indicated by dots apply to Scotland only.

Six months (three months) (one year) after etc. As to the computation of time, see s 119 ante, as applied by s 186 post. See also the note "Within six months . . ." to s 5 ante.

Election under the local government Act. See the note to s 202 post.

Witness. As to witnesses' expenses, see s 143 ante.

High Court. See the notes to ss 39 and 120 ante.

Person who . . . entered into a recognisance. Ie under s 136 ante.

Prescribed officer. See the note to s 138 ante.

Dealt with as if forfeited by the Crown Court. The provisions of the Powers of Criminal Courts Act 1973, ss 31, 32, Vol 12, title Criminal Law, accordingly apply.

Parish and community elections; municipal elections in City of London. See the notes to s 67 ante.

European Assembly elections. See the note to s 154 ante.

Definitions. For "parliamentary election petition", see s 120 ante; for "respondent", see s 121(2) or 128(2) ante; for "local government Act", see s 203(1) post.

Fines Act (Ireland) 1851. 14 & 15 Vict c 90; not printed in this work.

---

156 Further provisions as to costs

(1) Where upon the trial of an election petition it appears to the election court—

  (a) that a corrupt practice has not been proved to have been committed in reference to the election by or with the knowledge and consent of the respondent to the petition, and

  (b) that the respondent took all reasonable means to prevent corrupt practices being committed on his behalf,

[the court may, subject to the provisions of subsection (5) below, make such order with respect to the whole or part of the costs of the petition as is mentioned in that subsection].

(2)–(4) . . .

(5) If it appears to the court that any person or persons is or are proved, whether by providing money or otherwise, to have been extensively engaged in corrupt practices, or to have encouraged or promoted extensive corrupt practices in reference to the

election, the court may, after giving that person or those persons an opportunity of being heard by counsel or solicitor and examining and cross-examining witnesses to show cause why the order should not be made—

(a) order the whole or part of the costs to be paid by that person, or those persons or any of them, and

(b) order that if the costs cannot be recovered from one or more of those persons they shall be paid by some other of those persons or by either of the parties to the petition.

(6) Where any person appears to the court to have been guilty of a corrupt or illegal practice, the court may, after giving that person an opportunity of making a statement to show why the order should not be made, order the whole or any part of the costs of or incidental to any proceeding before the court in relation to that offence or to that person to be paid by that person to such person or persons as the court may direct.

NOTES

Sub-ss (1), (5), (6) contain provisions formerly in the Representation of the People Act 1949, s 136, as amended, in the case of s 136(3), by the Local Government Reorganisation (Consequential Provisions) (Northern Ireland) Order 1973, SI 1973/2095, arts 2(5), 5(2), Sch 2.

The words in square brackets in sub-s (1) were substituted by the Representation of the People Act 1985, s 24, Sch 4, para 51(a), as from 1 October 1985, and sub-ss (2)–(4) were repealed by ss 24, 28(1) of, and Sch 4, para 51(b), Sch 5 to, that Act, as from that date.

Sub-s (1): Corrupt practice. See the note "Corrupt practices" to s 122 ante.

Knowledge. See the note "Knows" to s 60 ante.

Consent. See the note to s 75 ante.

Costs. For other provisions as to costs, see s 154 ante and the notes thereto.

Sub-s (6): Corrupt or illegal practice. See the notes "Corrupt practices" and "Illegal practice" to s 122 ante.

Parish and community elections; municipal elections in City of London. See the notes to s 67 ante; and see, in particular, as to municipal elections in the City, s 196 post.

European Assembly elections. See the note to s 154 ante.

Definitions. For "respondent", see s 121(2) or 128(2) ante; for "costs" and "money", see s 185 post; for "election", "election court", "election petition" and "person", see s 202(1) post.

157 Appeals and jurisdiction

(1) No appeal lies without the special leave of the High Court from the decision of the High Court on any question of law, whether on appeal or otherwise, under the foregoing provisions of this Part of this Act, and if leave to appeal is granted the decision of the Court of Appeal in the case shall be final and conclusive.

(2) Subject to the provisions of this Act and of the rules made under it, the principles, practice and rules on which committees of the House of Commons used to act in dealing with election petitions shall be observed, so far as may be, by the High Court and election court in the case of election petitions, and in particular the principles and rules with regard to—

(a) agency,

(b) evidence,

(c) a scrutiny, and

(d) declaring any person elected in place of any other person declared not to have been duly elected,

shall be observed, as far as may be, in the case of a petition questioning an election under the local government Act as in the case of a parliamentary election petition.

(3) The High Court has, subject to the provisions of this Act, the same powers, jurisdiction and authority with respect to an election petition and the proceedings on it as if the petition were an ordinary action within its jurisdiction.

(4) The duties to be performed in relation to parliamentary elections by the prescribed

officer under this Part shall be performed by such one or more of the masters of the Supreme Court (Queen's Bench Division) as the Lord Chief Justice may determine.

(5) There shall be awarded to those masters respectively, in addition to their salaries payable apart from this subsection, such remuneration for the performance of their duties in relation to parliamentary elections under this Part as the Lord Chief Justice with the Treasury's consent may determine.

(6) The duties to be performed in relation to elections under the local government Act by the prescribed officer under this Part shall be performed by the prescribed officer of the High Court.

(7) (*Applies to Scotland only.*)

(8) Subsection (1) above does not apply in Northern Ireland and, in the application of subsections (4) and (5) to Northern Ireland, the references to the Lord Chief Justice are references to the Lord Chief Justice of Northern Ireland and the reference to any master of the Supreme Court (Queen's Bench Division) is a reference to an officer of the Supreme Court of Judicature of Northern Ireland.

NOTES

Sub-s (1)–(3), (6), (8) contain provisions formerly in the Representation of the People Act 1949, s 137(1)–(3), (5), (7), respectively. Sub-ss (4), (5) contain provisions formerly in s 137(4) of that Act.

Sub-s (1): No appeal lies, etc. Sub-s (1) applies whether the decision sought to be challenged is of a final or of an interlocutory nature (*Everett v Griffiths (No 3)* [1923] 1 KB 138, 92 LJKB 290). See also *Pontefract Case, Shaw v Reckitt* [1893] 2 QB 59, 62 LJQB 375 (the divisional court rescinded an order made by a judge not on the rota and so not authorised to make it; an appeal from this rescission was dismissed by the Court of Appeal on the ground that, as leave to appeal had not been granted, no appeal lay).

High Court. See the note to s 39 ante.

Or otherwise. Ie under s 146 ante.

Foregoing provisions of this Part. Ie ss 120–156 ante.

Court of Appeal. Ie Her Majesty's Court of Appeal in England; see the Interpretation Act 1978, s 5, Sch 1, Vol 41, title Statutes. For the constitution of the court, see the Supreme Court Act 1981, s 2, and for its two divisions, see s 3 of that Act, Vol 11, title Courts.

Election under the local government Act. See the note to s 202 post.

Sub-s (2): Subject to the provisions of this Act and of the rules made under it. Sub-s (2) must be read subject, in particular, to the Election Petition Rules 1960, SI 1960/543 (having effect under s 182 post), r 2(4), as construed in accordance with the Interpretation Act 1978, ss 17(2)(*a*), 23(2), Vol 41, title Statutes, which provides that, subject to this Act and those rules, the practice and procedure of the High Court, including the rules relating to the discovery and inspection of documents and the delivery of interrogatories, shall apply to a petition under those rules as if it were an ordinary action within its jurisdiction, notwithstanding any different practice, principle or rule on which the committees of the House of Commons used to act in dealing with election petitions.

Agency. Cf the note "By his agents" to s 159 post.

Scrutiny. As to scrutiny generally, see 15 Halsbury's Laws (4th edn) paras 924 et seq.

Sub-s (3): Subject to the provisions of this Act. Cf the note to s 123 ante.

Sub-s (5): Parliamentary elections. See the note "Parliamentary election" to s 1 ante.

Sub-s (5): Treasury. See the note to s 29 ante.

Sub-s (6): Prescribed officer. By the Election Petition Rules 1960, SI 1960/543, r 2(3), as construed in accordance with the Interpretation Act 1978, ss 17(2)(*a*), 23(2), Vol 41, title Statutes, the Master of the Supreme Court (Queen's Bench Division) who is nominated under sub-s (4) above as the prescribed officer in relation to parliamentary elections is also to be the prescribed officer in relation to elections under the local government Act.

Sub-s (8): Sub-s (1) above does not apply, etc. See, however, the Judicature (Northern Ireland) Act 1978, s 35(2)(*h*), Vol 31, title Northern Ireland (Pt 2), which provides that no appeal to the Court of Appeal shall lie from the decision of the High Court on any question of law, whether on appeal or otherwise, under ss 120–156 ante.

Parish and community elections; municipal elections in City of London. See the notes to s 67 ante.

European Assembly elections. This section is applied to such elections by the European Assembly Elections Regulations 1984, SI 1984/137, reg 3(1), Sch 1, subject to the substitution for sub-s (2) above of the following subsection:

"(2) Subject to the provisions of this Act and the rules made under it, the principles, practice and rules on which election courts act in dealing with parliamentary election petitions shall be observed, so far as may be, by the High Court and election court in the case of Assembly election petitions."

See further the Introductory Note to this Act.

Definitions. For "parliamentary election petition", see s 120 ante; for "prescribed", see s 185 post; for "election court" and "election petition", see s 202(1) post; for "local government Act", see s 203(1) post.

Consequences of finding by election court of corrupt or illegal practice

158 Report as to candidate guilty of a corrupt or illegal practice

(1) The report of an election court under section 144 or section 145 above shall state whether any corrupt or illegal practice has or has not been proved to have been committed by or with the knowledge and consent of any candidate at the election, and the nature of the corrupt or illegal practice.

(2) For the purposes of sections 159 and 160 below—

   (*a*) if it is reported that a corrupt practice other than treating or undue influence was committed with the knowledge and consent of a candidate, he shall be treated as having been reported personally guilty of that corrupt practice, and

   (*b*) if it is reported that an illegal practice was committed with the knowledge and consent of a candidate at a parliamentary election, he shall be treated as having been reported personally guilty of that illegal practice.

(3) The report shall also state whether any of the candidates has been guilty by his agents of any corrupt or illegal practice in reference to the election; but if a candidate is reported guilty by his agents of treating, undue influence or any illegal practice, and the court further reports that the candidate has proved to the court—

   (*a*) that no corrupt or illegal practice was committed at the election by the candidate or his election agent and the offences mentioned in the report were committed contrary to the orders and without the sanction or connivance of the candidate or his election agent, and

   (*b*) that the candidate and his election agent took all reasonable means for preventing the commission of corrupt and illegal practices at the election, and

   (*c*) that the offences mentioned in the report were of a trivial, unimportant and limited character, and

   (*d*) that in all other respects the election was free from any corrupt or illegal practice on the part of the candidate and of his agents,

then the candidate shall not be treated for the purposes of section 159 as having been reported guilty by his agents of the offences mentioned in the report.

In relation to an election where candidates are not required to have election agents, for paragraphs (*a*) and (*b*) above the following paragraphs shall be substituted—

   "(*a*) that no corrupt or illegal practice was committed at the election by the candidate or with his knowledge or consent and the offences mentioned in the report were committed without the sanction or connivance of the candidate, and

   (*b*) that all reasonable means for preventing the commission of corrupt and illegal practices at the election were taken by and on behalf of the candidate, ".

NOTES

Sub-ss (1), (2) contain provisions formerly in the Representation of the People Act 1949, s 138(1), (2). Sub-s (3) contains provisions formerly in s 138(3), (4) of that Act.

Report . . . shall state, etc. As to the contents of a report under s 144 or 145 ante, see also s 160(1) post; and as to laying the report before the Attorney General, see s 160(3) post.

Corrupt or illegal practice. For the corrupt and illegal practices created by this Act, see the notes to ss 168 and 169 post, respectively; and for the consequences of a report by an election court that a candidate or other person is guilty of a corrupt or illegal practice, see ss 159, 160(4), (5) post.

An illegal practice excused under s 86 ante, or s 167 or Sch 4, para 7 post, ceases ipso facto to be illegal and need not be reported (*Northumberland, Hexham Division, Case, Hudspeth and Lyall v Clayton* (1892) 4 O'M & H 143).

Knowledge. See the note "Knows" to s 60 ante.

Consent; connivance. See the notes to s 75 ante.

Treating. For the acts constituting treating, see s 114 ante.

Undue influence. For the acts constituting undue influence, see s 115 ante.

Parliamentary election. See the note to s 1 ante.

Guilty by his agents. For the discussion of the law of liability, see the note "By his agents" to s 159 post. Sub-s (3) does not apply where there has been bribery by an agent nor to a case of personation (*Pontefract Case, Shaw v Reckitt* (1893) 4 O'M & H 200).

Has proved to the court. The onus of proof lies on the candidate (*Rochester Borough Case, Barry and Varrall v Davis* (1892) 4 O'M & H 156).

Election agent. As to the appointment of election agents, see s 67 ante and the notes thereto.

Took all reasonable means. In *Southampton Borough Case, Austin and Rowland v Chamberlayne and Simeon* (1895) 5 O'M & H 17, the court refused relief to a candidate who had taken part in a disorderly procession round the town in which it was satisfied that a great deal of drinking took place, and that he must have known of the danger of treating occurring. In the same case it was held that if there is a joint candidature (which may still be the case in local government elections) relief could be granted to one candidate and refused to the other.

Election where candidates are not required to have election agents. See s 71 ante.

Parish and community elections; municipal elections in City of London. See the notes to s 67 ante.

European Assembly elections. This section is applied to such elections by the European Assembly Elections Regulations 1984, SI 1984/137, reg 3(1), Sch 1. See further the Introductory Note to this Act.

As to provisions relating to such elections in Northern Ireland, see the Introductory Note to this Act.

Definitions. For "candidate", see, by virtue of s 185 post, s 118 ante; for "election" and "election court", see s 202(1) post.

159 Candidate reported guilty of corrupt or illegal practice

(1) If a candidate who has been elected is reported by an election court personally guilty or guilty by his agents of any corrupt or illegal practice his election shall be void.

(2) A candidate at a parliamentary election shall also be incapable from the date of the report of being elected to and sitting in the House of Commons for the constituency for which the election was held or any constituency which includes the whole or any part of the area of the first-mentioned constituency as constituted for the purposes of the election—

    (*a*) if reported personally guilty of a corrupt practice, for ten years;

    (*b*) if reported guilty by his agents of a corrupt practice or personally guilty of an illegal practice, for seven years;

    (*c*) if reported guilty by his agents of an illegal practice, during the Parliament for which the election was held.

(3) A candidate at an election under the local government Act shall also be incapable from the date of the report of holding any corporate office in the local government area for which the election was held, or in any local government area which includes the whole or any part of the area of the first-mentioned local government area as constituted for the purposes of the election, or, if the election was in Scotland, of holding any corporate office in Scotland—

    (*a*) if reported personally guilty of a corrupt practice, for ten years,

    (*b*) if reported guilty by his agents of a corrupt practice, for three years,

    (*c*) if reported personally guilty or guilty by his agents of an illegal practice, during the period for which the candidate was elected to serve or for which if elected he might have served,

and if at the date of the report he holds any such corporate office, then the office shall be vacated as from that date.

In this subsection "corporate office" in England and Wales means the office of chairman, mayor or councillor of a county, London borough, district or parish or community council or of chairman of a parish or community meeting; and in Scotland the office of councillor of any local authority.

(4) The provisions of this section as to the consequences of the report that a candidate was guilty by his agents of a corrupt or illegal practice have effect subject to the express provisions of this Act relating to particular acts which are declared to be corrupt or illegal practices.

NOTES

Sub-ss (1)–(3) contain provisions formerly in the Representation of the People Act 1949, s 139, as partly repealed, in the case of s 139(3), by the Local Government Act 1972, s 272(1), Sch 30. Sub-s (4) contains provisions formerly in s 138(5) of that Act.

Reported. Ie under ss 144 or 145 ante.

Personally guilty. As to when a person is to be treated as having been reported personally guilty of a corrupt or illegal practice, see s 158(2) ante.

By his agents. For the position of sub-agents, see s 68(2) ante; and as to when a candidate is not to be treated as having been reported guilty by his agents, see s 158(3) ante.

The term "agents" in relation to election law includes agents other than election agents and sub-agents. Payment for his services is not necessary to constitute a person an agent (*Bewdley Case* (1869) 19 LT 676), nor need he be actually appointed by the candidate or by his election agent or sub-agent (*Harwich Borough Case, Tomline v Tyler* (1880) 44 LT 187). A person may be an agent of a candidate although not in his capacity as a candidate, namely, a land agent to a landowner who is adopted as a candidate (*Tamworth Case, Hill and Walton v Peel and Bulmer* (1869) 20 LT 181); such agency is not within this section; the agency to which this section relates is agency for a person in his capacity as candidate and acting with reference to the election.

Committees, canvassers, political associations, and other associations and supporters are not necessarily agents of a candidate by reason of concerning themselves with an election. For the circumstances in which they become agents and the evidence necessary to prove agency, see the following cases:

(i) Committees: *Staleybridge Case, Ogden, Woolley and Buckley v Sidebottom* (1869) 20 LT 75; *Westminster Borough Case* (1869) 20 LT 238; *Dublin City Case* (1869) 1 O'M & H 270; *Windsor Case, Herbert v Gardiner* (1874) 31 LT 133; *Wakefield Case* (1874) 2 O'M & H 100; *Durham Borough Case* (1874) 2 O'M & H 134; *Maidstone Borough Case, Evans v Viscount Castlereagh* (1906) 5 O'M & H 200.

(ii) Canvasser: *Westbury Case, Eyers' Case* (1869) 20 LT 16; *Westminster Borough Case* (1869) 20 LT 238; *Shrewsbury Case* (1870) 2 O'M & H 36; *Bolton Case, Ormerod v Cross* (1874) 31 LT 194; *Tewkesbury Case, Collins v Price* (1880) 44 LT 192.

(iii) Political associations: *Wigan Case* (1869) 21 LT 122; *Wakefield Case* (1874) 2 O'M & H 100; *Westminster Borough Case* (1869) 20 LT 238; *Gravesend Case, Truscott v Bevan* (1880) 44 LT 64; *Chester City Case, Heywood, Dodd, Jones and Davies v Dodson and Lawley* (1880) 44 LT 285; *Westbury Case* (1880) 3 O'M & H 78; *Bewdley Case, Spencer v Harrison* (1880) 44 LT 283; *Northumberland, Hexham Division Case, Hudspeth and Lyal v Clayton* (1892) 4 O'M & H 143; *Worcester Borough Case, Glaszard and Turner v Allsopp* (1892) 4 O'M & H 153; *Tower Hamlets, St George's Division Case, Benn v Marks* (1896) 5 O'M & H 89.

(iv) Other associations: *Walsall Borough Case, Hateley, Moss and Mason v James* (1892) 4 O'M & H 123.

(v) Supporters: *Great Yarmouth Borough Case, White v Fell* (1906) 5 O'M & H 176; *Hartlepools Case* (1910) 6 O'M & H 1.

For a candidate to be legally affected by the conduct of another person acting as his agent, there must be some assent, express or implied, on the candidate's part to that person acting as his agent in relation to the election or some ratification or adoption of work done by him. For the consideration of the legal nature of the relationship between a candidate and his agents and his liability in respect of their acts and omissions, see the following cases: *Norwich Case, Tillett v Stracey* (1869) 19 LT 615; *Westminster Borough Case* (1869) 20 LT 238; *Taunton Borough Case, Marshall and Brannan v James* (1874) 30 LT 125; *Boston Borough Case, Malcolm v Parry* (1874) LR 9 CP 610; *Harwich Borough Case, Tomline v Tyler* (1880) 44 LT 187; *Aylesbury Case* (1886) 4 O'M & H 59; *Northumberland, Hexham Division, Case* (1892) (published as Parliamentary Paper No 25 of 1893); and *Great Yarmouth Borough Case, White v Fell* (1906) 5 O'M & H 176.

For the distinction between general and special agency, see *Westbury Case, Laverton v Phipps, Harrop's Case* (1869) 20 LT 16; *Bodmin Case* (1869) 20 LT 989; *Hereford Borough Case, Thomas v Clive and Wyllie* (1869) 21 LT 117; *Harwich Borough Case, Tomline v Tyler* (1880) 44 LT 187; and *Wigan Case, Spencer and Prestt v Powell* (1881) 4 O'M & H 1.

For the position of an agent of an agent, see *Cooper v Slade* (1858) 6 HL Cas 746, 27 LJQB 449; *Barnstable Case* (1874) 2 O'M & H 105; and *Plymouth Case, Latimer and Barratt v Bates* (1880) 3 O'M & H 107.

See further as to evidence of agency, examples of kinds of agents and termination of agency, 15 Halsbury's Laws (4th edn) paras 698–704.

Corrupt or illegal practice. For the corrupt and illegal practices created by this Act, see the notes to ss 168 and 169 post, respectively.

Shall be void. As to the consequences of a local election being declared void, see s 135 ante; and see generally, as to a candidate's liability to have his election avoided under the doctrines of election agency, 15 Halsbury's Laws (4th edn) para 697. For an exception from sub-s (1) above, see s 189(2) post.

Parliamentary election; constituency. See the notes to s 1 ante.

Shall also be incapable, etc. For further incapacities, see s 160(4), (5) post; and as to mitigation and remission of incapacities, see s 174 post.

By the Local Government Act 1972, s 80(1)(e), Vol 25, title Local Government, a person is disqualified for being elected or being a member of a local authority if he is disqualified under this Part of this Act for being a member of that authority. See also the Land Drainage Act 1976, Sch 1, paras 5(1)(e), 8(1)(e), Vol 22, title Land Drainage, as construed in accordance with the Interpretation Act 1978, s 17(2)(a), Vol 41, title Statutes, concerning vacation of office by, and disqualification for appointment as, a member of a regional or local land drainage committee if a person is disqualified for being a member of a local authority under this Part.

Election under the local government Act. See the note to s 202 post.

England; Wales. See the note to s 4 ante.

County, London borough, district. See the note "County council" to s 31 ante, and the notes "London borough" and "Council of every district" to s 8 ante.

Parish or community council (meeting). As to parishes and communities and their meetings and councils, see the Local Government Act 1972, ss 1(6)–(9), 9 et seq, 20(4), 27 et seq, Sch 1, Pts IV, V, Sch 4, Pt III, Vol 25, title Local Government.

Express provisions ... relating to particular acts, etc. See, eg, s 61(7)(b), 75(5)(ii), 78(3)(b) and 106(2)(a) ante, and 189(2) and Sch 4, para 1(2) post.

Parish and community elections; municipal elections in City of London. See the notes to s 67 ante.

European Assembly elections. This section is applied to such elections by the European Assembly Elections Regulations 1984, SI 1984/137, reg 3(1), Sch 1, subject to:

(1) the substitution in sub-s (2) above for the words "House of Commons" of the word "Assembly"; and

(2) the substitution in sub-s (2)(c) above, for the words "during the Parliament for which the election was held", of the words "until the next general election of representatives to the Assembly".

See further the Introductory Note to this Act.

As to provisions relating to such elections in Northern Ireland, see the Introductory Note to this Act.

Definitions. For "candidate", see, by virtue of s 185 post, s 118 ante; for "election court", see s 202(1) post; for "local government Act" and "local government area", see s 203(1) post.

---

160 Persons reported personally guilty of corrupt or illegal practices

(1) The report of the election court under section 144 or section 145 above shall state the names of all persons (if any) who have been proved at the trial to have been guilty of any corrupt or illegal practice . . ., but in the case of someone—

(a) who is not a party to the petition, or

(b) who is not a candidate on behalf of whom the seat or office is claimed by the petition,

the election court shall first cause notice to be given to him, and if he appears in pursuance of the notice shall give him an opportunity of being heard by himself and of calling evidence in his defence to show why he should not be so reported.

(2) . . .

[(3) The report shall be laid before the Director of Public Prosecutions.]

(4) Subject to the provisions of section 174 below, a candidate or other person reported by an election court personally guilty of a corrupt practice shall for five years from the date of the report be incapable—

(a) of being registered as an elector or voting at any parliamentary election in the United Kingdom or at any election in Great Britain to any public office, and

(b) of being elected to and sitting in the House of Commons, and

(c) of holding any public or judicial office,

and, if already elected to the House of Commons or holding such office, shall from that date vacate the seat or office.

(5) Subject to the provisions of section 174, a candidate or other person reported by

an election court personally guilty of an illegal practice shall for five years from the date of the report be incapable of being registered as an elector or voting at any parliamentary election or at any election to a public office held—

(a) if the offence was committed in reference to a parliamentary election, for or within the constituency for which it was held or for or within any constituency or local government area wholly or partly within the area of the first-mentioned constituency as constituted for the purposes of the election;

(b) if the offence was committed in reference to an election under the local government Act, for or within the local government area for which the election was held or for or within any constituency or local government area wholly or partly within the area of the first-mentioned local government area as constituted for the purposes of the election.

. . . . . .

(6) Without prejudice to the generality of the provisions of section 205(2) below, nothing in subsection (4) or subsection (5) above affects matters relating to the Northern Ireland Assembly or local elections or holding office in Northern Ireland.

(7) The provisions of this section as to the consequences of the report that a candidate was guilty by his agents of a corrupt or illegal practice have effect subject to the express provisions of this Act relating to particular acts which are declared to be corrupt or illegal practices.

NOTES

Sub-s (1) contains provisions formerly in the Representation of the People Act 1949, s 140(1). Sub-ss (4)–(6) contain provisions formerly in s 140(3)–(5), respectively, of that Act, as amended, in the case of s 140(5), by the Northern Ireland (Modification of Enactments—No 1) Order 1973, SI 1973/2163, art 14(1), Sch 5, para 15(b). Sub-s (7) contains provisions formerly in s 138(5) of the 1949 Act.

The words omitted from sub-s (1), and the whole of sub-s (2), were repealed, and sub-s (3) was substituted, by the Representation of the People Act 1985, ss 24, 28(1), Sch 4, para 52, Sch 5, as from 1 October 1985.

The words omitted from sub-s (5) where indicated by dots apply to Scotland only.

Sub-s (1): Corrupt or illegal practice. For the corrupt and illegal practices created by this Act, see the notes to ss 168 and 169 post, respectively.

Notice. As to the service of notices, see s 184 post.

By himself. If the person on whom the notice is served is desirous of appearing and showing cause against being reported, he can only be heard in person; counsel or solicitor may not be heard on his behalf; see *R v Mansel Jones* (1889) 23 QBD 29, 60 LT 860. Notwithstanding this decision election courts have exercised a discretion of allowing persons so showing cause to appear by counsel; see 3 Halsbury's Laws (4th edn) para 1168, note 3.

Sub-s (3): Director of Public Prosecutions. See the note to s 148 ante.

Sub-s (4): Personally guilty. As to when a person is to be treated as personally guilty of a corrupt or illegal practice, see s 158(2) ante.

The provisions of sub-ss (4) and (5) above apply only to individuals personally guilty. Persons guilty by an agent are liable to lose office under s 159(2), (3) ante, but they do not incur other penalties and in particular they do not lose the franchise (*Morris v Shrewsbury Town Clerk* [1909] 1 KB 342, 78 LJKB 234).

If on an election petition the judges declare an election void and render an ambiguously worded report which fails to distinguish between personal default of a candidate and default by an agent, the ambiguity will be resolved in his favour and he will retain his vote (*Grant v Pagham Overseers* (1877) 3 CPD 80, 47 LJQB 59).

Shall . . . be incapable, etc. For further incapacities, see s 159(2), (3) ante; and as to mitigation and remission of incapacities, see s 174 post. The incapacities under sub-ss (4) and (5) above are applied to persons convicted of corrupt or illegal practices by s 173 post.

Registered as an elector. As to the registration of electors, see ss 9 et seq ante.

Parliamentary election. See the note to s 1 ante.

United Kingdom. See the note to s 6 ante.

Great Britain. Ie England, Scotland and Wales; see the Union with Scotland Act 1706, preamble, Art I, Vol 10, title Constitutional Law (Pt 1), as read with the Interpretation Act 1978, s 22(1), Sch 2, para 5(a), Vol 41, title Statutes.

Sub-s (5): Personally guilty; shall . . . be incapable etc. See the notes to sub-s (4) above.

Constituency. See the note to s 1 ante.

Election under the local government Act. See the note to s 202 post.

Sub-s (6): Northern Ireland Assembly. This assembly was established by the Northern Ireland Assembly Act 1973, and further relevant provisions are contained in the Northern Ireland Constitution Act 1973, Pts II, IV, both Vol 31, title Northern Ireland (Pt 2). The Assembly, elected under s 2 of the first-mentioned Act, was dissolved by the Northern Ireland Assembly (Dissolution) Order 1975, SI 1975/422 (made under the Northern Ireland Act 1974, s 1(1), Vol 31, title Northern Ireland (Pt 2)). Under Sch 1, para 1, to the 1974 Act, laws for Northern Ireland may be made by Order in Council during the interim period as defined by s 1(4) of that Act. By para 1(7) of that Schedule, references to Measures of the Northern Ireland Assembly include references to such Orders in Council.

A new Assembly has now been elected by virtue of an election held on 20 October 1982 (ie the day appointed by the Northern Ireland Assembly (Day of Election) Order 1982, SI 1982/1078, made under the Northern Ireland Constitution Act 1973, s 27(7), as applied by s 1(1) of the 1974 Act). Provision for the general or partial suspension of the system of direct rule introduced by Sch 1 to the 1974 Act may now be made by Order in Council made under the Northern Ireland Act 1982, Vol 31, title Northern Ireland (Pt 2), and the effect of any such Order is set out in Sch 1 to that Act. See also, in particular, s 3 of the 1982 Act, as to matters which may be considered by the Assembly pending general suspension of direct rule; s 5 as to the dissolution of the Assembly and revocation of Orders in Council made under s 2 of the Act; and s 6 and Sch 2 for amendments of the 1973 Acts.

Sub-s (7): By his agents; express provisions ... relating to particular acts, etc. See the notes to s 159 ante.

Parish and community elections; municipal elections in City of London. See the notes to s 67 ante.

European Assembly elections. This section is applied to such elections by the European Assembly Elections Regulations 1984, SI 1984/137, reg 3(1), Sch 1, subject to:

(1) the insertion in sub-s (4) above, after the word "parliamentary", of the words "or Assembly", and after the words "House of Commons" (in both places), of the words "or Assembly"; and
(2) the insertion in sub-s (5) above, after the words "any parliamentary", of the words "or Assembly".

See further the Introductory Note to this Act; but note that by virtue of reg 3(1) of, and Sch 1 to, the above-mentioned regulations, reg 3(5)(a) of those regulations, which is set out in that note, does not operate so as to convert the words "any parliamentary election" in sub-s (4) to "any Assembly election" nor to convert the words "parliamentary election" in sub-s (5), except para (a) thereof, to "Assembly election".

As to provisions relating to such elections in Northern Ireland, see the Introductory Note to this Act.

Definitions. For "judicial office" and "public office", see s 185 post; for "candidate", see, by virtue of s 185 post, s 118 ante; for "election court", "elector", "person" and "vote", see s 202(1) post; for "local government Act" and "local government area", see s 203(1) post.

Director of Public Prosecutions' duty to report corrupt practice

161 Justice of the Peace

Where a justice of the peace is reported by an election court to have been guilty of any corrupt practice in reference to an election, ... [the court shall] report the case to the Lord Chancellor [or, in the case of a justice of the peace for any area in Scotland, the Secretary of State] with such evidence as may have been given of the corrupt practice.

NOTES

This section, as originally enacted, contained provisions formerly in the Representation of the People Act 1949, s 141(1).

The words omitted were repealed by the Representation of the People Act 1985, s 28(1), Sch 5, as from 1 October 1985, and the words in square brackets were substituted or inserted by s 24 of, and Sch 4, para 53 to, that Act, as from that date.

Reported. Ie under ss 144 or 145 ante.

Corrupt practice. For the corrupt practices created by this Act, see the note to s 168 post.

Parish and community elections; municipal elections in City of London. See the notes to s 67 ante.

European Assembly elections. This section and ss 162–164 post, are applied to such elections by the European Assembly Elections Regulations 1984, SI 1984/137, reg 3(1), Sch 1. See further the Introductory Note to this Act.

As to provisions relating to such elections in Northern Ireland, see the Introductory Note to this Act.

Definitions. For "election" and "election court", see s 202(1) post.

162 Member of legal and certain other professions

Where a barrister, advocate, solicitor or any person who belongs to any profession the admission to which is regulated by law is reported by an election court to have been guilty of any corrupt practice in reference to an election, . . .—

> (a) [the court shall] bring the matter before the Inn of Court, [Faculty of Advocates], High Court or tribunal having power to take cognizance of any misconduct of the person in his profession; and
> (b) the Inn of Court, [Faculty of Advocates], High Court or tribunal may deal with him as if the corrupt practice were misconduct by him in his profession.

NOTES

This section, as originally enacted, contained provisions formerly in the Representation of the People Act 1949, s 141(2).

The words omitted were repealed by the Representation of the People Act 1985, s 28(1), Sch 5, as from 1 October 1985, and the words in square brackets were substituted or inserted by s 24 of, and Sch 4, para 54 to, that Act, as from that date.

Reported. Ie under ss 144 or 145 ante.

Corrupt practices. For the corrupt practices created by this Act, see the note to s 168 post.

High Court. See the note to s 39 ante.

Parish and community elections; municipal elections in City of London. See the notes to s 67 ante.

European Assembly elections. See the note to s 161 ante.

Definitions. For "election" and "election court", see s 202(1) post.

163 Holder of licence or certificate under Licensing Acts

(1) If it appears to an election court that a person holding a licence or certificate under the Licensing Acts has knowingly permitted any bribery or treating in reference to any election to take place upon his licensed premises—

> (a) the court shall, after affording him such rights as are conferred on those about to be reported under section 160(1) above, report the fact; and
> (b) ... [the court shall] bring the report before the licensing authority from whom, or on whose certificate, that person obtained his licence, and the licensing authority shall cause the report to be entered in the proper register of licences.

(2) The entry of the report in that register shall be taken into consideration by the licensing authority in determining whether they will or will not grant a renewal of the licence or certificate of the person reported and may be a ground, if the authority think fit, for refusing renewal.

NOTES

This section contains provisions formerly in the Representation of the People Act 1949, s 141(3), (4).

The words omitted were repealed by the Representation of the People Act 1985, s 28(1), Sch 5, as from 1 October 1985, and the words in square brackets were substituted by s 24 of, and Sch 4, para 55 to, that Act, as from that date.

Licence or certificate under the Licensing Acts. In England and Wales this refers, in particular, to a justices' licence as defined by the Licensing Act 1964, s 1, Vol 24, title Licensing and Liquor Duties, and a special hours certificate granted under s 77 or 78 of that Act in the same title.

Knowingly. See the note "Knows" to s 60 ante.

Bribery or treating. As to these offences, see ss 113 and 114 ante.

Licensed premises. This expression is defined by the Licensing Act 1964, s 200(1), Vol 24, title Licensing and Liquor Duties.

Such rights as are conferred on those about to be reported, etc. These rights are set out in s 160(1) ante.

Licensing authority. In England and Wales this refers to the licensing justices constituted by the Licensing Act 1964, s 2(2), (5), Sch 1, Pt I, Vol 24, title Licensing and Liquor Duties.

Proper register of licences. This is the register kept under the Licensing Act 1964, s 30, Vol 24, title Licensing and Liquor Duties.

Parish and community elections; municipal elections in City of London. See the notes to s 67 ante.

European Assembly elections. See the note to s 161 ante.

Definitions. For "Licensing Acts", see s 185 post; for "election" and "election court", see s 202(1) post.

Further provision as to avoidance of elections and striking off votes

164 Avoidance of election for general corruption etc

(1) Where on an election petition it is shown that corrupt or illegal practices or illegal payments, employments or hirings committed in reference to the election for the purpose of promoting or procuring the election of any person at that election have so extensively prevailed that they may be reasonably supposed to have affected the result—

    (a) his election, if he has been elected, shall be void, and

    (b) he shall be incapable of being elected to fill the vacancy or any of the vacancies for which the election was held.

(2) An election shall not be liable to be avoided otherwise than under this section by reason of general corruption, bribery, treating or intimidation.

(3) An election under the local government Act may be questioned on the ground that it is avoided under this section.

NOTES

This section contains provisions formerly in the Representation of the People Act 1949, s 142.

Corrupt or illegal practices. For the corrupt and illegal practices created by this Act, see the notes to ss 168 and 169 post, respectively.

Illegal payments, employments or hirings. See the corresponding notes to s 175 post.

For the purpose of promoting, etc. Cf the notes "With a view to" and "Promoting or procuring the election of a candidate" to s 75 ante.

So extensively prevailed, etc. Note that the report of an election court must state whether corrupt or illegal practices have extensively prevailed at the election; see ss 144(4) and 145(3) ante.

Shall be void. For the purposes of ss 122 and 129 ante, an allegation that an election is avoided under this section must be deemed to be an allegation of corrupt practices notwithstanding that the offences alleged are or include offences other than corrupt practices; see sub-ss (7) and (8) of those sections respectively.

Shall not be liable to be avoided. Ie it can be no longer avoided at common law in respect of the matters specified in sub-s (2). Personation is not mentioned in that subsection, and it has been judicially held that there was no rule for avoidance of an election on account of general personation (*Belfast Borough Western Division, Case* (1886) 4 O'M & H 105).

General bribery. In each case the court should look to the circumstances of the case to see if the result might have been obtained by bribery. For a discussion of the common law, see *Bradford Case (No 2), Storey and Garnett v Forster* (1869) 19 LT 723; *Drogheda Borough Case* (1869) 21 LT 402; and *Ipswich Case, Packard v Collings and West* (1886) 54 LT 619. For the offence of bribery, see s 113 ante.

General treating. For a discussion of the common law, see *Bradford Case (No 2), Storey and Garnett v Forster* (1869) 19 LT 723, and *Ipswich Case, Packard v Collings and West* (1886) 54 LT 619. For the offence of treating, see s 114 ante.

General intimidation. The essence of general intimidation is that freedom of election has ceased to exist in the particular constituency or area for which the election is held. A localised intimidation will not necessarily affect the result (*Drogheda Borough Case* (1869) 21 LT 402). Persons of ordinary courage and intelligence must have been prevented from voting as they wished (*Cheltenham Case, Gardner v Samuelson* (1869) 19 LT 816; *Salford Case, Anderson, Bryant and Harding v Cawley and Charley, Balderstone's Case* (1869) 20 LT 120; *Nottingham Borough Case* (1869) 1 O'M & H 245).

For spiritual intimidation see *South Meath Case, Dalton v Fullam* (1892) Day 132; *North Meath Case* (1892) Day 141.

Election under the local government Act. See the note to s 202 post.

May be questioned. As to the questioning of elections under the local government Act, see ss 127 et seq ante.

Parish and community elections; municipal elections in City of London. See the notes to s 67 ante.

European Assembly elections. See the note to s 161 ante.

Definitions. For "election" and "election petition", see s 202(1) post; for "local government Act", see s 203(1) post.

165 Avoidance of election for employing corrupt agent

(1) If at a parliamentary or local government election a candidate or his election agent personally engages as a canvasser or agent for the conduct or management of the election any person whom he knows or has reasonable grounds for supposing to be subject to an incapacity to vote at the election by reason—

(*a*) of his having been convicted or reported of any corrupt or illegal practice within the meaning of this Act or of the law relating to elections for the Northern Ireland Assembly, or

(*b*) of his having been convicted more than once of an offence under the Public Bodies Corrupt Practices Act 1889,

the candidate shall be incapable of being elected to fill the vacancy or any of the vacancies for which the election is held.

(2) A local government election may be questioned on the ground that the person whose election is questioned was, at the time of the election, by virtue of this section incapable of being elected.

(3) A vote given for a person who, at the time of the election, was by virtue of this section incapable of being elected shall not, by reason of that incapacity, be deemed to be thrown away so as to entitle another candidate to be declared elected, unless given at a poll consequent on the decision of an election court that he was so incapable.

NOTES

Sub-s (1) contains provisions formerly in the Representation of the People Act 1949, s 143(1), as amended by the Northern Ireland (Modification of Enactments—No 1) Order 1973, SI 1973/2163, art 14(1), Sch 5, para 15(*c*). Sub-ss (2), (3) contain provisions formerly in s 143(2) of the 1949 Act.

Parliamentary . . . election. See the note to s 1 ante.

Election agent. As to the appointment of election agents, see s 67 ante and the notes thereto.

Personally engages. For the canvasser or agent to be personally engaged it is sufficient for him to be engaged with the knowledge and consent of the candidate or election agent; see *North Norfolk Case* (1869) 1 O'M & H 236 at 238, and *Norwich Case* (1871) 2 O'M & H 38 at 40.

Conduct or management of the elections. It is not necessary that the agent should be an agent for the management of the whole election; it is sufficient if he is agent for part of the election. He must be not simply an agent who might be employed to such an extent as might make the candidate answerable for corrupt or illegal practices committed by him, but employed in the way of managing a portion of the election; see *North Norfolk Case* (1869) 1 O'M & H 236 at 239.

Knows. See the note to s 60 ante.

Incapacity to vote. Such an incapacity is imposed by s 160(4)(*a*) or (5) ante, and by those provisions as applied by s 173 post, and may be imposed under the Public Bodies Corrupt Practices Act 1889, s 2(*d*), Vol 12, title Criminal Law.

Convicted or reported. Ie convicted under s 168 or 169 post, or reported under s 144 or 145 ante.

Corrupt or illegal practice. For the corrupt and illegal practices created by this Act, see the notes to ss 168 and 169 post, respectively.

Northern Ireland Assembly. See the note to s 160 ante.

May be questioned. As to the questioning of local government elections, see ss 127 et seq ante.

Parish and community elections; municipal elections in City of London. See the notes to s 67 ante.

European Assembly elections. This section is applied to such elections by the European Assembly Elections Regulations 1984, SI 1984/137, reg 3(1), Sch 1, subject to the insertion in sub-s (1) above after the words "this Act" of the words "(as it applies to parliamentary and local government elections and as applied by regulations under the European Assembly Elections Act 1978)". See further the Introductory Note to this Act.

As to provisions relating to such elections in Northern Ireland, see the Introductory Note to this Act.

Definitions. For "candidate", see, by virtue of s 185 post, s 118 ante; for "election court" and "vote", see s 202(1) post; for "local government election", see s 203(1) post.

Public Bodies Corrupt Practices Act 1889. See Vol 12, title Criminal Law.

166 Votes to be struck off for corrupt or illegal practices

(1) Where, on a parliamentary election petition claiming the seat for any person, a candidate is proved to have been guilty by himself, or by any person on his behalf, of bribery, treating or undue influence in respect of any person who voted at the election there shall, on a scrutiny, be struck off from the number of votes appearing to have been given to the candidate one vote for every person who voted at the election and is proved to have been so bribed, treated or unduly influenced.

(2) If any person who is guilty of a corrupt or illegal practice or of illegal payment, employment or hiring at an election votes at the election, his vote shall be void.

(3) If any person who is subject under any enactment relating to corrupt or illegal practices to an incapacity to vote at a parliamentary election or an election to any public office votes at that election, his vote shall be void.

NOTES

This section contains provisions formerly in the Representation of the People Act 1949, s 144.
Bribery, treating or undue influence. As to these offences, see ss 113–115 ante.
There shall, on a scrutiny, be struck off, etc. It is not necessary for this purpose to go into the question of how the person bribed had actually voted (*Boston Borough Case, Malcolm v Parry* (1874) LR 9 CP 610; *Down County Case* (1880) 3 O'M & H 115; *West Bromwich Case, Hazel v Viscount Lewisham* (1911) 6 O'M & H 256 at 266). If, however, it appears that the voter deliberately spoilt his ballot paper the election court may refuse to strike off a vote (*West Bromwich Case* cited above). In the case of bribery it appears necessary to prove not only the giving of the bribe with a corrupt motive but also that the person receiving it acted corruptly (*Boston Borough Case* cited above; *Down County Case* cited above).
There is no power to add a vote for the candidate for whom the voter would have voted but for intimidation (*Oldham Case, Cobbett v Hibbert and Platt* (1869) 20 LT 302).
As to scrutiny generally, see 15 Halsbury's Laws (4th edn) paras 924 et seq.
So bribed etc. "So bribed" means bribed by the candidate or any person on his behalf (*Boston Borough Case, Malcolm v Parry* (1874) LR 9 CP 610).
Corrupt or illegal practice. For the corrupt and illegal practices created by this Act, see the notes to ss 168 and 169 post, respectively. As to the votes of persons guilty of personation and of persons impersonated, see 15 Halsbury's Laws (4th edn) para 928.
Illegal payment, employment or hiring. See the note to s 175 post.
Shall be void. Accordingly the vote mentioned in sub-s (2) or (3) above may be struck off on a scrutiny.
Incapacity to vote. See the note to s 165 ante.
Parliamentary election. See the note to s 1 ante.
Parish and community elections; municipal elections in City of London. See the notes to s 67 ante.
European Assembly elections. This section and ss 167–171, 173–176, 178–186 post, are applied to such elections by the European Assembly Elections Regulations 1984, SI 1984/137, reg 3(1), Sch 1. See further the Introductory Note to this Act.
As to provisions relating to such elections in Northern Ireland, see the Introductory Note to this Act.
Definitions. For "parliamentary election petition", see s 120 ante; for "public office", see s 185 post; for "candidate", see, by virtue of s 185 post, s 118 ante; for "election" and "vote", see s 202(1) post.

Power to except innocent act from being illegal practice, payment, employment or hiring

167 Application for relief

(1) An application for relief under this section may be made to the High Court or an election court or else, if in respect of a payment made in contravention of section 78(1) or (2) above, or of paragraph 1 of Schedule 4 to this Act, to a county court.

[(1A) Where a person makes an application under this section he shall notify the Director of Public Prosecutions of the application and the Director or his assistant or representative may attend the hearing of the application and make representations at the hearing in respect of it.]

(2) If it is shown to the court by such evidence as to the court seems sufficient—

   (*a*) that any act or omission of any person would apart from this section by reason of being in contravention of this Act be an illegal practice, payment, employment or hiring,

   (*b*) that the act or omission arose from inadvertence or from accidental miscalculation or from some other reasonable cause of a like nature, and in any case did not arise from any want of good faith, and

   (*c*) that such notice of the application has been given in the constituency or, as the case may be, the area of the authority for which the election was held, as to the court seems fit,

and under the circumstances it seems to the court to be just that either that or any other person should not be subject to any of the consequences under this Act of the act or omission, the court may make an order allowing the act or omission to be an exception from the provisions of this Act making it an illegal practice, payment, employment or hiring and upon the making of the order no person shall be subject to any of the consequences under this Act of that act or omission.

(3) (*Applies to Scotland only.*)

(4) Except in Scotland, the jurisdiction vested by the above provisions of this section in the High Court in matters relating to parliamentary elections shall, subject to rules of court, be exercised by—

   (*a*) one of the judges for the time being on the rota for the trial of parliamentary election petitions,

   (*b*) in Northern Ireland, one of the judges of the High Court or the Court of Appeal for the time being selected under section 108 of the Judicature (Northern Ireland Act 1978,

sitting either in court or at chambers but shall not be exercisable by a master.

(5) The jurisdiction vested by this section in a county court may, except in Northern Ireland, be exercised otherwise than in open court, and, in Northern Ireland, shall be exercised in accordance with rules of court.

An appeal lies to the High Court from any order of a county court made under this section.

NOTES

This section, as originally enacted, contained provisions formerly in the Representation of the People Act 1949, s 145, as partly repealed in the case of s 145(4), by the Representation of the People Act 1969, s 24(4), Sch 3, Pt I, and as amended, in the case of s 145(4), by the Judicature (Northern Ireland) Act 1978, s 122(1), Sch 5, Pt II.

Sub-s (1A) was inserted by the Representation of the People Act 1985, s 24, Sch 4, para 56, as from 1 October 1985.

Sub-s (1): Application for relief. Application may be made at any time; see *Ex p Kyd* (1897) 14 TLR 64 (before the election); *Re County Councillors' Elections* (1889) 5 TLR 203 (petition threatened; relief granted); *Lichfield Case* (1892) Day 76 (application made after withdrawal of petition; relief granted); *Nichol v Fearby* [1923] 1 KB 480, [1922] All ER Rep 790 (application made after issue of writ claiming penalties). If a prosecution has been commenced, an adjournment may be granted in order to allow application for relief to be made (*Re Huntingdon Borough Municipal Election, ex p Clark* (1885) 52 LT 260). If an election petition has been presented, the court will usually decline to adjudicate upon an application by the successful candidate whose election is questioned by the petition, and the court may either refuse it or adjourn the hearing until the petition has been heard (*Ex p Wilks* (1885) 16 QBD 114, 50 JP 487; *Re County Council Elections, Evans' Case* (1889) 5 TLR 206; *Re County Councils' Elections, Hempson's Case* (1889) 5 TLR 220). In some cases, especially where the act complained of is trivial and not likely in itself to have affected the result of the election, the court will be prepared to adjudicate even though the result is that the grant of relief puts an end to the petition (*Ex p Forster* (1903) 89 LT 18, 19 TLR 525).

High Court. See the notes to ss 39 and 120 ante; and note sub-s (4) above.

County court. See the note to s 30 ante; and note sub-s (5) above.

Sub-s (1A): Director of Public Prosecutions. See the note to s 148 ante.

Sub-s (2): By such evidence as . . . seems sufficient. Mere assertions are insufficient; evidence must be forthcoming (*Ex p Perry* (1884) 48 JP 824). Cf the note "On production of such evidence, etc" to s 86 ante.

The applicant must swear an affidavit. If there is more than one applicant there should be a joint affidavit by all (*Re Andrews, Re Streatham Vestry* (1899) 68 LJQB 683). The court will not act on an unsworn medical certificate that a candidate is too ill to swear an affidavit (*Re County Councillors' Elections, Lord Dinevor's Case* (1889) 5 TLR 220 (application adjourned)). If affidavits contradict other evidence given, and the contradiction is not explained, or if the affidavit of an opponent contradicts the affidavit of an applicant, the court will be inclined to take no action, particularly so if there are other proceedings pending in which the legality or illegality of the acts in question can be decided (*Re Pembroke CC Case, Re Ramsgate Election, ex p Hobbs* (1889) 5 TLR 272).

Illegal practice, payment, employment or hiring. For the illegal practices created by this Act, see the note to s 169 post, and as to illegal payments, employments and hirings, see the note thereon to s 175 post.

Inadvertence. "Inadvertence is a word which is capable of several interpretations and which has been interpreted in various ways not always I think consistent with one another. It may mean mere thoughtlessness, it may mean what is equivalent to a mere mistake, but in this case it was also an ignorance of the law ... Persons might be fairly described as acting inadvertently because they did not know the law ... inadvertence does not cover a case where in the immediate duty which he is performing he ought to have a full knowledge of the law"; see *West Bromwich Case, Hazel v Viscount Lewisham* (1911) 6 O'M & H 256 at 287 per Ridley J. "Inadvertence ... may be either that the party was not aware of what was done, or that he did not know that it was wrong ... Now as to the payments for the banners. The election agent might fairly say that the payments were inadvertent in the sense that he did not know that they were wrong"; see *Stepney Borough Case, Rushmere v Isaacson* (1892) Day 116 at 120 per Cave J.

The court will not be disposed to favour persons who have made no effort to discover what their legal obligations may be, except perhaps persons who have not on previous occasions been candidates or concerned in conducting an election campaign (see the note "Order for allowing an authorised excuse" to s 86 ante). If a non-qualified person consults a legally qualified person and receives bad advice, he is not to be penalised for that, but if he asks the opinion of unqualified persons and acts hoping that his action is legal and it is not, he is liable to be refused relief for taking the risk (*Re School Board Election, ex p Montefiore* (1888) 5 TLR 78). If any person, whether legally qualified or not, reads the text of an Act or regulations and fails to comprehend an obscure or difficult point he may receive exemption, but it is otherwise if matters are clear (*Ex p Walker* (1889) 22 QBD 384, 58 LJQB 190, CA). Consultation of inaccurate and misleading text books may also be acceptable as a good excuse (see per Baron Huddleston in *Re County Councillors' Elections, Birley's Case* (1889) 5 TLR 220: "Mr Birley had been a member of the bar but only for two years and that a long time ago. The imposing appearance of the text book and its large type might have led him to believe that it contained all that was necessary"). See also *Re Preston, Fishwick Ward Councillor, Re Hubberstey* (1899) 43 Sol Jo 826, cited in the note "Illegal practice" to s 78 ante, and *Re Shipston-on-Stour Rural District Council Election* (1953) Times, 9 June, cited in the note "Illegal practice" to s 110 ante.

In short, carelessness will not prevent relief being granted provided it does not approach recklessness (*Re Bedwellty Constituency Parliamentary Election, ex p Finch* (1965) 109 Sol Jo 514).

Some other reasonable cause. In *Ipswich Case* (1887) 3 TLR 397, the illness of an unpaid agent was accepted as a good excuse for failure to render returns within the prescribed time limit; in *Re St Matthew's Ward, Cambridge Borough Case, ex p Hawkins and French* (1899) 44 Sol Jo 102, relief was granted to an applicant who asserted that he was misled by his parliamentary experience and had not appreciated a difference existing between parliamentary and municipal election law.

For a provision declaring certain matters to constitute a "reasonable cause" for the purposes of this section, see s 77(3) ante.

Such notice of the application ... as seems fit. The court is judge of the sufficiency of notice, but want of adequate notice is good ground for refusal to adjudicate. Notice should be given to the candidates and to the returning officer, and there should be advertisement for the constituency or local government area (as may be applicable). Advertisement in newspapers will not be regarded as sufficient (*Ex p Perry* (1884) 48 JP 824). However, when application is made to an election court less notice is required and notice in court to the interested parties will do (*Hexham Case* (1892) Day 77; *Stepney Borough Case, Rushmere v Isaacson* (1892) Day 116). Although failure to give proper notice is a ground for refusing relief (*Re County Councillors' Elections, New Swindon Case, ex p Hinton* (1889) 5 TLR 195) the fact that one particular voter does not receive notice is no ground for subsequent objection by him if an order granting relief has been made (*Re Wigan Case* (1885) 2 TLR 159).

Want of precision in a notice claiming relief is good ground for awarding costs to an opponent (*Re County Councillors' Elections, Keatinge and Wynn's Case* (1889) 5 TLR 195). An application should not be hypothetical, ie in respect of certain acts "if found to be illegal" (*Walsall Case, Hateley, Moss and Mason v James* (1892) Day 106).

Constituency. See the note to s 1 ante.

Consequences ... of the act or omission. See, in particular, ss 158–160 ante, as to the consequences of a finding by an election court of illegal practice, ss 158–160 ante, and as to prosecutions for illegal practices, s 169 post.

Exception from the provisions of this Act. For decisions on specific offences, see the notes to s 73 ante (expenses paid otherwise than through an election agent); s 76 ante (expenditure in excess of maximum amount); s 78 ante (payment of claim made out of time); s 101 ante (hiring of vehicles to convey voters); s 108 ante (illegal hiring of premises); s 110 ante (printer's name omitted from publications); and s 111 ante (use of paid canvassers).

No person shall be subject to any of the consequences, etc. The grant of an order legalises the act complained of, whereas under s 86(7) ante only the applicant for an order is excused.

Sub-s (4): Parliamentary elections. See the note "Parliamentary election" to s 1 ante.

Rules of court. As to such rules, see s 182 post and the notes thereto.

Rota. As to the selection of judges for the rota for the trial of parliamentary election petitions, see the Supreme Court Act 1981, s 142, Vol 11, title Courts.

Costs. An applicant must pay his own costs of obtaining relief. Trivial offences do not justify opposition, but the court will grant costs if there is a point of substance (*Ex p Kyd* (1897) 14 TLR 154). Candidates and returning officers are regarded as proper opposers, but the court is inclined to disfavour opposition by other persons; see *Re County Council Elections* (1889) 53 JP 263, where costs were refused; cf *Re Pembroke CC Case, Re Ramsgate Election, ex p Hobbs* (1889) 5 TLR 272, where costs were granted. See also *Re County Councillors' Elections, Keatinge and Wynn's Case* (1889) 5 TLR 195, cited in the second paragraph of the note "Such notice of the application . . . as seems fit" above.

Appeal to Court of Appeal. The Court of Appeal will be prepared to reverse a Divisional Court's decision on an application under this section if facts are brought before it which arose subsequently to the hearing in the Divisional Court (*Ex p Thomas* (1889) 60 LT 728) or which were not available to the Divisional Court (*Ex p Birtwhistle* (1889) 5 TLR 321, CA), or where there are conflicting decisions of Divisional Courts (*Ex p Walker* (1889) 22 QBD 384, 58 LJQB 190, CA).

Parish and community elections; municipal elections in City of London. See the notes to s 67 ante.

European Assembly elections. See the note to s 166 ante.

Definitions. For "parliamentary election petition", see s 120 ante; for "election" and "election court", see s 202(1) post.

Judicature (Northern Ireland) Act 1978, s 108. See Vol 31, title Northern Ireland (Pt 2).

Prosecutions for corrupt or illegal practices

168 Prosecutions for corrupt practices

[(1) A person who is guilty of a corrupt practice shall be liable—

(*a*) on conviction on indictment—

(i) in the case of a corrupt practice under section 60 above, to imprisonment for a term not exceeding two years, or to a fine, or to both,

(ii) in any other case, to imprisonment for a term not exceeding one year, or to a fine, or to both;

(*b*) on summary conviction, to imprisonment for a term not exceeding 6 months, or to a fine not exceeding the statutory maximum, or to both.]

(5), (6) . . .

(7) If it appears to the court by which any person holding a licence or certificate under the Licensing Acts is convicted of the offence of bribery or treating that the offence was committed on his licensed premises—

(*a*) the court shall direct the conviction to be entered in the proper register of licences, and

(*b*) the entry shall be taken into consideration by the licensing authority in determining whether they will or will not grant a renewal of the licence or certificate, and may be a ground, if the authority think fit, for refusing its renewal.

NOTES

Sub-s (7) contains provisions formerly in the Representation of the People Act 1949, s 146(6).

Sub-s (1) was substituted for the original sub-ss (1)–(4) by the Representation of the People Act 1985, s 23, Sch 3, para 8, as from 1 October 1985, and sub-ss (5), (6) were repealed by ss 24, 28(1) of, and Sch 4, para 57, Sch 5 to, that Act, as from that date.

Corrupt practice. For the offences constituting corrupt practices, see s 60 ante (personation), s 75(5) ante (expenses not authorised by election agent), s 82(6) ante (false declaration of expenses), ss 113–115 ante (bribery, treating and undue influence), and Sch 4, para 5 post (false declaration of expenses at certain local elections in England and Wales).

Shall be liable, etc; Conviction on indictment; fine. See the notes to s 65 ante.

Summary conviction. See the note to s 62 ante.

The court. Ie the election court; for meaning, see s 202(1) post.

Sub-s (7): Licence or certificate under the Licensing Acts; licensed premises; licensing authority. See the notes to s 163 ante.

Bribery or treating. As to these offences, see ss 113 and 114 ante.

Proper register of licences. This is the register kept under the Licensing Act 1964, s 30, Vol 24, title Licensing and Liquor Duties. Entry in that register of a conviction of bribery and treating in pursuance of sub-s (7) above is a ground for refusing the renewal or transfer of an old on-licence; see s 12(2) of that Act in the same title.

Related provisions. A person charged with a corrupt practice may under s 170 post be found guilty of an illegal practice. The time limit for prosecutions is fixed by s 176 post, and provisions as to venue in certain cases are contained in ss 177 and 178 post. For the criminal liability of members of associations or bodies of persons, where the offence is committed by that association or body, see s 179 post. For the duties of the Director of Public Prosecutions in relation to any offence under this Act, see s 181(1) post. As to evidence by certificate of the returning officer, see s 180 post. See also the note "Corrupt practice" to s 60 ante.

Welsh Sunday polls. This section and ss 169, 170 and 173 post, so far as they relate to specified offences prosecuted on indictment or in a magistrates' court, apply to a poll under the Licensing Act 1964, s 66 (Sunday closing in Wales), Vol 24, title Licensing and Liquor Duties, as if it were a poll at an ordinary election of district councillors; see s 67(5)(d) of the 1964 Act. See also, as to ss 169 and 173 post, s 67(6) of that Act.

Parish and community elections; municipal elections in City of London. See the notes to s 67 ante.

European Assembly elections. See the note to s 166 ante.

Definitions. For "Licensing Acts", see s 185 post; for "person" and "statutory maximum", see s 202(1) post.

169 Prosecutions for illegal practices

A person guilty of an illegal practice shall on summary conviction . . . be [liable to a fine not exceeding level 5 on the standard scale; and] on a prosecution for an illegal practice it shall be sufficient to allege that the person charged was guilty of an illegal practice.

NOTES

This section, as originally enacted, contained provisions formerly in the Representation of the People Act 1949, s 147, as affected by the Criminal Justice Act 1982, ss 37(1), (2), 38(1), (6), (8), 46(1).

The words omitted were repealed by the Representation of the People Act 1985, s 28(1), Sch 5, as from 1 October 1985, and those in square brackets were substituted by s 23 of, and Sch 3, para 9 to, that Act, as from that date.

Illegal practice. For the offences constituting illegal practices, see s 61(7) ante (voting offences); s 75(5) ante (failure to deliver or send declaration or return of expenses required to be authorised by election agent); s 78(3) ante (payment of claims); s 84 ante (failure to make return and declaration of expenses); s 90(2) ante (incurring expense at certain local elections); s 92(2) ante (broadcasting from outside United Kingdom); s 93 ante (broadcasting in United Kingdom); s 94 ante (use of imitation poll cards); s 97(1) ante (disturbances at meetings); s 102 ante (payments for conveyance of voters); s 106(1) ante (making false statements as to candidates); s 109(2) ante (payment for exhibition of election notices); s 110(3) ante (use of literature without printer's imprint); s 175(2) post (illegal payment, employment or hiring); s 189(1) post (voting at certain local elections when barred); and Sch 4, para 5 post (failure to make return and declaration of expenses at certain local elections in England and Wales).

Summary conviction. See the note to s 62 ante.

Related provisions. Under s 170 post, a person charged with an illegal practice may be found guilty of that offence notwithstanding that the act concerned amounted to a corrupt practice. The time limit for prosecutions is fixed by s 176 post, and provisions as to venue in certain cases are contained in ss 177 and 178 post. A prosecution may be barred by the allowance of an authorised excuse under s 86 or an exception under s 167 ante. For the criminal liability of members of associations or bodies of persons where the offence is committed by that association or body, see s 179 post. For the duties of the Director of Public Prosecutions in relation to offences under this Act, see s 181(1) post. As to evidence by certificate of the returning officer, see s 180 post. See also the note "Illegal practice" to s 61 ante.

Welsh Sunday polls. See the note to s 168 ante.

Parish and community elections; municipal elections in City of London. See the notes to s 67 ante.

European Assembly elections. See the note to s 166 ante.

Definitions. For "person" and "standard scale", see s 202(1) post.

170 Conviction of illegal practice on charge of corrupt practice etc

A person charged with a corrupt practice may, if the circumstances warrant such finding, be found guilty of an illegal practice (which offence shall for that purpose be an indictable offence), and a person charged with an illegal practice may be found guilty of that offence notwithstanding that the act constituting the offence amounted to a corrupt practice.

NOTES

This section contains provisions formerly in the Representation of the People Act 1949, s 148.
Person. For meaning, see s 202(1) post.
Corrupt practice. See the note to s 168 ante.
Indictable offence. For meaning, see the Interpretation Act 1978, s 5, Sch 1, Vol 41, title Statutes.
Illegal practice. See the notes to s 169 ante.
Welsh Sunday polls. See the note to s 168 ante.
Parish and community elections; municipal elections in City of London. See the notes to s 67 ante.
European Assembly elections. See the note to s 166 ante.

171, 172   *(Repealed by the Representation of the People Act 1985, ss 24, 28(1), Sch 4, paras 58, 59, Sch 5, as from 1 October 1985.)*

173 Incapacities on conviction of corrupt or illegal practice

Subject to the provisions of section 174 below, but in addition to any punishment as provided by the above provisions—

  (a) a person convicted of a corrupt practice . . . shall be subject to the incapacities imposed by section 160(4) above as if at the date of the conviction he had been reported personally guilty of that corrupt practice; and
  (b) a person convicted of an illegal practice shall be subject to the incapacities imposed by section 160(5) as if at the date of the conviction he had been reported personally guilty of that illegal practice.

NOTES

This section contains provisions formerly in the Representation of the People Act 1949, s 151, as partly repealed by the Criminal Law Act 1967, s 10, Sch 3, Pt III.
The words omitted from para (a) were repealed by the Representation of the People Act 1985, ss 24, 28(1), Sch 4, para 60, Sch 5, as from 1 October 1985.
Subject to . . . s 174. This section should be read subject also to ss 61(7)(a) and 92(2) ante.
Punishment as provided by the above provisions. See, in particular, ss 168 and 169 ante.
Corrupt practice; Welsh Sunday polls. See the notes to s 168 ante.
Illegal practice. See the note to s 169 ante.
Parish and community elections; municipal elections in City of London. See the notes to s 67 ante.
European Assembly elections. See the note to s 166 ante.

Mitigation and remission of incapacities

174 Mitigation and remission etc

  (1) Where—
  (a) any person is subject to any incapacity by virtue of the report of an election court, and
  (b) he or some other person in respect of whose acts the incapacity was imposed is on a prosecution acquitted of any of the matters in respect of which the incapacity was imposed,

the court may order that the incapacity shall thenceforth cease so far as it is imposed in respect of those matters.

(2) Where any person who is subject to any incapacity as mentioned above is on a prosecution convicted of any such matters as are mentioned above, no further incapacity shall be taken to be imposed by reason of the conviction, and the court shall have the like power (if any) to mitigate or remit for the future the incapacity so far as it is imposed by section 160 above in respect of the matters of which he is convicted, as if the incapacity had been imposed by reason of the conviction.

(3) A court exercising any of the powers conferred by subsections (1) and (2) above shall make an order declaring how far, if at all, the incapacities imposed by virtue of the relevant report remain unaffected by the exercise of that power, and that order shall be conclusive for all purposes.

(4) Where a person convicted of a corrupt or illegal practice is subsequently reported to have been guilty of that practice by an election court, no further incapacity shall be imposed on him under section 160 by reason of the report.

(5) Where any person is subject to any incapacity by virtue of a conviction or of the report of an election court, and any witness who gave evidence against that person upon the proceeding for the conviction or report is convicted of perjury in respect of that evidence, the incapacited person may apply to the High Court, and the court, if satisfied that the conviction or report so far as respects that person was based upon perjury, may order that the incapacity shall thenceforth cease.

(6) Except in Scotland, the jurisdiction vested in the High Court by subsection (5) above in matters relating to parliamentary elections shall, subject to rules of court, be exercised—

(a) by one of the judges for the time being on the rota for the trial of parliamentary election petitions,

(b) in Northern Ireland, by one of the judges of the High Court or the Court of Appeal for the time being selected under section 108 of the Judicature (Northern Ireland) Act 1978,

either in court or at chambers, or by a master of the Supreme Court in manner directed by and subject to an appeal to those judges.

NOTES

This section contains provisions formerly in the Representation of the People Act 1949, s 152, as partly repealed, in the case of s 152(1) and (6), by the Representation of the People Act 1969, s 24(4), Sch 3, Pt I and, as amended, in the case of s 152(6), by the Judicature (Northern Ireland) Act 1978, s 122(1), Sch 5, Pt II.

Sub-s (1): Subject to any incapacity by virtue of the report of an election court. The incapacities in question are those specified in ss 159(2), (3) and 160(4), (5) ante.

Prosecution. Ie a prosecution under s 168 or 169 ante.

Sub-s (2): Like power (if any) to mitigate or remit, etc. It is thought that this refers to powers such as those conferred by ss 61(7)(a) and 92(2) ante.

Sub-s (4): Corrupt or illegal practice. See the notes "Corrupt practice" to s 168 ante, and "Illegal practice" to s 169 ante.

Reported . . . by an election court. Ie under s 144 or 145 ante, in conjunction with s 160(1) ante.

Sub-s (5): Subject to any incapacity by virtue of a conviction or of the report of an election court. The incapacities in question are those specified in s 159(2), (3) and 160(4), (5) ante, and in s 160(4) as applied by s 173 ante.

Perjury. As to this offence, see the Perjury Act 1911, s 1, Vol 12, title Criminal Law.

High Court. See the notes to ss 39 and 120 ante; and note sub-s (6) above.

Sub-s (6): Parliamentary elections. See the note "Parliamentary election" to s 1 ante.

Rules of court. As to such rules, see s 182 post and the notes thereto.

Rota. See the note to s 167 ante.

Parish and community elections; municipal elections in City of London. See the notes to s 67 ante.

European Assembly elections. See the note to s 166 ante.

Definitions. For "parliamentary election petition", see s 120 ante; for "election court", see s 202(1) post.

Judicature (Northern Ireland) Act 1978, s 108. See Vol 31, title Northern Ireland (Pt 2).

Illegal payments, employments or hirings

175 Illegal payments etc

(1) A person guilty of an offence of illegal payment, employment or hiring shall, on summary conviction, be [liable to a fine not exceeding level 5 on the standard scale; and] on a prosecution for such an offence it shall be sufficient to allege that the person charged was guilty of an illegal payment, employment or hiring as the case may be.

(2) A candidate or election agent who is personally guilty of an offence of illegal payment, employment or hiring shall be guilty of an illegal practice, and if an offence of illegal payment, employment or hiring is committed with the candidate's knowledge and consent at an election where candidates are not required to have election agents, the candidate shall be guilty of an illegal practice.

(3) Any person charged with an offence of illegal payment, employment or hiring may be found guilty of that offence, notwithstanding that the act constituting the offence amounted to a corrupt or illegal practice.

NOTES

This section contains provisions formerly in the Representation of the People Act 1949, s 153, as affected, in the case of s 153(1), by the Criminal Justice Act 1982, ss 37(1), (2), 38(1), (6), (8), 46(1).

The words in square brackets in sub-s (1) were substituted by the Representation of the People Act 1985, s 23, Sch 3, para 10, as from 1 October 1985.

Illegal payment, employment or hiring. For the provisions creating the offence of illegal payment, see ss 107 and 112 ante; for the offence of illegal employment, see s 111 ante; and for the offences of illegal hiring, see ss 101 and 108 ante.

Summary conviction. See the note to s 62 ante.

Election agent. As to the appointment of election agents, see s 67 ante and the notes thereto.

Illegal practice. See the note to s 61 ante.

Knowledge. See the note "Knows" to s 60 ante.

Consent. See the note to s 75 ante.

Election where candidates are not required to have election agents. For these elections, see s 71 ante.

Corrupt or illegal practice. For the offences constituting corrupt practices, see the note "Corrupt practice" to s 168 ante, and for those constituting illegal practices, see the note "Illegal practice" to s 169 ante.

Further provisions. The time limit for prosecutions is fixed by s 176 post, and provisions as to venue in certain cases are contained in ss 177, 178 post. A prosecution may be barred by the allowance of an exception under s 167 ante. For the criminal liability of members of associations or bodies of persons where the offence is committed by that association or body, see s 179 post. For the duties of the Director of Public Prosecutions in relation to charges of illegal practice, see s 181(1) post. As to evidence by certificate of the returning officer, see s 180 post.

Parish and community elections; municipal elections in City of London. See the notes to s 67 ante.

European Assembly elections. See the note to s 166 ante.

Definitions. For "candidate" see, by virtue of s 185 post, s 118 ante; for "election", "person" and "standard scale", see s 202(1) post.

General provisions as to prosecutions

176 Time limit for prosecutions

(1) A proceeding against a person in respect of [any offence under any provision contained in or made under this Act] shall be commenced within one year after the offence was committed, and the time so limited by this section shall, in the case of any proceedings under the Magistrates' Courts Act 1980 (or, in Northern Ireland, the Magistrates' Courts (Northern Ireland) Order 1981) for any such offence ... be substituted for any limitation of time contained in that Act or Order.

[(2) For the purposes of this section—

    (*a*) in England and Wales, the laying of an information;

    (*b*) (*applies to Scotland only*); and

    (*c*) in Northern Ireland, the making of a complaint,

shall be deemed to be the commencement of a proceeding.]

  (3) . . .

NOTES

This section, as originally enacted, contained provisions formerly in the Representation of the People Act 1949, s 154, as partly repealed, in the case of s 154(1), by the Representation of the People Act 1969, s 24(4), Sch 3, Pt I.

The words in square brackets in sub-s (1) were substituted and sub-s (2) was substituted by the Representation of the People Act 1985, s 24, Sch 4, para 61(*a*), (*b*), and the words omitted from sub-s (1), and the whole of sub-s (3), were repealed by ss 24, 28(1) of, and Sch 4, para 61(*c*), Sch 5 to that Act.

Person. For meaning, see s 202(1) post.

Within one year after, etc. As to the computation of time, see, by virtue of s 186 post, s 119 ante. Note also sub-s (2) above and see also the note "Within six months . . ." to s 5 ante.

Parish and community elections; municipal elections in City of London. See the notes to s 67 ante.

European Assembly elections. See the note to s 166 ante.

Magistrates' Courts Act 1980. For the limitation of time, see s 127 of that Act, Vol 27, title Magistrates.

Magistrates' Courts (Northern Ireland) Order 1981. SI 1981/1675.

177 Local election offence punishable summarily

A prosecution for any offence punishable summarily committed in reference to an election under the local government Act—

    (*a*) may be instituted before any magistrates' court in the county in which the local government area for which the election was held is situated or which it adjoins; and

    (*b*) the offence shall be deemed for all purposes to have been committed within the jurisdiction of that court.

This section does not apply in Scotland.

NOTES

This section contains provisions formerly in the Representation of the People Act 1949, s 159(5), as partly repealed by the Representation of the People Act 1969, s 21(2).

Election under the local government Act. See the note to s 202 post.

County. See the note to s 22 ante.

Parish and community elections; municipal elections in City of London. See the notes to s 67 ante.

Definitions. For "local government Act" and "local government area", see s 202(1) post.

[178 Prosecution of offences committed outside the United Kingdom

Proceedings in respect of an offence under this Act alleged to have been committed outside the United Kingdom by a Commonwealth citizen or citizen of the Republic of Ireland may be taken, and the offence may for all incidental purposes be treated as having been committed, in any place in the United Kingdom.]

NOTES

This section was substituted by the Representation of the People Act 1985, s 24, Sch 4, para 62, as from 1 October 1985.

Offence . . . alleged to have been committed outside the United Kingdom. It is not clear to what extent this Act has extra-territorial operation though s 92 ante, in particular, has effect outside the United Kingdom. The Representation of the People Act 1918, s 38 (repealed), declared that "where any person commits out of the United Kingdom any act which if that act had been committed in the United Kingdom would have rendered that person liable to prosecution and punishment under the Ballot Act 1872 or the Corrupt and Illegal Practices Prevention Act 1883 (as amended by any subsequent Act), or under this Act, that person shall be liable to be proceeded against and punished as though the act had been committed in the United Kingdom at any place where that person may for the time being be". This section, however, contains no express provision corresponding to that repealed section stating what acts done outside the United Kingdom constitute offences against the Act. See also the note "United Kingdom" to s 6 ante.

Commonwealth citizen; Republic of Ireland. See the notes to s 1 ante.

Parish and community elections; municipal elections in City of London. See the notes to s 67 ante.

European Assembly elections. See the note to s 166 ante; and see further the European Assembly Elections Act 1978, s 4(2) ante.

179 Offences by associations

Where—

(a) any corrupt or illegal practice or any illegal payment, employment or hiring, or

(b) any offence under section 110 above,

is committed by any association or body of persons, corporate or unincorporate, the members of the association or body who have taken part in the commission of the offence shall be liable to any fine or punishment imposed for that offence by this Act.

NOTES

This section contains provisions formerly in the Representation of the People Act 1949, s 156.

Corrupt or illegal practice. See the notes "Corrupt practice" to s 168 ante, and "Illegal practice" to s 169 ante.

Illegal payment, employment or hiring. See the note to s 175 ante.

Members of the association or body who have taken part, etc. For provisions relating to the prosecution of officers of associations or bodies for certain offences, see ss 75(6) and 92(3) ante.

Parish and community elections; municipal elections in City of London. See the notes to s 67 ante.

European Assembly elections. See the note to s 166 ante.

180 Evidence by certificate of holding of elections

On—

(a) any prosecution for a corrupt or illegal practice or for any illegal payment, employment or hiring, and

(b) any proceedings for a penalty under section 85 above or paragraph 4 of Schedule 4 to this Act,

the certificate of the returning officer at an election—

(i) that the election mentioned in the certificate was duly held, and

(ii) that the person named in the certificate was a candidate at the election,

shall be sufficient evidence of the facts stated in it.

NOTES

This section contains provisions formerly in the Representation of the People Act 1949, s 158.

Corrupt or illegal practice. See the notes "Corrupt practice" to s 168 ante, and "Illegal practice" to s 169 ante.

Illegal payment, employment or hiring. See the note to s 175 ante.

Returning officer. As to returning officers, see ss 24, 26–28 and 35 ante.

Proof of election. The court has taken judicial notice of the holding of a general parliamentary election (*Coventry Case, Berry v Eaton and Hill* (1869) 20 LT 405 at 406).

Parish and community elections; municipal elections in City of London. See the notes to s 67 ante.

European Assembly elections. See the note to s 166 ante.

Definitions. For "candidate", see, by virtue of s 185 post, s 118 ante; for "election", see s 202(1) post.

181 Director of Public Prosecutions

(1) Where information is given to the Director of Public Prosecutions that any [offence under this Act has been committed], it is his duty to make such inquiries and institute such prosecutions as the circumstances of the case appear to him to require.

(2) The Director by himself or by his assistant or by his representative appointed under subsection (3) below [may and, if the election court so requests him, shall] attend the trial of every election petition.

(3) The Director may nominate . . . a barrister or solicitor . . . to be his representative for the purposes of this Part of this Act . . .

(4) The Director in performing any duty under this Act shall act in accordance with regulations under the Prosecution of Offences Act 1979, and subject to them in accordance with the directions (if any) given to him by the Attorney General; and any assistant or representative of the Director in performing any duty under this Part shall act in accordance with those regulations and directions (if any) and with the directions given to him by the Director.

(5) There shall be allowed to the Director and his assistant or representative for the purposes of this Part (other than his general duties under subsection (1) above) such allowances for expenses as the Treasury may approve.

(6) The costs incurred in defraying the expenses of the Director incurred for those purposes (including the remuneration of his representative) shall, in the first instance, be paid by the Treasury, and . . . shall be deemed to be expenses of the election court; but if for any reasonable cause it seems just to the court so to do, the court shall order all or part of those costs to be repaid to the Treasury by the parties to the petition, or such of them as the court may direct.

(7) (*Applies to Scotland only.*)

(8) In the application of this section to Northern Ireland, the reference to the Prosecution of Offences Act 1979 does not apply.

NOTES

Sub-ss (1)–(6), (8), as originally enacted, contained provisions formerly in the Representation of the People Act 1949, s 159(1)–(4), (6), (7), (9), respectively, as amended, in the case of s 159(4) and (9), by the Prosecution of Offences Act 1979, s 11(1), Sch 1.

The words in square brackets in sub-ss (1), (2) were substituted, and the words omitted from sub-ss (3), (6) were repealed, by the Representation of the People Act 1985, ss 24, 28(1), Sch 4, para 63, Sch 5, as from 1 October 1985.

Sub-s (1): Director of Public Prosecutions. See the note to s 148 ante.

Prosecutions. As to prosecutions for corrupt and illegal practices, see ss 168 and 169 ante.

Sub-s (2): Trial. As to the trial of election petitions, see s 139 ante.

Sub-s (3): This Part of this Act. Ie Pt III (ss 120–186).

Sub-s (4): Duty under this Act. For particular duties of the Director under this Act see, in addition to sub-ss (1) and (2) above, ss 140(6), 148(4) ante.

Sub-s (5): Treasury. See the note to s 29 ante.

Sub-s (6): For any reasonable cause . . . the court shall order . . . those costs to be repaid, etc. For the circumstances in which an order will or will not be made for payment of the Director's costs by a party to the petition, see *Norwich Case, Birkbeck v Bullard* (1886) 54 LT 625 (order refused); *Lambeth, Kennington Division, Case, Crossman v Davis* (1886) 54 LT 628 (petition dismissed as utterly unfounded and petitioner ordered for that reason to pay Director's costs); *Devonport Case, Pascoe v Puleston* (1886) 54 LT 733 (leave to withdraw petition granted; court held that it had no jurisdiction to order payment as there had been no trial of the petition) (followed in *Re Lichfield Case* (1892) 9 TLR 92); *Northumberland, Hexham Division, Case, Hudspeth and Lyal v Clayton* (1892) 4 O'M & H 143 (respondent ordered to pay costs where his conduct and that of his agent had rendered them necessary); *Worcester Borough Case, Glaszard and Turner v Allsopp* (1892) 4 O'M & H 153 (costs allowed); *Islington, West Division Case, Medhurst v Lough and Gasquet* (1901) 17 TLR

230 (costs refused; reasons not given in the report); *Monmouth Boroughs Case, Embrey and Sweeting v Harris* (1901) 5 O'M & H 166 (costs refused); *Cheltenham Case* (1911) 6 O'M & H 227 (costs refused); *West Bromwich Case, Hazel v Viscount Lewisham* (1911) 6 O'M & H 256 (costs refused). Decisions on the question of costs for the Director are not as a general rule fully reported, though it may be because the court assigned no reasons. The general principle is that costs will be refused as a matter of course unless a good case for granting them be made out, and the mere fact that the Director is under a statutory obligation to attend the trial in person or by a representative is not regarded as establishing any claim to costs on his part.

As to costs generally, see s 183 post.

Parish and community elections; municipal elections in City of London. See the notes to s 67 ante.

European Assembly elections. See the note to s 166 ante.

Definitions. For "costs", see s 185 post; for "election", "election court" and "election petition", see s 202(1) post.

Prosecution of Offences Act 1979. See Vol 12, title Criminal Law. As to the making of regulations, see s 9 of that Act (repealed by the Prosecution of Offences Act 1985, s 31(6), Sch 2, as from a day to be appointed under s 31(2) thereof, and re-enacted in s 29 of that Act, Vol 12, title Criminal Law).

Supplemental

182 Rules of procedure

(1) The authority having for the time being power to make rules of court for the Supreme Court may make rules for the purposes of Part II and this Part of this Act.

(2) In relation to the power conferred by subsection (1) above to make rules—

(*a*) that power shall be exercisable by statutory instrument, and be treated for the purposes of the Statutory Instruments Act 1946 as if conferred on a Minister of the Crown; and

(*b*) a statutory instrument containing rules under subsection (1) shall be subject to annulment in pursuance of a resolution of either House of Parliament.

(3) (*Applies to Scotland only.*)

(4) This section does not apply to Northern Ireland.

NOTES

Sub-ss (1), (2) contain provisions formerly in the Representation of the People Act 1949, s 160(1), (2).

Authority having ... power to make rules of court. Ie the Supreme Court Rule Committee constituted under the Supreme Court Act 1981, s 85, Vol 11, title Courts.

Part II. Ie ss 67–119 ante.

This Part. Ie Pt III (ss 120–186).

Statutory instrument; subject to annulment. See the note to s 36 ante.

Parish and community elections; municipal elections in City of London. See the notes to s 67 ante.

European Assembly elections. See the note to s 166 ante.

Statutory Instruments Act 1946. See Vol 41, title Statutes.

Rules under this section. Up to 1 August 1985 no rules had been made under this section but by virtue of the Interpretation Act 1978, s 17(2)(*b*), Vol 41, title Statutes, the Election Petition Rules 1960, SI 1960/543, as amended by SI 1979/543, SI 1985/1278, have effect as if so made. Those rules are applied by the Greater London (Elections) Order 1964, SI 1964/346 (made under the London Government Act 1963, s 84, Vol 26, title London). In addition the European Assembly Election Petition Rules 1979, SI 1979/521, have effect as if made under this section as applied to elections to the European Assembly (see the note "European Assembly elections" to s 166 ante). See also, as to the exercise of the jurisdiction of the High Court under the Representation of the People Acts, RSC Ord 94, r 5; and note s 157(2) ante as to the principles, practice and rules which are to be observed by the High Court and election courts in the case of election petitions.

Northern Ireland. In relation to Northern Ireland the corresponding power to make rules is that contained in the Judicature (Northern Ireland) Act 1978, s 55, Vol 31, title Northern Ireland (Pt 2); cf the definition of "prescribed" in s 185 post.

183 Costs

(1) The rules of the Supreme Court with respect to costs to be allowed in actions, causes and matters in the High Court shall in principle and so far as practicable apply to the costs of petition and other proceedings under Part II or this Part of this Act, and the taxing officer shall not allow any costs higher than would be allowed in any action, cause or matter in the High Court on a common fund basis.

(2) Where any costs or other sums are, under the order of an election court or otherwise under this Part, to be paid by any person, those costs or sums shall be due from that person to the person or persons to whom they are to be paid and, if payable to the Treasury, shall be a debt due to Her Majesty and in either case may be recovered accordingly.

(3) (*Applies to Scotland only.*)

NOTES

This section contains provisions formerly in the Representation of the People Act 1949, s 161.
Rules ... with respect to costs. The rules referred to are in RSC Ord 62.
High Court. See the note to s 39 ante.
Part II. Ie ss 67–119 ante.
This Part. Ie Pt III (ss 120–186).
Common fund basis. As to the common fund basis for taxation of costs, see RSC Ord 62, r 28(4).
Order of an election court. As to orders made by an election court concerning costs, see s 154 ante.
Treasury. See the note to s 29 ante.
Debt due to Her Majesty. As to civil proceedings by the Crown in the High Court or county court to recover Crown debts, see the Crown Proceedings Act 1947, ss 13, 15, Vol 13, title Crown Proceedings. As to execution by the Crown, see s 26 of that Act, in the same title.
Parish and community elections; municipal elections in City of London. See the notes to s 67 ante.
European Assembly elections. See the note to s 166 ante.
Definitions. For "costs", see s 185 post, for "election court" and "person", see s 202(1) post.

184 Service of notices

(1) Any summons, notice or document required to be served on any person with reference to any proceeding respecting an election for the purpose of causing him to appear before the High Court, the county court, or any election court, or otherwise or of giving him an opportunity of making a statement, or showing cause, or being heard by himself before any court for any purpose of this Part of this Act may be served—

(a) by delivering it to that person, or by leaving it at, or sending it by post by a registered letter or by the recorded delivery service, to his last known place of abode in the constituency or, as the case may be, the area of the authority for which the election was held; or

(b) if the proceeding is before any court in such other manner as the court may direct.

(2) In proving service by post under this section it shall be sufficient to prove that the letter was prepaid, properly addressed, and registered or recorded with the Post Office.

NOTES

This section contains provisions formerly in the Representation of the People Act 1949, s 162, as affected by the Recorded Delivery Service Act 1962, s 1, Schedule, and as amended, in the case of s 162(2), by the Post Office Act 1969, s 76, Sch 4, Pt II, para 47(2).
Summons. This section does not apply to the summoning of witnesses under s 140(1) ante.
Causing him to appear; showing cause. Eg under s 87(1) or 156(5) ante.
High Court. See the note to s 39 ante.
County court. See the note to s 30 ante.
Being heard by himself. This covers a proceeding referred to in s 160(1) ante.
This Part of this Act. Ie Pt III (ss 120–186).

May be served. It is thought that service by post otherwise than by registered post or recorded delivery will be insufficient, but subject to this, as sub-s (1) is permissive only it is clear that where a notice is served in a different manner and is received this contitutes good service; see *Sharpley v Manby* [1942] 1 KB 217, sub nom *Re Sharpley's and Manby's Arbitration* [1942] 1 All ER 66, CA, and *Stylo Shoes Ltd v Prices Tailors Ltd* [1960] Ch 396, [1959] 3 All ER 901. See also RSC Ord 65, r 5, and the notes thereto in the Supreme Court Practice.

Last known place of abode. Though as a general rule an address which the person concerned is known to have left is not a proper address for service (*White v Weston* [1968] 2 QB 647, [1968] 2 All ER 842, CA) the position is otherwise where the use of the last known address is expressly authorised (*Re Follick, ex p Trustee* [1907] 97 LT 645). For other relevant cases, see *Hanrott's Trustees v Evans* (1887) 4 TLR 128; *R v Farmer* [1892] 1 QB 637, [1891–4] All ER Rep 921, CA; *R v Webb* [1896] 1 QB 487; *Berry v Farrow* [1914] 1 KB 632; *Stylo Shoes Ltd v Prices Tailors Ltd* [1960] Ch 396, [1959] 3 All ER 901; and *McGlynn v Stewart* 1974 SLT 230.

Constituency. See the note to s 1 ante.

In proving service, etc. Sub-s (2) above appears to exclude the operation of the Interpretation Act 1978, s 7, Vol 41, title Statutes.

Parish and community elections; municipal elections in City of London. See the notes to s 67 ante.

European Assembly elections. See the note to s 166 ante.

Definitions. For "election", "election court" and "person", see s 202(1) post.

185 Interpretation of Part III

In this Part of this Act, unless the context otherwise requires—

"appropriate officer" has the same meaning as in section 67(7) above;

"candidate" has the same meaning as in Part II of this Act and the saving in section 117(1) above applies in relation to this Part as in relation to Part II;

"costs" includes charges and expenses;

"date of the allowance of an authorised excuse" has the meaning assigned to it by section 86(8) above or paragraph 7 of Schedule 4 to this Act, as the case may be;

"declaration as to election expenses" means a declaration made under section 82 above or, as the case may be, paragraph 3 of Schedule 4 to this Act;

"judicial office" includes the office of justice of the peace;

"Licensing Acts" means the Licensing Act 1964 and the Acts amending that Act, or the corresponding enactments forming part of the law of Scotland or Northern Ireland;

"money" and "pecuniary reward" shall be deemed to include—

(a) any office, place or employment, and

(b) any valuable security or other equivalent of money, and

(c) any valuable consideration,

and expressions referring to money shall be construed accordingly;

"payment" includes any pecuniary or other reward;

"prescribed" means prescribed by rules of court, or, in Northern Ireland, such rules under section 55 of the Judicature (Northern Ireland) Act 1978;

"public office" means any office—

(a) under the Crown, or

(b) under the charter of a city or borough, or

(c) under the Acts relating to local government or public health or public education,

whether the office is that—

(i) of mayor, provost, chief magistrate, chairman, alderman, councillor, member of a board, commission or other local authority in any local government or other area; or

(ii) of proper officer or other officer under a council, board, commission or other authority; or

(iii) of any other office to which a person is elected or appointed under any such charter or enactment as is mentioned above, including any other municipal or parochial office;

"return as to election expenses" means a return made under section 81 above or, as the case may be, paragraph 3 of Schedule 4 to this Act;

"Speaker" includes Deputy Speaker and, where the office of Speaker is vacant, Clerk of the House of Commons, or any other officer for the time being performing the duties of Clerk of the House of Commons.

NOTES

This section contains provisions formerly in the Representation of the People Act 1949, s 163, as partly repealed by the Courts Act 1971, s 56(4), Sch 11, Pt IV, as affected by the Local Government Act 1972, s 251(1), Sch 29, para 4(1), and as amended by the Judicature (Northern Ireland) Act 1978, s 122(1), Sch 5, Pt II.

This Part of this Act. Ie Pt III (ss 120–186).

Candidate. For the meaning of this expression in Pt II of this Act, see s 118 ante.

Rules of court. Ie rules of court under s 182 ante.

Parish and community elections; municipal elections in City of London. See the notes to s 67 ante.

European Assembly elections. See the note to s 166 ante.

Definitions. For "proper officer", see s 202(1) post; for "local government area", see s 203(1) post.

Licensing Act 1964. See Vol 24, title Licensing and Liquor Duties.

Judicature (Northern Ireland) Act 1978, s 55. See Vol 31, title Northern Ireland (Pt 2).

186 Computation of time for purposes of Part III

Section 119 above applies in computing any period of time for the purposes of this Part of this Act as for the purposes of Part II of this Act.

NOTES

This section contains provisions formerly in the Representation of the People Act 1949, s 164.

This Part. Ie ss 120–186.

Part II. Ie ss 67–119.

Parish and community elections; municipal elections in City of London. See the notes to s 67 ante.

European Assembly elections. See the note to s 166 ante.

PART IV

SPECIAL PROVISIONS AS TO OTHER LOCAL ELECTIONS

England and Wales, and Scotland

187 Application of Act to certain local elections

(1) The following provisions of this Act—

(*a*) in Part I, sections . . . 60 and 66,
(*b*) Parts II and III,
(*c*) in this Part, section 189,

so far as they apply to an election in England and Wales of—

(i) . . . parish or community councillors, or
(ii) the chairman of a . . . parish or community council or a parish meeting,

have effect subject to such adaptations, modifications and exceptions as may be made by rules under section 36 above, but nothing in this subsection affects the operation of section 96 or section 100 above.

(2) Sections 48(1) and (2) and [63] above have effect as if any reference in them to a local government election included a reference to any other election under the local government Act.

NOTES

Sub-s (1) contains provisions formerly in the Representation of the People Act 1949, s 165(1), as amended by the Local Government Act 1972, s 45, Sch 6, para 11. Sub-s (2) contains provisions formerly in s 54 of the 1949 Act.

The words omitted from sub-s (1) were repealed by the Representation of the People Act 1985, ss 24, 28(1), Sch 4, para 64(*a*), Sch 5, as from 1 October 1985, and the reference to "64" in sub-s (2) was substituted by s 24 of, and Sch 4, para 64(*b*) to, that Act, as from that date.

Parts II and III. Ie ss 67–119 (Pt II) and ss 120–186 (Pt III).

England; Wales. See the note to s 4 ante.

Such adaptations ... as may be made by rules under s 36. The only adaptations, etc, made as mentioned in sub-s (1) above are those made by—

(i) the Local Elections (Parishes and Communities) Rules 1973, SI 1973/1910, r 4, as amended by SI 1974/84 and SI 1983/1153; that rule provides that in the application of the provisions referred to in sub-s (1) above to an election of the chairman and councillors of a parish or community council for any reference to the proper officer of the authority there shall be substituted a reference to the returning officer and that in s 136(2)(*b*) ante, for the words "such amount not exceeding £500" there shall be substituted the words "an amount of £50 or such smaller amount or such larger amount not exceeding £300".

(ii) the Parish and Community Meetings (Polls) Rules 1973, SI 1973/1911, r 4, as amended by SI 1983/1151; that rule provides that in the application of the provisions referred to in sub-s (1) above, other than s 66 ante, to the election of a chairman of a parish meeting at a parish meeting the adaptations etc set out in that rule shall have effect. These adaptations (which also apply to a poll consequent on a parish or community meeting; see the note "Application of this Act to polls consequent on parish or community meetings" below) are as follows:

    (*a*) where the poll is to be taken on any question other than that of the election of the chairman of the parish meeting or of an appointment to any other office only the following of the aforesaid provisions apply, namely, ss 60, 113–115, 168, 173 (except para (*b*)), 176, 179–181 and 186 ante;

    (*b*) references to the proper officer of the authority for which the election was held are to be taken as references to the returning officer;

    (*c*) references to the authority for which the election was held are to be taken as references to the parish and references to the area thereof are to be construed accordingly except in s 130(6) ante, where the expression "the area of the authority for which the election was held" means the district (as defined in the Local Government Act 1972, s 270, Vol 25, title Local Government) in which the parish is situate;

    (*d*) in sections ss 60(2), 99(1) and 100(1) ante, for the expression "local government election" there is substituted the expression "election under the Local Government Act";

    (*e*) in s 136(2)(*b*) ante, for the words "such amount not exceeding £500" there are substituted the words "an amount of £50 or such smaller amount or such larger amount not exceeding £300";

    (*f*) references to an election under the Local Government Act are deemed to include a reference to the election of the chairman of a parish meeting at a parish meeting and to a poll consequent on a parish or community meeting.

Election under the local government Act. See the note to s 202 post.

Application of this Act to polls consequent on parish or community meetings. By the Local Government Act 1972, Sch 12, paras 18(5), 34(5), Vol 25, title Local Government, the enactments mentioned in sub-s (1) above apply in the case of a poll consequent on a parish or community meeting as if it were a poll for the election of parish or community councillors subject to any adaptations, alterations or exceptions made by rules made by the Secretary of State. The Parish and Community Meetings (Polls) Rules 1973, SI 1973/1911, r 4, as amended by SI 1983/1151, accordingly provides that in the application of the enactments mentioned in sub-s (1) above, other than s 66 ante, to a poll consequent on a parish or community meeting the adaptations set out in that rule shall have effect (these adaptations are reproduced in head (ii) of the note "Such adaptations ... as may be made by rules under s 36" above) and r 5 of those rules as so amended provides that in the application of s 66 ante, and the Local Elections (Parishes and Communities) Rules 1973, SI 1973/1910 (having effect under s 36 ante) to a poll consequent on a parish or community meeting adaptations etc shall be made so that they read as set out in the Schedule to SI 1973/1911 as amended by SI 1976/2067 and SI 1983/1151.

Isles of Scilly. See the note to s 8 ante.

Definitions. For "local government Act" and "local government election", see s 203(1) post.

188 (*Applies to Scotland only.*)

189 Voting offences at certain local elections

(1) If a person—

(a) votes, or induces or procures any person to vote, at an election under the local government Act which is not a local government election,

(b) knowing that he or that person is prohibited by any enactment from voting at that election,

he shall be guilty of an illegal practice.

(2) A candidate shall not be liable nor shall his election be avoided for any illegal practice under subsection (1) above committed without his knowledge or consent.

NOTES

This section contains provisions formerly in the Representation of the People Act 1949, s 168(1).

Procures. See the note "Aids, abets, counsels or procures" to s 60 ante.

Election under the local government Act; local government election. See the note "Election under the local government Act" to s 202 post.

Knowing; knowledge. See the note "Knows" to s 60 ante.

Prohibited ... from voting. For such prohibitions, see ss 160(5)(b) and 173(b) ante, and the Public Bodies Corrupt Practices Act 1889, s 2(d), Vol 12, title Criminal Law.

Illegal practice. See the note to s 61 ante.

Candidate. Cf the definition in s 118 ante.

Nor shall his election be avoided. As to the avoidance of the election of a candidate who has been reported guilty of an illegal practice, see s 159(1) ante.

Consent. See the note to s 75 ante.

Parish and community elections. This section applies to elections of the chairman of a parish or community council or parish meeting subject to any exceptions, modifications and adaptations made by rules under s 36 ante; see s 187(1) ante, and the rules noted thereto.

Municipal elections in the City of London. As to the application of this section to such elections, see s 191(1) post.

Definitions. For "person" and "vote", see s 202(1) post; for "local government Act" and "local government election", see s 203(1) post.

190 (*Repealed by the Representation of the People Act 1985, ss 24, 28(1), Sch 4, para 65, Sch 5, as from 1 October 1985.*)

The City

191 Municipal elections in the City

(1) For the purposes of—

(a) sections . . . 60 and 61 in Part I of this Act,

(b) the whole of Part II of this Act except sections 96 and 99,

(c) the whole of Part III of this Act,

(d) section 189 above and sections [193] to 198 below, and

(e) the whole of Part V of this Act,

"local government election" and "election under the local government Act" include a municipal election in the City (that is, an election to the office of mayor, alderman, common councilman or sheriff and also the election of any officer elected by the mayor, aldermen and liverymen in common hall),

"corporate office" includes each of those offices,

"local government area" includes the City,

"clerk of the authority" means in relation to the City, the town clerk of the City,

"electoral area" means in relation to a ward election, the ward, and in relation to any other municipal election in the City, the City.

In relation to municipal elections in the City those enactments have effect subject to the modifications mentioned in sections [193] to 196 below.

(2) Schedule 6 to this Act has effect as regards the operation of Part II (ward elections) of the City of London (Various Powers) Act 1957.

NOTES

Sub-s (1) contains provisions formerly in the Representation of the People Act 1949, s 167(1). Sub-s (2) contains provisions formerly in the Representation of the People Act 1969, s 23(1).

The word omitted from sub-s (1)(*a*) was repealed by the Representation of the People Act 1985, s 28(1), Sch 5, as from 1 October 1985, and the references to "193" in that subsection were substituted by s 24 of, and Sch 4, para 66 to, that Act, as from that date.

Part II; Part III; Part V. Ie ss 67–119 (Pt II), ss 120–186 (Pt III) and ss 199–207 (Pt V).

Local government election; local government Act; local government area; electoral area. For the general definitions of these expressions, see s 203(1) post.

City. Ie the City of London; see s 202(1) post.

Modifications mentioned in ss 193 to 196. See also ss 197 and 198 post.

Ward elections. By the City of London (Various Powers) Act 1957, s 8, Vol 26, title London, certain provisions of this Act, in addition to the provisions which apply by virtue of this section and ss 193–196 post, apply with modifications to ward elections in the City of London. See also s 197(1), (3) post.

City of London (Various Powers) Act 1957, Part II. See Vol 26, title London.

192 (*Repealed by the Representation of the People Act 1985, s 28(1), Sch 5, as from 1 October 1985.*)

193 Personation and other voting offences

In relation to municipal elections in the City—

    (*a*) in sections 60 and 61 above "vote" does not include voting otherwise than on a poll; and

    (*b*) in section 61(2), paragraph (*a*)(ii) does not apply.

NOTES

This section contains provisions formerly in the Representation of the People Act 1949, s 167(3).

Municipal elections in the City. As to the application of provisions of this Act to such elections, see s 191 ante and the notes thereto.

Definitions. For "municipal election in the City", see s 191(1) ante; for "the City" and "vote", see s 202(1) post.

194 Broadcasting

In relation to municipal elections in the City—

    (*a*) neither section 92 nor section 93 above apply by virtue of section 191 above to municipal elections in the City other than ward elections; and

    (*b*) for the purposes of section 93(1) a ward election shall be deemed to be pending during the period beginning—

        (i) in the case of an annual election three weeks before the day fixed for the election, and

        (ii) in other cases with the day on which the precept is issued,

        and ending in all cases with the day of the poll (or, if no poll is taken, with the day fixed for the election).

NOTES

This section contains provisions formerly in the Representation of the People Act 1969, s 9(6).

Municipal elections in the City. As to the application of provisions of this Act to such elections, see s 191 ante and the notes thereto.

Definitions. For "municipal election in the City", see s 191(1) ante; for "the City", see s 202(1) post.

195 Disturbances at meetings

In relation to municipal elections in the City—

(a) in section 97 above the reference to the day of election shall be taken as a reference to the day fixed for the election and (where a poll is taken) any day after that up to and including the day of the poll; but

(b) in relation to a meeting held with reference to an election other than an annual election that section does not apply to an offence committed on or before the day on which the precept is issued.

NOTES

This section contains provisions formerly in the Representation of the People Act 1969, s 167(6).

Municipal elections in the City. As to the application of provisions of this Act to such elections, see s 191 ante and the notes thereto.

Definitions. For "municipal election in the City", see s 191(1) ante; for "the City", see s 202(1) post.

196 Costs or expenses

In relation to municipal elections in the City, any costs or expenses directed to be paid under section 132 . . . above by the authority for which the election was held shall—

(a) if incurred in respect of a ward election, be paid out of the general rate; and

(b) in any other case, be paid by the chamberlain of the City out of the City's cash.

NOTES

This section contains provisions formerly in the Representation of the People Act 1949, s 167(7), as amended by the City of London (Various Powers) Act 1961, s 44.

The words omitted were repealed by the Representation of the People Act 1985, s 28(1), Sch 5, as from 1 October 1985.

Municipal elections in the City. As to the application of provisions of this Act to such elections, see s 191 ante and the notes thereto.

Definitions. For "municipal election in the City", see s 191(1) ante; for "the City", see s 202(1) post.

197 Candidate's expenses: ward, and liverymen in common hall, elections

(1) For a candidate at a ward election in the City the maximum amount of election expenses is £120 together with an additional 2.4p for every elector (taken according to the enumeration of the ward list to be used at the election); but the provision made by section 76(6) above for increasing the maximum amount of election expenses in the event of a candidate's death applies to the maximum amount under this subsection.

(2) A candidate at an election by liverymen in common hall need not have an election agent, his maximum amount of election expenses is [15p for every elector on the common hall register to be used at the election], and section 90 above and Schedule 4 to this Act apply at such an election as they apply to an election of parish councillors, but the form of declaration as to election expenses shall be such as may be prescribed by Act of Common Council [and in this subsection "common hall register" means the list prepared under section 4 of the City of London Ballot Act 1887].

(3) The Secretary of State may by order vary a maximum amount of the candidate's election expenses specified in subsection (1) or subsection (2) above where in his opinion there has been a change in the value of money since the last occasion on which that amount was [fixed (whether by such an order or otherwise)], and the variation shall be such as in his opinion is justified by that change.

An order under this subsection shall not be made unless a draft of the order has been laid before, and approved by resolution of, each House of Parliament; and the power to make the order is exercisable by statutory instrument.

NOTES

Sub-s (1) contains provisions formerly in the Representation of the People Act 1949, s 167(4), as substituted by the Representation of the People Act 1977, s 1(2), and amended by the Representation of the People (Variation of Limits of Candidates' Election Expenses) Order 1982, SI 1982/363, art 5. Sub-s (2) contains provisions formerly in s 167(5) of the 1949 Act, as amended by art 6 of the 1982 Order. Sub-s (3) contains provisions formerly in the Representation of the People Act 1978, s 2.

The words in square brackets in sub-ss (2), (3) were substituted or inserted by the Representation of the People Act 1985, s 24, Sch 4, para 67, as from 1 October 1985.

Candidate; election expenses. For the meanings of these expressions in Pt II of this Act, see s 118 ante.

Maximum amount of election expenses. As to the election expenses generally, see ss 72 et seq ante; and as to the limitation of expenses, see, in particular, ss 76 and 77 ante, as applied by s 191(1) ante.

Ward list. This list is prepared under the City of London (Various Powers) Act 1957, s 7, Vol 26, title London.

Election agent. As to election agents, see s 67 ante and the notes thereto.

Secretary of State. Cf the note to s 4 ante. The Secretary of State here concerned is the Secretary of State for the Home Department.

Last occasion. By virtue of s 206 and Sch 7, para 6 post, for the purposes of sub-s (3) above, the last occasion on which the maximum amount of candidates' expenses was varied by order was, in the case of the amounts specified in sub-ss (1), (2) above, 12 March 1982; see the Representation of the People (Variation of Limits of Candidates' Election Expenses) Order 1982, SI 1982/363.

Laid before ... Parliament. For meaning, see the Laying of Documents before Parliament (Interpretation) Act 1948, s 1(1), Vol 41, title Statutes.

Statutory instrument. For provisions as to statutory instruments generally, see the Statutory Instruments Act 1946, Vol 41, title Statutes.

Definitions. For "the City" and "elector", see s 202(1) post.

Orders under this section. Up to 1 August 1985 no order had been made under sub-s (3) above and none has effect thereunder by virtue of the Interpretation Act 1978, s 17(2)(b), Vol 41, title Statutes.

City of London Ballot Act 1887, s 4. 50 & 51 Vict c xiii; not printed in this work.

198 Effect of avoidance of election to corporate office

In relation to the City, where a candidate who has been elected to a corporate office is—

(*a*) by a certificate of an election court, or

(*b*) by a decision of the High Court,

declared not to have been duly elected, acts done by him in execution of the office before the time when the certificate or decision is certified to the clerk of the authority for which the election was held shall not be invalidated by reason of that declaration.

NOTES

This section contains provisions formerly in the Representation of the People Act 1949, s 118(2), as repealed except in its application to the City of London by the Local Authorities etc (Miscellaneous Provisions) (No 2) Order 1974, SI 1974/595, art 3(22), Sch 1, Pt I.

Candidate. For the meaning of this expression in Pt III of this Act, see, by virtue of s 185 ante, s 118 ante.

Certificate of an election court. Ie a certificate given under s 145(1), (2) ante, as applied by s 191(1) ante.

High Court. See the note to s 39 ante.

Certified to the clerk of the authority. Ie under s 145(6) or 146(3) ante.

Definitions. For "corporate office" and "clerk of the authority", see s 191(1) ante; for "the City" and "election court", see s 202(1) post.

PART V

GENERAL AND SUPPLEMENTAL

Supplemental

199 (*Repealed by the Representation of the People Act 1985, ss 22(2), 28(1), Sch 5, as from 1 October 1985.*)

200 Public notices, and declarations

[(1) A public notice required by or under this Act to be given by a returning officer for a parliamentary election shall be given by posting the notice in some conspicuous place or places in the constituency and may also be given in such other manner as he thinks desirable for publicising it.

(1A) A public notice required by or under this Act to be given by the proper officer of a local authority at a local government election shall be given by posting the notice in some conspicuous place or places in the local government area and may also be given in such other manner as he thinks desirable for publicising it.]

(2) Any person before whom a declaration is authorised to be made under this Act may take the declaration.

NOTES

This section, as originally enacted, contained provisions formerly in the Representation of the People Act 1949, s 171(3), (4).

Sub-ss (1), (1A) were substituted for the original sub-s (1) by the Representation of the People Act 1985, s 24, Sch 4, para 68, as from 1 October 1985.

Returning officer. As to returning officers for parliamentary elections, see ss 24, 26–28 ante.

Parliamentary election; constituency. See the note to s 1 ante.

European Assembly elections. This section is applied to such elections by the European Assembly Elections Regulations 1984, SI 1984/137, reg 3(1), Sch 1. See further the Introductory Note to this Act.

As to provisions relating to such elections in Northern Ireland, see the Introductory Note to this Act.

Definitions. For "local authority", "local government area" and "local government election", see s 203(1) post; for "proper officer", see s 202(1) post.

201 Regulations

(1) Any power conferred by this Act to make regulations shall, except where this Act otherwise provides, be a power exercisable by the Secretary of State by statutory instrument.

(2) A statutory instrument containing regulations so made shall not come into force unless or until it is approved by resolution of each House of Parliament; but this subsection does not apply to—

(a) rules made under sections 36 and 42 above;

(b) regulations made under section 199 above and section 203(4) below.

NOTES

Sub-s (1) contains provisions formerly in the Representation of the People Act 1949, s 171(5), the Electoral Registers Act 1949, s 1(5), and the Elections (Welsh Forms) Act 1964, s 1(1). Sub-s (2) contains provisions formerly in the first and second above-mentioned enactments.

Prospective amendment. The following subsection is substituted for sub-s (2) above by the Representation of the People Act 1985, s 24, Sch 4, para 69 post, as from a day to be appointed under s 29(2) of that Act:

"(2) No regulations shall be made under this Act by the Secretary of State otherwise than under section 203(4) below unless a draft of the regulations has been laid before and approved by a resolution of each House of Parliament.".

Secretary of State. Cf the note to s 4 ante.

Statutory instrument. See the note to s 197 ante.

Interpretation

202 General provisions as to interpretation

(1) In this Act, unless the context otherwise requires—

"Attorney General" includes the Solicitor General in cases where the Attorney General is interested or otherwise unable to act;

"the City" means the City of London;

"Clerk of the Crown" means Clerk of the Crown in Chancery;

"Common Council" means the Common Council of the City;

"dwelling house" includes any part of a house where that part is occupied separately as a dwelling house;

"election" means a parliamentary election or an election under the local government Act;

"election court" means—

    (*a*) in relation to a parliamentary election petition, the judges presiding at the trial;

    (*b*) in relation to a petition questioning an election under the local government Act, the court constituted under this Act for the trial of that petition;

"election petition" means a petition presented in pursuance of Part III of this Act;

"elector" in relation to an election, means any person whose name is for the time being on the register to be used at that election, but does not include those shown in the register as below voting age on the day fixed for the poll;

"legal incapacity" includes (in addition to any incapacity by virtue of any subsisting provision of the common law) any disqualification imposed by this Act or any other Act;

"parliamentary election petition" means an election petition questioning a parliamentary election or return;

"parliamentary elections rules" means the parliamentary elections rules in Schedule 1 to this Act;

"person" includes (without prejudice to the provisions of the Interpretation Act 1978) an association corporate or unincorporate;

"prescribed" except in Part III of this Act means prescribed by regulations;

"proper officer" means in England and Wales one within the meaning of section 270(3) and (4) of the Local Government Act 1972 . . .;

.   .   .   .   .

"service voter" means a person who has made a service declaration and is registered or entitled to be registered in pursuance of it;

"standard scale" has the meaning given by section 75 of the Criminal Justice Act 1982;

"statutory maximum" has the meaning given by section 74 of the Criminal Justice Act 1982;

"sub-agent" has the meaning given by section 68(1) above;

"voter" means a person voting at an election and includes a person voting as proxy and, except in the parliamentary elections rules, and the rules under section 36 and 42 above, a person voting by proxy, and "vote" (whether noun or verb) shall be construed accordingly, except that in those rules any reference to an elector voting or an elector's vote shall include a reference to an elector voting by proxy or an elector's vote given by proxy.

(2) For the purposes of the Representation of the People Acts a person shall be deemed not to have attained a given age until the commencement of the relevant anniversary of the day of this birth.

NOTES

Sub-s (1) contains provisions formerly in the Representation of the People Act 1949, s 171(1), as amended and partly repealed by the Representation of the People Act 1969, s 24(1), (4), Sch 2, para 21, Sch 3, Pt I, and is also derived from the Local Government Act 1972, s 270(3), (4), and the Criminal Justice Act 1982, ss 74, 75. Sub-s (2) contains provisions formerly in the Representation of the People Act 1969, s 1(5).

The words omitted from the definition of "proper officer" apply to Scotland only.

The other words omitted were repealed by the Representation of the People Act 1985, ss 24(1), 28, Sch 4, para 70, Sch 5, as from 1 October 1985.

Prospective amendment. The following definitions are inserted in the appropriate places in sub-s (1) by the Representation of the People Act 1985, s 11, Sch 2, Pt I, para 3 post, as from a day to be appointed under s 29(2) of that Act:—

"'the absent voters list' means, in relation to any election, the list kept under section 7 of the Representation of the People Act 1985 for that election."

"'the list of proxies' has, in relation to any election, the meaning given by section 7 of the Representation of the People Act 1985."

The following definition is also inserted in this section, by s 4(5) of the 1985 Act post, as from a day to be appointed under s 29(2) of that Act:—

"'overseas elector's declaration' has the meaning given by section 2 of the Representation of the People Act 1985."

"Attorney General" includes the Solicitor General, etc. The definition of "Attorney General" should be compared with the Law Officers Act 1944, s 1, Vol 10, title Constitutional Law (Pt 4) which provides for the functions of the Attorney General to be discharged by the Solicitor General in certain cases.

Parliamentary election. See the note to s 1 ante.

Election under the local government Act. Ie under the Local Government Act 1972 or the Local Government Act 1985, Pt III, both Vol 25, title Local Government; see s 203(1) post. The following are such elections: the election of the chairman of a county or district council (ss 3(1) and 22(1) of the 1972 Act), and of county and district councillors (ss 6(1) and 25(1) of the 1972 Act), the election of the mayor and councillors of a London borough (s 8(1) of, and Sch 2, paras 2(1), 6(1) to, the 1972 Act), the election of the chairman and councillors of a parish or community council (ss 15(1), 16(2), 34(1) and 35(1) of the 1972 Act) and the election of the members of the Inner London Education Authority (s 19 of the 1985 Act). The expression "election under the local government Act" therefore has a wider meaning than "local government election" (as defined by s 203(1) post), since it includes the election by councils of members of the council such as the chairman and mayor as well as elections of councillors by the electorate. Note also that by s 191(1) ante the expression "election under the local government Act" includes municipal elections in the City of London for the purposes of certain provisions of this Act, and that by s 203(4) post this Act applies, subject to certain exceptions, in relation to the Isles of Scilly as if the council of those isles were a county council.

Election court. For the constitution of courts for the trial of election petitions, see s 123 ante (parliamentary elections) and s 130 ante (local elections).

Part III of this Act. Ie ss 120–186 ante.

Register. As to the registration of electors, see ss 8 et seq ante.

Incapacity by virtue of . . . the common law. The common law incapacities to vote are considered in 15 Halsbury's Laws (4th edn) para 410; the main incapacities are those which disqualify peers for voting at parliamentary elections and which disqualify persons suffering from severe mental illness except during lucid intervals.

Disqualification imposed by this Act or any other Act. See, in particular, s 3 ante, as to the disfranchisement of offenders in prison, etc; ss 160(4)(a), (5) and 173 ante, as to the disqualification of offenders against election law; the Peerage Act 1963, s 6, Vol 33, title Peerages and Dignities, which disqualifies peeresses in their own right for voting at parliamentary elections; and the Public Bodies Corrupt Practices Act 1889, s 2(d), Vol 12, title Criminal Law, under which the court convicting a person of corruption for the second time may disqualify him for voting for five years.

As to parliamentary and local government franchise generally, see ss 1–7 ante.

England; Wales. See the note to s 4 ante.

Service voter. As to service qualifications and declarations, see ss 14–17 ante.

Person shall be deemed not to have attained a given age, etc. Sub-s (2) above is similar to the provision made for general purposes by the Family Law Reform Act 1969, s 9, Vol 6, title Children.

European Assembly elections. This section is applied to such elections by the European Assembly Elections Regulations 1984, SI 1984/137, reg 3(1), Sch 1, subject to:

(1) the omission from sub-s (1) of the definitions of "elector" and "parliamentary election rules"; and
(2) the insertion in sub-s (1) in the definition of "registration duties", after the words "the duties", of the words "in connection with an Assembly election".

See further the Introductory Note to this Act.

As to provisions relating to such elections in Northern Ireland, see the Introductory Note to this Act.

Definitions. For "voting age", see s 1(1)(c) or 2(1)(c) ante; for "registration officer", see s 8(1) ante; for parliamentary election petition", see s 120 ante; for "local government Act", see s 203(1) post.

Interpretation Act 1978. For the meaning of "person", see s 5 of, and Sch 1 to, that Act, Vol 41, title Statutes.

Local Government Act 1972, s 270(3), (4). See Vol 25, title Local Government.

Criminal Justice Act 1982, ss 74, 75. See Vol 27, title Magistrates. Section 74 defines "standard scale" as the scale set out in s 37(2) of that Act. The scale, as amended by art 2(4) of, and Sch 4 to, the Criminal Penalties etc (Increase) Order 1984, SI 1984/447 (made under the Magistrates' Courts Act 1980, s 143, Vol 27, title Magistrates) is: level 1: £50; level 2: £100: level 3: £400; level 4: £1000; level 5: £2000.

Section 75 of the 1982 Act defines "statutory maximum" as the "prescribed sum" within the meaning of the Magistrates' Courts Act 1980, s 32; that section has been amended by art 2(1) of, and Sch 1 to, the 1984 Order which specifies £2000 as that sum.

Representation of the People Acts. For the Acts which may be cited by this collective title, see the Introductory Note to the Representation of the People Act 1948 ante.

203 Local government provisions as to England and Wales

(1) In this Act, unless the context otherwise requires, in relation to England and Wales—

["council" includes the Inner London Education Authority and, "councillors" includes members of that Authority;]

["electoral area" means any electoral division or ward or, in the case of a parish or community in which there are no wards, the parish or community, for which the election of councillors is held under the local government Act;]

"local authority" means a county council, . . . a district council, a London borough council [the Inner London Education Authority] or a parish or community council;

"local government Act" means the Local Government Act 1972 [or Part III of the Local Government Act 1985];

"local government area" means a county, London borough, [the Inner London Education Area] district, parish or community;

'local government election" means the election of councillors for any electoral area.

(2) Subject to any express provision contained in Part I of this Act, that Part, so far as it has effect for the purpose of parliamentary elections [or of elections of members of the Inner London Education Authority] . . . applies in relation to the City as if it were a London borough, and as if the Common Council were a London borough council.

For the purposes of this subsection the Inner Temple and the Middle Temple shall be treated as forming part of the City.

(3) The modifications made by subsection (2) above do not affect section 52(4) above.

(4) This Act applies in relation to the Isles of Scilly as if those isles were a county and as if the council of those isles were a county council, except that—

(a) [the council shall appoint an officer of the council to be registration officer for the isles and] paragraph 1(1) of Schedule 2 . . . shall apply as if the isles were a district and the council were a district council;

(b) the provisions of Part I relating to the conduct of local government elections shall have effect in relation to those isles subject to such adaptations as the Secretary of State may by regulations prescribe.

(5) For the purposes of section 265 of the Local Government Act 1972 (application to Isles of Scilly) the provisions of this Act as to rules made by the Secretary of State under section 36 above shall be deemed to be contained in a public general Act relating to local government.

NOTES

Sub-s (1), as originally enacted, contained provisions formerly in the Representation of the People Act 1949, s 172(1), as partly repealed by the London Government Act 1963, s 93(1), Sch 18, Pt II, and as further partly repealed by the Local Government Act 1972, s 272(1), Sch 30, and as amended by the Local Authorities etc (Miscellaneous Provisions) (No 2) Order 1974, SI 1974/595, art 3(7), and in s 270(1) of the 1972 Act. Sub-ss (2), (3) contain provisions formerly in s 172(3) of the 1949 Act, as amended by the London Government Act 1963, s 8(1), Sch 3, para 33(2), and as partly repealed by the City of London (Various Powers) Act 1968, s 3(4)(b), and as affected by s 8(1) of, and Sch 3, para 21 to, the 1963 Act, and as further partly repealed by s 272(1) of, and Sch 30 to, the 1972 Act. Sub-s (4) contains provisions formerly in s 172(4) of the 1949 Act, as affected by the Secretary of State for the Environment Order 1970, SI 1970/1681, and in the Representation of the People Act 1969, s 26(3)(c). Sub-s (5) is derived from s 265 of the 1972 Act.

The words omitted from the definition of "local authority" in sub-s (1), and from sub-s (2), were repealed by the Local Government Act 1985, s 102(2), Sch 17, as from 1 April 1986 ("the abolition date" within the meaning of s 1(2) of that Act), and the definition of "council" in sub-s (1), together with the words in square brackets in the definitions of "local authority", "local government Act" and "local government area" in that subsection, and in sub-s (2), were inserted by s 19 of, and Sch 9, Pt I, para 1(10), (11) to, that Act, as from 1 September 1985 (see the Local Government Act 1985 (New Authorities) (Appointed Days) Order 1985, SI 1985/1263).

The definition of "electoral area" in sub-s (1) was substituted by the Representation of the People Act 1985, s 24, Sch 4, para 71(a), as from 1 October 1985, and the words in square brackets in sub-s (4)(a) were substituted and the words omitted from that paragraph were repealed, by ss 24, 28(1) of, and Sch 4, para 71(b), Sch 5 to, that Act, as from that date.

Sub-s (1): England; Wales. See the note to s 4 ante.

Inner London Education Authority. See the note to s 31 ante.

Electoral area; local government area; local government election. For the purposes of certain provisions of this Act these definitions are extended by s 191(1) ante in relation to the City of London.

The definition of "local government election" is narrower than the expression "election under the local government Act", which is also used in this Act; see the note on the latter expression to s 202 ante.

Electoral division. See the note to s 22 ante.

London borough; London borough council. See the note "London borough" to s 8 ante.

District; district council. See the note "Council of every district" to s 8 ante.

Parish; community; parish or community council. As to the parishes in England and the communities in Wales and their meetings and councils, see the Local Government Act 1972, ss 1(6)–(9), 9 et seq, 20(4), 27 et seq, Sch 1, Pts IV, V, Sch 4, Pt III, Vol 25, title Local Government.

County council; county. See the note "County council" to s 31 ante.

Inner London Education Area. Ie Greater London exclusive of the outer London boroughs; see the Local Government Act 1985, s 18(3), Vol 25, title Local Government.

Sub-s (2): Part I of this Act. Ie ss 1–66 ante.

Parliamentary elections. See the note "Parliamentary election" to s 1 ante.

Sub-s (4): Council of those isles. The Council of the Isles of Scilly is continued in being by the Local Government Act 1972, s 265(1), Vol 25, title Local Government, and is now constituted by the Isles of Scilly Order 1978, SI 1978/1844, art 4 (made under s 265(2) of that Act).

Provisions . . . relating to the conduct of local government elections. See, in particular, ss 35 et seq ante.

Secretary of State. Cf the note to s 4 ante. The Secretary of State concerned with sub-s (4)(b) above is the Secretary of State for the Environment.

Sub-s (5): Secretary of State. See the note to s 36 ante.

Definitions. For "registration officer", see s 8(1) ante; for "the City" and "Common Council", see s 202(1) ante.

Local Government Act 1972. See Vol 25, title Local Government. As to the Isles of Scilly Order 1978, SI 1978/1844 (made under s 265(2) of that Act), arts 5(2), 6(4), Schedule, see the notes "Isles of Scilly" to ss 8 and 36 ante.

Local Government Act 1985, Part III. See Vol 25, title Local Government.

Regulations under this section. Up to 1 August 1985, no regulations had been made under sub-s (4)(b) above and none have effect thereunder by virtue of the Interpretation Act 1978, s 17(2)(b), Vol 41, title Statutes.

For general provisions as to regulations, see s 201 ante.

204 (*Applies to Scotland only.*)

Scotland and Northern Ireland

205 General application to Northern Ireland

(1) This section has (in addition to any express application elsewhere in the Act) effect for the general application of this Act to Northern Ireland, and accordingly—

[(*a*) a reference to the Attorney General refers to the Attorney General for Northern Ireland;

(*aa*) a reference to the Director of Public Prosecutions refers to the Director of Public Prosecutions for Northern Ireland;]

(*b*) subject to subsection (2) below, a reference to any enactment shall be construed as a reference to that enactment as it applies in Northern Ireland.

(2) Nothing in this Act affects the law relating to local government in Northern Ireland.

NOTES

This section, as originally enacted, contained provisions formerly in the Representation of the People Act 1949, s 174(1), (2), as partly repealed, in the case of s 174(1), by the Northern Ireland Act 1962, s 30(2), Sch 4, Pt IV, and as further partly repealed, in the case of s 174(1), by the Northern Ireland (Modification of Enactments—No 1) Order 1973, SI 1973/2163, art 14(2), Sch 6, and in the case of s 174(2), by the Northern Ireland Constitution Act 1973, s 41(1), Sch 6, Pt I.

Sub-s (1)(*a*), (*aa*) were substituted for the original sub-s (1)(*a*) by the Representation of the People Act 1985, s 24, Sch 4, para 72, as from 1 October 1985.

Attorney General for Northern Ireland. By the Northern Ireland Constitution Act 1973, s 10(1), Vol 31, title Northern Ireland (Pt 2), the Attorney General for England and Wales is ex officio the Attorney General for Northern Ireland also; and by s 10(2), (3) of that Act, the functions of the Attorney General for Northern Ireland may be discharged by the Solicitor General for England and Wales in certain cases.

Cf also the definition of "Attorney General" in s 202(1) ante.

Director of Public Prosecutions for Northern Ireland. Provision for the appointment of the Director of Public Prosecutions for Northern Ireland and a deputy Director is made by the Prosecution of Offences (Northern Ireland) Order 1972, SI 1972/538, art 4, as amended by the Northern Ireland Constitution Act 1973, s 34.

Nothing in this Act affects, etc. See also s 160(6) ante.

European Assembly elections. Certain provisions of this Act and of the Representation of the People (Northern Ireland) Regulations 1983, SI 1983/436, are applied to European Assembly elections in Northern Ireland; see the Introductory Note to this Act.

Operation

206 Transitional and saving provisions, amendments and repeals

In Schedule 7 to this Act—

> (*a*) Part I has effect as to its transitional and saving provisions, and
> (*b*) Part II has effect as to its provisions relating to the interpretation of other Acts,

and subject to that Schedule—

> (i) the enactments and order specified in Schedule 8 to this Act have effect subject to the amendments consequent on this Act specified in that Schedule; and
> (ii) the enactments and orders specified in Schedule 9 to this Act (of which those in Part I are obsolete) are repealed or revoked to the extent specified in the third column of that Schedule.

207 Citation and commencement

(1) This Act may be cited as the Representation of the People Act 1983, and is included among the Acts which may be cited as the Representation of the People Acts.

(2) This Act shall come into force on such day as the Secretary of State may by order made by statutory instrument appoint.

NOTES

Secretary of State. Cf the note to s 4 ante. The Secretary of State here concerned is the Secretary of State for the Home Department.

Statutory instrument. For provisions as to statutory instruments generally, see the Statutory Instruments Act 1946, Vol 41, title Statutes.

Representation of the People Acts. For the Acts which may be cited by this collective title, see the Introductory Note to the Representation of the People Act 1948 ante.

Order under this section. The Representation of the People Act 1983 (Commencement) Order 1983, SI 1983/153 (bringing this Act into force on 15 March 1983).

SCHEDULES

SCHEDULE 1

PART I

PROVISIONS AS TO TIME

Timetable

1. The proceedings at the election shall be conducted in accordance with the following Table.

TIMETABLE

Proceeding	*Time*	
Issue of writ.	In the case of a general election, as soon as practicable after the issue of the proclamation summoning the new Parliament.	In the case of a by-election, as soon as practicable after the issue of the warrant for the writ.
Publication of notice of election.	In the case of a general election or by-election, not later than 4 in the afternoon on the second day after that on which the writ is received.	
Delivery of nomination papers.	In the case of a general election, between the hours of 10 in the morning and 4 in the afternoon on any day after the date of publication of the notice of election, but not later than the sixth day after the date of the proclamation summoning the new Parliament.	In the case of a by-election, the same as in the case of a general election, except that the last day shall be a day fixed by the returning officer and shall be not earlier than the third day after the date of publication of the notice of election nor later than the seventh day after that on which the writ is received.
Delivery of notices of withdrawals of candidature.	Within the time for the delivery of nomination papers at the election.	
The making of objections to nomination papers.	In the case of a general election or a by-election, during the hours allowed for delivery of nomination papers on the last day for their delivery and the hour following; but—	

(a) no objection may be made in the afternoon of that last day except to a nomination paper delivered within 24 hours of the last time for its delivery, and in the case of a nomination paper so delivered no objection may be so made to the sufficiency or nature of the particulars of the candidate unless made at or immediately after the time of the delivery of the nomination paper; and

(b) the foregoing provisions do not apply to objections made in pursuance of rule 15(2).

| Publication of statement of persons nominated. | In the case of a general election or a by-election, at the close of the time for making objections to nomination papers or as soon afterwards as any objections are disposed of. | |
| Polling. | In the case of a general election, between the hours of 7 in the morning and 10 at night on the *tenth* day after the last day for delivery of nomination papers. | In the case of a by-election, between the hours of 7 in the morning and 10 at night on the day fixed by the returning officer, which shall not be earlier than the *eighth* nor later than the *tenth* day after the last day for delivery of nomination papers. |

NOTES

This rule contains provisions formerly in the Representation of the People Act 1949, Sch 2, r 1, as amended and partly repealed by the Representation of the People Act 1969, ss 14, 24(4), Sch 1, Pt II, para 2, Sch 3, Pt II, and as further amended by the Representation of the People Act 1981, s 3, Schedule, para 1.

Prospective amendment. In the second column of the entry relating to polling for the word "tenth", the word "eleventh" is substituted, and in the third column of that entry, for the words "eighth" and "tenth" the words "ninth" and "eleventh" are substituted, respectively, by the Representation of the People Act 1985, s 24, Sch 4, para 73 post, as from a day to be appointed under s 29(2) of that Act.

Issue of writ. For the form and manner of issue of writs, see r 3 post.

Publication of notice of election. See r 5 post.

4 in the afternoon; 10 in the morning, etc. Ie by Greenwich mean time or by summer time as the case may be; see the Interpretation Act 1978, s 9, Vol 41, title Statutes, or the Summer Time Act 1972, s 3, Vol 45, title Time.

Delivery of nomination papers. Provision concerning the latest time of delivery of nomination papers is mandatory. If a nomination paper is delivered after that time and accepted and the candidate nominated is elected, his electon is void (*Cutting v Windsor* (1924) 40 TLR 395, 22 LGR 345). Delivery must be made to the returning officer; see r 10 post.

The time for delivery of nomination papers where a poll has been countermanded owing to the death of a candidate is determined, with the necessary modification as to the date on which the writ is received, in accordance with the third column in the Timetable in this rule; see r 60(1)(*b*) post.

Returning officer. As to returning officers, see ss 24, 26–28 ante.

Withdrawals of candidature. For the procedure, see r 13 post.

Objections to nomination papers. As to decisions on objections to nomination papers, see r 12 post.

Polling. The time for polling where a poll has been countermanded owing to the death of a candidate is determined, with the necessary modification as to date on which the writ is received, in accordance with the third column in the Timetable in this rule; see r 60(1)(*b*) post.

Close of poll. In *Islington West Division Case, Medhurst v Lough and Gasquet* (1901) 17 TLR 210, the election court was of opinion that ballot papers could not be issued after the hour fixed for the closure of the poll but that ballot papers issued before that hour might be filled in and deposited in the ballot box after that time. This decision is contrary to the decision of the House of Commons Committee in *Ipswich Case* (1835) Kn & Omb 332, 380, 382 (when a vote cast after the time for voting was declared void) and contrary to the Irish case of *Gribbin v Kirker* (1873) IR 7 CL 30 in which an election was declared void because votes were received after the close of the poll. Under s 23(3) ante, irregular reception of votes is not in itself sufficient to render an election invalid "if it appears to the tribunal . . . that—(*a*) the election was so conducted as to be substantially in accordance with the law as to elections; and (*b*) the act or omission did not affect its result". The construction adopted in *Islington West Division Case* cited above is liberal, but generally speaking the construction applied by the courts to election law is strict (see the cases noted to r 6 post).

As to the construction of the expression "close of poll" with respect to polls adjourned because of riots, see r 42(2)(*b*) post.

Computation of time. See r 2 post.

Riot or open violence. As to the adjournment of nomination proceedings or the poll in case of riot or open violence, see rr 16 and 42 post.

European Assembly elections. This rule is applied to such elections by the European Assembly Elections Regulations 1984, SI 1984/137, reg 3(1), Sch 1, subject to the substitution of the following timetable:

"Timetable

Proceeding	*Time*
Publication of notice of election.	Not later than the twenty-fifth day before the date of the poll.
Delivery of nomination papers.	Between the hours of 10 am and 4 pm on any day after the date of the publication of the notice of the election but not later than the nineteenth day before the date of the poll.
Delivery of notices of withdrawals of candidature.	Within the time for the delivery of nomination papers at the election.
The making of objections to nomination papers.	During the hours allowed for delivery of nomination papers on the last day for their delivery and the hour following; but—
	(*a*) no objection may be made in the afternoon of that last day except to a nomination paper delivered within 24 hours of the last time for its delivery, and in the case of a nomination paper so delivered no objection may be so made to the sufficiency or nature of the particulars of the candidate unless made at or immediately after the time of the delivery of the nomination paper; and
	(*b*) the foregoing provisions do not apply to objections made in pursuance of rule 15(2) below.
Publication of statement of persons nominated.	At the close of the time for making objections to nomination papers or as soon afterwards as any objections are disposed of.
Polling.	Between the hours of 7 am and 10 pm on the day of the poll.".

See further the Introductory Note to this Act.

As to provisions relating to such elections in Northern Ireland, see the Introductory Note to this Act.

Computation of time

2.—(1) In computing any period of time for the purposes of the Timetable—

(*a*) a Saturday or Sunday,

(*b*) *a day of the Christmas break, of the Easter break or of a bank holiday break*, or

(*c*) a day appointed for public thanksgiving or mourning,

shall be disregarded, and any such day shall not be treated as a day for the purpose of any proceedings up to the completion of the poll nor shall the returning officer be obliged to proceed with the counting of the votes on such a day.

(2) In this rule "bank holiday" means—

(*a*) in relation to a general election, a day which is a bank holiday under the Banking and Financial Dealings Act 1971 in any part of the United Kingdom,

(*b*) in relation to a by-election, a day which is a bank holiday under that Act in that part of the United Kingdom in which the constituency is situated,

but at a general election sub-paragraph (*b*) and not sub-paragraph (*a*) of this paragraph applies in relation to any proceedings—

(i) commenced afresh by reason of a candidate's death; and

(ii) extending, by reason of riot or open violence, beyond the time laid down by the Timetable.

(3) In this rule—

"bank holiday break" means any bank holiday not included in the Christmas break or the Easter break and the period beginning with the last weekday before that bank holiday and ending with the next weekday which is not a bank holiday,

"Christmas break" means the period beginning with the last weekday before Christmas Day and ending with the first weekday after Christmas Day which is not a bank holiday,

"Easter break" means the period beginning with the Thursday before and ending with the Tuesday after Easter Day,

"weekday" does not include a Saturday,

but so much of this paragraph as includes in a bank holiday break a period before and after a bank holiday does not apply to bank holidays other than New Year's Day which are not bank holidays in England and Wales.

NOTES

This rule contains provisions formerly in the Representation of the People Act 1969, Sch 2, r 2, as amended by the Representation of the People Act 1969, s 18(2), and as affected by the Banking and Financial Dealings Act 1971, s 4(1), and further amended by the Representation of the People Act 1981, s 3, Schedule, para 2.

Prospective amendment. Para (3) is repealed, and the following sub-paragraph is substituted for sub-para (1)(*b*) above by the Representation of the People Act 1985, ss 19(5), 28(1), Sch 5 post, as from a day to be appointed under s 29(2) of that Act:—

"(*b*) a Christmas Eve, Christmas Day, Maundy Thursday, Good Friday or a bank holiday."

Timetable. See r 1 ante.

Returning officer. As to returning officers, see ss 24, 26–28 ante.

Counting of votes. For procedure, see rr 44–49 post.

United Kingdom. See the note to s 6 ante.

Constituency. See the note to s 1 ante.

Proceedings . . . commenced afresh by reason of a candidate's death. This refers to proceedings mentioned in r 60 post.

European Assembly elections. This rule is applied to such elections by the European Assembly Elections Regulations 1984, SI 1984/137, reg 3(1), Sch 1. See further the Introductory Note to this Act.

As to provisions relating to such elections in Northern Ireland, see the Introductory Note to this Act.

Banking and Financial Dealings Act 1971. See Vol 45, title Time.

PART II

STAGES COMMON TO CONTESTED AND UNCONTESTED ELECTIONS

ISSUE OF WRIT AND NOTICE OF ELECTION

Issue of writ

3.—(1) Writs for parliamentary elections shall continue to be sealed and issued in accordance with the existing practice of the office of the Clerk of the Crown.

(2) Each writ shall be in the form in the Appendix and shall be directed to the returning officer by the title of his office as returning officer (and not by his name) and conveyed to him.

(3) Her Majesty may by Order in Council—

(*a*) specify the manner in which writs are to be conveyed, whether by post, by an officer appointed by the Lord Chancellor or, as regards Northern Ireland, the Secretary of State, or otherwise, and make different provision for different classes of writs; and

(*b*) provide for the giving of receipts for writs by persons to whom they are delivered or who may receive them in the course of their conveyance.

(4) Delivery of the writ to a person for the time being authorised by law to act as deputy for the officer who by virtue of his office is returning officer shall be as good as delivery to the returning officer.

(5) An Order in Council under this rule—

(*a*) may require a returning officer to provide an address to which writs are to be conveyed and any change of that address; and

(*b*) may provide for recording those addresses; and

(*c*) may provide that the delivery of a writ to a person found in and for the time being in charge of a place so recorded as the office of a returning officer shall be as good as delivery to that returning officer.

(6) The person to whom the writ is delivered shall endorse the date of receipt on the writ in the form shown in the Appendix.

(7) A draft of an Order in Council under this rule shall be laid before Parliament, and any such Order may provide for any incidental or supplemental matter.

NOTES

This rule contains provisions formerly in the Representation of the People Act 1949, Sch 2, r 3, as partly repealed by the Local Government Act 1972, s 272(1), Sch 30, and by the Returning Officers (Scotland) Act 1977, s 3(2), and as affected by the Northern Ireland Constitution Act 1973, s 40(1), Sch 5, para 4(1).

Parliamentary elections. See the note "Parliamentary election" to s 1 ante.

Clerk of the Crown. Ie the Clerk of the Crown in Chancery; see s 202(1) ante.

Returning officer. As to returning officers, see ss 24, 26–28 ante; and note paras (4) and (5)(*c*) above. It should be noted that by s 28(2)(*a*) ante registration officers acting as returning officers may not exercise the duties imposed on returning officers by this rule; but see r 4 post as to conveyance of the writ to the acting returning officer.

Secretary of State. See the note to s 4 ante.

Laid before Parliament. For meaning, see the Laying of Documents before Parliament (Interpretation) Act 1948, s 1(1), Vol 41, title Statutes.

Orders in Council under this rule. The Parliamentary Writs Order 1983, SI 1983/605; the Parliamentary Writs (Northern Ireland) Order 1983, SI 1983/606.

The power to make Orders in Council is exercisable by statutory instrument, see the Statutory Instruments Act 1946, s 1(1), Vol 41, title Statutes.

Conveyance of writ to acting returning officer

4.—(1) For an election in a constituency in England and Wales the writ shall (notwithstanding anything in rule 3 above) be conveyed to the acting returning officer if the returning officer—

(*a*) has so requested by notice in the form prescribed by an Order in Council under rule 3 and received by the Clerk of the Crown one month or more before the issue of the writ; and

(*b*) has not revoked it by a further notice in the form so prescribed and received within such time as is mentioned above.

(2) A notice under this rule has effect in relation to all constituencies—

(*a*) of which the person giving it is returning officer at the time of giving it; or

(*b*) of which he or a successor in office becomes returning officer by virtue of that office.

(3) Where by virtue of this rule writs are conveyed to the acting returning officer paragraph (5) of rule 3 applies in relation to him as it applies in relation to a returning officer.

NOTES

This rule contains provisions formerly in the Representation of the People Act 1949, Sch 2, r 4(1), (2), (4), as partly repealed, in the case of r 4(2), by the Local Government Act 1972, s 272(1), Sch 30.

Constituency. See the note to s 1 ante.

England; Wales. See the note to s 4 ante.

Acting returning officer. As to the discharge of the returning officer's functions by the registration officer; see s 28 ante.

Returning officer. Cf the note to r 3 ante.

Month. Ie a calendar month; see the Interpretation Act 1978, s 5, Sch 1, Vol 41, title Statutes.

Notice of election

5.—(1) The returning officer shall publish notice of the election . . ., stating—

  (*a*) the place and times at which nomination papers are to be delivered, and
  (*b*) the date of the poll in the event of a contest,

and the notice shall state that forms of nomination paper may be obtained at that place and those times.

(2) The notice of election shall state the date by which—

  (*a*) applications to *be treated as an absent voter*, and
  (*b*) other applications and notices about postal or proxy voting,

must reach the registration officer in order that they may be effective for the election.

(3) . . .

NOTES

Para (1) contains provisions formerly in the Representation of the People Act 1949, Sch 2, r 6. Para (2) contains provisions formerly in the Representation of the People Act 1969, s 6(6).

The words omitted from para (1), and the whole of para (3), were repealed by the Representation of the People Act 1985, ss 24, 28(1), Sch 4, para 74, Sch 5, as from 1 October 1985.

Prospecive amendment. For the words in italics in para (2)(*a*) above, the words "vote by post or by proxy" are substituted by the Representation of the People Act 1985, s 11, Sch 2, Pt I, para 4 post, as from a day to be appointed under s 29(2) of that Act.

Returning officer. As to returning officers, see ss 24, 26–28 ante.

Publish notice. As to public notices by the returning officer, see s 200(1) ante.

Place and times at which nomination papers are to be delivered. As to these, see r 10 post (place for delivery) and r 1 ante (time of delivery).

Applications to be treated as an absent voter. As to these, see s 20 ante, the Representation of the People Regulations 1983, SI 1983/435, reg 38, and the Representation of the People (Northern Ireland) Regulations 1983, SI 1983/436, reg 23.

Other applications and notices about postal or proxy voting. As to these, see ss 19 et seq ante, the Representation of the People Regulations 1983, SI 1983/435, regs 39 et seq, and the Representation of the People (Northern Ireland) Regulations 1983, SI 1983/436, regs 24 et seq. Note, however, that ss 19 et seq ante are repealed by the Representation of the People Act 1985, s 28(1), Sch 4, as from a day to be appointed under s 29(2) of that Act, and replaced, as from that date, by ss 8, 9 of that Act. It is thought therefore that both of the 1983 instruments will be amended accordingly.

Registration officer. For meaning, see s 8(1) ante.

Constituency. See the note to s 1 ante.

European Assembly elections. This rule is applied to such elections by the European Assembly Elections Regulations 1984, SI 1984/137, reg 3(1), Sch 1. See further the Introductory Note to this Act.

As to provisions relating to such elections in Northern Ireland, see the Introductory Note to this Act.

NOMINATION

Nomination of candidates

6.—(1) Each candidate shall be nominated by a separate nomination paper, in the form in the Appendix delivered—

  (*a*) by the candidate himself, or
  (*b*) by his proposer or seconder,

to the returning officer at the place fixed for the purpose, but the paper may be so delivered on the candidate's behalf by his election agent if the agent's name and address have been previously given to the returning officer as required by section 67 of this Act or are so given at the time the paper is delivered.

(2) The nomination paper shall state the candidate's—

    (a) full names,
    (b) home address in full, and
    (c) if desired, description,

and the surname shall be placed first in the list of his names.

(3) The description, if any, shall not exceed 6 words in length, and need not refer to his rank, profession or calling so long as, with the candidate's other particulars, it is sufficient to identify him.

NOTES

Para (1) contains provisions formerly in the Representation of the People Act 1949, Sch 2, r 7(1), and in the Representation of the People Act 1969, Sch 1, Pt II, para 5(1)(a). Paras (2), (3) contain provisions formerly in Sch 2, r 7(2), (3) to, the 1949 Act, as amended by s 12(1) of the 1969 Act.

Form in the Appendix. See also the note "Welsh versions of forms" to the Appendix post.

Proposer or seconder. See r 7 post.

Returning officer. As to returning officers, see ss 24, 26–28 ante.

Place fixed. See r 10 post.

Election agent. As to election agents, see s 67 ante and the notes thereto.

Full names. Initials will not suffice; cf *Mather v Brown* (1876) 1 CPD 596, 45 LJQB 547 (name of "Robert V Mather" inserted on nomination paper full name being "Robert Vicars Mather"; held, insufficient description). A nomination paper would not be liable to rejection under r 12 post on account of the use of a contraction for a Christian name such as "Wm" for "William" (cf *R v Bradley* (1861) 3 E & E 634, 30 LJQB 180; *Henry v Armitage* (1883) 12 QBD 257, 53 LJQB 111, CA), nor on account of a misspelling (*Miller v Everton* (1895) 64 LJQB 692, 72 LT 839 ("Millar" for "Miller")), if there was no reasonable doubt in each case as to the person intended to be described. It is sufficient if the names given accurately describe the candidate for the purpose for which he needs to be identified on the nomination paper (ie for standing for election to Parliament), even if it is known that the candidate uses also other names (*Greenway-Stanley v Paterson* [1977] 2 All ER 663, (1976) 75 LGR 367). See also as to misdescriptions, s 50 ante; and see, further, 15 Halsbury's Laws (4th edn) para 562, note 1.

Home address in full. The forerunner of para (2) above continued to refer to "place of residence" (rather than "home address in full") though the form of nomination paper prescribed by the Representation of the People Act 1949, Sch 2, Appendix was amended by the Representation of the People Act 1969, s 14, Sch 1, Pt II, para 5(2), so that it referred to "home address in full" instead of "place of residence". The text of r 6(2) has now been brought into line with the form of nomination paper though no specific amendment to the 1949 Act authorised this.

A person's home address is the place where he lives with his family and sleeps at night and is not his place of business (*Re v Hammond* (1852) 17 QB 772, 21 LJQB 153). The object of the statutory provisions is to give one address by which the candidate can be easily identified (*Allen v Greensill* (1874) 4 CB 100, 16 LJCP 142; *R v Hammond* (1852) 17 QB 772, 21 LJQB 153). If a wrong home address is given the nomination paper is invalid (*R v Election Court, ex p Sheppard* [1975] 2 All ER 723, [1975] 1 WLR 1319; *R v Coward* (1851) 16 QB 819, 20 LJQB 359; *R v Deighton* (1844) 5 QB 896, 13 LJQB 241), but an incorrect description of a true home address would not invalidate the nomination paper if the description were such as to be commonly understood (s 50 ante; and see *Soper v Basingstoke Corpn* (1877) 2 CPD 440, 46 LJQB 422; *R v Gregory* (1853) 1 E & B 600, 22 LJQB 120).

European Assembly elections. This rule is applied to such elections by the European Assembly Elections Regulations 1984, SI 1984/137, reg 3(1), Sch 1, subject to the addition at the end of the rule of the following paragraph:

"(4) A nomination paper may consist of a single sheet, or of two or more sheets securely fastened together."

See further the Introductory Note to this Act.

As to provisions relating to such elections in Northern Ireland, see the Introductory Note to this Act.

Subscription of nomination paper

7.—(1) The nomination paper shall be subscribed by two electors as proposer and seconder, and by eight other electors as assenting to the nomination.

(2) Where a nomination paper bears the signatures of more than the required number of persons as proposing, seconding or assenting to the nomination of a candidate, the signature or signatures (up to the required number) appearing first on the paper in each category shall be taken into account to the exclusion of any others in that category.

(3) The nomination paper shall give the electoral number of each person subscribing it.

(4) The returning officer—

(a) shall supply any elector with a form of nomination paper at the place and during the time for delivery of nomination papers, and

(b) shall at any elector's request prepare a nomination paper for signature,

but it is not necessary for a nomination to be on a form suppied by the returning officer.

(5) A person shall not subscribe more than one nomination paper at the same election and, if he does, his signature shall be inoperative on any paper other than the one first delivered, but he shall not be prevented from subscribing a nomination paper by reason only of his having subscribed that of a candidate who has died or withdrawn before delivery of the first mentioned paper.

(6) In this rule—

"elector" means a person—

(a) who is registered as a parliamentary elector in the constituency in the register to be used at the election, or

(b) who, pending the publication of that register, appears from the electors lists for that register as corrected by the registration officer to be entitled to be so registered,

and accordingly includes a person shown in the register or electors lists as below voting age if it appears from it that he will be of voting age on the day fixed for the poll, but not otherwise; and

"electoral number" means—

(i) a person's number in that register, or

(ii) pending the publication of the register, his number (if any) in the electors lists for that register.

NOTES

This rule contains provisions formerly in the Representation of the People Act 1949, Sch 2, r 8, as amended by the Representation of the People Act 1969, s 24(1), Sch 2, para 23(1).

Subscribed. For decisions of the courts on the subscription of nomination papers, see 15 Halsbury's Laws (4th edn) para 563, text and notes 4–6, 9–11.

Returning officer. As to returning officers, see ss 24, 26–28 ante.

Place and . . . time for delivery of nomination papers. As to these, see r 10 post (place of delivery) and r 1 ante (time of delivery).

Registered as a parliamentary elector. As to the registration of parliamentary electors, see ss 9 et seq ante.

Constituency. See the note to s 1 ante.

Register to be used at the election. See s 13(1) ante.

Electors lists . . . as corrected. Electors lists are to be prepared under s 10(b) ante. As to their correction, see the Representation of the People Regulations 1983, SI 1983/435, regs 19 et seq, and the Representation of the People (Northern Ireland) Regulations 1983, SI 1983/436, reg 14.

European Assembly elections. This rule is applied to such elections by the European Assembly Elections Regulations 1984, SI 1984/137, reg 3(1), Sch 1, subject to:

(1) the substitution in para (1) of the words "twenty-eight" for the word "eight"; and

(2) the substitution in para (6) for the definition of "elector" of the following definition:

"'elector' means a person—

(a) who is registered in any of the registers to be used at the election in the Assembly constituency (excluding any person not registered at an address within the Assembly constituency); or

(b) who, pending the publication of those registers, appears from the electors lists for those registers (as corrected by the registration officer) to be entitled to be so registered at an address within the Assembly constituency;

and accordingly includes a person shown in any of those registers or electors lists as below voting age if it appears from those registers or lists that he will be of voting age on the day of the poll, but not otherwise;".

See further the Introductory Note to this Act.

As to provisions relating to such elections in Northern Ireland, see the Introductory Note to this Act.

Definitions. For "voting age", see s 1(1)(c) ante; for "registration officer", see s 8(1) ante. Note as to "elector" and "electoral number", para (6) above.

Consent to nomination

8.—(1) A person shall not be validly nominated unless his consent to nomination—

(a) is given in writing on or within one month before the day fixed as the last day for the delivery of nomination papers,

(b) is attested by one witness, and

(c) is delivered at the place and within the time for the delivery of nomination papers,

subject to paragraph (2) below.

(2) If the returning officer is satisfied that owing to the absence of a person from the United Kingdom it has not been reasonably practicable for his consent in writing to be given as mentioned above, a telegram (or any similar means of communication) consenting to his nomination and purporting to have been sent by him shall be deemed for the purposes of this rule to be consent in writing given by him on the day on which it purports to have been sent, and attestation of his consent shall not be required.

(3) A candidate's consent given under this rule—

(a) shall state the day, month and year of his birth; and

(b) shall state—

(i) that he is aware of the provisions of the House of Commons Disqualification Act 1975; and

(ii) that to the best of his knowledge and belief he is not disqualified for membership of the House of Commons.

NOTES

This rule contains provisions formerly in the Representation of the People Act 1949, Sch 2, r 9, as amended by the House of Commons Disqualification Act 1975, s 10(2), and by the Representation of the People Act 1981, s 3, Schedule, para 3.

Writing. See the note "Written" to s 28 ante.

Within one month before, etc. Cf the note "Within six months . . ." to s 5 ante.

Last day for the delivery of nomination papers; place and ... time for the delivery of nomination papers. As to these, see r 10 post (place of delivery), and r 1 ante (time of delivery).

Returning officer. As to returning officers, see ss 24, 26–28 ante.

United Kingdom. See the note to s 6 ante.

Telegram (or any similar means of communication). The forerunner of para (2) above mentioned only a telegram; see, further, the note to s 38 ante.

European Assembly elections. This rule is applied to such elections by the European Assembly Elections Regulations 1984, SI 1984/137, reg 3(1), Sch 1, subject to the substitution in para (3)(b) above for the words "the House of Commons Disqualification Act 1975" of the words "paragraph 5 of Schedule 1 to the Act of 1978" and for the words "membership of the House of Commons" of the words "the office of representative to the Assembly". See further the Introductory Note to this Act.

As to provisions relating to such elections in Northern Ireland, see the Introductory Note to this Act.

House of Commons Disqualification Act 1975. See Vol 32, title Parliament.

Deposit

9.—(1) A person shall not be validly nominated unless the sum of [£500] is deposited by him or on his behalf with the returning officer at the place and during the time for delivery of nomination papers.

(2) The deposit may be made either—

(a) by the deposit of any legal tender, or

(b) by means of a banker's draft, or

(c) with the returning officer's consent, in any other manner,

but the returning officer may refuse to accept a deposit sought to be made by means of a banker's draft if he does not know that the drawer carries on business as a banker in the United Kingdom.

[(3) Where the deposit is made on behalf of the candidate, the person making the deposit shall at the time he makes it give his name and address to the returning officer (unless they have previously been given to him under section 67 of this Act or rule 6(1) above).]

NOTES

This rule, as originally enacted, contained provisions formerly in the Representation of the People Act 1949, Sch 2, r 10.

The reference to "£500" in para (1) was substituted by the Representation of the People Act 1985, s 13(*a*), as from 1 October 1985, and para (3) was added by s 24 of, and Sch 4, para 75 to, that Act, as from that date.

Returning officer. As to returning officers, see ss 24, 26–28 ante.

Place and . . . time for delivery of nomination papers. As to these, see r 10 post (place of delivery), and r 1 ante (time of delivery).

United Kingdom. See the note to s 6 ante.

Return or forfeiture of deposit. See r 53 post.

European Assembly elections. This rule is applied to such elections by the European Assembly Elections Regulations 1984, SI 1984/137, reg 3(1), Sch 1, subject to the substitution in para (1) above of "£600" for "£500". See further the Introductory Note to this Act.

As to provisions relating to such elections in Northern Ireland, see the Introductory Note to this Act.

Place for delivery of nomination papers

10.—(1) The returning officer shall fix the place at which nomination papers are to be delivered to him, and shall attend there during the time for their delivery and for the making of objections to them.

(2) Except in Scotland, the place shall be in—

    (*a*) the constituency; or

    (*b*) the registration area which includes the constituency; or

    (*c*) unless the constituency is a borough constituency, in a district adjoining the constituency or registration area.

For the purposes of paragraph (*b*) above "registration area" means—

    (i) in England and Wales, the area of two or more constituencies which have the same registration officer;

    (ii) in Northern Ireland, the county borough of Belfast and each county.

(3) (*Applies to Scotland only.*)

NOTES

This rule contains provisions formerly in the Representation of the People Act 1949, Sch 2, r 11, as amended by the Local Government (Scotland) Act 1973, s 11(3), Sch 3, para 17.

Returning officer. As to returning officers, see ss 24, 26–28 ante.

Time for their delivery and for the making of objections. See r 1 ante.

Constituency; borough constituency. See the note to s 24 ante.

District. See the note "Council of every district", to s 8 ante.

England; Wales. See the note to s 4 ante.

Constituencies which have the same registration officer. As to the areas for which registration officers act, see s 8(2) ante; and for the meaning of "registration officer", see s 8(1) ante.

European Assembly elections. Para (1) above is applied to such elections by the European Assembly Elections Regulations 1984, SI 1984/137, reg 3(1), Sch 1, subject to the insertion after the word "place" of the words "in the Assembly constituency". See further the Introductory Note to this Act.

As to provisions relating to such elections in Northern Ireland, see the Introductory Note to this Act.

Right to attend nomination

11.—(1) Except for the purpose of delivering a nomination paper or of assisting the returning officer, and subject to paragraph (4) below, no person is entitled to attend the proceedings during the time for delivery of nomination papers or for making objections to them unless he is—

    (*a*) a person standing nominated as a candidate, or

    (*b*) the election agent, proposer or seconder of such a person,

but where a candidate acts as his own election agent he may name one other person who shall be entitled to attend in place of his election agent.

(2) Where a person stands nominated by more than one nomination paper, only the persons subscribing as proposer and seconder—

    (*a*) to such one of those papers as he may select, or

(b) in default of such a selection, to that one of those papers which is first delivered, shall be entitled to attend as his proposer and seconder.

(3) The right to attend conferred by this rule includes the right—

(a) to inspect, and
(b) to object to the validity of,

any nomination paper.

(4) A candidate's wife or husband is entitled to be present at the delivery of the candidate's nomination, and may afterwards, so long as the candidate stands nominated, attend the proceedings referred to in paragraph (1) above, but without any such right as is conferred by paragraph (3) above.

NOTES

Paras (1)–(3) contain provisions formerly in the Representation of the People Act 1949, Sch 2, r 12. Para (4) contains provisions formerly in the Representation of the People Act 1969, Sch 1, r 5(1)(b).

Returning officer. As to returning officers, see ss 24, 26–28 ante.

Time for delivery of nomination papers or for making objections. See r 1 ante.

Election agent. As to election agents, see s 67 ante and the notes thereto.

Proposer or seconder. Ie the persons subscribing the nomination paper as proposer and seconder under r 7 ante.

Candidate acts as his own election agent. Ie by virtue of s 67(2) or 70 ante.

Object to the validity. As to decisions as to the validity of nomination papers, see r 12 post.

European Assembly elections. This rule is applied to such elections by the European Assembly Elections Regulations 1984, SI 1984/137, reg 3(1), Sch 1. See further the Introductory Note to this Act.

As to provisions relating to such elections in Northern Ireland, see the Introductory Note to this Act.

Decisions as to validity of nomination papers

12.—(1) Where a nomination paper and the candidate's consent to it are delivered and a deposit is made in accordance with these rules, the candidate shall be deemed to stand nominated unless and until—

(a) the returning officer decides that the nomination paper is invalid; or
(b) proof is given to the returning officer's satisfaction of the candidate's death; or
(c) the candidate withdraws.

(2) The returning officer is entitled to hold a nomination paper invalid only on one of the following grounds—

(a) that the particulars of the candidate or the persons subscribing the paper are not as required by law;
(b) that the paper is not subscribed as so required; and
(c) that the candidate is disqualified by the Representation of the People Act 1981.

(3) The returning officer shall give his decision on any objection to a nomination paper as soon as practicable after it is made.

(4) Where he decides that a nomination paper is invalid, he shall endorse and sign on the paper the fact and the reasons for his decision.

(5) The returning officer's decision that a nomination paper is valid shall be final and shall not be questioned in any proceeding whatsoever.

(6) Subject to paragraph (5) above nothing in this rule prevents the validity of a nomination being questioned on an election petition.

NOTES

This rule contains provisions formerly in the Representation of the People Act 1969, Sch 2, r 13, as amended by the Representation of the People Act 1981, s 3, Schedule, para 4.

Nomination paper and ... consent ... are delivered. Ie in accordance with rr 1, 6(1), 8(1), (2) and 10 ante.

Deposit is made. Ie in accordance with r 9 ante.

Returning officer. As to returning officers, see ss 24, 26–28 ante.

Candidate withdraws. As to the withdrawal of candidates, see r 13 post.

Returning officer is entitled to hold a nomination paper invalid, etc. Subject to para (2)(c) above, the duty of the returning officer is limited to deciding the question of the validity of a nomination by an examination of the nomination paper itself and he has no jurisdiction to enquire into the eligibility of a candidate nominated, which is a question for an election court; see *Watson v Ayton* [1946] KB 297, 115 LJKB 213, where the election was held void. Moreover the returning officer is only concerned to see that the nomination paper is good in form and he is not required to determine whether the particulars given are correct; see *R v Election Court, ex p Sheppard* [1975] 2 All ER 723, [1975] 1 WLR 1319, and *Greenway-Stanley v Paterson* [1977] 2 All ER 663 (1976) 75 LGR 367.

The fact that the nomination paper is worded in a language spoken in a specific area in the United Kingdom does not of itself invalidate it if it is in all other respects in conformity with these rules; see *Evans v Thomas* [1962] 2 QB 350, [1962] 3 All ER 108. Forms in Welsh for use at elections in Wales have now been prescribed (see the Welsh Language Act 1967, s 2, Vol 41, title Statutes) and these include a Welsh version of a nomination paper for a parliamentary election.

When accepted by the returning officer as valid a nomination paper becomes unimpeachable under para (5) above, but the validity of a nomination may be questioned on an election petition (para (6)). In *R v Election Court, ex p Sheppard* [1975] 2 All ER 723, [1975] 1 WLR 1319, Lord Widgery CJ said that the combined effect of paras (5) and (6) was that if the returning officer made a pronouncement on the form of the nomination paper and pronounced it to be valid as to form in accordance with his duty under para (2) then his decision was final and that could not be questioned. But if and in so far as the nomination paper was to be attacked on grounds other than form, other than objections apparent on the returning officers' investigation, then para (6) allowed such a matter of complaint to be raised.

Particulars of the candidate ... are not as required by law. The particulars of the candidate mentioned in para (2)(*a*) are those specified in r 6(2), (3) ante.

Persons subscribing; subscribed as so required. As to the subscription of nomination papers, see r 7 ante.

Election petition. As to the questioning of a parliamentary election as an election petition, see ss 120 et seq, 136 et seq ante.

European Assembly elections. This rule is applied to such elections by the European Assembly Elections Regulations 1984, SI 1984/137, reg 3(1), Sch 1, subject to the insertion in para (2)(*c*) after the words "Act 1981" of the words "(which applies in respect of the office of representative to the Assembly by virtue of paragraph 5(1)(*a*) of Schedule 1 to the Act of 1978)". See further the Introductory Note to this Act.

As to provisions relating to such elections in Northern Ireland, see the Introductory Note to this Act.

Representation of the People Act 1981. The relevant provisions of that Act are ss 1 and 2, Vol 32, title Parliament, which relate to the disqualification of certain offenders for membership of the House of Commons. By s 2(1) of that Act it is provided that if a person disqualified by the Act is nominated for election his nomination shall be void. Para (2)(*c*) above should be read together with r 15 post.

Withdrawal of candidates

13.—(1) A candidate may withdraw his candidature by notice of withdrawal—

   (*a*) signed by him and attested by one witness, and
   (*b*) delivered to the returning officer at the place for delivery of nomination papers.

(2) Where a candidate is outside the United Kingdom, a notice of withdrawal signed by his proposer and accompanied by a written declaration also so signed of the candidate's absence from the United Kingdom shall be of the same effect as a notice of withdrawal signed by the candidate; but where the candidate stands nominated by more than one nomination paper a notice of withdrawal under this paragraph shall be effective if, and only if—

   (*a*) it and the accompanying declaration are signed by all the proposers except any who is, and is stated in that declaration to be, outside the United Kingdom; or
   (*b*) it is accompanied, in addition to that declaration, by a written statement signed by the candidate that the proposer giving the notice is authorised to do so on the candidate's behalf during his absence from the United Kingdom.

NOTES

This rule contains provisions formerly in the Representation of the People Act 1949, Sch 2, r 14.

Returning officer. As to returning officers, see ss 24, 26–28 ante.

Place for delivery of nomination papers. See r 10 ante.

United Kingdom. See the note to s 6 ante.

Written. See the note to s 28 ante.

Proposers. As to the subscription of a nomination paper by a proposer, etc, see r 7 ante.

European Assembly elections. This rule is applied to such elections by the European Assembly Elections Regulations 1984, SI 1984/137, reg 3(1), Sch 1. See further the Introductory Note to this Act.

As to provisions relating to such elections in Northern Ireland, see the Introductory Note to this Act.

Publication of statement of persons nominated

14.—(1) The returning officer shall prepare and publish a statement showing the persons who have been and stand nominated and any other persons who have been nominated, with the reason why they no longer stand nominated.

(2) The statement shall show the names, addresses and descriptions of the persons nominated as given in their nomination papers, together with the names of the persons subscribing those papers.

(3) The statement shall show the persons standing nominated arranged alphabetically in order of their surnames, and, if there are two or more of them with the same surname, of their other names.

(4) In the case of a person nominated by more than one nomination paper, the returning officer shall take the particulars required by the foregoing provisions of this rule from such one of the papers as the candidate (or the returning officer in default of the candidate) may select, but if the election is contested a candidate standing nominated may require the returning officer to include in the statement the names of the persons subscribing a second and third nomination.

NOTES

This rule contains provisions formerly in the Representation of the People Act 1949, Sch 2, r 15.

Returning officer. As to returning officers, see ss 24, 26–28 ante.

Statement. The statement of persons nominated is to include a notice of the poll (r 23(1) post) and in an uncontested election is to declare the person standing nominated to be elected (r 50(2) post).

Stand nominated. A candidate stands nominated except in the cases mentioned in r 12(1) ante.

Names . . . as given in their nomination papers. Ie under r 6(2), (3) ante.

Persons subscribing. Ie under r 7 ante.

Second and third nomination. These words at the end of para (4) above should read "second and third nomination paper".

European Assembly elections. This rule is applied to such elections by the European Assembly Elections Regulations 1984, SI 1984/137, reg 3(1), Sch 1, subject to the insertion at the end of paras (2) and (4) above of the words "as proposer and seconder". See further the Introductory Note to this Act.

As to provisions relating to such elections in Northern Ireland, see the Introductory Note to this Act.

Disqualification by Representation of the People Act 1981

15.—(1) If it appears to the returning officer that any of the persons nominated might be disqualified by the Representation of the People Act 1981 he shall, as soon as practicable after the expiry of the time allowed for the delivery of nomination papers, prepare and publish a draft of the statement required under rule 14 above.

(2) The draft shall be headed "Draft statement of persons nominated" and shall omit the names of the persons subscribing the papers but shall contain a notice stating that any person who wishes to object to the nomination of any candidate on the ground that he is disqualified for nomination under the Representation of the People Act 1981 may do so between the hours of 10 in the morning and 4 in the afternoon on the day and at the place specified in the notice; and the day so specified shall be the day next after the last day for the delivery of nomination papers.

NOTES

This rule contains provisions formerly in the Representation of the People Act 1949, Sch 2, r 15A, as inserted by the Representation of the People Act 1981, s 3, Schedule, r 5.

Returning officer. As to returning officers, see ss 24, 26–28 ante.

Time allowed (last day) for the delivery of nomination papers. See r 1 ante.

10 in the morning; 4 in the afternoon. See the corresponding note to r 1 ante.

European Assembly elections. This rule is applied to such elections by the European Assembly Elections Regulations 1984, SI 1984/137, reg 3(1), Sch 1, subject to the insertion in para (1) after the words "Act 1981" of the words "(which applies in respect of the office of representation to the Assembly by virtue of paragraph 5(1)(*a*) of Schedule 1 to the Act of 1978)". See further the Introductory Note to this Act.

As to provisions relating to such elections in Northern Ireland, see the Introductory Note to this Act.

Representation of the People Act 1981. See the note to r 12 ante. As to the invalidation of a nomination paper where the candidate is disqualified by that Act, see r 12(2)(*c*) ante.

Adjournment of nomination proceedings in case of riot

16.—(1) Where the proceedings for or in connection with nomination are on any day interrupted or obstructed by riot or open violence—

(a) the proceedings shall be abandoned for that day, and

(b) if that day is the last day for the delivery of nomination papers, the proceedings shall be continued on the next day as if that were the last day of such delivery,

and that day shall be treated for the purposes of these rules as being the last day for such delivery (subject to any further application of this rule in the event of interruption or obstruction on that day).

(2) Where proceedings are abandoned by virtue of this rule nothing—

(a) may be done after they are continued if the time for doing it had passed at the time of the abandonment;

(b) done before the abandonment shall be invalidated by reason of the abandonment.

NOTES

This rule contains provisions formerly in the Representation of the People Act 1949, Sch 2, r 16, as partly repealed by the Representation of the People Act 1981, s 3, Schedule, para 7(a).

Last day for the delivery of nomination papers. See r 1 ante.

European Assembly elections. This rule and rr 17–21 post are applied to such elections by the European Assembly Elections Regulations 1984, SI 1984/137, reg 3(1), Sch 1. See further the Introductory Note to this Act.

As to provisions relating to such elections in Northern Ireland, see the Introductory Note to this Act.

Method of election

17.—(1) If the statement of persons nominated shows more than one person standing nominated, a poll shall be taken in accordance with Part III of these rules.

(2) If the statement of persons nominated shows only one person standing nominated, that person shall be declared to be elected in accordance with Part IV of these rules.

NOTES

This rule contains provisions formerly in the Representation of the People Act 1949, Sch 2, r 17.

Statement of persons nominated. This is to be prepared under r 14 ante.

Part III; Part IV. Ie rr 18–49 (Pt III) and rr 50–53 (Pt IV).

European Assembly elections. See the note to r 16 ante.

PART III

CONTESTED ELECTIONS

GENERAL PROVISIONS

Poll to be taken by ballot

18. The votes at the poll shall be given by ballot, the result shall be ascertained by counting the votes given to each candidate and the candidate to whom the majority of votes have been given shall be declared to have been elected.

NOTES

This rule contains provisions formerly in the Representation of the People Act 1949, Sch 2, r 18.

Votes. For the meaning of "vote", see s 202(1) ante.

Shall be declared, etc. This provision is imperative; the validity of the candidate's election is a matter for an election court to decide under Pt III (ss 120–186) of this Act not the returning officer (*Pritchard v Bangor Corpn* (1888) 13 App Cas 241, 57 LJQB 313, HL). As to the declaration, see r 50 post.

European Assembly elections. See the note to r 16 ante.

The ballot papers

19.—(1) The ballot of every voter shall consist of a ballot paper, and the persons shown in the statement of persons nominated as standing nominated, and no others, shall be entitled to have their names inserted in the ballot paper.

(2) Every ballot paper shall be in the form in the Appendix, and shall be printed in accordance with the directions in that Appendix, and—

> (a) shall contain the names and other particulars of the candidates as shown in the statement of persons nominated;
> (b) shall be capable of being folded up;
> (c) shall have a number printed on the back;
> (d) shall have attached a counterfoil with the same number printed [on it].

(3) The order of the names in the ballot paper shall be the same as in the statement of persons nominated.

NOTES

This rule contains provisions formerly in the Representation of the People Act 1949, Sch 2, r 19.

The words in square brackets in para (2)(d) were substituted by the Representation of the People Act 1985, s 24, Sch 4, para 76, as from 1 October 1985.

Voter. For meaning, see s 202(1) ante.

Statement of persons nominated. This is to be prepared under r 14 ante.

Misdescriptions. As to misdescriptions in ballot papers, see s 50 ante.

European Assembly elections. See the note to r 16 ante.

The official mark

20.—(1) Every ballot paper shall be marked with an official mark, which shall perforate the ballot paper.

(2) The official mark shall be kept secret, and an interval of not less than seven years shall intervene between the use of the same official mark at elections for the same constituency.

(3) The official mark used for ballot papers issued for the purpose of voting by post shall not be used at the same election for ballot papers issued for the purpose of voting in person.

NOTES

This rule contains provisions formerly in the Representation of the People Act 1949, Sch 2, r 20, as amended by the Representation of the People Act 1969, s 14, Sch 1, Pt II, para 4.

Constituency. See the note to s 1 ante.

Voting by post. As to postal ballot papers, see r 24 post.

European Assembly elections. See the note to r 16 ante.

Prohibition of disclosure of vote

21. No person who has voted at the election shall, in any legal proceeding to question the election or return, be required to state for whom he voted.

NOTES

This rule contains provisions formerly in the Representation of the People Act 1949, Sch 2, r 21.

Voted. For the meaning of "vote", see s 202(1) ante.

Legal proceedings to question the election or return. As to questioning parliamentary elections, see Pt III (ss 120–186) of this Act ante.

To state for whom he voted. See *Finsbury Central Division Case, Penton v Naoroji* (1892) 4 O'M & H 171, 176 (request to voter to identify his ballot paper). As to questions put to a voter concerning his political opinions, see *North Durham County Case, Glahom and Storey v Elliot* (1874) 31 LT 321, and *Harwich Borough Case, Tomline v Tyler* (1880) 44 LT 187 (elector should not be asked political views unless he has previously avowed them).

European Assembly elections. See the note to r 16 ante.

Use of schools and public rooms

22.—(1) The returning officer may use, free of charge, for the purpose of taking the poll—

(*a*) a room in a school to which this rule applies;

(*b*) a room the expense of maintaining which is payable out of any rate.

This rule applies—

(i) in England and Wales, to a school maintained or assisted by a local education authority or a school in respect of which grants are made out of moneys provided by Parliament to the person or body of persons responsible for the management of the school;

(ii) (*applies to Scotland only*);

(iii) in Northern Ireland, to a school in receipt of a grant out of moneys appropriated by Measure of the Northern Ireland Assembly.

(2) The returning officer shall make good any damage done to, and defray any expense incurred by the persons having control over, any such room as mentioned above by reason of its being used for the purpose of taking the poll.

(3) The use of a room in an unoccupied house for that purpose does not render a person liable to be rated or to pay any rate for the house.

(4) In Northern Ireland this rule does not apply to any school adjoining or adjacent to any church or other place of worship nor to any school connected with a nunnery or other religious establishment.

NOTES

This rule contains provisions formerly in the Representation of the People Act 1949, Sch 2, r 22(1)–(4), as amended, in the case of r 22(1), by the Local Government Act 1958, s 62, Sch 8, para 31(4), and as affected, in the case of r 22(1), by the Northern Ireland Constitution Act 1973, s 40(1), Sch 5, para 2(1).

Returning officer. As to returning officers, see ss 24, 26–28 ante.

England; Wales. See the note to s 4 ante.

Local education authority. See the note to s 108 ante.

Measure of the Northern Ireland Assembly. By the Northern Ireland Act 1974, s 1(3), Sch 1, para 1(7), Vol 31, title Northern Ireland (Pt 2), this includes an Order in Council under para 1 of Sch 1 to the 1974 Act. See also the note "Northern Ireland Assembly" to s 160 ante.

European Assembly elections. This rule is applied to such elections by the European Assembly Elections Regulations 1984, SI 1984/137, reg 3(1), Sch 1, subject to the insertion in paras (1) and (2) above after the words "taking the poll" of the words "counting the votes or verifying the ballot paper accounts, as the case may be". See further the Introductory Note to this Act.

As to provisions relating to such elections in Northern Ireland, see the Introductory Note to this Act.

ACTION TO BE TAKEN BEFORE THE POLL

Notice of poll

23.—(1) The returning officer shall in the statement of persons nominated include a notice of the poll, stating the day on which and hours during which the poll will be taken.

(2) The returning officer shall also give public notice (which may be combined with the statement of persons nominated) of—

(*a*) the situation of each polling station;

(*b*) the description of voters entitled to vote there; . . .

(*c*) . . .

[and he shall as soon as practicable after giving such notice give a copy of it to each of the election agents].

(3) . . .

NOTES

Paras (1) and (2), as originally enacted, contained provisions formerly in the Representation of the People Act 1949, Sch 2, r 23(1), (2).

The words omitted from para (2), and the whole of para (3), were repealed, and the words in square brackets in para (2) were added, by the Representation of the People Act 1985, ss 24, 28(1), Sch 4, para 77, Sch 5, as from 1 October 1985.

Returning officer. As to returning officers, see ss 24, 26–28 ante.
Statement of persons nominated. This is to be prepared under r 14 ante.
Day on which and hours during which the poll will be taken. See r 1 ante.
Public notice. For the method of giving public notice, see s 200(1) ante.
Polling station. As to the provision of polling stations, see r 25 post.
Election agents. As to election agents, see s 67 ante and the notes thereto.
European Assembly elections. This rule is applied to such elections by the European Assembly Elections Regulations 1984, SI 1984/137, reg 3(1), Sch 1, subject to the omission of para (2) above. See further the Introductory Note to this Act.
As to provisions relating to such elections in Northern Ireland, see the Introductory Note to this Act.
Definitions. For "voter" and "vote", see s 202(1) ante.

Postal ballot papers

24. The returning officer shall as soon as practicable [and in no event later than any date which may be prescribed as the last date for the purpose] send to those entitled to vote by post, at the addresses *provided by them for the purpose*, a ballot paper and a declaration of identity in the prescribed form, together with an envelope for their return.

NOTES

This rule contains provisions formerly in the Representation of the People Act 1949, Sch 2, r 25.
The words in square brackets were inserted by the Representation of the People Act 1985, s 24, Sch 4, para 78, as from 1 October 1985.
Prospective amendment. The words "shown in the absent voters list" are substituted for the words in italics by the Representation of the People Act 1985, s 11, Sch 2, Pt I, para 5 post, as from a day to be appointed under s 29(2) of that Act.
Returning officer. As to returning officers, see ss 24, 26–28 ante.
Those entitled to vote by post; addresses provided. See, in particular, ss 19(4) and 22(2) ante (prospectively repealed); and as to the issue and receipt of postal ballot papers, see the Representation of the People Regulations 1983, SI 1983/435, Pt V, and the Representation of the People (Northern Ireland) Regulations 1983, SI 1983/436, Pt V.
Prescribed form. As to the forms of postal ballot paper and identity, see the Representation of the People Regulations 1983, SI 1983/435, regs 49, 50, Sch 3, Form H, and the Representation of the People (Northern Ireland) Regulations 1983, SI 1983/436, regs 34, 35, Sch 3, Form E.
Return. As to when a postal ballot paper is to be deemed duly returned, see r 45(2) post.
Official mark. As to the official mark which is to be used for ballot papers, see r 20 ante.
European Assembly elections. This rule and r 25 post, are applied to such elections by the European Assembly Elections Regulations 1984, SI 1984/137, reg 3(1), Sch 1. See further the Introductory Note to this Act.
As to provisions relating to such elections in Northern Ireland, see the Introductory Note to this Act.
Definitions. For "prescribed" and "vote", see s 202(1) ante.

Provision of polling stations

25.—(1) The returning officer shall provide a sufficient number of polling stations and, subject to the following provisions of this rule, shall allot the electors to the polling stations in such manner as he thinks most convenient.

(2) One or more polling stations may be provided in the same room.

(3) The polling station alloted to electors from any polling district shall be in the polling place for that district.

(4) (*Applies to Scotland only.*)

(5) The returning officer shall provide each polling station with such number of compartments as may be necessary in which the voters can mark their votes screened from observation.

NOTES

This rule contains provisions formerly in the Representation of the People Act 1949, Sch 2, r 26, as partly repealed by the Representation of the People Act 1969, s 14, Sch 1, Pt I.
Returning officer. As to returning officers, see ss 24, 26–28 ante.
Polling district; polling place. As to polling districts and places, see s 18 ante.
Compartments. As to the sufficiency of a compartment provided, see *Nicolson v Wick Magistrates* 1922

SC 374 (the compartment need not wholly enclose the voter; a compartment which provides secrecy to an ordinary careful user thereof complies with legal requirements).

European Assembly elections. See the note to r 24 ante.

Definitions. For "elector", "voter" and "vote", see s 202(1) ante.

Appointment of presiding officers and clerks

26.—(1) The returning officer shall appoint and pay a presiding officer to attend at each polling station and such clerks as may be necessary for the purposes of the election, but he shall not appoint any person who has been employed by or on behalf of a candidate in or about the election.

(2) The returning officer may, if he thinks fit, preside at a polling station and the provisions of these rules relating to a presiding officer shall apply to a returning officer so presiding with the necesary modifications as to things to be done by the returning officer to the presiding officer or by the presiding officer to the returning officer.

(3) A presiding officer may do, by the clerks appointed to assist him, any act (including the asking of questions) which he is required or authorised by these rules to do at a polling station except order the arrest, exclusion or removal of any person from the polling station.

NOTES

This rule contains provisions formerly in the Representation of the People Act 1949, Sch 2, r 27.

This rule is amended in relation to Northern Ireland; see the note "Northern Ireland" below.

Returning officer. As to returning officers, see ss 24, 26–28 ante.

Presiding officer; clerks. For the penalty for the breach of duty by presiding officers and clerks, see s 63 ante.

European Assembly elections. This rule is applied to such elections by the European Assembly Elections Regulations 1984, SI 1984/137, reg 3(1), Sch 1, and in the case of such elections the following rule is added after this rule by the same provisions:

"Appointment of verifying officers and clerks

26A.—(1) The returning officer shall appoint and pay verifying officers to attend at such places as he deems necessary for the verification of the ballot paper accounts and such clerks as may be necessary for the purposes of the verification, but he shall not appoint a person who has been employed by or on behalf of a candidate in or about the election.

(2) The returning officer may, if he thinks fit, act as a verifying officer and the provisions of these rules relating to a verifying officer shall apply to a returning officer so acting, with the necessary modifications as to things to be done by the returning officer to the verifying officer or by the verifying officer to the returning officer.

(3) A verifying officer may do, by the clerks appointed to assist him, any act which he is required or authorised by these rules to do.".

See further the Introductory Note to this Act.

As to provisions relating to such elections in Northern Ireland, see the Introductory Note to this Act.

Northern Ireland. At the end of para (3) above the words "or refuse to deliver a ballot paper under paragraph (1C) of rule 37 (including that paragraph as applied by rule 38, 39 or 40)." are added by the Elections (Northern Ireland) Act 1985, s 2(2) post, as from 6 August 1985.

Special lists

27. The registration officer shall as soon as practicable prepare the following special lists—

(a) a list (in these rules referred to as "the absent voters list") giving the name and number on the register of every person entitled to vote at the election as an absent voter;

(b) a list (in these rules referred to as "the list of proxies") giving—

(i) the names and numbers on the register of the electors for whom proxies have been appointed (omitting any of those electors who are registered as service voters and entitled to vote by post); and

(ii) the names and addresses of the persons appointed;

(c) a list of any persons entitled to vote by post as proxy at the election.

NOTES

This rule contains provisions formerly in the Representation of the People Act 1949, Sch 2, r 28.

Prospective repeal. This rule is repealed by the Representation of the People Act 1985, s 28(1), Sch 5 post, as from a day to be appointed under s 29(2) of that Act. Most of the provisions referred to in the notes to this rule are also prospectively repealed by the 1985 Act.

Absent voters list; list of proxies; list of persons entitled to vote by post as proxy. As to the form and publication of these lists, see s 53(1)(a) ante, the Representation of the People Regulations 1983, SI 1983/435, reg 45, and the Representation of the People (Northern Ireland) Regulations 1983, SI 1983/436, reg 30; and as to misdescription, see s 50 ante.

As to the questions on which the above-mentioned lists are conclusive, see s 49(3) ante.

See also, as to records of absent voters, proxies and postal proxies, ss 20(5), 21(8) and 22(8) ante.

Register. As to the register of electors, see ss 9 et seq ante, the Representation of the People Regulations 1983, SI 1983/435, Pt III, and the Representation of the People (Northern Ireland) Regulations 1983, SI 1983/436, Pt III.

Person entitled to vote ... as an absent voter. For these persons, see s 19(1) ante; and see s 20 ante, as to application to be treated as an absent voter.

Electors for whom proxies have been appointed. As to the electors who may vote by proxy, see s 19(2), (3), (5) ante; and as to the appointment of proxies, see s 21 ante.

Registered as service voters and entitled to vote by post. For the meaning of "service voter", see s 202(1) ante; as to service qualifications and declarations, see ss 14–17 ante; and as to the service voters who are entitled to vote by post, see s 19(4) ante.

Persons entitled to vote by post as proxy. As to when a proxy may vote by post, see s 22(2), (3) ante.

European Assembly elections. This rule is applied to such elections by the European Assembly Elections Regulations 1984, SI 1984/137, reg 3(1), Sch 1, subject to:

(1) the insertion after the words "registration officer" of the words "for any area wholly or partly comprised in an Assembly constituency";

(2) the addition at the end of the rule of the words "and supply such lists to the returning officer".

See further the Introductory Note to this Act.

As to provisions relating to such elections in Northern Ireland, see the Introductory Note to this Act.

Definitions. For "registration officer", see s 8(1) ante; for "elector", "service voter" and "vote", see s 202(1) ante.

Issue of official poll cards

28.—(1) The returning officer shall as soon as practicable send to electors and their proxies an official poll card, but a card need not be sent to any person—

(a) as an elector if he is placed on the absent voters list for the election; or

(b) as a proxy if *his application to vote as such by post is allowed for the election.*

(2) An elector's official poll card shall be sent or delivered to his qualifying address, and a proxy's to his address as shown in the list of proxies.

(3) The official poll card shall be in the prescribed form and shall set out—

(a) the name of the constituency;

(b) the elector's name, qualifying address and number on the register;

(c) the date and hours of the poll and the situation of the elector's polling station.

(4) Paragraph (6) of rule 7 above applies for the interpretation of this rule.

NOTES

This rule contains provisions formerly in the Representation of the People Act 1949, Sch 2, r 29.

Prospective amendment. The words "he is entitled to vote by post as proxy at the election" are substituted for the words in italics in para (1)(b) above, by the Representation of the People Act 1985, s 11, Sch 2, Pt I, para 6 post, as from a day to be appointed under s 29(2) of that Act, and at the end of that paragraph the words "and a card shall not be sent to any person registered, or to be registered, in pursuance of an overseas elector's declaration" are inserted by s 4(6) of the 1985 Act post, as from a day to be appointed under s 29(2) of that Act.

Returning officer. As to returning officers, see ss 24, 26–28 ante.

Proxies. See the note "Electors for whom proxies have been appointed" to r 27 ante.

Official poll card. For the prohibition of imitation poll cards, see s 94 ante.

Application to vote as such by post. As to applications by proxies to vote by post, see s 22(2), (3) ante.

Qualifying address. This expression is not defined in this Act, but cf s 1(1)(a) ante.

Prescribed form. For the prescribed forms of official poll card, see the Representation of the People Regulations 1983, SI 1983/435, reg 69, Sch 3, Forms E, F and the Representation of the People (Northern Ireland) Regulations 1983, SI 1983/436, reg 54, Sch 3, Forms B, C. Welsh versions of the said Forms E and F are prescribed by the Elections (Welsh Forms) Regulations 1975, SI 1975/1329 (as to which, see the last note to s 53 ante).

Constituency. See the note to s 1 ante.

Register. See the note to r 27 ante.

Date and hours of the poll. See r 1 ante.

Polling station. As to polling stations, see r 25 ante.

European Assembly elections. This rule and r 29 post, are applied to such elections by the European Assembly Elections Regulations 1984, SI 1984/137, reg 3(1), Sch 1. See further the Introductory Note to this Act.

As to provisions relating to such elections in Northern Ireland, see the Introductory Note to this Act.

Definitions. For "elector", see, by virtue of para (4) above, r 7(6) ante; for "absent voters list" and "list of proxies", see r 27(a), (b) ante (prospectively repealed); "prescribed", see s 202(1) ante.

Equipment of polling stations

29.—(1) The returning officer shall provide each presiding officer with such number of ballot boxes and ballot papers as in the returning officer's opinion may be necessary.

(2) Every ballot box shall be so constructed that the ballot papers can be put in it, but cannot be withdrawn from it, without the box being unlocked.

(3) The returning officer shall provide each polling station with—

(a) materials to enable voters to mark the ballot papers;

(b) instruments for stamping on them the official mark;

(c) copies of the register of electors or such part of it as contains the names of the electors allotted to the station;

(d) the parts of any special lists prepared for the election corresponding to the register of electors or the part of it provided under sub-paragraph (c) above.

(4) A notice in the form in the Appendix, giving directions for the guidance of the voters in voting, shall be printed in conspicuous characters and exhibited inside and outside every polling station.

(5) In every compartment of every polling station there shall be exhibited *a notice as follows*—

(a) "The voter may vote for only one candidate"; or

(b) "The voter may vote for not more than one candidate".

NOTES

This rule contains provisions formerly in the Representation of the People Act 1949, Sch 2, r 30, as amended by the Representation of the People Act 1969, s 14, Sch 1, Pt II, para 13(2).

Prospective amendment. The words "the notice 'Vote for one candidate only. Put no other mark on the ballot paper, or your vote may not be counted'" are substituted for the words in italics in para (5) above by the Representation of the People Act 1985, s 24, Sch 4, para 79 post, as from a day to be appointed under s 29(2) of that Act.

Returning officer. As to returning officers, see ss 24, 26–28 ante.

Presiding officer. This officer is appointed under r 26(1) ante.

Ballot boxes and ballot papers. As to postal ballot papers, see r 24 ante, and the notes thereto; and as to the provision of a postal voters' ballot box or boxes, see the Representation of the People Regulations 1983, SI 1983/435, reg 58, and the Representation of the People (Northern Ireland) Regulations 1983, SI 1983/436, reg 43.

Official mark. As to this, see r 20 ante.

European Assembly elections. See the note to s 28 ante.

Appointment of polling and counting agents

30.—(1) Each candidate may, before the commencement of the poll, appoint—

(a) polling agents to attend at polling stations for the purpose of detecting personation; and

(b) counting agents to attend at the counting of the votes.

(2) The returning officer may limit the number of counting agents, so however that—

(a) the number shall be the same in the case of each candidate; and (*b*) the number allowed to a candidate shall not (except in special circumstances) be less than the number obtained by dividing the number of clerks employed on the counting by the number of candidates.

(3) Notice in writing of the appointment, stating the names and addresses of the persons appointed, shall be given by the candidate to the returning officer and shall be so given not later than the second day (computed like any period of time in the Timetable) before the day of the poll.

(4) If an agent dies, or becomes incapable of acting, the candidate may appoint another agent in his place, and shall forthwith give to the returning officer in writing of the name and address of the agent appointed.

(5) The foregoing provisions of this rule shall be without prejudice to the requirements of section 72(1) of this Act as to the appointment of paid polling agents, and any appointment authorised by this rule may be made and the notice of appointment given to the returning officer by the candidate's election agent, instead of by the candidate.

(6) In the following provisions of these rules references to polling and counting agents shall be taken as references to agents—

(*a*) whose appointments have been duly made and notified; and
(*b*) where the number of agents is restricted, who are within the permitted number.

(7) Any notice required to be given to a counting agent by the returning officer may be delivered at or sent by post to the address stated in the notice of appointment.

(8) A candidate may himself do any act or thing which any polling or counting agent of his, if appointed, would have been authorised to do, or may assist his agent in doing any such act or thing.

(9) A candidate's election agent may do or assist in doing anything which a polling or counting agent of his is authorised to do; and anything required or authorised by these rules to be done in the presence of the polling or counting agents may be done in the presence of a candidate's election agent instead of his polling agent or counting agents.

(10) Where by these rules any act or thing is required or authorised to be done in the presence of the polling or counting agents, the non-attendance of any agents or agent at the time and place appointed for the purpose shall not, if the act or thing is otherwise duly done, invalidate the act or thing done.

NOTES

Paras (1)–(8), (10) contain provisions formerly in the Representation of the People Act 1949, Sch 2, r 31, as amended and partly repealed by the Representation of the People Act 1969, s 24(1), Sch 2, para 25(2). Para (9) contains provisions formerly in s 11(5) of the 1969 Act.

Polling agents. As to the appointment of paid polling agents, see s 72(1) ante; and note para (5) above.

It has been held that an agreement not to employ polling agents should not be enforced by the courts (*Ainsworth v Lord Muncaster* (1885) 2 TLR 108).

Personation. This is punishable under s 60 ante.

Counting of the votes. As to the counting of votes, see rr 44 et seq post.

Returning officer. As to returning officers, see ss 24, 26–28 ante.

Writing. See the note "Written" to s 28 ante.

Timetable. This is set out in r 1 ante.

Forthwith. See the note to s 67 ante.

Election agent. As to election agents, see s 67 ante and the notes thereto.

May be delivered, etc. As this provision is permissive only, it is clear that, where a notice is served in a different manner and is received, this constitutes good service; see *Sharpley v Manby* [1942] 1 KB 217, sub nom *Re Sharpley's and Manby's Arbitration* [1942] 1 All ER 66, CA, and *Stylo Shoes Ltd v Prices Tailors Ltd* [1960] Ch 396, [1959] 3 All ER 901.

Sent by post. This provision brings into operation the provisions of the Interpretation Act 1978, s 7, Vol 41, title Statutes, to the effect that service is deemed to be effected by properly addressing, prepaying and posting a letter containing the document and, unless the contrary is proved, to have been effected at the time at which the letter would be delivered in the ordinary course of post.

Service by post may be effected by ordinary or registered letter; see *T O Supplies (London) Ltd v Jerry Creighton Ltd* [1952] 1 KB 42, [1951] 2 All ER 992. It follows that it is also permissible to use the recorded delivery service.

European Assembly elections. This rule is applied to such elections by the European Assembly Elections Regulations 1984, SI 1984/137, reg 3(1), Sch 1, subject to:

(1) the insertion in para (1)(*b*) above after the words "counting agents to attend at" of the words "the verification of the ballot paper accounts and"; and

(2) the insertion in para (2) above after the words "returning officer" of the words "or, as the case may be verifying officer", and after the words "the counting" of the words "or, as the case may be, the verification of the ballot paper accounts".

See further the Introductory Note to this Act.

As to provisions relating to such elections in Northern Ireland, see the Introductory Note to this Act.

Declaration of secrecy

31.—(1) Before the opening of the poll a declaration of secrecy in the form in paragraph (4) of this rule, or in a form as near to it as circumstances admit, shall be made by—

(*a*) *the returning officer and the presiding officers;*

(*b*) *every clerk authorised to attend at a polling station or the counting of the votes;*

(*c*) *every candidate attending at a polling station or at the counting of the votes and every election agent so attending;*

(*d*) *every candidate's wife or husband attending at the counting of the votes;*

(*e*) *every polling agent and counting agent;*

(*f*) *every person permitted by the returning officer to attend at the counting of the votes, though not entitled to do so,*

but the constables on duty at polling stations or at the counting of the votes shall not be required to make the declaration of secrecy.

(2) Notwithstanding anything in paragraph (1) above, the following persons atending at the counting of the votes—

(*a*) *any candidate,*

(*b*) *any election agent, or any candidate's wife or husband attending by virtue of the rule authorising election agents and candidates' wives or husbands to attend as such,*

(*c*) *any person permitted by the returning officer to attend, though not entitled to do so,*

(*d*) *any clerk making the declaration in order to attend at the counting of the votes,*

need not make the declaration before the opening of the poll but shall make it before he or she is permitted to attend the counting, and a polling or counting agent appointed after the opening of the poll shall make the declaration before acting as such an agent.

(3) The returning officer shall make the declaration in the presence of a justice of the peace, and any other person shall make the declaration in the presence either of a justice of the peace or of the returning officer, and subsections (1), (2), (3) and (6) of section 66 of this Act shall be read to the declarant by the person taking the declaration or shall be read by the declarant in the presence of that person; but—

(*a*) *in England and Wales the declaration may be made by the returning officer or any other person before a person who is chairman of . . . a county council or a district council or mayor of a London borough, and may be made by a person other than the returning officer before a person who is the proper officer of any such council; and*

(*b*) *(applies to Scotland only);*

(*c*) *in Northern Ireland the declaration may be made by a person other than the returning officer before the clerk of a district council.*

(4) The declaration shall be as follows—

"I solemnly promise and declare that I will not do anything forbidden by subsections (1), (2), (3) and (6) of section 66 of the Representation of the People Act 1983, which have been read to [by] me."

NOTES

This rule contains provisions formerly in the Representation of the People Act 1949, Sch 2, r 32, as amended and partly repealed by the Representation of the People Act 1969, s 24(1), Sch 2, para 26(1), and as affected by the Local Government Act 1972, s 251(1), Sch 29, Pt I, para 4(1), and amended by the Local Government Reorganisation (Consequential Provisions) (Northern Ireland) Order 1973, SI 1973/2095, art 2(6). Paras (1)–(3) are also partly derived from Sch 1, para 8 to the 1969 Act as amended by art 2(6) of the 1973 Order.

The words omitted from sub-para (3)(*a*) were repealed by the Local Government Act 1985, s 102(1), Sch 17, as from 1 April 1986 ("the abolition date" within the meaning of s 1(2) of that Act).

Prospective substitution. The rule set out below is substituted for this rule by the Representation of the People Act 1985, s 24, Sch 4, para 31 post, as from a day to be appointed under s 29(2) of that Act:

"Notification of requirement of secrecy

31. The returning officer shall make such arrangements as he thinks fit to ensure that—

    (*a*) every person attending at a polling station (otherwise than for the purpose of voting or assisting a blind voter to vote or as a constable on duty there) has been given a copy in writing of the provisions of subsections (1), (3) and (6) of section 66 of this Act; and

    (*b*) every person attending at the counting of the votes (other than any constable on duty at the counting) has been given a copy in writing of the provisions of subsections (2) and (6) of that section."

Returning officer. As to returning officers, see ss 24, 26–28 ante.

Presiding officers. These officers are appointed under r 26(1) ante.

Authorised to attend at a polling station or the counting of the votes. For the persons who are authorised so to attend, see rr 32(1), (2) and 44(2) post.

Election agent. As to election agents, see s 67 ante and the notes thereto.

Polling agent; counting agent. As to the appointment of these agents, see r 30 ante.

Constables. See the note "Constable" to s 19 ante.

Rule authorising election agents and candidates' wives or husbands to attend. See r 44(2)(*b*), (*c*) post.

England; Wales. See the note to s 4 ante.

County council. See the note to s 31 ante.

District council; London borough. See the corresponding notes to s 8 ante.

Welsh version of declaration. For the Welsh version of the declaration of secrecy set out in para (4) above, see the Elections (Welsh Forms) Order 1970, SI 1970/616, Schedule, Form 1 (made under the Welsh Language Act 1967, s 2(1), Vol 41, title Statutes).

European Assembly elections. This rule is applied to such elections by the European Assembly Elections Regulations 1984, SI 1984/137, reg 3(1), Sch 1, subject to the following modifications:

    (1) In paragraph (1)—

        (*a*) before the words "the counting", in each place where they occur, there are inserted the words "the verification of the ballot paper accounts or";

        (*b*) in sub-para (*a*), after the words "returning officer" there are inserted the words "the verifying officers", and

        (*c*) for sub-para (*f*), there is substituted:

        "(*f*) every person permitted by the verifying officer to attend at the verification of the ballot paper accounts or by the returning officer to attend at the counting of the votes, though not entitled to do so,".

    (2) In para (2)—

        (*a*) before the words "the counting", in each place where they occur, there are inserted the words "the verification of the ballot paper accounts or";

        (*b*) in sub-para (*c*), after the words "returning officer" there are inserted the words "or, as the case may be, verifying officer"; and

        (*c*) in sub-para (*d*), after the word "clerk" there are inserted the words "or verifying officer".

    (3) In paras (3) and (4), after "(2)" there is inserted "(2A)".

See further the Introductory Note to this Act.

It would appear that when the substitution of this rule, as noted above, is brought into force, new modifications will be made in relation to its application to European Assembly elections.

As to provisions relating to such elections in Northern Ireland, see the Introductory Note to this Act.

Definitions. For "proper officer" and "vote", see s 202(1) ante.

THE POLL

Admission to polling station

32.—(1) The presiding officer shall regulate the number of voters to be admitted to the polling station at the same time, and shall exclude all other persons except—

    (*a*) the candidates and their election agents;

    (*b*) the polling agents appointed to attend at the polling station;

    (*c*) the clerks appointed to attend at the polling station;

    (*d*) the constables on duty; and

    (*e*) the companions of blind voters.

(2) Not more than one polling agent shall be admitted at the same time to a polling station on behalf of the same candidate.

(3) A constable or person employed by a returning officer shall not be admitted to vote in

person elsewhere than at his own polling station under the relevant provision of this Act, except on production and surrender of a certificate as to his employment, which shall be in the prescribed form and signed by the prescribed officer of police or by the returning officer, as the case may be.

(4) Any certificate surrendered under this rule shall forthwith be cancelled.

NOTES

This rule contains provisions formerly in the Representation of the People Act 1949, Sch 2, r 33, as amended by the Representation of the People Act 1969, s 24(1), Sch 2, para 27.

Presiding officer; clerks. These officers are appointed under r 26(1) ante.

Election agents. As to election agents, see s 67 ante and the notes thereto.

Polling agents. As to the appointment of polling agents, see r 30 ante.

Constables. See the note "Constable" to s 19 ante.

Companions of blind voters. As to these, see r 39 post.

Returning officer. As to returning officers, see ss 24, 26–28 ante.

His own polling station. As to the allotment of electors to polling stations, see r 25(1) ante.

Prescribed form; prescribed officer of police. These are prescribed by the Representation of the People Regulations 1983, SI 1983/435, reg 47, Sch 3, Form G, as amended by SI 1984/137, and the Representation of the People (Northern Ireland) Regulations 1983, SI 1983/436, reg 32, Sch 3, Form D, as amended by SI 1984/198.

Forthwith. See the note to s 67 ante.

European Assembly elections. This rule and rr 33 and 34 post, are applied to such elections by the European Assembly Elections Regulations 1984, SI 1984/137, reg 3(1), Sch 1. See further the Introductory Note to this Act.

As to provisions relating to such elections in Northern Ireland, see the Introductory Note to this Act.

Definition. For "prescribed" and "voter", see s 202(1) ante.

Keeping of order in station

33.—(1) It is the presiding officer's duty to keep order at his polling station.

(2) If a person misconducts himself in a polling station, or fails to obey the presiding officer's lawful orders, he may immediately, by the presiding officer's order, be removed from the polling station—

(a) by a constable in or near that station, or

(b) by any other person authorised in writing by the returning officer to remove him,

and the person so removed shall not, without the presiding officer's permission, again enter the polling station during the day.

(3) Any person so removed may, if charged with the commission in the polling station of an offence, be dealt with as a person taken into custody by a constable for an offence without a warrant.

(4) The powers conferred by this rule shall not be exercised so as to prevent a voter who is otherwise entitled to vote at a polling station from having an opportunity of voting at that station.

NOTES

This rule contains provisions formerly in the Representation of the People Act 1949, Sch 2, r 34.

Presiding officer. This officer is appointed under r 26(1) ante.

Constable. See the note to s 19 ante.

Writing. See the note "Written" to s 28 ante.

Returning officer. As to returning officers, see ss 24, 26–28 ante.

Dealt with as a person taken into custody ... without a warrant. Cf the note "Without warrant arrest him" to s 97 ante.

European Assembly elections. See the note to r 32 ante.

Definitions. For "voter" and "vote", see s 202(1) ante.

Sealing of ballot boxes

34. Immediately before the commencement of the poll, the presiding officer shall show the ballot box empty to such persons, if any, as are present in the polling station, so that they may see

that it is empty, and shall then lock it up and place his seal on it in such a manner as to prevent its being opened without breaking the seal, and shall place it in his view for the receipt of ballot papers, and keep it so locked and sealed.

NOTES

This rule contains provisions formerly in the Representation of the People Act 1949, Sch 2, r 35.
Presiding officer. This officer is appointed under r 26(1) ante.
European Assembly elections. See the note to r 32 ante.

Questions to be put to voters

35.—(1) The presiding officer may, and if required by a candidate or his election or polling agent shall, put to any person applying for a ballot paper at the time of his application, but not afterwards, the following questions, or either of them—

(*a*) in the case of a person applying as an elector—

(i) "Are you the person registered in the register of parliamentary electors for this election as follows?" (*read the whole entry from the register.*)

(ii) "Have you already voted, here or elsewhere, at this by-election [general election], otherwise than as proxy for some other person?"

(*b*) in the case of a person applying as proxy—

(i) "Are you the person whose name appears as A.B. in the list of proxies for this election as entitled to vote as proxy on behalf of C.D.?"

(ii) "Have you already voted here or elsewhere at this by-election [general election] as proxy on behalf of C.D.?"

(2) In the case of a person applying as proxy, the presiding officer may, and if required as mentioned above shall, put the following additional question—

"Are you the husband [wife], parent, grandparent, brother [sister], child or grandchild of C.D.?"

and if that question is not answered in the affirmative the following question—

"Have you at this election already voted in this constituency on behalf of two persons of whom you are not the husband [wife], parent, grandparent, brother [sister], child or grandchild?"

(3) A ballot paper shall not be delivered to any person required to answer the above questions or any of them unless he has answered the questions or question satisfactorily.

(4) Save as by this rule authorised, no inquiry shall be permitted as to the right of any person to vote.

NOTES

This rule contains provisions formerly in the Representation of the People Act 1949, Sch 2, r 36.
Presiding officer. This officer is appointed under r 26(1) ante.
Election or polling agent. As to election agents, see s 67 ante and the notes thereto. Polling agents are appointed under r 30 ante.
Proxy. As to proxies at parliamentary elections, see ss 21 and 22 ante. Those sections are repealed by the Representation of the People Act 1985, s 28(1), Sch 5 post, as from a day to be appointed under s 29(2) of that Act, and new provision is made as to proxies, as from that date, by ss 8, 9 of that Act.
Welsh versions of questions. For the Welsh versions of the questions to be put under this rule, see the Elections (Welsh Forms) Order 1970, SI 1970/616, Schedule, Forms 2–4 (made under the Welsh Language Act 1967, s 2(1), Vol 41, title Statutes).
European Assembly elections. This rule is applied to such elections by the European Assembly Elections Regulations 1984, SI 1984/137, reg 3(1), Sch 1, subject to the omission from para (1)(*a*)(i) above of the word "parliamentary". See further the Introductory Note to this Act.
As to provisions relating to such elections in Northern Ireland, see the Introductory Note to this Act.
Definitions. For "elector" and "vote", see s 202(1) ante.

Challenge of voter

36.—(1) *If at the time a person applies for a ballot paper for the purpose of voting in person, or after he has applied for a ballot paper for that purpose and before he has left the polling station, a candidate or his election or polling agent—*

(a) *declares to the presiding officer that he has reasonable cause to believe that the applicant has committed an offence of personation, and*

(b) *undertakes to substantiate the charge in a court of law,*

the presiding officer may order a constable to arrest the applicant, and the order of the presiding officer shall be sufficient authority for the constable so to do.

(2) *A person against whom a declaration is made under this rule shall not by reason of it be prevented from voting.*

(3) *A person arrested under the provisions of this rule shall be dealt with as a person taken into custody by a constable for an offence without a warrant.*

NOTES

This rule contains provisions formerly in the Representation of the People Act 1949, Sch 2, r 37.

Prospective repeal. This rule is repealed by the Police and Criminal Evidence Act 1984, ss 26(1), 119(2), Sch 7, Pt I, Vol 12, title Criminal Law, as from a day to be appointed under s 121(1) of that Act, Vol 12, title Criminal Law.

Election or polling agent. See the note to r 35 ante.

Presiding officer. This officer is appointed under r 26(1) ante.

Offence of personation. This is punishable under s 60 ante.

Constable. See the note to s 19 ante.

Arrest; dealt with as a person taken into custody ... without a warrant. Cf the note "Without warrant arrest him" to s 97 ante.

European Assembly elections. This rule and rr 37–42 post, are applied to such elections by the European Assembly Elections Regulations 1984, SI 1984/137, reg 3(1), Sch 1. See further the Introductory Note to this Act.

As to provisions relating to such elections in Northern Ireland, see the Introductory Note to this Act.

Voting procedure

37.—(1) A ballot paper shall be delivered to a voter who applies for one, and immediately before delivery—

(*a*) the ballot paper shall be stamped with the official mark;

(*b*) the number [and name] of the elector as stated in the copy of the register of electors shall be called out;

(*c*) the number of the elector shall be marked on the counter-foil;

(*d*) a mark shall be placed in the register of electors against the number of the elector to denote that a ballot paper has been received but without showing the particular ballot paper which has been received; and

(*e*) in the case of a person applying for a ballot paper as proxy, a mark shall also be placed against his name in the list of proxies.

(2) The voter, on receiving the ballot paper, shall forthwith proceed into one of the compartments in the polling station and there secretly mark his paper and fold it up so as to conceal his vote, and shall then show to the presiding officer the back of the paper, so as to disclose the official mark, and put the ballot paper so folded up into the ballot box in the presiding officer's presence.

(3) The voter shall vote without undue delay, and shall leave the polling station as soon as he has put his ballot paper into the ballot box.

NOTES

This rule contains provisions formerly in the Representation of the People Act 1949, Sch 2, r 38, as partly repealed by the Representation of the People Act 1969, s 24(4), Sch 3, Pt II.

The words in square brackets in para (1)(*b*) were substituted by the Representation of the People Act 1985, s 24, Sch 4, para 81, as from 1 October 1985.

This rule is amended in relation to Northern Ireland; see the note "Northern Ireland" below.

Official mark. As to this, see r 20 ante.

Number ... of the elector ... shall be called out. It has been said that the calling out of the elector's name, number and description is in order that polling agents and others present may be able to identify the elector in case of alleged personation; see *Re Gloucestershire, Thornbury Division, Election Petition, Ackers v Howard* (1886) 16 QBD 739, 55 LJQB 273. This would not, however, apply to a person voting as proxy.

Register of electors. See the note "Register" to r 27 ante.

Proxy. As to proxies at parliamentary elections, see ss 21 and 22 ante (both prospectively repealed).

List of proxies. This is to be prepared under r 27(*b*) ante (prospectively repealed).

Forthwith. See the note to s 67 ante.

Presiding officer. This officer is appointed under r 26(1) ante.

European Assembly elections. See the note to r 36 ante.

Definitions. For "elector", "voter" and "vote", see s 202(1) ante; for "list of proxies", see s 27(*b*) ante.

Northern Ireland. As from 6 August 1985 the words "Subject to paragraphs (1A) to (1G) below, a" are substituted in para (1) above for the word "A" by the Elections (Northern Ireland) Act 1985, s 2(3)(*a*), and by s 1(2) thereof, the following paragraphs are inserted after para (1):

"(1A) A ballot paper shall not be delivered to a voter unless he has produced a specified document to the presiding officer or a clerk.

(1B) Where a voter produces a specified document, the presiding officer or clerk to whom it is produced shall deliver a ballot paper to the voter unless the officer or clerk decides that the document raises a reasonable doubt as to whether the voter is the elector or proxy he represents himself to be.

(1C) Where a voter produces a specified document to a presiding officer and he so decides, he shall refuse to deliver a ballot paper to the voter.

(1D) Where a voter produces a specified document to a clerk and he so decides, he shall refer the matter and produce the document to the presiding officer who shall proceed as if the document had been produced to him in the first place.

(1E) For the purposes of this rule a specified document is one which for the time being falls within the following list:

(*a*) a current licence to drive a motor vehicle granted under Part III of the Road Traffic Act 1972 (excluding a provisional licence), or under Article 12 of the Road Traffic (Northern Ireland) Order 1981 or any corresponding enactment for the time being in force;

(*b*) a current passport issued by the Government of the United Kingdom or by the Government of the Republic of Ireland;

(*c*) a current book for the payment of allowances, benefits or pensions issued by the Department of Health and Social Services for Northern Ireland;

(*d*) a medical card issued by the Northern Ireland Central Services Agency for the Health and Social Services;

(*e*) a certified copy, or extract, of an entry of marriage issued by a Registrar General, where the voter producing the copy or extract is a woman married within the period of two years ending with the day of the poll concerned.

In sub-paragraph (*e*) above "a Registrar General" means the Registrar General for England and Wales, the Registrar General of Births, Deaths and Marriages for Scotland or the Registrar General for Northern Ireland.

(1F) Regulations may make provision varying the list in paragraph (1E) above (whether by adding or deleting documents or varying any description of document).

(1G) References in this rule to producing a document are to producing it for inspection.".

Votes marked by presiding officer

38.—(1) The presiding officer, on the application of a voter—

(*a*) who is incapacited by blindness or other physical cause from voting in manner directed by these rules, or

(*b*) who declares orally that he is unable to read,

shall, in the presence of the polling agents, cause the voter's vote to be marked on a ballot paper in manner directed by the voter, and the ballot paper to be placed in the ballot box.

(2) The name and number on the register of electors of every voter whose vote is marked in pursuance of this rule, and the reason why it is so marked, shall be entered on a list (in these rules called "the list of votes marked by the presiding officer").

In the case of a person voting as proxy for an elector, the number to be entered together with the voter's name shall be the elector's number.

NOTES

This rule contains provisions formerly in the Representation of the People Act 1949, Sch 2, r 39, as partly repealed by the Representation of the People Act 1981, s 3, Schedule, para 7(*b*).

This rule is amended in relation to Northern Ireland; see the note "Northern Ireland" below.

Presiding officer. This officer is appointed under r 26(1) ante.

Blindness. As to voting by blind persons, see also r 39 post.

In the presence of the polling agents. Polling agents are appointed under r 30 ante. As to things which are to be done in their presence, note the provisions of paras (9) and (10) of that rule.

Register of electors. See the note "Register" to r 27 ante.

Proxy. As to proxies at parliamentary elections, see ss 21 and 22 ante. Those sections are repealed by the Representation of the People Act 1985, s 28(1), Sch 5, as from a day to be appointed under s 29(2) of that Act, and new provision is made as to proxies, as from that date, by ss 8, 9 of that Act.

European Assembly elections. See the note to r 36 ante.

Definitions. For "elector", "voter" and "vote", see s 202(1) ante.

Northern Ireland. As from 6 August 1985 in para (1) above the words "Subject to paragraph (1A) below, the" are substituted for the word "The" by the Elections (Northern Ireland) Act 1985, s 2(3)(*b*); and by s 1(3) thereof the following paragraph is inserted after para (1):

> "(1A) Paragraphs (1A) to (1G) of rule 37 shall apply in the case of a voter who applies under paragraph (1) above as they apply in the case of a voter who applies under rule 37(1), but reading references to delivering a ballot paper to a voter as references to causing a voter's vote to be marked on a ballot paper.".

Voting by blind persons

39.—(1) If a voter makes an application to the presiding officer to be allowed on the ground of blindness to vote with the assistance of another person by whom he is accompanied (in these rules referred to as "the companion"), the presiding officer shall require the voter to declare orally whether he is so incapacitated by his blindness as to be unable to vote without assistance.

(2) If the presiding officer—

(*a*) is satisfied that the voter is so incapacitated, and

(*b*) is also satisfied by a written declaration made by the companion (in these rules referred to as "the declaration made by the companion of a blind voter") that the companion—

(i) is a qualified person within the meaning of this rule, and

(ii) has not previously assisted more than one blind person to vote at the election,

the presiding officer shall grant the application, and then anything which is by these rules required to be done to or by that voter in connection with the giving of his vote may be done to, or with the assistance of, the companion.

(3) For the purposes of this rule, a person shall be qualified to assist a blind voter to vote, if that person is either—

(*a*) a person who is entitled to vote as an elector at the election; or

(*b*) the father, mother, brother, sister, husband, wife, son or daughter of the blind voter and has attained the age of 18 years.

(4) The name and number in the register of electors of every voter whose vote is given in accordance with this rule and the name and address of the companion shall be entered on a list (in these rules referred to as "the list of blind voters assisted by companions").

In the case of a person voting as proxy for an elector, the number to be entered together with the voter's name shall be the elector's number.

(5) The declaration made by the companion—

(*a*) shall be in the form in the Appendix;

(*b*) shall be made before the presiding officer at the time when the voter applies to vote with the assistance of a companion and shall forthwith be given to the presiding officer who shall attest and retain it.

(6) No fee or other payment shall be charged in respect of the declaration.

NOTES

This rule contains provisions formerly in the Representation of the People Act 1949, Sch 2, r 40, as amended by the Representation of the People Act 1969, s 24(1), Sch 2, para 28.

This rule is amended in relation to Northern Ireland; see the note "Northern Ireland" below.

Presiding officer. This officer is appointed under r 26(1) ante.

Blindness. As to voting by blind persons, see also r 38 ante.

Written. See the note to s 28 ante.

Person who is entitled to vote as an elector. See, in particular, s 1 ante.

Attained the age of 18. As to when a person attains a given age, see s 202(2) ante.

Register of electors. See the note "Register" to r 27 ante.

Proxy. As to proxies at parliamentary elections, see ss 21 and 22 ante. Those sections are repealed by the Representation of the People Act 1985, s 28(1), Sch 5, as from a day to be appointed under s 29(2) of that Act, and new provision is made as to proxies, as from that date, by ss 8, 9 of that Act.

Form in the Appendix. See also the note "Welsh versions of forms" to the Appendix post.

Forthwith. See the note to s 67 ante.

European Assembly elections. See the note to r 36 ante.

Definitions. For "elector", "voter" and "vote", see s 202(1) ante. Note as to "the companion", para (1) above and as to "qualified person", para (3) above.

Northern Ireland. As from 6 August 1985 in para (2) above the words "Subject to paragraph (2A) below, if" are substituted for the word "If" by the Elections (Northern Ireland) Act 1985, s 2(3)(c); and by s 1(4) thereof the following paragraph is inserted after para (2):

"(2A) Paragraphs (1A) to (1G) of rule 37 shall apply in the case of a voter who applies under paragraph (1) above as they apply in the case of a voter who applies under rule 37(1), but reading references to delivering a ballot paper to a voter as references to granting a voter's application.".

Tendered ballot papers

40.—(1) If a person, representing himself to be—

(a) a particular elector named on the register and not named in the absent voters list, or

(b) a particular person named in the list of proxies as proxy for an elector and not *named in the list of persons* entitled to vote by post as proxy,

applies for a ballot paper after another person has voted in person either as the elector or his proxy, the applicant shall, on satisfactorily answering the questions permitted by law to be asked at the poll, be entitled, subject to the following provisions of this rule, to mark a ballot paper (in these rules referred to as "a tendered ballot paper") in the same manner as any other voter.

(2) A tendered ballot paper shall—

(a) be of a colour differing from the other ballot papers;

(b) instead of being put into the ballot box, be given to the presiding officer and endorsed by him with the name of the voter and his number in the register of electors, and set aside in a separate packet.

(3) The name of the voter and his number on the register of electors shall be entered on a list (in these rules referred to as the "tendered votes list").

(4) In the case of a person voting as proxy for an elector, the number to be endorsed or entered together with the voter's name shall be the number of that elector.

NOTES

This rule contains provisions formerly in the Representation of the People Act 1949, Sch 2, r 41.

This section is amended in relation to Northern Ireland; see the note "Northern Ireland" below.

Prospective repeal. The words in italics in para (1)(b) are repealed by the Representation of the People Act 1985, ss 11, 28(1), Sch 2, Pt I, para 7, Sch 5 post, as from a day to be appointed under s 29(2) of that Act.

Register. See the note to r 27 ante.

Absent voters list; list of proxies; list of persons entitled to vote by post as proxy. These lists are to be prepared under r 27 ante (prospectively repealed).

Proxy. As to proxies at parliamentary elections, see ss 21 and 22 ante. Those sections are repealed by the Representation of the People Act 1985, s 28(1), Sch 5 post, as from a day to be appointed under s 29(2) of that Act, and new provision as to proxies is made, as from that date, by ss 8, 9 of that Act.

Questions permitted . . . to be asked. For these, see r 35 ante.

Presiding officer. This officer is appointed under r 26(1) ante.

European Assembly elections. See the note to r 36 ante.

Definitions. For "elector", "voter" and "vote", see s 202(1) ante; for "absent voters list" and "list of proxies", see r 27 ante (prospectively repealed). Note as to "tendered ballot paper", para (1) above.

Northern Ireland. The following amendments are made by the Elections (Northern Ireland) Act 1985, ss 1(5), (6), 2(4) respectively as from 6 August 1985:

after para (1) above there are inserted the following paragraphs:

"(1A) Paragraphs (1A) to (1G) of rule 37 shall apply in the case of a person who seeks to mark a tendered ballot paper under paragraph (1) above as they apply in the case of a voter who applies for a ballot paper under rule 37(1).

(1B) Paragraph (1C) below applies where a presiding officer refuses to deliver a ballot paper to a person under paragraph (1C) of rule 37 (including that paragraph as applied by rule 38 or 39 of this rule).

(1C) The person shall, on satisfactorily answering the questions permitted by law to be asked at the poll, nevertheless be entitled, subject to the following provisions of this rule, to mark a ballot paper (in these rules referred to as "a tendered ballot paper") in the same manner as any other voter."

after para (4) above there are inserted the following paragraphs:

"(5) A person who marks a tendered ballot paper under paragraph (1C) above shall sign the paper, unless it was marked after an application was refused under rule 38 or 39.

(6) A paper which is required to be signed under paragraph (5) above and is not so signed shall be void."

after this rule there is inserted the following rule:

"Refusal to deliver ballot paper

40A.—(1) This rule applies where a presiding officer refuses to deliver a ballot paper under paragraph (1C) of rule 37 (including that paragraph as applied by rule 38, 39 or 40).

(2) The refusal shall be subject to review on an election petition but, subject to that, shall be final and shall not be questioned in any proceeding whatsoever.".

Spoilt ballot papers

41. A voter who has inadvertently dealt with his ballot paper in such manner that it cannot be conveniently used as a ballot paper may, on delivering it to the presiding officer and proving to his satisfaction the fact of the inadvertence, obtain another ballot paper in the place of the ballot paper so delivered (in these rules referred to as "a spoilt ballot paper"), and the spoilt ballot paper shall be immediately cancelled.

NOTES

This rule contains provisions formerly in the Representation of the People Act 1949, Sch 2, r 42.
Voter. For meaning, see s 202(1) ante.
Presiding officer. This officer is appointed under r 26(1) ante.
Spoilt ballot paper. See also, as to spoilt postal ballot papers, the Representation of the People Regulations 1983, SI 1983/435, reg 60, and the Representation of the People (Northern Ireland) Regulations 1983, SI 1983/436, reg 45.
European Assembly elections. See the note to r 36 ante.

Adjournment of poll in case of riot

42.—(1) Where the proceedings at any polling station are interrupted or obstructed by riot or open violence, the presiding officer shall adjourn the proceedings till the following day and shall forthwith give notice to the returning officer.

(2) Where the poll is adjourned at any polling station—

(a) the hours of polling on the day to which it is adjourned shall be the same as for the original day; and

(b) references in this Act to the close of the poll shall be construed accordingly.

NOTES

This rule contains provisions formerly in the Representation of the People Act 1949, Sch 2, r 43.
Presiding officer. This officer is appointed under r 26(1) ante.
Forthwith. See the note to s 67 ante.
Returning officer. As to returning officers, see ss 24, 26–28 ante.
Hours of polling. See r 1 ante.
European Assembly elections. See the note to r 36 ante.

Procedure on close of poll

43.—(1) As soon as practicable after the close of the poll, the presiding officer shall, in the presence of the polling agents, make up into separate packets, sealed with his own seal and the seals of such polling agents as desire to affix their seals—

(a) each ballot box in use at the station, sealed so as to prevent the introduction of additional ballot papers and unopened, but with the key attached,

(b) the unused and spoilt ballot papers placed together,

(c) the tendered ballot papers,

(d) the marked copies of the register of electors and of the list of proxies,

(e) the counterfoils of the used ballot papers and the certificates as to employment on duty on the day of the poll,

(f) the tendered votes list, the list of blind voters assisted by companions, the list of votes marked by the presiding officer, a statement of the number of voters whose votes are so marked by the presiding officer under the heads "physical incapacity" and "unable to read", and the declarations made by the companions of blind voters,

and shall deliver the packets or cause them to be delivered to the returning officer to be taken charge of by him; but if the packets are not delivered by the presiding officer personally to the returning officer, the arrangements for their delivery shall require the returning officer's approval.

(2) The marked copies of the register of electors and of the list of proxies shall be in one packet but shall not be in the same packet as the counterfoils of the used ballot papers and the certificates as to employment on duty on the day of the poll.

(3) The packets shall be accompanied by a statement (in these rules referred to as "the ballot paper account") made by the presiding officer showing the number of ballot papers entrusted to him, and accounting for them under the heads of ballot papers issued and not otherwise accounted for, unused, spoilt and tendered ballot papers.

NOTES

This rule contains provisions formerly in the Representation of the People Act 1949, Sch 2, r 44, as amended by the Representation of the People Act 1969, s 14(1), Sch 1, Pt II, paras 9, 10(1), and as partly repealed by the Representation of the People Act 1981, s 3, Schedule, para 7(c).

Presiding officer. This officer is appointed under r 26(1) ante.

In the presence of the polling agents. See the note to r 38 ante.

Make up into separate packets. For a case of non-observance of this rule which did not affect the validity of the votes in question, see *Woodward v Sarsons* [1875] LR 10 CP 733, [1874–80] All ER Rep 262.

Marked copies of the register . . . and . . . list of proxies. This refers to the marks placed in the register and list of proxies under r 37(1)(d), (e) ante.

Certificates as to employment on duty. As to these certificates, see r 32(3) ante.

Returning officer. As to returning officers, see ss 24, 26–28 ante.

Disposal, production, etc, of documents. See rr 54 et seq post.

European Assembly elections. This rule is applied to such elections by the European Assembly Elections Regulations 1984, SI 1984/137, reg 3(1), Sch 1, subject to the substitution in para (1) above for the words "returning officer", in each place where they occur, of the words "verifying officer". In the case of such elections the following rules are added after this rule by the same provisions:

"Attendance at verification of ballot paper accounts

43A.—(1) The verifying officer shall make arrangements for the verification of the ballot paper accounts in the presence of the counting agents as soon as practicable after the close of the poll, and shall give the counting agents notice in writing of the time and place at which he will begin such verification.

(2) No person other than—

(a) the returning officer,

(b) the verifying officer and his clerks,

(c) the candidates and their spouses,

(d) the election agents, and

(e) the counting agents,

may attend the verification of the ballot paper accounts, unless permitted by the verifying officer to attend; and the verifying officer shall not permit a person to attend unless he is satisfied that the efficient verification of the ballot paper accounts will not be impeded.

(3) The verifying officer shall allow the counting agents all such reasonable facilities for observing the proceedings, and all such information with respect to them, as he can give them consistently with the orderly conduct of the proceedings and the discharge of his duties in connection with them.

Procedure at verification of ballot paper accounts

43B.—(1) The verifying officer shall in the presence of the counting agents—

(a) open each ballot box and, taking out the ballot papers in it, count and record the number of them and verify each ballot paper account; and

(b) count such of the postal ballot papers as have been duly returned and record the number counted.

(2) A postal ballot paper shall not be deemed to be duly returned unless it is returned in the proper envelope so as to reach the returning officer before the close of the poll and is accompanied by the declaration of identity duly signed and authenticated.

(3) The verifying officer shall not count any tendered ballot paper.

(4) The verifying officer, while counting and recording the number of ballot papers, shall keep the ballot papers with their faces downwards.

(5) The verifying officer shall verify each ballot paper account forwarded to him by comparing it with the number of ballot papers recorded by him, the unused and spoilt ballot papers in his possession and the tendered votes list (opening and resealing the packets containing the unused and spoilt ballot papers and the tendered votes list) and shall draw up a statement as to the result of the verification, which any counting agent present may copy.

(6) The verifying officer shall, subject to the directions of the returning officer, determine the hours during which the procedure under this rule is proceeded with.

(7) The verifying officer shall take proper precautions for the security of the ballot papers and documents.

(8) On completion of the procedure under this rule the verifying officer shall, subject to the directions of the returning officer, make up into packets the ballot papers counted by him, seal them up in containers endorsing on each a description of the area to which the ballot papers relate, and, subject to paragraph (10) below, deliver or cause to be delivered the containers to the returning officer together with a list of them and of the contents of each container and a statement of his verification of the ballot paper accounts.

(9) At the same time as the verifying officer delivers, or causes to be delivered, to the returning officer the containers referred to in paragraph (8) above, he shall also deliver, or cause to be delivered, to the returning officer the remaining packets referred to in rule 43(1) of these rules.

(10) Paragraphs (8) and (9) above do not apply where the verification of the ballot paper accounts takes place at the same place as the counting of the votes.".

See further the Introductory Note to this Act.

As to provisions relating to such elections in Northern Ireland, see the Introductory Note to this Act.

Definitions. For "voter" and "vote", see s 202(1) ante; for "list of proxies", see r 27(*b*) ante (prospectively repealed); for "list of votes marked by the presiding officer", see r 38(2) ante; for "declaration made by the companion of a blind voter", see r 39(2)(*b*) ante; for "list of blind voters assisted by companions", see r 39(4) ante; for "tendered ballot paper", see r 40(1) ante; for "tendered votes list", see r 40(3) ante; for "spoilt ballot paper", see r 41 ante; as to "close of the poll", see r 42(2)(*b*) ante.

COUNTING OF VOTES

Attendance at counting of votes

44.—(1) The returning officer shall make arrangements for counting the votes in the presence of the counting agents as soon as practicable after the close of the poll, and shall give to the counting agents notice in writing of the time and place at which he will begin to count the votes.

(2) No person other than—

    (*a*) the returning officer and his clerks,
    (*b*) the candidates and their wives or husbands,
    (*c*) the election agents,
    (*d*) the counting agents,

may be present at the counting of the votes, unless permitted by the returning officer to attend.

(3) A person not entitled to attend at the counting of the votes shall not be permitted to do so by the returning officer unless he—

    (*a*) is satisfied that the efficient counting of the votes will not be impeded; and
    (*b*) has either consulted the election agents or thought it impracticable to do so.

(4) The returning officer shall give the counting agents all such reasonable facilities for overseeing the proceedings, and all such information with respect to them, as he can give them consistently with the orderly conduct of the proceedings and the discharge of his duties in connection with them.

(5) In particular, where the votes are counted by sorting the ballot papers according to the candidate for whom the vote is given and then counting the number of ballot papers for each candidate, the counting agents shall be entitled to satisfy themselves that the ballot papers are correctly sorted.

NOTES

Paras (1), (2), (4), (5) contain provisions formerly in the Representation of the People Act 1949, Sch 2, r 45. Para (3) contains provisions formerly in the Representation of the People Act 1969, Sch 1, Pt II, para 11.

Returning officer. As to returning officers, see ss 24, 26–28 ante.

In the presence of the counting agents. Counting agents are appointed under r 30 ante. As to things which are to be done in their presence, note the provisions of paras (9) and (10) of that rule.

Writing. See the note "Written" to s 28 ante.

Clerks. These are appointed under r 26(1) ante.

Election agents. As to election agents, see s 67 ante and the notes thereto.

European Assembly elections. This rule is applied to such elections by the European Assembly Elections Regulations 1984, SI 1984/137, reg 3(1), Sch 1, subject to:

(1) the substitution in para (1) above for the words "close of the poll" of the words "material time"; and
(2) the addition at the end of para (1) above of the following words:

"For the purposes of this paragraph the "material time" means—

(a) in the case of a general election of representatives, the time when the counting of votes becomes permissible under Article 9(2) of the Act referred to in section 8(2)(a) of the Act of 1978 (counting not to begin until close of polling in the member State whose electors are the last to vote within the period referred to in Article 9(1));
(b) in the case of a by-election the close of the poll.".

See further the Introductory Note to this Act.

As to provisions relating to such elections in Northern Ireland, see the Introductory Note to this Act.

Definitions. For "vote", see s 202(1) ante; as to "close of the poll", see r 42(2)(b) ante.

The count

45.—[(1) The returning officer shall—

(a) in the presence of the counting agents open each ballot box and count and record the number of ballot papers in it;
(b) in the presence of the election agents verify each ballot paper account; and
(c) count such of the postal ballot papers as have been duly returned and record the number counted.

(1A) The returning officer shall not count the votes given on any ballot papers until—

(a) in the case of postal ballot papers, they have been mixed with the ballot papers from at least one ballot box, and
(b) in the case of ballot papers from a ballot box, they have been mixed with the ballot papers from at least one other ballot box.]

(2) A postal ballot paper shall not be deemed to be duly returned unless it is returned in the proper envelope so as to reach the returning officer before the close of the poll and is accompanied by the declaration of identity duly signed and authenticated.

(3) The returning officer shall not count any tendered ballot paper.

(4) The returning officer, while counting and recording the number of ballot papers and counting the votes, shall keep the ballot papers with their faces upwards and take all proper precautions for preventing any person from seeing the numbers printed on the back of the papers.

(5) The returning officer shall verify each ballot paper account by comparing it with the number of ballot papers recorded by him, and the unused and spoilt ballot papers in his possession and the tendered votes list (opening and resealing the packets containing the unused and spoilt ballot papers and the tendered votes list) and shall draw up a statement as to the result of the verification, which any election agent may copy.

(6) The returning officer shall so far as practicable proceed continuously with the votes, allowing only time for refreshment, except that he may, in so far as he and the agents agree, exclude the hours between 7 in the evening and 9 on the following morning.

For the purposes of this exception the agreement of a candidate or his election agent shall be as effective as the agreement of his counting agents.

(7) During the time so excluded the returning officer shall—

(a) place the ballot papers and other documents relating to the election under his own seal and the seals of such of the counting agents as desire to affix their seals; and (*b*) otherwise take proper precautions for the security of the papers and documents.

NOTES

This rule, as originally enacted, contained provisions formerly in the Representation of the People Act 1949, Sch 2, r 46, as amended by the Representation of the People Act 1969, s 24(1), Sch 2, para 29. Para (1) is also partly derived from Sch 1, Pt II, para 10(2) to, the 1969 Act.

Paras (1), (1A) were substituted for the original para (1) by the Representation of the People Act 1985, s 24, Sch 4, para 82, as from 1 October 1985.

Returning officer. As to returning officers, see ss 24, 26–28 ante.

In the presence of the counting agents. See the note to r 44 ante.

Election agents. As to election agents, see s 67 ante and the notes thereto.

Postal ballot papers; proper envelope; declaration of identity. As to these, see r 24 ante.

7 in the evening; 9 on the following morning. See the note "4 in the afternoon; 10 in the morning, etc" to r 1 ante.

Excepted days. Under r 2(1) ante, the returning officer is not obliged to proceed with the counting of votes on a Saturday, Sunday, bank holiday, etc.

European Assembly elections. This rule is applied to such elections by the European Assembly Elections Regulations 1984, SI 1984/137, reg 3(1), Sch 1, subject to:

(1) the substitution for paras (1)–(3) above of the following paragraph:

"(1) Where the verifying officer has made the ballot papers up into packets in accordance with rule 43B(8) above, the returning officer shall open all such packets and mix together all the ballot papers received.";

(2) the omission from para (4) above of the words "counting and recording the number of ballot papers and"; and

(3) the omission of para (5) above.

See further the Introductory Note to this Act.

As to provisions relating to such elections in Northern Ireland, see the Introductory Note to this Act.

Definitions. For "vote", see s 202(1) ante; for "tendered ballot paper", see r 40(1) ante; for "tendered votes list", see r 40(3) ante; for "spoilt ballot paper", see r 41 ante; for "ballot paper account", see r 43(3) ante; as to "close of the poll", see r 45(2)(*b*) ante.

Re-count

46.—(1) A candidate or his election agent may, if present when the counting or any re-count of the votes is completed, require the returning officer to have the votes re-counted or again re-counted but the returning officer may refuse to do so if in his opinion the request is unreasonable.

(2) No step shall be taken on the completion of the counting or any re-count of votes until the candidates and election agents present at its completion have been given a reasonable opportunity to exercise the right conferred by this rule.

NOTES

This rule contains provisions formerly in the Representation of the People Act 1949, Sch 2, r 47.

General Note. The failure of the returning officer to hold a re-count will not invalidate the election where there has been no substantial irregularity and the absence of the re-count has made no difference at all to the result of the election; see s 23(3) ante, and *Levers v Morris* [1972] 1 QB 221, [1971] 3 All ER 1300.

Election agent. As to election agents, see s 67 ante and the notes thereto.

Votes. For meaning, see s 202(1) ante.

Returning officer. As to returning officers, see ss 24, 26–28 ante.

European Assembly elections. This rule and rr 47–49 post, are applied to such elections by the European Assembly Elections Regulations 1984, SI 1984/137, reg 3(1), Sch 1. See further the Introductory Note to this Act.

As to provisions relating to such elections in Northern Ireland, see the Introductory Note to this Act.

Rejected ballot papers

47.—(1) Any ballot paper—

(*a*) which does not bear the official mark, or

(*b*) on which votes are given for more than one candidate, or

(*c*) on which anything is written or marked by which the voter can be identified except the printed number on the back, or

(d) which is unmarked or void for uncertainty,

shall, subject to the provisions of the next following paragraph, be void and not counted.

(2) A ballot paper on which the vote is marked—

(a) elsewhere than in the proper place, or
(b) otherwise than by means of a cross, or
(c) by more than one mark,

shall not for such reason be deemed to be void if an intention that the vote shall be for one or other of the candidates clearly appears, and the way the paper is marked does not itself identify the voter and it is not shown that he can be identified by it.

(3) The returning officer shall endorse the word "rejected" on any ballot paper which under this rule is not to be counted, and shall add to the endorsement the words "rejection objected to" if an objection is made by a counting agent to his decision.

(4) The returning officer shall draw up a statement showing the number of ballot papers rejected under the several heads of—

(a) want of official mark;
(b) voting for more than one candidate;
(c) writing or mark by which voter could be identified;
(d) unmarked or void for uncertainty.

NOTES

This rule contains provisions formerly in the Representation of the People Act 1949, Sch 2, r 48, as partly repealed by the Representation of the People Act 1969, s 24(1), Sch 2, para 30.

Official mark. As to this, see r 20 ante. A defective application of the official mark will not invalidate a ballot paper if the court can satisfy itself that the proper officer did intend to apply it to the ballot paper (*Gloucester County, Cirencester Division, Case, Lawson v Chester-Master* (1893) 9 TLR 255; *Re South Newington (Kingston-upon-Hull) Municipal Election Petition, Lewis v Shepperdson* [1948] 2 All ER 503, 112 JP 357).

Written. See the note to s 28 ante.

By which the voter can be identified. Voters' initials on a ballot paper will invalidate it (*Re South Newington (Kingston-upon-Hull) Municipal Election Petition, Lewis v Shepperdson* [1948] 2 All ER 503, 112 JP 357).

The mere fact that a voter has written the name of the candidate on his ballot paper does not of itself invalidate the paper under para (1)(c) above since a ballot paper is only invalidated if the voter can be clearly identified from what is written. Where the voter's identity cannot be discovered and he has made his intention clear it is valid under para (2) above (*Ruffle v Rogers* [1982] 1 QB 1220, [1982] 3 All ER 157, CA; not following *Woodward v Sarsons* (1875) LR 10 CP 733, [1874–80] All ER Rep 267 and *Exeter Case, Duke v St Maw* (1911) 6 O'M & H 228).

See, further, as to the rejection of ballot papers under para (1)(c), 15 Halsbury's Laws (4th edn) para 634, and the cases there cited.

Unmarked or void for uncertainty; vote is marked . . . elsewhere than in the proper place, etc. A vote is void for uncertainty where it is upon the face of the ballot paper doubtful whether the voter intended to vote for one candidate or another (*Gloucester County, Cirencester Division, Case* (1893) cited above). See, further, as to paras (1)(d) and (2) above, 15 Halsbury's Laws (4th edn) para 635, and the cases there cited.

Returning officer. As to returning officers, see ss 24, 26–28 ante.

Counting agent. These are appointed under r 30 ante.

Shall . . . be void. If the name of a person entitled to vote be inaccurately entered on the register but the entry is intended to refer to him and he votes, the vote is valid so long as it is within the scope of s 50 ante (*R v Thwaites* (1853) 1 E & B 704, 22 LJQB 238). See also *R v Fox* (1887) 16 Cox CC 166, cited in the note "Person shall be guilty, etc" to s 60 ante.

As to the striking off or avoidance of votes for corrupt or illegal practices, see s 166 ante.

Votes received after close of poll. For the discussion of the legal position, see the note "Close of poll" to r 1 ante.

Votes cast away. If at an election votes are cast for a candidate who is disqualified absolutely for election because of a personal incapacity, and that fact is made known to the electors who vote for him in spite of notice of the disqualification, their votes are cast away and the rival candidate though numerically in a minority must be declared elected (*Re Tipperary Cases, Morton v Cahalan, Moore v Scully and Cahalan* (1875) IR 9 CL 217).

A candidate does not become automatically disqualified for election by reason of corrupt or illegal practice. His election if regular is valid until set aside by an election court. Consequently where an elected candidate was unseated on election petition, votes cast for him were not treated as cast away so as to entitle the other candidate to be regarded as elected; the fact that the electorate was given notice of the corrupt practice which led to the election petition was held to be immaterial (*Re Launceston Case, Drinkwater v Deakin* (1874) LR 9 CP 626, 43 LJCP 355). If a candidate's nomination has been accepted as valid and he is disqualified for election but the disqualification is not apparent on the nomination paper and there has been no notification to the electorate, then should he receive a majority of votes the election is merely void; votes cast for him are not thrown away so as to entitle anyone else to claim to be elected (*Hobbs v Morey* [1904] 1 KB 74, 73 LJKB 47).

A candidate desirous of taking advantage of the law concerning votes thrown away consequent upon receipt of notice of disqualification of the person to whom such votes are given should see that his notice is given in unambiguous terms precisely defining the nature of the disqualification objected to and the circumstances in which it arises. He should also give notice before the poll begins. In *R v Blizard* (1866) LR 2 QB 55, 36 LJQB 18, on a quo warranto information (since abolished by the Administration of Justice (Miscellaneous Provisions) Act 1938, s 9, Vol 13, title Crown Proceedings) the court declined costs of the rule to the relator although it made the rule absolute, because it was of opinion that the notice of disqualification issued by him was ambiguous. In the subsequent proceeding, *R v Tewkesbury Corporation* (1868) LR 3 QB 629, 37 LJQB 288, application was made for a mandamus to oblige the corporation to accept the relator in *R v Blizard* (1866) above as a councillor. The court declined to adjudge the applicant as elected on the basis that votes given to the disqualified candidate had been cast away. The main ground of its decision was that though the electors might know the facts, namely, that the mayor was both returning officer and candidate, knowledge of the legal consequences could not be attributed to them. The claim failed generally on the ground of insufficiency of notice.

As to votes given to a disqualified candidate, see also 15 Halsbury's Laws (4th edn) paras 573, 930.

Votes subsequently discovered. For the circumstances in which ballot papers discovered after declaration of the result of the poll must be included, see *Re Derbyshire North-Eastern Case, Holmes v Lee and Cleaver* (1923) 39 TLR 423.

European Assembly elections. See the note to r 46 ante.

Definitions. For "voter" and "vote", see s 202(1) ante.

Decisions on ballot papers

48. The decision of the returning officer on any question arising in respect of a ballot paper shall be final, but shall be subject to review on an election petition.

NOTES

This rule contains provisions formerly in the Representation of the People Act 1949, Sch 2, r 49.

Returning officer. As to returning officers, see ss 24, 26–28 ante.

Question arising in respect of a ballot paper. This refers to questions of validity arising under r 47 ante. The validity or invalidity of votes arising from other causes, such as want of legal capacity in the voter or want of qualification to be elected in a candidate, must be raised on election petition. See also the note "Votes cast away" to r 47 ante.

Election petition. For definition, see s 202(1) ante; and as to election petitions, see Pt III (ss 120–186) of this Act ante.

European Assembly elections. See the note to s 46 ante.

Equality of votes

49. Where, after the counting of the votes (including any re-count) is completed, an equality of votes is found to exist between any candidates and the addition of a vote would entitle any of those candidates to be declared elected, the returning officer shall forthwith decide between those candidates by lot, and proceed as if the candidate on whom the lot falls had received an additional vote.

NOTES

This rule contains provisions formerly in the Representation of the People Act 1949, Sch 2, r 50.

Votes. For meaning, see s 202(1) ante.

Returning officer. As to returning officers, see ss 24, 26–28 ante.

Forthwith. See the note to s 67 ante.

Decide between those candidates by lot. Any such decision is also effective for the purposes of an election petition; see s 139(6)(*a*) ante.

European Assembly elections. See the note to r 46 ante.

Part IV

Final Proceedings in Contested and Uncontested Elections

Declaration of result

50.—(1) In a contested election, when the result of the poll has been ascertained, the returning officer shall forthwith—

(*a*) declare to be elected the candidate to whom the majority of votes has been given;

(*b*) return his name to the Clerk of the Crown; and

(*c*) give public notice of his name and of the total number of votes given for each candidate together with the number of rejected ballot papers under each head shown in the statement of rejected ballot papers.

(2) In an uncontested election, the statement of persons nominated, in addition to showing the person standing nominated, shall also declare that person elected, and the returning officer shall forthwith return his name to the Clerk of the Crown.

NOTES

This rule contains provisions formerly in the Representation of the People Act 1949, Sch 2, r 51, as amended by the Representation of the People Act 1969, s 14, Sch 1, Pt II, para 13(4).

Returning officer. As to returning officers, see ss 24, 26–28 ante. It should be noted that by s 28(2)(*b*) ante, registration officers acting as returning officers may not exercise any duty imposed on a returning officer by this rule which the person holding that office reserves to himself and undertakes to perform in person.

A returning officer does not possess the functions of an election court, and his duty is limited to declaring the result of the poll, leaving objection to the successful candidate to be taken by election petition, nor is it his function to adjudicate upon questions as to the personal capacity of voters; this is a matter for an election court (*Pritchard v Bangor Corporation* (1888) 13 App Cas 241, 57 LJQB 313, HL).

Forthwith. See the note to s 67 ante.

Public notice. For the method of giving public notice, see s 200(1) ante.

Rejected ballot papers; statement of rejected ballot papers. As to these, see r 47 ante.

Statement of persons nominated. This is to be prepared under r 14 ante.

European Assembly elections. This rule is applied to such elections by the European Assembly Elections Regulations 1984, SI 1984/137, reg 3(1), Sch 1, subject to:

(1) the substitution for para (1)(*b*) above of the following sub-paragraph:

"(*b*) notify his name to the Secretary of State;" and

(2) the substitution in para (2) above for the words "return his name to the Clerk of the Crown" of the words "notify his name to the Secretary of State".

See further the Introductory Note to this Act.

As to provisions relating to such elections in Northern Ireland, see the Introductory Note to this Act.

Definitions. For "Clerk of the Crown" and "vote", see s 202(1) ante (and see also as to "Clerk of the Crown", r 51(5) post).

Return to the writ

51.—(1) The returning officer shall return the name of the member elected by endorsing on the writ a certificate in the form in the Appendix.

(2) Any rule of law or enactment as to the effect of, or manner of dealing with, the return of a member to serve in Parliament applies to the certificate.

(3) The returning officer may, on receiving a receipt, deliver the writ with the certificate endorsed on it to the postmaster of the principal post office of the place of election or the postmaster's deputy.

(4) The postmaster or his deputy shall send the writ so endorsed by the first post, free of charge, under cover to the Clerk of the Crown with the words "Election Writ and Return" endorsed on it.

(5) Any reference in the foregoing provisions of this Part of these rules to the Clerk of the Crown shall be taken, in relation to an election for a constituency in Northern Ireland, as a reference to the Clerk of the Crown for Northern Ireland, but any writ returned to the Clerk of the Crown for Northern Ireland shall be transmitted by him to the Clerk of the Crown in

England and the return shall be certified to the House of Commons in the same manner as returns for elections for constituencies in Great Britain.

(6) A copy of each writ returned to the Clerk of the Crown for Northern Ireland and of the certificate endorsed on it shall be attested by the Secretary of State, shall be kept in the office of the Clerk of the Crown for Northern Ireland and may be given in evidence if the originals are lost.

NOTES

This rule contains provisions formerly in the Representation of the People Act 1949, Sch 2, r 52, as affected by the Northern Ireland Constitution Act 1973, s 40(1), Sch 5, para 4(1).

Returning officer. As to returning officers, see ss 24, 26–28 ante.

Writ. As to the issue of the writ and its conveyance to the returning officer, see rr 3, 4 ante.

Clerk of the Crown. Ie the Clerk of the Crown in Chancery; see s 202(1) ante. Note, however, para (5) above.

Constituencies. See the note "Constituency" to s 1 ante.

Great Britain. See the note to s 160 ante.

Secretary of State. See the note to s 4 ante.

Record of returns at Crown Office

52.—(1) The Clerk of the Crown shall from the certificate on each writ returned to him enter the name of the member returned in a book to be kept by him at the Crown Office.

(2) The Clerk of the Crown shall also enter in the book any alteration or amendment made by him in the certificate endorsed on any writ.

(3) The book shall be open to public inspection at reasonable times and any person may, on payment of a reasonable fee, take copies from the book.

NOTES

This rule contains provisions formerly in the Representation of the People Act 1949, Sch 2, r 53.

Clerk of the Crown. Ie the Clerk of the Crown in Chancery; see s 202(1) ante.

Certificate on each writ returned. Ie the certificate endorsed under r 51(1) ante.

At reasonable times. See the note "At all reasonable times" to s 89 ante.

Return or forfeiture of candidate's deposit

53.—(1) The deposit made under rule 9 of these rules shall either be returned to the person making it or his personal representatives or be forfeited to Her Majesty.

(2) Except in the cases mentioned below in this rule, the deposit shall be returned [not later than the next day after that on which] the result of the election is declared.

[(2A) For the purposes of paragraph (2) above—

(a) a day shall be disregarded if it would be disregarded under rule 2 above in computing any period of time for the purposes of the timetable for an election of the kind in question; and

(b) the deposit shall be treated as being returned on a day if a cheque for the amount of the deposit is posted on that day.]

(3) If the candidate is not shown as standing nominated in the statement of persons nominated, or if the poll is countermanded or abandoned by reason of his death, the deposit shall be returned as soon as practicable after the publication of the statement or after his death, as the case may be.

(4) Subject to paragraph (3) above the deposit shall be forfeited if a poll is taken and, after the counting of the votes by the returning officer (including any re-count) is completed, the candidate is found not to have polled more than [one-twentieth] of the total number of votes polled by all the candidates.

(5) Notwithstanding anything in paragraphs (2) to (4) above, if at a general election a candidate is shown as standing nominated in more than one constituency in the statements of persons nominated, not more than one of the deposits shall be returned and, if necessary, the Treasury shall direct which it is to be.

NOTES

This rule, as originally enacted, contained provisions formerly in the Representation of the People Act 1949, Sch 2, r 54, as amended by the Representation of the People Act 1969, s 24(1), Sch 2, para 31.

The words in square brackets in para (2) were substituted, and para (2A) was inserted, by the Representation of the People Act 1985, s 24, Sch 4, para 83, as from 1 October 1985, and the words in square brackets in para (4) were substituted by s 13(*b*) of that Act, as from that date.

Result . . . is declared. Ie under r 50 ante.

Statement of persons nominated. This is to be prepared under r 14 ante.

Poll is countermanded . . . by reason of his death. Ie under r 60 post.

Returning officer. As to returning officers, see ss 24, 26–28 ante.

Constituency. See the note to s 1 ante.

Treasury. See the note to s 29 ante.

European Assembly elections. This rule and r 54 post, are applied to such elections by the European Assembly Elections Regulations 1984, SI 1984/137, reg 3(1), Sch 1. See further the Introductory Note to this Act.

As to provisions relating to such elections in Northern Ireland, see the Introductory Note to this Act.

PART V

DISPOSAL OF DOCUMENTS

Sealing up of ballot papers

54.—(1) On the completion of the counting at a contested election the returning officer shall seal up in separate packets the counted and rejected ballot papers.

(2) The returning officer shall not open the sealed packets of tendered ballot papers or of counterfoils and certificates as to employment on duty on the day of the poll, or of marked copies of the register of electors and lists of proxies.

NOTES

This rule contains provisions formerly in the Representation of the People Act 1949, Sch 2, r 55(1), (3).

Counting. See rr 44–49 ante.

Returning officer. As to returning officers, see ss 24, 26–28 ante.

Rejected ballot papers. As to these, see r 47 ante.

Sealed packets of tendered ballot papers, etc. As to the sealed packets mentioned in para (2), see r 43 ante.

European Assembly elections. See the note to r 53 ante.

Definitions. For "list of proxies", see r 27(*b*) ante (prospectively repealed); for "tendered ballot paper", see r 40(1) ante.

Delivery of documents to Clerk of the Crown

55.—(1) The returning officer shall then forward to the Clerk of the Crown the following documents—

(*a*) the packets of ballot papers in his possession,

(*b*) the ballot paper accounts and the statements of rejected ballot papers and of the result of the verification of the ballot paper accounts,

(*c*) the tendered votes lists, the lists of blind voters assisted by companions, the lists of votes marked by the presiding officer and the related statements, and the declarations made by the companions of blind voters,

(*d*) the packets of counterfoils and certificates as to employment on duty on the day of the poll,

(*e*) the packets containing marked copies of registers and of lists of proxies,

endorsing on each packet a description of its contents, the date of the election to which they relate and the name of the constituency for which the election was held.

(2) The returning officer may forward the documents either by delivering them by himself or his agent to the Clerk of the Crown or his deputy or by sending them by post in like manner as he may send the writ by post; but if he sends them by post—

(*a*) he shall send a letter to the Clerk of the Crown by the same post, specifying the number and description of the documents so sent;

(*b*) a copy of the receipt given him by the postmaster or deputy postmaster shall be signed by him and retained by the postmaster or deputy postmaster.

(3) The Clerk of the Crown shall on receiving the documents give a receipt to the person delivering them, and shall register them in books of the Crown Office specifying the date and time of receipt.

(4) Any receipt to be given for the documents shall show the date and time of their receipt.

NOTES

This rule contains provisions formerly in the Representation of the People Act 1949, Sch 2, r 56.
Returning officer. As to returning officers, see ss 24, 26–28 ante.
Packets of ballot papers. These are to be made up under r 54(1) ante.
Statements of rejected ballot papers. These are to be drawn up under r 47(4) ante.
Statements . . . of the result of the verification of the ballot paper accounts. These are to be drawn up under r 45(5) ante.
Packets of counterfoils, etc; packets containing marked copies, etc. As to the packets mentioned in para (1)(*d*) and (*e*), see r 43 ante.
Constituency. See the note to s 1 ante.
Sending them by post in like manner as . . . the writ. Ie in the manner provided by the Order in Council noted to r 3 ante.
European Assembly elections. Para (1) above is applied to such elections by the European Assembly Elections Regulations 1984, SI 1984/137, reg 3(1), Sch 1, subject to:

(1) the substitution for the words "then forward to the Clerk of the Crown" of the word "retain"; and
(2) the omission of the words from "the date of the election" to the end of the paragraph.

See further the Introductory Note to this Act.
As to provisions relating to such elections in Northern Ireland, see the Introductory Note to this Act.
Definitions. For "Clerk of the Crown", see s 202(1) ante, and r 59 post; for "list of proxies", see r 27(*b*) ante (prospectively repealed); for "list of votes marked by the presiding officer", see r 38(2) ante; for "declaration made by the companion of a blind voter", see r 39(2)(*b*) ante; for "list of blind voters assisted by companions", see r 39(4) ante; for "tendered votes list", see r 40(3) ante; for "ballot paper account", see r 43(3) ante.

Orders for production of documents

56.—(1) An order—

(*a*) for the inspection or production of any rejected ballot papers in the custody of the Clerk of the Crown, or
(*b*) for the opening of a sealed packet of counterfoils and certificates as to employment on duty on the day of the poll or the inspection of any counted ballot papers in his custody,

may be made—

(i) by the House of Commons; or
(ii) if satisfied by evidence on oath that the order is required for the purpose of instituting or maintaining a prosecution for an offence in relation to ballot papers, or for the purpose of an election petition, by the High Court or a county court.

(2) An order for the opening of a sealed packet of counterfoils and certificates or for the inspection of any counted ballot papers in the Clerk of the Crown's custody may be made by an election court.

(3) An order under this rule may be made subject to such conditions as to—

(*a*) persons,
(*b*) time,
(*c*) place and mode of inspection,
(*d*) production or opening,

as the House of Commons or court making the order may think expedient; but in making and carrying into effect an order for the opening of a packet of counterfoils and certificates or for the inspection of counted ballot papers, care shall be taken that the way in which the vote of any particular elector has been given shall not be disclosed until it has been proved—

(i) that his vote was given; and
(ii) that the vote has been declared by a competent court to be invalid.

(4) An appeal lies to the High Court from any order of a county court under this rule.

(5) Any power given under this rule—

(a) to the High Court or, except in Northern Ireland, to a county court, may be exercised by any judge of the court otherwise than in open court; and

(b) in Northern Ireland to a county court, may be exercised in such manner as may be provided by rules of court.

(6) Where an order is made for the production by the Clerk of the Crown of any document in his possession relating to any specified election—

(a) the production by him or his agent of the document ordered in such manner as may be directed by that order shall be conclusive evidence that the document relates to the specified election; and

(b) any endorsement on any packet of ballot papers so produced shall be prima facie evidence that the ballot papers are what they are stated to be by the endorsement.

(7) The production from proper custody of a ballot paper purporting to have been used at any election, and of a counterfoil marked with the same printed number and having a number marked on it in writing, shall be prima facie evidence that the elector whose vote was given by that ballot paper was the person who at the time of the election had affixed to his name in the register of electors the same number as the number written on the counterfoil.

(8) Save as by this rule provided, no person shall be allowed to inspect any rejected or counted ballot papers in the possession of the Clerk of the Crown or to open any sealed packets of counterfoils and certificates.

NOTES

This rule contains provisions formerly in the Representation of the People Act 1949, Sch 2, r 57.

Rejected ballot paper. As to these, see r 47 ante.

Sealed packet of counterfoils, etc. As to the packet mentioned in para (1)(b) above, see r 43 ante. In *Petersfield Case, Stowe v Jolliffe* (1874) LR 9 CP 446, 43 LJCP 173, the Court of Common Pleas granted an order authorising the opening of such packet for the purposes of examining the marked register of voters which had been placed therein.

Prosecution for an offence in relation to ballot papers. As to tampering with ballot papers, see s 65 ante. Dereliction of duty in counting ballot papers is an "offence in relation to ballot papers" for the purposes of para (1)(ii) above (*McWhirter v Platten* [1970] 1 QB 508, [1969] 1 All ER 172). As to offences under this Act generally, see s 63 ante.

For the purpose of an election petition. This means for the purpose of a petition actually presented or proposed to be presented (*Re Lancashire, Darwen Division, Case* (1885) 2 TLR 220).

By the High Court or a county court. The House of Commons may under para (1)(i) of this rule make an order for such reason as it thinks fit, but the power of the High Court or of a county court under para (1)(ii) is exercisable only for either of the two purposes mentioned therein.

As to election petitions, see Pt III (ss 120–186) of this Act ante.

High Court. See the note to s 39 ante.

County court. See the note to s 30 ante.

Order . . . may be made by an election court. It should be noted that the powers of an election court under para (2) above do not include power to order inspection or production of rejected ballot papers; cf para (1)(a) above.

Persons; time; etc. It is thought that sub-paras (a)–(d) of para (3) above do not accurately reproduce the effect of the corresponding passage in the repealed legislation, which read "persons, time, place and mode of inspection, production or opening" without division into sub-paragraphs and that para (3) can only be properly understood if it is read as if this redrafting had not been introduced.

Writing. See the note "Written" to s 28 ante.

European Assembly elections. This rule is applied to such elections by the European Assembly Elections Regulations 1984, SI 1984/137, reg 3(1), Sch 1, subject to:

(1) the substitution in para (1) above for the words "Clerk of the Crown" of the words "returning officer";

(2) the omission of para (1)(i) above;

(3) the substitution in para (2) above for the words "Clerk of the Crown's" of the words "returning officer's";

(4) the omission from para (3) above of the words "House of Commons or"; and

(5) the substitution in paras (6) and (8) above for the words "Clerk of the Crown", in each place where they occur, of the words "returning officer".

See further the Introductory Note to this Act.

As to provisions relating to such elections in Northern Ireland, see the Introductory Note to this Act.
Definitions. For "Clerk of the Crown", "election court", "election petition", "elector" and "vote", see s 202(1) ante (and see also as to "Clerk of the Crown", r 59 post).

Retention and public inspection of documents

57.—(1) The Clerk of the Crown shall retain for a year all documents relating to an election forwarded to him in pursuance of these rules by a returning officer, and then, unless otherwise directed by order of the House of Commons or the High Court, shall cause them to be destroyed.

(2) Those documents, except ballot papers, counterfoils and certificates as to employment on duty on the day of the poll, shall be open to public inspection at such time and subject to such conditions as may be prescribed by the Clerk of the Crown with the consent of the Speaker of the House of Commons.

(3) The Clerk of the Crown shall, on request, supply copies of or extracts from the documents open to public inspection on payment of such fees and subject to such conditions as may be sanctioned by the Treasury.

NOTES

This rule contains provisions formerly in the Representation of the People Act 1949, Sch 2, r 58.
Clerk of the Crown. Ie the Clerk of the Crown in Chancery; see s 202(1) ante. See, however, para 59 post.
Documents ... forwarded ... by a returning officer. As to the documents which are to be so forwarded, see r 55 ante. Note that by s 75(4) ante this rule also applies to copies of returns and declarations as to expenses required to be authorised by the election agent, which are to be sent to the Clerk of the Crown under that subsection.
High Court. See the note to s 39 ante.
Except ballot papers, etc. The excepted documents mentioned in para (2) may be inspected on the order of the House of Commons, High Court, county court or election court under r 56 ante.
Certificates as to employment on duty. As to these certificates, see r 32(3) ante.
Treasury. See the note to s 29 ante.
European Assembly elections. This rule is applied to such elections by the European Assembly Elections Regulations 1984, SI 1984/137, reg 3(1), Sch 1, subject to:

(1) the substitution in para (1) above for the words "Clerk of the Crown" of the words "returning officer" and for the words "forwarded to him in pursuance of these rules by a returning officer" of the words "to which rule 55(1) of these rules applies";
(2) the omission from para (1) above of the words "the House of Commons or";
(3) the substitution in para (2) above for the words from "Clerk of the Crown" to the end of the paragraph of the words "returning officer";
(4) the substitution in para (3) above for the words "Clerk of the Crown" of the words "returning officer" and for the words "the Treasury" of the words "the local authority by which he is employed".

See further the Introductory Note to this Act.
As to provisions relating to such elections in Northern Ireland, see the Introductory Note to this Act.

58 (*Applies to Scotland only.*)

Disposal of documents in Northern Ireland

59. In relation to an election for a constituency in Northern Ireland, any reference in this Part of these rules to the Clerk of the Crown shall be taken as a reference to the Clerk of the Crown for Northern Ireland.

NOTES

This rule contains provisions formerly in the Representation of the People Act 1949, Sch 2, r 60.
Constituency. See the note to s 1 ante.
This Part of these rules. Ie Pt V (rr 54–59).

Part VI

Death of Candidate

Countermand or abandonment of poll on death of candidate

60.—(1) If at a contested election proof is given to the returning officer's satisfaction before the result of the election is declared that one of the persons named or to be named as candidate in the ballot papers has died, then the returning officer shall countermand notice of the poll or, if polling has begun, direct that the poll be abandoned, and all proceedings with reference to the election shall be commenced afresh in all respects as if the writ had been received 28 days after the day on which proof was given to the returning officer of the death except that—

(a) no fresh nomination shall be necessary in the case of a person shown in the statement of persons nominated as standing nominated, and

(b) in the case of a general election, as in the case of a by-election, the time for delivery of nomination papers and the time for polling shall be determined in accordance with the third column in the Timetable in rule 1 of these rules (with the necessary modification of any reference to the date on which the writ is received).

(2) Where the poll is abandoned by reason of a candidate's death the proceedings at or consequent on that poll shall be interrupted, and the presiding officer at any polling station shall take the like steps (so far as not already taken) for the delivery to the returning officer of ballot boxes and of ballot papers and other documents as he is required to take on the close of the poll in due course, and the returning officer shall dispose of ballot papers and other documents in his possession as he is required to do on the completion in due course of the counting of the votes, but—

(a) it shall not be necessary for any ballot paper account to be prepared or verified; and

(b) the returning officer, without taking any step or further step for the counting of the ballot papers or of the votes shall seal up all the ballot papers, whether the votes on them have been counted or not, and it shall not be necessary to seal up counted and rejected ballot papers in separate packets.

(3) The provisions of these rules as to the inspection, production, retention and destruction of ballot papers and other documents relating to a poll at an election apply to any such documents relating to a poll abandoned by reason of a candidate's death, with the following modifications—

(a) ballot papers on which the votes were neither counted nor rejected shall be treated as counted ballot papers; and

(b) no order shall be made for the production or inspection of any ballot papers or for the opening of a sealed packet of counterfoils or certificates as to employment on duty on the day of the poll unless the order is made by a court with reference to a prosecution.

NOTES

This rule contains provisions formerly in the Representation of the People Act 1969, s 13(1)–(3).
Returning officer. As to returning officers, see ss 24, 26–28 ante.
Notice of the poll. This is to be given under r 5 ante.
Proceedings ... shall be commenced afresh, etc. Ie in accordance with r 1 ante, subject to the exceptions in para (1)(a) and (b) above.
28 days after, etc. In calculating this period the day from which it runs is to be excluded; see 45 Halsbury's Laws (4th edn) para 1134.
Statement of persons nominated. This statement is to be prepared under r 14 ante.
Presiding officer. This officer is appointed under r 26 ante.
Delivery ... of ballot boxes, etc. This is governed by r 43 ante.

Dispose of ballot papers, etc. This is governed by rr 54, 55 ante.

Ballot paper account. This is generally to be prepared under r 43(3) ante, and to be verified under r 45 ante.

Seal up counted and rejected ballot papers in separate packets. This is generally to be done under r 54(1) ante. As to rejected ballot papers, see r 47 ante.

Inspection, production . . . of ballot papers, etc. See rr 56, 57 ante.

No order shall be made, etc. As to the making of orders for production or inspection of documents, see r 56 ante.

European Assembly elections. This rule is applied to such elections by the European Assembly Elections Regulations 1984, SI 1984/137, reg 3(1), Sch 1, subject to:

(1) the substitution in para (1) above for the words "as if the writ had been received 28 days" of the words "as if the day appointed by order under paragraph 3 of Schedule 1 to the Act of 1978 was the first Thursday after the expiry of 45 days";
(2) the omission of para (1)(b) above;
(3) the insertion at the end of para (1) above of the words "and the period of 45 days shall be calculated in accordance with rule 2 of these rules"; and
(4) the insertion in para (2) alter the words "in due course" (in the first place where they occur) of the words "to the verifying officer".

See further the Introductory Note to this Act.

As to provisions relating to such elections in Northern Ireland, see the Introductory Note to this Act.

Definitions. As to "close of the poll", see r 42(2)(b) ante; for "ballot paper account", see r 43(3) ante.

APPENDIX OF FORMS

Note.—The forms contained in this Appendix may be adapted so far as circumstances require.

Form of writ

★Elizabeth the Second by the Grace of God of the United Kingdom of Great Britain and Northern Ireland and of Our other Realms and Territories Queen Head of the Commonwealth Defender of the Faith to the Returning Officer for the   Constituency Greeting

★ The name of the sovereign may be altered when necessary.

†Whereas by the advice of Our Council We have ordered a Parliament to be holden at Westminister on the   day of   next We Command you that due notice being first given you do cause election to be made according to law of a Member to serve in Parliament for the said   Constituency [‡in the place of   ] And that you do cause the name of such Member when so elected, whether he be present or absent, to be certified to Us in Our Chancery without delay

† This preamble to be omitted except in case of a general election.
‡ Except in a general election insert here *in the place of A B, deceased* or otherwise, stating the cause of vacancy.

Witness Ourself at Westminster the   day of   in the   year of Our Reign, and in the year of Our Lord 19

Label or direction of writ

To the Returning Officer for the   Constituency.
A writ of a new election of a Member for the said Constituency.

Endorsement

Received the within Writ on the   day of   , 19   .

(Signed)

Returning Officer (*or as the case may be.*)

Certificate endorsed on writ

I hereby certify, that the Member elected for the   Constituency in pursuance of the within
written Writ is   of   in the County of
(Signed)

Returning Officer (*or as the case may be.*)

.   .   .   .   .

Form of nomination paper

ELECTION OF A MEMBER to serve in Parliament for the   Constituency.
We, the undersigned, being electors for the said Constituency, do hereby nominate the under-
mentioned person as a candidate at the said election.

Candidate's surname	Other names in full	Description	Home address in full
BROWN	John Edward ...	Merchant	52, George Street, Bristol

Signatures	Electoral Number (see Note 3)	
	Distinctive letter	Number
Proposer...	....	....
Seconder	....	....
We, the undersigned, being electors for the said Constituency, do hereby assent to the foregoing nomination.		
1	....	....
2	....	....
3	....	....
4	....	....
5	....	....
6	....	....
7	....	....
8	....	....

NOTE

1. The attention of candidates and electors is drawn to the rules for filling up nomination papers and other provisions relating to nomination contained in the parliamentary elections rules in Schedule 1 to the Representation of the People Act 1983.

2. Where a candidate is commonly known by some title he may be described by his title as if it were his surname.

3. A person's electoral number is his number in the register to be used at the election (including the distinctive letter of the parliamentary polling district in which he is registered) except that before publication of the register his number (if any) in the electors lists for that register shall be used instead.

4. An elector may not subscribe more than one nomination paper for the same election.

5. A person whose name is entered in the register or electors lists may not subscribe a nomination paper if the entry gives as the date on which he will become of voting age a date later than the day fixed for the poll.

Form of Ballot Paper

Form of Front of Ballot Paper

			Counterfoil No.
1	**BROWN** (JOHN EDWARD Brown, of 52, George Street, Bristol, merchant.)		*The counterfoil is to have a number to correspond with that on the back of the Ballot Paper.*
2	**BROWN** (THOMAS WILLIAM Brown, of 136, London Road, Swindon, salesman.)		
3	**JONES** (William David Jones, of High Elms, Wilts, gentleman.)		
4	**MERTON** (Hon. George Travis, commonly called Viscount Merton, of Swansworth, Berks.)		
5	**SMITH** (Mary Smith, of 72, High Street, Bath, married woman.)		

Form of Back of Ballot Paper

No.

Election for the   Constituency
on   19

Note.—The number on the ballot paper is to correspond with that on the counterfoil.

Directions as to printing the ballot paper

1. Nothing is to be printed on the ballot paper except in accordance with these directions.

2. So far as practicable, the following arrangements shall be observed in the printing of the ballot paper—

    (*a*) no word shall be printed on the face except the particulars of the candidates;

    (*b*) no rule shall be printed on the face except the horizontal rules separating the particulars of the candidates from one another and the vertical rules separating those particulars from the numbers on the left-hand side and the spaces on the right where the vote is to be marked;

    (*c*) the whole space between the top and bottom of the paper shall be equally divided between *the candidates by the rules separating their particulars.*

3. The surname of each candidate shall in all cases be printed by itself in large capitals, and his full particulars shall be set out below it and shall be printed in ordinary type except that small capitals shall be used—

    (*a*) if his surname is the same as another candidate's, for his other names; and

(b) if his other names are also the same as the other candidate's, either for his home address or for his description unless each of them is the same as that of another candidate with the same surname and other names.

4. The number on the back of the ballot paper shall be printed in small characters.

Form of directions for the guidance of the voters in voting

1. The voter should see that the ballot paper, before it is handed to him, is stamped with the official mark.

2. The voter will go into one of the compartments and, with the pencil provided in the compartment, place a cross on the right-hand side of the ballot paper, opposite the name of the candidate for whom he votes, thus X.

3. The voter will then fold up the ballot paper so as to show the official mark on the back, and leaving the compartment will, without showing the front of the paper to any person, show the official mark on the back to the presiding officer, and then, in the presence of the presiding officer, put the paper into the ballot box, and forthwith leave the polling station.

4. If the voter inadvertently spoils a ballot paper he can return it to the officer, who will, if satisfied of such inadvertence, give him another paper.

5. If the voter votes for more than one candidate, or places any mark on the paper by which he may afterwards be identified his ballot paper will be void, and will not be counted.

6. If the voter fraudulently takes a ballot paper out of a polling station or fraudulently puts into the ballot box any paper other than the one given to him by the officer, he will be liable on conviction to imprisonment for a term not exceeding six months.

Form of declaration to be made by the companion of a blind voter

I, *A.B.*, of   , having been requested to assist *C.D.*, (*in the case of a blind person voting as proxy add* voting as proxy for *M.N.*) whose number on the register is   to record his vote at the election now being held in this constituency, hereby declare that [I am entitled to vote as an elector at the said election] [I am the   ★   of the said voter and have attained the age of 18 years], and that I have not previously assisted any blind person [except *E.F.*, of   ] to vote at the said election.

(Signed) *A.B.*,

day of   19   .

I, the undersigned, being the presiding officer for the   polling station for the   Constituency, hereby certify that the above declaration, having been first read to the above-named declarant, was signed by the declarant in my presence.

(Signed) *G.H.*,

day of   19   .
minutes past   o'clock [a.m.][p.m.]

NOTE.—If the person making the above declaration knowingly and wilfully makes therein a statement false in a material particular, he will be guilty of an offence.
★State the relationship of the companion to the voter.

NOTES

This Appendix contains provisions formerly in the Representation of the People Act 1949, Sch 2, Appendix, as amended and partly repealed by the Representation of the People Act 1969, ss 14, 24(1), Sch 1, Pt II, paras 5(2), 13(2)(c), Sch 2, paras 32, 33, 37, and as further partly repealed by the Local Government Act 1972, s 272(1), Sch 30, and amended by the Representation of the People Act 1981, s 3, Schedule, para 6.

The form of notice of election was repealed as indicated by dots at the top of p 707 ante by the Representation of the People Act 1985, s 28(1), Sch 5, as from 1 October 1985.

Prospective amendment. The following amendments are made to the Appendix by the Representation of the People Act 1985, s 24, Sch 4, paras 84 to 86 post, as from a day or days to be appointed under s 29(2) of that Act:

At the top of the form of the grant of a ballot paper, the words "VOTE FOR ONE CANDIDATE ONLY" in large capitals are inserted.

In the directions as to printing the ballot paper—

in para 2(a), the words "the direction 'VOTE FOR ONE CANDIDATE ONLY' and" are inserted after the word "except";
in para 2(b), the words "the horizontal rule separating the direction mentioned in paragraph (a) above from the particulars of the candidates and" are inserted after the word "except";
in para 2(c), the words "the direction mentioned in paragraph (a) above and each of the candidates by the horizontal rules mentioned in paragraph (b) above" are substituted for the words printed in italics;
after paragraph 2, "2A. The direction mentioned in paragraph 2(a) above shall be printed in large capitals." is inserted.

The following form is substituted for the form in italics:
"Form of directions for the guidance of the voters in voting
GUIDANCE FOR VOTERS

1. When you are given a ballot paper make sure it is stamped with the official mark.

2. Go to one of the compartments. Mark a cross (X) in the box on the right hand side of the ballot paper opposite the name of the candidate you are voting for.

3. Fold the ballot paper in two. Show the official mark to the presiding officer, but do not let anyone see your vote. Put the ballot paper in the ballot box and leave the polling station.

4. Vote for one candidate only. Put no other mark on the ballot paper, or your vote may not be counted.

5. If by mistake you spoil a ballot paper, show it to the presiding officer and ask for another one.".

Welsh versions of forms. For the Welsh versions of the forms of nomination paper and of declaration to be made by the companion of a blind voter set out in this Appendix, see the Elections (Welsh Forms) Order 1970, SI 1970/616, Schedule, Forms 5, 6 (made under the Welsh Language Act 1967, s 2(1), Vol 41, title Statutes).

European Assembly elections. The form of nomination paper, the form of ballot paper (including directions as to printing the ballot paper), the form of directions for the guidance of the voters in voting and the form of declaration to be made by the companion of a blind voter are applied to such elections by the European Assembly Elections Regulations 1984, SI 1984/137, reg 3(1), Sch 1, subject to the substitution in para 1 of the form of notice of election, and in the form of nomination paper, for the word "Parliament" of the words "the European Assembly" and to the extension of the nomination paper to allow for the signatures of 28 assentors. See further the Introductory Note to this Act.

As to provisions relating to such elections in Northern Ireland, see the Introductory Note to this Act.

SCHEDULE 2
Section 53
PROVISIONS WHICH MAY BE CONTAINED IN REGULATIONS AS TO REGISTRATION ETC

1.—(1) Provisions prescribing the arrangements to be made for the carrying out of his registration duties by a registration officer for part of a constituency, where the constituency is not coterminous with or wholly situated in a district or London borough.

(2) Provisions authorising a registration officer to require persons to give information required for the purpose of his registration duties.

2. Provisions imposing on registration officers the duty of requiring persons to give information required for the purpose of the officer's duty under section 3(1) of the Juries Act 1974.

3. Provisions laying down a timetable for the preparation of the register and other matters, and providing that notices and other documents received by the registration officer out of time may be or shall be disregarded either altogether or for the purposes of a particular register or election.

4. Provisions as to the manner in which service declarations, and applications and notices from service voters, are to be transmitted to the registration officer.

5.—(1) Provisions as to the evidence which shall or may be required, or be deemed sufficient or conclusive evidence, of a person's service declaration having ceased to be in force.

(2) Provisions as to the evidence of age or nationality which may be required in connection with a person's registration otherwise than as a service voter or with his appointment as a proxy.

(3) Provisions requiring any fee payable in connection with the making for the purpose of the regulations of any statutory declaration to be paid by the registration officer.

(4) Provisions as to the evidence which shall or may be required, or be deemed sufficient or conclusive evidence in connection with a person's application to be treated as an absent voter—

(a) of his being subject to any physical incapacity and as to its probable duration; or

(b) of his being bound to any religious observance and of the nature and times of the observance; or

(c) of the fact that he is acting as returning officer at any election; or

(d) of his employment as a constable or by a returning officer, mayor or person acting as mayor and the circumstances of that employment.

6. Provisions as to the cases in which a claim or objection may be determined by the registration officer without a hearing, and as to a person's right in any such cases to make written representations to him.

7. Provisions authorising a registration officer to require any person's evidence at a hearing before him to be given on oath and to administer oaths for the purpose.

[8. Provisions requiring the registration officer to prepare a special list of those persons entitled to be registered whose addresses are not required to be shown on the electors lists or of any class of such persons, showing the addresses of the person concerned.]

9. . . .

10. Provisions requiring copies of the electors lists, register and other documents or prescribed parts of them to be available for inspection by the public at such places as may be prescribed.

11. Provisions authorising or requiring the registration officer to supply to such persons as may be prescribed copies of the electors lists, register and other documents or prescribed parts of them, whether free of charge or on payment of a prescribed fee.

[11A.—(1) Provisions authorising or requiring registration officers who are data users to supply data, or documents containing information extracted from data and in such form as may be prescribed, to such persons as may be prescribed on payment of a prescribed fee.

(2) In this paragraph "data user" and "data" have the same meanings as in section 1 of the Data Protection Act 1984.]

12. Provisions as to the proceedings in connection with the issue and receipt of ballot papers for voting by post (including provisions as to the persons who are to be entitled or may be allowed to attend and the rights and obligations of persons attending), and provisions as to the steps to be taken to ensure the secrecy of the voting and the safe custody (before and after the count) of the ballot papers returned and other documents.

13.—(1) Provisions imposing pecuniary [penalties (not exceeding level 3 on the standard scale for any offence)] on persons summarily convicted—

(a) of having failed to comply with, or given false information in pursuance of, any such requisition of the registration officer as is mentioned in paragraph 1 or paragraph 2 above.

(b) of having, without lawful authority, destroyed, mutilated, defaced or removed any notice published by the registration officer in connection with his registration duties, or any copies of a document which have been made available for inspection in pursuance of those duties.

(2) Any other provisions incidental or supplemental to those mentioned in the foregoing paragraphs of this Schedule.

NOTES

Para 1(1) contains provisions formerly in the Representation of the People Act 1949, Sch 4, para 1, as substituted by the Local Government Act 1972, s 45, Sch 4, para 1. Para 1(2) contains provisions formerly in Sch 4, para 2, to the 1949 Act, as amended by the Representation of the People Act 1969, s 24(1), Sch 2, para 38(1). Para 2 contains provisions formerly in Sch 4, para 2A, to the 1949 Act as inserted by the Criminal Justice Act 1972, s 26(1), and amended by the Juries Act 1974, s 3(3). Paras 3, 4 contain provisions formerly in paras 3, 4 of Sch 4 to the 1949 Act. Para 5 contains provisions formerly in para 5 of Sch 4 to the 1949 Act, as amended and partly repealed by the Representation of the People Act 1969, ss 7(3), 24(1), (4), Sch 2, para 38(2), (3), Sch 3, Pt II. Paras 6, 7 contain provisions formerly in paras 6, 7 of Sch 4 to the 1949 Act. Paras 10, 11, 12 contain provisions formerly in paras 9–11 of Sch 4 to the 1949 Act. Para 13 contains provisions formerly in para 12 of Sch 4 to the 1949 Act, as amended by the Criminal Justice Act 1972, s 26(1), and the Juries Act 1974, s 3(3), and affected by the Criminal Justice Act 1982, ss 37(1), (2), 40(1), (5), (8), 46(1).

Para 8 was substituted and para 11A was inserted by the Representation of the People Act 1985, s 24, Sch 4, para 85(a), (c), respectively, as from 1 October 1985. Para 9 was repealed by ss 24, 28(1) of, and Sch 4, para 85(b), Sch 5 to, that Act, as from that date. The words in square brackets in para 13(1) were substituted by s 23 of, and Sch 3, para 11 to, that Act, as from that date.

Prospective amendment. As from a day or days to be appointed under the Representation of the People Act 1985, s 29(2) post, the following amendments are made as set out below:

Paras 4(2), 5(1A) are inserted by s 4(7)(a), (b) of that Act:

"(2) Provisions as to the manner in which overseas electors' declarations, and applications from persons making such declarations, are to be transmitted to the registration oficer."

"(1A) Provisions as to the evidence which shall or may be required, or be deemed sufficient or conclusive evidence, of a person satisfying any of the requirements for qualifying as an overseas elector in respect of any constituency.".

Para 5A is inserted, and para 5(4) is repealed by s 11 of, and Sch 2, Pt I, para 8 to, that Act:

"5A—(1) Provision requiring applications under section 6 or 7 of the Representation of the People Act 1985 to be attested and limiting the number of such applications that a person may attest.

(2) Provision requiring a person applying under section 7 of the Representation of the People Act 1985 to do so in person, producing a document of a prescribed description.

(3) Provision as to the evidence which shall or may be required, or be deemed sufficient or conclusive evidence, in connection with a person's application to vote by proxy or to vote by post as elector or as proxy.

(4) Provision authorising or requiring registration officers—

    (a) to make inquiries of persons included in the record kept under section 6(3) of the Representation of the People Act 1985 for the purpose of determining whether there has been a material change of circumstances, and

    (b) to treat failure to respond to such inquiries as sufficient evidence of such a change."

Para 1: Constituency. See the note to s 1 ante.

District; London borough. See the notes "Council of every district" and "London borough" to s 8 ante; and note, in relation to the Isles of Scilly, s 203(4)(a) ante.

Para 3: Register. As to registers of electors, see ss 9 et seq ante.

Para 4: Service declarations; service voters. As to these, see ss 14–17 ante.

Para 5: Appointment as a proxy. As to the appointment of proxies at parliamentary elections, see s 21 ante, and as to proxies at local government elections, see s 34 ante. Those sections are repealed by the Representation of the People Act 1985, s 28(1), Sch 5 post, as from a day to be appointed under s 29(2), and new provision is made as from that date in relation to voting other than in person by ss 6–9 of that Act.

Statutory declaration. Ie a declaration made by virtue of the Statutory Declarations Act 1835, Vol 17, title Evidence; see the Interpretation Act 1978, s 5, Sch 1, Vol 41, title Statutes.

Application to be treated as an absent voter. Ie under s 20 ante (parliamentary elections) or s 33 ante (local government elections). Those sections are repealed by the Representation of the People Act 1985, s 28(1), Sch 5 post, as from a day to be appointed under s 29(2), and new provision is made as from that date in relation to voting other than in person by ss 6–9 of that Act.

Returning officer. As to returning officers, see ss 24, 26–28 and 35 ante.

Para 6: Written. See the note to s 28 ante.

Para 7: Oath. This includes affirmation and declaration; see the Interpretation Act 1978, s 5, Sch 1, Vol 41, title Statutes. As to oaths, affirmations and declarations, see the Oaths Act 1978, Vol 17, title Evidence, and the relevant enactments noted to s 1 of that Act.

Para 9: Special provision about residence applying to merchant seamen. See s 6 ante.

Para 10: Electors lists. These lists are to be prepared under s 10(b) ante.

Para 12: Voting by post. As to the persons who may vote by post, see ss 19(4), 22(2), 32(4) and 34(4) ante. Those sections are repealed by the Representation of the People Act 1985, s 28(1), Sch 5 post, as from a day to be appointed under s 29(2), and new provision is made as from that date in relation to voting other than in person by ss 6–9 of that Act.

Para 13: Summarily convicted. See the note "Summary conviction" to s 62 ante.

False. See the note to s 62 ante.

Definitions. For "registration officer", see s 8(1) ante; for "election", "prescribed", "service voter" and "standard scale", see s 202(1) ante.

Juries Act 1974, s 3(1). See Vol 22, title Juries.

Data Protection Act 1984. See Vol 6, title Civil Rights and Liberties.

Regulations. See the last note to s 53 ante for regulations made under that section and this Schedule.

SCHEDULE 3

Sections 81, 82

RETURN AND DECLARATIONS AS TO ELECTION EXPENSES
FORM OF RETURN

Election in the   .   .   .   .
constituency (*for a local government election substitute* county of   district of
        , *or as the case may be*).
Date of publication of notice of election .   .   .   .
Name of candidate   .   .   .   .

1. I am the election agent of the person named above as a candidate at this election [am the person named above as a candidate at this election and was my own election agent].

(*Where there has been a change of election agent suitable variations may be introduced here and elsewhere in the return.*)

2. I hereby make the following return of the candidate's [my] election expenses at this election.

Receipts

(*Include all money, securities or equivalent of money received in respect of expenses incurred on account of or in connection with or incidental to the above election*).

Received of the above-named candidate (*or, if the candidate is his own election agent*, paid
    by me)   ...   .   £
Received of (*set out separately the name and description of each person, club, society or
    association and the amount received from him or them*) ...   .   £

Expenditure

NOTE.—*The return shall deal under a separate heading or sub-heading with any expenses included in it as respects which a return is required to be made by section 75 of this Act.*

Candidate's personal expenses—
    paid by him [by me as candidate]   ...   .   £
    paid by me [by me acting as my election agent]   ...   .   £
Received by me for my services as election agent (*omit if candidate is his own election
    agent*) ...   .   £
Paid to * as sub-agent of the polling district of ...   .   £
Paid to *† as polling agent   ...   .   £
Paid to *§ as clerk [messenger] for   days services ...   .   £
Paid to the following persons in respect of goods supplied or work and labour done—
    to *§ (*set out the nature of the goods supplied or work and labour done thus*
            [*printing*], [*advertising*], [*stationery*])   ...   .   £
Paid to *§ as a speaker at a public meeting at   on   19 , as
    remuneration [expenses]   ...   .   £
Paid for the hire of rooms—
    for holding public meetings—
    paid to *§ for hire of (*identify the rooms by naming or describing them*)   ...   ...   £
    for committee rooms—
    paid to *§ for hire of (*identify the rooms by naming or describing them*)   ...   ...   £
Paid for postage ...   .   £
Paid for telegrams (or any similar means of communication) ...   .   £
Paid for miscellaneous matters—
    to *§ (*set out the reason for the payment*)   ...   .   £
    In addition to the above I am aware (*unless the candidate is his own election agent add* as election agent for the above-named candidate) of the following disputed and unpaid claims—
Disputed claims—
    by ‡ for (*set out the goods, work and labour, or other matter on the ground of which the
        claim is based*)   ...   .   £
Unpaid claims allowed by the   court to be paid after the proper time or in respect of which application has been or is about to be made to the   court (*state in each case whether the High Court or some other court*)—
    by ‡ for (*set out the goods, work and labour, or other matter on the ground of which the
        claim is due*) ...   .   £

Signature of person making return . . . .

* *Set out separately the name and description of each person with the amount paid to him.*
† *These particulars may be set out in a separate list annexed to and referred to in the account thus "Paid to (polling agent) as per annexed list £.........................".*
‡ *Set out separately the name and description of each person with the amount paid to or claimed by him.*
§ *These particulars may be set out in a separate list annexed to and referred to in the account.*

FORM OF DECLARATIONS

Election in the . . . . constituency (*for a local government election substitute* county of   , district of , *or as the case may be*).

Date of publication of notice of election . . . .

Name of candidate . . . .

I solemnly and sincerely declare as follows:—

1. I am the person named above as a candidate at this election [and was my own election agent] *or* was at this election the election agent of the person named above as a candidate.

2. I have examined the return of election expenses [about to be] [delivered] by my election agent [by me] to the returning officer, (*at a local government election, substitute* appropriate officer) of which a copy is now shown to me and marked   , and to the best of my knowledge and belief it is a complete and correct return as required by law.

3. To the best of my knowledge and belief, all expenses shown in the return as paid were paid by my election agent [by me], except as otherwise stated in relation to my [the candidate's] personal expenses.

4. I understand that the law does not allow any election expenses not mentioned in this return to be defrayed except in pursuance of a court order.

Signature of declarant . . . .
Signed and declared by the above named declarant on the   day of   , before me,

(Signed) . . . .
Justice of the Peace (*or as the case may be*) for . . . .

(NOTE.—*Where there has been a change of election agent, suitable variations may be introduced into the declaration as to expenses.*)

NOTES

This Schedule contains provisions formerly in the Representation of the People Act 1949, Sch 5, as amended by the Representation of the People Act 1969, s 24(1), Sch 2, para 39.

The word "delivered" in square brackets in para 2 of the Form of Declarations was substituted by the Representation of the People Act 1985, s 24, Sch 4, para 88, as from 1 October 1985.

Parish and community elections; municipal elections in City of London. See the notes to s 67 ante.

European Assembly elections. This Schedule is applied to such elections by the European Assembly Elections Regulations 1984, SI 1984/137, reg 3(1), Sch 1. See further the Introductory Note to this Act.

As to provisions relating to such elections in Northern Ireland, see the Introductory Note to this Act.

SCHEDULE 4

Sections 90, 197

ELECTION EXPENSES AT CERTAIN LOCAL ELECTIONS IN ENGLAND AND WALES

1.—(1) Any claim against any person in respect of any election expenses incurred by or on behalf of a candidate which is not sent in within 14 days after the day of election shall be barred and not paid, and all election expenses incurred as mentioned above shall be paid within 21 days after the day of election and not otherwise.

(2) If any person makes a payment in contravention of this paragraph he shall be guilty of an illegal practice, but a candidate shall not be liable, nor shall his election be avoided, for any illegal practice committed under this sub-paragraph without his consent or connivance.

2. Every agent of a candidate at the election shall, within 23 days after the day of election, make a true return to the candidate in writing of all election expenses incurred by the agent and if he fails so to do he shall be liable on summary conviction to a fine not exceeding level 3 on the standard scale.

3. Within 28 days after the day of election every candidate shall [deliver] to the proper officer of the authority for which the election is held a return of all election expenses incurred by the candidate or his agents vouched (except in the case of sums under [£10]) by bills stating the particulars and receipts and accompanied by a declaration by the candidate as to election expenses.

4.—(1) After the expiry of the time for making the return and declaration, the candidate, if elected, shall not, until he has made the return and declaration or until the date of the allowance of any authorised excuse under paragraph 7 below, sit or vote in the council and if he does so—

(a) he shall forfeit £50 for every day on which he so sits or votes; or

(b) instead of civil proceedings for a penalty, proceedings may be instituted in a magistrates' court, and he shall be liable on conviction to a fine of an amount not exceeding the amount of the penalty which would be recoverable in civil proceedings.

[(2) Civil proceedings for a penalty under this paragraph shall be commenced within the period of one year beginning with the day in respect of which the penalty is alleged to have been incurred.

(3) For the purposes of sub-paragraph (2) above] the issue of a writ or other process shall be deemed to be a commencement of a proceeding, where the service or execution of the same on or against the alleged offender is prevented by the absconding or concealment or act of the alleged offender, but save as mentioned above the service or execution of the same on or against the alleged offender, and not its issue, shall be deemed to be the commencement of the proceeding.

5. If the candidate fails to make that return and declaration he shall be guilty of an illegal practice, and, if he knowingly makes that declaration falsely, he shall be guilty of a corrupt practice.

6. The High Court, an election court or the county court may, on application either of the candidate or a creditor, allow any claim to be sent in and any expense to be paid after the time limited by this Schedule, and a return of any sum so paid shall forthwith after payment be sent to the proper officer of the authority.

7.—(1) If the candidate applies to the High Court, an election court or the county court and shows that the failure to make that return and declaration or either of them or any error or false statement in them has arisen by reason of—

(a) his illness or absence, or

(b) the absence, death, illness or misconduct of any agent, clerk or officer, or

(c) inadvertence or any reasonable cause of a like nature,

and not by reason of any want of good faith on the applicant's part, the court may—

(i) after such notice of the application as it considers fit, and

(ii) on production of such evidence of the grounds stated in the application, and of the applicant's good faith, and otherwise, as it considers fit,

make such order allowing the authorised excuse for the failure, error or false statement as it considers just.

(2) The order may make the allowance conditional upon compliance with such terms as to the court seem best calculated for carrying into effect the objects of this Schedule, and the order shall relieve the applicant from any liability or consequence under this Act in respect of the matters excused by the order.

(3) The date of the order, or, if conditions and terms are to be complied with, the date on which the applicant fully complies with them, is referred to in this Act as the date of the allowance of the excuse.

8.—(1) The return and declaration shall be kept at the office of the proper officer of the authority and shall at all reasonable times during the twelve months next after they are received by him be open to inspection by any person on payment of the prescribed fee and the proper officer shall, on demand, provide copies of them, or of any part of them, at the prescribed price.

(2) After the expiry of twelve months the proper officer of the authority may cause the return and declaration to be destroyed or, if the candidate so requires, shall return them to him.

9. For the purposes of this Schedule—

    (*a*) the jurisdiction vested by paragraph 7 in a county court may be exercised otherwise than in open court; and

    (*b*) an appeal lies to the High Court from any order of a county court made by virtue of that paragraph.

NOTES

Para 1 contains provisions formerly in the Representation of the People Act 1949, Sch 6, para 1. Para 2 contains provisions formerly in Sch 6, para 2, to the 1949 Act, as affected by the Criminal Justice Act 1982, ss 37(1), (2), 38(1), (6), (8), 46(1). Para 3 contains provisions formerly in Sch 6, para 3, to the 1949 Act, as affected by the Decimal Currency Act 1969, s 10(1), and by the Local Government Act 1972, s 251(1), Sch 29, para 4(1). Paras 4 (as originally enacted), 5 contain provisions formerly in Sch 6, paras 4, 5, to the 1949 Act. Para 6 contains provisions formerly in Sch 6, para 6, to the 1949 Act, as affected by s 251(1) of, and Sch 2, para 4(1) to, the 1972 Act. Para 7 contains provisions formerly in Sch 6, para 7, to the 1949 Act. Para 8 contains provisions formerly in Sch 6, para 8, to the 1949 Act, as amended by the Representation of the People Act 1969, s 8(6), and as affected by s 251(1) of, and Sch 29, para 4(1) to, the 1972 Act. Para 9 contains provisions formerly in Sch 6, para 9, to the 1949 Act.

The word in square brackets in para 3 and the reference to "£10" in that paragraph, and the words in square brackets in para 4, were substituted by the Representation of the People Act 1985, ss 14(6), 24, Sch 4, para 89, as from 1 October 1985.

Para 1: Within 14(21) days after, etc. For the computation of time, see s 119 ante. See also the note "Within six months . . ." to s 5 ante.

The time limits in para 1 above must be read subject to para 6 above.

Illegal practice. See the notes to ss 61 and 78 ante.

Consent; connivance. See the notes to s 75 ante.

Para 2: Agent. For the circumstances establishing agency, see the note "By his agents" to s 159 ante.

Election. For the elections to which this Schedule applies, see ss 90(1) and 197(2) ante.

Within 23 days after, etc. See the corresponding note to para 1 above.

Writing. See the note "Written" to s 28 ante.

Summary conviction. See the note to s 62 ante. The obligation imposed by para 2 above is absolute and since, unlike an offence against para 1 above, an offence against para 2 is not an illegal practice, there is no right to apply for relief under s 167 ante.

Para 3: Within 28 days after, etc. See the corresponding note to para 1 above.

Declaration. As to the form of declaration, see s 90(1)(*b*) or 197(2) ante.

Para 4: Time for making the return and declaration. This refers to the time prescribed by para 3 above.

Forfeit. The penalty belongs to the Crown since this Act does not give it to any other person (*Bradlaugh v Clarke* (1883) 8 App Cas 354, [1881–5] All ER Rep 1002).

As to evidence in proceedings for penalties under para 4 above, see s 180 ante.

Council. Ie the parish or community council (s 90(1) ante) or the Common Council of the City of London (s 197 ante).

Magistrates' court. For meaning, see, by virtue of the Interpretation Act 1978, s 5, Sch 1, Vol 41, title Statutes, the Magistrates' Courts Act 1980, s 148, Vol 27, title Magistrates.

Conviction. Ie summary conviction, as to which, see the note to s 62 ante.

Within one year after, etc. See the note "Within 14(21) days after, etc" to para 1 above.

Para 5: That return and declaration. Ie that required by para 3 ante.

Illegal practice. See the note to s 61 ante; and note also the provision for relief in para 7 above.

Knowingly. See the note "Knows" to s 60 ante.

Falsely. See the note "False" to s 62 ante.

Corrupt practice. See the note to s 60 ante.

Para 6: High Court. See the note to s 39 ante.

County court. See the note to s 30 ante.

Time limited by this Schedule. Ie limited by para 1 above.

Forthwith. See the note to s 67 ante.

Para 7: Applies to the High Court, etc. Cf the note "Apply for relief" to s 86 ante (to which para 7 above corresponds).

Notice of the application; on production of such evidence, etc; order allowing the authorised excuse. Cf the corresponding notes to s 86 ante.

Order shall relieve the applicant. This provision is similar to s 86(7) ante. Contrast s 167 ante, by which an order under that section relieves any person whether the applicant or not.

Liability or consequence under this Act. See, in particular, paras 4 and 5 above and the notes thereto.

Para 8: At all reasonable times. See the note to s 89 ante.

Months. This means calendar months; see the Interpretation Act 1978, s 5, Sch 1, Vol 41, title Statutes.

Prescribed fee; prescribed price. By the Representation of the People Regulations 1983, SI 1983/435, reg 70(2), (3), the fee for inspection is £1 and the price of a copy is 10p for each side of each page.

Definitions. For "candidate" and "election expenses", see s 118 ante; for "election court", "person", "prescribed", "proper officer" and "standard scale", see s 202(1) ante.

SCHEDULE 5

Section 95

Uꜱᴇ ꜰᴏʀ Pᴀʀʟɪᴀᴍᴇɴᴛᴀʀʏ Eʟᴇᴄᴛɪᴏɴ Mᴇᴇᴛɪɴɢꜱ ᴏꜰ Rᴏᴏᴍꜱ ɪɴ Sᴄʜᴏᴏʟ Pʀᴇᴍɪꜱᴇꜱ ᴀɴᴅ ᴏꜰ Mᴇᴇᴛɪɴɢ Rᴏᴏᴍꜱ

1.—(1) Any arrangements for the use of a room in school premises shall be made with the local education authority maintaining the school.

(2) Any question as to the rooms in school premises which a candidate in any constituency is entitled to use, or as to the times at which he is entitled to use them, or as to the notice which is reasonable, shall be determined by the Secretary of State.

2.—(1) Every local education authority shall prepare and revise for their area lists of the rooms in school premises which candidates in any constituency are entitled to use.

(3) The list shall include the rooms in premises outside, as well as those in premises in, the constituency.

3.—(1) Every district and London borough council shall prepare and revise for their area lists of the meeting rooms which candidates in any constituency are entitled to use.

(2) The list shall indicate the person to whom applications for the use of the room are to be made in each case.

(3) The list shall not include any room if the person maintaining it disputes the right of candidates in the constituency to use it.

4. The lists of rooms in school premises and of meeting rooms prepared for each constituency shall be kept by the registration officer, and those lists and particulars of any change made on their revision shall (where necessary) be forwarded to him accordingly.

5. In the event of a dissolution, or of a vacancy occurring in the seat for the constituency, any person stating himself to be, or to be authorised by, a candidate or his election agent shall be entitled at all reasonable hours to inspect those lists or a copy of them.

6. (*Applies to Scotland only.*)

NOTES

This Schedule contains provisions formerly in the Representation of the People Act 1949, Sch 7, as amended, in the case of para 1(2), by the Secretary of State for Education and Science Order 1964, SI 1964/490, art 3(2)(a), and as partly repealed, in the case of para 3(1), by the London Government Act 1963, s 93(1), Sch 18, Pt II, and as further affected, in the case of para 1(2), by the Transfer of Functions (Wales) Order 1970, SI 1970/1536, art 6(4), and further amended, in the case of para 3(1), by the Local Government Act 1972, s 45(1), Sch 6, para 13.

Para 1: School premises. Ie premises in a school mentioned in s 95(2)(a) ante; see also s 95(7) ante.

Local education authority. See the note to s 108 ante.

Secretary of State. Cf the note to s 4 ante. The Secretary of State here concerned is the Secretary of State for Education and Science or, as respects Wales, the Secretary of State for Wales.

Para 2: Constituency. See the note to s 1 ante.

Para 3: District and London borough council. See the notes "Council of every district" and "London borough" to s 8 ante.

Meeting rooms. Ie meeting rooms mentioned in s 95(3) ante; see also s 95(7) ante.

Para 5: Election agent. As to election agents, see s 67 ante and the notes thereto.

At all reasonable hours. See the note "At all reasonable times" to s 89 ante.

European Assembly elections. Paras 1 and 5 of this Schedule are applied to such elections by the European Assembly Elections Regulations 1984, SI 1984/137, reg 3(1), Sch 1, subject to the substitution in para 5 above for the word "dissolution" of the words "general election of representatives" and for the words "those lists" of the words "the lists of rooms and school premises and of meeting rooms prepared under this Schedule as it has effect for parliamentary elections". See further the Introductory Note to this Act.

As to provisions relating to such elections in Northern Ireland, see the Introductory Note to this Act.

Isles of Scilly. See the note to s 8 ante.

Definitions. For "registration officer", see s 8(1) ante; for "school premises", "meeting room" and "room", see s 95(7) ante; for "candidate", see s 118 ante.

SCHEDULE 6

Section 191(2)

WARD ELECTIONS IN THE CITY

1. Without prejudice to the application of any provision of this Act to elections in the City by virtue of sections 191 to 196 of this Act, this Schedule has effect as regards the operation of Part II of the City of London (Various Powers) Act 1957 (referred to in this Schedule as "the City Act").

2. Notwithstanding anything in section 6(1) of the City Act—

   (a) a person qualified (age apart) to vote as an elector at a ward election shall be entitled to do so if he is of the age of 18 years or over on the date of the poll, except that,

   (b) a person registered in the ward list to be used at a ward election shall not be entitled to vote as an elector at the election if his entry in the ward list gives a date later than the date of the poll as the date on which he will attain the age of 18 years.

3. Ward lists and provisional ward lists shall give for any elector the date which it appears to the town clerk of the City that the elector will attain the age of 18 years, if that date is after the 16th November in the year in which the ward lists are to be published.

4. Claims and objections asking for the omission, insertion or alteration of a date in a ward list as that on which an elector will attain that age may be made as in the case of claims and objections relating to the inclusion of a person's name in the list, and sections 7(4) and 9 of the City Act shall with any necessary modifications apply accordingly.

5. Any power under this Act to prescribe the form of service declaration may be exercised so as to take account of the difference between the qualifying date under this Act and the qualifying date under the City Act.

6. Nothing in this Act affects the operation of subsections (3) and (4) and paragraph (a) of subsection (5) of section 5 of the Representation of the People Act 1949 (which contain provisions relating to the yearly value of lands and premises and to cases of their joint occupation) in relation to their application by section 4(2) of the City Act.

NOTES

Paras 1, 5, 6 contain provisions formerly in the Representation of the People Act 1969, s 23(1), (3), (4), respectively. Paras 2–4 contain provisions formerly in s 23(2) of the 1969 Act, as affected by the City of London (Various Powers) Act 1968, s 3(2).

Person qualified ... to vote ... at a ward election. For these persons, see the City of London (Various Powers) Act 1957, s 6, Vol 26, title London.

Age of 18 years or over. As to when a person attains a given age, see s 202(2) ante.

Ward lists; provisional ward lists. These are to be prepared under the City of London (Various Powers) Act 1957, s 7, Vol 26, title London.

Power ... to prescribe the form of service declaration. See s 16 ante.

Qualifying date. As to the qualifying date under this Act, see s 4 ante, and as to that under the City of London (Various Powers) Act 1957, see s 6(2) of that Act, Vol 26, title London.

Definitions. For "the City", "elector" and "vote", see s 202(1) ante. Note as to "the City Act", para 1 above.

City of London (Various Powers) Act 1957, Part II, ss 4(2), 6(1), 7(4), 9. See Vol 26, title London.

Representation of the People Act 1949, s 5. That section was repealed with a saving by the Representation of the People Act 1969, s 24(4), (5), Sch 3, Pt II (repealed).

So much of it as is saved by para 6 above is printed in the notes to the City of London (Various Powers) Act 1957, s 4(2), Vol 26, title London.

SCHEDULE 7

Section 206

TRANSITIONAL AND SAVING PROVISIONS AND INTERPRETATION OF OTHER ACTS

PART I

TRANSITIONAL AND SAVING PROVISIONS

General

1. Where a period of time specified in an enactment repealed by this Act is current at its commencement, this Act has effect as if the provision corresponding to that enactment had been in force when that period began to run.

2. The imposition or subsistence of an incapacity is not affected by the repeal by this Act of any enactment, and any such incapacity shall for the purposes of this Act be treated as having been imposed under the corresponding provision of this Act.

Electoral Law Act (Northern Ireland) 1962

3. Notwithstanding the repeal by this Act of section 1(3) of the Representation of the People Act 1977, the amendments by that section 1(3) of the Electoral Law Act (Northern Ireland) 1962 continue to have the same effect as they had immediately before the coming into force of this Act.

Licensing Act 1964

4. Notwithstanding the repeal by this Act of section 24(2) of the Representation of the People Act 1969, the amendments by that section 24(2) of the Licensing Act 1964 continue to have the same effect as they had immediately before the coming into force of this Act.

Northern Ireland Constitution Act 1973

5. So far as sections 8(4) and 26 of this Act reproduce any provision derived from the exercise of the power under section 38 of the Northern Ireland Constitution Act 1973 to make an Order in Council that provision has effect as if it were contained in an Order in Council so made.

Variation of limits of candidates' election expenses

6. Notwithstanding the revocation by this Act of the Representation of the People (Variation of Limits of Candidates' Election Expenses) Order 1981 and the Representation of the People (Variation of Limits of Candidates' Election Expenses) Order 1982, on the commencement of this Act the coming into operation of those orders shall for the purposes of sections [76A(1)] and 197(3) of this Act be taken (as the case may be) as the last occasion on which the maximum amount of the candidates' expenses was [fixed] by order.

Section 254 of the Local Government Act 1972

7. Any power exercisable under section 254 of the Local Government Act 1972 (consequential and supplementary provision) in relation to a provision of that Act repealed and re-enacted by this Act is exercisable in relation to that provision as so re-enacted to the extent that it would have been exercisable immediately before such repeal.

8, 9. ...

NOTES

The reference to "76A(1)" and the word "fixed" in para 6 were substituted, and paras 8, 9 were repealed, by the Representation of the People Act 1985, ss 24, 28(1), Sch 4, para 90, Sch 5, as from 1 October 1985.

Enactment repealed by this Act. See s 206 ante, and Sch 9 post.

Commencement; coming into force of this Act. This Act was brought into force on 15 March 1983 by the order noted to s 207 ante.

Representation of the People Act 1977, s 1(3); Representation of the People Act 1969, s 24(2). Repealed by s 206 ante, and Sch 9, Pt II post.

Electoral Law Act (Northern Ireland) 1962. 1962 c 14 (NI); not printed in this work. It is thought that the words "that section 1(3) of the Electoral Law Act (Northern Ireland) 1962" in para 3 above should read "that subsection to section 42(1) of the Electoral Law Act (Northern Ireland) 1962".

Licensing Act 1964. It is thought that the words "that section 24(2) of the Licensing Act 1964" in para 4 above should read "that subsection to Schedule 8 to the Licensing Act 1964". For Sch 8 to the 1964 Act, see Vol 24, title Licensing and Liquor Duties.

Northern Ireland Constitution Act 1973, s 38. See Vol 31, title Northern Ireland (Pt 2).

Representation of the People (Variation of Limits of Candidates' Election Expenses) Order 1981. SI 1981/191. That order came into operation on 13 January 1981.

Representation of the People (Variation of Limits of Candidates' Election Expenses) Order 1982. SI 1982/363. That order came into operation on 12 March 1982.

Local Government Act 1972, s 254. See Vol 25, title Local Government.

PART II

INTERPRETATION OF OTHER ACTS

Register, electors, etc.

10.—(1) A reference in any Act (whenever passed) to—

(*a*) the register of parliamentary and local government electors, or
(*b*) the register of parliamentary electors, or
(*c*) the register of local government electors, or
(*d*) the electors lists for such a register,

shall be taken as a reference to—

(i) the register kept under this Act, or
(ii) that register so far as it relates to parliamentary electors, or
(iii) that register so far as it relates to local government electors, or
(iv) the electors lists for such a register,

as the case may be, and references in any Act to a parliamentary or local government elector shall be construed accordingly.

(2) In relation to a person shown in a register or electors list as attaining voting age on a specified date the references in sub-paragraph (1) above do not apply except for the purposes of an election at which the day fixed for the poll falls on or after that date.

Registration and returning officers

11. A reference in any Act (whenever passed) to—

(*a*) the registration officer for the registration of parliamentary or local government electors, or
(*b*) the returning officer for a parliamentary election or constituency,

shall be taken respectively as a reference to the registration officer or returning officer appointed under this Act.

Registration expenses

12. A reference in any Act (whenever passed) to registration expenses in connection with the registration of parliamentary or local government electors shall be taken as a reference to registration expenses under this Act.

Supplemental

13.—(1) Subject to this paragraph, the provisions of paragraphs 10 to 12 of this Schedule apply to a reference—

(*a*) to any of the matters mentioned in those provisions, whatever the terms used in that reference; and
(*b*) to any other matter which was to be construed as a reference to any of those matters by virtue of an enactment repealed by the Representation of the People Act 1948.

(2) Those provisions so far as they relate to this Act or any other Act passed after that Act of 1948 do not apply where the context otherwise requires.

(3) Those provisions so far as they relate to Acts passed before that Act of 1948 may be excluded in whole or in part by an order of the Secretary of State in any particular case where they appear to him to be inappropriate.

(4) That order may make such change in the law which this Act reproduces from the Representation of the People Act 1949 as might have been made before its commencement under paragraph 8(1)(*c*) of Part I of Schedule 10 to that Act of 1948.

(5) The provisions of paragraphs 10 to 12 may be supplemented by an order made by the Secretary of State in relation to an Act passed previous to the Representation of the People Act 1948—

(*a*) where, in any particular case, such an order appears to him necessary for harmonising the previous Act with the provisions of this Act; and (*b*) to the extent that the provisions of this Act re-enact such provisions of the Representation of the People Act 1949 as re-enacted provisions of that Act of 1948.

(6) A power conferred by this paragraph to make an order shall be exercisable by statutory instrument, and any such instrument shall be subject to annulment by resolution of either House of Parliament.

(7) Nothing in paragraphs 10 to 12 shall be taken to prejudice the operation in relation to this Act of any provision of the Interpretation Act 1978 as to repeals.

NOTES

Para 10 contains provisions formerly in the Representation of the People Act 1949, Sch 8, para 1(1), as amended by the Representation of the People Act 1969, s 24(1), Sch 2, para 40. Para 11 contains provisions formerly in Sch 8, para 2 to the 1949 Act, as amended by the Local Authorities etc (Miscellaneous Provision) (No 2) Order 1974, SI 1974/595, art 3(7). Para 12 contains provisions formerly in Sch 8, para 3, to the 1949 Act, as partly repealed by the Election Commissioners Act 1949, s 21, Schedule. Para 13(1)–(4) contain provisions formerly in Sch 8, para 7(1)–(3), to the 1949 Act. Para 13(5)–(7) contain provisions formerly in s 169(2), (3) and (1), respectively, of that Act.

Para 10: Register. As to the registers of electors, see ss 9–13 ante.

Parliamentary electors; local government electors. For these, see ss 1 and 2 ante, respectively.

Electors lists. These are to be prepared under s 10(*b*) ante.

Attaining voting age. For the meaning of "voting age", see s 1(1)(*c*) or 2(1)(*c*) ante, and as to when a person attains that age, see s 202(2) ante.

Para 11: Registration officer. These officers are appointed under s 8 ante.

Returning officer. As to these officers, see ss 24, 26–28 and 35 ante.

Para 12: Registration expenses. As to these, see s 54 ante.

Para 13: Secretary of State. Cf the note to s 4 ante. The Secretary of State here concerned is the Secretary of State for the Home Department.

Statutory instrument; subject to annulment. See the note to s 36 ante.

Definitions. For "voting age", see s 1(1)(*c*) or 2(1)(*c*) ante; for "registration officer", see s 8(1) ante.

Representation of the People Act 1948. Sch 10, Pt I, para 8(1), to that Act was repealed by the SLR Act 1953. The 1948 Act was passed, ie received the Royal Assent, on 30 July 1948.

Representation of the People Act 1949. That Act was repealed by s 206 ante, and Sch 9, Pt II post.

Interpretation Act 1978. For the provisions of that Act as to repeals, see ss 15–17 thereof, Vol 41, title Statutes.

Orders under this Part of this Schedule. Up to 1 August 1985, no order had been made under para 13(3) or (5) above and none has effect thereunder by virtue of the Interpretation Act 1978, s 17(2)(*b*), Vol 41, title Statutes.

(*Sch 8: para 1 adds the Public Meeting Act 1908, s 1(4), Vol 12, title Criminal Law; paras 2–4 amend the City of London (Various Powers) Act 1957, ss 4, 8, 9(4), respectively, Vol 26, title London; para 5 amends the City of London (Various Powers) Act 1960, s 39, Vol 26, title London; para 6 amends the London Government Act 1963, Sch 3, Pt II, paras 22, 23, Vol 26, title London; paras 7–10 amend the Licensing Act 1964, ss 12(2), 67(5), (6), Sch 8, paras 1, 5, Vol 24, title Licensing and Liquor Duties; para 11 amends the Post Office Act 1969, s 72(1), Vol 34, title Post Office; paras 12–14 amend the Local Government Act 1972, ss 6(1), 9(5), 11(3)(b), 16(2), 25(1), 28(2), 29(3)(b), 35(1), 80(1)(e), 86(b), 89(b), Sch 2, para 6(1), Sch 12, paras 18(5), 34(5), Vol 25, title Local Government; paras 15, 16, 23 apply to Scotland only; para 17 amends the Juries Act 1974, s 3(1), Vol 22, title Juries; paras 18–20 amend the House of Commons Disqualification Act 1975, ss 6(3), Sch 1, Pt III and substitute s 10 of that Act, Vol 32, title Parliament; paras 21, 22 amend the European Assembly Elections Act 1978, ss 4(2), 7(2), respectively ante; paras 24, 25 amend the Judicature (Northern Ireland) Act 1978, ss 35(2)(h), 108(1), respectively, Vol 31, title Northern Ireland (Pt 2); para 26 amends the Supreme Court Act 1981, s 142(1), Vol 11, title Courts; para 27 amends the Mental Health (Amendment) Act 1982, s 70(2), Vol 28, title Mental Health; para 28 amends the Legal Aid, Advice and Assistance (Northern Ireland) Order 1981, SI 1981/228, Sch 1, Pt II, para 5.)*

SCHEDULE 9

Section 206

REPEALS AND REVOCATIONS
PART I
REPEALS OF OBSOLETE PROVISIONS

Chapter	Short Title	Extent of Repeal
7 & 8 Geo 5 c 64	The Representation of the People Act 1918	Sections 19 and 43.
12, 13 & 14 Geo 6 c 68	The Representation of the People Act 1949	In paragraph (*b*) of section 45(11), from the beginning to the words "appeals thereunder, and". In section 111(2)— (*a*) paragraph (*a*); (*b*) in paragraph (*b*), the words "whose clerk is registration officer". In section 116(2), the word "gaolers". Section 132. In section 161(2), the words "a simple contract debt". In section 163, in the definition of "public office", the word "municipal" where it first occurs and the word "bailie". In section 168(2), the words "where the poll is taken by means of voting papers". Section 170. In section 174(1), paragraphs (*b*) and (*c*). In Schedule 2— (*a*) in Part II, rule 4(3); (*b*) in Part IV; in rule 53(2), the words "double return and any". In paragraph 1(1) of Schedule 8, the words "and local government electors registered under this Act" to the end.
1968 c xxxvii	The City of London (Various Powers) Act 1968	In section 3— (*a*) in subsection (3), the entry relating to the Representation of the People Act 1949; (*b*) subsection (4). Section 4.
1969 c 39	The Age of Majority (Scotland) Act 1969	In paragraph 2 of Schedule 2, the words "The Representation of the People Acts (and any regulations, rules or other instruments thereunder) and".
1969 c 46	The Family Law Reform Act 1969	In paragraph 2 of Schedule 2, the words "The Representation of the People Acts (and any regulations, rules or other instruments thereunder)" and the words "and any statutory provision" to the end.

Chapter	Short Title	Extent of Repeal
1973 c xx	The City of London (Various Powers) Act 1973	Section 9.
1973 c 65	The Local Government (Scotland) Act 1973	In section 11— (a) subsection (2); (b) in subsection (3), the words "Representation of the People Acts and other" and "and local government"; (c) subsection (4). In Schedule 2, paragraph 2(4), (5).
1979 c 40	The Representation of the People Act 1979	The whole Act.

PART II

CONSEQUENTIAL REPEALS

Chapter	Short Title	Extent of Repeal
12, 13 & 14 Geo 6 c 68	The Representation of the People Act 1949	The whole Act, so far as unrepealed.
12, 13 & 14 Geo 6 c 86	The Electoral Registers Act 1949	The whole Act.
2 & 3 Eliz 2 c 8	The Electoral Registers Act 1953	The whole Act.
6 & 7 Eliz 2 c 55	The Local Government Act 1958	In Schedule 8, paragraph 31(2) to (4).
6 & 7 Eliz 2 c 64	The Local Government and Miscellaneous Financial Provisions (Scotland) Act 1958	In Part I of Schedule 4, paragraph 16(2).
1961 c xxviii	The City of London (Various Powers) Act 1961	Section 44.
1963 c 33	The London Government Act 1963	In Schedule 3— (a) in Part I, paragraph 16; (b) in Part III, paragraphs 27, 31 to 33 and 35.
1964 c 31	The Elections (Welsh Forms) Act 1964	The whole Act.
1968 c 64	The Civil Evidence Act 1968	In the Schedule, the entry relating to the Representation of the People Act 1949.
1969 c 15	The Representation of the People Act 1969	The whole Act.
1969 c 48	The Post Office Act 1969	In Part II of Schedule 4, paragraph 47.
1971 c 23	The Courts Act 1971	In Part II of Schedule 8, paragraph 30.
1971 c 36 (NI)	The Civil Evidence Act (Northern Ireland) 1971	In the Schedule, the entry relating to the Representation of the People Act 1949.
1972 c 70	The Local Government Act 1972	Part III. In section 243— (a) in subsection (2), the words "section 42 above or"; (b) in subsection (4), the words "section 44(1) or". Schedule 6.
1973 c 65	The Local Government (Scotland) Act 1973	Sections 6 to 10. In Schedule 3, paragraphs 2 to 18, and 20 to 23.
1974 c 23	The Juries Act 1974	Section 3(3).

Chapter	Short Title	Extent of Repeal
1975 c 21	The Criminal Procedure (Scotland) Act 1975	In Schedule 7A, item 6.
1975 c 24	The House of Commons Disqualification Act 1975	Section 10(1).
1976 c 29	The Representation of the People (Armed Forces) Act 1976	The whole Act.
1976 c 52	The Armed Forces Act 1976	In Schedule 9, paragraph 19.
1976 c 63	The Bail Act 1976	In Schedule 2, paragraph 12.
1977 c 9	The Representation of the People Act 1977	The whole Act.
1977 c 14	The Returning Officers (Scotland) Act 1977	The whole Act.
1977 c 45	The Criminal Law Act 1977	In Schedule 1, item 9. In Schedule 12, the entry relating to the Representation of the People Act 1949.
1978 c 4	The Local Government (Scotland) Act 1978	In the Schedule, paragraph 2.
1978 c 23	The Judicature (Northern Ireland) Act 1978	In Part II of Schedule 5, the entry relating to the Representation of the People Act 1949.
1978 c 32	The Representation of the People Act 1978	The whole Act.
1979 c 31	The Prosecution of Offences Act 1979	In Schedule 1, the entry relating to the Representation of the People Act 1949.
1980 c 3	The Representation of the People Act 1980	The whole Act.
1981 c 34	The Representation of the People Act 1981	Section 3 and the Schedule.
1982 c 51	The Mental Health (Amendment) Act 1982	Section 69(5). In section 70(2) the words— (*a*) "62 and"; (*b*) "and Schedule 2 to this Act". Schedule 2.

Part III
Consequential Revocations

Year and Number	Title	Extent of Revocation
SI 1973/2095	Local Government Reorganisation (Consequential Provisions) (Northern Ireland) Order 1973	Article 2(4) to (6).
SI 1973/2163	Northern Ireland (Modification of Enactments—No 1) Order 1973	In Schedule 5, paragraph 15.
SI 1974/595	Local Authorities etc (Miscellaneous Provision) (No 2) Order 1974	Article 3(7).
SI 1977/293	Local Authorities etc (Miscellaneous Provision) Order 1977	Article 4(2).
SI 1981/191	Representation of the People (Variation of Limits of Candidates' Election Expenses) Order 1981	The whole Order.
SI 1982/363	Representation of the People (Variation of Limits of Candidates' Election Expenses) Order 1982	The whole Order.

DESTINATION TABLE

This table shows in column (1) the enactments repealed by the Representation of the People Act 1983, and in column (2) the provisions of that Act corresponding to the repealed provisions.

In certain cases the enactment in column (1), though having a corresponding provision in column (2) is not, or is not wholly, repealed, as it is still required, or partly required for the purposes of other legislation.

(1)	(2)	(1)	(2)
Representation of the People Act 1918 (c 64)	Representation of the People Act 1983 (c 2)	Representation of the People Act 1949 (c 68)	Representation of the People Act 1983 (c 2)
s 19, 43	Applied to Scotland	s 12 (7)	Rep, 1972 c 70, s 272 (1), Sch 30 and SI 1973/ 2095, art 5 (2), Sch 2
Representation of the People Act 1949 (c 68)		(8)	s 19 (8)
——————		13 (1)–(3)	20 (1)–(3)
s 1 (1)	s 1 (1), (3), (4)	(4)	(5)
(2)	(2)	14 (1), (2)	21 (1), (2)
(3)	(4)	(3)–(7)	(4)–(8)
2 (1)	2 (1)	15 (1), (2)	22 (1), (2)
proviso	(2), (3) (b)	(3)	Rep, 1972 c 70, s 272 (1), Sch 30 and SI 1973/ 2095, art 5 (2), Sch 2
(2)	(3) (a)		
3	Rep, 1949 c 86, s 5, Sch 3	(4)–(8)	s 22 (4)–(8)
4 (1), (2)	s 5 (1), (2)	16	23
(3)	5 (3), 7 (1)	17 (1)	Rep, 1972 c 70, s 272 (1), Sch 30
(4)	14 (2)	(2)	Applied to Scotland
5	Rep, 1969 c 15, s 24 (4), Sch 3, Pt II (but see Sch 6, para 6)	(3)	Rep, SI 1973/2095, art 5 (2), Sch 2
6 (1)	s 8 (1)	(4)–(6)	s 27
(2)	Rep, 1972 c 70, s 272 (1), Sch 30	18 (1)	28 (1)
(3)	Applied to Scotland	(1A)	(2)
(4)	Rep, SI 1973/2095, art 5 (2), Sch 2	(1B)	(6)
		(2)–(4)	(3)–(5)
7 (1), (2)	s 9 (1), (2)	(5)	Rep, 1972 c 70, s 272 (1), Sch 30
(3)	Rep, 1949 c 86, s 5, Sch 3	19	Rep, SI 1973/2095, art 5 (2), Sch 2
8 (1), (2)	s 12 (1), (2)		
(2A), (2B)	(3), (4)	20 (1)	s 29 (1), (2)
(3)	Rep, 1980 c 3, s 3 (2), Schedule	(2)–(4)	(3)–(5)
		(5), (6)	(7), (8)
9 (1)	s 10	(7)–(10)	30
(2)	Rep, SI 1973/2095, art 5 (2), Sch 2	21	Rep, SI 1973/2095, art 5 (2), Sch 2
(3)–(6)	s 11	22 (1)	s 31 (1)
10 (1)	14 (1)	(1A)	(2)
(2), (3)	15 (1)	(2)	Rep, 1963 c 33, s 93 (1), Sch 18, Pt I
(3A)–(3C)	(2)–(4)	(3)	s 31 (3)
(4)	(5)	23 (1)–(4)	32 (1)–(4)
(5)	16	(5)	Rep, 1969 c 15, s 24 (4), Sch 3, Pt II
(6), (7)	17		
(8), (9)	15 (6), (7)	(6)–(8)	s 32 (7)–(9)
(10)	Rep, 1969 c 15, s 24 (4), Sch 3, Pt II	(9)	Rep, 1972 c 70, s 272 (1), Sch 30
11 (1), (2)	s 18 (1), (2)	24	s 33
(3)–(8)	(4)–(9)	25	34
12 (1)–(4)	19 (1)–(4)	26, 27	Rep, 1972 c 70, s 272 (1), Sch 30
(5)	Rep, 1969 c 15, s 24 (4), Sch 3, Pt II		
(6)	s 19 (7)		

(1) Representation of the People Act 1949 (c 68)	(2) Representation of the People Act 1983 (c 2)	(1) Representation of the People Act 1949 (c 68)	(2) Representation of the People Act 1983 (c 2)
s 28	Rep, 1963 c 33, s 93 (1), Sch 18, Pt I	s 45 (6)	Rep, 1971 c 23, s 56 (4), Sch 11, Pt IV
29	Rep, 1972 c 70, s 272 (1), Sch 30	(7)	s 56 (6)
30–32	Rep, 1973 c 65, s 237, Sch 29	(8)–(10)	Applied to Scotland
33	s 46	(11)	s 58
34	Rep, 1972 c 70, s 272 (1), Sch 30	46 (1)	59 (1)
35 (1), (2)	s 47	(2)	Rep, 1981 c 55, s 28 (2), Sch 5, Pt I
(3)	Rep, 1963 c 33, s 93 (1), Sch 18, Pt I	(3), (4)	s 59 (2), (3)
(4)	Applied to Scotland	(4A)	(4)
36 (1)	Rep, 1972 c 70, s 272 (1), Sch 30 and 1973 c 65, s 237, Sch 29	(5)	(3)
(2)	s 39 (5)	47–53	60–66
(3)	Rep, 1973 c 65, s 237, Sch 29	54	187 (2)
(4)	s 39 (6)	55 (1)–(4)	67 (1)–(4)
37 (1), (2)	48 (1), (2)	(5), (6)	(6), (7)
(3)	Rep, 1972 c 70, s 272 (1), Sch 30 and 1973 c 65, s 237, Sch 29	56	68
(4)	Applied to Scotland	57 (1)	69 (1)
38	Rep, 1969 c 15, s 24 (4), Sch 3, Pt II	(2)	Rep, 1969 c 15, s 24 (4), Sch 3, Pt II
39 (1)–(3)	s 49 (1)–(3)	(3)	s 69 (3)
(3A)	(4)	58 (1)–(4)	70 (1)–(4)
(4)	(5)	(5)	(6)
(5)	50	(6)	Applied to Scotland
40	51	59–63	s 71–75
41 (1), (2)	52 (1), (2)	64 (1), (2)	76 (1), (2)
(3)	Rep, 1972 c 70, s 272 (1), Sch 30	(3), (4)	(4), (5)
(4), (5)	s 52 (3), (4)	(4A)	(6)
(5A)	Applied to Scotland	(5)	Rep, 1957 c 43, s 1
(6)	Rep, SI 1973/2095, art 5 (2), Sch 2	65–69	s 77–81
42	s 53	70 (1)	82 (1)
43 (1)–(3)	54 (1)–(3)	(2)	(2), (3)
(4)	Rep, 1972 c 70, s 272 (1), Sch 30 and SI 1973/2095, art 5 (2), Sch 2	(3), (4)	(5), (6)
(5)	s 54 (4)	71	83
(6)	Rep, 1972 c 70, s 272 (1), Sch 30	72	84
(7)	s 54 (5)	73 (1), (2)	85 (1), (2)
(8)	Rep, 1973 c 65, s 237, Sch 29	(3)	(3)–(5)
44 (1)	s 55 (1)	74 (1)–(9)	86 (1)–(9)
(2)	Rep, 1972 c 70, s 272 (1), Sch 30	(10)	(10), (11)
(3)–(5)	s 55 (2)–(4)	75	87
(6)	Rep, SI 1973/2095, art 5 (2), Sch 2	76	See s 88
45 (1)–(5)	s 56 (1)–(5)	77 (1)	s 89 (1)
		(2)	(2), (3)
		78–80	90–92
		81–85	94–98
		86 (1)	99 (1)
		(2)	Applied to Scotland
		(3), (4)	Rep, 1972 c 14, s 3 (2)
		87 (1)	s 100 (1), (2)
		(2)	Rep, 1969 c 15, s 24 (4), Sch 3, Pt I
		(3)	s 100 (3)
		88	Rep, 1958 c 9, s 1
		89 (1)	s 101 (1), (3)
		(2)	(2)
		(3)	102
		(4)	103 (2)
		90 (1)	(1)

(1) Representation of the People Act 1949 (c 68)	(2) Representation of the People Act 1983 (c 2)	(1) Representation of the People Act 1949 (c 68)	(2) Representation of the People Act 1983 (c 2)
s 90 (2), (3)	s 104	s 124 (2)–(5)	s 144 (4)–(7)
(4)	105 (1), (2)	125	145
(5)	Applied to Scotland	126 (1)	146 (1)–(3)
91 (1)	s 106 (1), (2)	(2)	(4)
(2)	(3)	(3)	Applied to Scotland
(3)	Applied to Scotland	(4)	Rep, 1962 c 30, s 30 (2), Sch 4, Pt II
(4)	s 106 (5), (6)	127–131	s 147–151
(5)–(7)	(7)–(9)	132	Obsolete
92	107	133	s 152
93 (1)	108 (1), (2)	134 (1)	153 (1), (2)
(2), (3)	(3), (4)	(2)	(3), (4)
94–96	109–111	(3)	Applied to Scotland
97	Rep, 1969 c 15, s 24 (4), Sch 3, Pt II	135 (1)	s 154 (1), (2)
98–101	s 112–115	(2)	155
102	Rep, 1969 c 15, s 24 (4), Sch 3, Pt II	(3)	Applied to Scotland
103	s 118	136 (1)–(3)	s 156 (1)–(3)
104	117	(4), (5)	(5), (6)
105	116	137 (1)–(3)	157 (1)–(3)
106–110	119–123	(4)	(4), (5)
111 (1)	Rep, 1971 c 23, s 56 (4), Sch 11, Pt IV and 1978 c 23, s 122 (2), Sch 7, Pt I	(5)	(6)
		(6)	Applied to Scotland
		(7)	s 157 (8)
(2)	124 (b)	138 (1), (2)	158 (1), (2)
(3)	(a)	(3), (4)	(3)
(4)	Rep, 1971 c 23, s 56 (4), Sch 11, Pt IV and 1978 c 23, s 122 (2), Sch 7, Pt I	(5)	159 (4), 160 (7)
		139	159 (1)–(3)
		140 (1)	160 (1), (2)
(5)–(7)	s 126	(2)–(5)	(3)–(6)
(8)	Applied to Scotland	141 (1)	161
112–114	s 127–129	(2)	162
115 (1)	130 (1)	(3), (4)	163
(2), (3)	(2)	142	164
(4)–(8)	(3)–(7)	143 (1)	165 (1)
116 (1)	131 (1)	(2)	(2), (3)
(2), (3)	(2)	144	166
(4)	(3)	145	167
(5)	132	146 (1)–(5)	168 (1)–(5)
(6), (7)	133	(6)	(7)
117	Applied to Scotland	(7)	Rep, 1969 c 15, s 24 (4), Sch 3, Pt I
118 (1)	s 135 (1), (2)	147	s 169
(2)	198	148	170
(3)	135 (3)	149 (1)–(9)	171 (1)–(9)
119 (1), (2)	136 (1), (2)	(10)	Rep, 1960 c 65, s 19 (2), Sch 4
(3)	(3), (5)	(11)	s 171 (10)
(4)–(8)	(4)–(8)	150 (1)–(4)	Rep, 1952 c 48, s 18 (1), Schedule
120–122	137–139	(5)	Applied to Scotland
123 (1)–(6)	140 (1)–(6)	(6), (7)	Rep, 1968 c 10 (NI), s 11, Schedule
(7)	141 (1)–(3)	151–154	s 173–176
(8)	(4)	155	178
(9), (10)	142	156	179
(11)	143	157	Rep, 1967 c 58, s 10 (2), Sch 3, Pt III
(12)	Applied to Scotland		
124 (1)	s 144 (1)–(3)		

(1) Representation of the People Act 1949 (c 68)	(2) Representation of the People Act 1983 (c 2)	(1) Representation of the People Act 1949 (c 68)	(2) Representation of the People Act 1983 (c 2)
s 158	s 180	Sch 2, parliamentary elections rules—	
159 (1)–(4)	181 (1)–(4)	r 4 (3)	Obsolete
(5)	177	(4)	Sch 1, r 4 (3)
(6), (7)	181 (5), (6)	5	Rep, 1969 c 15, s 14, Sch 1, Pt I
(8)	Applied to Scotland	6	Sch 1, r 5 (1)
(9)	s 181 (8)	7 (1)–(3)	6
160 (1), (2)	182 (1), (2)	(4)	Rep, 1969 c 15, s 24 (4), Sch 3, Pt II
(3)	Applied to Scotland	8	Sch 1, r 7
(4)	Rep, 1978 c 23, s 122 (2), Sch 7, Pt I	9 (1)	8 (1), (2)
161–164	s 183–186	(2), (3)	(3)
165 (1)	187 (1)	10	9
(2)–(4)	Rep, 1972 c 70, s 272 (1), Sch 30	11	10
166	Applied to Scotland	12	11 (1)–(3)
167 (1)	s 191	13–15	12–14
(2)	192	15A	15
(3)	193	16–21	16–21
(4), (5)	197 (1), (2)	22 (1)–(4)	22
(6)	195	(5)	Rep, 1977 c 14, s 3 (2)
(7)	196	23 (1), (2)	Sch 1, r 23 (1), (2)
168 (1)	189	(3), (4)	Rep, 1969 c 15, s 14, Sch 1, Pt I
(2)	Applied to Scotland	24	Rep, 1969 c 15, s 24 (4), Sch 3, Pt II
169 (1)	Sch 7, para 13 (7)	25–30	Sch 1, r 24–29
(2)	para 13 (5)	31 (1)	30 (1), (2)
(3)	para 13 (6)	(2)–(7)	(3)–(8)
170	Obsolete	(8)	(10)
171 (1)	s 202 (1)	32	31
(2)	——	33 (1)	32 (1)
(3), (4)	200	(1A)	(2)
(5)	201	(2), (3)	(3), (4)
172 (1)	203 (1)	34–44	33–43
(2)	Rep, 1972 c 70, s 272 (1), Sch 30	45 (1), (2)	44 (1), (2)
(3)	s 203 (2), (3)	(3), (4)	(4), (5)
(4)	(4)	46 (1)–(4)	45 (1)–(4)
173	Applied to Scotland	(4A)	(5)
174 (1), (2)	s 205	(5), (6)	(6), (7)
(3)	Rep, 1973 c 36, s 41 (1), Sch 6, Pt I	47–54	46–53
175 (1)	Rep, SLRA 1953	55 (1)	54 (1)
(2), (3)	——	(2)	Rep, 1969 c 15, s 24 (4), Sch 3, Pt II
(4)	Sch 7, para 2	(3)	Sch 1, r 54 (2)
(5)–(7)	——	56–58	55–57
176		59	Applied to Scotland
Sch 1	Rep, 1949 c 86, s 5 (3), Sch 3	60	Sch 1, r 59
2, parliamentary elections rules—		Appendix	Appendix
r 1	Sch 1, r 1	Sch 2, local elections rules	Rep, 1972 c 70, s 272 (1), Sch 30
2 (1), (2)	2 (1), (2)	3	Rep, 1973 c 65, s 237 (1), Sch 29
(2A), (3)	(3)	4, para 1, 2	Sch 2, para 1
3 (1)–(4)	3 (1)–(4)	para 2A	para 2
(5)	Rep, 1977 c 14, s 3 (2)	para 3, 4	para 3, 4
(6)–(8)	Sch 1, r 3 (5)–(7)		
4 (1), (2)	4 (1), (2)		

(1)	(2)	(1)	(2)
Representation of the People Act 1949 (c 68)	Representation of the People Act 1983 (c 2)	Electoral Registers Act 1949 (c 86)	Representation of the People Act 1983 (c 2)
Sch 4, para 5 (1)	Sch 2, para 5 (1)	s 5 (1), (2)	
para 5 (2)	para 5 (2), (3)	(3)	Rep, SLRA 1953
para 5 (3)	para 5 (4)	Sch 1	Rep, 1969 c 15, s 24 (4), Sch 3, Pt II
para 6–8	para 6–8		
para 9–12	para 10–13	2	Rep, 1972 c 71, s 64 (2), Sch 6, Pt I
5	3		
6	4	3	Rep, SLRA 1953
7, para 1	5, para 1		
para 2 (1), (2)	para 2 (1), (2)	Electoral Registers Act 1953 (c 8)	
para 2 (3)	para 2 (1)		
para 3 (1), (2)	para 3 (1), (2)	s 1 (1)	s 4, 13 (1)
para 3 (3)	para 3 (1)	(2)–(4)	Rep, 1969 c 15, s 24 (4), Sch 3, Pts I, II
para 3 (4)	para 3 (3)		
para 4, 5	para 4, 5	2	
para 6	Applied to Scotland	Schedule	Rep, 1957 c 56, s 191 (1), Sch 11, 1958 c 9, s 1, 1963 c 33, s 93 (1), Sch 18, Pt II, and 1969 c 15, s 24 (4), Sch 3, Pt II
8, para 1 (1)	Sch 7, para 10		
para 1 (2)	Rep, 1949 c 90, s 21, Schedule		
para 2, 3	Sch 7, para 11, 12		
para 4	Rep, 1949 c 90, s 21, Schedule	Local Government Act 1958 (c 55)	
para 5 (1)	Rep, 1949 c 90, s 21, Schedule, 1956 c 43, s 2 (1) (a), Sch 2, Pt I, para 4, 1963 c 33, s 93 (1), Sch 18, Pt I, 1972 c 11, s 29 (4), Sch 8, 1972 c 70, s 272 (1), Sch 30 and 1973 c 65, s 237 (1), Sch 29	Sch 8, para 31 (2)	s 54 (3)
		para 31 (3)	55 (2)
		para 31 (4)	Sch 1, r 22 (1)
		City of London (Various Powers) Act 1961 (c xxviii)	
para 5 (2), (3)	Rep, 1972 c 70, s 272 (1), Sch 30		
para 5 (4)–(6)	Rep, 1973 c 65, s 237 (1), Sch 29	s 44	s 196
para 6	Rep, 1963 c 33, s 93 (1), Sch 18, Pt II	London Government Act 1963 (c 33)	
para 7 (1), (2)	Sch 7, para 13 (1), (2)	Sch 3, para 16	31 (4)
para 7 (3)	para 13 (3), (4)	para 27 (1)	(1)
para 7 (4)		para 27 (2)	(5)
9	Rep, SLRA 1953	para 31	122 (3)
		para 32	
Electoral Registers Act 1949 (c 86)		para 33 (1)	
		para 33 (2)	203 (2)
s 1 (1), (2)	s 13 (1)	para 35	
(3), (4)	4	Elections (Welsh Forms) Act 1964 (c 31)	
(5)	13 (2), 201		
(6)	13 (3), (4)	s 1 (1)	199 (1), 201 (1)
(7)	Rep, 1969 c 15, s 24 (4), Sch 3, Pt I	(2), (3)	199 (2), (3)
2	Rep, 1969 c 15, s 24 (4), Sch 3, Pt II	2	
3 (1)	Rep, 1972 c 71, s 64 (2), Sch 6, Pt I	Criminal Law Act 1967 (c 58)	
(2)	Rep, SLRA 1953		
4	Rep, 1953 c 8, s 1 (3)	s 1†	65 (3), 99 (1), 168 (3)

† Not repealed

(1)	(2)
Civil Evidence Act 1968 (c 64)	Representation of the People Act 1983 (c 2)
Schedule*	s 141 (1), (2)
City of London (Various Powers) Act 1968 (c xxxvii)	
s 3 (3)*, (4)	} Obsolete
4	
Representation of the People Act 1969 (c 15)	
s 1 (1)	s 1 (1), 2 (1)
(2)	12 (5)
(3)	21 (3), 34 (3)
(4)	Sch 1, r 39 (3)
(5)	s 202 (2)
2 (1), (2)	Rep, 1976 c 29, s 1 (1)
(3)	s 14 (1)
(4)	Rep, 1976 c 29, s 3 (8)
3 (1)	s 6
(2)	Sch 2, para 9
4	s 3
5 (1)	19 (1), 32 (1)
(2)	19 (5), 32 (5)
(3)	20 (4), 33 (3)
6 (1)	Rep, 1972 c 70, s 272 (1), Sch 30 and SI 1973/ 2095, art 5 (2), Sch 2
(2)	s 19 (1)
(3)	19 (6), 32 (6)
(4)	See ss 22, 34
(5)	———
(6)	Sch 1, r 5(2), (3)
(7)	———
7 (1)	s 9 (3)
(2)	Rep, 1980 c 3, s 3 (2), Schedule
(3)	———
8 (1)	Rep, 1977 c 9, s 1 (4), Schedule, Pt I
(2)	s 76 (6)
(3)	Rep, 1977 c 9, s 1 (4), Schedule, Pt I
(4)	s 82 (4)
(5)	88
(6)	89 (1), Sch 4, para 8 (1)
9 (1), (2)	93 (1), (2)
(3)	———
(4)	75 (1)
(5)	92 (1)
(6)	194
10	———
11 (1)	67 (5)
(2)	68 (1)
(3)	69 (2)

(1)	(2)
Representation of the People Act 1969 (c 15)	Representation of the People Act 1983 (c 2)
s 11 (3A)	Applied to Scotland
(4)	Sch 1, r 30 (3), (5), 32 (2)
(5)	1, r 30 (9)
(6)	
12 (1)	1, r 6 (2), (3)
(2)	Rep, 1971 c 7, s 3 (2) and 1973 c 65, s 237 (1), Sch 29
13 (1)	s 38 (2), Sch 1, r 60 (1)
(2), (3)	Sch 1, r 60 (2), (3)
(4)	Rep, 1972 c 70, s 272 (1), Sch 30 and 1973 c 65, s 237 (1), Sch 29
(5)	———
14	
15–17	Rep, 1972 c 70, s 272 (1), Sch 30
18 (1)	Rep, 1972 c 70, s 272 (1), Sch 30
(2)	Sch 1, r 2 (1), (3)
(3)–(5)	Rep, 1972 c 70, s 272 (1), Sch 30
19 (1)	s 48 (3)
(2)–(4)	Rep, 1972 c 70, s 272 (1), Sch 30
20	s 29 (6)
21	———
22 (1)	———
(2)	139 (3)
23 (1)	191 (2), Sch 6, para 1
(2)	Sch 6, para 2–4
(3), (4)	para 5, 6
24 (1)	———
(2)	See Sch 7, para 4
(3)	Rep, 1972 c 70, s 272 (1), Sch 30
(4), (5)	———
25	
26 (1)	———
(2)	Rep, 1972 c 70, s 272 (1), Sch 30
(3)	s 203 (4)
(4)	205 (1)
(5)	———
27, 28	———
Sch 1, Pt I	
Pt II—	
para 1 (1)	Rep, 1972 c 70, s 272 (1), Sch 30
para 1 (2)	Passim
para 2	Sch 1, r 1
para 3	Rep, 1973 c 65, s 237 (1), Sch 29
para 4	Sch 1, r 20 (1), (3)
para 5 (1)	6 (1), 11 (4)

* Repealed in part

(1)	(2)	(1)	(2)
Representation of the People Act 1969 (c 15)	Representation of the People Act 1983 (c 2)	Representation of the People Act 1969 (c 15)	Representation of the People Act 1983 (c 2)
Sch 1, Pt II—		Sch 2, para 23 (2)	Rep, 1973 c 65, s 237 (1), Sch 29
para 5 (2)	Sch 1, Appendix		
para 6 (1)	s 38 (1)	para 24	Rep, 1972 c 70, s 272 (1), Sch 30
para 6 (2)	Rep, 1973 c 65, s 237 (1), Sch 29	para 25 (1)	Rep, 1973 c 65, s 237 (1), Sch 29
para 7	Rep, 1973 c 65, s 237 (1), Sch 29	para 25 (2)	Sch 1, r 30 (5)
para 8 (1), (2)	Sch 1, r 31 (1), (3)	para 26 (1)	31
para 8 (3)	(3)	para 26 (2)	Rep, 1972 c 70, s 272 (1), Sch 30
para 9	43 (1)	para 26 (3)	Rep, 1973 c 65, s 237 (1), Sch 29
para 10 (1)	43 (3)		
para 10 (2)	45 (1)	para 27	Sch 1, r 32 (2)
para 11	44 (3)	para 28	39 (3)
para 12 (1)	23 (3)	para 29 (1)	45 (1), (5)
para 12 (2)	Rep, 1972 c 70, s 272 (1), Sch 30	para 29 (2)	Rep, 1973 c 65, s 237 (1), Sch 29
para 13 (1)	Rep, 1972 c 70, s 272 (1), Sch 30	para 30	——
para 13 (2)	Sch 1, r 29 (4), (5), Appendix	para 31	Sch 1, r 53 (3)
para 13 (3)	Rep, 1973 c 65, s 237 (1), Sch 29	para 32, 33	Appendix
para 13 (4)	Sch 1, r 50 (1)	para 34–36	Rep, 1973 c 65, s 237 (1), Sch 29
para 13 (5)	Rep, 1973 c 65, s 237 (1), Sch 29	para 37	Sch 1, Appendix
2, para 1	s 1 (1), 2 (1)	para 38 (1)	2, para 1 (2)
para 2 (1)	Rep, 1976 c 29, s 3 (8)	para 38 (2), (3)	para 5 (3), (4)
para 2 (2)	——	para 39	3
para 3	s 10	para 40	7, para 10 (2)
para 4 (1)	14 (1)	3, 4	——
para 4 (2)	16		
para 4 (3)	Rep, 1976 c 29, s 3 (8)	**Family Law Reform Act 1969 (c 46)**	
para 4 (4)	——		
para 5	s 19 (1)	Sch 2, para 2★	Obsolete
para 6 (1)	21 (2)		
para 6 (2)	(6)	**Post Office Act 1969 (c 48)**	
para 7	22 (2), (5)–(7)		
para 8 (1)	32 (1)	Sch 4, para 47 (1)	s 91 (1), (3)
para 8 (2)	(4)	para 47 (2)	184 (2)
para 9	33 (2)		
para 10	34 (3)	**Courts Act 1971 (c 23)**	
para 11 (1)	49 (2)		
para 11 (2), (3)	(4), (5)	Sch 8, para 30 (1)	130 (2)
para 12	59 (3), (4)	para 30 (2)	140 (1)
para 13 (1)	61 (1)	para 30 (3)	155 (2)
para 13 (2)	(2), (3)		
para 14	68 (1), (2), (5)	**Civil Evidence Act (Northern Ireland) 1971 (c 36) (NI)**	
para 15	70 (4)		
para 16	76 (6)		
para 17	91 (4)	Schedule★	141 (1), (2)
para 18	119 (2), (3)		
para 19	122 (3), (4)	**Local Government Act 1972 (c 70)**	
para 20 (1)	Rep, 1977 c 9, s 1 (4), Schedule, Pt I		
para 21	s 202 (1)	s 39	8 (2)
para 22	Rep, 1972 c 70, s 272 (1), Sch 30	40 (1), (2)	24 (1)
para 23 (1)	Sch 1, r 7 (6)	(3)	28 (1), (2), (6)

★ Repealed in part

(1)	(2)
Local Government Act 1972 (c 70)	Representation of the People Act 1983 (c 2)
s 40 (4)	s 28 (6)
(5)	24 (2)
41	35
42 (1)	36 (1)
(2)	——
(3)–(8)	36 (2)–(7)
43	37
44 (1)–(4)	39 (1)–(4)
(5)–(8)	(6)–(9)
45	——
243 (1)†, (2)★	40 (1)
(3)†	(2)
(4)★, (5)†	(3)
265†	See s 203 (5)
266 (1)†	s 24 (1) (c), (e), 36 (7)
	(a), 37
270 (1)†	40 (1), 203 (1)
(3)†	67 (7), 202 (1)
(4)†	202 (1)
Sch 6, para 1	52 (3)
para 2	54 (1), (4)
para 3	156 (4)
para 4	——
para 5 (1), (2)	18 (2)
para 5 (3)	(5)
para 6	19 (4), 22 (3)
para 7	28 (3)
para 8	31 (1)
para 9	——
para 10	39 (5), (6)
para 11	187 (1)
para 12	Sch 2, para 1 (1)
para 13	5, para 3 (1)
para 14	s 69 (2)
City of London (Various Powers) Act 1973 (c xx)	
s 9	Obsolete
Local Government Reorganisation (Consequential Provisions) (Northern Ireland) Order 1973, SI 1973/2095	
art 2 (4)	s 19 (4)
(5)	156 (3)
(6)	82 (4), Sch 1, r 31 (3)
Northern Ireland (Modification of Enactments—No 1) Order 1973, SI 1973/2163	
Sch 5, para 15 (a)	18 (7), 58
para 15 (b)	160 (6)
para 15 (c)	165 (1)

(1)	(2)
Juries Act 1974 (c 23)	Representation of the People Act 1983 (c 2)
s 3 (3)	Sch 2, para 2
Local Authorities etc (Miscellaneous Provision) (No 2) Order 1974, SI 1974/595	
art 3 (7) (a)	s 39 (5)
(b)	203 (1)
(c)	Sch 7, para 11
House of Commons Disqualification Act 1975 (c 24)	
s 10 (1)	Sch 1, r 8 (3)
Representation of the People (Armed Forces) Act 1976 (c 29)	
s 1 (1)	——
(2)	s 15 (2)–(4)
2	14 (1)
3 (1)	——
(2), (3)	Rep, 1980 c 3, s 3 (2), Schedule
(4)	s 16
(5)	17 (1)
(6)	15 (7)
(7), (8)	——
4	——
Armed Forces Act 1976 (c 52)	
Sch 9, para 19	3 (2)
Bail Act 1976 (c 63)	
Sch 2, para 12	171 (7)
Representation of the People Act 1977 (c 9)	
s 1 (1)	76 (2)
(2)	197 (1)
(3)	See Sch 7, para 3
(4)	——
2	——
Schedule	——
Criminal Law Act 1977 (c 45)	
s 28 (2)†	s 168 (4)
31 (6)†	65 (4), 97 (3)
32 (1)†	65 (5), 149, 168 (2)
Sch 1, item 9	62 (1)
12★	171 (9)

★ Repealed in part   † Not repealed

(1)	(2)
Local Authorities etc (Miscellaneous Provision) Order 1977, SI 1977/293	Representation of the People Act 1983 (c 2)
art 4 (2)	s 32 (8)
Judicature (Northern Ireland) Act 1978 (c 23)	
Sch 5, Part II*	78 (6), 86 (9), 122 (8), 123 (1), 140 (1), 146 (4), 148 (6), 167 (4), 174 (6), 185
Representation of the People Act 1978 (c 32)	
s 1	76 (2)
2	76 (3), 197 (3)
3, 4	—
Prosecution of Offences Act 1979 (c 31)	
Sch 1*	181 (4), (8)
Representation of the People Act 1979 (c 40)	
s 1–3 Schedule	} Obsolete
Representation of the People Act 1980 (c 3)	
s 1 (1)	s 12 (3), (4)
(2)	16, 17 (2)
(3)	—
2 (1)	11 (1)–(4)
(2)	56 (1)
(3)	—
3	—
Schedule	—
Representation of the People Act 1981 (c 34)	
s 3	—
Schedule, para 1	Sch 1, r 1
para 2	2 (1), (3)
para 3	8 (3)
para 4	12 (2)
para 5	15
para 6	Appendix
para 7	—
Representation of the People (Variation of Limits of Candidates' Election Expenses) Order 1981, SI 1981/191	
art 1	—

(1)	(2)
Representation of the People (Variation of Limits of Candidates' Election Expenses) Order 1981, SI 1981/191	Representation of the People Act 1983 (c 2)
art 2	s 76 (2)
Criminal Justice Act 1982 (c 48)	
s 37 (1)†, (2)†	s 62 (1), 63 (1), 64 (1), 65 (4), 97 (3), 100 (2), 110 (3), 169, 175 (1), Sch 2, para 13 (1), Sch 4, para 2
38 (1)†, (6)†, (8)†	63 (1), 64 (1), 100 (2), 110 (3), 169, 175 (1), Sch 4, para 2
40 (1)†, (5)†, (8)† 46 (1)†	Sch 2, para 13 (1) s 62 (1), 63 (1), 64 (1), 65 (4), 97 (3), 100 (2), 110 (3), 169, 175 (1), Sch 2, para 13 (1), Sch 4, para 2
74†, 75†	202 (1)
Mental Health (Amendment) Act 1982 (c 51)	
s 62 (1)	5 (3), 7 (1)
(2)	—
69 (5)	—
70 (2)*	—
Sch 2, para 1	7 (2)
para 2	(3)
para 3 (1)–(6)	(4)
para 3 (7), (8)	(5), (6)
para 3 (9)	(2)
para 4	(7), (8)
para 5	(9)
para 6	62 (1)
para 7 (1)	19 (1) (f), (4), 32 (1) (e), (4)
para 7 (2)	20 (2), 33 (2)
para 7 (3)	20 (1), 33 (1)
para 8	—
Representation of the People (Variation of Limits of Candidates' Election Expenses) Order 1982, SI 1982/363	
art 1	—
2–4	76 (2)
5, 6	197 (1), (2)
7	—

* Repealed in part   † Not repealed

ELECTIONS (NORTHERN IRELAND) ACT 1985

(1985 c 2)

ARRANGEMENT OF SECTIONS

An Act to make further provision for preventing personation at elections in Northern Ireland
[24 January 1985]

Parliamentary elections

1 Voters to produce specified documents

(1) In the Representation of the People Act 1983 ("the 1983 Act") Schedule 1 (parliamentary elections rules) shall be amended as follows.

(2) The following shall be inserted after rule 37(1) (ballot paper to be delivered to voter on application)—

"(1A) A ballot paper shall not be delivered to a voter unless he has produced a specified document to the presiding officer or a clerk.

(1B) Where a voter produces a specified document, the presiding officer or clerk to whom it is produced shall deliver a ballot paper to the voter unless the officer or clerk decides that the document raises a reasonable doubt as to whether the voter is the elector or proxy he represents himself to be.

(1C) Where a voter produces a specified document to a presiding officer and he so decides, he shall refuse to deliver a ballot paper to the voter.

(1D) Where a voter produces a specified document to a clerk and he so decides, he shall refer the matter and produce the document to the presiding officer who shall proceed as if the document had been produced to him in the first place.

(1E) For the purposes of this rule a specified document is one which for the time being falls within the following list:—

(*a*) a current licence to drive a motor vehicle granted under Part III of the Road Traffic Act 1972 (excluding a provisional licence), or under Article 12 of the Road Traffic (Northern Ireland) Order 1981 or any corresponding enactment for the time being in force;

(*b*) a current passport issued by the Government of the United Kingdom or by the Government of the Republic of Ireland;

(*c*) a current book for the payment of allowances, benefits or pensions issued by the Department of Health and Social Services for Northern Ireland;

(*d*) a medical card issued by the Northern Ireland Central Services Agency for the Health and Social Services;

(*e*) a certified copy, or extract, of an entry of marriage issued by a Registrar General, where the voter producing the copy or extract is a woman married within the period of two years ending with the day of the poll concerned.

In sub-paragraph (*e*) above "a Registrar General" means the Registrar General for England and Wales, the Registrar General of Births, Deaths and Marriages for Scotland or the Registrar General for Northern Ireland.

(1F) Regulations may make provision varying the list in paragraph (1E) above (whether by adding or deleting documents or varying any description of document).

(1G) References in this rule to producing a document are to producing it for inspection."

(3) The following shall be inserted after rule 38(1) (incapacitated voter's vote to be marked on ballot paper on application)—

"(1A) Paragraphs (1A) to (1G) of rule 37 shall apply in the case of a voter who applies under paragraph (1) above as they apply in the case of a voter who applies under rule 37(1), but reading references to delivering a ballot paper to a voter as references to causing a voter's vote to be marked on a ballot paper."

(4) The following shall be inserted after rule 39(2) (blind voter to be allowed assistance of companion on application)—

"(2A) Paragraphs (1A) to (1G) of rule 37 shall apply in the case of a voter who applies under paragraph (1) above as they apply in the case of a voter who applies under rule 37(1), but reading references to delivering a ballot paper to a voter as references to granting a voter's application."

(5) The following shall be inserted after rule 40(1) (person entitled to mark tendered ballot paper after another has voted)—

"(1A) Paragraphs (1A) to (1G) of rule 37 shall apply in the case of a person who seeks to mark a tendered ballot paper under paragraph (1) above as they apply in the case of a voter who applies for a ballot paper under rule 37(1).

(1B) Paragraph (1C) below applies where a presiding officer refuses to deliver a ballot paper to a person under paragraph (1C) of rule 37 (including that paragraph as applied by rule 38 or 39 or this rule).

(1C) The person shall, on satisfactorily answering the questions permitted by law to be asked at the poll, nevertheless be entitled, subject to the following provisions of this rule, to mark a ballot paper (in these rules referred to as "a tendered ballot paper") in the same manner as any other voter."

(6) The following shall be inserted after rule 40(4)—

"(5) A person who marks a tendered ballot paper under paragraph (1C) above shall sign the paper, unless it was marked after an application was refused under rule 38 or 39.

(6) A paper which is required to be signed under paragraph (5) above and is not so signed shall be void."

NOTES

Commencement. This section and ss 2, 3 post, so far as they are necessary to give effect to s 5(1) post, came into force on 24 January 1985, which was the date on which this Act was passed; see, s 7(3) post. For all other purposes, this section and ss 2, 3 post, were brought into force on 6 August 1985 by the Elections (Northern Ireland) Act 1985 (Commencement) Order 1985, SI 1985/1221, made under s 7(2) post.

Sub-s (2): Presiding officer. This officer is appointed under the Representation of the People Act 1983, s 23, Sch 1, r 26(1) ante.

Proxy. As to proxies at parliamentary elections, see the Representation of the People Act 1983, ss 21, 22 ante. Those sections are repealed by the Representation of the People Act 1985, s 28(1), Sch 5 post, as from a date to be appointed under s 29(2) of that Act. For new provisions as to proxies, see, as from that date, ss 8, 9 of that Act.

Current passport issued, etc. United Kingdom passports are issued, under the royal prerogative, by the Foreign and Commonweath Office or by diplomatic representatives outside the United Kingdom; see further 18 Halsbury's Laws (4th edn) para 1412.

United Kingdom. Ie Great Britain and Northern Ireland; see the Interpretation Act 1978, s 5, Sch 1, Vol 41, title Statutes.

Republic of Ireland. Ie that part of Ireland previously officially known in this country as Eire and originally called the Irish Free State; see the Ireland Act 1949, s 1(1), (3), Vol 7, title Commonwealth and Other Territories (Pt 3(c)) in conjunction with the Eire (Confirmation of Agreements) Act 1938, s 1 (repealed).

Within the period of two years ending with, etc. As a general rule the effect of defining a period in such a manner is to include the day on which the event in question occurs.

Sub-s (5): Questions permitted by law to be asked, etc. As to these, see the Representation of the People Act 1983, s 23, Sch 1, r 35 ante.

Sub-s (6): Sign. See, as to whether a mark in lieu of signature is sufficient, on the one hand, *Morton v French* 1908 SC 171 (mark held insufficient) and, on the other hand, *Re Gill* (1920) CR Rep 63 (mark held sufficient).

Elections other than parliamentary elections. Provisions corresponding to those in this section or ss 2, 3 post may be contained in orders made under the Northern Ireland Constitution Act 1973, s 38(1), Vol 31, title Northern Ireland (Pt 2), and the Northern Ireland Assembly Act 1973, s 2(5), Vol 31, title Northern Ireland (Pt 2); see s 5(1), (2) post.

In relation to European Assembly elections, note that the European Assembly Elections Act 1978, Sch 1, para 2(1) ante, has effect subject to anything in regulations made under that paragraph which applies or corresponds to any of the provisions in this section or ss 2, 3 post; see s 5(3) post.

Definitions. For "voter" and "elector", see the Representation of the People Act 1983, s 202(1) ante. Note as to "specified document", "a Registrar General" and "producing a document", s 23, Sch 1, r 37(1E), (1F), (1G) to the 1983 Act as inserted by sub-s (2) above, and note as to "a tendered ballot paper", s 23, Sch 1, r 40(1C) to that Act as inserted by sub-s (5) above.

Representation of the People Act 1983. See this title ante.

Road Traffic Act 1972, Part III. Ie ss 84–111 of that Act, see Vol 38, title Road Traffic.

Road Traffic (Northern Ireland) Order 1981. SI 1981/154 (NI 1).

Regulations. Up to 1 August 1985 no regulations had been made for the purposes of the Representation of the People Act 1983, s 23, Sch 1, r 37(1F), as inserted by sub-s (2) above.

For general provisions as to regulations made under the 1983 Act, see s 201 thereof ante.

---

2 Further provisions

(1) Schedule 1 to the 1983 Act shall be further amended as mentioned in subsections (2) to (4).

(2) At the end of rule 26(3) (clerks may do what presiding officer may do, with exceptions) there shall be inserted "or refuse to deliver a ballot paper under paragraph (1C) of rule 37 (including that paragraph as applied by rule 38, 39 or 40)."

(3) The following minor amendments shall be made—

    (*a*) in rule 37(1) for "A" there shall be substituted "Subject to paragraphs (1A) to (1G) below, a";

    (*b*) in rule 38(1) for "The" there shall be substituted "Subject to paragraph (1A) below, the";

    (*c*) in rule 39(2) for "If" there shall be substituted "Subject to paragraph (2A) below, if".

(4) After rule 40 there shall be inserted—

"Refusal to deliver ballot paper

40A—(1) This rule applies where a presiding officer refuses to deliver a ballot paper under paragraph (1C) of rule 37 (including that paragraph as applied by rule 38, 39 or 40).

(2) The refusal shall be subject to review on an election petition but, subject to that, shall be final and shall not be questioned in any proceeding whatsoever."

(5) The following shall be inserted after section 61(6) of the 1983 Act (voting offences)—

"(6A) Where a person is alleged to have committed an offence under subsection (2)(*a*)(i) or (3)(*a*)(i) above by voting on a second or subsequent occasion at a parliamentary election, he shall not be deemed by virtue of subsection (6) above to have voted by applying on a previous occasion for a ballot paper for the purpose of voting in person unless he then marked a tendered ballot paper under rule 40(1C) of the parliamentary elections rules."

NOTES

Commencement. See the note to s 1 ante.

Sub-s (4): Presiding officer. See the note to s 1(2) ante.

Sub-s (5): Parliamentary election. Ie an election of a Member to serve in Parliament for a constituency; see the Interpretation Act 1978, s 5, Sch 1, Vol 41, title Statutes.

Elections other than parliamentary elections. See the note to s 1 ante.

Definitions. For "election petition" and "parliamentary elections rules", see the Representation of the People Act 1983, s 202(1) ante; and for "tendered ballot paper", see s 23 of, and Sch 1, r 40(1C) to, that Act, as inserted by s 1(5) of this Act ante.

1983 Act. Ie the Representation of the People Act 1983 ante; see s 1(1) ante.

3 Offences relating to specified documents

(1) A person commits an offence if, on the day of or the day next preceding the poll for a parliamentary election, he has possession of a document to which this section applies, with the intention of committing or of enabling another person to commit the offence of personation at the election.

(2) This section applies to—

    (*a*) a document which is not, but purports to be, a specified document within the meaning of rule 37 of the parliamentary elections rules in Schedule 1 to the 1983 Act, and

    (*b*) a specified document within the meaning of that rule which either falsely bears the name of the person in possession or does not bear that name.

(3) If a constable has reasonable grounds for suspecting that a person has possession of a document in contravention of subsection (1), the constable may—

    (*a*) search that person, and detain him for the purpose of searching him;

    (*b*) search any vehicle in which the constable suspects that the document may be found, and for that purpose require the person in control of the vehicle to stop it;

    (*c*) seize and retain, for the purpose of proceedings for an offence under subsection (1), any document found in the course of the search if there are reasonable grounds for suspecting that it is a document to which this section applies.

(4) If a resident magistrate is satisfied by complaint on oath that there are reasonable grounds for suspecting that a person has possession on any premises of a document in contravention of subsection (1), he may grant a warrant authorising any constable—

    (*a*) to enter, if need be by force, the premises named in the warrant,

    (*b*) to search the premises and any person found there, and

    (*c*) to seize and retain, for the purpose of proceedings for an offence under subsection (1), any document found in the course of the search if there are reasonable grounds for suspecting that it is a document to which this section applies.

(5) A person commits an offence if he—

(a) intentionally obstructs a constable in the exercise of his powers under this section, or

(b) conceals from a constable acting in the exercise of those powers any document to which this section applies.

(6) A constable may arrest without warrant a person who has committed, or whom the constable has reasonable grounds for suspecting to have committed, an offence under subsection (1) or (5) if—

(a) he has reasonable grounds for believing that that person will abscond unless arrested,

(b) the name and address of that person are unknown to, and cannot be ascertained by, him, or

(c) he is not satisfied that a name and address furnished by that person as his name and address are true.

(7) A person is guilty of a corrupt practice if he commits or aids, abets, counsels or procures the commission of an offence under subsection (1); and the provisions of the 1983 Act relating to corrupt practices shall apply in such a case, but reading for the words "one year" in section [168(1)(a)(ii)] (penalty on indictment) the words "two years".

(8) A person guilty of an offence under subsection (5) shall be liable on summary conviction to a fine not exceeding level 5 on the standard scale (as provided by Article 5 of the Fines and Penalties (Northern Ireland) Order 1984) or to imprisonment for a term not exceeding 6 months or to both.

(9) A prosecution shall not be instituted in respect of an offence under subsection (1) except by or with the consent of the Director of Public Prosecutions for Northern Ireland.

(10) In this section—

"premises" includes any place and, in particular, includes any moveable structure, and

"vehicle" means a vehicle intended or adapted for use on land (however propelled, and including a caravan or other vehicle intended or adapted to be drawn).

NOTES

The reference to "168(1)(a)(ii)" in sub-s (7) was substituted by the Representation of the People Act 1985, s 25(2), as from 1 October 1985.

Commencement. See the note to s 1 ante.

Sub-s (1): Parliamentary election. See the note to s 2 ante.

Personation. See, as to the offence of personation, the Representation of the People Act 1983, s 60 ante.

Sub-s (3): Reasonable grounds for suspecting. It is submitted that these words require not only that the person in question has reasonable grounds for suspecting but also that he does actually suspect; see *R v Banks* [1916] 2 KB 621, [1916–17] All ER Rep 356, and *R v Harrison* [1938] 3 All ER 134, 159 LT 95; and see also *Nakkuda Ali v Jayaratne* [1951] AC 66, PC.

The existence of the reasonable grounds and of the suspicion founded on it is ultimately a question of fact to be tried on evidence and the grounds on which the person acted must be sufficient to induce in a reasonable person the required suspicion; see in particular, *McArdle v Egan* (1933) 150 LT 412, [1933] All ER Rep 611, CA; *Nakkuda Ali v Jayaratne* supra; *Registrar of Restrictive Trading Agreements v W H Smith & Son Ltd* [1969] 3 All ER 1065 at 1070, [1969] 1 WLR 1460 at 1468, CA per Lord Denning MR; and *IRC v Rossminster Ltd* [1980] AC 952, [1980] 1 All ER 80 at 84, 92, 103, 104, HL.

Search. A magistrate has no power to inquire into the reasonableness or unreasonableness of the search, unless he finds it was a mere pretence by the officer (*Anderson v Reid* (1902) 86 LT 713).

Sub-s (4): Oath. This includes affirmation and declaration; see the Interpretation Act 1978, s 5, Sch 1, Vol 41, title Statutes. As to oaths, affirmations and declarations, see the Oaths Act 1978, Vol 17, title Evidence, and the relevant enactments noted to s 1 of that Act.

Sub-s (5): Intentionally obstructs. Obstruction need not involve physical violence; see, especially, *Borrow v Howland* (1896) 74 LT 787, and *Hinchliffe v Sheldon* [1955] 3 All ER 406, [1955] 1 WLR 1207. In fact there is authority for saying that anything which makes it more difficult for a person to carry out his duty amounts to obstruction; see *Hinchliffe v Sheldon* supra at 408 per Lord Goddard CJ. Thus merely giving a warning to some other person may amount to obstruction of the person carrying out his duty; see *Green v Moore* [1982] QB 1044, [1982] 1 All ER 428, and *Moore v Green* [1983] 1 All ER 663. Yet standing by and doing nothing is not obstruction unless there is a legal duty to act; see *Swallow v LCC* [1916] 1 KB 224, [1914–15] All ER Rep 403; and contrast *Baker v Ellison* [1914] 2 KB 762; but see *Rice v Connolly* [1966] 2 QB 414, [1966] 2 All ER 649. However, a positive act does not cease to be obstructive just because it is lawful in itself; see *Dibble v Ingleton* [1972] 1 QB 480 sub nom *Ingleton v Dibble* [1972] 1 All ER 275.

Obstruction must, however, to be an offence under this section, be intentional; and an act is done intentionally if it is deliberate and wilful, not accidental or inadvertent, but so that the mind of the person who does the act goes with it; cf *R v Senior* [1899] 1 QB 283 at 290, 291, [1895–9] All ER Rep 511 at 514 per Lord Russell of Killowen. It is therefore necessary for the prosecution to prove that the act in question was done with the intention of obstructing, and intervention with the intention of assisting the person obstructed is not an offence; see *Willmott v Atack* [1977] QB 498, [1976] 3 All ER 794. Provided, however, that the person charged intended to do an act, which amounted to obstruction or that his actions were not aimed primarily at the person obstructed; it is immaterial that he did not appreciate that what he did amounted in law to obstruction; see *Moore v Green* supra; *Hills v Ellis* [1983] QB 680, [1983] 1 All ER 667, and *Lewis v Cox* [1984] 3 All ER 672. See also *R v Walker* (1934) 24 Cr App Rep 117; *Eaton v Cobb* [1950] 1 All ER 1016, 114 JP Jo 271; *Arrowsmith v Jenkins* [1963] 2 QB 561, [1963] 2 All ER 210; *Rice v Connolly* supra; *Dibble v Ingleton* supra; *Wershof v Metropolitan Police Comr* [1978] 3 All ER 540, (1978) 122 Sol Jo 279, and *R v Sheppard* [1981] AC 394, [1980] 3 All ER 899, HL.

Sub-s (6): Reasonable grounds for believing. Cf the note "Reasonable grounds for suspecting" to sub-s (3) above.

Sub-s (7): Aids, abets, counsels or procures. As to the difference between "aid and abet" and "counsel and procure", see *Ferguson v Weaving* [1951] 1 KB 814 at 819, [1951] 1 All ER 412 at 413.

Inaction, when positive conduct to prevent the commission of the offence is a duty in the circumstances, may amount to aiding and abetting; see *Du Cros v Lambourne* [1907] 1 KB 40; *Rubie v Faulkner* [1940] 1 KB 571, [1940] 1 All ER 285; and *Tuck v Robson* [1970] 1 All ER 1171, [1970] 1 WLR 741. Yet, mere negligence in the performance of a duty, in consequence of which the opportunity for committing the offence is created, does not of itself constitute aiding and abetting; see *Callow v Tillstone* (1900) 83 LT 411. To be convicted as an aider and abettor a person must know all the circumstances which constitute the offence, but whether he realises that these circumstances constitute an offence is immaterial; see *Ackroyd's Air Travel Ltd v DPP* [1950] 1 All ER 933 at 936, 48 LGR 398; and *Thomas v Lindop* [1950] 1 All ER 966 at 968, [1950] WN 227, per Lord Goddard CJ.

"Procure" has been defined as "obtain by care and effort" and, it has been said, "can be more simply paraphrased as 'see to it'"; see *Re Royal Victoria Pavilion, Ramsgate, Whelan v FTS (Great Britain) Ltd* [1961] Ch 581 at 587, [1961] 3 All ER 83 at 86. Similarly it has been held that "to procure means to produce by endeavour. You procure a thing by setting out to see that it happens and taking the appropriate steps to produce that happening"; see *A-G's Reference (No 1 of 1975)* [1975] QB 773 at 779, [1975] 2 All ER 684 at 686, CA; applied in *R v Broadfoot* [1976] 3 All ER 753, [1977] Crim LR 690, CA.

Sub-s (8): Shall be liable on summary conviction. Summary jurisdiction and procedure in Northern Ireland and principally dealt with by the Magistrates' Courts (Northern Ireland) Order 1981, SI 1981/1675 (NI 26).

Sub-s (9): Consent of the Director of Public Prosecutions for Northern Ireland. Provision for the appointment of the Director of Public Prosecutions for Northern Ireland and a deputy Director is made by the Prosecution of Offences (Northern Ireland) Order 1972, SI 1972/538, art 4, as amended by the Northern Ireland Constitution Act 1973, s 34. As to arrest, remand, etc, where the consent of the Director has not yet been given, see the Criminal Jurisdiction Act 1975, s 12, Vol 31, title Northern Ireland (Pt 2); and as to evidence of such consent, see art 7(6) of the 1972 Order.

Elections other than parliamentary elections. See the note to s 1 ante.

1983 Act. Ie the Representation of the People Act 1983 ante; see s 1(1) ante. As to the provisions of that Act relating to corrupt practices, see, in particular, in connection with this section, ss 168–170, 173 thereof.

Fines and Penalties (Northern Ireland) Order 1984. SI 1984/703 (NI 3). Art 5 of that Order makes provision for a standard scale of fines for offences punishable on summary conviction. A fine of level 5 on that scale, as amended by the Criminal Penalties etc (Increase) Order (Northern Ireland) 1984, SR 1984/253 (made under art 17(1) of the Fines and Penalties (Northern Ireland) Order 1984, SI 1984/703 (NI 3)), is the sum of £2,000.

4 Effect on the franchise

The provisions of the Representation of the People Acts stating who is entitled to vote at parliamentary elections shall have effect subject to the provisions contained in the parliamentary elections rules by virtue of sections 1 and 2 above.

NOTES

Commencement. This section was brought into force on 6 August 1985 by the Elections (Northern Ireland) Act 1985 (Commencement) Order 1985, SI 1985/1221, made under s 7(2) post.

Representation of the People Acts. For the Acts which may be cited by this collective title, see the Introductory Note to the Representation of the People Act 1948 ante.

Other elections

5 Elections other than parliamentary

(1) Without prejudice to the generality of section 38(1) of the Northern Ireland Constitution Act 1973 (power by Order in Council to provide for local authority elections, but not the franchise) an Order in Council under it may contain provisions corresponding to any of those of sections 1 to 3 of this Act; and in section 38(1)(*a*) the words "(but not the franchise)", and the Electoral Law Act (Northern Ireland) 1962, shall have effect subject to that.

(2) Without prejudice to the generality of section 2(5) of the Northern Ireland Assembly Act 1973 (power to make by order provision concerning elections to Assembly, including provision as to franchise) an order under it may contain provisions corresponding to any of those of sections 1 to 3 of this Act.

(3) Paragraph 2(1) of Schedule 1 to the European Assembly Elections Act 1978 (person entitled to vote if he would be entitled at parliamentary or local election) shall have effect subject to anything in regulations under paragraph 2 (conduct of elections) which applies or corresponds to any of the provisions of sections 1 to 3 of this Act; but otherwise those provisions, and any provision corresponding to any of them, shall be ignored in construing paragraph 2(1).

NOTES

Commencement. Sub-s (1) of this section came into force on 24 January 1985 which was the date on which this Act was passed (ie received the Royal Assent); see s 7(3) post. Sub-ss (2), (3) were brought into force on 6 August 1985 by the Elections (Northern Ireland) Act 1985 (Commencement) Order 1985, SI 1985/1221, made under s 7(2) post.

Order in Council. The power to make Orders in Council is exercisable by statutory instrument; see the Statutory Instruments Act 1946, s 1(1), Vol 41, title Statutes.

Northern Ireland Constitution Act 1973. See Vol 31, title Northern Ireland (Pt 2).

Electoral Law Act (Northern Ireland) 1962. 1962 c 14 (NI); not printed in this work.

Northern Ireland Assembly Act 1973. See Vol 31, title Northern Ireland (Pt 2).

European Assembly Elections Act 1978. See this title ante.

General

6 Expenses

Any increase attributable to this Act in the sums to be paid out of, or charged on and paid out of, the Consolidated Fund under any other enactment shall be paid out of, or charged on and paid out of, that Fund.

NOTES

Commencement. This section came into force on 24 January 1985 which was the date on which this Act was passed (ie received the Royal Assent); see s 7(3) post.

Consolidated Fund. Ie the Consolidated Fund of the United Kingdom which was established by the Consolidated Fund Act 1816, s 1, Vol 30, title Money (Pt 1). By the Finance Act 1954, s 34(3), Vol 30, title

Money (Pt 1), any charge on the Fund extends to the growing produce thereof. See also, as to payment out of the Fund, the Exchequer and Audit Departments Act 1866, s 13, in conjunction with the Exchequer and Audit Departments Act 1957, s 2, and the Finance Act 1975, s 56, all Vol 30, title Money (Pt 1).

7 Citation, commencement and extent

(1) This Act may be cited as the Elections (Northern Ireland) Act 1985, and shall be included among the Acts that may be cited as the Representation of the People Acts.

(2) Subject to subsection (3), this Act shall come into force on such day as the Secretary of State may appoint by order made by statutory instrument.

(3) Section 5(1), section 6 and this section (and sections 1 to 3 so far as necessary to give effect to section 5(1)) shall come into force on the day on which this Act is passed.

(4) This Act extends to Northern Ireland only.

NOTES

Representation of the People Acts. For the Acts that may be cited by this collective title, see the Representation of the People Act 1948 ante.

Secretary of State. Ie one of Her Majesty's Principal Secretaries of State; see the Interpretation Act 1978, s 5, Sch 1, Vol 41, title Statutes. The Secretary of State here concerned is the Secretary of State for Northern Ireland.

Statutory instrument. For provisions as to statutory instruments generally, see the Statutory Instruments Act 1946, Vol 41, title Statutes.

Day on which this Act is passed. This Act was passed, ie received the Royal Assent, on 24 January 1985.

Order under this section. The Elections (Northern Ireland) Act 1985 (Commencement) Order 1985, SI 1985/1221, which brought into force on 6 August 1985 those provisions of this Act which were not already in force by virtue of sub-s (3) above.

REPRESENTATION OF THE PEOPLE ACT 1985

(1985 c 50)

ARRANGEMENT OF SECTIONS

(For s 20, see Vol 32, title Parliament.)

An Act to amend the law relating to parliamentary elections in the United Kingdom and local government elections in Great Britain, to provide for combining polls taken on the same date at such elections and elections to the Assembly of the European Communities, to extend the franchise at elections to that Assembly, to amend the law relating to the effect of the demise of the Crown on the summoning and duration of a new Parliament and to repeal section 21(3) of the Representation of the People Act 1918   [16 July 1985]

Commencement. This Act came into force, or is to come into force, on dates appointed by order; see s 29 post, the note "Orders under this section" thereto, and the "Commencement" notes throughout the Act. **Northern Ireland.** This Act applies to the extent specified in s 29(4), (5) post.

Extension of franchise to British citizens overseas

1 Extension of parliamentary franchise

(1) Subject to section 1(3) of the principal Act, a person is entitled (notwithstanding anything in section 1(2) of that Act) to vote as an elector at a parliamentary election in any constituency if—

(*a*) he qualifies as an overseas elector in respect of that constituency on the qualifying date, and

(*b*) on that date and on the date of the poll he is not subject to any legal incapacity to vote and is a British citizen.

(2) For the purposes of this and the principal Act, a person qualifies as an overseas elector in respect of a constituency on the qualifying date if—

(*a*) on that date he is not resident in the United Kingdom, and

(*b*) he satisfies the following conditions.

(3) Those conditions are that—

(*a*) he was included in a register of parliamentary electors in respect of an address at a place that is situated within the constituency concerned,

(*b*) on the date by reference to which the register was prepared, he was resident or treated for the purposes of registration as resident at that address.

(c) that date fell within the period of five years ending immediately before the qualifying date, and

(d) if he was included in any register of parliamentary electors prepared by reference to a date later than the date referred to in paragraph (b) above, he was not resident or treated for the purposes of registration as resident at an address in the United Kingdom on that later date.

(4) The reference in subsection (1) above to a person being subject to a legal incapacity to vote on the qualifying date does not include a reference to his being below the age of 18 on that date.

NOTES

Commencement. Up to 1 August 1985, no order had been made under s 29(2) post, bringing this section into force.

General Note. This section and s 2 post implement proposals made in the Government Reply to the First Report from the Home Affairs Committee Session 1982–83 on the Representation of the People Acts HC 32–1 (Cmnd 9140) to extend the parliamentary franchise to certain British citizens living abroad.

The Representation of the People Act 1983, s 1(3) ante restricts entitlement to vote to those persons who are registered in the register of parliamentary electors for a constituency in the United Kingdom. Electoral registers are prepared annually by reference to residence in the constituency on the qualifying date (currently 10 October for the entire country excluding Northern Ireland where the qualifying date is at present 15 September; see s 4 of the 1983 Act. Hitherto persons living abroad were not entitled to be registered to vote since they could not fulfil the residence qualification, although special provision was made for members of the armed forces and certain Crown servants. This section together with s 2 post, enables persons who qualify as overseas electors thereunder to make a declaration entitling them to be included in a parliamentary register under s 12 of the 1983 Act.

Although Commonwealth citizens and citizens of the Irish Republic may be registered as parliamentary electors if resident in the United Kingdom the franchise is extended by this section only to those overseas electors who are British citizens (sub-s (1)(b)) in keeping with the recommendation made by para 2.3 of the White Paper. Since the basis of the parliamentary system is the representation of constituencies it was considered unacceptable by the Government to extend the franchise to those who had no connection with any United Kingdom constituency (see para 2.4 of the Government Reply). Accordingly sub-s (3) above confines qualification as an overseas elector to persons who have previously been included in a register of parliamentary electors. The Government proposed to limit the period within which a person may qualify as an overseas elector to seven years after departure from the United Kingdom (para 2.10 of the Reply) but this limit was reduced to five years during the passage of the Bill through Parliament (sub-s (3)(c)).

Sub-s (1): Entitled . . . to vote as an elector. For the persons entitled to vote at parliamentary elections apart from the provisions of this Act, see the Representation of the People Act 1983, s 1 ante.

The resolution of a committee of the House of Commons cannot deprive anyone of a right to vote conferred by statute; see *Bulmer v Norris* (1860) 9 CBNS 19.

Parliamentary election. Ie an election of a member to serve in Parliament for a constituency; see the Interpretation Act 1978, s 5, Sch 1, Vol 41, title Statutes.

Constituency. For definition, see the House of Commons (Redistribution of Seats) Act 1949, s 4 ante. The present constituencies are described in the Representation of the People Act 1948, Sch 1 ante.

Qualifying date. For this date, see the Representation of the People Act 1983, s 4 ante.

British citizen. As to British citizenship, see the British Nationality Act 1981, Pt I, s 36, Sch 2, paras 2–5, Vol 31, title Nationality and Immigration.

Sub-s (2): Resident. By virtue of s 27(2) post, the Representation of the People Act 1983, ss 5, 6, 7(1) ante, which contain provisions as to residence, apply for the purposes of this section and ss 2, 3 post. See further the notes to s 5 of the 1983 Act.

For certain presumptions as to residence etc in relation to this section, see s 2(6) post.

United Kingdom. Ie Great Britain and Northern Ireland; see the Interpretation Act 1978, s 5, Sch 1, Vol 41, title Statutes. See also the note "Great Britain" to s 3 post.

Sub-s (3): Register of parliamentary electors. As to the preparation and publication of registers of parliamentary electors and of local government electors, see the Representation of the People Act 1983, ss 9–13 ante. See also s 2 post.

Resident or treated . . . as resident. See the note "Resident" above.

Sub-s (4): Below the age of 18. As to the attainment of a given age for the purposes of this Act, see by virtue of s 27(2) post, the Representation of the People Act 1983, s 202(2) ante.

Definitions. For "elector", "legal incapacity" and "vote", see, by virtue of s 27(2) post, the Representation of the People Act 1983, s 202(1) ante.

Principal Act. Ie the Representation of the People Act 1983 ante.

2 Registration of British citizens overseas

(1) A person may not be registered in any register as mentioned in section 12(1) of the principal Act on the ground that he may be entitled by virtue of section 1 of this Act to vote at parliamentary elections for which the register is to be used except—

    (a) in pursuance of a declaration made by him under and in accordance with this section (an "overseas elector's declaration"), and

    (b) in the register for the constituency or part of the constituency within which is situated the place in the United Kingdom specified in the declaration in accordance with subsection (4) below as having been the address in respect of which he was registered;

and may not be so registered on that ground unless the registration officer concerned is satisfied that, on the qualifying date, he qualifies as an overseas elector in respect of the constituency for which that register is prepared.

(2) An overseas elector's declaration must be made with a view to registration in the register of electors for a particular year and with reference to the qualifying date for that register and must be made within the twelve months ending with that date.

(3) An overseas elector's declaration must state—

    (a) the date of the declaration,

    (b) that the declarant is a British citizen,

    (c) that the declarant will not be resident in the United Kingdom on the qualifying date,

    (d) when he ceased to be so resident or, in the case of a person relying on registration in pursuance of a service declaration, when he ceased to have a service qualification or, if later, ceased to be so resident, and

    (e) that the declarant does not intend to reside permanently outside the United Kingdom,

and must contain such other information and satisfy such other requirements (which may include requirements for declarations to be attested and for the charging of fees in respect of their attestation) as may be prescribed.

(4) An overseas elector's declaration must specify the address in respect of which he was registered and may not specify more than one such address; and if the declarant makes more than one such declaration bearing the same date and specifying different addresses in the United Kingdom as the address in respect of which he was registered the declarations shall be void.

(5) An overseas elector's declaration may be cancelled at any time by the declarant and such a declaration bearing a later date shall, without any express cancellation, cancel an overseas elector's declaration bearing an earlier date which was made with reference to the same qualifying date.

(6) For the purposes of section 1 of this Act and Part I of the principal Act, where a person is registered in a register of parliamentary electors for any constituency or part of a constituency in pursuance of an overseas elector's declaration, it shall be conclusively presumed—

    (a) that the address specified in the declaration in accordance with subsection (4) above is at a place that is situated within that constituency or, as the case may be, part, and

    (b) that he was not resident in the United Kingdom on the qualifying date;

and for the purposes of section 1 of this Act, section 49(1)(a) of the principal Act (register conclusive as to residence) does not apply in relation to a person's previous registration in a register of parliamentary electors unless he is registered in pursuance of an overseas elector's declaration by virtue of that previous registration.

NOTES

Commencement. Up to 1 August 1985, no order had been made under s 29(2) post, bringing this section into force.

General Note. This section contains provisions concerning the procedure for making an overseas elector's declaration and gives effect to proposals contained in para 2.11 of the Government Reply to the First Report from the Home Affairs Committee Session 1982–83 on the Representation of the People Acts HC 32–1 (Cmnd 9140). Concern was expressed during the passage of the Bill through Parliament that the franchise should not extend to those persons who intend to sever their connections with the United Kingdom permanently and sub-s (3)(*e*) was inserted to exclude for example those who leave the country to avoid the payment of taxes. In other respects the requirements of this section are modelled on the provisions of the Representation of the People Act 1983, s 15 ante, relating to service declarations.

Sub-s (1): Parliamentary elections; constituency; United Kingdom; qualifying date. See the corresponding notes to s 1 ante.

Registration officer. As to the appointment of registration officers, see the Representation of the People Act 1983, s 8 ante.

Qualifies as an overseas elector, etc. Ie in accordance with s 1(2), (3) ante.

Sub-s (2): Months. This means calendar months; see the Interpretation Act 1978, s 5, Sch 1, Vol 41, title Statutes.

Sub-s (3): British citizen; resident. See the notes to s 1 ante.

Service declaration. For the provisions as to service voters generally, see (by virtue of s 27(2) post) the Representation of the People Act 1983, ss 14 et seq ante.

Prescribed. Ie prescribed by regulations; see, by virtue of s 27(2) post, the Representation of the People Act 1983, s 202(1) ante. Up to 1 August 1985 no regulations had been made prescribing information or requirements for the purposes of sub-s (3) above.

As to regulations under this Act generally see, by virtue of s 27(2) post, s 201 of the 1983 Act, which is amended by s 24, Sch 4, para 69 post, as from a day to be appointed under s 29(2) post.

Offences. For offences connected with overseas elector's declarations and the penalty therefor, see s 12(1), (2), (4) post.

Definitions. For "elector" and "prescribed", see by virtue of s 27(2) post, the Representation of the People Act 1983, s 202(1) ante. Note as to "overseas elector's declaration", sub-s (1)(*a*) above.

Principal Act. Ie the Representation of the People Act 1983 ante; see s 27(1) post.

---

3 Extension of franchise for European Assembly elections

(1) The reference in paragraph 2(1)(*a*) of Schedule 1 to the European Assembly Elections Act 1978 to persons registered in the register of parliamentary electors at an address within an Assembly constituency (only persons registered there entitled to vote at Assembly elections in the constituency) includes a reference to any person so registered in pursuance of an overseas elector's declaration where the address specified in the declaration in accordance with section 2(4) of this Act is at a place that is situated within the constituency.

(2) A peer is entitled by virtue of this section to vote as elector at an Assembly election in any constituency if—

    (*a*) he qualifies under this section in respect of that constituency on the qualifying date,

    (*b*) on that date and on the day appointed for the election he is not subject to any legal incapacity to vote and is a British citizen, and

    (*c*) he is registered in the constituency in the register under this section to be used at the election.

(3) For the purposes of subsection (2) above, a peer qualifies under this section in respect of a constituency on the qualifying date if—

    (*a*) on that date he is not resident in the United Kingdom, and

    (*b*) he satisfies the following conditions.

(4) Those conditions are that—

    (*a*) he was included in a register of local government electors in respect of an address at a place that is situated within the constituency concerned,

(b) on the date by reference to which the register was prepared, he was resident or treated for the purposes of registration as resident at that address,

(c) that date fell within the period of five years ending immediately before the qualifying date, and

(d) if he was included in any register of local government electors prepared by reference to a date later than the date referred to in paragraph (b) above, he was not resident or treated for the purposes of registration as resident at an address in the United Kingdom on that later date.

(5) Regulations under this section may provide for the registration, subject to prescribed exceptions and on satisfying prescribed conditions, of those peers who (apart from the requirement of registration) may be entitled by virtue of this section to vote as electors at Assembly elections.

(6) Such regulations shall require each registration officer to prepare and publish, in respect of any year for which any peers are to be registered under this section, a register of the peers so registered, and any such register shall so far as practicable be combined with the registers of parliamentary electors and of local government electors, the names of peers registered under this section being marked to indicate that fact.

(7) Such regulations—

(a) may require a person seeking registration under this section to make a declaration for the purpose, being a declaration of the prescribed facts and containing the prescribed information, and may require such declarations to be attested and provide for the charging of fees in respect of their attestation, and

(b) may apply with such modifications or exceptions as may be prescribed any provision in respect of the registration of parliamentary or local government electors made by or under the principal Act or this Act and, in Northern Ireland, by or under the Electoral Law Act (Northern Ireland) 1962.

(8) In this section—

"legal incapacity" has the same meaning—

(a) in relation to Great Britain as it has in the principal Act for the purposes of local government elections, and

(b) in relation to Northern Ireland as it has in the Electoral Law Act (Northern Ireland) 1962 for the purposes of local elections,

but the reference in subsection (2)(b) above to a person being subject to a legal incapacity to vote on the qualifying date does not include a reference to his being below the age of 18 on that date;

"local election" has the same meaning as in the Electoral Law Act (Northern Ireland) 1962, and

"qualifying date" means, in relation to an Assembly election in Great Britain, the date which would be the qualifying date if that election were a local government election and, in relation to an Assembly election in Northern Ireland, the date which would be the qualifying date if that election were a local election,

and references to the register of local government electors include a reference to the register of electors prepared in accordance with the Electoral Law Act (Northern Ireland) 1962.

(9) For the purposes of this section, section 49(2)(a) of the principal Act (registers conclusive as to residence) does not apply in relation to a person's previous registration

in a register of local government electors unless he is registered under this section by virtue of that previous registration.

NOTES

Commencement. Up to 1 August 1985, no order had been made under s 29(2) post, bringing this section into force.

General Note. Following the proposals set out in para 2.9 of the Government Reply to the First Report from the Home Affairs Committee Session 1982–83 on the Representation of the People Acts HC 32–1 (Cmnd 9140) this section is enacted to give British citizens resident abroad the right to vote at European Parliament elections. It is included as an interim measure pending the outcome of deliberations by the Council of Ministers of the European Community relating to the introduction of a uniform electoral procedure to guarantee all Community nationals the right to vote at European Parliament elections irrespective of their place of residence within the Community.

Sub-s (1): Register of parliamentary electors. See the note to s 1 ante.

Assembly constituency. As to these constituencies, see the European Assembly Elections Act 1978, s 3, Sch 1, para 1, Sch 2 ante.

Sub-s (2): Qualifying date; British citizen. See the notes to s 1 ante.

Sub-s (3): Resident; United Kingdom. See the notes to s 1 ante.

Sub-s (4): Register of local government electors. See the note "Register of parliamentary electors" to s 1 ante; and note also the final provision of sub-s (8) above.

Resident or treated . . . as resident. See the note "Resident" to s 1 ante.

Sub-s (8): Great Britain. Ie England, Scotland and Wales; see the Union with Scotland Act 1706, preamble, Art I, Vol 10, title Constitutional Law (Pt 1), as read with the Interpretation Act 1978, s 22(1), Sch 2, para 5(a), Vol 41, title Statutes.

Below the age of 18. See the note to s 1 ante.

Definitions. For "overseas elector's declaration", see s 2(1)(a) ante; for "Assembly" and "Assembly election", see s 27(1) post; by virtue of s 27(2) post for "elector", "prescribed" and "vote", see the Representation of the People Act 1983, s 202(1) ante, and for "local government election", see s 203(1) of that Act. Note as to "legal incapacity", "local election", "qualifying date" and "register of local government electors" sub-s (8) above.

European Assembly Elections Act 1978, Sch 1, para 2(1)(a). See this title ante.

Principal Act. Ie the Representation of the People Act 1983 ante; see s 27(1) post.

Electoral Law Act (Northern Ireland) 1962. 1962 c 14 (NI); not printed in this work.

Regulations under this section. Up to 1 August 1985 no regulations had been made under this section. As to regulations under this Act generally, see, by virtue of s 27(2) post, the Representation of the People Act 1983, s 201 ante, which is amended by s 24, Sch 4, para 69 post, as from a day to be appointed under s 29(2) post.

4 Extension of franchise: consequential amendments

(1) In section 9(2) of the principal Act (combined register to indicate those registered only as local government electors) after the words "only as" there shall be inserted the words "parliamentary electors or".

(2) In section 10 of that Act (preparation of registers)—

(a) in paragraph (a) (inquiry as to persons entitled to be registered except in pursuance of service declaration) after the word "declaration" there shall be inserted the words "patient's declaration or overseas elector's declaration"; and

(b) in paragraph (b) (preparation of lists of those entitled to be registered together with their qualifying addresses) for the words "together with" there shall be substituted the words "and, subject to any prescribed exceptions".

(3) In section 12(1) of that Act (right to be registered, subject to exceptions) in paragraph (a) after the word "qualification" there shall be inserted—

"(aa) section 2(1) of the Representation of the People Act 1985".

(4) In section 49 of that Act (effect of registers) in subsection (5) in paragraph (a) and paragraph (i) after the word "Ireland" there shall be inserted the words "or, in the case of a person registered as a parliamentary elector in pursuance of an overseas elector's declaration, a British citizen".

(5) In section 202 of that Act (interpretation) before the definition of "parliamentary election petition" there shall be inserted the following definition—

"'overseas elector's declaration' has the meaning given by section 2 of the Representation of the People Act 1985".

(6) In Schedule 1 to that Act in rule 28 (issue of poll cards) at the end of paragraph (1) there shall be inserted the words "and a card shall not be sent to any person registered, or to be registered, in pursuance of an overseas elector's declaration".

(7) In Schedule 2 to that Act (regulations as to registration)—

(*a*) at the end of paragraph 4 there shall be inserted—

"(2) Provisions as to the manner in which overseas electors' declarations, and applications from persons making such declarations, are to be transmitted to the registration officer."; and

(*b*) after paragraph 5(1) there shall be inserted—

"(1A) Provisions as to the evidence which shall or may be required, or be deemed sufficient or conclusive evidence, of a person satisfying any of the requirements for qualifying as an overseas elector in respect of any constituency.".

NOTES

Commencement. Up to 1 August 1985, no order had been made under s 29(2) post, bringing this section into force.

Sub-s (4): British citizen. See the note to s 1 ante.

Sub-s (7): Conclusive evidence. The tendering of evidence declared by statute to be conclusive precludes evidence to the contrary unless the evidence adduced is inaccurate on the face of it or fraud is shown, but other evidence to the same effect is not made inadmissible; see 17 Halsbury's Laws (4th edn) para 28.

Constituency. See the note to s 1 ante.

Definitions. For "elector", "overseas elector's declaration" and "prescribed", see the Representation of the People Act 1983, s 202(1) ante, as amended by sub-s (5) above; for "patient's declaration", cf s 7(2) of that Act.

Principal Act. Ie the Representation of the People Act 1983 ante.

Voting at parliamentary elections in the United Kingdom and local government elections in Great Britain

5 Manner of voting at parliamentary and local government elections

(1) This section applies to determine the manner of voting of a person entitled to vote as an elector at a parliamentary or local government election.

(2) He may vote in person at the polling station allotted to him under the appropriate rules, unless he is entitled as an elector to an absent vote at the election.

(3) He may vote by post if he is entitled as an elector to vote by post at the election.

(4) If he is entitled to vote by proxy at the election, he may so vote unless, before a ballot paper has been issued for him to vote by proxy, he applies at the polling station allotted to him under the appropriate rules for a ballot paper for the purpose of voting in person, in which case he may vote in person there.

(5) If he is not entitled as an elector to an absent vote at the election but cannot reasonably be expected to go in person to the polling station allotted to him under the appropriate rules by reason of the particular circumstances of his employment, either as a constable or by the returning officer, on the date of the poll for a purpose connected with the election, he may vote in person at any polling station in the constituency, or, as the case may be, electoral area.

(6) For the purposes of the provisions of this and the principal Act, a person entitled

to vote as an elector at a parliamentary or local government election is entitled as an elector to vote by post or entitled to vote by proxy at the election if he is shown in the absent voters list for the election as so entitled; and references in those provisions to entitlement as an elector to an absent vote at a parliamentary or local government election are references to entitlement as an elector to vote by post or entitlement to vote by proxy at the election.

(7) In this section and sections 6 to 9 of this Act—

"appropriate rules" means—

(a) in the case of a parliamentary election, the parliamentary elections rules, and

(b) in the case of a local government election, rules made (or having effect as if made) under section 36 or, as the case may be, 42 of the principal Act, and

"local government election" means a local government election in Great Britain.

NOTES

Commencement. Up to 1 August 1985, no order had been made under s 29(2) post, bringing this section into force.

General Note. This section and ss 6, 7 post contain new provisions which simplify and rationalise the provisions of the Representation of the People Act 1983, ss 19, 20, 32, 33 (repealed by s 28, Sch 5 post, as from a day to be appointed under s 29(2) post), relating to absent voting at parliamentary elections and local government elections.

Hitherto an absent vote was in general exercisable only by post although this depended on the elector supplying an address in the United Kingdom to which a ballot paper could be sent. Those unable to comply with this requirement were obliged to vote by proxy. The Government in its Reply to the First Report from the Home Affairs Committee Session 1982–83 on the Representation of the People Acts HC 32-1 (Cmnd 9140) considered that proxy voting was generally unpopular and proposed that the provision which prevented postal ballot papers from being sent abroad should be repealed (see para 3.19 of the Reply). Ss 6(1) and 7(1) post allow an elector entitled to an absent vote to choose between voting by post or by proxy subject to requirements to be prescribed by regulations. In order to accommodate postal voters abroad the parliamentary election timetable is extended by one day; see the Representation of the People Act 1983, Sch 1, r 1 ante, as amended by s 24 and Sch 4, para 73 post, as from a day to be appointed under s 29(2) post.

See also the General Note to s 7 post.

Sub-s (1): Person entitled to vote as an elector at a parliamentary or local government election. As to the persons entitled to vote at such elections, see the Representation of the People Act 1983, ss 1, 2 ante, and see also, as to parliamentary elections, s 1 ante. See also the note "Parliamentary election" to s 1 ante.

Sub-s (2): Polling station allotted to him, etc. As to the allocation of polling stations for a parliamentary election, see r 25 of the Parliamentary Elections Rules contained in the Representation of the People Act 1983, Sch 1 ante; and as respects local government elections see the Local Elections (Principal Areas) Rules 1973, SI 1973/79, Sch 2, r 21 (for elections of councillors of Greater London and London boroughs, and counties and districts in England and Wales), and the Local Elections (Parishes and Communities) Rules 1973, SI 1973/1910, Sch 1, r 20 (for elections of parish councillors in England and community councillors in Wales).

Entitled as an elector to an absent vote. For provisions governing entitlement to an absent vote see ss 6, 7 post.

Sub-s (4): Entitled to vote by proxy. For further provisions relating to voting by proxy, see ss 8, 9 post.

Sub-s (5): Polling station. In sub-s (5) above this expression does not include a reference to a special polling station in Northern Ireland; see s 10 and Sch 1, para 29 post.

Constable. This means any person holding the office of constable (as to which, see 36 Halsbury's Laws (4th edn) paras 201 et seq), not a member of a police force holding the rank of constable. As to the attestation of constables, see the Police Act 1964, s 18, Sch 2, Vol 33, title Police, and as to their jurisdiction, see s 19 of that Act.

Returning officer. As to the designation of such officers for parliamentary elections in England and Wales, see the Representation of the People Act 1983, s 24 ante, or as respects Northern Ireland, s 26 of that Act. As to returning officers for local government elections in England and Wales, see s 35 of the 1983 Act.

Sub-s (7): Great Britain. See the note to s 3 ante.

Offence. For an offence connected with this section and the penalty therefor, see s 12(3), (4) post.

Definitions. By virtue of s 27(2) post for "the absent voters list", "elector", "parliamentary elections rules" and "vote", see the Representation of the People Act 1983, s 202(1) ante, as amended by s 11 and Sch 2, para 3(a) post, as from a day to be appointed under s 29(2) post, and for "electoral area" and "local government election", see s 203(1) of the 1983 Act. Note also as to "appropriate rules" and "local government election" sub-s (7) above; and note as to "entitlement as an elector to an absent vote", sub-s (6) above.

Principal Act. Ie the Representation of the People Act 1983 ante; see s 27(1) post.

Rules. Rules made, or having effect as if made, under the Representation of the People Act 1983, s 36 ante, are noted to that section; see also the first note to sub-s (2) above. S 42 of the 1983 Act applies to Scotland only and is not printed in this work.

6 Absent vote at elections for an indefinite period

(1) Where a person applies to the registration officer to vote by post, or to vote by proxy, at parliamentary elections, at local government elections or at both for an indefinite period, the registration officer shall grant the application (subject to subsection (6) below) if—

(a) he is satisfied that the applicant is eligible for an absent vote at elections to which the application relates for an indefinite period,

(b) he is satisfied that the applicant is or will be registered in the register for such elections, and

(c) the application meets the prescribed requirements.

(2) For the purposes of this section, a person is eligible for an absent vote at parliamentary or local government elections for an indefinite period—

(a) if he is or will be registered as a service voter,

(b) if he cannot reasonably be expected—

(i) to go in person to the polling station allotted or likely to be allotted to him under the appropriate rules, or

(ii) to vote unaided there,

by reason of blindness or other physical incapacity,

(c) if he cannot reasonably be expected to go in person to that polling station by reason of the general nature of his occupation, service or employment or that of his spouse, or

(d) if he cannot go in person from his qualifying address to that polling station without making a journey by air or sea,

and is also eligible for an absent vote at parliamentary elections for an indefinite period if he is or will be registered in pursuance of an overseas elector's declaration.

(3) The registration officer shall keep a record of those whose applications under this section have been granted showing—

(a) whether their applications were in respect of parliamentary elections, local government elections or both,

(b) in the case of those who may vote by post, the addresses provided by them in their applications as the addresses to which their ballot papers are to be sent, and

(c) in the case of those who may vote by proxy, the names and addresses of those appointed as their proxies.

(4) The registration officer shall remove a person from the record kept under subsection (3) above—

(a) if he applies to the registration officer to be removed,

(b) in the case of any registered person, if he ceases to be registered or registered at the same qualifying address or ceases to be, or becomes, registered as a service voter or in pursuance of an overseas elector's declaration, or

(c) if the registration officer gives notice that he has reason to believe there has been a material change of circumstances.

(5) A person shown in the record kept under subsection (3) above as voting by post or, as the case may be, voting by proxy may subsequently alter his choice (subject to

subsection (6) below) on an application to the registration officer that meets the prescribed requirements and the registration officer shall amend the record accordingly.

(6) A person applying to vote by post must provide an address in the United Kingdom as the address to which his ballot paper is to be sent.

NOTES

Commencement. Up to 1 August 1985, no order had been made under s 29(2) post, bringing this section into force.

General Note. See the General Note to s 5 ante.

Sub-s (1): Parliamentary elections. See the corresponding note to s 1 ante.

Prescribed. Ie prescribed by regulations; see, by virtue of s 27(2) post, the Representation of the People Act 1983, s 202(1) ante. Up to 1 August 1985 no regulations had been made prescribing matters for the purposes of this Act.

As to regulations under this Act generally see, by virtue of s 27(2) post, s 201 of the 1983 Act ante, as amended by s 24 and Sch 4, para 69 post, as from a day to be appointed under s 29(2) post.

Sub-s (2): Service voter. For provisions as to service voters generally, see, by virtue of s 27(2) post, the Representation of the People Act 1983, ss 14–17 ante.

Polling station allotted . . . to him, etc. See the note to s 5 ante.

General nature of his occupation. In order to qualify as an absent voter on the ground of the general nature of his occupation under previous legislation, an elector's inability to attend his polling station had to be due to a fundamental condition of his employment and be liable to recur throughout the continuance of that employment (*Daly v Watson* 1960 SLT 271). A minister of the Church of Scotland summoned to General Assembly (*Craig v Mitchell* 1955 SLT 369) and a managing director having to attend conferences (*Daly v Watson* supra) were accordingly registered as absent voters. But such registration was refused in *Keay v Macleod* 1953 SLT 144, where the circumstances were considered as accidental and extrinsic to the applicants' occupation.

Qualifying address. This expression is not defined in this Act or in the Representation of the People Act 1983 ante, but cf ss 1(1)(a) and 2(1)(a) of that Act.

Sub-s (3): Shall keep a record. For provisions relating to breach of official duty, see the Representation of the People Act 1983, s 63 ante.

Addresses to which their ballot papers are to be sent. A person entitled to a postal vote for an indefinite period under this section may apply to the registration officer for his ballot paper to be sent to a different address in the United Kingdom or to vote by proxy in respect of a particular parliamentary or local government election; see s 7(2) post.

Sub-s (6): United Kingdom. See the note to s 1 ante.

Offence. For offences connected with this section and the penalty therefor, see s 12(3), (4) post.

Definitions. For "appropriate rules", see s 5(7) ante; by virtue of s 27(2) post for "registration officer" see the Representation of the People Act 1983, s 8(1) ante, for "election", "prescribed", "service voter" and "vote", see s 202(1) of that Act, and for "local government election", see s 203(1) of that Act (and see also s 5(7) ante).

Transitional provisions. For transitional provisions relating to electors entitled to an absent vote before the commencement of this section and ss 7–9 post, see s 11 and Sch 2, Pt II post.

7 Absent vote at a particular election and absent voters list

(1) Where a person applies to the registration officer to vote by post, or to vote by proxy, at a particular parliamentary or local government election, the registration officer shall grant the application (subject to subsection (5) below) if—

(a) he is satisfied that the applicant's circumstances on the date of the poll will be or are likely to be such that he cannot reasonably be expected to vote in person at the polling station allotted or likely to be allotted to him under the appropriate rules,

(b) he is satisfied that the applicant is or will be registered in the register of parliamentary or, as the case may be, local government electors, and

(c) the application meets the prescribed requirements.

(2) Subsection (1) above does not apply to a person who is included in the record kept under section 6 of this Act in respect of elections of the kind in question, but such a person may, in respect of a particular parliamentary or local government election, apply to the registration officer—

(a) for his ballot paper to be sent to a different address in the United Kingdom, or

(b) to vote by proxy,

if he is shown in the record so kept as voting by post at elections of the kind in question.

(3) The registration officer shall grant an application under subsection (2) above if it meets the prescribed requirements.

(4) The registration officer shall, in respect of each parliamentary or local government election, keep a special list ("the absent voters list") consisting of—

(a) a list of—

(i) those whose applications under subsection (1) above to vote by post at the election have been granted, together with the addresses provided by them in their applications as the addresses to which their ballot papers are to be sent, and

(ii) those who are for the time being shown in the record kept under section 6 of this Act as voting by post at elections of the kind in question (excluding those so shown whose applications under subsection (2) above to vote by proxy at the election have been granted), together with the addresses provided by them in their applications under that section or, as the case may be, subsection (2) above as the addresses to which their ballot papers are to be sent, and

(b) a list ("the list of proxies") of those whose applications under this section to vote by proxy at the election have been granted or who are for the time being shown in the record kept under section 6 of this Act as voting by proxy at elections of the kind in question, together with the names and addresses of those appointed as their proxies.

(5) A person applying to vote by post must provide an address in the United Kingdom as the address to which his ballot paper is to be sent.

NOTES

Commencement. Up to 1 August 1985, no order had been made under s 29(2) post, bringing this section into force.

General Note. This section implements recommendations contained in para 3.12 of the Government Reply to the First Report from the Home Affairs Committee Session 1982–83 on the Representation of the People Acts HC 32–1 (Cmnd 9140). It simplifies the procedure for obtaining an absent vote at a particular election by replacing the various provisions previously governing eligibility for such a vote with the single requirement that any elector who cannot reasonably be expected to vote in person at his polling station on the date of the election is entitled to an absent vote (sub-s (1)(a)). It is envisaged that this significant change will permit holidaymakers in particular to qualify for an absent vote for the first time. It will also cover those whose employment requires their absence from their constituency on polling day where the general nature of their occupation is not such that they are eligible for an absent vote for an indefinite period under s 6 ante. Persons caring for sick relatives and others with genuine reasons for non-attendance at their polling station will also benefit. In each case an applicant must satisfy the registration officer that he is entitled to an absent vote and the section confers power for further requirements to be imposed by regulations.

See also the General Note to s 5 ante.

Sub-s (1): Parliamentary . . . election. See the note to s 1 ante.

Polling station allotted . . . to him, etc. See the note to s 5 ante.

Prescribed. See the note to s 6 ante.

Sub-s (2): Elections of the kind in question. Applications under s 6 ante may be made in respect of either parliamentary or local government elections or both.

United Kingdom. See the note to s 1 ante.

Offence. For offences connected with this section and the penalty therefor, see s 12(3), (4) post.

Definitions. For "appropriate rules", see s 5(7) ante; by virtue of s 27(2) post for "registration officer", see, the Representation of the People Act 1983, s 8(1) ante, for "election", "prescribed" and "vote", see s 202(1) of the 1983 Act, and for "local government election", see s 203(1) of that Act (and see also s 5(7) ante).

Transitional provisions. See the note to s 6 ante.

Northern Ireland. This section may be modified in its application to Northern Ireland; see s 10(2), (5) post.

8 Proxies at elections

(1) Subject to the provisions of this section, any person is capable of being appointed proxy to vote for another (in this section and section 9 of this Act referred to as "the elector") at any parliamentary or local government election and may vote in pursuance of the appointment.

(2) The elector cannot have more than one person at a time appointed as proxy to vote for him at parliamentary elections (whether in the same constituency or elsewhere).

(3) A person is not capable of being appointed to vote, or voting, as proxy at a parliamentary or local government election—

(a) if he is subject to any legal incapacity (age apart) to vote at that election as an elector, or

(b) if he is neither a Commonwealth citizen nor a citizen of the Republic of Ireland.

(4) A person is not capable of voting as proxy at any such election unless on the date of the poll he has attained the age of eighteen.

(5) A person is not entitled to vote as proxy at the same parliamentary election in any constituency, or at the same local government election in any electoral area, on behalf of more than two electors of whom that person is not the husband, wife, parent, grandparent, brother, sister, child or grandchild.

(6) Where the elector applies to the registration officer for the appointment of a proxy to vote for him at parliamentary elections, at local government elections or at both for an indefinite period, the registration officer shall make the appointment if the application meets the prescribed requirements and he is satisfied that the elector is or will be—

(a) registered in the register of electors for elections in respect of which the application is made, and

(b) shown in the record kept under section 6 of this Act as voting by proxy at such elections,

and that the proxy is capable of being and willing to be appointed to vote as proxy at such elections.

(7) Where the elector applies to the registration officer for the appointment of a proxy to vote for him at a particular parliamentary or local government election, the registration officer shall make the appointment if the application meets the prescribed requirements and he is satisfied that the elector is or will be—

(a) registered in the register of parliamentary or, as the case may be, local government electors for that election, and

(b) entitled to vote by proxy at that election by virtue of an application under section 7 of this Act,

and that the proxy is capable of being and willing to be appointed.

(8) The appointment of a proxy under this section is to be made by means of a proxy paper issued by the registration officer.

(9) The appointment may be cancelled by the elector by giving notice to the registration officer and shall also cease to be in force—

(a) where the appointment related to a parliamentary election or parliamentary elections, on the issue of a proxy paper appointing a different person to vote for him at a parliamentary election or parliamentary elections (whether in the same constituency or elsewhere), and

(b) where the appointment related to a local government election or local government elections, on the issue of a proxy paper appointing a different person to vote for him at a local government election or local government elections in the same electoral area.

(10) Subject to subsection (9) above, the appointment shall remain in force—

(a) in the case of an appointment for a particular election, for that election, and

(b) in any other case, while the elector is shown as voting by proxy in the record kept under section 6 of this Act in pursuance of the same application under that section.

(11) Stamp duty is not chargeable on any instrument appointing a proxy under this section.

NOTES

Commencement. Up to 1 August 1985, no order had been made under s 29(2) post, bringing this section into force.

Sub-s (1): Appointed proxy to vote for another. For provisions governing applications to vote by proxy, see ss 6, 7 ante.

Parliamentary . . . election. See the note to s 1 ante.

Sub-s (2): Constituency. See the note to s 1 ante.

Sub-s (3): Commonwealth citizen. In Acts passed after 1982 this means a person who has the status of a Commonwealth citizen under the British Nationality Act 1981; see s 51(2) of the 1981 Act, Vol 31, title Nationality and Immigration, and for the persons who have that status, see s 37 of, and Sch 3 to, that Act.

Republic of Ireland. Ie that part of Ireland previously officially known in this country as Eire and originally called the Irish Free State; see the Ireland Act 1949, s 1(1), (3), Vol 7, title Commonwealth and Other Territories (Pt 3(c)) in conjunction with the Eire (Confirmation of Agreements) Act 1938, s 1 (repealed).

Sub-s (4): Attained the age of eighteen. See the note "Below the age of 18" to s 1 ante.

Sub-s (6): Prescribed. See the note to s 6 ante.

Offence. For an offence connected with this section and the penalty therefor, see s 12(3), (4) post.

Definitions. By virtue of s 27(2) post, for "registration officer", see the Representation of the People Act 1983, s 8(1) ante, for "election", "elector", "legal incapacity", "prescribed" and "vote", see s 202(1) of the 1983 Act, and for "electoral area" and "local government election", see s 203(1) of that Act (and see also as to "local government election", s 5(7) ante). Note as to "the elector" sub-s (1) above.

Transitional provisions. See the note to s 6 ante.

---

9 Voting as proxy

(1) A person entitled to vote as proxy at a parliamentary or local government election may do so in person at the polling station allotted to the elector under the appropriate rules unless he is entitled to vote by post as proxy for the elector at the election, in which case he may vote by post.

(2) Where a person is entitled to vote by post as proxy for the elector at any election, the elector may not apply for a ballot paper for the purpose of voting in person at the election.

(3) For the purposes of this and the principal Act, a person entitled to vote as proxy for another at a parliamentary or local government election is entitled so to vote by post if he is included in the list kept under subsection (9) below in respect of the election.

(4) Where a person applies to the registration officer to vote by post as proxy at parliamentary elections, at local government elections or at both for an indefinite period, the registration officer shall (subject to subsections (10) and (12) below) grant the application if—

(a) the applicant is included in any record kept under section 6 of this Act in respect of a constituency, or electoral area, for the whole or any part of which the registration officer acts, or

(b) the address provided by the applicant in his application as the address to which his ballot paper is to be sent is not in the same area as the elector's qualifying address or, where the elector is registered in pursuance of an overseas elector's declaration, the address specified in the declaration in accordance with section 2(4) of this Act,

and the application meets the prescribed requirements.

(5) For the purposes of this section, two addresses are in the same area only if—

(a) both addresses are in the same parliamentary constituency in Greater London or in the same parliamentary constituency in a metropolitan county in England,

(b) both addresses are in the same electoral division of a non-metropolitan county in England and, if either address is in a parish, both are in the same parish,

(c) both addresses are in the same electoral division of a county in Wales and in the same community,

(d) *(applies to Scotland only)*, or

(e) both addresses are in the same ward in Northern Ireland.

(6) The registration officer shall keep a record of those whose applications under subsection (4) above have been granted showing—

(a) whether their applications were in respect of parliamentary elections, local government elections or both, and

(b) the addresses provided by them in their applications as the addresses to which their ballot papers are to be sent.

(7) Where a person applies to the registration officer to vote by post as proxy at a particular election and the application meets the prescribed requirements, the registration officer shall (subject to subsections (10) and (12) below) grant the application if—

(a) he is satisfied that the applicant's circumstances on the date of the poll will be or are likely to be such that he cannot reasonably be expected to vote in person at the polling station allotted or likely to be allotted to the elector under the appropriate rules, or

(b) the applicant is, or the registration officer is satisfied that he will be, included in respect of the constituency or, as the case may be, electoral area for the whole or any part of which the registration officer acts in any of the absent voters lists for that election.

(8) Where, in the case of a particular election, a person included in the record kept under subsection (6) above in respect of elections of the kind in question applies to the registration officer for his ballot paper to be sent to a different address in the United Kingdom, the registration officer shall grant the application if it meets the prescribed requirements.

(9) The registration officer shall, in respect of each parliamentary or local government election, keep a special list of—

(a) those who are for the time being included in the record kept under subsection (6) above in respect of elections of the kind in question, together with the addresses provided by them in their applications under that subsection or, as the case may be, subsection (8) above as the addresses to which their ballot papers are to be sent, and

(b) those whose applications under subsection (7) above have been granted in respect of the election concerned, together with the addresses provided by them in their applications as the addresses to which their ballot papers are to be sent.

(10) The registration officer shall not grant any application under this section unless—

(a) he is satisfied that the elector is or will be registered in the register of parliamentary electors, local government electors or both (as the case may be), and

(b) there is in force an appointment of the applicant as the elector's proxy to vote for him at elections of the kind in question or, as the case may be, the election concerned.

(11) The registration officer shall remove a person from the record kept under subsection (6) above—

(a) if he applies to the registration officer to be removed,

(b) where he was included in the record on the ground mentioned in subsection (4)(a) above, if he ceases to be included in any record kept under section 6 of this Act in respect of a constituency, or electoral area, for the whole or any part of which the registration officer acts or becomes so included in pursuance of a further application under that section,

(c) if the elector ceases to be registered as mentioned in subsection (10)(a) above, or

(d) if the appointment of the person concerned as the elector's proxy ceases to be in force (whether or not he is re-appointed).

(12) A person applying to vote by post as proxy must provide an address in the United Kingdom as the address to which his ballot paper is to be sent.

NOTES

Commencement. Up to 1 August 1985, no order had been made under s 29(2) post, bringing this section into force.

Sub-s (1): Entitled to vote as proxy. As to the capacity of persons to vote as proxies, see s 8 ante.

Parliamentary . . . election. See the note to s 1 ante.

Polling station allotted to the elector, etc. See the note "Polling station allotted to him, etc" to s 5 ante.

Sub-s (4): Constituency. See the note to s 1 ante.

Qualifying address; prescribed. See the notes to s 6 ante.

Sub-s (5): Greater London. Ie the London boroughs, the City of London and the Inner and Middle Temples; see the London Government Act 1963, s 2(1), Vol 26, title London.

Metropolitan county; non-metropolitan county; county. As to the metropolitan and non-metropolitan counties in England and the counties in Wales, see the Local Government Act 1972, ss 1(1), (2), 20(1), (2), Sch 1, Pts I, II, Sch 4, Pt I, Vol 25, title Local Government.

England; Wales. For meanings, see the Interpretation Act 1978, s 5, Sch 1, Vol 41, title Statutes.

Electoral division. As to the division of counties into electoral divisions for the purposes of the election of councillors, see the Local Government Act 1972, ss 6(2)(a), 25(2)(a), Vol 25, title Local Government.

Parish. As to the parishes in England, see the Local Government Act 1972, s 1(6)–(9), Sch 1, Pts IV, V, Vol 25, title Local Government.

Community. As to the communities in Wales, see the Local Government Act 1972, s 20(4), Sch 4, Pt III, Vol 25, title Local Government.

Sub-s (8): United Kingdom. See the note to s 1 ante.

Offence. For an offence connected with this section and the penalty therefor, see s 12(3), (4) post.

Definitions. For "appropriate rules", see s 5(7) ante; for "the elector", see s 8(1) ante; by virtue of s 27(2) post for "registration officer", see the Representation of the People Act 1983, s 8(1) ante, for "the absent voters list", "election", "overseas elector's declaration", "prescribed" and "vote", see s 202(1) of the 1983 Act, as amended by s 11 and Sch 2, para 3(a) post, as from a day to be appointed under s 29(2) post, and for "electoral area" and "local government election", see s 203(1) of that Act (and see also as to "local government election", s 5(7) ante).

Principal Act. Ie the Representation of the People Act 1983 ante; see s 27(1) post.

Transitional provisions. See the note to s 6 ante.

10 Voting at special polling stations in Northern Ireland

(1) Schedule 1 to this Act makes provision for those—

(a) whose circumstances on the date of the poll at a particular parliamentary election in Northern Ireland will be or are likely to be such that they cannot reasonably be expected to vote in person as electors at the polling stations allotted or likely to be allotted to them under the parliamentary elections rules, but

(b) who on that date will be in Northern Ireland.

(2) The Secretary of State may by order made by statutory instrument bring that Schedule into force if he is satisfied that it is necessary to do so in order to prevent serious abuse of the system of voting by post in the case of ballot papers for elections in Northern Ireland sent to addresses there in pursuance of applications granted under section 7(1) of this Act.

(3) That Schedule shall cease to be in force if the Secretary of State so provides by order made by statutory instrument (without prejudice to his power to make a further order under subsection (2) above), and an order under this subsection may include such transitional provisions as the Secretary of State considers necessary or expedient.

(4) No order under this section shall be made unless a draft of the order has been laid before and approved by each House of Parliament.

(5) While that Schedule is in force, section 7(5) of this Act shall have effect as if it required a person applying under section 7(1) of this Act to vote by post at a particular parliamentary election in Northern Ireland to provide an address in Great Britain as the address to which his ballot paper is to be sent.

NOTES

Commencement. Up to 1 August 1985, no order had been made under s 29(2) post, bringing this section into force, but as to the operation of Sch 1 post, see sub-ss (2)–(4) above.

Sub-s (1): Parliamentary election. See the note to s 1 ante.

Polling station allotted . . . to them, etc. Cf the note "Polling station allotted to him, etc" to s 5 ante.

Sub-s (2): Secretary of State. Ie one of Her Majesty's Principal Secretaries of State; see the Interpretation Act 1978, s 5, Sch 1, Vol 41, title Statutes. The Secretary of State here concerned is the Secretary of State for Northern Ireland.

Statutory instrument. For provisions as to statutory instruments generally, see the Statutory Instruments Act 1946, Vol 41, title Statutes.

Satisfied. Statutory powers are often conferred in subjective terms, the competent authority being entitled to act, eg, when it is "satisfied" or it "appears" to it that, or when in its "opinion", a prescribed state of affairs exists, but the inherent jurisdiction of the courts to determine whether such powers have been exceeded is not readily ousted by the use of such language; see, further, 1 Halsbury's Laws (4th edn), para 22.

Applications granted under section 7(1) of this Act. Ie applications to vote by post or by proxy at a particular parliamentary election.

Sub-s (4): Laid . . . before Parliament. For meaning, see the Laying of Documents before Parliament (Interpretation) Act 1948, s 1(1), Vol 41, title Statutes.

Sub-s (5): Great Britain. See the note to s 3 ante.

Definitions. For "elector", "parliamentary election rules" and "vote", see, by virtue of s 27(2) post, the Representation of the People Act 1983, s 202(1) ante.

Orders under this section. Up to 1 August 1985 no order had been made under sub-s (2) above.

Northern Ireland. This section applies to Northern Ireland only; see s 29(4) post.

11 Manner of voting: supplementary provision

Schedule 2 to this Act (which—

(*a*) in Part I, makes amendments of the principal Act consequential on the provisions of sections 5 to 9 of this Act,

(*b*) in Part II, makes transitional provision in relation to absent voters, and

(*c*) in Part III, makes provision as to absent voting at municipal elections in the City)

shall have effect.

NOTES

Commencement. Up to 1 August 1985, no order had been made under s 29(2) post, bringing this section into force.

Municipal election in the City. Ie an election to the office of mayor, alderman, common councilman or sheriff and also the election of any officer elected by the mayor, aldermen and liverymen in common hall.

"The City" means the City of London; see, by virtue of s 27(2) post, the Representation of the People Act 1983, s 202(1) ante.

Principal Act. Ie the Representation of the People Act 1983 ante; see s 27(1) post.

Offences as to declarations, etc

12 Offences as to declarations, etc

(1) A person who makes an overseas elector's declaration or a declaration purporting to be an overseas elector's declaration—

    (*a*) when he knows that he is subject to a legal incapacity to vote at parliamentary elections (age apart), or

    (*b*) when he knows that it contains a statement which is false,

is guilty of an offence.

(2) A person who attests an overseas elector's declaration or a declaration purporting to be an overseas elector's declaration when he knows—

    (*a*) that he is not authorised to attest such a declaration, or

    (*b*) that it contains a statement which is false,

is guilty of an offence.

(3) A person who makes a statement which he knows to be false in any declaration or form used for any of the purposes of sections 5 to 9 of this Act or attests an application under section 6 or 7 of this Act when he knows that he is not authorised to do so or that it contains a statement which is false is guilty of an offence.

(4) A person guilty of an offence under this section shall be liable on summary conviction to a fine not exceeding level 5 on the standard scale.

NOTES

Commencement. Up to 1 August 1985, no order had been made under s 29(2) post, bringing this section into force.

Knows. Knowledge is an essential ingredient of the offence and must be proved by the prosecution; see, in particular, *Gaumont British Distributors Ltd v Henry* [1939] 2 KB 711, [1939] 2 All ER 808.

Knowledge includes the state of mind of a person who shuts his eyes to the obvious; see *James & Son Ltd v Smee* [1955] 1 QB 78 at 91, [1954] 3 All ER 273 at 278 per Parker J. Moreover, there is authority for saying that where a person deliberately refrains from making inquiries the results of which he might not care to have, this constitutes in law actual knowledge of the facts in question; see *Knox v Boyd* 1941 JC 82 at 86, and *Taylor's Central Garages (Exeter) Ltd v Roper* (1951) 115 JP 445 at 449, 450, [1951] WN 383, per Devlin J; and see also, in particular, *Mallon v Allon* [1964] 1 QB 385 at 394, [1963] 3 All ER 843 at 847. Yet mere neglect to ascertain what could have been found out by making reasonable inquiries is not tantamount to knowledge; *Taylor's Central Garages (Exeter) Ltd v Roper* supra per Devlin J, and cf *London Computator Ltd v Seymour* [1944] 2 All ER 11; but see also *Mallon v Allon* supra.

Parliamentary elections. See the corresponding note to s 1 ante.

False. A statement may be false on account of what it omits even though it is literally true; see *R v Lord Kylsant* [1932] 1 KB 442, [1931] All ER Rep 179, and *R v Bishirgian* [1936] 1 All ER 586; and cf *Curtis v Chemical Cleaning and Dyeing Co Ltd* [1951] 1 KB 805 at 808, 809, [1951] 1 All ER 631 at 634, CA. Whether or not gain or advantage accrues from the false statement is irrelevant; see *Jones v Meatyard* [1939] 1 All ER 140; *Stevens & Steeds Ltd and Evans v King* [1943] 1 All ER 314; *Clear v Smith* [1981] 1 WLR 399, [1980] Crim LR 246; and *Barrass v Reeve* [1980] 3 All ER 705, [1981] 1 WLR 408.

Summary conviction. Summary jurisdiction and procedure are mainly governed by the Magistrates' Courts Act 1980, Vol 27, title Magistrates, and by rules made under s 144 of that Act.

Definitions. For "overseas elector's declaration", see s 2(1)(*a*) ante; for "legal incapacity", "standard scale" and "vote", see, by virtue of s 27(2) post, the Representation of the People Act 1983, s 202(1) ante.

13, 14 (*S 13 amends the Representation of the People Act 1983, Sch 1, rr 9(1) 53(4) ante; s 14 amends ss 73(2), 74(1), 75(1), 90(1) of, and Sch 4, para 3 to, that Act, and inserts s 76A in that Act ante.*)

Combination and timing of polls

15 Combination of polls at parliamentary, European Assembly and local elections

(1) Where the polls at—

(a) a parliamentary general election and an Assembly general election;

(b) an ordinary local government election and a parliamentary general election; or

(c) an ordinary local government election and an Assembly general election,

are to be taken on the same date, they shall be taken together.

(2) Where the polls at elections for related areas are to be taken on the same date but are not required by subsection (1) above or section 36 of the principal Act to be taken together, they may nevertheless be so taken if the returning officer for each election thinks fit.

(3) In subsection (2) above the reference to elections includes Assembly elections but does not include elections under the local government Act which are not local government elections; and for the purposes of that subsection two areas are related if one is coterminous with or situated wholly or partly within the other.

(4) Where the polls at any elections are combined under this section the cost of taking the combined polls (excluding any cost solely attributable to one election) and any cost attributable to their combination shall be apportioned equally among the elections.

(5) The Secretary of State may by regulations make such provision as he thinks fit in connection with the combining of polls at any elections under this section including provision modifying the Representation of the People Acts in relation to such elections.

NOTES

Commencement. Up to 1 August 1985, no order had been made under s 29(2) post, bringing this section into force.

Sub-s (1): Parliamentary general election. Cf the note "Parliamentary election" to s 1 ante.

Sub-s (2): Returning officer. See the note to s 5 ante.

Thinks fit. See the note "Satisfied" to s 10 ante.

Sub-s (5): Secretary of State. Ie one of Her Majesty's Principal Secretaries of State; see the Interpretation Act 1978, s 5, Sch 1, Vol 41, title Statutes. The Secretary of State here concerned is the Secretary of State for the Home Department.

Definitions. For "Assembly general election", see s 27(1) post; by virtue of s 27(2) post for "election", see the Representation of the People Act 1983, s 202(1) ante, and for "local government Act" and "local government election", see s 203(1) of the 1983 Act ante. Note also as to "election" and "related areas", sub-s (3) above.

Principal Act. Ie the Representation of the People Act 1983 ante; see s 27(1) post.

Representation of the People Acts. For the Acts which may be cited by this collective title, see s 29(1) post and the Introductory Note to the Representation of the People Act 1948 ante.

Regulations under this section. Up to 1 August 1985 no regulations had been made under sub-s (5) above.

As to regulations under this Act generally, see, by virtue of s 27(2) post, the Representation of the People Act 1983, s 201 ante, as amended by s 24 and Sch 4, para 69 post, as from a day to be appointed under s 29(2) post.

Northern Ireland. This section does not apply to Northern Ireland; see s 29(4), (5) post.

16 Postponement of poll at parish or community council elections

(1) Where the date of the poll at a parliamentary general election or an Assembly general election is the same as the ordinary day of election of councillors for local government areas in England and Wales—

(a) any poll at an election of parish or community councillors to be held in England and Wales on that date shall be postponed for three weeks;

(b) the date to which any such poll is so postponed shall be taken to be the ordinary day of election for the purposes of sections 16(3) and 35(2) of the Local Government Act 1972 and the day of election for the purposes of any rules concerning the conduct of elections of such councillors made (or having effect as if made) under section 36 of the principal Act; and

(c) any expenses of any returning officer for an election at which the poll is postponed under this subsection which are attributable to the postponement shall be charged on and paid out of the Consolidated Fund.

(2) In subsection (1) of section 40 of the principal Act (timing of local elections) after the words "section 39 above" there shall be inserted the words "or section 16 of the Representation of the People Act 1985".

NOTES

Commencement. Up to 1 August 1985, no order had been made under s 29(2) post, bringing this section into force.

Parliamentary . . . election. See the note to s 1 ante.

Ordinary day of election. Ie the first Thursday in May or such other day as the Secretary of State may by order appoint; see, by virtue of s 27(2) post, the Representation of the People Act 1983, s 37 ante. Note however s 18(1) post which makes special provision for local elections in 1986.

Parish; community; England; Wales. See the notes to s 9 ante.

Returning officer. See the note to s 5 ante.

Consolidated Fund. Ie the Consolidated Fund of the United Kingdom which was established by the Consolidated Fund Act 1816, s 1, Vol 30, title Money (Pt 1). By the Finance Act 1954, s 34(3), in the same title, any charge on the Fund extends to the growing produce thereof. See also, as to payment out of the Fund, the Exchequer and Audit Departments Act 1866, s 13, in conjunction with the Exchequer and Audit Departments Act 1957, s 2, and the Finance Act 1975, s 56, all Vol 30, title Money (Pt 1).

Definitions. For "Assembly general election", see s 27(1) post; for "local government area", see, by virtue of s 27(2) post, the Representation of the People Act 1983, s 203(1) ante.

Local Government Act 1972, ss 16(3), 35(2). See Vol 25, title Local Government.

Principal Act. Ie the Representation of the People Act 1983 ante; see s 27(1) post.

Northern Ireland. This section does not apply; see s 29(4), (5) post.

17 (*Substitutes the Representation of the People Act 1983, s 36(3), (3A)–(3C) ante for the original sub-s (3).*)

18 Ordinary day of local elections

(1) Notwithstanding sections 37 and 43 of the principal Act (which provide respectively for the ordinary day of local elections in England and Wales and the day of ordinary local elections in Scotland), in 1986 the ordinary day of election of councillors for local government areas in England and Wales and the day of ordinary local election of councillors for local government areas in Scotland shall be 8th May.

(2) . . .

NOTES

Sub-s (2) amends the Representation of the People Act 1983, s 37(*b*) ante.

Commencement. This section was brought into force on 1 October 1985 by the Representation of the People Act 1985 (Commencement No 1) Order 1985, SI 1985/1185, made under s 29(2) post.

Ordinary day of election. Cf the note to s 16 ante.

England; Wales. See the note to s 9 ante.

Local government area. For meaning, see, by virtue of s 27(2) post, the Representation of the People Act 1983, s 203(1) ante.

Principal Act. Ie the Representation of the People Act 1983 ante; see s 27(1) post. S 43 of that Act applies to Scotland only and is not printed in this work.

Northern Ireland. This section does not apply; see s 29(4), (5) post.

19 Timing of elections

(1) In section 40(1) of the principal Act (days to be disregarded for the purpose of the timing of local elections in England and Wales)—

(a) for the words "Sunday, day of the Christmas break, of the Easter break or of a bank holiday break" there shall be substituted the words "Saturday, Sunday, Christmas Eve, Christmas Day, Maundy Thursday, Good Friday, bank holiday"; and

(b) the words from "In this subsection" onwards shall cease to have effect.

(2) In section 39 of that Act (local elections void etc in England and Wales) in subsection (1) (period within which elections to fill vacancies to be held) for the words "42 days" there shall be substituted the words "35 days".

(3) (*Applies to Scotland only.*)

(4) In section 119 of that Act (computation of time for purposes of Part II) for subsections (2) and (3) there shall be substituted—

"(2) The days referred to in subsection (1) above are Saturday, Sunday, Christmas Eve, Christmas Day, Maundy Thursday, Good Friday, a bank holiday or a day appointed for public thanskgiving or mourning.

(3) In this section 'bank holiday', in relation to any election, means a day which is a bank holiday in the part of the United Kingdom in which the constituency or, as the case may be, electoral area is situated.".

(5) In Schedule 1 to the principal Act (parliamentary elections rules), in rule 2 (computation of time)—

(a) in paragraph (1) for sub-paragraph (b) there shall be substituted—

"(b) a Christmas Eve, Christmas Day, Maundy Thursday, Good Friday or a bank holiday";

and

(b) paragraph (3) shall cease to have effect.

(6) In the Local Government Act 1972—

(a) ...;

(b) for the purposes of subsection (4) of that section, subsection (1) of that section shall have effect as if for the words from "Sunday" to "bank holiday break" there were substituted the words "Saturday, Sunday, Christmas Eve, Christmas Day, Maundy Thursday, Good Friday or bank holiday"; and

(c) in section 89(1) (period within which elections to fill casual vacancies in office of councillor for principal area to be held) for the words "forty-two days", in both places where they occur, there shall be substituted the words "thirty-five days".

NOTES

Sub-s (6)(a) amends the Local Government Act 1972, s 243(3), Vol 25, title Local Government.

Commencement. Sub-s (6)(a) was brought into force on 1 October 1985 by the Representation of the People Act 1985 (Commencement No 1) Order 1985, SI 1985/1185, made under s 29(2) post. Up to 1 August 1985, no order had been made under s 29(2), bringing the remainder of this section into force.

Sub-s (4): Bank holiday. As to the bank holidays in the United Kingdom, see the Banking and Financial Dealings Act 1971, s 1, Sch 1, Vol 45, title Time.

United Kingdom; constituency. See the notes to s 1 ante.

Electoral area. For meaning, see the Representation of the People Act 1983, s 203(1) ante.

Sub-s (6): That section. Ie s 243 of the 1972 Act.

Principal Act. Ie the Representation of the People Act 1983 ante; see s 27(1) post.

Local Government Act 1972, s 89(1). See Vol 25, title Local Government.

Miscellaneous and supplemental

20 (*See Vol 32, title* Parliament.)

21 Ordinary elections of parish and community councillors: insufficient nominations

(1) This section applies where, at an ordinary election of parish or community councillors in England and Wales, an insufficient number of persons are or remain validly nominated to fill the vacancies in respect of which the election is held.

(2) Unless the number of newly elected members of the council in question is less than the number that constitutes a quorum for meetings of the council—

(a)   those members may co-opt any person or persons to fill the vacancy or vacancies remaining unfilled,

(b)   the district council may exercise the powers conferred by section 39(4) of the principal Act (power of district council by order to do anything necessary for the proper holding of an election etc) in relation to any such vacancy or vacancies as are not so filled, and

(c)   section 39(1) of that Act (duty of returning officer to order an election) shall not apply;

but the powers mentioned in paragraph (b) above shall not be exercised before the expiry of the period of 35 days (computed according to section 40 of that Act) beginning with the day on which the election was held.

(3) Subsection (7) of section 39 of that Act (parishes in different districts grouped) shall apply for the purposes of subsection (2) above as it applies for the purposes of subsections (4) and (6) of that section and section 40(3) of that Act (computation of time) shall apply for the purposes of subsection (2) above as it applies for the purposes of section 39.

NOTES

Commencement. Up to 1 August 1985, no order had been made under s 29(2) post, bringing this section into force.

Ordinary election of parish or community councillors. As to when such elections take place, see the Local Government Act 1972, ss 16(3), 25(2), Vol 25, title Local Government.

England; Wales. See the note to s 9 ante.

District council. As to the districts in England and Wales and their councils, see the Local Government Act 1972, ss 1(1), (3), (4), 2(2), (3), 20(1), (3), 21(2), (3), Sch 1, Pt I, Sch 4, Pt II, Vol 25, title Local Government.

Principal Act. Ie the Representation of the People Act 1983 ante; see s 27(1) post.

Northern Ireland. This section does not apply; see s 29(4), (5) post.

---

22 Welsh versions of forms

(1) In section 2(1) of the Welsh Language Act 1967 (power to prescribe Welsh version of forms, etc specified in enactments passed either before or after that Act) the reference to any enactment passed either before or after that Act shall include regulations made under the principal Act or this Act and rules made (or having effect as if made) under section 36 of the principal Act.

(2) ...

NOTES

Sub-s (2) repeals the Representation of the People Act 1983, s 199.

Commencement. This section was brought into force on 1 October 1985 by the Representation of the People Act 1985 (Commencement No 1) Order 1985, SI 1985/1185, made under s 29(2) post.

Passed either before or after that Act. The Welsh Language Act 1967 was passed (ie received Royal Assent) on 27 July 1967.

Welsh Language Act 1967, s 2(1). See Vol 41, title Statutes.
Principal Act. Ie the Representation of the People Act 1983 ante; see s 27(1) post.
Northern Ireland. This section does not apply; see s 29(4), (5) post.

23 Increase in penalties for offences under principal Act, etc

Schedule 3 to this Act shall have effect for the purpose of increasing the penalties applying in respect of certain offences under the principal Act and otherwise amending the provisions in that Act concerning such penalties.

NOTES

Commencement. This section was brought into force on 1 October 1985 by the Representation of the People Act 1985 (Commencement No 1) Order 1985, SI 1985/1185, made under s 29(2) post.
Principal Act. Ie the Representation of the People Act 1983 ante; see s 27(1) post.

24 Miscellaneous amendments of principal Act

The principal Act shall have effect subject to the amendments specified in Schedule 4 to this Act (being miscellaneous amendments including amendments consequential on the provisions of this Act).

NOTES

Commencement. This section was brought into force on 1 October 1985 by the Representation of the People Act 1985 (Commencement No 1) Order 1985, SI 1985/1185, made under s 29(2) post; but note that by s 29(3) post the amendment made by Sch 4, para 18 post, came into force on the passing of this Act on 16 July 1985.
Principal Act. Ie the Representation of the People Act 1983 ante; see s 27(1) post.

25 Amendment of other enactments

(1) Section 26 of the Police and Criminal Evidence Act 1984 (repeal of statutory powers of arrest) shall not apply to rule 36 in Schedule 1 to the principal Act (power of presiding officer to order constable to arrest person suspected of personation) and, accordingly, in Schedule 2 to the 1984 Act (preserved powers of arrest) there shall be inserted at the appropriate place—

"1983 c 2   Rule 36 in Schedule 1 to the Representa-
                                    tion of the People Act 1983".

(2) ...

NOTES

Sub-s (2) amends the Elections (Northern Ireland) Act 1985, s 3(7) ante, as from 1 October 1985.
Commencement. Sub-s (1) came into force on the passing of this Act on 16 July 1985; see s 29(3)(a) post.
Police and Criminal Evidence Act 1984, s 26, Sch 2. See Vol 12, title Criminal Law.
Principal Act. Ie the Representation of the People Act 1983 ante; see s 27(1) post.

26 Expenses

(1) There shall be charged on and paid out of the Consolidated Fund any increase attributable to this Act in the sums to be charged on and paid out of that Fund under any other Act.

There shall be paid out of money provided by Parliament—

(a) any increase attributable to this Act in the sums to be paid out of money so provided under any other Act, and

(b) any administrative expenses incurred by the Secretary of State by virtue of this Act.

NOTES

Commencement. This section was brought into force on 1 October 1985 by the Representation of the People Act 1985 (Commencement No 1) Order 1985, SI 1985/1185, made under s 29(2) post.
Consolidated Fund. See the note to s 16 ante.
Secretary of State. See the note to s 15 ante.

27 Interpretation

(1) In this Act—

"Assembly" means the Assembly of the European Communities,
"Assembly election" means an election of a representative to the Assembly and "Assembly general election" means a general election of such representatives, and
"principal Act" means the Representation of the People Act 1983.

(2) The principal Act and sections 1 to 12, 15 to 18 and 21 of and Schedule 1 to this Act shall have effect as if those sections and that Schedule were contained in Part I of that Act, and sections 5, 6 and 7(1) of the principal Act (residence) apply for the purposes of sections 1 to 3 of this Act as they apply for the purposes of sections 1 and 2 of that Act.

(3) References in any enactment other than an enactment contained in this or the principal Act to Part I of that Act include a reference to sections 1 to 12, 15 to 18 and 21 of and Schedule 1 to this Act.

NOTES

Commencement. Sub-s (1) of this section came into force on the passing of this Act on 16 July 1985; see s 29(3)(a) post. Sub-ss (2), (3) were brought into force on 1 October 1985 by the Representation of the People Act 1985 (Commencement No 1) Order 1985, SI 1985/1185, made under s 29(2) post.
Assembly of the European Communities. Ie the one common Assembly which has served the European Communities since the establishment of the European Economic Community and the European Atomic Energy Community in 1958; see the Convention on Common Institutions, arts 1, 2(1), in conjunction with ECSC Treaty, arts 20–25, EEC Treaty, arts 137–144, and Euratom Treaty, arts 107–114. The Assembly is also known as the European Parliament, although under the treaties it exercises only advisory and supervisory, and not legislative, powers. The Act annexed to the Decision of the Council of the European Communities concerning the Election of Representatives of the Assembly by Direct Universal Suffrage, 76/787/ECSC, EEC, Euratom, makes new provisions for the composition of the Assembly and for the election of the members thereof and accordingly provides for the lapse of the provisions of the above-mentioned Treaties concerning the composition of the Assembly, viz, ECSC Treaty, art 21(1), (2), EEC Treaty, art 138(1), (2), and Euratom Treaty, art 108(1), (2).
Representation of the People Act 1983. See this title ante.

28 Repeals

(1) The enactments mentioned in Schedule 5 to this Act are hereby repealed to the extent specified in column 3 of that Schedule.

(2) Section 21(3) of the Representation of the People Act 1918 (time appointed for meeting of Parliament not to be less than twenty clear days after proclamation summoning it) shall cease to have effect.

(3) Article 2(1), (2) and (3) of the Local Government Reorganisation (Consequential Provisions) (Northern Ireland) Order 1973 (which provides for the Chief Electoral Officer for Northern Ireland to be electoral registration officer for constituencies in Northern Ireland and returning officer for parliamentary elections in such constituencies and is superseded by provision made in this Act) is hereby revoked.

29 Citation, commencement and extent

(1) This Act may be cited as the Representation of the People Act 1985 and shall be included among the Acts that may be cited as the Representation of the People Acts.

(2) This Act (except the provisions mentioned in subsection (3) below) shall come into force on such day as the Secretary of State may by order made by statutory instrument appoint, and different days may be appointed for different provisions and for different purposes.

(3) Those provisions are—

(*a*) sections 25(1) and 27(1) of this Act, this section, the amendment made by paragraph 18 of Schedule 4 to this Act and the repeal made by the entry in Schedule 5 to this Act relating to the Police and Criminal Evidence Act 1984 (which come into force on the day on which this Act is passed), and

(*b*) Schedule 1 to this Act (which may be brought into force under section 10 of this Act).

(4) This Act, except the provisions mentioned in subsection (5) below, extends to Northern Ireland; and section 10 of and Schedule 1 to this Act extend to Northern Ireland only.

(5) Those provisions are sections 15 to 18, 21 to 22 of this Act and any amendment or repeal by this Act of an enactment not extending to Northern Ireland.

SCHEDULES

SCHEDULE 1

Section 10

SPECIAL POLLING STATIONS IN NORTHERN IRELAND

PART I

RIGHT TO VOTE AT SPECIAL POLLING STATIONS

1.—(1) Where, in the case of a person entitled to vote as an elector at a parliamentary election in Northern Ireland, the absent voters list shows that a special polling station is allotted to him he may, notwithstanding anything in section 5 of this Act, vote only in person at that polling station.

(2) Where a person applies to the Chief Electoral Officer for Northern Ireland (in this Schedule referred to as "the electoral officer") to vote at a particular parliamentary election in Northern Ireland at a special polling station, the electoral officer shall grant the application if—

    (a) he is satisfied that the applicant's circumstances on the date of the poll will be or are likely to be such that he cannot reasonably be expected to vote in person at the polling station allotted or likely to be allotted to him under the parliamentary elections rules,

    (b) he is satisfied that the applicant is or will be registered in the register of parliamentary electors, and

    (c) the application meets the prescribed requirements.

(3) The electoral officer shall allot a special polling station to any person whose application under this paragraph is granted and shall send him a notice setting out the situation of the special polling station allotted to him and giving such other information as may be prescribed.

(4) There shall be included in the absent voters list in respect of each parliamentary election in Northern Ireland a list of persons whose applications under this paragraph have been granted, setting out, in the case of each person, the situation of the special polling station allotted to him and giving such other information as may be prescribed.

(5) For the purposes of this paragraph, the electoral officer—

    (a) shall designate special polling places and may by further designations from time to time alter any designation under this paragraph,

    (b) shall publish such notice as he thinks is required of the situation of any place or places currently designated under this paragraph, and

    (c) shall in respect of each parliamentary election, provide a special polling station in each special polling place, unless he is satisfied that the number of persons likely to vote there at that election does not justify it.

(6) Sub-paragraph (5) above has effect notwithstanding anything in section 18 of the principal Act.

NOTES

Commencement. See s 29(2), (3)(b) ante, in conjunction with s 10(2) ante and the note "Orders under this section" thereto.

Person entitled to vote as an elector at a parliamentary election in Northern Ireland. As to the persons entitled to vote at such elections, see the Representation of the People Act 1983, s 1 ante, and s 1 ante. See also the note "Parliamentary election" to s 1 ante.

Applies. The Representation of the People Act 1983, Sch 2, para 5A, as inserted by s 11 ante and Sch 2, para 8 post, as from a day to be appointed under s 29(2) ante, applies to applications under this paragraph; see para 28 of this Schedule post.

Chief Electoral Officer for Northern Ireland. This officer is appointed under the Electoral Law Act (Northern Ireland) 1962, s 14 (not printed in this work) as substituted by the Electoral Law (Northern Ireland) Order 1972, SI 1972/1264, art 6(1). The Representation of the People Acts are modified in respect of the functions of the electoral officer under this Schedule by para 24 post.

Satisfied. See the note to s 10 ante.

Register of parliamentary electors. Ie the register prepared pursuant to the Representation of the People Act 1983, s 9 ante, as amended by s 4(1) ante, as from a day to be appointed under s 29(2) ante.

Prescribed. See the note to s 6 ante.

Publish such notice. Cf, as to public notices by virtue of s 27(2) post, the Representation of the People Act 1983, s 200(1) ante, as read with para 24(b) of this Schedule post.

Offence. For an offence connected with this paragraph and the penalty therefor, see s 12(3), (4) ante, as applied by para 30 of this Schedule post.

Definitions. for "the absent voters list", "parliamentary elections rules", "prescribed" and "vote", see, by virtue of s 27(2) ante, the Representation of the People Act 1983, s 202(1) ante, as amended by s 11 ante and Sch 2, para 3(a) post as from a day to be appointed under s 29(2) ante. Note as to "the electoral officer", sub-para (2) above.

Principal Act. Ie the Representation of the People Act 1983 ante; see s 27(1) ante.

Northern Ireland. This Part of this Schedule applies to Northern Ireland only; see s 29(4) ante.

PART II

RULES RELATING TO SPECIAL POLLING STATIONS

2. The following paragraphs in this Part of this Schedule shall have effect for all purposes as additional rules in Schedule 1 to the principal Act.

3. The official mark on the ballot paper of those voting in respect of a constituency at a special polling station—

(a) shall be different from the official mark on the ballot papers of those voting at the same election in respect of the constituency at polling stations allotted to them under the parliamentary elections rules, and

(b) shall be kept secret;

and an interval of seven years shall intervene between the use of the same official mark on ballot papers of those voting at special polling stations.

4.—(1) The electoral officer shall provide each presiding officer at a special polling station with a list (in this Schedule referred to as "the special polling list") of those electors to whom the special polling station has been allotted, showing for each elector—

(a) the constituency in respect of which he is or appears from the electors lists concerned to be entitled to be registered, and

(b) his electoral number.

(2) Rule 7(6) of the parliamentary elections rules applies for the purposes of this paragraph.

5.—(1) The electoral officer may, after such consultation as appears to him to be desirable, appoint persons (including candidates and their election agents) to attend special polling stations as observers, and each appointment of an observer—

(a) shall be made in writing, and

(b) shall indicate the polling station or polling stations to which he is assigned.

(2) References in this Schedule to observers are references to observers appointed under this paragraph.

6.—(1) When the electoral officer has received the ballot boxes and packets from all the special polling stations, he shall in the presence of each candidate wishing to attend or (if a candidate so chooses) his agent—

(a) open each ballot box and count and record the number of ballot papers in it,

(b) verify each ballot paper account, and

(c) in the case of a general election or two or more by-elections, sort the ballot papers into separate packets for each constituency.

(2) The electoral officer shall give notice in writing to the candidates of the time and place at which he will begin to count the ballot papers under this paragraph, and no person other than the candidates or (where they so choose) their agents may be present unless permitted by the electoral officer.

(3) A person not entitled to attend at the counting of ballot papers under this paragraph shall not be permitted to do so unless the electoral officer—

(a) is satisfied that the efficient counting of the ballot papers will not be impeded, and

(b) has either consulted the candidates or, as the case may be, their agents or thought it impracticable to do so.

(4) The electoral officer shall give to the candidates or, as the case may be, their agents all such reasonable facilities for overseeing the proceedings, and all such information with respect to them, as he can give them consistently with the orderly conduct of the proceedings and the discharge of his duties in connection with them.

(5) The electoral officer shall verify each ballot paper account by comparing it with the number of ballot papers recorded by him, and the unused and spoilt ballot papers in his possession and the tendered votes list (opening and resealing the packets containing unused and spoilt ballot papers) and shall draw up a statement as to the result of the verification, which any candidate or, as the case may be, his agent may copy.

(6) In the case of a general election or two or more by-elections, each packet of ballot papers for a constituency, accompanied by a statement of the number of ballot papers, shall be sent to the place where the votes for that constituency are to be counted and the votes given on the ballot papers may, when—

(a) in the presence of the counting agents appointed under rule 30 of the parliamentary elections rules, the number of ballot papers in the packet has been counted and compared with the statement, and

(b) those ballot papers have been mixed with the ballot papers from at least one ballot box not used at a special polling station,

be counted in accordance with the parliamentary elections rules (other than rule 45(1), (1A) and (5)).

(7) In any other case, the votes given on any ballot papers counted under this paragraph may, when they have been mixed with the ballot papers from at least one ballot box not used at a special polling station, be counted in accordance with the parliamentary elections rules (other than rule 45(1), (1A) and (5)).

(8) References in this paragraph to a candidate's agent are references to his election agent or to his counting agent appointed under rule 30 of the parliamentary elections rules to attend at the counting of the votes.

7.—(1) On the completion of the counting at a contested election, the electoral officer shall, in relation to votes cast at special polling stations, forward to the Clerk of the Crown for Northern Ireland—

(a) the ballot paper accounts and the statements of rejected ballot papers and of the result of the verification of the ballot paper accounts,
(b) the tendered votes list, the list of votes marked by the presiding officer and the related statements,
(c) the packets of counterfoils, and
(d) the special polling lists,

endorsing on each packet a description of its contents and the date of the election to which they relate.

(2) Rules 55(2) to (4) and 59 of the parliamentary elections rules apply for the purposes of this paragraph.

NOTES

Commencement. See s 29(2), (3)(b) ante in conjunction with s 10(2) ante and the note "Orders under this section" thereto.

Para 2: Rules in Schedule 1 to the principal Act. Ie the parliamentary elections rules contained in the Representation of the People Act 1983, Sch 1 ante. Those rules are applied with modifications in relation to special polling stations by Part III of this Schedule post.

Para 3: Official mark. Every ballot paper must be marked with an offical mark which perforates the ballot paper; see r 20(1) of the parliamentary elections rules ante.

Constituency. See the note to s 1 ante.

Special polling station. For the duty of the electoral officer to provide special polling stations, see para 1(5)(c) of this Schedule ante.

Para 4: Presiding officer. As to the appointment etc of these officers, see r 26 of the parliamentary elections rules ante.

Para 5: Consultation. See the note "Consulted" below.

Observers. The requirement of secrecy imposed by the Representation of the People Act 1983, s 66(1) ante, applies with modifications to observers within the meaning of this Schedule; see para 27 of this Schedule post.

Writing. Unless the contrary intention appears this includes other modes of representing or reproducing words in a visible form; see the Interpretation Act 1978, s 5, Sch 1, Vol 41, title Statutes.

Para 6: Packets. Ie the packets required to be made-up by the presiding officer in accordance with r 43 of the parliamentary elections rules ante.

Consulted. On what constitutes consultation, see, in particular, *Fletcher v Minister of Town and Country Planning* [1947] 2 All ER 496, (1947) 111 JP Jo 542; *Rollo v Minister of Town and Country Planning* [1948] 1 All ER 13, [1948] LJR 817, CA; *Re Union of Whippingham and East Cowes Benefices, Derham v Church Comrs for England* [1954] AC 245, [1954] 2 All ER 22, PC; and *Agricultural, Horticultural and Forestry Industry Training Board v Aylesbury Mushrooms Ltd* [1972] 1 All ER 280, [1972] 1 WLR 190.

Offences. For offences in connection with tampering with ballot papers etc, see, by virtue of s 27(2) ante, the Representation of the People Act 1983, s 65 ante, as modified by para 26 of this Schedule post.

Definitions. For "parliamentary elections rules", see, by virtue of s 27(2) ante, the Representation of the People Act 1983, s 202(1) ante; for "the electoral officer", see para 1(2) of this Schedule ante; by virtue of para 8 of this Schedule post for "tendered votes list" and "ballot paper account", see rr 40(3) and 43(3), respectively, of the parliamentary elections rules ante. Note as to "special polling list" para 4(1) above and as to "observer" para 5(2) above.

Principal Act. Ie the Representation of the People Act 1983 ante; see s 27(2) ante.

Northern Ireland. This Part of this Schedule applies to Northern Ireland only; see s 29(4) ante.

Part III
Modifications of Parliamentary Elections Rules

8. Subject to the rules in Part II of this Schedule, the parliamentary elections rules shall have effect in relation to special polling stations so far as applicable to them, but subject to the modifications made by this Part of this Schedule.

9. References to the election shall in the case of a general election or two or more by-elections be read as references to the elections in all the constituencies concerned in Northern Ireland and references to candidates at the election shall be construed accordingly.

10. References to a candidate's polling agent appointed to attend at a polling station shall be read as references to an observer assigned to that station.

11. References to the register of parliamentary electors for an election shall be read as references to the special polling list for that election.

12. Rule 5(2) shall apply to applications to vote at a special polling station and to other applications and notices about voting at such stations.

13. Rule 20(2) and (3) shall not apply.

14. Rules 23, 24 and 25(1) to (4) shall not apply.

15. Rules 28 and 29(3)(*c*) and (*d*) shall not apply.

16. Rule 30(1) to (9) shall not apply.

17. Rule 31 shall have effect as if—

    (*a*) the reference to counting the votes were a reference to counting the ballot papers under this Schedule, and

    (*b*) references to provisions of section 66 of the principal Act were references to those provisions as they have effect by virtue of paragraph 27 below.

18. In rule 32—

    (*a*) paragraph (1)(*a*) and (*e*), and
    (*b*) paragraphs (2), (3) and (4),

shall not apply and the presiding officer shall not admit a person to a special polling station as observer except on production of his appointment.

19. Rule 35(1) shall have effect as if the question that may be put under sub-paragraph (*a*)(i) were—"Are you the person shown in the special polling list for this election as follows?" (*read the whole entry from the list.*)

20. Rule 36(1) shall have effect as if the reference to a candidate or his election agent were omitted.

21. Rule 39 shall not apply.

22. Rule 40(1) shall apply as if, for sub-paragraphs (*a*) and (*b*), there were substituted a reference to a particular elector named in the special polling list.

23. Rules 44 and 45 shall not apply.

NOTES

Commencement. See s 29(2), (3)(*b*) ante in conjunction with s 10(2) ante and the note "Orders under this section" thereto.

Para 8: Part II of this Schedule. Ie paras 2–7 of this Schedule ante.

Parliamentary elections rules. Ie the rules contained in the Representation of the People Act 1983, Sch 1 ante; see by virtue of s 27(2) ante, s 202(1) of the 1983 Act ante.

Special polling stations. For the duty of the electoral officer to provide these, see para 1(5)(*c*) of this Schedule ante.

This Part of this Schedule. Ie Part III of this Schedule.

Definitions. For "special polling list", see para 4(1) of this Schedule ante; for "observer", see para 5(2) of this Schedule ante.

Northern Ireland. This Part of this Schedule applies to Northern Ireland only; see s 29(4) ante.

Part IV

Modification of Representation of the People Acts

24. The Representation of the People Acts shall have effect as if the functions of the electoral officer under this Schedule were—

(a) in the case of functions under paragraph 1(2) and (4) above, functions as registration officer, and

(b) in any other case, functions as returning officer.

25. The reference in section 53(1)(c) of the principal Act to voting by post or proxy includes a reference to voting at a special polling station.

26. Section 65(3) of the principal Act shall have effect as if the reference to counting the votes included a reference to counting the ballot papers under this Schedule.

27. Section 66 of the principal Act shall have effect as if—

(a) the duty imposed by subsection (1) were imposed also on observers,

(b) the references to the register of electors included a reference to the special polling list, and

(c) references to the counting of the votes included a reference to counting the ballot papers under this Schedule.

28. Paragraph 5A of Schedule 2 to the principal Act shall apply to applications under paragraph 1 above.

29. The second reference in section 5(5) of this Act to a polling station does not include a reference to a special polling station.

30. The references in section 12(3) of this Act to section 7 of this Act include a reference to paragraph 1 above.

NOTES

Commencement. See s 29(2), (3)(b) ante in conjunction with s 10(2) ante and the note "Orders under this section" thereto.

Returning officer. See the note to s 5 ante.

Definitions. For "registration officer", see, by virtue of s 27(2) ante, the Representation of the People Act 1983, s 8(1) ante; for "the electoral officer", see para 1(2) of this Schedule ante; for "the special polling list", see para 4(1) of this Schedule ante; for "observer", see para 5(2) of this Schedule ante.

Representation of the People Acts. See the note to s 15 ante.

Principal Act. Ie the Representation of the People Act 1983 ante; see s 27(2) ante.

Northern Ireland. This Part of this Schedule applies to Northern Ireland only; see s 29(4) ante.

SCHEDULE 2

Section 11

Manner of Voting

Part I

Consequential Amendments of Principal act

1. In section 56 (registration appeals: England and Wales) in subsection (1)(b), for the words "be treated as an absent voter" there shall be substituted the words "vote by proxy or by post as elector".

2. In section 61 (voting offences)—

(a) in subsection (1)(a) for the words from "be treated" to the end there shall be substituted the words "vote by proxy or by post as elector, at a parliamentary or local government election, or at parliamentary or local government elections, knowing that he is subject to a legal incapacity to vote at the election or, as the case may be, at elections of that kind; or";

(b) in subsection (1)(b) for the words from "parliamentary" to the end there shall be substituted the words "any parliamentary or local government election or at parliamentary or local government elections knowing that he or the person to be appointed is subject to a legal incapacity to vote at the election or, as the case may be, at elections of that kind; or";

(c) in subsection (1)(c) the words "or applies to vote by post" shall cease to have effect;

(d) in subsection (2)(d) the words "not being a service voter" shall cease to have effect, after the word "elections" there shall be inserted the words "in any constituency" and after the word "force" and the words "an appointment" there shall be inserted the words "in respect of that or another constituency";

(e) subsection (3)(c) shall cease to have effect; and

(f) in subsection (4) after the word "constituency" there shall be inserted the words "or at a local government election in any electoral area".

3. In section 202 (interpretation)—

(a) before the definition of "Attorney General" there shall be inserted the following definition—

"'the absent voters list' means, in relation to any election, the list kept under section 7 of the Representation of the People Act 1985 for that election"; and

(b) after the definition of "legal incapacity" there shall be inserted the following definition—

"'the list of proxies' has, in relation to any election, the meaning given by section 7 of the Representation of the People Act 1985".

4. In Schedule 1 in rule 5(2)(a) (notice of election to specify time for applying for an absent vote) for the words from "be" to "voter" there shall be substituted the words "vote by post or by proxy".

5. In Schedule 1 in rule 24 (postal ballot papers) for the words "provided by them for the purpose" there shall be substituted the words "shown in the absent voters list".

6. In Schedule 1 in rule 28 (issue of poll cards) in paragraph (1)(b) for the words from "his application" to the end there shall be substituted the words "he is entitled to vote by post as proxy at the election".

7. In Schedule 1 in rule 40 (tendered ballot papers) in paragraph (1)(b) the words "named in the list of persons" shall cease to have effect.

8. In Schedule 2 (regulations as to registration) paragraph 5(4) shall cease to have effect and at the end of that paragraph there shall be inserted—

"5A.—(1) Provision requiring applications under section 6 or 7 of the Representation of the People Act 1985 to be attested and limiting the number of such applications that a person may attest.

(2) Provision requiring a person applying under section 7 of the Representation of the People Act 1985 to do so in person, producing a document of a prescribed description.

(3) Provision as to the evidence which shall or may be required, or be deemed sufficient or conclusive evidence, in connection with a person's application to vote by proxy or to vote by post as elector or as proxy.

(4) Provision authorising or requiring registration officers—

(a) to make inquiries of persons included in the record kept under section 6(3) of the Representation of the People Act 1985 for the purpose of determining whether there has been a material change of circumstances, and

(b) to treat failure to respond to such inquiries as sufficient evidence of such a change."

NOTES

Commencement. Up to 1 August 1985, no order had been made under s 29(2) ante bringing this Part into force.

Para 2: Parliamentary . . . election; constituency. See the notes to s 1 ante.

Para 8: Conclusive evidence. See the note to s 4 ante.

Definitions. By virtue of s 27(2) ante: for "registration officer", see the Representation of the People Act 1983, s 8(1) ante; for "absent voters list", "elector", "legal incapacity" and "prescribed", see s 202(1) of the 1983 Act, as amended by para 3 above; for "electoral area" and "local government election", see s 203(1) of the 1983 Act.

Principal Act. Ie the Representation of the People Act 1983 ante; see s 27(2) ante.

Regulations. Up to 1 August 1985 no regulations had been made containing the provisions specified in the Representation of the People Act 1983, Sch 2, para 5A as inserted by para 8 above.

Northern Ireland. In so far as it relates to the amendment of provisions which do not extend to Northern Ireland, this Part of this Schedule does not apply to Northern Ireland; see s 29(4), (5) ante.

PART II

TRANSITIONAL PROVISION FOR ABSENT VOTERS

9.—(1) In relation to any person who, immediately before the commencement date, was entitled, in pursuance of an application or applications to be treated as an absent voter for an indefinite period, to vote by post or by proxy at parliamentary elections, local government elections or both, sections 6 to 9 of this Act shall have effect—

(a) as if an application by him under section 6 of this Act so to vote at elections of the kind or kinds in question had been granted on that date,

(b) where, immediately before that date, an appointment of a person to vote for him as proxy at parliamentary elections or at parliamentary and local government elections was in force, as if the appointment had been made under section 8 of this Act on that date in respect of elections of the kind or kinds in question, and

(c) where the application treated as granted by virtue of paragraph (a) above is an application to vote by post, as if he had specified in the application as the address to which his ballot paper is to be sent the address provided by him for the purpose under section 19 of the principal Act.

(2) Sub-paragraph (1) above does not apply to a person who applied to be treated as an absent voter by virtue of section 19(1)(e) of the principal Act.

10. In relation to any person who, immediately before the commencement date, was entitled to vote by proxy at any election by virtue of section 19(2) or 32(2) of the principal Act or would have been so entitled but for an application to vote by post under section 19(4), sections 6 to 9 of this Act shall have effect—

(a) as if an application by him under section 6 of this Act to vote by proxy at both parliamentary and local government elections or, as the case may be, at local government elections had been granted on that date, and

(b) where, immediately before that date, an appointment of a person to vote for him as proxy at parliamentary elections, local government elections or both was in force, as if the appointment had been made under section 8 of this Act on that date in respect of elections of the kind or kinds in question.

11.—(1) Where an appointment of a person to vote as proxy for another at parliamentary elections, local government elections or both is treated by virtue of paragraph 9 or 10 above as made under section 8 of this Act and immediately before the commencement date the proxy was entitled, in pursuance of an application or applications for an indefinite period, so to vote by post at elections of the kind or kinds in question, section 9 of this Act shall have effect—

(a) where the proxy's application or applications were based on his entitlement as elector to vote by post, as if an application by him under section 9(4)(a) of this Act to vote by post as proxy at elections of the kind or kinds in question had been granted on that date, and

(b) where the proxy's application was based on the situation of the address to which his ballot paper was to be sent, as if an application by him under section 9(4)(b) of this Act to vote by post as proxy at parliamentary elections had been granted on that date.

12. In this Part of this Schedule—

"commencement date" means the date of commencement of sections 5 to 9 of this Act; and "local government election" has the same meaning as in those sections;

but this Part of this Schedule shall have effect, in relation to a person who, immediately before the commencement date, is entitled to vote by post as elector or as proxy at local government elections other than elections of parish or community councillors, as if he were then entitled so to vote at all local government elections.

NOTES

Commencement. Up to 1 August 1985, no order had been made under s 29(2) ante, bringing this Part into force.

Para 9: Parliamentary elections. See the corresponding note to s 1 ante.

Para 12: Date of commencement of sections 5 to 9 of this Act. See the "Commencement" notes to those sections.

This Part of this Schedule. Ie Pt II (paras 9–12) of this Schedule.

Principal Act. Ie the Representation of the People Act 1983 ante; see s 27(2) ante. Ss 19 and 32 of that Act are repealed by s 28 ante and Sch 5 post.

PART III

VOTING AT MUNICIPAL ELECTIONS IN THE CITY

13.—(1) The City of London (Various Powers) Act 1957 shall be amended as follows.

(2) In section 8(1), the words from "section 32" to "(proxies at local government elections)" shall be omitted.

(3) For section 8(2) and (3) there shall be substituted—

"(2) Subject as hereinafter provided, sections 5 to 9 and 12(3) and (4) of the Representation of the People Act 1985 shall apply to and in respect of ward elections, but as if any reference to the polling station allotted or likely to be alloted to any person under rules made (or having effect as if made) under section 36 of the Representation of the People Act 1983 were a reference to the polling station provided or likely to be provided by the returning officer.".

(4) In section 8(4) after the words "Act of 1983" there shall be inserted the words "or the Act of 1985" and after the words "subsection (1)" (where they first appear) there shall be inserted the words "or (2)".

(5) In section 8(5) after the words "Act of 1983" there shall be inserted the words "or the Act of 1985" and after the words "subsection (1)" there shall be inserted the words "or (2)".

NOTES

Commencement. Up to 1 August 1985, no order had been made under s 29(2) ante, bringing this Part into force.

Ward elections. For meaning, see the City of London (Various Powers) Act 1957, s 4(1), Vol 26, title London.

City of London (Various Powers) Act 1957. See Vol 26, title London.

(Sch 3: para 1 amends the Representation of the People Act 1983, s 62(1) ante; para 2 substitutes s 65(3), (4) for s 65(3)–(5) of that Act; para 3 amends s 66(6) of that Act; para 4 substitutes s 99(2) of that Act; paras 5–7 amend ss 100(2), 110(3), 149 of that Act respectively; para 8 substitutes s 168(1) for s 168(1)–(4) of that Act; paras 9–11 amend ss 169, 175(1) of, Sch 2, para 13(1) to, that Act respectively.)

SCHEDULE 4

Section 24

MISCELLANEOUS AMENDMENTS OF THE PRINCIPAL ACT

Part I (parliamentary and local government franchise and its exercise)

1–6. . . .

7. Section 38 (nominations and candidate's death in local election in England and Wales) shall cease to have effect.

8. . . .

9. Section 44 (candidate's death in local election in Scotland) shall cease to have effect.

10–19. . . .

NOTES

Paras 1–6, 12–14, 16–18 amend the Representation of the People Act 1983, ss 3(1), 11, 15(7), 18, 26, 28, 52–54, 56, 58, 62(1)(b)(ii) respectively ante; paras 8, 10, 11, 15 repeal ss 39(8), 49(1)(d), (2)(c), 51, 55 of that Act respectively; para 19 substitutes s 63 for ss 63, 64 of that Act.

Commencement. This Part was brought into force on 1 October 1985, by the Representation of the People Act 1985 (Commencement No 1) Order 1985, SI 1985/1185, made under s 29(2) ante, except para 18, which came into force on the passing of this Act on 16 July 1985 (see s 29(3)(a) ante), and paras 7, 9 above which, up to 1 August 1985, had not been brought into force by order made under s 29(2) ante.

Principal Act. Ie the Representation of the People Act 1985 ante; see s 27(1) ante.

Part II (the election campaign)

20–33. . . .

34. For subsection (1) of section 91 (candidate's right to send election address post free) there shall be substituted—

"(1) A candidate at a parliamentary election is, subject to Post Office regulations, entitled to send free of charge for postage either—

(a) one unaddressed postal communication, containing matter relating to the election only and not exceeding 60 grammes in weight, to each place in the constituency which, in accordance with those regulations, constitutes a delivery point for the purposes of this subsection; or

(b) one such postal communication addressed to each elector.".

35–43. . . .

NOTES

Paras 20–24, 26–33, 35–39, 42, 43 amend the Representation of the People Act 1983, ss 67(4), 68(3), 69(1)(a), 70, 75, 78(1), (4), 79(1), (4), 81, 82, 85–89, 93(2)(b), 94–96, 97(2)(b), 108, 118 ante; paras 25, 40, 41 repeal ss 76(3), 103(2), 106(4) of that Act respectively.

Commencement. This Part was brought into force on 1 October 1985 by the Representation of the People Act 1985 (Commencement No 1) Order 1985, SI 1985/1185, made under s 29(2) ante, except para 34 above which, up to 1 August 1985, had not been brought into force by order made under that subsection.

Parliamentary election. See the note to s 1 ante.

Post Office. This public authority is constituted by the Post Office Act 1969, s 6, Sch 1, Vol 34, title Post Office.

Regulations. These regulations are not made by statutory instrument and are not noted in this work.

Free of charge. See, however, as to the remuneration of the Post Office out of the Consolidated Fund, the Post Office Act 1969, s 72, Vol 34, title Post Office.

Definitions. For "candidate", see the Representation of the People Act 1983, s 118 ante; for "election" and "elector", see s 202(1) of that Act.

44–67 (Pts III, IV). *(Paras 44, 45, 47–49, 51–56, 60–64, 66, 67 amend the Representation of the People Act 1983, ss 122(4), 124, 126(3), 136, 140, 156, 160–162, 163(1)(b), 167, 173(a), 176, 178, 181, 187, 191, 197 respectively ante; paras 46, 50, 57–59, 65 repeal ss 125(a), 141(3), (4), 142, 168(5), (6), 171, 172 of that Act respectively ante.)*

Part V (general and supplemental)

68. . . .

69. For subsection (2) of section 201 (regulations) there shall be substituted—

"(2) No regulations shall be made under this Act by the Secretary of State otherwise than under section 203(4) below unless a draft of the regulations has been laid before and approved by a resolution of each House of Parliament.".

70–72. . . .

NOTES

Paras 68, 71, 72 amend the Representation of the People Act 1983, ss 200(1), 203, 205 respectively ante. Para 70 repeals s 202 of that Act.

Secretary of State. See the note to s 15 ante.

Laid before . . . Parliament. See the note to s 10 ante.

Schedule 1 (parliamentary elections rules)

73. In Schedule 1 in rule 1 (timetable)—

   (*a*) in the second column of the entry relating to polling (general elections) for the word "tenth" there shall be substituted the word "eleventh"; and

   (*b*) in the third column of that entry (by-elections) for the words "eighth" and "tenth" there shall be substituted respectively the words "ninth" and "eleventh".

74–78. . . .

79. In Schedule 1 in rule 29(5) (alternative forms of notice to be exhibited in compartments at polling stations) for the words from "a notice" onwards there shall be substituted the words "the notice 'Vote for one candidate only. Put no other mark on the ballot paper, or your vote may not be counted.'".

80. In Schedule 1 for rule 31 there shall be substituted—

"Notification of requirement of secrecy

   31. The returning officer shall make such arrangements as he thinks fit to ensure that—

   (*a*) every person attending at a polling station (otherwise than for the purpose of voting or assisting a blind voter to vote or as a constable on duty there) has been given a copy in writing of the provisions of subsections (1), (3) and (6) of section 66 of this Act; and

   (*b*) every person attending at the counting of the votes (other than any constable on duty at the counting) has been given a copy in writing of the provisions of subsections (2) and (6) of that section.".

81–83. . . .

84. In Schedule 1 in the Appendix of forms the form of the front of a ballot paper shall be amended by the insertion at the top of the words "VOTE FOR ONE CANDIDATE ONLY" in large capitals.

85. In Schedule 1 in the Appendix of forms in the directions as to printing the ballot paper—

   (*a*) in paragraph 2(*a*), after the word "except" there shall be inserted the words "the direction "VOTE FOR ONE CANDIDATE ONLY" and";

   (*b*) in paragraph 2(*b*) after the word "except" there shall be inserted the words "the horizontal rule separating the direction mentioned in paragraph (*a*) above from the particulars of the candidates and";

   (*c*) in paragraph 2(*c*) for the words from "the candidates" onwards there shall be substituted the words "the direction mentioned in paragraph (*a*) above and each of the candidates by the horizontal rules mentioned in paragraph (*b*) above"; and

   (*d*) after paragraph 2 there shall be inserted—

   "2A. The direction mentioned in paragraph 2(*a*) above shall be printed in large capitals.".

86. In Schedule 1 in the Appendix of forms, for the form of directions for the guidance of the voters in voting there shall be substituted—

"Form of directions for the guidance of the voters in voting

GUIDANCE FOR VOTERS

1. When you are given a ballot paper make sure it is stamped with the official mark.

2. Go to one of the compartments. Mark a cross (X) in the box on the right hand side of the ballot paper opposite the name of the candidate you are voting for.

3. Fold the ballot paper in two. Show the official mark to the presiding officer, but do not let anyone see your vote. Put the ballot paper in the ballot box and leave the polling station.

4. Vote for one candidate only. Put no other mark on the ballot paper, or your vote may not be counted.

5. If by mistake you spoil a ballot paper, show it to the presiding officer and ask for another one.".

NOTES

Paras 74–78, 81–83 amend the Representation of the People Act 1983, Sch 1, rr 5, 9, 19(2)(*d*), 23, 24, 37(1)(*b*), 45, 53, respectively ante.

Returning officer. See the note to s 5 ante.

Writing. Unless the contrary intention appears this includes other modes of representing or reproducing words in a visible form; see the Interpretation Act 1978, s 5, Sch 1, Vol 41, title Statutes.

Other Schedules

87–90. (*Amend the Representation of the People Act 1983, Schs 2, 3, 4, 7, respectively, ante.*)

SCHEDULE 5

Section 28

REPEALS

Chapter	Short Title	Extent of Repeal
1797 c 127	The Meeting of Parliament Act 1797	Sections 3 to 5.
7 & 8 Geo 5 c 64	The Representation of the People Act 1918	The whole Act, so far as otherwise unrepealed.
5 & 6 Eliz 2 c x	The City of London (Various Powers) Act 1957	In section 8(1), the words from "section 32" to "(proxies at local government elections)".
1972 c 70	The Local Government Act 1972	In section 243(3), the words "of election or" in the second place where they occur and the words "as the case may be".
1983 c 2	The Representation of the People Act 1983	In section 18, in subsection (2)(*b*) the words "in the case of a county constituency" and in subsection (6) paragraph (*b*) and the word "and" immediately preceding it.
		Sections 19 to 22.
		Sections 32 to 34.
		Section 38.
		Section 39(8).
		In section 40(1), the words from "In this subsection" onwards.
		In section 43(2)(*b*), the words ", or section 44(2)".
		Section 44.
		In section 49, subsections (1)(*d*), (2)(*c*) and (3).
		Section 51.
		In section 52(2), the words "by the Secretary of State or, in Scotland".
		Section 53(2).
		Section 55.
		Section 56(1)(*c*) and (6).
		In section 61, in subsection (1)(*c*) the words "or applies to vote by post", in sub-section (2)(*d*) the words "not being a service voter" and subsection (3)(*c*).
		Section 76(3).
		Section 103(2).
		In section 104(*b*), the words "except section 103(2)".

Chapter	Short Title	Extent of Repeal
1983 c 2—*cont*	The Representation of the People Act 1983—*cont*	Section 106(4). In section 108, subsection (3) and in subsection (4) the word "also". In section 124, in paragraph (*a*) the words "receiving the judges and" and paragraph (*b*). In section 125, paragraph (*a*). In section 126(3), the words "and Northern Ireland". In section 136, in subsection (4) the words from "not" to "notice", subsection (5) and in subsection (7) the words "not exceeding five days". In section 140, subsection (5) and in subsection (7) the words from "and shall give" to the end of the subsection. Section 141(3) and (4). Section 142. In section 148(4)(*a*) the words "(appointed with the Attorney General's approval)". Section 156(2) to (4). Section 160, in subsection (1) the words "and whether" to "indemnity" and subsection (2). In section 161, the words from "whether" to "not". In section 162, the words from "whether" to "not". In section 163(1)(*b*), the words from "whether" to "not". Section 168(5) and (6). In section 169, the words from "(including" to "court)". Sections 171 and 172. In section 173(*a*), the words "on indictment or by an election court". In section 176, in subsection (1) the words from "whether" to "otherwise" and subsection (3). In section 181, in subsection (3) the words from "with" to "approval", from "of not" to "standing" and from "and" onwards and in subsection (6) the words from "so far" to "defendant". In section 187(1), the word "51(2)" and the word "district" in both places where it occurs. Section 190. In section 191(1)(*a*), the word "51(2)". Section 192.

Chapter	Short Title	Extent of Repeal
1983 c 2—*cont*	The Representation of the People Act 1983—*cont*	In section 196, the words "or under section 156(2)". Section 199. In section 202(1), the definition of "registration duties". In section 203(4)(*a*), the words from "and any" to "officer". In Schedule 1, rule 2(3). In Schedule 1, in rule 5, in paragraph (1) the words "in the form in the Appendix" and paragraph (3). In Schedule 1, in rule 23, paragraph (2)(*c*) and the word "and" immediately preceding it and paragraph (3). In Schedule 1, rule 27. In Schedule 1, in rule 40(1)(*b*) the words "named in the list of persons". In Schedule 1, in the Appendix of Forms, the form of notice of election. In Schedule 2, paragraphs 5(4) and 9. In Schedule 7, paragraphs 8 and 9. In Schedule 8, in paragraph 3(*a*)(ii), the words from "section 32" to "(proxies at local government elections)" and paragraph 3(*b*) and (*c*).
1984 c 60	The Police and Criminal Evidence Act 1984	In Schedule 7, in Part I, in column 3 of the entry relating to the Representation of the People Act 1983, the words "In Schedule 1, paragraph 36".

NOTES

Commencement. Up to 1 August 1985, no order had been made under s 29(2) ante bringing into force the repeals relating to the City of London (Various Powers) Act 1957 or the Representation of the People Act 1983, ss 19 to 22, 32 to 34, 38, 40(1), 49(3), 61, Sch 1, rr 2(3), 27, 40(1)(*b*), Sch 2, para 5(4), Sch 8. The entry relating to the Police and Criminal Evidence Act 1984 came into force on the passing of this Act on 16 July 1985; see s 29(3)(*a*) ante. The remainder of this Schedule was brought into force on 1 October 1985 by the Representation of the People Act 1985 (Commencement No 1) Order 1985, SI 1985/1185, made under s 29(2) ante.

Northern Ireland. In so far as it relates to the repeal of enactments which do not extend to Northern Ireland, this Schedule does not apply to Northern Ireland; see s 29(4), (5) ante.

ELECTRICITY

Table of Contents

Cross References

For Compulsory Acquisition of Land	*See title*	Compulsory Acquisition
Dishonest Dealing with Electricity	,,	Criminal Law
Electric Railways	,,	Railways, Inland Waterways and Pipelines
Employment, Conditions of	,,	Employment; Health and Safety at Work
Finance for Nationalised Industries	,,	Money (Pt 1)
Income Tax of Electricity Boards	,,	Taxation
Local Authorities	,,	Local Government; London
Public Lighting	,,	London; Public Health; Road Traffic
Rating of Electricity Boards	,,	Rating
Telecommunications	,,	Telecommunications and Broadcasting

Preliminary Note

The Electricity Act 1947 nationalised the electricity supply industry as from 1 April 1948. The situation immediately prior to nationalisation was, briefly, as follows: the Electricity Commissioners exercised general supervisory powers over electricity supply under the Minister of Fuel and Power; the supply of electricity to undertakers through the "grid" system was the responsibility of the Central Electricity Board; the supply of electricity to ordinary consumers under statutory powers was in the hands partly of company undertakers, partly of local authorities and partly of joint electricity authorities; the subsidiary powers of electricity undertakers were contained in the Schedule to the Electric Lighting (Clauses) Act 1899. The relevant legislation was the 1899 Act and the

Electricity (Supply) Acts 1882 to 1936 (as to which, see the Introductory Note to the Electric Lighting Act 1882). Although the 1947 Act changed the structure and ownership of the industry, much of the earlier legislation, as amended or modified by later Acts, is still of importance.

Changes introduced by the Electricity Act 1947

Under the 1947 Act, the assets of the Central Electricity Board and other authorised undertakers and of certain other bodies were vested in new statutory corporations created by that Act for purposes of electricity supply and with certain exceptions those bodies were themselves dissolved. The Electricity Commissioners were dissolved by order made under s 58. In general, those provisions of the earlier Acts which related to the authorisation of electricity supply by company undertakers or local authorities, to the creation of joint electricity authorities or to the functions of the Electricity Commissioners or the Central Electricity Board were repealed, while those provisions which related to the execution of works etc by undertakers were adapted so as to apply to the new statutory corporations.

Administration

The Electricity Act 1947, Pt I, provided for the establishment of certain new statutory corporations, namely, the British Electricity Authority (in the Act referred to as "the Central Authority") and the Area Boards (ss 1–3). The Electricity Reorganisation (Scotland) Act 1954 stripped the Central Authority of its functions in Scotland and dissolved the Scottish Area Boards, establishing in their place a South of Scotland Electricity Board. It also renamed the Central Authority the Central Electricity Authority (Sch 1, Pt II). The Electricity Act 1957 dissolved the Central Authority and established in its place a Central Electricity Generating Board (in the Act referred to as "the Generating Board") and an Electricity Council (ss 1 (repealed), 2 and 3), and provided for the transfer of the assets and liabilities of the Central Authority to the Electricity Council and the Generating Board (ss 25, 26 (repealed)), and for the payment of compensation to members and officers of the Authority (s 27). The Generating Board and the Area Boards (together with the North of Scotland Hydro-Electric Board established under the Hydro-Electric Development (Scotland) Act 1943 (largely repealed)) and the South of Scotland Electricity Board are referred to as "Electricity Boards" (s 1(3) of the 1947 Act and the Electricity Reorganisation (Scotland) Act 1954, Sch 1, Pt II).

The two Scottish boards now continue in existence by virtue of the Electricity (Scotland) Act 1979 (not printed in this work).

The main duty of the Generating Board is to develop and maintain an efficient, co-ordinated and economical system of supply of electricity in bulk for all parts of England and Wales, and for that purpose to generate or acquire supplies of electricity and to provide bulk supplies of electricity for the Area Boards for distribution by those Boards (Electricity Act 1957, s 2(5)). The main duty of the Electricity Council is to advise the Secretary of State on questions affecting the electricity supply industry and matters relating thereto and to promote and assist the maintenance and development by Electricity Boards in England and Wales of an efficient, co-ordinated and economical system of electricity supply (s 3(4) of the 1957 Act). The main duty of the Area Boards is to acquire bulk supplies of electricity from the Generating Board and to plan and carry out an efficient and economical distribution of those supplies to persons in the area who require them, though under s 6 of the 1957 Act they may themselves, with the approval of the Secretary of State, generate electricity. (The Energy Act 1983 makes provision for the manufacture and supply of electricity by persons other than Electricity Boards; see ss 2–11 of that Act.) Area Boards are established for the whole of Great Britain (except Scotland where the North of Scotland Hydro-Electric Board and the South of Scotland Electricity Board in general combine the functions elsewhere exercisable by the Generating Board and the Area Boards respectively). The areas of the Area Boards have been defined by order under s 4 of the 1947 Act, and by that section the Secretary of State is given power to vary their areas, including the power to dissolve existing or create new boards. S 7 of that Act provides for the formation in each area of a Consultative Council. The duties of each Council are, in general, to advise the appropriate Area Board, but in certain cases it has the right to make representations to the Electricity Council or the Secretary of State. For further provisions as to the powers, duties and liabilities of Electricity Boards, see also ss 1 and 9–11 of the 1947 Act and the Electricity Act 1957, ss 2–11.

Pt II of the 1947 Act (now largely repealed) deals with the acquisition of existing electricity undertakings by the Electricity Boards and the consequent payment of compensation.

The Electricity Consumers' Council was established by the Energy Act 1983, s 21 and Sch 2, to consider matters affecting the interests of consumers of electricity supplied by Electricity Boards in England and Wales and to report to the Secretary of State or the Electricity Council.

Miscellaneous provisions

The Schedule to the Electric Lighting (Clauses) Act 1899 was incorporated with the 1947 Act; see s 57(2) of, and Sch 4, Pt III to, that Act. It contains various provisions relating to the nature and mode of supply, the execution of works, the appointment of electric inspectors, the testing and inspection of mains and the use and certification of meters. It also incorporates provisions of the Electric Lighting Act 1882, the Gasworks Clauses Act 1847 and the Gasworks Clauses Act 1871. The Electric Lighting Act 1909 includes provisions relating to meters and electric lines. The Electricity (Supply) Act 1919 contains, inter alia, provisions relating to overhead wires and wayleaves; see also, in relation to wayleaves, s 11 of the Electricity (Supply) Act 1922 and s 44 of the Electricity (Supply) Act 1926. S 25 of the 1922 Act makes provision relating to the power of certain bodies to supply electricity. The Electricity Supply (Meters) Act 1936 deals with the appointment of meter examiners and the apparatus for meter testing; see also, in relation to meters, ss 49–59 of the Schedule to the 1899 Act, the Electricity Act 1957, s 30 and the Energy Act 1983, s 12.

The 1957 Act contains a number of miscellaneous provisions dealing, inter alia, with the supply of electricity to railways (s 28), the placing of electric lines above ground (s 32), and provisions as to public inquiries (s 34, Sch 2).

The rights of entry of electricity boards, (including power to enter property without consent in an emergency) are regulated by the Rights of Entry (Gas and Electricity Boards) Act 1954.

Provisions relating to finance, including fixing of tariffs, accounting matters and borrowing powers are contained in, inter alia, the Electricity Act 1947, ss 37, 45, 46, the Electricity Act 1957, ss 13–24, the Electricity and Gas Act 1963, the Gas and Electricity Act 1968, the Electricity Act 1972, the Energy Act 1976, s 16, the Nuclear Safeguards and Electricity (Finance) Act 1978, s 5, and the Energy Act 1983, ss 5–10, 17, 18, 35.

The Electricity (Amendment) Act 1961, as amended by the Nuclear Installations (Amendment) Act 1965, enables the Central Electricity Generating Board to produce radioactive material in a nuclear reactor for sale or supply to other persons.

The Energy Act 1976, s 7 enables the Secretary of State to give directions to the Electricity Boards and other undertakings requiring the holding of fuel stocks at or near electricity generating plant. S 14 of that Act requires that the Secretary of State be notified in writing of any proposal to install or convert electricity generating plant to burn crude liquid petroleum, petroleum products or natural gas or to enter into, or extend, arrangements for the supply of natural gas as a fuel for such a plant.

Secretary of State for Energy

The administrative functions under the Electric Lighting Acts 1882 to 1909 were in the hands of the Board of Trade. By the Electricity (Supply) Act 1919, which established the Electricity Commissioners, provision was made under s 39 for transferring all the functions of the Board of Trade (except that of appointing Electricity Commissioners), both under that Act and under the earlier legislation, to the Minister of Transport; those functions were so transferred by the Minister of Transport (Electricity Supply) Order 1920, SR & O 1920/58. The functions were transferred back to the Board of Trade by the Defence (Functions of Ministers) Regulations 1941, SR & O 1941/2057, and were transferred to the Minister of Fuel and Power by the Ministers of the Crown (Minister of Fuel and Power) Order 1942, SI 1942/1132; they were retained by that Minister by virtue of the Ministry of Fuel and Power Act 1945, s 1(2), Sch 1.

The Electricity Commissioners, to whom the Minister of Transport was formerly to refer for advice (Electricity (Supply) Act 1919, s 39(2) (repealed)), were dissolved by the Electricity Commissioners (Dissolution) Order 1948, SI 1948/1769 and their property and functions under the Electricity (Supply) Acts 1882 to 1919 were transferred by that Order to the Minister of Fuel and Power.

The Minister of Fuel and Power was restyled the Minister of Power by the Minister of Fuel and Power (Change of Style and Title) Order 1957, SI 1957/48.

The functions of the Minister of Fuel and Power, so far as they related to the generation and supply of electricity in Scotland and matters connected therewith and the giving of certain consents in relation to those functions, were transferred to the Secretary of State for Scotland, as were the functions of the Minister and the Secretary of State for Scotland acting jointly under the Hydro-Electric Development (Scotland) Act 1943, and, so far as they related exclusively to Scotland, the functions of the Minister and the Secretary of State for Scotland acting jointly under the Electricity Act 1947 (Electricity Reorganisation (Scotland) Act 1954, s 1(1), (2) (repealed by the Electricity (Scotland) Act 1979, s 46(2), Sch 12 and replaced by provisions of that Act not printed in this title)). By s 1(3) of the 1954 Act the functions of the Minister in relation to the making of regulations under the Electric Lighting Act 1888, s 4, and the Electricity Act 1947, s 60 were transferred to the Secretary of State and the Minister acting jointly. By s 15(1) of, and Sch 1, Pt III to, the 1954 Act, references to the Minister or the Board of Trade are, in general, in relation to the Scottish Boards, to be construed as references to the Secretary of State.

The Ministry of Power was dissolved, and the functions of the Minister of Power transferred to the Minister of Technology by the Minister of Technology Order 1969, SI 1969/1498. The functions of the Minister of Technology in relation to the electricity supply industry were transferred to the Secretary of State by the Secretary of State for Trade and Industry Order 1970, SI 1970/1537. These functions were subsequently transferred to the Secretary of State by the Secretary of State (New Departments) Order 1974, SI 1974/692, and are now in practice exercised by the Secretary of State for Energy.

ELECTRIC LIGHTING ACT 1882

(45 & 46 Vict c 56)

ARRANGEMENT OF SECTIONS

An Act to facilitate and regulate the supply of Electricity for Lighting and other purposes in Great Britain and Ireland **[18 August 1882]**

Electricity (Supply) Acts 1882 to 1936. By the Electricity Supply (Meters) Act 1936, s 5(1) post, the following Acts may be cited together by this collective title:—the Electric Lighting Act 1882 (this Act); the Electric Lighting Act 1888 post; the Electric Lighting Act 1909 post; the Electricity (Supply) Act 1919 post; the Electricity (Supply) Act 1922 post; the Electricity (Supply) Act 1926 post; the Electricity (Supply) Act 1928 (repealed); the Electricity (Supply) Act 1933 (repealed); the Electricity (Supply) Act 1935 (repealed); and the Electricity Supply (Meters) Act 1936 post.

See also as to laying before Parliament of reports with respect to performance of the functions of the Secretary of State under these Acts, the Electricity Act 1957, s 10(6) post.

Construction. The Electricity (Supply) Acts 1882 to 1936 are to be construed as one Act; see the Electricity Supply (Meters) Act 1936, s 5(1) post. See also the Electricity Act 1947, Sch 4, Pt I post, the Electricity Reorganisation (Scotland) Act 1954, s 17 post, the Electricity Act 1957, Sch 4, Pt II post, and the Electricity (Amendment) Act 1961, Schedule post.

Northern Ireland. This Act was repealed in relation to Northern Ireland by the Electricity Supply (Northern Ireland) Order 1972, SI 1972/1072.

1 Short title

This Act may be cited for all purposes as the Electric Lighting Act 1882.

2–11 (*Repealed by the Electricity Act 1947, s 57(7) Sch 5; for saving of provisional orders made under s 4, see the Electricity Act 1947, s 57(7), proviso (a) post; for saving of regulations made under s 6, see s 60(2) of that Act post.*)

12 Incorporation of certain provisions of Clauses Consolidation Acts

The provisions of the following Acts shall be incorporated with this Act; that is to say,

(1) The Lands Clauses Acts, except the enactments with respect to the purchase and taking of lands otherwise than by agreement, and except the enactments with respect to the entry upon lands by the promoters of the undertaking; and

(2) The provisions of the Gasworks Clauses Act 1847, with respect to breaking up streets for the purpose of laying pipes, and with respect to waste or misuse of the gas or injury to the pipes and other works, except so much thereof as relates to the use of any burner other than such as has been provided or approved of by the undertakers; and

(3) Sections thirty-eight to forty-two inclusive, and sections forty-five and forty-six, of the Gasworks Clauses Act 1871.

[For the purposes of this Act, in the construction of all the enactments incorporated by this section the "promoters" or "undertakers" means an Electricity Board and "the undertaking" means the business carried on by such a Board, and "the special

Act" means the Electricity (Supply) Acts 1882 to 1936 (including, as regards the North of Scotland Board, the Act of 1943), the Electricity Act 1947, and any local enactment (within the meaning of the last named Act) applicable to any such Board.]

In the construction of the said Lands Clauses Acts, "land" includes easements in or relating to lands.

In the construction of the said Gasworks Clauses Act 1847, and the Gasworks Clauses Act 1871, the said Acts shall be construed as if "gas" meant "electricity" and as if "pipe" meant electric line, and "works" meant "works" as defined by this Act, and as if "the limits of the special Act" meant [in relation to the [Generating Board], [the whole of England and Wales], in relation to any Area Board, the area for which that Board is for the time being established, and in relation to the North of Scotland Board, the North of Scotland District].

All offences, forfeitures, penalties, and damages under the said incorporated provisions of the said Acts or any of them may be prosecuted and may be recovered in manner by the said Acts respectively enacted in relation thereto, provided that sums recoverable under the provisions of section forty of the Gasworks Clauses Act 1871, shall not be recovered as penalties, but may be recovered summarily as civil debts.

NOTES

The words in the first and second pairs of square brackets were substituted by the Electricity Act 1947, s 57(1), Sch 4, Pt I, the words "Generating Board" were substituted by the Electricity Act 1957, s 42(1), Sch 4, Pt II, and the words "the whole of England and Wales" were substituted by the Electricity Reorganisation (Scotland) Act 1954, s 15(1), Sch 1, Pt III.

This section (with omissions) is embodied in the Electric Lighting (Clauses) Act 1899, Schedule, Appendix post.

North of Scotland Board. References to the North of Scotland Board include references to the South of Scotland Electricity Board; see the Electricity Reorganisation (Scotland) Act 1954, Sch 1, Pt III post.

North of Scotland District. References to the North of Scotland District include references to the district of the South of Scotland Electricity Board; see the Electricity Reorganisation (Scotland) Act 1954, Sch 1, Pt III post.

Generating Board. The reference is to the Central Electricity Generating Board established under the Electricity Act 1957, s 2 post.

England; Wales. For meaning, see the Interpretation Act 1978, ss 5, 22(1), Sch 1, Sch 2, para 5(a), Vol 41, title Statutes.

Summarily as civil debts. By the Magistrates' Courts Act 1980, s 58(1), Vol 27, title Magistrates, a magistrates' court has power to make an order on complaint for the payment of any money which is recoverable summarily as a civil debt; and by s 127(1) of that Act, the complaint may not be heard unless it was made within six months from the time when the matter of complaint arose.

Definitions. For "Area Board", see the Electricity Act 1947, s 1(3) post; for "electric line", "electricity", "Lands Clauses Acts", "street" and "works", see s 32 post; for "Electricity Board", see s 1(3) of the 1947 Act; for "North of Scotland Board" and "North of Scotland District", see s 67(1), (2) of the 1947 Act.

Gasworks Clauses Act 1847; Gasworks Clauses Act 1871. Repealed by the Gas Act 1948, s 76, Sch 4, and replaced by Sch 3 to that Act. The 1948 Act was repealed by the Gas Act 1972, s 49(3), Sch 8. The repeal of the incorporated Acts does not affect their operation as incorporated; see in particular, *R v Smith* (1873) LR 8 QB 146, 42 LJMC 46. The incorporated provisions (the Gasworks Clauses Act 1847, ss 6, 7, 18–20 and the Gasworks Clauses Act 1871, ss 38–42, 45, 46) are set out in the Electric Lighting (Clauses) Act 1899, Schedule, Appendix post, which is incorporated with the Electricity Act 1947 by s 57(2) of that Act post.

Electricity (Supply) Acts 1882 to 1936. For the Acts which may be cited by this collective title, see the Introductory Note to this Act.

Act of 1943. Ie the Hydro-Electric Development (Scotland) Act 1943 (c 32) (largely repealed by the Electricity (Scotland) Act 1979 (c 11) and replaced by provisions of that Act (not printed in this work)); see the Electricity Act 1947, s 67(1), (2) post.

Electricity Act 1947. See this title post.

13 Restriction on breaking up of private streets, railways, and tramways

Nothing in this Act or in any Act incorporated therewith shall authorise or empower [the North of Scotland Board or any Area Board] to break up any street which is not repairable by [the inhabitants at large] or any railway or tramway, without the consent of the authority, company, or person by whom such street, railway, or tramway is repairable, unless in pursuance of special powers in that behalf inserted in the license, order, or special Act, or with the written consent of the Board of Trade, and the Board of Trade shall not in any case . . . give any such consent until notice has been given to such authority, company, or person by advertisement or otherwise, as the Board of Trade may direct, and an opportunity has been given to such authority, company, or person to state any objections they may have thereto.

NOTES

The words in the first pair of square brackets were substituted, and the words omitted were repealed, by the Electricity Act 1947, s 57, Sch 4, Pt I. The words in the second pair of square brackets were substituted, with a saving, by the Public Utilities Street Works Act 1950, s 17(2)(a), Sch 5.

General Note. This section must be read in the light of the Public Utilities Street Works Act 1950, s 20(3), Vol 20, title Highways, Streets and Bridges (under which this section has no effect in relation to the breaking up of a street as to which no liability to repair subsists).

North of Scotland Board. See the note to s 12 ante.

Power to break up streets. See s 12(2) ante.

Board of Trade. The functions of the Board of Trade under this section are now exercised by the Secretary of State for Energy; see the Preliminary Note to this title.

Definitions. For "Area Board", see the Electricity Act 1947, s 1(3) post; for "company" and "street", see s 32 post.

14 Restrictions as to above-ground works

Notwithstanding anything in this Act or in any Act incorporated therewith, the undertakers shall not be authorised to place any electric line above ground, along, over, or across any street, without the express consent of the local authority, and the local authority may require the undertakers to forthwith remove any electric line placed by them contrary to the provisions of this section, or may themselves remove the same, and recover the expenses of such removal from the undertakers in a summary manner; and where any electric line has been placed above ground by the undertakers in any position, a court of summary jurisdiction, upon complaint made, if they are of opinion that such electric line is or is likely to become dangerous to the public safety, may, notwithstanding any such consent as aforesaid, make an order directing and authorising the removal of such electric line by such person and upon such terms as they may think fit.

NOTES

Above-ground works. As to consents necessary for the placing of works above ground, see also the Electric Lighting (Clauses) Act 1899, Schedule, s 10(b) and the Electricity (Supply) Act 1919, ss 21, 22 post.

For safety regulations concerning overhead lines, see the Electricity (Overhead Lines) Regulations 1970, SI 1970/1355.

Definitions. For "electric line" and "street", see s 32 post; for "local authority", see s 31 post; and see as to "undertakers", the Electricity Act 1947, Sch 4, Pt I post.

15 Power to undertakers to alter position of pipes and wires

Subject to the provisions of this Act and of the license, order, or special Act authorising them to supply electricity, . . . the undertakers may alter the position of any pipes or wires being under any street or place authorised to be broken up by them which may interfere with the exercise of their powers under this Act, on previously making or securing such compensation to the owners of such pipes or wires, and on complying with such conditions as to the mode of making such alterations as may before the commencement of such alterations be agreed upon between the undertakers and owners, or in case of difference as may be determined in manner prescribed by the license or provisional order authorising the undertakers to supply electricity, or where no such manner is prescribed as may be determined by arbitration, and any local or other public authority, company, or person may in like manner alter the position of any electric lines or works of the undertakers, being under any such street or place as aforesaid, which may interfere with the lawful exercise of any powers vested in such local or other public authority, company, or person in relation to such street or place, subject to the like provisions conditions, and restrictions as are in this section contained with reference to the alteration of the position of any pipes or wires by the undertakers.

NOTES

The words omitted were repealed by the Electricity Act 1947, s 57(1), Sch 4, Pt I.

This section was repealed with savings by the Public Utilities Street Works Act 1950, s 24(2)(a), Sch 5, Vol 20, title Highways, Streets and Bridges, so far as it relates to the alteration for the purposes of the authority's works, as defined in Pt II of that Act, of the position of any electric lines or other works in a street or in controlled land.

Alteration of pipes and wires. Cf the Electric Lighting (Clauses) Act 1899, Schedule, s 17 post.

Arbitration. See s 28 post.

Definitions. For "company", "electricity", "street" and "works", see s 32 post; and see as to "license, order, or special Act" and "undertakers", the Electricity Act 1947, Sch 4, Pt I post, in conjunction with the definition of "enactment" in s 67(1) of that Act post.

16 Clause for protection of canals

If at any time after [an Electricity Board or any undertakers whose undertaking has been transferred to any such Board] have placed any works under, in, upon, over, along or across any canal, any person having power to construct docks, basins or other works upon any land adjoining to or near such canal, constructs any dock, basin or work on such land, but is prevented by the works of [an Electricity Board or any undertakers whose undertaking has been transferred to any such Board] from forming a communication for the convenient passage of vessels with or without masts between such dock, basin or other work, and such canal; or if the business of such dock, basin or other work is interfered with by reason or in consequence of any such works of [an Electricity Board or any undertakers whose undertaking has been transferred to any such Board] then the undertakers at the request of such person, and on having reasonable facilities afforded them by him for placing works round such dock, basin or other work, under, in, upon, over, along or across land belonging to or under his control, shall remove and place their work accordingly. If any dispute arises between the undertakers and such person as to the facilities to be afforded to the undertakers, or as to the direction in which the works are to be placed, it shall be determined by arbitration.

NOTES

The words in square brackets in this section were substituted by the Electricity Act 1947, s 57(1), Sch 4, Pt I.

This section was repealed with a saving by the Public Utilities Street Works Act 1950, s 24(2)(a), Sch 5, Vol 20, title Highways, Streets and Bridges, so far as it relates to the removal for the purposes of the authority's works as defined in Pt II of that Act, of any works in a street or in controlled land.

Arbitration. See s 28 post.

Further provisions. See also the Electric Lighting (Clauses) Act 1899, Schedule, ss 15, 19 post; and see as to wayleaves, the Electricity (Supply) Act 1919, s 22 post.

Definitions. For "Electricity Board", see the Electricity Act 1947, s 1(3) post; for "works", see s 32, post; and see as to "undertakers" and "undertaking", Sch 4, Pt I, to the 1947 Act post.

17 Compensation for damage

In the exercise of the powers in relation to the execution of works given them under this Act, or any license, order, or special Act, the undertakers shall cause as little detriment and inconvenience and do as little damage as may be, and shall make full compensation to all bodies and persons interested for all damage sustained by them by reason or in consequence of the exercise of such powers, the amount and application of such compensation in case of difference to be determined by arbitration.

NOTES

Construction of section. The provisions of this section relate to payment of compensation for damage caused by the execution of works required to supply electricity and not to damage caused by their user when constructed; see *Shelfer v City of London Electric Lighting Co* [1895] 1 Ch 287, [1891–4] All ER Rep 838, CA.

Arbitration. See s 28 post.

Definitions. For "works", see s 32 post; and see as to "license, order, or special Act" and "undertakers", the Electricity Act 1947, Sch 4, Pt I post, in conjunction with the definition of "enactment", in s 67(1) of that Act.

18 Undertakers not to prescribe special form of lamp or burner

The undertakers shall not be entitled to prescribe any special form of [electrical fittings] to be used by any company or person, or in any way to control or interfere with the manner in which electricity supplied by them under this Act, and any license, order or special Act is used: Provided always that no local authority, company, or person shall be at liberty to use any form of [electrical fittings] or to use the electricity supplied to them for any purposes, or to deal with it in any manner so as to unduly or improperly interfere with the supply of electricity supplied to any other local authority, company, or person by the undertakers, and if any dispute or difference arises between the undertakers, and any local authority, company, or person entitled to be supplied with electricity under this Act, or any license, order, or special Act, as to the matters aforesaid, such dispute or difference shall be determined by arbitration.

NOTES

The words in square brackets were substituted by the Electricity Act 1947, s 57(1), Sch 4, Pt I.

Arbitration. See s 28 post.

Definitions. For "company" and "electricity", see s 32 post; for "electrical fittings", see the Electricity Act 1947, s 67(1), (2) post; for "local authority", see s 31 post; and see as to "license, order, or special Act" and "undertakers", the Electricity Act 1947, Sch 4, Pt I post, in conjunction with the definition of "enactment" in s 67(1) of that Act post.

19, 20 (*Repealed by the Electricity Act 1947, s 57(7), Sch 5.*)

21 Recovery of charges, etc

If any local authority, company, or person neglect to pay any charge for electricity or any other sum due from them to the undertakers in respect of the supply of electricity to such local authority, company, or person, the undertakers may cut off such supply, and for that purpose may cut or disconnect any electric line or other work through which electricity may be supplied, and may, until such charge or other sum, together with any expenses incurred by the undertakers in cutting off such supply of electricity as aforesaid, are fully paid, but no longer, discontinue the supply of electricity to such local authority, company, or person.

NOTES

Charge. As to fixing charges for electricity supply, see the Electricity Act 1947, s 37 post.

Provisions for the recovery of charges are contained in the Gasworks Clauses Act 1871, s 40 (incorporated by s 12 ante, and set out in the Electric Lighting (Clauses) Act 1899, Schedule, Appendix post).

Cut off. For further powers to undertakers to refuse to supply energy to persons where payments are in arrear, see the Electric Lighting Act 1909, s 18 post. See also as to notice to be given by consumers before quitting premises, s 17 of that Act post, and for power to recover charges for re-connection after supplies have been lawfully cut off, the Electricity (Supply) Act 1926, s 45 post.

Definitions. For "company", "electric line" and "electricity", see s 32 post; for "local authority", see s 31 post; and see as to "undertakers", the Electricity Act 1947, Sch 4, Pt I post.

22 Injuring works with intent to cut off supply of electricity

Any person who unlawfully and maliciously cuts or injures any electric line or work with intent to cut off any supply of electricity shall be guilty of felony, and be liable to be kept in penal servitude for any term not exceeding five years, or to be imprisoned with or without hard labour for any term not exceeding two years; but nothing in this section shall exempt a person from any proceeding for any offence which is punishable under any other provision of this Act, or under any other Act, or at common law, so that no person be punished twice for the same offence.

NOTES

Felony. The old common law classification of crimes as treasons, felonies and misdemeanours has been abolished, although certain offences against the security of the Crown and state remain treason. All distinctions between felonies and misdemeanours were abolished by the Criminal Law Act 1967, s 1(1), see Vol 12, title Criminal Law. Former felonies were thereafter to be treated as misdemeanours had been. By virtue of s 10 of the 1967 Act, in conjunction with Schs 2, 3 to that Act, all references in pre-1967 enactments to felonies are to be taken as being references to "offences".

Offences under this section are now triable either way by virtue of the Magistrates' Courts Act 1980, s 17, Sch 1, para 10, Vol 27, title Magistrates.

Penal servitude; hard labour. The courts now have no power to sentence a person to penal servitude or to imprisonment with hard labour; see the Criminal Justice Act 1948, s 1(1), (2), Vol 12, title Criminal Law. That section also provides that every enactment conferring power on a court to pass such sentence is to be construed as conferring power to pass a sentence of imprisonment for a similar term. Accordingly the maximum sentence under this section is five years' imprisonment.

Further provisions. For provisions as to penalties for damage to apparatus, see the Gasworks Clauses Act 1847, s 19, and the Gasworks Clauses Act 1871, s 38, both incorporated by s 12 ante, and set out in the Electric Lighting (Clauses) Act 1899, Schedule, Appendix post.

Definitions. For "electric lines", "electricity" and "works", see s 32 post.

23 (Repealed by the Larceny Act 1916, s 48, Schedule.)

24 Power to enter lands or premises for ascertaining quantities of electricity consumed, or to remove fittings, etc

Any officer appointed by the undertakers may at all reasonable times enter any premises to which electricity is or has been supplied [(whether by the undertakers or by any other person) directly through electric lines belonging to the undertakers], in order to inspect the electric lines, meters, accumulators, fittings, works, and apparatus for the supply of electricity belonging to the undertakers, and for the purpose of ascertaining the quantity of electricity consumed or supplied, or where a supply of electricity is no longer required, or where the undertakers are authorised to take away and cut off the supply of electricity from any premises, for the purpose of removing any electric lines, accumulators, fittings, works, or apparatus belonging to the undertakers, repairing all damage caused by such entry, inspection, or removal.

NOTES

The words in square brackets were substituted by the Energy Act 1983, s 14(1).

Extension. This section and s 25 post are extended by the Electric Lighting Act 1909, s 16 post. On the other hand, rights of entry for the purposes of an electricity board are restricted by the Rights of Entry (Gas and Electricity Boards) Act 1954 post.

Definitions. For "electric lines", "electricity" and "works", see s 32 post; and see as to "undertakers", the Electricity Act 1947, Sch 4, Pt I post.

25 Electric lines, etc not to be subject to distress in certain cases

Where any electric lines, meters, accumulators, fittings, works, or apparatus belonging to the undertakers are placed in or upon any premises not being in the possession of the undertakers for the purpose of [a supply of electricity (whether by the undertakers or any other person) directly through electric lines belonging to them], such electric lines, meters, accumulators, fittings, works, or apparatus shall not be subject to distress or to the landlord's remedy for rent of the premises where the same may be, nor to be taken in execution under any process of a court of law or equity, or any proceedings in bankruptcy against the person in whose possession the same may be.

NOTES

The words in square brackets were substituted by the Energy Act 1983, s 25, Sch 3, para 1.

Extension. See the note to s 24 ante.

Definitions. For "electric line", "electricity" and "works", see s 32 post; and see as to "undertakers", the Electricity Act 1947, Sch 4, Pt I post.

26 Protection of Postmaster-General

[The undertakers shall not make any alteration of any telecommunication apparatus kept installed for the purposes of a telecommunications code system except in accordance with the telecommunications code.

The undertakers shall not, in the exercise of the powers conferred by this Act, or by any licence, order, or special Act, lay down any electric line or do any other work for the supply of electricity whereby any telecommunication apparatus kept installed for the purposes of a telecommunications code system is or may be injuriously affected.

Before any such electric line is laid down or work (other than repairs) is done within ten yards of any such telecommunication apparatus, the undertakers or their agents shall, one month or (in the case of the laying of service lines to consumers' premises) seven clear days before commencing such work, give written notice to the operator of the telecommunications code system in question specifying the course and nature of the work, including the gauge of any electric lines.

The undertakers and their agents shall conform with such reasonable requirements, either general or special, as may from time to time be made by the operator of any telecommunications code system for the purpose of preventing any telecommunication apparatus kept installed for the purposes of that system from being injuriously affected by any work done within ten yards of that apparatus.

Any difference which arises between the operator of a telecommunications code system and the undertakers or their agents with respect to any of the requirements of the preceding provisions of this section shall be determined by arbitration.]

In the event of any contravention of or wilful non-compliance with this section by the undertakers or their agents the undertakers shall be liable to a fine not exceeding ten pounds for every day during which such contravention or non-compliance continues, or, if the [service provided by the telecommunications code system in question] is wilfully interrupted, not exceeding fifty pounds for every day on which such interruption continues.

Provided that nothing in this section shall subject the undertakers or their agents to a fine under this section, if they satisfy the court having cognizance of the case that the immediate execution of the work was required to avoid an accident, or otherwise was a work of emergency, and that they [forthwith served on the operator of the telecommunications code system in question] a notice of the execution thereof, stating the reason for executing the same without previous notice.

[For the purposes of this section telecommunication apparatus shall be deemed to be injuriously affected where the service provided by the telecommunication system for the purposes of which that apparatus is used is in any manner affected.

Paragraph 23 of the telecommunications code (which provides a procedure for certain cases where works involve the alteration of telecommunication apparatus) shall apply to the undertakers for the purposes of any works authorised by this Act.

Paragraph 1(2) of the telecommunications code (alteration of apparatus to include moving, removal or replacement of apparatus) shall apply for the purposes of this section as it applies for the purposes of that code.

The preceding provisions of this section shall not apply in relation to any telecommunication apparatus which is kept installed in a conduit or structure falling within subsection (6)(a) of section 98 of the Telecommunications Act 1984 (by virtue of which telecommunication apparatus may be installed in electricity conduits etc).]

NOTES

The words in square brackets were substituted by the Telecommunications Act 1984, s 109, Sch 4, para 6; accordingly the marginal note is obsolete.

Agents. An agent is a person who has the authority, express or implied, to act on behalf of another, and who consents to act (*Pole v Leask* (1863) 33 LJ Ch 155 at 161). See, further, 1 Halsbury's Laws (4th edn) para 701 and 16 Halsbury's Laws (4th edn) paras 501 et seq.

Written. Unless the contrary intention appears this includes other modes of representing or reproducing words in a visible form; see the Interpretation Act 1978, s 5, Sch 1, Vol 41, title Statutes.

From time to time. This means "as the occasion shall arise" or "as and when it is appropriate so to do"; see *Holliday v Wakefield Corpn* (1887) 57 LT 559 at 562, 563, per Mathew J, and *Re Von Dembinska, ex p The Debtor* [1954] 2 All ER 46 at 48, [1954] 1 WLR 748, CA, per Evershed MR.

Wilfully. This expression, in the words of Lord Russell of Killowen CJ, in *R v Senior* [1899] 1 QB 283 at 290, 291, [1895–9] All ER Rep 511 at 514, "means that the act is done deliberately and intentionally, not by accident or inadvertence, but so that the mind of the person who does the act goes with it". See also, in particular, *R v Walker* (1934) 24 Cr App Rep 117; *Eaton v Cobb* [1950] 1 All ER 1016, 114 JP 271; *Arrowsmith v Jenkins* [1963] 2 QB 561, [1963] 2 All ER 210; *Rice v Connolly* [1966] 2 QB 414, [1966] 2 All ER 649; *Dibble v Ingleton* [1972] 1 QB 480, sub nom *Ingleton v Dibble* [1972] 1 All ER 275; *Willmott v Atack* [1977] QB 498, [1976] 3 All ER 794; *Wershof v Metropolitan Police Comr* [1978] 3 All ER 540, [1978] Crim LR 424; and *R v Sheppard* [1981] AC 394, [1980] 3 All ER 899, HL.

Arbitration. See s 28 post.

Protection of telecommunication apparatus. See also the Electric Lighting Act 1888, s 4 post; the Electric Lighting (Clauses) Act 1899, Schedule, ss 14, 20, 69 post; the Electricity Act 1947, s 9(3) post; and the Electricity Act 1957, s 28(8) post.

Definitions. By virtue of the Telecommunications Act 1984, s 109, Sch 4, para 1(1), Vol 45, title Telecommunications and Broadcasting, for "telecommunication apparatus" see Sch 2, para 1(1) to the 1984 Act; for "telecommunication system", see s 4(1), (2) of that Act; for "the operator", "the telecommunications code", and "telecommunications code system", see Sch 4, para 1(1) to that Act; for "electricity", "electric line" and "works", see s 32 post; and see as to "licence, order, or special Act", and "undertakers", the Electricity Act 1947, Sch 4, Pt I post, in conjunction with the definition of "enactment" in s 67(1) of that Act post.

Telecommunications Act 1984, s 98(6)(a). See Vol 45, title Telecommunications and Broadcasting.

27 (*Repealed by the Electric Lighting Act 1888, s 2.*)

28 Arbitration

Where any matter is by this Act, or any license, order, or special Act, directed to be determined by arbitration, such matter shall, except as otherwise expressly provided, be determined by an engineer or other fit person to be nominated as arbitrator by the Board of Trade on the application of either party, and the expenses of the arbitration shall be borne and paid as the arbitrator directs.

Any license or provisional order granted under this Act shall be deemed to be a special Act within the meaning of the Board of Trade Arbitrations, etc, Act 1874.

NOTES

Directed to be determined by arbitration. See ss 15–17, 26 ante.

Board of Trade. The arbitrator will now be nominated by the Secretary of State for Energy; see the Preliminary Note to this title.

For application of provisions of the Arbitration Act 1950, Pt I, Vol 2, title Arbitration, see s 31 of that Act.

Board of Trade Arbitrations, etc, Act 1874. See Vol 36, title Railways, Inland Waterways and Pipelines.

29, 30 (*Repealed by the Electricity Act 1947, s 57, Sch 5.*)

[31 Definition of local authority, etc

In this Act, unless the context otherwise requires, the expression "local authority" means—

(*a*) in England and Wales the council of a . . . district or . . . borough and the Common Council of the City of London; and

(*b*) (*applies to Scotland only*).]

NOTES

This section was substituted by the Electricity Act 1947, s 57(1), Sch 4, Pt I.

The words omitted from para (*a*) in the first place were repealed by the Local Authorities etc (Miscellaneous Provision) (No 2) Order 1974, SI 1974/595, art 3(22), Sch 1, Pt I, and those omitted from that paragraph in the second place were repealed by the Local Authorities etc (Miscellaneous Provision) (No 3) Order 1975, SI 1975/1636, art 4(1).

England; Wales. For meaning, see the Interpretation Act 1978, ss 5, 22(1), Sch 1, Sch 2, para 5(*a*), Vol 41, title Statutes.

District. As to the districts in England and Wales and their councils, see the Local Government Act 1972, ss 1(1), (3), (4), 2(2), (3), 20(1), (3), 21(2), (3), Sch 1, Pt I, Sch 4, Pt II, Vol 25, title Local Government.

Borough. The boroughs, other than London boroughs, existing immediately before 1 April 1974 were abolished on that date by the Local Government Act 1972, ss 1(9), (10), 20(6), Vol 25, title Local Government, and the reference to a borough no longer has any effect.

Common Council of the City of London. Ie the mayor, aldermen and commons of the City of London in common council assembled; see the City of London (Various Powers) Act 1958, s 5, Vol 26, title London.

---

32 Interpretation

In this Act, unless the context otherwise requires—

The expression "electricity" means electricity, electric current, or any like agency:

The expression "electric line" means a wire or wires, conductor, or other means used for the purpose of conveying, transmitting, or distributing electricity with any casing, coating, covering, tube, pipe, or insulator enclosing, surrounding, or supporting the same, or any part thereof, or any apparatus connected therewith for the purpose of conveying, transmitting, or distributing electricity or electric currents:

The expression "works" means and includes electric lines, also any buildings, machinery, engines, works, matters, or things of whatever description required to supply electricity and to carry into effect the object of the undertakers under this Act:

The expression "company" means any body of persons corporate or unincorporate:

The expression "Lands Clauses Acts" means the Lands Clauses Consolidation Acts 1845, 1860, and 1869:

The expression "street" includes any square, court, or alley, highway, lane, road, thoroughfare, or public passage, or place, within the area in which the undertakers are authorised to supply electricity by this Act or any license, order, or special Act:

.   .   .   .   .

NOTES

The words omitted were repealed by the Post Office Act 1969, s 141(1), Sch 11, Pt II.

Electric line. A supporting tower is not within this definition; see *Central Electricity Generating Board v Jennaway* [1959] 3 All ER 409, [1959] 1 WLR 937.

This definition is applied by the Telecommunications Act 1984, s 98(9), Vol 45, title Telecommunications and Broadcasting.

Undertakers. See, as to construction, the Electricity Act 1947, Sch 4, Pt I post.

Lands Clauses Consolidation Acts 1845, 1860 and 1869. Ie the Lands Clauses Consolidation Act 1845 and the Lands Clauses Consolidation Act Amendment Act 1860, both Vol 9, title Compulsory Acquisition, and the Lands Clauses Consolidation Act 1869 (repealed).

33 For the protection of mines

Nothing in this Act shall limit or interfere with the rights of any owner, lessee, or occupier of any mines or minerals lying under or adjacent to any road along or across which any electric line shall be laid to work such mines and minerals.

NOTE

Electric line. For meaning, see s 32 ante.

34 Provision as to general Acts

Nothing in this Act shall exempt the undertakers or their undertaking from the provisions of any general Act relating to the supply of electricity which may be passed in this or any future session of Parliament.

NOTE

Definitions. For "electricity", see s 32 ante; and see as to "undertakers", the Electricity Act 1947, Sch 4, Pt I post.

35–37 *(S 35 repealed by the Post Office Act 1969, s 141(1), Sch 11, Pt II; s 36 applies to Scotland only; s 37 spent consequent upon the repeal of this Act in relation to Northern Ireland by the Electricity Supply (Northern Ireland) Order 1972, SI 1972/1072.)*

(Schedule repealed by the Electricity Act 1947, s 57(7), Sch 5.)

ELECTRIC LIGHTING ACT 1888

(51 & 52 Vict c 12)

An Act to amend the Electric Lighting Act 1882   [28 June 1888]

The whole Act is repealed by the Energy Act 1983, s 36, Sch 4, Pt I post as from a day to be appointed under s 37 of that Act.

Northern Ireland. The whole Act was repealed as to Northern Ireland by the Electricity Supply (Northern Ireland) Order 1972, SI 1972/1072.

1–3 *(Repealed by the Electricity Act 1947, s 57(7), Sch 5.)*

4 Restrictions as to placing of electric lines, etc

(1) *Where in any case any electric line or other work may have been laid down or erected in, over, along, across, or under any street, for the purpose of supplying electricity, or may have*

been laid down or erected in any other position for such purpose in such a manner as not to be entirely enclosed within any building or buildings, or where any electric line or work so laid down or erected may be used for such purpose otherwise than under and subject to the provisions of a licence, order, or special Act, the Board of Trade, if they think fit, may, by notice in writing under the hand of one of the secretaries or assistant secretaries of the Board of Trade, to be served upon the body or person owning or using or entitled to use such electric line or work, require that such electric line or work shall be continued and used only in accordance with such conditions and subject to such regulations for the protection of the public safety and [of any telecommunication apparatus kept installed for the purposes of a telecommunications code system or of any other telecommunication apparatus lawfully kept installed in any position], as the Board of Trade may by or in pursuance of such notice prescribe, and in case of non-compliance with the said regulations then the Board of Trade may require such body or person to remove such electric line or work: Provided that nothing in this subsection shall apply to any electric line or work laid down or erected by any body or person for the supply of electricity generated upon any premises occupied by such body or person to any other part of such premises.

(2) Where in any case any electric line or work is used for the supply of electricity in such a manner as to injuriously affect [any telecommunication apparatus kept installed for the purposes of a telecommunications code system or to affect the service provided by any such system, the Secretary of State may], by notice to be served upon the body or person owning or using or entitled to use such electric line or work, require that such supply be continued only in accordance with such conditions and regulations for the protection of [any telecommunication apparatus kept installed for the purposes of a telecommunications code system and the service provided by any such system as the Secretary of State may by or in pursuance of such notice prescribe; and in default of compliance with such conditions and regulations the Secretary of State may require] that the supply of electricity through such electric line or work shall be forthwith discontinued: Provided that nothing in this subsection shall apply to the supply of electricity through any electric line or work laid down or erected under and subject to the provisions of any licence, order, or special Act, or which may be used in accordance with any conditions or regulations prescribed by the Board of Trade by or in pursuance of any notice given by them under this section.

(3) If any body or person fails to comply with the requirements of any notice which may be served upon them or him under this section, such body or person shall be liable to a penalty not exceeding [level 2 on the standard scale] for every such offence, to be recovered summarily, and any court of summary jurisdiction, on complaint made, may make an order directing and authorising the removal of any electric line or work specified in such notice by such person and upon such terms as they may think fit.

(4) Any notice authorised to be served under this section upon any body or person may be served by the same being addressed to such body or person, and being left at or transmitted through the post to any office of such body or the usual or last known place of abode of such person; and any notice so served by post shall be deemed to have been served at the time when the letter containing the notice would be delivered in the usual course of post, and in proving such service it shall be sufficient to prove that the letter containing the notice was properly addressed and put into the post.

(5) In this section terms and expressions to which by the Electric Lighting Act 1882 meanings are assigned shall have the same respective meanings, provided that the term "street" shall include any square, court, or alley, highway, lane, road, thoroughfare, or public passage or place whatever . . .

(6) Nothing in this section shall apply [to any electric line, being an electric line kept installed solely for the purposes of a telecommunication system], except by way of protection, as in this section provided.

NOTES

The whole Act is prospectively repealed as noted in the Introductory Note.

The words in square brackets in sub-ss (1), (2), (6) were substituted, and the words omitted from sub-s (5) were repealed, by the Telecommunications Act 1984, s 109(1), (6), Sch 4, para 8, Sch 7, Pt I.

The reference in sub-s (3) to level 2 on the standard scale is substituted by virtue of the Criminal Justice Act 1982, s 46, Vol 27, title Magistrates. The maximum fine was previously increased to £50 by the Criminal Law Act 1977, s 31(6).

Board of Trade. The functions of the Board of Trade under this section are now exercised by the Secretary of State for Energy; see the Preliminary Note to this title.

Secretary of State. Ie one of Her Majesty's Principal Secretaries of State; see the Interpretation Act 1978, s 5, Sch 1, Vol 41, title Statutes. The Secretary of State here concerned is the Secretary of State for Energy.

Standard scale. By the Criminal Justice Act 1982, ss 37(3), 75, Vol 27, title Magistrates, this means the standard scale set out in s 37(2) of that Act as amended by order made under the Magistrates' Courts Act 1980, s 143(1), in the same title. The scale as amended by the Criminal Penalties etc (Increase) Order 1984, SI 1984/447, art 3(4), Sch 4, is: level 1: £50; level 2: £100; level 3: £400; level 4: £1,000; and level 5: £2,000.

Recovered summarily. Summary jurisdiction and procedure are mainly governed by the Magistrates' Courts Act 1980, Vol 27, title Magistrates, and by rules made under s 144 of that Act.

Protection of telecommunication apparatus. See also the Electric Lighting Act 1882, s 26 ante, the Electric Lighting (Clauses) Act 1899, Schedule, ss 14, 20, 69 post, the Electricity Act 1947, s 9(3) post, and the Electricity Act 1957, s 28(8) post.

Liability for escape of electricity. The principle of *Rylands v Fletcher* (1868) LR 3 HL 330, [1861–73] All ER Rep 1, has been applied to the case of a man who creates an electric current for his own use, and who discharges it into the earth beyond his control (*National Telephone Co v Baker* [1893] 2 Ch 186, 62 LJ Ch 699); but see *Collingwood v Home and Colonial Stores Ltd* [1936] 3 All ER 200, 155 LT 550, CA, as to electricity used for domestic purposes; and see, generally, 16 Halsbury's Laws (4th edn) paras 213 et seq.

Definitions. For "electric line", "electricity", "street" and "work", see the Electric Lighting Act 1882, s 32 ante, in conjunction with sub-s (5) above; and see as to "license, order or special Act", the Electricity Act 1947, Sch 4, Pt I post in conjunction with the definition of "enactment" in s 67(1) of that Act post. By virtue of the Telecommunications Act 1984, s 109, Sch 4, para 1(1), Vol 45, title Telecommunications and Broadcasting, for "telecommunication apparatus" see Sch 2, para 1(1) to the 1984 Act; for "telecommunication system", see s 4(1), (2) of that Act; and for "telecommunications code system", see Sch 4, para 1(1) to that Act.

Regulations under this section. The Electricity Supply Regulations 1937 (El C 12B) were prescribed by the Electricity Commissioners (who exercised the power by virtue of the Electricity (Supply) Act 1919, s 2 (repealed)) and reprinted by HM Stationery Office in 1972.

5 Short title

This Act may be cited as the Electric Lighting Act 1888; and the Electric Lighting Act 1882 and this Act shall be read and construed together as one Act, and may be cited together for all purposes as the Electric Lighting Acts 1882 and 1888.

NOTES

The whole Act is prospectively repealed as noted in the Introductory Note.

Construction. The Electricity (Supply) Acts 1882 to 1936 (as to which, see the next note) are to be construed as one Act; see the Electricity Supply (Meters) Act 1936, s 5(1) post. See also the Electricity Act 1947, Sch 4, Pt I post; the Electricity Reorganisation (Scotland) Act 1954, s 17 post; and the Electricity Act 1957, Sch 4, Pt II post.

Electric Lighting Acts 1882 and 1888. For the Acts (including these Acts) which may be cited together as the Electricity (Supply) Acts 1882 to 1936, see the Introductory Note to the Electric Lighting Act 1882 ante.

Electric Lighting Act 1882. See this title ante.

ELECTRIC LIGHTING (CLAUSES) ACT 1899

(62 & 63 Vict c 19)

ARRANGEMENT OF SECTIONS

An Act for incorporating in one Act certain provisions usually contained in Provisional Orders made under the Acts relating to Electric Lighting   [9 August 1899]

By the Electricity Act 1947, s 57(2) post the Schedule to this Act is incorporated with that Act and has effect, as so incorporated, subject to the adaptations and modifications specified in Sch 4, Pt III to that Act. The Schedule to this Act, as so incorporated, is further adapted or modified by the Electricity Reorganisation (Scotland) Act 1954, s 15(1), Sch 1, Pt III post. All these adaptations and modifications are incorporated in the text of the Schedule as printed post.

Northern Ireland. The whole Act was repealed as to Northern Ireland by the Electricity Supply (Northern Ireland) Order 1972, SI 1972/1072.

1 Provisions in schedule to be incorporated in Electric Lighting Orders

.   .   .   .   .

The expression "Electric Lighting Acts" means in this Act the Electric Lighting Acts 1882 and 1888, and, so far as respects Scotland, the Electric Lighting Acts 1882 and 1888, and the Electric Lighting (Scotland) Act 1890.

.   .   .   .   .

NOTES

The words omitted from this section were repealed by the Electricity Act 1947, s 57(7), Sch 5. The marginal note is no longer applicable in view of such repeal.

Electric Lighting Acts 1882 and 1888. For the Acts (including these Acts) which may be cited as the Electricity (Supply) Acts 1882 to 1936, and which are to be construed as one Act, see the Introductory Note to the Electric Lighting Act 1882 ante.

Electric Lighting (Scotland) Act 1890. Repealed by the Electricity Act 1947, s 57(7), Sch 5.

2 Short title, extent, and commencement

(1) This Act may be cited as the Electric Lighting (Clauses) Act 1899.

(2), (3) . . .

NOTE

Sub-ss (2), (3) were repealed by the Electricity Act 1947, s 57(7), Sch 5.

SCHEDULE

1 Interpretation

The provisions of this schedule are to be read and construed subject in all respects to the provisions of the Electric Lighting Acts, and of any other Acts or parts of Acts incorporated therewith [and of the Electricity Act 1947 and, in relation to the North of Scotland District, of the Act of 1943], and those Acts and parts of Acts are in this schedule collectively referred to as "the principal Act"; and the several words, terms, and expressions to which by the principal Act meanings are assigned, shall have in this schedule the same respective meanings, provided that in this schedule—

.   .   .   .   .

The expression "energy" means electrical energy, and for the purposes of applying the provisions of the principal Act to [this Schedule] electrical energy shall be deemed to be an agency within the meaning of electricity as defined in the Electric Lighting Act 1882:

The expression "power" means electrical power or the rate per unit of time at which energy is supplied:

The expression "main" means any electric line ... through which energy may be supplied or intended to be supplied by the Undertakers for the purposes of general supply:

The expression "service line" means any electric line through which energy may be supplied or intended to be supplied by the Undertakers to a consumer either from any main or directly from the premises of the Undertakers:

The expression "distributing main" means the portion of any main which is used for the purpose of giving origin to service lines for the purposes of general supply:

The expression "general supply" means the general supply of energy to ordinary consumers, and includes, unless otherwise specially agreed with the local authority, the general supply of energy to the public lamps, ... but shall not include the supply of energy to any one or more particular consumers under special agreement:

.   .   .   .   .

The expression "county council" means the county council of the county in which the area of supply is situated:

The expression "consumer" means any body or person supplied or entitled to be supplied with energy by the Undertakers:

The expression "consumer's terminals" means the ends of the electric lines situate upon any consumer's premises ... at which the supply of energy is delivered from the service lines:

.   .   .   .   .

The expression "railway" includes any tramroad, that is to say, any tramway other than a tramway as herein-after defined:

The expression "tramway" means any tramway laid along any street:

The expression "daily penalty" means a penalty for each day on which any offence is continued after conviction therefor:

[The expression "Electricity regulations" means any regulations made [under section 60 of the Electricity Act 1947 or section 16 of the Energy Act 1983]].

.   .   .   .   .

The expression "plan" means a plan drawn to a horizontal scale of at least one inch to eighty-eight feet, and where possible a section drawn to the same horizontal scale as the plan and to a vertical scale of at least one inch to eleven feet, or to such other scale as [the Minister of Power] may approve of for both plan and section, together with such detail plan and sections as may be necessary.

[the expression "private supplier" means a person other than an Electricity Board who supplies electricity generated otherwise than by an Electricity Board.]

[References in this Schedule to telecommunication apparatus shall not include references to any telecommunication apparatus which is kept installed in a conduit or structure falling within subsection (6)(a) of section 98 of the Telecommunications Act 1984 (by virtue of which telecommunication apparatus may be installed in electricity conduits etc.); and, for the purposes of this Schedule, telecommunication apparatus shall be deemed to be injuriously affected where the service provided by the telecommunication system for the purposes of which that apparatus is used is in any manner affected.]

NOTES

The definition "telegraphic line" was repealed by the Telecommunications Act 1984, s 109(6), Sch 7, Pt I; the other words omitted were repealed, the words in the first pair of square brackets were inserted, and the words in square brackets in the definition "energy" were substituted, by the Electricity Act 1947, s 57(2), Sch 4, Pt III.

The definition "Electricity regulations" was substituted by the Electricity Act 1947, s 57(2), Sch 4, Pt III and the words in the inner pair of square brackets in that definition were substituted by the Energy Act 1983, s 25, Sch 3, para 2(2).

The words in square brackets in the definition "plan" were substituted by the Minister of Fuel and Power (Change of Style and Title) Order 1957, SI 1957/48 (see further the note below).

The definition "private supplier" was added by the Energy Act 1983, s 15, Sch 1, para 2.

The final paragraph in square brackets was added by the Telecommunications Act 1984, s 109(1), Sch 4, para 9(2).

North of Scotland District. References in this Schedule to the North of Scotland District and to the North of Scotland Board also include references to the South of Scotland District and the South of Scotland Board; see the Electricity Reorganisation (Scotland) Act 1954, Sch 1, Pt III post.

Undertakers. For meaning, see s 2 of this Schedule post.

County council. As to the counties in England and Wales and their councils, see the Local Government Act 1972, ss 1(1), (2), 2(1), (3), 20(1), (2), 21(1), (3), Sch 1, Pts I, II, Sch 4, Pt I, Vol 25, title Local Government.

Consumer's terminals. See *A-G v Gravesend Corpn* [1936] Ch 550, [1935] All ER Rep 706.

Daily penalty. See *Chepstow Electric Light and Power Co v Chepstow Gas and Coke Consumers' Co* [1905] 1 KB 198, 74 LJKB 28.

Minister of Power. The functions of the Minister of Power under this section are now exercised by the Secretary of State for Energy; see the Preliminary Note to this title.

Electricity Board. For meaning, see the Electricity Act 1947, s 1(3) post.

Telecommunication apparatus; telecommunication system. For meaning see, by virtue of the Telecommunications Act 1984, Sch 4, para 1(1), Vol 45, title Telecommunications and Broadcasting, Sch 2 to that Act and s 4(1), (2) of that Act respectively.

Electric Lighting Acts. For definition, see s 1 ante.

Electricity Act 1947; Energy Act 1983, s 16. See this title post.

The Act of 1943. Ie the Hydro-Electric Development (Scotland) Act 1943 (c 32) (largely repealed by the Electricity (Scotland) Act 1979 (c 11) and replaced by provisions of that Act (not printed in this work)); see the Electricity Act 1947, s 67(1), (2) post.

Electric Lighting Act 1882. For definition of "electricity", see s 32 of that Act ante.

Telecommunications Act 1984, s 98(6)(a). See Vol 45, title Telecommunications and Broadcasting.

Provisions as to Undertakers

2 Description of Undertakers

[The expression "Undertakers" means any Electricity Board, except that in sections twenty-one to thirty, thirty-nine to ... , sixty and eighty-one, the said expression does not include the [Generating Board], and the said section eighty-one shall not apply to anything done or omitted to be done by the North of Scotland Board in operating a generating station.]

NOTES

This section was substituted by the Electricity Act 1947, s 57(2), Sch 4, Pt III. The words omitted were repealed by the Energy Act 1983, ss 15, 36, Sch 1, para 3, Sch 4, Pt I and the words "Generating Board" were substituted by the Electricity Act 1957, s 42(1), Sch 4, Pt II.

North of Scotland Board. See the note "North of Scotland District" to s 1 of this Schedule ante.

Definitions. For "Electricity Board", see the Electricity Act 1947, s 1(3) post. By virtue of s 1 of this Schedule, for "the Generating Board" and "generating station", see s 67(1) of the 1947 Act post.

3 (*Repealed by the Electricity Act 1947, s 57(7), Sch 5.*)

Area of Supply

4 Area of supply and prohibition of supply beyond area

[The expression "the area of supply" means—

    (*a*) in relation to the [Generating Board], [the whole of England and Wales];

    (*b*) in relation to any Area Board the area for which the Board is for the time being established; and

    (*c*) in relation to the North of Scotland Board, the North of Scotland District];

    [(*d*) in relation to the South of Scotland Board, the South of Scotland District].

NOTES

This section was substituted by the Electricity Act 1947, s 57(2), Sch 4, Pt III. The words in square brackets in para (*a*) were substituted by the Electricity Reorganisation (Scotland) Act 1954, s 15(1), Sch 1, Pt III, and the Electricity Act 1957, s 42(1), Sch 4, Pt II. Para (*d*) was added by s 15(1) of, and Sch 1, Pt III to, the 1954 Act. The marginal note is no longer wholly applicable.

North of Scotland Board, etc. See the note "North of Scotland District" to s 1 of this Schedule ante.

Definitions. For "Area Board", see the Electricity Act 1947, s 1(3) post. By virtue of s 1 of this Schedule, for "the Generating Board" see s 67(1) of the 1947 Act post.

5–9 (*Repealed by the Electricity Act 1947, s 57(7), Sch 5.*)

Nature and Mode of Supply

10 Systems and mode of supply

Subject to the provisions of [this Schedule] and the principal Act, the Undertakers may supply energy within the area of supply for all . . . purposes . . . provided as follows:—

    (a) *The energy shall be supplied only by means of some system approved in writing by [the Minister of Power], and subject to the [Electricity regulations]; and*

    (b) The Undertakers shall not, [without the express consent and authorisation of [the Minister of Power] and the express consent of the local authority also], place any electric line [other than a service line] above ground except within premises in the sole occupation or control of the Undertakers, . . . ; *and*

    (c) *The Undertakers shall not permit any part of any circuit to be connected with earth except so far as may be necessary for carrying out the provisions of the [Electricity regulations], unless the connexion is for the time being approved by [the Minister of Power], . . . and is made in accordance with the conditions, if any, of that approval.*

NOTES

The words "the Minister of Power" were substituted by the Minister of Fuel and Power (Change of Style and Title) Order 1957, SI 1957/48 (see further the note below).

The words "other than a service line" in para (*b*) were inserted by the Electricity Act 1957, s 31, and the words omitted from that paragraph were repealed by ss 31, 42(3) of, and Sch 5, Pt I to, that Act.

The words in the first pair of square brackets in this section and the words in the first (outer) pair of square brackets in para (*b*) were substituted, and the words omitted in the first and second places from the beginning of this action were repealed, by the Electricity Act 1947, s 57(2), Sch 4, Pt III.

The words omitted from para (*c*) were repealed by the Telecommunications Act 1984, s 109(1), Sch 4, para 9(2).

Prospective amendment. The words in italics are repealed by the Energy Act 1983, s 36, Sch 4, Pt I, as from a day to be appointed under s 37(1) of that Act post.

System approved etc. For power to require the remedying of defects in the system or works, see s 69 of this Schedule post.

Minister of Power. The functions of the Minister of Power under this section are now exercised by the Secretary of State for Energy; see the Preliminary Note to this title.

Express consent and authorisation etc. For provisions as to applications for consent or authorisation of the Secretary of State, see the Electricity Act 1957, s 32 post, and for provisions as to public inquiries, see s 34 of that Act and Sch 2 thereto post.

Express consent of the local authority. Under the Electricity Supply Act 1919, s 21 post, the consent of the local authority is not required where the consent or authorisation of the Secretary of State is obtained; see *National Trust for Places of Historic Interest or Natural Beauty v Midlands Electricity Board* [1952] Ch 380, [1952] 1 All ER 298, CA.

See also *Central Electricity Generating Board v Jennaway* [1959] 3 All ER 409, [1959] 1 WLR 937.

Above ground. See also the Electric Lighting Act 1882, s 14 ante; the Electricity (Supply) Act 1919, s 22 post; and the Electricity (Supply) Act 1926, s 44 post.

Nuisance. The obtaining of the necessary consent and authorisation under para (*b*) above will not exempt the Undertakers from liability for nuisance; see s 81 post, and *Midwood & Co Ltd v Manchester Corpn* [1905] 2 KB 597, 74 LJKB 884, CA.

Definitions. For "area of supply", see s 4 of this Schedule ante. By virtue of s 1 of this Schedule ante, for "electric line", see the Electric Lighting Act 1882, s 32 ante, and for "local authority", see s 31 of the 1882 Act. For "Electricity regulations", "energy", "principal Act" and "service line", see s 1 of this Schedule ante, and for "undertakers", see s 2 of this Schedule ante.

Works

11 Additional provisions as to works

The provisions of [this Schedule] as to works shall be in addition but subject to those of the principal Act, and in particular those of the Gasworks Clauses Act 1847, with respect to breaking up streets, incorporated in the principal Act and set out in the Appendix to this schedule.

NOTES

The words in square brackets were substituted by the Electricity Act 1947, s 57(2), Sch 4, Pt III.

Definitions. For "the principal Act" see s 1 of this Schedule ante. By virtue of the same section, for "street" and "works", see the Electric Lighting Act 1882, s 32 ante.

Gasworks Clauses Act 1847. Cf the note to the Electric Lighting Act 1882, s 12 ante.

12 Powers for execution of works

[The provisions of this Schedule relating to the execution of works in, under, along or across any street or part of a street not repairable by the [inhabitants at large], or over or under any railway or tramway, shall, in the case of the North of Scotland Board, or any Area Board, only apply to streets, railways or tramways (if any), or parts thereof, which the Board are specially authorised to break up by any local enactment applicable to the Board, or to the breaking up of which the Minister has consented under section 13 of the Electric Lighting Act 1882, but save as aforesaid nothing in this Schedule shall authorise any such Board to break up or interfere with any such street, railway or tramway without the consent of the authority or person by whom it is repairable.]

NOTES

This section was substituted by the Electricity Act 1947, s 57(2), Sch 4, Pt III, and the words "inhabitants at large" were substituted by the Public Utilities Street Works Act 1950, s 15(3)(a), Sch 5.

North of Scotland Board. See the note to the Electric Lighting Act 1882, s 12 ante.

Street . . . not repairable etc. Apparently, if a street is repairable neither by the local authority nor by any other person, an Area Board has no power to break it up, even with the consent of the Minister under the Electric Lighting Act 1882, s 13 ante, unless it is specially authorised to do so by a local enactment; see *Andrews v Abertillery UC* [1911] 2 Ch 398, 80 LJ Ch 724, CA.

See, however, the Electricity (Supply) Act 1919, s 22 post, as to wayleaves.

Definitions. For "Area Board", see the Electricity Act 1947, s 1(3) post. By virtue of s 1 of this Schedule ante, for "local enactment" and "Minister", see s 67(1) of the 1947 Act; and for "street" and "works", see the Electric Lighting Act 1882, s 32 ante. For "North of Scotland Board", see s 67(1), (2) of the 1947 Act; and for "railway" and "tramway", see s 1 of this Schedule ante.

Electric Lighting Act 1882, s 13. See this title ante.

13 Street boxes

(1) Subject to the provisions of the principal Act, and [this Schedule], and the [Electricity regulations], the Undertakers may construct in any street such boxes as may be necessary for purposes in connexion with the supply of energy, including apparatus for the proper ventilation of the boxes: Provided that . . . no such box or apparatus shall be placed above ground, except with the consent of the authority, body, or person, by whom the street is repairable.

(2) Every such box shall be for the exclusive use of the Undertakers and under their sole control, except so far as [the Minister of Power] otherwise orders, and shall be used by the Undertakers only for the purpose of leading off service lines and other distributing conductors, or for examining, testing, regulating, measuring, directing, or controlling, the supply of energy, or for examining or testing the condition of the mains or other portions of the works, or for other like purposes connected with the undertaking, and the Undertakers may place therein meters, switches, and any other suitable and proper apparatus, for any of the above purposes.

(3) Every such box, including the upper surface or covering thereof, shall be constructed of such materials, and shall be constructed and maintained by the Undertakers in such manner, as not to be a source of danger, whether by reason of inequality of surface or otherwise.

(4) . . . the local authority . . . may, with the approval of [the Minister of Power] prescribe the hours during which the Undertakers are to have access to the boxes, and if the Undertakers during any hours not so prescribed remove or displace or keep removed or displaced the upper surface or covering of any box without the consent of the local authority, they shall be liable for each offence to a penalty not exceeding [level 1 on the standard scale], and to a daily penalty not exceeding five pounds: Provided that the Undertakers shall not be subject to any such penalties as aforesaid if the court are of opinion that the case was one of emergency, and that the Undertakers complied with the requirements of this section so far as was reasonable under the circumstances.

NOTES

The words in square brackets in sub-s (1) were substituted, and the words omitted from that subsection and from sub-s (4) were repealed, by the Electricity Act 1947, s 57(2), Sch 4, Pt III.

The words "the Minister of Power" were substituted by the Minister of Fuel and Power (Change of Style and Title) Order 1957, SI 1957/48, art 1(2) (see further the note below).

The reference in sub-s (4) to level 1 on the standard scale is substituted by virtue of the Criminal Justice Act 1982, s 46, Vol 27, title Magistrates. The maximum fine was previously increased to £25 by the Criminal Law Act 1977, s 31(6).

Street boxes. A street box is a "building structure or work" within the London Building Act 1930, s 161, Vol 26, title London; see *County of London Electric Supply Co Ltd v Perkins* (1908) 98 LT 870, 72 JP 133.

As to placing such works in disused burial grounds, see *St Nicholas Acons (Rector and Churchwardens) v LCC* [1928] AC 469, [1928] All ER Rep 240, PC, and *Re St Peter the Great, Chichester* [1961] 2 All ER 513, [1961] 1 WLR 907.

Minister of Power. The functions of the Minister of Power under this section are now exercised by the Secretary of State for Energy; see the Preliminary Note to this title.

Standard scale. By the Criminal Justice Act 1982, ss 37(3), 75, Vol 27, title Magistrates, this means the standard scale set out in s 37(2) of that Act as amended by order made under the Magistrates' Courts Act 1980, s 143(1), in the same title. The scale as amended by the Criminal Penalties etc (Increase) Order 1984, SI 1984/447, art 3(4), Sch 4, is: level 1: £50; level 2: £100; level 3: £400; level 4: £1,000; and level 5: £2,000.

Definitions. For "Electricity regulations", "energy", "main", "the principal Act" and "service line", see s 1 of this Schedule ante. By virtue of the same section, for "local authority", see the Electric Lighting Act 1882, s 31 ante; and for "street" and "works", see s 32 of that Act. For "Undertakers", see s 2 of this Schedule ante.

14 Notice of works, with plan, to be served on Postmaster-General and local authority

(1) Where the exercise of any of the powers of the Undertakers in relation to the execution of any works (including the construction of boxes) will involve the placing of any works in, under, along or across any street or public bridge, the following provisions shall have effect:—

(a) One month [or in the case of service lines, seven days] before commencing the execution of the works (not being repairs, renewals, or amendments of existing works of which the character and position are not altered), the Undertakers shall serve a notice [upon the local authority and any relevant telecommunications operator] describing the proposed works, together with a plan of the works showing the mode and position in which the works are intended to be executed, and the manner in which it is intended that the street or bridge, or any sewer, drain, or tunnel, therein or thereunder, is to be interfered with, and shall, upon being required to do so [by the local authority or that operator give the authority or that operator any such further information as the authority or that operator desires].
No part of the month of August shall be included in calculating the above-mentioned period of one month.

(b) [The local authority or the relevant telecommunications operator may, in the discretion of the authority or that operator] approve any such works or plan, subject to such amendments or conditions as may seem fit, or may disapprove them, and may give notice of that approval or disapproval to the Undertakers.

(c) [Where the local authority or the relevant telecommunications operator approves] any such works or plan, subject to any amendments or conditions with which the Undertakers are dissatisfied, or [disapproves] any such works or plan, the Undertakers may appeal to [the Minister of Power] and [the Minister of Power] may inquire into the matter, and allow or disallow the appeal, and may approve any such works or plan, subject to such amendments or conditions as seem fit, or may disapprove them.

(d) [If the local authority or the relevant telecommunications operator fails] to give such notice of approval or disapproval to the Undertakers within one month after the service of the notice upon them, [the local authority or that operator] shall be deemed to have approved the works and plan.

(e) Notwithstanding anything in [this Schedule] or the principal Act, the Undertakers shall not be entitled to execute any such works as above specified, except so far as they may be of a description and in accordance with a plan which has been approved or is to be deemed to have been [approved by the local authority or the relevant telecommunications operator], or by [the Minister of Power], as above-mentioned; but where any such works, description, and plan are so approved, or to be deemed to be approved, the Undertakers may cause those works to be executed in accordance with the description and plan, subject in all respects to the provisions of [this Schedule] and the principal Act.

(f) If the Undertakers make default in complying with any of the requirements or restrictions of this section, they shall (in addition to any other compensation which they may be liable to make under the provisions of [this Schedule] or the principal Act) make full [compensation to the local authority or the relevant telecommunications operator for any loss or damage which the authority or that operator] may incur by reason thereof, and in addition thereto they shall be liable for each default to a penalty not exceeding [level 1 on the standard scale], and to a daily penalty not exceeding five pounds: Provided that the Undertakers shall not be subject to any such penalty as aforesaid if the court are of opinion that the case was one of emergency, and that the Undertakers complied with the requirements of this section so far as was reasonable under the circumstances.

[(1A) In the application of this subsection to a street or public bridge references to a relevant telecommunications operator are references to the operator of any telecommunications code system for the purposes of which any telecommunication apparatus is kept installed in, under, along or across that street or bridge.]

(2) In the application of this section to a street or public bridge (not within a county borough) which is repairable by the county council, a reference to the county council shall be substituted for a reference to the local authority.

(3) ...

(4) Nothing in this section shall exempt the Undertakers from any penalty or obligation to which they may be liable under [this Schedule] or otherwise by law in the event of any [telecommunication apparatus kept installed for the purposes of any telecommunications code system being] at any time injuriously affected by the Undertakers' works or their supply of energy.

NOTES

The words in the first pair of square brackets in sub-s (1) were inserted by the Electricity (Supply) Act 1926, s 43, Sch 5.

The words "this Schedule" wherever they occur in this section were substituted, and sub-s (3) was repealed, by the Electricity Act 1947, s 57, Sch 4, Pt III.

Sub-s (1A) was inserted by the Telecommunications Act 1984, s 109, Sch 4, para 9.

The words "the Minister of Power" wherever they occur in this section were substituted by the Minister of Fuel and Power (Change of Style and Title) Order 1957, SI 1957/48, art 1(2) (see further the note below).

The reference in sub-s (1)(f) to level 1 on the standard scale is substituted by virtue of the Criminal Justice Act 1982, s 46, Vol 27, title Magistrates. The maximum fine was previously increased to £25 by the Criminal Law Act 1977, s 31(6).

The remaining words in square brackets in this section were substituted by the Telecommunications Act 1984, s 109, Sch 4, para 9.

This section was repealed by the Public Utilities Street Works Act 1950, s 15(3), Sch 5, Vol 20, title Highways, Streets and Bridges, so far as it requires a notice and plan of works to be served on a local authority within the meaning of this Schedule or on a county council.

Postmaster General. Notice is now to be served on the local authority and any relevant telecommunications operator; see sub-s (1)(a) above. Accordingly the reference in the marginal note to the Postmaster General no longer has any effect.

Serve a notice. For provisions as to service, see the Electricity Act 1947, s 63 post, in conjunction with s 57(2) of that Act post.

Plan. As to contents, cf East Molesey Local Board v Lambeth Waterworks Co [1892] 3 Ch 289, 62 LJ Ch 82.

Tunnel. It appears that this does not include a railway tunnel (see Caledonian Rly Co v Glasgow Corpn 1901 3 F(Ct of Sess) 526, 8 SLT 457). See also Schweder v Worthing Gas Light and Coke Co [1912] 1 Ch 83, 81 LJ Ch 102.

Minister of Power. The functions of the Minister of Power under this section are now exercised by the Secretary of State for Energy; see the Preliminary Note to this title.

Standard scale. See the note to s 13 of this Schedule ante.

Protection of telecommunication apparatus. See also ss 20, 69 of this Schedule post; the Electric Lighting Act 1882, s 26 ante; the Electric Lighting Act 1888, s 4 ante; the Electricity Act 1947, s 9(3) post; and the Electricity Act 1957, s 28(8) post.

Extension. This section, so far as it relates to the operator of any telecommunications code system, is incorporated with the Electricity (Supply) Act 1919, s 22 post, by sub-s (4) of that section, and is applied by the Electricity Act 1947, s 9(3) post.

Definitions. For "county council", "daily penalty", "energy", "plan", "the principal Act" and "service line", see s 1 of this Schedule ante. By virtue of the same section, for "local authority", see the Electric Lighting Act 1882, s 31 ante; and for "street" and "works", see s 32 of the 1882 Act. For "Undertakers", see s 2 of this Schedule ante. For "telecommunications operator" see, by virtue of the Telecommunications Act 1984, s 109, Sch 4, para 1(1), Vol 45, title Telecommunications and Broadcasting, s 9(3) of that Act, and note sub-s (1A) above; for "telecommunication apparatus", see, by virtue of s 109 of, and Sch 4, para 1(1) to, the 1984 Act, Sch 2 to that Act, and note the final paragraph of s 1 of this Schedule; and for "telecommunciations code system", see Sch 4, para 1(1) to the 1984 Act.

15 As to streets not repairable by local authority, railways, tramways, and canals

Where the exercise of the powers of the Undertakers in relation to the execution of any works will involve the placing of any works in, under, along, or across any street or part of a street not repairable by the local authority, including where the area of supply is not wholly in a county borough, the county council, or over or under any railway, tramway, or canal, the following provisions shall have effect unless otherwise agreed between the parties interested:—

(a) One month before commencing the execution of the works (not being repairs, renewals, or amendments of existing works of which the character and position are not altered) the Undertakers shall, in addition to any other notices which they may be required to give under [this Schedule], or the principal Act, serve a notice upon the body or person liable to repair the street or part of a street, or the body or person for the time being entitled to work the railway or tramway, or the owners of the canal (as the case may be), in this section referred to as the "owners," describing the proposed works, together with a plan of the works showing the mode and position in which the works are intended to be executed and placed, and shall, upon being required to do so by any such owners, give them any such further information in relation thereto as they desire.

(b) Every such notice shall contain a reference to this section, and direct the attention of the owners to whom it is given to the provisions thereof.

(c) Within three weeks after the service of any such notice and plan upon any owners, those owners may, if they think fit, serve a requisition upon the Undertakers requiring that any question in relation to the works, or to compensation in respect thereof, and any other question arising upon the notice or plan, shall be settled by arbitration; and thereupon that question, unless settled by agreement, shall be determined by arbitration accordingly.

(d) In settling any question under this section an arbitrator shall have regard to any duties or obligations which the owners may be under in respect of the street, railway, tramway, or canal, and may, if he thinks fit, require the Undertakers to execute any temporary or other works so as to avoid any interference with any traffic, so far as may be possible.

(e) Where no such requisition as in this section mentioned is served upon the Undertakers, or where after any such requisition has been served upon them any question required to be settled by arbitration has been so settled, the Undertakers may, upon paying or securing any compensation which they may be required to pay or secure, cause to be executed the works specified in such notice and plan as aforesaid and may repair, renew, and amend them (provided that their character and position are not altered), but subject in all respects to the provisions of [this Schedule] and the principal Act, and only in accordance with the notice and plan so served by them as aforesaid, or such modifications thereof respectively as may have been determined by arbitration as herein-before mentioned, or as may be agreed upon between the parties.

(f) All works to be executed by the Undertakers under this section shall be carried out to the reasonable satisfaction of the owners, and those owners shall have the right to be present during the execution of the works.

(g) Where the repair, renewal, or amendment of any existing works, of which the character or position is not altered, will involve any interference with any railway or with any tramway over or under which those works have been placed, the Undertakers shall, unless it is otherwise agreed between the parties, or in cases of emergency, give to the owners not less than twenty-four hours' notice before commencing to effect the repair, renewal or amendment, and the owners shall be entitled by their officer to superintend the works, and the Undertakers shall conform to such reasonable requirements as may be made by the owners or that officer. The notice shall be in addition to any other notices which the Undertakers may be required to give under [this Schedule] or the principal Act.

(h) If the Undertakers make default in complying with any of the requirements or restrictions of this section they shall (in addition to any other compensation which they may be liable to make under the provisions of [this Schedule] or the principal Act) make full compensation to the owners affected thereby for any loss or damage which they may incur by reason thereof, and in addition thereto they shall be liable for each default to a penalty not exceeding [level 1 on the standard scale] and to a daily penalty not exceeding five pounds: Provided that the Undertakers shall not be subject to any such penalty as aforesaid if the court are of opinion that the case was one of emergency, and that the Undertakers complied with the requirements of this section so far as was reasonable under the circumstances.

NOTES

The reference in para (h) to level 1 on the standard scale is substituted by virtue of the Criminal Justice Act 1982, s 46, Vol 27, title Magistrates. The maximum fine was previously increased to £25 by the Criminal Law Act 1977, s 31(6). The other words in square brackets in this section were substituted by the Electricity Act 1947, s 57, Sch 4, Pt III.

This section was repealed as to code-regulated works by the Public Utilities Street Works Act 1950, s 15(3), Sch 5, Vol 20, title Highways, Streets and Bridges.

County borough. The boroughs, other than London boroughs, existing immediately before 1 April 1974 were abolished on that date by the Local Government Act 1972, ss 1(9), (10), 20(6), Vol 25, title Local Government, and the reference to a county borough no longer has any effect.

Serve a notice. For provisions as to service, see the Electricity Act 1947, s 63 post, in conjunction with s 57(2) of that Act post.

Plan. See the note to s 14 of this Schedule ante.

Within three weeks after. The general rule in cases where an act is to be done within a specified time is that the day from which it runs is not to be counted; see *Goldsmiths' Co v West Metropolitan Rly Co* [1904] 1 KB 1, [1900–3] All ER Rep 667, CA; *Stewart v Chapman* [1951] 2 KB 792, [1951] 2 All ER 613.

Twenty-four hours' notice. As to exclusion of Sunday etc, see s 62(4) of this Schedule post.

Standard scale. See the note to s 13 of this Schedule ante.

Extension. This section and ss 16, 17, 19, 20 and 77 of this Schedule post are applied in relation to wayleaves by the Electricity (Supply) Act 1919, s 22(2) post.

Definitions. For "area of supply", see s 4 of this Schedule ante. For "county council", "daily penalty", "plan", "the principal Act"; "railway" and "tramway", see s 1 of this Schedule ante. By virtue of the same section, for "local authority", see the Electric Lighting Act 1882, s 31 ante, and the Electricity Act 1947, s 67(1) post; and for "street" and "works", see s 32 of the 1882 Act. For "Undertakers", see s 2 of this Schedule ante. Note as to "the owners" para (a) above.

16 Street authority, etc, may give notice of desire to break up streets, etc, on behalf of Undertakers

Any body or person for the time being liable to repair any street or part of a street or entitled to work any railway or tramway which the Undertakers are empowered to break up . . . may, if they think fit, serve a notice upon the Undertakers stating that they desire to exercise or discharge all or any part of any of the powers or duties of the Undertakers as therein specified in relation to the breaking up, filling-in, re-instating, or making good any streets, bridges, sewers, drains, tunnels, or other works vested in or under the control or management of that body or person, and may amend or revoke any such notice by another notice similarly served.

Where any such body or person (in this section referred to as the "givers of the notice") have given notice that they desire to exercise or discharge any such specified powers and duties of the Undertakers, then so long as that notice remains in force the following provisions shall have effect, unless it is otherwise agreed between the parties interested:—

(a) The Undertakers shall not be entitled to proceed themselves to exercise or discharge any such specified powers or duties as aforesaid, except where they have required the givers of the notice to exercise or discharge those powers or duties, and the givers of the notice have refused or neglected to comply with that requisition, as herein-after provided, or in cases of emergency.

(b) In addition to any other notices which they are required to give under the provisions of [this Schedule] or the principal Act, the Undertakers shall, not more than four days and not less than two days before the exercise or discharge of any such powers or duties so specified as aforesaid is required to be commenced, serve a requisition upon the givers of the notice stating the time when that exercise or discharge is required to be commenced, and the manner in which any such powers or duties are required to be exercised or discharged.

(c) Upon receipt of any such requisition as last aforesaid, the givers of the notice may proceed to exercise or discharge any such powers or duties as required by the Undertakers, subject to the like restrictions and conditions, so far as they are applicable, as the Undertakers would themselves be subject to in that exercise or discharge.

(d) If the givers of the notice decline or, for twenty-four hours after the time when any such exercise or discharge of any powers or duties is by any requisition required to be commenced, neglect to comply with the requisition, the Undertakers may themselves proceed to exercise or discharge the powers or duties therein specified in like manner as they might have done if such notice as aforesaid had not been given to them by the givers of the notice.

(e) In any case of emergency the Undertakers may themselves proceed at once to exercise or discharge so much of any such specified powers or duties as aforesaid as may be necessary for the actual remedying of any defect from which the emergency arises without serving any requisition on the givers of the notice; but in that case the Undertakers shall, within twelve hours after they begin to exercise or discharge such powers or duties as aforesaid, give information thereof in writing to the givers of the notice.

(f) If the Undertakers exercise or discharge any such specified powers or duties as aforesaid otherwise than in accordance with the provisions of this section, they shall be liable for each offence to a penalty not exceeding [level 1 on the standard scale], and to a daily penalty not exceeding five pounds: Provided that the Undertakers shall not be subject to any such penalties as aforesaid if the court are of opinion that the case was one of emergency, and that the Undertakers complied with the requirements of this section so far as was reasonable under the circumstances.

(g) All expenses properly incurred by the givers of the notice in complying with any requisition of the Undertakers under this section shall be repaid to them by the Undertakers, and may be recovered summarily.

(h) . . .

Provided that nothing in this section shall in any way affect the rights of the Undertakers to exercise or discharge any powers or duties conferred or imposed upon them by [this Schedule] or the principal Act in relation to the execution of any works beyond the actual breaking up, filling in, reinstating or making good any such street or part of a street, or any such bridges, sewers, drains, tunnels, or other works, or railway or tramway as in this section mentioned.

NOTES

The reference in para (f) to level 1 on the standard scale is substituted by virtue of the Criminal Justice Act 1982, s 46, Vol 27, title Magistrates. The maximum fine was previously increased to £25 by the Criminal Law Act 1977, s 31(6). The other words in square brackets in this section were substituted, and the words omitted were repealed, by the Electricity Act 1947, s 57(2), Sch 4, Pt III.

This section was repealed by the Public Utilities Street Works Act 1950, s 15(3), Sch 5, Vol 20, title Highways, Streets and Bridges, so far as it related to works which if executed by the undertakers would be code-regulated works.

Serve a notice. For provisions as to service, see the Electricity Act 1947, s 63 post, in conjunction with s 57(2) of that Act post.

Not more than four days etc. As to exclusion of Sunday etc, see s 62(4) of this Schedule post.

Standard scale. See the note to s 13 of this Schedule ante.

Extension. See the note to s 15 of this Schedule ante.

Third party liability as between Undertakers and local authority. As to liability of Undertakers for injury to third parties when a local authority have exercised the option conferred on them by this section to do works, see *Pearce v County of London Electric Supply Co Ltd* (1935) 34 LGR 349.

Cf *Cressy v South Metropolitan Gas Co* (1906) 94 LT 790, 70 JP 405; *Brame v Commercial Gas Co* [1914] 3 KB 1181, 84 LJKB 570; and *Rider v Metropolitan Water Board* [1949] 2 KB 378, [1949] 2 All ER 97.

Definitions. For "daily penalty", "the principal Act", "railway" and "tramway", see s 1 of this Schedule ante. By virtue of the same section, for "street" and "works", see the Electric Lighting Act 1882, s 32 ante. For "Undertakers", see s 2 of this Schedule ante. Note as to "givers of the notice", the second paragraph above.

17 As to alteration of pipes, wires, etc under streets

The Undertakers may alter the position of any pipes (except . . . any pipe forming part of any sewer of the local authority), or any wires being under any street or place authorised to be broken up by them, which may interfere with the exercise of their powers under the principal Act or [this Schedule]; and any body or person may in like manner alter the position of any electric lines or works of the Undertakers, being under any such street or place as aforesaid, which may interfere with the lawful exercise of any powers vested in that body or person in relation to that street or place, subject to the following provisions, unless it is otherwise agreed between the parties interested:—

(a) One month before commencing any such alterations the Undertakers, or the body or person (as the case may be), in this section referred to as the "operators," shall serve a notice upon the body or person for the time being entitled to the pipes, wires, electric lines, or works (as the case may be), in this section referred to as the "owners," describing the proposed alterations, together with a plan showing the manner in which it is intended that the alterations shall be made, and shall, upon being required to do so by any such owners, give them any such further information in relation thereto as they may desire.

(b) Within three weeks after the service of any such notice and plan upon any owners those owners may, if they think fit, serve a requisition upon the operators requiring that any question in relation to the works or to compensation in respect thereof or any other question arising upon such notice or plan as aforesaid shall be settled by arbitration; and thereupon that question, unless settled by agreement, shall be determined by arbitration accordingly.

(c) In settling any question under this section an arbitrator shall have regard to any duties or obligations which the owners may be under in respect of the pipes, wires, electric lines, or works, and may, if he thinks fit, require the operators to execute any temporary or other works, so as to avoid interference with any purpose for which the pipes, wires, electric lines, or works are used so far as possible.

(d) Where no such requisition as in this section mentioned is served upon the operators, the owners shall be held to have agreed to the notice or plan served on them as aforesaid, and in that case, or where, after any such requisition has been served upon them, any question required to be settled by arbitration has been so settled, the operators, upon paying or securing any compensation which they may be required to pay or secure, may cause the alterations specified in such notice and plan as aforesaid to be made, but subject in all respects to the provisions of the principal Act and [this Schedule], and only in accordance with the notice and plan so served by them as aforesaid, or such modifications thereof respectively as may have been determined by arbitration as herein-before mentioned or as may be agreed upon between the parties.

(e) At any time before any operators are entitled to commence any such alterations as aforesaid, the owners may serve a statement upon the operators, stating that they desire to execute the alterations themselves, and where any such statement has been served upon the operators, they shall not be entitled to proceed themselves to execute the alterations, except where they have notified to the owners that they require them to execute the alterations, and the owners have refused or neglected to comply with the notification as herein-after provided.

(f) Where any such statement as last aforesaid has been served upon the operators, they shall, not more than forty-eight hours and not less than twenty-four hours before the execution of the alterations is required to be commenced, serve a notification upon the owners stating the time when the alterations are required to be commenced, and the manner in which the alterations are required to be made.

(g) Upon receipt of any such notification as last aforesaid, the owners may proceed to execute the alterations as required by the operators, subject to the like restrictions and conditions, so far as they are applicable, as the operators would themselves be subject to in executing the alterations.

(h) If the owners decline or, for twenty-four hours after the time when any such alterations are required to be commenced, neglect to comply with the notification, the operators may themselves proceed to execute the alterations in like manner as they might have done if no such statement as aforesaid had been served upon them.

(*i*) All expenses properly incurred by any owners in complying with any notification of any operators under this section shall be repaid to them by the operators, and may be recovered summarily.

(*j*) ...

(*k*) If the operators make default in complying with any of the requirements or restrictions of this section they shall (in addition to any other compensation which they may be liable to make under the provisions of [this Schedule] or the principal Act) make full compensation to the owners affected thereby for any loss, damage, or penalty which they may incur by reason thereof, and in addition thereto they shall be liable for each default to a penalty not exceeding [level 1 on the standard scale], and to a daily penalty not exceeding five pounds: Provided that the operators shall not be subject to any such penalty as aforesaid if the court are of opinion that the case was one of emergency, and that the operators complied with the requirements of this section so far as was reasonable under the circumstances.

NOTES

The reference in para (*k*) to level 1 on the standard scale is substituted by virtue of the Criminal Justice Act 1982, s 46, Vol 27, title Magistrates. The maximum fine was previously increased to £25 by the Criminal Law Act 1977, s 31(6). The other words in square brackets were substituted, and the words omitted were repealed, by the Electricity Act 1947, s 57(2), Sch 4, Pt III.

This section was repealed by the Public Utilities Street Works Act 1950, s 15(3), Sch 5, Vol 20, title Highways, Streets and Bridges, so far as it related to the alteration, for the purpose of authority's works, of the position of any electric lines or other works in a street or in controlled land.

Alteration of pipes, wires etc. Cf the Electric Lighting Act 1882, s 15 ante.

Serve a notice. For provisions as to service, see the Electricity Act 1947, s 63 post, in conjunction with s 57(2) thereof post.

Within three weeks after. See the note to s 15 of this Schedule ante.

Not more than forty-eight hours, etc. As to the exclusion of Sunday etc, see s 62(4) of this Schedule post.

May be recovered summarily. By the Magistrates' Courts Act 1980, s 58(1), Vol 27, title Magistrates, a magistrates' court has power to make an order on complaint for the payment of any money which is recoverable summarily as a civil debt, and by s 127(1) of that Act, the complaint may not be heard unless it was made within six months from the time when the matter of complaint arose.

Standard scale. See the note to s 13 of this Schedule ante.

Exclusion. The provisions of this section are excluded by the Highways Act 1980, s 181(6), Vol 20, title Highways, Streets and Bridges.

Extension. See the note to s 15 of this Schedule ante.

Definitions. For "daily penalty", "plan" and "the principal Act", see s 1 of this Schedule ante. By virtue of the same section, for "electric line", "street" and "works", see the Electric Lighting Act 1882, s 32 ante; and for "local authority", see s 31 of that Act. For "Undertakers", see s 2 of this Schedule ante. Note as to "operators" and "owners", para (*a*) above.

18 Laying of electric lines, etc near sewers, etc or gas or water pipes, or other electric lines

(1) Where the Undertakers require to dig or sink any trench for laying down or constructing any new electric lines (other than service lines) or other works near to which any sewer, drain, watercourse, defence, or work under the jurisdiction or control of the local authority, or any main, pipe, syphon, electric line, or other work belonging to any gas, electric supply, or water company has been lawfully placed, or where any gas or water company required to dig or sink any trench for laying down or constructing any new mains or pipes (other than service pipes) or other works near to which any lines or works of the Undertakers have been lawfully placed, the Undertakers or the gas or water company (as the case may be), in this section referred to as the "operators," shall, unless it is otherwise agreed between the parties interested, or in case of sudden emergency, give to the local authority, or to the gas, electric supply, or water company, or to the Undertakers (as the case may be), in this section referred to as the "owners," not less than three days' notice before commencing to dig or sink such trench as aforesaid, and those owners shall be entitled by their officer to superintend the work, and the operators shall conform with such reasonable requirements as may be made by the owners or the officer for protecting from injury every such sewer, drain, watercourse, defence, main, pipe, syphon, electric line, or work, and for securing access thereto, and they shall also, if required by the owners thereof, repair any damage that may be done thereto.

(2) Where the operators find it necessary to undermine but not alter the position of any pipe, electric line, or work, they shall temporarily support it in position during the execution of their works, and before completion provide a suitable and proper foundation for it where so undermined.

(3) Where the operators (being the Undertakers) lay any electric line, crossing or liable to touch any mains, pipes, lines, or services belonging to any gas, electric supply, or water company, the conducting portion of the electric line shall be effectively insulated in a manner approved by [the Minister of Power]; and the Undertakers shall not, except with the consent of the gas, electric supply, or water company, as the case may be, and of [the Minister of Power], lay their electric lines so as to come into contact with any such mains, lines, pipes, or services, or, except with the like consent, employ any such mains, pipes, lines, or services as conductors for the purposes of their supply of energy.

(4) Any question or difference which may arise under this section shall be determined by arbitration.

(5) If the operators make default in complying with any of the requirements of this section they shall make full compensation to all owners affected thereby for any loss, damage, penalty, or costs which they may incur by reason thereof; and in addition thereto they shall be liable for each default to a penalty not exceeding [level 1 on the standard scale], and to a daily penalty not exceeding five pounds: Provided that the operators shall not be subject to any such penalty if the court are of opinion that the case was one of emergency, and that the operators complied with the requirements of this section so far as was reasonable under the circumstances, or that the default in question was due to the fact that the operators were ignorant of the position of the sewer, drain, watercourse, defence, main, pipe, syphon, electric line, or work affected thereby, and that that ignorance was not owing to any negligence on the part of the operators.

(6) For the purposes of this section the expression "gas company" shall mean any body or person lawfully supplying gas; the expression "water company" shall mean any body or person lawfully supplying water or water power; and the expression "electric supply company" shall mean any body or person supplying energy in pursuance of the principal Act, but not in pursuance of [this Schedule].

(7) . . .

NOTES

The words in square brackets in sub-s (3) were substituted by the Minister of Fuel and Power (Change of Style and Title) Order 1957, SI 1957/48, art 1(2) (see further the note below).

The reference in sub-s (5) to level 1 on the standard scale is substituted by virtue of the Criminal Justice Act 1982, s 46, Vol 27, title Magistrates. The maximum fine was previously increased to £25 by the Criminal Law Act 1977, s 31(6).

The words in square brackets in sub-s (6) were substituted, and sub-s (7) was repealed, by the Electricity Act 1947, s 57, Sch 4, Pt III.

Electricity supply company. As to powers of persons other than undertakers, as defined by s 2 of this Schedule ante, to supply electricity, see the Energy Act 1983 post.

Not less than three days' notice. For provisions as to service, see the Electricity Act 1947, s 63 post in conjunction with s 57(2) of that Act post. As to exclusion of Sunday etc, see s 62(4) of this Schedule post.

Minister of Power. The functions of the Minister of Power under this section are now exercised by the Secretary of State for Energy ; see the Preliminary Note to this title.

Standard scale. See the note to s 13 of this Schedule ante.

Penalty. An award of compensation does not bar the right to proceed for penalties under this section; see *Chepstow Electric Light and Power Co v Chepstow Gas and Coke Consumers' Co* [1905] 1 KB 198, 74 LJKB 28.

Definitions. For "daily penalty", "energy", "main", "the principal Act" and "service line", see s 1 of this Schedule ante. By virtue of that section, for "electric line" and "works", see the Electric Lighting Act 1882, s 32 ante, and for "local authority", see s 31 of that Act. For "Undertakers", see s 2 of this Schedule ante. Note as to "electric supply company", "gas company" and "water company", sub-s (6), and as to "operators" and "owners", sub-s (1), above.

---

19 For protection of railway and canal companies

In the exercise of any of the powers of [this Schedule] relating to the execution of works, the Undertakers shall not in any way injure the railways, tunnels, arches, works, or conveniences belonging to any railway or canal company, nor obstruct or interfere with the working of the traffic passing along any railway or canal.

NOTES

The words in square brackets were substituted by the Electricity Act 1947, s 57(2), Sch 4, Pt III.

Railway or canal company. Railway and canal undertakings were vested in the British Railways Board and the British Waterways Board respectively by the Transport Act 1947 (repealed) and the Transport Act 1962, Vol 36, title Railways, Inland Waterways and Pipelines.

Extension. See the note to s 15 of this Schedule ante.

Definitions. For "railway", see s 1 of this Schedule ante; and for "Undertakers", see s 2 of this Schedule ante. By virtue of s 1 of this Schedule, for "works", see the Electric Lighting Act 1882, s 32 ante.

20 For protection of telegraphic and telephonic wires

(1) The Undertakers shall take all reasonable precautions in constructing, laying down, and placing their electric lines and other works of all descriptions, and in working their undertaking so as not injuriously to affect, whether by induction or otherwise, the working of any wire or line used for the purpose of [telecommunications] [or electrical control of railways], or the currents in that wire or line, whether that wire or line be or be not in existence at the time of the laying down or placing of the electric lines or other works.

If any question arises between the Undertakers and the owner of any such wire or line as to whether the Undertakers have constructed, laid down, or placed their electric lines or other works or worked their undertaking in contravention of this sub-section, and as to whether the working of that wire or line or the current therein is or is not injuriously affected thereby, that question shall be determined by arbitration; and the arbitrator (unless he is of opinion that the wire or line, not having been so in existence at such time as aforesaid, has been placed in unreasonable proximity to the electric lines or works of the Undertakers) may direct the Undertakers to make any alterations in, or additions to, their system, so as to comply with the provisions of this section, and the Undertakers shall make those alterations or additions accordingly.

(2) Seven days before commencing to lay down or place any electric line, or to use any electric line in any manner whereby [telecommunications] [or electrical control of railways] through any wire or line lawfully laid down or placed in any position may be injuriously affected, the Undertakers shall, unless otherwise agreed between the parties interested, give to the owner of the wire or line notice in writing specifying the course, nature, and gauge of the electric line, and the manner in which the electric line is intended to be used, and the amount and nature of the currents intended to be transmitted thereby, and the extent to and manner in which (if at all) earth returns are proposed to be used; and any owner entitled to receive that notice may serve a requisition on the Undertakers requiring them to adopt such precautions as may be therein specified in regard to the laying, placing, or user of the electric line for the purpose of preventing the injurious affection; and the Undertakers shall conform with such reasonable requirements as may be made by the owner for the purpose of preventing the communication through the wire or line from being injuriously affected as aforesaid.

If any difference arises between any such owner and the Undertakers with respect to the reasonableness of any requirements so made, that difference shall be determined by arbitration.

Provided that nothing in this sub-section shall apply to repairs or renewals of any electric line so long as the course, nature, and gauge of the electric line, and the amount and nature of the current transmitted thereby, are not altered.

(3) If in any case the Undertakers make default in complying with the requirements of this section, they shall make full compensation to every such owner as aforesaid for any loss or damage which he may incur by reason thereof, and in addition thereto they shall be liable for each default to a penalty not exceeding [level 1 on the standard scale], and to a daily penalty not exceeding [two pounds]: Provided that the Undertakers shall not be subject to any such penalty as aforesaid if the court are of opinion that the case was one of emergency and that the Undertakers complied with the requirements of this section so far as was reasonable under the circumstances, or that the default was due to the fact that the Undertakers were ignorant of the position of the wire or line affected thereby, and that the ignorance was not owing to any negligence on the part of the Undertakers.

(4) Nothing in this section contained shall be held to deprive any owner of any existing rights to proceed against the Undertakers by indictment, action, or otherwise, in relation to any of the matters aforesaid.

[(5) References in this section to the owner of any wire or line used for the purpose of telecommunications shall include references to any person who is running, or is authorised by a licence under section 7 of the Telecommunications Act 1984 to run, any telecommunication system for the purposes of which that wire or line is kept installed.]

NOTES

The words in the first pair of square brackets in sub-s (1) and those in the first pair of square brackets in sub-s (2) were substituted, and sub-s (5) was added, by the Telecommunications Act 1984, s 109(1), Sch 4, para 9(5).

The words in the second pair of square brackets in sub-s (1) and those in the second pair of square brackets in sub-s (2) were inserted by the Electricity Act 1947, s 57(2), Sch 4, Pt III.

The reference in sub-s (3) to level 1 on the standard scale is substituted by virtue of the Criminal Justice Act 1982, s 46, Vol 27, title Magistrates. The maximum fine was previously increased to £25 by the Criminal Law Act 1977, s 31(6). The words in the second pair of square brackets in sub-s (3) are substituted by virtue of the Decimal Currency Act 1969, s 10(1), Vol 10, title Constitutional Law (Pt 3).

Notice. For provisions as to service, see the Electricity Act 1947, s 63 post, in conjunction with s 57(2) of that Act post.

Standard scale. See the note to s 13 of this Schedule ante.

Protection of telecommunication apparatus. See also the Electric Lighting Act 1882, s 26 ante; the Electric Lighting Act 1888, s 4 ante; s 14 of this Schedule ante; s 69 of this Schedule post; the Electricity Act 1947, s 9(3) post and the Electricity Act 1957, s 28(8) post.

Extension. See the note to s 15 of this Schedule ante.

Definitions. For "daily penalty" and "railway", see s 1 of this Schedule ante. By virtue of the same section, for "electric line" and "works", see the Electric Lighting Act 1882, s 32 ante. For "Undertakers", see s 2 of this Schedule ante.

Telecommunications Act 1984, s 7. See Vol 45, title Telecommunications and Broadcasting.

Compulsory Works

21 Mains, etc to be laid down in streets specified in Special Order and in remainder of area of supply

(1) ...

(2) ... the Undertakers shall, at any time after the expiration of eighteen months after the [vesting date], lay down suitable and sufficient distributing mains for the purposes of general supply throughout every ... street or part of a street [or along any other route] within the area of supply, upon being required to do so in manner provided by [this Schedule].

All such mains as last above mentioned (unless already laid down) shall be laid down by the Undertakers within six months after any requisition in that behalf served upon them in accordance with the provisions of [this Schedule] has become binding upon them, or within such further time as may in any case be approved by [the Minister of Power].

(3) When any such requisition is made in respect of any street not repairable by the local authority, which the Undertakers are not specially authorised to break up by [a local enactment], the Undertakers shall (unless the authority, or person by whom that street is repairable, consent to the breaking up thereof) forthwith apply to [the Minister of Power] under section thirteen of the Electric Lighting Act 1882 for the written consent of [the Minister of Power] authorising and empowering the Undertakers to break up that street, and the requisition shall not be binding upon them if [the Minister of Power] refuse [his] consent in that behalf.

NOTES

The words "the Minister of Power" wherever they occur in this section were substituted by the Minister of Fuel and Power (Change of Style and Title) Order 1957, SI 1957/48, art 1(2) (see further the note below). The other words in square brackets in this section were substituted and the words omitted were repealed by the Electricity Act 1947, s 57(2), Sch 4, Pt III; the marginal note is no longer applicable in view of the repeal of sub-s (1).

Requisition served in accordance with provisions of this Schedule. See s 24 of this Schedule post. For provisions as to service, see the Electricity Act 1947, s 63 post, in conjunction with s 57(2) of that Act post.

Minister of Power. The functions of the Minister of Power under this section are now exercised by the Secretary of State for Energy; see the Preliminary Note to this title.

Definitions. For "area of supply", see s 4 of this Schedule ante; and for "distributing main" and "general supply", see s 1 of this Schedule ante. By virtue of the same section, for "local authority", see the Electric Lighting Act 1882, s 31 ante; for "street", see s 32 of that Act; and for "local enactment", see the Electricity Act 1947, s 67(1) post. For "Undertakers", see s 2 of this Schedule ante.

Electric Lighting Act 1882, s 13. See this title ante.

22 As to laying of electric line under special agreement

... the Undertakers shall, twenty-eight days at the least before commencing to lay in any street any electric line which is intended for supplying energy to any particular consumer, and not for the purposes of general supply, serve upon the local authority, and upon the owner or occupier of all premises abutting on so much of the street as lies between the points of origin and termination of the electric line so to be laid, a notice stating that the Undertakers intend to lay the electric line, and setting forth the effect of this section, and if within that period any two or more of those owners or occupiers require in accordance with the provisions of [this Schedule] that a supply shall be given to their premises, the necessary distributing main shall be laid by the Undertakers at the same time as the electric line intended for the particular consumer.

NOTES

The words in square brackets were substituted, and the words omitted were repealed, by the Electricity Act 1947, s 57(2), Sch 4, Pt III.

Twenty-eight days. These are exclusive of the day of service and the day when the work is begun; see, in particular, *R v Turner* [1910] 1 KB 346, 79 LJKB 176 and *Re Hector Whaling Ltd* [1936] Ch 208, [1935] All ER Rep 302; but see also *Schnabel v Allard* [1967] 1 QB 627, [1966] 3 All ER 816, CA.

Serve etc. For provisions as to service, see the Electricity Act 1947, s 63 post, in conjunction with s 57(2) of that Act post.

Definitions. For "consumer", "distributing main", "energy" and "general supply", see s 1 of this Schedule ante. By virtue of the same section, for "electric line" and "street", see the Electric Lighting Act 1882, s 32 ante; and for "local authority", see s 31 of that Act. For "Undertakers", see s 2 of this Schedule ante.

23 If Undertakers fail to lay down mains, etc, Order may be revoked

(1) If the Undertakers ... make default in laying down any distributing mains in accordance with the provisions of [this Schedule] within the periods prescribed in that behalf respectively, they shall be liable for each default to a penalty not exceeding five pounds for each day during which the default continues ...

(2), (3) ...

NOTES

The words in square brackets were subsituted, and the words omitted were repealed, by the Electricity Act 1947, s 57(2), Sch 4, Pt III. The marginal note is no longer applicable in view of such amendment.

Definitions. For "distributing main", see s 1 of this Schedule ante; and for "Undertakers", see s 2 of this Schedule ante.

24 Manner in which requisition is to be made

(1) Any requisition requiring the Undertakers to lay down [a distributing main] for the purposes of general supply throughout any street or part of a street [or along any other route] may be made by six or more owners or occupiers of premises along that street or part of a street [or within reasonable proximity of such route] or, where the local authority ... have the control and management of the public lamps in that street or part of a street, by the local authority.

(2) Every such requisition shall be signed by the persons making it, or by the local authority (as the case may be), and shall be served upon the Undertakers.

(3) Forms of requisition shall be kept by the Undertakers at their office and a copy shall, on

application, be supplied free of charge to any owner or occupier of premises within the area of supply and, where necessary, to the local authority, and any requisition so supplied shall be deemed valid in point of form.

NOTES

The words in square brackets were added or substituted, and the words omitted were repealed, by the Electricity Act 1947, s 57(2) and Sch 4, Pt III.

Requisition. As to duty of Undertakers to comply with requisition, see s 21 of this Schedule ante. For power of Undertakers to impose terms, see ss 25, 26 of this Schedule post. For provisions as to service, see the Electricity Act 1947, s 63 post, in conjunction with s 57(2) of that Act post.

Definitions. For "areas of supply", see s 4 of this Schedule ante, and for "distributing main" and "general supply", see s 1 of this Schedule ante. By virtue of s 1 of this Schedule ante, for "local authority", see the Electric Lighting Act 1882, s 31 ante, and for "street", see s 32 of that Act ante. For "Undertakers", see s 2 of this Schedule ante.

25 Provisions on requisition by owners or occupiers

(1) Where any such requisition is made by any such owners or occupiers as aforesaid, the Undertakers (if they think fit) may, within fourteen days after the service of the requisition upon them, serve a notice on all the persons by whom the requisition is signed, stating that they decline to be bound by the requisition unless those persons or some of them will bind themselves to take, or will guarantee that there shall be taken, a supply of energy for a period of three years at the least, of such amount in the aggregate (to be specified by the Undertakers in the notice) as will, at the rates of charge for the time being charged by the Undertakers for a supply of energy from distributing mains to ordinary consumers within the area of supply, produce annually such reasonable sum as is specified by the Undertakers in the notice: Provided that in the notice the Undertakers shall not, without the authority of [the Minister of Power] specify any sum exceeding twenty per centum upon the expense of providing and laying down the required distributing mains and any other mains or additions to existing mains which may be necessary for the purpose of connecting those distributing mains with the nearest available source of supply.

(2) Where such a notice is served the requisition shall not be binding on the Undertakers unless within fourteen days after the service of the notice on all the persons signing the requisition has been effected, or in case of difference within fourteen days after the delivery of the arbitrator's award, there be tendered to the Undertakers an agreement severally executed by those persons or some of them, binding them to take or guaranteeing that there shall be taken a supply of energy for a period of three years at the least of such amount as will in the aggregate at the rates of charge above specified produce an annual sum amounting to the sum specified in the notice or determined by arbitration under this section, nor unless sufficient security for the payment to the Undertakers of all moneys which may become due to them from those persons under the agreement is offered to the Undertakers (if required by them by such notice as aforesaid) within the period limited for the tender of the agreement as aforesaid.

(3) If the Undertakers consider that the requisition is unreasonable, or that, under the circumstances of the case, the provisions of this section ought to be varied, they may, within fourteen days after the service of the requisition upon them, appeal to [the Minister of Power] and that [Minister], after such inquiry (if any) as [he thinks] fit, may, by order, either determine that the requisition is unreasonable, and shall not be binding upon the Undertakers, or may authorise the Undertakers by their notice to require a supply of energy to be taken for such longer period than three years, and to specify such sum or percentage, whether calculated as hereinbefore provided or otherwise, as is fixed or directed by the order, and the terms of the abovementioned agreement shall be varied accordingly.

(4) In case of any appeal to [the Minister of Power] under this section, any notice by the Undertakers under this section may be served by them within fourteen days after the decision of [the Minister of Power].

(5) If any difference arises between the Undertakers and any persons signing any such requisition as to any such notice or agreement, that difference shall, subject to the provisions of this section and to the decision of [the Minister of Power] upon any such appeal as aforesaid, be determined by arbitration.

NOTES

The words "the Minister of Power" wherever they occur in this section were substituted by the Minister of Fuel and Power (Change of Style and Title) Order 1957, SI 1957/48, art 2(1) (see further the note below). The other words in square brackets were substituted by the Electricity Act 1947, s 57(2), Sch 4, Pt III.

Such requisition. See s 24 of this Schedule ante.

Serve a notice. For provisions as to service, see the Electricity Act 1947, s 63 post, in conjunction with s 57(2) of that Act post.

Minister of Power. The functions of the Minister of Power under this section are now exercised by the Secretary of State for Energy; see the Preliminary Note to this title.

Sufficient security. As to the nature and amount, see s 71 of this Schedule post.

Definitions. For "area of supply", see s 4 of this Schedule ante. For "consumer", "distributing main", "energy" and "main", see s 1 of this Schedule ante. For "Undertakers", see s 2 of this Schedule ante.

26 Provisions on requisition by local authority

Where any such requisition is made by the local authority it shall not be binding on the Undertakers, unless at the time when the service is effected, or within fourteen days thereafter, there be tendered to the Undertakers (if required by them) an agreement executed by the local authority, and binding them to take for a period of three years at the least a supply of energy for lighting such public lamps in the street or part of a street in respect of which the requisition is made as may be under their management or control.

NOTES

Such requisition. See s 24 of this Schedule ante.

Definitions. For "energy", see s 1 of this Schedule ante. By virtue of the same section, for "local authority", see the Electric Lighting Act 1882, s 31 ante; and for "street", see s 32 of that Act. For "Undertakers", see s 2 of this Schedule ante.

Supply

27 Undertakers to furnish sufficient supply of energy to owners and occupiers within the area of supply

(1) The Undertakers shall, upon being required to do so by the owner or occupier of any premises situate within fifty yards from any distributing main of the Undertakers in which they are, for the time being, required to maintain or are maintaining a supply of energy for the purposes of general supply to private consumers under [this Schedule] or the [Electricity regulations], give and continue to give a supply of energy for those premises in accordance with the provisions of [this Schedule] and of the said regulations, and they shall furnish and lay any electric lines that may be necessary for the purpose of supplying the maximum power with which any such owner or occupier is entitled to be supplied under [this Schedule] subject to the conditions following; (that is to say),—

The cost of so much of any electric line for the supply of energy to any owner or occupier as may be laid upon the property of that owner or in the possession of that occupier, and of so much of any such electric lines as it may be necessary to lay for a greater distance than sixty feet from any distributing main of the Undertakers, although not on that property, shall, if the Undertakers so require, be defrayed by that owner or occupier.

[(1A) Subsection (1) of this section shall not apply in relation to premises to which a supply of energy is already given, directly from electric lines belonging to the Undertakers, by a private supplier.]

(2) Every owner or occupier of premises requiring a supply of energy shall—

    (*a*) Serve a notice upon the Undertakers specifying the premises in respect of which the supply is required and the maximum power required to be supplied, and the day (not being an earlier day than a reasonable time after the date of the service of the notice) upon which the supply is required to commence; and

    (*b*) If required by the Undertakers, enter into a written contract with them to continue to receive and pay for a supply of energy for a period of at least two years of such an amount that the payment to be made for the supply, at the rate of charge for the time being charged by the Undertakers for a supply of energy to ordinary consumers within the area of supply, shall not be less than twenty per centum per annum on the outlay incurred by the Undertakers in providing any electric lines required under this section to be provided by them for the purpose of the supply, and if required by the Undertakers give to them security for the payment to them of all moneys which may become due to them by the owner or occupier in respect of any electric lines to be furnished by the Undertakers, and in respect of energy to be supplied by them.

(3) Provided always, that the Undertakers may, after they have given a supply of energy in respect of any premises, by notice in writing, require the owner or occupier of those premises, within seven days after the date of the service of the notice, to give to them security for the payment of all moneys which may become due to them in respect of the supply, in case the owner or occupier has not already given that security, or in case any security given has become invalid or is insufficient; and in case any such owner or occupier fail to comply with the terms of the notice, the Undertakers may, if they think fit, discontinue to supply energy for the premises as long as the failure continues.

(4) Provided also, that if the owner or occupier of any such premises as aforesaid uses any form of [electrical [plant or] fittings] or uses the energy supplied to him by the Undertakers for any purposes, or deals with it in any manner so as to interfere unduly or improperly with the efficient supply of energy to any other body or person by the Undertakers, the Undertakers may, if they think fit, discontinue to supply energy to those premises so long as the [electrical [plant or] fittings] is so used, or the energy is so used or dealt with.

(5) Provided also, that the Undertakers shall not be compelled to give a supply of energy to any premises unless they are reasonably satisfied that the electric lines, [plant,] fittings, and apparatus therein are in good order and condition, and not calculated to affect injuriously the use of energy by the Undertakers or by other persons.

(6) If any difference arises under this section as to any improper use of energy or as to any alleged defect in any electric lines, [plant,] fittings, or apparatus, that difference shall be determined by arbitration.

NOTES

The words in square brackets in sub-s (1) were substituted by the Electricity Act 1947, s 57(2), Sch 4, Pt III.

Sub-s (1A) and the words in square brackets in sub-ss (5), (6) were inserted by the Energy Act 1983, ss 13, 25, Sch 3, para 2(3)(*b*).

In sub-s (4), the words "plant or" in both cases where they occur were inserted by the Energy Act 1983, s 25, Sch 3, para 2(3)(*a*); the other words in square brackets were substituted by the Electricity Act 1947, s 57(2), Sch 4, Pt III.

Occupier. This does not include someone whose original entry in the premises was unlawful and forcible; see *Woodcock v South Western Electricity Board* [1975] 2 All ER 545, [1975] 1 WLR 983.

Serve a notice. For provisions as to service, see the Electricity Act 1947, s 63 post, in conjunction with s 57(2) of that Act post.

Discontinuance for arrears. For power to discontinue supply when payment is in arrear, see the Electric Lighting Act 1882, s 21 ante and the Electric Lighting Act 1909, s 18 post.

Definitions. For "area of supply", see s 4 of this Schedule ante. For "consumer", "distributing main", "Electricity regulations", "energy" and "general supply", see s 1 of this Schedule ante. By virtue of the same section, for "electric line", see the Electric Lighting Act 1882, s 32 ante. For "electrical fittings" and "electrical plant", see the Electricity Act 1947, s 67(1), (2) post. For "Undertakers", see s 2 of this Schedule ante.

---

28 Maximum power

(1) The maximum power with which any consumer shall be entitled to be supplied shall be of such amount as he may require to be supplied with, not exceeding what may be reasonably anticipated as the maximum consumption on his premises: Provided that where any consumer has required the Undertakers to supply him with a maximum power of any specified amount, he shall not be entitled to alter that maximum except upon one month's notice to the Undertakers, and any expenses reasonably incurred by the Undertakers in respect of the service lines by which energy is supplied to the premises of that consumer, or any fittings or apparatus of the Undertakers upon those premises, consequent upon the alteration, shall be paid by him to the Undertakers, and may be recovered summarily as a civil debt.

(2) If any difference arises between any such owner or occupier and the Undertakers as to what may be reasonably anticipated as the consumption on his premises or as to the reasonableness of any expenses under this section, that difference shall be determined by arbitration.

NOTES

Notice. For provisions as to the service of notices, see the Electricity Act 1947, s 63 post, in conjunction with s 57(2) of that Act post.

Summarily as a civil debt. By the Magistrates' Courts Act 1980, s 58(1), Vol 27, title Magistrates, a magistrates' court has power to make an order on complaint for the payment of any money which is recoverable summarily as a civil debt, and by s 127(1) of that Act, the complaint may not be heard unless it was made within six months from the time when the matter of complaint arose.

Definitions. For "consumer", "energy" and "service line", see s 1 of this Schedule ante; and for "Undertakers", see s 2 of this Schedule ante.

29 Supply of energy to public lamps

. . . the Undertakers shall, upon receiving reasonable notice from the local authority requiring them to supply energy to any public lamps within the distance of seventy-five yards from any distributing main of the Undertakers in which they are for the time being required to maintain a current of energy for the purposes of general supply under [this Schedule], or the [Electricity regulations], give and continue to give a supply of energy to those lamps in such quantities as the local authority may require to be supplied.

NOTES

The words in square brackets were substituted, and the words omitted were repealed, by the Electricity Act 1947, s 57(2), Sch 4, Pt III.

Definitions. For "distributing main", "Electricity regulations", "energy" and "general supply", see s 1 of this Schedule ante. By virtue of the same section, for "local authority", see the Electric Lighting Act 1882, s 31 ante. For "Undertakers", see s 2 of this Schedule ante.

30 Penalty for failure to supply

(1) Whenever the Undertakers make default in supplying energy to any owner or occupier of premises to whom they may be and are required to supply energy under [this Schedule], they shall be liable in respect of each default to a penalty not exceeding [two pounds] for each day on which the default occurs.

(2) Where . . . the Undertakers make default in supplying energy to the public lamps to which they may be and are required to supply energy under [this Schedule], the Undertakers shall be liable in respect of each default to a penalty not exceeding [two pounds] for each lamp, and for each day on which the default occurs.

(3) Whenever the Undertakers make default in supplying energy in accordance with the terms of the [Electricity regulations] they shall be liable to such penalties as are prescribed by the regulations in that behalf.

(4) Provided that the penalties to be inflicted on the Undertakers under this section shall in no case exceed in the aggregate in respect of any defaults not being wilful defaults on the part of the Undertakers the sum of fifty pounds for any one day, and provided also that in no case shall any penalty be inflicted in respect of any default if the court are of opinion that the default was caused by inevitable accident or force majeure or was of so slight or unimportant a character as not materially to affect the value of the supply.

NOTES

The words in the second pair of square brackets in sub-s (1), and those in the second pair of square brackets in sub-s (2) are substituted by virtue of the Decimal Currency Act 1969, s 10(1), Vol 10, title Constitutional Law (Pt 3). The other words in square brackets were substituted, and the words omitted were repealed, by the Electricity Act 1947, s 57(2), Sch 4, Pt III.

Default. An action will not lie at common law for negligence in supply; see *Stevens v Aldershot Gas, Water and District Lighting Co (now Mid-Southern District Utility Co)* (1932) 102 LJKB 12, 31 LGR 48.

Force majeure. See *Hackney Borough Council v Doré* [1922] 1 KB 431, 91 LJKB 109 and *G Scammell and Nephew Ltd v Hurley* [1929] 1 KB 419, 98 LJKB 98, CA.

Definitions. For "Electricity regulations" and "energy", see s 1 of this Schedule ante; and for "Undertakers", see s 2 of this Schedule ante.

31–34 *(Repealed by the Electricity Act 1947, s 57(7), Sch 5.)*

Electric Inspectors

35 Appointment of electric inspectors

(1) . . . [the Minister of Power] . . . may appoint and keep appointed, one or more competent and impartial person or persons to be electric inspectors under [this Schedule].

(2) . . .

NOTES

The words "this Schedule" were substituted, and the words omitted were repealed, by the Electricity Act 1947, s 57(2), Sch 4, Pt III. The words "the Minister of Power" were substituted by the Minister of Fuel and Power (Change of Style and Title) Order 1957, SI 1957/48, art 1(2) (see further the note below).

Minister of Power. The functions of the Minister of Power under this section are now exercised by the Secretary of State for Energy; see the Preliminary Note to this title.

---

36 Duties of electric inspectors

(1) The duties of an electric inspector under [this Schedule] shall be as follows:—

(a) The inspection and testing, periodically and in special cases, of the [electric lines and works of persons who supply energy] and the supply of energy given by them;

(b) . . . ; and

(c) Such other duties [as the Secretary of State may determine].

[(2) The Minister may prescribe by regulations the manner in which and the times at which any such duties are to be performed by an electric inspector and also the fees to be taken by him, and any fees taken by an electric inspector shall be paid by him to the Minister.]

NOTES

The words "this Schedule" in sub-s (1) and the whole of sub-s (2) were substituted by the Electricity Act 1947, s 57(2), Sch 4, Pt III. The words in the second and third pairs of square brackets in sub-s (1) were substituted by the Energy Act 1983, ss 14(2), 25, Sch 3, para 2(4), and the words omitted from that subsection were repealed by the Electricity Supply (Meters) Act 1936, s 5(2).

Secretary of State; Minister. The powers under this section are now exercised by the Secretary of State for Energy; see the Preliminary Note to this title.

Definitions. By virtue of s 1 of this Schedule ante, for "electric lines" and "works", see the Electric Lighting Act 1882, s 32 ante; and for "Minister", see the Electricity Act 1947, s 67(1) post. For "Electricity regulations" and "energy", see s 1 of this Schedule ante; and for "Undertakers", see s 2 of this Schedule ante.

Regulations under this section. No regulations had been made under this section up to 1 August 1985.

---

37 *(Repealed by the Electricity Act 1947, s 57(7), Sch 5.)*

38 Notice of accidents and inquiries by [Minister of Power]

(1) *The Undertakers shall send to [the Minister of Power] notice of any accident by explosion, or fire, and also of any other accident of such kind as to have caused, or to be likely to have caused, loss of life, or personal injury which has occurred in any part of the Undertakers' works or their circuits, or in connection with those works or circuits, and also notice of any loss of life or personal injury occasioned by any such accident. The notice shall be sent by the earliest practicable post after the accident occurs, or, as the case may be, after the loss of life or personal injury becomes known to the Undertakers.*

If the Undertakers fail to comply with the provisions of this sub-section they shall be liable, for each default, to a penalty not exceeding [level 2 on the standard scale].

(2) *[The Minister of Power] may also, if [he deems] it necessary, appoint any electric inspector or other fit person to inquire and report as to the cause of any accident affecting the safety of the public, which may have been occasioned with or in connexion with the Undertakers' works, whether notice of the accident has or has not been received from the Undertakers, or as to the manner and extent in and to which the provisions of [this Schedule] and the principal Act, and of the [Electricity regulations], so far as those provisions affect the safety of the public, have been complied with by the Undertakers; and any person appointed under this section, not being an electric inspector, shall for the purposes of his appointment have all the powers of an electric inspector under [this Schedule].*

NOTES

The words "the Minister of Power" were substituted by the Minister of Fuel and Power (Change of Style and Title) Order 1957, SI 1957/48 art 1(2), and the marginal note has been adjusted accordingly (see further the note below).

The reference in sub-s (1) to level 2 on the standard scale is substituted by virtue of the Criminal Justice Act 1982, s 46, Vol 27, title Magistrates. The maximum fine was previously increased to £50 by the Criminal Law Act 1977, s 31(6).

The words in the other pairs of square brackets in sub-s (2) were substituted by the Electricity Act 1947, s 57(2), Sch 4, Pt III.

Prospective repeal. This section is repealed by the Energy Act 1983, s 36, Sch 4, Pt I post as from a day to be appointed under s 37(1) of that Act.

Notice. Accidents may in certain cases be notifiable under the Notification of Accidents and Dangerous Occurrences Regulations 1980, SI 1980/804.

For provisions as to service, see the Electricity Act 1947, s 63 post, in conjunction with s 57(2) of that Act post.

Minister of Power. The functions of the Minister of Power under this section are now exercised by the Secretary of State for Energy; see the Preliminary Note to this title.

Standard scale. See the note to s 13 of this Schedule ante.

Definitions. For "Electricity regulations" and "the principal Act", see s 1 of this Schedule ante; and for "Undertakers", see s 2 of this Schedule ante. By virtue of s 1 of this Schedule ante, for "works", see the Electric Lighting Act 1882, s 32 ante.

Testing and Inspection

39 Testing of mains

On the occasion of the testing of any main of the Undertakers reasonable notice thereof shall be given to the Undertakers by the electric inspector, and the testing shall be carried out at such suitable hours as, in the opinion of the inspector, will least interfere with the supply of energy by the Undertakers, and in such manner as the inspector thinks expedient, but, except [with the written authority given] in each case in that behalf by [the Minister of Power], he shall not be entitled to have access to or interfere with the mains of the Undertakers at any points other than those at which the Undertakers have reserved for themselves access to the said mains: Provided that the Undertakers shall not be held responsible for any interruption in the supply of energy which may be occasioned by or required by the inspector for the purpose of any such testing as aforesaid. Provided also that the testings shall not be made in regard to any particular portion of a main oftener than once in any three months, unless in pursuance of [a written authority given] in each case in that behalf by [the Minister of Power].

NOTES

The words "the Minister of Power" were substituted by the Minister of Fuel and Power (Change of Style and Title) Order 1957, SI 1957/48, art 1(2) (see further the note below). The other words in square brackets were substituted by the Electricity Act 1947, s 57(2), Sch 4, Pt III.

Minister of Power. The functions of the Minister of Power under this section are now exercised by the Secretary of State for Energy; see the Preliminary Note to this title.

Application. This section and ss 42–48 post are applied to suppliers of electricity other than Electricity Boards by the Energy Act 1983, s 14(3) post.

40 Testing of works and supply on consumer's premises

An electric inspector, if and when required to do so by any consumer, shall, on payment by the consumer of the prescribed fee, test the variation of electric pressure at the consumer's terminals, or make such other inspection and testing of the service lines, apparatus, and works of the Undertakers upon the consumer's premises as may be necessary for the purpose of determining whether the Undertakers have complied with the provisions of [this Schedule] and the [Electricity regulations].

NOTES

The words in square brackets were substituted by the Electricity Act 1947, s 57(2), Sch 4, Pt III.

Prescribed fee. For power to make regulations prescribing fees, see s 36(2) of this Schedule, ante.

Definitions. For "consumer", "consumer's terminals", "Electricity regulations" and "service line", see s 1 of this Schedule ante. For "Undertakers", see s 2 of this Schedule ante. By virtue of s 1 of this Schedule, for "works", see the Electric Lighting Act 1882, s 32 ante.

41 Undertakers, not being local authority, to establish testing stations

(1) . . . the Undertakers shall at such places, within a reasonable distance from a distributing main, establish at their own cost and keep in proper condition such reasonable number of testing stations, as [the Minister thinks] proper and sufficient for testing the supply of energy by the Undertakers through the main, and shall place thereat proper and suitable instruments of a pattern to be approved by [the Minister], and shall connect those stations by means of proper and sufficient electric lines with the mains, and supply energy thereto for the purpose of the testing.

(2), (3) . . .

NOTES

In sub-s (1), the words in square brackets were substituted and the words omitted were repealed and sub-ss (2), (3) were also repealed, by the Electricity Act 1947, s 57(2), Sch 4, Pt III; the marginal note is therefore no longer wholly applicable.

Minister of Power. The functions of the Minister of Power under this section are now exercised by the Secretary for Energy; see the Preliminary Note to this title.

Definition. For "distributing main", "energy" and "main", see s 1 of this Schedule ante. By virtue of the same section, for "electric line", see the Electric Lighting Act 1882, s 32 ante; and for "Minister", see the Electricity Act 1947, s 67(1) post. For "Undertakers", see s 2 of this Schedule ante.

42 Undertakers to keep instruments on their premises

The Undertakers shall set up and keep upon all premises from which they supply energy by any distributing mains such suitable and proper instruments of such pattern and construction as may be approved or prescribed by [the Minister of Power], and shall take and record, and keep recorded such observations as [the Minister of Power] may prescribe, and any observations so recorded shall be receivable in evidence.

NOTES

The words in square brackets were substituted by the Minister of Fuel and Power (Change of Style and Title) Order 1957, SI 1957/48, art 1(2) (see further the note below).

Minister of Power. The functions of the Minister of Power under this section are now exercised by the Secretary of State for Energy; see the Preliminary Note to this title.

Application. See the note to s 39 of this Schedule ante.

Definitions. For "distributing main" and "energy", see s 1 of this Schedule ante; and for "Undertakers", see s 2 of this Schedule ante.

43 Readings of instruments to be taken

(1) The Undertakers shall keep in efficient working order all instruments which they are required by or under [this Schedule] to place, set up, or keep at any testing station or on their own premises, and any electric inspector appointed under [this Schedule] may examine and record the readings of those instruments, and any readings so recorded shall be receivable in evidence.

(2) . . .

NOTES

The words in square brackets were substituted, and sub-s (2) was repealed, by the Electricity Act 1947, s 57(2), Sch 4, Pt III.

Undertakers. For meaning, see s 2 of this Schedule ante.

Application. See the note to s 39 of this Schedule ante.

44 Electric inspector may test Undertakers' instruments

Any electric inspector appointed under [this Schedule] shall have the right to have access at all reasonable hours to the testing stations and premises of the Undertakers for the purpose of testing the electric lines and instruments of the Undertakers, and ascertaining if they are in order, and in case they are not in order he may require the Undertakers forthwith to have them put in order.

NOTES

The words in square brackets were substituted by the Electricity Act 1947, s 57(2), Sch 4, Pt III.

Application. See the note to s 39 of this Schedule ante.

Definitions. By virtue of s 1 of this Schedule ante, for "electric line", see the Electric Lighting Act 1882, s 32 ante. For "Undertakers", see s 2 of this Schedule ante.

45 Representation of Undertakings at testings

The Undertakers may, if they think fit, on each occasion of the testing of any main or service line, or the testing or inspection of any instruments of the Undertakers by any electric inspector, be represented by some officer or other agent, but that officer or agent shall not interfere with the testing or inspection.

NOTES

Application. See the note to s 39 of this Schedule ante.

Definitions. For "main", and "service line", see s 1 of this Schedule ante, and for "Undertakers", see s 2 of this Schedule ante.

46 Undertakers to give facilities for testing

The Undertakers shall afford all facilities for the proper execution of [this Schedule] with respect to inspection and the testing and readings and inspection of instruments, and shall comply with all the requirements of or under [this Schedule] in that behalf; and in case the Undertakers make default in complying with any of the provisions of this section they shall be liable in respect of each default to a penalty not exceeding [level 1 on the standard scale], and to a daily penalty not exceeding one pound.

NOTES

The words in the first and second pairs of square brackets were substituted by the Electricity Act 1947, s 57(2), Sch 4, Pt III.

The reference to level 1 on the standard scale is substituted by virtue of the Criminal Justice Act 1982, s 46, Vol 27, title Magistrates. The maximum fine was previously increased to £25 by the Criminal Law Act 1977, s 31(6).

Standard scale. See the note to s 13 of this Schedule ante.

Application. See the note to s 39 of this Schedule ante.

Definitions. For "daily penalty" see s 1 of this Schedule ante; and for "Undertakers", see s 2 of this Schedule ante.

47 Report of results of testing

(1) Every electric inspector shall, on the day immediately following that on which any testing has been completed by him under [this Schedule], make and deliver a report of the results of his testing to the . . . person by whom he was required to make the testing, and to the Undertakers, and that report shall be receivable in evidence.

(2) If the Undertakers or any such ... person are or is dissatisfied with any report of any electric inspector, they or he may appeal to [the Minister of Power] against the report, and thereupon [the Minister of Power] shall inquire into and decide upon the matter of the appeal, and [his] decision shall be final and binding on all parties.

NOTES

The words in the first pair of square brackets in sub-s (1) were substituted, and the words omitted were repealed, by the Electricity Act 1947, s 57(2), Sch 4, Pt III, and the word in the third pair of square brackets in sub-s (2) was substituted by virtue of those provisions.

The words in the first and second pairs of square brackets in sub-s (2) were substituted by the Minister of Fuel and Power (Change of Style and Title) Order 1957, SI 1957/48, art 1(2) (see further the note below).

Undertakers. For definition, see s 2 of this Schedule ante.

Minister of Power. The functions of the Minister of Power under this section are now exercised by the Secretary of State for Energy; see the Preliminary Note to this title.

48 Expenses of electric inspector

(1) Save as otherwise provided by [this Schedule] or by the [Electricity regulations], all fees and reasonable expenses of an electric inspector shall, unless agreed, be ascertained ... by [the Minister of Power], and shall be paid by the Undertakers, and ... may be recovered summarily as a civil debt.

(2) Provided that where the report of an electric inspector, or the decision of [the Minister of Power], shows that any consumer was guilty of any default or negligence, the fees and expenses shall, on being ascertained as above mentioned, be paid by the consumer as ... [the Minister of Power] ..., having regard to the report or decision, [directs], and may be recovered summarily as a civil debt.

(3) Provided also, that in any proceedings for penalties under [this Schedule] the fees and expenses of an electric inspector incurred in connection with the proceedings shall be payable by the complainant or defendant as the court direct.

NOTES

The words "the Minister of Power" were substituted by the Minister of Fuel and Power (Change of Style and Title) Order 1957, SI 1957/48, art 1(2) (see further the note below). The other words in square brackets were substituted by the Electricity Act 1947, s 57(2), Sch 4, Pt III. The words omitted were repealed by the last-mentioned provisions.

Fees and reasonable expenses of inspector. These do not include his salary or the general expenses of his laboratory (*Crawford v City of London Electric Lighting Co* (1898) 67 LJQB 942, 78 LT 841).

Minister of Power. The functions of the Minister of Power under this section are now exercised by the Secretary of State for Energy; see the Preliminary Note to this title.

Summarily as a civil debt. See the note to s 28 of this Schedule ante.

Definitions. For "consumer" and "Electricity regulations", see s 1 of this Schedule ante; and for "Undertakers", see s 2 of this Schedule ante.

Meters

[49 Meters to be used except by agreement

(1) This section applies to—

(a) a supply by the Undertakers to an ordinary consumer, and

(b) a supply by a private supplier to a person (other than the Undertakers) who takes the supply directly from electric lines belonging to the Undertakers,

unless otherwise agreed between the Undertakers and (in a case within paragraph (a) above), the consumer or (in a case within paragraph (b) above) the private supplier.

(2) The value of a supply to which this section applies shall be ascertained by means of an appropriate meter duly certified under the provisions of this Schedule, and fixed and connected with the Undertakers' lines in some manner approved by the Secretary of State.

(3) References in this section and the following sections to the value of a supply are references to the amount of energy supplied or (according to the method of charging) the electrical quantity contained in the supply.]

NOTES

This section was substituted by the Energy Act 1983, s 15, Sch 1, para 4.

Secretary of State. Ie the Secretary of State for Energy; see the Preliminary Note to this title.

Definitions. For "consumer", "energy" and "private supplier", see s 1 of this Schedule ante; for "Undertakers", see s 2 of this Schedule ante; and for "electric line", see the Electric Lighting Act 1882, s 32 ante.

[50 Meter to be certified

A meter shall be considered to be duly certified under the provisions of [this Schedule] if it be certified by an [authorised person] to be a meter capable of ascertaining the value of the supply within such limits of error as may, as respects meters of the class to which the meter belongs, be allowed by [the Minister of Power], and to be of some construction and pattern approved by [the Minister of Power] and every such meter is hereinafter referred to as a "certified meter": Provided that where any alteration is made in any certified meter, that meter shall cease to be a certified meter unless and until it is again certified as a certified meter under the provisions of [this Schedule].]

NOTES

This section was substituted by the Electric Lighting Act 1909, s 11, Sch 2, with possible modifications if incorporated in enactments then existing.

The words "authorised person" were substituted by the Energy Act 1983, s 15, Sch 1, para 5; the words "the Minister of Power" were substituted by the Minister of Fuel and Power (Change of Style and Title) Order 1957, SI 1957/48, art 1(2) (see further the note below); the words "this Schedule" were substituted by the Electricity Act 1947, s 57(2), Sch 4, Pt III.

Minister of Power. The functions of the Minister of Power under this section are now exercised by the Secretary of State for Energy; see the Preliminary Note to this title.

Certification of meters. For further provisions as to the certification of meters, see the Electricity Act 1957, s 30 post.

Definitions. For "the value of a supply", see s 49 of this Schedule ante; and for "authorised person" see s 50A(1) of this Schedule post.

[50A Persons authorised to certify meters

(1) The reference in section 50 above to an authorised person is a reference to—

(a) a meter examiner appointed under the Electricity Supply (Meters) Act 1936, or

(b) a person authorised by the Secretary of State under this section.

(2) The Secretary of State may authorise a person who manufactures or repairs meters to certify, in accordance with section 50 above, meters manufactured or repaired by him.

(3) An authorisation under this section may be given subject to such conditions as the Secretary of State thinks fit and may be withdrawn before the end of the period for which it is given if any of those conditions is not satisfied.

(4) The Secretary of State may make regulations prescribing fees to be paid to him by applicants for or holders of authorisations under this section towards administrative expenses incurred by him by virtue of this section; and different fees may be prescribed in relation to different areas and different cases.]

NOTES

This section was inserted by the Energy Act 1983, s 15, Sch 1, para 6.

Secretary of State. Ie the Secretary of State for Energy; see the Preliminary Note to this title.

Thinks fit. Statutory powers are often conferred in subjective terms, the competent authority being entitled to act, eg, when it "thinks fit", or when it is "satisfied" or it "appears" to it that a prescribed state of affairs exists, but the inherent jurisdiction of the courts to determine whether such powers have been exceeded is not readily ousted by the use of such language; see further 1 Halsbury's Laws (4th edn) para 22.

Certification of meters. For further provisions as to the certification of meters, see the Electricity Act 1957, s 30 post.

Regulations under this section. No regulations had been made under this section up to 1 August 1985.

Electricity Supply (Meters) Act 1936. See this title post.

[50B Uncertified meters—Offences

(1) If the Undertakers or a private supplier install a meter for the purpose of ascertaining the value of a supply to which section 49 above applies and that meter, at the time when it is installed, is not a certified meter, the Undertakers or the supplier shall be guilty of an offence.

(2) Where a meter used for the purpose of ascertaining the value of a supply to which section 49 above applies ceases to be a certified meter, the person providing the supply shall as soon as practicable take all reasonable steps either for causing the meter to be recertified or for causing it to be removed or (if its removal is not reasonably practicable) for ceasing to supply energy through it.

(3) A person who fails to take the steps required of him by subsection (2) above shall be guilty of an offence unless he shows that the meter ceased to be a duly certified meter by reason only of its being altered or moved without his knowledge.

(4) A person guilty of an offence under this section shall be liable on summary conviction to a fine not exceeding level 2 on the standard scale (within the meaning of section 75 of the Criminal Justice Act 1982).

(5) Proceedings for an offence under this section shall not, in England and Wales, be instituted except by or with the consent of the Secretary of State or the Director of Public Prosecutions.]

NOTES

This section was inserted by the Energy Act 1983, s 15, Sch 1, para 6.

Person. Unless the contrary intention appears this includes a body of persons corporate or unincorporate; see the Interpretation Act 1978, s 5, Sch 1, Vol 41, title Statutes.

Reasonably practicable. The meaning of this expression and the difference between "reasonably practicable" and the stricter standard of "practicable" have been most often considered judicially in relation to safety legislation. See further, 20 Halsbury's Laws (4th edn) para 553.

Summary conviction. Summary jurisdiction and procedure are mainly governed by the Magistrates' Courts Act 1980, Vol 27, title Magistrates, and by rules made under s 144 of that Act.

Standard scale. See the note to s 13 of this Schedule ante.

England; Wales. For meanings, see the Interpretation Act 1978, s 5, Sch 1, Vol 41, title Statutes.

Consent of the Secretary of State or the Director of Public Prosecutions. The Secretary of State here concerned is the Secretary of State for Energy.

Provision for the appointment of the Director of Public Prosecutions and Assistant Directors is currently made by the Prosecution of Offences Act 1979, s 1, Vol 12, title Criminal Law; by sub-s (4) of that section an Assistant Director may do any act or thing which the Director is required or authorised to do. See also, in particular, s 6 of that Act, as to arrest, remand, etc, where the consent of the Director has not yet been given, and s 7, as to evidence of such consent.

The 1979 Act is repealed by the Prosecution of Offences Act 1985, Vol 12, title Criminal Law, as from a day to be appointed under s 31(2) thereof. New provision is made as to the establishment of a Crown Prosecution Service for England and Wales by ss 1–10. In particular, by s 1(6), every Crown Prosecutor has all the powers of the Director as to the institution and conduct of proceedings but exercises those powers under his direction.

Provisions re-enacting ss 6 and 7 of the 1979 Act are contained in ss 25 and 26 of the 1985 Act, respectively.

Consent should be proved before the summons is issued, and the point that consent is lacking cannot be taken for the first time after the case for the prosecution has been closed; see *Price v Humphries* [1958] 2 QB 353, [1958] 2 All ER 725.

Certification of meters. For further provisions as to the certification of meters, see the Electricity Act 1957, s 30 post.

Definitions. For "certified meter", see s 50 of this Schedule ante; for "energy", see s 1 of this Schedule ante; for "Undertakers", see s 2 of this Schedule ante; and for "value of a supply", see s 49 of this Schedule ante.

Criminal Justice Act 1982, s 75. See Vol 27, title Magistrates.

[51 Inspector to certify meter

An electric inspector, on being required to do so by the Undertakers [, the person supplied with energy or, where the supply is by a private supplier, that supplier], and on payment of the prescribed fee by the party so requiring him, shall examine any meter used or intended to be used for ascertaining the value of [a supply to which section 49 above applies], and shall certify it as a certified meter if he considers it entitled to be so certified, and the inspector shall, on the like requisition and payment, examine the manner in which any such meter has been fixed and connected with the [Undertakers'] lines, and shall certify that it has been fixed and connected with the [Undertakers'] lines in some manner approved by [the Minister of Power], if he considers that it is entitled to be so certified.]

NOTES

This section was substituted by the Electric Lighting Act 1909, s 11, Sch 2, with possible modifications if incorporated in enactments then existing.

The words "the Minister of Power" were substituted by the Minister of Fuel and Power (Change of Style and Title) Order 1957, SI 1957/48, art 1(2) (see further the note below); the other words in square brackets were substituted by the Energy Act 1983, s 15, Sch 1, para 7.

Electric inspector. The powers of electric inspectors under this section have been transferred by the Electricity Supply (Meters) Act 1936, s 1(4) post to meter examiners appointed under that section.

Prescribed fee. See the Electricity Supply (Meters) Act 1936, s 1(3) post.

Minister of Power. The functions of the Minister of Power under this section are now exercised by the Secretary of State for Energy; see the Preliminary Note to this title.

Definitions. For "Undertakers", see s 2 of this Schedule ante; for "energy" and "private supplier", see s 1 ante; and for "certified meter", see s 50 ante.

52 Undertakers to supply meters if required to do so

Where the value of [a supply by the Undertakers] is under [this Schedule] required to be ascertained by means of an appropriate meter, the Undertakers shall, if required by any consumer supply him with an appropriate meter, and shall, if required, fix it upon the premises of the consumer and connect the service lines therewith and procure the meter to be duly certified under the provisions of [this Schedule], ... ; provided that previously to supplying any such meter the Undertakers may require the consumer to pay to them a reasonable sum in respect of the price of the meter, or to give security therefor, or (if he desires to hire the meter) may require him to enter into an agreement for the hire of the meter as herein-after provided.

NOTES

The words in the first pair of square brackets were substituted, and the words omitted were repealed, by the Energy Act 1983, ss 15, 20, 36, Sch 1, para 8, Sch 4, Pt I. The words in the second and third pairs of square brackets were substituted by the Electricity Act 1947, s 57(2), Sch 4, Pt III.

Certified under provisions of this Schedule. See s 51 of this Schedule ante; and see also the Electricity Act 1957, s 30 post.

Security. As to the nature and amount, see s 71 of this Schedule post.

Agreement for the hire. See s 55 of this Schedule post.

Definitions. For "consumer" and "service line", see s 1 of this Schedule ante; for "Undertakers", see s 2 of this Schedule ante; and for "the value of a supply", see s 49 of this Schedule ante.

[53 Meters not to be connected or disconnected without notice

(1) No meter used or to be used for ascertaining the value of a supply to which section 49 above applies shall be connected with, or disconnected from, any electric line belonging to the Undertakers by the Undertakers, the person supplied (or to be supplied) with energy or, where the supply is by a private supplier, that supplier unless the person intending to connect or disconnect the meter has given to the other person or persons mentioned above not less than forty-eight hours' notice in writing of the intention to do so.

(2) A person who contravenes this section shall be guilty of an offence and liable on summary conviction to a fine not exceeding level 2 on the standard scale (within the meaning of section 75 of the Criminal Justice Act 1982).]

NOTES

This section was substituted by the Energy Act 1983, s 15, Sch 1, para 9.

Not less than forty-eight hours notice. For provisions as to the service of notices, see the Electricity Act 1948, s 63 post in conjunction with s 57(2) of that Act post. As to exclusion of Sunday etc, see s 62(4) of this Schedule post.

Person; summary conviction. See the notes to s 50B of this Schedule ante.

Writing. Unless the contrary intention appears this includes other modes of representing or reproducing words in a visible form; see the Interpretation Act 1978, s 5, Sch 1, Vol 41, title Statutes.

Standard scale. See the note to s 13 of this Schedule ante.

Definitions. For "energy", see s 1 of this Schedule ante. By virtue of the same section, for "electric line", see the Electric Lighting Act 1882, s 32 ante. For "private supplier", see s 1 of this Schedule ante; for "Undertakers", see s 2 of this Schedule ante; and for "the value of a supply", see s 49 of this Schedule ante.

Criminal Justice Act 1982, s 75. See Vol 27, title Magistrates.

54 Consumer to keep his meter in proper order

(1) Every consumer shall at all times at his own expense keep all meters belonging to him, whereby the value of [a supply by the Undertakers] is to be ascertained, in proper order for correctly registering that value, and in default of his so doing the Undertakers may cease to supply energy through the meter.

(2) ...

NOTES

The words in square brackets were substituted, and sub-s (2) was repealed, by the Energy Act 1983, ss 15, 20, 36, Sch 1, para 10, Sch 4, Pt I.

Definitions. For "consumer" and "energy", see s 1 of this Schedule ante; for "Undertakers", see s 2 of this Schedule ante; and for "the value of a supply", see s 49 of this Schedule ante.

55 Power to the Undertakers to let meters

The Undertakers may let for hire any meter for ascertaining the value of [a supply of energy], and any fittings thereto, for such remuneration in money and on such terms with respect to the repair of the meter and fittings, and for securing the safety and return to the Undertakers of the meter and fittings, as may be agreed upon between the hirer and the Undertakers, or, in case of difference, determined by [the Minister of Power] and that remuneration shall be recoverable by the Undertakers summarily as a civil debt.

NOTES

The words in the first pair of square brackets were substituted by the Energy Act 1983, s 15, Sch 1, para 11. The words in the second pair of square brackets were substituted by the Minister of Fuel and Power (Change of Style and Title) Order 1957, SI 1957/48, art 1(2) (see further the note below).

Minister of Power. The functions of the Minister of Power under this section are now exercised by the Secretary of State for Energy; see the Preliminary Note to this title.

Summarily as a civil debt. See the note to s 28 of this Schedule ante.

Protection of meters. As to protection of meters from distress, execution and proceedings in bankruptcy while on the consumer's premises, see the Electric Lighting Act 1882, s 25 ante, and the Electric Lighting Act 1909, s 16 post.

Definitions. For "energy", see s 1 of this Schedule ante; for "Undertakers", see s 2 of this Schedule ante; and for "the value of a supply", see s 49 of this Schedule ante.

56 Undertakers to keep meters let for hire in repair

The Undertakers shall, unless the agreement for hire otherwise provides, at all times, at their own expense, keep all meters let for hire by them to any consumer, whereby the value of [a supply by the Undertakers] is ascertained, in proper order for correctly registering that value, and in default of their doing so the consumer shall not be liable to pay rent for the meters during such time as the default continues. The Undertakers shall, for the purposes aforesaid, have access to and be at liberty to remove, test, inspect, and replace any such meter at all reasonable times: Provided that the expenses of procuring any such meter to be again duly certified, where that re-certifying is thereby rendered necessary, shall be paid by the Undertakers.

NOTES

The words in square brackets were substituted by the Energy Act 1983, s 15, Sch 1, para 12.

Definitions. For "consumer", see s 1 of this Schedule ante; for "Undertakers", see s 2 of this Schedule ante; and for "the value of a supply", see s 49 of this Schedule ante.

[57 Questions as to correctness of meter to be determined by meter examiner

(1) Any question—

    (*a*) whether a meter, by which there is ascertained the value of a supply to which section 49 above applies, is in proper order for correctly registering that value, or

    (*b*) whether the value of such a supply has been correctly registered by any meter,

may be referred by any of the persons concerned to a meter examiner appointed under the Electricity Supply (Meters) Act 1936 for determination by him; and in this section "the persons concerned" means the Undertakers, the person supplied and, where the supply is by a private supplier, that supplier.

(2) Before determining a question referred to him under this section, the meter examiner shall give notice to the other person or persons concerned; and his decision shall be final and binding upon all the persons concerned.

(3) A meter examiner determining a question referred to him under this section may make awards of costs or expenses as between the persons concerned.

(4) In the case of a supply by the Undertakers the register of the meter used to ascertain the value of the supply shall, except as provided by this section, be conclusive evidence in the absence of fraud of that value.

(5) The Secretary of State may by regulations—

    (*a*) prescribe a fee to be paid to the Secretary of State by a person other than the Undertakers referring a question for determination under this section;

    (*b*) specify circumstances in which the fee may be refunded; and

    (*c*) make provision requiring the Undertakers to pay sums determined by the Secretary of State towards any administrative expenses incurred by him (and not recovered as mentioned in paragraph (*a*) above) in connection with the determination of questions under this section.]

NOTES

This section was substituted by the Energy Act 1983, s 15, Sch 1, para 13.

General Note. In *Hendon Electric Supply Co Ltd v Banks* (1917) 87 LJKB 790, 118 LT 544, it was held that, where no electric inspector had been appointed under s 35 of this Schedule ante and in consequence differences could not be determined as provided by this section (before it was replaced), no cause of action arose against a consumer disputing the accuracy of his meter for the value of electricity claimed to have been supplied; see also *Joseph v East Ham Corpn* [1936] 1 KB 367, 105 LJKB 410, CA.

Person. See the note to s 50B of this Schedule ante.

Secretary of State. Ie one of Her Majesty's Principal Secretaries of State; see the Interpretation Act 1978, s 5, Sch 1, Vol 41, title Statutes. The Secretary of State here concerned is the Secretary of State for Energy; see the Preliminary Note to this title.

Definitions. For "private supplier", see s 1 of this Schedule ante; for "Undertakers", see s 2 of this Schedule ante; and for "value of a supply", see s 49 of this Schedule ante.

Electric Supply Meters Act 1936. See this title post.

Regulations under this section. No regulations had been made up to 1 August 1985.

58 Undertakers to pay expenses of providing new meters where method of charge altered

Where any consumer who is supplied with energy by the Undertakers from any distributing main is provided with a certified meter for the purpose of ascertaining the value of the supply and the Undertakers change the method of charging for energy supplied by them from the main, the Undertakers shall pay to that consumer the reasonable expenses to which he may be put in providing a new meter for the purpose of ascertaining the value of the supply according to the new method of charging, and those expenses may be recovered by the consumer from the Undertakers summarily as a civil debt.

NOTES

Summarily as a civil debt. See the note to s 28 of this Schedule ante.
Definitions. For "consumer", "distributing main", "energy" and "main", see s 1 of this Schedule ante; for "Undertakers", see s 2 of this Schedule ante; and for "the value of the supply", see s 49 of this Schedule ante.

[59 Undertakers may place meters to measure supply or to check measurement

(1) Subject to subsection (2) below, the Undertakers may place upon the premises of any person supplied with energy directly from electric lines belonging to them such meter or other apparatus (in addition to any meter to ascertain the value of the supply) as they may desire for the purpose of ascertaining or regulating the amount of energy supplied to him, the number of hours during which the supply is given, the maximum power taken by him or any other quantity or time connected with the supply.

(2) A meter or apparatus placed upon premises under this section—

(a) shall be of a construction and pattern approved by the Secretary of State and shall be fixed and connected with the Undertakers' lines in a manner so approved;

(b) shall, where the supply of energy is by the Undertakers, be supplied and maintained entirely at the cost of the Undertakers; and

(c) shall be placed between the Undertakers' mains and the ends of the Undertakers' lines at which the supply of energy is delivered unless otherwise agreed between the Undertakers, the person supplied with energy and, where the supply is by a private supplier, that supplier.]

NOTES

This section was substituted by the Energy Act 1983, s 15, Sch 1, para 14.
Person. See the note to s 50B of this Schedule ante.
Secretary of State. Ie one of Her Majesty's Principal Secretaries of State; see the Interpretation Act 1978, s 5, Sch 1, Vol 41, title Statutes. The Secretary of State here concerned is the Secretary of State for Energy; see the Preliminary Note to this title ante.
Definitions. For "energy", "main" and "private supplier", see s 1 of this Schedule ante; for "the Undertakers", see s 2 of this Schedule ante; for "the value of a supply", see s 49 of this Schedule ante; and for "electric line", see the Electric Lighting Act 1882, s 32 ante.

Maps

60 Map of area of supply to be made

(1) *The Undertakers shall [within a period of twelve months beginning with the vesting date] cause a map to be made of the area of supply, and shall cause to be marked thereon the line and the depth below the surface of all their then existing mains, service lines, and other underground works and street boxes, and shall once in every year cause that map to be duly corrected so as to show the then existing lines. The Undertakers shall also, if so required by [the Minister of Power] or [British Telecommunications], cause to be made sections showing the level of all their existing mains and underground works other than service lines. The said map and sections shall be made on such scale or scales as [the Minister of Power] [prescribes].*

(2) *Every map and section so made or corrected, or a copy thereof, marked with the date when it was so made or last corrected, shall be kept by the Undertakers at their principal office within the area of supply [or, in the case of the North of Scotland Board, at their offices most convenient to the area of supply], and shall at all reasonable times be open to the inspection of all applicants, and those applicants may take copies of it or any part thereof. The undertakers may demand and take from every such applicant such fee not exceeding [5p] for each inspection of the map, section, or copy, and such further fee not exceeding [25p] for each copy of it, or any part thereof, taken by the applicant, as they prescribe.*

(3) *The Undertakers shall, if required by [the Minister of Power] or [British Telecommunications], or . . . by the local authority, supply to them or him a copy of any such map or section and cause that copy to be duly corrected so as to agree with the original or originals thereof as kept for the time being at the office of the Undertakers.*

[Provided that a local authority shall only be entitled to require a copy of so much of any such map as relates to the area of that local authority.]

(4) *If the Undertakers fail to comply with any of the requirements of this section they shall for each default be liable to a penalty not exceeding [level 1 on the standard scale], and to a daily penalty not exceeding two pounds.*

NOTES

The words "the Minister of Power" in sub-ss (1), (3) were substituted by the Minister of Fuel and Power (Change of Style and Title) Order 1957, SI 1957/48, art 1(2) (see further the note "Minister of Power" below); the references to "British Telecommunications" in those subsections are substituted by virtue of the British Telecommunications Act 1981, s 87, Sch 3, Pt II, para 7(*c*) Vol 45, title Telecommunications and Broadcasting (but see the note "British Telecommunications " below); and the figures in square brackets in sub-s (2) are substituted by virtue of the Decimal Currency Act 1969, s 10(1), Vol 10, title Constitutional Law (Pt 3).

The reference in sub-s (4) to level 1 on the standard scale is substituted by virtue of the Criminal Justice Act 1982, s 46, Vol 27, title Magistrates. The maximum fine was previously increased to £25 by the Criminal Law Act 1977, s 31(6).

The other words in square brackets in this section were substituted or added, and the words omitted were repealed, by the Electricity Act 1947, s 57(2), Sch 4, Pt III.

Prospective repeal. This section is repealed by the Energy Act 1983, s 36, Sch 4, Pt I, post, as from a day to be appointed under s 37(1) of that Act.

Twelve months beginning with, etc. The use of the words "beginning with" makes it clear that in computing this period the day from which it runs is to be included; see *Hare v Gocher* [1962] 2 QB 641, [1962] 2 All ER 763, and *Trow v Ind Coope (West Midlands) Ltd* [1967] 2 QB 899 at 909, [1967] 2 All ER 900, CA. See also *Dodds v Walker* [1981] 2 All ER 609, [1981] 1 WLR 1027, HL, as to the day of expiry of periods of a month or a specified number of months.

Minister of Power. The functions of the Minister of Power under this section are now exercised by the Secretary of State for Energy; see the Preliminary Note to this title.

British Telecommunications. These references now have effect as references to the operator of any telecommunications code system; see the Telecommunications Act 1984, s 109(1), Sch 4, paras 1(1), 9(6), Vol 45, title Telecommunications and Broadcasting; see also s 109(4) of, and Sch 5, Pt II, para 45 to, that Act.

Standard scale. See the note to s 13 of this Schedule ante.

Definitions. For "area of supply", see s 4 of this Schedule ante. For "daily penalty", "main" and "service line", see s 1 of this Schedule ante. By virtue of the same section, for "local authority", see the Electric Lighting Act 1882, s 31 ante; and for "works", see s 32 of the 1882 Act ante. For "North of Scotland Board", see s 67(1), (2) of the 1947 Act post.

Notices, etc

61 Notices, etc, may be printed or written

Notices, orders, and other documents under [this Schedule] may be in writing or in print, or partly in writing and partly in print, and where any notice, order, or document requires authentication by the local authority, the signature thereof by the clerk or surveyor to the local authority shall be sufficient authentication.

NOTES

The words in square brackets were substituted by the Electricity Act 1947, s 57(2), Sch 4, Pt III.

Writing. Unless the contrary intention appears this includes other modes of representing or reproducing words in a visible form; see the Interpretation Act 1978, s 5, Sch 1, Vol 41, title Statutes.

Local authority. By virtue of s 1 of this Schedule, for meaning, see the Electric Lighting Act 1882, s 31 ante.

62 Service of notices, etc

(1)–(3) . . .

(4) Subject to the provisions of [this Schedule] as to cases of emergency, where the interval of

time between the service of any notice or document under the provisions of [this Schedule] and the execution of any works, or the performance of any duty or act, is less than seven days, the following days shall not be reckoned in the computation of that time; that is to say, Sunday, Christmas Day, Good Friday, any bank holiday under and within the meaning of the Bank Holiday Act 1871, and any Act amending that Act, and any day appointed for public fast, humiliation, or thanksgiving.

NOTES

Sub-ss (1)–(3) were repealed, and the words in square brackets in sub-s (4) were substituted, by the Electricity Act 1947, s 57, Sch 4, Pt III.

Service of notices. For further provisions as to service of notices, see, by virtue of the Electricity Act 1947, s 57(2) post, s 63 of that Act.

Bank Holiday Act 1871. Repealed by the Banking and Financial Dealings Act 1971, s 4(5), Sch 2, Pt II; for statutory holidays, see now Sch 1 to that Act, Vol 45, title Time.

63–68   (*Repealed by the Electricity Act 1947, s 57(7), Sch 5.*)

General

69 Remedying of system and works

(1) If at any time it is established to the satisfaction of [the Minister of Power]—

  (*a*) that the Undertakers *are supplying energy otherwise than by means of a system which has been approved by [the Minister of Power] or (except in accordance with the provisions of [this Schedule] have permitted any part of their circuits to be connected with earth or* placed any electric line above ground; *or*

  (*b*) *that any electric lines or works of the Undertakers are defective, so as not to be in accordance with the provisions of [this Schedule] or the [Electricity regulations]; or*

  (*c*) *that any work of the Undertakers or their supply of energy is attended with danger to the public safety, or injuriously affects [any telecommunication apparatus kept installed for the purposes of a telecommunications code system];*

[the Minister of Power] may by order specify the matter complained of, and require the Undertakers to abate or discontinue it within such period as is therein limited in that behalf, and if the Undertakers make default in complying with the order they shall be liable to a penalty not exceeding twenty pounds for every day during which the default continues.

(2) [The Minister of Power] may also if [he thinks] fit by the same or any other order forbid the use of any electric line *or work* as from such date as may be specified in that behalf until the order is complied with, or for such time as may be so specified, and if the Undertakers make use of any such electric line *or work* while the use thereof is so forbidden they shall be liable to a penalty not exceeding one hundred pounds for every day during which the user continues.

(3) . . .

NOTES

The words "the Minister of Power" wherever they occur in this section were substituted by the Minister of Fuel and Power (Change of Style and Title) Order 1957, SI 1957/48, art 1(2) (see further the note below), and the words in the first pair of square brackets in sub-s (1)(*c*) were substituted by the Telecommunications Act 1984, s 109(1), Sch 4, para 9(7). The other words in square brackets were substituted by, or by virtue of, and sub-s (3) was repealed by, the Electricity Act 1947, s 57(2), Sch 4, Pt III.

Prospective repeal. The words in italics are repealed by the Energy Act 1983, s 36, Sch 4, Pt I post, as from a day to be appointed under s 37(1) of that Act.

Minister of Power. The functions of the Minister of Power under this section are now exercised by the Secretary of State for Energy; see the Preliminary Note to this title.

Established to the satisfaction; thinks fit. Statutory powers are often conferred in subjective terms, the competent authority being entitled to act, eg, when it "thinks fit", or when it is "satisfied" or it "appears" to it that a prescribed state of affairs exists, but the inherent jurisdiction of the courts to determine whether such powers have been exceeded is not readily ousted by the use of such language; see further 1 Halsbury's Laws (4th edn) para 22.

Unauthorised systems. See, as to restrictions on systems and modes of supply, s 10 of this Schedule ante.

Protection of telecommunication apparatus. See also the Electric Lighting Act 1882, s 26 ante; the

Electric Lighting Act 1888, s 4 ante; ss 14 and 20 of this Schedule ante; the Electricity Act 1947, s 9(3) post and the Electricity Act 1957, s 28(8) post.

Definitions. By virtue of s 1 of this Schedule ante, for "electric line" and "works", see the Electric Lighting Act 1882, s 32 ante. For "Electricity regulations", "energy" and "telegraphic line", see s 1 of this Schedule ante; and for "Undertakers", see s 2 of this Schedule ante. For "telecommunications code system", see the Telecommunications Act 1984, Sch 4, para 1(1), Vol 45, title Telecommunications and Broadcasting, and by virtue of that paragraph, for "telecommunication apparatus", see Sch 2 to that Act.

70 *(Repealed by the Electricity Act 1947, s 57(7), Sch 5.)*

71 Nature and amount of security

Where any security is required under [this Schedule] to be given to ... the Undertakers, that security may be by way of deposit or otherwise, and of such amount as may be agreed upon between the parties, or as in default of agreement may be determined on the application of either party, by a court of summary jurisdiction, and that court may also order by which of the parties the costs of the proceedings before them shall be paid, and the decision of the court shall be final and binding on all parties: Provided that where any such security is given by way of deposit the party to whom the security is given shall pay interest at the rate of four per centum per annum on every sum of [50p] so deposited for every six months during which it remains in their hands.

NOTES

The words in the first pair of square brackets were substituted, and the words omitted repealed, by the Electricity Act 1947, s 57(2), Sch 4, Pt III.

The words in the second pair of square brackets are substituted by virtue of the Decimal Currency Act 1969, s 10(1), Vol 10, title Constitutional Law (Pt 3).

Security. See as to the giving of security, ss 25 and 27 of this Schedule ante.

Undertakers. For meaning, see s 2 of this Schedule ante.

72 *(Repealed by the Ministry of Fuel and Power Act 1945, s 7(3), Sch 3.)*

73 Approval or consent of [Minister of Power]

(1) Where [this Schedule] provides for any consent or approval of [the Minister of Power, the Minister] may give that consent or approval subject to terms or conditions, or may withhold [his] consent or approval, as in [his] discretion [he] may think fit.

(2) All costs and expenses of or incident to any approval, consent, certificate, or order of [the Minister of Power] or of any inspector or person appointed by [the Minister of Power], including the cost of any inquiry or tests for the purpose of determining whether the same should be given or made, to such an amount as [the Minister of Power certifies] to be due, shall be borne and paid by the applicant therefor.

Provided that where any approval is given by [the Minister of Power] to any plan, pattern, or specification, [he] may require such copies of the plan, pattern, or specification as [he thinks] fit to be prepared and deposited at [his] office at the expense of the applicant, and may, as [he thinks] fit, revoke any approval so given, or permit the approval to be continued, subject to such modifications as [he thinks] necessary.

NOTES

The words "the Minister of Power" were substituted wherever they occur in this section by the Minister of Fuel and Power (Change of Style and Title) Order 1957, SI 1957/48, art 1(2) (see further the note below). The other words in square brackets were substituted by, or by virtue of, the Electricity Act 1947, s 57(2), Sch 4, Pt III.

Minister of Power. The functions of the Minister of Power under this section are now exercised by the Secretary of State for Energy; see the Preliminary Note to this title.

74, 75 *(Repealed by the Electricity Act 1947, s 57(7), Sch 5.)*

76 Recovery and application of penalties

(1) All penalties, fees, expenses, and other moneys recoverable under [this Schedule], or under the [Electricity regulations], the recovery of which is not otherwise specially provided for, may be recovered summarily in manner provided by the Summary Jurisdiction Acts.

(2) . . .

(3) Any penalty recovered on prosecution by any other body or person, or any part thereof, may, if the court so direct, be paid to that body or person.

NOTES

The words in square brackets were substituted, and sub-s (2) was repealed, by the Electricity Act 1947, s 57(2), Sch 4, Pt III.

Electricity regulations. For definition, see s 1 of this Schedule ante.

Recovered summarily. By the Magistrates' Courts Act 1980, s 58(1), Vol 27, title Magistrates, a magistrates' court has power to make an order on complaint for the payment of any money which is recoverable summarily as a civil debt, and by s 127(1) of that Act, the complaint may not be heard unless it was made within six months from the time when the matter of complaint arose.

Summary Jurisdiction Acts. Repealed; for provisions as to recovery of penalties, see the previous note.

77 Undertakers to be responsible for all damages

The Undertakers shall be answerable for all accidents, damages, and injuries happening through the act or default of the Undertakers, or of any person in their employment, by reason of or in consequence of any of the Undertakers' works, and shall save harmless all authorities, bodies, and persons by whom any street is repairable, and all other authorities, companies, and bodies collectively and individually, and their officers and servants, from all damages and costs in respect of those accidents, damages, and injuries.

NOTES

Extent of liability. See *Heard v Brymbo Steel Co Ltd* [1947] KB 692, [1948] LJR 372; and see generally as to liability under this section, 16 Halsbury's Laws (4th edn) para 216.

Extension. See the note to s 15 of this Schedule ante.

Definitions. By virtue of s 1 of this Schedule ante, for "company", "street" and "works", see the Electric Lighting Act 1882, s 32 ante. For "Undertakers", see s 2 of this Schedule ante.

78 (*Repealed by the Electricity Act 1947, s 57(7), Sch 5.*)

[79

Nothing in this Schedule shall affect any right or remedy conferred by or in accordance with the telecommunications code on the operator of a telecommunications code system or otherwise prejudice the provisions of that code.]

NOTES

This section was substituted by the Telecommunications Act 1984, s 109(1), Sch 4, para 9(8).

Definitions. By virtue of the Telecommunications Act 1984, Sch 4, para 1(1), Vol 45, title Telecommunications and Broadcasting, for "the operator" and "telecommunications code system", see that paragraph, and for "the telecommunciations code", see Sch 2 to the 1984 Act.

80 Saving rights of the Crown in the foreshore

Although any shore, bed of the sea, river, channel, creek, bay, or estuary is included in the area of supply, nothing in [this Schedule] shall authorise the Undertakers to take, use, or in any manner interfere with any portion of that shore or bed of the sea, or of the river, channel, creek, bay, or estuary, or any right in respect thereof belonging to the Queen's most Excellent Majesty in right of Her Crown, and under the management of the Board of Trade, without the previous consent in writing of the Board of Trade on behalf of Her Majesty (which consent the Board of Trade may give), neither shall anything in [this Schedule] contained extend to take away, prejudice, diminish, or alter any of the estates, rights, privileges, powers, or authorities vested in or enjoyed or exerciseable by the Queen's Majesty.

NOTES

The words in square brackets were substituted by the Electricity Act 1947, s 57(2), Sch 4, Pt III.

Undertakers. For meaning, see s 2 of this Schedule ante.

Board of Trade. The Crown Estate Commissioners are now responsible for the management of the Crown foreshore and, it is thought, also have the power to give consents under this section; see the Minister of Shipping (Transfer of Functions) Order 1939, SR & O 1939/1470, the Ministers of the Crown (Minister of War Transport) Order 1941, SR & O 1941/654, the Minister of War Transport (Dissolution) Order 1946, SR & O 1946/375, the Coast Protection Act 1949, ss 37, 38(2), 40(1) (repealed), the Crown Estate Act 1956, s 1 (repealed), and the Crown Estate Act 1961, s 1, Vol 10, title Constitutional Law (Pt 2).

81 Undertakers not exempted from proceedings for nuisance

Nothing in [this Schedule or any local enactment] shall exonerate the Undertakers from any indictment, action, or other proceedings for nuisance in the event of any nuisance being caused or permitted by them.

NOTES

The words in square brackets were substituted by the Electricity Act 1947, s 57(2), Sch 4, Pt III.

Nuisance. See *Manchester Corpn v Farnworth* [1930] AC 171, [1929] All ER Rep 90, HL; and see generally 16 Halsbury's Laws (4th edn) para 214.

See also the Electricity (Supply) Act 1919, s 10 post, as to the exclusion of remedy by injunction in cases falling within that section.

Definitions. By virtue of s 1 of this Schedule ante, for "local enactment", see the Electricity Act 1947, s 67(1) post. For "Undertakers", see s 2 of this Schedule ante.

82–84 *(S 82 repealed by the Electricity Act 1947, s 57(7), Sch 5; s 83 applies to Scotland only; s 84 (application to Ireland) spent on repeal of this Act in relation to Northern Ireland by the Electricity Supply (Northern Ireland) Order 1972, SI 1972/1072.)*

APPENDIX

Section 12 of the Electric Lighting Act 1882 (45 & 46 Vict c 56)

12 Incorporation of certain provisions of Clauses Consolidation Acts

The provisions of the following Acts shall be incorporated with this Act; that is to say,

*   *   *   *   *

    (2) The provisions of the Gasworks Clauses Act 1847 with respect to breaking up streets for the purpose of laying pipes, and with respect to waste or misuse of the gas or injury to the pipes and other works, except so much thereof as relates to the use of any burner other than such as has been provided or approved of by the undertakers; and

    (3) Sections thirty-eight to forty-two inclusive, and sections forty-five and forty-six, of the Gasworks Clauses Act 1871.

[For the purposes of this Act, in the construction of all the enactments incorporated by this section the "promoters" or "undertakers" means an Electricity Board and "the undertaking" means the business carried on by such a Board and "the special Act" means the Electricity (Supply) Acts 1882 to 1936 (including, as regards the North of Scotland Board, the Act of 1943), the Electricity Act 1947, and any local enactment (within the meaning of the last named Act) applicable to any such Board.]

        *   *   *   *   *

In the construction of the said Gasworks Clauses Act 1847, and the Gasworks Clauses Act 1871, the said Acts shall be construed as if "gas" meant "electricity" and as if "pipe" meant electric line, and "works" meant "works" as defined by this Act, and as if "the limits of the special Act" meant [in relation to the [Generating Board], the whole of Great Britain except the North of Scotland District, in relation to any Area Board, the area for which that Board is for the time being established, and in relation to the North of Scotland Board, the North of Scotland District.]

All offences, forfeitures, penalties, and damages under the said incorporated provisions of the said Acts or any of them may be prosecuted and may be recovered in manner by the said Acts respectively enacted in relation thereto, provided that sums recoverable under the provisions of section forty of the Gasworks Clauses Act 1871 shall not be recovered as penalties, but may be recovered summarily as civil debts.

NOTES

The words in square brackets were substituted by the Electricity Act 1947, s 57(1), (2), Sch 4, Pts I, III, and in these words, the words "Generating Board" were substituted by the Electricity Act 1957, s 42(1), Sch 4, Pt II.

The substitution of the words "the whole of England and Wales" for the words "the whole of Great Britain except the North of Scotland District" in s 12 of the 1882 Act does not apply to the section as it appears above.

Recovered summarily etc; Generating Board; North of Scotland Board; North of Scotland District. See the notes to this section, p 784 ante.

Definitions. For "Area Board", see the Electricity Act 1947, s 1(3) post; for "electric line", "electricity", "street" and "works", see s 32 of the 1882 Act ante; for "Electricity Board", see s 1(3) of the 1947 Act, in conjunction with the Electricity Reorganisation (Scotland) Act 1954, Sch 1, Pt II post; and for "North of Scotland Board" and "North of Scotland District", see s 67(1), (2) of the 1947 Act.

Gasworks Clauses Act 1847. For the relevant sections of that Act, see this Appendix post.

Gasworks Clauses Act 1871, ss 38–42, 45, 46. See this Appendix post.

Electricity (Supply) Acts 1882 to 1936. For the Acts which may be cited by this collective title, see the Introductory Note to the Electric Lighting Act 1882 ante.

Act of 1943. Ie the Hydro-Electric Development (Scotland) Act 1943 (c 32) (largely repealed by the Electricity (Scotland) Act 1979 (c 11) and replaced by provisions of that Act (not printed in this work)); see the Electricity Act 1947, s 67(1), (2) post.

Electricity Act 1947. See this title post.

Sections of the Gasworks Clauses Act 1847 (10 & 11 Vict c 15), incorporated

And with respect to the breaking up of streets for the purpose of laying pipes, be it enacted as follows:—

6 Power to break up streets, etc, under superintendence, and to open drains

The Undertakers ... may open and break up the soil and pavement of the several streets and bridges within the limits of the special Act, and may open and break up any sewers, drains, or tunnels within or under such streets and bridges, and lay down and place within the same limits pipes, conduits, service pipes, and other works, and from time to time repair, alter, or remove the same, and also make any sewers that may be necessary for carrying off the washings and waste liquids which may arise in the making of the gas, and for the purposes aforesaid may remove and use all earth and materials in and under such streets and bridges, and they may, in such streets, erect any pillars, lamps, and other works, and do all other acts which the Undertakers shall from time to time deem necessary for supplying gas to the inhabitants of the district included within the said limits, doing as little damage as may be in the execution of the powers hereby or by the special Act granted, and making compensation for any damage which may be done in the execution of such powers.

NOTES

The words omitted were repealed by the Public Utilities Street Works Act 1950, s 15(3)(*a*), Sch 5.

Definitions. For "Undertakers", see the Electric Lighting Act 1882, s 12, in this Appendix ante; and see as to "gas", "the limits of the special Act" and "pipe", the same section.

7 Not to enter on private land without consent

Provided always that nothing herein shall authorise or empower the Undertakers to lay down or place any pipe or other works into, through, or against any building, or in any land, not dedicated to public use without the consent of the owners and occupiers thereof; except that the Undertakers may at any time enter upon and lay or place any new pipe in the place of any existing pipe, in any land wherein any pipe hath been already lawfully laid down or placed in pursuance of this or the special Act or any other Act of Parliament, and may repair or alter any pipe so laid down.

NOTE

Definitions. For "Undertakers", see the Electric Lighting Act 1882, s 12, in this Appendix ante; and see as to "pipe" and "works", the same section.

8–12 (*Repealed by the Public Utilities Street Works Act 1950, s 15(3)(a), Sch 5.*)

★   ★   ★   ★   ★

And with respect to waste or misuse of the gas, or injury to the pipes or other works, be it enacted as follows:—

18 Penalty for fraudulently using the gas of the Undertakers

Every person who shall lay or cause to be laid any pipe to communicate with any pipe belonging to the Undertakers without their consent, or shall fraudulently injure any such meter as aforesaid, or who, in case the gas supplied by the Undertakers is not ascertained by meter, shall use any burner *other than such as has been provided or approved of by the Undertakers, or* of larger dimensions than he has contracted to pay for or shall keep the lights burning for a longer time than he has contracted to pay for, or who shall otherwise improperly use or burn such gas . . . shall forfeit to the Undertakers the sum of five pounds for every such offence, and also the sum of [two pounds] for every day such pipe shall so remain, or such works or burner shall be so used, or such excess be so committed or continued, . . . ; and the Undertakers may take off the gas from the house and premises of the persons so offending, notwithstanding any contract which may have been previously entered into.

NOTES

The words omitted were repealed by the Electricity Act 1957, ss 29(5), 42(1) and Sch 4, Pt II. The words relating to the provision or approval of burners are in italics because the Electric Lighting Act 1882, s 12, as set out in this Appendix ante, excludes so much of the Gasworks Clauses Act 1847 as relates to the use of other than approved burners. The words in square brackets are substituted by virtue of the Decimal Currency Act 1969, s 10(1), Vol 10, title Constitutional Law (Pt 3).

Five pounds. For a possible increase in the fine which may be imposed under this section and under ss 19, 20 post and the Gasworks Clauses Act 1871 post, see the Criminal Law Act 1977, s 31(5), (6), and the Criminal Justice Act 1982, s 46, both Vol 27, title Magistrates.

Definitions. For "Undertakers", see the Electric Lighting Act 1882, s 12, in this Appendix ante; and see as to "gas" and "pipe", the same section.

19 Penalty for wilfully damaging pipes

Every person who shall wilfully remove, . . . any pipe, pillar, post, plug, lamp, or other work of the Undertakers for supplying gas, or who shall wilfully extinguish any of the public lamps or lights, or waste or improperly use any of the gas supplied by the Undertakers, shall for each such offence forfeit to the Undertakers any sum not exceeding five pounds, in addition to the amount of the damage done.

NOTES

The words omitted were repealed by the Criminal Damage Act 1971, s 11(8), Schedule, Pt II.

Five pounds. See the note to the Gaswork Clauses Act 1847, s 18, in this Appendix ante.

Definitions. For "Undertakers", see the Electric Lighting Act 1882, s 12, in this Appendix ante; and see as to "gas" and "pipe", the same section.

20 Satisfaction for accidentally damaging pipes

Every person who shall carelessly or accidentally break, throw down, or damage any pipe, pillar, or lamp belonging to the Undertakers or under their control, shall pay such sum of money by way of satisfaction to the Undertakers for the damage done, not exceeding five pounds, as any two justices or the sheriff shall think reasonable.

NOTE

Five pounds. See the note to the Gaswork Clauses Act 1847, s 18, in this Appendix ante.

Sections of the Gasworks Clauses Act 1871 (34 & 35 Vict c 41), incorporated

*　　*　　*　　*　　*

38 Penalty for injuring meters

Every person who wilfully, fraudulently, or by culpable negligence injures or suffers to be injured any pipes, meter or fittings belonging to the Undertakers, or alters the index to any meter, or prevents any meter from duly registering the quantity of gas supplied, . . . shall (without prejudice to any other right or remedy for the protection of the Undertakers or the punishment of the offender) for every such offence forfeit and pay to the Undertakers a sum not exceeding five pounds, and the Undertakers may in addition thereto recover the amount of any damage by them sustained; and in any case in which any person has wilfully or fraudulently injured or suffered to be injured any pipes, meter, or fittings belonging to the Undertakers, or altered the index to any meter, or prevented any meter from duly registering the quantity of gas supplied, the Undertakers may also, until the matter complained of has been remedied, but no longer, discontinue the supply of gas to the person so offending (notwithstanding any contract previously existing); and the existence of artificial means for causing such alteration or prevention, . . . when such meter is under the custody or control of the consumer, shall be primâ facie evidence that such alteration, prevention, . . . as the case may be, has been fraudulently, knowingly and wilfully caused by the consumer using such meter.

NOTES

The words omitted were repealed by the Theft Act 1968, s 33(3), Sch 3, Pt I, the repeals having effect for the purposes of this Schedule as incorporated with the Electricity Act 1947 post, or any other enactment.

Five pounds. See the note to the Gaswork Clauses Act 1847, s 18, in this Appendix ante.

Definitions. For "Undertakers", see the Electric Lighting Act 1882, s 12, in this Appendix ante; and see as to "gas" and "pipe", the same section.

Recovery of Gas Rents

39 Incoming tenants not liable to pay arrears of gas rents, etc

In case any consumer of gas supplied by the Undertakers leaves the premises where such gas has been supplied to him without paying the gas rent or meter rent due from him, the Undertakers shall not be entitled to require from the next tenant of such premises the payment of the arrears left unpaid by the former tenant, unless such incoming tenant has undertaken with the former tenant to pay or exonerate him from the payment of such arrears.

NOTE

Definitions. For "Undertakers", see the Electric Lighting Act 1882, s 12, in this Appendix ante; and see as to "gas", the same section.

40 Recovery of rents, etc

If any person supplied with gas or with any gas meter or fittings by the Undertakers, neglects to pay to the Undertakers the rent due for such gas, or the rent or money due to the Undertakers for the hire or fixing of such meter, or any expenses lawfully incurred by the Undertakers in cutting off the gas from the premises of such person, the Undertakers may recover the sum so due in like manner as a penalty under this Act.

NOTE

Definitions. For "Undertakers", see the Electric Lighting Act 1882, s 12, in this Appendix ante; and see as to "gas", the same section.

41 Recovery of sums due to Undertakers

Whenever any person neglects to pay any rent or sum due and payable by him to the Undertakers, the Undertakers may recover the same, with full costs of suit, in any court of competent jurisdiction, and the remedy of the Undertakers under this enactment shall be in addition to their other remedies for the recovery of such rent or sum.

NOTE

Undertakers. For meaning, see the Electric Lighting Act 1882, s 12, in this Appendix ante.

Legal Proceedings

42 Contents of summons or warrant

Any summons or warrant issued for any of the purposes of this Act may contain, in the body thereof, or in a schedule thereto, several names and several sums.

★   ★   ★   ★   ★

45 Service of notice by Undertakers

Every notice which the Undertakers are by this Act required to serve upon any person shall be served by being delivered to the person for whom it is intended, or by being left at his usual or last-known place of abode, or sent by post addressed to such persons, or if such person or his address be not known to the Undertakers, and cannot after due inquiry be found or ascertained, then by being affixed for three days to some conspicuous part of the premises to which such notice relates.

NOTE

Undertakers. For meaning, see the Electric Lighting Act 1882, s 12, in this Appendix ante.

46 Liability to gas rent not to disqualify justices from acting

No justice or judge of any county court or quarter sessions shall be disqualified from acting in the execution of this Act by reason of his being liable to the payment of any gas rent or other charge under this Act.

NOTE

Gas. See, as to construction, the Electric Lighting Act 1882, s 12, in this Appendix ante.

ELECTRIC LIGHTING ACT 1909

(9 Edw 7 c 34)

ARRANGEMENT OF SECTIONS

An Act to amend the Acts relating to Electric Lighting   [25 November 1909]

Northern Ireland. This Act, except ss 22, 25, 27(1), was repealed in relation to Northern Ireland by the Electricity Supply (Northern Ireland) Order 1972, SI 1972/1072 (NI 9), art 54(2), Sch 7.

1 *(Repealed by the Electricity Act 1947, s 57(7), Sch 5; see proviso (a) to that subsection for saving of orders made under the repealed provision.)*

2 Construction of generating station on land acquired by agreement

It shall not be lawful for [the Generating Board or any Area Board] after the passing of this Act, except with the consent of the Board of Trade [(which consent may be subject to such conditions as the Minister may impose)], to construct [or extend] any generating station on any land . . . , and the Board of Trade shall not in any case give such consent until notice has been given, by advertisement or otherwise, as the Board of Trade may direct, to the local authority of the district in which the land is situate, [to the local planning authority (within the meaning of the Town and Country Planning Act 1947) in whose area that land is situate] and to owners and lessees of land situate within three hundred yards of the land upon which the generating station is to be constructed [or extended], and an opportunity has been given to such local authority, [local planning authority] owners and lessees, of stating any objections they may have thereto [and, in the case of an extension of any generating station, the Minister may, if the extension appears to him to be of a minor character, dispense with the giving of a notice and of an opportunity for stating objections as aforesaid.] . . .

NOTES

The words in square brackets were added or substituted by the Electricity Act 1947, s 57(1), Sch 4, Pt I, and the Electricity Act 1957, s 42(1), Sch 4, Pt II. The words omitted were repealed by the Electricity Act 1947, s 57(1), Sch 4, Pt I.

General Note. This section must be read in conjunction with the Electricity Act 1957, s 33 post (under which, where under this section notice, and an opportunity of stating objections, are required to be given to the local authority of the district in which the land in question is situated, the like requirements as to notice, and as to an opportunity of stating objections, apply in relation to the local planning authority in whose area the land is situated, and an application for the consent of the Secretary of State under this section is to be in writing and to describe by reference to a map the land in relation to which the consent is required).

See also as to public inquiries in respect of applications for consent under this section, s 34 of, and Sch 2 to, the 1957 Act post.

Generating Board. Ie the Central Electricity Generating Board established under the Electricity Act 1957, s 2 post.

Board of Trade; Minister. The functions of the Board of Trade and the Minister under this section are now exercised by the Secretary of State for Energy; see the Preliminary Note to this title.

Saving. This section is not affected by the Energy Act 1976, s 14 post (fuelling of new and converted power stations); see sub-s (6) thereof.

Definitions. For "Area Board", see the Electricity Act 1947, s 1(3) post. By virtue of the Electricity (Supply) Act 1919, s 40(2) post, for "generating station", see s 36 of that Act post; and for "local authority", see the Electricity Act 1882, s 31 ante.

Town and Country Planning Act 1947. The reference to a local planning authority within the meaning of that Act is now to be construed as a reference to such an authority within the meaning of the Town and Country Planning Act 1971, s 1, Sch 3, Vol 46, title Town and Country Planning; see the Interpretation Act 1978, s 17(2)(*a*), Vol 41, title Statutes.

3–10 (*Ss 3–9 repealed by the Electricity Act 1947, s 57(7), Sch 5; s 10 repealed by the Electricity (Supply) Act 1922, s 22(6).*)

11 Certification of meters

(1) The sections set out in the Second Schedule to this Act shall be substituted for sections forty-nine, fifty, fifty-one, and fifty-three of the schedule to the Electric Lighting (Clauses) Act 1899, as incorporated with any Act or Order passed or confirmed after the commencement of this Act.

(2) The provisions contained in the sections so set out shall, subject to such adaptations (if any) as may be necessary, be substituted for any corresponding provisions as to the use, examination, and certification of meters, and their connection and disconnection with electric lines, contained in or incorporated with any special Act or Provisional Order relating to the supply of electricity passed or confirmed before the commencement of this Act.

NOTES

Electric lines. By virtue of s 27(2) post, for meaning, see the Electric Lighting Act 1882, s 32 ante.
Further provisions. For further provisions as to the certification of meters, see the Electricity Act 1957, s 30 post.
Electric Lighting (Clauses) Act 1899. See this title ante.

12–15 (*Ss 12–14 repealed by the Electricity Act 1947, s 57(7), Sch 5; s 15 repealed by the Electricity (Supply) Act 1922, s 23(2).*)

16 Electric lines, etc, let on hire, though fixed to premises, to remain the property of undertakers

All electric lines, fittings, apparatus, and appliances let by any undertakers on hire or belonging to any undertakers, but being in or upon premises of which the undertakers are not in possession, shall, whether they be or be not fixed or fastened to any part of any premises in or upon which they may be situate, or to the soil under any such premises, at all times continue to be the property of, and be removable by the undertakers, and sections twenty-four and twenty-five of the Electric Lighting Act 1882, shall extend and apply to all such electric lines, fittings, apparatus, and appliances: Provided that such electric lines, fittings, apparatus, or appliances have upon them respectively a distinguishing metal plate affixed to a conspicuous part thereof, or a distinguishing brand or other mark conspicuously impressed or made thereon, sufficiently indicating the undertakers as the actual owners thereof.

For the purposes of this section, electric lines, fittings, apparatus, and appliances disposed of by the undertakers on terms of payment by instalments shall, until the whole of the instalments have been paid, be deemed to be electric lines, fittings, apparatus, and appliances let on hire by the undertakers.

Nothing in this section shall affect the amount of the assessment for rating of any premises upon which any electric lines, fittings, apparatus or appliances are or shall be fixed.

NOTES

Let on hire. For power to let equipment, see the Electric Lighting (Clauses) Act 1899, Schedule, s 55 ante, and the Electricity Act 1947, s 2(4) post.

Definitions. By virtue of s 27(2) post, for "electric line" see the Electric Lighting Act 1882, s 32 ante. See as to "undertakers", the Electricity Act 1947, Sch 4, Pt I post.

Electric Lighting Act 1882, ss 24, 25. See this title ante.

17 Notice to be given to undertakers before removing

(1) Twenty-four hours' notice in writing shall be given to the undertakers by every consumer before he quits any premises supplied with electrical energy by the undertakers, and, in default of such notice, the consumer so quitting shall be liable to pay to the undertakers the money accruing due in respect of such supply up to the next usual period for ascertaining the register of the meter on such premises, or the date from which any subsequent occupier of such premises may require the undertakers to supply electrical energy to such premises, whichever shall first occur.

(2) Notice to the effect of this section shall be endorsed upon any demand note for charges for electrical energy.

NOTES

Writing. Unless the contrary intention appears this includes other modes of representing or reproducing words in a visible form; see the Interpretation Act 1978, s 5, Sch 1, Vol 41, title Statutes.

Undertakers. See, as to construction, the Electricity Act 1947, Sch 4, Pt I post.

Liable to pay. See, as to recovery of charges, the Electric Lighting Act 1882, s 21 ante.

18 Power to refuse to supply electrical energy in certain cases

The undertakers may refuse to supply electrical energy to any person whose payments for the supply of electrical energy are for the time being in arrear (not being the subject of a bonâ fide dispute), whether any such payments be due to the undertakers in respect of a supply to the premises in respect of which such supply is demanded or in respect of other premises.

NOTES

Undertakers. See, as to construction, the Electricity Act 1947, Sch 4, Pt I post.

May refuse to supply. See also, as to discontinuance of supply as a remedy for non-payment of charges, the Electric Lighting Act 1882, s 21 ante.

Bonâ fide dispute. For an illustration of a bonâ fide dispute, see *Joseph v East Ham Corpn* [1936] 1 KB 367, 105 LJKB 410, CA.

19 Exemption of agreements for the supply of electricity from stamp duty

Electrical energy shall be deemed to be goods, wares, or merchandise for the purposes of section fifty-nine of the Stamp Act 1891 (which makes certain contracts chargeable with stamp duty as conveyances on sale) . . .

NOTES

The words omitted were repealed by the Finance Act 1970, s 36(8), Sch 8, Pt IV.

General Note. This section settles doubts expressed in *County of Durham Electrical Power Distribution Co v IRC* [1909] 2 KB 604, 78 LJKB 1158, CA, as to whether electrical energy is "goods, wares or merchandise" for the purposes of the Stamp Act 1891, Vol 41, title Stamp Duties.

Stamp Act 1891, s 59. See Vol 41, title Stamp Duties.

20, 21 (*S 20 repealed by the Electricity Act 1947, s 57(7), Sch 5; s 21 repealed by the Local Government Act 1933, s 307(1), Sch 11, Pt IV, and (as to London) by the London Government Act 1939, s 207(1), Sch 8.*)

22 For the protection of the Commissioners of Works

(1) With a view to the protection of the royal palaces, parks, and gardens, museums, and other public buildings, and their contents (in this section referred to as "the protected premises"), the Commissioners of Works and their engineer, or other officer duly authorised in writing under the hand of their secretary, may from time to time enter upon and inspect any generating station of any undertakers, and, if on such inspection it should appear to the Commissioners that proper precautions are not being adopted for the due consumption of smoke, and for preventing as far as reasonably practicable the evolution of oxides of sulphur, and generally for the prevention of nuisance in relation to the protected premises, they may, without prejudice to any other remedy, require the undertakers forthwith to carry out such works and to do such things as are necessary in the circumstances.

(2) The undertakers shall give all reasonable facilities for such inspection to the Commissioners and their engineer or other officer as aforesaid.

(3) Any dispute arising between the Commissioners and the undertakers in relation to any of the provisions of this section shall be determined by arbitration.

This section shall not apply to the station of the Westminster Electric Supply Corporation, Limited, at Horseferry Road, in the city of Westminster.

NOTES

Commissioners of Works. By the Ministry of Works (Transfer of Powers) (No 1) Order 1945, SR & O 1945/991, the functions of the Commissioners of Works were transferred to the Minister of Works, and any reference to them in any enactment is, so far as necessary for the purpose or in consequence of such transfer, to be construed as a reference to the Minister, who was renamed the Minister of Public Buildings and Works by the Minister of Works (Change of Style and Title) Order 1962, SI 1962/1549. The functions of the Minister of Public Buildings and Works under this section are transferred to the Secretary of State by virtue of the Secretary of State for the Environment Order 1970, SI 1970/1681, art 2(1).

Definitions. By virtue of the Electricity (Supply) Act 1919, s 40(2) post, for "generating station", see s 36 of that Act post. See as to "undertakers", the Electricity Act 1947, Sch 4, Pt I post; and note as to "the protected premises", sub-s (1) above.

Northern Ireland. See the Introductory Note to this Act.

23, 24 (*S 23 repealed by the Energy Act 1983, ss 1, 36, Sch 4, Pt I; s 24 repealed by the Electricity Act 1947, s 57(7), Sch 5.*)

25 Definitions

In this Act, unless the context otherwise requires,—

.   .   .   .   .

The expression "Electric Lighting Acts" means—

    (*a*) As respects England and Ireland, the Electric Lighting Acts 1882 and 1888; and

    (*b*) As respects Scotland, the Electric Lighting Acts 1882 and 1888, the Electric Lighting (Scotland) Act 1890, and the Electric Lighting (Scotland) Act 1902:

.   .   .   .   .

The expression "road" includes any street as defined by the Electric Lighting Act 1882:

.   .   .   .   .

NOTES

The words omitted were repealed by the Electricity Act 1947, s 57(1), Sch 4, Pt I.

Electric Lighting Acts 1882 and 1888. For the Acts (including these Acts) which may be cited as the Electricity (Supply) Acts 1882 to 1936, see the Introductory Note to the Electric Lighting Act 1882 ante.

Electric Lighting (Scotland) Act 1890; Electric Lighting (Scotland) Act 1902. Repealed by the Electricity Act 1947, s 57(7), Sch 5.
Northern Ireland. See the Introductory Note to this Act.

26 (*Sub-s (1) repealed by the Electricity Act 1947, s 57, Sch 4, Pt I; sub-s (2) repealed by the SLR Act (Northern Ireland) 1954.*)

27 Short title, construction, and commencement

(1) This Act may be cited as the Electric Lighting Act 1909.

(2) This Act and the Electric Lighting Acts shall be construed together as one Act, and may be cited as the Electric Lighting Acts 1882 to 1909.

(3) This Act shall come into operation on the first day of April, nineteen hundred and ten.

NOTES

Construction. The Electricity (Supply) Acts 1882 to 1936 (as to which, see the next note), are to be construed as one Act; see the Electricity Supply (Meters) Act 1936, s 5(1) post. See also the Electricity Act 1947, Sch 4, Pt I post; the Electricity Reorganisation (Scotland) Act 1954, s 17 post; and the Electricity Act 1957, Sch 4, Pt II post.
Electric Lighting Acts 1882 to 1909. For the Acts (including these Acts) which may be cited as the Electricity (Supply) Acts 1882 to 1936, see the Introductory Note to the Electric Lighting Act 1882 ante.
Northern Ireland. See the Introdutory Note to this Act.

(*Sch 1 repealed by the Electricity Act 1947, s 57(7), Sch 5; Sch 2 substituted ss 49, 51, 53 in the Schedule to the Electric Lighting (Clauses) Act 1899 ante.*)

ELECTRICITY (SUPPLY) ACT 1919

(9 & 10 Geo 5 c 100)

ARRANGEMENT OF SECTIONS

GENERATING STATIONS

An Act to amend the Law with respect to the supply of electricity   [23 December 1919]

Northern Ireland. The whole Act was repealed as to Northern Ireland by the Electricity Supply (Northern Ireland) Order 1972, SI 1972/1072.

1–8 (*Ss 1–4 repealed by the Electricity Commissioners (Dissolution) Order 1948, SI 1948/ 1769 (made under the Electricity Act 1947, s 58); ss 5–8 repealed by s 57(7) of, and Sch 5 to, the 1947 Act.*)

GENERATING STATIONS

9   (*Repealed by the Electricity Act 1947, s 57(7), Sch 5.*)

10 Right to use for generating stations land acquired for that purpose

Where . . . any authorised undertakers are authorised by order made after the passing of this Act to acquire or use any land for the purpose of a generating station, no person shall be entitled to restrain the use of the land for that purpose.

NOTES

The words omitted were repealed by the Electricity Act 1947, s 57, Sch 4, Pt I.
Liability for nuisance. This section frees undertakers from liability to injunction, but, it would appear, not from liability to damages for nuisance; see *Farnworth v Manchester Corpn*, [1929] 1 KB 533, 98 LJKB 224, CA, per Scrutton LJ; affd sub nom *Manchester Corpn v Farnworth* [1930] AC 171, [1929] All ER Rep 90, HL; and see also the Electric Lighting (Clauses) Act 1899, Schedule, s 81 ante.
Definitions. For "generating station", see s 36 post; and see as to "authorised undertakers", the Electricity Act 1947, Sch 4, Pt I post.

11–19 (*S 11 repealed by the Energy Act 1983, ss 1, 36, Sch 4, Pt I; ss 12, 13, 16–19 repealed by the Electricity Act 1947, s 57(7), Sch 5; for saving of rights under s 16, see s 55(6) of the 1947 Act post; s 14 repealed by the Electricity (Supply) Act 1922, s 17(3); s 15 repealed by the Water Resources Act 1963, s 136(2), Sch 14, Pt II.*)

AMENDMENTS OF ELECTRIC LIGHTING ACTS

20   (*Repealed by the Electricity Act 1947, s 57(7), Sch 5.*)

21 Overhead wires

Where the consent [or authorisation] of the Board of Trade is obtained to [or for] the placing of any electric line above ground in any case, the consent of the local authority [(including a county council)] shall not be required, anything in the Electric Lighting Acts, or in any order or special Act relating to the undertaking to the contrary notwithstanding, but the Board of Trade before giving their consent [or authorisation] shall give the local authority [and the local planning authority within the meaning of the Town and Country Planning Act 1947] [and (where it is proposed to place the line along or across any county bridge or any main road vested in a county council) the county council] [not being the local planning authority] an opportunity of being heard.

NOTES

The words in square brackets were inserted by the Electricity (Supply) Act 1926, s 50, Sch 6, the Town and Country Planning Act 1947, s 113(1), Sch 8, and the Electricity Act 1947, s 57(1), Sch 4, Pt I.

General Note. This section must be read in the light of the Public Utilities Street Works Act 1950, s 17(5), Vol 20, title Highways, Streets and Bridges (under which a consent obtained for the purposes of this section to the placing of an electric line of which a plan and section have been the subject of a declaration by an arbitrator under s 4(7) of that Act is deemed to extend to the placing of any such line of which another plan and section are submitted in exercise of the right in that behalf reserved to the undertakers by that subsection).

Consent. Notwithstanding the Electric Lighting (Clauses) Act 1899, Schedule, s 10(b) ante, this section permits the consent of the local authority to be dispensed with; see *National Trust for Places of Historic Interest or Natural Beauty v Midlands Electricity Board* [1952] Ch 380, [1952] 1 All ER 298, CA. See also, as to procedure under this section and s 22 post, the Electricity (Supply) Act 1926, s 44 post.

Board of Trade. The functions of the Board of Trade under this section are now exercised by the Secretary of State for Energy; see the Preliminary Note to this title.

Definitions. For "Electric Lighting Acts", see s 36 post. By virtue of s 40(2) post, for "electric line", see the Electric Lighting Act 1882, s 32 ante; and for "local authority", see s 31 of that Act.

Town and Country Planning Act 1947. See the note to the Electric Lighting Act 1909, s 2 ante.

22 Wayleaves

(1) . . . any authorised undertakers may place any electric line below ground across any land, and above ground across any land other than land covered by buildings or used as a garden or pleasure ground in cases where the placing of such lines above ground is otherwise lawful, and where any line has been so placed across any land the . . . undertakers may enter on the land for the purpose of repairing or altering the line:

Provided that, before placing any such line across any land, the . . . undertakers shall serve on the owner and occupier of the land notice of their intention, together with a description of the nature and position of the lines proposed to be so placed; and if, within twenty-one days after the service of the notice, the owner and occupier fail to give their consent or attach to their consent any terms or conditions or stipulations to which . . . the undertakers object, it shall not be lawful to place the line across that land without the consent of the Board of Trade; and the Board of Trade may, if after giving all parties concerned an opportunity of being heard they think it just, give their consent either unconditionally or subject to such terms, conditions, and stipulations as they think just; and in deciding whether to give or withhold their consent, or to impose any terms, conditions, or stipulations (including the carrying of any portion of the line underground) the Board shall, among other considerations, have regard to the effect, if any, on the amenities or value of the land of the placing of the line in the manner proposed.

(2) The power of placing lines across land conferred by this section shall include the power of placing a line across or along any railway, canal, inland navigation, dock or harbour, subject to the rights of the owners thereof and to the following conditions:—

   (a) In respect of any electric lines placed or proposed to be placed across any line of railway from side to side thereof sections fifteen, sixteen, nineteen, twenty, and seventy-seven of the schedule to the Electric Lighting (Clauses) Act 1899 shall, without prejudice to any protection given to the railway company by the Electric Lighting Acts and this Act, apply as though the said electric lines were placed or proposed to be placed in accordance with powers contained in a [local enactment (as defined by the Electricity Act 1947) applicable to the Electricity Board]:

   (b) In respect of any electric lines placed or proposed to be placed across any canal or inland navigation from side to side thereof, whether by being carried above or below ground, sections fifteen, nineteen, and seventy-seven of the schedule to the Electric Lighting (Clauses) Act 1899 shall, without prejudice to any protection given to the owners of the canal by the Electric Lighting Acts and this Act, apply as though the said electric lines were placed in accordance with powers contained in a [local enactment (as defined by the Electricity Act 1947) applicable to the Electricity Board]:

(c) In respect of any electric lines placed or proposed to be placed over or upon or under any line of railway along its course, the provisions contained in the proviso to subsection (1) of this section shall not apply, and in lieu thereof the following conditions shall apply:—

(i) Failing agreement between the ... authorised undertakers proposing to place such electric lines and the railway company, the ... authorised undertakers may apply to the Board of Trade, who may decide either that the lines shall not be so placed or may refer the question to the Railway and Canal Commission, and that Commission may, ... make an order for the placing of the electric lines, subject to such pecuniary terms as the Commission think just, or refusing to allow such lines to placed ... ;

(ii) The ... authorised undertakers shall, upon receiving notice in writing from the railway company, remove or alter within a reasonable time, and to the reasonable satisfaction of the railway company, any such electric lines which shall interfere with the existing or any proposed works of the railway company or the traffic thereon: Provided that, if within twenty-one days after receipt of such notice the ... authorised undertakers object to the removal or alteration required by such notice, a difference shall be deemed to have arisen, which shall be referred to and determined by the Railway and Canal Commission;

(iii) Save as herein provided, sections fifteen, sixteen, nineteen, twenty, and seventy-seven of the schedule to the Electric Lighting (Clauses) Act 1899 shall, without prejudice to any protection given to the railway company by the Electric Lighting Acts and by this Act, apply as though the said electric lines were placed in accordance with powers contained in a [local enactment (as defined by the Electricity Act 1947) applicable to the Electricity Board]:

(d) In respect of any electric lines placed or proposed to be placed over or upon or under any canal or inland navigation along its course, the provisions contained in the proviso to subsection (1) of this section shall not apply, and in lieu thereof the following conditions shall apply:—

(i) The provisions of paragraphs (c)(i) and (c)(ii) of this subsection shall apply as in the case of railways and for that purpose the expression "railway company" shall mean the owners of the canal or inland navigation:

(ii) Save as herein provided, sections fifteen, sixteen, nineteen, and seventy-seven of the schedule to the Electric Lighting (Clauses) Act 1899 shall, without prejudice to any protection given to the owners of canals by the Electric Lighting Acts and this Act, apply as though the said electric lines were placed in accordance with powers contained in a [local enactment (as defined by the Electricity Act 1947) applicable to the Electricity Board]:

(e) No electric line shall be placed in the tunnels of any tube railway within the Metropolitan Police area, except with the consent of the company owning such railway:

(*f*) In respect of any electric lines placed or proposed to be placed across any lands or works forming part of any dock or harbour undertaking regulated by Act of Parliament, whether by being carried above ground or below ground, sections fifteen, sixteen, seventeen, nineteen, and seventy-seven of the schedule to the Electric Lighting (Clauses) Act 1899 shall, without prejudice to any protection given to the authority owning or managing the undertaking by the Electric Lighting Acts and this Act, apply as though the said electric lines were placed in accordance with powers contained in a [local enactment (as defined in the Electricity Act 1947) applicable to the Electricity Board]:

(*g*) The sections of the schedule to the Electric Lighting (Clauses) Act 1899, by this subsection applied to canals, inland navigations, docks and harbours, and lands or works forming part thereof, shall apply thereto as if references in those sections to streets and persons liable to repair streets and to canals and canal companies included, respectively, canals, inland navigations, docks and harbours, and lands and works forming part of a dock or harbour, and the authority owning or managing the same.

(3) For the purposes of this section, any company or body or person entitled by virtue of any Act of Parliament to receive tolls or dues in respect of the navigation on or use of any canal, inland navigation, dock or harbour shall be deemed to be owners of such canal, inland navigation, dock or harbour.

(4) Section fourteen of the schedule to the Electric Lighting (Clauses) Act 1899, [so far as it relates to the operator of any telecommunications code system, shall be] incorporated with this section, and shall apply to the execution of any works which will involve the placing of lines across or along any land, whether below ground or above ground, under this section in like manner as it applies to the execution of works which will involve the placing of lines in, under, along, or across any street or public bridge.

[(5) Nothing in this section shall—

(*a*) affect any rights conferred by or in accordance with the telecommunications code on the operator of a telecommunications code system; or

(*b*) affect any determination under that code or any agreement entered into for the purposes of that code; or

(*c*) operate in such manner as to interfere with or involve any additional expense in the exercise of any such rights.]

(6) A notice under this section may be served on the owner or occupier of any land by delivering it to him, or by leaving it or forwarding it by post addressed to him at his usual or last known place of abode, and may be addressed by the description of the owner or occupier of the lands (naming them) without further name or description.

NOTES

The words omitted from sub-s (1), in the first and second places from sub-s (2)(*c*)(i) and from sub-s (2)(*c*)(ii) were repealed, and the words in square brackets in sub-s (2) were substituted, by the Electricity Act 1947, s 57(1), Sch 4, Pt I. The words omitted in the third and fourth places from sub-s (2)(*c*)(i) were repealed by the Railway and Canal Commission (Abolition) Act 1949, s 8(2), Schedule. The words in square brackets in sub-s (4) and the whole of sub-s (5) were substituted by the Telecommunications Act 1984, s 109(1), Sch 4, para 13.

General Note. The grant of a wayleave under this section implies a grant of any additional right necessary for the enjoyment thereof, eg, a right to erect steel supporting towers; see *Central Electricity Generating Board v Jennaway* [1959] 3 All ER 409, [1959] 1 WLR 937.

As to procedure under this section, see the Electricity (Supply) Act 1926, s 44 post, which permits concurrent applications under this section and s 21 ante, and the Electricity (Compulsory Wayleaves) (Hearings Procedure) Rules 1967, SI 1967/450. For power of Electricity Boards, where wayleaves have originally been granted by agreement, to retain their lines in position on termination of such agreement, see the Electricity (Supply) Act 1922, s 11 post, which applies this section. See also as to the power of Electricity Boards to purchase compulsorily land required for any purpose connected with the discharge of their functions, the Electricity Act 1947, s 9 post.

For restrictions on the placing of lines above ground, see s 21 ante; the Electric Lighting Act 1882, s 14 ante; and the Electric Lighting (Clauses) Act 1899, Schedule, s 10(*b*) ante.

Sub-s (1): Pleasure ground. For discussion of the meaning of this phrase, see *Central Electricity Generating Board v Dunning* [1970] Ch 643, [1970] 1 All ER 897.

Board of Trade. The functions of the Board of Trade under this section are now exercised by the Secretary of State for Energy; see the Preliminary Note to this title.

Consent. The Secretary of State has no power to attach pecuniary terms to his consent or to award compensation (which may be determined by arbitration under the Electric Lighting Act 1882, ss 17, 28 ante) (*West Midlands Joint Electricity Authority v Pitt* [1932] 2 KB 1, [1932] All ER Rep 861).

See also *Porter v Ipswich Corpn* [1922] 2 KB 145, 91 LJKB 962 (poles in highway; consent of owner of subsoil not necessary).

Sub-s (2): Railway and Canal Commission. The functions of the Commission, which has been abolished, are now exercised by the High Court, and references to the Commission are to be construed as references to that Court; see the Railway and Canal Commission (Abolition) Act 1949, s 1(1), Vol 36, title Railways, Inland Waterways and Pipelines.

Definitions. By virtue of s 40(2) post, for "company", "electric line", "street" and "works", see the Electric Lighting Act 1882, s 32 ante. For "Electric Lighting Acts", "railway" and "railway company", see s 36 post; for "Electricity Board", see the Electricity Act 1947, s 1(3) post, in conjunction with the Electricity Reorganisation (Scotland) Act 1954, Sch 1, Pt II post; and see as to "authorised undertakers", Sch 4, Pt I, to the 1947 Act post. By virtue of the Telecommunications Act 1984, Sch 4, para 1(1), Vol 45, title Telecommunications and Broadcasting, for "the operator" and "telecommunications code system", see that paragraph; and for "the telecommunications code", see Sch 2 to that Act.

Electric Lighting (Clauses) Act 1899. See this title ante.

Electricity Act 1947. For definition of "local enactment" in that Act, see s 67(1) thereof post.

23–30 (*Ss 23, 24, 26–28, 30 repealed by the Electricity Act 1947, s 57(7), Sch 5; s 25 repealed by the Telecommunications Act 1984, s 109(6), Sch 7, Pt I; s 29(1) repealed by the Electricity Commissioners (Dissolution) Order 1948, SI 1948/1769 (made under s 58 of the 1947 Act); s 29(2) repealed by s 57(1) of, and Sch 4, Pt I to, the 1947 Act; s 29(3), (4) repealed by the Electricity Act 1957, s 42(3), Sch 5, Pt I.*)

GENERAL

31–33 (*S 31 repealed by the Industrial Relations Act 1971, ss 133, 169(b), Sch 9; s 32 repealed by the Electricity Act 1947, s 57(7), Sch 5; s 33 repealed by the Electricity Commissioners (Dissolution) Order 1948, SI 1948/1769 (made under s 58 of the 1947 Act).*)

34 Power to make rules

(1) The Board of Trade . . . may . . . make rules in relation to applications and other proceedings before them under this Act, and to the payments to be made in respect thereof, and to the publication of notices and advertisements and the manner in which and the time within which representations or objections with reference to any application or other proceeding are to be made, and to the holding of inquiries in such cases as they may think it advisable, and to the costs of such inquiries, and to any other matters arising in relation to their powers and duties under this Act.

(2) Any rules made in pursuance of this section shall be laid before Parliament as soon as may be after they are made, and shall have the same effect as if enacted in this Act.

NOTES

The words omitted were repealed by the Electricity Commissioners (Dissolution) Order 1948, SI 1948/1769 (made under the Electricity Act 1947, s 58 post).

General Note. This section must be read in the light of the Electricity Act 1957, Sch 2, para 5 post (under which, where any regulations made under s 34 of that Act post, or under Sch 2 thereto post, are for the time being in force, any rules made under this section, in so far as they relate to applications to which the regulations apply, have effect subject to those regulations).

Board of Trade. The functions of the Board of Trade under this section are now exercised by the Secretary of State for Energy; see the Preliminary Note to this title.

Laid before Parliament. For meaning, see the Laying of Documents before Parliament (Interpretation) Act 1948, s 1(1), Vol 41, title Statutes.

Shall have effect as if enacted in this Act. See, as to this expression, *Patent Agents Institute v Lockwood*

[1894] AC 347, 63 LJPC 75; cf *Glasgow Insurance Committee v Scottish Insurance Comrs* 1915 SC 504, 52 SCLR 378; *Minister of Health v R, ex p Yaffe* [1931] AC 494, [1931] All ER Rep 343.

Rules under this section. The Electricity (Ministry of Transport) Costs and Expenses Rules 1922, SR & O 1922/1165. Other rules made under this section are now spent.

35 (*Repealed by the Electricity Act 1947, s 57(7), Sch 5.*)

36 Definitions

In this Act, unless the context otherwise requires—

The expression "Electric Lighting Acts" means the Electric Lighting Acts 1882 to 1909:

. . . . .

The expression "generating station" means any station for generating electricity, including any buildings and plant used for the purpose, and the site thereof, and a site intended to be used for a generating station, but does not include any station for transforming, converting, or distributing electricity:

The expression "railway generating station" means a station for generating electricity for use solely or mainly by a railway company for the purposes of their undertaking:

. . . . .

The expression "main transmission lines" means all extra high-pressure cables and overhead lines (not being an essential part of an authorised undertaker's distribution system or the distribution system of a railway company or the owners of a dock undertaking) transmitting electricity from a generation station to any other generating station, or to a sub-station, together with any step-up and step-down transformers and switch-gear necessary to, and used for, the control of such cables or overhead lines, and the buildings or such part thereof as may be required to accommodate such transformers and switch-gear:

The expressions "railway company" and "railway" have the same meaning as in the Regulation of Railways Act 1873:

Other expressions have the same meaning as in the Electric Lighting Act 1909.

References to orders under the Electric Lighting Acts shall include references to deeds of transfer executed in pursuance of powers conferred by those orders.

NOTES

The definitions omitted were repealed by the Electricity Act 1947, s 57(1), Sch 4, Pt I and the Energy Act 1983, s 36, Sch 4, Pt I.

Generating station. The Clean Air Act 1956, s 10 Vol 35, title Public Health (which relates to the height of chimneys) does not apply to the erection or extension of a generating station as defined in this section other than a private generating station as so defined; see sub-s (4) of that section.

Electric Lighting Acts 1882 to 1909. For the Acts (including these Acts), which may be cited as the Electricity (Supply) Acts 1882 to 1936, and which are to be construed as one Act, see the Introductory Note to the Electric Lighting Act 1882 ante.

Regulation of Railways Act 1873. For definitions of "railway" and "railway company" in that Act, see s 3 thereof, Vol 36, title Railways, Inland Waterways and Pipelines.

Electric Lighting Act 1909. See this title ante.

37, 38 (*S 37 applies to Scotland only; s 38 (application to Ireland) is spent consequent upon the repeal in relation to Northern Ireland of this Act noted in the Introductory Note.*)

39 Transfer of powers of Board of Trade to Minister of Transport

(1) All the powers and duties of the Board of Trade under this Act or the Electric Lighting Acts, or the orders and regulations made thereunder, or any local Act relating to the supply of electricity, or any enactment relating to matters incidental to such supply shall, as from such date as His Majesty in Council may fix, be transferred to the Minister of Transport, and accordingly references to the Board of Trade in any such Acts, orders, regulations, or enactments shall be construed as references to the Minister of Transport: . . .

(2) . . .

NOTES

The words omitted from sub-s (1) were repealed by the Ministry of Fuel and Power Act 1945, s 7(1), Sch 3. Sub-s (2) was repealed by the Electricity Commissioners (Dissolution) Order 1948, SI 1948/1769.

Minister of Transport. The functions of the Minister of Transport in relation to electricity undertakings and the supply of electricity are now exercised by the Secretary of State for Energy; see the Preliminary Note to this title.

Electric Lighting Acts. See s 36 ante and the notes thereto.

Orders under this section. No orders made under this section are in force as at 1 August 1985.

40 Short title and construction

(1) This Act may be cited as the Electricity (Supply) Act 1919, and the Electric Lighting Acts 1882 to 1909 and this Act may be cited together as the Electricity (Supply) Acts 1882 to 1919.

(2) This Act shall be construed as one with the Electric Lighting Acts.

NOTES

Construed as one. Ie the enactments in question are to be construed as if they were contained in one Act, unless there is some manifest discrepancy; see eg *Phillips v Parnaby* [1934] 2 KB 299 at 302. Accordingly, definitions in the earlier Act may be relevant to the construction of provisions of this Act (see *Solomons v R Gertzenstein Ltd* [1954] 2 QB 243, [1954] 2 All ER 625, CA; *Crowe (Valuation Officer) v Lloyds British Testing Co Ltd* [1960] 1 QB 592, [1960] 1 All ER 411, CA).

The Electricity (Supply) Acts 1882 to 1936 (as to which see the next note) are to be construed as one Act; see the Electricity Supply (Meters) Act 1936, s 5(1) post. See also the Electricity Act 1947, Sch 4, Pt I post; the Electricity Reorganisation (Scotland) Act 1954, s 17 post; and the Electricity Act 1957, Sch 4, Pt II post.

Electric Lighting Acts 1882 to 1909. For the Acts (including these Acts) which may be cited as the Electricity (Supply) Acts 1882 to 1936, see the Introductory Note to the Electric Lighting Act 1882 ante.

(*Schedule repealed by the Electricity Act 1947, s 57(7), Sch 5.*)

ELECTRICITY (SUPPLY) ACT 1922

(12 & 13 Geo 5 c 46)

An Act to amend the law with respect to the supply of electricity　　　　　　[4 August 1922]

Northern Ireland. This Act does not apply; see s 31(2) post.

1–10 (*Repealed by the Electricity Act 1947, s 57(7), Sch 5.*)

11 Power to continue wayleaves

Where any . . . authorised undertakers have under any terminable agreement or arrangement, whether made before or after the passing of this Act, placed above or below ground any electric line which could have been so placed under the provisions of section twenty-two of [the Electricity (Supply) Act 1919], the . . . authorised undertakers may, notwithstanding the termination of such agreement or arrangement, retain the line in position, on the same terms and subject to the same conditions as were previously applicable thereto, unless and until objection is made by the owner or occupier of any land over or under which it is placed, but, in the event of any such objection being made, the line shall only be retained if the provisions of section twenty-two of [the Electricity (Supply) Act 1919] regulating the placing of a new line are complied with, and subject to the provisions of that section applicable to lines placed across land in pursuance of that section:

Provided that the . . . authorised undertakers may, at any time whilst a line is so retained, apply to the Minister of Transport for a revision of the said terms and conditions, in which event the provisions of section twenty-two of [the Electricity (Supply) Act 1919] shall apply as if the retention of the line in position where the placing of an electric line across land, and the . . . undertakers shall not be required to remove the line pending the decision upon such application.

NOTES

The words in square brackets were substituted, and the words omitted were repealed, by the Electricity Act 1947, s 57(1), Sch 4, Pt I.

Minister of Transport. The functions of the Minister of Transport in relation to electricity undertakings and the supply of electricity are now exercised by the Secretary of State for Energy; see the Preliminary Note to this title.

Definitions. By virtue of s 31(1) post, for "electric line", see the Electric Lighting Act 1882, s 32 ante. See as to "authorised undertakers", the Electricity Act 1947, Sch 4, Pt I post.

Electricity (Supply) Act 1919, s 22. See this title ante.

12–24 (*Ss 12–22, 24 repealed by the Electricity Act 1947, s 57(7), Sch 5; s 23 repealed by the Energy Act 1983, ss 17(1), 36, Sch 4, Pt I.*)

25 Power of persons not being undertakers to supply electricity

(1) Notwithstanding anything to the contrary contained in any special Act or order, it shall be lawful for the owners or lessees of any railway generating station, or of any generating station erected under statutory authority for the purpose of working tramways or light railways, to supply electricity therefrom upon such terms and conditions as may be agreed—

[(*a*) to the owners or lessees of any other railway generating station; or
(*b*) to any Electricity Board; or
(*c*) to any consumer, subject to the consent of the Area Board in whose area the premises to be supplied are situated or, if they are situated in the North of Scotland District, the North of Scotland Board] . . .

Provided also that nothing contained in this section shall limit or derogate from any powers already conferred on or exercisable by any owners or lessees of any railway generating station, or of any generating station erected under statutory authority for the purpose of working tramways or light railways, or apply to any agreement already or hereafter entered into in pursuance of any such powers.

(2) The Electricity Commissioners may, subject to the provisions of the Electricity (Supply) Acts 1882 to 1919 and of the Schedules to the Electric Lighting (Clauses) Act 1899, by order authorise the breaking up of such roads, railways, and tramways as may be necessary for the purpose of such a supply.

(3) The provisions of the Electricity (Supply) Acts 1882 to 1919 and of the Schedule to the Electric Lighting (Clauses) Act 1899, so far as they relate to the [protection of the operator of a telecommunications code system shall] apply to any works for the supply

of electricity under this section, and, in the application of those provisions, the owners or lessees mentioned in subsection (1) of this section shall be deemed to be the undertakers, and nothing in this section shall [affect any right or remedy conferred by or in accordance with the telecommunications code].

NOTES

The words in square brackets in sub-s (1) were substituted, and the words omitted were repealed, by the Electricity Act 1947, s 57(1), Sch 4, Pt I. The words in square brackets in sub-s (3) were substituted by the Telecommunications Act 1984, s 109, Sch 4, para 15.

North of Scotland Distict; North of Scotland Board. See the notes to the Electric Lighting Act 1882, s 12 ante.

Electricity Commissioners. The functions of the Electricity Commissioners under this section are now exercised by the Secretary of State for Energy; see the Preliminary Note to this title.

Definitions. For "Area Board", see the Electricity Act 1947, s 1(3) post. By virtue of s 31(1) post, for "electricity" and "works", see the Electric Lighting Act 1882, s 32 ante; for "generating station", "railway" (defined with "railway company") and "railway generating station", see the Electricity (Supply) Act 1919, s 36 ante, for "Electricity Board", see s 1(3) of the 1947 Act, in conjunction with the Electricity Reorganisation (Scotland) Act 1954, Sch 1, Pt II post. For "North of Scotland Board" and "North of Scotland District", see s 67(1), (2) of the 1947 Act. By virtue of the Electricity (Supply) Act 1926, s 52(1) post, for "owner", see s 51 of that Act. See as to "special Act or order", the Electricity Act 1947, Sch 4, Pt I post, in conjunction with the definition of "enactment" in s 67(1) of that Act post. By virtue of the Telecommunications Act 1984, Sch 4, para 1(1), Vol 45, title Telecommunications and Broadcasting, for "the operator", and "telecommunications code system", see that paragraph, and for "the telecommunications code", see Sch 2 of that Act.

Electricity (Supply) Acts 1882 to 1919. For the Acts (including these Acts) which may be collectively cited as the Electricity (Supply) Acts 1882 to 1936, see the Introductory Note to the Electric Lighting Act 1882 ante. For provisions relating to the breaking up of streets etc, see ss 12, 13 of the 1882 Act. For provisions relating to the protection of telecommunication apparatus, see s 26 of that Act ante, and the Electric Lighting Act 1888, s 4 ante.

Electric Lighting (Clauses) Act 1899. See this title ante. As to execution of works, see ss 11 et seq of the Schedule to that Act. For provisions relating to the protection of telecommunication apparatus, see ss 14, 20, 69 of that Schedule.

26–30 (*Repealed by the Electricity Act 1947, s 57(7), Sch 5.*)

31 Short title, construction, and extent

(1) This Act may be cited as the Electricity (Supply) Act 1922, and the Electricity (Supply) Acts 1882 to 1919 and this Act shall be construed together as one Act and may be cited as the Electricity (Supply) Acts 1882 to 1922.

(2) This Act shall not extend to Ireland.

NOTES

Construed . . . as one. Ie the enactments in question are to be construed as if they were contained in one Act, unless there is some manifest discrepancy; see eg *Phillips v Parnaby* [1934] 2 KB 299 at 302. Accordingly, definitions in the earlier Act may be relevant to the construction of provisions of this Act (see *Solomons v R Gertzenstein Ltd* [1954] 2 QB 243, [1954] 2 All ER 625, CA; *Crowe (Valuation Officer) v Lloyds British Testing Co Ltd* [1960] 1 QB 592, [1960] 1 All ER 411, CA).

The Electricity (Supply) Acts 1882 to 1936 (as to which see the next note) are to be construed as one Act; see the Electricity Supply (Meters) Act 1936, s 5(1) post. See also the Electricity Act 1947, Sch 4, Pt I post; the Electricity Reorganisation (Scotland) Act 1954, s 17 post; and the Electricity Act 1957, Sch 4, Pt II post.

Electricity (Supply) Acts 1882 to 1922. For the Acts (including these Acts) which may be cited as the Electricity (Supply) Acts 1882 to 1936, see the Introductory Note to the Electric Lighting Act 1882 ante.

(*Schedule repealed by the Electricity Act 1947, s 57(7), Sch 5.*)

ELECTRICITY (SUPPLY) ACT 1926

(16 & 17 Geo 5 c 51)

ARRANGEMENT OF SECTIONS

An Act to amend the law with respect to the supply of electricity   [15 December 1926]

Northern Ireland. This Act does not apply; see s 52(2) post.

1–23 *(Repealed by the Electricity Act 1947, s 57(7), Sch 5; for saving of rights under s 15 of this Act, see ss 55(6), 57(7) of the 1947 Act post.)*

24 Protection of Government observatories, etc

(1) *[An Electricity Board] shall not provide, construct, equip, or alter or use any generating station, sub-station, transformer station, building, plant, machinery, electric main, appliance work or apparatus, or use or permit to be used, transmit, convert, or transform any electrical energy either under this Act or otherwise in such a manner as to affect injuriously in any respect whatever either by vibration or obstruction or smoke or by electric or electromagnetic action or influence, or by any means whatsoever whether similar to those enumerated or not any Government observatory or laboratory existing at the passing of this Act or any instrument or apparatus in or adjacent thereto, and used in or in connection therewith.*

(2) . . .

NOTES

The words in square brackets in sub-s (1) were substituted by the Electricity Act 1947, s 57(1), Sch 4, Pt I; sub-s (2) was repealed by the Post Office Act 1969, s 141(1), Sch 11, Pt II.

Prospective repeal. This section is repealed by the Energy Act 1983, s 36, Sch 4, Pt I post, as from a day to be appointed under s 37(1) of that Act.

Definitions. By virtue of the Electricity Act 1947, Sch 4, Pt I post, for "Electricity Board", see s 1(3) of that Act post, in conjunction with the Electricity Reorganisation (Scotland) Act 1954, Sch 1, Pt II post. By virtue of s 52(1) post, for "generating station", see the Electricity (Supply) Act 1919, s 36 ante.

25–30 *(Repealed by the Electricity Act 1947, s 57(7), Sch 5.)*

MISCELLANEOUS PROVISIONS

31–33 *(Ss 31, 32 repealed by the Electricity Act 1947, s 57(7), Sch 5; s 33 repealed by the SL(R) Act 1981.)*

34 Power to lop trees and hedges obstructing electric lines

(1) Where any tree or hedge obstructs or interferes with the construction, maintenance, or working of any ... electric line which is being constructed or is owned by any authorised undertakers, or will interfere with the maintenance or working of such a line, the authorised undertakers may give notice to the owner or occupier of the land on which the tree or hedge is growing requiring him to lop or cut it so as to prevent the obstruction or interference, subject to the payment to him by the authorised undertakers of the expenses reasonably incurred by him in complying with the notice:

Provided that, in any case where such a notice is served upon a person who, although the occupier of the land on which the tree or hedge is growing, is not the owner thereof, a copy of the notice shall also be served upon the owner thereof, if known.

(2) If within twenty-one days from the giving of such notice the requirements of the notice are not complied with, and neither the owner nor occupier of the land gives such a counter notice as is hereinafter mentioned, the authorised undertakers may cause the tree or hedge to be lopped or cut so as to prevent such obstruction or interference as aforesaid.

(3) If, within twenty-one days from the giving of such notice, the owner or occupier of the land on which the tree or hedge is growing gives a counter notice to the authorised undertakers objecting to the requirements of the notice, the matter shall, unless the counter notice is withdrawn, be referred to the Minister of Transport, who, after giving the parties an opportunity of being heard, may make such order as he thinks just, and any such order may empower the authorised undertakers (after giving such reasonable previous notice to any person by whom such counter notice was given of the commencement of the work as the order may direct) to cause the tree or hedge to be lopped or cut so as to prevent such obstruction or interference as aforesaid, and may determine any question as to what compensation (if any) and expenses are to be paid.

(4) The authorised undertakers shall issue instructions to their officers and servants with a view to securing that trees and hedges shall be lopped or cut in a woodmanlike manner and so as to do as little damage as may be to trees, fences, hedges, and growing crops, and shall cause the boughs lopped to be removed in accordance with the directions of the owner or occupier, and shall make good any damage done to the land.

(5) Any compensation or expenses payable to the owner or occupier by the authorised undertakers under this section shall be recoverable summarily as a civil debt.

(6) Where for the purpose of the construction or maintenance of a transmission line it is necessary to fell any trees, this section shall apply to the felling of trees in like manner as it applies to the lopping of trees.

(7) ...

NOTES

The words omitted from sub-s (1) and the whole of sub-s (7) were repealed by the Electricity Act 1947, s 57(1), Sch 4, Pt I.

Minister of Transport. The powers of the Minister of Transport under this section are now exercised by the Secretary of State for Energy; see the Preliminary Note to this title.

Summarily as a civil debt. By the Magistrates' Courts Act 1980, s 58(1), Vol 27, title Magistrates, a magistrates' court has power to make an order on complaint for the payment of any money which is recoverable summarily as a civil debt, and by s 127(1) of that Act, the complaint may not be heard unless it was made within six months from the time when the matter of complaint arose.

Definitions. By virtue of s 52(1) post, for "electric line", see the Electric Lighting Act 1882, s 32 ante. For "transmission line", see s 51 post; and see as to "authorised undertakers", the Electricity Act 1947, Sch 4, Pt I post.

35 Protection of county bridges

(1) Unless and except so far as may be otherwise agreed between any county council (in this section referred to as "the county council") and [an Electricity Board], the following provisions shall have effect (that is to say)—

(a) Nothing in this Act shall in any way limit or affect the powers of the county council to rebuild, alter, widen or repair the structure of any bridge upon which any [work of an Electricity Board] shall be constructed, or impose upon the county council any liability which was not by law imposed upon them prior to the commencement of this Act;

(b) . . .

(c) When the rebuilding, altering, widening or repairing of such bridge shall have been completed the Board shall have the same rights and powers with regard to such bridge and its approaches as they had before the works were carried out;

(d) If any dispute arises between the county council and the Board with regard to this section the same shall be determined by an arbitrator to be appointed on the application of either party by the Minister of Transport.

(2) (*Applies to Scotland only.*)

NOTES

The words in square brackets were substituted by the Electricity Act 1947, s 57(1), Sch 4, Pt I. Sub-s (1)(*b*) was repealed by the Public Utilities Street Works Act 1950, s 15(3)(*b*), Sch 5.

County council. As to the counties in England and Wales and their councils, see the Local Government Act 1972, ss 1(1), (2), 2(1), (3), 20(1), (2), 21(1), (3), Sch 1, Pts I, II, Sch 4, Pt I, Vol 25, title Local Government.

Minister of Transport. The powers of the Minister of Transport under this section are now exercised by the Secretary of State for Energy; see the Preliminary Note to this title.

Definitions. For "Electricity Board", see the Electricity Act 1947, s 1(3) post. By virtue of s 52(1) post, for "work", see the Electric Lighting Act 1882, s 32 ante. Note as to "the county council", sub-s (1) above.

AMENDMENTS OF THE ELECTRICITY SUPPLY ACTS

36–42 (*Repealed by the Electricity Act 1947, s 57(7), Sch 5.*)

43 Amendment of Schedule to 62 & 63 Vict c 19

(1) The Schedule to the Electric Lighting (Clauses) Act 1899, as incorporated with any special Act or Order passed or confirmed whether before or after the commencement of this Act, shall have effect subject to the amendments specified in the Fifth Schedule to this Act.

(2) Any special Act or Order relating to the supply of electricity passed or confirmed before the commencement of this Act which does not incorporate the provisions of the Schedule to the Electric Lighting (Clauses) Act 1899, which are amended by the Fifth Schedule to this Act, but contains corresponding provisions, shall have effect as if the like amendments were made in those corresponding provisions.

NOTES

Definitions. By virtue of s 52(1) post, for "electricity", see the Electric Lighting Act 1882, s 32 ante. See as to "special Act or Order", the Electricity Act 1947, Sch 4, Pt I post, in conjunction with the definition of "enactment" in s 67(1) of that Act post.

Electric Lighting (Clauses) Act 1899, Schedule. See this title ante.

44 Amendment of s 21 of the Electricity (Supply) Act 1919

(1) Where [application is] made by any authorised undertakers for consent to the placing of any electric line above ground and wayleaves have not been agreed with the owners or occupiers of any land proposed to be crossed by a line, the undertakers may serve notice in accordance with the provisions of section twenty-two of the Electricity (Supply) Act 1919 of their proposal to place the line [or, as the case may be, may commence proceedings under the Acquisition of Land (Authorisation Procedure) Act 1946, as applied by section nine of the Electricity Act 1947, to purchase compulsorily a right to place the line], and the Minister of Transport may proceed concurrently under sections twenty-one and twenty-two of the Electricity (Supply) Act 1919 [or, as the case may be, under the said section twenty-one and under the said Act of 1946 as so applied].

(2) Where . . . any authorised undertakers have in pursuance of powers conferred on them under section twenty-two of the Electricity (Supply) Act 1919 [or, in the case of the North of Scotland Board, under the provisions of the Act of 1943], erected on any land supports for an electric line above ground, the . . . undertakers shall, for the purposes of section eight of the Mines (Working Facilities and Support) Act 1923, be deemed to be persons having an interest in the land on which such supports are erected.

(3) Where an application has been made to the Minister of Transport for his consent to the placing of any electric line above ground, and representations are made that the line will prejudically affect any ancient monument within the meaning of [the Ancient Monuments and Archaeological Areas Act 1979], the Minister of Transport, in determining whether to give or withhold his consent, or to impose conditions, shall take into consideration any recommendations made to him by the Commissioners of Works with a view to preventing the ancient monument being prejudicially affected.

NOTES

The words in square brackets in sub-ss (1), (2) were added or substituted, and the words omitted from sub-s (2) were repealed, by the Electricity Act 1947, s 57(1), Sch 4, Pt I; the words in square brackets in sub-s (3) were substituted by the Ancient Monuments and Archaeological Areas Act 1979, s 64(2), Sch 4, para 1.

Application . . . for consent. See the Electric Lighting (Clauses) Act 1899, Schedule, s 10(b) ante; and see also the Electric Lighting Act 1882, s 14 ante.

Minister of Transport. The functions of the Minister of Transport in relation to electricity undertakings and the supply of electricity are now exercised by the Secretary of State for Energy; see the Preliminary Note to this title.

Concurrently. See also the Electricity Act 1957, s 34(7) post.

North of Scotland Board. See the note to the Electric Lighting Act 1882, s 12 ante.

Commissioners of Works. See the note to the Electric Lighting Act 1909, s 22 ante.

Definitions. By virtue of s 52(1) post, for "electric line", see the Electric Lighting Act 1882, s 32 ante. For "North of Scotland Board", see the Electricity Act 1947, s 67(1), (2) post; and see as to "authorised undertakers", the Electricity Act 1947, Sch 4, Pt I post.

Electricity (Supply) Act 1919, ss 21, 22. See this title ante.

Acquisition of Land (Authorisation Procedure) Act 1946. Repealed by the Acquisition of Land Act 1981, s 34, Sch 6, Pt I, Vol 9, title Compulsory Acquisition, and replaced as noted in the destination table to that Act.

Electricity Act 1947, s 9. See this title post.

Act of 1943. Ie the Hydro-Electric Development (Scotland) Act 1943 (c 32) (largely repealed by the Electricity (Scotland) Act 1979 (c 11) and replaced by provisions of that Act (not printed in this work)); see the Electricity Act 1947, s 67(1), (2) post.

Mines (Working Facilities and Support) Act 1923, s 8. By virtue of the Mines (Working Facilities and Support) Act 1966, s 15(4), the reference to s 8 of the 1923 Act is now to be construed as a reference to s 7 of the 1966 Act, Vol 29, title Mines, Minerals and Quarries.

Ancient Monuments and Archaeological Areas Act 1979. See Vol 32, title Open Spaces and Historic Buildings (Pt 2).

45 Power to recover charge for reconnection

Any expenses reasonably incurred by any authorised undertakers in reconnecting any electric line or other work through which electricity may be supplied which may have been lawfully cut off or disconnected by reason of any default of the consumer may be recovered by the authorised undertakers in like manner as expenses lawfully incurred by them in such cutting off or disconnecting.

NOTES

General Note. For power of undertakers to cut off and disconnect lines, see the Electric Lighting Act 1882, s 21 ante. As to recovery of charges incurred in disconnecting, see the notes to that section.

Definitions. By virtue of s 52(1) post, for "electric line" and "electricity", see the Electric Lighting Act 1882, s 32 ante. See as to "authorised undertakers", the Electricity Act 1947, Sch 4, Pt I post.

46–49 (*Repealed by the Electricity Act 1947, s 57(7), Sch 5.*)

50 Minor amendments

The amendments specified in the second column of the Sixth Schedule to this Act (which relate to minor details) shall be made in the provisions of the Electricity (Supply) Acts 1882 to 1922, specified in the first column of that Schedule.

GENERAL

51 Interpretation

(1) For the purposes of this Act, unless the context otherwise requires—

. . . . .

The expression "transmission line", when used with reference to a line which is a main transmission line within the meaning of the Electricity (Supply) Act 1919 shall include all such works as are mentioned in that definition, and, when used with reference to a line which is not such a main transmission line, shall include any works necessary to and used for the control of the transmission line and the transmission of electricity thereby and the buildings or such part thereof as may be required to accommodate those works;

The expression "owners" in relation to a generating station includes lessees or occupiers of the station operating the station;

. . . . .

(2)–(5) . . .

NOTES

The words omitted from sub-s (1) and the whole of sub-ss (2)–(5) were repealed by the Electricity Act 1947, s 57(1), Sch 4, Pt I.

Electricity (Supply) Act 1919. For definition of "main transmission lines" in that Act, see s 36 thereof ante.

52 Short title, construction and extent

(1) This Act may be cited as the Electricity (Supply) Act 1926, and shall be construed as one with the Electricity (Supply) Acts 1882 to 1922, and those Acts and this Act may be cited as the Electricity (Supply) Acts 1882 to 1926.

(2) This Act shall not extend to Northern Ireland.

NOTES

Construed as one. Ie the enactments in question are to be construed as if they were contained in one Act, unless there is some manifest discrepancy; see eg *Phillips v Parnaby* [1934] 2 KB 299 at 302. Accordingly, definitions in the earlier Act may be relevant to the construction of provisions of this Act (see *Solomons v R*

Gertzenstein Ltd [1954] 2 QB 243, [1954] 2 All ER 625, CA; *Crowe (Valuation Officer) v Lloyds British Testing Co Ltd* [1960] 1 QB 592, [1960] 1 All ER 411, CA).

The Electricity (Supply) Acts 1882 to 1936 (as to which see the next note), are to be construed as one Act; see the Electricity Supply (Meters) Act 1936, s 5(1) post. See also the Electricity Act 1947, Sch 4, Pt I post; the Electricity Reorganisation (Scotland) Act 1954, s 17 post; and the Electricity Act 1957, Sch 4, Pt II post.

Electricity (Supply) Acts 1882 to 1922. For the Acts (including these Acts) which may be cited as the Electricity (Supply) Acts 1882 to 1936, see the Introductory Note to the Electric Lighting Act 1882 ante.

(Schs 1–4, 7 repealed by the Electricity Act 1947, s 57(7), Sch 5; Sch 5 repealed in part by the Electricity Act 1947, s 57(7), Sch 5; the remainder amends s 14 of the Schedule to the Electric Lighting (Clauses) Act 1899 ante; Sch 6 repealed in part by the Electricity Act 1947, s 57(7), Sch 5, the Water Resources Act 1963, s 136(2), Sch 14 and the SL(R) Act 1978; the remainder amends the Electricity (Supply) Act 1919, s 21 ante.)

ELECTRICITY SUPPLY (METERS) ACT 1936
(26 Geo 5 & 1 Edw 8 c 20)

An Act to make better provision for the measurement of electricity supplied by authorised undertakers   [29 May 1936]

Northern Ireland. This Act does not apply; see s 5(3) post.

1 Appointment of examiners, etc

(1) . . . the Electricity Commissioners shall appoint and . . . keep appointed a sufficient number of competent and impartial persons as meter examiners who shall be charged with [such duties as the Secretary of State may determine in connection with] the examination and certifying of meters used or intended to be used in connection with the supply of electricity . . . , and such meter examiners shall comply with any directions given by the Electricity Commissioners as to the exercise and performance of their powers and duties.

(2) . . .

(3) The Electricity Commissioners may prescribe the fees to be paid to meter examiners . . . in respect of the certifying or examination of any meter and may prescribe different fees in relation to different areas: . . .

(4) Subject as hereinafter provided, meter examiners appointed under this Act shall have the powers and duties in relation to meters which are conferred or imposed on electric inspectors by sections fifty, fifty-one and fifty-seven of the Schedule of 1899 and such powers and duties shall cease to be exercised by electric inspectors accordingly, and the said sections fifty, fifty-one and fifty-seven shall have effect in relation to meters as if references to a meter examiner appointed under this Act were substituted for references to an electric inspector under the Special Order, to an electric inspector appointed under the Special Order or to an electric inspector: . . .

NOTES

The words omitted in the first and second places from sub-s (1), and the whole of sub-s (2), were repealed by the SL(R) Act 1971; the other words omitted from sub-s (1), and the words omitted in the first place from sub-s (3), were repealed, and the words in square brackets in sub-s (1) were inserted, by the Energy Act 1983, ss 15, 36, Sch 1, para 15, Sch 4, Pt I. The words omitted in the second place from sub-s (3) were repealed by the Electricity Commissioners (Dissolution) Order 1948, SI 1948/1769. The words omitted from sub-s (4) were repealed by the Electricity Act 1947, s 57(1), Sch 4, Pt I.

General Note. S 49 of the Schedule to the Electric Lighting (Clauses) Act 1899 ante, as originally enacted, required the amount of energy supplied by undertakers to any ordinary consumer or the electrical quantity contained in the supply to be ascertained (in the absence of agreement to the contrary between consumer and undertakers) by a duly certified meter. S 51 of that Schedule provides for the certification of meters by electric inspectors. By s 57 of that Schedule, which makes provision for the settlement of differences between consumer and undertakers as to the correctness of any meter, the register of a meter is, subject to such provisions, to be conclusive evidence in the absence of fraud of the value of the supply. In practice, before this Act was passed, the provisions of the Electric Lighting (Clauses) Act 1899, Schedule, ss 49–51 ante, were not in all cases complied with; and in *Joseph v East Ham Corpn* [1936] 1 KB 367, 105 LJKB 410, CA, it was held that the register of an uncertified meter was not conclusive evidence of the value of the supply; see also *Hendon Electric Supply Co Ltd v Banks* (1917) 87 LJKB 790, 118 LT 544.

This Act, therefore, by this section, provided for the appointment of a new class of officials, namely, meter examiners, who were to take over the duties previously imposed on electric inspectors with regard to the examining and certification of meters. By s 2 post, it provided for the provision of apparatus for meter testing.

Electricity Commissioners. The functions of the Electricity Commissioners are now exercised by the Secretary of State for Energy; see the Preliminary Note to this title.

Prescription of fees. No fees have been prescribed under this section as at 1 August 1985.

Persons authorised to certify meters. See also the Electric Lighting (Clauses) Act 1899, Schedule, s 50A ante.

Uncertified meters. As to offences in relation to uncertified meters, see the Electric Lighting (Clauses) Act 1899, Schedule, s 50B ante.

Definitions. By virtue of s 5(1) post, for "electricity", see the Electric Lighting Act 1882, s 32 ante. See as to "authorised undertakers" and "special order", the Electricity Act 1947, Sch 4, Pt I post, in conjunction with the definition of "enactment" in s 67(1) of that Act post.

Schedule of 1899. Ie the Schedule to the Electric Lighting (Clauses) Act 1899 (as amended); see s 4(1) post. For ss 50, 51, 57 of that Schedule, see this title ante.

2 Apparatus for meter testing, etc

(1) Subject as hereinafter provided, it shall be the duty of any authorised undertakers to provide, and to maintain in proper condition, such suitable apparatus as may be prescribed or approved by the Electricity Commissioners for the examination, testing and regulating of meters used or intended to be used in connection with the supply of electricity [(whether by the undertakers or by another person) directly through lines belonging to the undertakers], and to afford to meter examiners appointed under this Act all necessary facilities for the use of the said apparatus for the purpose of the exercise and performance of their powers and duties in relation to such meters as aforesaid:

Provided that the Electricity Commissioners, if satisfied with respect to any authorised undertakers that any such apparatus provided by some other person is available for the purpose of the examination, testing and regulating of such meters as aforesaid, and that satisfactory arrangements have been or are about to be made for the use of the apparatus for that purpose by the said undertakers, may by order direct that this subsection shall not apply to those undertakers; and any such order may be revoked by a subsequent order of the Commissioners without prejudice to the making of a new order.

(2) Any two or more authorised undertakers may with the approval of, and shall if required by, the Electricity Commissioners enter into and carry into effect arrangements—

(a) for the provision of such apparatus as aforesaid by one or more of the parties to the arrangements for the use of the parties thereto or any of them; and

(b) for the examination, testing and regulating, by the party providing any apparatus as aforesaid, of meters used or intended to be used in connection with the supply of electricity [through lines belonging to the other parties] or any of them;

and may enter into, and carry into effect, arrangements for the repairing and reconditioning by any party to the arrangements of meters used or intended to be used in connection with the supply of electricity [through lines belonging to the other parties] or any of them.

Any such arrangements as aforesaid shall be made on such terms and conditions as may be agreed between the parties or, if the arrangements are entered into in pursuance of a requirement of the Electricity Commissioners, on such terms and conditions as may, in default of such agreement, be settled by the Commissioners.

(3) So long as there are in force any such arrangements as aforesaid for the provision of apparatus by any authorised undertakers, those undertakers shall have the same duties under subsection (1) of this section in relation to the meters which they are required by the arrangements to examine, test and regulate, as they have under that subsection in relation to meters used or intended to be used in connection with the supply of electricity [through lines belonging to the other parties] themselves.

(4) . . .

NOTES

The words in square brackets in sub-ss (1)–(3) were substituted by the Energy Act 1983, s 15, Sch 1, para 16.

Sub-s (4) was repealed by the Electricity Act 1947, s 57(1), Sch 4, Pt I.

Electricity Commissioners. See the note to s 1 ante.

Definitions. By virtue of s 5(1) post, for "electricity", see the Electric Lighting Act 1882, s 32 ante. See as to "authorised undertakers", the Electricity Act 1947, Sch 4, Pt I post.

3 *(Repealed by the SL(R) Act 1971.)*

4 Definitions

(1) In this Act unless the context otherwise requires—

.   .   .   .   .

"The Schedule of 1899" means the Schedule to the Electric Lighting (Clauses) Act 1899 (as amended by any subsequent Act) as incorporated with any Act or Order passed or confirmed whether before or after the passing of this Act.

(2) Any reference in this Act to the Schedule of 1899 or to any provision of that Schedule shall be construed as including a reference to any corresponding provision of any Act or Order which does not incorporate that Schedule or that provision thereof, as the case may be.

NOTES

The words omitted were repealed by the SL(R) Act 1971.

Electric Lighting (Clauses) Act 1899, Schedule. See this title ante, where that Schedule is printed as amended.

Orders under this section. The Electricity Supply Meters Act 1936 (Appointed Day) Orders 1938, ie the Electricity Supply (Meters) Act 1936 (Appointed Day) Order 1938, SR & O 1938/484, and the Electricity Supply (Meters) Act 1936 (Appointed Day) Order (No 2) 1938, SR & O 1938/513.

5 Short title, citation, repeal and extent

(1) This Act may be cited as the Electricity Supply (Meters) Act 1936, and shall be construed as one with the Electricity (Supply) Acts 1882 to 1935, and those Acts and this Act may be cited together as the Electricity (Supply) Acts 1882 to 1936.

(2) . . .

(3) This Act shall not extend to Northern Ireland.

NOTES

Sub-s (2) amends the Electric Lighting (Clauses) Act 1899, Schedule, ss 36(1), 57 ante.

Construed as one. Ie the enactments in question are to be construed as if they were contained in one Act, unless there is some manifest discrepancy; see eg *Phillips v Parnaby* [1934] 2 KB 299 at 302. Accordingly, definitions in the earlier Act may be relevant to the construction of provisions of this Act (see *Solomons v R*

Gertzenstein Ltd [1954] 2 QB 243, [1954] 2 All ER 625, CA; *Crowe (Valuation Officer) v Lloyds British Testing Co Ltd* [1960] 1 QB 592, [1960] 1 All ER 411, CA).

See also the Electricity Act 1947, Sch 4, Pt I post; the Electricity Reorganisation (Scotland) Act 1954, s 17 post; and the Electricity Act 1957, Sch 4, Pt II post.

Electricity (Supply) Acts 1882 to 1936. For the Acts which may be cited by this collective title, see the Introductory Note to the Electric Lighting Act 1882 ante.

ELECTRICITY ACT 1947

(10 & 11 Geo 6 c 54)

ARRANGEMENT OF SECTIONS

PART I

CENTRAL ELECTRICITY AUTHORITY AND AREA ELECTRICITY BOARDS

PART II

ACQUISITION OF ELECTRICITY UNDERTAKINGS

Vesting of Assets

Compensation to Local Authorities

PART III

FINANCIAL PROVISIONS

PART IV

MISCELLANEOUS AND GENERAL

Further Provisions relating to Electricity Supply

Conditions of Employment and Pension Rights

An Act to provide for the establishment of a British Electricity Authority and Area Electricity Boards and for the exercise and performance by that Authority and those Boards and the North of Scotland Hydro-Electric Board of functions relating to the supply of electricity and certain other matters; for the transfer to the said Authority or any such Board as aforesaid of property, rights, obligations and liabilities of electricity undertakers and other bodies; to amend the law relating to the supply of electricity; to make certain consequential provision as to income tax; and for purposes connected with the matters aforesaid

[13 August 1947]

Electricity Acts 1947 to 1961. This Act and the Electricity Act 1957 post, may, by virtue of s 43(1) of that Act post, be cited together as the Electricity Acts 1947 and 1957, and those Acts and the Electricity (Amendment) Act 1961 post, may, by virtue of s 2(2) of that Act post, be cited together as the Electricity Acts 1947 to 1961.

See as to construction in this Act of references to the Act of 1957, the Electricity (Amendment) Act 1961, Schedule post.

Northern Ireland. This Act does not apply; see s 69(2) post.

PART I

[Central Electricity Authority] and Area Electricity Boards

1 Main functions of Electricity Boards

(1) There shall be established an Authority, to be known as the [Central Electricity Authority] . . .

[(1A) . . .]

(2) There shall be established Boards, to be known by the names mentioned in the first column of the First Schedule to this Act, for the areas which are described in general terms in the second column of that Schedule and are to be defined by orders made under this Part of this Act, and it shall be the duty of every such Board . . . to acquire from the [Generating Board] bulk supplies of electricity and to plan and carry out an efficient and economical distribution of those supplies to persons in their area who require them.

(3) In this Act and in any amendment made by this Act in any other enactment the [Central Electricity Authority] is referred to as "the Central Authority" and the Boards established under the last foregoing subsection are referred to as "Area Boards" and the [Generating Board] and the Area Boards, together with the North of Scotland Board, are referred to as "Electricity Boards".

(4) Any Area Board may—

(a) by agreement with any other Area Board and [after consultation with the Generating Board], give to or acquire from that other Area Board bulk supplies of electricity;

[(b) by agreement with any person other than an Electricity Board, acquire supplies of electricity from that person]; and

(c) by agreement with any other Area Board, [or in compliance with a request under section 5 of the Energy Act 1983] supply electricity to consumers in the area of that other Area Board.

If any Area Board are unable to obtain the agreement of another Area Board under paragraph (c) of this subsection, they may apply to the [Electricity Council] for an authorisation to supply electricity to consumers in such part of the area of that other Area Board as may be specified in the authorisation, and, if the [Electricity Council] gives such an authorisation, the first-named Area Board shall have power to supply electricity in accordance therewith.

(5) [Paragraphs (a) and (c)] of the last foregoing subsection shall apply in relation to the North of Scotland Board and the North of Scotland District as if that Board were an Area Board and that District were the area of an Area Board, subject to the modification that . . . any authorisation for the supply of electricity by an Area Board to consumers in the North of Scotland District shall be given by the Secretary of State.

[Provided that nothing in the provisions of this or the last foregoing subsection shall affect the operation of section sixteen of the Act of 1943 in relation to transactions between the North of Scotland Board and the South of Scotland Board.]

(6) In exercising and performing their functions the Electricity Boards shall, subject to and in accordance with any directions given by the Minister or Secretary of State under this Part of this Act [or under the Electricity Act 1957]—

(a) promote the use of all economical methods of generating, transmitting and distributing electricity;

(b) secure, so far as practicable, the development, extension to rural areas and cheapening of supplies of electricity;

(c) avoid undue preference in the provision of such supplies [and in complying with requests under section 5 of the Energy Act 1983];

(d) promote the simplification and standardisation of methods of charge for such supplies;

(e) promote the standardisation of systems of supply and types of electrical fittings;

and shall also promote the welfare, health and safety of persons in the employment of the Boards.

(7) (Applies to Scotland only.)

NOTES

The words in square brackets in sub-ss (1), (5), and those in the first pair of square brackets in sub-s (3), were substituted or inserted by the Electricity Reorganisation (Scotland) Act 1954, s 15(1), Sch 1, Pt II.

The words omitted from sub-ss (1), (2), and sub-s (1A) (which was inserted by s 15(1) of, and Sch 1, Pt II to, the 1954 Act), were repealed by the Electricity Act 1957, s 42(3), Sch 5, Pt I.

Sub-s (4)(b) was substituted, and the words in square brackets in sub-ss (4)(c), (6)(c) were inserted, by the Energy Act 1983, s 25, Sch 3, para 3.

The remaining words in square brackets were substituted or inserted by s 42(1) of, and Sch 4, Pt I to, the 1957 Act.

General Note. Provision is made for the supply of electricity to the Central Electricity Generating Board by the North of Scotland Hydro-Electric Board or the South of Scotland Electricity Board by virtue of the Electricity (Scotland) Act 1979, s 8(1) (not printed in this work). Provision is made for the supply of electricity to the Scottish Boards by the Generating Board by virtue of the Electricity Act 1957, s 2(6)(a) post. See also as to collaboration between the Scottish Electricity Boards, the Electricity Council, the Central

Electricity Generating Board and the Area Boards, s 17 of the Hydro-Electric Development (Scotland) Act 1943 (not printed in this work). A supply of electricity to meet the requirements for haulage or traction of railway undertakers in England and Wales may be provided by the South of Scotland Electricity Board with the approval of the Central Electricity Generating Board; see the Electricity (Scotland) Act 1979, ss 3, 47(3), Sch 3, para 1(*b*) (not printed in this work).

Sub-s (1): Central Electricity Authority. The Authority was dissolved by the Electricity Act 1957, s 1 (repealed) and replaced by the Central Electricity Generating Board (see s 2 of the 1957 Act post) and the Electricity Council (see s 3 of the 1957 Act post).

Sub-s (2): Defined by orders under this Part of Act. As to definition of areas of Area Boards, see s 4(1) post, and the orders noted to that section. For power of the Secretary of State to vary such areas and to establish new, and dissolve existing boards, see sub-ss (3)–(6) of that section.

Sub-s (3): North of Scotland Board. The references to the North of Scotland Board and the North of Scotland District in this Act (except in sub-s (7) above and in s 67 post), include references to the South of Scotland Board and the South of Scotland District, respectively; see the Electricity Reorganisation (Scotland) Act 1954, Sch 1, Pt II post.

Sub-s (4): Consultation. On what constitutes consultation, see, in particular, *Fletcher v Minister of Town and Country Planning* [1947] 2 All ER 496, (1947) 111 JP Jo 542; *Rollo v Minister of Town and Country Planning* [1948] 1 All ER 13, [1948] LJR 817, CA; *Re Union of Whippingham and East Cowes Benefices, Derham v Church Comrs for England* [1954] AC 245, [1954] 2 All ER 22, PC; and *Agricultural, Horticultural and Forestry Industry Training Board v Aylesbury Mushrooms Ltd* [1972] 1 All ER 280, [1972] 1 WLR 190.

Electricity Council. See the Electricity Act 1957, s 3 post.

Sub-s (5): North of Scotland District. See the note "North of Scotland Board" above.

Undue preference. For prohibition of undue preference in the fixing of tariffs by Area Boards, see s 37(8) post.

Methods of charge. As to fixing and variation of tariffs, see s 37 post.

Welfare, health and safety of employees. As to the application of the Factories Act 1961, to electricity stations, see s 123 of that Act, Vol 19, title Health and Safety at Work.

Balancing of revenue accounts. For general duty of the Generating Board and the Area Boards to balance revenue accounts, see the Electricity Act 1957, s 13 post.

Borrowing powers. For borrowing powers of the Generating Board and the Area Boards, see the Electricity Act 1957, s 15 post, and the Gas and Electricity Act 1968, s 2 post.

Generation of electricity. For provisions as to the generation of electricity by Area Boards, see the Electricity Act 1957, s 6 post.

Compensation for loss of office. Compensation for loss of office may be paid to a member of an Electricity Board in accordance with the Electricity and Gas Act 1963, s 3 post.

Pipelines. For exclusion of application of the Pipelines Act 1962, Vol 36, title Railways, Inland Waterways and Pipelines, to and in relation to Electricity Boards, see s 58 of that Act. See also the note "Rating" below.

Applications for nuclear licences. Notice of an application for a nuclear licence in respect of a generating station by an Electricity Board may not be required by virtue of the Nuclear Installations Act 1965, s 3(3), Vol 47, title Trade and Industry (Pt 2(b)); see s 3(4) of that Act.

Rating. For provisions as to the rating of premises occupied by an Electricity Board, see the General Rate Act 1967, s 34 and Sch 7, Vol 36, title Rating. See also as to pipelines, s 21 of, and Sch 3, para 5 to, that Act.

Furnishing of overseas aid by electricity authorities. For provisions as to the furnishing of overseas aid by electricity authorities, see the Overseas Development and Co-operation Act 1980, s 2(1)–(3), (6), Sch 1, Pt I, Vol 7, title Commonwealth and Other Territories (Pt 4).

Compensation for area boards for losses due to price restraint. For provisions relating to such compensation, see the Statutory Corporations (Financial Provisions) Act 1975, s 1, Sch 1, Vol 30, title Money (Pt 1).

Definitions. For "bulk supplies", "electrical fittings", "employment", "functions", "the Generating Board", "Minister", "North of Scotland Board" and "North of Scotland district", see s 67(1) post.

Energy Act 1983, s 5. See this title post.

Act of 1943. Ie the Hydro-Electric Development (Scotland) Act 1943 (c 32) (largely repealed by the Electricity (Scotland) Act 1979 (c 11) and replaced by provisions of that Act (not printed in this work)), see s 67(1) post.

Electricity Act 1957. See this title post.

2 Additional functions of Electricity Boards

(1) . . .

(2) It shall be the duty of the [Generating Board] and every Area Board, in consultation with any organisation appearing to them to be appropriate, to make provision for advancing the skill of persons employed by them and for improving the efficiency of their equipment and the manner in which that equipment is to be used, including provision by them and the assistance of the provision by others of facilities for training and education.

(3) . . .

(4) Any Area Board shall have power—

    (a) to sell, hire or otherwise supply electrical fittings and to instal, repair, maintain or remove any electrical fittings; and

    (b) to carry on all such other activities as it may appear to the Board to be requisite, advantageous or convenient for them to carry on for or in connection with the exercise and performance of their functions . . . or with a view to making the best use of any assets vested in them by or under this Act:

Provided that nothing in this subsection shall empower an Area Board to [manufacture electrical fittings or to manufacture, sell, hire or otherwise supply electrical plant].

(5) The [Generating Board] and any Area Board shall have power to do any thing and to enter into any transaction (whether or not involving the expenditure, the borrowing in accordance with the provisions of this Act or the lending of money, the acquisition of any property or rights or the disposal of any property or rights not in their opinion required for the proper exercise or performance of their functions) which in their opinion is calculated to facilitate the proper [exercise or performance of any of their functions . . .] . . . , or is incidental or conducive thereto, ...

(6) . . .

(7) Any Electricity Board may, by agreement with any other Electricity Board, use for the purposes of any of their functions any works, plant or other property of that other Board, and, if it appears to the Minister that such use cannot be obtained by agreement and is required for the purpose of securing efficient and economical services, he may by order authorise such use on such terms and conditions (including the payment of money) as he may determine.

(8) . . .

[(8A) Where an order under subsection (7) of this section affects [any of the Electricity Boards in England and Wales] and a Scottish Electricity Board, that order shall be made by the Minister and the Secretary of State jointly.]

(9) For the avoidance of doubt it is hereby declared that the foregoing provisions of this Act [and the provisions of section two of the Electricity Act 1957, as to the functions of the Generating Board] relate only to the capacity of Electricity Boards as statutory corporations, and nothing in those provisions shall be construed as authorising the disregard by any such Board of any enactment or rule of law.

NOTES

Sub-ss (1), (3), (6) were repealed by the Electricity Act 1957, s 42(3), Sch 5, Pt II, and the words in square brackets in sub-ss (2), (5), (9) were substituted or inserted by s 42(1) of, and Sch 4, Pt I to, that Act.

The words omitted from sub-ss (4), (5) were repealed, and the words in square brackets in sub-s (4) were substituted, by the Energy Act 1983, ss 25, 36, Sch 3, para 4(3), (4), Sch 4, Pt I.

Sub-s (8) was repealed by the Electricity (Scotland) Act 1979, s 46, Sch 10, para 8, Sch 12.

Sub-s (8A) was inserted by the Electricity Reorganisation (Scotland) Act 1954, s 15(1), Sch 1, Pt II.

Sub-s (2): It shall be the duty etc. Sub-s (2) must be read in conjunction with the Electricity Act 1957, s 12(4) post.

Consultation. See the note to s 1(4) ante.

Sub-s (5): Borrowing. See now the Electricity Act 1957, s 15 post, and the Gas and Electricity Act 1968, s 2 post.

Acquisition of any property. For power of compulsory purchase, see s 9 post.

Sub-s (7): By order. For provisions as to orders generally, see s 64 post.

Sub-s (8A): Secretary of State. See the note to s 4 post.

Extensions. Sub-s (5) is applied to the Electricity Council by the Electricity Act 1957, s 3(6) post (see also s 3(8) thereof). Sub-s (9) is extended by s 6(3) of the same Act post, and the Electricity (Amendment) Act 1961, s 1(2) post.

Definitions. For "Area Board" and "Central Authority", see s 1(3) ante; for "electrical fittings", "electrical plant", "employed", "enactment", "functions" and "the Generating Board", see s 67(1) post; and for "Electricity

Board", see s 1(3) ante, in conjunction with the Electricity Reorganisation (Scotland) Act 1954, Sch 1, Pt II post. By virtue of s 57(1), Sch 4, Pt I post, for "electricity" and "works", see the Electric Lighting Act 1882, s 32 ante. By virtue of the Electricity Reorganisation (Scotland) Act 1954, s 17 post, for "Scottish Electricity Board", see s 14(1) of that Act post.

Electricity Act 1957, s 2. See this title post. See also the Electricity (Amendment) Act 1961, Schedule post.

3 Constitution of Central Authority and Area Boards

(1) The [Generating Board] and every Area Board shall be a body corporate with perpetual succession and a common seal . . .

(2) . . .

(3) Every Area Board shall be constituted as follows:—

> (a) the chairman and not less than five or more than seven other members shall be appointed by the Minister . . . from amongst persons appearing to the Minister to be qualified as having had experience of, and having shown capacity in, electricity supply, local government, industrial, commercial, agricultural or financial matters, applied science, administration, or the organisation of workers; and
>
> (b) there shall be one other member who shall be the person for the time being holding the office of chairman of the Consultative Council established under the following provisions of this Part of this Act for the area of the Area Board:

. . . .

(4) . . .

(5) The Minister shall . . . appoint one of the members of each of the Area Boards to be deputy chairman of that Board.

(6) There shall be paid to the members of the [Generating Board] and to the members of each of the Area Boards such remuneration (whether by way of salaries or fees) and such allowances as may be determined by the Minister with the approval of the Treasury, and, on the retirement or death of any member in whose case it may be so determined to make such provision, such a pension to or in respect of that member as may be so determined.

Any such remuneration, allowances and pensions as aforesaid shall be paid by the [Generating Board] or, as the case may be, the Area Board concerned.

(7) The Minister may make regulations with respect to—

> (a) the appointment of, and the tenure and vacation of office by, the members of the [Generating Board] and any Area Board;
>
> (b) the quorum, proceedings, meetings and determinations of the [Generating Board] and any Area Board;
>
> (c) the execution of instruments and the mode of entering into contracts by and on behalf of the [Generating Board] or any Area Board, and the proof of documents purporting to be executed, issued or signed by the [Generating Board] or any Area Board or a member or officer thereof; and
>
> (d) any other matters supplementary or incidental to the matters aforesaid for which provision appears to the Minister to be necessary or expedient.

(8) Subject to the provisions of any regulations made under the last foregoing subsection, the [Generating Board] and every Area Board shall have power to regulate their own procedure.

NOTES

The words omitted from sub-s (1) were repealed by the Charities Act 1960, s 48(2), Sch 7, Pt II.

Sub-s (2) was repealed, and the words in square brackets in sub-ss (1), (6), (7), (8) were substituted, by the Electricity Act 1957, s 42(1), (3), Sch 4, Pt I, Sch 5, Pt II. The words omitted from sub-s (3)(*a*), and those omitted from sub-s (5), were repealed by s 42(3) of, and Sch 5, Pt II to, that Act.

The proviso to sub-s (3) was repealed by the SL(R)Act 1977.

Sub-s (4) was repealed by the House of Commons Disqualification Act 1957, s 14(1), Sch 4.

The marginal note is no longer accurate.

General Note. This section must be read in conjunction with the Electricity Act 1957, s 4 post, as to whole-time appointments. See also as to the status of the Generating Board and Area Boards, s 38 of the same Act post.

Consultative Council. See s 7 post.

Remuneration. See also the Statutory Corporations (Financial Provisions) Act 1975, s 6(1), Sch 3, para 2(*b*) title Money (Pt 1).

Extensions. Sub-ss (1), (6)–(8) are applied to the Electricity Council by the Electricity Act 1957, s 3(6) post. See also s 3(7) of that Act.

Definitions. For "Area Board", see s 1(3) ante; for "the Generating Board" and "Minister", see s 67(1) post.

Regulations under this section. The Electricity (Central Authority and Area Boards) Regulations 1947, SR & O 1947/1750, as amended by SI 1957/1382 and SI 1968/1780.

Transitional provisions. See, in relation to sub-s (6) above, the Electricity Act 1957, Sch 3, para 12 post.

4 Definition of and variation of areas

(1) The Minister shall before the vesting date by order made after consultation with the Central Authority define the areas for which Area Boards are established under this Act, and each area shall be so defined by reference to a map, and copies of the map of each area shall be available for inspection at such places and at such times as may be specified in a notice published by the Minister in the London Gazette and, in the case of an area in Scotland, the Edinburgh Gazette, and (in all cases) in such newspapers circulating in the area as the Minister thinks fit.

(2) The Minister may, after consultation with the [Electricity Council] and after giving to each Area Board concerned an opportunity to make representations, by order vary the areas for which Area Boards are established under this Act, and such variation may involve not only the variation of the boundaries of existing areas but also the formation of a new area from any part of an existing area or parts of existing areas or the amalgamation of an existing area with any other such area or part thereof.

Any such order shall define by reference to a map the new areas or new boundaries constituted by the order, and copies of any such map shall be available for inspection in like manner as copies of the maps defining the original areas.

(3) If any question arises as to the exact boundary of any area, as defined by any order made under this section, it shall be determined by the Minister, after giving to the Area Boards concerned an opportunity to make representations on such question.

(4) An order made under subsection (2) of this section the effect of which is to increase or reduce the total number of such areas as aforesaid, or to constitute a new area for which a new Area Board is required to be established under the next following subsection, shall not be made unless a draft thereof has been laid before Parliament and has been approved by resolution of each House of Parliament.

(5) An order made under subsection (2) of this section shall state whether the areas affected by the order are to be regarded as the areas of existing Area Boards, or whether any such area is to be regarded as a new area for which a new Area Board is required to be established, and in the latter case a new Board shall be established in accordance with the foregoing provisions of this Act and those provisions shall apply to that Board accordingly, and it shall be known by such name as may be specified in the order.

(6) An order under subsection (2) of this section shall, so far as it appears to the Minister to be necessary or expedient in consequence of the variation of areas or the establishment of a new Area Board, provide—

(a) for the transfer of property, rights, liabilities and obligations from one Area Board to another;

(b) for the modification of agreements for the purpose of giving effect to the transfer of rights, liabilities and obligations thereunder from one Area Board to another and, in a case where part only of the rights, liabilities and obligations under any agreement are transferred, for substituting for that agreement separate agreements in the requisite terms, and for any apportionments and indemnities consequent thereon;

(c) for the purpose of transferring part of the land comprised in any lease vested in any such Board to another such Board, for the severance of that lease, and for apportionments and indemnities consequent thereon;

(d) for dissolving any Area Board the whole of whose functions are to be exercised by another Area Board or Boards, and for winding up the affairs of the Board to be dissolved; and

(e) for such other financial adjustments between the Boards concerned as may be required in consequence of any such transfer, and for any other matter supplementary to or consequential on the matters aforesaid, including the continuation of legal proceedings.

[(7) The foregoing provisions of this section, except subsection (1) shall apply to the Scottish Electricity Boards and to the districts of these Boards as if these Boards were Area Boards and these Districts were the areas of Area Boards, subject to the modification that an order or determination affecting either Board or District shall be made by the Secretary of State and in relation to the South of Scotland Board and the South of Scotland District any reference to this Act shall include a reference to the Electricity Reorganisation (Scotland) Act 1954.

(8) Where an Area Board and their area and a Scottish Electricity Board and their district are both affected by an order or determination under this section, any such order or determination shall be made by the Minister and the Secretary of State jointly.]

NOTES

Sub-ss (7), (8) were substituted by the Electricity Reorganisation (Scotland) Act 1954, s 15(1), Sch 1, Pt II. The words in square brackets in sub-s (2) were substituted by the Electricity Act 1957, s 42(1), Sch 4, Pt I.

Sub-s (1): Vesting date. See the note to s 22(2) post.

Central Authority. See the note "Central Electricity Authority" to s 1 ante.

Area Boards. A list of the Area Boards and a description of their areas in general terms is contained in Sch 1 post.

Sub-s (2): Consultation. See the note to s 1(4) ante.

Electricity Council. See the Electricity Act 1957, s 3 post.

Sub-s (6): Transfers of property. Cf the provisions of s 19 post, as to transfers of property between Electricity Boards. As to exemption from stamp duty on transfers, see s 11(2) post. For consequential power to modify the application of local enactments, see s 57(6) post.

Secretary of State. Anything which, by virtue of this section, s 2 ante, or s 19, 54, 55 or 60 post is required to be done jointly by the Minister and the Secretary of State is to be done jointly by the Secretary of State for the time being discharging the functions expressed to be conferred on the Minister by this Act and the Secretary of State for Scotland; see the Trade and Industry Order 1970, SI 1970/1537, art 6(1), Sch 2, para 3. The Minister here concerned is the Secretary of State for Energy.

Definitions. For "Area Board", see s 1(3) ante; and for "functions", "lease", "Minister", "South of Scotland Board" and "South of Scotland District", see s 67(1) post. By virtue of the Electricity Reorganisation (Scotland) Act 1954, s 17 post, for "Scottish Electricity Board", see s 14(1) of that Act post.

Electricity Reorganisation (Scotland) Act 1954. See this title post.

Orders under this section. The Electricity (Areas of Area Boards) Order 1947, SI 1947/2465; the Electricity Area (Congleton) Order 1950, SI 1950/819; the Electricity Area (Gleadless and Base Green) Order 1953, SI 1953/679; the Electricity (Essex Undertakings) (Variation of Areas and Transfer) Order 1963, SI 1963/555; and the Electricity Areas (Peterborough New Town) Order 1973, SI 1973/2050.

5, 6 (*Repealed by the Electricity Act 1957, s 42(3), Sch 5, Pt II.*)

7 Consultative Councils

(1) A Consultative Council shall be established for the purposes mentioned in this section for the area of every Area Board.

[(2) Each of the said Councils shall consist of a chairman appointed by the Minister and of not less than twenty or more than thirty other persons so appointed of whom—

    (a) not less than two-fifths or more than three-fifths shall be appointed from a panel of persons nominated by such associations as appear to the Minister to represent local authorities in the area;

    (b) the remainder shall be appointed, after consultation with such bodies as the Minister thinks fit, to represent agriculture, commerce, industry, labour, and the general interests of consumers of electricity and other persons or organisations interested in the development of electricity in the area.

(2A) In the appointment of any person under paragraph (a) of the last foregoing subsection the Minister shall have particular regard to his ability to exercise a wide and impartial judgment on the matters to be dealt with by the Council generally; and in making appointments under paragraph (b) of that subsection the Minister shall have particular regard to any nominations made to him, by the bodies mentioned in that paragraph, of persons who are recommended by them as having both adequate knowledge of the requirements of the interests to be represented and also the ability to exercise a wide and impartial judgment on the matters to be dealt with by the Council generally.]

(3) . . .

(4) Each of the said Councils shall be charged with the duties—

    (a) of considering any matter affecting the distribution of electricity in the area, including the variation of tariffs and the provision of new or improved services and facilities within the area, being a matter which is the subject of a representation made to them by consumers or other persons requiring supplies of electricity in that area, or which appears to them to be a matter to which consideration ought to be given apart from any such representation, and where action appears to them to be requisite as to any such matter, of notifying their conclusions to the Area Board; and

    (b) of considering and reporting to the Area Board on any such matter which may be referred to them by that Board;

    [(c) of considering any matter affecting the variation of any tariff regulating the charges for the provision of bulk supplies of electricity by the Generating Board for distribution in the area, being a matter which is either the subject of a representation made to them by consumers or other persons requiring supplies of electricity in the area, or which appears to them to be a matter to which consideration ought to be given apart from any such representation, and, where after consultation with the Area Board action appears to them to be requisite as to any such matter, of notifying their conclusions to the Generating Board;

    (d) of considering and reporting to the Generating Board on any such matter as is mentioned in the last foregoing paragraph which may be referred to them by the Generating Board.]

[(4A) Each of the said Councils—

    (a) may make representations to the Electricity Consumers' Council on any matter which has been considered by them under subsection (4) of this section and affects the interests of consumers or prospective consumers of electricity in the area or of any class of those consumers, and

    (b) shall consider and report to the Electricity Consumers' Council on any matter which may be referred to them by that Council.]

(5) Each of the said Councils shall be informed by the Area Board of that Board's general plans and arrangements for exercising and performing their functions under this Act and may make representations thereon to that Board.

[(6) The Area Board or the Generating Board, as the case may be, shall consider any conclusions, reports or representations notified or made to them by a Consultative Council under subsection (4) or subsection (5) of this section; and the Council may, after consultation with the Area Board, and, in the case of any conclusion or report notified or made to the Generating Board, after consultation with that Board also, make representations to the Electricity Council on matters arising thereout.

(7) Where representations have been made to the Electricity Council under the last foregoing subsection with respect to one of the Electricity Boards, and it appears to that Council, after consultation with the Board in question and with the Consultative Council making the representations, that a defect is disclosed in that Board's general plans and arrangements for the exercise and performance of their functions, the Electricity Council may give to that Board such advice as they think fit for remedying the defect.

(8) A Consultative Council may, after consultation with the Electricity Council, make representations to the Minister on any matters arising out of representations made by them under subsection (6) of this section with respect to one of the Electricity Boards; and if it appears to the Minister, after consultation with that Board and with the Consultative Council making the representations, that a defect is disclosed in that Board's general plans and arrangements for the exercise and performance of their functions, he may give such directions to the Board as he thinks necessary for remedying the defect.

(8A) Where representations, relating to any such matter as is mentioned in paragraph (a) or paragraph (c) of subsection (4) of this section, have been made to a Consultative Council, and the Consultative Council do not consider any action to be requisite with respect thereto, the Council shall notify their conclusions to the person making the representations; and if that person submits those representations to the Electricity Council, then—

> (a) if it appears to the Electricity Council, after consultation with the Electricity Board to whom the representations relate and with the Consultative Council, that a defect is disclosed in that Board's general plans and arrangements for the exercise and performance of their functions, the Electricity Council may give to that Board such advice as they think fit for remedying the defect;
>
> (b) the Electricity Council may make representations to the Minister on any matters arising out of advice given by them to an Electricity Board under the foregoing paragraph; and
>
> (c) if it appears to the Minister, after consultation with the Board and with the Electricity Council, that a defect is disclosed in that Board's general plans and arrangements for the exercise and performance of their functions, he may give such directions to the Board as he thinks necessary for remedying the defect.]

(9) Every Consultative Council shall prepare and submit to the Minister a scheme for the appointment by them of committees or individuals to be local representatives of the Council in such localities as may be specified in the scheme, and it shall be the duty of such committees and individuals to consider the particular circumstances and requirements of those localities with respect to the distribution of electricity and to make representations to the Council thereon, and to be available for receiving on behalf of the Council representations from consumers in those localities; and, if the scheme is approved by the Minister, the Consultative Council shall put it into effect.

A member of a Consultative Council shall be eligible for appointment under such a scheme, either as a member of a committee or as an individual, but membership of the Council shall not be a necessary qualification for such an appointment.

(10)–(11A) . . .

(12) Where, in consequence of the variation of the areas of Area Boards under the foregoing provisions of this Part of this Act, it is necessary to establish new Consultative Councils under this section, the Minister may by order provide for dissolving and winding up the affairs of any Consultative Council who cease to exercise or perform functions by reason of the variation.

[(13) The Minister may make provision by regulations in relation to Consultative Councils in England and Wales for any matters for which provision may be made by regulations under section three of this Act in relation to Area Boards, and for the appointment of persons to act in the place of the chairmen of such Councils.

Subject to the provisions of any such regulations, the said Councils shall have power to regulate their own procedure.]

(14) . . .

NOTES

Sub-s (3) was repealed by the House of Commons Disqualification Act 1957, s 14(1), Sch 4.

Sub-s (4A) was inserted by the Energy Act 1983, s 22(3).

Sub-ss (10)–(11A) were repealed by the Statutory Corporations (Financial Provisions) Act 1975, s 7(2), Sch 5.

Sub-ss (2), (2A), (4)(c), (d), (6)–(8A), (13) were substituted or added by the Electricity Act 1957, s 5(1), Sch 1, Pt I, and sub-s (14) was repealed by s 42(3) of, and Sch 5, Pt I to, that Act.

Sub-s (1): Area of every Area Board. As to establishment of Area Boards, see s 1(2) ante. As to definition of areas, see s 4 ante.

Sub-s (4): Tariffs. As to fixing and variation, see s 37 post.

Sub-s (4A): Electricity Consumers' Council. As to the constitution and functions of this body, see the Energy Act 1983, s 21 post.

Sub-s (6): Electricity Council. See the Electricity Act 1957, s 3 post.

Sub-s (8): Consultation. See the note to s 1(4) ante.

Sub-s (12): Variation of areas of Area Boards. For power of the Secretary of State to vary the areas of Area Boards and to establish new and dissolve existing Boards, see s 4 ante.

Financial and administrative provisions. For various financial and administrative provisions relating to Consultative Councils, see the Statutory Corporations (Financial Provisions) Act 1975, s 6(1), (3), Sch 3, paras 1–4, 6–9, Vol 30, title Money (Pt 1).

Disabled persons. In the appointing of members to the Consultative Councils, the desirability should be considered of including at least one person with experience of disabled persons; see the Chronically Sick and Disabled Persons Act 1970, s 14(1), Vol 34, title Post Office.

Definitions. For "Area Board", see s 1(3) ante; and for "bulk supply", "functions", "the Generating Board", "local authority", "Minister" and "officer", see s 67(1) post. By virtue of s 57(1), Sch 4, Pt I post, for "electricity", see the Electric Lighting Act 1882, s 32 ante. For "Electricity Board", see s 1(3) ante, in conjunction with the Electricity Reorganisation (Scotland) Act 1954, Sch 1, Pt II post.

Orders under this section. The Electricity (Consultative Council) (Areas) Regulations 1948, SI 1948/898, as amended by SI 1958/1 and SI 1977/710.

7A, 8 (S 7A (which was added by the Electricity Act 1957, s 5(2), Sch 1, Pt II) was repealed by the Electricity (Scotland) Act 1979, s 46(2), Sch 12; s 8 repealed by the Electricity Act 1957, s 42(3), Sch 5 (see now s 10 of that Act post).)

9 Compulsory purchase of land

(1) The Minister may authorise any Electricity Board to purchase compulsorily any land which they require for any purpose connected with the discharge of their functions, and the [Acquisition of Land Act 1981] shall apply, in relation to any such compulsory purchase, . . .

(2) In this section the expression "land" includes easements and other rights over land, and an Electricity Board may be authorised under this section to purchase compulsorily

a right to place an electric line across land, whether above or below ground, and to repair and maintain the line, without purchasing any other interest in the land.

In relation to the compulsory purchase of any such right to place an electric line across land, the said Acquisition of Land (Authorisation Procedure) Act 1946 ... and the enactments incorporated therewith shall have effect as if references (whatever the terms used) to the land comprised in the compulsory purchase order were construed, where the context so requires, as references to the land across which the line is to be placed, and references to the obtaining or taking possession of the first-mentioned land were construed as references to the exercise of the said right.

(3) Section fourteen of the Schedule to the Electric Lighting (Clauses) Act 1899 (as incorporated with this Act), so far as the said section [relates to the operator of a telecommunications code system shall] apply to the placing of an electric line in pursuance of any right purchased under this section in like manner as it applies to the execution of works involving the placing of lines in, under, along, or across any street or public bridge.

(4) (*Applies to Scotland only.*)

NOTES

The words in square brackets in sub-s (1) were substituted, and the words omitted from sub-ss (1), (2) were repealed, by the Acquisition of Land Act 1981, s 34, Sch 4, para 1, Sch 6, Pts I, II.

Purchase of right to place line. The Secretary of State's power to authorise such purchase supplements his power to consent to a compulsory wayleave under the Electricity (Supply) Act 1919, s 22 ante.

Placing of lines above ground. As to restrictions on overhead lines, see the Electric Lighting Act 1882, s 14 ante; the Electric Lighting (Clauses) Act 1899, Schedule, s 10(*b*) ante; and the Electricity (Supply) Act 1919, s 21 ante.

Procedure. The Minister may deal concurrently with an application for leave to place a line above ground under the Electricity (Supply) Act 1919, s 21 ante, and an application for consent to a compulsory wayleave under s 22 of that Act ante, or to the compulsory purchase of the right to place a line under this section; see the Electricity (Supply) Act 1926, s 44(1) ante.

Definitions. For "Electricity Board", see s 1(3) ante in conjunction with the Electricity Reorganisation (Scotland) Act 1954, Sch 1, Pt II post; and for "electric line", "functions" and "Minister", see s 67(1) post. Note as to "land", sub-s (2) above. By virtue of the Telecommunications Act 1984, Sch 4, para 1(1), Vol 45, title Telecommunications and Broadcasting, for "operator" and "telecommunications code system", see that paragraph.

Acquisition of Land Act 1981. See Vol 9, title Compulsory Acquisition.

Acquisition of Land (Authorisation Procedure) Act 1946. By virtue of the amendment made to sub-s (1), it would appear that the reference in sub-s (2) to the 1946 Act should be read as a reference to the Acquisition of Land Act 1981. Section 2 of that Act was repealed by the SL(R) Act 1953 and accordingly the reference to that section has no effect.

Electric Lighting (Clauses) Act 1899. See this title ante.

10 Power of Electricity Boards to promote and oppose Bills

The [Electricity Council, the Generating Board] and any Area Board may, with the consent of the Minister, and the North of Scotland Board may, with the consent of the Secretary of State, promote Bills in Parliament [and the Electricity Council] and any Electricity Board may oppose any Bill in Parliament, and this power shall be in lieu of any power to promote or oppose Bills which an Electricity Board might otherwise possess under any of the provisions of this Act as successors to any authorised undertakers.

NOTES

The words in square brackets were substituted or inserted by the Electricity Act 1957, s 42(1), Sch 4, Pt I.

Electricity Council. See the Electricity Act 1957, s 3 post.

North of Scotland Board. See the note to s 1 ante.

Definitions. For "Area Board", see s 1(3) ante; for "authorised undertakers", "the Generating Board", "Minister" and "North of Scotland Board", see s 67(1) post; and for "Electricity Board", see s 1(3) ante in conjunction with the Electricity Reorganisation (Scotland) Act 1954, Sch 1, Pt II post.

11 Electricity Boards not to be exempt from taxation, etc

(1) Subject to the provisions of subsection (2) of this section, nothing in this Act shall be deemed to exempt any Electricity Board from any liability for any tax, duty, rate, levy or other charge whatsoever whether general or local.

(2) For the purposes of section fifty-two of the Finance Act 1946 (which exempts from stamp duty certain documents connected with nationalisation schemes) any transfers of property from one Electricity Board to another effected by an order made under this Act shall be deemed to be part of the initial putting into force of such a scheme.

NOTES

Taxes and rates. For provisions as to income tax and corporation tax, see the Income and Corporation Taxes Act 1970, s 349, title Taxation.

For provisions as to rating, see the General Rate Act 1967, s 34, Sch 7, Vol 36, title Rating.

Transfers of property between Electricity Boards. For power to the Minister to effect such transfers, see s 4(6) ante.

Electricity Board. For meaning, see s 1(3) ante, in conjunction with the Electricity Reorganisation (Scotland) Act 1954, Sch 1, Pt II post.

Finance Act 1946, s 52. See Vol 41, title Stamp Duties.

12 (*Repealed by the Law Reform (Limitation of Actions, &c) Act 1954, ss 1, 8(3), Schedule.*)

PART II

ACQUISITION OF ELECTRICITY UNDERTAKINGS

Vesting of Assets

13 Bodies to whom Part II of Act applies

(1) This Part of this Act applies to—

(*a*) the bodies specified in the Second Schedule to this Act (hereafter in this Act referred to as "authorised undertakers") being the bodies who fall within the class described in the next following subsection;

(*b*) every company (hereafter in this Act referred to as a "power station company") who are not authorised undertakers but whose business wholly or mainly consists in the construction, owning or operating of a generating station or stations for the supply of electricity to authorised undertakers; and

(*c*) every company (hereafter in this Act referred to as an "electricity holding company") who—

(i) are not authorised undertakers, or a power station company,

(ii) had at the date of the last audited balance sheet of the electricity holding company before the first day of January, nineteen hundred and forty-six, one or more subsidiary companies, being authorised undertakers or power station companies, and

(iii) at the said date held securities of, or rights in respect of moneys owed by, the said subsidiary companies, the value of which, as shown in that balance sheet, amounted to not less than three-quarters of the total amount of all the assets of the holding company as so shown:

Provided that any company who are not authorised undertakers, a power station company or an electricity holding company but who hold securities of, or rights in respect of monies owed by, authorised undertakers or power station companies amounting to a substantial proportion of the assets of the first mentioned company, may serve on the Minister, not later than two months after the passing of this Act, a notice stating that they wish to be treated as an electricity holding company, and the Minister may, on the service of such notice, if he thinks fit, by order direct that this Act is to have effect, and be deemed always to have had effect, as if the company were an electricity holding company, and this Act shall have effect accordingly.

(2) The class of bodies referred to in paragraph (*a*) of the last foregoing subsection are—

    (i) bodies who supply electricity, under the authority of any enactment, in any area of supply in Great Britain; and

    (ii) bodies who supply electricity, under the authority of an enactment, to the bodies mentioned in paragraph (i) hereof or to the Central Electricity Board:

Provided that the said class does not include—

    (*a*) the North of Scotland Board;

    (*b*) any body, other than a local authority, whose business as suppliers of electricity consists wholly or mainly in the supply of electricity for consumption by themselves or by a company of whom they are a subsidiary company;

    (*c*) any local authority who supply electricity for the purposes of a transport undertaking carried on by them and do not supply electricity for other purposes to any substantial extent; or

    (*d*) any body, other than a local authority, who carry on a transport undertaking and who do not supply electricity under any provisional or special order made under the Electricity (Supply) Acts 1882 to 1936.

(3) Where a special order made under section twenty-six of the Electricity (Supply) Act 1919, comes into force between the passing of this Act and the vesting date and provides for the transfer of the undertaking or any part of the undertaking of any authorised undertakers to another body, the order may—

    (*a*) if the body from whom the undertaking or part thereof is transferred no longer falls within the class described in subsection (2) of this section, provide that this Part of this Act shall not apply to that body;

    (*b*) if by reason of the transfer, the body to whom the undertaking or part thereof is transferred falls within the said class, provide that this Part of this Act shall apply to that body;

and this Act shall have effect in accordance with any such direction.

(4) Any such special order may, for the purpose of giving effect to a transfer of the undertaking or part thereof, revoke or amend any enactment relating to the powers of the body from whom the undertaking or part thereof is transferred.

(5) For the purposes of paragraph (*c*) of subsection (1) of this section, where the value of any such securities or rights as are therein mentioned is not separately shown in the balance sheet therein mentioned, by reason that they are grouped with other assets of the company and the balance sheet shows the value of the group as a whole, the value placed on the said securities or rights in the books of the company and used in arriving at the value of the group of assets as so shown shall have effect as if it had been shown separately in the balance sheet.

(6) Where an agreement under section eighteen of the Act of 1943 for the transfer to the North of Scotland Board of the whole or any part of the undertaking of any undertakers comes into force between the passing of this Act and the vesting date, and the undertakers thereupon cease to fall within the class described in subsection (2) of this section, this Part of this Act shall not apply to them.

NOTES

Sub-s (1): Passing of this Act. This Act was passed, ie received the Royal Assent, on 13 August 1947.

Sub-s (2): Area of supply. See the Electric Lighting (Clauses) Act 1899, Schedule, s 4 ante.

Central Electricity Board. This body was set up under the Electricity (Supply) Act 1926, s 1 (repealed), for the purpose of establishing the electricity "grid" system and of supplying electricity in bulk to authorised undertakers. It was one of the bodies to which this section applied (see sub-s (1) above and Sch 2 post) and was dissolved by s 14(11) (repealed).

Sub-s (6): Vesting date. See the note to s 22(2) post.

Definitions. For "company", "enactment", "generating station", "holding company", "local authority", "Minister", "North of Scotland Board", "securities" and "subsidiary company", see s 67(1) post. Note as to "authorised undertakers", "electricity holding company" and "power station company", sub-s (1) above.

Electricity (Supply) Acts 1882 to 1936. For the Acts which may be cited by this collective title, see the Introductory Note to the Electric Lighting Act 1882 ante.

Electricity (Supply) Act 1919, s 26. Repealed by s 57(7) and Sch 5. Two special orders were made under that section to take advantage of sub-ss (3) and (4) above, namely, the Letchworth and District Electricity Special Order 1947, and the Pontefract Electricity Special Order 1947, which amend Sch 2 to this Act post.

Act of 1943. Ie the Hydro-Electric Development (Scotland) Act 1943 (c 32) (largely repealed by the Electricity (Scotland) Act 1979 (c 11) and replaced by provisions of that Act (not printed in this work)); see s 67(1) post.

Orders under this section. Orders under this section, being local, are not noted in this work.

14–18 (*Ss 14–16 repealed by the SL(R) Act 1977; ss 17, 18 repealed by the Electricity Act 1957, s 42(3), Sch 5, Pt I.*)

19 Subsequent transfer of property from one Electricity Board to another

(1) The Minister may, whether on the application of any of the Electricity Boards [in [England and Wales]] concerned or without any such application, provide by order—

(a) for the transfer to any [such Electricity Board] of any property, rights, liabilities and obligations vested . . . in another such Board;

(b) for the modification of agreements so far as necessary for giving effect to the transfer of rights, liabilities and obligations thereunder from one such Board to another and, in a case where part only of the rights, liabilities and obligations under any agreement are transferred, for substituting for the agreement separate agreements in the requisite terms, and for any apportionments and indemnities consequent thereon;

(c) for the purpose of transferring part of the land comprised in any lease vested in any such Board to another such Board, for the severance of that lease, and for apportionments and indemnities consequent thereon;

(d) for such other financial adjustments between the Boards concerned as may be required in consequence of any such order, and for any other matters supplementary to or consequential on the matters aforesaid for which provision appears to the Minister to be necessary or expedient:

Provided that the Minister shall consult the [Electricity Council] before making any such order.

[(2) The provisions of the last foregoing subsection shall apply to the Scottish Electricity Boards with the substitution for any reference to the Minister of a reference to the Secretary of State, and for the reference to the [Electricity Council] of a reference to these Boards . . .

(3) An order under this section may relate to transfers as aforesaid between [any of the Electricity Boards in England and Wales] and a Scottish Electricity Board:

Provided that any such order shall be made by the Minister and the Secretary of State jointly after consultation with the [Electricity Council] and with the Scottish Electricity Board concerned.]

NOTES

The words omitted from sub-ss (1)(*a*), (2) were repealed by the Electricity Act 1972, ss 3, 4(3), Schedule.

The words in the first pair of square brackets in sub-s (1) were inserted, and sub-ss (2), (3) were substituted by the Electricity Reorganisation (Scotland) Act 1954, s 15(1), Sch 1, Pt II; the words "England and Wales" and the other words in square brackets were substituted by the Electricity Act 1957, s 42(1), Sch 4, Pt I.

England; Wales. For meaning, see the Interpretation Act 1978, ss 5, 22(1), Sch 1, Sch 2, para 5(*a*), Vol 41, title Statutes.

Consult; consultation. See the note "Consultation" to s 1(4) ante.

Electricity Council. See the Electricity Act 1957, s 3 post.

Transfers between Boards. Cf the provisions of s 4(6) ante as to transfers of property and modification of agreements and financial adjustments on variation of the areas of Area Boards.

As to exemption from stamp duty on transfers, see s 11(2) ante. For consequential power to modify the application of local enactments, see s 57(6) post.

Secretary of State. See the note to s 4 ante.

Definitions. For "Electricity Board", see s 1(3) ante in conjunction with the Electricity Reorganisation (Scotland) Act 1954, Sch 1, Pt II post; and for "lease" and "Minister", see s 67(1) post. By virtue of the Electricity Reorganisation (Scotland) Act 1954, s 17 post, for "the Scottish Electricity Boards", see s 14(1) of that Act post.

Orders under this section. The Electricity (Rugeley) (Transfer) Order 1949, SI 1949/322; the Electricity (South Wales) (Transfer) Order 1949, SI 1949/569; the Electricity House Ltd (Transfer) Order 1949, SI 1949/658; the Electricity (Falmouth, Dartmouth and Kingswear) (Transfer) Order 1949, SI 1949/1181; the Electricity (Dundee-Abernethy Transmission) (Transfer) Order 1949, SI 1949/1952; the Electricity (Central London Electricity Accessories) (Transfer) Order 1949, SI 1949/2288; the Electricity (Transmission Lines, England and Wales) (Transfer) Order 1952, SI 1952/595; the Electricity (Transmission Lines, Scotland) (Transfer) Order 1952, SI 1952/596; the Electricity (Metropolitan Undertakings) (Transfer) Order 1955, SI 1955/597; the Electricity (Kent and Surrey Undertakings) (Transfer) Order 1963, SI 1963/252; the Electricity (Essex Undertakings) (Variation of Areas and Transfer) Order 1963, SI 1963/555; the Electricity (Transfer of Transmission Assets) (East Midlands Electricity Board) Order 1973, SI 1973/1348; the Electricity (Transfer of Transmission Assets) (South Western Electricity Board) Order 1974, SI 1974/1092; the Electricity (Transfer of Transmission Assets) (London Electricity Board) Order 1974, SI 1974/1445; the Electricity (Transfer of Transmission Assets) (North Eastern Electricity Board) Order 1974, SI 1974/1951; the Electricity (Transfer of Transmission Assets) (Southern Electricity Board) Order 1975, SI 1975/831; the Electricity (Transfer of Transmission Assets) (South Eastern Electricity Board) Order 1975, SI 1975/1150; the Electricity (Transfer of Transmission Assets) (Midland Electricity Board) Order 1975, SI 1975/1896; the Electricity (Transfer of Transmission Assets) (South Wales Electricity Board) Order 1975, SI 1975/1897; the Electricity (Transfer of Transmission Assets) (Yorkshire Electricity Board) Order 1975, SI 1975/2245; the Electricity (Transfer of Transmission Assets) (Eastern Electricity Board) Order 1976, SI 1976/131; the Electricity (Transfer of Transmission Assets) (Merseyside and North Wales Electricity Board) Order 1976, SI 1976/1138; the Electricity (Transfer of Transmission Assets) (North Western Electricity Board) Order 1977, SI 1977/504.

20, 21 (*Repealed by the SL(R) Act 1977.*)

Compensation to Local Authorities

22 Compensation to local authorities

(1) The Central Authority shall, by way of compensation for the vesting in them or in any other Electricity Board of property and rights of any local authority, and in lieu of any other compensation in respect of that vesting, make payments to the authority in accordance with this and the two next following sections.

(2) Where the local authority have raised a loan wholly or partly for the purposes of their functions as authorised undertakers or have advanced money for those purposes out of any consolidated loans fund or mortgage loans pool established by them or out of any other moneys held by them, and, in pursuance of the arrangements in force immediately before the vesting date for the redemption of the loan and the payment of interest thereon or, as the case may be, for the repayment of the advance and the payment of interest thereon, any amounts would, but for this Act, have fallen, on or after the vesting date, to be debited in the accounts of the local authority in their capacity as authorised undertakers, the Central Authority shall, subject to the provisions of this section, pay those amounts to the local authority at the times at which, but for this Act,

those amounts would have fallen to be debited in the accounts of the local authority in their capacity aforesaid.

(3) Where the local authority have before the vesting date made arrangements for the making of financial adjustments, as between the accounts of the local authority in their capacity as authorised undertakers and any other account of the local authority, in respect of any other transaction or matter affecting both their functions as authorised undertakers and other functions of the authority, and in pursuance of those arrangements any amounts would, but for this Act, have fallen, on or after the vesting date, to be debited or credited in the accounts of the local authority in their capacity as authorised undertakers and credited, or, as the case may be, debited, in some other account of the local authority, the Central Authority shall, subject to the provisions of this section, pay those amounts to the local authority or be entitled to receive those amounts from the authority, as the case may be, at the times at which, but for this Act, those amounts would have fallen to be debited or credited in the accounts of the local authority in their capacity aforesaid:

Provided that this subsection shall not apply in relation to any apportionment of establishment charges between the accounts of the local authority in their capacity aforesaid and other accounts of the authority.

(4) The Central Authority and the local authority may agree or the Minister of Health may, on the application of either party in default of such agreement, determine that, having regard to the circumstances in which any such arrangements were made and the circumstances arising under this Act, the last foregoing subsection shall not apply to those arrangements or shall apply thereto with such modifications as to the payments to be made by the Central Authority or the local authority as may be so agreed or determined, and the said subsection shall have effect subject to any such agreement or determination.

Any other question arising under either of the two last foregoing subsections as to the payments to be made thereunder shall, in default of agreement, be determined by the Minister of Health.

(5) Any payment made by the Central Authority or the local authority under the foregoing provisions of this section which would, but for this Act, have been debited or credited as a capital payment, or any payment made in respect of the liability for the redemption of a loan or the repayment of an advance, shall be deemed to be a capital payment, and any other such payment shall be deemed to be an annual payment.

NOTES

General Note. This section must be read in conjunction with the Electricity Act 1957, s 23(1) post (under which sums payable by or to the Central Authority under this section are now payable by or to the Electricity Council). See also the Electricity Reorganisation (Scotland) Act 1954, s 10(2) (not printed in this work), and s 23(2) of the 1957 Act post.

Sub-s (1): Central Authority. See the note "Central Electricity Authority" to s 1 ante.

Sub-s (2): Vesting date. By virtue of s 14 of this Act (repealed), the vesting date was 1 April 1948.

Sub-s (4): Minister of Health. The functions of the Minister of Health under this section were transferred to the Minister of Housing and Local Government except that his functions as they applied to Wales were transferred to the Secretary of State; see the Transfer of Functions (Minister of Health and Minister of Local Government and Planning) (No 1) Order 1951, SI 1951/172, in conjunction with the Minister of Local Government and Planning (Change of Style and Title) Order 1951, SI 1951/1900, and the Secretary of State for Wales and Minister of Land and Natural Resources Order 1965, SI 1965/319. The functions of the Minister of Housing and Local Government were transferred to the Secretary of State by the Secretary of State for the Environment Order 1970, SI 1970/1681.

Definitions. For "authorised undertakers", see s 13(1)(a) ante; for "Central Authority", see s 1(3) ante; for "Electricity Board", see s 1(3) ante, in conjunction with the Electricity Reorganisation (Scotland) Act 1954, Sch 1, Pt II post; for "functions", "loan" and "local authority", see s 67(1) post.

23–35 (*Ss 23–26, 29, 30, 34 repealed by the Electricity Act 1957, s 42(3), Sch 5, Pt I; ss 27, 28, 31–33, 35 repealed by the SL(R) Act 1977.*)

PART III

FINANCIAL PROVISIONS

36 (*Repealed by the Electricity Act 1957, s 42(3), Sch 5, Pt II.*)

37 Fixing and variation of tariffs

[(1) The prices to be charged by the Generating Board for the supply of electricity by them to Area Boards shall be in accordance with such tariffs as may be fixed from time to time by the Generating Board after consultation with the Electricity Council; the different tariffs may be fixed for different Area Boards.]

[(1A) The prices to be charged by the Generating Board for any supply of electricity given in compliance with a request under section 5 of the Energy Act 1983 shall be in accordance with such tariffs as may be fixed from time to time by the Generating Board after consultation with the Electricity Council.]

(2) The tariffs fixed under [subsection (1) or (1A) of this section] shall be so framed as to show the methods by which and the principles on which the charges are to be made as well as the prices which are to be charged, and shall be published in such manner as in the opinion of the [Generating Board] will secure adequate publicity for them.

(3) [Subject to the provisions of the Electricity Act 1957 with respect to railways, the prices to be charged by an Area Board for the supply of electricity by them shall be in accordance with such tariffs as may be fixed from time to time by them after consultation with the Consultative Council established for their area and with the Electricity Council], and those tariffs shall be so framed as to show the methods by which and the principles on which the charges are to be made as well as the prices which are to be charged, and shall be published in such manner as in the opinion of the Area Board will secure adequate publicity for them:

Provided that—

    (*a*) the tariffs in force immediately before the vesting date in the area of supply or any part of the area of supply of any authorised undertakers shall remain in force, until varied or replaced by tariffs fixed in accordance with this section, and apply to the supply of electricity by the Area Board within whose area the said area of supply or part thereof is comprised; and

    (*b*) nothing in this subsection shall affect any agreement in force immediately before the vesting date.

(4) A tariff fixed by an Area Board under the last foregoing subsection may include a rent or other charge in respect of electrical fittings provided by the Board ....

[(4A) Tariffs fixed under this section may include charges in respect of the availability of a supply of electricity, and such a charge may vary according to the extent to which the supply is taken up.

(4B) Where the Electricity Council is consulted as to a tariff which includes a charge of the kind referred to in subsection (4A) of this section, the Council shall consult the Secretary of State as to the methods by which and the principles on which the charge is to be made.]

(5), (6) ...

(7) Notwithstanding anything in the foregoing provisions of this section, [a Board] may enter into an agreement with any [person] for the supply of electricity to him on such terms as may be specified in the agreement:

Provided that [a Board], in exercising their powers under this subsection, shall—

(a) secure that such agreements are only made in cases where the tariffs in force are not appropriate owing to special circumstances; and

(b) . . .

(8) [A Board], in fixing tariffs and making agreements under this section [and in proposing prices in accordance with section 6(2) of the Energy Act 1983], shall not show undue preference to any person or class of persons and shall not exercise any undue discrimination against any person or class of persons . . .

NOTES

Sub-s (1), the words in the second pair of square brackets in sub-s (2), and the words in square brackets in sub-s (3) were substituted, and sub-ss (5), (6) and the words omitted from sub-ss (7), (8) were repealed, by the Electricity Act 1957, ss 14(2), 42(1), (3), Sch 4, Pt I, Sch 5, Pt II; for a saving, see Sch 3, para 3(5) to that Act post.

Sub-ss (1A), (4A), (4B) were inserted, the words in the first pair of square brackets in sub-s (2) and the words in square brackets in sub-ss (7), (8) were substituted, and the words omitted from sub-s (4) were repealed, by the Energy Act 1983, ss 17(1), 25, 36, Sch 3, para 5, Sch 4, Pt I.

Sub-s (1): Consultation. See the note to s 1 ante.

Electricity Council. See the Electricity Act 1957, s 3 post.

Sub-s (3): Vesting date. By virtue of s 14 of this Act (repealed), the vesting date was 1 April 1948.

Sub-s (4): Rent in respect of electrical fittings. For power of Area Boards to supply electrical fittings, see s 2(4)(a) ante.

Sub-s (7): Owing to special circumstances. It would appear that, in deciding whether such circumstances existed, the factors to be taken into account would include the amount of energy consumed, the expense of supplying it and getting payment, the uniformity of demand and the time when the energy was required; cf *Metropolitan Electric Supply Co Ltd v Ginder* [1901] 2 Ch 799, 70 LJ Ch 862 (meaning of "similar circumstances" in the Electric Lighting Act 1882, s 19 (repealed)).

Sub-s (8): Undue preference. Cf s 1(6)(c) ante. For relevant cases, see, in particular, *South of Scotland Electricity Board v British Oxygen Co Ltd* [1956] 3 All ER 199, [1956] 1 WLR 1069, HL and *South of Scotland Electricity Board v British Oxygen Co Ltd (No 2)* [1959] 2 All ER 255, [1959] 1 WLR 587, HL.

Undue discrimination. See *London Electricity Board v Springate* [1969] 3 All ER 289, [1969] 1 WLR 524, CA.

Definitions. For "Area Boards", see s 1(3) ante. By virtue of s 57(1), Sch 4, Pt I post, for "area of supply", see the Electric Lighting (Clauses) Act 1899, Schedule, s 4 ante; and for "railway", see the Electricity (Supply) Act 1919, s 36 ante. For "authorised undertakers", see s 13(1)(a) ante; for "electrical fittings" and "the Generating Board", see s 67(1) post.

Energy Act 1983, ss 5, 6(2). See this title post.

Electricity Act 1957. For provisions of that Act with respect to railways, see s 28 thereof post.

38–44 (*S 38 repealed by the Electricity (Scotland) Act 1979, Sch 10, para 13, Sch 12; ss 39, 41–44 repealed by the Electricity Act 1957, s 42(3), Sch 5, Pt II; s 40 repealed by the SL(R) Act 1977 (sub-ss (1), (2), (4) previously repealed by the Electricity Act 1957, s 42(3), Sch 5, Pt II).*)

45 Sums which are to be chargeable to revenue account

(1) The [Generating Board] [the South of Scotland Board] and the Area Boards shall charge to revenue account in every year all charges which are proper to be made to revenue account, including, in particular, proper allocations [in the case of the Generating Board, to the generating reserve fund, in the case of the South of Scotland Board, to the general reserve fund established under section eleven A of the Act of 1943, and, in the case of an Area Board, to the area reserve fund maintained by the Board], proper provision for the redemption of capital and proper provision for depreciation of assets or for renewal of assets, and all payments (including the payments which are by the relevant provision of this Act, or by any other relevant enactment, to be deemed to be capital payments) which fall to be made in that year to any local authority under Part II of this Act in respect of any loan of that local authority, and references in this Act to outgoings properly chargeable to revenue account shall be construed accordingly.

[(2) . . .]

46 Accounts and audit of Central Authority and Area Boards

(1) The [Electricity Council, the Generating Board] and each Area Board shall keep proper accounts and other records in relation to the business of that [Council] or the business of that Board, as the case may be, and shall prepare in respect of each financial year a statement of accounts in such form as the Minister, with the approval of the Treasury, may direct, being a form which shall conform with the best commercial standards.

(2) The form of the said statement shall be such as to secure the provision of separate information as respects the generation of electricity, the distribution of electricity, and each of the main other activities of the Electricity Board concerned, and to show as far as may be the financial and operating results of each such activity.

(3) The accounts of the [Electricity Council, the Generating Board] and of every Area Board shall be audited by auditors to be appointed in respect of each financial year by the Minister:

Provided that no person shall be qualified to be so appointed unless he is a member of one or more of the following bodies:—

> The Institute of Chartered Accountants in England and Wales;
> The Society of Incorporated Accountants and Auditors;
> The Society of Accountants in Edinburgh;
> The Institute of Accountants and Actuaries in Glasgow;
> The Society of Accountants in Aberdeen;
> The Association of Certified and Corporate Accountants, Limited.

[(4) The Electricity Council, the Generating Board and every Area Board shall, as soon as their accounts have been audited, send a copy of the statement thereof referred to in subsection (1) of this section to the Minister and (in the case of the Generating Board or an Area Board) to the Electricity Council, together with a copy of any report made by the auditors on that statement or on those accounts, and copies of those statements and of every such report shall be made available to the public at a reasonable price.]

(6) The Minister shall lay a copy of every such statement and report before each House of Parliament.

47 *(Repealed by the Electricity (Scotland) Act 1979, s 46(2), Sch 12.)*

PART IV

MISCELLANEOUS AND GENERAL

48 *(Repealed by the Electricity Act 1957, s 42(3), Sch 5, Pt I.)*

Further Provisions relating to Electricity Supply

49 *(Repealed by the Electricity Act 1957, s 42(3), Sch 5, Pt I.)*

50 Use of heat from generating stations

[(1) It shall be the duty of every Electricity Board to adopt and support schemes—

  (*a*) for the combined production of heat and electricity, and
  (*b*) for the use of heat produced in combination with electricity, or incidentally from its generation, for the heating of buildings or for other useful purposes.

(2) Nothing in subsection (1) of this section—

  (*a*) shall remove the need for an Area Board to obtain the approval of the Secretary of State under section 6 of the Electricity Act 1957 to proposals for the generation of electricity by the Board, or
  (*b*) shall require an Electricity Board to undertake expenditure in connection with a scheme which does not meet the financial criteria applied by the Board in relation to other expenditure of the Board.]

(3) Any Electricity Board may, in accordance with a scheme submitted by them to the Minister and approved by order of the Minister, exercise for the purposes mentioned in [subsection (1) of this section] any powers of that Board under this Act (including any enactments incorporated therewith) or the Electricity (Supply) Acts 1882 to 1936, or any local enactment, being powers relating to the breaking-up of streets, railways and tramways, in like manner and subject to the like provisions and restrictions as they are exercisable for the purposes of the supply of electricity, subject to such adaptations as may be prescribed by the order:

Provided that, in the case of a scheme of the North of Scotland Board, the scheme shall be submitted to, and approved by order of, the Secretary of State.

(4) Any order made under this section shall be subject to special parliamentary procedure.

  [(5) . . .]

NOTES

Sub-ss (1), (2), and the words in square brackets in sub-s (3) were substituted by the Energy Act 1983, s 19(1); sub-s (5) (which was added by the Electricity Reorganisation (Scotland) Act 1954, s 15(1), Sch 5, Pt I) was repealed by the Electricity Act 1957, s 42(3), Sch 5, Pt I.

Enactments incorporated therewith. By s 57(2) post, the Schedule to the Electric Lighting (Clauses) Act 1899 ante is incorporated with this Act. That Act is the only Act containing powers of breaking up streets etc which is so incorporated; see ss 11 et seq of the Schedule to that Act ante.

Local enactment. For provisions for the adaptation of local enactments, see s 57(3), (7) post.

Special parliamentary procedure. This procedure is regulated by the Statutory Orders (Special Procedure) Acts 1945 and 1965, Vol 41, title Statutes.

Definitions. For "Electricity Board", see s 1(3) ante; for "enactment", "local enactment", "Minister" and "North of Scotland Board", see s 67(1) post.

Electricity Act 1957. See this title post.

Electricity (Supply) Acts 1882 to 1936. For the Acts which may be cited by this collective title, see the Introductory Note to the Electric Lighting Act 1882 ante.

Order under this section. The London Electricity Board Heating Scheme Order 1972, SI 1972/152.

---

51 Power to break up streets for certain purposes

(1) Where any Area Board or the North of Scotland Board—

(a) acquire a bulk supply of electricity which is received by them outside their area or, as the case may be, outside the North of Scotland District; or

(b) provide a supply of electricity outside their area or, as the case may be, outside the North of Scotland District,

the Board may, in accordance with proposals submitted by them to the Minister and approved by him, exercise for the purpose of such acquisition or the provision of such supply any powers of that Board under this Act (including any enactment incorporated therewith) or the Electricity (Supply) Acts 1882 to 1936, or any local enactment, being powers relating to the breaking up of streets, railways and tramways which would not otherwise be so exercisable:

Provided that, in the case of the North of Scotland Board, the proposals shall be submitted to and approved by the Secretary of State, and the references to the enactments aforesaid shall include a reference to the Act of 1943.

(2) The powers conferred by this section shall be exercisable in like manner and subject to the like provisions and restrictions as they are exercisable by the Board concerned for the purpose of the supply of electricity in the area or District of the Board.

[(3) This section shall apply to the [Generating Board] as it applies to an Area Board.]

NOTES

Sub-s (3) was added by the Electricity Reorganisation (Scotland) Act 1954, s 15(1), Sch 1, Pt II, and the words in square brackets within that subsection were substituted by the Electricity Act 1957, s 42(1), Sch 4, Pt I.

Supply of electricity between areas. As to the power of Area Boards to acquire electricity from one another, and to supply to consumers in one another's area, see s 1(4) ante.

Enactment incorporated therewith. See the note "Enactments incorporated therewith" to s 50 ante.

Local enactment. For provisions for the adaptation of local enactments, see s 57(3), (7) post.

Definitions. For "Area Board", see s 1(3) ante; and for "bulk supply", "enactment", "the Generating Board", "local enactment", "Minister", "North of Scotland Board" and "North of Scotland District", see s 67(1) post. By virtue of s 57(1), Sch 4, Pt I post, for "electricity", see the Electric Lighting Act 1882, s 32 ante.

Electricity (Supply) Acts 1882 to 1936. See the notes to s 50 ante.

Act of 1943. Ie the Hydro-Electric Development (Scotland) Act 1943 (not printed in this work); see s 67(1) post.

---

52 (*Repealed by the SL(R) Act 1971.*)

Conditions of Employment and Pension Rights

53 (*Repealed by the Electricity Act 1957, s 42(3), Sch 5, Pt I.*)

54 Provisions as to pension rights

(1) The Minister and the Secretary of State may make joint regulations for all or any of the following purposes, that is to say—

(a) for providing pensions to or in respect of persons who are or have been in the employment of an Electricity Board [or the Electricity Council] or a Consultative Council, or persons who have been members of the Central Electricity Board or have been employed by any body to whom Part II of this Act applies or have been employed whole-time for the purpose of administering undertakings or parts of undertakings of authorised undertakers, but who have not been taken into the employment of an Electricity Board [or the Electricity Council] as aforesaid;

(b) for the establishment and administration of pension schemes and pension funds for the purposes of the foregoing paragraph, for the continuance, amendment, repeal or revocation of existing pension schemes relating in whole or in part to the like purposes [(whether the schemes in question came into existence before or after the vesting date)] and of enactments relating thereto and of trust deeds, rules or other instruments made for the purposes thereof, for the transfer in whole or in part, or for the extinguishment, of liabilities under any such existing pension schemes, and for the transfer in whole or in part, or winding up, of pension funds held for the purposes of any such existing pension schemes, so, however, that nothing in this paragraph shall be construed as authorising the diversion of any such funds to purposes other than those of the foregoing paragraph;

(c) for making any provision consequential on any such provision as aforesaid including provision for the dissolution or winding up of bodies, whether incorporated or not, the continued existence whereof is unnecessary having regard to the regulations.

(2) Where provision is made by any such regulations for the amendment, repeal or revocation of any existing pension scheme or of any enactment relating thereto or any trust deed, rules or other instrument made for the purposes thereof, or for the transfer or extinguishment of any liability under any pension scheme or for the transfer or winding up of any pension fund held for the purposes of any such scheme, the regulations shall be so framed as to secure that persons having pension rights under the scheme, whether such persons as are mentioned in paragraph (a) of the last foregoing subsection or not, are not placed in any worse position by reason of the amendment, repeal, revocation, transfer, extinguishment or winding up:

Provided that this subsection shall have effect subject to such limitations as may be prescribed for meeting cases in which, in connection with any provision made by this Act or in anticipation of the making of any such provision, pension rights have been created otherwise than in the ordinary course.

(3) Regulations made under this section shall not be invalid by reason that in fact they do not secure that persons having pension rights are not placed in any worse position by reason of any such amendment, repeal, revocation, transfer, extinguishment or winding up as is mentioned in the last foregoing subsection, but if the Minister and the Secretary of State are satisfied or it is determined as hereinafter mentioned that any such regulations have failed to secure that result, the Minister and the Secretary of State shall as soon as possible make the necessary amending regulations.

Any dispute arising as to whether or not the said result has been secured by any regulations made under this section shall be referred to a referee or board of referees appointed by [the Secretary of State], after consultation with the Lord Chancellor or, where the proceedings are to be held in Scotland, after consultation with the Secretary of State, for his or their determination thereon, . . .

(4) Without prejudice to the generality of the foregoing provisions of this section, regulations made under this section may contain provisions authorising any person who, being a participant in any pension scheme to which the regulations relate, becomes a member of an Electricity Board [or the Electricity Council] being treated as if his service as a member of the Board [or Council] were service in the employment of the Board [or Council], and the pension rights of any such person resulting from the operation of any such provision shall not be affected by any provision of this Act [(including any such provision as applied to the Electricity Council by the Electricity Act 1957)] which requires that the pensions, if any, which are to be paid in the case of members of the Board [or Council] are to be determined by the Minister with the approval of the Treasury.

(5) Subject to any regulations made under this section, the provisions of this Act which vest liabilities and obligations of a body to whom Part II of this Act applies in an Electricity Board shall apply in relation to customary obligations of the body in respect of pensions, notwithstanding that the body was under no legal obligation in respect of those pensions, and if any question arises as to the existence or extent of any such customary obligation, the question shall, in default of agreement, be referred to a referee or board of referees appointed by [the Secretary of State], after consultation with the

Lord Chancellor, or where the proceedings are to be held in Scotland, after consultation with the Secretary of State, . . . and the Electricity Board shall give effect to that decision.

(6) . . .

(7) Regulations made under this section may contain such supplementary and consequential provisions as the Minister and the Secretary of State think necessary, including provisions as to the manner in which questions arising under the regulations are to be determined and provisions adapting, modifying or repealing enactments, whether of general or special application.

(8) Regulations made for the purposes of this section may be made so as to have effect from a date prior to the making thereof, so, however, that so much of any regulations as provides that any provision thereof is to have effect from a date prior to the making thereof shall not place any person other than an Electricity Board [or the Electricity Council] in a worse position than he would have been if the regulations had been made to have effect only as from the date of the making thereof.

NOTES

The words in square brackets in sub-ss (1), (4), (8) were inserted by the Electricity Act 1957, s 42(1), Sch 4, Pt I. The words omitted from sub-ss (3), (5) were repealed by the Tribunals and Inquiries Act 1958, s 15, Sch 2, Pt II. The words in square brackets in sub-ss (3), (5) were substituted by the Secretary of State for Employment and Productivity Order 1968, SI 1968/729. Sub-s (6) was repealed by the Statute Law (Consequential Repeals) Act 1965, s 1(1), Schedule.

Secretary of State. See the note to s 4 ante.

Electricity Council. See the Electricity Act 1957, s 3 post.

Consultative Council. As to establishment and functions, see s 7 ante.

Central Electricity Board. This body was established under the Electricity (Supply) Act 1926, s 1 (repealed), for the purpose of carrying out the electricity "grid" scheme. It is one of the authorised undertakers who are listed in Sch 2 post, and to whom Pt II of this Act applied (see s 13(1) ante), and was dissolved under s 14(11) of this Act (repealed).

By the Electricity (Supply) Act 1926, s 33 (repealed) the Board was given power to adopt the provisions of the Local Government Superannuation Act 1937 (repealed with a saving by the Superannuation Act 1972, s 29(2), (4), Schs 7, 8, para 5, Vol 33, title Pensions and Superannuation).

Body to whom Part II of this Act applies. See s 13(1) ante.

Transfer of financial liability. For a power to transfer financial liabilities incurred under this section in certain cases, see the Statutory Corporations (Financial Provisions) Act 1975, s 6(1), (3), Sch 3, paras 8, 9(2), Vol 30, title Money (Pt 1).

Referee or board of referees. Any question which, by virtue of this section or regulations under s 55 post or that section as applied by the Electricity Act 1957, s 27 post, is to be determined by a referee or board of referees must be referred to an industrial tribunal; see the Employment Protection (Consolidation) Act 1978, s 130, Sch 10, para 7, Vol 16, title Employment.

Provision which requires pensions to be determined by Minister. The reference in sub-s (4) above is to s 3(6) ante.

Provisions which vest liabilities in Electricity Board. Such provision was made by s 14 of this Act (repealed).

Definitions. For "authorised undertakers", "employed" (and "employment"), "enactment", "Minister", "pension", "pension fund", "pension rights", "pension scheme", "prescribed" and "regulations", see s 67(1) post; for "Electricity Board", see s 1(3) ante, in conjunction with the Electricity Reorganisation (Scotland) Act 1954, Sch 1, Pt II post, and the Electricity Act 1957, Sch 3, para 11 post.

Electricity Act 1957. See this title post.

Regulations under this section. The Electricity (Pension Scheme) Regulations 1948, SI 1948/226, as amended by SI 1950/359, SI 1957/2226 and SI 1971/936; the Electricity (Pension Rights) Regulations 1948, SI 1948/2172, as amended by SI 1950/359, SI 1951/1079 and SI 1957/2226; the Electricity (Pension Rights) (Particular Schemes) Regulations 1951, SI 1951/1079; the Electricity Supply (Staff) Superannuation Scheme and the Electricity Supply (Industrial Staff) Superannuation Scheme (Winding Up) Regulations 1983, SI 1983/353; and regulations classified as local not noted in this work.

See also the National Insurance (Modification of Electricity Superannuation Schemes) Regulations 1961, SI 1961/306.

55 Compensation to officers in connection with transfers

(1) The Minister and the Secretary of State jointly shall by regulations require every Electricity Board to pay, in such cases and to such extent as may be specified in the

regulations, compensation to officers of any body whose property, rights, liabilities and obligations vest by virtue of this Act in the Board and officers employed whole-time for the purpose of administering undertakings or parts of undertakings of authorised undertakers, being officers who suffer loss of employment or loss or diminution of emoluments or pension rights or whose position is worsened in consequence of the vesting, or in consequence of the subsequent transfer to another Electricity Board or the subsequent disposal in any other manner, of any such property, rights, liabilities or obligations.

(2) The Minister shall also, in such cases and to such extent as may be specified in the regulations, by regulations require the Central Authority to pay compensation to—

    (a) members of the Central Electricity Board, and

    (b) Electricity Commissioners and officers of the Electricity commissioners,

who suffer loss of employment or loss or diminution of emoluments or pension rights or whose position is worsened in consequence of the dissolution of the Central Electricity Board or, as the case may be, the Electricity Commissioners, by or under this Act.

(3) Regulations made under subsection (1) or subsection (2) of this section shall, in such cases and to such extent as may be specified in the regulations, extend to persons who would have been within the said subsection (1) or, as the case may be, the said subsection (2) but for any war service in which they have been engaged.

In this subsection the expression "war service" means service in any of His Majesty's forces and such other employment as may be specified in the regulations.

(4) Different regulations may be made under this section in relation to different classes of persons, and any such regulations may be so framed as to have effect as from a date prior to the making thereof, so, however, that so much of any regulations as provides that any provision thereof is to have effect as from a date earlier than the making thereof shall not place any person other than an Electricity Board in a worse position than he would have been in if the regulations has been made to have effect only as from the date of the making thereof.

(5) Regulations made under this section—

    (a) shall prescribe the procedure to be followed in making claims for compensation, and the manner in which and the person by whom the question whether any or what compensation is payable is to be determined; and

    (b) may in particular contain provisions enabling appeals from any determination as to whether any or what compensation is payable to be brought, in such cases and subject to such conditions as may be prescribed by the regulations, before a referee or board of referees appointed by [the Secretary of State], after consultation with the Lord Chancellor or where the proceedings are to be held in Scotland, after consultation with the Secretary of State,

.   .   .   .   .

(6) Nothing in this section shall be construed as enabling regulations to be made prejudicing the rights of any person under section sixteen of the Electricity (Supply) Act 1919, or under section fifteen of and the Fourth Schedule to the Electricity (Supply) Act 1926, or under the Compensation of Displaced Officers (War Service) (Electricity Undertakings) Order 1946, being rights arising in consequence of events which occurred before the vesting date.

References to the said sections and Schedule shall be construed as including references to those sections and that Schedule as applied by any other enactment, with or without modifications and adaptations.

(7) No regulations shall be made under this section unless a draft thereof has been laid before Parliament and has been approved by resolution of each House of Parliament.

(8) [The Secretary of State] may, with the consent of the Treasury, pay out of moneys provided by Parliament—

    (*a*) to any referee or to the members of any board of referees appointed by him under this section or the last foregoing section such fees and allowances as he may with the consent of the Treasury determine; and

    (*b*) to persons giving evidence before any such referee or board such allowances as he may with the consent of the Treasury determine.

NOTES

The words omitted at the end of sub-s (5) were repealed by the Tribunal and Inquiries Act 1958, s 15, Sch 2, Pt II. The words in square brackets is sub-ss (5), (8) were substituted by the Secretary of State for Employment and Productivity Order 1968, SI 1968/729 for words themselves substituted by the Minister of Labour Order 1959, SI 1959/1769.

Sub-s (1): Secretary of State. See the note to s 4 ante.

Body whose property etc, vest in Board. S 14 (repealed) vested in Electricity Boards, in the manner set out in that section and subject to ss 15, 17 (repealed), the property, rights, etc, of authorised undertakers, power station companies and electricity holding companies as defined by s 13 ante.

Subsequent transfer to another Board. Property may be transferred from one Electricity Board to another under ss 4(2), (6), 19 ante.

Sub-s (2): Central Authority. See the note "Central Electricity Authority" to s 1 ante.

Central Electricity Board. See the note to s 54 ante.

Electricity Commissioners. See the General Note to s 58 post.

Sub-s (5): Making claims. As to penalties for false claims, see s 61 post.

Referee or board of referees. See the note to s 54 ante.

Sub-s (6): Vesting date. See the note to s 22(2) ante.

Set-off of redundancy payments. By the Redundancy Payments Statutory Compensation Regulations 1965, SI 1965/1988, the amount of compensation under regulations made under this section or the Electricity Act 1957, s 27 post is to be reduced by the amount of redundancy payments under the Redundancy Payments Act 1965 (repealed by the Employment Protection (Consolidation) Act 1978, and replaced by provisions of that Act).

Extensions. Sub-ss (3)–(6), (8) above are applied by the Electricity Act 1957, s 27(3) post.

Definitions. For "authorised undertakers", see s 13(1)(*a*) ante; for "Electricity Board", see s 1(3) ante; for "emoluments", "employed", "enactment", "Minister", "officer", "pension rights" and "regulations", see s 67(1) post.

Electricity (Supply) Act 1919, s 16. Repealed by s 57(7) of, and Sch 5 to, this Act; but cf proviso (*b*) to s 57(7) post, with sub-s (6) above. The repealed section provided for compensation to officers or servants who had suffered loss of employment, diminution of salary, etc, as a result of transfers of undertakings etc effected under or in consequence of that Act.

Electricity (Supply) Act 1926, s 15, Sch 4. Repealed by s 57(7) of, and Sch 5 to, this Act; but cf proviso (*b*) to s 57(7) post, with sub-s (6) above. The repealed provisions applied (with modifications) the Electricity (Supply) Act 1919, s 16 (as to which see the note above), to officers or servants of authorised undertakers affected by the closing of generating stations, etc, under or in consequence of the Electricity (Supply) Act 1926.

Compensation of Displaced Officers (War Service) (Electricity Undertakings) Order 1946. SR & O 1946/2176 (spent).

Regulations under this section. The Electricity (Staff Compensation) Regulations 1949, SI 1949/460; the Electricity (Commissioners and Others) (Compensation) Regulations 1950, SI 1950/965.

56 Arbitration Acts not to apply to proceedings before referees or boards of referees

Nothing in the Arbitration Acts 1889 to 1934 shall be construed as applying to any proceedings before a referee or board of referees appointed under either of the two last foregoing sections by [the Secretary of State].

NOTES

The words in square brackets were substituted by the Secretary of State for Employment and Productivity Order 1968, SI 1968/729.

Referee or board of referees. See the note to s 54 ante.

Arbitration Acts 1889 to 1934. Repealed; see now the Arbitration Act 1950, Vol 2, title Arbitration.

Consequential Amendment of Statutory Provisions

57 Application, amendment and repeal of enactments relating to electricity supply

(1) As from the vesting date, the Electricity (Supply) Acts 1882 to 1936, and any other enactment to which any provision of Part I of the Fourth Schedule to this Act applies, shall have effect subject to the adaptations and modifications specified in Part I of that Schedule, and the Act of 1943 shall have effect subject to the adaptations and modifications specified in Part II of that Schedule, being adaptations, and modifications required for the purpose of applying the said Acts and enactments to Electricity Boards and otherwise required in consequence of the provisions of this Act.

(2) The Schedule to the Electric Lighting (Clauses) Act 1899 shall, as from the vesting date, be incorporated with this Act, and shall have effect, as so incorporated, subject to the adaptations and modifications specified in Part III of the said Fourth Schedule.

(3) All local enactments in force at the vesting date and applicable to any authorised undertakers except enactments applicable to local authorities or composite companies otherwise than in their capacity as authorised undertakers, shall, as from the vesting date, have effect—

(*a*) as if for references to the undertakers there were substituted references to the appropriate Board;

(*b*) as if for any reference (however worded and whether expressed or implied) to the undertaking or any part of the undertaking or to the area of supply or any part of the area of supply of the undertakers there were substituted a reference to so much of the business carried on by the appropriate Board as corresponds to that undertaking or part thereof or, as the case may be, a reference to the area constituting the said area of supply or part thereof immediately before the vesting date;

and shall also have effect, as from such date as may be prescribed which may be prior to the making of the regulations but not to the vesting date, with such other adaptations and modifications (if any) as may be prescribed, being adaptations and modifications required in consequence of the provisions of this Act (including the foregoing provisions of this section) or of the Act of 1943:

Provided that the provisions of any such local enactment shall, in so far as they are inconsistent with or rendered redundant by the provisions of this Act (including the foregoing provisions of this section) or of the Act of 1943 cease to have effect, as from the vesting date.

In this subsection the expression "the appropriate Board"—

(*a*) in relation to undertakers all of whose property, rights, liabilities and obligations vest by virtue of this Act in a single Electricity Board, means that Board;

(*b*) in relation to undertakers, in whose case generating stations and main transmission lines vest by virtue of this Act in the Central Authority, and other parts of the undertaking vest as aforesaid in an Area Board, means—

(i) the Central Authority, as respects any enactment applicable only to the part of the undertaking vested in that Authority;

(ii) the Area Board, as respects any enactment applicable only to other parts of the undertaking;

(iii) both the said Authority and Board, as respects any enactment applicable both to the part vested in the Authority and to other parts of the undertaking.

(4) For the purpose of securing, so far as reasonably practicable, a uniform statutory

code applicable throughout the area of each Area Board and the North of Scotland District, the Minister may, as respects local enactments applicable to an Area Board, and the Secretary of State may, as respects local enactments applicable to the North of Scotland Board, by order provide for the repeal or amendment of any such enactment or for its extension to the whole of the area concerned, and for such matters consequential on or incidental to any such repeal, amendment or extension for which the Minister or the Secretary of State considers it necessary or expedient to provide.

An order under this subsection shall be subject to special parliamentary procedure.

(5) Where an order made under this Act provides for the transfer of property, rights, liabilities and obligations from any Electricity Board to another such Board, that order or a subsequent order may provide for the application to the last named Board of the provisions of any local enactment applicable to the first named Board, so far as appears to the Minister or Ministers by whom the order is made necessary or expedient in consequence of the said transfer.

(6) Where the undertaking of any person authorised by any enactment to supply electricity does not vest by virtue of this Act in any Electricity Board, the Minister or Secretary of State, as the case may be, may by order provide for the continued application to the undertaking, subject to such adaptations and modifications as may be necessary, of any enactments which would otherwise cease to apply to the undertaking in consequence of this section, including enactments repealed by this section.

(7) . . . where any local enactment incorporates (with or without adaptations or modifications) any provisions of the Schedule to the Electric Lighting (Clauses) Act 1899, repealed by this subsection, or contains any provisions substantially corresponding therewith, those provisions shall cease to have effect:

Provided that—

  (a) the repeal of any provision under which any special order or other order was made, being an order which would be applicable to an Electricity Board by virtue of subsection (3) of this section, shall not affect that order;

  (b) the repeal of the provisions of section sixteen of the Electricity (Supply) Act 1919, and section fifteen of and the Fourth Schedule to the Electricity (Supply) Act 1926, and of the Fifth Schedule to the Act of 1943 (so far as it applies the provisions aforesaid) shall not affect the rights of any person arising under any of those provisions in consequence of any event occurring before the vesting date; and

  (c) the repeal of section forty-two of and the First Schedule to the Civil Defence Act 1939 shall not prevent the disposal of plant, equipment and property, and the application of the proceeds thereof, in accordance with Part II of the said Schedule.

NOTES

The words omitted from sub-s (7) were repealed by the SLR Act 1950.

Sub-s (1): Vesting date. See the note to s 22(2) ante.

Sub-s (2): All local enactments. Sub-s (3) must now be read in conjunction with the Electricity Act 1957, s 42(2) post (under which, in effect, the reference to the Central Authority is to be taken as a reference to the Central Electricity Generating Board and the power to prescribe other adaptations and modifications of local enactments is extended).

Composite companies. By s 17(1) of this Act (repealed), this means a company specified in Sch 2, Pt II post.

Sub-s (4): North of Scotland District; North of Scotland Board. See the note "North of Scotland Board" to s 1 ante.

Special parliamentary procedure. See the Statutory Orders (Special Procedure) Acts 1945 and 1965, Vol 41, title Statutes.

Sub-s (6): Where the undertaking etc. As to undertakings excepted from the vesting provisions of this Act, see s 13(2) ante.

Definitions. For "Area Boards" and "Central Authority", see s 1(3) ante; for "authorised undertakers", "enactment", "generating station", "local authority", "local enactment", "main transmission lines", "Minister", "North of Scotland Board", "North of Scotland District", "prescribed" and "regulations", see s 67(1) post; for Electricity Boards, see s 1(3) ante, in conjunction with the Electricity Reorganisation (Scotland) Act 1954, Sch 1, Pt II post. Note as to "the appropriate board", sub-s (3) above.

Electricity (Supply) Acts 1882 to 1936. For the Acts which may be cited by this collective title, see the Introductory Note to the Electric Lighting Act 1882 ante.

Act of 1943. Ie the Hydro-Electric Development (Scotland) Act 1943 (c 32) (largely repealed by the Electricity (Scotland) Act 1979 (c 11) and replaced by provisions of that Act (not printed in this work)); see s 67(1) post.

Electric Lighting (Clauses) Act 1899, Schedule. See this title ante.

Electricity (Supply) Act 1919, s 16; Electricity (Supply) Act 1926, s 15, Sch 4. See the notes to s 55 ante.

Civil Defence Act 1939, s 42, Sch 1. The section referred to authorised the Central Electricity Board to set up a pool of plant and equipment for use in the event of damage consequent upon hostile attack. Pt II of the Schedule referred to authorised the disposal of such plant and equipment.

Orders under this section. The orders made under this section are now spent.

58 Power to dissolve Electricity Commissioners

(1) The Minister may by order provide—

(*a*) for dissolving the Electricity Commissioners;

(*b*) for transferring to the Minister all property, rights, liabilities and obligations of the Electricity Commissioners, and for the modification of agreements so far as necessary for giving effect to the transfer of rights, liabilities and obligations thereunder;

(*c*) for transferring to the Minister, the Secretary of State, the Central Authority or the North of Scotland Board any functions previously exercisable by the Electricity Commissioners under any enactment or for extinguishing any such functions;

(*d*) for transferring from the Minister to the Central Authority or the North of Scotland Board such of the property, rights, liabilities and obligations transferred to him from the Electricity Commissioners as appear to the Minister to relate any functions of the Commissioners so transferred;

(*e*) for the adaptation, modification or repeal of enactments relating to the Electricity Commissioners; and

(*f*) for matters incidental or supplementary to the matters aforesaid for which it appears to the Minister to be necessary or expedient to provide.

(2) Any order made under this section shall secure that the pension rights of persons who have been Electricity Commissioners or officers of the Electricity Commissioners are not prejudiced by the order, and any pension payable in satisfaction of those rights shall be paid out of moneys provided by Parliament and shall be repaid to the Treasury by the [Electricity Council] and the North of Scotland Board on demand to such extent as the Treasury may determine.

NOTES

The words in square brackets in sub-s (2) were substituted by the Electricity Act 1957, s 42(1), Sch 4, Pt I.

General Note. The Electricity Commissioners were established under the Electricity (Supply) Act 1919, s 1 (repealed by the order mentioned in the last note below) for the purpose of promoting, supervising and regulating the supply of electricity.

The Commissioners were dissolved on 1 August 1948 by order under this section; see the note below.

As to compensation to the Commissioners and their officers on dissolution, see s 55(2) ante.

Electricity Council. See the Electricity Act 1957, s 3 post.

Definitions. For "Central Authority", see s 1(3) ante; and for "enactment", "functions", "Minister", "North of Scotland Board", "officer", "pension" and "pension rights", see s 67(1) post.

Order under this section. The Electricity Commissioners (Dissolution) Order 1948, SI 1948/1769.

59 (*Repealed by the SL(R) Act 1971.*)

General

60 Power to make regulations relating to efficiency of supply and safety

(1) *The Minister [and the Secretary of State] may make such [joint] regulations as [they think] fit for the purpose of securing that any supply of electricity furnished to any consumer by an Electricity Board is regular and efficient, and that the public is so far as practicable protected from any personal injury, fire or other dangers arising from [the supply or] the use of electricity so furnished.*

(2) *Any regulations made under section six of the Electric Lighting Act 1882 and in force immediately before the vesting date shall continue in force, notwithstanding the repeal by this Act of the said section six, and shall have effect as if they had been made under this section.*

NOTES

The words in square brackets in sub-s (1) in the first to third places were inserted or substituted by the Electricity Reorganisation (Scotland) Act 1954, s 15(1), Sch 1, Pt II. The words in square brackets in sub-s (1) in the fourth place were inserted by the Electricity Act 1957, s 42(1), Sch 4, Pt I.

Prospective repeal. This section is repealed by the Energy Act 1983, s 36, Sch 4, Pt I post, as from a date to be appointed under s 37(1) of that Act.

Secretary of State. See the note to s 4 ante.

Definitions. By virtue of s 57(1) ante, and Sch 4, Pt I post, for "electricity", see the Electric Lighting Act 1882, s 32 ante. For "Electricity Board", see s 1(3) ante, in conjunction with the Electricity Reorganisation (Scotland) Act 1954, Sch 1, Pt II post; and for "Minister" and "regulations", see s 67(1) post.

Electric Lighting Act 1882, s 6. Repealed by s 57(1) of, and Sch 5 to, this Act. The proviso to that section conferred powers on the Minister (as successor to the functions relating to electricity supply of the Board of Trade) which were broadly similar to those conferred by sub-s (1) above. Such powers were exercised by means of regulations made by the Electricity Commissioners; as to such regulations, see the note below.

Regulations under this section. The Electricity (Overhead Lines) Regulations 1970, SI 1970/1355. By virtue of sub-s (2), the Electricity Supply Regulations 1937 (copies of which are obtainable from HM Stationery Office) continue in force under this section.

61 Penalties

(1) If any person, in giving any information, making any claim or giving any notice for the purposes of any provision of this Act or of any regulation thereunder, makes any statement which he knows to be false in a material particular, or recklessly makes any statement which is false in a material particular, he shall be liable on summary conviction to imprisonment for a term not exceeding three months or to a fine not exceeding [the prescribed sum], or to both such imprisonment and such fine, or on conviction on indictment to imprisonment for a term not exceeding two years or to a fine ... or to both such imprisonment and such fine.

(2) Regulations made under any provision of this Act may provide that persons offending against the regulations shall be liable on summary conviction to a fine not exceeding [level 3 on the standard scale] and, if the offence in respect of which he is so convicted is continued after the conviction, he shall be guilty of a further offence and liable in respect thereof on summary conviction to a fine not exceeding five pounds for each day on which the offence is so continued.

NOTES

The words in square brackets in sub-s (1) are substituted by virtue of the Magistrates' Courts Act 1980, s 32, Vol 27, title Magistrates and the words "not exceeding five hundred pounds" are omitted, as indicated by dots, by virtue of the Criminal Law Act 1977, s 32(1), Vol 12, title Criminal Law (see further the note "Fine" below). The reference to level 3 on the standard scale in sub-s (2) is substituted by virtue of the Criminal Justice Act 1982, ss 40, 46, Vol 27, title Magistrates.

General Note. For provisions as to prosecutions under this section and as to offences by corporations, see s 62 post.

Knows. Knowledge is an essential ingredient of the offence and must be proved by the prosecution; see, in particular, *Gaumont British Distributors Ltd v Henry* [1939] 2 KB 711, [1939] 2 All ER 808.

Knowledge includes the state of mind of a person who shuts his eyes to the obvious; see *James & Son Ltd v Smee* [1955] 1 QB 78 at 91, [1954] 3 All ER 273 at 278 per Parker J. Moreover, there is authority for saying that where a person deliberately refrains from making inquiries the results of which he might not care to have, this constitutes in law actual knowledge of the facts in question; see *Knox v Boyd* 1941 JC 82 at 86, and *Taylor's Central Garages (Exeter) Ltd v Roper* (1951) 115 JP 445 at 449, 450 per Devlin J, [1951] WN 383; and see also, in particular, *Mallon v Allon* [1964] 1 QB 385 at 394, [1963] 3 All ER 843 at 847. Yet mere neglect to ascertain what could have been found out by making reasonable inquiries is not tantamount to knowledge; *Taylor's Central Garages (Exeter) Ltd v Roper* supra per Devlin J, and cf *London Computator Ltd v Seymour* [1944] 2 All ER 11; but see also *Mallon v Allon* supra.

As to when the knowledge of an employee or agent may be imputed to his employer or principal, see 11 Halsbury's Laws (4th edn) para 54.

False. A statement may be false on account of what it omits even though it is literally true; see *R v Lord Kylsant* [1932] 1 KB 442, [1931] All ER Rep 179, and *R v Bishirgian* [1936] 1 All ER 586; and cf *Curtis v Chemical Cleaning and Dyeing Co Ltd* [1951] 1 KB 805 at 808, 809, [1951] 1 All ER 631 at 634, CA. Whether or not gain or advantage accrues from the false statement is irrelevant; see *Jones v Meatyard* [1939] 1 All ER 140; *Stevens & Steeds Ltd and Evans v King* [1943] 1 All ER 314; *Clear v Smith* [1981] 1 WLR 399, [1980] Crim LR 246; and *Barrass v Reeve* [1980] 3 All ER 705, [1981] 1 WLR 408.

Material particular. A particular may be material on the ground that it renders another statement more credible; see *R v Tyson* (1867) LR 1 CCR 107. As to whether evidence should be adduced to show why a piece of information was a material particular, see *R v Mallett* [1978] 3 All ER 10, [1978] 1 WLR 820, CA.

Recklessly. In *R v Caldwell* [1982] AC 341, [1981] 1 All ER 961, HL (applied in *R v Lawrence* [1982] AC 510, [1981] 1 All ER 974, HL; and see also *R v Pigg* [1982] 2 All ER 591, CA; revsd on another point [1983] 1 All ER 56, HL, and *Elliott v C* [1983] 2 All ER 1005, [1983] 1 WLR 939; and *Goldman v Thai Airways International Ltd* [1983] 3 All ER 693) it was held that when used in criminal enactments, the term "reckless" was used not as a term of legal art but in the popular or dictionary sense of meaning "careless, regardless or heedless of the possible harmful consequences of one's acts". As such the term encompassed both a decision to ignore a risk of harmful consequences flowing from an act which the accused had recognised as existing and also a failure to give any thought to whether there was any risk in circumstances where, if any thought were given to the matter, it would be obvious that there was. On the meaning of "recklessly", see also 11 Halsbury's Laws (4th edn) para 14, and 4 Words and Phrases (2nd edn) 272, 273, and the cases there cited.

Summary conviction. Summary jurisdiction and procedure are mainly governed by the Magistrates' Courts Act 1980, Vol 27, title Magistrates, and by rules made under s 144 of that Act.

Prescribed sum. Ie the prescribed sum within the meaning of the Magistrates Courts Act 1980, s 32, Vol 27, title Magistrates; see the Criminal Justice Act 1982, s 74(1), in the same title. By s 32(9) of the 1980 Act, as amended, the prescribed sum is £2,000 but a different amount may be substituted by order under s 143(1) of that Act.

Conviction on indictment. All proceedings on indictment are to be brought before the Crown Court; see the Supreme Court Act 1981, s 46(1), Vol 11, title Courts. As to the trial of indictments generally, see 11 Halsbury's Laws (4th edn) paras 225 et seq.

Fine. There is no specific limit to the amount of the fine which may be imposed on conviction on indictment, but the fine should be within the offender's capacity to pay; see, in particular, *R v Churchill (No 2)* [1967] 1 QB 190, [1966] 2 All ER 215, CCA; revsd on other grounds sub nom *Churchill v Walton* [1967] 2 AC 224, [1967] 1 All ER 497, HL; and see also the Bill of Rights (1688), s 1, Vol 10, title Constitutional Law (Pt 1).

Standard scale. By the Criminal Justice Act 1982, ss 37(3), 75, Vol 27, title Magistrates, this means the standard scale set out in s 37(2) of that Act as amended by order made under the Magistrates' Courts Act 1980, s 143(1), in the same title. The scale as amended by the Criminal Penalties etc (Increase) Order 1984, SI 1984/447, art 3(4), Sch 4, is: level 1: £50; level 2: £100; level 3: £400; level 4: £1,000; and level 5: £2,000.

Regulations. For definition, see s 67(1) post.

---

62 Provisions as to prosecutions and as to offences by corporations

(1) Proceedings for an offence under the last foregoing section or any regulation made under this Act shall not, in England and Wales, be instituted except by or with the consent of the Minister or by the Director of Public Prosecutions.

(2) Where an offence under the last foregoing section or any regulation made under this Act has been committed by a body corporate, every person who at the time of the commission of the offence was a director, general manager, secretary or other similar officer of the body corporate, or was purporting to act in any such capacity, shall be deemed to be guilty of that offence unless he proves that the offence was committed without his consent or connivance and that he exercised all such diligence to prevent the commission of the offence as he ought to have exercised having regard to the nature of his functions in that capacity and to all the circumstances.

NOTES

England; Wales. For meaning, see the Interpretation Act 1978, ss 5, 22(1), Sch 1, Sch 2, para 5(*a*), Vol 41, title Statutes.

Director of Public Prosecutions. Provision for the appointment of the Director of Public Prosecutions and Assistant Director is currently made by the Prosecution of Offences Act 1979, s 1, Vol 12, title Criminal Law; by sub-s (4) of that section an Assistant Director may do any act or thing which the Director is required or authorised to do.

The 1979 Act is repealed by the Prosecution of Offences Act 1985, Vol 12, title Criminal Law, as from a day to be appointed under s 31(2) thereof. New provision is made as to the establishment of a Crown Prosecution Service for England and Wales by ss 1–10. In particular, by s 1(6), every Crown Prosecutor has all the powers of the Director as to the institution and conduct of proceedings but exercises those powers under his direction.

Definitions. For "Minister" and "officer", see s 67(1) post.

63 Service of notices, etc

Any notice or other document required or authorised to be given, delivered or served under this Act or regulations or orders made thereunder or under any enactment applied by or incorporated with this Act [or the Electricity Act 1957] [or Part I of the Energy Act 1983 or regulations made thereunder] may be given, delivered or served either—

(*a*) by delivering it to the person to whom it is to be given or delivered or on whom it is to be served; or

(*b*) by leaving it at the usual or last known place of abode of that person; or

(*c*) by sending it in a prepaid registered letter addressed to that person at his usual or last known place of abode; or

(*d*) in the case of an incorporated company or body, or the arbitration tribunal, by delivering it to the secretary or clerk of the company, body or tribunal at their registered or principal office or sending it in a prepaid registered letter addressed to the secretary or clerk of the company, body or tribunal at that office; or

(*e*) if it is not practicable after reasonable enquiry to ascertain the name or address of a person to whom it should be given or delivered, or on whom it should be served, as being a person having any interest in land, by addressing it to him by the description of the person having that interest in the premises (naming them) to which it relates, and delivering it to some person on the premises, or, if there is no person on the premises to whom it can be delivered, affixing it, or a copy of it, to some conspicuous part of the premises.

NOTES

The words in the first pair of square brackets were inserted by the Electricity Act 1957, s 42(1), Sch 4, Pt I; the words in the second pair of square brackets were substituted by the Energy Act 1983, s 25, Sch 3, para 6.

Enactment applied by or incorporated with this Act. As to application and incorporation of enactments, see s 57 ante.

The Electric Lighting (Clauses) Act 1899, Schedule, ss 61 and 62(4) ante, contains further provisions as to notices under that Schedule.

Extension. This section is applied by the Rights of Entry (Gas and Electricity Boards) Act 1954, s 2(3) post.

Definitions. For "arbitration tribunal", "company" and "enactment", see s 67(1) post.

Electricity Act 1957; Energy Act 1983. See this title post.

64 Provisions as to regulations and orders

(1) Any power conferred by this Act [or by Part I of the Energy Act 1983] to make regulations or orders shall include power to provide by those regulations or orders for the determination of questions of fact or of law which may arise in giving effect to the regulations or orders and for regulating (otherwise than in relation to any court proceedings) any matters relating to the practice and procedure to be followed in

connection with the determination of such questions, including provision as to the mode of proof of any matters and provision as to parties and their representation for the right to appear and be heard (as well in court proceedings as otherwise) of the Minister [or, as the case may be, the Secretary of State] or other authorities, and as to awarding costs of proceedings for the determination of such questions, determining the amount thereof and the enforcement of awards thereof.

(2) Any power conferred by this Act [or by Part I of the Energy Act 1983] to prescribe by regulations or orders a period within which things are to be done shall include power to provide by those regulations or orders for extending the period so prescribed.

(3) All orders and regulations made under this Act, not being orders or regulations required to be laid before Parliament in draft or orders subject to special parliamentary procedure, shall be laid before Parliament immediately after they are made and if either House, within a period of forty days beginning with the day on which any such order or regulations is or are so laid before it, resolves that the order or regulations be annulled, the order or regulations shall thereupon cease to have effect, but without prejudice to the validity of anything previously done thereunder or to the making of any new order or regulations.

(4) In reckoning for the purposes of the last foregoing subsection any such period of forty days, no account shall be taken of any time during which Parliament is dissolved or prorogued, or during which both Houses are adjourned for more than forty days.

(5) Notwithstanding anything in subsection (4) of section one of the Rules Publication Act 1893, orders and regulations made under this Act shall be deemed not to be, or to contain, statutory rules to which that section applies.

(6) In the case of orders defining or varying the areas for which Area Boards are established under this Act, copies of the maps by reference to which those areas are defined by the orders shall be made available, during the period for which the orders or drafts thereof are laid before Parliament, for inspection by members of each House of Parliament.

(7) Any order made under any such power may be revoked or varied by a subsequent order made in the like manner and subject to the like conditions.

NOTES

The words in the first pair of square brackets in sub-s (1) and the words in square brackets in sub-s (2) were substituted by the Energy Act 1983, s 25, Sch 3, para 7; the words in the second pair of square brackets in sub-s (1) were substituted by the Electricity Reorganisation (Scotland) Act 1954, s 15(1), Sch 1, Pt II.

Laid before Parliament. For meaning, see the Laying of Documents before Parliament (Interpretation) Act 1948, s 1(1), Vol 41, title Statutes.

Special parliamentary procedure. This procedure is regulated by the Statutory Orders (Special Procedure) Acts 1945 and 1965, Vol 41, title Statutes.

Sub-s (6): Orders defining or varying the areas etc. See s 4 ante.

Definitions. For "Area Boards", see s 1(3) ante; and for "Minister" and "regulations", see s 67(1) post.

Rules Publication Act 1893, s 1(4). Repealed by the Statutory Instruments Act 1946, s 12(1).

65 Expenses of the Minister

Any administrative expenses incurred by the Minister or any other Minister of the Crown or Government department under this Act shall be paid out of moneys provided by Parliament, and any sums received by the Minister or by any other Minister of the Crown or Government department under or by virtue of this Act shall be paid into the Exchequer.

NOTE

Minister. The functions of the Minister are now exercised by the Secretary of State for Energy; see the Preliminary Note to this title.

66 Inquiries

(1) The Minister or the Secretary of State may cause an inquiry to be held in any case when he deems it advisable to do so in connection with any matter arising under this Act (including any enactment incorporated therewith) or the Electricity (Supply) Acts 1882 to 1936, or the Act of 1943 [or the Electricity Reorganisation (Scotland) Act 1954] [or the Electricity Act 1957] [or Part I of the Energy Act 1983].

(2) Subsections (2) to (5) of section two hundred and ninety of the Local Government Act 1933 shall apply to any inquiry held by the Minister in England and Wales in pursuance of this section, and shall have effect as if the expression "department" included the Minister, and the provisions of the Sixth Schedule to the Act of 1943 shall apply to any inquiry held in Scotland, whether by the Minister or the Secretary of State, in pursuance of this section in like manner as those provisions apply to any inquiry held by the Secretary of State for the purposes of that Act:

Provided that no local authority shall be ordered to pay costs under subsection (4) of the said section two hundred and ninety in the case of any inquiry unless they are a party thereto.

NOTES

In sub-s (1), the words in the first pair of square brackets were inserted by the Electricity Reorganisation (Scotland) Act 1954, s 15(1), Sch 1, Pt II, the words in the second pair of square brackets were inserted by the Electricity Act 1957, s 42(1), Sch 4, Pt I, and the words in the third pair of square brackets were inserted by the Energy Act 1983, s 25, Sch 3, para 8.

Inquiry. Inquiries held under this section are subject to the Tribunals and Inquiries Act 1971, ss 1, 11, Vol 10, title Constitutional Law (Pt 4); see the Tribunals and Inquiries (Discretionary Inquiries) Order 1975, SI 1975/1379, art 3, Schedule, Pt II.

Enactment incorporated therewith. The Schedule to the Electric Lighting (Clauses) Act 1899 ante is incorporated with this Act by s 57(2) ante.

... shall apply etc. Sub-s (2) is extended by the Electricity Act 1957 post; see Sch 2, para 2, thereto post.

Definitions. For "enactment", "local authority" and "Minister", see s 67(1) post.

Electricity (Supply) Acts 1882 to 1936. For the Acts which may be cited by this collective title, see the Introductory Note to the Electric Lighting Act 1882 ante.

Act of 1943. Ie the Hydro-Electric Development (Scotland) Act 1943 (c 32) (largely repealed by the Electricity (Scotland) Act 1979 (c 11) and replaced by provisions of that Act (not printed in this work)); see s 67(1) post.

Local Government Act 1933, s 290. Repealed by the Local Government Act 1972, and replaced by s 250 of that Act, Vol 25, title Local Government. The provisions applied relate to the attendance of witnesses at inquiries, the taking of evidence thereat and the costs thereof.

Electricity Reorganisation (Scotland) Act 1954; Electricity Act 1957; Energy Act 1983. See this title post.

67 Interpretation

(1) In this Act, except where the context otherwise requires, the following expressions have the meanings hereby respectively assigned to them, that is to say—

"the Act of 1943" means the Hydro-Electric Development (Scotland) Act 1943;

"arbitration tribunal" means the tribunal established under section thirty-one of this Act;

"Area Board" has the meaning assigned to it by section one of this Act;

"authorised undertakers" means the bodies specified in the Second Schedule to this Act, and any reference in this Act to the capacity of a local authority or a composite company as authorised undertakers shall be construed as a reference to their capacity as a body authorised by any enactment to supply electricity in an area of supply;

"bulk supply" means a supply of electricity to be used for the purposes of distribution;

"Central Authority" has the meaning assigned to it by section one of this Act;

"company" means a company incorporated by any enactment and a company within the meaning of the Companies Act 1929;

"Electricity Board" has the meaning assigned to it by section one of this Act;

"electricity holding company" has the meaning assigned to it by section thirteen of this Act;

"electrical fittings" means electric lines, fittings, apparatus and appliances designed for use by consumers of electricity for lighting, heating, motive power and other purposes for which electricity can be used;

"electric line" has the same meaning as in the Electric Lighting Act 1882;

"electrical plant" means any plant, equipment, apparatus and appliances used for the purposes of generating, transmitting and distributing electricity, but not including any electrical fittings;

"emoluments" includes any allowances, privileges or benefits, whether obtaining legally or by customary practice;

"employed" means employed as an officer and "employment" shall be construed accordingly;

"enactment" means a public general Act, a local private or personal Act, a provisional order confirmed by an Act, and any regulation or order made under any enactment, or any provision, contained in any such Act, provisional order, regulation or order, and also includes any deed of transfer whereby statutory powers have been transferred to any authorised undertakers;

"financial year,"—

    (a) in relation to [either of the Scottish Electricity Boards], means the financial year determined by the Secretary of State under section fifteen of the Act of 1943;

    (b) in relation to any other Electricity Board [or to the Electricity Council], means a period of twelve months ending with a day to be prescribed, so however that the first financial year [(except in relation to the Electricity Council and the Generating Board)] shall be the period beginning with the passing of this Act and ending with the first occurrence of the prescribed day, and, in case of any alteration of the prescribed day, the duration of the financial year as to which the alteration is first to have effect shall be shortened or extended as may be prescribed, by not more than six months, so as to end on the new prescribed day; and

    (c) in relation to any body to whom Part II of this Act applies, other than a local authority, means the period of twelve months for which the accounts of the body are normally made up;

"functions" means duties and powers;

["the Generating Board" means the Central Electricity Generating Board constituted under the Electricity Act 1957];

"generating station" has the same meaning as in the Electricity (Supply) Act 1919;

"holding company" shall be construed in accordance with the definition contained in the Companies Act 1947;

"joint board of local authorities" means a joint board constituted under section eight of the Electric Lighting Act 1909, or by a local enactment;

"lease" includes an agreement for a lease and any tenancy agreement;

"loan", in relation to a local authority, means a loan raised by the issue of securities or by a mortgage created under Part IX of the Local Government Act 1933, or any similar enactment, and a loan advanced by the Public Works Loan Commissioners on the security of a mortgage;

"local authority" means the council of a ... district or ... borough, and the Common Council of the City of London, and includes, in section seven of this Act, the council of a county, and also includes in any other provision of this Act except the said section seven any joint board of local authorities having functions as authorised undertakers and also other functions;

"local enactment" means any enactment except a public general Act;

"main transmission lines" has the same meaning as in the Electricity (Supply) Act 1919;

"Minister" means [the Minister of Power];

"net revenue", in relation to any body, means the revenue of that body, after deducting therefrom all charges which are proper to be made to revenue account, including, in particular, proper provision for the redemption of capital and proper provision for depreciation of assets or for renewal of assets, but not including provision for interest on debentures and debenture stock;

"North of Scotland Board" means the North of Scotland Hydro-Electric Board constituted under the Act of 1943;

"North of Scotland District" means the area defined in the Second Schedule to the Act of 1943, subject to any order made under Part I of this Act varying that area;

"officer" includes a managing director and a director whose functions are substantially those of an employee but not any other director, and also includes a servant;

"pension", in relation to any person, means a pension, whether contributory or not, of any kind whatsoever payable to or in respect of him, and includes a gratuity so payable and a return of contributions to a pension fund, with or without interest thereon or any other addition thereto;

"pension fund" means a fund established for the purposes of paying pensions;

"pension rights" includes, in relation to any person, all forms of right to or eligibility for the present or future payment of a pension to or in respect of that person, and any expectation of the accruer of a pension to or in respect of that person under any customary practice and includes a right of allocation in respect of the present or future payment of a pension;

"pension scheme" includes any form of arrangements for the payment of pensions, whether subsisting by virtue of an Act, trust, contract or otherwise;

"power station company" has the meaning assigned to it by section thirteen of this Act;

"prescribed" means prescribed by regulations;

"railway undertakers" means any body authorised by any enactment to carry goods and passengers by railway;

"regulations" means regulations made by the Minister;

"securities", in relation to a body corporate, means any shares, stock, debentures and debenture stock of the body corporate, and also includes any mortgages of the body which were quoted in the Stock Exchange Official Daily List (within the meaning of section twenty of this Act) on all six of the dates first mentioned in subsection (2) of that section, and "holder of securities", in relation to any body to whom Part II of this Act applies, means, except in the provisions relating to the appointment of the stockholders' representative, a person who, immediately before the vesting date, was the holder of securities of that body, or his successor in title;

["South of Scotland Board" means the South of Scotland Electricity Board constituted under the Electricity Reorganisation (Scotland) Act 1954;

"South of Scotland District" means the district referred to in subsection (1) of section two of the Electricity Reorganisation (Scotland) Act 1954];

"stockholders' representative" has the meaning assigned to it by section twenty-one of this Act;

"subsidiary company" shall be construed in accordance with the definition contained in the Companies Act 1947;

"vesting date" has the meaning assigned to it by subsection (1) of section fourteen of this Act.

(2) The definitions of "the Act of 1943", "electrical fittings", "the North of Scotland Board" and "the North of Scotland District" shall apply for the purposes of any amendment made by this Act in any other enactment.

(3) References in this Act to any other enactment shall be construed as references to that enactment as amended by or under any other enactment including this Act.

NOTES

The words in square brackets in para (a) of the definition of "financial year" were substituted and the definitions of "South of Scotland Board" and "South of Scotland District" were inserted by the Electricity Reorganisation (Scotland) Act 1954, s 15(1), Sch 1, Pt II. The words in square brackets in para (b) of the definition of "financial year", and the definition of "the Generating Board", were inserted by the Electricity Act 1957, s 42(1), Sch 4, Pt I. In the definition of "local authority", the words omitted in the first place were repealed by the Local Authorities etc (Miscellaneous Provision) Order 1974, SI 1974/595, art 3(22), Sch 1, Pt I, and those omitted in the second place were repealed by the Local Authorities etc (Miscellaneous Provision) (No 3) Order 1975, SI 1975/1636, art 4(2).

As to the definition of "Minister", see the note below. The words in square brackets in that definition were substituted by the Minister of Fuel and Power (Change of Style and Title) Order 1957, SI 1957/48.

Authorised undertakers. For the meaning of "authorised undertaker", see also s 13(1), (2) ante.

Central Authority. See the note "Central Electricity Authority" to s 1 ante.

Enactment. The grant of powers of electricity supply by means of a provisional order confirmed by an Act was authorised by the Electric Lighting Act 1882, s 4 (repealed). Special orders, made by the Electricity Commissioners, Ministerially confirmed and approved by resolution of both Houses of Parliament, were substituted for provisional orders by the Electricity (Supply) Act 1919, s 26 (repealed). In the early days of the electricity industry powers granted by provisional orders were not infrequently transferred, or purported to be transferred, by deed.

Financial year. The Scottish Electricity Boards means the North of Scotland Board and the South of Scotland Board; see, by virtue of the Electricity Reorganisation (Scotland) Act 1954, s 17 post, s 14(1) of that Act.

The day prescribed in relation to the Electricity Council and any Electricity Board other than the Scottish Electricity Boards is 31 March; see the Electricity (Financial Years) Regulations 1948, SI 1948/747, as amended by SI 1958/509.

District. As to the districts in England and Wales and their councils, see the Local Government Act 1972, ss 1(1), (3), (4), 2(2), (3), 20(1), (3), 21(2), (3), Sch 1, Pt I, Sch 4, Pt II, Vol 25, title Local Government.

Borough. The boroughs, other than London boroughs, existing immediately before 1 April 1974 were abolished on that date by the Local Government Act 1972, ss 1(9), (10), 20(6), Vol 25, title Local Government, and the reference to a borough no longer has any effect.

A district may have the status and title of borough conferred on it by royal charter; see the Local Government Act 1972, s 245, Vol 25, title Local Government.

Common Council of the City of London. Ie the mayor, aldermen and commons of the City of London in common council assembled; see the City of London (Various Powers) Act 1958, s 5, Vol 26, title London.

County. The counties existing immediately before 1 April 1974 were abolished on that date by the Local Government Act 1972, ss 1(10), 20(6), Vol 25, title Local Government, and by virtue of s 179(1), (2) of that Act, the reference to a county is to be construed as a county established by ss 1(1), (2), 20(1), (2) of, and Sch 1, Pts I, II, Sch 4, Pt I to, the 1972 Act.

Minister of Power. The functions of the Minister of Power under this Act are now exercised by the Secretary of State for Energy; see the Preliminary Note to this title.

Securities. As to the bodies to whom Pt II of this Act applies, see s 13 ante.

Hydro-Electric Development (Scotland) Act 1943. 6 & 7 Geo 6 c 32; largely repealed by the Electricity (Scotland) Act 1979 (c 11) and replaced by provisions of that Act (not printed in this work).

Companies Act 1929. Repealed; see now for definition of "company", the Companies Act 1985, s 735(1)(a), Vol 8, title Companies.

Electric Lighting Act 1882. For definition of "electric line" in that Act, see s 32 thereof ante.

Electricity Act 1957. The Central Electricity Generating Board is constituted under s 2 of that Act post.

Electricity (Supply) Act 1919. For definition of "generating station" and of "main transmission line" in that Act, see s 36 thereof ante.

Companies Act 1947. See now for meanings of "holding company" and "subsidiary", the Companies Act 1985, s 736, Vol 8, title Companies.

Electric Lighting Act 1909, s 8. Repealed by s 57(7) of, and Sch 5 to, this Act.
Local Government Act 1933, Part IX. Repealed by the Local Government Act 1972, s 272(1), Sch 30, Vol 25, title Local Government, and replaced by Sch 13 to that Act.

68 (*Applies to Scotland only.*)

69 Short title and extent

(1) This Act may be cited as the Electricity Act 1947.

(2) This Act shall not extend to Northern Ireland.

SCHEDULES

FIRST SCHEDULE

Section 1

AREA ELECTRICITY BOARDS

Name of Area Board	*Description of Area*
The London Electricity Board.	The administrative County of London and parts of Essex, Kent, Middlesex and Surrey.
The South Eastern Electricity Board.	Parts of Kent, Middlesex, Surrey and Sussex.
The Southern Electricity Board.	Berkshire, Hampshire, the Isle of Wight, Wiltshire and parts of Buckinghamshire, Dorsetshire, Gloucestershire, Middlesex, Oxfordshire, Somersetshire, Surrey and Sussex.
The South Western Electricity Board.	Cornwall (including the Isles of Scilly), Devonshire and parts of Dorsetshire, Gloucestershire (including Bristol) and Somersetshire.
The Eastern Electricity Board.	Cambridgeshire, Hertfordshire, Huntingdonshire, the Isle of Ely, Norfolk, Suffolk and parts of Bedfordshire, Buckinghamshire, Essex, Middlesex, Oxfordshire and the Soke of Peterborough.
The East Midlands Electricity Board.	Leicestershire, Northamptonshire, Rutland and parts of Bedfordshire, Buckinghamshire, Derbyshire, Lincolnshire, Nottinghamshire, the Soke of Peterborough, Staffordshire and Warwickshire.
The Midlands Electricity Board.	Herefordshire, Worcestershire and parts of Gloucestershire, Oxfordshire, Shropshire, Staffordshire and Warwickshire (including Birmingham).
The South Wales Electricity Board.	Brecknockshire, Carmarthenshire, Glamorganshire, Monmouthshire, Pembrokeshire, Radnorshire and part of Cardiganshire.
The Merseyside & North Wales Electricity Board.	Anglesey, Caernarvonshire, Denbighshire, Flintshire, Merionethshire, Montgomeryshire and parts of Cardiganshire, Cheshire, Lancashire (including Liverpool) and Shropshire.
The Yorkshire Electricity Board.	Parts of Derbyshire, Lincolnshire, Nottinghamshire and of the East and West Ridings of Yorkshire.
The North Eastern Electricity Board.	Durham, Northumberland, the North Riding of Yorkshire and parts of the East and West Ridings of Yorkshire (including York).
The North Western Electricity Board.	Cumberland, Westmorland and parts of Cheshire, Derbyshire, Lancashire (including Manchester) and of the West Riding of Yorkshire.

.   .   .   .   .

NOTES

The words omitted were repealed by the Electricity Reorganisation (Scotland) Act 1954, ss 3(2), 14(1), 15(2), Sch 2, Pt I.

Note that the counties existing immediately before 1 April 1974 were abolished on that date by the Local Government Act 1972, ss 1(10), 20(6), Vol 25, title Local Government, and as to the new counties established by that Act, see (as to England) Sch 1, and (as to Wales) Sch 4, to that Act.

SECOND SCHEDULE

AUTHORISED UNDERTAKERS TO WHOM PART II OF ACT APPLIES

PART I

Public and Local Authorities and Companies (other than Composite Companies)

Aberayron and District Electricity Supply and Power Co Ltd.

Aberdare Urban District Council.

Aberdeen Corporation.

Abertillery Urban District Council.

Aberystwyth Corporation.

Accrington Corporation.

Adwick-le-Street Urban District Council.

Airdrie Corporation.

Aldeburgh Electric Supply Co Ltd.

Alderley Edge & Wilmslow Electricity Board.

Aldershot Corporation.

Alton District Electricity Co Ltd.

Altrincham Electric Supply, Ltd.

Amble Urban District Council.

Ammanford Urban District Council.

Ashbourne Urban District Council.

Ashford Urban District Council.

Ashton-in-Makerfield Urban District Council.

Ashton-under-Lyne Corporation.

Askrigg & Reeth Electric Supply Co Ltd.

Atherton Urban District Council.

Aylesbury Corporation.

Ayrshire Electricity Board.

Bacup Corporation.

Bangor Corporation.

Barking Corporation.

Barnes Corporation.

Barnoldswick Urban District Council.

Barnsley Corporation.

Barnstaple Corporation.

Barrow-in-Furness Corporation.

Barry Corporation.

Basingstoke Corporation.

Bath Corporation.

Batley Corporation.

Battersea Borough Council.

Beckenham Corporation.

Bedford Corporation.

Bedfordshire, Cambridgeshire & Huntingdonshire Electricity Co.

Bedwas and Machen Urban District Council.

Bedwellty Urban District Council.

Bermondsey Borough Council.

Bethesda Urban District Council.

Bethnal Green Borough Council.

Bexhill Corporation.

Bexley Corporation.

Bideford & District Electricity Supply Co Ltd.

Bingley Urban District Council.

Birkenhead Corporation.

Birmingham Corporation.

Blackburn Corporation.

Blackpool Corporation.

Blandford Forum & District Electric Supply Co Ltd.

Bolsover Urban District Council.

Bolton Corporation.

Borrowstounness Corporation.

Borth & Ynyslas Electric Supply Co Ltd.

Boston & District Electric Supply Co Ltd.

Bournemouth Corporation.

Bournemouth & Poole Electricity Supply Co Ltd.

Bradford Corporation.

Bredbury and Romiley Urban District Council.

Brentford & Chiswick Corporation.

Brentford Electric Supply Co Ltd.

Brentwood District Electric Co Ltd.

Bridgend Urban District Council.

Bridgwater & District Electric Supply & Traction Co Ltd.

Bridlington Corporation.

Bridport Corporation.

Brierfield Urban District Council.

Brighouse Corporation.

Brighton Corporation.

Bristol Corporation.

Bromley Corporation.

Buckie Corporation.

Buckrose Light & Power Co Ltd.

Bude Electric Supply Co Ltd.

Burford Electric Light & Power Co Ltd.

Burgess Hill Electricity Ltd.

Burnham & District Electric Supply Co Ltd.

Burnley Corporation.

Burton-upon-Trent Corporation.

Bury Corporation.

Buxton Corporation.

Caernarvon Corporation.

Caerphilly Urban District Council.

Calne Corporation.
Cambridge Electric Supply Co Ltd.
Campbeltown and Mid-Argyll Electric Supply Co Ltd.
Cannock Urban District Council.
Canterbury Corporation.
Cardiff Corporation.
Cardiff Rural District Council.
Cark & District Electricity Co Ltd.
Carlisle Corporation.
Carmarthen Electric Supply Co Ltd.
Castleford Urban District Council.
Central Electricity Board.
Central London Electricity Ltd.
Central Sussex Electricity Ltd.
Chasetown & District Electricity Co Ltd.
Cheadle & Gatley Urban District Council.
Cheltenham Corporation.
Chepstow Electric Lighting & Power Co Ltd.
Chesham Electric Light & Power Co Ltd.
Chester Corporation.
Chesterfield Corporation.
Chichester Corporation.
Chislehurst Electric Supply Co Ltd.
Chudleigh Electric Light & Power Co Ltd.
City of London Electric Lighting Co Ltd.
Clacton Urban District Council.
Cleethorpes Corporation.
Clitheroe Corporation.
Clyde Valley Electrical Power Co.
Coatbridge Corporation.
Colchester Corporation.
Colne Corporation.
Colne Valley Electric Supply Co Ltd.
Colne Valley Urban District Council.
Colwyn Bay Corporation.
Congleton Corporation.
Connah's Quay Urban District Council.
Conway Corporation.
Cornwall Electric Power Co.
County of London Electric Supply Co Ltd.
Coventry Corporation.
Craven Hydro-Electric Supply Co Ltd.
Crewe Corporation.
Crieff Electric Supply Co Ltd.
Crook and Willingdon Urban District Council.
Croydon Corporation.

Culm Valley Electric Supply Co Ltd.
Cwmbran Urban District Council.
Darlington Corporation.
Dartford Corporation.
Darwen Corporation.
Dawlish Electric Light & Power Co Ltd.
Dearne District Electricity Board.
Denny & Dunipace Corporation.
Derby Corporation.
Derbyshire & Nottinghamshire Electric Power Co.
Dewsbury Corporation.
Dolgelly Urban District Council.
Doncaster Corporation.
Dorchester Corporation.
Dover Corporation.
Dumbarton Corporation.
Dumfries Corporation.
Dumfriesshire County Council.
Dunbartonshire County Council.
Dundee Corporation.
Dunoon & District Electricity Supply Co Ltd.
Ealing Corporation.
Earby Urban District Council.
East Anglian Electric Supply Co Ltd.
East Dereham Urban District Council.
East Devon Electricity Co Ltd.
East Grinstead Urban District Council.
East Ham Corporation.
East Retford Corporation.
East Suffolk Electricity Distribution Co Ltd.
Eastbourne Corporation.
Ebbw Vale Urban District Council.
Eccles Corporation.
Edinburgh Corporation.
Egham & Staines Electricity Co Ltd.
Electric Supply Corporation, Ltd.
Electrical Distribution of Yorkshire, Ltd.
Electricity Distribution of North Wales & District, Ltd.
Elland Urban District Council.
Epsom & Ewell Corporation.
Erith Corporation.
Eston Urban District Council.
Exe Valley Electricity Co Ltd.
Exeter Corporation.
Falkirk Corporation.
Fareham Urban District Council.

Farnworth Corporation.
Faversham Corporation.
Felixstowe Urban District Council.
Fife Electric Power Co.
Finchley Corporation.
First Garden City, Ltd.
Fleetwood Corporation.
Folkestone Electricity Supply Co Ltd.
Foots Cray Electricity Supply Co Ltd.
Formby Urban District Council.
Fort William Corporation.
Frinton-on-Sea & District Electric Light & Power Co Ltd.
Fulham Borough Council.
Gainsborough Urban District Council.
Galloway Water Power Co.
Gellygaer Urban District Council.
Gillingham Corporation.
Glasgow Corporation.
Gloucester Corporation.
Gorseinon Electric Light Co Ltd.
Grampian Electricity Supply Co.
Grange Urban District Council.
Gravesend Corporation.
Great Yarmouth Corporation.
Greenock Corporation.
Grimsby Corporation.
Guildford Corporation.
Guisborough Urban District Council.
Hackney Borough Council.
Halifax Corporation.
Hamilton Corporation.
Hammersmith Borough Council.
Hampstead Borough Council.
Harrogate Corporation.
Harwich Corporation.
Haslingden Corporation.
Hastings Corporation.
Hawarden Rural District Council.
Hawes Electric Lighting Co Ltd.
Hazel Grove & Bramhall Urban District Council.
Hebden Royd Urban District Council.
Heckmondwike Urban District Council.
Helensburgh Corporation.
Herne Bay & District Electricity Supply Co Ltd.
Hertford Corporation.
Heston & Isleworth Corporation.

Heywood Corporation.
High Wycombe Corporation.
Hindley Urban District Council.
Hitchin Urban District Council.
Holmfirth Urban District Council.
Holsworthy Electric Supply Co Ltd.
Holyhead Urban District Council.
Horley & District Electricity Supply Co Ltd.
Hornsey Corporation.
Horsham Urban District Council.
Horwich Urban District Council.
Hove Corporation.
Hoylake Urban District Council.
Huddersfield Corporation.
Ilford Corporation.
Ilfracombe Electric Light & Power Co Ltd.
Ilkley Urban District Council.
Inverness Corporation.
Ipswich Corporation.
Isle of Wight Electric Light & Power Co Ltd.
Islington Borough Council.
Keighley Corporation.
Kendal Corporation.
Kent Electric Power Co.
Keswick Electric Light Co Ltd.
Kettering Corporation.
King's Lynn Corporation.
Kingston-upon-Hull Corporation.
Kingston-upon-Thames Corporation.
Kirkcaldy Corporation.
Kirkcudbright County Council.
Lanarkshire County Council.
Lanarkshire Hydro-Electric Power Co.
Lancashire Electric Power Co.
Lancaster Corporation.
Leeds Corporation.
Leek Urban District Council.
Leicester Corporation.
Leicestershire & Warwickshire Electric Power Co.
Leigh Corporation.
Lerwick Corporation.
Lewes & District Electric Supply Co Ltd.
Leyton Corporation.
Lichfield Corporation.
Lincoln Corporation.
Littleborough Urban District Council.

Liverpool Corporation.
Llandrindod Wells Urban District Council.
Llandudno Urban District Council.
Llanelly & District Electric Supply Co Ltd.
Llanfairfechan Urban District Council.
Llangollen Urban District Council.
Loch Leven Electricity Supply Co Ltd.
London & Home Counties Joint Electricity Authority.
London Electric Supply Corporation Ltd.
London Power Co Ltd.
Long Eaton Urban District Council.
Lossiemouth and Brandenburgh Corporation.
Lothians Electric Power Co.
Loughborough Corporation.
Louth Corporation.
Lowestoft Corporation.
Luton Corporation.
Lyme Regis Corporation.
Lynton & Lynmouth Electric Light Co Ltd.
Lytham St Anne's Corporation.
Macclesfield Corporation.
Machynlleth Electric Supply Co Ltd.
Maesteg Urban District Council.
Maidenhead Corporation.
Maidstone Corporation.
Malvern Urban District Council.
Manchester Corporation.
Mansfield Corporation.
Margate, Broadstairs & District Electricity Board.
Market Drayton Electric Light & Power Co Ltd.
Marlborough Corporation.
Marple Urban District Council.
Melton Mowbray Electric Light Co Ltd.
Menai Bridge Urban District Council.
Mersey Power Co Ltd.
Merthyr Electric Traction & Lighting Co Ltd.
Metropolitan Electric Supply Co Ltd.
Mexborough Urban District Council.
Mid-Cheshire Electricity Supply Co Ltd.
Mid-Cumberland Electricity Co Ltd.
Mid-Lincolnshire Electric Supply Co Ltd.
Mid-Somerset Electric Supply Co Ltd.
Middlesbrough Corporation.
Middleton Corporation.
Midland Electric Corporation for Power Distribution Ltd.
Midland Electric Light & Power Co Ltd.

Milford-on-Sea Electric Supply Co Ltd.
Milford Haven Urban District Council.
Millom Rural District Council.
Milnrow Urban District Council.
Milton & Barton-on-Sea (Hants) Electricity Supply Co Ltd.
Minehead Electric Supply Co Ltd.
Mirfield Urban District Council.
Mold Urban District Council.
Monmouth Electricity Co Ltd.
Morecambe & Heysham Corporation.
Morley Corporation.
Motherwell & Wishaw Corporation.
Mountain Ash Urban District Council.
Musselburgh & District Electric Light & Traction Co Ltd.
Mynyddislwyn Urban District Council.
Neath Corporation.
Neath Rural District Council.
Nelson Corporation.
New Mills Urban District Council.
Newark Corporation.
Newcastle & District Electric Lighting Co Ltd.
Newcastle-under-Lyme Corporation.
Newcastle-upon-Tyne Corporation.
Newmarket Electric Light Co Ltd.
Newport Corporation (Mon.).
Newton-le-Willows Urban District Council
Normanton Urban District Council.
North Berwick Corporation.
North-Eastern Electric Supply Co Ltd.
North Lincolnshire & Howdenshire Electricity Co Ltd.
North of Scotland Electric Light & Power Co Ltd.
North Somerset Electric Supply Co Ltd.
North Wales and South Cheshire Joint Electricity Authority.
North Wales Power Co Ltd.
North West Midlands Joint Electricity Authority.
Northampton Electric Light & Power Co Ltd.
Northmet Power Co.
Northwood Electric Light & Power Co Ltd.
Norwich Corporation.
Notting Hill Electric Lighting Co Ltd.
Nottingham Corporation.
Nuneaton Corporation.
Oban Corporation.
Ogmore & Garw Urban District Council.
Oldham Corporation.
Ormskirk Electric Supply Co Ltd.

Ossett Corporation.
Oswestry Corporation.
Oxford Corporation.
Padiham Urban District Council.
Paignton Electric Light & Power Co Ltd.
Paisley Corporation.
Peacehaven Electric Light & Power Co Ltd.
Penarth Urban District Council.
Penmaenmawr Urban District Council.
Penrith Electric Supply Co Ltd.
Penybont Rural District Council.
Perth Corporation.
Peterborough Corporation.
Peterhead Electricity Co Ltd.
Petersfield Electric Light & Power Co Ltd.
Plymouth Corporation.
Plympton St Mary Rural District Council.
Pontardawe Rural District Council.
Pontypool Electric Light & Power Co Ltd.
Pontypridd Urban District Council.
Poplar Borough Council.
Port Talbot Corporation.
Porthcawl Electricity Co Ltd.
Portland Urban District Council.
Portsmouth Corporation.
Prestatyn Urban District Council.
Preston Corporation.
Pudsey Corporation.
Radcliffe Corporation.
Ramsgate & District Electric Supply Co Ltd.
Rawtenstall Corporation.
Reading Corporation.
Redcar Corporation.
Reigate Corporation.
Rhondda Urban District Council.
Rhyl Urban District Council.
Richmond (Surrey) Electric Light & Power Co Ltd.
Richmond (Yorks) Corporation.
Ringmer & District Electricity Co Ltd.
Ringwood Electric Supply Co Ltd.
Risca Urban District Council.
Rochdale Corporation.
Rotherham Corporation.
Rugby Corporation.
Rushden & District Electric Supply Co Ltd.
Ruthin Corporation.

St Austell & District Electric Lighting & Power Co Ltd.
St Helens Corporation.
St Marylebone Borough Council.
St Pancras Borough Council.
Sale Corporation.
Salford Corporation.
Salisbury Electric Light & Supply Co Ltd.
Scarborough Corporation.
Scottish Central Electric Power Co.
Scottish Midlands Electricity Supply Ltd.
Scottish Southern Electric Supply Co Ltd.
Scunthorpe Corporation.
Seaford & Newhaven Electricity Ltd.
Seaham Urban District Council.
Seaton and District Electric Light Co Ltd.
Sedbergh Electricity Supply Co Ltd.
Settle and District Electricity Co Ltd.
Sevenoaks & District Electricity Co Ltd.
Sheerness & District Electric Supply Co Ltd.
Sheffield Corporation.
Shipley Urban District Council.
Shoreditch Borough Council.
Shoreham & District Electric Lighting & Power Co Ltd.
Shropshire, Worcestershire & Staffordshire Electric Power Co.
Skelmorlie Electric Supply Co Ltd.
Skelton and Brotton Urban District Council.
Skipton Urban District Council.
Sleaford Urban District Council.
Slough & Datchet Electric Supply Co Ltd.
South Cumberland Electricity Supply Co Ltd.
South-East Kent Electric Power Co Ltd.
South-East Yorkshire Light & Power Co Ltd.
South London Electric Supply Corporation Ltd.
South Metropolitan Electric Light & Power Co Ltd.
South Shields Corporation.
South Somerset & District Electricity Co Ltd.
South Wales Electric Power Co.
Southampton Corporation.
Southend-on-Sea Corporation.
Southport Corporation.
Southwark Borough Council.
Spalding Urban District Council.
Spenborough Urban District Council.
Stafford Corporation.
Stalybridge, Hyde, Mossley & Dukinfield Transport & Electricity Board.
Stanley Urban District Council.

Stepney Borough Council.

Steyning Electricity Ltd.

Stirling Corporation.

Stockport Corporation.

Stockton-on-Tees Corporation.

Stoke Newington Borough Council.

Stoke-on-Trent Corporation.

Stone Urban District Council.

Stornoway Electric Supply Co Ltd.

Strathclyde Electricity Supply Co Ltd.

Stretford & District Electricity Board.

Stroud Electric Supply Co Ltd.

Sunderland Corporation.

Sussex Electricity Supply Co Ltd.

Sutton Coldfield Corporation.

Swansea Corporation.

Swindon Corporation.

Swinton & Pendlebury Corporation.

Tadcaster Electricity Co Ltd.

Tamworth District Electric Supply Co Ltd.

Taunton Corporation.

Teignmouth Electric Lighting Co Ltd.

Thornbury & District Electricity Co Ltd.

Thornton Cleveleys Urban District Council.

Thurrock Urban District Council.

Thurso & District Electric Supply Co Ltd.

Tiverton Corporation.

Todmorden Corporation.

Tonbridge Urban District Council.

Torquay Corporation.

Towyn, Aberdovey and District Electricity Co Ltd.

Tredegar Urban District Council.

Trent Valley & High Peak Electricity Co Ltd.

Tunbridge Wells Corporation.

Turton Urban District Council.

Tynemouth Corporation.

Ulverston Urban District Council.

Urban Electric Supply Co Ltd.

Uttoxeter Urban District Council.

Uxbridge & District Electric Supply Co Ltd.

Wakefield Corporation.

Wallasey Corporation.

Walsall Corporation.

Walthamstow Corporation.

Walton and Weybridge Urban District Council.

Warmley Rural District Council.

Warrington Corporation.
Watford Corporation.
Weald Electricity Supply Co Ltd.
Wellingborough Electric Supply Co Ltd.
Wellington District Electricity Co Ltd.
Welwyn Garden City Electricity Supply Co Ltd.
Wessex Electricity Co.
West Bromwich Corporation.
West Cambrian Power Co Ltd.
West Devon Electric Supply Co Ltd.
West Gloucestershire Power Co Ltd.
West Ham Corporation.
West Hampshire Electricity Co Ltd.
West Hartlepool Corporation.
West Kent Electric Co Ltd.
West Lothian County Council.
West Midlands Joint Electricity Authority.
West Riding Automobile Co Ltd.
Westmorland and District Electricity Supply Co Ltd.
Weston-super-Mare & District Electric Supply Co Ltd.
Weymouth and Melcombe Regis Corporation.
Whitby Urban District Council.
Whitehaven Corporation.
Whitstable Electric Co Ltd.
Whitworth Urban District Council.
Wick Corporation.
Wickford & District Electricity Supply Co Ltd.
Wigan Corporation.
Wigtownshire Electricity Co Ltd.
Willesden Corporation.
Wilton Electricity Supply Co Ltd.
Wimbledon Corporation.
Winchester Corporation.
Windermere & District Electricity Supply Co Ltd.
Windsor Electrical Installation Co Ltd.
Wisbech Electric Light & Power Co Ltd.
Witney Urban District Council.
Woking Electric Supply Co Ltd.
Wolverhampton Corporation.
Woodstock & District Electrical Distribution Co Ltd.
Woolwich Borough Council.
Worcester Corporation.
Workington Corporation.
Worksop Corporation.
Worthing Corporation.
Wrexham Corporation.

Yale Electric Power Co Ltd.

York Corporation.

Yorkshire Electric Power Co.

PART II

Composite Companies

Ascot District Gas & Electricity Co.

Bognor & District Gas & Electricity Co.

Brixham Gas & Electricity Co.

Bungay Gas & Electricity Co.

Farnham Gas & Electricity Co.

Guildford Gas Light & Coke Co.

Mid Southern Utility Co.

Oakham Gas & Electricity Co Ltd.

Salcombe Gas & Electricity Co Ltd.

Whitchurch (Hants) Gas & Electricity Co Ltd.

Uckfield Gas & Electricity Co.

Yorktown (Camberley) Gas & Electricity Co.

NOTES

By the Letchworth and District Electricity Special Order 1947, having effect under s 13(3) ante, Pt II of this Act is not to apply to First Garden City Ltd and the name of Letchworth Electricity Ltd is to be deemed to have been inserted in this Schedule instead of the name of First Garden City Ltd.

By the Pontefract Electricity Special Order 1947 having effect under s 13(3) ante, Pt II of this Act is not to apply to the West Riding Automobile Co Ltd and the name of the Pontefract Electricity Company Ltd is to be deemed to have been inserted in this Schedule instead of the name of the West Riding Automobile Co Ltd.

(Sch 3 repealed by the SL(R) Act 1977.)

FOURTH SCHEDULE

Section 57

ADAPTATIONS AND MODIFICATIONS OF ENACTMENTS

PART I

ENACTMENTS OTHER THAN THE ELECTRIC LIGHTING (CLAUSES) ACT 1899 AND THE HYDRO-ELECTRIC DEVELOPMENT (SCOTLAND) ACT 1943

General Adaptations

Subject to any specific adaptation or modification made by this Schedule, references in any of the provisions of the Electricity (Supply) Acts 1882 to 1936, or any other enactment (except the Electric Lighting (Clauses) Act 1899, the Act of 1943, or any local enactment)—

    (*a*) to any body or person authorised by any enactment or licence to supply electricity in any area (whatever expression may be used to describe such a body or person);

    (*b*) to the undertaking of any such body or person; and

    (*c*) to any enactment or licence authorising such supply (whatever expression may be used);

shall be construed as referring only to an Electricity Board, to the business carried on by any such Board, and to any local enactment applicable to any such Board, respectively.

References in any of the provisions of the Electricity (Supply) Acts 1882 to 1936 to those Acts, and any reference therein to one or more of those Acts, being a reference which, by virtue of the construction of those Acts as one, is to be construed as a reference to all the said Acts, shall be construed as including a reference to this Act and, as regards the North of Scotland Board, to the Act of 1943.

In their application to the North of Scotland District, the Electricity (Supply) Acts 1882 to 1936 shall have effect with the additional modification that there shall be substituted (except in section four of the Electric Lighting Act 1888, sections one to four, twenty-nine and thirty-nine of the Electricity (Supply) Act 1919, and the Electricity Supply (Meters) Act 1936) for references to the Minister or the Electricity Commissioners, references to the Secretary of State.

(Remainder repealed in part by the Electricity Reorganisation (Scotland) Act 1954, s 15(2), Sch 2, the Water Resources Act 1963, s 136(2), Sch 14, Pt II, the Post Office Act 1969, s 141, Sch 11, Pt II, the SL(R) Act 1978 and the Energy Act 1983, s 36, Sch 4, Pt I, and, so far as not repealed, amends the Electric Lighting Act 1882, ss 12, 13, 15, 16, 18, 31, 36 ante; the Electric Lighting Act 1909, ss 2, 25 ante; the Electricity (Supply) Act 1919, ss 10, 11, 21, 22, 36 ante; the Electricity (Supply) Act 1922, ss 11, 25 ante; the Electricity (Supply) Act 1926, ss 24, 34, 35, 44, 51 ante; the Electricity Supply (Meters) Act 1936, ss 1, 2, 5 ante.)

NOTES

Authorised by licence to supply electricity. The Electric Lighting Act 1882, s 3 (repealed), provided for the grant of licences by the Board of Trade to supply electricity for periods not exceeding seven years at a time. So far as known, there were no licences in force at the vesting date for the purposes of this Act.

Local enactment. Provisions for the adaptation of local enactments are contained in s 57(3)–(7) ante.

Including a reference to this Act. Also including a reference to the Electricity Act 1957 post; see Sch 4, Pt II, thereto post.

Definitions. For "Electricity Board", see s 1(3) ante; and for "enactment", "local enactment", "Minister", "North of Scotland Board" and "North of Scotland District", see s 67(1) ante.

Electricity (Supply) Acts 1882 to 1936. For the Acts which may be cited by this collective title, see the Introductory Note to the Electric Lighting Act 1882 ante. Those Acts are to be construed as one; see the Electricity Supply (Meters) Act 1936, s 5(1) ante.

Electric Lighting (Clauses) Act 1899. See this title ante. Adaptations and modifications of that Act are contained in Pt III of this Schedule.

Act of 1943. Ie the Hydro-Electric Development (Scotland) Act 1943 (c 32) (largely repealed by the Electricity (Scotland) Act 1979 (c 11) and replaced by provisions of that Act (not printed in this work)); see s 67(1) ante.

(Pt II repealed with savings by the Electricity (Scotland) Act 1979, Sch 10, para 13, Sch 12 (not printed in this work).)

Part III

The Schedule to the Electric Lighting (Clauses) Act 1899

General Adaptation

Subject to any specific adaptation or modification, for the words "the Special Order", wherever they occur throughout the Schedule, there shall be substituted the words "this Schedule".

Any words limiting any provision of the Schedule to cases where the local authority are not the undertakers shall be omitted.

For references to the Board of Trade, wherever they occur throughout the Schedule, except in section eighty, there shall be substituted references to the Minister, and for the words "Board of Trade regulations", wherever they so occur, there shall be substituted the words "Electricity regulations".

Provided that in relation to the North of Scotland District, for the said references to the Board of Trade (except in section ten, subsection (3) of section eighteen, sections thirty-five, thirty-eight, thirty-nine, forty-one, forty-two, forty-seven to fifty-one, fifty-nine and sixty-nine), there shall be substituted references to the Secretary of State.

(Remainder repealed by the Electricity Reorganisation (Scotland) Act 1954, s 15(2), Sch 2, Pt I and the Energy Act 1983, s 36, Sch 4, Pt I and, so far as not repealed, amends the Electric Lighting (Clauses) Act 1899, Schedule, ss 1, 2, 4, 10, 12, 14, 16, 17, 18, 20, 21, 23, 24, 27, 35, 36, 39, 41, 43, 47, 48, 60, 62, 69, 71, 76, 81, 83 and Appendix ante.)

NOTES

North of Scotland District. See the note "North of Scotland Board" to s 1 ante.
Definitions. For "local authority", "Minister" and "North of Scotland District", see s 67(1) ante.

(Sch 5 repealed by the SLR Act 1950.)

RIGHTS OF ENTRY (GAS AND ELECTRICITY BOARDS) ACT 1954

(2 & 3 Eliz 2 c 21)

An Act to regulate the exercise of statutory rights of entry by or on behalf of Gas Boards and Electricity Boards, and for purposes connected with the matter aforesaid
[18 March 1954]

Northern Ireland. This Act does not apply; see s 4(2) post.

1 Restriction on exercise of rights of entry

(1) No right of entry to which this Act applies shall be exercisable in respect of any premises except—

(*a*) with consent given by or on behalf of the occupier of the premises, or
(*b*) under the authority of a warrant granted under the next following section:

Provided that this subsection shall not apply where entry is required in a case of emergency.

(2) This Act applies to all rights of entry conferred by [the Gas Act 1972 or regulations made thereunder, by any other enactment relating to gas], by the enactments relating to electricity, or by any local enactment, in so far as those rights are exercisable for the purposes of [the British Gas Corporation or an Electricity Board].

(3) No person shall be liable to a penalty, under any enactment relating to obstruction of the exercise of a right of entry to which this Act applies, by reason only of his refusing admission to a person who seeks to exercise the right of entry without a warrant granted under the next following section.

NOTES

The words in square brackets in sub-s (2) were substituted by the Gas Act 1972, s 49(1), Sch 6, para 5(1).

Occupier. The meaning of this word may vary according to the purposes of the legislation in which it is used, but it seems that in general a person is an occupier if he has a sufficient degree of control over the state of the premises or over the activities of persons thereon, and that, in order to be an occupier, it is not necessary for a person to have entire control over the premises, but it is sufficient for him to share the control with others (*Wheat v Lacon & Co Ltd* [1966] AC 552, [1966] 1 All ER 582, HL; see also *H & N Emanuel Ltd v GLC* [1971] 2 All ER 835, 115 Sol Jo 226, CA; *Harris v Birkenhead Corpn* [1976] 1 All ER 341, [1976] 1 WLR 279, CA; and *Jackson v Hall* [1980] AC 854, [1980] 1 All ER 177, HL). The expression "occupier" includes a person who has a licence entitling him to possession (*Stevens v London Borough of Bromley* [1972] Ch 400, [1972] 1 All ER 712, CA; *R v Tao* [1976] 3 All ER 65, [1976] 3 WLR 25, CA) and a statutory tenant (*Brown v Ministry of Housing and Local Government* [1953] 2 All ER 1385), but not, it is thought, a person whose entry on the premises was unlawful and forcible (*Woodcock v South Western Electricity Board* [1975] 2 All ER 545, [1975] 1 WLR 983). See, further, 4 Words and Phrases (2nd edn) 12 et seq.

Any other enactment relating to gas. See the Gas Act 1965, ss 6(3), (4), 20, Sch 6, Vol 19, title Gas.

Enactments relating to electricity. See the Electric Lighting Act 1882, s 24 ante in conjunction with the Electric Lighting Act 1909, s 16 ante. See also the Electricity Act 1957, s 35 post.

British Gas Corporation. As to the establishment of the British Gas Corporation and its powers and duties, see the Gas Act 1972, ss 1 et seq, Vol 19, title Gas.

Definitions. For "case of emergency", see s 3(3) post; for "enactment", "local enactment", "premises" and "right of entry", see s 3(1) post. For "Electricity Board" see, by virtue of s 3(1) post, the Electricity Act 1947, s 1 ante.

Gas Act 1972. Rights of entry are conferred by s 27 of, and Sch 4 to, that Act, Vol 19, title Gas, and as to regulations, see s 31 of that Act.

2 Warrant to authorise entry

(1) Where it is shown to the satisfaction of a justice of the peace, on sworn information in writing—

(*a*) that admission to premises specified in the information is reasonably required by [the Corporation or an] Electricity Board, or by an employee of [the Corporation or] such a Board, for a purpose so specified;

(*b*) that [the Corporation or Board] or their employee, as the case may be, would, apart from the preceding section, be entitled for that purpose to exercise in respect of the premises a right of entry to which this Act applies; and

(*c*) that the requirements (if any) of the relevant enactment have been complied with,

then subject to the provisions of this section the justice may by warrant under his hand authorise [the Corporation or Board] or their employee, as the case may be, to enter the premises, if need be by force.

(2) If, in a case to which the preceding subsection applies, the relevant enactment does not require notice of an intended entry to be given to the occupier of the premises, the justice shall not grant a warrant under this section in respect of the right of entry in question unless he is satisfied—

(*a*) that admission to the premises for the purpose specified in the information was sought by a person lawfully requiring entry in the exercise of that right, and was so sought after not less than twenty-four hours' notice of the intended entry had been given to the occupier; or

(*b*) that admission to the premises for that purpose was sought in a case of emergency and was refused by or on behalf of the occupier; or

(*c*) that the premises are unoccupied; or

(*d*) that an application for admission to the premises would defeat the object of the entry.

(3) Where paragraph (*a*) of the last preceding subsection applies, [section 44 of the Gas Act 1972 (if entry is required for the purposes of the Corporation)] or section sixty-three of the Electricity Act 1947 (if entry is required for the purposes of an Electricity Board) shall apply to the service of the notice required by that paragraph.

(4) Every warrant granted under this section shall continue in force until the purpose for which the entry is required has been satisfied.

(5) Any person who, in the exercise of a right of entry under the authority of a warrant granted under this section, enters any premises which are unoccupied, or premises of which the occupier is temporarily absent, shall leave the premises as effectually secured against trespassers as he found them.

(6) Where a warrant is granted under this section in respect of a right of entry, then for the purposes of any enactment whereby—

(*a*) an obligation is imposed to make good damage, or to pay compensation, or to take any other step, in consequence of the exercise of the right of entry, or

(*b*) a penalty is imposed for obstructing the exercise of that right,

any entry effected, or sought to be effected, under the authority of the warrant shall be treated as an entry effected, or sought to be effected, in the exercise of that right of entry.

(7) (*Applies to Scotland only.*)

NOTES

The words in square brackets in sub-ss (1), (3) were substituted or inserted by the Gas Act 1972, s 49(1), Sch 6, para 5(2)–(4).

Justice of the peace. A justice of the peace may be either a lay justice or a stipendiary magistrate. The main provisions relating to justices of the peace (including stipendiary magistrates), covering such matters as appointment, removal and organisation, will be found in the Justices of the Peace Act 1979, Vol 27, title Magistrates, and the office and jurisdiction of justices are considered generally in 29 Halsbury's Laws (4th edn) paras 201 et seq.

Writing. Unless the contrary intention appears this includes other modes of representing or reproducing words in a visible form; see the Interpretation Act 1978, s 5, Sch 1, Vol 41, title Statutes.

Occupier. See the note to s 1 ante.

Definitions. For "case of emergency", see s 3(3) post; for "the Corporation", "employee", "enactment", "premises" and "right of entry", see s 3(1) post. For "Electricity Board", see, by virtue of s 3(1) post, the Electricity Act 1947, s 1 ante. See also as to "person lawfully requiring entry", s 3(2)(a) post, and as to "relevant enactments" and "requirements" of the relevant enactment, s 3(2)(b) post.

Gas Act 1972, s 44. See Vol 19, title Gas.

Electricity Act 1947, s 63. See this title ante.

---

3 Interpretation

(1) In this Act the following expressions have the meanings hereby assigned to them respectively, that is to say,—

> ["the Corporation" means the British Gas Corporation;]
> "Electricity Board" has the same meaning as in the Electricity Act 1947;
> ["employee", in relation to the Corporation or to an Electricity Board, means an officer, servant or agent of the Corporation or of the Board;]
> "enactment" includes a local enactment;

> .   .   .   .   .

> "local enactment" means a local or private Act, or an order made under, or confirmed by, an Act (whether a public general Act or a local or private Act);
> "premises" means a building or a part of a building;
> "right of entry" includes a power of entry.

(2) In this Act—

> (a) references to a person lawfully requiring entry to premises in the exercise of a right of entry to which this Act applies are references to a person seeking admission to those premises by virtue of that right and in accordance with the requirements (if any) of the relevant enactment; and
> (b) references to the relevant enactment, in relation to a right of entry, are references to the enactment conferring that right, and references to the requirements of the relevant enactment are references to any requirements of that enactment as to the giving of notices or the taking of any other step before, or at the time of, the exercise of the right.

(3) References in this Act to a case of emergency are references to a case in which a person lawfully requiring entry to the premises in question, in the exercise of a right of entry to which this Act applies, has reasonable cause to believe that circumstances exist which are likely to endanger life or property, and that immediate entry to the premises is necessary to verify the existence of those circumstances or to ascertain their cause or to effect a remedy.

NOTES

The definitions "the Corporation" and "employee" were inserted and substituted, respectively, and the definition "Gas Board" was repealed, by the Gas Act 1972, s 49(1), (3), Sch 6, para 5(5), Sch 8.

British Gas Corporation. See the note to s 1 ante.

Electricity Act 1947. See this title ante. For the meaning of "Electricity Board" in that Act, see s 1(3) of that Act.

4 Short title, extent and commencement

(1) This Act may be cited as the Rights of Entry (Gas and Electricity Boards) Act 1954.

(2) This Act shall not extend to Northern Ireland.

(3) This Act shall come into operation at the expiration of the period of one month beginning with the day on which it is passed.

NOTE

One month beginning with, etc. "Month" means calendar month; see the Interpretation Act 1978, s 5, Sch 1, Vol 41, title Statutes. In calculating this period the day (ie 18 March 1954) on which this Act was passed is to be reckoned; see *Hare v Gocher* [1962] 2 QB 641, [1962] 2 All ER 763, and *Trow v Ind Coope (West Midlands) Ltd* [1967] 2 QB 899 at 909, [1967] 2 All ER 900, CA. Accordingly this Act came into force on 18 April 1954.

ELECTRICITY REORGANISATION (SCOTLAND) ACT 1954

(2 & 3 Eliz 2 c 60)

ARRANGEMENT OF SECTIONS

PART I

REORGANISATION

An Act to transfer the functions of the Minister of Fuel and Power in Scotland in relation to electricity to the Secretary of State; to establish the South of Scotland Electricity Board; to transfer the functions of the British Electricity Authority in the south of Scotland and of the Scottish Area Boards to that Board; to amend the Hydro-Electric Development (Scotland) Act 1943; and for purposes connected therewith   **[25 November 1954]**

Part I

Reorganisation

1 Transfer of the functions of the Minister of Fuel and Power to the Secretary of State

(1), (2) ...

(3) *On the vesting date the functions of the Minister in relation to the making of regulations under section four of the Electric Lighting Act 1888, and under section sixty of the Act of 1947 (which empower the Minister to make regulations relating to safety and the efficiency of supply of electricity) shall be transferred to the Secretary of State and the Minister acting jointly.*

(4) ...

NOTES

Sub-ss (1), (2), (4) were repealed by the Electricity (Scotland) Act 1979, s 46(1), (2), Schs 10, 12 and replaced by provisions of that Act (not printed in this work).

Prospective repeal. Sub-s (3) is repealed by the Energy Act 1983, s 36, Sch 4, Pt I post, as from a day to be appointed under s 37(1) of that Act.

Definitions. By virtue of the Electricity Act 1947, s 57(1), Sch 4, Pt I ante (so far as applicable), and s 17 post, for "electricity", see the Electric Lighting Act 1882, s 32 ante, and for "functions" and "Minister", see the Electricity Act 1947, s 67(1) ante. For "the Act of 1947" and "the vesting date", see s 14(1) post.

Electric Lighting Act 1888, s 4. See this title ante.

2–10 *(Ss 2, 10(3) repealed by the Electricity (Scotland) Act 1979, s 46(1), (2), Schs 10, 12, and replaced by provisions of that Act (not printed in this work); ss 3–9 repealed by the SL(R) Act 1977; s 10(1) repealed by the Electricity Act 1957, s 42(3), Sch 5, Pt I; s 10(2) applies to Scotland only.)*

Part IV

Miscellaneous and General

11–13 *(Repealed by the Electricity (Scotland) Act 1979, s 46(1), (2), Schs 10, 12, and replaced by provisions of that Act (not printed in this work); s 13 repealed by the SL(R) Act 1978.)*

14 Interpretation

(1) In this Act unless the context otherwise requires the following expressions have the meanings hereby respectively assigned to them—

"the Act of 1947" means the Electricity Act 1947;

. . . . .

"the Scottish Electricity Boards" means the North of Scotland Board and the South of Scotland Board; and

"the vesting date" means the first day of April, nineteen hundred and fifty-five.

(2) References in this Act to any enactment shall, unless the context otherwise requires, be construed as references to that enactment as amended by or under any other enactment including this Act.

NOTES

The words omitted from sub-s (1) are spent.

Electricity Act 1947. See this title ante.

South of Scotland Board. See the note to Sch 1, Pt II to this Act post.

North of Scotland Board. For meaning, see, by virtue of s 17 post, the Electricity Act 1947, s 67(1) ante.

15 Adaptation of enactments and repeals

(1) As from the vesting date any enactment to which any provision of the First Schedule to this Act applies shall have effect subject to the adaptations and modifications specified in that Schedule, being adaptations and modifications required for the purpose of applying the said enactments to the South of Scotland Board or otherwise required in consequence of the provisions of this Act or relating to matters of minor detail:

Provided that the said First Schedule, so far as it relates to the First Schedule to the Act of 1943, and to section twelve of that Act, so far as the provisions of that section are necessary for enabling the South of Scotland Board to borrow for the payment of administrative and preliminary expenses, shall come into operation on the passing of this Act.

(2) . . .

NOTES

Sub-s (2) was repealed by the SL(R) Act 1972.
South of Scotland Board. This Board was established by s 2(1) of this Act (repealed). See now the Electricity (Scotland) Act 1979, ss 1, 2(1), Sch 2, para 2 (not printed in this work).
Definitions. By virtue of s 17 post, for "enactment", see the Electricity Act 1947 s 67(1) ante. For "the vesting date", see s 14(1) ante.
Act of 1943. Ie the Hydro-Electric Development (Scotland) Act 1943 (c 32) (largely repealed by the Electricity (Scotland) Act 1979 (c 11) and replaced by provisions of that Act (not printed in this work)).

16 Savings

(1) Nothing done by or in relation to the Minister, or the Minister and the Secretary of State acting jointly, before the vesting date, shall be invalidated by the passing of this Act.

(2) Anything in process of being done by or in relation to the Minister, or the Minister and the Secretary of State acting jointly, in connection with any functions transferred under Part I of this Act at the vesting date (and, in particular, legal proceedings then pending to which the Minister is a party) may be continued by or in relation to the Secretary of State.

(3) Authorities and appointments given or made by the Minister in connection with any functions as aforesaid, other than an appointment to an Electricity Board or Consultative Council dissolved by subsection (2) of section three of this Act, shall on the vesting date, continue in force as if made or given by the Secretary of State:

Provided that nothing in this subsection shall prevent any authority or appointment being terminated as from the coming into operation of this Act.

(4) . . .

(5) Any Act of Parliament or instrument shall, so far as may be necessary for or in consequence of the transfers effected by this Act, have effect as if references to, or references which are to be construed as references to, the Minister, his Department or any of his officers, were references to the Secretary of State or to the Department of, or to the corresponding officers of, the Secretary of State.

(6) The last foregoing subsection applies to all Acts of Parliament and instruments whether passed, executed, made or given before or after the passing or coming into operation of this Act, except that—

    (a) it does not apply to Acts of Parliament passed after the coming into operation of this Act; and (*b*) in relation to Acts of Parliament or instruments passed, executed, made or given after the passing of this Act, it has effect subject to any contrary intention which appears from the Act or instrument.

NOTES

Sub-s (4) is spent by virtue of the repeal of the Electricity Act 1947, s 53.

Definitions. By virtue of s 17 post, for "Electricity Board", see s 1(3) of the Electricity Act 1947 ante, in conjunction with Sch 1, Pt II post, and for "functions" and "Minister", see s 67(1) of that Act ante. For "the vesting date", see s 14(1) ante.

17 Short title and citation

This Act may be cited as the Electricity Reorganisation (Scotland) Act 1954, and shall be construed as one with the Act of 1947, and the Act of 1943, the Act of 1947, as it applies to Scotland, the Hydro-Electric Development (Scotland) Act 1952, and this Act may be cited together as the Electricity (Scotland) Acts 1943 to 1954.

NOTES

Act of 1947. Ie the Electricity Act 1947 ante; see s 14 ante.

Act of 1943. Ie the Hydro-Electric Development (Scotland) Act 1943; largely repealed and replaced by the Electricity (Scotland) Act 1979 (not printed in this work).

Hydro-Electric Development (Scotland) Act 1952. Repealed by the Electricity (Borrowing Powers) Act 1959, s 2(2), Schedule.

SCHEDULES

FIRST SCHEDULE

Section 15

ADAPTATION OF ENACTMENTS

(Pt I repealed by the Electricity (Scotland) Act 1979, s 46(1), (2), Schs 10, 12, and replaced by provisions of that Act (not printed in this work).)

PART II

THE ELECTRICITY ACT 1947

General Adaptation

The Authority established by section one shall be known by the name of the Central Electricity Authority and that name shall be substituted for the words "British Electricity Authority" wherever occurring.

Subject to any specific adaptations or modifications made by this Schedule, any reference to the North of Scotland Board or to the North of Scotland District (except in subsection (7) of section one, in subsections (1) to (6) and subsection (8) of section forty-seven, and section sixty-seven) shall include a reference to the South of Scotland Board or to the South of Scotland District respectively.

.   .   .   .   .

NOTES

The words omitted amend the Electricity Act 1947, ss 1, 2, 19, 45, 60, 64, 67 ante, are repealed by the Electricity Act 1972, s 4(3), Schedule or the SL(R) Act 1978, or are spent.

South of Scotland Board; South of Scotland District. The South of Scotland Board was established under s 2(1) of this Act (repealed) with responsibility for the South of Scotland District. See now the Electricity (Scotland) Act 1979, ss 1, 2(1), Sch 2, para 2 (not printed in this work).

Definitions. By virtue of s 17 ante, for "North of Scotland Board" and "North of Scotland District", see the Electricity Act 1947, s 67(1) ante.

Electricity Act 1947. See this title ante.

PART III

ENACTMENTS OTHER THAN THE HYDRO-ELECTRIC DEVELOPMENT (SCOTLAND) ACT 1943 AND THE ELECTRICITY ACT 1947

General Adaptation

Subject to any specific adaptations or modifications made by this Schedule, references in any of the provisions of the Electricity (Supply) Acts 1882 to 1926, the Schedule to the Electric Lighting (Clauses) Act 1899, as incorporated with the Act of 1947, and Part V of the Local Government Act 1948—

(a) to the Minister or the Board of Trade (except in relation to sections forty-nine to fifty-four and fifty-seven to fifty-nine of the Schedule to the Electric Lighting (Clauses) Act 1899, as incorporated with the Act of 1947, and the reference to the Board of Trade in section eighty of that Schedule) shall, in relation to the Districts of the Scottish Electricity Boards and these Boards, be construed as references to the Secretary of State; and

(b) to the North of Scotland Board (except in section ninety-nine of the Local Government Act 1948) shall include a reference to the South of Scotland Board.

Subject to any specific adaptations or modifications made by this Schedule, references in any of the provisions of the aforesaid enactments, other than Part V of the Local Government Act 1948, to the North of Scotland District shall include a reference to the South of Scotland District.

.   .   .   .   .

NOTES

The words omitted were repealed in part by the Electricity Act 1957, s 42(3), Sch 5, Pt I; the remainder are spent or amend the Electric Lighting Act 1882, s 12 ante.

South of Scotland Board; South of Scotland District. See the note to Pt II of this Schedule ante.

Definitions. By virtue of s 17 ante, for "Minister", "North of Scotland Board" and "North of Scotland District", see the Electricity Act 1947, s 67(1) ante. For "the Scottish Electricity Boards", see s 14(1) ante.

Electricity (Supply) Acts 1882 to 1926. For the Acts (including these Acts) which may be cited as the Electricity (Supply) Acts 1882 to 1936, see the Introductory Note to the Electric Lighting Act 1882 ante.

Electric Lighting (Clauses) Act 1899, Schedule. See this title ante.

Act of 1947. Ie the Electricity Act 1947 ante; see s 14(1) ante.

Local Government Act 1948, Part V. The relevant provisions of that Part are all repealed.

(Sch 2 repealed by the SL(R) Act 1974.)

ELECTRICITY ACT 1957

(5 & 6 Eliz 2 c 48)

ARRANGEMENT OF SECTIONS

Reorganisation

An Act to provide for the dissolution of the Central Electricity Authority and the establishment of a Central Electricity Generating Board and an Electricity Council, and for the transfer of functions of the said Authority to that Board or Council or to the Minister of Power; to make further provision as to other matters relating to the supply of electricity; and for purposes connected with the matters aforesaid   [17 July 1957]

Northern Ireland. The Act does not apply; see s 43(5) post.

Reorganisation

1 *(Repealed by the SL(R) Act 1977.)*

2 Establishment, constitution and functions of Central Electricity Generating Board

(1) There shall be established a Board, to be called the Central Electricity Generating Board (in this Act referred to as "the Generating Board"), who shall, as from the vesting date, perform the functions assigned to them by or under this Act, together with such functions of the Central Authority under the Electricity Act 1947 (in this Act referred to as "the principal Act"), and other enactments, as by virtue of this Act are transferred to the Generating Board.

(2) The Generating Board shall consist of a chairman appointed by the Minister and such number of other members so appointed, not being less than seven or more than nine, as the Minister may from time to time determine.

(3) All the members of the Generating Board shall be appointed by the Minister from amongst persons appearing to him to be qualified as having had experience of, and having shown capacity in, the generation or supply of electricity, industrial, commercial or financial matters, applied science, administration, or the organisation of workers.

(4) The Minister shall appoint one or more members of the Generating Board to be deputy chairman or deputy chairmen of the Board.

(5) Without prejudice to any other functions assigned or transferred to them as mentioned in subsection (1) of this section, it shall as from the vesting date be the duty of the Generating Board to develop and maintain an efficient, co-ordinated and economical system of supply of electricity in bulk for all parts of England and Wales, and for that purpose—

(*a*) to generate or acquire supplies of electricity; and
(*b*) to provide bulk supplies of electricity for the Area Boards for distribution by those Boards.

(6) In accordance with any agreement made in that behalf by the Generating Board with the person or body of persons to be supplied, the Generating Board may provide bulk supplies of electricity—

(*a*) for either of the Scottish Electricity Boards, or
(*b*) for any person or body of persons carrying on an electricity undertaking outside Great Britain,

and may provide supplies of electricity (whether in bulk or otherwise) for any other person or body of persons for whom the Generating Board may for the time being be authorised by the Minister to provide such supplies.

(7) The Generating Board shall have power—

(*a*) to manufacture anything required by the Generating Board or by any Area Board for purposes of research or development or for the repair or maintenance of their equipment;
[(*aa*) to produce radioactive material in a nuclear reactor at any of the Generating Board's generating stations for the purpose of selling or otherwise supplying it to other persons, and to sell or otherwise supply radioactive material produced in any such nuclear reactor;]
(*b*) to sell, hire or otherwise supply electrical plant, and to instal, repair, maintain or remove any electrical plant and electrical fittings; and
(*c*) to carry on all such other activities as it may appear to the Generating Board to be requisite, advantageous or convenient for them to carry on for or in

connection with the performance of their functions … or with a view to making the best use of any assets vested in them:

Provided that nothing in paragraph (c) of this subsection, or in the principal Act, shall be construed as authorising the Generating Board to manufacture anything except as mentioned in paragraph (a) [or paragraph (aa)] of this subsection, or to sell, hire or otherwise supply electrical fittings.

(8) For the purposes of any enactment (including the principal Act and this Act) the Generating Board shall be included among the Boards referred to as Electricity Boards, or as Electricity Boards in England and Wales.

[(9) In this section "radioactive material" and "nuclear reactor" have the meanings assigned to them respectively by subsection (6) of section one of the Electricity (Amendment) Act 1961, and any reference to producing radioactive material shall be construed in accordance with that subsection.]

NOTES

The words in square brackets in sub-s (7) were inserted, and sub-s (9) was added, by the Electricity Amendment Act 1961, s 1(3), Schedule. The words omitted from sub-s (7) were repealed by the Energy Act 1983, ss 25, 36, Sch 3, para 10, Sch 4, Pt I.

Central Electricity Generating Board. By the Electricity Act 1947, s 3(1) ante, the Board is a body corporate with perpetual succession and a common seal. See also as to remuneration, appointment etc of members, proceedings etc of the Board, s 3(6)–(8) of the 1947 Act, and for regulations applicable to the Board, the Electricity (Central Authority and Area Boards) Regulations 1947, SR & O 1947/1750, as amended by SI 1957/1382 and by SI 1968/1780.

Vesting date. By virtue of s 1 of this Act (repealed), the vesting date was 1 January 1958.

Central Authority. Ie the Central Electricity Authority, which was established under the Electricity Act 1947, s 1(1) ante as the British Electricity Authority and re-named the Central Electricity Authority by the Electricity Reorganisation (Scotland) Act 1954, s 15(1), Sch 1, Pt II ante.

Chairman. The chairman must be a whole-time member of the Board; see s 4(1) post. As to term of office etc, see the note "Members" below.

Members. For provisions as to appointment of whole-time members other than the chairman, see s 4(2) post. As to term of office and re-appointment of members appointed under sub-s (2), see the Electricity (Central Authority and Area Boards) Regulations 1947, SR & O 1947/1750, reg 1(1), (2), as substituted by SI 1957/1382.

To provide bulk supplies etc. Under the Electricity Act 1947, s 1(2) ante, the Area Boards are under a corresponding duty to acquire bulk supplies of electricity from the Generating Board.

Great Britain. Ie England, Scotland and Wales; see the Union with Scotland Act 1706, preamble, Art I, Vol 10, title Constitutional Law (Pt 1), as read with the Interpretation Act 1978, s 22(1), Sch 2, para 5(a), Vol 41, title Statutes.

Savings. As is made clear by the Electricity Act 1947, s 2(9) ante, this section relates only to the capacity of the Generating Board as a statutory corporation and nothing therein is to be construed as authorising the disregard by the Board of any enactment or rule of law.

Application for nuclear licences; balancing of revenue accounts; borrowing powers; compensation for loss of office; compensation for losses due to price restraint; pipelines; rating; furnishing of overseas aid by electricity authorities. See the notes to the Electricity Act 1947, s 1 ante.

Definitions. By virtue of s 40(1) post, for "Area Board" and "the Central Authority", see the Electricity Act 1947, s 1(3) ante, and for "bulk supply", "electrical fittings", "electrical plant", "enactment", "functions" and "Minister", see s 67(1) of that Act ante. For "perform" and "performance", see s 40(1) post. By virtue of s 40(1) post, and the Electricity Reorganisation (Scotland) Act 1954, s 17 ante, for "the Scottish Electricity Boards", see s 14(1) of that Act ante. Note as to "the Generating Board" and "the principal Act", sub-s (1) above.

Electricity Act 1947. See this title ante.

Electricity (Amendment) Act 1961, s 1(6). See this title post.

3 Establishment, constitution and functions of Electricity Council

(1) There shall be established a Council, to be called the Electricity Council, who shall, as from the vesting date, perform the functions assigned to them by or under this Act, together with such functions of the Central Authority under the principal Act and other enactments as by virtue of this Act are transferred to the Electricity Council.

(2) The Electricity Council shall be constituted as follows:—

(*a*) the Minister shall appoint a person to be the chairman of the Council, and shall appoint two other persons to be deputy chairmen of the Council, and may (in addition to the members so appointed) appoint as members of the Council such number, not exceeding three, of other persons (being persons appearing to the Minister to be qualified as mentioned in subsection (3) of the last preceding section) as he may from time to time determine;

(*b*) three other members shall be the person for the time being holding office as chairman of the Generating Board, and such other members of that Board as may be designated by that Board; and

(*c*) the remaining members shall be the persons for the time being holding the office of chairman of an Area Board:

Provided that the deputy chairman of an Area Board shall be entitled to attend meetings of the Electricity Council in place of the chairman of that Board during any vacancy in the office of chairman or in the event of the chairman being unable to attend owing to illness or absence from Great Britain; and any member of the Generating Board designated by the Board in that behalf shall be entitled to attend meetings of the Electricity Council—

(i) in place of the chairman of the Generating Board, during any vacancy in the office of chairman of that Board, or

(ii) in place of any of the members of the Council referred to in paragraph (*b*) of this subsection, in the event of any inability of that member to attend owing to illness or absence from Great Britain,

and any person attending a meeting of the Electricity Council by virtue of this proviso in place of another person shall, in relation to that meeting, have the same rights, powers and duties as the person in whose place he attends.

(3) A person who is for the time being a member of an Electricity Board shall not be eligible to be appointed by the Minister by virtue of paragraph (*a*) of the last preceding subsection to be a member of the Electricity Council, whether as chairman, deputy chairman or otherwise; and, notwithstanding anything in the last preceding section or in any other enactment, a person who is for the time being a member of the Electricity Council so appointed shall not be eligible for appointment as a member of an Electricity Board.

(4) Without prejudice to any other functions assigned or transferred to the Electricity Council as mentioned in subsection (1) of this section, it shall as from the vesting date be the duty of that Council—

(*a*) to advise the Minister on questions affecting the electricity supply industry and matters relating thereto; and

(*b*) to promote and assist the maintenance and development by Electricity Boards in England and Wales of an efficient, co-ordinated and economical system of electricity supply.

(5) The Electricity Council shall have power, if so authorised by all the Electricity Boards in England and Wales, or by any group of those Boards, to perform services for, or act on behalf of, the Boards concerned in relation to matters of common interest to those Boards.

(6) Subsection (5) of section two of the principal Act (which confers ancillary powers on Electricity Boards), and subsections (1), (6), (7) and (8) of section three of that Act (which relate respectively to the incorporation of Electricity Boards, to the remuneration, allowances and pensions of members of Electricity Boards, to the power of the Minister to make regulations with respect to Electricity Boards, and to the regulation of their procedure subject to any such regulations) shall apply in relation to the Electricity Council as they apply in relation to any of the Electricity Boards in England and Wales.

(7) The power to make regulations under subsection (7) of section three of the principal Act, as applied in relation to the Electricity Council by the last preceding subsection, shall be exercisable by statutory instrument; and any instrument containing any such regulations shall be subject to annulment in pursuance of a resolution of either House of Parliament.

(8) For the avoidance of doubt it is hereby declared that the provisions of this section as to the functions of the Electricity Council (including the provisions of subsection (5) of section two of the principal Act as applied to that Council) relate only to the capacity of the Electricity Council as a statutory corporation; and nothing in those provisions shall be construed as authorising the disregard by that Council of any enactment or rule of law.

NOTES

Vesting date. See the note to s 2 ante.

Central Authority. See s 2 ante.

Chairman. The chairman must be a whole-time member of the Council; see s 4(1) post. As to term of office etc, see the note "Members" below.

Members. For provisions as to the appointment of whole-time members other than the chairman, see s 4(2) post. As to term of office and re-appointment of members appointed under sub-s (2)(a), see the Electricity (Central Authority and Area Boards) Regulations 1947, SR & O 1947/1750, reg 1(1), (2), as substituted by SI 1957/1382.

Great Britain. See the note to s 2 ante.

Statutory instrument; subject to annulment. For provisions as to statutory instruments generally, see the Statutory Instruments Act 1946, Vol 41, title Statutes, and as to statutory instruments which are subject to annulment, see ss 5(1), 7(1) of that Act.

Borrowing powers. For borrowing powers of the Electricity Council, see s 15 post, and the Gas and Electricity Act 1968, s 2 post. As to the power of the Electricity Council to borrow in currencies other than sterling, see the Statutory Corporations (Financial Provisions) Act 1975, s 5(1), Sch 2, Vol 30, title Money (Pt 1).

Compensation for loss of office. Compensation for loss of office may be paid to a member of the Electricity Council in accordance with the Electricity and Gas Act 1963, s 3 post.

Furnishing of overseas aid by electricity authorities. For provisions as to the furnishing of overseas aid by electricity authorities, see the Overseas Development and Co-operation Act 1980, s 2(1)–(3), (6), Sch 1, Pt I, Vol 7, title Commonwealth and Other Territories (Pt 4).

Pensions. The Consultative Council may, if the Secretary of State determines that they should do so, assume in respect of payment of certain pensions the functions of the Electricity Council; see the Statutory Corporations (Financial Provisions) Act 1975, s 5(1), Sch 2, Vol 30, title Money (Pt 1).

Definitions. By virtue of s 40(1) post, for "Area Board" and "the Central Authority", see the Electricity Act 1947, s 1(3) ante; for "Electricity Board", see s 1(3) of the 1947 Act, in conjunction with the Electricity Reorganisation (Scotland) Act 1954, Sch 1, Pt II ante; and for "enactment", "functions" and "Minister", see s 67(1) of that Act ante. For "the Generating Board", see s 2(1) ante; for "perform", see s 40(1) post.

Principal Act. Ie the Electricity Act 1947; see s 2(1) ante. For ss 2(5), 3(1), (6), (7), (8) of that Act, see this title ante. See also for regulations, the Electricity (Central Authority and Area Boards) Regulations 1947, SR & O 1947/1750, as amended by SI 1957/1382 and SI 1968/1780.

4 Whole-time members of Generating Board, Electricity Council and Area Boards

(1) The office of chairman of the Generating Board or of the Electricity Council shall not be held except by a person appointed as a whole-time member of the Board or Council.

(2) Subject to the preceding subsection, in the exercise of his powers of appointing members of the Generating Board or of the Electricity Council in accordance with sections two and three of this Act, or of appointing members of an Area Board in accordance with section three of the principal Act, the Minister shall secure that as many of the members so appointed as he may consider requisite for the efficient performance of the functions of the Council or Board shall be appointed as whole-time members of the Council or Board.

5 Consultative Councils

(1) Section seven of the principal Act (under which a Consultative Council is established for the area of each Area Board) shall, in its application to England and Wales, have effect subject to the amendments specified in Part I of the First Schedule to this Act.

(2) (*Applies to Scotland only.*)

Generation of electricity by Area Boards, and provision for research

6 Generation of Electricity by Area Boards

(1) If it appears to an Area Board to be expedient that the Board should generate electricity for the purpose of distribution to consumers whom they are required or authorised to supply, the Board, after consultation with the Generating Board and the Electricity Council, may formulate proposals for the generation of electricity by them for that purpose and may submit those proposals to the Minister.

(2) Where any proposals under this section have been submitted to the Minister and have been approved by him, with or without modifications, the Area Board submitting the proposals shall have power to generate electricity in accordance with those proposals as so approved.

(3) Subsection (9) of section two of the principal Act (which relates to the construction of provisions conferring powers on Electricity Boards) shall have effect in relation to the provisions of this section as it has effect in relation to the provisions referred to in that subsection.

7 Research

(1) It shall be the duty of the Electricity Council to settle from time to time, in consultation with the Minister, a general programme of research into matters affecting the supply of electricity and other matters affecting the functions of Area Boards, the Generating Board or the Electricity Council.

(2) It shall be the duty of the Electricity Council to secure the carrying out of any

general programme settled by them under the preceding subsection; and for that purpose they may themselves conduct research into any of the matters mentioned in that subsection and may make arrangements with any other persons, including any of the Electricity Boards, for the conduct of such research by them.

(3) Any of the Area Boards or the Generating Board may conduct research in accordance with arrangements made by the Electricity Council under this section, and may also, after consultation with the Electricity Council, conduct research into such matters affecting the functions of the Board as are not for the time being included in the general programme settled by the Council.

NOTES

Electricity Council. See s 3 ante.

Consultation. See the note to s 6 ante.

Definitions. By virtue of s 40(1) post, for "Area Board" and "Electricity Boards", see the Electricity Act 1947, s 1(3) ante, in conjunction with the Electricity Reorganisation (Scotland) Act 1954, Sch 1, Pt II ante; and for "functions" and "Minister", see s 67(1) of that Act ante. For "the Generating Board", see s 2(1) ante.

Provisions as to administration, and as to conditions of employment

8 Powers of Minister in relation to Electricity Council and Electricity Boards

(1) The Minister may give to the Electricity Council, or to any of the Electricity Boards in England and Wales, such directions of a general character as to the performance by that Council or Board of their functions as appear to the Minister to be requisite in the national interest.

(2) Before giving any directions to the Electricity Council under the preceding subsection the Minister shall consult the Council; and before giving any directions to an Electricity Board under that subsection, the Minister shall consult that Board and the Electricity Council.

(3) The Minister may, after consultation with the Electricity Council, give directions to any of the Electricity Boards in England and Wales as to the use or disposal of any assets vested in the Board which are not connected with the generation, transmission or distribution of electricity.

(4) In carrying out such measures of reorganisation or such works of development as involve substantial outlay on capital account, each of the Electricity Boards in England and Wales shall act in accordance with a general programme settled by the Board from time to time after consultation with the Electricity Council and approved by the Minister.

(5) The Electricity Council shall furnish the Minister with such returns, accounts and other information as he may require with respect to the property and activities of the Council and of Electricity Boards in England and Wales and shall afford to him facilities for verifying such information, in such manner and at such times as he may reasonably require.

(6) Each of the Electricity Boards in England and Wales shall afford to the Electricity Council, and, if the Minister so requires, to the Minister, facilities for obtaining information with respect to the property and activities of the Board, and shall furnish the Electricity Council, and, if he so requires, the Minister, with returns, accounts and other information with respect thereto, and shall afford to the Electricity Council and the Minister facilities for verifying such information, in such manner and at such times as the Council or the Minister may reasonably require.

9 Representations by Electricity Boards to Electricity Council

(1) Any of the Electricity Boards in England and Wales may make representations to the Electricity Council on any matter relating to the performance of the functions of any other of those Boards:

Provided that an Electricity Board, before making any representations under this subsection with respect to any matter relating to the functions of another Electricity Board, shall consult that Board with respect to that matter.

(2) Where any representations are made to the Electricity Council under the preceding subsection, and, after consultation with the Board making the representations and with the Board to whom the representations relate, it appears to the Council that a defect is disclosed in the general plans and arrangements of either or both of those Boards for the performance of their functions, the Electricity Council may give to that Board or those Boards such advice as they think fit for remedying the defect.

(3) The Electricity Council may make representations to the Minister on any matters arising out of advice given by them to an Electricity Board under this section; and if it appears to the Minister, after consultation with that Board and with the Electricity Council, that a defect is disclosed in that Board's general plans and arrangements for the performance of their functions, he may give such directions to that Board as he thinks necessary for remedying the defect.

10 Annual reports

(1) Every Area Board and the Generating Board shall, as soon as possible after the end of each financial year, make to the Minister a report on the performance by them of their functions during that year and on their policy and programmes; and every Area Board and the Generating Board shall, as soon as their report has been made to the Minister, send a copy thereof to the Electricity Council.

(2) As soon as possible after copies of the reports of the Generating Board and all the Area Boards for any financial year have been received by the Electricity Council, the Council shall make to the Minister a report consisting of—

    (a) a report on the performance by the Council of their functions during that year, and on the policy and programmes of the Council, and

(b) a general review of the activities and progress during that year of the electricity supply industry in England and Wales, taking that industry as a whole.

(3) Every report made under this section by an Area Board, the Generating Board or the Electricity Council for any year shall set out any directions given by the Minister to the Board or Council during that year, except any direction in the case of which the Minister has notified to the Board or Council his opinion that it should be omitted in the interests of national security.

(4) The Minister may give directions as to the form of the reports to be made under the preceding provisions of this section.

(5) A Consultative Council for the area of any Area Board may, in respect of any financial year of the Board, make to the Board a report on the performance by the Council of their functions during that year; and any such report shall be made to the Board as soon as possible after the end of the financial year in question, and the Board shall include that report in the report made by them under this section.

(6) The Minister shall lay before each House of Parliament a copy of the report made for each financial year by each Area Board, the Generating Board and the Electricity Council, and shall at the same time lay before each House of Parliament a report with respect to the performance of his functions during that year under the principal Act and this Act and the Electricity (Supply) Acts 1882 to 1936, except as regards matters which in his opinion it is against the interests of national security to disclose.

NOTES

Electricity Council. See s 3 ante.

Shall lay, etc. For provisions as to the laying of documents before Parliament, see the Laying of Documents before Parliament (Interpretation) Act 1948, s 1(1), Vol 41, title Statutes.

Definitions. By virtue of s 40(1) post, for "Area Board", see the Electricity Act 1947, s 1(3) ante, and for "financial year", "functions" and "Minister", see s 67(1) of the same Act ante. For "the Generating Board", see s 2(1) ante, and for "performance", see s 40(1) post. See also as to directions, s 40(2) post.

Electricity (Supply) Acts 1882 to 1936. For the Acts which may be cited by this collective title, see the Introductory Note to the Electric Lighting Act 1882 ante.

11 Consolidated statements of accounts

(1) In addition to the statements of accounts required by section forty-six of the principal Act, the Electricity Council shall prepare, in respect of each financial year beginning on or after the vesting date, a consolidated statement of accounts of the Council, the Generating Board and the Area Boards for that year in such form as the Minister, with the approval of the Treasury, may direct, being a form which shall conform with the best commercial standards.

(2) The form of a consolidated statement under this section shall be such as to provide separate information with respect to the generation of electricity, the distribution of electricity, and each of the other main activities of the electricity supply industry in England and Wales, and to show as far as may be the financial and operating results of each such activity.

(3) The consolidated statement prepared under this section for a financial year shall be submitted to the auditors appointed by the Minister to audit the accounts of the Electricity Council for that year, and those auditors shall make a report on the statement.

(4) As soon as the auditors have made a report on a consolidated statement prepared under this section, the Electricity Council shall send a copy of the statement and of that

report to the Minister; and copies of the statement and report shall be made available to the public at a reasonable price.

(5) The Minister shall lay before each House of Parliament a copy of every statement prepared under this section and of the report of the auditors thereon.

NOTES

   Principal Act. Ie the Electricity Act 1947; see s 2(1) ante. For s 46 of that Act, see this title ante.
   Vesting date. By virtue of s 1 of this Act (repealed), the vesting date was 1 January 1958.
   Electricity Council. See s 3 ante.
   Shall lay, etc. See the note to s 10 ante.
   Definitions. By virtue of s 40(1) post, for "Area Boards", see the Electricity Act 1947, s 1(3) ante, and for "financial year" and "Minister", see s 67(1) of that Act ante. For "Generating Board", see s 2(1) ante.

12 Machinery for settling terms and conditions of employment

(1) Except in so far as they are satisfied that adequate machinery exists for achieving the purposes of this section, it shall be the duty of the Electricity Council and the Scottish Electricity Boards to seek joint consultations with any organisation appearing to them to be appropriate, with a view to the conclusion between the Council, those Boards and that organisation of such joint agreements as appear to the parties to be desirable with respect to the establishment and maintenance of machinery for—

   (a) the settlement by negotiation of terms and conditions of employment of persons employed by the Electricity Council or by Electricity Boards, with provision for reference to arbitration in default of such settlement in such cases as may be determined by or under the agreements; and

   (b) the promotion, improvement and encouragement of measures affecting the safety, health, welfare, education and training of persons employed by the Electricity Council or by Electricity Boards, and the discussion of other matters of mutual interest to that Council or those Boards and persons so employed, including efficiency in the operation of the services of the Council or the Boards.

(2) Before entering into any agreement in pursuance of the preceding subsection, the Electricity Council shall consult the Generating Board and each of the Area Boards.

(3) It shall be the duty of the Generating Board and of each of the Area Boards to comply with any agreement concluded in pursuance of subsection (1) of this section.

(4) In so far as the Generating Board or any Area Board are required by subsection (2) of section two of the principal Act to consult with any organisation appearing to them to be appropriate with respect to the performance of their duty under that subsection to provide, or assist the provision of, facilities for training and education, the Board, in determining what organisation is appropriate, shall have regard to any machinery established for the purposes of paragraph (b) of subsection (1) of this section.

(5) The Electricity Council and each of the Scottish Electricity Boards shall send to the Minister, the Secretary of State and the Minister of Labour and National Service a copy of any agreement concluded for the purposes of this section to which the Council or that Board, as the case may be, are a party.

NOTES

   Electricity Council. See s 3 ante.
   Employment; employed. It is clear that these expressions do not have here the narrow meaning assigned to them by the Electricity Act 1947, s 67(1), which is applicable by virtue of s 40(1) post.
   Consult. See the note "Consultation" to s 6 ante.
   Principal Act. Ie the Electricity Act 1947; see s 2(1) ante. For s 2(2) of that Act, see this title ante.
   Definitions. By virtue of s 40(1) post, for "Area Boards", see the Electricity Act 1947, s 1(3) ante, for "Electricity Boards", see s 1(3) of the 1947 Act, in conjunction with the Electricity Reorganisation (Scotland)

Act 1954, Sch 1, Pt II ante; and for "Minister", see s 67(1) of the 1947 Act ante. For "the Generating Board", see s 2(1) ante. By virtue of s 40(1) post, and the Electricity Reorganisation (Scotland) Act 1954, s 17 ante, for "the Scottish Electricity Boards", see s 14(1) of that Act ante. For "performance", see s 40(1) post.

Finances of Electricity Boards and Electricity Council

13 General duty of Boards to balance revenue account

It shall be the duty of the Generating Board and of each of the Area Boards so to perform their functions as to secure that the revenues of the Board are not less than sufficient to meet the outgoings of the Board properly chargeable to revenue account, taking one year with another.

NOTE

Definitions. By virtue of s 40(1) post, for "Area Boards", see the Electricity Act 1947, s 1(3) ante, and for "functions", see s 67(1) of that Act ante. For "the Generating Board", see s 2(1) ante; for "perform", see s 40(1) post.

14 Tariffs and special agreements

(1), (2) . . .

(3) Where a consumer has requested an Area Board to enter into an agreement with him under subsection (7) of the said section thirty-seven (under which Area Boards are empowered to enter into special agreements with consumers), or to renew an agreement entered into under that subsection, or to vary the terms of such an agreement, and the Board—

- (a) have refused to comply with that request, or
- (b) have refused to comply with it except on terms which are not acceptable to the consumer,

the consumer may refer the matter to the Consultative Council established for the area of that Board.

(4) The grounds on which a consumer may refer a matter to a Consultative Council under the last preceding subsection are as follows, that is to say,—

- (a) where the consumer's request to the Board to enter into or renew an agreement has been refused, that, owing to special circumstances, the tariffs in force in the area are not appropriate to him;
- (b) where the consumer's request to the Board to vary the terms of an agreement have been refused, that, owing to a change of circumstances since the agreement was made, its terms have ceased to be reasonable;
- (c) in any other case, that the terms proposed by the Board are unreasonable.

(5) Where a matter is referred to a Consultative Council under subsection (3) of this section, then, without prejudice to any functions of the Consultative Council or of the Electricity Council under section seven of the principal Act,—

- (a) if it appears to the Consultative Council that the consumer has established to their satisfaction the grounds on which the matter was referred to them, the Council shall notify their conclusions to the consumer and to the Area Board;
- (b) if it appears to the Consultative Council that the consumer has not so established those grounds, the Council shall notify their conclusions to the consumer;
- (c) if the consumer is dissatisfied with the conclusions of the Consultative Council, or if (in a case falling within paragraph (a) of this subsection) he claims that the Area Board have failed to give effect to those conclusions, he may refer the matter to the Electricity Council, on the same grounds as those

on which the matter was referred to the Consultative Council, subject to any modifications which may be appropriate in view of any subsequent proposal of the Area Board; and

(d) if it appears to the Electricity Council, after consultation with the Area Board and with the Consultative Council, that the consumer has established to the satisfaction of the Electricity Council the grounds on which the matter was referred to them, the Electricity Council may give to the Area Board such advice as they may consider appropriate in the circumstances.

(6) Any reference in this section to a refusal to comply with a request includes a reference to a failure to comply with it within a reasonable time after the request is made.

NOTES

Sub-ss (1), (2) amend the Electricity Act 1947, s 37(1), (3) ante.

Said section 37. Ie s 37 of the Electricity Act 1947 ante.

Principal Act. Ie the Electricity Act 1947; see s 2(1) ante. For s 7 of that Act, see this title ante.

May refer. See also the Electricity (Consultative Council) (Areas) Regulations 1948, SI 1948/898, reg 6, as substituted by SI 1958/1.

Consultative Council. See the Electricity Act 1947, s 7 ante.

Electricity Council. See s 3 ante.

Consultation. See the note to s 6 ante.

Definitions. By virtue of s 40(1) post, for "Area Board", see the Electricity Act 1947, s 1(3) ante, and for "functions", see s 67(1) of the 1947 Act ante. Note as to "refused", sub-s (6) above.

---

15 Borrowing powers of Electricity Council, Generating Board and Area Boards

(1) The Electricity Council, the Generating Board or any Area Board, with the consent of the Minister and with the approval of the Treasury, or in accordance with the terms of any general authority issued by the Minister with the approval of the Treasury, may borrow temporarily, by way of overdraft or otherwise, such sums as the borrowing Council or Board may require for meeting their obligations or performing their functions.

(2) The Electricity Council, with the consent of the Minister and the approval of the Treasury, may borrow money by the issue of British Electricity Stock, for all or any of the following purposes, that is to say,—

(a) the redemption of any British Electricity Stock;

(b) the repayment of [Government advances] made to the Central Authority or to the Electricity Council;

(c) the provision of money for meeting any expenditure incurred by the Electricity Council, the Generating Board or any Area Board in connection with any works the cost of which is properly chargeable to capital account;

(d) the provision of any working capital required by the Electricity Council, the Generating Board or any Area Board;

(e) any other purpose for which capital moneys are properly applicable by the Electricity Council, the Generating Board or any Area Board, including the repayment of money temporarily borrowed by them for any of the purposes mentioned in this subsection;

(f) any other payment which the Electricity Council, the Generating Board or any Area Board are authorised to make and which ought, in the opinion of the Electricity Council, to be spread over a term of years.

(3) The Electricity Council may raise money, for all or any of the purposes mentioned in [either of the preceding subsections], by the taking of [Government advances] from the Minister.

[(3A) The Electricity Council, with the consent of the Secretary of State and the approval of the Treasury, may borrow money in sterling from the Commission of the European Communities or from the European Investment Bank for all or any of the purposes mentioned in subsection (2) of this section.]

(4) The Generating Board or any Area Board, after consultation with the Electricity Council, and with the consent of the Minister and the approval of the Treasury, may borrow money by the issue of stock, for all or any of the following purposes, that is to say,—

    (a) the redemption of any stock issued by the Board;

    (b) the provision of money for meeting any expenditure incurred by the Board in connection with any works the cost of which is properly chargeable to capital account;

    (c) the provision of any working capital required by the Board;

    (d) the discharge of any responsibility allocated to the Board in respect of British Electricity Stock or [Government advances], in so far as that responsibility is attributable to the principal of that Stock or of those advances;

    (e) any other purpose for which capital moneys are properly applicable by the Board, including the repayment of any money temporarily borrowed by the Board for any of the purposes mentioned in this subsection;

    (f) any other payment which the Board are authorised to make and which ought in their opinion to be spread over a term of years.

(5) The aggregate of the amounts outstanding in respect of—

    (a) the principal of any British Electricity Stock issued by the Central Authority, otherwise than for the purpose of paying compensation under Part II of the principal Act whether in stock or cash, and

    (b) the principal of any [Government advances] [(whether temporary or otherwise)] made to the Central Authority or to the Electricity Council, and

    (c) the principal of any stock issued under this Act, and

    [(cc) the principal of any money borrowed by the Electricity Council under subsection (3A) of this section, and]

    (d) any temporary loans raised by the Central Authority, the Electricity Council, the Generating Board or any Area Board,

shall not at any time exceed the sum of [£5200 million or such greater sum, not exceeding £6500 million, as the Secretary of State may by order specify]:

Provided that nothing in this subsection shall prevent the Electricity Council, the Generating Board or any Area Board from borrowing for the purpose of redeeming any stock which they are required or entitled to redeem, or of repaying [Government advances], or of repaying any money temporarily borrowed by them.

(6) Neither the Electricity Council nor the Generating Board nor any Area Board shall borrow any money except in accordance with the preceding provisions of this section.

(7) In this Act "[Government advances]" means advances made under section forty-two of the Finance Act 1956 (which provides for the making of [Government advances] to nationalised industries and undertakings) [or under section 2 of the Electricity and Gas Act 1963 (which makes similar provision in respect of certain bodies including the Electricity Council)].

NOTES

Sub-ss (3A), (5)(cc) were inserted by the Statutory Corporations (Financial Provisions) Act 1974, s 4, Sch 2. The words "Government advances" wherever they occur were substituted by the National Loans Act 1968, s 2, Sch 1. The words in the first pair of square brackets in sub-s (3) were substituted, the words in square brackets in sub-s (5)(b) were inserted, and the words in the third pair of square brackets in sub-s (7) were added, by the Electricity and Gas Act 1963, ss 1(2), 2(2), Sch 1. The words in the third pair of square brackets in sub-s (5) were substituted by the Electricity Act 1972, s 1(1).

Sub-s (1): Electricity Council. See s 3 ante.

Treasury. Ie the Commissioners of HM Treasury; see the Interpretation Act 1978, s 5, Sch 1, Vol 41, title Statutes.

Sub-s (2): British Electricity Stock. For further provisions as to such stock, see s 16 post.

Sub-s (3A): Secretary of State. Ie the Secretary of State for Energy; see the Preliminary Note to this title.

Commission of the European Communities. For the establishment of the Commission, see the Merger Treaty, art 9.

European Investment Bank. This bank was established under the EEC Treaty, art 129, and its functions are set out in art 130 of that Treaty. Art 18(3) of the Protocol on the Statute of the European Investment Bank annexed to the EEC Treaty, provides that when granting a loan to an undertaking other than a Member State, the bank must make the loan conditional either on a guarantee from the Member State in whose territory the project will be carried out or on other adequate guarantees.

Sub-s (4): Consultation. See the note to s 6 ante.

Sub-s (5): British Electricity Stock issued by the Central Authority. See s 16(1) post, and the note "British Electricity Stock" to that section.

Principal Act. Ie the Electricity Act 1947 ante; see s 2(1) ante.

Treasury guarantees etc. For provisions as to Treasury guarantees, see s 17 post, and for provisions as to estimates of Electricity Boards' borrowing requirements and allocations to them of liabilities, see s 18 post.

Borrowing of foreign currency by Electricity Council. For provisions as to the borrowing of foreign currency by the Electricity Council, see the Gas and Electricity Act 1968, s 2 post.

Expenditure to promote employment. The Electricity Act 1972, s 2 post empowers the Secretary of State to make grants to the Electricity Council or any Electricity Board towards expenditure intended to promote employment.

Definitions. By virtue of s 40(1) post, for "Area Board" and "the Central Authority", see the Electricity Act 1947, s 1(3) ante, and for "functions" and "Minister", see s 67(1) of that Act ante. For "the Generating Board", see s 2(1) ante; for "perform", see s 40(1) post. Note as to "Government advances", sub-s (7) above.

Finance Act 1956, s 42. Repealed by the Electricity and Gas Act 1963, s 4(2), Sch 2; see now s 2 of that Act post.

Electricity and Gas Act 1963, s 2. See this title post.

Order under this section. The Electricity (Borrowing Powers) Order 1974, SI 1974/1295 (specifying a sum of £6,500 million).

---

16 Issue of stock

(1) The Electricity Council may create and issue any stock required for the purpose of exercising their powers under the last preceding section; and any stock so created and issued shall, in common with any British Electricity Stock issued by the Central Authority under the principal Act, be known as British Electricity Stock, and shall be included in the stock referred to by that name in any enactment (including the principal Act and this Act).

(2) The Generating Board or any Area Board may create and issue any stock required for the purpose of exercising their powers under the last preceding section; and any stock so created and issued by one of those Boards shall be known by the name of that Board followed by the word "Stock".

(3) . . . British Electricity Stock shall be issued, transferred, dealt with and redeemed upon such terms and in accordance with such provisions as may be prescribed by regulations made by the Minister with the approval of the Treasury; and any such regulations may, in relation to any such stock, apply (with or without modifications) any provisions of the Local Loans Act 1875 or of any enactments relating to stock issued by a local authority.

(4) For the purposes of issues of stock by the Generating Board or by Area Boards, provision may be made by regulations made by the Minister with the approval of the Treasury—

    (*a*) for empowering the Board issuing any such stock to charge the stock and the interest thereon upon the revenues of the Board, with or without power to charge the stock and the interest thereon upon the undertaking of the Board;

    (*b*) for treating the obligations of such a Board under the following provisions of this Act in respect of payments to the Electricity Council, and contributions to the central guarantee fund, as a charge upon the revenues and undertaking of the Board, and for determining how that charge shall rank in relation to any charge upon those revenues or that undertaking created by the Board in connection with any such issue of stock;

(c) for prescribing (subject to any provision made by virtue of the last preceding paragraph) the terms upon which any such stock may be issued, transferred, dealt with or redeemed;

(d) for applying (with or without modifications) any provisions of the Local Loans Act 1875 or of any enactments relating to stock issued by a local authority;

and different provision may be made by any such regulations in relation to different Boards or in relation to different issues of stock by the same Board.

(5) The power to make regulations under this section shall be exercisable by statutory instrument; and any instrument containing such regulations shall be subject to annulment in pursuance of a resolution of either House of Parliament.

NOTES

The words omitted from sub-s (3) were repealed by the SL(R) Act 1977.

Sub-s (1): Electricity Council. See s 3 ante.

Stock. Stocks guaranteed by the Treasury and issued under this Act or the 1947 Act are exempted from capital gains tax in accordance with the Capital Gains Tax Act 1979, s 67(1), title Taxation.

Central Authority. See s 2 ante.

British Electricity Stock. Under the Electricity Act 1947, s 40(1), which was repealed by s 42(3) of, and Sch 5, Pt II to, this Act (repealed), this expression, in effect, meant stock created and issued under that Act by the Central Electricity Authority.

Treasury. See the note to s 15 ante.

Regulations under sub-s (3). For the exercise of the power to make regulations or orders under sub-s (3) permitting the transfer of specified securities through a computer-based system, see the Stock Transfer Act 1982, s 1, Vol 30, title Money (Pt 1), as from a day to be appointed under s 6(2) of that Act.

Sub-s (4): Central guarantee fund. See s 19 post.

Sub-s (5): Statutory instrument; subject to annulment. See the note to s 3 ante.

Treasury guarantees etc. For provisions as to Treasury guarantees, see s 17 post, and for provisions as to estimates of Electricity Boards' borrowing requirements and allocations to them of liabilities, see s 18 post.

Definitions. By virtue of s 40(1) post, for "Area Board" and "the Central Authority", see the Electricity Act 1947, s 1(3) ante, and for "enactment", "local authority" and "the Minister", see s 67(1) of that Act ante. For "the Generating Board", see s 2(1) ante.

Local Loans Act 1875. See Vol 30, title Money (Pt 3).

Regulations under this section. The Electricity (Stock) Regulations 1957, SI 1957/2228, as amended by the Family Law Reform Act 1969, s 1(3), Sch 1, Pt II, Vol 6, title Children and SI 1981/1763.

17 Treasury guarantees

(1) The Treasury may guarantee, in such manner and on such conditions as they think fit, the redemption or repayment of, [the payment of interest on and the discharge of any other financial obligation in connection with]

(a) any British Electricity Stock, or

(b) any temporary loan raised by the Electricity Council, the Generating Board or any Area Board, [or

(c) any money borrowed by the Electricity Council under section 15(3A) of this Act].

(2) Any sums required by the Treasury for fulfilling any guarantee given under the preceding subsection, or under section forty-two of the principal Act, shall be charged on and issued out of the Consolidated Fund; and all such sums, together with interest thereon at such rate as the Treasury may determine, shall be repaid to the Treasury by the Electricity Council in such manner and over such period as the Treasury, after consultation with the Minister, may determine.

(3) Immediately after a guarantee is given under this section, the Treasury shall lay a statement of the guarantee before each House of Parliament.

(4) Where any sum is issued out of the Consolidated Fund under this section, the Treasury shall forthwith lay before each House of Parliament a statement that that sum has been issued.

(5) Any sums repaid to the Treasury under subsection (2) of this section shall be paid into the Exchequer.

NOTES

The words in the first pair of square brackets in sub-s (1) were substituted by the Miscellaneous Financial Provisions Act 1983, s 4, Sch 2; the words in the second pair of square brackets in that subsection were inserted by the Statutory Corporations (Financial Provisions) Act 1975, s 5(2).

Treasury. See the note to s 15 ante.

British Electricity Stock. See s 16(1) ante. This section and s 18(1)–(3) post, have effect, by virtue of the Gas and Electricity Act 1968, s 2(3) post, as if references to the British Electricity Stock included references to sums borrowed or securities issued under that section.

Electricity Council. See s 3 ante.

Consolidated Fund. Ie the Consolidated Fund of the United Kingdom which was established by the Consolidated Fund Act 1816, s 1, Vol 30, title Money (Pt 1).

Shall be repaid etc. Cf as to the central guarantee fund, s 19 post.

Shall lay, etc; shall forthwith lay, etc. See the note "Shall lay, etc" to s 10 ante.

Definitions. By virtue of s 40(1) post, for "Area Board", see the Electricity Act 1947, s 1(3) ante. For "the Generating Board", see s 2(1) ante.

Principal Act. Ie the Electricity Act 1947; see s 2(1) ante. S 42 of that Act was repealed by s 42(3) of, and Sch 5, Pt II to, this Act (repealed).

18 Estimates of Board's requirements and allocations to them of liabilities in respect of stock

(1) The Generating Board and each Area Board shall submit to the Electricity Council, at such times as the Council may direct, periodical estimates of the sums that they will require to be provided by means of borrowing by the issue of British Electricity Stock, and shall provide therewith such information as the Electricity Council may require as to the purposes for which those sums will be required; and the Electricity Council shall not proceed to exercise any powers exercisable by them of borrowing for the purpose of defraying expenditure incurred by any such Board in carrying out reorganisation or development unless the Council are satisfied that the reorganisation or development will be in accordance with a general programme settled by the Board and approved by the Minister under subsection (4) of section eight of this Act.

(2) Where the Electricity Council borrow money by the issue of British Electricity Stock, they shall determine, in accordance with a scheme from time to time settled by the Council with the Minister, after giving to the Generating Board and each Area Board an opportunity to make representations thereon to him, the shares in which the ultimate responsibility for meeting obligations in respect of that issue of stock is to be borne; and the scheme shall provide—

> (a) for allocating to the Electricity Council responsibility in respect of stock issued for the provision of money required by the Council for the performance of their functions, and for allocating to the Generating Board and the Area Boards responsibility in respect of all other stock issued for the purpose of borrowing money, having regard to the extent to which the money is borrowed for the purposes of the respective Boards;
>
> (b) for allocating to the Generating Board, the Area Boards and the Electricity Council responsibility in respect of any stock issued for the purpose of redeeming or converting British Electricity Stock, in the same proportions as responsibility was allocated in respect of the stock to be redeemed or converted.

(3) The Generating Board and each Area Board shall, at such times as may be directed by the Electricity Council, pay to the Council—

(a) such sums as may be necessary to enable the Council to make any payments, or to refund to themselves any payments made, in respect of interest on or the redemption of British Electricity Stock, including payments into a sinking fund, in so far as the payments are attributable to stock for which the Generating Board or Area Board, as the case may be, are ultimately responsible under this section, and

(b) such contributions towards the expenses incurred by the Electricity Council in issuing any British Electricity Stock, and in managing that stock, as bear to the total expenses so incurred the same proportion as the amount of the stock in respect of which the Board in question are ultimately responsible under this section bears to the total amount of the stock.

(4) The preceding provisions of this section shall apply in relation to the raising of money by the taking of [Government advances] as they apply in relation to the borrowing of money by the issue of British Electricity Stock; and accordingly references in those provisions to borrowing money, to British Electricity Stock or an issue of such stock, to issuing such stock, or to redeeming or converting such stock, shall be construed as including references to the raising of money, to [Government advances], to the taking of such advances, or to repaying such advances, as the case may be.

NOTES

The words in square brackets in sub-s (4) were substituted by the National Loans Act 1968, s 2, Sch 1.

Electricity Council. See s 3 ante.

Sums that they will require etc. Cf s 15(2) ante; but see also s 15(4) ante.

British Electricity Stock. See s 16(1) ante and the note to s 17 ante.

Any powers exercisable by them etc. See s 15(2) ante.

Extension. Sub-ss (1)–(3) above apply in relation to borrowing by the Electricity Council under s 15(3A) ante as they are applied by sub-s (4) above to borrowing by means of Government advances; see the Statutory Corporations (Financial Provisions) Act 1975, s 5(2), Vol 30, title Money (Pt 1).

Definitions. By virtue of s 40(1) post, for "Area Board", see the Electricity Act 1947, s 1(3) ante, and for "functions" and "Minister", see s 67(1) of that Act ante. For "the Generating Board", see s 2(1) ante; for "Government advances", see s 15(7) ante; and for "performance", see s 40(1) post. See also as to "in the same proportions as responsibility was allocated" etc, Sch 3, para 4(2) post.

19 Central guarantee fund

(1) The Electricity Council shall establish and maintain a fund, which shall be known as the central guarantee fund, for the following purposes, that is to say:—

(a) in the event of any temporary inability on the part of the Electricity Council, the Generating Board or any Area Board to discharge their obligations in respect of the payment of interest on, or the redemption or repayment of, any British Electricity Stock or [Government advances] or [any temporary or other loan], for enabling the payment in question to be made out of the fund;

(b) for repaying to the Treasury any payments made by them for the purpose of fulfilling any guarantee given by the Treasury under section seventeen of this Act, or under section forty-two of the principal Act;

and the moneys in the central guarantee fund shall not be applied for any other purposes.

(2) The Generating Board and each of the Area Boards shall in each financial year contribute to the central guarantee fund such sums as the Electricity Council, with the approval of the Minister and the Treasury, may from time to time determine, including any sums required to make good payments out of the fund for the purposes mentioned in the preceding subsection:

Provided that—

(a) the aggregate of the sums standing to the credit of the central guarantee fund shall not at any time exceed the sum of twenty million pounds;

(b) the aggregate of the sums contributed to the central guarantee fund, excluding any sums required to make good payments out of the fund, shall not in any financial year exceed the sum of four million pounds.

(3) If the Electricity Council propose to determine any sums to be contributed under the last preceding subsection, but the Minister and the Treasury do not approve the proposal, the Minister, with the approval of the Treasury, may himself determine the sums to be so contributed.

(4) The Electricity Council, for the purpose of correcting from time to time, having regard to changed circumstances, the extent of the contributions made by the Electricity Boards to the central guarantee fund under this section, may, with the approval of the Minister and the Treasury, repay out of the fund to any such Board any part of those contributions previously made by that Board.

(5) All moneys in the central guarantee fund, which are not for the time being required to be applied for the purposes of the fund, shall be invested in such securities of Her Majesty's Government in the United Kingdom, or such securities guaranteed by the Treasury, as may be determined by the Electricity Council with the approval of the Minister and the Treasury.

(6) Any interest arising from the investment of moneys in the fund shall be paid into the fund, except when the sums standing to the credit of the fund have reached the sum of twenty million pounds, and shall in that case be distributed among the Generating Board and the Area Boards in such shares as may be determined by the Electricity Council, having regard to the extent of their respective contributions to the fund.

(7) If the Generating Board or any Area Board fail to discharge their obligations in respect of any such payments as are referred to in paragraph (a) of subsection (1) of this section, or in respect of contributions which they are required to make to the central guarantee fund, the Electricity Council, with the approval of the Minister, may give directions to that Board with respect to the management or policy of the Board, including tariffs and other financial matters, during such period as the Minister after consultation with the Electricity Council and the Board may determine, being a period which extends at least until those obligations (including any contributions required to be made to the central guarantee fund in respect of the default) have been met.

NOTES

The words in the first pair of square brackets in sub-s (1) were substituted by the National Loans Act 1968, s 2, Sch 1; the words in the second pair of square brackets in sub-s (1) were substituted by the Statutory Corporations (Financial Provisions) Act 1975, s 5(2).

Sub-s (1): Electricity Council. See s 3 ante.

British Electricity Stock. See s 16(1) ante.

Sub-s (7): Consultation. See the note to s 6 ante.

Definitions. By virtue of s 40(1) post, for "Area Boards", see the Electricity Act 1947, s 1(3) ante; for "Electricity Boards", see s 1(3) of the 1947 Act in conjunction with the Electricity Reorganisation (Scotland) Act 1954, Sch 1, Pt II ante, and for "financial year" and "Minister", see s 67(1) of the 1947 Act. For "the Generating Board", see s 2(1) ante, and for "Government advances", see s 15(7) ante. See also as to directions, s 40(2) post.

Principal Act. Ie the Electricity Act 1947; see s 2(1) ante. S 42 of that Act was repealed by s 42(3) of, and Sch 5, Pt II to, this Act (repealed).

20 Reserve funds

(1) The Generating Board shall establish and maintain a general reserve fund for the purposes of that Board, which shall be known as the generating reserve fund.

(2) Every Area Board shall establish and maintain (or, in the case of a fund established before the coming into operation of this section, shall continue to maintain) a general

reserve fund for the purposes of the Board, which shall be known as an area reserve fund.

(3) Subject to the following provisions of this section, the Generating Board shall contribute to the generating reserve fund, and each Area Board shall contribute to the area reserve fund maintained by them, to such extent as the Board maintaining the fund may from time to time determine.

(4) The management of the generating reserve fund, and of every area reserve fund, and the application of the moneys comprised therein, shall, subject to the next following subsection, be as the Board maintaining the fund may determine:

Provided that no part of any such fund shall be applied otherwise than for the purposes of the Board maintaining the fund.

(5) The power of the Minister under section eight of this Act to give directions to any of the Electricity Boards in England and Wales as to the performance of their functions shall extend to the giving to them of directions (whether of a general or a specific character) as to—

(a) any matter relating to the establishment or management of a fund which the Board are required to maintain under this section, or

(b) the making of contributions to such a fund, or

(c) the application of any moneys comprised in such a fund;

but no directions shall be given by the Minister as to a matter falling within paragraph (a), paragraph (b) or paragraph (c) of this subsection except with the approval of the Treasury.

(6) The preceding provisions of this section shall be without prejudice to the power of the Generating Board or any Area Board to establish appropriate reserves for replacements or other purposes; but with respect to the management and application of any such reserves the Generating Board or an Area Board shall act in accordance with any directions given by the Minister after consultation with the Treasury.

(7) It is hereby declared that one of the purposes of the generating reserve fund and the area reserve funds is the prevention of frequent fluctuations in the charges made by the Generating Board and the Area Boards, and the powers of those Boards in relation to those funds shall be exercised accordingly.

(8) . . .

NOTES

Sub-s (8) was repealed by the SL(R) Act 1977.

Sub-s (5): Treasury. See the note to s 15 ante.

Sub-s (6): Consultation. See the note to s 6 ante.

Definitions. By virtue of s 40(1) post, for "Area Board", see the Electricity Act 1947, s 1(3) ante; for "Electricity Boards", see s 1(3) of the 1947 Act, in conjunction with the Electricity Reorganisation (Scotland) Act 1954, Sch 1, Pt II ante; and for "functions" and "Minister", see s 67(1) of that Act. For "the Generating Board", see s 2(1) ante; for "performance", see s 40(1) post. See also as to directions, s 40(2) post.

---

21 Contributions by Electricity Boards to expenses of Electricity Council

(1) The Electricity Council may require any of the Electricity Boards in England and Wales from time to time to contribute such sums as the Council, with the approval of the Minister, may determine, towards meeting the expenses of the Council; and every Electricity Board shall comply with any requirement of the Electricity Council under this subsection.

(2) Without prejudice to the generality of the preceding subsection, the expenses

referred to in that subsection shall be taken to include the satisfaction of any obligations of the Electricity Council in respect of—

(*a*) compensation to members and officers of the Central Authority;

(*b*) payments under Part V of the Local Government Act 1948 for the benefit of local authorities;

[(*c*) corporation tax;]

(*d*) payments to local authorities in pursuance of section twenty-three of this Act.

NOTES

Sub-s (2)(*c*) was substituted for the words "income tax or profits tax" in relation to years of assessment and companies' accounting periods ending after 5 April 1970 by the Finance Act 1969, s 60, Sch 20, paras 28(2), 30(1).

Electricity Council. See s 3 ante.

Definitions. By virtue of s 40(1) post, for "the Central Authority", see the Electricity Act 1947, s 1(3) ante; for "Electricity Boards", see s 1(3) of the 1947 Act, in conjunction with the Electricity Reorganisation (Scotland) Act 1954, Sch 1, Pt II ante; and for "local authority", "Minister" and "officer", see s 67(1) of the 1947 Act.

Local Government Act 1948, Part V. See Vol 36, title Rating.

22 Application of surplus revenues of Electricity Boards

(1) Any excess, for any financial year, of the revenues of any of the Electricity Boards in England and Wales over their outgoings for that year properly chargeable to revenue account shall, subject to the following provisions of this section, be applied for such purposes of the Board as the Board may determine.

(2) The power of the Minister under section eight of this Act to give directions to any of the Electricity Boards in England and Wales as to the performance of their functions shall extend to the giving to them, with the approval of the Treasury, of directions (whether of a general or a specific character) as to the application of any such excess of revenues over outgoings.

NOTE

Treasury. See the note to s 15 ante.

Definitions. By virtue of s 40(1) post, for "Electricity Boards", see the Electricity Act 1947, s 1(3) ante, in conjunction with the Electricity Reorganisation (Scotland) Act 1954, Sch 1, Pt II ante; and for "financial year", "functions" and "Minister", see s 67(1) of the 1947 Act. For "performance", see s 40(1) post.

23 Compensation to local authorities

(1) Any sum which, if the Central Authority had continued to exist, would, at a time on or after the vesting date, have become payable by or to that Authority under section twenty-two of the principal Act (which relates to compensation to local authorities in respect of the undertakings transferred to Electricity Boards under that Act) shall be payable by the Electricity Council, or to that Council, as the case may be.

(2) The provisions of subsections (4) and (5) of the said section twenty-two (which contain supplementary provisions for the purposes of that section) shall apply in relation to payments under this section as, in the circumstances mentioned in subsection (1) of this section, they would have applied to the payments to be made by or to the Central Authority.

NOTES

Vesting date. By virtue of s 1 of this Act (repealed), the vesting date was 1 January 1958.

Shall be payable etc. For provisions as to contributions by Electricity Boards, see s 21 ante.

Electricity Council. See s 3 ante.

Definitions. By virtue of s 40(1) post, for "the Central Authority", see the Electricity Act 1947, s 1(3) ante.

Principal Act. Ie the Electricity Act 1947; see s 2(1) ante. For s 22 of that Act, see this title ante.

24 *(Repealed by the Income and Corporation Taxes Act 1970, s 538(1), Sch 16.)*

Transfer of undertaking of Central Authority to Electricity Council and Generating Board

25 Transfer of assets and liabilities of Central Authority

(1), (2) . . .

(3) . . . As from the vesting date subsection (4) of section forty-two of the Finance Act 1956 (which relates to the repayment of, and payment of interest on, advances made under that section) shall apply in relation to [Government advances] made to the Central Authority as if they had been made to the Electricity Council, and the provisions of that section as to sums received under the said subsection (4) shall apply accordingly.

(4)–(6) . . .

NOTES

Sub-ss (1), (2), (4)–(6) and the words omitted from sub-s (3) were repealed by the SL(R) Act 1977; the words in square brackets in sub-s (3) were substituted by the National Loans Act 1968, s 2, Sch 1.

Vesting date. By virtue of s 1 of this Act (repealed), the vesting date was 1 January 1958.

Electricity Council. See s 3 ante.

Definitions. By virtue of s 40(1) post, for "the Central Authority", see the Electricity Act 1947, s 1(3) ante. For "Government advances", see s 15(7) ante.

Finance Act 1956, s 42. Repealed by the Electricity and Gas Act 1963, s 4(2), Sch 2.

26 *(Repealed by the SL(R) Act 1977.)*

27 Compensation to members and officers of Central Authority and Area Boards

(1) The Minister shall, with the approval of the Treasury, require the Electricity Council to make to any person holding office as a member of the Central Authority immediately before that Authority ceases to exist, being a person who suffers loss of employment or loss or diminution of emoluments or pension rights or whose position is worsened in consequence of the dissolution of the Central Authority, payment of such compensation for loss of office as the Minister may, with the approval of the Treasury, determine.

(2) The Minister shall by regulations require the Electricity Council to pay, in such cases and to such extent as may be specified in the regulations, compensation to officers of the Central Authority or any Area Board who suffer loss of employment or loss or diminution of emoluments or pension rights or whose position is worsened in consequence of this Act.

(3) . . . the provisions of subsections (3) to (6) and subsection (8) of section fifty-five of the principal Act (which relates to the payment of compensation to officers of electricity undertakings transferred under that Act) shall apply to any regulations made under this section as if those regulations had been made under subsection (1) of the said section fifty-five, and as if, in subsection (4) of that section, the reference to an Electricity Board included a reference to the Electricity Council.

(4), (5) . . .

(6) The power to make regulations under this section shall be exercisable by statutory instrument; and no regulations shall be made under this section unless a draft of the regulations has been laid before Parliament and has been approved by a resolution of each House of Parliament.

NOTES

Sub-ss (4), (5) and the words omitted from sub-s (3) were repealed by the Tribunals and Inquiries Act 1958, s 15, Sch 2, Pt II.

Electricity Council. See s 3 ante.

Treasury. See the note to s 15 ante.

Statutory instrument; laid before … Parliament. For provisions as to statutory instruments generally, see the Statutory Instruments Act 1946, Vol 41, title Statutes; and as to statutory instruments, drafts of which are required to be laid before Parliament, see s 6 of that Act, and the Laying of Documents before Parliament (Interpretation) Act 1948, Vol 41, title Statutes.

Pension rights of persons not entitled to compensation. For provisions as to pension payments to, or in respect of, former members of the Central Authority who are not entitled to compensation under sub-s (1) above, see Sch 3, para 12 post.

Set-off of redundancy payments. See the note to the Electricity Act 1947, s 55 ante.

Definitions. By virtue of s 40(1) post, for "Area Board" and "the Central Authority", see the Electricity Act 1947, s 1(3) ante; and for "emoluments", "employment", "officer", "Minister" and "pension rights", see s 67(1) of that Act.

Principal Act. Ie the Electricity Act 1947; see s 2(1) ante. For s 55 of that Act, see this title ante. As to regulations made under the Electricity Act 1947, s 55 ante, as applied by this section, see the note "Referee or board of referees" to s 54 of the 1947 Act.

Regulations under this section. The Electricity (Staff Compensation) Regulations 1959, SI 1959/1322.

Miscellaneous and supplementary provisions

28 Supply of electricity to railways

(1) Subject to the provisions of this section, it shall be the duty of the Generating Board to provide in England and Wales, and it shall be the duty of the Scottish Electricity Boards to provide in their respective Districts, a supply of electricity to meet the requirements for haulage or traction of railway undertakers.

(2) A supply of electricity to railway undertakers may be provided—

(*a*) in England or Wales by the South Scotland Board with the approval of the Generating Board;

(*b*) in the South of Scotland District by the Generating Board with the approval of the South of Scotland Board; or

(*c*) in the District of either of the Scottish Electricity Boards by the other of them, with the approval of the Board in whose District the supply is provided.

(3) An Area Board shall not, except with the approval of the Generating Board, supply electricity to railway undertakers for purposes of haulage or traction.

(4) Nothing in the last preceding subsection shall be construed as authorising an Area Board to supply electricity to railway undertakers in the area of another Area Board, or in the District of a Scottish Electricity Board, except with the agreement of that Board or an authorisation given by the Electricity Council or the Secretary of State (in accordance with the provisions of subsections (4) and (5) of section one of the principal Act), as well as the approval of the Generating Board as required by the last preceding subsection.

(5) The terms and conditions on which electricity is supplied by an Electricity Board to any railway undertakers for the purposes of haulage or traction shall be such as may be agreed between the Board and the undertakers or, in default of such agreement, as may be determined by the appropriate Ministers:

Provided that any terms and conditions so agreed or determined shall be such as, in the opinion of the Board, or of the appropriate Ministers, as the case may be, will not cause a financial loss to result to the Board from the provision of the supply.

(6) Where the terms and conditions on which electricity is supplied by an Electricity Board to any railway undertakers for purposes of haulage or traction are determined by the appropriate Ministers, that determination—

(*a*) shall not extend to the terms and conditions on which any electricity so supplied may be used by the undertakers for other purposes, and

(*b*) shall not be taken to preclude the Board and the undertakers from subsequently varying the terms and conditions so determined by agreement between them.

(7) An Electricity Board may enter into an agreement with any railway undertakers, to whom the Board are to supply electricity for purposes of haulage or traction, whereby any of that electricity may be used by the undertakers for other purposes, on such terms and conditions as may be specified in the agreement.

[(8) Without prejudice to any other enactment providing for the protection of telecommunication apparatus kept installed for the purposes of a telecommunications code system (and subject to the terms of any agreement made under section 98 of the Telecommunications Act 1984 with respect to the keeping of any telecommunication apparatus in a conduit or structure falling within subsection (6)(*a*) of that section (electricity conduits)), any electricity supplied under this section to any railway undertakers shall be used in such manner as not to cause, or to be likely to cause, any interference (whether by induction or otherwise) with any telecommunication apparatus kept installed for the purposes of any such system, or with the service provided by any such system.]

(9) In this section "the appropriate Ministers", in relation to Electricity Boards in England and Wales, means the Minister and [the Minister of Transport] acting jointly, and, in relation to Scottish Electicity Boards, means the Secretary of State and [the Minister of Transport] acting jointly, . . .

NOTES

Sub-s (8) was substituted, and the words omitted from sub-s (9) were repealed, by the Telecommunications Act 1984, s 109(1), (6), Sch 4, para 34, Sch 7, Pt I. The words in square brackets in sub-s (9) were substituted by the Minister of Aviation Order 1959, SI 1959/1768.

Sub-s (8): Any other enactment etc. Cf the Electric Lighting Act 1882, s 26 ante; the Electric Lighting Act 1888, s 4 ante; the Electric Lighting (Clauses) Act 1899, Schedule, ss 14, 20, 69 ante; and the Electricity Act 1947, s 9(3) ante.

Sub-s (9): Minister of Transport. The functions of the Minister of Transport under this section are now exercised by the Secretary of State for Energy; see the Preliminary Note to this title ante.

Definitions. By virtue of s 40(1) post, for "Area Board", see the Electricity Act 1947, s 1(3) ante; for "Electricity Boards", see s 1(3) of the 1947 Act, in conjunction with the Electricity Reorganisation (Scotland) Act 1954, Sch 1, Pt II ante; and for "enactment", "Minister", "railway undertakers", "South of Scotland Board" and "South of Scotland District", see s 67(1) of the 1947 Act. For "the Generating Board", see s 2(1) ante. By virtue of s 40(1) post, and the Electricity Reorganisation (Scotland) Act 1954, s 17 ante, for "the Scottish Electricity Board", see s 14(1) of that Act. Note as to "the appropriate Ministers", sub-s (9) above. By virtue of the Telecommunications Act 1984, Sch 4, para 1(1), Vol 45, title Telecommunications and Broadcasting, for "telecommunications code system", see that paragraph, and for "telecommunication apparatus", see Sch 2 to that Act.

Principal Act. Ie the Electricity Act 1947; see s 2(1) ante. For s 1(4), (5) of that Act, see this title ante.

Telecommunications Act 1984, s 98. See Vol 45, title Telecommunications and Broadcasting.

---

29 Maximum charges for reselling electricity supplied by Electricity Boards

(1) An Area Board, . . . may publish a notice fixing maximum charges in consideration of which electricity supplied by the Board may be resold by persons to whom it is so supplied, or by any class of such persons specified in the notice.

(2) Any notice under this section shall be published in such manner as in the opinion of the Board will secure adequate publicity for it; and the maximum charges fixed by any such notice may be varied by a subsequent notice published by the Board in accordance with this subsection.

(3) Different maximum charges may be fixed by a Board under this section for different classes of cases, whether by reference to different parts of the area . . . of the

Board or to different tariffs under which electricity is supplied by the Board or to any other relevant circumstances.

(4) If any person, in consideration of the resale of any electricity supplied by an Area Board . . . in circumstances to which a notice published by the Board under this section applies, requires the payment of charges exceeding the maximum charges applicable thereto in accordance with the notice, the amount of the excess shall be recoverable by the person to whom the electricity is resold.

(5) So much of section eighteen of the Gasworks Clauses Act 1847, as incorporated with the Electric Lighting Act 1882, as provides for a penalty to be imposed on persons who supply persons with electricity supplied to them, shall cease to have effect.

NOTES

The words omitted were repealed by the Electricity (Scotland) Act 1979, s 46(2), Sch 12.

Definitions. By virtue of s 40(1) post, for "Area Board", see the Electricity Act 1947, s 1(3) ante.

Gasworks Clauses Act 1847, s 18. See the Appendix to the Electric Lighting (Clauses) Act 1899, Schedule.

Electric Lighting Act 1882. See this title ante. S 12 of that Act incorporates, inter alia, certain provisions of the Gasworks Clauses Act 1847, which was repealed by the Gas Act 1948, s 76, Sch 4.

30 Certification of meters

(1) With regard to the certification of meters under the provisions of the Schedule to the Electric Lighting (Clauses) Act 1899, as incorporated with the principal Act (in this Act referred to as "the Schedule of 1899"), the Minister may by order provide, either in relation to meters generally or in relation to meters of any class specified in the order,—

(a) that, where a meter is certified under the provisions of the Schedule of 1899 after the date on which the order comes into operation, that certification (if it has not previously ceased to have effect) shall cease to have effect at the end of such period, beginning with the date of the certification, as may be specified in the order;

(b) that the certification of a meter under those provisions, where it was effected before the passing of this Act, or thereafter but before the date on which the order comes into operation, shall cease to have effect (if it has not previously ceased to have effect) either on the date on which the order comes into operation, or at the end of such period beginning with the date of the certification as may be specified in the order, whichever is the later;

(c) that, notwithstanding the proviso to section fifty of the Schedule of 1899 (under which, if a certified meter is altered, it ceases to be certified until re-certified), the making in a meter of an alteration of a description specified in the order (being a description of alteration appearing to the Minister to be such as not to affect the ascertainment of the value of [a supply]) shall not cause the meter to cease to be a certified meter;

(d) that, where a certified meter is moved in circumstances specified in the order, the certification of the meter shall thereupon cease to have effect, notwithstanding that the move does not involve any alteration of the meter.

(2) Any order made under the preceding subsection may be revoked or varied by a subsequent order thereunder; and the power to make orders under that subsection shall be exerciseable by statutory instrument, and any instrument containing such an order shall be laid before Parliament.

(3) The Minister may give directions to Electricity Boards—

(a) as to the examination and testing of meters by those Boards, by the use of apparatus provided in accordance with section two of the Electricity Supply

(Meters) Act 1936, before submitting the meters to a meter examiner for certification;

(b) as to the making of reports by those Boards on meters examined and tested by them, and as to the information to be included in such reports;

(c) as to the sealing and unsealing of meters, and, in particular, as to the custody and use of apparatus for sealing meters and the keeping of records in connection therewith.

(4) A meter examiner may certify a meter under the provisions of the Schedule of 1899, notwithstanding that he has not himself examined or tested it, if—

(a) the meter is submitted to him for certification by an Electricity Board, together with a report stating that the Board have examined and tested the meter in accordance with directions given by the Minister under the last preceding subsection, and containing the information required by those directions;

(b) the information contained in the report is such as to indicate, in the opinion of the meter examiner, that the meter is entitled to be certified;

(c) the meter is one of a number submitted to the meter examiner together at the same time by the same Electricity Board; and

(d) the meter examiner, by the use of apparatus provided in accordance with section two of the said Act of 1936, has himself examined and tested such number of those meters as he may consider sufficient to constitute a reasonable test of all the meters submitted to him by the Board for certification on that occasion.

[(4A) Where a person other than an Electricity Board submits a meter examiner for certification under the provisions of the Schedule of 1899, the meter examiner may certify the meter, notwithstanding that he has not himself examined or tested it, if—

(a) the meter was manufactured or repaired by the person submitting it;

(b) that person has obtained the consent of the Secretary of State to the submission; and

(c) any conditions subject to which the consent was given have been satisfied.]

(5)–(8) . . .

(9) In this section "the value of [a supply]" has the same meaning as in the Schedule of 1899, and "meter examiner" has the same meaning as in the Electricity Supply (Meters) Act 1936.

NOTES

The words in square brackets in sub-s (1)(c) and sub-s (9) were substituted, and sub-s (4A) was inserted, by the Energy Act 1983, s 15, Sch 1, para 17(2), (3), (5). Sub-ss (5)–(8) were repealed by ss 15, 30 of, and Sch 1 to, that Act, with a saving in respect of offences committed before 1 June 1983; see the Energy Act 1983 (Commencement No 1) Order 1983, SI 1983/790.

Passing of this Act. Ie 17 July 1957, the date of the Royal Assent.

Statutory instrument; laid before Parliament. See the note to s 27 ante.

Directions. See also s 40(2) post.

Definitions. By virtue of s 40(1) post, for "Electricity Boards", see the Electricity Act 1947, s 1(3) ante, in conjunction with the Electricity Reorganisation (Scotland) Act 1954, Sch 1, Pt II ante, and for "Minister", see s 67(1) of the 1947 Act ante. Note as to "the value of a supply", sub-s (9) above.

Electric Lighting (Clauses) Act 1899, Schedule. See this title ante. For the provisions of that Schedule as to certification of meters, see ss 50, 50A, 51 thereof ante; and for the meaning of "the value of a supply", see s 49 of that Schedule.

Principal Act. Ie the Electricity Act 1947; see s 2(1) ante. For incorporation of the Electric Lighting (Clauses) Act 1899, Schedule ante, see s 57(2) of the 1947 Act ante.

Electricity Supply (Meters) Act 1936. See this title ante. For meter examiners under that Act, see s 1 thereof ante.

Orders under this section. The Meters (Permitted Alterations) Order 1958, SI 1958/1061; the Meters (Periods of Certification) Order 1982, SI 1982/1442.

31 (*Amends s 10 of the Schedule to the Electric Lighting (Clauses) Act 1899 ante.*)

32 Further provisions as to placing of electric lines

(1) Every application for the consent or authorisation of the Minister under paragraph (*b*) of section ten of the Schedule of 1899 (in this section referred to as "section ten (*b*)")—

(*a*) shall be in writing;

(*b*) shall describe by reference to a map the land across which the electric line is proposed to be placed; and

(*c*) shall state whether all necessary wayleaves have been agreed with owners and occupiers of land proposed to be crossed by the line.

(2) Where such an application made by an Electricity Board states that all necessary wayleaves have not been agreed as mentioned in paragraph (*c*) of the preceding subsection, the Minister, if he thinks fit, may give notice to the Board that he does not propose to proceed with the application until he is satisfied, with respect to all the land over which wayleaves have not been agreed, that the Board have taken such action on their part as is mentioned in subsection (1) of section forty-four of the Electricity (Supply) Act 1926 (which enables applications for consent or authorisation under section ten (*b*) and applications in respect of wayleaves to be taken concurrently); and where the Minister gives such a notice under this subsection—

(*a*) the Minister shall not be required to proceed with the application until he is satisfied that the Board have taken all the requisite action in accordance with the notice, and

(*b*) the provisions of subsection (1) of the said section forty-four as to concurrent proceedings shall apply accordingly.

(3) Where an application for consent or authorisation under section ten (*b*) states that all necessary wayleaves have not been agreed, but the Minister does not proceed concurrently as mentioned in subsection (1) of the said section forty-four, the Minister, if he gives his consent or authorisation under section ten (*b*), may give it subject to the condition (either in respect of the whole of the line or in respect of any part of it specified in the consent or authorisation) that the work is not to proceed until the Minister gives his permission; and in determining at any time whether to give permission for the work to proceed, either generally or in respect of a part of the line, the Minister—

(*a*) shall have regard to the extent to which the necessary wayleaves have been agreed by that time, and

(*b*) in so far as any such wayleaves have not then been agreed in respect of any part of the line, shall take into account any prejudicial effect which, in his opinion, the giving of permission (whether in respect of that part or of any adjacent part of the line) might have on any subsequent proceedings relating to the outstanding wayleaves.

(4) (*Applies to Scotland only.*)

NOTES

Definitions. By virtue of s 40(1) post, for "Electricity Board", see the Electricity Act 1947, s 1(3) ante, and for "Minister", see s 67(1) of that Act.

Schedule of 1899. Ie the Schedule to the Electric Lighting (Clauses) Act 1899, as incorporated with the Electricity Act 1947; see s 30(1) ante, in conjunction with s 2(1) ante.

Electricity (Supply) Act 1926, s 44(1). See this title ante.

33 Provisions as to construction or extension of generating stations

(1) Where under section two of the Electric Lighting Act 1909 (which relates to the construction or extension of generating stations), notice, and an opportunity of stating objections, are required to be given to the local authority of the district in which the land in question is situated, the like requirements as to notice, and as to an opportunity

of stating objections, shall apply in relation to the local planning authority in whose area the land is situated.

(2) An application for the consent of the Minister or of the Secretary of State under the said section two shall be in writing, and shall describe by reference to a map the land in relation to which the consent is required.

(3) In this and the next following section "local planning authority", in relation to England and Wales, has the same meaning as in the Town and Country Planning Act 1947, and, in relation to Scotland, has the same meaning as in the Town and Country Planning (Scotland) Act 1947.

NOTES

Definitions. By virtue of s 40(1) post, for "local authority" and "the Minister", see the Electricity Act 1947, s 67(1) ante; and note as to "local planning authority", sub-s (3) above.

Electric Lighting Act 1909, s 2. See this title ante.

Town and Country Planning Act 1947. The provisions referred to are repealed by the Town and Country Planning Act 1971, s 292, Sch 25; see now as to "local planning authority", s 1 of the 1971 Act, Vol 46, title Town and Country Planning and, as to such authorities in Greater London, see the Local Government Act 1985, s 3, Vol 25, title Local Government.

Town and Country Planning (Scotland) Act 1947. Most of this Act was repealed and replaced by the Town and Country Planning (Scotland) Act 1972 (not printed in this work).

---

34 Special provisions as to public inquiries

(1) Where an application has been made to the Minister for his consent or authorisation under paragraph (*b*) of section ten of the Schedule of 1899, or for his consent under section two of the Electric Lighting Act 1909, and the local planning authority have notified the Minister that they object to the application, and that objection of the local planning authority has not been withdrawn, the Minister (either in addition to, or in lieu of, any other hearing or opportunity of stating objections) shall cause a public inquiry to be held, and, before determining whether to give his consent or authorisation, shall consider the objection and the report of the person who held the inquiry:

Provided that this subsection shall not apply where the Minister proposes to accede to the application subject to such modifications or conditions as will give effect to the objection of the local planning authority.

(2) In relation to applications for consent under section two of the Electric Lighting Act 1909, and to applications for consent or authorisation under paragraph (*b*) of section ten of the Schedule of 1899 in respect of the placing of high voltage lines, the Minister shall make provision by regulations for securing—

    (*a*) that (in addition to any notice required to be given under section two of the said Act of 1909) notice of every such application shall be published in such manner as may be specified in the regulations;

    (*b*) that (in addition to any notice required to be given under the said section two, and to the publication of notices in accordance with the preceding paragraph) notice of any such application shall, where the Minister so directs, be served upon such persons as may be specified in the directions;

    (*c*) that every notice published or served in pursuance of the regulations shall state the time within which, and the manner in which, objections to the application can be made by persons other than those to whom (under the said section two, or under section twenty-one of the Electricity (Supply) Act 1919) an opportunity of being heard or of stating objections is required to be given, and that the time so stated shall not be less than such minimum period as may be specified in the regulations; and (*d*) that, in so far as any such notice requires objections to be sent to any person other than the Minister, copies of the objections shall be sent to the Minister by that person:

Provided that, in relation to applications for consent under the said section two to the extension of generating stations, any regulations made under this subsection may include provision for enabling the Minister to give directions dispensing with the requirements of the regulations, in cases where in accordance with that section the Minister dispenses with the giving of notices thereunder.

(3) Where, in the case of any such application as is mentioned in the last preceding subsection,—

(*a*) the Minister is not required by virtue of subsection (1) of this section to cause a public inquiry to be held, but
(*b*) objections or copies of objections have been sent to the Minister in pursuance of regulations made under the last preceding subsection,

the Minister shall consider those objections, together with all other material considerations, with a view to determining whether a public inquiry should be held with respect to the application, and, if he thinks it appropriate to do so, shall cause a public inquiry to be held, either in addition to, or in lieu of, any other hearing or opportunity of stating objections to the application.

(4) Where in accordance with any of the preceding provisions of this section a public inquiry is to be held in respect of an application by an Electricity Board, the Minister shall inform the Board accordingly; and the Board shall in two successive weeks publish a notice stating—

(*a*) the fact that the application has been made, and the purpose thereof, together with a description of the land to which it relates;
(*b*) a place in the locality where a copy of the application, and of the map referred to therein, can be inspected; and
(*c*) the place, date and time of the public inquiry.

(5) A notice under the last preceding subsection shall be published in one or more local newspapers circulating in the locality in which the land in question is situated, or circulating respectively in the several localities in which different parts of that land are situated, as the Board publishing the notice may consider appropriate.

(6) If it appears to the Minister that, in addition to the publication of a notice in accordance with subsections (4) and (5) of this section, further notification of the public inquiry should be given (either by the service of notices, or by advertisement, or in any other way) in order to secure that the information specified in paragraphs (*a*) to (*c*) of subsection (4) of this section is sufficiently made known to persons in the locality, the Minister may direct the Board to take such further steps for that purpose as may be specified in the direction.

(7) Where in accordance with this section a public inquiry is to be held in respect of an application for the consent or authorisation of the Minister under paragraph (*b*) of section ten of the Schedule of 1899, and (whether in pursuance of subsection (2) of section thirty-two of this Act or otherwise) the Minister is proceeding concurrently as mentioned in subsection (1) of section forty-four of the Electricity (Supply) Act 1926, the public inquiry shall extend to all the matters arising in those concurrent proceedings, and any notice of the inquiry (in addition to any other matters required to be stated therein) shall indicate the extent of the inquiry accordingly.

(8) The provisions of the Second Schedule to this Act shall have effect for the purposes of this section.

(9) (*Applies to Scotland only.*)

(10) In this section "high voltage line" means an electric line for conveying or transmitting electricity at or above a voltage of one hundred and thirty-two thousand.

NOTES

General Note. This section is additional to, and not in derogation of, the Electricity Act 1947, s 66 ante. See also Sch 2, para 3 post.

Public inquiry. Inquiries held under sub-s (3) are subject to the Tribunals and Inquiries Act 1971, ss 1, 11, 12, Vol 10, title Constitutional Law (Pt 4); see the Tribunals and Inquiries (Discretionary Inquiries) Order 1975, SI 1975/1379, arts 3, 4, Schedule, Pt I.

Definitions. By virtue of s 40(1) post, for "electric line", "generating station", "Minister" and "regulations", see the Electricity Act 1947, s 67(1) post, and for "Electricity Board", see s 1(3) of that Act, in conjunction with the Electricity Reorganisation (Scotland) Act 1954, Sch 1, Pt II ante. For "local planning authority", see s 33(3) ante. Note as to "high voltage line", sub-s (10) above.

Schedule of 1899. See the note to s 32 ante.

Electric Lighting Act 1909, s 2; Electricity (Supply) Act 1919, s 21; Electricity (Supply) Act 1926, s 44(1). See this title ante.

Regulations under this section. The Electricity (Publication of Applications) Regulations 1957, SI 1957/2227 and the Electricity Generating Stations and Overhead Lines (Inquiries Procedure) Rules 1981, SI 1981/1841.

Note as to regulations under this section, Sch 2, paras 4, 5 post.

35 Entry on land for purposes of exploration

(1) Without prejudice to any other rights of entry exercisable by Electricity Boards, an Electricity Board, or any person duly authorised in writing by an Electricity Board, may, at any reasonable time, enter upon and survey any land, other than land covered by buildings or used as a garden or pleasure ground, for the purpose of ascertaining whether the land would be suitable for use for the purposes of any functions of the Board.

(2) Subsections (4), (5) and (9) of section one hundred and three of the Town and Country Planning Act 1947 (which contain supplementary provisions relating to the right of entry conferred by that section) shall apply in relation to the powers conferred by this section as they apply in relation to the powers conferred by that section:

Provided that—

(*a*) subsection (4) of that section (which requires twenty-four hours' notice to be given of an intended entry upon any occupied land) shall so apply as if for the words "twenty-four hours" there were substituted the words "twenty-eight days"; and

(*b*) subsection (9) of that section (which relates to power to search and bore for the purpose of ascertaining the nature of the subsoil or the presence of minerals therein) shall so apply as if the words "or the presence of minerals therein" were omitted.

(3) Where in the exercise of any power conferred by this section any damage is caused to land or to chattels, any person interested in the land or chattels may recover compensation in respect of that damage from the Electricity Board by whom or on whose behalf the power is exercised; and where in consequence of the exercise of any such power any person is disturbed in his enjoyment of any land or chattels, he may recover from that Electricity Board compensation in respect of the disturbance.

(4) Subsection (1) of section one hundred and ten of the Town and Country Planning Act 1947 (which provides for the determination of disputes as to compensation under that Act), shall apply to any question of disputed compensation under this section.

(5) . . .

NOTES

Sub-s (5) was repealed by the Electricity (Scotland) Act 1979, s 46(2), Sch 12.

Enter upon and survey any land. The unlawful obstruction of such a survey may constitute a breach of the peace; see *R v Chief Constable of the Devon and Cornwall Constabulary, ex p Central Electricity Generating Board* [1981] 3 All ER 826, [1981] 3 WLR 967, CA, where it was held that the board was entitled to use the common law remedy of self-help to remove obstructing protesters.

Functions of the Board. Ie duties and powers; see, by virtue of s 40(1) post, the Electricity Act 1947, s 67(1) ante.

Town and Country Planning Act 1947, ss 103(4), (5), (9), 110(1). Repealed by the Town and Country Planning Act 1962; see now the Town and Country Planning Act 1971, ss 280, 281, Vol 46, title Town and Country Planning.

---

36 *(Repealed by the Town and Country Planning Act 1968, s 108, Sch 11 and the Town and Country Planning (Scotland) Act 1969, s 107, Sch 11.)*

37 Preservation of amenity

In formulating or considering any proposals relating to the functions of the Generating Board or of any of the Area Boards (including any such general programme as is mentioned in subsection (4) of section eight of this Act), the Board in question, the Electricity Council and the Minister, having regard to the desirability of preserving natural beauty, of conserving flora, fauna and geological or physiographical features of special interest, and of protecting buildings and other objects of architectural or historic interest, shall each take into account any effect which the proposals would have on the natural beauty of the countryside or on any such flora, fauna, features, buildings or objects.

NOTES

Electricity Council. See s 3 ante.

Definitions. By virtue of s 40(1) post, for "Area Boards", see the Electricity Act 1947, s 1(3) ante, and for "functions" and "Minister", see s 67(1) of that Act. For "the Generating Board", see s 2(1) ante.

---

38 Status of Electricity Council, Generating Board and Area Boards

It is hereby declared for the avoidance of doubt that neither the Electricity Council nor the Generating Board nor any of the Area Boards are to be regarded as the servant or agent of the Crown or as enjoying any status, immunity or privilege of the Crown, and no property of the Council or of any of those Boards is to be regarded as property of, or held on behalf of, the Crown.

NOTES

It is hereby declared etc. Even apart from this section there could be little, if any, doubt that the position is as stated in this section; see *Tamlin v Hannaford* [1950] 1 KB 18, [1949] 2 All ER 327, CA.

Electricity Council. See s 3 ante.

Definitions. By virtue of s 40(1) post, for "Area Boards", see the Electricity Act 1947, s 1(3) ante. For "the Generating Board", see s 2(1) ante.

---

39 *(Repealed by the SL(R) Act 1978.)*

40 Interpretation

(1) In this Act the following expressions have the meanings hereby assigned to them respectively, that is to say:—

"[Government advances]" has the meaning assigned to it by section fifteen of this Act;

"the Generating Board" has the meaning assigned to it by section two of this Act;

"performance", in relation to functions, includes the exercise of powers as well as the performance of duties, and "perform" shall be construed accordingly;

"the principal Act" means the Electricity Act 1947;

"the Schedule of 1899" has the meaning assigned to it by section thirty of this Act;

"the vesting date" has the meaning assigned to it by section one of this Act;

and, except in so far as the context otherwise requires, other expressions used in this Act and in the principal Act have the same meanings in this Act as in that Act.

(2) Any provision of this Act conferring a power to give directions, if it does not expressly provide that the directions shall be of a general character, shall be construed as conferring a power to give directions either of a general or of a specific character; and every provision of this Act conferring a power to give directions shall be construed as imposing, on any person to whom directions are given thereunder, a duty to comply with those directions.

(3) Except in so far as the context otherwise requires, any reference in this Act to an enactment shall be construed as a reference to that enactment as amended by or under any other enactment, including this Act.

NOTES

The words in square brackets in sub-s (1) were substituted by the National Loans Act 1968, s 2, Sch 1.

Functions; enactment. By virtue of sub-s (1) above, for meanings, see the Electricity Act 1947, s 67(1) ante.

Power to give directions. Sub-s (2) also applies in relation to directions given by the Secretary of State to Electricity Boards in respect of matters arising out of representations made to him by the Electricity Consumers' Council under the Energy Act 1983, s 21 post; see sub-s (8) of that section.

Electricity Act 1947. See this title ante.

41 Transitional provisions

The transitional provisions contained in the Third Schedule to this Act shall have effect for the purposes of this Act.

42 Amendment and adaptation of enactments, and repeals

(1) Without prejudice to the amendments and adaptations of enactments having effect by virtue of the preceding provisions of this Act, the enactments specified in the Fourth Schedule to this Act, and all other enactments (including local enactments) to which any general provisions of Part II of that Schedule apply, shall have effect subject to the amendments and adaptations specified in that Schedule, being—

(a) amendments and adaptations for transferring functions of the Central Authority to the Electricity Council, the Generating Board or the Minister, or for applying to the Electricity Council, the Generating Board or the Minister provisions which apply to the Central Authority;

(b) amendments and adaptations consequential on the preceding provisions of this Act or on the amendments and adaptations referred to in the preceding paragraph;

(c) other amendments of a minor character.

(2) In so far as any reference in a local enactment to any authorised undertakers, or to any matter relating to any authorised undertakers,—

(a) has effect as adapted or modified by virtue of subsection (3) of section fifty-seven of the principal Act, and

(b) as so adapted or modified, has effect as a reference to the Central Authority, or to any matter relating to the Central Authority, that reference shall have effect as a reference to the Generating Board, or to the corresponding matter relating to the Generating Board, as the case may be; and so much of the said subsection (3) as confers power to prescribe other adaptations and modifications of local enactments shall apply in relation to the provisions of this Act (including the preceding provisions of this subsection) as it applies in relation to the provisions mentioned in that subsection.

(3) . . .

NOTES

Sub-s (3) was repealed by the SL(R) Act 1974.
Electricity Council. See s 3 ante.
Definitions. By virtue of s 40(1) ante, for "the Central Authority", see the Electricity Act 1947, s 1(3) ante, and for "authorised undertakers", "enactments", "functions", "local enactment" and "Minister", see s 67(1) of that Act. For "the Generating Board", see s 2(1) ante.
Principal Act. Ie the Electricity Act 1947 ante; see s 40(1) ante.

43 Short title, citation, commencement and extent

(1) This Act may be cited as the Electricity Act 1957; and the Electricity Act 1947 and this Act may be cited together as the Electricity Acts 1947 and 1957.

(2) (*Applies to Scotland only.*)

(3) Sections five to twenty-two, section twenty-four, section twenty-eight and section forty-two of this Act shall come into operation on the vesting date.

(4) (*Applies to Scotland only.*)

(5) This Act shall not extend to Northern Ireland.

NOTES

Vesting date. By virtue of s 1 of this Act (repealed), the vesting date was 1 January 1958.
Electricity Act 1947. See this title ante.

SCHEDULES

(*Sch 1, Pt I, paras 1–3, 5, 6 amend the Electricity Act 1947, s 7 ante; para 4 is spent on the repeal of sub-s (10) of that section; Sch 1, Pt II aplies to Scotland only.*)

SECOND SCHEDULE

Section 34

SUPPLEMENTARY PROVISIONS AS TO PUBLIC INQUIRIES

1. In the case of an application for the consent or authorisation of the Minister under paragraph (*b*) of section ten of the Schedule of 1899, where in accordance with any of the provisions of section thirty-four of this Act a public inquiry is to be held, and the application relates to land in the areas of two or more local planning authorities,—

    (*a*) the application shall not be the subject of a public inquiry in so far as it relates to land in the area of a local planning authority who have not notified the Minister that they object to the application, unless the Minister otherwise directs having regard to objections by other persons of which he has notice;

    (*b*) in so far as the application is to be the subject of a public inquiry in relation to land in the areas of two or more local planning authorities, the Minister may direct that separate public inquiries shall be held in the area of each of those authorities;

and, where the Minister gives any such directions, the provisions of the said section thirty-four shall apply with the necessary modifications:

Provided that for the purposes of sub-paragraph (*a*) of this paragraph a local planning authority who have notified the Minister that they object to the application shall be treated as not having done so if the Minister proposes to accede to the application subject to such modifications or conditions as will give effect to the objection.

2. Subsection (2) of section sixty-six of the principal Act (which relates to inquiries under that Act) shall apply in relation to inquiries held in pursuance of section thirty-four of this Act as it applies in relation to inquiries held in pursuance of the said section sixty-six.

3. For the purposes of section thirty-four of this Act the Minister may make regulations limiting the time within which notification of objections may be made to the Minister by local planning authorities, and providing that objections which are not notified within the time so limited may be disregarded for those purposes.

4. Any power to make regulations under section thirty-four of this Act, or under this Schedule, shall be exercisable by statutory instrument, and any instrument containing such regulations shall be subject to annulment in pursuance of a resolution of either House of Parliament; and different provision may be made by any such regulations in relation to different classes of applications or otherwise in relation to different classes of cases.

5. Where any regulations made under section thirty-four of this Act, or under this Schedule, are for the time being in force, any rules made under section thirty-four of the Electricity (Supply) Act 1919, in so far as they relate to applications to which the regulations apply, shall have effect subject to those regulations.

6. (*Applies to Scotland only.*)

7. In this Schedule "local planning authority" has the same meaning as in section thirty-four of this Act.

NOTES

Para 1: Minister. See, by virtue of s 40(1) ante, the Electricity Act 1947, s 67(1) ante.

Para 4: Statutory instrument; laid before Parliament. See the note to s 27 ante.

Para 7: Local planning authority. For meaning of "local planning authority" in s 34 ante, see s 33(3) ante and the note thereto.

Schedule of 1899. Ie the Schedule to the Electric Lighting (Clauses) Act 1899, as incorporated with the Electricity Act 1947; see s 30(1) ante, in conjunction with s 2(1) ante.

Principal Act. Ie the Electricity Act 1947; see s 2(1) ante.

Electricity Supply Act 1919, s 34. See this title ante.

Regulations under this Schedule. No regulations had been made under this Schedule up to 1 August 1985.

Note as to such regulations, paras 4, 5 above.

THIRD SCHEDULE

Section 41

Transitional Provisions

Consultative Councils

1.—(1) ...

(2) Any regulations made by virtue of the said section seven which are in force immediately before the vesting date, in so far as they relate to matters for which provision could be made by regulations under that section as amended by this Act, or under the said new section seven A, as the case may be, shall continue to have effect after that date, until revoked, as if they had been made under the said section seven as so amended, or under the said section seven A, as the case may be.

NOTES

Sub-para (1) was repealed by the SL(R) Act 1977.

Said section seven. Ie the Electricity Act 1947, s 7 ante.

Vesting date. By virtue of s 1 of this Act (repealed), the vesting date was 1 January 1958.

Any regulations etc. The regulations made under the Electricity Act 1947, s 7 ante, relating to England and Wales and in force up to the vesting date were the Electricity (Consultative Council) (Areas) Regulations

1948, SI 1948/898, which were amended by SI 1958/1 and SI 1977/710 and were still in force on 1 September 1985.

Section 7A. This section, which related to Scotland only, was repealed by the Electricity (Scotland) Act 1979, s 46(2), Sch 12.

Machinery for settling employment conditions

2.—(1) This paragraph applies to any agreement entered into by the Central Authority under section fifty-three of the principal Act (which made provision for purposes similar to those of section twelve of this Act), being an agreement which is in force immediately before the vesting date.

(2) Any such agreement relating to employed persons generally or to any class of employed persons—

(a) shall continue in operation on and after the vesting date until it is superseded by an agreement made in relation to employed persons generally or to that class of employed persons, as the case may be, under the corresponding provisions of section twelve of this Act, and

(b) while it so continues in operation, shall, subject to the following provisions of this paragraph, have effect, in relation to any time on or after the vesting date, as if the Electricity Council had been a party to the agreement and as if, in the provisions of the agreement, references (however expressed) to the Central Authority were references to the Electricity Council or to the Generating Board or to both of them, as the case may require.

(3) In so far as any agreement to which this paragraph applies provides for the constitution of a national organisation (that is to say, a council or other organisation whose functions under the agreement extend to the whole of Great Britain or the whole of England and Wales), the agreement shall have effect, in relation to any time on or after the vesting date, subject to the following provisions, that is to say,—

(a) any power for the Central Authority to appoint members of the organisation to represent the Authority generally shall be construed as a power for the Electricity Council to appoint members to represent the Council; and any member of the organisation so appointed by the Central Authority shall be treated as if he had been appointed by the Electricity Council to represent the Council;

(b) any other power for the Central Authority to appoint a member of the organisation shall be construed as if it were a power for the Electricity Council to appoint such a member, and as if any reference in that power to a division of the Authority were a reference to the corresponding division of the Generating Board; and any member of the organisation appointed by the Central Authority in the exercise of such a power shall be treated as if he had been appointed by the Electricity Council in the exercise of that power as modified by this provision.

(4) In so far as any agreement to which this paragraph applies provides for the constitution of an organisation other than a national organisation, the agreement shall have effect, in relation to any time on or after the vesting date, subject to the following provisions, that is to say,—

(a) any power for the Central Authority, or a division of the Central Authority, to appoint any members of the organisation shall be construed as a power for the Generating Board, or the corresponding division of the Generating Board, as the case may be, to appoint those members;

(b) any members of the organisation appointed by the Central Authority, or a division of the Central Authority, shall be treated as if they had been appointed by the Generating Board, or the corresponding division of the Generating Board, as the case may be.

(5) It shall be the duty of the Generating Board and of each of the Area Boards to comply with any agreement to which this paragraph applies, while it continues in operation in accordance with this paragraph.

(6) Subsection (1) of section twenty-six of this Act shall not apply to any agreement to which this paragraph applies.

NOTES

Vesting date. See the note to para 1 of this Schedule ante.

Employed. It is clear that this expression does not have here the narrow meaning assigned to it by the Electricity Act 1947, s 67(1) ante, which is applicable by virtue of s 40(1) ante.

Great Britain. See the note to s 2 ante.

Definitions. By virtue of s 40(1) ante, for "Area Board" and "the Central Authority", see the Electricity Act 1947, s 1(3) ante. For "the Generating Board", see s 2(1) ante.

Principal Act. Ie the Electricity Act 1947; see s 2(1) ante. S 53 of that Act was repealed by s 42(3) of, and Sch 5, Pt I to, this Act (repealed).

Tariffs

3.—(1)–(4) . . .

(5) Nothing in subsection (2) of section fourteen of this Act shall be construed as affecting any agreement in force immediately before the vesting date, being an agreement entered into by an Area Board under the provisions of subsection (7) of section thirty-seven of the principal Act (under which Area Boards are empowered to enter into special agreements with consumers).

NOTES

Sub-paras (1)–(4) were repealed by the SL(R) Act 1977.

Vesting date. See the note to para 1 of this Schedule ante.

Principal Act. Ie the Electricity Act 1947 ante; see s 2(1) ante.

Liabilities in respect of British Electricity Stock and [Government advances]

4.—(1) In respect of British Electricity Stock issued before the vesting date, the Electricity Council shall prepare a scheme for determining, as between the Electricity Council, the Generating Board and the Area Boards, the shares in which the ultimate responsibility for meeting obligations in respect of that stock is to be borne, and for allocating to the Council, to the Generating Board, and to each of the Area Boards respectively, responsibility in respect of stock so issued in accordance with the shares determined under that scheme.

(2) In paragraph (*b*) of subsection (2) of section eighteen of this Act, the reference to the proportions in which responsibility was allocated in respect of the stock to be redeemed or converted shall be construed, where the stock to be redeemed or converted is stock issued before the vesting date, as a reference to the proportions in which responsibility for that stock was allocated under the preceding sub-paragraph.

(3) Subsection (3) of section eighteen of this Act shall apply in relation to stock for which responsibility is allocated under this paragraph as it applies in relation to stock for which responsibility is allocated in accordance with that section.

NOTES

The words in square brackets in the heading were substituted by the National Loans Act 1968, s 2, Sch 1.

British Electricity Stock. See s 16(1) ante.

Vesting date. See the note to para 1 of this Schedule ante.

Electricity Council. See s 3 ante.

Scheme. For further provisions, see para 6 of this Schedule post.

Definitions. By virtue of s 40(1) ante, for "Area Boards", see the Electricity Act 1947, s 1(3) ante. For "the Generating Board", see s 2(1) ante.

5.—(1) The Electricity Council shall prepare a scheme for determining, as between the Electricity Council, the Generating Board and the Area Boards, the shares in which the ultimate responsibility is to be borne for meeting obligations in respect of [Government advances] made to the Central Authority, and for allocating to the Council, to the Generating Board, and to each of the Area Boards respectively, responsibility in respect of such [Government advances] in accordance with the shares determined under that scheme.

(2) Paragraph (*b*) of subsection (2) of section eighteen of this Act shall apply to British Electricity Stock issued by the Electricity Council for the purpose of repaying [Government advances] made to the Central Authority, with the substitution, for the words "stock to be redeemed or converted" of the words "[Government advances] to be repaid".

(3) Subsection (3) of section eighteen of this Act shall apply in relation to payments in respect of interest on, or the repayment of, [Government advances] made to the Central Authority as it applies in relation to payments in respect of interest on or the redemption of stock, as if any reference therein to responsibility under that section were a reference to responsibility under a scheme made by virtue of this paragraph.

NOTES

The words in square brackets were substituted by the National Loans Act 1968, s 2, Sch 1.
Electricity Council. See s 3 ante.
British Electricity Stock etc. See ss 15(2), 16(1) ante.
Scheme. For further provisions, see para 6 of this Schedule post.
Definitions. By virtue of s 40(1) ante, for "Area Boards" and "the Central Authority", see the Electricity Act 1947, s 1(3) ante, and for "Minister", see s 67(1) of that Act. For "the Generating Board", see s 2(1) ante, and for "Government advances", see s 15(7) ante.

6. Any scheme prepared by the Electricity Council under paragraph 4 or paragraph 5 of this Schedule shall not have effect until it has been settled by the Council with the Minister, after giving to the Generating Board and each of the Area Boards an opportunity to make representations thereon to him.

NOTES

Electricity Council. See s 3 ante.
Definitions. By virtue of s 40(1) ante, for "Area Boards", see the Electricity Act 1947, s 1(3) ante, and for "Minister", see s 67(1) of that Act ante. For "the Generating Board", see s 2(1) ante.

7–10. *(Repealed by the SL(R) Act 1977.)*

Pension rights

11. Notwithstanding any amendment of the principal Act having effect by virtue of this Act, in section fifty-four of that Act (which relates to pensions for former employees) any reference to an Electricity Board shall continue on and after the vesting date to include a reference to the Central Authority.

NOTES

Notwithstanding any amendment etc. This refers to the amendment of the Electricity Act 1947, s 1(3) ante, made by s 42(1) ante, Sch 4, Pt I, to this Act.
Electricity Board. Under the Electricity Act 1947, s 1(3), as previously in force, the expression "Electricity Boards" included the Central Authority.
Vesting date. See the note to para 1 of this Schedule ante.
Definitions. By virtue of s 40(1) ante, for "the Central Authority" and "Electricity Board", see the Electricity Act 1947, s 1(3) ante.
Principal Act. Ie the Electricity Act 1947; see s 2(1) ante. For s 54 of that Act, see this title ante.

12. Notwithstanding any amendment by this Act of subsection (6) of section three of the principal Act (which relates to the remuneration and pensions of members of the Central Authority and of Area Boards),—

(a) the provisions of that subsection (except so much of those provisions as requires the payments thereunder to be made by the Central Authority) shall continue on and after the vesting date to have effect in relation to persons who were members of the Central Authority at any time before the vesting date, other than persons to whom compensation becomes payable by virtue of subsection (1) of section twenty-seven of this Act;

(b) any liability arising by virtue of the said subsection (6) (in so far as that subsection has effect in accordance with the preceding sub-paragraph) to pay any pension on or after the vesting date to or in respect of persons who were members of the Central Authority shall be treated for the purposes of section twenty-six of this Act as if it had been a liability of the Central Authority subsisting immediately before the vesting date.

NOTES

Notwithstanding any amendment etc. This refers to the amendment made by s 42(1) ante, Sch 4, Pt I, to this Act.

Central Authority. See the note to s 2 ante.

Vesting date. See the note to para 1 of this Schedule ante.

Definitions. By virtue of s 40(1) ante, for "the Central Authority", see the Electricity Act 1947, s 1(3) ante, and for "pension", see s 67(1) of that Act ante.

Principal Act. Ie the Electricity Act 1947; see s 2(1) ante. For s 3(6) of that Act, see this title ante.

13, 14. *(Repealed by the SL(R) Act 1977.)*

FOURTH SCHEDULE

Section 42

AMENDMENT AND ADAPTATION OF ENACTMENTS

(Pt I repealed in part by the Electricity Act 1972, s 4, Schedule, the SL(R) Act 1977 and the Energy Act 1983, s 36, Sch 4, Pt I; the remainder amends the Electricity Act 1947, ss 1–4, 10, 19, 37, 45, 46, 51, 54, 58, 60, 63, 66, 67, Sch 3 ante.)

PART II

AMENDMENTS AND ADAPTATIONS OF OTHER ENACTMENTS

General amendments and adaptations

Subject to any specific amendment or adaptation made by the following provisions of this Schedule, the words "Generating Board" shall be substituted for the words "Central Authority", "Central Electricity Authority" or "British Electricity Authority" wherever those words occur in any enactment (including any local enactment) other than the Electricity Act 1947, and the enactments relating to income tax and the profits tax.

In the provisions of the Electricity (Supply) Acts 1882 to 1936, any reference to those Acts, or to one or more of those Acts, being a reference which by virtue of Part I of the Fourth Schedule to the principal Act is to be construed as including a reference to the principal Act, shall be construed as also including a reference to this Act.

Where any local enactment refers to any provisions of the principal Act which are amended by this Act, or, being provisions relating to the Central Authority, are re-enacted (with or without modifications) in this Act in the form of corresponding provisions relating to the Generating Board or the Electricity Council, the reference shall be construed as a reference to the provisions in question as amended by this Act, or to the corresponding provisions of this Act, as the case may be.

In any amendment made in any other enactment by the preceding provisions of this Part of this Schedule, or by the following provisions thereof, "the Generating Board" means the Central Electricity Generating Board constituted under this Act.

(Remainder repealed in part by the Local Government Act 1958, s 67, Sch 9, Pts II, V; the Tribunals and Inquiries Act 1958, s 15, Sch 2, Pt II; the Gas Act 1960, s 3(2); the General Rate Act 1967, s 117, Sch 14, Pt I; the House of Commons Disqualification Act 1975, Sch 3; the Electricity (Scotland) Act 1979, s 46(2), Sch 12; the Energy Act 1983, s 36, Sch 4, Pt I; amends the Gas Works Clauses Act 1847, s 18, incorporated with the Electric Lighting Act 1882 by virtue of s 12 thereof ante; the

Electric Lighting (Clauses) Act 1899, Schedule ante; the Electric Lighting Act 1909, s 2 ante; the Finance Act 1956, s 42 (repealed); or applies to Scotland only.)

(Sch 5 repealed by the SL(R) Act 1974.)

ELECTRICITY (AMENDMENT) ACT 1961
(9 & 10 Eliz 2 c 8)

An Act to empower the Central Electricity Generating Board to produce radioactive material in a nuclear reactor at any of the Board's generating stations for sale or supply to other persons, and to sell or supply radioactive material produced in any such reactor; and for purposes connected therewith   [2 March 1961]

Northern Ireland. This Act does not apply; see s 2(3) post.

1 Extension of Powers of Central Electricity Generating Board

(1) Notwithstanding anything in the proviso to subsection (7) of section two of the Electricity Act 1957 (which limits the powers of the Central Electricity Generating Board in respect of manufacture), the Central Electricity Generating Board shall have power (subject to the next following subsection) to produce radioactive material in a nuclear reactor at any of the Board's generating stations for the purpose of selling or otherwise supplying it to other persons; and the Board shall have power to sell or otherwise supply radioactive material produced in any such nuclear reactor.

(2) Subsection (9) of section two of the Electricity Act 1947 (which provides that the powers conferred on Electricity Boards by that Act and by section two of the said Act of 1957 shall not authorise those Boards to disregard any enactment or rule of law) shall apply to any power exercisable by virtue of the preceding subsection.

(3) In accordance with the preceding subsections, the Electricity Acts 1947 and 1957 shall have effect subject to the amendments and adaptations specified in the Schedule to this Act.

(4) . . .

(5) References in this Act to any enactment shall, except where the context otherwise requires, be construed as references to that enactment as amended or extended by or under any other enactment, including this Act.

(6) In this Act—

"radioactive material" means a substance produced by a process of nuclear fission or by any other process whereby a substance is subjected to bombardment by neutrons or is otherwise subjected to ionising radiations;
["nuclear reactor" has the same meaning as in the Nuclear Installations (Amendment) Act 1965]; and
"substance" means any natural or artificial substance, whether in solid or liquid form or in the form of a gas or vapour;

and for the purposes of this Act, and of section two of the Electricity Act 1957, a substance possessing radioactivity which is wholly or partly attributable to a process shall be taken to be a substance produced by that process, and any reference to producing radioactive material shall be construed accordingly.

NOTES

Sub-s (4) was repealed by the National Loans Act 1968, s 24(2), Sch 6, Pt I.

The definition in square brackets in sub-s (6) was substituted by the Nuclear Installations (Amendment) Act 1965, s 17(2).

Central Electricity Generating Board. This Board was established by the Electricity Act 1957, s 2 ante.

Electricity Act 1957, s 2; Electricity Act 1947, s 2(9). See this title ante.

Electricity Acts 1947 and 1957. Ie the Electricity Act 1947 ante and the Electricity Act 1957 ante; see s 43(1) of the 1957 Act ante.

Nuclear Installations (Amendment) Act 1965. Repealed, so far as concerns this definition, by the Nuclear Installations Act 1965, s 29(1). See now s 26(1) of the 1965 Act, Vol 47, title Trade and Industry (Pt 2(b)).

2 Short title, citation and extent

(1) This Act may be cited as the Electricity (Amendment) Act 1961.

(2) The Electricity Act 1947 and 1957 and this Act may be cited together as the Electricity Acts 1947 to 1961.

(3) This Act shall not extend to Scotland or to Northern Ireland.

NOTE

Electricity Acts 1947 and 1957. See the note to s 1 ante.

SCHEDULE

Section 1

AMENDMENT AND ADAPTATIONS

The Electricity Act 1947

The reference in subsection (9) of section two to the Electricity Act 1957, and (except where the context otherwise requires) any other reference to that Act, shall be construed as a reference to that Act as amended by this Act.

.   .   .   .   .   .

NOTE

The words omitted amend the Electricity Act 1957, s 2 ante.

Electricity Act 1957, s 2(9). See this title ante.

ELECTRICITY AND GAS ACT 1963

(1963 c 59)

An Act to increase the statutory limits imposed on the amounts outstanding in respect of borrowings by the Electricity Council and Electricity Boards and the Gas Council and Area Gas Boards; to make further provision for Exchequer advances to certain of those bodies; to provide in certain cases for compensating members of those bodies for loss of office; and for purposes connected with the matters aforesaid   [18 December 1963]

Northern Ireland. This Act does not apply.

1 *(Repealed by the Electricity Act 1972, s 4(3), Schedule.)*

2 Exchequer advances to Electricity and Gas Councils and to Scottish Electricity Boards

(1) The Minister of Power (in this section referred to as "the Minister") may with the approval of the Treasury advance to the Electricity Council . . . any sums which, within the limits imposed by the relevant enactments, the Council . . . have power to borrow.

(2) The enactments specified in Schedule 1 to this Act shall have effect subject to the amendments specified in that Schedule, in addition to those made by section 1 of this Act . . .

(3) Any advances made by the Minister . . . under this section shall be repaid to him at such times and by such methods, and interest thereon shall be paid to him at such rates and at such times, as he may with the approval of the Treasury from time to time direct.

(4) The Treasury may issue out of the [National Loans Fund] to the Minister . . . such sums as are necessary to enable them to make advances under this section.

(5) . . .

(6) Any sums received by the Minister . . . under subsection (3) of this section shall be paid into the [National Loans Fund], . . .

(7) In respect of each financial year the Minister . . . shall each prepare, in such form and manner as the Treasury may direct, an account of sums issued to him under this section and of the sums to be paid into the [National Loans Fund] under subsection (6) of this section and of the disposal by him of those sums respectively, and shall send it to the Comptroller and Auditor General not later than the end of November following that financial year; and the Comptroller and Auditor General shall examine, certify and report on the account and lay copies of it, together with his report, before each House of Parliament.

(8) Any account prepared under subsection (7) of this section—

    (a) (spent)
    (b) in any case, shall include any sums received by the Minister, or, as the case may be, the Secretary of State, under subsection (4) of that section in respect of the financial year to which the account relates;

and neither the Minister nor the Secretary of State shall be required to prepare an account under that section in respect of the year 1963–1964 or any subsequent year.

(9) In relation to the making of advances to any of the Councils . . . mentioned in subsection (1) of this section after the passing of this Act, this section shall have effect in substitution for the provisions of section 42 of the Finance Act 1956; but (except as provided by subsection (8) of this section) this section shall have effect without prejudice to the operation of any provisions of that section in relation to advances made before the passing of this Act.

NOTES

The words omitted in the first place from sub-s (1) were in part repealed by the Electricity (Scotland) Act 1979, s 46(2), Sch 12, and in part repealed by the Gas Act 1972, s 49(3), Sch 8; the words omitted in the second place from that subsection were repealed by the Electricity (Scotland) Act 1979, s 46(2), Sch 12.

The words omitted from sub-s (2) were repealed by the Electricity Act 1972, s 1(5).

The words omitted from sub-ss (3), (4), (7)–(9), and the words omitted in the first place from sub-s (6), were repealed by the Electricity (Scotland) Act 1979, s 46(2), Sch 12.

The words in square brackets in sub-ss (4), (6), (7) were substituted, and sub-s (5) and the words omitted in the second place from sub-s (6) were repealed, by the National Loans Act 1968, s 2, Sch 1.

Sub-s (1): Minister of Power. The functions of the Minister of Power under this Act are now exercised by the Secretary of State for Energy; see the Preliminary Note to this title.

Treasury. Ie the Commissioners of HM Treasury; see the Interpretation Act 1978, s 5, Sch 1, Vol 41, title Statutes.

Electricity Council. See the Electricity Act 1957, s 3 ante.

Limits imposed by the relevant enactments. This is to be taken as a reference to all relevant limits on borrowing for the time being in force under the enactments relating to electricity; see the Electricity Act 1972, s 1(5) post.

Sub-s (3): Interest. The rate of interest is to be determined in accordance with the National Loans Act 1968, Vol 30, title Money (Pt 3); see s 5 of, and Sch 1 to, that Act, as amended by the Finance Act 1982, s 153(2).

Sub-s (4): National Loans Fund. See the National Loans Act 1968, s 1, Vol 30, title Money (Pt 3).

Finance Act 1956, s 42. That section was repealed by s 4(2) of, and Sch 2 to, this Act.

3 Payments to members of Councils and Boards of compensation for loss of office

(1) Where, after the passing of this Act, a person ceases, otherwise than on the expiry of his term of office, to be a member of a Council or Board to which this section applies, and it appears to the appropriate Minister that there are special circumstances which make it right that that person should receive compensation, that Minister may with the approval of the Treasury require that Council or Board to make to that person a payment of such amount as may be determined by the appropriate Minister with the approval of the Treasury.

(2) This section applies to the following Councils and Boards, that is to say—

    (a) the Electricity Council;
    (b) the Central Electricity Generating Board;
    (c) Area Boards within the meaning of the Electricity Act 1947;
    (d)–(g) . . .

(3) In this section "the appropriate Minister" . . . means the Minister of Power . . .

NOTES

Sub-s (2)(d), (e), and the words omitted from sub-s (3), were repealed by the Electricity (Scotland) Act 1979, s 46(2), Sch 12. Sub-s (2)(f), (g) were repealed by the Gas Act 1972, s 49(3), Sch 8.

Passing of this Act. The Act was passed, ie received the Royal Assent, on 18 December 1963.

Appropriate Minister. Note sub-s (3) above and the note "Minister of Power" to s 2 ante.

Treasury. See the note to s 2 ante.

Electricity Council. See the Electricity Act 1957, s 3 ante.

Central Electricity Generating Board. See the Electricity Act 1957, s 2 ante.

Electricity Act 1947. The Area Boards within the meaning of that Act are the Boards established under s 1(2) thereof ante, viz, the Boards mentioned in Sch 1 thereto ante; see s 1(3) thereof.

4 Short title, repeal and consequential provision

(1) This Act may be cited as the Electricity and Gas Act 1963.

(2) The enactments specified in Schedule 2 to this Act are hereby repealed to the extent specified in the third column of that Schedule:

Provided that (without prejudice to section 2(8) of this Act) the repeal of section 42 of the Finance Act 1956 shall not affect the operation of any provisions of that section in relation to advances made thereunder before the passing of this Act.

(3) ...

___

NOTES

Sub-s (3) was repealed by the Electricity (Scotland) Act 1979, s 46(2), Sch 12.
Passing of this Act. See the note to s 3 ante.

___

(*Sch 1 repealed in part by the Gas Act 1972, s 49(3), Sch 8, the Electricity (Scotland) Act 1979, s 46(2), Sch 12; remainder amends the Electricity Act 1957, s 15 ante; Sch 2 repealed by the SL(R) Act 1974; Sch 3 repealed by the Electricity (Scotland) Act 1979, s 46(2), Sch 12.*)

NUCLEAR INSTALLATIONS (AMENDMENT) ACT 1965

(1965 c 6)

An Act to make new provision in place of or amend certain provisions of the Nuclear Installations (Licensing and Insurance) Act 1959 so as to give effect to certain international agreements; to make other amendments to that Act; and for connected purposes [23 March 1965]

(*Whole Act except s 17(2) repealed by the Nuclear Installations Act 1965, s 29(1); s 17(2) amends the Electricity (Amendment) Act 1961, s 1(6) ante.*)

GAS AND ELECTRICITY ACT 1968

(1968 c 39)

An Act to increase the statutory limits on the amounts outstanding in respect of borrowings by the Gas Council and Area Gas Boards; to provide for the borrowing by the Electricity Council, the Scottish Electricity Boards and the Gas Council of money in foreign currency; to enable the said Councils and Boards and other electricity authorities to furnish overseas aid; to increase the number of members of the Gas Council; and for connected purposes [30 July 1968]

Northern Ireland. This Act does not apply.

1 (*Repealed by the Gas Act 1972, s 49(3), Sch 8.*)

2 Power of Electricity Council to borrow foreign currency by issue of securities

(1) Subject to the provisions of this section, the Electricity Council may [with the consent of the Secretary of State (which shall require the approval of the Treasury), borrow] any sums of foreign currency ... for all or any of the purposes mentioned in section 15(2) of the Electricity Act 1957 [or for the purposes of the repayment of the principal of sums borrowed by them under this section or of] the redemption of securities previously issued under this section, and they may create and issue securities required for the purpose of borrowing money in manner aforesaid.

(2) The amount outstanding in respect of the principal of any [sums borrowed] under this section shall be included in the aggregate of the amounts outstanding in respect of loans raised by the Electricity Council and Electricity Boards in England and Wales which is subject to the limit imposed by section 15(5) of the Electricity Act 1957; but this subsection shall not prevent the Electricity Council from borrowing in excess of the said limit for the purpose of [repaying the principal of any sums borrowed by them under this section or for the purpose of] redeeming any securities issued under this section which they are required or entitled to redeem.

(3) Section 17 (Treasury guarantees), [and section] 18(1) to (3) (estimates of Boards' requirements and allocations to them of liabilities in respect of British Electricity Stock) . . . of the Electricity Act 1957 shall have effect as if references to British Electricity Stock included references to [sums borrowed or] securities issued under this section.

(4) The prohibition contained in subsection (6) of section 15 of the Electricity Act 1957 of borrowing except in accordance with the provisions of that section shall not apply to borrowing under this section.

(5) Nothing in this section shall be taken as exempting the Electricity Council from the provisions of any order under section 1 of the Borrowing (Control and Guarantees) Act 1946 or from the provisions of the Exchange Control Act 1947.

NOTES

The words in the first pair of square brackets in sub-s (1) and those in the first pair of square brackets in sub-s (3) were substituted, and the words omitted from sub-s (3) were repealed, by the Statutory Corporations (Financial Provisions) Act 1975, s 7(1), (2), Sch 4, para 4, Sch 5; the other words in square brackets in sub-ss (1), (3) and the words in square brackets in sub-s (2) were substituted, and the words omitted from sub-s (1) were repealed, by the Statutory Corporations (Financial Provisions) Act 1974, s 4, Sch 2.

Electricity Council. See the Electricity Act 1957, s 3 ante.

Secretary of State. Ie one of Her Majesty's Principal Secretaries of State; see the Interpretation Act 1978, s 5, Sch 1, Vol 41, title Statutes. The Secretary of State here concerned is the Secretary of State for Energy; see the Preliminary Note to this title.

Treasury. Ie the Commissioners of HM Treasury; see the Interpretation Act 1978, s 5, Sch 1, Vol 41, title Statutes.

Foreign currency. Ie currency other than sterling; see s 7(1) post.

Electricity Boards in England and Wales. See, by virtue of the Electricity Act 1947, ss 1(3), 67(1) ante, s 1(2) of that Act.

Electricity Act 1957, ss 15, 17, 18. See this title ante.

Borrowing (Control and Guarantees) Act 1946, s 1; Exchange Control Act 1947. See Vol 30, title Money (Pt 1).

3–6 *(S 3 repealed by the Statutory Corporations (Financial Provisions) Act 1975, s 7(2), Sch 5 and the Electricity (Scotland) Act 1979, s 46(1), Sch 10, para 9; ss 4, 6 repealed by the Gas Act 1972, s 49(3), Sch 8; s 5 repealed by the Overseas Development and Co-operation Act 1980, s 18(1), Sch 2, Pt I, and replaced by s 2(1)–(3), (6) of, and Sch 1, Pt I to, that Act, Vol 7, title* Commonwealth and Other Territories (Pt 4).*)*

7 Interpretation

(1) In this Act, except where the context otherwise requires—

"the Minister" means the Minister of Power; and
"foreign currency" means any currency other than sterling.

(2) Except where the context otherwise requires, any reference in this Act to any other enactment is a reference to that enactment as amended by any subsequent enactment, and includes a reference to it as applied by any subsequent enactment.

NOTE

　Minister of Power. The functions of the Minister of Power are now exercised by the Secretary of State for Energy; see the Preliminary Note to this title.

8 Short title

This Act may be cited as the Gas and Electricity Act 1968.

ELECTRICITY ACT 1972

(1972 c 17)

An Act to increase the statutory limits imposed on the amounts outstanding in respect of borrowings by the Electricity Council and Electricity Boards, to authorise contributions by the Secretary of State to expenditure intended to promote employment and to make further provision for the transfer of property between Electricity Boards 　　[23 March 1972]

　Northern Ireland. This Act does not apply.

1 Borrowing powers of electricity authorities

　(1), (2) . . .

　(3) Any power to make an order which is exercisable by virtue of this section includes power to revoke or vary any such order by a subsequent order.

　(4) Any such power shall be exercisable by statutory instrument, and no order shall be made in the exercise of any such power unless a draft of the order has been laid before the Commons House of Parliament and has been approved by resolution of that House.

　(5) The reference in section 2(1) of the Electricity and Gas Act 1963 (Government advances) to the limits on borrowing imposed by the relevant enactments shall be taken as a reference to all relevant limits on borrowing for the time being in force under the enactments relating to electricity . . .

NOTES

　Sub-s (1) amends the Electricity Act 1957, s 15(5) ante. Sub-s (2) repealed by the Electricity (Scotland) Act 1979, s 46(2), Sch 12. The words omitted from sub-s (5) were repealed by the Gas Act 1972, s 49(3), Sch 8.

　Revoke or vary. The express power to revoke or vary orders is necessary because the Interpretation Act 1978, s 14, Vol 41, title Statutes, does not extend to powers to make such instruments contained in Acts passed before 1 January 1979; see s 22(1) of, and Sch 2, para 3 to, that Act.

　Statutory instrument; laid before ... Parliament. For provisions as to statutory instruments generally, see the Statutory Instruments Act 1946, Vol 41, title Statutes; and as to statutory instruments, drafts of which are required to be laid before Parliament, see s 6 of that Act, and the Laying of Documents before Parliament (Interpretation) Act 1948, Vol 41, title Statutes.

　Electricity and Gas Act 1963, s 2(1). See this title ante.

　Order under this section. The Electricity (Borrowing Powers) Order 1974, SI 1974/1295 (specifying a sum of £6,500 million).

2 Contributions by Secretary of State towards expenditure intended to promote employment

　(1) There may be defrayed out of moneys provided by Parliament such sums not in the aggregate exceeding [£45 million] as may be required by the Secretary of State for the purpose of making with the approval of the Treasury contributions towards expenses to which this section applies.

(2) This section applies—

    (a) to expenses incurred by the Electricity Council or any Electricity Board in or in connection with the carrying out of any project which is commenced before 1st April 1974 and which, pursuant to an agreement entered into with the Secretary of State with a view to promoting employment (whether or not in the electricity industry) is, in whole or in part, commenced or carried out earlier than it would have been but for the agreement, and

    (b) to expenses incurred by any of those bodies in or by reason of the purchase before that date of materials for any project, being a purchase which, pursuant to any such agreement, was effected earlier than it would have been but for the agreement.

(3) This section applies to expenses incurred before as well as after the passing of this Act.

(4) In this section "Electricity Board" has the same meaning as in the Electricity Act 1947.

NOTES

The words in square brackets in sub-s (1) were substituted by the Energy Act 1976, s 16.

Secretary of State. Ie one of Her Majesty's Principal Secretaries of State; see the Interpretation Act 1978, s 5, Sch 1, Vol 41, title Statutes. The Secretary of State here concerned is the Secretary of State for Energy; see the Preliminary Note to this title ante.

Treasury. Ie the Commissioners of HM Treasury; see the Interpretation Act 1978, s 5, Sch 1, Vol 41, title Statutes.

Electricity Council. See the Electricity Act 1957, s 3 ante.

Electricity Act 1947. See this title ante. For the meaning of "Electricity Board", see s 1 of that Act.

3 (*Repealed by the SL(R) Act 1978.*)

4 Citation, construction and repeals

(1) This Act may be cited as the Electricity Act 1972 . . .

(2) Except where the context otherwise requires, references in this Act to any enactment are references thereto as amended by any other enactment, including any enactment contained in this Act.

(3) . . .

NOTES

The words omitted from sub-s (1) were repealed by the Electricity (Scotland) Act 1979, s 46(2), Sch 12. Sub-s (3) was repealed by the SL(R) Act 1978.

(*Schedule repealed by the SL(R) Act 1978.*)

ENERGY ACT 1976

(1976 c 76)

An Act to make further provision with respect to the nation's resources and use of energy
[22 November 1976]

Northern Ireland. The provisions of this Act printed in this title do not apply; see s 23(3) post, and cf, as respects s 16 post, the Electricity Act 1972, s 2 ante.

1–5 (*See Vol 47, title* Trade and Industry (Pt 1).)

Maintenance of fuel reserves

6 (*See Vol 47, title* Trade and Industry (Pt 1).)

7 Fuel stocks at power stations

(1) Directions under this section may be given—

(*a*) to the Central Electricity Generating Board, an Area Electricity Board, the North of Scotland Hydro-Electric Board or the South of Scotland Electricity Board;

(*b*) to any person who has the means of generating electricity for the purposes of an undertaking carried on by him.

(2) In respect of any electricity generating station the Secretary of State may direct any of those Boards and, in respect of a station of a capacity of 100 megawatts or more, he may direct any such person as is referred to in subsection (1)(*b*)—

(*a*) to make such arrangements with respect to fuel stocks held at or near that generating station for the purposes of its operation as will—

(i) enable those stocks to be brought within a specified time to, and thereafter maintained at, a specified level, and

(ii) ensure that they do not fall below that level, except as may be permitted by the terms of the direction or by authority of the Secretary of State;

(*b*) to create such stocks and make such arrangements with respect to them.

(3) The amount of fuel stocks may be specified by reference to the period for which it would enable the generating station to be maintained in operation.

(4) In this section "specified" means specified by the Secretary of State's direction and a direction may specify—

(*a*) the cases and circumstances in which fuel stocks are to be treated as held at or near any generating station;

(*b*) the extent to which the direction may be treated as complied with where access can be had to stocks held for the use of a number of consumers, under arrangements made or approved by the Secretary of State;

(*c*) the manner in which the period mentioned in subsection (3) above is to be calculated.

NOTES

Directions. For power to revoke or vary a direction and provide by order for the same purpose as a direction, see s 17(2), (5) of this Act, Vol 47, title Trade and Industry (Pt 1).

Central Electricity Generating Board. The Board was established by the Electricity Act 1957, s 2 ante.

Area Electricity Board. Area Electricity Boards were established by the Electricity Act 1947, s 1(2), Sch 1 ante.

Secretary of State. Ie one of Her Majesty's Principal Secretaries of State for the time being; see the Interpretation Act 1978, s 5, Sch 1, Vol 41, title Statutes. The Secretary of State here concerned is the Secretary of State for Energy; see the Preliminary Note to this title.

Offences and penalties. See ss 18(2), (4), (5), 19(1), (2) of this Act, Vol 47, title Trade and Industry (Pt 1).

Administration and enforcement. See s 18(1) of, and Sch 2 to, this Act, Vol 47, title Trade and Industry (Pt 1).

Definitions. For "undertaking", see s 21 post. Note as to "specified", sub-s (4) above.

Orders. Up to 1 August 1985, no order had been made under this section by virtue of s 17(5) of this Act, Vol 47, title Trade and Industry (Pt 1).

8–11 (*S 8 repealed by the Oil and Gas (Enterprise) Act 1982, ss 12(2), 37(2), Sch 4; for s 9 (which was substituted for the original ss 9–11), see Vol 19, title Gas.*)

Other measures for controlling energy sources and promoting economy

12, 13 (*For s 12, see Vol 19, title Gas; s 13 repealed by the Gas Act 1980, s 1(4).*)

14 Fuelling of new and converted power stations

(1) A person who proposes to carry out works—

    (*a*) for the establishment of an electricity generating station to be fuelled by crude liquid petroleum, any petroleum product or natural gas; or

    (*b*) for the conversion of an electricity generating station with a view to its being so fuelled,

shall, unless his case is one excepted by order of the Secretary of State under subsection (4), give written notice of the proposal to him.

(2) A person who proposes—

    (*a*) to enter into contractual or other arrangements for obtaining a supply of natural gas as fuel for an electricity generating station; or

    (*b*) to extend the duration of any such arrangements (whether made before or after the passing of this Act),

shall, unless the arrangements fall within the scope of a general authority granted by the Secretary of State by order under subsection (5), give written notice of the proposal to him.

(3) The Secretary of State may, if he thinks it expedient having regard to current energy policies, direct that a proposal notified to him under this section be not carried out, or be carried out in accordance with conditions specified in the direction.

(4) The Secretary of State may by order prescribe cases in which notice under subsection (1) above need not be given; and the cases prescribed may be those where—

    (*a*) the plant is of less than specified capacity or is used only for specified purposes; or

    (*b*) such other circumstances obtain as make it unnecessary in the Secretary of State's opinion for him to be given notice under the subsection.

(5) The Secretary of State may by order grant authority for the purposes of subsection (2) above for fuel supply arrangements of any description specified in the order.

(6) This section does not affect—

    (*a*) section 2 of the Electric Lighting Act 1909;

    (*b*) . . .

    (*c*) section 21 of the Control of Pollution Act 1974;

    (*d*) section 11 of the Local Government (Miscellaneous Provisions) Act 1976,

(all of which operate so as, in certain circumstances, to require the Secretary of State's consent for power station construction etc.).

NOTES

Sub-s (6)(*b*) was repealed by the Energy Act 1983, s 36, Sch 4, Pt I.

Secretary of State. See the note to s 7 ante.

Written. Expressions referring to writing are, unless the contrary intention appears, to be construed as including references to other modes of representing or reproducing words in a visible form; see the Interpretation Act 1978, s 5, Sch 1, Vol 41, title Statutes.

Direct. For power to revoke or vary a direction and provide by order for the same purpose as a direction, see s 17(2), (5) of this Act, Vol 47, title Trade and Industry (Pt 1).

Offences and penalties. See ss 18(2), (4), (5), 19(1), (2) of this Act, Vol 47, title Trade and Industry (Pt 1).

Administration and enforcement. See s 18(1) of, and Sch 2 to, this Act, Vol 47, title Trade and Industry (Pt 1).

Definitions. For "natural gas" and "petroleum products", see s 21 post.

Electric Lighting Act 1909, s 2. See this title ante.

Control of Pollution Act 1974, s 21. See Vol 35, title Public Health.

Local Government (Miscellaneous Provisions) Act 1976, s 11. See Vol 25, title Local Government.

Orders under this section. Up to 1 August 1985 no order had been made under sub-s (4) or (5) above or under sub-s (3) above by virtue of s 17(5) of this Act, Vol 47, title Trade and Industry (Pt 1).

For general provisions as to orders, see s 17(1)–(4) of this Act, Vol 47, title Trade and Industry (Pt 1).

15 (*See Vol 47, title* Trade and Industry (Pt 1).)

16 Finance for power projects

The limit on the aggregate of the sums payable out of money provided by Parliament under section 2(1) of the Electricity Act 1972 (projects advanced in the programme with a view to promoting employment) is increased from £25 million to £45 million.

NOTE

Electricity Act 1972, s 2(1). See this title ante.

17–20 (*For ss 17, 18(1), (2), (4), (5), 19, 20, see Vol 47, title* Trade and Industry (Pt 1); *for s 18(3), see Vol 19, title* Gas.)

21 Interpretation

In this Act—

> . . . . . .

> "natural gas" means any gas derived from natural strata;
> "petroleum products" means the following substances produced directly or indirectly from crude, that is to say, fuels, lubricants, bitumen, wax, industrial spirits and any wide-range substance (meaning a substance whose final boiling point at normal atmospheric pressure is more than 50 degrees C higher than its initial boiling point);

> . . . . . .

> "undertaking" includes a business, and also any activity carried on by a body of persons, whether corporate or unincorporate; and

> . . . . .

NOTE

The definitions omitted from this section where indicated by dots, are not relevant to the provisions of this Act printed in this title, and are printed in Vol 47, title Trade and Industry (Pt 1).

22 (*See Vol 47, title* Trade and Industry (Pt 1).)

23 Citation, commencement and extent

(1) This Act may be cited as the Energy Act 1976.

(2) This Act shall come into operation on a day appointed by order of the Secretary of State, and different days may be so appointed for different provisions and for different purposes.

(3) This Act, except sections 7 to 11, 13 and 14 and paragraph 5 of Schedule 2, extends to Northern Ireland.

(4) (*See Vol 47, title* Trade and Industry (Pt 1).)

NOTES

Secretary of State. See the note to s 7 ante.

Orders under this section. The Energy Act 1976 (Commencement No 1) Order 1976, SI 1976/1964 (bringing this section into force on 30 November 1976); the Energy Act 1976 (Commencement No 2)

Order 1976, SI 1976/2127 (bringing ss 7, 14, 16 ante and s 21 ante, so far as it relates to those sections, into force on 1 January 1977); and the Energy Act 1976 (Commencement No 3) Order 1977, SI 1977/652 (which relates to provisions not set out in this title).

(*For Schs 1–4, see Vol 47, title* Trade and Industry (Pt 1).)

NUCLEAR SAFEGUARDS AND ELECTRICITY (FINANCE) ACT 1978

(1978 c 25)

An Act to make provision for giving effect to an International Agreement for the application of Safeguards in the United Kingdom in connection with the Treaty on the Non-Proliferation of Nuclear Weapons; and to authorise contributions by the Secretary of State to expenditure by the Central Electricity Generating Board in connection with the construction of the second stage of the Board's generating station at Drax [30 June 1978]

Northern Ireland. S 5 post does not apply; see s 6(2) post.

1–4 (*See Vol 47, title* Trade and Industry (Pt 2(b).)

Contributions in connection with Drax power Station

5 Contributions by Secretary of State towards expenditure in connection with stage two of Drax power station

(1) There may be defrayed out of money provided by Parliament such sums not in the aggregate exceeding £50 million as may be required by the Secretary of State for the purpose of making, with the approval of the Treasury, contributions towards expenditure incurred by the Central Electricity Generating Board in or in connection with the execution of Drax works, being contributions made by him in consideration of the Board commencing, at his request, the construction of the second stage of their coal-fired electricity generating station at Drax in the county of North Yorkshire earlier than they would otherwise have done.

(2) In this section "Drax works" means—

(*a*) works for the construction of the second stage of the Board's said generating station; and

(*b*) other works which the Board consider requisite in connection with the construction of the second stage of that station.

(3) The reference in subsection (1) above to expenditure incurred by the Board includes expenditure incurred as there mentioned before as well as after the passing of this Act.

NOTES

Secretary of State. Ie one of Her Majesty's Principal Secretaries of State; see the Interpretation Act 1978, s 5, Sch 1, Vol 41, title Statutes. The Secretary of State here concerned is the Secretary of State for Energy; see the Preliminary Note to this title.

Treasury. Ie the Commissioners of HM Treasury; see the Interpretation Act 1978, s 5, Sch 1, Vol 41, title Statutes.

Central Electricity Generating Board. For the establishment, constitution and functions of the Central Electricity Generating Board, see the Electricity Act 1957, s 2 ante.

Supplemental

6 Short title and extent

(1) This Act may be cited as the Nuclear Safeguards and Electricity (Finance) Act 1978.

(2) This Act extends to Northern Ireland.

ENERGY ACT 1983

(1983 c 25)

ARRANGEMENT OF SECTIONS

PART I

ELECTRICITY

Private generation and supply

Miscellaneous and general

PART II

NUCLEAR INSTALLATIONS

PART III

GENERAL

An Act to amend the law relating to electricity so as to facilitate the generation and supply of electricity by persons other than Electricity Boards, and for certain other purposes; and to amend the law relating to the duties of persons responsible for nuclear installations and to compensation for breach of those duties   [9 May 1983]

Commencement. This Act, with the exception of certain repeals made by Sch 4, Pt I came into force on 1 June 1983 or 1 September 1983; see s 37(1), the orders noted thereto and the "Commencement" notes throughout the Act. No order had been made bringing the remainder of the Act into force up to 1 September 1985.

Northern Ireland. Pt I of this Act (except Sch 2, para 11) and Sch 4, Pt I do not extend to Northern Ireland, but otherwise this Act applies; see s 38(2) post.

PART I

ELECTRICITY

Private generation and supply

1 (*Repeals the Electric Lighting Act 1909, s 23 and the Electricity (Supply) Act 1919, s 11.*)

2 Notice of construction or extension of generating stations

(1) Subject to subsection (5) below, any person other than an Electricity Board or a local authority who proposes—

(*a*) to construct or extend an electricity generating station having plant with a rating exceeding 10 megawatts, or

(*b*) to extend an existing electricity generating station in such a way that it will have plant with such a rating,

shall give written notice of his proposal to the Area Board for the area in which the station is or will be or, if it is or will be within the district of a Scottish Board, to that Board.

(2) The Secretary of State may make regulations as to the time when a notice under this section is to be given and the particulars which it is to contain.

(3) A person who is required to give a notice under this section shall be guilty of an offence if the work of construction or extension begins without the required notice having been given.

(4) A person guilty of an offence under this section shall be liable—

(*a*) on conviction on indictment, to a fine, or

(*b*) on summary conviction, to a fine not exceeding the statutory maximum.

(5) (*Applies to Scotland only.*)

(6) References in this section to extending a generating station are references to increasing the rating of its plant.

NOTES

Commencement. This Part (ss 1–26), except ss 21, 22 post was brought into force on 1 June 1983, and ss 21, 22 post were brought into force on 1 September 1983, by the Energy Act 1983 (Commencement No 1) Order 1983, SI 1983/790, made under s 37(1) post.

Sub-s (1): Person. Unless the contrary intention appears this includes a body of persons corporate or unincorporate; see the Interpretation Act 1978, s 5, Sch 1, Vol 41, title Statutes.

Written. Expressions referring to writing are, unless the contrary intention appears, to be construed as including references to other modes of representing or reproducing words in a visible form; see the Interpretation Act 1978, s 5, Sch 1, Vol 41, title Statutes.

Sub-s (2): Secretary of State. Ie one of Her Majesty's Principal Secretaries of State; see the Interpretation Act 1978, s 5, Sch 1, Vol 41, title Statutes. The Secretary of State here concerned is the Secretary of State for Energy; see the Preliminary Note to this title.

Sub-s (3): Person . . . guilty of an offence. Except when the penalty is inappropriate or where, by the nature of the offence, it must be committed by an individual, a corporation may be convicted for the criminal acts (including those requiring mens rea) of the directors and managers who represent the directing mind and will of the corporation and control what it does (*DPP v Kent and Sussex Contractors Ltd* [1944] KB 146, [1944] 1 All ER 119; *R v ICR Haulage Ltd* [1944] KB 551 [1944] 1 All ER 691, CCA; *Tesco Supermarkets Ltd v Nattrass* [1972] AC 153, [1971] 2 All ER 127, HL), but it cannot be convicted for the criminal acts of its inferior servants or agents unless the offence is one for which an employer or principal may be vicariously liable (*John Henshall (Quarries) Ltd v Harvey* [1965] 2 QB 233, [1965] 1 All ER 725; *Tesco Supermarkets Ltd v Nattrass* supra; *R v Andrews-Weatherfoil Ltd* [1972] 1 All ER 65, CA). See further, on the criminal liability of corporations, 9 Halsbury's Laws (4th edn) para 1379 and 11 Halsbury's Laws (4th edn) para 34, and as to vicarious liability, 11 Halsbury's Laws (4th edn) paras 51 et seq.

As to proceedings for offences, and the liability of officers of a body corporate, see s 23 post.

Sub-s (4): Conviction on indictment. All proceedings on indictment are to be brought before the Crown Court; see the Supreme Court Act 1981, s 46(1), Vol 11, title Courts. As to the trial of indictments generally, see 11 Halsbury's Laws (4th edn) paras 225 et seq.

Fine. There is no specific limit to the amount of the fine which may be imposed on conviction on indictment, but the fine should be within the offender's capacity to pay; see, in particular, *R v Churchill (No 2)* [1967] 1 QB 190, [1966] 2 All ER 215, CCA; revsd on other grounds sub nom *Churchill v Walton* [1967] 2 AC 224, [1967] 1 All ER 497, HL; and see also the Bill of Rights (1688), s 1, Vol 10, title Constitutional Law (Pt 1).

Summary conviction. Summary jurisdiction and procedure are mainly governed by the Magistrates' Courts Act 1980, Vol 27, title Magistrates, and by rules made under s 144 of that Act.

Definitions. For "Electricity Board", "local authority" and "statutory maximum", see s 26 post; and, by virtue of s 26 post, for "Area Board", see the Electricity Act 1947, s 1(3) ante. Note as to references to extending a generating station, sub-s (6) above.

Regulations under this section. The Electricity (Private Generating Stations and Requests by Private Generators and Suppliers) Regulations 1984, SI 1984/136, reg 2, Sch 1.

For general provisions as to regulations, see s 24 post.

3 Nuclear-powered generating stations

(1) Subject to subsection (5) below, no person shall construct, extend or become the operator of a nuclear-powered generating station without the consent of the Secretary of State.

(2) A consent given for the purposes of this section may be subject to such conditions as the Secretary of State thinks fit.

(3) A person who contravenes subsection (1) above, or any condition of a consent given for the purposes of this section, shall be guilty of an offence.

(4) A person guilty of an offence under this section shall be liable—

(*a*) on conviction on indictment, to a fine, or

(*b*) on sumary conviction, to a fine not exceeding the statutory maximum.

(5) This section shall not apply to the construction, extension or operation of a generating station by an Electricity Board.

(6) In this section "nuclear-powered generating station" means an electricity generating station the operation of which requires a licence under section 1 of the Nuclear Installations Act 1965; and references to extending a generating station are references to increasing the rating of its plant.

NOTES

Commencement. See the note to s 2 ante.

Person; Secretary of State. See the notes to s 2 ante.

Thinks fit. Statutory powers are often conferred in subjective terms, the competent authority being entitled to act, eg, when it "thinks fit", or when it is "satisfied" or it "appears" to it that a prescribed state of affairs exists, but the inherent jurisdiction of the courts to determine whether such powers have been exceeded is not readily ousted by the use of such language; see further 1 Halsbury's Laws (4th edn) para 22.

Person . . . guilty of an offence; Conviction on indictment; fine; summary conviction. See the notes to s 2 ante.

Definitions. For "Electricity Board" and "statutory maximum", see s 26 post. Note as to "nuclear-powered generating station", and references to extending a generating station, sub-s (6) above.

Nuclear Installations Act 1965, s 1. See Vol 47, title Trade and Industry (Pt 2(b)).

4 (*Applies to Scotland only.*)

5 Private generators and Electricity Boards

(1) In this section "private generator or supplier" means a person other than an Electricity Board or local authority who—

(*a*) generates electricity, or

(*b*) supplies electricity generated otherwise than by an Electicity Board or local authority.

(2) Where a private generator or supplier requests an Electricity Board—

(*a*) to give and continue to give a supply of electricity to premises where he generates electricity or from which he supplies electricity to others, or

(*b*) to purchase electricity generated by him, or

(*c*) to permit him to use the Board's transmision and distribution system for the purpose of giving a supply of electricity to any premises,

the Board shall offer to comply with the request unless on technical grounds it would not be reasonably practicable to do so.

(3) Subject to sections 6 to 8 below, an offer under this section may include such reasonable terms and may be made subject to such reasonable conditions as the Board may determine, including—

(*a*) terms requiring security to be given for the payment of any sums that may become payable to the Board, and

(*b*) the condition that any necessary planning or other consents are obtained (including, in the case of an offer by the Central Electricity Generating Board, the consent of the Secretary of State under section 2(6) of the Electricity Act 1957).

(4) Every offer under this section shall include such reasonable terms and conditions as the Board may consider necessary to secure that the control by Electricity Boards of the operation of the electricity supply system is not impaired.

(5) If, before a request under this section can be complied with, it is necessary for any electric lines or other electrical plant to be provided, or for any other works to be carried out, the terms of an offer under this section—

(*a*) shall include an undertaking by the Board to provide the lines or other plant or carry out the works, and

(b) may require the person making the request to make payments to the Board in respect of any expenditure incurred by the Board in carrying out the undertaking.

(6) A request under this section shall contain such particulars, and shall be in such form, as may be prescribed by regulations made by the Secretary of State; and such regulations may make provision for the payment to the Board by the person making the request of fees to meet the Board's administrative expenses in dealing with the request.

NOTES

Commencement. See the note to s 2 ante.

Person. See the note to s 2 ante.

Reasonably practicable. The meaning of this expression and the difference between "reasonably practicable" and the stricter standard of "practicable" have been most often considered judicially in relation to safety legislation. See further, 20 Halsbury's Laws (4th edn) para 553.

May determine. See the note "Thinks fit" to s 3 ante.

Central Electricity Generating Board. As to the establishment, constitution and functions of this body, see the Electricity Act 1957, s 2 ante.

Secretary of State. See the note to s 2 ante.

Further provisions. See, in particular, s 6 post (charges for electricity supplied in compliance with requests); s 7 post (duty of Electricity Boards to fix tariffs of prices to be paid for electricity purchases); s 8 post (tariffs of charges for use of transmission and distribution systems); s 9 post (resolution of disputes arising under this section); s 10 post (further provisions as to charges under ss 7, 8 post); s 11 post (arrangements between Electricity Boards arising out of requests under this section); and s 16 post (power of Secretary of State to make regulations relating to supply and safety).

Definitions. For "Electricity Board" and "local authority", see s 26 post; and by virtue of s 26 post, for "electric line", see the Electric Lighting Act 1882, s 32 ante, and for "electrical plant", see the Electricity Act 1947, s 67(1) ante. Note as to "private generator or supplier", sub-s (1) above.

Electricity Act 1957, s 2(6). See this title ante.

Regulations under this section. The Electricity (Private Generating Stations and Requests by Private Generators and Suppliers) Regulations 1984, SI 1984/136, regs 3, 4, Sch 2.

For general provisions as to regulations, see s 24 post.

6 Charges for supplies by Electricity Boards

(1) Subject to subsection (2) below, the price to be paid for electricity supplied by an Electricity Board in compliance with requests under section 5 above shall be in accordance with tariffs fixed under section 37 of the Electricity Act 1947 or section 22 of the Electricity (Scotland) Act 1979.

(2) Where, owing to special circumstances, the tariffs fixed under section 37 of the Electricity Act 1947 or section 22 of the Electricity (Scotland) Act 1979 are not appropriate to a supply requested under section 5 above, the terms of the Board's offer under section 5 shall specify the price proposed by the Board and any arrangements proposed for its revision.

NOTES

Commencement. See the note to s 2 ante.

Electricity Board. For meaning, see s 26 post.

Electricity Act 1947, s 37. See this title ante.

Electricity (Scotland) Act 1979. 1979 c 11; not printed in this work.

7 Charges for purchases by Electricity Board

(1) Each Electricity Board other than the Central Electricity Generating Board shall as soon as practicable after the commencement of this section fix tariffs of prices that will be paid by the Board for electricity purchased by it in compliance with requests under section 5 above.

(2) In the case of any purchase in respect of which—

(*a*) there is no tariff in force under this section which is applicable, or

(*b*) the tariff applicable is not appropriate owing to special circumstances,

the terms of the offer made by the Board under section 5 above shall specify the price proposed by the Board and any arrangements proposed for its revision.

(3) The principles on which tariffs are fixed and prices proposed by an Electricity Board in accordance with this section shall include the principle that a purchase by the Board in compliance with a request under section 5 above should be on terms which—

(*a*) will not increase the prices payable by customers of the Board for electricity supplied to them by the Board, and

(*b*) will reflect the costs that would have been incurred by the Board but for the purchase.

(4) The terms of an offer to purchase electricity in compliance with a request under section 5 above may include a requirement that the vendor shall make to the Board from time to time such reasonable payments as the Board may determine in respect of the costs of maintenance, operation and depreciation of the assets employed, and of the administrative expenses incurred, by the Board in complying with the request.

(5) The amount of the payments to be made to the Board in accordance with subsection (4) above may include an amount designed to give the Board a return of the assets there referred to (taking into account any payment of the kind referred to in section 5(5) above) which is not greater than any return that the Board expects to receive on comparable assets.

NOTES

Commencement. See the note to s 2 ante.
Electricity Board. For meaning, see s 26 post.
Central Electricity Generating Board. See the note to s 5 ante.
Tariffs. As to the framing of tariffs fixed under this section, see s 10 post.
Specify the price. As to a requirement of prior consultation with the Electricity Council, see s 10(5) post.
Reasonable payments. As to the determination of disputes as to the reasonableness of payments, see s 9 post.
May determine. See the note "Thinks fit" to s 3 ante.

8 Charges for use of transmission and distribution systems

(1) Each Electricity Board shall as soon as practicable after the commencement of this section prepare tariffs of charges that will be made by the Board to persons permitted to use the Board's transmission and distribution system in pursuance of requests under section 5 above.

(2) In any case where—

(*a*) there is no tariff in force under this section which is applicable to the use requested, or

(*b*) the tariff applicable is not appropriate owing to special circumstances,

the terms of the offer made by the Board under section 5 above shall specify the charge proposed by the Board and any arrangements proposed for its revision.

(3) The principles on which tariffs are fixed and charges proposed by an Electricity Board in accordance with this section shall include the principle that chrages should be no more than sufficient to provide a return on the relevant assets (taking into account any payments of the kind referred to in section 5(5) above) comparable to any return that the Board expects to receive on comparable assets; and for this purpose "relevant assets" means the assets employed by the Board in complying with requests for permission to use the Board's transmission and distribution system.

NOTES
Commencement. See the note to s 2 ante.
Electricity Board. For the meaning, see s 26 post.
Tariffs. As to the framing of tariffs fixed under this section, see s 10 post.
Persons. See the note "Person" to s 2 ante.
Specify the charge. As to a requirement of prior consultation with the Electricity Council, see s 10(5) post.

9 Disputes as to offers under section 5 etc

(1) Any dispute as to—

(a) whether it would be reasonably practicable for an Electricity Board to comply with a request made to it under section 5 above, or

(b) whether a tariff which is applicable in the case of any supply, purchase or use requested under section 5 above is appropriate to that case, or

(c) the price or charge proposed by an Electricity Board in a case in which no tariff is applicable and appropriate, or

(d) the reasonableness of any other term or condition of an offer made by the Board under section 5 above, or

(e) the reasonableness of any payment demanded by an Electricity Board in accordance with section 7(4) above,

may be referred to the Secretary of State for determination by him or, if he thinks fit, by an arbitrator (or in Scotland an arbiter) appointed by him.

(2) The Secretary of State may make regulations as to the conduct of proceedings for the determination of disputes under this section; and the Arbitration Act 1950 and the Arbitration Act 1979 shall, in their application to disputes determined by an arbitrator appointed under this section, have effect subject to the provisions of such regulations.

(3) Regulations under this section relating to the determination of disputes by the Secretary of State may include provision—

(a) enabling the Secretary of State to require a party to the dispute to pay a sum determined by the Secretary of State towards any administrative expenses incurred by him in connection with the determination of the dispute, and

(b) as to awards of costs or expenses as between the parties to the dispute.

(4) Any sums paid to the Secretary of State by virtue of this section shall be paid into the Consolidated Fund.

(5)–(8) (*Apply to Scotland only.*)

NOTES
Commencement. See the note to s 2 ante.
Reasonably practicable. See the note to s 5 ante.
Electricity Board. For meaning, see s 26 post.
Secretary of State. See the note to s 2 ante.
Thinks fit. See the note to s 3 ante.
Consolidated Fund. Ie the Consolidated Fund of the United Kingdom which was established by the Consolidation Fund Act 1816, s 1 Vol 30, title Money (Pt 1).
Arbitration Act 1950; Arbitration Act 1979. See Vol 2, title Arbitration.
Regulations under this section. The Electricity (Conduct of Proceedings for the Determination of Disputes) Regulations 1984, SI 1984/135 (made under sub-ss (2), (3) above).
For general provisions as to regulations, see s 24 post.

10 Further provisions as to charges under sections 7 and 8

(1) The tariffs fixed under section 7 or 8 above shall be so framed as to show the methods by which and the principles on which the charges are to be made as well as

their amount, and shall be published in such manner as in the opinion of the Electricity Board concerned will secure adequate publicity.

(2) Tariffs fixed under section 7 or 8 above by an Electricity Board other than a Scottish Board shall be fixed after consultation with the Electricity Council, which shall consult the Secretary of State as to the methods by which and the principles on which charges are to be made.

(3) (*Applies to Scotland only.*)

(4) The tariffs required by sections 7 or 8 above may be altered or replaced from time to time, and need not be exhaustive.

(5) Before proposing a price in accordance with section 7(2) above or a charge in accordance with section 8(2) above an Electricity Board other than a Scottish Board shall consult the Electricity Council.

(6) An Electricity Board, in fixing tariffs and proposing prices or charges in accordance with section 7 or 8 above, shall not show undue preference to any person or class of persons and shall not exercise any undue discrimination against any person or class of persons.

NOTES

Commencement. See the note to s 2 ante.
Opinion. See the note "Thinks fit" to s 3 ante.
Electricity Board. For meaning, see s 26 post.
Consultation. On what constitutes consultation, see, in particular, *Fletcher v Minister of Town and Country Planning* [1947] 2 All ER 496, (1947) 111 JP Jo 542; *Rollo v Minister of Town and Country Planning* [1948] 1 All ER 13, [1948] LJR 817, CA; *Re Union of Whippingham and East Cowes Benefices, Derham v Church Comrs for England* [1954] AC 245, [1954] 2 All ER 22, PC; and *Agricultural, Horticultural and Forestry Industry Training Board v Aylesbury Mushrooms Ltd* [1972] 1 All ER 280, [1972] 1 WLR 190.
Electricity Council. As to the new establishment, constitution and functions of this Council, see the Electricity Act 1957, s 3 ante.
Secretary of State. See the note to s 2 ante.

11 Arrangements between Electricity Boards

(1) Where a request is made to an Electricity Board under section 5 above and that Board ("the first Board") considers that the request could more appropriately be met by another Electricity Board ("the second Board"), the first Board may propose to the second Board that the second Board meet the request.

(2) If the second Board does not agree to a proposal under subsection (1) above, the first Board may refer the dispute to the Secretary of State for determination by him.

(3) If—

    (*a*) the second Board agrees to a proposal under subsection (1) above; or
    (*b*) the Secretary of State, on a reference under subsection (2) above, determines that the request is to be met by the second Board,

the request shall be treated as if it had been made to the second Board.

NOTES

Commencement. See the note to s 2 ante.
Secretary of State. See the note to s 2 ante.
Definitions. For "Electricity Board", see s 26 post. Note as to "the first Board" and "the second Board", sub-s (1) above.

12 Meters to be of approved pattern

(1) Subject to subsection (5) below, no person shall use a meter for measuring the amount of electrical energy supplied by him to another person, or the electrical quantity contained in the supply, unless it is of an approved pattern.

(2) A meter is of an approved pattern for the purposes of this section if it is of a pattern for the time being approved by the Secretary of State or by a person who, for the purpose of implementing any Community obligation, is responsible for giving pattern approval in a member State other than the United Kingdom.

(3) A person who uses a meter in contravention of this section shall be guilty of an offence unless he believes, on reasonable grounds, that the meter is of an approved pattern.

(4) A person guilty of an offence under this section shall be liable on summary conviction to a fine not exceeding level 2 on the standard scale.

(5) This section shall not apply—

    (a) in relation to a supply by Electricity Board, or
    (b) in relation to a meter installed before (and not moved since) the commencement of this section.

NOTES
Commencement; Person; Secretary of State. See the notes to s 2 ante.
Community obligation. For meaning, see the European Communities Act 1972, Sch 1, Pt II, Vol 17, title European Communities, as applied by the Interpretation Act 1978, s 5, Sch 1, Vol 41, title Statutes.
Member State. Ie a State which is a member of the European Communities; see the European Communities Act 1972, s 1(2), Sch 1, Pt II, Vol 17, title European Communities, as applied by the Interpretation Act 1978, s 5, Sch 1, Vol 41, title Statutes.
United Kingdom. Ie Great Britain and Northern Ireland; see the Interpretation Act 1978, s 5, Sch 1, Vol 41, title Statutes.
Believes, on reasonable grounds. The existence of the reasonable grounds, and of the belief founded on it, is ultimately a question of fact to be tried on evidence and the grounds on which the person acted must be sufficient to induce in a reasonable person the required belief; see in particular, *McArdle v Egan* (1933) 150 LT 412, [1933] All ER Rep 611, CA; *Nakkuda Ali v Jayaratne* [1951] AC 66, PC; *Registrar of Restrictive Trading Agreements v W H Smith & Son Ltd* [1969] 2 All ER 1065 at 1070, [1969] 1 WLR 1460 at 1468, CA per Lord Denning MR; and *IRC v Rossminster Ltd* [1980] AC 952, [1980] 1 All ER 80, HL.
Person . . . guilty of an offence; summary conviction. See the notes to s 2 ante.
Definitions. For "Electricity Board" and "standard scale", see s 26 post.

13 (*Amends s 27 of the Schedule to the Electric Lighting (Clauses) Act 1899 ante.*)

14 Inspection and testing of lines etc

(1), (2) . . .

(3) Sections 39 and 42 to 48 of that Schedule (which make further provision as to testing and inspection, including provision giving inspectors the right of access to the premises of suppliers for the purpose of testing electric lines and instruments and provision penalising suppliers who fail to comply with the Schedule's requirements) shall apply in relation to suppliers of electricity other than Electricity Boards as they apply in relation to Area Boards and Scottish Boards.

(4) References in this section to the Schedule to the Electric Lighting (Clauses) Act 1899 are references to that Schedule as incorporated with the Electricity Act 1947.

NOTES

Sub-s (1) amends the Electric Lighting Act 1882, s 24 ante; sub-s (2) amends the Electric Lighting (Clauses) Act 1899, Schedule, s 36(1)(a) ante.

Commencement. See the note to s 2 ante.

Definitions. For "Electricity Board", see s 26 post; by virtue of s 26 post, for "Area Board", see the Electricity Act 1947, s 1(3) ante; and for "electric line", see the Electric Lighting Act 1882, s 32 ante; and by virtue of the Electric Lighting (Clauses) Act 1899, Schedule, s 1 ante, for "electricity", see s 32 of the 1882 Act ante.

That Schedule. Ie the Schedule to the Electric Lighting (Clauses) Act 1899 ante, as incorporated with the Electricity Act 1947 ante by s 57(2) of that Act, subject to the modifications and adaptations specified in Sch 4, Pt III to that Act.

Miscellaneous and general

15 Amendments relating to meters

The enactments mentioned in Schedule 1 to this Act shall have effect subject to the amendments specified in that Schedule.

NOTE

Commencement. See the note to s 2 ante.

16 Regulations relating to supply and safety

(1) The Secretary of State may make such regulations as he thinks fit for the purpose of—

    (a) securing that supplies of electricity by Electricity Boards or other persons are regular and efficient; and

    (b) eliminating or reducing the risks of personal injury, or damage to property or interference with its use, arising from the supply of electricity by an Electricity Board or any other person, from the use of electricity so supplied or from the installation, maintenance or use of any electrical plant.

(2) Without prejudice to the generality of subsection (1) above, regulations under this section may—

    (a) make provision for relieving an Electricity Board from any obligation to supply or purchase electricity, or to permit the use of the Board's transmission and distribution system, in cases where electrical plant or fittings or their use do not comply with the regulations;

    (b) prohibit the supply of electricity except by means of a system approved by the Secretary of State;

    (c) make provision requiring compliance with notices given by the Secretary of State specifying action to be taken in relation to any electrical plant or fittings for the purpose of—

        (i) preventing or ending a breach of regulations under this section, or

        (ii) eliminating or reducing a risk of personal injury or damage to property or interference with its use;

    (d) make provision requiring notice to be given to the Secretary of State, in such cases as may be specified in the regulations, of accidents and of failures of supplies of electricity;

    (e) make provision as to the keeping, by persons who supply electricity, of maps, plans and sections and as to their production (on payment, if so required, of a reasonable fee) for inspection or copying;

(f) provide for particular requirements of the regulations to be deemed to be complied with in the case of electrical plant or fittings complying with specified standards or requirements;

(g) provide for the granting of exemptions from any requirement of the regulations.

(3) Regulations under this section may provide that any person who contravenes any specified circumstances, shall be guilty of an offence under this section.

(4) A person guilty of an offence under this section shall be liable on summary conviction to a fine not exceeding level 5 on the standard scale.

NOTES

Commencement; Secretary of State. See the notes to s 2 ante.
Thinks fit. See the note to s 3 ante.
Persons. See the note "Person" to s 2 ante.
Person . . . guilty of an offence; summary conviction. See the notes to s 2 ante.
Definitions. For "Electricity Board" and "standard scale", see s 26 post; by virtue of s 26 post, for "electrical fittings" and "electrical plant", see the Electricity Act 1947, s 67(1) ante.
Regulations under this section. Up to 1 August 1985, no regulations had been made under sub-s (1) above.

For general provisions as to regulations, see s 24 post.

17 (*S 17(1) adds sub-ss (4A), (4B) to s 37 of the Electricity Act 1947 ante and repeals the Electricity (Supply) Act 1922, s 23; s 17(2) applies to Scotland only.*)

18 Purchases by Electricity Boards from local authorities

(1) This section applies to any purchase of electricity by an Electricity Board in accordance with arrangements made in pursuance of—

(*a*) section 21(2) of the Control of Pollution Act 1974 (production of heat and electricity from waste etc), or

(*b*) section 11(2) of the Local Government (Miscellaneous Provisions) Act 1976 (production of heat etc by local authorities).

(2) The price at which a purchase to which this section applies is made shall be the same as it would be by virtue of section 7 above if the purchase were made in compliance with a request under section 5 above; and subsections (4) and (5) of section 7 shall apply to a purchase to which this section applies as they apply to a purchase made in compliance with such a request.

(3) Section 9 above shall apply to a dispute as to—

(*a*) the price at which a purchase to which this section applies is to be made, or

(*b*) the reasonableness of any payment demanded by an Electricity Board in accordance with section 7(4) above as applied by this section,

as it applies to disputes within section 9(1)(*a*) to (*e*).

NOTES

Commencement. See the note to s 2 ante.
Electricity Board. For meaning, see s 26 post.
Control of Pollution Act 1974, s 21(2). See Vol 35, title Public Health.
Local Government (Miscellaneous Provisions) Act 1976, s 11(2). See Vol 25, title Local Government.

19, 20 (*S 19(1), (2) amends the Electricity Act 1947, s 50 ante; s 19(3) applies to Scotland only; s 20 amends ss 52, 54 of the Schedule to the Electric Lighting (Clauses) Act 1899 ante.*)

21 The Electricity Consumers' Council

(1) There shall be a consumers' council for England and Wales (in this section referred to as "the Council") to be known as the Electricity Consumers' Council.

(2) The Council shall consist of a chairman appointed by the Secretary of State, and not more than thirty other members made up of—

    (*a*) the chairman for the time being of the Consultative Councils established under section 7 of the Electricity Act 1947 for the areas of Area Boards, and

    (*b*) such other persons as the Secretary of State may appoint.

(3) It shall be the duty of the Council to consider any matter affecting the interests of consumers generally of electricity supplied by Electricity Boards in England and Wales, or of any class of such consumers, being a matter which—

    (*a*) is referred to the Council by the Secretary of State or the Electricity Council, or

    (*b*) is the subject of a report or representations made to the Council by one of the Consultative Councils mentioned in subsection (2) above, or

    (*c*) appears to the Council to be a matter to which consideration ought to be given apart from any such reference, report or representations.

(4) The Council shall report to the Secretary of State or, as the case may be, the Electricity Council on any matter considered by them by virtue of subsection (3)(*a*) above, and where it appears to them that action ought to be taken concerning any other matter considered by them under subsection (3) they shall make representations to the Electricity Council on that matter.

(5) The Council may, after consulting the Electricity Council, make representations to the Secretary of State on any matter considered by them under this section otherwise than on a reference by the Secretary of State.

(6) The Council shall consider any plans, arrangements or proposals of which they are informed under section 22 below and may make representations on them to the Electricity Council.

(7) The Council may refer to any of the Consultative Councils mentioned in subsection (2) above any matter which affects the interests of consumers of electricity in the area for which the Consultative Councils established or the interests of any class of those consumers.

(8) The Secretary of State may, after consultation with the Board concerned and with the Electricity Council, give such directions as he thinks fit to an Electricity Board in England or Wales with respect to matters arising out of representations made to him by the Council under this section, and shall send to the Council a copy of any such directions; and section 40(2) of the Electricity Act 1957 shall apply in relation to such directions as it applies in relation to directions under that Act.

(9) The Council shall make to the Secretary of State, as soon as possible after the end of each financial year of the Electricity Council, a report on the performance by the Council of their functions during that year; and the Secretary of State shall lay a copy of the report before each House of Parliament.

(10) In this section references to consumers of electricity include references to prospective consumers.

(11) Schedule 2 to this Act shall have effect with respect to the Council.

NOTES

    Commencement. See the note to s 2 ante.

    Sub-s (1): England; Wales. For meanings, see the Interpretation Act 1978, s 5, Sch 1, Vol 41, title Statutes.

    Sub-s (2): Secretary of State. See the note to s 2 ante.

Sub-s (3): It shall be the duty, etc. As to the remedies for failure to perform a statutory duty, see generally the Preliminary Note to the title Statutes, Vol 41, 1 Halsbury's Laws (4th edn) paras 99, 195, 205, and 44 Halsbury's Laws (4th edn) paras 941 et seq.

Electricity Council. See the note to s 10 ante.

Appears. See the note "Thinks fit" to s 3 ante.

Sub-s (5): Consulting. See the note "Consultation" to s 10 ante.

Sub-s (6): Thinks fit. See the note to s 3 ante.

Sub-s (9): Lay ... before ... Parliament. For meaning, see the Laying of Documents before Parliament (Interpretation) Act 1948, s 1(1), Vol 41, title Statutes.

Definitions. For "Electricity Board", see s 26 post, and, by virtue of s 26 post, for "Area Board", see the Electricity Act 1947, s 1(3) ante. Note as to "the Council" sub-s (1) above, and as to "consumers of electricity" sub-s (10) above.

Electricity Act 1947, s 7; Electricity Act 1957, s 40(2). See this title ante.

22 Functions of other bodies in relation to Electricity Consumers' Council

(1) It shall be the duty of the Electricity Council to inform the Electricity Consumers' Council of the general plans and arrangements of the Electricity Council and of the Central Electricity Generating Board for performing their functions in relation to the supply of electricity, and in particular of any proposal of the Central Electricity Generating Board to vary a tariff.

(2) The Electricity Council may refer any matter to the Electricity Consumers' Council and shall consider any representations or report made to them by the Electricity Consumers' Council.

(3) ...

NOTES

Sub-s (3) inserts the Electricity Act 1947, s 7(4A) ante.

Commencement. See the note to s 2 ante.

It shall be the duty etc. See the note to s 21 ante.

Electricity Council. See the note to s 10 ante.

Inform the Electricity Consumers' Council etc. The Council, which is established by s 21 ante, is required to consider any plans, arrangements or proposals of which they are informed under this section; see s 21(6) ante.

Central Electricity Generating Board. See the note to s 5 ante.

Electricity Act 1947, s 7(4). See this title ante.

23 Offences

(1) Proceedings for an offence under this Part of this Act shall not, in England and Wales, be instituted except by or with the consent of the Secretary of State or the Director of Public Prosecutions.

(2) Where an offence committed by a body corporate under this Part of this Act is proved to have been committed with the consent or connivance of, or to be attributable to any neglect on the part of, any director, manager, secretary or other similar officer of the body corporate or any person who was purporting to act in any such capacity, he as well as the body corporate shall be guilty of that offence and shall be liable to be proceeded against and punished accordingly.

(3) Where the affairs of a body corporate are managed by its members, subsection (2) above shall apply in relation to acts and defaults of a member in connection with his functions of management as if he were a director of the body corporate.

NOTES

Commencement. See the note to s 2 ante.

This Part of this Act. Ie Pt I (ss 1–26) of this Act.

England; Wales. See the note to s 21 ante.

Secretary of State. See the note to s 2 ante.

Director of Public Prosecutions. Provision for the appointment of the Director of Public Prosecutions and Assistant Directors is currently made by the Prosecution of Offences Act 1979, s 1, Vol 12, title Criminal Law; by sub-s (4) of that section an Assistant Director may do any act or thing which the Director is required or authorised to do. See also, in particular, s 6 of that Act, as to arrest, remand etc, where the consent of the Director has not yet been given, and s 7 thereof, ibid, as to evidence of such consent.

The 1979 Act is repealed by the Prosecution of Offences Act 1985, Vol 12, title Criminal Law, as from a day to be appointed under s 31(2) thereof. New provision is made as to the establishment of a Crown Prosecution Service for England and Wales by ss 1–10. In particular, by s 1(6), every Crown Prosecutor has all the powers of the Director as to the institution and conduct of proceedings but exercises those powers under his direction.

Provisions re-enacting ss 6 and 7 of the 1979 Act are contained in ss 25 and 26 of the 1985 Act, respectively.

Consent should be proved before the summons is issued, and the point that consent is lacking cannot be taken for the first time after the case for the prosecution has been closed; see *Price v Humphries* [1958] 2 QB 353, [1958] 2 All ER 725.

Offence committed by a body corporate. See the note "Person . . . guilty of an offence" to s 2 ante; and for the general law relating to corporations, see 9 Halsbury's Laws (4th Edn), paras 1201 et seq.

Consent. There is authority for saying that this presupposes knowledge; see *Re Caughey, ex p Ford* (1876) 1 Ch D 521 at 528, CA, per Jessel MR, and *Lamb v Wright & Co* [1924] 1 KB 857 at 864, [1924] All ER Rep 220 at 223. It is thought, however, that actual knowledge is not necessary; cf *Knox v Boyd* 1941 JC 82 at 86; *Taylor's Central Garages (Exeter) Ltd v Roper* (1951) 115 JP 445 at 449, 450, per Devlin J, [1951] WN 383; *James & Son Ltd v Smee* [1955] 1 QB 78 at 91, [1954] 3 All ER 273 at 278 per Parker J; and *Mallon v Allon* [1964] 1 QB 385 at 394, [1963] 3 All ER 843 at 847.

Connivance. Though there are many decisions on the meaning of this word in matrimonial law (see *Godfrey v Godfrey* [1965] AC 444, [1964] 3 All ER 154, HL, especially the speech of Lord Guest in which earlier decisions are reviewed), there is little authority as to its meaning in the context in which it appears in this section (see *Gregory v Walker* (1912) 77 JP 55, 29 TLR 51, and Glanville Williams, Criminal Law: The General Part, para 222). It is thought that the word implies knowledge of, and acquiescence in, the offence committed. Yet it seems that here again positive knowledge is not necessary and that suspicion is enough although mere negligence or inattention is not; see *Rogers v Rogers* (1830) 3 Hag Ecc 57 (but note the express reference to neglect in this section).

Neglect. This word implies failure to perform a duty of which the person knows or ought to know; see *Re Hughes, Rea v Black* [1943] Ch 296 at 298, [1943] 2 All ER 269 at 271 per Simonds J. For circumstances in which an offence was held to be attributable to neglect on the part of a director, see *Crickitt v Kursaal Casino Ltd (No 2)* [1968] 1 All ER 139 at 146, 147, [1968] 1 WLR 53, HL, and for circumstances in which the opposite was held, see *Huckerby v Elliott* [1970] 1 All ER 189, (1969) 113 Sol Jo 1001.

Purporting to act. The reference to any person who was purporting to act in any such capacity is introduced in view of *Dean v Hiesler* [1942] 2 All ER 340, where a director who had not been duly appointed was held not liable for an offence committed by the company.

24 Regulations: general

Any power to make regulations conferred on the Secretary of State by this Part of this Act—

(a) shall include power to make different provision for different areas or in relation to different cases or circumstances; and

(b) shall be exercisable by statutory instrument, which shall be subject to annulment in pursuance of a resolution of either House of Parliament.

NOTES

Commencement. See the note to s 2 ante.

Secretary of State. See the note to s 2 ante.

This Part of this Act. Ie Pt I (ss 1–26) of this Act.

Statutory instrument; subject to annulment. For provisions as to statutory instruments generally, see the Statutory Instruments Act 1946, Vol 41, title Statutes, and as to statutory instruments which are subject to annulment, see ss 5(1), 7(1) of that Act.

25 Amendments

The enactments mentioned in Schedule 3 to this Act shall have effect subject to the amendments specified in that Schedule (being minor amendments and amendments consequential on the preceding provisions of this Part of this Act).

NOTES

Commencement. See the note to s 2 ante.
This Part of this Act. Ie Pt I (ss 1–26) of this Act.

26 Interpretation of Part I

In this Part of this Act—

"Area Board" has the same meaning as in the Electricity Act 1947;

"electrical fittings" and "electrical plant" have the same meanings as in the Electricity Act 1947;

"electric line" has the same meaning as in the Electric Lighting Act 1882;

"Electricity Board" means an Area Board, a Scottish Board or the Central Electricity Generating Board;

"local authority" means any of the following—

(a) a county or district council in England or Wales, . . . a London borough council, the Common Council of the City of London, and the Council of the Isles of Scilly;

(b) (applies to Scotland only);

. . . . . .

"standard scale" has the meaning given by section 75 of the Criminal Justice Act 1982;

"statutory maximum" has the meaning given by section 74 of the Criminal Justice Act 1982.

NOTES

The words omitted from the definition of "local authority" were repealed as from 1 April 1986 by the Local Government Act 1985, s 102(2), Sch 17.

The definition omitted where indicated by dots applies to Scotland only.

Commencement. See the note to s 2 ante.

This Part of this Act. Ie Pt I (ss 1–26) of this Act.

Central Electricity Generating Board. See the note to s 5 ante.

County council. As to the counties in England and Wales and their councils, see the Local Government Act 1972, ss 1(1), (2), 2(1), (3), 20(1), (2), 21(1), (3), Sch 1, Pts I, II, Sch 4, Pt I, Vol 25, title Local Government.

District council. As to the districts in England and Wales and their councils, see the Local Government Act 1972, ss 1(1), (3), (4), 2(2), (3), 20(1), (3), 21(2), (3), Sch 1, Pt I, Sch 4, Pt II, Vol 25, title Local Government.

London borough. For definition, see the Interpretation Act 1978, s 5, Sch 1, Vol 41, title Statutes; and as to the London boroughs and their councils, see the London Government Act 1963, s 1, Sch 1, Vol 26, title London, and the Local Government Act 1972, s 8, Sch 2, Vol 25, title Local Government.

Common Council of the City of London. Ie the mayor, aldermen and commons of the City of London in common council assembled; see the City of London (Various Powers) Act 1958, s 5, Vol 26, title London.

Council of the Isles of Scilly. The Council of the Isles of Scilly is continued in being by the Local Government Act 1972, s 265(1), Vol 25, title Local Government, and is now constituted by the Isles of Scilly Order 1978, SI 1978/1844, art 4 (made under s 265(2) of that Act).

Application. An Electricity Board within the meaning of Pt I of this Act is also an "electricity authority" for the purposes of the Telecommunications Act 1984, s 98, Vol 45, title Telecommunications and Broadcasting; see sub-s (9) thereof.

Electricity Act 1947. For the meaning of "Area Board", see s 1(3) of that Act ante; and for "electrical fittings" and "electrical plant", see s 67(1) of that Act ante.

Electric Lighting Act 1882. For the meaning of "electric line", see s 32 of that Act ante.

Criminal Justice Act 1982, ss 74, 75. See Vol 27, title Magistrates. Section 74 defines "standard scale" as the scale set out in s 37(2) of that Act. The scale, as amended by art 2(4) of, and Sch 4 to, the Criminal Penalties etc (Increase) Order 1984, SI 1984/447 (made under the Magistrates' Courts Act 1980, s 143, Vol 27, title Magistrates) is: level 1: £50; level 2: £100: level 3: £400; level 4: £1000; level 5: £2000.

Section 75 of the 1982 Act defines "statutory maximum" as the "prescribed sum" within the meaning of the Magistrates' Courts Act 1980, s 32; that section has been amended by art 2(1) of, and Sch 1 to, the 1984 Order which specifies £2000 as that sum.

PART II

NUCLEAR INSTALLATIONS

27 Limitation of operators' liability

(1)–(7) ...

(8) Subsection (1) above shall not affect liability in respect of any occurrence before (or beginning before) the commencement of this section; and where the amount applicable under section 16(1) of the 1965 Act to the licensee of a site is increased by virtue of subsection (1) above, then for the purposes of section 19 of that Act the cover period relating to him as licensee of that site and current at the commencement of this section shall end and a new cover period shall begin.

NOTES

Sub-ss (1)–(7) amend the Nuclear Installations Act 1965, ss 13(5), 16, 19, 20(1), 26(1), Vol 47, title Trade and Industry (Pt 2(b)).

Commencement. Pt II (ss 27–34) of this Act was brought into force on 1 September 1983 by the Energy Act 1983 (Commencement No 1) Order 1983, SI 1983/790, made under s 37(1) post.

Definitions. For "cover period", see the Nuclear Installations Act 1965, s 19(2), Vol 47, title Trade and Industry (Pt 2(b)), and for "licensee" and "occurrence" see s 26(1) of that Act.

The 1965 Act. Ie the Nuclear Installations Act 1965, Vol 47, title Trade and Industry (Pt 2(b)).

28–32 (*Ss 28, 29 amend the Nuclear Installations Act 1965, ss 17, 18, 21, Vol 47, title* Trade and Industry (Pt 2(b)) *in respect of occurrences beginning after 1 September 1983; s 30 inserts ss 25A, 25B in the 1965 Act; s 31 amends s 17 of that Act; s 32 amends s 26(1) of that Act.*)

33 Extension to territories outside United Kingdom

The provisions in respect of which the power conferred by section 28 of the 1965 Act is exercisable shall include the provisions of that Act as amended by this Act.

NOTES

Commencement. See the note to s 27 ante.

1965 Act. Ie the Nuclear Installations Act 1965, Vol 47 title Trade and Industry (Pt 2(b)).

34 (*Repeals the Atomic Energy Authority Act 1954, s 5(3).*)

PART III

GENERAL

35 Financial provisions

There shall be paid out of money provided by Parliament—

(*a*) any administrative expenses of the Secretary of State attributable to this Act, and

(*b*) any increase attributable to this Act in the sums payable out of money so provided under the Nuclear Installations Act 1965.

NOTES

Commencement. Para (*a*) above was brought into force on 1 June 1983, and para (*b*) was brought into force on 1 September 1983, by the Energy Act 1983 (Commencement No 1) Order 1983, SI 1983/790, made under s 37(1) post.

Secretary of State. See the note to s 2 ante.

Nuclear Installations Act 1965. See Vol 47, title Trade and Industry (Pt 2(b)).

36 Repeals

The enactments mentioned in Schedule 4 to this Act are hereby repealed to the extent specified in the third column of that Schedule.

NOTE

Commencement. As to the commencement of provisions relating to Sch 4, see the notes to that Schedule post.

37 Commencement

(1) This Act shall come into force on such day as the Secretary of State may appoint by order made by statutory instrument, and different days may be so appointed for different purposes.

(2) An order under subsection (1) above may make such transitional provision and savings as appear to the Secretary of State to be necessary or expedient.

(3) If section 17(5) of the Nuclear Installations Act 1965 has not been brought into force under section 30(2) of that Act before the day appointed under subsection (1) above for the coming into force of section 31 of this Act, it shall come into force on that day.

NOTES

Commencement. Sub-ss (1), (2) above were brought into force on 1 June 1983, and sub-s (3) was brought into force on 1 September 1983, by the Energy Act 1983 (Commencement No 1) Order 1983, SI 1983/790, made under sub-s (1) above.

Secretary of State. See the note to s 2 ante.

Statutory instrument. For provisions as to statutory instruments generally, see the Statutory Instruments Act 1946, Vol 41, title Statutes.

Nuclear Installations Act 1965, ss 17(5), 30(2). See Vol 47, title Trade and Industry (Pt 2(b)). The order noted below brought s 31 of this Act into force on 1 September 1983 and, as no date had been previously appointed for the commencement of s 17(5) of the 1965 Act, that subsection came into force on the same day by virtue of sub-s (3) above.

Order under this section. The Energy Act 1983 (Commencement No 1) Order 1983, SI 1983/790 (bringing certain provisions of this Act into force on 1 June 1983 or 1 September 1983 as shown in the "Commencement" notes to this Act and making transitional provisions and savings in relation to the amendments made by Sch 1, paras 9, 13, 17 to this Act.

38 Short title and extent

(1) This Act may be cited as the Energy Act 1983.

(2) The following provisions of this Act, namely

(*a*) Part I (except paragraph 11 of Schedule 2), and
(*b*) Part I of Schedule 4,

do not extend to Northern Ireland; but otherwise this Act does extend there.

SCHEDULES

(Sch 1, paras 1–14 amend the Electric Lighting (Clauses) Act 1899, Schedule, ss 1, 2, 50–52, 54–56, ante, substitute ss 49, 53, 57, 59, and insert ss 50A, 50B in the Schedule to that Act, paras 15, 16 amend the Electricity Supply (Meters) Act 1936, ss 1, 2 ante; para 17 amends the Electricity Act 1957, s 30 ante.)

SCHEDULE 2

THE ELECTRICITY CONSUMERS' COUNCIL (S 21)

The chairman

1. If the Secretary of State so determines, there shall be paid to the chairman of the Council such remuneration as the Secretary of State may determine.

2. If the Secretary of State so determines in the case of a person who has been remunerated under paragraph 1 above, a pension shall be paid to or in respect of that person, or payments towards the provision of a pension to or in repsect of that person shall be made, in accordance with the determination.

3. If a person in receipt of remuneration under paragraph 1 above as chairman ceases to hold that office, and it appears to the Secretary of State that there are special circumstances which make it right that that person should receive compensation, he shall be paid by way of compensation a sum of such amount as the Secretary of State may determine.

Administration, personnel, etc

4. The Council may, subject to the approval of the Secretary of State as to numbers, appoint such officers as appear to the Council to be requisite for the performance of their functions.

5. The Secretary of State shall provide the Council with funds—

    (*a*) with which to pay—

        (i) to their members, such travelling and other allowances as the Secretary of State may determine; and

        (ii) to their officers, such remuneration and such travelling and other allowances, as the Council may with the approval of the Secretary of State determine; and

    (*b*) with which to defray such other expenses in connection with the Council's functions as the Secretary of State may determine to be appropriate.

6. The Secretary of State may make arrangements for the Council to be provided with office accommodation.

7.—(1) There shall be paid such pensions, or arrangements shall be made for the payment of such pensions, as the Secretary of State may determine to or in respect of such persons who are or have been officers of the Council as the Secretary of State may determine.

(2) The Secretary of State shall provide the Council with funds with which to pay any such pension or to finance any such arrangements.

Constitution and procedure

8.—(1) The Secretary of State may make regulations with respect to—

    (*a*) the appointment of, and the tenure and vacation of office by, members of the Council;

    (*b*) the appointment of one or more members of the Council as deputy chairman or deputy chairmen;

    (*c*) the quorum, proceedings, meetings and determinations of the Council;

    (*d*) the execution of documents and the mode of entering into contracts by and on behalf of the Council, and the proof of documents purporting to be executed, issued or signed by the Council or a member or officer of the Council; and

    (*e*) any other matters supplementary or incidental to those mentioned in paragraphs (*a*) to (*d*) for which provision appears to him to be necessary or expedient.

(2) Subject to any regulations made under this paragraph, the Council shall have power to regulate their own procedure.

9. The validity of any proceedings of the Council shall not be affected by any vacancy amongst the members or by any defect in the appointment of a member.

Amendment of other Acts

10, 11. . . .

12. The consent of the Treasury shall be required for any determination or approval by the Secretary of State under this Schedule.

13. Any payments to be made under paragraphs 1 to 3 above shall be made by the Secretary of State, and they and any other payments made by him under this Schedule shall be defrayed out of money provided by Parliament.

14. In this Schedule "pension" includes an allowance or gratuity payable on retirement or otherwise.

NOTES

Para 10 amends the Chronically Sick and Disabled Persons Act 1970, s 14(1), Vol 34, title Post Office; para 11 amends the House of Commons Disqualification Act 1975, Sch 1, Pt III, Vol 32, title Parliament.

Commencement. This Schedule was brought into force on 1 September 1983 by the Energy Act 1983 (Commencement No 1) Order 1983, SI 1983/790, made under s 37(1) ante.

Para 1: Secretary of State. See the note to s 2 ante.

May determine. See the note "Thinks fit" to s 3 ante.

Para 8: Quorum. "The word 'quorum' in its ordinary signification has reference to the existence of a complete body of persons, of whom a certain specified number is competent to transact the business of the whole"; see *Faure Electric Accumulator Co Ltd v Phillipart* (1888) 58 LT 525 at 527.

Para 12: Treasury. Ie the Commissioners of HM Treasury, see the Interpretation Act 1978, s 5, Sch 1, Vol 41, title Statutes.

Regulations under this Schedule. The Electricity (Consumers' Council) Regulations 1983, SI 1983/1129, as amended by SI 1983/1748 (made under para 8 above).

(*Sch 3: para 1 amends the Electric Lighting Act 1882, s 25 ante; para 2 amends the Electric Lighting (Clauses) Act 1899, Schedule, ss 1, 27, 36 ante; paras 3–8 amend the Electricity Act 1947, ss 1, 2, 37, 63, 64, 66, respectively ante; para 9 amends the Clean Air Act 1956, s 10(4), Vol 35, title* Public Health; *para 10 amends the Electricity Act 1957, s 2(7) ante; para 11 amends the Clean Air Act 1968, s 6(10), Vol 35, title* Public Health; *paras 12–17 apply to Scotland only.*)

SCHEDULE 4

Section 36

Enactments Repealed

Part I

Electricity

Chapter	Short Title	Extent of Repeal
51 & 52 Vict c 12	The Electric Lighting Act 1888	The whole Act.
62 & 63 Vict c 19	The Electric Lighting (Clauses) Act 1899	In the Schedule (as incorporated with the Electricity Act 1947 or any other enactment)— in section 2, the words from "forty-nine" to "fifty-eight"; in section 10, paragraph (*a*), paragraph (*c*) and the word "and" immediately preceding paragraph (*c*); section 38; in section 52, the words from "and for those purposes" to "acts";

Chapter	Short Title	Extent of Repeal
62 & 63 Vict c 19—*cont*	The Electric Lighting (Clauses) Act 1899—*cont*	section 54(2); section 60; in section 69(1), in paragraph (*a*) the words from "are" to "Schedule" and the words from "permitted" to "earth or", paragraph (*b*) (and the word "or" preceding it) and paragraph (*c*); in section 69(2), the words "or work" in each place where they occur.
9 Edw 7 c 34	The Electric Lighting Act 1909	Section 23.
9 & 10 Geo 5 c 100	The Electricity (Supply) Act 1919	Section 11. In section 36, the definition of "private generating station".
12 & 13 Geo 5 c 46	The Electricity (Supply) Act 1922	Section 23.
16 & 17 Geo 5 c 51	The Electricity (Supply) Act 1926	Section 24
26 Geo 5 & 1 Edw 8 c 20	The Electricity Supply (Meters) Act 1936	In section 1(1) the words "by authorised undertakers". In section 1(3), the words "by any consumer or the undertakers as the case may be".
9 & 10 Geo 6 c 49	The Acquisition of Land (Authorisation Procedure) Act 1946	In Schedule 4, the entry relating to the Electricity (Supply) Act 1919.
10 & 11 Geo 6 c 54	The Electricity Act 1947	In section 2(4)(*b*), the words "under the foregoing section". In section 2(5), the words from "under" where it first occurs to "this section" and the words from "but" to the end. In section 37(4), the words "on the premises of the consumer". Section 60. In Schedule 4— in Part I, the entries relating to section 23 of the Electric Lighting Act 1909, section 11 of the Electricity (Supply) Act 1919 and section 24 of the Electricity (Supply) Act 1926; and in Part III, the entries relating to sections 49 and 60 of the Schedule to the Electric Lighting (Clauses) Act 1899.
2 & 3 Eliz 2 c 60	The Electricity Reorganisation (Scotland) Act 1954	Section 1(3). In Part III of Schedule 1, the entry relating to the Electric Lighting Act 1888.
4 & 5 Eliz 2 c xciv	The South of Scotland Electricity Order Confirmation Act 1956	Section 40.
5 & 6 Eliz 2 c 48	The Electricity Act 1957	In section 2(7)(*c*), the words "under the preceding provisions of this section". Section 30(5) to (8).

Chapter	Short Title	Extent of Repeal
5 & 6 Eliz 2 c 48— *cont*	The Electricity Act 1957—*cont*	In Schedule 4— in Part I, the entries relating to sections 50 and 60 of the Electricity Act 1947; and in Part II, the entry relating to the Electricity (Supply) Act 1919.
7 Eliz 2 c ii	The North of Scotland Electricity Order Confirmation Act 1958	Section 27.
1969 c 48	The Post Office Act 1969	In Schedule 4— in paragraph 8, sub-paragraph (*b*), in sub-paragraph (*c*) the references to sections 10, 60 and 69 of the Schedule to the Electric Lighting (Clauses) Act 1899 and sub-paragraph (*g*); paragraph 11.
1976 c 76	The Energy Act 1976	Section 14(6)(*b*).
1979 c 11	The Electricity (Scotland) Act 1979	In section 7(3), the words "under this Act". In section 9(2), the words from "but" to the end. In section 22(3), the words "on the premises of the consumer". In section 35(1), the word "private" in both places where it occurs and the word "new". Section 35(2). In paragraph 13 of Schedule 10, the reference to section 60 of the Electricity Act 1947.
1981 c 67	The Acquisition of Land Act 1981	In paragraph 1 of Schedule 4, the entry relating to the Electricity (Supply) Act 1919.

NOTE

Commencement. By the Energy Act 1983 (Commencement No 1) Order 1983, SI 1983/790, made under s 37(1) ante, the following repeals in this Part of this Schedule were brought into force on 1 June 1983, viz, the repeals relating to the Electric Lighting (Clauses) Act 1899, Schedule, ss 2, 52, 54(2); the Electric Lighting Act 1909; the Electricity (Supply) Act 1919; the Electricity (Supply) Act 1922; the Electricity Supply (Meters) Act 1936; the Acquisition of Land (Authorisation Procedure) Act 1946; the Electricity Act 1947 (except for s 60, in Sch 4, Pt I, the entry relating to the Electricity (Supply) Act 1926, s 24, and in Sch 4, Pt III, the entry relating to the Electric Lighting (Clauses) Act 1899, Schedule, s 60); the South of Scotland Electricity Order Confirmation Act 1956; the Electricity Act 1957 (except in Sch 4, Pt I, the entry relating to the Electricity Act 1947, s 60); the North of Scotland Electricity Order Confirmation Act 1958; the Post Office Act 1969, Sch 4, para 11; the Energy Act 1976, s 14(6)(*b*); the Electricity (Scotland) Act 1979 (except for the reference to the Electricity Act 1947, s 60, in Sch 10, para 13); and the Acquisition of Land Act 1981. That order also provides under s 37(2) ante, that the Electricity Act 1957, s 30(5)–(8), shall continue to have effect for the purposes of offences committed prior to 1 June 1983. As at 1 August 1985, no order bringing the remaining repeals in this Part of this Schedule into force had been made under s 37(1).

Part II

Nuclear Installations

Chapter	Short Title	Extent of Repeal
2 & 3 Eliz 2 c 32	The Atomic Energy Authority Act 1954	Section 5(3).
1965 c 57	The Nuclear Installations Act 1965	In section 17(3)(b)(ii), the words "not being less than £2,100,000".
1969 c 18	The Nuclear Installations Act 1969	Section 2.

NOTE

Commencement. This Part of this Schedule was brought into force on 1 September 1983 by the Energy Act 1983 (Commencement No 1) Order 1983, SI 1983/790, made under s 37(1) ante.

INDEX

advowson
university or college—
  gratuitous transfer of, 89
  power to sell, 86–8
  purchase of, 88

age
birth certificate, registrar supplying, 171
compulsory school, 134
evidence of, 172
presumption of, 210
school-leaving, date of attaining, 223

area board. *See also* **electricity board**
accounts—
  consolidated statement of, 927
  keeping, 878
amenity, preserving, 948
annual report, 926
area reserve fund—
  allocations to, 877
  establishment and maintenance, 936
areas of—
  definition, 865
  list of, 896
  new, 865
  variation, 865
assets, best use of, 863
audit, 878
body corporate, 864
borrowing powers, 930, 962
chairman—
  appointing, 864
  deputy, 864
  Electricity Council, attending meetings of, 922
constitution of, 864
Consultative Council—
  annual report, 927
  consideration of conclusions of, 868
  duties of, 867
  establishment of, 867, 924
  local representatives, 868
  Minister, representations to, 868
  new, establishing, 869
  procedure, rules of, 869
  special agreement, reference to, 929
  transitional provisions, 951
consumers in another area, supplying, 861
electrical fittings, powers on, 863
electricity supplies, acquiring, 861
employment, compliance with agreement on, 928
establishment of, 860
estimate of requirements, issuing, 934
generation of electricity by, 924
meetings, 864
members—
  appointment, 864
  compensation for loss of office, 959
  remuneration, 864
names of, 896
new, constituting, 865
officers, compensation to, 939
procedure, rules on, 864
railway—
  supply of electricity to, 940
    charge for, 876

area board—*continued*
resale of electricity, charge for, 941
research by, 925
revenue account, balancing, 929
special agreement on supply—
  appropriate, where, 876
  Consultative Council, reference to, 929
status of, 948
stock, issuing, 931–2
streets, power to break up, 879
tariff. *See* **electricity board**
Treasury guarantee of loan, 933

army school
educational endowments, schemes for, 104
meaning, 105

benefice
college headship, severance from, 89
university or college—
  augmentation by, 87
  endowment, substitution of lands, 88

Board of Education
transfer of powers to, 3

Boundary Commissions
assessors, 460
assistant Commissioners, 456
chairman, 456
constituency, meaning, 454
constitution of, 451, 456
deputy chairman, 460
electoral quota—
  meaning, 461
  observing, 458
establishment of, 451
expenses, 457
local inquiry, holding, 457, 461
members, 456
officers, 456
Orders in Council, provisions on, 453
parliamentary counties and boroughs, effect of
  disappearance of, 454
procedure, 457
recommendations—
  publishing, 457
  revision of, 461
redistribution of seats—
  periodical reports on, 452
  rules for, 458
report—
  European Assembly constituencies, on, 471
  general provisions, 453
  intervals between, 460
  publication of, 452
secretary, 457

British Electricity Authority
Central Electricity Authority, substitution of, 917

British Electricity Stock
Electricity Council issuing, 930
expenses of issue, 935
issue of, 932
obligations in respect of, shares in, 934